SPARKNOTES
101

Literature

SPARK PUBLISHING

Spark Publishing
A Division of Barnes & Noble Publishing
120 Fifth Avenue
New York, NY 10011
www.sparknotes.com

ISBN-10: 1-4114-0026-7
ISBN-13: 978-1-4114-0026-9

Please submit comments and questions or report errors to www.sparknotes.com/errors

Printed and bound in the United States

CONTENTS

CONTENTS

CONTENTS

WELCOME TO SPARKNOTES 101: LITERATURE

Thanks for choosing *Sparknotes: 101 Literature*! Whether you're studying for a test, brushing up on a few novels, writing a paper, or even trudging through four years of English classes, *SparkNotes 101: Literature* will provide a helping hand.

Before you dive in, here are a few quick tips and explanations that will help you get the most out of this book.

THE BOOKS

To make navigation easy, the entries are arranged alphabetically by book title. If you want to see the books listed by date of publication or alphabetically by author, turn to page 915 and consult the indexes.

QUICK SUMMARIES

If you're in a rush or just want to refresh your memory about a certain book, check out the quick summary at the top of each entry for a one-sentence rundown. For example, the quick summary of Canterbury Tales is:

> *A group of travelers making a pilgrimage to Canterbury tell each other stories that are by turns crude, hilarious, creepy, gruesome, and pious.*

KEY FACTS

Note that Key Facts for plays don't list tone, point of view, or tense, since these categories usually only apply to novels.

CHARACTER LISTS

Characters are listed alphabetically by last name. If characters have a frequently-used nickname, you'll see that in parenthesis next to the character's full name. For example, one character from *Ulysses* is listed as *Marion Bloom (Molly)*.

If a certain character is never identified by name in the novel, he or she will be identified by role in the character list. For example, one character in *A Clockwork Orange* is identified in the character list as *Prison Chaplain*. Such characters are alphabetized by the first word of their role. *Prison Chaplain*, for example, is listed after the character named *Pete*.

QUOTATIONS

After each quotation, you'll see three categories: location, speaker, and context. These will give you some quick context. Location tells you where the quotation comes from; Speaker tells you who says the quotation; Context tells you what's going on at this point in the book. For example, one quotation entry from *Moby-Dick* looks like this:

Location: Chapter 41
Speaker: Ishmael
Context: Ishmael describes Ahab's feelings about Moby Dick

We hope *SparkNotes 101: Literature* helps you, comforts you, and occasionally saves your butt!

SPARKNOTES
101

Literature

1984

George Orwell

A citizen of the totalitarian country Oceania rebels against the ruling Party and is tortured and brainwashed as a result.

THE LIFE OF GEORGE ORWELL

Born Eric Blair in India in 1903, George Orwell was educated as a scholarship student at prestigious boarding schools in England. Because of his background—he famously described his family as "lower-upper-middle class"—he never quite fit in. He felt oppressed and outraged by the dictatorial control that the schools he attended exercised over students' lives. His painful experiences with snobbishness and social elitism at Eton, as well as his familiarity with British imperialism in India, made him deeply suspicious of the class system in English society. After graduating from Eton, Orwell decided to forego college in order to work as a British Imperial Policeman in Burma. He hated his duties in Burma, where he was required to enforce the strict laws of a political regime he despised. Orwell's bad health, which troubled him throughout his life, caused him to return to England on convalescent leave. Once back in England, he quit the Imperial Police and dedicated himself to becoming a writer.

Inspired by Jack London's 1903 book *The People of the Abyss*, which detailed Jack London's experience in the slums of London, Orwell bought ragged clothes from a secondhand store and went to live among the very poor in London. He published a book about this experience entitled *Down and Out in Paris and London*. Orwell later lived among destitute coal miners in northern England, an experience that inspired him to give up on capitalism in favor of democratic socialism. In 1936, Orwell went to report on the Civil War in Spain, where he witnessed nightmarish atrocities committed by fascist political regimes. As the dictators Adolf Hitler and Joseph Stalin rose to power, Orwell's hatred of totalitarianism and political authority intensified. Orwell devoted his energy to writing politically charged novels, first *Animal Farm* in 1945, then *1984* in 1949.

1984 IN CONTEXT

1984, one of Orwell's most expertly crafted novels, is still a powerful warning against the dangers of a totalitarian society. *1984* reflects Orwell's experiences in Spain, Germany, and the Soviet Union, where advanced technology worsened the danger of absolute political authority. *1984*, a close cousin to Aldous Huxley's novel *Brave New World* (1932), is one of the most famous novels of the negative utopian, or dystopian, genre. Whereas a utopian novel portrays a perfect human society, a dystopian novel portrays the worst human society imaginable. Dystopian novels aim to show readers the horror of societal degradation. *1984* was published at the dawn of the nuclear age and before the television had become a fixture in the family home, but Orwell's vision of a post-atomic dictatorship in which every individual would be monitored ceaselessly by means of the telescreen still seemed terrifyingly possible.

The world that Orwell envisioned in *1984* did not materialize in full. The Cold War ended with the triumph of democracy, as evidenced by the fall of the Berlin Wall and the disintegration of the Soviet Union in the early 1990s. However, some of the dire predictions of *1984* have come to pass, particularly the intrusive role of government and the ability of machines (computers, it turns out, not televisions) to spy on their users.

1984: KEY FACTS

Time and place written: England, 1947–1949

Date of first publication: 1949

Publisher: Harcourt Brace Jovanovich, Inc.

Type of work: Novel

Genre: Dystopia

Language: English	

Language: English

Setting (time): 1984

Setting (place): London, England (known as "Airstrip One" in the novel's alternate reality)

Tense: Past

Tone: Dark, frustrated, pessimistic

Narrator: Third-person, limited

Point of View: Winston Smith's

Protagonist: Winston Smith

Antagonist: The Party; Big Brother

1984: PLOT OVERVIEW

Winston Smith is a low-ranking member of the ruling Party in London, a city in the nation of Oceania. Everywhere Winston goes, even his own home, the Party watches him through telescreens. Everywhere Winston looks, he sees the face of the Party's seemingly omniscient leader, a figure known only as Big Brother. The Party controls everything in Oceania, even the people's history and language. Currently, the Party is forcing the implementation of an invented language called Newspeak, which will eliminate all words related to political rebellion in an attempt to prevent actual political rebellion. Even thinking rebellious thoughts is illegal. Thoughtcrime is, in fact, the worst of all crimes.

As the novel opens, Winston feels frustrated by the oppression and rigid control of the Party, which prohibits free thought, sex, and any expression of individuality. Winston has illegally purchased a diary, intending to record his criminal thoughts in it. He is fixated on a powerful Party member named O'Brien, whom Winston believes is a secret member of the Brotherhood—the mysterious, legendary group that works to overthrow the Party.

Winston works in the Ministry of Truth, where he alters historical records according to the Party's specifications. One day he notices a beautiful dark-haired co-worker staring at him. Winston worries that she is an informant who will turn him in for his thoughtcrime. Privately, Winston is troubled by the Party's control of history. The Party claims that Oceania has always been allied with Eastasia in a war against Eurasia, but Winston remembers a time when this was not true. The Party also claims that Emmanuel Goldstein, the alleged leader of the Brotherhood, is the most dangerous man alive, but this does not seem plausible to Winston. Winston spends his evenings wandering through the poorest neighborhoods in London, where the proletarians, or proles, live squalid lives relatively free of Party monitoring.

One day, Winston receives a note from the dark-haired girl that reads "I love you." The girl's name is Julia. Winston and Julia begin a covert affair, keeping a careful lookout for signs that the Party is monitoring them. Eventually they rent a room above the secondhand store in the prole district where Winston bought the diary. As the relationship continues, Winston is sure they will be caught and punished sooner or later. He knows he has been doomed since he wrote his first diary entry. Julia is more pragmatic and optimistic than Winston, whose hatred for the Party grows increasingly intense. At last, Winston receives the message he has been waiting for: O'Brien wants to see him.

Winston and Julia travel to O'Brien's apartment. As a member of the powerful Inner Party (Winston belongs to the Outer Party), O'Brien leads a life of incredible luxury. He tells Winston and Julia that, like them, he hates the Party, and says that he works against it as a member of the Brotherhood. He accepts Winston and Julia into the Brotherhood and gives Winston a copy of Emmanuel Goldstein's book, the manifesto of the Brotherhood. Back in the room above the store, Winston reads the book—an amalgam of several class-based twentieth-century social theories—to Julia. Suddenly, soldiers barge in and seize them. Mr. Charrington, the proprietor of the store, is a member of the Thought Police.

Torn away from Julia and taken to a place called the Ministry of Love, Winston finds out that O'Brien is a Party spy. He pretended to be a member of the Brotherhood in order to trick Winston into committing an open act of rebellion against the Party. For months, O'Brien tortures and brainwashes Winston, who struggles to resist. At last, O'Brien sends Winston to the dreaded Room 101, the final destination for anyone who opposes the Party. O'Brien tells Winston that he will be forced to confront his worst fear. Throughout the novel, Winston has had recurring nightmares about rats. O'Brien straps a cage full of rats onto Winston's head and prepares to allow the rats to eat his face. Winston gives in and pleads with O'Brien to hurt Julia, not him.

All along, O'Brien wanted Winston to give up Julia. His spirit broken, Winston is released to the outside world. He meets Julia, but no longer feels anything for her. She admits that under torture, she begged for her pain to be shifted to him. Winston has accepted the Party entirely and learned to love Big Brother.

CHARACTERS IN *1984*

Big Brother The perceived ruler of Oceania. Though he never appears in the novel, and though he may not actually exist, Big Brother is a crucial figure. Everywhere Winston looks, he sees posters of Big Brother's face bearing the message "BIG BROTHER IS WATCHING YOU." Big Brother's image is stamped on coins and broadcast on the unavoidable telescreens. It haunts Winston's life and fills him with hatred and fascination.

O'Brien A mysterious, powerful, and sophisticated member of the Inner Party. O'Brien tricks Winston into thinking he is a member of the Brotherhood, the legendary group of anti-Party rebels.

Mr. Charrington An old man who runs a secondhand store in the prole district. Kindly and encouraging, Mr. Charrington seems to share Winston's interest in the past. He also seems to support Winston's rebellion against the Party and his relationship with Julia, renting Winston a room without a telescreen in which to carry out his affair. Despite appearances, Mr. Charrington is a member of the Thought Police.

Emmanuel Goldstein A legendary leader of the Brotherhood, at least according to the Party. Like Big Brother, Goldstein exerts influence on the novel without ever appearing in it. It seems he was a Party leader who fell out of favor with the regime. The Party describes him as the most dangerous and treacherous man in Oceania.

Julia Winston's lover. Julia is a beautiful dark-haired girl who works in the Fiction Department at the Ministry of Truth. Julia, who enjoys sex, says she has had affairs with many Party members. Julia is pragmatic and optimistic. She rebels against the Party for her own enjoyment. Her rebellion is small and personal, in contrast to Winston's ideological rebellion.

Parsons A fat, obnoxious, dull Party member who lives near Winston and works at the Ministry of Truth. Parsons has a dull wife and suspicious, ill-mannered children who work for the Junior Spies.

Winston Smith The protagonist of the novel. Winston, a minor member of the ruling Party, is a thin, frail, contemplative intellectual, and fatalistic thirty-nine-year-old. He hates the totalitarian government that controls and represses the citizens. Winston longs for revolution.

Syme An intelligent, outgoing man who works with Winston at the Ministry of Truth. Syme specializes in language. As the novel opens, he is working on a new edition of the Newspeak dictionary. Winston believes Syme is too intelligent to stay in the Party's favor.

THEMES IN *1984*

THE DANGERS OF TOTALITARIANISM In 1949, the Cold War had not yet escalated, many American intellectuals supported communism, and the relationships between democratic and communist nations were ambiguous. In the American press, the Soviet Union was often portrayed as a great moral experiment. However, Orwell was deeply disturbed by the cruelty and oppression he had seen in communist countries, and with 1984 he wanted to warn Western readers about the dangers of totalitarian government. The fact that the novel is set in the year 1984, a mere thirty-five years after its publication, was meant to show readers that if totalitarianism flourished unchecked, the world of the novel could quickly become a reality.

PSYCHOLOGICAL AND PHYSICAL MANIPULATION The Party barrages citizens with psychological stimuli designed to overwhelm their capacity for independent thought. In every citizen's room, a giant telescreen broadcasts a constant stream of propaganda designed to recast the failures and shortcomings of the Party as triumphant successes. Authorities constantly monitor people's behavior via telescreen. Omnipresent signs reading "BIG BROTHER IS WATCHING YOU" remind the citizens that the authorities are watching them. The Party inducts children into an organization called the Junior Spies, brainwashing them and encouraging them to spy on their parents and report any instance of disloyalty to the Party. The Party also forces individuals to suppress their sexual desires, treating sex as a procreative duty useful for the creation of new Party members. The Party encourages people to channel their frustration and emotion into ferocious displays of hatred against the Party's political enemies, many of whom are invented. The Party also monitors and controls the bodies of its subjects, constantly watching for signs of disloyalty. Even a tiny facial twitch can result in an arrest. The Party forces its members to undergo mass morning exercises called the Physical Jerks, and then to work long, grueling days. Anyone who does manage to defy the Party is punished and "reeducated" through systematic torture. After he is subjected to weeks of re-education, Winston concludes that nothing is more powerful than physical pain—no emotional loyalty or moral conviction can overcome it.

CONTROL OF HISTORY AND LANGUAGE The Party manages and rewrites newspapers and histories, manipulating history to justify the present. It claims that the past was a time of misery and slavery, and that the Party has liberated the human race. It also deliberately weakens people's memories and forbids them to keep mementos from the past. If no one can remember life before the Revolution, then no one can say that the Party has failed mankind by forcing people to live in poverty, filth, ignorance, and hunger. The Party also controls language, replacing English with Newspeak. In Newspeak, there are no words to describe disobedience or rebellion. If we cannot capture a feeling in words, the Party believes, that feeling does not exist.

SYMBOLS IN *1984*

BIG BROTHER Big Brother's face symbolizes the omnipresence of the Party. All over London, he appears on posters that read "BIG BROTHER IS WATCHING YOU." Big Brother's name cunningly suggests warmth and protection. Despite the soothing connotations of his name, Big Brother does not protect so much as terrify and threaten. Big Brother also symbolizes the vague way the higher ranks of the Party present themselves. They do not want people to know who really rules Oceania or what life is like for the rulers. The Party tells the citizens that Big Brother is the leader of the nation and the head of the Party, but Winston can never determine whether or not he actually exists.

THE TELESCREENS The omnipresent telescreens symbolize the Party's constant monitoring of its subjects. In their dual capability to blare constant propaganda and observe citizens, the telescreens also suggest that totalitarian governments abuse technology for their own ends instead of using technology to improve civilization.

IMPORTANT QUOTATIONS FROM *1984*

> *WAR IS PEACE*
> *FREEDOM IS SLAVERY*
> *IGNORANCE IS STRENGTH*

Location: Book One, Chapter I
Speaker: Party slogans
Context: We see the Party slogan carved into a pyramid

These words, the official slogans of the Party, typify doublethink—the ability to hold two contradictory ideas in one's mind at the same time. They are inscribed in massive letters on the white pyramid of the Ministry of Truth. Weakened by fear and assaulted by propaganda, the citizens believe everything the Party tells them, even when the Party's assertions are completely illogical. At the Hate Week rally, for instance, the Party suddenly announces that the nation it has been at war with is now its ally, and its former ally is its new enemy. The people in the crowd accept this reversal immediately and are ashamed to find they have made the wrong signs for the event. In the same way, people accept the Party ministries' names, though they contradict their functions: the Ministry of Plenty oversees economic shortages, the

Ministry of Peace wages war, the Ministry of Truth spreads propaganda and revises history, and the Ministry of Love carries out torture and punishment. The national slogan of Oceania, a mass of contradictions, shows the psychological control that lies at the heart of the Party's power. The Party convinces citizens that "War Is Peace" because having a common enemy keeps the people of Oceania united, and that "Freedom Is Slavery" because the independent man is doomed to fail. But the final line of the slogan reveals the Party's true attitude: "Ignorance Is Strength" because the inability of the people to recognize contradictions cements the power of the authoritarian regime.

And perhaps you might pretend, afterwards, that it was only a trick and that you just said it to make them stop and didn't really mean it. But that isn't true. At the time when it happens you do mean it. You think there's no other way of saving yourself and you're quite ready to save yourself that way. You want it to happen to the other person. You don't give a damn what they suffer. All you care about is yourself.

Location: Book Three, Chapter VI
Speaker: Julia to Winston
Context: A discussion of what happened in Room 101

Julia tells Winston that she wanted her torture to be shifted to him, and he confesses he felt exactly the same way. Julia and Winston have betrayed each other, which means the Party has won. In the end, Julia and Winston realize that no moral conviction or fellow feeling is strong enough to withstand torture. Physical pain will always cause people to betray their convictions in order to end their suffering. The principles of doublethink inform the Party's conviction that control over the body equates with control of the mind.

Who controls the past controls the future. Who controls the present controls the past.

Location: Book One, Chapter III, and Book Three, Chapter II
Speaker: Party slogans
Context: In Book One, Winston thinks about the Party's control of memory and history. In Book Three, Winston, now imprisoned, talks to O'Brien about the nature of the past

---

In the end the Party would announce that two and two made five, and you would have to believe it. It was inevitable that they should make that claim sooner or later: the logic of their position demanded it. Not merely the validity of experience, but the very existence of external reality was tacitly denied by their philosophy.

Location: Book One, Chapter VII
Speaker: Winston's thoughts
Context: Winston looks at a children's history book and marvels at the Party's control of the mind

---

And when memory failed and written records were falsified—when that happened, the claim of the Party to have improved the conditions of human life had got to be accepted, because there did not exist, and never again could exist, any standard against which it could be tested.

Location: Book One, Chapter VIII
Speaker: Winston's thoughts
Context: Winston has just had a frustrating conversation with an old man about life before the Revolution

THE AENEID

Virgil

A Trojan destined to found Rome, undergoes many trials on land and sea during his journey to Italy, finally defeating the Latin Turnus and avenging the murder of Pallas.

THE LIFE OF VIRGIL

Virgil, the preeminent poet of the Roman Empire, was born Publius Vergilius Maro on October 15, 70 B.C., near Mantua, a city in northern Italy. The son of a farmer, Virgil studied in Cremona, then in Milan, and finally in Rome. Around 41 B.C., he returned to Mantua to begin work on his *Eclogues*, which he published in 37 B.C. Soon afterward, civil war forced him to flee south to Naples, where seven years later he finished his second work, the *Georgics*, a long poem on farming. Virgil's writing brought him public recognition, wealth from patrons, and the favor of the emperor.

For much of Virgil's life internal strife plagued the Roman government. During Virgil's youth, the First Triumvirate—Julius Caesar, Pompey, and Crassus—governed the Roman Republic. When Crassus was killed around 53 B.C., Caesar began a civil war against Pompey. After defeating Pompey, Caesar reigned alone until the Ides of March in 44 B.C., when Brutus and Cassius, two senators, assassinated him. Civil war erupted between the assassins and the Second Triumvirate—Octavian, Antony, and Lepidus. By 36 B.C., only Octavian and Antony remained. They began warring against each other. At the Battle of Actium in 31 B.C., Octavian defeated Antony and his ally Cleopatra of Egypt, finally consolidating power for himself. Four years later, Octavian assumed the title Augustus. His reign marked the height of the first age of the Roman Empire.

THE *AENEID* IN CONTEXT

Immediately after finishing the *Georgics*, Virgil began his masterwork, the *Aeneid*. He was fortunate to enter the good graces of Augustus, and in part, the *Aeneid* legitimizes Augustus's reign. The *Aeneid* tells the story of the Trojan hero Aeneas, who made a perilous flight from Troy to Italy following the Trojan War. Later, Aeneas's descendents found Rome in Italy. In the epic, Virgil repeatedly foreshadows the coming of Augustus, perhaps to silence critics who claimed that Augustus achieved power through violence and treachery. The easiest way to justify the recent brutal events in Rome was to claim that the civil wars and the changes in leadership were fated, part of a preordained plan to usher in the reign of the great Augustus. Whether or not Virgil was sincere in the praise he heaped on Augustus is a matter of debate. The *Aeneid* is by no means a purely political work; its subject stands on its own as a story for all time.

Virgil did not invent the story that Rome descended from Troy. In writing the *Aeneid*, he relied on already existing tales about Aeneas that extended from the ancient Greek poet Homer through the contemporary Roman historian Livy. Ancient accounts of Aeneas's postwar wanderings vary. Greek art from the sixth century B.C. portrays Aeneas carrying his father, Anchises, out from the burning ruins of Troy. Archaeological evidence suggests that as early as the sixth century B.C., the myth of Aeneas was often depicted in art on the Italian mainland. Before Virgil, several poets had connected Dido and Aeneas, but Virgil was the first to tie all the elements of Aeneas's story together in epic form.

After working on the *Aeneid* for eleven years, Virgil still did not consider it fit for publication. He planned to spend three years editing it, but fell ill while returning from a trip to Greece. Just before his death on September 21, 19 B.C., he ordered the manuscript of the *Aeneid* burned, because he considered it unfinished. Augustus intervened, however, and had the poem published against Virgil's wishes.

Virgil's masterful and meticulously crafted poetry earned him a reputation as the greatest poet in the Latin language. Throughout the Middle Ages and into the Renaissance, his fame grew. He inspired poets of many nationalities, including Dante, an Italian; Milton, an Englishman; and an anonymous French poet who reinterpreted the *Aeneid* as medieval romance, *Le Roman d'Eneas*. As the culture became Christian, Virgil was viewed as a pagan prophet of Christianity because several lines in his works can be interpreted as predictions of the coming of Christ. Writers of the Renaissance applauded Virgil for the fluidity of his rigorously structured poetry and the vividness of his portrayals of human emotion.

Modern critics, on the other hand, have been less kind to Virgil. They often compare Virgil's poetry unfavorably to that of his Greek predecessors, especially the *Iliad* and the *Odyssey*, epics attributed to Homer that portray the Trojan War and its aftermath. Most contemporary scholars believe Virgil's poetry pales in comparison to Homer's. Virgil himself often compared his poetry to Homer's. In the *Aeneid*, he expressed a desire to surpass Homer while still borrowing heavily from him. The *Aeneid* shares with the *Iliad* and the *Odyssey* a tone of ironic tragedy, as characters act against their own wishes, submit to fate, and often meet dark ends. Most scholars agree that Virgil distinguished himself within the epic tradition of antiquity by representing the broad spectrum of emotion felt by characters living through dislocation and war.

THE AENEID: ESSENTIAL FACTS

Time and place written: Around 20 B.C.; probably in Rome and the north of Italy, and perhaps in Greece

Date of first publication: Sometime after Virgil's death in 19 B.C.

Type of work: Epic poem

Genre: Heroic epic, mythological story

Language: Latin

Setting (time): The aftermath of the Trojan War, about 1000 B.C.

Setting (place): The Mediterranean, including the north coast of Asia Minor, Carthage, and Italy

Tense: Usually past, sometimes switching to present to increase the immediacy of a scene. Virgil also uses the future tense for prophecy and prediction

Tone: Solemn and honorific when discussing the glory of Rome; tragic and sympathetic when depicting the victims of history

Narrator: The poet Virgil, and the character Aeneas in Books II and III

Point of view: When Virgil narrates, the point of view includes the actions of the gods as well as the human story; when Aeneas narrates, the point of view is solely his

Protagonist: Aeneas

Antagonist: Juno, Turnus

THE *AENEID*: PLOT OVERVIEW

On the Mediterranean Sea, Aeneas and his fellow Trojans flee from their home city of Troy, which has been destroyed by the Greeks. They sail for Italy, where Aeneas is destined to found Rome. As they near their destination, a fierce storm throws them off course and lands them in Carthage. Dido, Carthage's founder and queen, welcomes them. Aeneas tells Dido the long and painful story of his group's travels thus far.

Aeneas tells of the sack of Troy that ended the Trojan War after ten years of Greek siege. In the final campaign, the Trojans allowed a wooden horse to pass into their city walls. Unbeknown to them, the horse hid several Greek soldiers in its hollow belly. Aeneas escaped the burning city with his father, Anchises; his son, Ascanius; and the hearth gods that represent the fallen city of Troy. Assured by the gods that a glorious future awaited him in Italy, he set sail with a fleet bearing the surviving citizens of Troy. Twice they attempted to build a new city, only to be driven away by bad omens and plagues. Harpies (creatures that are part woman and part bird) cursed them, but they also had unexpected encounters with friendly countrymen. Finally, after the loss of Anchises and a bout of terrible weather, they made their way to Carthage.

Impressed by Aeneas's exploits and sympathetic to his suffering, Dido, a Phoenician princess who fled her home and founded Carthage after her brother murdered her husband, falls in love with Aeneas. They live together as lovers until the gods remind Aeneas of his duty to found a new city. He decides to set sail once again. Dido, devastated by his departure, orders a huge pyre built with Aeneas's castaway possessions, climbs on it, and stabs herself to death with the sword Aeneas left behind.

As the Trojans make for Italy, bad weather blows them to Sicily, where they hold funeral games for the dead Anchises. The women, tired of the voyage, begin to burn the ships, but a downpour puts the fires out. Some of the travel-weary stay behind. Aeneas, reinvigorated after his father visits him in a dream, takes the rest of his countrymen on toward Italy. Once there, Aeneas descends into the underworld, guided by the Sibyl of Cumae, to visit his father. He is shown a pageant of the future history and heroes of Rome, which helps him understand the importance of his mission. Aeneas returns from the underworld, and the Trojans continue up the coast to the region of Latium.

The arrival of the Trojans in Italy begins peacefully. King Latinus, the Italian ruler, extends his hospitality. He hopes Aeneas will turn out to be the foreigner who will fulfill a prophecy by marrying the king's daughter Lavinia. But King Latinus's wife, Amata, wants Lavinia to marry Turnus, a local suitor. Meanwhile, Ascanius hunts a stag that was a pet of the local herdsmen. A fight breaks out, and several people are killed. Turnus, riding this current of anger, begins a war.

Aeneas, at the suggestion of the river god Tiberinus, sails north up the Tiber to seek military support from the neighboring tribes. During this voyage, Aeneas's mother, Venus, descends to give him a new set of weapons made by Vulcan. While Aeneas is away, Turnus attacks. Aeneas returns to find his countrymen embroiled in battle. Pallas, the son of Aeneas's new ally Evander, is killed by Turnus. Aeneas flies into a violent fury, and many more are slain by the day's end.

The two sides agree to a truce so they can bury the dead, and the Latin leaders decide that Aeneas and Turnus should settle the conflict by fighting a hand-to-hand duel. When the two leaders face off, however, the other men begin to quarrel, and full-scale battle resumes. Aeneas is wounded in the thigh, but eventually the Trojans begin to prevail. Turnus rushes out to meet Aeneas, who wounds Turnus badly. Aeneas nearly spares Turnus but then, remembering the slain Pallas, kills him.

CHARACTERS IN THE *AENEID*

MORTALS

Aeneas The protagonist of the *Aeneid*. Aeneas is a survivor of the siege of Troy and the future founder of Rome. He subordinates all other concerns to his destiny to found the Roman race in Italy. Aeneas's defining characteristic is piety—that is, respect for the will of the gods. A fearsome warrior and a leader able to motivate his men even in hard times, Aeneas is also capable of great compassion and sorrow.

Achates A Trojan and a friend of Aeneas.

Amata Queen of Laurentum (a region of Latium, in Italy) and wife of Latinus. Amata opposes the marriage of Lavinia, her daughter, to Aeneas. Amata is loyal to Turnus, Lavinia's original suitor. Once it becomes clear that Aeneas will win the battle, Amata kills herself.

Anchises Aeneas's father and a reminder of Aeneas's Trojan heritage. Although Anchises dies during the journey from Troy to Italy, his spirit continues to help Aeneas fulfill fate's decrees, especially by guiding Aeneas through the underworld and showing him what fate has in store for his descendants.

Ascanius Aeneas's young son by his first wife, Creusa. Though still a child, Ascanius (also called Iulus) often displays bravery and leadership. He leads a procession of boys on horseback during the games in Book V and helps defend the Trojan camp from Turnus's attack while his father is away. Ascanius is most significant as a symbol of Aeneas's destiny: to found the Roman race.

Camilla The leader of the Volscians, a race of warrior maidens. Camilla is perhaps the only strong female mortal in the epic.

Creusa Aeneas's wife at Troy and Ascanius's mother. In the flight from Troy, Creusa is lost and killed. When Aeneas returns to search for her, he meets her shade, or spirit, which tries to comfort him by saying that a new home and wife await him in Hesperia.

Dido The queen of Carthage, a city in northern Africa in what is now Libya. Dido left the land of Tyre when Pygmalion, her brother, murdered her husband. Although Dido is strong, she becomes a pawn of the gods in their struggle for Aeneas's destiny. Her love for Aeneas, provoked by Venus, is her downfall. After Aeneas abandons Dido, she constructs a funeral pyre and stabs herself with Aeneas's sword.

Drances A Latin leader who desires an end to the Trojan-Latin struggle. Drances questions Turnus's motives at the council of the Latins, infuriating Turnus.

Evander King of Pallanteum (a region of Arcadia, in Italy) and father of Pallas. Evander is a sworn enemy of the Latins. Aeneas befriends him and secures his assistance in the battles against Turnus.

Juturna Turnus's sister. Provoked by Juno, Juturna induces a full-scale battle between the Latins and the Trojans by disguising herself as an officer and goading the Latins.

Latinus The king of the Latins, the people of what is now central Italy, around the Tiber River. Latinus allows Aeneas into his kingdom and encourages him to woo his daughter, Lavinia. Latinus respects the gods and fate. His command over his people is not firm.

Lavinia King Latinus's daughter. Virgil does not develop Lavinia's character; she is important only as the impetus for the Trojan-Latin struggle. The question of who will marry Lavinia—Turnus or Aeneas—is crucial to future relations between the Latins and the Trojans and therefore to the *Aeneid*'s entire historical scheme.

Pallas Son of Evander. Evander entrusts Pallas to Aeneas's care and tutelage. Pallas eventually dies in battle at the hands of Turnus, causing Aeneas and Evander great grief. To avenge Pallas's death, Aeneas slays Turnus.

Sinon A Greek youth who persuades the Trojans to accept the wooden horse as an offering to Minerva, then lets out the warriors hidden inside the horse's belly.

Turnus The ruler of the Rutulians in Italy. Turnus is brash and fearless, a capable soldier who values his honor more than his life. Turnus is Aeneas's major mortal antagonist. Until Aeneas arrives, Turnus is Lavinia's leading suitor. Turnus's fury at Aeneas incites him to wage war against the Trojans even though he knows he cannot change fate.

GODS AND GODDESSES

Aeolus The god of the winds, enlisted to help Juno create bad weather for the Trojans in Book I.

Allecto One of the Furies (deities who avenge sins). In Book IV, Allecto is among the Furies Juno sends to incite the Latin people to war against the Trojans.

Apollo Son of Jupiter and god of the sun. Apollo was born at Delos and helps the Trojans in their voyage when they stop there. Because he is often portrayed as an archer, many characters invoke Apollo's name before they fire a shaft in battle.

Cupid A son of Venus and the god of erotic desire. In Book I, Cupid (Eros in Greek mythology) disguises himself as Ascanius, Aeneas's son, and causes Dido to fall in love with Aeneas.

Juno The queen of the gods, the wife and sister of Jupiter, and the daughter of Saturn. Juno (Hera in Greek mythology) hates the Trojans because the Trojan man Paris decided that Venus, not Juno, is the most beautiful goddess. Juno, a patron of Carthage, knows that Aeneas's Roman descendants are destined to destroy Carthage. Throughout the epic, Juno takes out her anger on Aeneas. She is his primary divine antagonist.

Jupiter The king of the gods and the son of Saturn. The gods often struggle against one another in battles of will, but Jupiter's will reigns supreme. The *impersonal force of fate* refers to Jupiter's will. Therefore, Jupiter (also known as Jove, and called Zeus in Greek mythology) directs the general progress of Aeneas's destiny, ensuring that Aeneas is never permanently thrown off his course toward Italy. Jupiter is controlled and levelheaded compared to the volatility of Juno and Venus.

Mercury The messenger god. The other gods often send Mercury (Hermes in Greek mythology) on errands to Aeneas.

Minerva The goddess who protects the Greeks during the Trojan War and helps them conquer Troy. Like Juno, Minerva (Pallas Athena in Greek mythology) dislikes the Trojans because Paris judged Venus the most beautiful goddess.

Neptune God of the sea and generally an ally of Venus and Aeneas. Neptune (Poseidon in Greek mythology) calms the storm that opens the epic and conducts Aeneas safely on the last leg of his voyage.

Saturn The father of the gods. Saturn (Chronos in Greek mythology) was king of Olympus until his son Jupiter overthrew him.

Tiberinus The river god associated with the Tiber River, where Rome will eventually be built. At Tiberinus's suggestion, Aeneas travels upriver to make allies of the Arcadians.

Venus The goddess of love and the mother of Aeneas. Venus (Aphrodite in Greek mythology) is a benefactor of the Trojans. She helps her son whenever Juno tries to hurt him, causing conflict among the gods. Venus is also referred to as Cytherea, after the island Cythera where she was born and where her shrine is located.

Vulcan God of fire and the forge, and husband of Venus. Venus urges Vulcan (Hephaestus in Greek mythology) to craft a superior set of arms for Aeneas. The arms serve Aeneas well in his battle with Turnus.

CHARACTERS FROM HOMER'S *ILIAD* RELEVANT TO THE *AENEID*

Achilles The greatest of the Greek warriors. Achilles slew the Trojan hero Hector during the war. He is the tragic hero of the *Iliad*.

Agamemnon The leader of the Greek army at Troy and the king of Argos, a city in Greece. Upon his return from the war, Agamemnon is killed by his adulterous wife, Clytemnestra.

Andromachë Hector's wife. Andromachë survives the siege of Troy. She meets Aeneas in his wanderings, tells him her story, and advises him about his course to Italy.

Hector The greatest of the Trojan warriors. Hector is killed at Troy. Because Hector defends his native city to the death, he is a figure similar to Turnus.

Helen The most beautiful mortal woman. Helen is the wife of Menelaus. When Paris abducts her, he sparks the Trojan War.

Menelaus A Greek king who weds Helen, making a pact with her other suitors to fight anyone who tries to steal her. When Paris abducts Helen, the pact is invoked and the Trojan War begins.

Paris A Trojan prince. Paris is the son of Priam and Hecuba, and the brother of Hector. The handsomest of men, Paris is asked to judge which goddess is most beautiful: Venus, Juno, or Minerva. Venus promises to give him Helen as his wife in exchange for judging in her favor, so Paris selects Venus. The judgment of Paris makes Juno permanently furious at the Trojans. Paris sets off the Trojan War by stealing Helen from her Greek husband, Menelaus.

Priam The king of Troy. Priam is slain before Aeneas's eyes as the Greeks sack Troy.

Pyrrhus The son of Achilles. Pyrrhus, also called Neoptolemus, appears in Aeneas's account of the siege of Troy as the brutal murderer of Priam and Priam's sons.

Ulysses The hero of Homer's *Odyssey* and one of the captains of the Greek army that takes Troy. Ulysses (Odysseus in Greek lore), like Aeneas, must make a long and treacherous voyage before he finds home again. In the *Aeneid*, Virgil situates Aeneas by comparing his wanderings to Ulysses'.

THEMES IN THE *AENEID*

THE PRIMACY OF FATE Aeneas's course is preordained. His various sufferings and glories over the course of the epic merely postpone his unchangeable destiny. Often, fate is equated with the will of Jupiter, the most powerful of the gods. The development of characters in the epic has to do with how eagerly or reluctantly they submit to fate. Juno and Turnus first fight fate and eventually resign themselves to it, which allows the epic to arrive at its destined end. Dido desires Aeneas and cannot submit to fate, which dictates that she cannot be with him. Because she refuses to accept fate, she dies. Aeneas preserves his sanity as well as his own life and his men's lives by subordinating his desires to the demands of fate and the rules of piety. Virgil's Roman audience viewed fate as a religious principle that determines the course of history.

THE SUFFERING OF WANDERERS In ancient culture, familial loyalty and geographic origin were of crucial importance. Homeland was the source of identity. For ancient people, homelessness meant an instable life and identity. Homelessness, therefore, is itself a form of suffering. Virgil adds to the sufferings of the wandering Trojans by putting them in dangerous situations. On the sea, storms buffet their fleet. On land, the Trojans do not know where they are or if they belong. These long wanderings serve as a metaphor for life, which is a kind of constant wandering. Like gods, we and Virgil's Roman audience know what fate has in store for the Trojans, but the wandering characters themselves do not, just as we do not know what fate has in store for us.

THE GLORY OF ROME   Virgil intended the *Aeneid* to be a myth of Rome's origins. He wanted it to emphasize the grandeur of Rome and legitimize the success of an empire that had conquered most of the known world. Virgil works backward, suggesting that the political and social situation of his own day derive from the traditions of the Greek gods and heroes. In the *Aeneid*, order and good government triumph emphatically over the Italian people, whose world prior to the Trojans' arrival is characterized by war, chaos, and irrationality. Virgil connects Aeneas the conqueror with Augustus, whose empire was generally peaceful and well-ordered.

SYMBOLS IN THE *AENEID*

FLAMES   Fire symbolizes both destruction and erotic desire or love. Virgil suggests that destruction and love are connected. For example, Paris's desire for Helen eventually leads to the fires of the siege of Troy. When Dido confesses her love for Aeneas to her sister, she says, "I recognize / the signs of the old flame, of old desire" (IV.31–32). Dido also recalls her previous marriage in "the thought of the torch and the bridal bed" (IV.25). The flames that she sees now do not keep her warm, as the flames of her marriage did, but consume her mind. She finally dies "enflamed and driven mad" (IV.965).

HEARTH GODS   The hearth gods of Troy, or Penates, symbolize locality and ancestry. These tribal gods, who are associated specifically with the city of Troy, reside in the household hearth. Aeneas gathers them up along with his family when he departs from his devastated home.

IMPORTANT QUOTATIONS FROM THE *AENEID*

Roman, remember by your strength to rule
Earth's peoples—for your arts are to be these:
To pacify, to impose the rule of law,
To spare the conquered, battle down the proud.

Location: VI.1151–1154
Speaker: Anchises
Context: Anchises talks to his son Aeneas in the underworld, explaining the destiny of Rome

Virgil places his own political ideals in the mouth of Anchises, the wise father, who warns his son that even in its conquests, the Roman nation should be more merciful than violent. Anchises' words echo Virgil's beliefs about the values that should guide Rome—the same values he believes have guided him in his own life. Anchises justifies the Roman Empire's imperialism in the same way Aeneas and the Trojans justify settling in Rome: by arguing that they bring justice and law to the conquered. Modern critics and readers have interpreted such passages as propaganda for the Augustan regime. Virgil does voice the opinions of the regime, but he truly shared those opinions. For that reason, the line between propaganda and art in the *Aeneid* is a blurry one.

When two bulls lower heads and horns and charge
In deadly combat . . .

. . .

[They g]ore one another, bathing necks and humps
In sheets of blood, and the whole woodland bellows.
Just so Trojan Aeneas and the hero

Son of Daunus, battering shield on shield,
Fought with a din that filled the air of heaven.

Location: XII.972–982
Speaker: The narrator
Context: Virgil describes Aeneas and Turnus locked together in the heat of battle

This passage uses a literary device Virgil employs throughout the poem: the epic simile. Epic similes make extended comparisons between an element of action or a character and an abstract or external image or concept. Virgil often draws his similes from rural landscapes and farm life, and often uses the phrase "just so" as a connector. These similes give Virgil's writing a descriptive richness, lingering at great length on some detail that might seem inconsequential. Often, Virgil uses the similes to flesh out his characters. This particular epic simile describes the intense battle between Aeneas and Turnus. By comparing these two warriors to bulls, Virgil conveys the potent, animalistic nature of their struggle.

I sing of warfare and a man at war.
From the sea-coast of Troy in early days
He came to Italy by destiny,
To our Lavinian western shore,
A fugitive, this captain, buffeted
. . .
Till he could found a city and bring home
His gods to Laetium, land of the Latin race,
The Alban lords, and the high walls of Rome.
Tell me the causes now, O Muse, how galled
. . .
From her old wound, the queen of gods compelled him—
. . .
To undergo so many perilous days
And enter on so many trials. Can anger
Black as this prey on the minds of heaven?

Location: I.1–19
Speaker: The narrator
Context: In the opening lines of the epic, Virgil establishes himself as Homer's heir and introduces
　　Aeneas

Did you suppose, my father,
That I could tear myself away and leave you?
Unthinkable; how could a father say it?
Now if it pleases the powers about that nothing
Stand of this great city; if your heart
Is set on adding your own death and ours
To that of Troy, the door's wide open for it.

Location: II.857–863
Speaker: Aeneas
Context: Aeneas speaks these words before fleeing Troy with his father on his back. In these lines, he
　　expresses his loyalty to his father, Anchises

Amata tossed and turned with womanly
Anxiety and anger. Now [Allecto]

Plucked one of the snakes, her gloomy tresses,
And tossed it at the woman, sent it down
Her bosom to her midriff and her heart,
. . .
Slipping between her gown and her smooth breasts
. . .
While the infection first, like dew of poison
Fallen on her, pervaded all her senses,
Netting her bones in fire.

Location: VII. 474–490
Speaker: The narrator
Context: Virgil describes the way Allecto incites Amata's rage against Aeneas

AGAMEMNON

Aeschylus

Upon returning from a victory in Troy, a warrior is killed by his wife.

THE LIFE OF AESCHYLUS

Aeschylus was born in Greece near the end of the sixth century B.C., probably in 525 B.C. The Persian Wars raged during his lifetime, and Aeschylus fought in a number of the important engagements, including Marathon and the battle of Salamis, when the Greeks turned back the invaders. Aeschylus began writing tragedies at an early age. In 484 B.C., he won his first victory at the annual competition at Athens. Of the Greek dramatists whose work has survived, Aeschylus is the earliest, preceding both Sophocles and Euripides. Many critics believe he largely invented what we know as tragic drama. Prior to Aeschylus, plays still consisted of just a single actor and a chorus. Aeschylus is credited with adding more actors, thus opening up a new range of dramatic possibilities.

Aeschylus won first prize a remarkable thirteen times. He is said to have written more than seventy plays, of which only seven have come down to us, including such widely known works as *Prometheus Bound* and *The Seven Against Thebes*. The play *Agamemnon* is the first installment of a trilogy, the *Oresteia*. The second and third parts of the trilogy are *The Libation-Bearers* and *The Eumenides*. Some critics consider this trilogy the greatest Athenian tragedy ever written, most notably for the fineness of its poetry and the strength of its characters. Aeschylus died in 456 B.C. in the Greek colony at Gela, Sicily.

AGAMEMNON IN CONTEXT

The events of *Agamemnon* are rooted in stories of Agamemnon's history and of the Trojan War, stories that would have been familiar to the Athenian audience of Aeschylus's day. The vengefulness that suffuses the play is due to Agamemnon's history: Agamemnon's father, Atreus, cruelly murdered the children of his own brother, Thyestes, and then served them as food to the unwitting Thyestes. Only one of Thyestes's children, Aegisthus, survived. Thyestes cursed the house of Atreus. Agememnon's personal history is also bound up in the Trojan War, which began when a treacherous Trojan prince stole Helen, the wife of Agamemnon's brother. Before sailing to Troy, Agamemnon sacrificed his daughter, Iphigenia, to obtain favorable winds for his fleet. When the play begins, Agamemnon has just triumphed after ten long years of leading the Greeks in their war against the Trojans.

Aeschylus's play is far more than a new arrangement of a well-established tale. Most Greek authors worked with existing legends, but each invented and reinterpreted as he saw fit. For example, the poet Homer writes of Agamemnon's fate, but he never mentions Atreus's crime or the sacrifice of Iphigenia—aspects of the story that Aeschylus stresses. By showing us what motivates Agamemnon, Aeschylus creates a complex moral drama about compelling, sophisticated characters.

The next play in the *Oresteia* trilogy, *The Libation-Bearers*, continues Agamemnon's story. In it, Agamemnon's son, Orestes, returns to Argo and avenges his father by killing his mother, his mother's lover, and Agamemnon's cousin. In the final installment, *The Eumenides*, the Furies pursue Orestes, trying to punish him for his matricide. Orestes finds refuge in Athens, where the goddess Athena calls off the Furies and gives Orestes a trial by jury.

AGAMEMNON: KEY FACTS

Time and place written: Fifth century B.C. Athens	
Date of first publication: First produced in 458 B.C.	
Publisher: Unknown	
Type of Work: Play	
Genre: Tragedy	

Language: Ancient Greek	
Setting (time): The end of the Trojan War	
Setting (place): Argos, Greece	
Tone: Dramatic, stylized, formal	
Protagonist: Clytemnestra	
Antagonist: Agamemnon, Clytemnestra, Aegisthus	

AGAMEMNON: PLOT OVERVIEW

A watchman is on duty on the roof of the palace at Argos, waiting for a signal announcing the fall of Troy to the Greek armies. A beacon flashes, and the watchman joyfully runs to tell the news to Queen Clytemnestra. When he is gone, the Chorus, made up of the old men of Argos, enters and tells the story of how Paris, the Trojan prince, stole Helen, the wife of the Greek king Menelaus, leading to ten years of war between Greece and Troy. The Chorus recalls how Clytemnestra's husband, Agamemnon, (Menelaus's brother) sacrificed their daughter, Iphigenia, to the god Artemis to obtain a favorable wind for the Greek fleet.

The queen appears, and the Chorus asks her why she has ordered sacrifices in thanks. She tells them the news: Troy fell last night. The Chorus give thanks to the gods. A herald appears and confirms the tidings, describing the army's sufferings at Troy and giving thanks for a safe homecoming. Clytemnestra tells him to go back to Agamemnon and ask him to return swiftly, but before he departs, the Chorus asks him for news of Menelaus. The herald replies that a terrible storm engulfed the Greek fleet on the way home, and Menelaus and many others are missing.

The Chorus sings of the terrible destructive power of Helen's beauty. Agamemnon enters, riding in his chariot with Cassandra, a Trojan princess whom he has taken as his slave and concubine. Clytemnestra welcomes him, professing her love, and orders a carpet of purple robes spread in front of him as he enters the palace. Agamemnon is cold toward her. He says that to walk on the carpet would be an act of hubris, but she badgers him into walking on the robes.

The Chorus expresses a sense of foreboding. Clytemnestra comes outside to order Cassandra inside. The Trojan princess will not speak, and the queen leaves her in frustration. Then Cassandra does speak, uttering incoherent prophecies about a curse on the house of Agamemnon. She tells the Chorus that their king will die, that she will die, and that an avenger will come. Resigned to her fate, she enters the house. The Chorus hears Agamemnon cry out in pain. As they debate what to do, the doors open, and Clytemnestra appears, standing over the corpses of her husband and Cassandra, both of whom she has killed. She says she has killed Agamemnon to avenge Iphigenia. Her lover, Aegisthus, joins her. He is Agamemnon's cousin. (Aegisthus's siblings were killed and cooked by Atreus, Agamemnon's father.) Clytemnestra and Aegisthus take over the government. The Chorus declares that Clytemnestra's son Orestes will return from exile to avenge his father.

CHARACTERS IN *AGAMEMNON*

Aegisthus Agamemnon's cousin and Clytemnestra's lover. Aegisthus's father and Agamemnon's father were rivals for the throne. Agamemnon's father cooked his rival's children—Aegisthus's brothers—and served them to him for dinner. Aegisthus survived and went into exile, waiting to take revenge for the terrible crime.

Agamemnon The King of Argos and the commander of the Greek armies during the siege of Troy. Agamemnon is Clytemnestra's husband and Menelaus's older brother. A great warrior, Agamemnon sacrificed his daughter, Iphigenia, in order to obtain a favorable wind to carry the Greek fleet to Troy. Agamemnon makes a brief appearance on stage, during which he behaves arrogantly.

Cassandra A Trojan princess. Agamemnon captures Cassandra and carries her to Argos as his slave and mistress. Cassandra was once Apollo's lover. He gave her the gift of prophecy, but when she refused to bear his child, Apollo punished her by making all around her disbelieve her predictions.

Chorus The elder citizens of Argos who were too old to fight in the Trojan War. They advised Queen Clytemnestra during Agamemnon's absence and provide commentary on the action of the play.

Clytemnestra   The play's protagonist. Clytemnestra is Agamemnon's wife and has ruled Argos in his absence. She plans his murder with ruthless determination and feels no guilt after committing it. She is convinced she is right to kill the man who killed her daughter. Although she is a sympathetic character, her crime is tainted by her entanglement with Aegisthus.

The Herald   The man who tells the Chorus of Agamemnon's homecoming. An ardent patriot, the Herald is ecstatic to see the home he thought he had left forever. He provides vivid descriptions of the horrors of the war against Troy.

The Watchman   The man who speaks the opening lines of the play. He is joyful at his king's return, but also gripped with a sense of foreboding.

THEMES IN *AGAMEMNON*

THE IMPOSSIBILITY OF UNDERSTANDING CAUSE AND EFFECT   Aeschylus portrays his characters as links in a long chain of cause and effect that they cannot understand. Their actions cannot be interpreted as discrete but must be viewed in the context of what comes before and after them. Thyestes's curse on the house of Atreus soured the fortunes of Agamemnon and his family. Clytemnestra kills her husband to avenge the death of Iphigenia—and possibly to vent her jealousy of Cassandra. Aegisthus longs to avenge the deaths of his siblings, perpetrated by Agamemnon's father. Orestes will kill his mother and uncle to avenge the death of Agamemnon. The Furies will chase Orestes, seeking vengeance. Everything the characters do is either the effect or the cause of a murder.

The audience understands the past, present, and future of these characters in a way that the characters themselves do not. The characters, who cannot see their own place in the chain, seem innocent and misguided. They long to end the cycle of violence, and they commit murder in part because they think this murder will be the one to end the cycle. Clytemnestra believes that once she has killed Agamemnon, she will have settled their score and wiped the slate clean. After the murder, she says she will now rest "content / that [she] swept from these halls / the murder, the sin, and the fury," and optimistically wonders "[i]f this is the end of suffering." Likewise, Aegisthus thinks he has closed a chapter by finally punishing Agamemnon for the horrific crimes of his father. Because the audience knows the violence will continue, the hopefulness of Clytemnestra and Agamemnon seems tragic.

THE ROLE OF WOMEN   Characters object when Clytemnestra murders Agamemnon partly because such a deed is "unwomanly." The confusion of gender roles began when Agamemnon left his wife in charge of ruling his kingdom in his absence. Although the Chorus presents his entrustment of power as due tradition—"For when the man is gone and his throne void, his right / falls to the prince's lady, and honor must be given"—a strong current of feeling runs against this official line, presenting Clytemnestra's rule as backward and undesirable. In the opening speech of the play, given by the watchman, we get the sense that people consider Clytemnestra perverse. The watchman looks forward to ending "a lady's / male strength of heart," as if Clytemnestra should not posses strength, a male attribute. References to Clytemnestra's unfitness for the job punctuate the text. For example, the Chorus argues that flawed, flighty judgment is a woman's trait. Clytemnestra is aware of this perception and tries to reassure her people of her femininity. She calls herself "a woman merely," as if to suggest how meek she considers her gender. To the point of exaggeration, she says the whole of her happiness as a wife depends on the return of her husband. By drawing upon and seeming to agree with conventional ideas about womanhood, Clytemnestra masks her bloody intentions.

THE DIFFICULTY OF NEGOTIATING PUBLIC AND PRIVATE SPHERES   Aeschylus demonstrates the difficulties of negotiating public and private spheres—a particular challenge for the leaders of men. Agamemnon is especially terrible at juggling his public and private roles. After Paris steals Helen, Agamemnon lets his private life motivate him, leading the youth of Greece in battle for a personal cause: the recovery of his brother's wife. The outspoken Chorus sullenly reminds us that Agamemnon put the needs of his family over the needs of his people, in the end losing countless men for the sake of one woman. After committing himself to this private cause, Agamemnon chooses the public over the private, sacrificing his daughter, Iphigenia, for the sake of his fleet. Yet this civic-minded decision might hurt Greece more than it helps it, for it leads to Agamemnon's death, which deprives Greece of a strong leader.

Aeshchylus admits that it is impossible for Agamemnon to negotiate the public and the private successfully, but he judges Clytemnestra more harshly. When she murders her husband, she settles a private score instead of thinking of her kingdom, depriving her people of a strong—not to mention legitimate—ruler. Aegisthus, whom she installs as leader, comes off less than heroic. He is also troubling from a dynastic standpoint. At the end of the play, he receives nothing but the Chorus's scorn.

SYMBOLS IN *AGAMEMNON*

NETS   References to nets recur constantly in *Agamemnon*, from fishing nets, to spider webs, to woven robes, to a viper's encircling coils. Nets stand for Clytemnestra's stratagems. She boasts, "as fishermen cast their huge circling nets, I spread / deadly abundance of rich robes and caught [Agamemnon] fast." Nets also symbolize fate, which entangles people in a scheme they cannot see.

HARE   Recounting the events that led up to Iphigenia's sacrifice, the Chorus notes that eagles "tore a hare, ripe, bursting with young unborn yet." The violation of the hare angered the goddess Artemis, who, "sick at the eagles' feasting," demanded recompense from Agamemnon. The hare with its young cruelly torn from it symbolizes Clytemnestra. Aeschylus also associates Clytemnestra with other animals, including the entangling viper, the ever-vigilant watchdog, and the lion mistakenly thought tame until it erupts in violence.

IMPORTANT QUOTATIONS FROM *AGAMEMNON*

The citizens speak: their voice is dull with hatred.
The curse of the people must be paid for.
There lurks for me in the hooded night
terror of what may be told me.
The gods fail not to mark
those who have killed many.
The black Furies stalking the man
fortunate beyond all right
wrench back again the set of his life
and drop him down to darkness. There among
the ciphers there is no more comfort
in power. And the vaunt of high glory
is bitterness; for God's thunderbolts
crash on the towering mountains.

Location: Lines 456–470
Speaker: The Chorus
Context: The Chorus concludes a long description of the tragic losses of the Trojan War

In a bitter speech "dull with hatred," the Chorus indicts its king, Agamemnon. Because of one foreign woman who happens to be Agamemnon's sister-in-law, Agamemnon has sent the young men of Greece to their deaths. The Chorus threatens Agamemnon, saying "[t]he curse of the people must be paid for"—implying that the payment for the curse must be the life of the man who brought it upon the people. Because of this threat, it is possible to argue that by murdering Agamemnon, Clytemnestra carries out not only her own will, but the will of the people. It is even possible to argue that the gods approve of what Clytemnestra does. As the Chorus says, "[t]he gods fail not to mark / those who have killed many."

The Chorus also suggests that life is not any better for kings than it is for peasants. Being close to the gods might seem ideal, but it means that you are an easy target for their wrath.

Now it is I you doom to be cast out from my city
with men's hate heaped and curses roaring in my ears.

Yet look upon this dead man; you would not cross him once
when with no thought more than as if a beast had died,
when his ranged pastures swarmed with the deep fleece of flocks,
he slaughtered like a victim his own child, my pain
grown into love, to charm away the winds of Thrace.
Were you not then bound to hunt him then clear of this soil
for the guilt stained upon him?

Location: Lines 1412–1420
Speaker: Clytemnestra
Context: Clytemnestra defends her murder of Agamemnon to the Chorus

With great eloquence and confidence, Clytemnestra justifies killing Agamemnon on the grounds that he sacrificed their daughter, Iphigenia. Instead of accepting the guilt the Chorus attributes to her, she says Agamemnon is the guilty one. Then she goes on the offensive, accusing her listeners of wrongfully allowing his crime to go unpunished. This speech is typical of Clytemnestra. Throughout the play, she is unflappable, implacable, regal, and surefooted. Instead of jeopardizing her vengeance by becoming excited, fearful, or reluctant when Agamemnon returns, she calmly and rationally proceeds step by step. Her careful approach reinforces the nets' symbolism, indicating that she has laid her plan with patience. Nothing could be further from the images of wild beasts with which the Chorus and Cassandra associate her. In this passage, Clytemnestra's attitude contrasts with Agamemnon's easy slaughter of Iphigenia. In describing how and why Iphigenia was sacrificed ("to charm away the winds of Thrace"), Clytemnestra either knowingly or unknowingly links her daughter to the countless others who were sacrificed to the trivial cause of retrieving Helen—an association guaranteed to stir the sympathy of the Chorus, which hates Agamemnon for sacrificing so many men.

I ask the gods some respite from the weariness
of this watchtime measured by years. I lie awake
elbowed upon the Atreidae's roof dogwise to mark
the grand processionals of all the stars of night
burdened with winter and again with heat for me,
dynasties in their shining blazoned on the air,
these stars, upon their wane and when the rest arise.

I wait; to read the meaning in that beacon light,
a blaze of fire to carry out of Troy the rumor
and outcry of its capture; to such end a lady's
male strength of heart in its high confidence ordains.

Location: Lines 1–11
Speaker: The watchman
Context: The watchman begins the play, speaking of Agamemnon's return

---

Daughter of Leda, you who kept my house for me,
there is one way your welcome matched my absence well.
You strained it to great length. Yet properly to praise
me thus belongs by right to other lips, not yours.
And all this—do not try in woman's ways to make
me delicate, nor, as if I were some Asiatic
bow down to earth and with wide mouth cry out to me,
nor cross my path with jealousy by strewing the ground
with robes. Such state becomes the gods, and none beside.

I am a mortal, a man. . .

Location: Lines 914–923
Speaker: Agamemnon
Context: Agamemnon responds to his wife's flattering welcome

Look there, see what is hovering above the house,
so small and young, imaged as in the shadow of dreams,
like children almost, killed by those most dear to them,
and their hands filled with their own flesh, as food to eat.
I see them holding out the inward parts, the vitals,
oh pitiful, that meat their father tasted of . . .
I tell you: There is one that plots vengeance for this,
the strengthless lion rolling in his master's bed,
who keeps, ah me, the house against his lord's return;
my lord too, now that I wear the slave's yoke on my neck.

Location: Lines 1217–1226
Speaker: Cassandra
Context: Cassandra tells the Chorus what she sees of the past and future

ALICE IN WONDERLAND

Lewis Caroll

A girl falls asleep and dreams of a series of adventures.

THE LIFE OF LEWIS CARROLL

Charles Lutwidge Dodgson, who gained fame under the pen name Lewis Carroll, was born on January 27, 1832, near the remote village of Daresbury, Cheshire, in central England. Carroll began his formal education as a boarder at nearby Richmond School. Later, he attended the famous Rugby School, where he achieved academic success but disliked the rough and tumble life. In 1851, Carroll moved to Oxford to continue his studies at Christ Church, where he excelled. Taking a vow of celibacy, Carroll was ordained as a deacon in 1861. He never proceeded to the priesthood, partly because of a slight stammer that affected his speaking.

In 1855, Carroll was appointed mathematical lecturer at Christ Church, a post he held until 1881. During those years, Carroll pursued two favorite diversions: photography and theater. Photography was a new and complicated process at the time, but Carroll mastered this mystery of chemistry and art and produced some of the finest amateur images of the period. He attended hundreds of theatrical performances in his lifetime, filling his frequent trips to London with plays. He counted among his friends many theatrical luminaries, including the actress Ellen Terry (1848–1928) and her family, and he helped launch the theater careers of several young girls by introducing them to actors and managers.

Carroll's publishing career proceeded along two tracks. Under his real name, Charles Dodgson, he wrote books on mathematics and logic, and penned articles on parliamentary representation and other serious topics. Under his pen name, Lewis Carroll, he wrote stories and poems, and invented games and puzzles. In a series of comic pamphlets that he wrote on Oxford controversies, he succeeded in combining his sense of humor with his interest in the college and university. Carroll's best-selling works were *Alice in Wonderland* (1865) and its 1872 sequel, *Through the Looking-Glass and What Alice Found There*.

Carroll's "child-friends" (his own term) brought him great joy. For them, he wrote letters, told stories, drew pictures, and even gave lessons in logic. They were frequent models for his photography, and a few of them posed nude for his photos. Child nudity was seen differently in the Victorian age than it is in ours; nude children were a symbol of purity and a popular image in Victorian art. Even so, some Victorians felt that a nude photograph was more dangerous than a drawing, and some believed that images of nude children worsened the problem of child prostitution in urban areas. Carroll was aware of the delicate issues surrounding nude photography, and he never took such photos without the mother's consent and the child's enthusiasm.

These nude photos coupled with Carroll's many friendships with children have prompted some people to wonder if Carroll engaged in pedophilic behavior. The nature of his relationships with young girls remains uncertain, debated to this day by contemporary scholars. Some critics cite his unusual relationship with Alice Liddell as the main reason for suspicion, especially because Alice's mother abruptly ended her daughter's relationship with Carroll in 1863, when Alice was eleven years old. Mrs. Liddell also destroyed all correspondence between Carroll and the girl. It is not known why she acted as she did.

Carroll continued to befriend young girls, many of whom wrote enthusiastically of his loving, concerned manner and suggested nothing about a sexual relationship. The term child-friend coined by Carroll himself, may be particularly misleading. Some of these child-friends were in their twenties and thirties. However, some of Carroll's child-friends ceased to be of interest to him once they reached the age of twelve. Carroll's most lasting legacy is his thorough understanding of and respect for the child psyche. Carroll died in Guildford, England in 1898. He was mourned by his friends and family, and by a world of children who had grown to love his writings.

ALICE IN WONDERLAND IN CONTEXT

In 1856, Carroll met the children of Henry George Liddell (1811–1898), the new Dean of Christ Church. He was especially taken with Liddell's four-year-old daughter, Alice (1852–1934), and in the ensuing years, the Liddell children became his frequent companions. He posed them for photographs, keeping them still for the long exposure periods by telling stories, and he took them for walks around Oxford.

On July 4, 1862, Carroll took Alice Liddell and her sisters, Lorina (1849–1930) and Edith (1854–1876), on a rowing trip on the River Thames. On the trip, he told them the story of *Alice's Adventures Under Ground*, which Alice begged him to write down. Carroll, whose previous literary output had primarily consisted of verse and stories in newspapers and comic magazines, showed friends the manuscript of *Alice's Adventures*, which he had illustrated with his own drawings. His friends encouraged him to have the manuscript published. Carroll rewrote the story, removing some private references and adding several episodes, and in 1865 published it under the pseudonym Lewis Carroll as *Alice's Adventures in Wonderland*. He replaced his own illustrations with those of the professional cartoonist John Tenniel (1820–1914). It became one of the best-loved novels ever published.

ALICE IN WONDERLAND: KEY FACTS

Full title: Alice's Adventures in Wonderland	
Time and place written: 1862–1865; Oxford, England	
Date of first publication: 1865	
Publisher: Macmillan	
Type of work: Novel	
Genre: Fiction, children's novel, fantasy	
Language: English	
Setting (time): 1859	
Setting (place): A riverbank in England, and the dream world of Wonderland	
Tense: Past	
Tone: Friendly, indulgent, serious, satirical	
Narrator: Anonymous omniscient narrator in the third person	
Point of view: The narrator's	
Protagonist: Alice	
Antagonist: The Queen of Hearts	

ALICE IN WONDERLAND: PLOT OVERVIEW

Alice sees a White Rabbit carrying a watch and worrying aloud about his lateness. She follows him down a rabbit-hole into a strange world. She drinks from a bottle labeled "DRINK ME" and shrinks. She eats a cake labeled "EAT ME" and grows until she is nine feet tall. Alice longs to get through a tiny door and to the garden she can see through it, but she cannot because of her great height. In her dismay, she cries. She fans herself with a fan dropped by the White Rabbit, which causes her to shrink again. Now tiny, Alice swims in a pool of her own tears. Along with a band of birds and animals, she swims ashore. The animals run a chaotic Caucus-Race in order to dry off.

The White Rabbit reappears and mistakes Alice for his housemaid, sending her on an errand to his house. In the White Rabbit's house, Alice drinks from another bottle and becomes so huge that she fills up the house. The Rabbit and his servants, believing her to be a monster, pelt her with pebbles that turn into cakes. Alice eats one, shrinks again, and escapes. She encounters a caterpillar smoking a hookah on top of a mushroom. The Caterpillar demands to know who she is, and Alice realizes that, after all of the changes she has endured, she has no idea how to answer his question. The Caterpillar tells her that the mushroom can help her get back to her old size: one side will make her smaller, and the other will make her larger. Alice nibbles at one side and grows a little bigger.

In a nearby house, Alice finds an ugly Duchess abusing her baby. She also meets a grinning Cheshire Cat. Alice rescues the squealing baby, who promptly turns into a pig. The Cheshire Cat suddenly appears in a tree. His body, head, and smile appear and disappear one at a time and without warning, but otherwise he seems reasonable enough. The cat directs Alice to the houses of the Mad Hatter and the March Hare. The Hare and Hatter, along with a sleepy Dormouse, are having a tea party, which Alice joins despite their assertions that there is "no room." The partygoers and Alice exchange various nonsensical remarks and insults before Alice gets offended and walks off. She ends up back in the long hall where her adventure started. She eats some mushroom and shrinks enough to go through the little door into the garden.

The garden belongs to the Queen of Hearts, who arrives with a procession of cards and the nervous-looking White Rabbit. The Queen invites Alice to play croquet. The game is difficult, since the balls are made of hedgehogs and the mallets of flamingoes. The Queen constantly orders that the players be beheaded. The Duchess arrives and acts artificially sweet to Alice, clinging to her uncomfortably. The game ends when the Queen has sentenced all the players to death except herself, the King, and Alice — although the King quietly pardons the criminals. The Queen orders a Gryphon to take Alice to see the Mock Turtle, a melancholy creature who tells Alice about his schooldays beneath the sea.

The Gryphon takes Alice to the courthouse for the trial of the Knave of Hearts, who has been accused of stealing a tray of tarts. Over the course of the trial, Alice begins growing again. The Queen decides to sentence the Knave before the jury has reached a verdict, but Alice, now full grown, tells her she can't do that. When the Queen orders her beheaded, Alice declares she is not afraid of a pack of cards, and the cards come flying at her. She awakens to find that her sister is brushing leaves out of her face. She tells her sister about her dream. Alice's sister thinks about how Alice will someday delight her own children with fanciful stories.

CHARACTERS IN *ALICE IN WONDERLAND*

Ada An acquaintance of Alice's. Ada does not appear in the book, but Alice refers to her when confused about her own identity. Alice reasons that she could not be Ada, because Ada has ringlets, and she does not.

Alice The protagonist of the novel. An English girl of about seven, Alice first feels bewildered in Wonderland but gradually gains self-confidence. Class-conscious and fond of showing off her knowledge, Alice is also polite, kindhearted, and curious.

Bill A lizard. The White Rabbit sends Bill down the chimney in an attempt to remove the overgrown Alice from it. Alice kicks him into the sky, but the other creatures revive him with brandy.

Caterpillar A hookah-smoking creature who sits atop a mushroom and questions Alice. The Caterpillar is severe and somewhat discourteous, but he does offer Alice advice.

Cheshire Cat The Duchess's grinning cat. The Cheshire Cat claims to be mad, but it is one of the more reasonable creatures in Wonderland.

Cook A servant of the Duchess's. The Cook makes soup with vast amounts of pepper and then hurls pots and dishes at the Duchess and her Baby.

Dodo The leader of the Caucus-race. Dodo is loosely based on the author, whose slight stammer caused him to pronounce his last name "Do-Do-Dodgson."

Duchess A violent, horribly ugly woman. The Duchess enjoys finding nonsensical morals in everything.

Hatter A guest at the tea party hosted by the March Hare. Because of a quarrel with Time, it is always six o'clock (tea-time) for the Hatter. At the knave's trial, the March Hare offers disjointed and nonsensical testimony.

King of Hearts The nervous husband of the Queen of Hearts. The King makes an incompetent judge at the trial of the Knave. He is self-centered, stubborn, and generally unlikable.

March Hare The host of the tea party. His name derives from the expression "mad as a March hare." He is combative and somewhat mournful.

Queen of Hearts The dictatorial, violent ruler of Wonderland. She solves all problems by ordering a beheading, but we learn from the Gryphon that she never actually executes anyone.

White Rabbit A nervous character of moderately important rank in Wonderland. At first he is hurried and flustered, worried that he is keeping the Duchess waiting, but later he seems comfortable in the presence of royalty.

THEMES IN *ALICE IN WONDERLAND*

THE DIFFICULTY OF MATURATION Alice repeatedly expresses confusion about who she is. As she tells the Caterpillar, she knew who she was when she woke up in the morning, but she has been through so many changes since then that she's not sure anymore. The physical changes Alice endures—suddenly growing to nine feet tall or folding up like a telescope to become as small as a mouse—reflect the unpredictable, often baffling physical changes that a child goes through as she enters adolescence—changes that often throw the child's notion of identity into disorder. During one of her tall phases, Alice begins to think about something she will do when she grows up and then realizes, to her dismay, that she is already as "grown up" as she'll ever be. Like many adolescents whose bodies mature before their minds do, Alice does not feel ready to be grown up.

THE SILLINESS OF DIDACTIC CHILDREN'S LITERATURE In the Victorian era, when the *Alice* novels were written, most literature for children was extremely didactic. Children's stories were meant to teach a moral lesson, not to delight or amuse. In these stories, virtuous children and animals were rewarded, while bad or disobedient children were punished with extremely gruesome and painful deaths. These stories were preachy, sentimental, and often badly written. Carroll's stories about Alice achieved such popularity in part because they avoid the formula of didactic literature. Carroll makes irreverent jokes; never talks down to children; refuses to teach any moral lessons; portrays grownups as baffling, violent, absurd creatures; and creates a heroine who is often selfish, sulky, judgmental, and disobedient.

Carroll makes his distaste for didactic literature clear by parodying many of its then-famous elements. Many of the poems in the *Alice* novels—"How Doth the Little Crocodile" and "You Are Old, Father William," for example—are direct, irreverent parodies of sentimental poems that children like Alice were often forced to memorize. Characters like the Duchess, who insists on finding a moral in everything, reveal Carroll's scorn for preaching to children. Carroll suggests that the Victorian stories of his day are utterly ineffective as educational tools. When Alice is confronted with a bottle labeled "DRINK ME," she remembers the cautionary tales she has read in which children die from drinking poison, but she cheerfully decides that since the bottle is not marked "Poison," it must be safe to drink from it.

THE RELATIONSHIP BETWEEN SOUND AND SENSE Much of the misunderstanding and humor in *Alice in Wonderland* comes from the discrepancy between the sound of a phrase and its sense, or meaning. The creatures who live in Wonderland constantly manipulate, change, and misunderstand the meaning of words, phrases, proverbs, and poems. This is partially because the creatures are irrational and absurd, but it is also because absurdity is inherent in language. A great deal of idiomatic English is based on rules and meaning whose origins, if any, have been lost. Words and phrases—especially idioms and proverbs—that seem unremarkable to native speakers of English often seem completely bizarre to someone who is learning English. When the Wonderland creatures speak to Alice, they demonstrate the arbitrary relationships between sound and sense, frequently suggesting that if two words sound the same ("lessen" and "lesson," for example), they must have the same meaning. They also insist on absurdly literal interpretations of almost all words and concepts. For example, the White Queen insists that her lady's maid can have jam tomorrow and yesterday but never today, because today is never tomorrow or yesterday.

SYMBOLS IN *ALICE IN WONDERLAND*

THE CAUCUS-RACE The Caucus-Race symbolizes the state of modern politics. In *Alice in Wonderland*, it is a pointless race with no end, no beginning, and prizes for everyone who participates, which suggests that political processes often disintegrate into a lot of people running around and getting excited for no reason, and insisting on being rewarded for it. The race also suggests all strange adult practices that seem pointless and illogical to children.

THE GRYPHON Carroll describes neither the Gryphon nor the Mock Turtle in the text. In the case of the Gryphon, he instructs the reader to "look at the picture." Tenniel's drawing shows the mythical beast with the head of an eagle and the body of a lion. In medieval times, gryphons symbolized Christ's embodiment of both man and God. Gryphons, who also symbolized vigilant attention, are the emblem of Trinity College, a college of Oxford, where Carroll lived and worked.

IMPORTANT QUOTATIONS FROM *ALICE IN WONDERLAND*

"I—I hardly know, Sir, just at present—at least I know who I was when I got up this morning, but I think I must have been changed several times since then."

Location: Chapter V
Speaker: Alice
Context: The Caterpillar asks who Alice is

In response to the Caterpillar's imperious questioning, Alice says she hardly knows who she is. In one sense, this passage reveals Alice's somewhat childish idea that identity and appearance are inextricably linked. Earlier, she decided that she couldn't possibly be her friend Ada, because Ada has ringlets in her hair and Alice does not. As Alice will discover, this method of determining identity is not very useful in Wonderland. The word *changed* means both physical change and mental change. By combining the two meanings, Carroll plays with words, as creatures in Wonderland do.

"If there's no meaning in it," said the King, "that saves a world of trouble, you know, as we needn't find any. And yet I don't know . . . I seem to see some meaning in them, after all. '—said I could not swim—' you can't swim, can you?" . . . The Knave shook his head sadly. . . . "All right, so far . . . 'We know it to be true'—that's the jury, of course— 'If she should push the matter on'—that must be the Queen— 'What would become of you?' —What, indeed! . . .Then again—'before she had this fit'—you never had fits, my dear, I think?" he said to the Queen.
"Never!" said the Queen, furiously, throwing an inkstand at the Lizard as she spoke.

Location: Chapter XII
Speaker: The narrator
Context: The King interprets the Knave's verses

At moments, the King is startlingly like a parody of modern-day literary critics. Carroll could not have predicted the various and sometimes wild ways critics would interpret his work—*Alice* has been subjected to every kind interpretation imaginable, from economic to feminist to psychedelic—but if he had, he might have answered them by writing a character like the King, who projects his own agenda onto texts, interpreting them in the way that best suits his interests. After hearing verses read out in court, verses flush with ambiguous pronouns and phrases, the King comes up with an interpretation that is clearly absurd. Carroll emphasizes that the King's interpretive work stems not from a faithful reading of the verses, but from the King's own agenda. When the King comes to the line "before she had this fit," a line that applies perfectly to the Queen, he pulls up short, unwilling to apply the insulting line to his temperamental wife. Her immediate fit emphasizes the silliness of the King's reading.

"If everybody minded their own business," the Duchess said, in a hoarse growl, "the world would go round a deal faster than it does."
"Which would not be an advantage," said Alice, who felt very glad to get an opportunity of showing off a little of her knowledge. "Just think what work it would make with the day and night! You see the earth takes twenty-four hours to turn round on its axis—"

"Talking of axes," said the Duchess, *"chop off her head!"*

Location: Chapter VI
Speaker: The narrator
Context: Alice visits the Duchess

"And how many hours a day did you do lessons?" said Alice, in a hurry to change the subject.
"Ten hours the first day," said the Mock Turtle, *"nine the next, and so on."*
"What a curious plan!" exclaimed Alice.
"That's the reason they're called lessons," the Gryphon remarked, *"because they lessen from day to day."*

Location: Chapter IX
Speaker: The narrator
Context: The Gryphon explains his childhood, punning in the process

ALL QUIET ON THE WESTERN FRONT

Erich Maria Remarque

A young German soldier loses his idealism, his friends, and finally his own life fighting on the French front during World War I.

THE LIFE OF ERICH MARIA REMARQUE

Erich Maria Remarque was born in Osnabrück, Germany, in 1898. In 1916, he was drafted into the German army to fight in World War I, in which he was badly wounded. Ten years after the war ended, he published *Im Westen Nichts Neues*, translated into English a year later and published as *All Quiet on the Western Front*.

After Adolf Hitler's rise to power in Germany in the early 1930s, the fiercely nationalistic Nazi regime attacked *All Quiet on the Western Front* and Remarque as unpatriotic. Despite Nazi hostilities toward him, in 1931 Remarque published a sequel to *All Quiet on the Western Front* entitled *The Road Back*, which is about the postwar experience of German citizens. This work provoked further hostility from the Nazis, and in 1932 Remarque fled to Switzerland with his wife, Jutta Zambona. In 1933, the Nazis banned Remarque's two novels and held a bonfire to burn copies of the books.

In 1939, Remarque immigrated to the United States. He obtained American citizenship in 1947. The Nazis killed Remarque's sister during World War II, in part because of her relationship to him. In 1951, Remarque and his wife divorced. In the Unites States, Remarque had a tempestuous affair with the actress Marlene Dietrich, which inspired his novel *Arch of Triumph*. In 1958, he married the film star Paulette Goddard. Remarque and Goddard eventually left the United States and moved to Porto Ranco, Switzerland, where Remarque died in 1970.

ALL QUIET ON THE WESTERN FRONT IN CONTEXT

When Remarque wrote *All Quiet on the Western Front*, the overwhelmingly majority of literary war stories in print romanticized combat. Very few novels, most notably Stephen Crane's *The Red Badge of Courage* (1895), had explored the violence and brutality of war in a realistic light. In the staunchly antiwar *All Quiet on the Western Front*, Remarque strips the typical romanticism from the war narrative and presents a grimly realistic version of a soldier's experience.

All Quiet on the Western Front won critical acclaim and immediately became an international success. An American film based on the book was released in 1930. None of Remarque's other works have approached the popularity of *All Quiet on the Western Front*. The novel and its first film adaptation are still influential as antiwar works and important chronicles of World War I. One of the remarkable aspects of the novel's success in England and America is that *All Quiet on the Western Front* deals with the experiences of German soldiers—detested enemies of the English and Americans during World War I and World War II. The positive American and English reception suggests that the novel speaks for all soldiers who suffered through the horrors of World War I.

ALL QUIET ON THE WESTERN FRONT: KEY FACTS

Time and place written: Late 1920s; Berlin

Date of first publication: 1928

Publisher: A. G. Ullstein in Germany; Little, Brown in the United States

Type of work: Novel

Genre: War novel, historical novel, social protest novel

Language: German

Setting (time): Late World War I: 1917–1918

Setting (place): The German/French front

Tense: Present; occasionally past during flashbacks. The unnamed narrator at the end of the novel uses the past tense

Tone: Empathetic, melancholy, disillusioned

Narrator: First person; third person during the two paragraphs following Paul's death

Point of view: Paul Bäumer's

Protagonist: Paul Bäumer

Antagonist: Patriotism; war

ALL QUIET ON THE WESTERN FRONT: PLOT OVERVIEW

Paul Bäumer, a young German man of nineteen, is a soldier in the German army, fighting on the French front in World War I. He voluntarily joined the army along with his friends after listening to the stirring, patriotic speeches of his teacher, Kantorek. Paul and his friends endured ten weeks of brutal training at the hands of the petty, cruel Corporal Himmelstoss. Eventually, they realized that the ideals of nationalism and patriotism that inspired them to enlist are simply empty clichés. They no longer believe that war is glorious or honorable, and they live in constant physical terror.

Paul's company receives a short reprieve after two weeks of fighting. Of the original 150-man company, only eighty are still alive. Paul and his friends visit Kemmerich, a former classmate who recently had a leg amputated after contracting gangrene. Kemmerich is slowly dying. Müller, another former classmate, wants Kemmerich's boots for himself. Paul tries to believe that this request is not insensitive. Like the other soldiers, Müller sees a dying man and has the pragmatic realization that dead men don't need boots. Surviving the agony of war, Paul thinks, forces you to remove yourself from emotions like grief, sympathy, and fear. Soon after, Paul returns to Kemmerich's bedside. Kemmerich asks Paul to take his boots to Müller. Paul goes to find a doctor, and when he comes back, Kemmerich is dead.

A group of new recruits comes to reinforce the company. Paul's friend Kat produces a beef and bean stew that impresses them. Kat says that if all the men in an army, including the officers, were paid the same wage and given the same food, wars would end immediately. Kropp, another of Paul's former classmates, says the leaders of nations should fight out their disagreements with clubs. They discuss the way petty, insignificant people become powerful and arrogant during war. Tjaden, a member of Paul's company, announces that the cruel Corporal Himmelstoss has been ordered to fight at the front as punishment for torturing recruits.

At night, the men go on a harrowing mission to lay barbed wire at the front. Pounded by artillery, they hide in a graveyard, where the force of the shelling causes buried corpses to emerge from their graves. The soldiers who survive return to their camp, where they think about what they will do at the end of the war. Paul worries that if the war did end, he wouldn't know what to do with himself. The men see Himmelstoss; Tjaden moons him.

The company is caught in a bloody battle with a group of Allied infantrymen. Men are blown apart, and limbs are severed from torsos. Giant rats pick at the dead and the wounded. Paul feels that he must become an animal in battle, trusting only his instincts. Only thirty-two of the eighty men in the company survive the battle. The men are given a short reprieve at a field depot. Paul and some of his friends go for a swim and meet some French girls. Paul desperately wishes to recapture his innocence with a woman who does not belong to an army brothel.

Paul receives seventeen days of leave and goes home to see his family. He feels awkward and oppressed in his hometown, unable to discuss his traumatic experiences with anyone. He learns that his mother is dying of cancer and that Kantorek, his patriotic teacher, has been conscripted as a soldier. Learning of his teacher's fate gives him a certain cold satisfaction. Paul visits Kemmerich's mother and lies, telling her Kemmerich's death was instant and painless. At the end of his leave, Paul spends some time at a training camp near a group of Russian prisoners of war. Paul feels that the Russians are people just like him.

Paul is sent back to his company and reunited with his friends. The Kaiser, the German emperor, pays a visit to the front. It disappoints the men to see that the Kaiser is merely a short man with a weak voice. In battle, Paul gets separated from his company and must hide in a shell hole. A French soldier jumps into the shell hole with him, and Paul instinctively stabs him. As the man dies slowly and painfully, Paul is overcome with remorse. He bandages the soldiers wounds and tells him he did not mean to kill him. Hours later, after the soldier has died, Paul looks through his things and finds that the soldier's name was Gérard Duval. Duval had a wife and child at home. When Paul returns to his company, he recounts the incident to his friends, who try to console him.

Paul and his friends are given an easy assignment: for three weeks, they are to guard a supply depot away from the fighting. When the next battle takes place, Paul and Kropp are wounded. At the hospital, Paul has surgery. Kropp's leg is amputated, and he becomes extremely depressed. Paul has a short leave at home before he returns to his company.

As the German army begins to give in to the unrelenting pressure of the Allied forces, Paul's friends are killed in combat one by one. Detering, one of Paul's close friends, attempts to desert but is caught and court-martialed. Kat is killed when a piece of shrapnel slices his head open while Paul is carrying him to safety. By the fall of 1918, Paul is the only one of his friends who has survived. Soldiers everywhere whisper that the Germans will soon surrender and peace will come. Paul is poisoned in a gas attack and given a short leave. He reflects that when the war ends, he will be ruined for peacetime. All he knows is the war. In October 1918, on a day with very little fighting, Paul is killed. The army report for that day reads simply: "All quiet on the Western Front." Paul's corpse wears a calm expression, as though relieved that the end has come at last.

CHARACTERS IN *ALL QUIET ON THE WESTERN FRONT*

Paul Bäumer A young German soldier fighting in the trenches during World War I. Paul is the protagonist and narrator of the novel. He is, at heart, a kind, compassionate, and sensitive young man, but the brutality of warfare teaches him to detach himself from his feelings. His account of the war is a bitter invective against sentimental, romantic ideas about combat.

Joseph Behm The first of Paul's classmates to die in the war. Behm did not want to enlist but caved under the pressure of the schoolmaster, Kantorek. His ugly, painful death shatters his classmates' trust in the authorities who convinced them to take part in the war.

Detering One of Paul's close friends in the Second Company. Detering is a young man who constantly longs for his wife and farm at home.

Gérard Duval A French soldier Paul kills in No Man's Land. Duval is a printer with a wife and child at home. He is the first person Paul kills in hand-to-hand combat.

Corporal Himmelstoss A noncommissioned training officer. Before the war, Himmelstoss was a postman. He is a petty, power-hungry little man who torments Paul and his friends during their training. After experiencing the horrors of trench warfare, he tries to make amends with them. ~

Stanislaus Katczinsky A soldier in Paul's company and Paul's best friend in the army. Kat, as he is known, is forty years old at the beginning of the novel and has a family at home. A resourceful, inventive man, he always manages to find food, clothing, and blankets.

Kantorek A pompous, ignorant, authoritarian schoolmaster in Paul's high school. Kantorek places intense pressure on Paul and his classmates to fulfill their "patriotic duty" by enlisting in the army.

Franz Kemmerich One of Paul's classmates and comrades in the war. After suffering a light wound, Kemmerich contracts gangrene, and his leg must be amputated. Kemmerich's death in Chapter Two is the first dramatic portrayal of the meaninglessness of death and the cheapness of life in wartime.

Kindervater A soldier in a neighboring unit. Kindervater is a bed wetter like Tjaden.

Albert Kropp A former classmate of Paul's who serves in the Second Company with Paul. An intelligent, speculative young man, Kropp is one of Paul's closest friends during the war. His interest in analyzing the causes of the war leads to one of the most articulate antiwar sentiments in the novel.

Leer One of Paul's classmates and close friends during the war. Leer serves with Paul in the Second Company. He was the first in Paul's class to lose his virginity.

Mittelstaedt One of Paul's classmates. Mittelstaedt becomes a training officer and enjoys tormenting Kantorek, his former schoolteacher, when Kantorek is conscripted as a soldier.

Müller One of Paul's former classmates. Müller, a hardheaded, practical young man, plies his friends in the Second Company with questions about their postwar plans.

Tjaden One of Paul's friends in the Second Company. Tjaden is a wiry young man with a voracious appetite. He bears a deep grudge against Corporal Himmelstoss.

Haie Westhus One of Paul's friends in the Second Company. A gigantic, burly man, Westhus was a peat-digger before the war. He plans to serve a full term in the army after the war ends, since he finds peat-digging so unpleasant.

THEMES IN *ALL QUIET ON THE WESTERN FRONT*

THE NUMBNESS OF SOLDIERS The soldiers fighting on the front are subject to constant physical danger. Primal, instinctive fear colors their every waking moment. The live in filthy, waterlogged ditches full of rats, decaying corpses, and lice. They frequently go without food and sleep, adequate clothing, or sufficient medical care. They watch their close friends die violent deaths. The cumulative effect of these conditions is overwhelming, and to cope with it the soldiers must disconnect themselves from their feelings. In Remarque's view, this emotional disconnection destroys the soldiers' humanity. Paul, for instance, cannot imagine a future without the war and cannot remember how he felt in the past. Soldiers stop mourning fallen friends and comrades. The living soldiers, however, feel intense bonds of loyalty and friendship as a result of the shared experience of war. These feelings, the only romanticized element of the novel, are virtually the only emotions the soldiers can still feel.

THE FOOLISHNESS OF NATIONALISM In many ways, nationalism was the precipitating cause of World War I. Nationalism is the idea that competing nation-states are a fundamental part of existence, that people owe their first loyalty to their nation, and that national identity is the primary component of identity. *All Quiet on the Western Front* is a scathing critique of nationalism, which is characterized as a hollow, hypocritical ideology, a tool used by those in power to control the masses. Nationalist ideas convince Paul and his friends to join the army, but the experience of fighting quickly teaches them that nationalism is an imaginary concept, a dream used to dupe the idealistic. Patriots like Kantorek and Himmelstoss are worthless on the battlefield. Those soldiers who succeed are the ones who fight not for the glory of their nation but for their own survival. Paul and his friends realize that the opposing armies are not real enemies. The real enemies are the men in power who sacrifice troops simply to increase their own power and glory.

THE EMPTINESS OF PATRIOTISM Remarque reserves his harshest criticism of nationalism for Kantorek, the teacher whose impassioned speeches convinced Paul and his friends to join the army. With idealistic, patriotic, and poetic rhetoric, Kantorek lauds national loyalty and glory. Paul and his friends become increasingly disgusted by the memory of Kantorek's speeches. The idealistic teacher did not understand that lofty ideals, which lead men into battle, become meaningless as soon as the battle is fought.

SYMBOLS IN *ALL QUIET ON THE WESTERN FRONT*

KEMMERICH'S BOOTS *All Quiet on the Western Front* doesn't employ a great deal of symbolism, but one important symbol in the novel is Kemmerich's boots, which represent the cheapening of human life during wartime. These high, supple boots are passed from soldier to soldier as each owner dies in sequence. Kemmerich took them from the corpse of a dead airman, Paul brings them to Müller when Kemmerich dies, and then he inherits them when Müller is shot to death. During the war, a good pair of boots is more valuable—and more durable—than a human life.

IMPORTANT QUOTATIONS FROM *ALL QUIET ON THE WESTERN FRONT*

> *This book is to be neither an accusation nor a confession, and least of all an adventure, for death is not an adventure to those who stand face to face with it. It will try simply to tell of a generation of men who, even though they may have escaped shells, were destroyed by the war.*

Location: Epigraph
Speaker: Remarque
Context: Before the narration begins, Remarque explains what his book is intended to be

In this passage, Remarque explains his project, setting his novel apart from the overblown, romanticized war novels that have come before his. He says his novel is not "an adventure." Unlike most war novels, it dispenses with romance and excitement and tells a stark, unsentimental story. Remarque points out that "death is not an adventure to those who stand face to face with it," suggesting that telling thrilling stories of war betrays the actual experience of soldiers. Remarque also says that war destroys men even when it does not actually kill them. He claims his novel is not an accusation—a partly inaccurate claim. *All Quiet on the Western Front* eviscerates war, powerful men, and ignorant patriots. It is hard to see the one-dimensional Kantorek, for example, as anything other than the object of accusation. The friction between realism and antiwar fervor is characteristic of the novel as a whole, in which Remarque tries to reconcile his hatred of the war with the need to create realistic characters who are more than mere punching bags.

> *At the sound of the first droning of the shells we rush back, in one part of our being, a thousand years. By the animal instinct that is awakened in us we are led and protected. It is not conscious; it is far quicker, much more sure, less fallible, than consciousness. . .. It is this other, this second sight in us, that has thrown us to the ground and saved us, without our knowing how. . .. We march up, moody or good-tempered soldiers—we reach the zone where the front begins and become on the instant human animals.*

Location: Chapter Four
Speaker: Paul
Context: As Paul and his comrades go to the front to lay barbed wire, Paul thinks about survival

Paul describes the psychological transformation soldiers undergo when they head into battle. They cease to be men ("moody or good-tempered soldiers") and instead become beasts ("human animals"). To survive, they must shut off the thoughtful, analytical part of their minds and rely entirely on animal instinct. Paul describes men who are walking thoughtlessly along and suddenly throw themselves to the ground just in time to avoid a shell. They were not consciously aware that a shell was approaching, but some instinct caused them to leap to safety. Paul says this "second sight" is the only thing that enables soldiers to survive a battle. The necessity of relying on instinct alone suggests that battles are animalistic and even subhuman.

> *The idea of authority, which they represented, was associated in our minds with a greater insight and a more humane wisdom. But the first death we saw shattered this belief. We had to recognize that our generation was more to be trusted than theirs. . .. The first bombardment showed us our mistake, and under it the world as they had taught it to us broke in pieces.*

Location: Chapter One
Speaker: Paul
Context: Paul reflects on the fact that the generation urging him and his friends to war never itself fought

Just as we turn into animals when we go up to the line . . . so we turn into wags and loafers when we are resting. . . .. We want to live at any price; so we cannot burden ourselves with feelings which, though they may be ornamental enough in peacetime, would be out of place here. Kemmerich is dead, Haie Westhus is dying . . . Martens has no legs anymore, Meyer is dead, Max is dead, Beyer is dead, Hammerling is dead . . . it is a damnable business, but what has it to do with us now—we live.

Location: Chapter Seven
Speaker: Paul
Context: Paul and his friends enjoy a moment of relaxation, and Paul thinks about the necessity of repressing pain

---

Comrade, I did not want to kill you. . . .. But you were only an idea to me before, an abstraction that lived in my mind and called forth its appropriate response. . . .. I thought of your hand-grenades, of your bayonet, of your rifle; now I see your wife and your face and our fellowship. Forgive me, comrade. We always see it too late. Why do they never tell us that you are poor devils like us, that your mothers are just as anxious as ours, and that we have the same fear of death, and the same dying and the same agony— Forgive me, comrade; how could you be my enemy?

Location: Chapter Nine
Speaker: Paul
Context: Paul speaks to Gérard Duval, the French soldier he has stabbed

ANIMAL FARM

George Orwell

A group of animals mount a successful rebellion against the farmer who rules them, but their dreams of equality for all are ruined when one pig seizes power.

THE LIFE OF GEORGE ORWELL

Born Eric Blair in India in 1903, George Orwell was educated as a scholarship student at prestigious boarding schools in England. Because of his background—he famously described his family as "lower-upper-middle class"—he never quite fit in. He felt oppressed and outraged by the dictatorial control that the schools he attended exercised over students' lives. His painful experiences with snobbishness and social elitism at Eton, as well as his familiarity with British imperialism in India, made him deeply suspicious of the class system in English society. After graduating from Eton, Orwell decided to forego college to work as a British Imperial Policeman in Burma. He hated his duties in Burma, where he was required to enforce the strict laws of a political regime he despised. Orwell's bad health, which troubled him throughout his life, caused him to return to England on convalescent leave. Once back in England, he quit the Imperial Police and dedicated himself to becoming a writer.

Inspired by Jack London's 1903 book *The People of the Abyss*, which detailed Jack London's experience in the slums of London, Orwell bought ragged clothes from a secondhand store and went to live among the very poor in London. He published a book about this experience entitled *Down and Out in Paris and London*. Orwell later lived among destitute coal miners in northern England, an experience that inspired him to give up on capitalism in favor of democratic socialism. In 1936, Orwell went to report on the Civil War in Spain, where he witnessed nightmarish atrocities committed by fascist political regimes. As the dictators Adolf Hitler and Joseph Stalin rose to power, Orwell's hatred of totalitarianism and political authority intensified. Orwell devoted his energy to writing politically charged novels, first *Animal Farm* in 1945, then *1984* in 1949.

ANIMAL FARM IN CONTEXT

Animal Farm, like *1984*, paints a terrifying picture of a world without personal freedom. A "fairy story" in the style of Aesop's fables, *Animal Farm* is an allegory of the history of Soviet communism in which animals on an English farm stand for Soviet leaders and people. Certain animals are based directly on Communist Party leaders: the pigs Napoleon and Snowball, for example, stand for Joseph Stalin and Leon Trotsky respectively. Because *Animal Farm* is such a strict allegory, it is useful to understand the rudiments of Soviet history under Communist Party rule.

In Russian society in the early twentieth century, a tiny minority controlled most of the country's wealth, while the vast majority of the country's inhabitants were impoverished and oppressed peasants. Communism arose in Russia when the nation's workers and peasants, assisted by a class of intellectuals known as the intelligentsia, rebelled against the wealthy capitalists and aristocrats. They hoped to establish a socialist utopia based on the principles of the German economic and political philosopher Karl Marx, whose *The Communist Manifesto* urged, "Workers of the world, unite!" Marx argued that when all property was commonly owned, everyone would be equal.

As a result of a profound economic and political crisis in the country, which was partially precipitated by the outbreak of World War I, Tsar Nicholas II, the monarch of Russia, abdicated the throne that his family had held for three centuries. Vladimir Ilych Lenin, a Russian intellectual revolutionary, seized power in the name of the Communist Party. The new regime took land and industry from private control and put them under government supervision. After Lenin died in 1924, Joseph Stalin and Leon Trotsky jockeyed for control of the newly formed Soviet Union. Stalin, a crafty and manipulative politician, soon banished Trotsky, a relentless proponent of international communism. Stalin ordered Trotsky expelled first from Moscow, then from the Communist Party, and finally from Russia altogether in 1936. Trotsky fled to Mexico, where he was assassinated on Stalin's orders in 1940. Stalin consolidated his power with brutal intensity, killing or imprisoning his perceived political enemies and later his collaborators, and overseeing the murders of approximately twenty million Soviet citizens.

As the Soviet government's economic planning faltered and failed, violence, fear, and starvation engulfed Russia. Stalin tried to unify the country by turning Trotsky into common national enemy. If there were people Stalin wanted to execute, he demonized them simply by linking them to Trotsky.

These events have direct parallels in *Animal Farm*. Like Stalin, Napoleon becomes a dictator, and like Trotsky, Snowball is never heard from again. Just as Stalin ousted Trotsky and then made him into a monster, Napoleon ousts Snowball from the farm and then uses him in his purges. *Animal Farm* was written as an attack on a specific government, but its general themes of oppression, suffering, and injustice are broad. Orwell's novel is a powerful attack on any political, rhetorical, or military power that seeks total control over the masses.

ANIMAL FARM: KEY FACTS

Full title: Animal Farm: A Fairy Story

Time and place written: 1943–1944; London

Date of first publication: 1946

Publisher: Harcourt Brace & Company

Type of work: Novella

Genre: Dystopian animal fable; satire; allegory; political roman á clef (French for "novel with a key"—a thinly veiled exposé of factual persons or events)

Language: English

Setting (time): Unspecified; possibly contemporaneous with the object of its satire, the Russian Revolution (1917–1945)

Setting (place): An imaginary farm in England

Tense: Past

Tone: Objective, ironic

Narrator: Anonymous narrator

Point of view: The common animals of Animal Farm

Protagonist: There is no clear central character in the novel, but Napoleon drives the action

Antagonist: All of the exploiting classes, including Mr. Jones, Napoleon, the pigs, and the neighboring humans

ANIMAL FARM: PLOT OVERVIEW

Old Major, a prize-winning boar, gathers the animals of the Manor Farm for a meeting in the big barn. He tells them he has had a dream of all animals living together without human beings oppressing them or controlling them. He tells the animals that they must work toward such a paradise and teaches them a song called "Beasts of England," which paints a picture of this ideal. The animals greet Old Major's vision with great enthusiasm. When Old Major dies only three nights after the meeting, three younger pigs—Snowball, Napoleon, and Squealer—work his main principles into a philosophy called Animalism. Late one night, the animals defeat the farmer, Mr. Jones, and run him off the land. They rename the property Animal Farm and dedicate themselves to achieving Old Major's dream. The cart-horse Boxer is particularly zealous. He commits his great strength to the prosperity of the farm and adopts the pledge "I will work harder" as his personal maxim.

At first, Animal Farm prospers. Snowball teaches the animals to read, and Napoleon educates a group of young puppies in the principles of Animalism. When Mr. Jones reappears to take back his farm, the animals defeat him again in what comes to be known as the Battle of the Cowshed. They take the farmer's abandoned gun as a token of their victory. As time passes, however, Napoleon and Snowball quibble more and more over the future of the farm. They begin to struggle with each other for power and influence among the other animals. Snowball concocts a scheme to build an electricity-generating windmill, but Napoleon opposes the plan. At a meeting about whether to take up the project, Snowball gives a passionate speech. Napoleon gives a brief reply and then makes a strange noise. Nine attack dogs—the puppies that Napoleon was educating—burst into the barn and chase Snowball from the farm. Napoleon assumes leadership of Animal Farm and says there will be no more meetings. From now on, he asserts, the pigs alone will make the decisions—for the good of every animal.

Napoleon quickly changes his mind and says the windmill should be built. The animals, especially Boxer, work hard to complete it. One day, after a storm, the animals find the windmill toppled. The human farmers in the area smugly say that the animals made the walls too thin, but Napoleon claims that Snowball returned to the farm to sabotage the windmill. He stages a great purge. Any animal who opposes Napoleon's uncontested leadership is accused of participating in Snowball's great conspiracy and instantly put to death, murdered by Napoleon's attack dogs. (Boxer takes up a second maxim: "Napoleon is always right.") With his leadership unquestioned, Napoleon begins expanding his powers, rewriting history to make Snowball a villain. Napoleon also begins to act more and more like a human being—sleeping in a bed, drinking whisky, and engaging in trade with neighboring farmers. The original Animalist principles strictly forbade such activities, but Squealer, Napoleon's propagandist, justifies every questionable action to the other animals, convincing them that Napoleon is a great leader and is making things better for everyone—despite the fact that the common animals are cold, hungry, and overworked.

Mr. Frederick, a neighboring farmer, cheats Napoleon in the purchase of some timber and then attacks the farm and dynamites the windmill, which had been rebuilt at great expense. A pitched battle ensues, and Boxer is badly wounded. The animals rout the farmers, but Boxer has been weakened by his injuries. Later, he falls while working on the windmill and senses his time has nearly come. One day, Squealer announces that Boxer was taken to the hospital, where he praised the Rebellion with his last breath and then died. The truth is that Napoleon has sold his most loyal and long-suffering worker to a glue maker in order to get money for whisky.

Years pass. The pigs become more and more like human beings. They walk upright, carry whips, and wear clothes. Eventually, the seven principles of Animalism, known as the Seven Commandments, are reduced to a single principle: "all animals are equal, but some animals are more equal than others." At a dinner, Napoleon entertains a human farmer named Mr. Pilkington and declares his intent to ally himself with the human farmers against the laboring classes of both the human and animal communities. He also changes the name of Animal Farm back to the Manor Farm, saying that this title is the "correct" one. Looking in at the party of elites through the farmhouse window, the common animals can no longer tell which are the pigs and which are the human beings.

CHARACTERS IN *ANIMAL FARM*

Benjamin An old donkey who refuses to feel inspired by the Rebellion. Benjamin believes life will remain unpleasant no matter who is in charge. Of all of the animals on the farm, he alone comprehends the changes that take place, but he seems either unwilling or unable to oppose the pigs.

Boxer A hard-working cart-horse. Boxer's incredible strength, dedication, and loyalty play a key role in the early prosperity of Animal Farm and the later completion of the windmill. Quick to help but rather slow-witted, Boxer shows great devotion to Animal Farm's ideals but little facility for independent thought. Boxer stands for trusting, idealistic Soviet workers.

Clover A good-hearted female cart-horse and Boxer's close friend. Clover often suspects the pigs of violating the Seven Commandments.

Jessie and Bluebell Two dogs, each of whom gives birth early in the novel. Napoleon confiscates their puppies, claiming he wants to educate them and then turning them into vicious attack dogs. Jessie and Bluebell stand for the mothers robbed of their children by brutal dictators.

Mr. Jones The farmer who runs the Manor Farm before the animals rebel. Mr. Jones is an unkind, often drunken master who indulges himself while his animals go hungry. He stands for Tsar Nicholas II, the leader ousted in the Russian Revolution.

Mr. Frederick The tough, shrewd operator of Pinchfield, a neighboring farm. Mr. Frederick stands for Adolf Hitler.

Minimus A poetic pig. Minimus writes verses about Napoleon and pens the banal patriotic song "Animal Farm, Animal Farm" to replace the earlier idealistic hymn "Beasts of England," which Old Major passes on to the animals. Minimus stands for the boot-licking, mediocre artists who thrive by pandering to dictators.

Mollie A vain, flighty mare. Mollie pulls Mr. Jones's carriage. She craves the attention of human beings and loves being groomed and pampered. When the animals take over Animal Farm, Mollie longs to wear ribbons in her mane and eat sugar cubes, as she did under human rule. Mollie represents the petit bourgeoisie that fled from Russia a few years after the Russian Revolution.

Moses A tame raven. Moses tells stories of Sugarcandy Mountain, the paradise to which animals supposedly go when they die. Moses plays only a small role in *Animal Farm*, but his stories suggest the way communism uses religion to pacify the oppressed.

Muriel The white goat who reads the Seven Commandments to Clover whenever Clover suspects the pigs of violating them.

Napoleon The pig who emerges as the leader of Animal Farm after the Rebellion. Napoleon uses military force in the form of nine loyal attack dogs to intimidate the other animals and consolidate his power. Napoleon, a supremely crafty and powerful pig, stands for Joseph Stalin.

Old Major The prize-winning boar whose vision of a socialist utopia inspires the Rebellion. Old Major stands for both the German political economist Karl Marx and the Russian revolutionary leader Vladimir Ilych Lenin.

Mr. Pilkington The easygoing gentleman farmer who runs Foxwood, a neighboring farm. Mr. Pilkington, Mr. Frederick's bitter enemy, represents the capitalist governments of England and the United States.

Snowball The pig who challenges Napoleon for control of Animal Farm after the Rebellion. Snowball is intelligent, passionate, and eloquent. He is less subtle and devious than Napoleon. Snowball stands for Leon Trotsky.

Squealer The pig who spreads Napoleon's propaganda to the other animals. Squealer justifies the pigs' monopolization of resources and cites false statistics pointing to the farm's success. Orwell uses Squealer to point out that powerful people use rhetoric to twist the truth and maintain control.

Mr. Whymper A solicitor. Napoleon hires Mr. Whymper to represent Animal Farm in human society. Mr. Whymper is the first human to make contact with the Animal Farm community, alarming the common animals.

THEMES IN *ANIMAL FARM*

THE TENDENCY TOWARD CLASS STRATIFICATION Orwell suggests that humans instinctively create class structures, even in societies allegedly based on total equality. As *Animal Farm* illustrates, classes that can unite in the face of a common enemy, as the animals do against the humans, will divide when that enemy is eliminated. The expulsion of Mr. Jones does not create equality—it creates a power vacuum. Soon a new oppressor assumes totalitarian control. The difference between intellectual and nonintellectual animals quickly turns into a new set of class divisions, with the "brainworkers" (as the pigs claim to be) using their superior intelligence to manipulate society. Orwell does not clarify whether it is simply the nature of all smart, ruthless beings to seek power. *Animal Farm* leaves room for the idea that while power sometimes corrupts, in the hands of a conscientious being it could be used for the good of all.

THE DANGER OF A NAÏVE WORKING CLASS Gullible, loyal, and hardworking, the animals of *Animal Farm* show how oppression comes about not just because of the oppressors, but because of the naiveté of the oppressed. When presented with a dilemma, for example, Boxer prefers not to puzzle out various possible actions but instead to repeat to himself, "Napoleon is always right." This kind of inability or unwillingness to question authority condemns the working class to subservience. The working class in *Animal Farm* relies on the ruling class to define their group identity, letting themselves be swayed by military awards, large parades, and new songs. They do not realize that the pigs are using language to manipulate them, distorting the rhetoric of socialist revolution to justify their behavior. By the end of the novella, the ruling principle of the farm is openly stated as "all animals are equal, but some animals are more equal than others."

SYMBOLS IN *ANIMAL FARM*

ANIMAL FARM   Animal Farm, known at the beginning and the end of the novel as the Manor Farm, symbolizes Russia and the Soviet Union under Communist Party rule. More generally, it symbolizes any human society, whether capitalist, socialist, fascist, or communist. Animal Farm has the internal structure of a nation, with a government (the pigs), a police force or army (the dogs), a working class (the other animals), and state holidays and rituals. Like any political entity, Animal Farm must worry about hostile neighbors (nearby farms).

THE BARN   The barn stands for the collective memory of a modern nation, which changes according to the dictates of the rulers. The pigs paint the Seven Commandments on the side of the barn and then alter them over and over again, convincing the other animals that the commandments have never changed. The working-class animals puzzle over these changes, but accept them. The ruling class constantly revises the commandments because it needs to change history in order to retain power. By rewriting a nation's origins and development, the ruling class gains control of the nation's very identity. The oppressed soon come to depend upon the authorities for their communal sense of self.

IMPORTANT QUOTATIONS FROM *ANIMAL FARM*

Beasts of England, beasts of Ireland,
Beasts of every land and clime,
Hearken to my joyful tiding
Of the golden future time.

Location: Chapter I
Speaker: Old Major
Context: Old Major recites the first verse of a song he heard in his dream

Like the communist anthem "Internationale," on which Old Major's song is based, "Beasts of England" stirs the emotions of the animals and fires their revolutionary idealism. The lofty optimism of the words "golden future time," which recur in the last verse, keep the animals focused on the Rebellion's goals and encourage them to ignore the suffering along the way. Later, once Napoleon has cemented his control over the farm, the song's revolutionary nature becomes a liability. Squealer chastises the animals for singing it, noting that it was the song of the Rebellion. Now that the Rebellion is over and a new regime has gained power, Squealer fears the power of such idealistic, hopeful lyrics. Wanting to discourage the animals' hope and vision, he orders Minimus to write a replacement for "Beasts of England" that praises Napoleon and emphasizes loyalty to the state over Animalist ideology.

At this there was a terrible baying sound outside, and nine enormous dogs wearing brass-studded collars came bounding into the barn. They dashed straight for Snowball, who only sprang from his place just in time to escape their snapping jaws.

Location: Chapter V
Speaker: The narrator
Context: Napoleon violently expels Snowball from Animal Farm

Napoleon's violent expulsion of Snowball from Animal Farm recreates the falling-out between Joseph Stalin and Leon Trotsky. Snowball, like Trotsky, wants to win popular support through his ideas and his eloquence—a tactic that appeals to the animals. Napoleon, like Stalin, prefers to work behind the scenes, building his power with secrecy and deception. Napoleon is losing the contest for the hearts and minds of the lower animals to his rival and must turn to his private police force of dogs to enforce his supremacy. This episode is the first of many in which the political positioning of the Rebellion's early days gives way to overt violence in a blatant reversal of the democratic principles that first animated Animal Farm.

"Four legs good, two legs bad."

Location: Chapter III
Speaker: Snowball
Context: Snowball condenses the Seven Commandments of Animalism into one sentence

---

All animals are equal, but some animals are more equal than others.

Location: Chapter X
Speaker: Abstractly, the pigs
Context: The Seven Commandments are finally boiled down to this one, nonsensical phrase

---

"If you have your lower animals to contend with," he said, "we have our lower classes!"

Location: Chapter X
Speaker: Mr. Pilkington
Context: Mr. Pilkington talks to Napoleon and his cabinet

ANNA KARENINA

Leo Tolstoy

After having an affair with a handsome military man, a woman kills herself.

THE LIFE OF LEO TOLSTOY

Lev (Leo) Nikolaevich Tolstoy was born into a large and wealthy Russian landowning family in 1828. Tolstoy's mother died when he was only two years old, and he idealized her throughout his life. When Tolstoy was nine, his family moved to Moscow. Shortly afterward, Tolstoy's father was murdered while traveling. Although Tolstoy was an intelligent child, he had little interest in academics. He failed his university entrance exam on his first attempt. Finally, he entered Kazan University at age sixteen and studied law and language. He developed an interest in the grand heroic cultures of Persia, Turkey, and the Caucasus—an interest that persisted throughout his life. Tolstoy was not popular at the university. In 1847, he left school without a degree.

After visiting his brother in the Russian army, Tolstoy decided to enlist. He served in the Crimean War (1854–1856), an experience he drew on to write *Sevastopol Stories* (1855). During his stint in the army, Tolstoy found time to write, producing a well-received autobiographical novel, *Childhood* (1852), followed by two others, *Boyhood* (1854) and *Youth* (1857).

In 1862, Tolstoy married Sofya Andreevna Behrs. He devoted most of the next two decades to raising a large family, managing his estate, and writing his two greatest novels, *War and Peace* (1865–1869) and *Anna Karenina* (1875–1877). Just before he married, Tolstoy had visited western Europe, partly to observe educational methods abroad. Upon returning to Russia, he founded schools for his peasants. Tolstoy came to believe that peasants possessed morality and camaraderie lacking in the upper classes.

Tolstoy lived during a period of intense development in Russia. By the time of his death in 1910, Russia had changed from an agricultural country to a major industrialized world power. The Slavophiles and the Westernizers, two intellectual groups, argued about Russia's direction. The Slavophiles believed Russia should reject modernization and cherish the traditional, Asiatic elements of its culture. The Westernizers believed Russia should join Europe in its march toward secular values and scientific thought. Political debates also raged in Russia, as a series of authoritarian tsars angered liberal and radical intellectuals who wanted constitutional rights.

By the 1890s, Tolstoy's reputation as a prophet of social thought had attracted disciples to his estate at Yasnaya Polyana. In 1898, Tolstoy published a radical essay called *What Is Art?*, in which he argues that moral instruction is the sole aim of great art and that by that standard Shakespeare's plays and Tolstoy's own novels are artistic failures. Frustrated by the disconnect between his philosophy and his wealth, and by his frequent quarrels with his wife, Tolstoy stole away from his estate in November 1910 at the age of eighty-two. Several days later, he died of pneumonia in a faraway railway station.

ANNA KARENINA IN CONTEXT

Tolstoy eventually turned to religion, a change that left an imprint on all his later writings. Many critics view *Anna Karenina* as the turning point in Tolstoy's career, the novel that marks his shift toward faith. The tension between Tolstoy's attraction to fiction and faith results in Anna, a complex character Tolstoy both disapproves of and loves. Levin emerges as the voice of faith in the novel.

Many elements of *Anna Karenina*'s plot come from Tolstoy's life. Levin's initial awkwardness, for example, might remind us of Tolstoy's unhappiness at his university. Tolstoy includes antimilitaristic sentiments in *Anna Karenina*, perhaps because of his experiences in the army. Levin's courtship of Kitty Shcherbatskaya is modeled on Tolstoy's own courtship of Sofya Andreevna, down to details such as the forgotten shirt that delays the wedding. The debate over Russia's destiny surfaces in *Anna Karenina*; Levin's peasants prefer simple wooden plows over more efficient, modern agricultural tools, which symbolizes Russia's rejection of the West. Tolstoy's ambivalent portrayal of the local elections in *Anna Karenina* reveals his uncertainty about the potential for democracy in Russia.

ANNA KARENINA: KEY FACTS

Time and place written: 1873–1877; the estate of Yasnaya Polyana, near Moscow

Date of first publication: 1873–1877 (serial publication)

Publisher: M. N. Katkov

Type of work: Novel

Genre: Novel of ideas; psychological novel

Language: Russian

Setting (time): 1870s

Setting (place): Moscow, St. Petersburg, and the Russian provinces, with brief interludes in Germany and Italy

Tense: Past

Tone: Impersonal, sympathetic

Narrator: Unnamed omniscient third-person narrator

Point of view: Anna Karenina and Konstantin Levin

Protagonist: Anna and Levin

Antagonist: For Anna, marital duty, social convention, maternal love, and passion for Vronsky; for Levin, identity and the mysteries of faith

ANNA KARENINA: PLOT OVERVIEW

Dolly Oblonskaya has caught her husband, Stiva, having an affair with their children's former governess, and threatens to leave him. Although somewhat remorseful, Stiva is primarily dazed and uncomprehending. Stiva's sister, Anna Karenina, wife of a government official, arrives at the Oblonskys' house in Moscow to mediate. Eventually, she manages to bring about a reconciliation.

Dolly's younger sister, Kitty, is being courted by two suitors: Konstantin Levin, an awkward landowner, and Alexei Vronsky, a dashing military man. After Kitty accepts Vronsky, he meets Anna Karenina and falls in love with her. Devastated, Kitty falls ill. Levin withdraws to his estate in the country to nurse his depression over Kitty's rejection. Anna returns to St. Petersburg.

Vronsky follows Anna to St. Petersburg, and their mutual attraction intensifies. Anna begins to mix with the freethinking social group of Vronsky's cousin, Betsy Tverskaya. At a party, Anna begs Vronsky to ask Kitty's forgiveness. In response, Vronsky tells Anna that he loves her. Karenin, Anna's husband, goes home from the party alone, sensing that something is amiss. Later that night, he tells Anna that he has suspicions about her and Vronsky, but she curtly dismisses his concerns.

Some time later, Vronsky participates in a military officers' horse race. Though an accomplished horseman, he makes an error during the race and inadvertently breaks his horse's back. Karenin notices his wife's intense interest in Vronsky during the race. He confronts Anna afterward, and she candidly admits that she is in love with Vronsky and is having an affair with him. Karenin is stunned.

Kitty attempts to recover her health at a spa in Germany, where she meets a pious Russian woman and her do-gooder protégé, Varenka. Kitty also meets Levin's sickly brother Nikolai, who is recovering at the spa.

Levin's half-brother, the intellectual Sergei Koznyshev, visits Levin in the country and criticizes him for quitting his job on the local administrative council. Levin says he found the work bureaucratic and useless. Levin works enthusiastically with the peasants on his estate, but their resistance to agricultural innovations frustrates him. He visits Dolly, who tempts him with talk of repairing his relationship with Kitty. Later, Levin meets Kitty at a dinner party. They get engaged and marry.

Karenin rejects Anna's request for a divorce, insisting that they should keep up appearances and stay together. Anna moves to the family's country home, away from her husband. She sees Vronsky often, but their relationship becomes troubled after Anna reveals she is pregnant. Vronsky considers resigning his military post, but his ambition changes his mind.

Karenin, catching Vronsky at the Karenin country home one day, finally agrees to a divorce. Anna is giving birth. In agony, she begs Karenin's forgiveness, and he suddenly grants it. He says she can decide about the divorce. Anna resents his generosity and does not ask for a divorce. Instead, Anna and Vronsky go to Italy, where they lead an aimless existence. Eventually, they return to Russia. Society spurns Anna because of her adulterous affair. Anna and Vronsky withdraw into seclusion, though Anna dares a birthday visit to her young son, who lives with Karenin. She feels jealous of Vronsky, who can freely participate in society while she must hide in the house.

Married life surprises Levin. Kitty is more helpful to Levin's dying brother Nikolai than Levin is. She greatly comforts Nikolai in his final days. Kitty discovers she is pregnant. Stiva visits and brings along a friend, Veslovsky, who irks Levin by flirting with Kitty. Dolly visits Anna and finds her radiant and happy. Anna's luxurious country home impresses Dolly, but her dependence on sedatives to sleep is disturbing. Anna is waiting for a divorce.

Levin and Kitty move to Moscow to await the birth of their baby. The expense of city life astonishes them. One day, Stiva takes Levin to visit Anna, whom Levin has never met. Anna enchants Levin. Anna is growing paranoid that Vronsky no longer loves her. Kitty has a son, an event that provokes conflicted emotions in Levin. Stiva goes to St. Petersburg to seek a cushy job and to beg Karenin to grant Anna a divorce. Karenin, following the advice of a questionable French psychic, refuses.

Anna picks a quarrel with Vronsky. When Vronsky leaves on an errand, Anna is tormented. She sends him a telegram urgently calling him home, and then sends a profusely apologetic note. In desperation, Anna drives to Dolly's to say goodbye, and then returns home. She resolves to meet Vronsky at the train station after his errand. At the station, despairing and dazed, Anna throws herself under a train and dies.

Two months later, Sergei's book is published to bad reviews. Sergei represses his disappointment by supporting the Slavic people trying to free themselves from Turkish rule. Sergei, Vronsky, and others board a train for Serbia to assist in the cause. Levin is skeptical. Unanswerable questions about the meaning of life obsess him. One day, a peasant remarks to Levin that the point of life is not to fill one's belly but to serve God and goodness. Levin receives this advice as gospel, and his life is suddenly transformed by faith.

Later that day, Levin, Dolly, and Dolly's children seek shelter from a sudden, violent thunderstorm. Levin realizes that Kitty and his son are still outside. He fears the worst, but his wife and child are safe. For the first time, Levin feels real love for his son, which pleases Kitty. Levin reflects again that the meaning of his life depends on his own goodness.

CHARACTERS IN *ANNA KARENINA*

A NOTE ON RUSSIAN NAMES

Russians have three names: a first name, a patronymic, and a surname. The patronymic is the father's first name with a suffix meaning "son of" or "daughter of": for example, Dmitrich (son of Dmitri) or Alexandrovna (daughter of Alexander). In formal address, people are called by both their first names and their patronymics (Konstantin Dmitrich, Ekaterina Alexandrovna). In informal address, people are sometimes called by nicknames, or diminutives. For instance, Konstantin Levin is sometimes called Kostya (the diminutive of Konstantin), and Alexei Vronsky is sometimes called Alyosha (the diminutive of Alexei). Surnames reflect gender. For example, the surname of Karenin's wife is Karenina, and the surname of Oblonsky's wife is Oblonskaya.

Varvara Andreevna (Varenka) A pure, high-minded young woman who becomes Kitty's friend at the German spa. Varenka is a protégé of Madame Stahl.

Countess Lydia Ivanovna A morally upright woman. Lydia Ivanovna, who is initially Anna's friend, eventually turns into her fiercest critic. She harbors a secret love for Karenin and convinces him to rely on psychics.

Alexei Alexandrovich Karenin A high-ranking government minister and one of the most important men in St. Petersburg. Karenin, Anna's husband, is formal and dutiful. He fulfills his family obligations as he does his social obligations—with thoroughness but little emotion.

Anna Arkadyevna Karenina A beautiful, aristocratic woman from St. Petersburg. Anna is intelligent, literate, and beautiful. Her adulterous affair with Vronsky results in social exile, misery, and finally suicide.

Sergei Alexeich Karenin (Seryozha) Karenin and Anna's young son. Karenin treats Seryozha coldly after learning of Anna's affair.

Fyodor Vassilyevich Katavasov An intellectual friend from Levin's university days.

Sergei Ivanovich Koznyshev Levin's half-brother. Koznyshev is a famed intellectual and writer whose thinking confuses Levin. Koznyshev, who embodies cold intellectualism, cannot embrace life fully.

Landau A French psychic who tells Karenin to reject Anna's plea for a divorce.

Konstantin Dmitrich Levin A socially awkward but generous landowner. Levin, an intellectual, philosophical man, aims to be sincere and productive in whatever he does. In many ways, Tolstoy modeled Levin on himself.

Nikolai Dmitrich Levin Levin's sickly brother. Freethinking Nikolai represents liberal social thought among certain Russian intellectuals of the period.

Agafya Mikhailovna Levin's former nurse and current housekeeper.

Marya Nikolaevna A former prostitute. After Nikolai Levin saves Marya, she becomes his companion.

Stepan Arkadyich Oblonsky (Stiva) Anna's brother. Stiva is a pleasure-loving aristocrat and minor government official whose affair with his children's governess nearly destroys his marriage. For Tolstoy, Stiva's moral laxity epitomizes the corruption of big-city life in St. Petersburg.

Darya Alexandrovna Oblonskaya (Dolly) Stiva's wife and Kitty's older sister. Dolly is one of the few people to treat Anna kindly after Anna's affair becomes public knowledge.

Ekaterina Alexandrovna Shcherbatskaya (Kitty) A beautiful young woman who marries Levin. The character of Kitty was inspired by Tolstoy's own wife. Sensitive and overprotected, Kitty is shocked by the crude realities of life. Although she is indifferent to intellectual matters, she is also courageous and compassionate.

Prince Alexander Dmitrievich Shcherbatsky The father of Kitty, Dolly, and Natalie. A practical aristocrat, Prince Shcherbatsky favors Levin over Vronsky as a potential husband for Kitty.

Princess Shcherbatskaya The mother of Kitty, Dolly, and Natalie. Princess Shcherbatskaya initially urges Kitty to choose Vronsky.

Madame Stahl A dubiously devout invalid woman whom the Shcherbatskys meet at a German spa.

Nikolai Ivanovich Sviyazhsky A friend of Levin. Sviyazhsky lives in a far-off province.

Elizaveta Fyodorovna Tverskaya (Betsy) A wealthy friend of Anna's and Vronsky's cousin. Betsy has a reputation for wild living and moral laxity.

Vasenka Veslovsky A young, pleasant, dapper man. Veslovsky lavishes attention on Kitty, making Levin jealous.

Alexander Kirillovich Vronsky Vronsky's brother.

Alexei Kirillovich Vronsky A wealthy, dashing military officer. Vronsky loves Anna passionately, but he is disappointed when their affair forces him to give up his dreams of career advancement.

Countess Vronsky Vronsky's judgmental mother.

Varvara Vronsky Alexander Vronsky's wife.

Yashvin Vronsky's wild army friend. Yashvin often gambles away large sums of money.

THEMES IN *ANNA KARENINA*

THE BLESSINGS OF FAMILY LIFE Tolstoy intended *Anna Karenina* to be a recognizable throwback to the "family novel," a genre that was once popular in Russia but had fallen out of fashion by the 1870s. The Russian family novel, which idealized domestic life, came under attack during the 1860s. Many social progressives attacked the institution of the family, calling it a backward and outmoded limitation on individual freedom and pointing out that families often used children as cheap laborers. In *Anna Karenina*, Tolstoy takes a pro-family position but writes candidly about the difficulties of family life, admitting that family life limits individual freedom. But, Tolstoy suggests, despite restrictions on personal liberty and despite the quarrels that plague every family, domestic life is a source of happiness and philosophical transcendence. Because Anna destroys a family, she dies in misery. Because Levin creates one, he finds meaning.

THE PHILOSOPHICAL VALUE OF FARMING Tolstoy devotes extensive sections of *Anna Karenina* to Levin's agricultural interests. This puzzles and frustrates some readers, who object to long passages about issues of mowing, peasant attitudes toward plows, and European agricultural reforms. However, these passages place *Anna Karenina* in a venerable genre that has existed since ancient times: the idyll. Idylls argue that farmers and shepherds are more fulfilled than their urban counterparts. In *Anna Karenina*, Tolstoy updates the idyll by making his spokesman, Levin, not only a devoted farmer but an impassioned philosopher—and the only character in the novel who achieves a clear vision of faith and happiness. Levin finds transcendence through farming. By working in the fields, he comes into close contact with the Russian peasants, supposedly the people who possess native Russian spirit, and his work involves him in a pursuit greater than himself. Because he farms, Levin is rooted in his nation and culture in a way that Europeanized aristocrats like Anna are not. Tolstoy stresses the importance of farming, making a farmer the bearer of Levin's epiphany and linking farming to Levin's statement about the meaning of life.

THE CONVENTIONAL RESPONSE TO ADULTERY *Anna Karenina* is best known as a novel about adultery. The mid-nineteenth century saw surging interest in adultery, as evidenced by works such as Nathaniel Hawthorne's *The Scarlet Letter* (1850) and Gustave Flaubert's *Madame Bovary* (1857). Although the guilty party in these works is always a woman who meets a bad end as a result of her wrongdoing, the nineteenth-century adultery novel is less moralizing than we might expect. For example, the moral atmosphere of *Anna Karenina* is not overwhelmingly Christian, despite its many biblical quotations. Many of the novel's devout Christian characters, such as Madame Stahl and Lydia Ivanovna, are repellent and hypocritical. Tolstoy even occasionally (and gently) mocks the church. Tolstoy portrays adultery as a social issue, not a religious or moral one. He suggests that adultery is devastating not because God disapproves of it, but because society does. Karenin objects to Anna's affair with Vronsky not because adultery is a sin, or even because adultery pains him, but because people will talk. Tolstoy condemns society's obsession with appearances more sternly than he condemns Anna's behavior.

SYMBOLS IN *ANNA KARENINA*

TRAINS In nineteenth-century western European novels, trains often symbolize progress and technological advancement. In Russian literature, however, they have a more ambiguous meaning. Tolstoy thought the railroad symbolized the spread of Western hyper-efficiency and rationalism, and the destruction of native traditions. At the end of the novel, Anna throws herself under a train. Here the train symbolizes Anna herself. With her affair, Anna derails traditions just as trains do. She finally kills herself with the symbol of herself.

VRONSKY'S RACEHORSE Frou-Frou, Vronsky's beautiful, expensive horse, symbolizes Anna. Like Vronsky's race on Frou-Frou, his affair with Anna is dangerous. Vronsky attempts to ride out both dangers—the horse race and the affair—with coolness and poise, and he succeeds for a while. But in the end, Vronsky's error leads to the death of Frou-Frou, just as his behavior is partly to blame for Anna's death.

IMPORTANT QUOTATIONS FROM *ANNA KARENINA*

"No, you're going in vain," she mentally addressed a company in a coach-and-four who were evidently going out of town for some merriment. "And the dog you're taking with you won't help you. You won't get away from yourselves."

Location: Part Seven, Chapter XXX
Speaker: Anna
Context: Ann rides to the train station, where she will commit suicide

Anna's thoughts on her final ride to the train station have become one of the most famous interior monologues in literature. As Anna looks at the people in a coach-and-four, she projects her own problems onto them, imagining that everyone is trying to escape themselves, as she is. Anna has sacrificed family and propriety in order to pursue her deepest personal desires, but ultimately the self for which she sacrificed everything becomes a burden and a torment. Like many people, Anna longs to get away from herself for a little while. Her longing is so intense it leads her to suicide.

"[M]y life now, my whole life, regardless of all that may happen to me, every minute of it, is not only not meaningless, as it was before, but has the unquestionable meaning of the good which it is in my power to put into it!"

Location: Closing lines
Speaker: Levin
Context: Levin reflects on the meaning of his life

Levin's exuberant affirmation of his new faith reminds us of Tolstoy's aim for his novel, which is philosophical as much as narrative. Most novelists might have ended their work with Anna's dramatic suicide, but Tolstoy concludes with an abstract philosophical statement. Levin lays claim to his "whole life . . . every minute of it" shortly after Anna has lost her life. Levin's gain corresponds precisely to Anna's loss, in a symmetry typical of Tolstoy's careful structure. Like Anna, Levin asserts the central place of the self. But unlike Anna, Levin thinks the self is nurturing, not punishing.

All happy families are alike; each unhappy family is unhappy in its own way.

Location: First sentences of the novel
Speaker: The narrator
Context: Tolstoy begins the novel in a philosophical vein

In that brief glance Vronsky had time to notice the restrained animation that played over her face and fluttered between her shining eyes and the barely noticeable smile that curved her red lips. It was as if a surplus of something so overflowed her being that it expressed itself beyond her will, now in the brightness of her glance, now in her smile.

Location: Part One, Chapter XVIII
Speaker: The narrator
Context: At the train station, Anna and Vronsky meet for the first time

"Respect was invented to cover the empty place where love should be. But if you don't love me, it would be better and more honest to say so."

Location: Part Seven, Chapter XXIV
Speaker: Anna
Context: Anna reproaches Vronsky for putting his mother's needs before hers

AS I LAY DYING

William Faulkner

In the 1920s in the American South, a deceased woman's husband and children undertake a difficult journey to Jefferson to bury her corpse.

THE LIFE OF WILLIAM FAULKNER
William Faulkner was born in New Albany, Mississippi, on September 25, 1897, the oldest of four sons in a southern family descended from Colonel William Clark Falkner, the great Civil War soldier, statesman, and railroad builder. A number of Faulkner's ancestors were involved in the Mexican-American War, the Civil War, and the Reconstruction, and were part of the local railroad industry and political scene. Faulkner showed signs of artistic talent from a young age but became bored with his classes and never finished high school.

Faulkner grew up in the town of Oxford, Mississippi, and eventually returned there in his later years and purchased his famous estate, Rowan Oak. Oxford and the surrounding area were Faulkner's inspiration for the fictional Yoknapatawpha County, Mississippi, and its town of Jefferson. These locales became the setting for a number of his works. Faulkner's "Yoknapatawpha novels" include *The Sound and the Fury* (1929), *As I Lay Dying* (1930), *Light in August* (1932), *Absalom, Absalom!* (1936), *The Hamlet* (1940), and *Go Down, Moses* (1942), and they feature some of the same characters and locations.

Faulkner was particularly interested in the decline of the Deep South after the Civil War. Many of his novels explore the deterioration of the Southern aristocracy after the destruction of its wealth and way of life during the Civil War and Reconstruction. Faulkner populates Yoknapatawpha County with the skeletons of old mansions and the ghosts of great men, patriarchs and generals from the past whose aristocratic descendents fail to live up to their family legacies. These families try to cling to old Southern values, codes, and myths that are corrupted and out of place in the reality of the modern world. The families in Faulkner's novels are characterized by failed sons, disgraced daughters, and smoldering resentments between whites and blacks.

Faulkner's reputation as one of the greatest novelists of the twentieth century is largely due to his highly experimental style. Faulkner was a pioneer in literary modernism, dramatically diverging from the forms and structures traditionally used in novels before his time. Faulkner often employs stream-of-consciousness narrative, nonchronological order, multiple narrators, shifts between the present and past tense, and impossibly long and complex sentences. Not surprisingly, these stylistic innovations make some of Faulkner's novels challenging to the reader. The innovations also had a deep impact on literature.

Although eventually he found critical success, Faulkner did not fare well financially. He was forced to work as a screenwriter in Hollywood to supplement his dwindling income. His fortunes were revived with the 1946 publication of *The Portable Faulkner*, which featured a large and varied selection of his writings. He was awarded the Nobel Prize in Literature in 1950. A pair of Pulitzer Prizes followed in 1955 and 1962. Faulkner continued to write until his death in 1962.

AS I LAY DYING IN CONTEXT
In the early twentieth century, a number of modernist writers experimented with narrative techniques that depended more on the exploration of individual consciousness than on plot to create a story. James Joyce's *Ulysses* (1922) and Marcel Proust's *In Search of Lost Time* (1913–1927) are among the most famous and successful of these experiments. Faulkner also made a substantial contribution to this movement. *As I Lay Dying* (1930) is one of the most vivid testaments to the power of this new style of experimentation with language and literary conventions.

The result is a novel of some daring, one that forgoes the unified perspective of a single narrator and fragments its text into fifty-nine segments told from fifteen different perspectives. Faulkner requires his readers to take an active part in constructing the story, allows for multiple and sometimes conflicting interpretations, and achieves remarkable levels of psychological insight.

In *As I Lay Dying*, Faulkner introduces Yoknapatawpha County—a fictional rendition of his native Lafayette County, Mississippi—which became the setting for most of his best-known works. The novels set in Yoknapatawpha County, with their recurring places, events, and families, may be read as one intricate tale.

Before Faulkner, the American South was often portrayed in literature as a backward, impossibly foreign land. Faulkner proved to be unusual in his ability to depict poor rural people with grace, dignity, and poetic grandeur, without whitewashing or ignoring their circumstances. The complexity and sophistication of the Yoknapatawpha novels changed many of the former perceptions of the South, and it is largely due to Faulkner that it is now considered one of the country's most fertile literary regions.

AS I LAY DYING: KEY FACTS

Time and place written: 1929–1930; Oxford, Mississippi

Date of first publication: October 6, 1930

Publisher: Jonathan Cape & Harrison Smith, Inc.

Type of work: Novel

Genre: Southern literature

Language: English

Setting (time): 1920s

Setting (place): A rural area in fictional Yoknapatawpha County, Mississippi

Tense: Present; occasionally past

Tone: Varies with narrator: tragic, comic, calm, hysterical, detached

Narrator: Interior monologues (first-person free narration) from the perspective of fifteen different characters

Point of view: Shifts between fifteen different characters, each with a distinct attitude toward the events of the novel

Protagonist: Darl Bundren

Antagonist: Dysfunction of the Bundren family, death of Addie Bundren, difficult journey to Jefferson, poverty, misunderstandings, fate

AS I LAY DYING: PLOT OVERVIEW

Addie Bundren, wife of Anse Bundren and the matriarch of a poor southern family, is very ill and is expected to die soon. Her oldest son, Cash, builds her coffin in front of her bedroom window. Although Addie's health is failing rapidly, two of her other sons, Darl and Jewel, leave town to make a delivery for the Bundrens' neighbor, Vernon Tull, whose wife and two daughters have been taking care of Addie. Shortly after Darl and Jewel leave, Addie dies. The youngest Bundren child, Vardaman, associates his mother's death with the death of a fish he caught and cleaned earlier that day. With some help, Cash completes the coffin just before dawn. Vardaman is troubled that his mother is nailed shut inside a box, and while the others sleep, he bores holes in the lid, two of which go through his mother's face. Addie's daughter, Dewey Dell, whose recent sexual liaisons with a local farmhand named Lafe have left her pregnant, is so overwhelmed by anxiety about her pregnancy that she barely mourns her mother's death. A funeral service is held on the following day.

Darl, who narrates much of this first section, returns to the house with Jewel a few days later. They realize their mother is dead when they see buzzards over their house. Darl sardonically reassures Jewel, who is widely perceived as ungrateful and uncaring, that he can be sure his beloved horse is not dead. Addie has made Anse promise to bury her in the town of Jefferson, and though an out-of-town burial is far more complicated than burying her at home, Anse's sense of obligation, combined with his desire to buy a set of false teeth, compels him to fulfill Addie's dying wish. Cash, who has broken his leg on a job site, helps the family heave the coffin into the wagon, but it is Jewel who ends up lifting it, almost single-handedly. On the trip, Jewel refuses to ride in the wagon and follows the rest of the family on his horse, which he bought when he was young with money he saved by secretly working nights on a neighbor's land.

On the first night of their journey, the Bundrens stay with a generous local family that regards the Bundrens' mission with skepticism. Because of severe flooding, the main bridges leading over the local river have been flooded or washed away, and the Bundrens are forced to turn around and attempt a river crossing. When a stray log interferes with the wagon, the coffin is knocked out, Cash's broken leg is reinjured, and the team of mules drowns. Vernon Tull sees the wreck and helps Jewel rescue the coffin and the wagon from the river. Together, the family members and Tull search the riverbed for Cash's tools.

Cora, Tull's wife, remembers Addie's unchristian inclination to respect her son Jewel more than she respected God. In one section of the novel, Addie herself recalls events from her life: her loveless marriage to Anse; her affair with the local minister, Whitfield, who is Jewel's biological father; and the births of her children. Whitfield recalls traveling to the Bundrens' house intending to confess the affair to Anse and eventually deciding not to say anything after all.

A horse doctor sets Cash's broken leg. Cash does not complain, although he faints from the pain. Anse purchases a new team of mules by mortgaging his farm equipment, spending his false teeth money as well as money that Cash was saving for a new gramophone, and trading in Jewel's horse. The family continues on its way. In the town of Mottson, residents react with horror to the stench coming from the Bundren wagon. Dewey Dell tries to buy a drug that will abort her unwanted pregnancy, but the pharmacist refuses to sell it to her, advising marriage instead. Darl creates a makeshift cement cast for Cash's broken leg, which fits poorly and only increases Cash's pain. The Bundrens spend the night at a local farm owned by a man named Gillespie. Darl, who has been skeptical of their mission for some time, burns down the Gillespie barn with the intention of incinerating the coffin and Addie's rotting corpse. Jewel rescues the animals in the barn, then risks his life to drag out Addie's coffin. Darl lies on his mother's coffin and cries.

The next day, the Bundrens arrive in Jefferson and bury Addie. Rather than face a lawsuit for Darl's arson, the Bundrens claim that Darl is insane and give him to a pair of men who commit him to a Jackson mental institution. Dewey Dell tries again to buy an abortion drug at the local pharmacy, where the cashier boy claims to be a doctor and tricks her into exchanging sexual services for what she soon realizes is not an abortion drug. In the morning, the children are greeted by their father, who sports a new set of false teeth and, with a mixture of shame and pride, introduces them to his new bride, a local woman he has met while borrowing shovels for Addie's burial.

CHARACTERS IN *AS I LAY DYING*

Armstid A farmer. The Bundrens stay with Armstid on the second night of their journey. Armstid offers to lend them a team of mules, but Anse repeatedly refuses the offer.

Addie Bundren The matriarch of the Bundren family. Addie's death sets the novel's action in motion. Addie is a former schoolteacher whose bitter, loveless life has caused her to despise her husband and to invest all of her love in her favorite child, Jewel.

Anse Bundren Addie's husband. Anse, a farmer, is poor, hunchbacked, and largely selfish. His children both hate and disrespect him, but he achieves all of his goals—he acquires false teeth, buries Addie in Jefferson, and remarries.

Darl Bundren The second oldest Bundren child. Of all the novel's characters, Darl is the closest to being a protagonist. He is the most sensitive and articulate of the surviving Bundrens and narrates more of the novel than anyone else.

Jewel Addie and Whitfield's bastard child. Proud and brooding, Jewel is the novel's greatest mystery. He is often considered selfish, but he becomes a determined protector of his mother's coffin.

Cash Bundren The eldest Bundren child. Cash is a skilled carpenter. Patient and selfless to the point of absurdity, Cash is the most stable major character. He never complains about his broken, festering leg, allowing the injury to worsen.

Dewey Dell Bundren The only Bundren daughter. Dewey Dell's pregnancy leaves her increasingly desperate, and she views all men with suspicion.

Vardaman Bundren The youngest Bundren child. Thoughtful and innocent, Vardaman has a lively imagination and memorably compares his mother to a fish.

Gillespie A farmer who houses the Bundrens late in their journey.

The Gillespie boy Gillespie's son. He helps Jewel save the animals from the burning barn.

Lafe Dewey Dell's sexual partner and the father of her baby. Lafe gives Dewey $10 to pay for an abortion. He does not appear in the novel.

MacGowan A despicable young employee at a Jefferson drugstore. MacGowan extorts a sexual favor from Dewey Dell in return for a fake abortion treatment.

Moseley A Mottson druggist. Moseley indignantly refuses Dewey Dell's request to help her abort. Moseley's stern lecture to Dewey Dell is both sanctimoniousness and, arguably, caring.

Peabody An obese rural doctor. Peabody attends to Addie and later to Cash. He is extremely critical of the way Anse treats his children.

Samson A farmer with whom the Bundrens spend the first night of their journey. Samson thinks that the Bundrens' problems are punishment for their behavior.

Cora Tull Vernon Tull's wife. A deeply religious woman, Cora stays with Addie during Addie's last hours. She frequently disapproves of Addie's behavior.

Vernon Tull The Bundrens' wealthier neighbor. Tull both criticizes and helps the Bundrens. He hires Darl, Jewel, and Cash for odd jobs and helps the Bundrens cross the river despite their overt hostility to him.

Whitfield The local minister. Whitfield has an affair with Addie and fathers Jewel.

THEMES IN *AS I LAY DYING*

THE INSTABILITY OF EXISTENCE AND IDENTITY Addie's death—the moment when she ceases to be—leads several characters to question her and their own existences and identities. Vardaman is bewildered by the transformation of a fish he cut into "pieces of not-fish," and associates that image with Addie's transformation, in death, from a person into a non-person. Darl believes that since the dead Addie is better described with the word "was" rather than the word "is," she must no longer exist. Since he has no mother, Darl reasons, he himself must also not exist.

These speculations are more than language and logic games. They have tangible, even terrible, consequences for the characters. Vardaman and Darl, for whom these questions are critical, both feel their holds on reality loosen as they explore such ideas. Early in the novel, Vardaman babbles senselessly; by the end of the novel, Darl is declared insane.

The instability of human identity is highlighted at the end of *As I Lay Dying*, when Anse introduces his new wife as Mrs. Bundren, a name that until recently has belonged to Addie. The quick usurpation of the title Mrs. Bundren suggests that identity is a transient or a vague concept.

THE TENSION BETWEEN WORDS AND THOUGHTS Addie's assertion that speech is made up of "just words," which perpetually fall short of the ideas and emotions they try to convey, reflects the novel's distrust of verbal communication. Even though the novel's interior monologues demonstrate that the characters have rich inner lives, few of their ideas or emotions are ever communicated to others. Conversations tend to be terse and halting, and do not reflect the characters' thoughts. The two presentations of the conversation between several local men and Cash about Cash's broken leg during Addie's funeral illustrates this point. The first presentation, printed in normal type, is simple and vague. It seems to be an account of the conversation that takes place aloud. The second version, in italics, is far more nuanced. Presumably, this second conversation is the one that the characters would have had if they dared to say what they think. One of the novel's most remarkable achievements is its portrayal of the emotional richness of a world in which verbal communication is ineffective or unreliable.

POINTLESS ACTS OF HEROISM Most of the novel's valiant struggles are thwarted and hence rendered ironic and absurd. The Bundrens' great effort to move their wagon across a flooded river is undermined by the problematic premise of the quest. The journey to Jefferson is impractical and is as much about Anse's false teeth as about Addie's dying wish. Cash's stoicism about his broken leg eventually becomes more ridiculous than noble. Jewel's rescue of Addie's coffin from the burning barn is heroic, but also invalidates Darl's arson of the barn—which, while criminal, is also arguably the most daring and noble act of all.

SYMBOLS IN *AS I LAY DYING*

ANIMALS After Addie dies, the Bundren children seize on animals to represent her. Vardaman declares that his mother is a fish, for like his fish, she has been transformed to a different state in death. Minutes after her mother's death, Dewey Dell mulls over her own pregnancy and calls the family cow a woman. The cow's swollen udders suggest Dewey Dell's unwanted burden. Darl says that Jewel's mother is his horse. For us, Jewel's love for his horse represents his love for his mother. For Jewel, the horse represents his hard-won freedom from the Bundren family.

ADDIE'S COFFIN Addie's coffin, heavy and awkward, embodies the enormous burden of dysfunction placed on the Bundren family, both by Addie's death and by their circumstances in life. Cash constructs the coffin with great care, but the absurdities mount: Addie's body is placed upside down in the coffin, and Vardaman drills holes in her face. Like the Bundrens' lives, the coffin is thrown off balance by Addie's corpse. Burying the coffin—the focal point of their difficulties—represents the return to normalcy for the family.

IMPORTANT QUOTATIONS EXPLAINED

I have seen it before in women. Seen them drive from the room them coming with sympathy and pity, with actual help, and clinging to some trifling animal to whom they never were more than pack-horses. That's what they mean by the love that passeth understanding: that pride, that furious desire to hide that abject nakedness which we bring here with us, . . . carry stubbornly and furiously with us into the earth again.

Location: Section 11
Speaker: Peabody
Context: Peabody comments on the dying Addie's love for her favorite son Jewel, who refuses to see her
  before he leaves even though she may die before his return

Peabody thinks that Addie's love for Jewel is unrequited and that her determination to continue loving him with such force is a sign of irrational stubbornness and pride. For us, Peabody's words are ironic. We know that Jewel is Addie and Whitfield's love child, which may explain her devotion to Jewel. It is also ironic that Peabody accuses Jewel of loving his mother no more than a "pack-horse," since Jewel adores his horse.
  Peabody's phrase "the love that passeth understanding" comes from the Bible, where it is used to describe love for Jesus (Ephesians 3:19). The biblical reference in this passage reveals the extent to which the characters consciously and unconsciously interpret their lives according to the values and explanations provided by the Bible.

"It's Cash and Jewel and Vardaman and Dewey Dell," pa says, kind of hangdog and proud too, with his teeth and all, even if he wouldn't look at us. "Meet Mrs Bundren," he says.

Location: Section 59, the novel's concluding words
Speaker: Cash
Context: Anse introduces his new wife to his children. This passage ends the novel

Anse's last line provides the novel's most ironic moment: on the day after his wife's burial—for which his children have braved fire, flood, and humiliation—Anse shows up with false teeth and a new wife, the woman who earlier loaned him shovels with which to bury the first Mrs. Bundren. The finale casts a shadow over the entire novel; all preceding events appear either farcical or tragic.

> *"Jewel's mother is a horse," Darl said.*
>   *"Then mine can be a fish, can't it, Darl?" I said.*
>   …
>   *"Then what is your ma, Darl?" I said.*
>   *"I haven't got ere one," Darl said. "Because if I had one, it is was. And if it was, it cant be is. Can it?"*

Location: Section 24
Speaker: Vardaman
Context: The Bundrens have loaded the coffin onto the wagon and are about to leave for Jefferson

---

> *[W]ords dont ever fit even what they are trying to say at…. [M]otherhood was invented by someone who had to have a word for it because the ones that had the children didn't care whether there was a word for it or not.*

Location: Section 40
Speaker: Addie
Context: In her only monologue, Addie gives her perspective on her life

---

> *Sometimes I think it aint none of us pure crazy and aint none of us pure sane until the balance of us talks him that-a-way. It's like it aint so much what a fellow does, but it's the way the majority of folks is looking at him when he does it.*

Location: Section 53
Speaker: Cash
Context: Cash discusses his family's decision to commit Darl to a mental institution after Darl burns down Gillespie's barn

THE AWAKENING

Kate Chopin

The wife of a New Orleans businessman drowns herself at sea after a series of awakenings leave her increasingly independent, aware of her desires, and alone.

THE LIFE OF KATE CHOPIN

Kate Chopin was born Catherine O'Flaherty on February 8, 1850, in St. Louis, Missouri. After her father's death in 1855, Chopin was raised by intelligent, independent women: her mother and grandmother, and the nuns at her Catholic boarding school. In 1870, two years after graduating at the top of her class, Chopin married Oscar Chopin, the son of a prominent Louisiana Creole family, and moved to New Orleans with him. Kate Chopin bore six children in the first ten years of marriage. With her husband's full support, she enjoyed many more liberties than other women of the era, from taking solitary walks to engaging in controversial political discussions. In 1879, plagued with financial problems, the Chopin family moved to Cloutierville, Louisiana, where Oscar Chopin owned some land. Three years later, he died suddenly of swamp fever. Chopin was devastated by her husband's death. During the next year, she was rumored to be having an affair with a married neighbor. When that relationship ended, Chopin and her children moved back to Missouri.

In 1889, Chopin began writing fiction, which enabled her to develop and express her strong views on women, sex, and marriage while simultaneously supporting her family. She enjoyed immediate success with stories about French Creoles and Cajuns. Chopin's stories were controversial, exploring themes of love, independence, passion, and freedom, but their specific setting allowed readers to interpret the emotions she described as curiosities of a particular culture rather truths about human nature.

The Awakening, Chopin's second and final novel, was published in 1899 at the height of her popularity. The tone of *The Awakening* revealed the author's sympathies for the behavior and emotions of Edna Pontellier, a sexually aware woman. Surprised and deeply hurt by the negative reception the novel received, Chopin published only three more short stories before she died of a brain hemorrhage in 1904.

THE AWAKENING IN CONTEXT

At the turn of the century, the feminist movement, which was just beginning to emerge in other parts of America, had not yet reached the conservative state of Louisiana, where by law women were considered the property of their husbands. In this environment, *The Awakening* was scorned for its open discussion of the emotional and sexual needs of women. It did not come into its own as a classic work of American fiction until it was rediscovered some fifty years later. Later generations have accepted the novel's depiction of female sexuality and equality and praised *The Awakening*'s realism and exploration of early American feminism.

Modern critics have noted the novel's rich detail and imagery, and have often analyzed and theorized about its ironic narrative voice. *The Awakening* has earned a place in the literary canon for the way it uses formal and structural techniques to explore themes of women's independence, desire, and sexuality.

THE AWAKENING: KEY FACTS

Time and place written: 1897–1899; St. Louis

Date of first publication: 1899

Publisher: Herbert S. Stone and Co.

Type of work: Novella

Genre: Bildungsroman, kunstlerroman

Language: English; certain phrases in French

Setting (time): 1899

Setting (place): Grand Isle (a vacation resort) and the French Quarter of New Orleans	
Tense: Immediate past	
Tone: Objective, sympathetic	
Narrator: Anonymous, third-person narrator	
Point of view: Edna Pontellier's	
Protagonist: Edna Pontellier	
Antagonist: The expectations and conventions of polite society	

THE AWAKENING: PLOT OVERVIEW

The Awakening opens at the end of the nineteenth century on Grand Isle, a summer holiday resort popular with the wealthy inhabitants of nearby New Orleans. Edna Pontellier is vacationing with her husband Léonce and their two sons at the cottages of Madame Lebrun. Léonce is kind and loving, but frequently goes away on business trips. Edna spends most of her time with her friend Adèle Ratignolle, a married Creole who epitomizes womanly elegance and charm. Through her friendship with the conservative but forthcoming Adèle, Edna learns a great deal about freedom of expression, beginning the process of self-discovery that constitutes the focus of the novella. Edna comes to know Robert Lebrun, Madame Lebrun's older son. The Grand Isle vacationers know Robert as a man who chooses one woman each year—often a married woman—and plays "attendant" to her all summer long. This summer, he devotes himself to Edna, and the two spend their days together lounging and talking by the shore.

As the summer progresses, Edna and Robert grow closer, and Robert's affections and attention inspire in Edna several internal revelations. She feels more alive than ever before, and she starts to paint again. She also learns to swim and becomes aware of her independence and sexuality. Edna and Robert never openly discuss their love for one another, but the time they spend alone together makes Edna remember the dreams and desires of her youth. Recognizing the intensity of his connection to Edna, Robert leaves Grand Isle to avoid consummating the relationship.

Back in New Orleans, Edna pursues her painting and ignores her social responsibilities. Worried about the changing attitude and increasing disobedience of his wife, Léonce seeks the guidance of the family physician, Doctor Mandelet. Doctor Mandelet suspects that Edna is having an affair. Instead of sharing his suspicions with Léonce, he recommends letting Edna's defiance run its course, arguing that attempts to control her would only fuel her rebellion. Accordingly, Léonce leaves Edna home alone while he is away on business. With both her husband and her children gone, Edna wholly rejects her former lifestyle. She moves into a home of her own and declares that she is independent, the possession of no one. Although she still loves Robert intensely, Edna pursues an affair with the town seducer, Alcée Arobin, who is able to satisfy her sexual needs. Edna maintains control throughout her affair with Arobin, never becoming emotionally attached to him.

The self-sufficient and unconventional old pianist Mademoiselle Reisz adopts Edna as a protégé, warning her of the sacrifices required of an artist. Edna is moved by Mademoiselle Reisz's piano playing and visits her often. She is also eager to read the letters that Robert sends to Mademoiselle Reisz, who is the only person who knows of Robert and Edna's secret love. Mademoiselle Reisz encourages Edna to admit to and act upon her feelings.

Unable to stay away, Robert returns to New Orleans. He finally admits his love for Edna but tells her they cannot possibly be together because she is married. Edna says she is now completely independent from her husband and wants to enjoy a happy life with Robert. But despite his love for Edna, Robert refuses to be with a married woman.

When Adèle goes into a difficult and dangerous labor, Edna leaves Robert's arms to go to her, pleading with him to wait for her return. Adèle urges Edna to "[t]hink of the children." While walking Edna home from Adèle's, Doctor Mandelet urges her to come see him, saying he is worried about the effects of her passionate but confused actions. Edna begins to think she has behaved selfishly.

Edna returns home to find that Robert has left, leaving behind a goodbye note. She has a devastating awakening. Haunted by thoughts of her children and realizing that eventually she would have found even Robert incapable of fulfilling her desires and dreams, Edna feels an overwhelming sense of solitude. Alone in a world to which she cannot belong, she returns to Grand Isle, the site of her first moments of emotional, sexual, and intellectual awareness, and goes into the sea. As she swims through the water, she thinks about her freedom from her husband and children, Robert's failure to understand her, Doctor Mandelet's words of wisdom, and Mademoiselle Reisz's courage. The text leaves open the question of whether Edna's suicide is a cowardly surrender or a liberating triumph.

CHARACTERS IN *THE AWAKENING*

Madame Antoine A friendly local on *Chênière Caminada*, the island where Edna and Robert attend mass.

Alcée Arobin Edna's lover. The playboy of the New Orleans Creole community, Alcée becomes Edna's lover while both her husband and Robert Lebrun, Edna's first lover, are away.

The Colonel Edna's father. A former Confederate officer in the Civil War, the Colonel is a strict Protestant and believes that husbands should manage their wives with authority and coercion.

Mrs. Highcamp A fashionable New Orleans matron. Mrs. Highcamp is instrumental in bringing together Edna and Alcée Arobin.

The Farival Twins Fourteen-year-old girls. The twins vacation at Grand Isle with their family. Associated with the Virgin Mary, they represent the ideal of chaste motherhood that adolescent Victorian girls are meant to attain eventually. They entertain guests by playing the piano and fulfill society's expectation that women should use art to delight others.

The Lady in Black The widowed lady in black is patient, resigned, solitary, and silent.

The Two Lovers Vacationers at the Lebrun cottages on Grand Isle who embody socially accepted forms of young love.

Madame Lebrun Robert and Victor's widowed mother. Madame Lebrun is the proprietor of the cottages on Grand Isle where the characters spend their summers.

Robert Lebrun The dramatic and passionate man with whom Edna falls in love. After courting many different women only half-seriously, Robert genuinely falls in love with Edna, a development that makes him feel torn between his desires and his sense of propriety.

Victor Lebrun Robert Lebrun's wayward younger brother. Victor spends his time chasing women and refuses to choose a career.

Doctor Mandelet Léonce and Edna's family physician. Doctor Mandelet sympathizes with Edna's dissatisfaction but worries about the possible consequences of her turmoil.

Margaret and Janet Edna's sisters. Margaret, the oldest, cared for her sisters after their mother died. Edna refuses to attend Janet's wedding.

Mariequita A young, pretty, flirtatious Spanish girl living on Grand Isle. Mariequita embodies the self-demeaning coquetry that Edna shuns.

Edna Pontellier The novel's protagonist. The twenty-eight-year-old wife of a New Orleans businessman, Edna finds herself dissatisfied with her marriage and limited lifestyle. In a series of awakenings over the course of the novel, she emerges from her semiconscious existence as a devoted wife and mother, discovering her own identity and acting on her desires for emotional and sexual satisfaction. Ultimately, her awakenings lead to isolation and suicide.

Léonce Pontellier Edna's husband. A wealthy, forty-year-old New Orleans businessman, Léonce is often away on business and spends little time with his family. Léonce is kind and loving but aloof.

Raoul and Etienne Pontellier Léonce and Edna's two sons.

Adèle Ratignolle Edna's close friend. Adèle epitomizes the conventional feminine ideal of the era. A foil for both Mademoiselle Reisz and the increasingly independent Edna, Adèle idolizes her children and worships her husband. Although Adèle leads a conservative life, her free manner of discourse and expression inspires Edna to abandon her reserve.

Mademoiselle Reisz A reclusive pianist. Mademoiselle Reisz's influence is instrumental in Edna's awakening. She is unmarried, childless, and focused on music, which is her passion. She warns Edna that a person who wants to be an artist must have a courageous and defiant soul.

THEMES IN *THE AWAKENING*

SOLITUDE AS THE CONSEQUENCE OF INDEPENDENCE For Edna Pontellier, social isolation comes as a direct consequence of newfound independence. By the end of the novel, Edna has become estranged from her family, and Adèle admonishes her for neglecting her children. Ultimately, Robert abandons Edna too, isolating her still more. The note Robert leaves for Edna makes it clear that she is alone in her awakening. Once Robert refuses to trespass the boundaries of societal convention, Edna is forced to acknowledge the profundity of her solitude.

MODES OF SELF-EXPRESSION During her awakening, Edna learns at least three new modes of expressing herself. From the Creole women on Grand Isle, she learns to speak frankly about what she thinks and feels. From Robert and Alcée, she learns how to express the love and passion she has kept secret for so long. From Mademoiselle Reisz, she learns to express herself through art. Mademoiselle Reisz's piano playing stirs Edna in a new way, touching her more deeply than music ever had before. Once Edna is aware of music's power to express emotion, she begins to paint in an entirely new way. Painting ceases to be a diversion and becomes a form of true expression.

SYMBOLS IN *THE AWAKENING*

BIRDS In *The Awakening*, caged birds symbolize Edna and other women entrapped by Victorian society. Madame Lebrun's parrot and mockingbird represent Edna and Madame Reisz, respectively. Just as the birds' movements are limited by their cages, the women's movements are limited by society—limited so severely that the women are unable to communicate with the world around them.

Edna's attempts to escape her husband, children, and society fail. Her efforts only land her in a house that is another cage. Edna may view it as a sign of her independence, but the new house, which is "two steps away" from her old home, only demonstrates her inability to leave her former life.

Critics who argue that Edna's suicide suggests defeat, both for her personally and for women in general, often point to the similarity between the bird imagery used by Mademoiselle Reisz and the bird imagery of the novel's final scene. Mademoiselle Reisz warns Edna that freedom is costly and difficult, saying, "[t]he bird that would soar above the level plain of tradition and prejudice must have strong wings. It is a sad spectacle to see the weaklings bruised, exhausted, fluttering back to earth." In the final pages, the narrator notes that "[a] bird with a broken wing was beating the air above, reeling, fluttering, circling disabled down, down to the water." This crippled bird might symbolize Edna, suggesting that her suicide is a gesture of defeat. But if the bird is a symbol not of Edna herself, but rather of Victorian womanhood, then its fall represents a triumph, suggesting that Edna's suicide has disabled convention just as the bird is disabled.

THE SEA The sea in *The Awakening* symbolizes freedom and escape. The sea is a vast expanse that Edna can brave only when she is solitary and only after she has discovered her own strength. Floating in the water, Edna is reminded of the depth of the universe and of her own role as a human being who exists in that depth. The sensuous sound of the surf constantly beckons to Edna throughout the novel.

Water, which is associated with cleansing and baptism, has long been a symbol of rebirth. In *The Awakening*, Chopin uses the sea to suggest that Edna's awakening is a rebirth of the spirit. Appropriately, Edna ends her life in the sea. With her suicide, a space of infinite potential becomes an enveloping void that carries both a promise and a threat. In its vastness, the sea also represents the strength, glory, and lonely horror of independence.

IMPORTANT QUOTATIONS FROM *THE AWAKENING*

In short, Mrs. Pontellier was beginning to realize her position in the universe as a human being, and to recognize her relations as an individual to the world within and about her. This may seem like a ponderous weight of wisdom to descend upon the soul of a young woman of twenty-eight—perhaps more wisdom than the Holy Ghost is usually pleased to vouchsafe to any woman."

But the beginning of things, of a world especially, is necessarily vague, tangled, chaotic, and exceedingly disturbing. How few of us ever emerge from such beginning! How many souls perish in its tumult!

The voice of the sea is seductive; never ceasing, whispering, clamoring, murmuring, inviting the soul to wander for a spell in abysses of solitude; to lose itself in mazes of inward contemplation.

The voice of the sea speaks to the soul. The touch of the sea is sensuous, enfolding the body in its soft, close embrace.

Location: Chapter VI
Speaker: The narrator
Context: On Grand Isle, Edna accepts Robert Lebrun's invitations to go swimming after initially refusing them

This passage describes the beginning of Edna's process of awakening. Most of the concepts explored in the novel are mentioned in this passage: independence and solitude, self-discovery, intellectual maturation, and sexual desire and fulfillment. With the remark "How few of us ever emerge from such beginning!" the narrator points out that Edna is unusual in her willingness to embark on a quest for autonomy, fulfillment, and self-discovery. The exclamation "How many souls perish in [the beginning's] tumult!" foreshadows the turmoil that results from Edna's growing awareness, suggesting that from the moment her awakening begins, Edna is marked for death. Additionally, the narrator's mention of the sea's sensual and inviting voice foreshadows Edna's eventual suicide. The sentence that begins "The voice of the sea" is repeated almost verbatim just before Edna's death.

"The years that are gone seem like dreams—if one might go on sleeping and dreaming—but to wake up and find—oh! well! Perhaps it is better to wake up after all, even to suffer, rather than to remain a dupe to illusions all one's life."

Location: Chapter XXXVIII
Speaker: Edna
Context: Doctor Mandelet walks Edna home and asks her about her frame of mind

The idea expressed in this quotation may be considered the overarching message, or even moral, of *The Awakening*. Even though Edna's awakening leads her to suffer, the year of joy and understanding that accompanies the awakening is worth more to Edna than a lifetime of the semiconscious submission that characterized her former existence.

She perceived that her will had blazed up, stubborn and resistant. She could not at that moment have done other than denied and resisted. She wondered if her husband had ever spoken to her like that before, and if she had submitted to his command. Of course she had; she remembered that she had. But she could not realize why or how she should have yielded, feeling as she then did.

Location: Chapter XI
Speaker: The narrator
Context: Edna has returned from her cathartic nighttime swim and lies on the porch hammock, ignoring her husband's entreaties to come to bed

---

"How many years have I slept?… The whole island seems changed. A new race of beings must have sprung up, leaving only you and me as past relics. How many ages ago did Madame Antoine and Tonie die? And when did our people from Grand Isle disappear from the earth?"

Location: Chapter XIII
Speaker: Edna to Robert Lebrun
Context: Edna has woken up from her nap at Madame Antoine's house

The pigeon-house pleased her. It at once assumed the intimate character of a home, while she herself invested it with a charm which it reflected like a warm glow. There was with her a feeling of having descended in the social scale, with a corresponding sense of having risen in the spiritual. Every step which she took toward relieving herself from obligations added to her strength and expansion as an individual. She began to look with her own eyes; to see and to apprehend the deeper undercurrents of life. No longer was she content to "feed upon opinion" when her own soul had invited her.

Location: Chapter XXXII
Speaker: The narrator
Context: With her husband and her children away, Edna has moved out of her home with her husband into a small house around the block

THE BELL JAR

Sylvia Plath

A young woman whose talent and intelligence have brought her close to achieving her dreams must overcome suicidal tendencies.

THE LIFE OF SYLVIA PLATH

Sylvia Plath was born to Otto and Aurelia Plath in 1932 and spent her early childhood in the seaport town of Winthrop, Massachusetts. Otto Plath died when Plath was eight years old. After her father's death, Plath moved with her mother, younger brother, and maternal grandparents to Wellesley, an inland suburb of Boston. Plath excelled in school and developed a strong interest in writing and drawing. In 1950, she won a scholarship to attend Smith College, where she majored in English. Like Esther, the protagonist of *The Bell Jar*, Plath was invited to serve as guest editor for a woman's magazine in New York. After returning to Wellesley for the remainder of the summer, she had a nervous breakdown and attempted suicide.

Plath completed a highly successful college career. She won the prestigious Fulbright scholarship to study at Cambridge University in England, where she met the English poet Ted Hughes. They married in 1956, and after a brief stint in the United States, where Plath taught at Smith, they moved back to England in 1959. Plath gave birth to her first child, Freda, the following year. The same year, she published *The Colossus*, her first volume of poetry. Her second child, Nicholas, was born in 1962. Hughes and Plath separated shortly after the birth of Nicholas. Plath's instability and Hughes's affair with another woman had placed great strain on their marriage. Plath and her children moved to a flat in London, where Plath continued to write poetry. The poems she wrote at this time were later published in a collection titled *Ariel* (1965). In February 1963, when Plath was thirty-one, she committed suicide by gassing herself in her kitchen.

Plath is primarily known not as a novelist but as an outstanding poet. *Ariel* cemented her reputation as a great artist. Her other volumes of poetry, published posthumously, include *Crossing the Water* (1971), *Winter Trees* (1971), and *The Collected Poems* (1981), which won the Pulitzer Prize.

Sylvia Plath's literary persona has always provoked extreme reactions. Onlookers tend to mythologize Plath either as a feminist martyr or a tragic heroine. Those who see her as a feminist martyr say that Plath was driven over the edge by her misogynist husband and sacrificed on the altar of pre-feminist, repressive 1950s America. Those who see her as a tragic heroine say that Plath was a talented but doomed young woman whose debilitating mental illness made her unable to deal with the pressures of society. Although neither myth presents a wholly accurate picture, truth exists in both.

THE BELL JAR IN CONTEXT

An autobiographical novel, *The Bell Jar* closely conforms to events in Plath's life. It recounts, in lightly fictionalized form, the summer and autumn after Plath's junior year of college. Plath most likely wrote a first draft of *The Bell Jar* in the late 1950s. In 1961, she received a fellowship that allowed her to complete the novel. *The Bell Jar* was published in London in January 1963 under the pseudonym Victoria Lucas. Plath used a pseudonym both to protect the people she portrayed in the novel and because she was uncertain of the novel's literary merit. The novel appeared posthumously in England under her own name in 1966, and in America, over the objections of her mother, in 1971. *The Bell Jar* has received moderate critical acclaim and has long been valued not only as a glimpse into the psyche of a major poet, but as a witty and harrowing American coming-of-age story.

THE BELL JAR: KEY FACTS

Time and place written: First draft as early as 1957, Cambridge, England; completed in 1962; Devon, England

Date of first publication: January 1963, under the pseudonym Victoria Lucas

Publisher: William Heinemann Limited (1963); Faber and Faber (first edition under Plath's name, 1966); Harper and Row (first American edition, 1971)

Type of work: Novel

Genre: Autobiographical fiction; bildungsroman

Language: English

Setting (time): June 1953–January 1954

Setting (place): New York City; the Boston suburbs

Tense: Past

Tone: Matter-of-fact, cynical, terse, detached, girlish

Narrator: Esther Greenwood

Point of view: First person

Protagonist: Esther Greenwood

Antagonist: The oppressive environment; encroaching madness

THE BELL JAR: PLOT OVERVIEW

Esther Greenwood, a college student from Massachusetts, travels to New York to work at a magazine for a month as a guest editor. Her boss is Jay Cee, a sympathetic but demanding woman. Esther lives in a women's hotel with the eleven other college girls chosen to work at the magazine. The sponsors of their trip wine and dine them, and shower them with presents. Esther knows she should be having the time of her life, but she feels deadened. The impending execution of the Rosenbergs—convicted in 1951 of conspiracy to commit espionage—worries Esther, and she can embrace neither the rebellious attitude of her friend Doreen nor the perky conformism of her friend Betsy. Esther attempts to lose her virginity with a U.N. interpreter, but he seems uninterested. On her last night in the city, she goes on a disastrous blind date with a man named Marco, who tries to rape her.

Esther wonders if she should marry and live a conventional domestic life or attempt to satisfy her ambition. Buddy Willard, her college boyfriend, is recovering from tuberculosis in a sanitarium and wants to marry Esther when he regains his health. To an outside observer, Buddy appears to be the ideal mate: handsome, gentle, intelligent, and ambitious. But he does not understand Esther's desire to write poetry. Buddy confesses that he slept with a waitress while dating Esther, and Esther decides he is a hypocrite and she cannot marry him. She sets out to lose her virginity as though in pursuit of the answer to an important mystery.

Esther returns to the Boston suburbs and discovers that she has not been accepted to a writing class she had planned to take. She makes vague plans to write a novel, learn shorthand, and start her senior thesis. A feeling of unreality soon takes over her life. Esther is unable to read, write, or sleep. She stops bathing. Her mother takes her to Dr. Gordon, a psychiatrist who prescribes electric shock therapy. Esther becomes more unstable than ever after this terrifying treatment and decides to kill herself. She tries to slit her wrists, but can only bring herself to slash her calf. She tries to hang herself, but cannot find a place to tie the rope in her low-ceilinged house. At the beach with friends, she attempts to drown herself, but she keeps floating to the surface of the water. Finally, she hides in a basement crawl space and takes a large quantity of sleeping pills.

Esther wakes up in the hospital. She has survived her suicide attempt with no permanent physical injuries. Once her body heals, she is sent to the psychiatric ward in the city hospital, where she is uncooperative, paranoid, and determined to end her life. Eventually, Philomena Guinea, the famous novelist who sponsors Esther's college scholarship, pays to move Esther to a private hospital. In this more enlightened environment, Esther comes to trust her new psychiatrist, a woman named Dr. Nolan. She slowly begins to improve with a combination of talk therapy, insulin injections, and properly administered electric shock therapy. She befriends Joan, a woman from her hometown. A large, horsy woman, Joan was a year ahead of Esther in college, and Esther envied her social and athletic success. Joan once dated Buddy. To Esther's disgust, Joan makes a sexual advance toward her.

As Esther improves, the hospital officials grant her permission to leave the hospital from time to time. During one of these excursions, she finally loses her virginity to a math professor named Irwin. She bleeds profusely and has to go to the emergency room. One morning, Joan, who seemed to be improving, hangs herself. Buddy comes to visit Esther. Both understand that their relationship is over. Esther will leave the mental hospital in time to start the winter semester at college. She believes she has regained a tenuous grasp on sanity, but knows that the bell jar of her madness could descend again at any time.

CHARACTERS IN *THE BELL JAR*

Betsy One of Esther's friends in New York. Betsy is a pretty, wholesome girl from Kansas. Esther feels she is more like Betsy than she is like Doreen, but she cannot relate to Betsy's cheerfulness and optimism.

Jay Cee Esther's boss at the magazine. Jay Cee is an ambitious career woman who encourages Esther to be ambitious. She treats Esther brusquely but kindly.

Constantin A U.N. simultaneous interpreter who takes Esther on a date. Handsome, thoughtful, and accomplished, Constantin seems sexually uninterested in Esther, who is willing to sleep with him.

Dodo Conway The Greenwoods' neighbor. Dodo is a Catholic woman with six children and a seventh on the way. She lives unconventionally, but everyone likes her.

Doreen One of Esther's friends in New York. Doreen is a blond, beautiful southern girl with a sharp tongue. Doreen rebels against convention in a way Esther admires but cannot entirely embrace.

Eric A past acquaintance of Esther's. Eric, a southern prep school boy, lost his virginity with a prostitute and now associates love with chastity and sex with debasement and shame.

Joan Gilling Esther's companion in the mental hospital. In the mental ward, Esther comes to think of Joan as her double. Esther does not particularly like Joan, but she feels an affinity for her.

Irwin A tall, intelligent, homely math professor at Harvard. Irwin, Esther's first lover, is charming and seductive but not particularly responsible or caring.

Doctor Gordon Esther's first psychiatrist. Dr. Gordon is good-looking and has an attractive family. Esther distrusts him and thinks him conceited. Dr. Gordon ends up doing Esther more harm than good.

Esther Greenwood The protagonist and narrator of the novel. Esther is attractive, talented, and lucky, but uncertainty plagues her. A sense of unreality clouds her existence.

Mrs. Greenwood Esther's mother. Mrs. Greenwood lost her husband when her children were still young and must struggle to make a living by teaching typing and shorthand. Practical and traditional, she loves Esther and worries about her future, but cannot understand her.

Philomena Guinea A famous, wealthy novelist. Philomena Guinea gives Esther a scholarship to attend college and pays for her stay in the private mental hospital. She is elderly, generous, and successful.

Jody A friend of Esther's. Esther was supposed to live with Jody during her summer writing course. Jody is friendly and tries to be helpful, but she cannot reach Esther.

Marco A tall, dark, well-dressed Peruvian. Marco takes Esther on a date to a country club. Although dashing and confident, Marco is also violent and sadistic. He thinks all women are sluts.

Doctor Nolan Esther's psychiatrist at the private mental hospital. Esther comes to trust and love Dr. Nolan, who acts as a kind and understanding surrogate mother. Progressive and unconventional, Dr. Nolan encourages Esther's unusual thinking.

Lenny Shepherd Doreen's love interest. Lenny is a New York deejay and smooth older man. He wears cowboy-style clothes and has a cowboy-style home.

Buddy Willard Esther's college boyfriend. Buddy is an athletic, intelligent, good-looking man who graduated from Yale and went to medical school. Buddy cares for Esther but has conventional ideas about women and fails to understand Esther's interest in poetry.

Mrs. Willard A friend of Esther's mother and the mother of Buddy Willard. Mrs. Willard, who feels protective of her son, has traditional ideas about the roles men and women should play.

Valerie A friend of Esther's in the private mental hospital. Valerie, who has had a lobotomy, is friendly and relaxed.

THEMES IN *THE BELL JAR*

THE EMPTINESS OF CONVENTION   Esther observes a gap between what society says she should experience and what she actually does experience. Consciousness of this gap intensifies her madness. Society expects women of Esther's age and station to act cheerful, flexible, and confident, and Esther feels she must repress her natural gloom, cynicism, and dark humor. She feels she cannot discuss or think about the dark spots in life that plague her: personal failure, suffering, and death. She knows the world of fashion she inhabits in New York should make her happy, but instead it strikes her as full of poison, drunkenness, and violence. Her relationships with men are supposed to be romantic and meaningful, but they are marked by misunderstanding, distrust, and brutality. Esther almost continuously feels that her reactions are wrong or that she is the only one to view the world as she does, and eventually these feelings make the world seem unreal. This sense of unreality grows until it becomes unbearable, and attempted suicide and madness follow.

THE RESTRICTED ROLE OF WOMEN IN 1950S AMERICA   Esther's alienation from the world around her comes from the expectations 1950s America places on her. Esther is torn between her desire to write and the pressure she feels to settle down and start a family. While Esther's intellectual talents earn her prizes, scholarships, and respect, many people assume that she longs to become a wife and mother. The girls at her college mock her studiousness and show respect for her only when she begins dating a handsome and well-liked boy. Esther's relationship with Buddy earns her mother's approval, and everyone expects Esther to marry him. Buddy assumes that Esther will drop her poetic ambitions as soon as she becomes a mother. The message sinks in, and Esther herself assumes she cannot be both mother and poet.

Esther longs for the adventures society denies her, particularly sexual adventures. She decides to reject Buddy for good when she realizes he represents a sexual double standard. He has an affair with a waitress while dating Esther, but expects Esther to remain a virgin until she marries him. Esther understands her first sexual experience as a crucial step toward independence and adulthood; she seeks this experience not for her own pleasure but to relieve herself of her burdensome virginity. Esther feels anxiety about her future because she can see only mutually exclusive choices: virgin or whore, submissive married woman or successful but lonely career woman. She dreams of a larger life, but the stress of even dreaming such a thing worsens her madness.

THE PERILS OF PSYCHIATRIC MEDICINE   *The Bell Jar* takes a critical view of the medical profession, particularly of psychiatric medicine. This critique begins with Esther's visit to Buddy's medical school, where Esther is troubled by the arrogance of the doctors and their lack of sympathy for the pain suffered by a woman in labor. When Esther meets her first psychiatrist, Dr. Gordon, she finds him self-satisfied and unsympathetic. He does not listen to her, but prescribes a traumatic and unhelpful shock therapy treatment. Joan, Esther's acquaintance in the mental hospital, tells a similar tale of the insensitivity of male psychiatrists. Some of the hospitals in which Esther stays are frighteningly sanitized and authoritarian. The novel does not paint an entirely negative picture of psychiatric care, however. When Esther goes to a more enlightened, luxurious institution, she begins to heal under the care of Dr. Nolan, a progressive female psychiatrist. Three methods of 1950s psychiatric treatment—talk therapy, insulin injections, and electroshock therapy—work for Esther under the attentive care of Dr. Nolan. Even properly administered therapy does not receive unmitigated praise, however. Shock therapy, for example, works by clearing the mind entirely. After one treatment, Esther finds herself unable to think about knives. This inability comes as a relief, but it also suggests that the therapy works by the dubious method of blunting Esther's sharp intelligence.

SYMBOLS IN *THE BELL JAR*

THE BELL JAR   The bell jar is an inverted glass jar generally used to display an object of scientific curiosity, contain a certain kind of gas, or maintain a vacuum. For Esther, the bell jar symbolizes madness. When gripped by insanity, she feels like she is inside an airless jar that distorts her perspective and prevents her from connecting with the people around her.

THE BEATING HEART   When Esther tries to kill herself, she finds that her body seems determined to live. Esther remarks that if it were up to her, she would die in no time, but her body sets up tricks and ruses to keep itself alive. The beating heart symbolizes this bodily desire for life. When Esther tries to drown herself, her heart beats, "I am I am I am." It repeats the same phrase when Esther attends Joan's funeral.

IMPORTANT QUOTATIONS FROM *THE BELL JAR*

When I was nineteen, pureness was the great issue. Instead of the world being divided up into Catholics and Protestants or Republicans and Democrats or white men and black men or even men and women, I saw the world divided into people who had slept with somebody and people who hadn't, and this seemed the only really significant difference between one person and another. I thought a spectacular change would come over me the day I crossed the boundary line.

Location: Chapter 7
Speaker: Esther
Context: Esther thinks about her desire to lose her virginity

Esther inhabits a world of limited sexual choices. Convention dictates that she must remain a virgin until she marries. If she chooses to have sex before marriage, she risks getting pregnant, displeasing her future husband, and ruining her own name. Esther sets out to defy conventional expectations by losing her virginity with someone she does not expect to marry. Despite this firm goal, she finds it difficult to gain an independent sexual identity. The men in her life provide little help: Buddy has traditional ideas about male and female roles even though he has transgressed by having an affair with a waitress; an acquaintance named Eric thinks sex is disgusting and will not have sex with a woman he loves; and Marco calls Esther a slut as he attempts to rape her. When Esther finally loses her virginity, she does not experience the "spectacular change" that she expected, although the experience does satisfy her in some ways. Esther only partially escapes the repressive ideas about sexuality that surround her. By losing her virginity, she frees herself of the oppressive expectation of purity, but she fails to find sexual pleasure or independence.

How did I know that someday—at college, in Europe, somewhere, anywhere—the bell jar, with its stifling distortions, wouldn't descend again?

Location: Chapter 20
Speaker: Esther
Context: Esther considers her tenuous new feelings of sanity

This quotation is the final word on Esther's supposed cure. The bell jar has lifted enough that Esther can function more or less normally. She no longer wants to kill herself, and she has begun to form tenuous connections with other people and with the outside world. But Esther still feels the bell jar hovering above her and worries that it will trap her again. Her madness does not obey reason, and though she feels grateful to have escaped from it temporarily, she does not believe that this escape is a fundamental or permanent change in her situation. If we read *The Bell Jar* as partly autobiographical, Plath's own life story confirms that the bell jar can descend again. Mental illness drove Plath to attempt suicide in her late teens, and recurring mental illness drove her to commit suicide in her early thirties.

Look what can happen in this country, they'd say. A girl lives in some out-of-the-way town for nineteen years, so poor she can't afford a magazine, and then she gets a scholarship to college and wins a prize here and a prize there and ends up steering New York like her own private car. Only I wasn't steering anything, not even myself. I just bumped from my hotel to work and to parties and from parties to my hotel and back to work like a numb trolleybus. I guess I should have been excited the way most of the other girls were, but I couldn't get myself to react. I felt very still and very empty, the way the eye of a tornado must feel, moving dully along in the middle of the surrounding hullabaloo.

Location: The first section of Chapter 1
Speaker: Esther
Context: Esther describes the disconnect between the way she is supposed to feel and the way she actually feels

---

[W]herever I sat—on the deck of a ship or at a street café in Paris or Bangkok—I would be sitting under the same glass bell jar, stewing in my own sour air.

Location: The beginning of Chapter 15
Speaker: Esther
Context: Esther explains what madness feels like

To the person in the bell jar, blank and stopped as a dead baby, the world itself is the bad dream.

Location: Chapter 20
Speaker: Esther
Context: Esther's mother has just suggested treating Esther's illness like a bad dream they can now forget

BELOVED

Toni Morrison

An ex-slave is haunted by the memory of the daughter she killed.

THE LIFE OF TONI MORRISON

Toni Morrison was born Chloe Anthony Wofford on February 18, 1931, in Lorain, Ohio, a small steel-mill city west of Cleveland. She was the second of four children. Her parents were George Wofford, who worked as a shipyard welder, and Rahmah Willis Wofford, whose parents had been sharecroppers.

Morrison excelled in high school and, in 1949, became the first woman in her family to go to college. She matriculated at Howard University, the esteemed, predominantly black institution in Washington, D.C. Morrison joined the college's drama club and during the summers traveled with the club through-out the South, performing for all-black audiences. At this time, Morrison began calling herself Toni, a shortened version of her middle name, Anthony.

After graduating from Howard with a bachelor's degree in English literature in 1953, Morrison earned a master's degree in English from Cornell University. In 1955, Morrison accepted her first teaching job at Texas Southern University, a predominantly black institution. Morrison has said that Texas Southern University instilled in her a sense of "black culture as a subject, an idea, as a discipline." She left Texas Southern after two years and returned to Howard University to join its English faculty. In Washington, she met Harold Morrison, a Jamaican architect. She married him in 1958. Three years later, Morrison gave birth to their first son, Harold Ford.

Morrison did not take an active part in the Civil Rights movement, which had electrified the Howard campus by the early 1960s. She was uncomfortable with the movement's philosophy of integration; she believed that integration would come only through the kind of black solidarity she had found at Texas Southern.

After the birth of their second son, Morrison and her husband divorced. Morrison took a job as a text-book editor at a subsidiary of Random House in Syracuse, New York. Eventually, she became a senior editor at Random House's New York City headquarters. She worked there for eighteen years, specializing in the literary works of black authors and collaborating on *The Black Book* (1974), a groundbreaking scrapbook of sorts that included photographs, documents, and articles collected from 300 years of Afri-can-American history and culture. Her goal as an editor was to help create a canon of African-American literature.

In the late 1960s, as Morrison's prominence as an editor grew, her literary career also began to flour-ish. Before leaving Syracuse, she had shown a short story to Alan Rancler, an editor, who encouraged her to expand the story into a full-length novel. Rancler published the resulting novel, *The Bluest Eye*, in 1970. Morrison's second novel, *Sula* (1973) was nominated for the National Book Award for Fiction in 1975. Her third novel, *Song of Solomon* (1977), which won the National Book Critics Circle Award, was the breakthrough work that made Morrison a household name in America. Morrison's other works include *Tar Baby* (1981), *Jazz* (1992), *Paradise* (1998), and *Beloved* (1987), which won the Pulitzer Prize in Fiction in 1988. In 1993, Morrison won the Nobel Prize in Literature, becoming the eighth woman and the first black woman to receive the honor.

BELOVED IN CONTEXT

Set during the Reconstruction era in 1873, *Beloved* centers on the powers of memory and history. For the former slaves in the novel, the past is a burden that they desperately and willfully try to forget. Yet for Sethe, the protagonist of the novel, memories of slavery are inescapable. They haunt her, literally, taking the form of the spirit of the daughter Sethe murdered to save her from a life of slavery. The events of *Beloved* are inspired by the real-life story of Margaret Garner, who, like Sethe, escaped from slavery in Kentucky and murdered her child when slave catchers caught up with her in Ohio.

One of Morrison's projects in *Beloved* is to investigate a history that had been lost to the ravages of forced silences and willed forgetfulness. *Beloved* also has a didactic element. Morrison uses Sethe's experience to suggest that before we can hope for stability, we must confront and understand the ghosts of the past. Morrison likens America to Sethe, arguing that contemporary Americans must confront the history of slavery in order to address its legacies: racial discrimination and discord.

BELOVED: KEY FACTS

Time and place written: 1980s; Albany, New York

Date of first publication: 1987

Publisher: Alfred A. Knopf

Type of work: Novel

Genre: Historical fiction; ghost story

Language: English

Tense: Immediate and distant past; also occasional present-tense passages

Tone: Mournful, regretful, dramatic

Setting (time): 1873, with frequent flashbacks to the early 1850s

Setting (place): Cincinnati, Ohio, Sweet Home plantation in Kentucky, and prison in Alfred, Georgia

Narrator: Varies

Protagonist: Sethe

Antagonist: Beloved; white racists

BELOVED: PLOT OVERVIEW

It is 1873 in Cincinnati, Ohio. Sethe, a former slave, lives at 124 Bluestone Road with her eighteen-year-old daughter, Denver. Sethe's mother-in-law, Baby Suggs, lived with them until her death eight years earlier. Just before Baby Suggs's death, Sethe's two sons, Howard and Buglar, ran away. Sethe believes they fled because of the abusive ghost that has haunted their house for years. Denver likes the ghost, which everyone believes to be the spirit of her dead sister.

On the day the novel begins, Paul D, whom Sethe has not seen since they were both enslaved on Mr. Garner's Sweet Home plantation in Kentucky approximately twenty years earlier, shows up at Sethe's house. His presence stirs up memories that Sethe has repressed for almost two decades. From this point on, the novel unfolds on two temporal planes. The present in Cincinnati constitutes one plane, and a series of events that took place around twenty years earlier constitutes the other.

Through a series of fragmented flashbacks, told from the various perspectives of the different characters, the following story emerges: Sethe was born in the South to an African mother she never knew. At age thirteen, she is sold to the Garners, who own Sweet Home and are comparatively benevolent. At Sweet Home, the other slaves, who are all men, lust after Sethe but never touch her. Sethe chooses to marry Halle, a generous man who has hired himself out on weekends and saved enough to buy his mother's freedom. Sethe and Halle have two sons, Howard and Buglar, and a baby daughter whose name we never learn. Mr. Garner dies, and the widowed Mrs. Garner asks her sadistic, vehemently racist brother-in-law to help her run the farm. He is known to the slaves as "schoolteacher." His oppressive presence makes life on the plantation unbearable. The slaves decide to run away.

Schoolteacher and his nephews anticipate the slaves' escape attempt and capture Paul D and Sixo. Schoolteacher kills Sixo and brings Paul D back to Sweet Home. Sethe, who is pregnant, has sent her children ahead to her mother-in-law Baby Suggs's house in Cincinnati. Invigorated by the recent capture, schoolteacher's nephews seize Sethe in the barn and violate her, drinking milk from her breasts. Halle, who is hiding secretly in a loft above, watches in horror. He goes mad. Paul D sees him sitting by a churn with butter slathered all over his face. Paul D is tortured, forced to wear an iron bit in his mouth.

Sethe runs away and collapses from exhaustion in a forest. A white girl, Amy Denver, finds her and nurses her back to health. Amy later helps Sethe deliver her baby in a boat. Sethe names this second daughter Denver. In Cincinnati, Sethe has twenty-eight wonderful days. On the last day, schoolteacher comes for Sethe and her children. Rather than surrender her children to a life of slavery, Sethe takes them to the woodshed and tries to kill them. She manages to kill her older daughter by slitting her throat.

Sethe later arranges for the baby's headstone to be carved with the word "Beloved." A group of white abolitionists, led by the Bodwins, fights to give Sethe her freedom. Sethe returns to the house at 124, where Baby Suggs has sunk into a deep depression. The community shuns the house, and the family lives in isolation.

Meanwhile, Paul D is sold to a man named Brandywine. After attempting to kill Brandywine, he is sentenced to work on a chain gang in Georgia. Paul D's traumatic experiences cause him to lock away his memories, emotions, and ability to love in the "tin tobacco box" of his heart. One day, a fortuitous rainstorm allows Paul D and the other chain gang members to escape. Years later, he ends up on Sethe's porch in Cincinnati.

Now Paul D chases away the house's ghost, which makes the lonely Denver resent him. One day, on their way home from a carnival, the three encounter a strange young woman sleeping near the steps of 124. Later, we learn that she is likely the embodied spirit of Sethe's dead daughter. Beloved moves into 124. Denver develops an obsessive attachment to Beloved, and Beloved becomes passionately attached to Sethe. Paul D and Beloved hate each other, and Beloved seduces Paul D against his will.

When Paul D learns the story of Sethe's "rough choice"—her infanticide—he leaves 124 and goes to stay in the basement of the local church. Sethe and Beloved's relationship grows more intense and exclusive. Beloved is increasingly abusive, manipulative, and parasitic, and Sethe is increasingly obsessed with satisfying Beloved's demands and making her understand why she murdered her. Denver leaves the premises of 124 for the first time in twelve years in order to seek help from Lady Jones, her former teacher. The community provides the family with food and eventually organizes to exorcise Beloved from 124. When they arrive at Sethe's house, they see Sethe on the porch with Beloved, who stands smiling at them, naked and pregnant. Mr. Bodwin, who has come to 124 to take Denver to her new job, arrives at the house. Mistaking him for schoolteacher, Sethe runs at Mr. Bodwin with an ice pick. She is restrained. In the confusion, Beloved disappears, never to return.

Afterward, Paul D comes back to Sethe, who has retreated to Baby Suggs's bed to die. Mourning Beloved, Sethe laments, "She was my best thing." Paul D replies, "You your best thing, Sethe." As time passes, the town and even the residents of 124 forget Beloved "[l]ike an unpleasant dream during a troubling sleep."

CHARACTERS IN *BELOVED*

Baby Suggs Halle's mother and Sethe's mother-in-law. Baby Suggs is a source of emotional and spiritual inspiration for Cincinnati's black residents. But after Sethe commits infanticide, Baby Suggs stops preaching and retreats to a sickbed to die. It is partially out of respect for Baby Suggs that the community responds to Denver's requests for support.

Beloved A mysterious visitor to 124. Beloved could be an ordinary woman traumatized by years of captivity, the ghost of Sethe's mother, or, most convincingly, the embodied spirit of Sethe's murdered daughter. On an allegorical level, Beloved represents the inescapable horror of slavery, which haunts its victims even after they escape it. Her presence catalyzes Sethe's, Paul D's, and Denver's processes of emotional growth.

Mr. and Miss Bodwin Siblings and white abolitionists. The Bodwins help Beloved win her freedom, and their intentions are always good, but there is something disconcerting about their brand of activism. Mr. Bodwin longs for the "heady days" of abolitionism, and Miss Bodwin wants to "experiment" on Denver by sending her to Oberlin College. In the Bodwins' house, Denver sees a slave figurine with the words "At Yo' Service."

Paul A, Paul F, and Sixo Slaves at Sweet Home. Paul A and Paul F are Paul D's brothers.

Paul D A former slave at Sweet Home. Because of his brutal experiences, Paul D represses his memories and tries not to love anything too much. He becomes Sethe's lover and, against his will, Beloved's.

Amy Denver An indentured servant. Amy is nurturing, compassionate, and flighty. She helps Sethe when she is ill and delivers baby Denver, whom Sethe names after her.

Denver Sethe's youngest child. Though intelligent, introspective, and sensitive, Denver has been stunted in her emotional growth by years of relative isolation. Beloved's malevolence forces Denver to overcome her fear of the world.

Ella A woman who was sexually brutalized by a white father and son who once held her captive. Ella organizes the women of the community to exorcise Beloved from 124.

Mr. and Mrs. Garner The owners of Sweet Home. The Garners are not violent, but they savage the slaves' spirits by treating them like subhuman beings.

Halle Sethe's husband and Baby Suggs's son. Halle is generous, kind, and sincere.

Lady Jones A teacher in Cincinnati. Lady Jones believes that everyone despises her for being a woman of mixed race.

Schoolteacher Mr. Garner's brother. Cold, sadistic, and vehemently racist, schoolteacher undertakes a "scientific" scrutiny of the slaves, which involves asking questions, taking physical measurements, and teaching lessons to his white pupils on the slaves' "animal characteristics."

Sethe The protagonist of the novel. Sethe is an independent and deeply maternal woman.

Stamp Paid An agent of the Underground Railroad. Stamp Paid helps Sethe to freedom and later saves Denver's life. Angered by the community's neglect of Sethe, Denver, and Paul D, Stamp questions the nature of a community's obligations to its members.

THEMES IN *BELOVED*

SLAVERY'S DESTRUCTION OF IDENTITY *Beloved* explores the physical, emotional, and spiritual devastation wrought by slavery. The most dangerous of slavery's effects is its denial of individual identity. Paul D is so alienated from himself that at one point he cannot tell whether the screaming he hears is his own or someone else's. As a person who was once traded like a piece of furniture, he worries that he could not possibly be a real man. In an attempt to shield himself from pain, Paul D locks away his feelings in the rusted "tobacco tin" of his heart. He believes that the key to survival is refusing to love too intensely. Sethe, like Paul D, is self-loathing and alienated from herself. She believes her children are the best part of herself. Some slaves—Jackson Till, Aunt Phyllis, and Halle—go insane, losing their selves completely.

Slavery does not destroy whites' identities, but it does dehumanize them, turning even the best of them into criminals. Stamp Paid says that slavery leaves whites "changed and altered . . . made . . . bloody, silly, worse than they ever wanted to be." Where slavery exists, everyone suffers a loss of humanity and compassion.

THE IMPORTANCE OF COMMUNITY SOLIDARITY *Beloved* suggests that individuals need the support of their communities in order to survive. Sethe is happiest during her twenty-eight days of freedom, when she becomes a part of the Cincinnati community. Denver discovers herself and grows up only when she leaves 124 and becomes a part of society. Paul D and his fellow prison inmates in Georgia escape by relying on each other, forced to move as one body because they are chained together. The community saves Sethe from mistakenly killing Mr. Bodwin and casting the shadow of another sin across her and her family's lives. When the support of the community falters, disaster results. The community, jealous of Sethe's and Baby Suggs's happiness, fails to alert Sethe to schoolteacher's approach. Therefore, the community is partly responsible for the death of Sethe's daughter. Baby Suggs never recovers from the community's betrayal. At the end of the novel, the community makes up for its past misbehavior by gathering at 124 to exorcise Beloved.

THE LIMITATIONS AND POWERS OF LANGUAGE At Sweet Home, whites wield language as a weapon against slaves. When Sixo turns schoolteacher's reasoning around, schoolteacher whips him to demonstrate that "definitions belong to the definers," not to the defined. Often, whites use language in boldly inaccurate ways. Mr. Garner constantly brags about allowing his slaves to live as "real men," even though he treats them like retarded children. The name "Sweet Home" itself is a cruel and ludicrous way to describe a place where humans are enslaved. Sixo eventually reacts to the hypocrisy of whites by abandoning English altogether, but other characters use English to redefine the world on their own terms. Baby Suggs and Stamp Paid rename themselves. Others manipulate language for their own purposes, making it impossible for the white slave owners to understand them. For example, Paul D and the Georgia prison inmates sing about their dreams and memories by "garbling . . . [and] tricking the words."

SYMBOLS IN *BELOVED*

RED Red has several symbolic meanings throughout the novel. Amy Denver longs for red velvet, which symbolizes her longing for a better life. Paul D's "red heart" represents emotion. The red roses that line the road to the carnival symbolize Sethe, Denver, and Paul D's new life together, but they also stink of death. The red rooster signifies manhood to Paul D, but manliness seems like an unattainable state to him. Perhaps most obviously, red symbolizes death. The central image of the novel is Sethe's bloody murder of her daughter.

TREES Trees symbolize healing, comfort, and life. Denver's "emerald closet" of boxwood bushes is a place of solitude and repose for her. The beautiful trees of Sweet Home mask the horror of the plantation in Sethe's memory. Paul D finds his freedom by following flowering trees to the North, and Sethe finds hers by escaping through a forest. By imagining the scars on Sethe's back as a "chokecherry tree," Amy Denver sublimates a site of trauma and brutality into one of beauty and growth. But as the sites of lynchings and of Sixo's death by burning, trees also symbolize murderousness.

IMPORTANT QUOTATIONS FROM *BELOVED*

Beloved *is divided into two parts, but not into chapters; we have imposed chapter numbers for ease of analysis.*

[I]f you go there—you who was never there—if you go there and stand in the place where it was, it will happen again; it will be there, waiting for you . . . [E]ven though it's all over—over and done with—it's going to always be there waiting for you.

Location: Part One, Chapter 3
Speaker: he narrator
Context: Denver remembers what Sethe once told her about the indestructible nature of the past

According to Sethe's theory of time, past traumas reenact themselves indefinitely, so it is possible to stumble into someone else's unhappy memory. Accordingly, although Sethe describes for Denver what "was" using the past tense, she turns to the future tense to tell her that the past will "always be there waiting for you." Sethe pictures the past as a physical presence, something that is "there," that fills a space. Beloved's arrival confirms the idea that history has physical being.

And if she thought anything, it was No. No. Nono. Nonono. Simple. She just flew. Collected every bit of life she had made, all the parts of her that were precious and fine and beautiful, and carried, pushed, dragged them through the veil, out, away, over there where no one could hurt them. Over there. Outside this place, where they would be safe.

Location: Part One, Chapter 18
Speaker: The narrator
Context: Sethe thinks of how she felt while trying to murder her children

Morrison describes Sethe's murderous frenzy as an unthinking, unconscious one. She writes "If [Sethe] thought anything," as if Sethe might have been beyond cognition. When she realized that schoolteacher was going to enslave her children, Sethe's instinctual reaction was to keep them safe, to put them in a place "where no one could hurt them." She killed her daughter from this desire to keep her safe, not in violence, anger, rebellion, or madness.

Sethe identifies her children as "the parts of her that were precious and fine and beautiful." For her to allow schoolteacher to take her children would be to allow him to destroy everything that is good in herself, to destroy all the life in her. Therefore, the murder of her daughter is also an act of self-defense.

124 was spiteful. Full of a baby's venom.

Location: The first words of Part One
Speaker: The narrator
Context: The narrator speaks of the ghost that haunts Sethe's house

---

White people believed that whatever the manners, under every dark skin was a jungle. Swift unnavigable waters, swinging screaming baboons, sleeping snakes, red gums ready for their sweet white blood. In a way . . . they were right . . . .But it wasn't the jungle blacks brought with them to this place. . . . It was the jungle whitefolks planted in them. And it grew. It spread . . . until it invaded the whites who had made it . . . . Made them bloody, silly, worse than even they wanted to be, so scared were they of the jungle they had made. The screaming baboon lived under their own white skin; the red gums were their own.

Location: Part Two, Chapter 19
Speaker: The narrator
Context: Stamp Paid considers the way slavery corrupts all who are involved in it

---

Saying more might push them both to a place they couldn't get back from. He would keep the rest where it belonged: in that tobacco tin buried in his chest where a red heart used to be. Its lid rusted shut.

Location: Part One, Chapter 7
Speaker: The narrator
Context: Paul worries that if he lets himself get attached to Sethe, his memories will overwhelm him

BEOWULF

Unknown

Beowulf, a great warrior, goes to Denmark on a successful mission to kill Grendel; he returns home to Geatland, where he becomes king and slays a dragon before dying.

BEOWULF IN CONTEXT

Beowulf is an archetypal Anglo-Saxon literary work and one of the cornerstones of modern literature. By the time *Beowulf* was composed by an unknown Anglo-Saxon poet around 700 A.D., much of its material had existed in oral narrative form for many years. Elements of *Beowulf*—including its setting and characters—date back to the period before the Anglo-Saxon and Scandinavian peoples invaded the island of Britain and settled there, bringing with them several closely related Germanic languages that would evolve into Old English. The action of the poem takes place around 500 A.D. Many of the characters in the poem, such as the Swedish and Danish royal family members, correspond to actual historical figures.

The Anglo-Saxon and Scandinavian invaders were originally pagan, but experienced a large-scale conversion to Christianity at the end of the sixth century. *Beowulf* is an old pagan story, but its poet tries to attribute Christian thoughts and motives to his characters, who frequently behave in distinctly un-Christian ways. The element of religious tension is common in Christian Anglo-Saxon writings, but the combination of a pagan story with a Christian narrator is fairly unusual.

Beowulf was composed in England. It is set in Scandinavia before the migration to Britain, and it tells the story of a bygone era. In the Scandinavian world of the story, tiny tribes of people rally around strong kings who protect their people from danger—especially from confrontations with other tribes. The warrior culture that results from this early feudal arrangement is extremely important both to the story and to our understanding of Saxon civilization. Strong kings demand bravery and loyalty from their warriors, whom they repay with treasures won in war. Mead-halls such as Heorot in *Beowulf* were places where warriors gathered in the presence of their lord to drink, boast, tell stories, and receive gifts. The early Middle Ages were a dangerous time, and Scandinavian society constantly feared invasion.

Only a single manuscript of *Beowulf* survived the Anglo-Saxon era. For many centuries, the manuscript was all but forgotten, and in the 1700s it was nearly destroyed in a fire. It was not until the nineteenth century that scholars and translators of Old English began to take an interest in the document. For the next hundred years, people were primarily interested in the poem as a source of information about the Anglo-Saxon era. Then, in 1936, the Oxford scholar J. R. R. Tolkien (who later wrote *The Hobbit* and *The Lord of the Rings*, works heavily influenced by *Beowulf*) published a groundbreaking paper entitled "*Beowulf*: The Monsters and the Critics." After the publication of this paper, *Beowulf* gained recognition as a serious work of art.

Beowulf, now widely taught, is often presented as the first important work of English literature. This might create the impression that *Beowulf* is the source of the English canon, but actually it had little impact on English literature until the twentieth century. It was not widely read until the 1800s and not regarded as an important work until the 1900s, so Chaucer, Shakespeare, Marlowe, Pope, Shelley, Keats, and most other important English writers before the 1930s had little or no knowledge of the epic. It was not until the mid-to-late twentieth century that *Beowulf* began to influence writers. Since then, it has had a marked impact on the work of many important novelists and poets, including W. H. Auden, Geoffrey Hill, Ted Hughes, and Seamus Heaney, the 1995 recipient of the Nobel Prize in literature who recently translated the epic.

BEOWULF: KEY FACTS

Time and place written: Between 700 and 1000 A.D.; England	
Date of first publication: Around 1000 A.D. in manuscript form	
Publisher: The original poem exists only in manuscript form	

Type of Work: Poem	
Genre: Alliterative verse, elegy, small-scale heroic epic	
Language: Anglo-Saxon (also called Old English)	
Setting (time): The main action of the story is set around 500 A.D.	
Setting (place): Denmark and Geatland (a region in what is now southern Sweden)	
Tense: Past, but with digressions into the distant past, and predictions of the future	
Tone: Enthusiastic, foreboding	
Narrator: A Christian man	
Point of view: Third-person limited omniscient	
Protagonist: Beowulf	
Antagonist: Grendel, Grendel's mother, the dragon	

BEOWULF: PLOT OVERVIEW

King Hrothgar of Denmark, a descendant of the great king Shield Sheafson, is enjoying a prosperous and successful reign. He builds a great mead-hall, Heorot, where his warriors gather to drink, receive gifts from their lord, and listen to stories sung by the *scops*, or bards. The jubilant noise from Heorot angers Grendel, a horrible demon who lives in the swamplands of Hrothgar's kingdom. Grendel terrorizes and kills the Danes every night. Because of Grendel, the Danes suffer many years of fear, danger, and death. Eventually, a young Geatish warrior named Beowulf hears of Hrothgar's plight. Inspired by the challenge, Beowulf sails to Denmark with a small company of men, determined to defeat Grendel.

Hrothgar, who once did a great favor for Beowulf's father, Ecgtheow, accepts Beowulf's offer to fight Grendel and holds a feast in the hero's honor. During the feast, an envious Dane named Unferth taunts Beowulf and says he is unworthy of his reputation. Beowulf responds by boasting about his past accomplishments. His confidence cheers the Danish warriors, and the feast continues into the night. At last Grendel arrives. Beowulf, though unarmed, is stronger than the demon. Grendel is terrified and struggles to escape. Beowulf tears off the monster's arm. Mortally wounded, Grendel slinks back into the swamp to die. The severed arm is hung high in the mead-hall as a trophy of victory.

Overjoyed, Hrothgar throws a feast in Beowulf's honor and showers him with gifts and treasure. As the feast goes on, Grendel's mother, a swamp-hag who lives in a desolate lake, comes to Heorot seeking revenge for her son's death. She murders Aeschere, one of Hrothgar's most trusted advisers, before slinking away. To avenge Aeschere's death, the company travels to the murky swamp, where Beowulf dives into the water and fights Grendel's mother in her underwater lair. He kills her with a sword forged for a giant. He finds Grendel's corpse, decapitates it, and brings the head to Hrothgar as a prize.

The Danes are again overjoyed, and Beowulf's fame spreads throughout the kingdom. Beowulf departs after bidding a sorrowful goodbye to Hrothgar, who has treated him like a son. He returns to Geatland, where he and his men are reunited with their king and queen, Hygelac and Hygd. Beowulf tells them of his adventures and hands over most of his treasure to Hygelac, who rewards him.

In time, Hygelac is killed in a war against the Shylfings, and, after Hygelac's son dies, Beowulf ascends to the throne of the Geats. He rules wisely for fifty years, bringing prosperity to Geatland. When Beowulf is an old man, a thief disturbs a barrow (mound) where a great dragon lies guarding a horde of treasure. Enraged, the dragon emerges from the barrow and begins unleashing fiery destruction upon the Geats. Sensing his own death approaching, Beowulf goes to fight the dragon. With the aid of Wiglaf, he succeeds in killing the beast. Before the dragon dies, it bites Beowulf in the neck, killing him with its fiery venom. The Geats fear that their enemies will attack them now that Beowulf is dead. Following Beowulf's wishes, they burn his body on a huge funeral pyre and then bury him with massive treasure in a barrow overlooking the sea.

CHARACTERS IN *BEOWULF*

PRINCIPAL CHARACTERS

Beowulf The protagonist of the epic. Beowulf, a Geatish hero, is incredibly strong and able. In his youth, he personifies all of the best values of the heroic culture. In his old age, he is a wise and effective ruler.

The Dragon An ancient, powerful serpent. The dragon, who guards a horde of treasure in a hidden mound, is Beowulf's final nemesis.

Grendel A demon descended from Cain. Grendel suffers for the sins of Cain, leading a ruthless and miserable existence because God seeks vengeance for Cain's murder of Abel.

Grendel's mother A swamp-hag. Grendel's mother possesses fewer human qualities than Grendel. Still, her terrorization of Heorot springs from her understandable anger over her son's death.

King Hrothgar The king of the Danes. A wise and aged ruler, Hrothgar leads in a different way than the youthful warrior Beowulf does. Hrothgar is a father figure for Beowulf and a model of the kind of king Beowulf will become.

OTHER DANES

Aeschere Hrothgar's trusted adviser.

Beow A Danish king. Beow was the son of Shield Sheafson and the father of Halfdane. The narrator suggests that Beow was a gift from God to a people in need of a leader.

Halfdane The father of Hrothgar, Heorogar, Halga, and an unnamed daughter who married a king of the Swedes. Halfdane succeeded Beow as ruler of the Danes.

Hrethric Hrothgar's elder son. Hrethric stands to inherit the Danish throne, but his older cousin Hrothulf eventually prevents him from doing so. Beowulf hosts Hrethric in Geatland and gives him guidance.

Hrothmund Hrothgar's second son.

Hrothulf Hrothgar's nephew. Hrothulf betrays his cousin, Hrethric, the rightful heir to the Danish throne.

Shield Sheafson The legendary Danish king from whom Hrothgar is descended. Shield Sheafson headed a long line of Danish rulers and embodied the Danish tribe's ideals of heroism and leadership. The poem opens with a brief account of his rise from orphan to warrior-king, concluding, "That was one good king."

Unferth A Danish warrior who is jealous of Beowulf. Unferth is unable or unwilling to fight Grendel.

Wealhtheow Hrothgar's wife, the gracious Queen of the Danes.

OTHER GEATS

Breca Beowulf's childhood friend. Beowulf once defeated Breca in a swimming match.

Ecgtheow Beowulf's father, Hygelac's brother-in-law, and Hrothgar's friend. Ecgtheow is dead by the time the poem begins, but he lives on through his reputation for nobility and his son's remembrances.

King Hrethel The Geatish king. Hrethel took Beowulf in after the death of Ecgtheow, Beowulf's father.

Hygd Hygelac's wife, the young, beautiful, and intelligent Queen of the Geats.

Hygelac Beowulf's uncle, king of the Geats, and husband of Hygd. Hygelac welcomes Beowulf back from Denmark.

Wiglaf A young kinsman and retainer of Beowulf. Wiglaf helps Beowulf in the fight against the dragon while all the other warriors run away.

OTHER FIGURES MENTIONED

King Heremod An evil king of legend.

Queen Modthryth A wicked queen of legend who punishes anyone who looks at her the wrong way.

Sigemund A figure from Norse mythology. Sigemund is famous for slaying a dragon.

THEMES IN *BEOWULF*

THE IMPORTANCE OF ESTABLISHING IDENTITY In *Beowulf*, identity is made up of ancestral heritage and individual reputation. In the world of the story, every male figure is known as his father's son. Characters cannot talk about their identity or even introduce themselves without referring to their family lineage. They take pride in ancestors who acted valiantly and try to live up to the standards their ancestors set. Heritage provides the foundation for identity, and reputation solidifies identity. While *Beowulf*'s pagan warrior culture does not have a concept of the afterlife, it sees fame as a way of living after death. The oral tradition plays a crucial role in identity, telling tales of the people and lineages of the past. The importance of oral communication explains the prevalence of bards' tales (such as the Heorot scop's relating of the Finnsburg episode) and warriors' boastings (such as Beowulf's telling of the Breca story).

TENSIONS BETWEEN THE HEROIC CODE AND OTHER VALUE SYSTEMS *Beowulf* articulates and illustrates the Germanic heroic code, which values strength, courage, and loyalty in warriors; hospitality, generosity, and political skill in kings; ceremoniousness in women; and good reputation in all people. This traditional, much-respected code helps the warrior society understand the world and the menaces in the world. All of the characters' moral judgments stem from the code. However, the code contradicts itself at some points. At several moments in *Beowulf*, the code offers no practical guidance on how to act or feel. One of these moments occurs when Danish Hildeburh marries the Frisian king. When the Danes and the Frisians start a war, both Hildeburh's Danish brother and her Frisian son are killed, and she must grieve for both men. The code also conflicts with medieval Christianity. The code says that honor comes from deeds performed during life, but Christianity says that glory comes in the afterlife. The code says that it is always better to retaliate than to mourn, but Christianity says that forgiving one's enemies is always best. Throughout *Beowulf*, the poet strains to accommodate these two sets of values. Though he is Christian, he cannot (and does not seem to want to) deny the fundamental pagan underpinnings of the story.

THE MEANING OF MONSTERS In Christian medieval culture, the word "monster" referred to someone with birth defects, which were interpreted as an ominous sign from God—a sign of transgression or of bad things to come. In keeping with this idea, the monsters Beowulf must fight in this Old English poem represent an inhuman or alien presence that must be exorcised for society's safety. The monsters are outsiders who exist beyond the boundaries of human realms. Grendel and his mother intrude on human society, wreaking havoc in Heorot, and Beowulf must kill them to restore order. To many readers, the three monsters that Beowulf slays have symbolic or allegorical meaning. Since Grendel is descended from the biblical figure Cain, who killed his own brother, Grendel has often been interpreted as a marauding killer, a particularly evil figure in Scandinavian society. The dragon, a traditional figure in medieval folklore and a common Christian symbol of sin, represents the malice a hero must conquer to prove his goodness. Because Beowulf's encounter with the dragon ends in mutual destruction, the dragon may also symbolize the inevitability of death.

SYMBOLS IN *BEOWULF*

THE GOLDEN TORQUE The collar or necklace that Wealhtheow gives Beowulf symbolizes the bond of loyalty between her people and Beowulf—and, by extension, the Geats. Hygelac dies in battle wearing the golden torque.

THE BANQUET The great banquet at Heorot after the defeat of Grendel represents the restoration of order and harmony. The preparation involves rebuilding the damaged mead-hall, which, along with the banquet itself, symbolizes the rebirth of the community.

IMPORTANT QUOTATIONS FROM *BEOWULF*

---

*So. The Spear-Danes in days gone by
and the kings who ruled them had courage and greatness.*

. . .

*There was Shield Sheafson, scourge of many tribes,
a wrecker of mead-benches, rampaging among foes.*

. . .

A foundling to start with, he would flourish later on

. . .

*In the end each clan on the outlying coasts
beyond the whale-road had to yield to him
and begin to pay tribute. That was one good king.*

Location: Lines 1–11
Speaker: The narrator
Context: The narrator sets the stage by introducing the Spear-Danes and some of their kings

These lines, which open the poem, establish the tone of Seamus Heaney's translation and introduce some of the poem's central ideas. Heaney's translation of the first word of the poem as "So" has provoked great debate. Previously, the first word had been translated into such poetic-sounding invocations as "Hark," "Lo," or, more casually, "Listen." In his introduction, Heaney explains his choice by pointing out that "so," as his relatives use it, "obliterates all previous discourse and narrative, and at the same time functions as an exclamation calling for immediate attention." From the first word, Heaney's translation has an inviting, conversational tone.

   The translation preserves many of the conventions of Anglo-Saxon poetry. Whenever possible, Heaney breaks his lines into two halves with a strong caesura, or pause (lines 4, 5, and 11, for example). He also uses alliteration, or repetition of consonant sounds, across the caesura to bind the half-lines together through sound ("foundling . . . flourish," for example). He replicates the poet's extensive use of multiple names to describe one person, referring to Shield Sheafson, for example, as "scourge of many tribes" and "wrecker of mead-benches." The compound word "whale-road," used here to refer to the sea, is one of the most famous examples of a kenning, an Anglo-Saxon rhetorical figure which replaces a noun with a metaphorical description of that noun.

   The opening lines introduce a number of important themes. The lines emphasize the value of ancestry, but also of heroic action—even a fatherless man with no known ancestry can make a name for himself if he behaves like a hero. They also emphasize the power of reputation. By establishing fame in his lifetime, an individual can hope to be remembered by subsequent generations—the only consolation death brings.

---

*Beowulf got ready,
donned his war-gear, indifferent to death;
his mighty, hand-forged, fine-webbed mail
would soon meet with the menace underwater.
It would keep the bone-cage of his body safe:*

. . .

*[His helmet] was of beaten gold,
princely headgear hooped and hasped*

by a weapon-smith who had worked wonders. . . .

Location: Lines 1442–1452
Speaker: The narrator
Context: Beowulf prepares to battle Grendel's mother

The treatment of weaponry and armor is of great importance to the *Beowulf* poet. In the poem, armor has a double history, just as a warrior does: one history of origin (as a warrior has family lineage) and another history of performance (as a warrior has deeds and reputation). These lines suggest that well-crafted armor and weapons will succeed in battle. This passage also sets forth a theory about fate—which, in the warrior culture of *Beowulf*, includes the idea that the present contains future events. The poet narrates in the past tense, but he often looks ahead to what will happen in the future. In these lines, for example, the poet reveals that Beowulf's armor "would keep the bone-cage of his body safe." This looking ahead may surprise readers used to the modern convention of building up suspense, but in a tradition that sees the future in the present, it would seem foolish to try to conceal what will happen.

And a young prince must be prudent like that,
giving freely while his father lives
so that afterwards in age when fighting starts
steadfast companions will stand by him
and hold the line. Behaviour that's admired
is the path to power among people everywhere.

Location: Lines 20–25
Speaker: The narrator
Context: The narrator explains the virtues of the early Danish king Beow

---

Wise sir, do not grieve. It is always better
to avenge dear ones than to indulge in mourning.
For every one of us, living in this world
means waiting for our end. Let whoever can
win glory before death. When a warrior is gone,
that will be his best and only bulwark.

Location: Lines 1384–1389
Speaker: Beowulf
Context: Grendel's mother has killed Aeschere, Hrothgar's trusted advisor, and Beowulf tries to comfort Hrothgar

---

O flower of warriors, beware of that trap.
eternal rewards. Do not give way to pride.
For a brief while your strength is in bloom
but it fades quickly; and soon there will follow
illness or the sword to lay you low,
or a sudden fire or surge of water
or jabbing blade or javelin from the air
or repellent age. Your piercing eye
will dim and darken; and death will arrive,

dear warrior, to sweep you away.

Location: Lines 1758–1768
Speaker: Hrothgar
Context: Hrothgar reaches the culmination of a long speech often referred to as "Hrothgar's sermon" in which Hrothgar warns Beowulf of the seductive dangers of success after Beowulf has defeated Grendel's mother

BILLY BUDD, SAILOR

Herman Melville

An innocent young sailor, kills an evil sailor in a moment of rage, a crime for which he is hanged.

THE LIFE OF HERMAN MELVILLE

Herman Melville, the third of eight children, was born in New York City in 1819. His parents were Maria Gansevoort Melville and Allan Melvill, a prosperous importer of foreign goods. When the family business failed at the end of the 1820s, the Melvills relocated to Albany in an attempt to revive their fortunes. Overwork drove Allan to an early grave, and Melville (the name was changed after his father's death) was forced to start working in a bank at age thirteen.

Before the age of nineteen, Melville worked as an elementary school teacher and a newspaper reporter. At nineteen, he made his first sea voyage, working as a merchant sailor on a ship bound for Liverpool, England. He returned to America the next summer to seek his fortune in the West. After briefly settling in Illinois, he went back East in the face of continuing financial difficulties. Twenty-one and desperate, Melville committed to a whaling voyage on board the *Acushnet*. In the summer of 1842, eighteen months after setting out from New York, Melville and another sailor abandoned ship in the South Seas. The two men found themselves in the Marquesas Islands, where they accidentally stumbled upon a tribe of cannibals. Lamed by an injury to his leg, Melville got separated from his companion and spent a month alone with the natives. This experience provided material for his first novel, *Typee: A Peep at Polynesian Life*, published in 1846. An indeterminate mixture of fact and fiction, the fanciful travel narrative was, during his lifetime, Melville's most popular and successful work.

Melville set out to write a series of novels detailing his adventures and his philosophy of life. *Typee* was the first in this series, followed by *Omoo* (1847) and *Mardi and a Voyage Thither* (1849). Melville went on to publish *Redburn* (1849) and *White-Jacket; or The World in a Man-of-War*. Today, Melville's first five novels are considered a prologue to his masterpiece, *Moby-Dick; or The Whale*, first published in 1851. A story set on a whaling ship, *Moby-Dick* is both a documentary of life at sea and a vast philosophical allegory of life in general. In the novel, Melville satirizes religion, moral values, and the literary and political figures of the day.

Moby-Dick got lukewarm reviews at first, which did not bother Melville. His next novel, *Pierre; or The Ambiguities* (1852), provoked critical outrage. The sole pastoral romance among Melville's works, *Pierre* features conflicted writing, incestuous themes, and dicey morals. After the disastrous reception of *Pierre*, Melville turned to short story writing. In the following five years, he published numerous fictional sketches in several prominent periodicals of the day. Most notable among these works are "Bartelby, The Scrivener" and "Benito Cereno." He also published *Israel Potter; or Fifty Years of Exile* (1855) and a bleak satire of trust titled *The Confidence Man: His Masquerade* (1857).

In the remaining thirty-five years of his life, Melville's literary production ground nearly to a halt. After a brief national lecture tour, he worked for almost twenty years as a customshouse inspector, finally retiring in the late 1880s. A volume of war poetry, *Battle-Pieces and Aspects of the War*, appeared in 1866, and Melville published the lengthy poem *Clarel: A Poem and Pilgrimage in the Holy Land* in 1876. Toward the end of his life, Melville produced two more volumes of verse, *John Marr and Other Sailors* (1888) and *Timoleon* (1891).

BILLY BUDD IN CONTEXT

At the time of his death in 1891, Melville had recently completed a novel. In 1924, the novel was published under the title *Billy Budd*. In the mid-twentieth century, when Melville began to gain wider acclaim, scholars and general readers started reading *Billy Budd* with serious care. Based in part on Melville's experiences at sea, *Billy Budd* also incorporates a historical incident involving Melville's first cousin, who arbitrated a controversy involving the trial and execution of two midshipmen on board the U.S.S. *Somers* in 1842.

Melville's first great proponent, Lewis Mumford, saw *Billy Budd* as proof of Melville's final acceptance of the injustices of life. According to Mumford, *Billy Budd* is the peaceful, patient last word of an aged man and an affirmation of true religious transcendence. Later critics, such as Lawrance Thompson, read *Billy Budd* as a bitter satire. According to Thompson, Melville's cynicism and defiance are actually exaggerated because Melville presents them subtly.

Although Melville finished a draft of *Billy Budd* before his death, he never prepared it for publication. The manuscript, undiscovered for more than thirty years after his death, was extremely rough, covered with innumerable notes for revision. Because of the indefinite state of the manuscript and the lapsed time between Melville's death and its discovery, there has been a longstanding controversy over how the book should be edited. As a result, widely varying editions of *Billy Budd* exist. Today, the Hayford/Sealts reading text is generally regarded as the best version of *Billy Budd*. Most commercially available editions are based on the Hayford/Sealts reading text.

BILLY BUDD: KEY FACTS

Full Title: Given in various editions as *Billy Budd*; *Billy Budd, Foretopman*; and *Billy Budd, Sailor (An Inside Narrative)*. The last seems to represent Melville's final intention

Time and place written: 1886–1891; New York City

Date of first publication: 1924

Publisher: Constable & Company, Ltd.

Type of work: Novel

Genre: Allegory

Language: English

Setting (time): Summer of 1797

Setting (Place): An English warship, the *Bellipotent*, somewhere on the Mediterranean Sea

Tense: Past

Tone: Ironic, disillusioned. Toward the end, either sincerely hopeful and optimistic or sarcastically hopeful and optimistic

Narrator: Omniscient third person

Point of view: Mainly Billy Budd; occasionally Claggart or Vere; briefly minor characters such as Captain Graveling

Protagonist: Billy Budd

Antagonist: Claggart

BILLY BUDD: PLOT OVERVIEW

It is the last decade of the eighteenth century. The British naval warship H.M.S. *Bellipotent* impresses (recruits) the young sailor Billy Budd, extracting him from the *Rights-of-Man*, a merchant ship. Captain Graveling, though reluctant to let one of his best men go, must bow to the superior ship's demands. Billy packs up his gear without protest and goes to the *Bellipotent*, where he settles in quickly. As foretopman (a sailor who sits atop the foremast or above), he is industrious and eager, and soon earns the affection of his fellow sailors.

Billy is deeply affected when he sees a crew member receive a violent lashing. Hoping to avoid a similar punishment, Billy tries to follow the rules carefully but finds himself under constant scrutiny. Puzzled by this persecution, Billy talks to the Dansker, an aged, experienced sailor. The Dansker says Claggart, the master-at-arms, has a grudge against Billy. Billy refuses to accept this theory.

One day at lunch, Billy accidentally spills his soup, which trickles to the feet of the passing Claggart, who makes a seemingly lighthearted remark about it. But Claggart, offended by the accident, takes it as proof of Billy's contempt for him. He fixates on the accident, and his assistant, Squeak, decides to persecute Billy still more to punish him.

One night, an anonymous figure wakes Billy and asks him to come to a remote quarter of the ship. Confused, Billy obeys. After some vague conversation, the unidentified man flashes two guineas and asks for a promise of cooperation. Billy realizes something is wrong. He raises his stuttering voice and threatens the man. The conspirator quickly slinks away, and Billy finds himself confronted by two curious sailors. Unsure of how to explain the situation, Billy says he came across a sailor who was in the wrong part of the ship and sent him back to his proper station with a rebuke.

Sometime later, after a skirmish with an enemy frigate, Claggart approaches Captain Vere with news of a rumored mutiny and names Billy Budd as the ringleader. Vere summons Billy to his cabin and tells Claggart to repeat his accusation. The accusation renders Billy speechless. Vere commands Billy to defend himself, but then, noticing Billy's stuttering, softens his approach. Furious at Claggart's lies, Billy strikes out in a fury, punching Claggart in the forehead.

The blow knocks Claggart unconscious. He lies bleeding from the nose and ears as Billy and Vere attempt to revive him. Abandoning the effort, Vere sends Billy to a neighboring stateroom until further notice. The ship's surgeon pronounces Claggart dead, and Captain Vere calls a drumhead court consisting of the captain of the marines, the first lieutenant, and the sailing master. Vere, as the main witness, reports on what happened. Then Billy is questioned. He admits to punching Claggart but says he did not intend to hurt him and is not plotting mutiny. The court dismisses Billy to the stateroom.

The jury seems deadlocked. Vere steps forward and says he thinks the rule of law must come before the reservations of conscience. He tells the jury it must acquit or condemn in strict accordance with the letter of military law. After further deliberation, the jury finds Billy Budd guilty as charged and sentences him to death by hanging on the following morning.

Captain Vere tells Billy of the decision. After a discussion we do not learn about directly, Vere leaves Billy by himself. Later that evening, Vere calls a general meeting of the ship's crew and explains the events of the day. Claggart is buried at sea. Billy spends his final hours in chains, guarded by a sentry. The ship's chaplain attempts to prepare Billy for his death, but Billy already seems to be in a state of perfect peace and resignation. As the chaplain leaves, he kisses Billy gently on the cheek as a token of goodwill.

The next morning, shortly after four o'clock, Billy is hanged in the mainyard of the ship. As the crew watches him being strung up, they hear him utter his last words: "God bless Captain Vere!" The assembled company automatically echoes this unexpected sentiment. Billy dies with surprising calm as dawn breaks over the horizon. After Billy's death, the crew begins to murmur, but the officers quickly send them off on various tasks. Whistles blow and the ship returns to regular business. In the ensuing days, sailors talk about Billy's fate and the mysterious circumstances of his death. On its return voyage, the *Bellipotent* falls in with a French warship, the *Athée*, or *Atheist*. Captain Vere, wounded in the skirmish, eventually dies in a Gibraltar hospital. His last words are, "Billy Budd, Billy Budd."

The legend of Billy Budd is recorded and institutionalized in naval circles. A newspaper reports the incident, implicating Billy Budd as the villainous assailant of the innocent Claggart. The sailors themselves, however, begin to revere Billy, treating the spar from his gallows as a holy object and composing laudatory verse in his memory.

CHARACTERS IN *BILLY BUDD*

Albert Captain Vere's hammock boy. Vere trusts Albert and sends him to summon Billy to the cabin on the day Claggart accuses him of mutinous plans.

Billy Budd The protagonist of the novel. Billy Budd, who was discovered on a doorstep as an infant, is now twenty-one years old and renowned for his good looks and gentle, innocent ways. Although much younger than most of the *Bellipotent*'s crewmen, Billy quickly becomes popular, earning the nickname "Baby Budd." Billy is unable to believe that other people could feel ill will toward him. He also stutters sometimes, and at certain crucial moments he is completely speechless.

Ship's Chaplain The man who reluctantly and unsuccessfully attempts to console Billy with words from the Bible on the eve of Billy's execution.

John Claggart The master-at-arms of the H.M.S. *Bellipotent* (an office equivalent to chief of police). Behind his back, the crew calls Claggart "Jemmy Legs." At age thirty-five, Claggart is lean and tall, with a protruding chin. His black hair contrasts with his pale complexion. Claggart entered the navy late in life, but advanced because of his sobriety, deference to authority, and patriotism. Claggart has a cruel streak, which the narrator explains as a natural tendency toward evil and depravity.

The Dansker Billy's acquaintance and confidante aboard the *Bellipotent*. A wizened old sailor with beady eyes, the Dansker occasionally gives inscrutable, oracular responses when Billy seeks out his confidence. Sometimes the Dansker is quiet and unhelpful.

Captain Graveling The captain of the *Rights-of-Man*. At fifty, Captain Graveling is a benign, conscientious shipmaster who is sorry to lose Billy Budd to the *Bellipotent*.

Ship's Purser A ruddy and rotund man. The purser thinks Billy's unusually peaceful death in the gallows might be evidence that he has superhuman powers.

Lieutenant Ratcliffe The brusque boarding officer of the *Bellipotent*.

Red Pepper The forecastleman. Red Pepper reproves Billy for not taking greater disciplinary action against the hidden man who offered him money.

Ship's Surgeon The man who pronounces Claggart dead. The surgeon thinks Vere's decision to call a drumhead court is hasty. Though unable to account for Billy's peaceful death, he refuses to believe that it had anything to do with the supernatural.

Squeak Claggart's most cunning corporal. Squeak supports Claggart's contempt for Billy and tries to make Billy's life miserable.

Captain the Honorable Edward Fairfax Vere The captain of the *Bellipotent*. A forty-year-old aristocratic bachelor, Vere is a distinguished sailor. His nickname, "Starry Vere," fits his abstraction and intellect. At sea, Vere often shuts himself up with his books. Vere is not haughty, but he is aloof and diffident.

The Red Whiskers Billy's adversary aboard the *Rights-of-Man*. When Billy strikes the Red Whiskers, his hatred of Billy turns to love.

THEMES IN *BILLY BUDD*

THE INDIVIDUAL VERSUS SOCIETY   In *Billy Budd*, Melville explores the way society forces people to repress their individuality. When the warship *Bellipotent* extracts Billy from the *Rights-of-Man*, the names of the ships ("Bellipotent" means "power of war") make the symbolism explicit: society forces men into war, thus robbing them of their natural rights. Society also requires people to separate their feelings from their social obligations. For example, Vere decides he must follow the letter of the law despite his feeling that Billy personifies goodness and innocence. Sometimes, leaders act against their own impulses in an effort to maintain society. Laws, not the dictates of individual conscience, govern society. A number of characters in *Billy Budd* have strong consciences, but fundamentally the people on the ship cannot trust one another. To combat the paranoia, life aboard the ship is governed by a strict set of rules, and everybody trusts the rules—not the honor or conscience of individuals—to maintain order. Melville finds this frightening. He suggests that the individual's attempt to assert himself in society ultimately will fail.

THE VULNERABILITY OF THE INNOCENT   Billy Budd does not represent goodness so much as he does innocence. The conflict between innocence and evil in this novel is different from the conflict between good and evil. Billy is not a hero in the traditional sense. Though he has the good looks and blithe attitude of the ideal Handsome Sailor, his defining characteristic is extreme naiveté, not moral strength or courage. Billy does not have a sufficient awareness of good and evil to choose goodness consciously, let alone champion it. Because he cannot recognize evil when it confronts him, he ultimately allows Claggart to draw him away from virtue and into violence. Billy wants only to be well liked. He assumes no one has cause to dislike him and takes everyone at face value. Claggart, who is full of deception, distrust, and malice, interprets Billy's placidity as a dangerous façade. Claggart destroys Billy because Billy is innocent. Dimly perceiving that Billy is somehow above the world of subterfuge and cruelty that he himself inhabits, Claggart becomes consumed with the desire to corrupt and destroy Billy. Evil exists to corrupt innocence, and even though Billy kills Claggart, in a sense Claggart achieves a double victory over Billy. Claggart forces Billy to fall from social and moral grace by committing murder, and Billy is killed as a consequence.

THE AMBIGUITY OF RELIGION Although the narrator rarely alludes to the Bible explicitly, *Billy Budd* creates a sustained parallel between Billy's story and the story of Christ's suffering and death on the cross. Like Christ, Billy is the innocent victim of a hostile society. Like Christ, he is put to death by a decent man. Vere plays the role of Pontius Pilate, the official who ignored his own conscience and followed the law, allowing Christ to be put to death. Claggart is a satanic figure, tempting Billy into evil and trying to destroy him. Claggart's temptation of Billy more closely mirrors the serpent's temptation of Adam and Eve in the Garden of Eden than anything in the Gospels. The narrator makes Claggart's connection to the serpent in Genesis explicit by comparing Claggart's dead body to the corpse of a snake. In addition to these obvious parallels, the novel makes innumerable Christian references. Critics are sharply divided over whether Melville includes religious imagery in *Billy Budd* as an embrace of religion or as a harsh critique of it.

SYMBOLS IN *BILLY BUDD*

THE SHIPS The *Rights-of-Man* symbolizes a natural state, a place where people maintain their individuality. The *Bellipotent* represents a military society under the threat of violence in which the rules of society infringe on the individual rights of men. The *Athée*, whose name means "the atheist" in French, symbolizes the antireligious aspects of a powerful society at war.

THE PURSER AND THE SURGEON The purser and the surgeon who debate Billy's story after his death represent faith and skepticism, two fundamentally opposed attitudes toward religious mysteries. The purser believes Billy's death was supernatural. The surgeon, maintaining a scientific viewpoint, refuses to acknowledge Billy's unusually peaceful death as more than a quirk of matter.

IMPORTANT QUOTATIONS FROM *BILLY BUDD*

Habitually living with the elements and knowing little more of the land than as a beach, or rather, that portion . . . set apart for dance-houses, doxies, and tapsters, in short what sailors call a "fiddler's green," his simple nature remained unsophisticated by those moral obliquities which are not in every case incompatible with that manufacturable thing known as respectability. But are sailors, frequenters of fiddlers' greens, without vices? No; but less often than with landsmen do their vices, so called, partake of crookedness of heart, seeming less to proceed from viciousness than exuberance of vitality after long constraint; frank manifestations in accordance with natural law. By his original constitution aided by the co-operating influences of his lot, Billy in many respects was little more than a sort of upright barbarian, much such perhaps as Adam presumably might have been ere the urbane Serpent wriggled himself into his company.

Location: Chapter 2
Speaker: The narrator
Context: The narrator describes the respectability of sailors

The narrator argues that sailors are less likely to be wicked than men on land, since they are not exposed to difficult moral situations. Sailors drink and visit prostitutes while on shore, sullying their reputations, but unlike people who spend most of their time on land, sailors do not commit vice out of "crookedness of heart" or "viciousness." Rather, they behave badly out of exuberance and energy after their long confinement at sea. Because he is a sailor, Billy is almost entirely ignorant of evil. He is an innocent, an "upright barbarian." He is the figure of natural or primitive man, ignorant of law and Christianity. The narrator describes the coming serpent as "urbane." Urbanity, or sophistication, is the opposite of innocence. Thus, Melville equates evil with experience.

With no power to annul the elemental evil in him, though readily enough he could hide it; apprehending the good, but powerless to be it; a nature like Claggart's, surcharged with energy as such natures almost invariably are, what recourse is left to it but to recoil upon itself and, like the scorpion for which the Creator alone is responsible, act out to the end the part allotted it.

Location: Chapter 12
Speaker: The narrator
Context: The narrator explains the innate, inexplicable origins of Claggart's evil

Claggart is unusual among literary villains, most of whom are evil either because of events that have corrupted them or because of deliberate, avoidable choices they have made. Claggart's evil has no identifiable cause. He simply embodies evil. Here Melville writes that Claggart can understand goodness, but is "powerless" to embrace it, just as he has no power to overcome his own "elemental evil." If Claggart is a prisoner of his own evil and has no choice but to act the part of the villain, then the question arises whether he is responsible for his actions.

"Baby Budd, Jemmy Legs is down on you." "Jemmy Legs!" ejaculated Billy, his welkin eyes expanding. "What for? Why, he calls me 'the sweet and pleasant young fellow,' they tell me." "Does he so?" grinned the grizzled one; then said, "Ay, Baby lad, a sweet voice has Jemmy Legs." "No, not always. But to me he has. I seldom pass him but there comes a pleasant word." "And that's because he's down upon you, Baby Budd."

Location: Chapter 9
Speaker: The Dansker and Billy
Context: Billy, baffled, seeks out Dansker's advice

For what can more partake of the mysterious than an antipathy spontaneous and profound such as is evoked in certain exceptional mortals by the mere aspect of some other mortal, however harmless he may be, if not called forth by this very harmlessness itself?

Location: Chapter 11
Speaker: The narrator
Context: The narrator diagnoses Claggart's evil

"Struck dead by an angel of God! Yet the angel must hang!"

Location: Chapter 20
Speaker: Vere
Context: Vere commits to pursuing the letter of the law despite his own feelings

BLACK BOY

Richard Wright

Richard Wright, author and protagonist, defies his cruel family and his racist society, and becomes a successful writer.

THE LIFE OF RICHARD WRIGHT

Richard Wright was born on September 4, 1908, on a farm near the river town of Natchez, Mississippi. He was the first of two sons born to Nathan Wright, an illiterate tenant farmer, and Ella Wilson Wright, a teacher. When Richard was about five years old, his father abandoned the family to live with another woman. Ella soon suffered a stroke that left her physically disabled for the rest of her life. Wright sometimes had to work to support the family, and his attendance at school was sporadic.

Despite his irregular schooling, Wright became an avid reader. When he was sixteen, he published a short story in a local black newspaper and began to dream of writing professionally. But his intensely religious household discouraged "idle" thoughts and creativity, and the dehumanizing Jim Crow South pronounced Wright and all black men unfit for anything but the lowliest work. In the late 1920s, Wright moved with his family to Chicago. As the Great Depression enveloped the country, Wright had to work several stultifying and exhausting jobs to support his family. Nevertheless, he began to write seriously in private.

In 1933, Wright published poetry in several leftist and revolutionary magazines. He joined the Communist Party in 1934. In 1937, Wright moved to New York and became Harlem editor of *The Daily Worker*, a Communist publication. The next eight years were a triumph for Wright. He published important essays such as "The Ethics of Living Jim Crow," acclaimed stories like "Fire and Cloud," and two very successful works: *Native Son* (1940) and the autobiography *Black Boy* (1945).

Wright abandoned the Communist Party in 1942 because he thought it was taking a soft stance on wartime racial discrimination. Wright moved to Paris in 1947, partly to protest the deep flaws he saw in American society. In Paris, he became interested in existentialism, the philosophical movement that attempted to understand individual existence in the context of an unfathomable universe. He often socialized with Jean-Paul Sartre and Simone de Beauvoir, two leading thinkers and writers of the existentialist movement. He also began corresponding with Frantz Fanon, the West Indian social philosopher, in the 1950s. Wright died of a heart attack in 1960. *Native Son* and *Black Boy* have secured Wright a place in the canon. Wright is remembered not merely as an intellectual but as a powerful American artist.

BLACK BOY IN CONTEXT

In his autobiography, *Black Boy*, Wright portrays his boyhood in the vicious Jim Crow South and his struggles with the Communist Party. Jim Crow laws, which took their cue from the infamous "separate but equal" ruling of *Plessy v. Ferguson* (1896), mandated segregation of black from white in restaurants, trains, movie theaters, and hospitals. It also prevented interracial marriage. The laws effectively created two separate societies with highly unequal distributions of wealth. These laws were not exclusive to the South, but they were most devastating in the South, likely because the South's history of slavery made it especially difficult for whites to accept black emancipation.

In the 1930s and 1940s, the stock market collapsed, industry stagnated, unemployment was rampant, and famine struck some parts of the United States. Many American intellectuals believed capitalism had caused these disasters. Communists believed in the dignity and agency of those people suffering during the Depression. The American Communist Party attracted many idealists, including Wright. Eventually, the American Communist Party suffered from the same internal bickering that plagued other American political organizations. The Party's increasingly authoritarian stance profoundly disappointed sensitive thinkers like Wright, who had joined the Party full of hope for a brighter future.

BLACK BOY: KEY FACTS

Time and place written: 1943–1944; New York City

Date of first publication: 1945

Publisher: Harper & Brothers

Full title: Black Boy (American Hunger): A Record of Childhood and Youth

Type of work: Autobiographical novel

Genre: Bildungsroman; existential novel; autobiographical novel; memoir

Language: English

Setting (time): Roughly 1912–1937

Setting (place): Mississippi, Arkansas, Tennessee, and Illinois, with detours to the Deep South and New York City

Tense: Past

Tone: Confessional, ironic, philosophical

Narrator: Richard Wright, the author, in the first person

Point of view: Richard Wright's

Protagonist: Richard Wright, the author and narrator

Antagonist: Richard's problematic individualism and intelligence; his stubbornness; the Jim Crow South; blacks and whites alike

BLACK BOY: PLOT OVERVIEW

Required to keep quiet while his grandmother lies ill in bed, four-year-old Richard Wright gets bored and plays with fire near the curtains. He accidentally burns down the family home in Natchez, Mississippi. His father, Nathan, finds him hiding under the burning house. His mother, Ella, beats him so severely that he loses consciousness and falls ill.

While Richard and his brother, Alan, are still very young, Nathan abandons the family. Without Nathan's financial support, the Wrights are poor and constantly hungry. For the next few years, Ella struggles to raise her children in Memphis, Tennessee. Richard and his brother are often unsupervised, and Richard gets into all sorts of trouble, becoming a regular at the local saloon—and an alcoholic—by the age of six. When Ella's bad health prevents her from working, Richard does whatever odd jobs he can to bring in some money for the family.

Life improves when Ella moves to Elaine, Arkansas, to live with her sister, Maggie, and her sister's husband, Hoskins. Hoskins runs a successful saloon, so there is always plenty of food to eat. But eventually white men, jealous of Hoskins's success, kill Hoskins and threaten the rest of his family. Ella and Maggie flee with the two boys to West Helena, Arkansas. Maggie soon goes to Detroit with her lover, Professor Matthews, and Ella takes her family to Jackson, Mississippi. Hard times return to the Wrights.

A paralytic stroke severely incapacitates Ella. Alan goes to live with Maggie in Detroit. Ella remains in Jackson. After a brief stay with kind Uncle Clark, Richard returns to his grandmother's home. Back at Granny's, Richard is hungry once more. Granny is a very strict Seventh-Day Adventist, and she thinks her strong-willed, dreamy, and bookish grandson is terribly sinful. Another of Richard's aunts, Addie, also dislikes Richard. Richard's obsession with reading and his lack of interest in religion make his home life an endless conflict. Granny forces him to attend the religious school where Aunt Addie teaches. One day in class, Aunt Addie beats Richard for no reason. When she tries to beat Richard again after school that day, he fends her off with a knife. Similar scenes frequently recur over the following months and years. One time, Richard dodges one of Granny's backhand slaps, causing her to fall off the porch and injure herself. Addie tries to beat Richard for this incident, but again he fends her off with a knife. Later, Richard's uncle Tom comes to live with the family. When Tom tries to beat Richard for his supposed insolence, Richard confronts him with razor blades.

Richard delights in his studies—particularly reading and writing—despite his family's hostility to such pursuits. To the bafflement and scorn of everyone, he publishes a story in a local black newspaper. He is valedictorian of his ninth grade class and insists on giving his own speech, defying his principal, friends, and family, who want him to give a speech that will appease the white audience.

As Richard enters the adult working world in Jackson, racism dogs him. Two white Southerners, Pease and Reynolds, run Richard off his job at an optical shop, saying such skilled work is not meant for blacks. Mr. Crane, the white Northerner who runs the company, hired Richard specifically because he wanted to teach a black man the optical trade, but he does little to defend Richard against the racists.

Richard resolves to leave for the North as soon as possible. He steals to raise the cash necessary for the trip. After swindling his boss at a movie theater, selling stolen fruit preserves, and pawning a stolen gun, Richard moves to Memphis, where the atmosphere is safer and where he can prepare to move to Chicago. In Memphis, Richard's kind, generous landlady, Mrs. Moss, wants Richard to marry her daughter, Bess. Richard takes a job at another optical shop, where Olin, a seemingly benevolent white coworker, tries to make Richard and Harrison, another young black worker, kill each other. Olin's trickery culminates in a grotesque boxing match between Richard and Harrison.

Falk, a kind white man who works at the optical shop, lets Richard use his library card to check out books from the whites-only library. Richard reads obsessively and grows more determined to write. Richard and Maggie go to Chicago. Ella and Alan will follow in a few months. In Chicago, Richard continues to struggle with racism, segregation, and poverty. He must cut corners and lie in order to protect himself and get ahead. He forces himself to work at a corrupt insurance agency that takes advantage of poor blacks. He also works for the Hoffmans, well-meaning Jewish storeowners. Irresponsibly, Richard soon quits to try to get a job in the post office.

As the Great Depression forces him and millions of others out of work, Richard begins to find Communism appealing, especially its emphasis on protecting the oppressed. He becomes a Communist Party member because he thinks his writing could help the Party cause. He finds various jobs through federal relief programs. To his mounting dismay, he finds that the Communist Party, like any other group, is beset by human fears and foibles. Other Communists distrust Richard because of his tendency to criticize Party pronouncements. They call him "intellectual" and "Trotskyite." Finally, after being physically assaulted during a May Day parade, Richard leaves the Party. He remains determined to make writing his link to the world.

CHARACTERS IN *BLACK BOY*

Aunt Addie   One of Ella's sisters. Addie lives with Granny in Jackson, Mississippi. She often beats and humiliates Richard. Addie, like Granny, is intensely religious.

Uncle Clark   One of Ella's brothers. Uncle Clark briefly houses Richard after Ella gets sick. Clark is a just, upright man, if a bit strict. He seems genuinely concerned for Richard's welfare.

Mr. Crane   A white Northerner who runs the optical shop where Richard works. Mr. Crane, a fair and unprejudiced man, is sad to see Richard forced out.

Ella (the schoolteacher)   A young schoolteacher who briefly rents a room in Granny's house. Bookish and dreamy, she introduces Richard to the pleasures of fiction by telling him the story of *Bluebeard and His Seven Wives*. Granny thinks Ella's stories are sinful and forces her to move out.

Falk   A white Irish Catholic worker at the optical shop in Memphis. Falk lets Richard borrow his library card. He seems pleased to learn that Richard is moving to Chicago to find a better life.

Granny   Richard's maternal grandmother. Austere and unforgiving, Granny is a strict Seventh-Day Adventist who thinks Richard is sinful. Granny's parents were slaves. Due to her partially white ancestry, she has light skin.

Grandpa   Richard's maternal grandfather and a former soldier in the Union Army during the Civil War. Sour and remote, Grandpa is forever bitter that a clerical error deprived him of his war pension. He keeps a loaded gun by his bed because he believes Civil War hostilities could pick up again at any moment.

Ed Green   A high-ranking black Communist. Green is suspicious of Richard's interviews with Ross. Green's rough, authoritative manner alienates Richard.

Griggs   One of Richard's boyhood friends. Griggs is intelligent and follows rules more willingly than Richard does. Griggs advises Richard on how to survive in the racist white world.

Harrison A young black man who works at a rival optical shop in Memphis. Richard and Harrison like each other, but Olin tricks them into quarreling.

Uncle Hoskins Maggie's first husband. Uncle Hoskins is a friendly man, but Richard stops trusting him after he pretends to drive his buggy into the river to frighten Richard. Local whites murder Hoskins.

The Hoffmans The white Jewish shopkeepers who employ Richard in Chicago. The Hoffmans respect Richard, but Richard assumes that they will act just like most Southern whites.

Aunt Maggie Ella's sister. Maggie, Richard's favorite aunt, occasionally lives with the Wrights.

Olin A white Southerner who works at the optical shop in Memphis, Tennessee. Racist and destructive, Olin pretends to be Richard's friend but secretly tries to get Richard and Harrison to kill each other.

"Professor" Matthews Maggie's second husband. The "Professor" is an outlaw. After Matthews apparently kills a white woman, he and Maggie flee to Detroit. Several years later, he deserts Maggie.

Pease and Reynolds Two white Southerners who run Richard off his job at the optical shop in Jackson, Mississippi.

Ross A black Communist. Richard wants to profile Ross for a series of biographical sketches.

Shorty The black elevator man in the building in Memphis where Richard works. Shorty is witty, intelligent, and confident, but he demeans himself to earn money.

Uncle Tom One of Ella's brothers. Like Aunt Addie, Uncle Tom dislikes Richard and leaps at any opportunity to beat or ridicule him.

Alan Wright Richard's younger brother. Born Leon Alan Wright, he goes by the name Alan.

Ella Wright Richard's mother. Although she is hard on Richard, Ella loves him. Despite her ill health and partial paralysis, Ella maintains an optimistic outlook on life.

Richard Wright Author, narrator, and protagonist of *Black Boy*. Richard is timid yet assured, tough yet compassionate, intelligent yet modest. Growing up in an abusive family in the racially segregated and violent American South, Richard finds salvation in reading, writing, and thinking.

Nathan Wright Richard's father. Nathan, although physically intimidating, is simple and weak. He abandons his family.

Comrade Young An escapee from a mental institution. Young shows up at a meeting of the John Reed Club, a revolutionary artists' organization Richard joins in Chicago.

THEMES IN *BLACK BOY*

THE EVIL EFFECTS OF RACISM   More than simply an autobiography, *Black Boy* is a passionate reflection on the racist world. Appropriately, the title of the work emphasizes the word "black." At every moment, Wright makes us acutely aware of skin color. In America, he is not merely growing up; he is growing up black. *Black Boy* portrays racism not only as an odious belief system held by odious people but also as a problem knit into the very fabric of society. People like Olin and Pease are evil, but they are just small threads in the vast social fabric of hatred, fear, and oppression. Richard believes that racism's roots in American culture are so deep that it might be impossible to destroy racism without destroying the culture itself. Racism destroys relations between whites and blacks and between blacks and blacks. Richard is so used to encountering racism that he meets kindness with suspicion.

THE INDIVIDUAL VERSUS SOCIETY   Richard, who is fiercely individualistic, wants to live in society on his own terms instead of doing as society wishes. Because of this desire, he must struggle against both white culture and black culture, neither of which knows how to handle a brilliant, strong-willed, self-respecting black man. Richard refuses to conform or to wilt. In Granny's home, he does not embrace barren, stifling spirituality. In school, he insists on reading his own speech. In Chicago, he defies the wishes of the Communist Party. Despite this constant refusal to conform, however, Richard feels spiritually connected to the rest of humanity. Therefore, as an artist, he struggles to show compassion for communities that say they do not want him.

THE REDEMPTIVE POWER OF ART   When Ella the schoolteacher furtively whispers the story of *Bluebeard and His Seven Wives* to Richard, Richard is transfixed. The story evokes his first "total emotional response." Throughout the novel, literature makes Richard feel that his life has texture and meaning. Such literature includes science-fiction and horror magazines, Wright's story of the Indian maiden, his discovery of H. L. Mencken, his story "The Voodoo of Hell's Half-Acre," and the writing he does for the Communist Party. The idea that life becomes meaningful through creative attempts to make sense of it is a central one in the history of philosophy, first articulated by Schopenhauer, refined by Nietzsche, and then taken up by the existentialists, with whom Wright grew fascinated. *Black Boy* itself is in part Wright's attempt to order the experiences of his life.

SYMBOLS IN *BLACK BOY*

ELLA'S ILLNESS   In Renaissance and Gothic literature, deformity or physical impairment often symbolizes an unhealthy or evil soul. This kind of symbolism implies that the universe is a sensible place that houses evil souls in mangled bodies. The universe of *Black Boy*, however, is a cruel one. Richard's mother, Ella, is kind and loving, yet she is rewarded with incurable ailments and paralytic legs. Equally unfairly, detestable family members have abundant strength. For Richard, Ella's infirmity symbolizes the unfair and random nature of the universe.

THE MEMPHIS OPTICAL SHOP WORKERS   The workers in the optical shop stand for different segments of a racially stratified society. Olin represents Southern white racists who terrorize black people for amusement. Falk represents Southern whites who sympathize with black people and want to help them. Shorty represents black workers who pander to whites but inwardly retain their racial and personal pride. The building's unnamed porter represents embittered black workers of the South. Several Ku Klux Klan members and Jews also populate the office.

IMPORTANT QUOTATIONS FROM *BLACK BOY*

I had . . . a conviction that the meaning of living came only when one was struggling to wring a meaning out of meaningless suffering. At the age of twelve I had an attitude toward life that was to . . . make me skeptical of everything while seeking everything, tolerant of all and yet critical . . . that could only keep alive in me that enthralling sense of wonder and awe in the face of the drama of human feeling which is hidden by the external drama of life.

Location: The end of Chapter 3
Speaker: Richard Wright
Context: Ella has had a second paralytic stroke

Many of Wright's major beliefs are articulated in this passage. Principal among these is his conviction that life is meaningful only when we struggle to make it so. Wright believes that life has no intrinsic significance, but that we can imbue it with significance by finding meaning where none exists. This idea recalls the theories of existentialist philosophers such as Jean-Paul Sartre, who Wright read and admired.

I concluded the book with the conviction that I had somehow overlooked something terribly important in life. I had once tried to write, had once reveled in feeling, had let my crude imagination roam, but the impulse to dream had been slowly beaten out of me by experience. Now it surged up again and I hungered for books, new ways of looking and seeing.

Location: The beginning of Chapter 13
Speaker: Richard Wright
Context: Richard has read H. L. Mencken's *A Book of Prefaces*

When Richard reads Mencken, he remembers he has an imagination, and his imagination is hungry. Throughout the novel, Richard reads with a passion that resembles physical appetite. Often, as in this passage, the desire to read and the desire to eat are closely allied. At times, the two desires mesh. This passage marks a turning point in Richard's life. Richard's direction was uncertain, but now Mencken sparks what will become a passionate devotion to the written word. Because Richard's life changes during it, this passage could be called the climax of the novel.

Our too-young and too-new America . . . insists upon seeing the world in terms of good and bad, the holy and the evil, the high and the low, the white and the black. . . It hugs the easy way of damning those whom it cannot understand, of excluding those who look different, and it salves its conscience with a self-draped cloak of righteousness. Am I damning my native land? No; for I, too, share these faults of character!

Location: The middle of Chapter 15
Speaker: Richard Wright
Context: Richard reflects on America's adolescent shortcomings

---

My life as a Negro in America had led me to feel . . . that the problem of human unity was more important than bread, more important than physical living itself; for I felt that without a common bond uniting men . . . there could be no living worthy of being called human.

Location: The beginning of Chapter 18
Speaker: Richard Wright
Context: Richard has attended, for the first time, a meeting of the John Reed Club

---

I would make his life more intelligible to others than it was to himself. I would reclaim his disordered days and cast them into a form that people could grasp, see, understand, and accept.

Location: The beginning of Chapter 19
Speaker: Richard Wright
Context: Richard describes his motivation for writing a biographical sketch of Ross

BRAVE NEW WORLD

Aldous Huxley

An outsider raised on the Reservation tries and fails to find love in the World State, a place where people are robbed of their humanity and sedated with the drug soma.

THE LIFE OF ALDOUS HUXLEY

Aldous Huxley was born in Surrey, England, on July 26, 1894, to an illustrious family deeply rooted in England's literary and scientific tradition. Huxley received an excellent education, first at home, then at Eton. He was an avid student, and during his lifetime he was renowned as a generalist—an intellectual who both had mastered the use of the English language and was informed about cutting-edge developments in science and other fields. Although much of Huxley's scientific understanding was superficial, he integrated current scientific findings into his novels and essays in a way that few other writers of his time could.

As a teenager, Huxley contracted an eye disease that left him almost blind. Because of his near blindness, he depended heavily on his first wife, Maria, to take care of him. Blindness and vision are motifs that permeate Huxley's writing. After graduating from Oxford in 1916, Huxley began to make a name for himself writing light satirical pieces about the British upper class. Huxley wrote prolifically as an essayist and journalist. He published four volumes of poetry. Beginning in 1921, Huxley produced a series of novels at an astonishing rate: *Crome Yellow* (1921), *Antic Hay* (1923), *Those Barren Leaves* (1925), and *Point Counter Point* (1928). Huxley left his early satires behind and wrote about subjects of philosophical and ethical significance. Much of Huxley's work deals with the conflict between the individual and society. Huxley explored this theme most successfully in *Brave New World* (1932).

In 1937, Huxley moved to California. An ardent pacifist, he was alarmed at the military buildup in Europe. Already famous as a writer of novels and essays, he tried to make a living as a screenwriter but had little success. Huxley never seemed to grasp the requirements of the form, and his erudite literary style did not translate well to the screen.

In the late 1940s, Huxley started to experiment with hallucinogenic drugs such as LSD and mescaline. He was interested in occult phenomena such as hypnotism and séances. Huxley wrote several books that had profound influences on the 1960s' counterculture. *The Doors of Perception*, a book about his experiences with mescaline, influenced Jim Morrison to name his band The Doors. (The phrase "the doors of perception" comes from a William Blake poem called *The Marriage of Heaven and Hell*.) In his last major work, *Island*, published in 1962, Huxley describes a doomed utopia called Pala that contrasts with the dystopia he imagined in *Brave New World*. Pala's ideal culture includes a hallucinogenic drug called "moksha." Huxley died on November 22, 1963, in Los Angeles.

BRAVE NEW WORLD IN CONTEXT

Brave New World, Huxley's most enduring work, imagines a fictional future in which free will and individuality have been sacrificed to complete social stability. The novel marked a new direction for Huxley, combining his skill for satire with his fascination with science to create a dystopian (anti-utopian) world in which a totalitarian government controls society with science and technology. *Brave New World* deals with themes similar to those in George Orwell's famous novel *1984*, but Huxley is perhaps a more gifted prophet than Orwell. Orwell wrote his novel in 1949, after World War II. He had seen totalitarian governments wreak havoc, and he was witnessing the Cold War and the arms race. Huxley, writing in 1932, predicted what Orwell had witnessed. One year after the publication of *Brave New World*, Hitler came to power. Six years after its publication, World War II broke out. Thirteen years after its publication, the U.S. dropped an atomic bomb, and the Cold War began. In many ways, Huxley's novel prophesizes the major themes and struggles of the second half of the twentieth century.

BRAVE NEW WORLD: KEY FACTS

Time and place written: 1931, England

Date of first publication: 1932

Publisher: Chatto and Windus, London

Type of work: Novel

Genre: Dystopia

Language: English

Setting (time): 2540 A.D.; referred to in the novel as 632 years "After Ford," meaning 632 years after the production of the first Model T car

Setting (place): England, Savage Reservation in New Mexico

Tense: Past

Tone: Satirical, ironic, silly, tragic, juvenile, pedantic

Narrator: Omniscient third person; free indirect narration (in which the narrator stays in third person but voices the thoughts of a particular character)

Point of View: Primarily Bernard or John; sometimes Lenina, Helmholtz Watson, or Mustapha Mond

Protagonists: Bernard Marx, Helmholtz Watson, John

Antagonist: Mustapha Mond; the State

BRAVE NEW WORLD: PLOT OVERVIEW

In the Central London Hatching and Conditioning Centre, the Director of the Hatchery and one of his assistants, Henry Foster, are giving a tour to a group of boys. The boys learn about how the Hatchery produces thousands of nearly identical human embryos. The embryos are conditioned to belong to one of five castes: Alpha, Beta, Gamma, Delta, or Epsilon. The Alpha embryos are destined to become the leaders and thinkers of the World State. In each succeeding caste, humans are slightly uglier and stupider. The Epsilons, stunted by oxygen deprivation and chemical treatments, are destined to perform menial labor.

The Director leads the boys to the Nursery, where they observe a group of Delta infants being reprogrammed to dislike books and flowers. The Director explains that this conditioning turns Deltas into docile and eager consumers. He explains the "hypnopaedic" (sleep-teaching) methods used to teach children the morals of the World State. Older children nap as a whispering voice repeats a lesson in "Elementary Class Consciousness."

Outside, hundreds of naked children are engaged in sexual play. Mustapha Mond, one of the ten World Controllers, introduces himself to the boys and explains the history of the World State, focusing on the State's successful efforts to remove strong emotions, desires, and human relationships from society. Meanwhile, inside the Hatchery, an employee named Lenina Crowne chats in the bathroom with Fanny Crowne (they have the same last name because only about ten thousand last names are used in the World State). Fanny scolds Lenina for going out with Henry Foster almost exclusively for four months. Lenina admits she is attracted to the strange, somewhat funny-looking Bernard Marx. In another part of the Hatchery, Bernard is enraged when he overhears a conversation between Henry and the Assistant Predestinator about "having" Lenina.

Bernard meets with Helmholtz Watson, a friend of his. Bernard is too small and weak for his caste, and Helmholtz is too intelligent for his job writing hypnopaedic phrases. In the next few days, Bernard asks his superior, the Director, for permission to visit the Savage Reservation with Lenina, who has agreed to go with him. The Director tells Bernard about visiting the Reservation with a woman twenty years earlier. During a storm, the woman was lost and never recovered. Later, Helmholtz tells Bernard that the Director thinks Bernard is difficult and unsocial, and plans to exile him to Iceland. Bernard is angry and distraught.

Lenina and Bernard are shocked to see aging and ill residents on the Reservation. No one in the World State has visible signs of aging. They witness a religious ritual in which a young man is whipped, and they find it abhorrent. After the ritual, they meet John, a fair-skinned young man who is isolated from the rest of the village. John's mother, Linda, was rescued by the villagers some twenty years ago. She was pregnant at the time. Bernard realizes that Linda is the woman the Director talked about and that it was the Director's child she carried. John says Linda was ostracized because she slept with all the men in the village. John learned to read using a book called *The Chemical and Bacteriological Conditioning of the Embryo* and *The Complete Works of Shakespeare*. Popé, one of Linda's lovers, gave her *The Complete Works of Shakespeare*. John is eager to see the "Other Place"—the "brave new world" that his mother has told him so much about. Bernard invites him to come to the World State. John agrees but insists that Linda be allowed to come too.

Lenina, disgusted with the Reservation, takes enough *soma* to knock her out for eighteen hours. Back on the Reservation, John breaks into the house where Lenina is lying intoxicated and unconscious, and barely suppresses his desire to touch her. Bernard, Lenina, John, and Linda fly to the World State. The Director is waiting to exile Bernard in front of his Alpha coworkers, but Bernard turns the tables by introducing John and Linda. The shame of being a "father"—the very word makes the onlookers laugh nervously—causes the Director to resign, leaving Bernard free to remain in London.

John is a hit in London society because of his strange life. The society John sees disturbs him. He is still attracted to Lenina, but he wants more than sex, which confuses him. Lenina wonders why John does not want to have sex with her. Bernard profits from discovering John, the "Savage." He takes advantage of his new status, sleeping with many women and hosting dinner parties with important guests, most of whom dislike Bernard but want to use him to meet John. One night John refuses to meet the guests, including the Arch-Community Songster, and Bernard's social standing plummets.

Bernard introduces John and Helmholtz, who quickly take to each other. John reads Helmholtz parts of *Romeo and Juliet*, and Helmholtz laughs at a serious passage about love, marriage, and parents—ideas that are ridiculous, almost scatological, in World State culture. Lenina becomes obsessed with John. She takes *soma* and tries to seduce him. He admits that he loves her, but when she tries to have sex with him, he panics and curses her. Someone calls John and tells him that Linda, who has been on permanent *soma*-holiday since her return, is dying.

After Linda dies in the hospital, John meets a group of Delta clones who are receiving their *soma* ration. He tells them to revolt and throws the *soma* out the window. A riot results. Bernard and Helmholtz rush to the scene and come to John's aid. After the police calm the rioters with *soma* vapor, John, Helmholtz, and Bernard are arrested and brought to the office of Mustapha Mond.

John and Mond debate the value of the World State's policies. John says they dehumanize people, and Mond says stability and happiness are more important than humanity. He says social stability requires the sacrifice of art, science, and religion. John protests that without these things, human life is not worth living. Mond says that Bernard and Helmholtz will be exiled to distant islands. Bernard reacts wildly and must be carried from the room. Helmholtz accepts the exile readily, thinking it will give him a chance to write.

John bids Helmholtz and Bernard goodbye. Mond refuses to let John follow them to the islands, so he retreats to a lighthouse in the countryside where he gardens and tries to purify himself by self-flagellation. Curious World State citizens soon catch him in the act, and reporters descend on the lighthouse to film news reports and a feely (movie). Hordes of people come and demand that John whip himself. Lenina comes and approaches John with her arms open. John brandishes his whip and screams, "Kill it! Kill it!" The intensity of the scene causes an orgy in which John takes part. The next morning, John hangs himself.

CHARACTERS IN *BRAVE NEW WORLD*

Fanny Crowne Lenina Crowne's friend. Fanny voices the conventional values of her caste and society.

Lenina Crowne A vaccination worker at the Central London Hatchery and Conditioning Centre. Sometimes Lenina acts in intriguingly unorthodox ways, but ultimately her values are those of conventional World State citizens.

The Director The administrator of the Central London Hatchery and Conditioning Centre. The Director is a threatening figure who has the power to exile people. He is secretly vulnerable because he fathered a child—a scandalous, obscene act in the World State.

Henry Foster One of Lenina's many lovers. Foster, a conventional Alpha male, casually discusses Lenina's body with his coworkers.

John The son of the Director and Linda. John is the only major character to have grown up outside the World State. After a life lived on the New Mexico Savage Reservation, he can't fit in to World State society.

Linda John's mother. After getting pregnant with the Director's son, Linda, a Beta, could not get an abortion on the Reservation and was too ashamed to return to the World State with a baby. Her promiscuity, normal in the World State, was a scandal on the Reservation. Linda desperately wants to return to the World State and to *soma*.

Bernard Marx An Alpha male and one of the novel's protagonists. Unlike most Alphas, Bernard is short. He has unorthodox views and can't fit into society, which makes him unhappy. Bernard's surname recalls Karl Marx. When threatened, Bernard can be petty and cruel.

Mustapha Mond The Resident World Controller of Western Europe, one of only ten World Controllers. Mond was once an ambitious scientist, but the State gave him the choice of going into exile or becoming a World Controller. He chose to give up science, and now he censors scientific discoveries and exiles people who have unorthodox beliefs. Mond keeps a collection of forbidden literature in his safe, including Shakespeare and religious writings.

Popé Linda's lover on the New Mexico Savage Reservation. Popé gave Linda a copy of *The Complete Works of Shakespeare*.

The Arch-Community-Songster The secular equivalent of an archbishop.

The Warden The talkative chief administrator for the New Mexico Savage Reservation. He is an Alpha.

Helmholtz Watson An Alpha lecturer at the College of Emotional Engineering. Helmholtz dislikes his meaningless work. Like Bernard, Helmholtz dislikes the World State, but whereas Bernard's complaints are petty, Helmholtz's are philosophical and intellectual. Helmholtz is often bored by Bernard's boastfulness and cowardice.

THEMES IN *BRAVE NEW WORLD*

THE USE OF TECHNOLOGY TO CONTROL SOCIETY In *Brave New World*, Huxley warns that it is dangerous to give the state control over new and powerful technologies. In the novel's dystopia, the State uses technology to force people to become avid consumers. It also uses technology to control reproduction, sterilizing two-thirds of the female population, forcing the rest to use contraceptives, and surgically removing ovaries when it needs to produce new humans. The State uses technology to produce *soma*, an addictive drug useful for pacifying the masses. The State censors and limits science because the fundamental project of science is the search for truth, which threatens the State's control. The State uses science solely in the service of technology. The State turns technology into a religion. Instead of referring to "Lord," as in the Christian God, people refer to "Ford," as in Henry Ford, the early twentieth-century industrialist and founder of the Ford Motor Company. They talk about "the year of our Ford" and exclaim "my Ford."

THE INCOMPATIBILITY OF HAPPINESS AND TRUTH Many characters in *Brave New World* strenuously avoid reality. Almost everyone uses *soma*, a drug that replaces reality with happy hallucinations. But even Shakespeare can be used to avoid facing the truth, as John demonstrates by his insistence on viewing Lenina through the lens of Shakespeare's world, first as a Juliet and later as an "impudent strumpet." According to Mustapha Mond, the World State believes that happiness is much more important than truth.

When Mond speaks of happiness, he means food, sex, drugs, nice clothes, and other consumer items. When he speaks of truth, he means scientific or empirical truth. He also means emotional truth such as love, friendship, and personal connection, all of which the government attempts to destroy. The search for truth, both scientific and emotional, involves a great deal of individual effort, of striving and fighting against odds.

THE DANGERS OF AN ALL-POWERFUL STATE Like George Orwell's *1984*, *Brave New World* depicts a dystopia in which an all-powerful state controls the people in order to preserve its own power. In *1984*, the government maintains control with constant surveillance, secret police, and torture, but in *Brave New World*, the State maintains control by actually changing what people want, rooting out their desires before they are born. The people of *1984* have human desires the government must suppress, but the people of *Brave New World* are so happy and superficially fulfilled that they don't care about their personal freedom. They have lost their dignity, morals, values, and emotions—in short, their humanity.

SYMBOLS IN *BRAVE NEW WORLD*

SOMA   The drug *soma* symbolizes the instant gratification the State uses to control the masses. It also symbolizes the powerful influence of science and technology on society. As a kind of sacrament, *soma* replaces religion in the World State.

IMPORTANT QUOTATIONS FROM *BRAVE NEW WORLD*

> *Mother, monogamy, romance. . . No wonder those poor pre-moderns were mad and wicked and miserable. Their world didn't allow them to take things easily, didn't allow them to be sane, virtuous, happy . . . they were forced to feel strongly. And feeling strongly (and strongly, what was more, in solitude, in hopelessly individual isolation), how could they be stable?*

Location: Chapter 3
Speaker: Mustapha Mond
Context: Mond explains the history of the World State to a group of boys touring the Hatchery

Mond's speech foreshadows John's preoccupations. "Mother, monogamy, romance" are precisely the issues that most concern John, and "feeling strongly" is what he values most highly. Mond claims that by doing away with such things as romance and feeling, the World State has brought stability and peace to humanity. But John argues that the absence of pain does not mean the presence of peace. That is, although romance and feeling may be painful, they are an essential part of our humanity. The World State has created a society in which people are machines who produce and consume. People are forced to be "happy" (if we equate happiness with stability) because they are forbidden to choose truth instead of the easy comfort of *soma*. But for those few not brainwashed and chemically altered before birth, like John, happiness is *not* the same thing as stability. The inability to find love or strong feeling in the World State eventually leads John to suicide.

> *Ford, we are twelve; oh, make us one,*
> *Like drops within the Social River;*
> *Oh, make us now together run*
> *As swiftly as thy shining Flivver.*
> *. . .*
> *Orgy-porgy, Ford and fun,*
> *Kiss the girls and make them One.*
> *Boys at one with girls at peace;*
> *Orgy-porgy gives release.*

Location: Chapter 5
Speaker: A synthetic bass voice
Context: The lines come from a song sung during the Solidarity Service

The trivial lyrics of this song reveal the banality of the "religion" the World State uses to make people conform. They also contrast with the richness of Shakespeare, which John quotes occasionally.

The "annihilating Twelve-in-One" is a metaphor for the whole of World State society, which creates humans identical to each other. The last stanza's phrase "orgy-porgy gives release" suggests that the World State has not succeeded in annihilating human nature altogether. People still need to release emotions that have not been entirely wiped out through conditioning. "Orgy-porgy gives release" also suggests that sex becomes boring when the government encourages it. Part of John's horror is that the government has managed to turn sex into a cheerful duty that is totally divorced from love and emotion.

Every one works for every one else. We can't do without any one. Even Epsilons are useful. We couldn't do without Epsilons. Every one works for every one else. We can't do without any one. . .

Location: Chapter 5
Speaker: The voice that whispers hypnopaedic rules
Context: Lenina remembers waking up as a small girl and, for the first time, hearing hypnopaedic messages whispered into her ear

---

A gramme is always better than a damn. . . A gramme in time saves nine. . . One cubic centimetre cures ten gloomy sentiments. . . Everybody's happy nowadays.... Every one works for every one else. . . .When the individual feels, the community reels. . . Never put off till to-morrow the fun you can have to-day. . . Progress is lovely

Location: Throughout the novel
Speaker: The voice that whispers hypnopaedic rules
Context: These phrases exemplify the hypnopaedic sayings that fill the novel

---

And if ever, by some unlucky chance, anything unpleasant should somehow happen, why, there's always soma to give you a holiday from the facts. And there's always soma to calm your anger, to reconcile you to your enemies, to make you patient and long-suffering. . . Anybody can be virtuous now. You can carry at least half your morality about in a bottle. Christianity without tears—that's what soma is.

Location: Chapter 17
Speaker: Mond
Context: As John and Mond talk, Mond tries to make the case for soma

▶

THE BROTHERS KARAMAZOV

Fyodor Dostoevsky

A bastard son kills his father; his three brothers—one passionate, one smart and skeptical, and one loving—share some of the moral culpability for the murder.

THE LIFE OF FYODOR DOSTOEVSKY

Fyodor Dostoevsky, one of the world's greatest novelists and literary psychologists, was born in Moscow in 1821. Dostoevsky was educated first at home and then at a boarding school. When he was a young boy, his father, a doctor, sent him to the St. Petersburg Academy of Military Engineering, from which he graduated in 1843. Dostoevsky's father was murdered—or so the traditionally held belief goes—at the hands of his ill-treated servants.

In St. Petersburg, Dostoevsky fell victim to a compulsive gambling habit that would dog him for most of his life. Eventually, he resigned his military commission and set to work on a novel, *Poor Folk* (1843), which received mostly harsh reviews. In April 1849, Dostoevsky was arrested and imprisoned in part because of his involvement with the Petrashevsky circle, a Socialist group that belligerently criticized Tsar Nicholas I (1796–1855). Dostoevsky was sentenced to death for his transgressions. At the last minute, as he stood in front of a firing squad, Tsar Nicholas commuted the sentence to four years of working in Siberian prison camps.

Dostoevsky's years in Siberia affected him profoundly. He lived in squalid conditions among petty thieves and murderers. For his entire sentence, his only reading material was the New Testament. In prison, Dostoevsky developed the first symptoms of the epilepsy from which he would suffer for the rest of his life. He became fascinated with the psychology of his fellow prisoners, who afforded him a first-hand glimpse into the inner workings of the criminal mind. He drew on these observations when writing Crime and Punishment and his other great post-exile works. The brutalities of his imprisonment made him shed much of the idealism of his youth, including his strong belief in radical Socialism. In its place, he developed a more conservative, reactionary, religious outlook.

Dostoevsky married Marya Isaeva (c. 1824–1864) and moved back to St. Petersburg. In the early months of 1864, Marya died of tuberculosis. Weeks later, Dostoevsky's brother Mikhail died unexpectedly. Dostoevsky began work on the first sections of *Crime and Punishment* (1866). A few months later, he finished *The Gambler* (1865). With his deadline looming, he hired a young woman, Anna Snitkina, to transcribe the manuscript. Anna and Dostoevsky married in 1867. Dostoevsky, enjoying a new stability, entered into the most prolific period of his career, completing five novels, including *The Brothers Karamazov* (1879).

Dostoevsky's fame expanded throughout Russia in the 1870s. He died on January 28, 1881. His funeral was attended by thousands of mourners, and he was buried with high religious honors in St. Petersburg's venerated Tikhvinsky cemetery.

THE BROTHERS KARAMAZOV IN CONTEXT

The Brothers Karamazov is perhaps Dostoevsky's greatest work. It is certainly his most complex examination of philosophical questions of human existence. The novel is a tale of harmony, disorder, and disintegration in a family and in the minds of the family's members. In its tragic depiction of a parricide, it shows the consequences of neglecting responsibility. The parricide of Fyodor Karamazov is not just the story of one man's death. It has been widely interpreted as a metaphor for the moral collapse of the Karamazov family, the turning of Russia on its Tsar, and the disrespect of humanity for God. Dostoevsky suggests that only when a father shows careful devotion to his children does he become blameless. If he does not show devotion, his children have a right to ask, "Father, why should I love you?"

THE BROTHERS KARAMAZOV: **KEY FACTS**

Time and place written: 1879–1880; Russia, primarily St. Petersburg

Date of first publication: 1879–1880

Publisher: The Russian Messenger

Type of work: Novel

Genre: Novel of ideas

Language: Russian

Setting (time): Mid-nineteenth century

Setting (place): A town in Russia

Tense: Past

Tone: Serious, comedic, warm, sardonic

Narrator: First person

Point of view: Alyosha, Ivan, Dmitri, and the unnamed narrator

Protagonist: Alyosha Karamazov

Antagonist: The philosophical conflict between religious faith and doubt

THE BROTHERS KARAMAZOV: **PLOT OVERVIEW**

In his youth, Fyodor Pavlovich Karamazov is a coarse, vulgar man devoted to making money and seducing young women. He has three sons: Dmitri, his son by his first wife, and Ivan and Alyosha, his sons by his second wife. After their mothers die, the children are sent away to relatives and friends, since Fyodor does not care about them. At the beginning of the novel, Dmitri Karamazov, who is now a twenty-eight-year-old soldier, has just returned to Fyodor's town to claim an inheritance his mother left to him. The men argue, and cold, intellectual Ivan, who knows neither his father nor his brother well, is eventually called in to help settle their dispute.

Kind, faithful Alyosha, who is about twenty, lives in the town at the monastery, where he studies with the renowned elder Zosima. He arranges a meeting between Zosima, Dmitri, and Fyodor. At the monastery, Fyodor and Dmitri embarrass themselves with displays of vulgarity and bad temper. It turns out that both Dmitri and Fyodor are in love with Grushenka, a beautiful young woman. Dmitri has left his fiancée, Katerina, to pursue Grushenka. He recently stole 3,000 rubles from Katerina in order to finance a lavish trip with Grushenka, and he is now desperate to pay the money back.

Many years previously, Fyodor impregnated a retarded mute girl. The girl died in childbirth, and Fyodor's servants took in Smerdyakov, the baby boy. Fyodor treats Smerdyakov as a servant, not a son. Smerdyakov develops a strange and malicious personality. He also suffers from epilepsy. Smerdyakov loves listening to Ivan discuss philosophy and repeats many of Ivan's ideas—particularly the idea that the soul is not immortal and that therefore morality does not exist.

After the humiliating scene in the monastery, Dmitri asks Alyosha to break off Dmitri's engagement to Katerina. Dmitri and Fyodor fight over Grushenka, and Dmitri threatens to kill his father. The next day, Alyosha visits Katerina. He finds Ivan with Katerina, and immediately perceives that the two are in love but are too proud and cold to act on it. Alyosha has dinner with Ivan, who explains that he cannot reconcile the idea of a loving God with the needless suffering of innocent children. He recites a poem he has written called "The Grand Inquisitor," which accuses Christ of placing an intolerable burden on humanity by giving people free will.

That evening, Alyosha returns to the monastery, where the frail Zosima is now on his deathbed. Right before he dies, Zosima emphasizes the importance of love and forgiveness in all human affairs. Zosima dies with his arms stretched out before him, as though to embrace the world. Many of the monks think a miracle will follow Zosima's death, because he was so holy, but in an unusually short amount of time, Zosima's corpse begins to stink. Zosima's critics says this proves he was corrupt in life. Alyosha is sickened by the injustice of seeing the wise and loving Zosima humiliated after his death. His friend Rakitin takes him to see Grushenka, hoping to corrupt him, but instead a bond of sympathy and understanding forms between Grushenka and Alyosha. Their friendship renews Alyosha's faith, and Alyosha helps Grushenka begin her own spiritual redemption. That night, Alyosha dreams about Zosima, who tells him he has done a good deed by helping Grushenka. Alyosha wakes and goes outside to kiss the ground.

Dmitri goes to Grushenka's house and finds that she is out. He rushes to Fyodor's house to look for her, but she is not there. Gregory, Fyodor's servant, sees Dmitri prowling and calls out "Parricide!" Dmitri strikes Gregory, leaving him bloody and unconscious. He flees to Grushenka's house, where the maid says Grushenka has gone to rejoin an old lover. Dmitri decides he must see Grushenka one more time and then kill himself.

Dmitri goes to a shop wearing a bloody shirt and holding and a large wad of cash. He buys food and wine and goes to see Grushenka and her lover. Grushenka realizes she loves Dmitri. The police suddenly burst in and arrest Dmitri on suspicion of murdering his father. Dmitri says the money he had was not stolen from Fyodor, but no one believes him. Dmitri is imprisoned.

Meanwhile, Alyosha befriends some of the local schoolboys, including a dying boy named Ilyusha. The schoolboys adore Alyosha and look to him for guidance.

Smerdyakov confesses to Ivan that he, not Dmitri, killed Fyodor. But he implicates Ivan in the crime because he taught Smerdyakov about the nonexistence of evil in a world without a God. Ivan's philosophies made Smerdyakov capable of committing murder. Ivan, consumed with guilt, goes home and has a breakdown. He sees a devil that relentlessly taunts him. Alyosha arrives and tells Ivan that Smerdyakov has hung himself.

At the trial, Ivan testifies that he is guilty of the murder. To clear Ivan's name, Katerina produces a letter from Dmitri in which he writes that he is afraid he might murder his father. Although most people in the courtroom believe Dmitri is innocent, the peasants on the jury find him guilty. After the trial, Katerina and Dmitri forgive each other, and she arranges for him to escape from prison and flee to America with Grushenka. Alyosha's friend Ilyusha dies. At the funeral, Alyosha tells the schoolboys that they must remember their love for each other. The schoolboys give Alyosha an enthusiastic cheer.

CHARACTERS IN *THE BROTHERS KARAMAZOV*

A NOTE ON RUSSIAN NAMES

Russians have three names: a first name, a patronymic, and a surname. The patronymic is the father's first name with a suffix meaning "son of" or "daughter of": for example, Fyodorovich (son of Fyodor). In formal address, people are called by both their first names and their patronymics (Dmitri Fyodorovich, for example). In informal address, people are sometimes called by nicknames, or diminutives. For instance, Alexei Karamazov is sometimes called Alyosha (the diminutive of Alexei), and Dmitri Karamazov is sometimes called Mitka (the diminutive of Dmitri). Surnames reflect gender.

In the list that follows, each character's most common nicknames are given in parentheses after the character's full name. If the character is frequently called by one of many nicknames, the frequently used name is italicized.

Father Ferapont A severe and ascetic monk who hates Zosima.

Fetyukovich A famous defense attorney from Moscow who represents Dmitri at the trial.

Alexei Fyodorovich Karamazov (Alyosha, Alyoshka, Alyoshenka, Alyoshechka, Alxeichick, Lyosha, Lyoshenka) The third son of Fyodor and the younger brother of Dmitri and Ivan. Kind, gentle, loving, and wise, Alyosha has faith in God and loves mankind. He is around twenty years old at the start of the novel.

Dmitri Fyodorovich Karamazov (Mitka, Mitya, Mitenka, Mitri Fyodorovich) Fyodor's oldest son. Dmitri is passionate and intemperate. He struggles to overcome his flaws and find spiritual redemption.

Fyodor Pavlovich Karamazov The wealthy father of Alyosha, Dmitri, Ivan, and Smerdyakov. Coarse, vulgar, greedy, and lustful, Fyodor devotes his life to pleasure and never thinks of others. Everyone who knows Fyodor loathes him.

Ivan Fyodorovich Karamazov (Vanya, Vanka, Vanechka) The second son of Fyodor and the brother of Dmitri and Alyosha. A brilliant student, Ivan cannot reconcile the existence of unjust suffering with the idea of a loving God, so religious doubt plagues him.

Katerina Ospovna Khokhlakov (Madame Khokhlakov) A wealthy gentlewoman in town. Madame Khokhlakov is somewhat shallow and self-centered.

Liza Khokhlakov (*Lise*) Madame Khokhlakov's daughter. Lise is a mischievous and capricious young girl. She and Alyosha make plans to marry when she is of age.

Ippolit Kirrillovich The prosecuting attorney at Dmitri's trial.

Nikolai Ivanov Krasotkin (*Kolya*) A bold, intelligent young boy who befriends Alyosha after Ilyusha becomes ill.

Lizaveta A young retarded girl usually called Stinking Lizaveta. Fyodor either seduces or rapes her, impregnating her with Smerdyakov.

Pyotr Alexandrovich Miusov A wealthy landowner, the cousin of Fyodor's first wife, and briefly the guardian of the young Dmitri. Miusov considers himself a political intellectual and despises Fyodor.

Pyotr Ilyich Perkhotin A friend of Dmitri's. Perkhotin is a young official who follows Dmitri on the night of Fyodor's murder.

Mikhail Osipovich Rakitin A young seminary student. Cynical and sarcastic, Rakitin adopts the fashionable philosophical theories of the moment, quoting Nietzsche and calling himself a socialist.

Kuzma Kuzmich Samsonov The old merchant who brings Grushenka to the town after her former lover betrays her.

Pavel Fyodorovich Smerdyakov The son of Lizaveta and Fyodor. Smerdyakov alternates between outright malice and the appearance of groveling servitude. He is not stupid, but he is overly impressionable, and Ivan's theories on amorality encourage him to murder Fyodor.

Ilyusha Snegiryov (Ilyushechka, Ilyushka) The young son of a military captain. Proud and unwilling to submit to the larger boys who pick on him, Ilyusha befriends Alyosha. He falls ill and dies toward the end of the novel.

Agrafena Alexandrovna Svetlov (Grushenka, Grusha, Grushka) A beautiful young woman. Proud, fiery, and headstrong, Grushenka is an object of desire among the men in the town. After she meets Alyosha, a hidden vein of gentleness and love begins to emerge in her character.

Gregory Kutuzov Vasilievich Fyodor Karamazov's servant. Gregory, along with his wife Marfa, raises Smerdyakov from birth.

Katerina Ivanovna Verkhovtsev (*Katya*, Katka, Katenka) Dmitri's fiancée. The proud and sensitive daughter of a military captain, Katerina is devastated when Dmitri leaves her for Grushenka. She acts martyred and insists on staying loyal to the people who hurt her.

Zosima The wise, saintly elder at the monastery. Zosima is Alyosha's mentor and teacher before his death in Book VI. Zosima preaches actively loving, forgiving the sins of others, and cherishing God's creation.

THEMES IN *THE BROTHERS KARAMAZOV*

THE CONFLICT BETWEEN FAITH AND DOUBT Dostoevsky does not present doubt and faith neutrally. He actively takes the side of faith, arguing that a life full of faith is far happier than a life full of doubt. Zosima and Alyosha have faith in God, which leads them to active love, kindness, and forgiveness. Ivan Karamazov is ruled by doubt. He tries to find the truth by examining evidence, a practice that leads to the rejection of God and conventional morality, and crippling inner despair. Doubt eventually results in Smerdyakov's murder of Fyodor and Ivan's breakdown. Despite his clear pro-faith stance, however, Dostoevsky examines the psychology of doubt with great objectivity and rigor. Ivan may be unhappy, but he makes a strong case for skepticism. In chapters such as "The Grand Inquisitor," Dostoevsky presents a convincing case against religion, the church, and God. He admits that those who embrace religious faith are taking a great philosophical risk and behaving in ways that defy logic.

THE BURDEN OF FREE WILL Everyone is free to form his or her own opinions about God's existence, conventional morality, and the pursuit of good and evil. Free will may seem to be a blessing, but

Ivan sees it as a hardship. Those characters like Ivan who doubt God's existence, a position free will allows, suffer terribly. Free will places a heavy burden on humanity, making it optional instead of voluntary to reject the comforts of the world and accept the uncertainties and hardships of religious belief. Most people are too weak to choose belief. The Grand Inquisitor Ivan imagines in Book V concludes that Christ should have taken away free will, thereby making people happy and secure. Dostoevsky sides with Alyosha and Zosima, who see free will as a necessary, if difficult, component of simple and satisfying faith.

THE IMPOSSIBILITY OF ASSIGNING SOLE BLAME   The Brothers Karamazov argues that people should forgive each another's sins and resist judging each other. Zosima explains that human lives are so interwoven that everyone bears some responsibility for the sins of everyone else. For a long time, Ivan insists he is not responsible for any actions but his own. But when Smerdyakov explains that Ivan's amoral philosophical beliefs made it possible for him to kill Fyodor, Ivan suddenly understands that he is complicit in the murder of his father.

SYMBOLS IN *THE BROTHERS KARAMAZOV*

CHARACTERS   The Brothers Karamazov is both realistic and philosophical. Characters are not only fully drawn, believable individuals, they are symbols of ideas. The drama acted out between the characters becomes the drama of ideas in conflict with each other. Alyosha stands for faith, Ivan for doubt, and Fyodor for selfishness and physical appetite.

ZOSIMA'S CORPSE   When Zosima's corpse begins to stink, Alyosha thinks that the corpse represents the indignity the world heaps on religious faith. The fate of Zosima's corpse suggests that faith is not justified by miracles. Rather, the person who chooses faith must do so despite the many convincing reasons to doubt.

IMPORTANT QUOTATIONS FROM *THE BROTHERS KARAMAZOV*

"Recall the first question; its meaning, though not literally, was this: 'You want to go into the world, and you are going empty-handed, with some promise of freedom, which they in their simplicity and innate lawlessness cannot even comprehend, which they dread and fear—for nothing has ever been more insufferable for man and for human society than freedom! But do you see these stones in this bare, scorching desert? Turn them into bread and mankind will run after you like sheep, grateful and obedient, though eternally trembling lest you withdraw your hand and your loaves cease for them.'"

Location: Book V, Chapter 5
Speaker: The Grand Inquisitor
Context: The Grand Inquisitor tells Christ he should have made bread from stones, as Satan suggested, and then won the obedience of mankind

The Grand Inquisitor argues that when Christ rejected the temptations of Satan, he placed an intolerable burden of free will on mankind. The Grand Inquisitor thinks Christ has done mankind a disservice by giving them freedom instead of safety. Satan was right, he says, and Christ was wrong.

"But hesitation, anxiety, the struggle between belief and disbelief—all that is sometimes such a torment for a conscientious man like yourself, that it's better to hang oneself. . . . I'm leading you alternately between belief and disbelief, and I have my own purpose in doing so. A new method, sir: when you've completely lost faith in me, then you'll immediately start convincing me to my face that I am not a dream but a reality—I know you know; and then my goal will be achieved. And it is a noble goal. I will sow a just a tiny seed of faith in you, and from it an oak will grow—and such an oak that you, sitting in

that oak, will want to join 'the desert fathers and the blameless women'; because secretly you want that ver-ry, ver-ry much.. . . ."

Location: Book XI, Chapter 9
Speaker: The devil
Context: Ivan has learned of his complicity in Fyodor's murder, and he hallucinates, seeing a taunting devil

In Ivan's hallucination, a devil mocks him with his former beliefs, pointing out that his logical positions clash with his inner desires. The devil shrewdly admits that he is deliberately toying with Ivan's belief, because he knows Ivan secretly wants to believe in him. Ivan's mind may advocate amorality, but his gut yearns for conventional morals and beliefs. The murder of Fyodor has made him even more secretly desperate for religious faith. This inner longing shames Ivan. In this passage, Ivan's psyche is stripped bare, revealing the emotional desolation that lies beneath his philosophical positions.

"Above all, do not lie to yourself. A man who lies to himself and listens to his own lie comes to a point where he does not discern any truth either in himself or anywhere around him, and thus falls into disrespect towards himself and others. Not respecting anyone, he ceases to love, and having no love, he gives himself up to the passions and coarse pleasures, in order to occupy and amuse himself, and in his vices reaches complete bestiality, and it all comes from lying continually to others and to himself."

Location: Book II, Chapter 2
Speaker: Zosima
Context: Zosima tells Fyodor about the importance of honesty

"Listen: if everyone must suffer, in order to buy eternal harmony with their suffering, pray tell me what have children got to do with it? It's quite incomprehensible why they should have to suffer, and why they should buy harmony with their suffering."

Location: Book V, Chapter 4
Speaker: Ivan
Context: Ivan explains to Alyosha why he cannot believe in God

---

"Very different is the monastic way. Obedience, fasting, and prayer are laughed at, yet they alone constitute the way to real and true freedom: I cut away my superfluous and unnecessary needs, through obedience I humble and chasten my vain and proud will, and thereby, with God's help, attain freedom of spirit, and with that, spiritual rejoicing!"

Location: Book VI, Chapter 3
Speaker: Zosima
Context: Zosima analyzes the nature of the Russian monk

THE CALL OF THE WILD

Jack London

A pampered dog adjusts to the harsh realities of life in the North as he struggles with his recovered wild instincts and finds a master who treats him right.

THE LIFE OF JACK LONDON

Jack London was born in San Francisco in 1876 to Flora Wellman, the rebellious daughter of an aristocratic family. London's father was a traveling astrologist named William Chaney who abandoned Flora. While Jack was still an infant, Flora married Civil War veteran John London, who gave Jack his last name. The impoverished family lived in Oakland.

Jack London left school after eighth grade, but remained a voracious reader and a frequent library visitor. His rough adolescence was full of adventures: a stint as a pirate in San Francisco Bay, sealing expeditions to the Far East, and a trip across America as a tramp, among other experiences. At the age of nineteen, London returned to Oakland to graduate from high school. He spent a semester at the University of California in Berkeley, but left college for the Yukon Territory in Canada in 1897 to join the Klondike gold rush.

The gold rush didn't make London rich, but it furnished him with plenty of material for his career as a writer. As a reporter, he covered the Russo-Japanese War of 1904 and the Mexican Revolution in the 1910s. Meanwhile, he published over fifty books and became, for a time, America's most famous and the world's most widely read author. He embodied the turn-of-the-century spirit of the American West. His portrayal of adventure and frontier life was a breath of fresh air in the world of nineteenth-century Victorian fiction, whose obsession with social norms had begun to seem trivial and irrelevant.

London was married twice—once in 1900, to his math tutor and friend Bess Maddern, and again in 1905, to his secretary Charmian Kittredge, whom he considered his true love. As the popularity of his works soared, he became a figure of contradictory values—he argued for socialist principles and women's rights but lived a life of luxury on his boat and his large California ranch; he preached equality and the brotherhood of man but celebrated violence, power, and brute force in novels such as *The Call of the Wild* (1903). London died at the age of forty in 1916. He had been plagued by alcoholism and other health problems for years, but many have suggested that his death was a suicide.

THE CALL OF THE WILD IN CONTEXT

The Call of the Wild, published in 1903, remains London's most famous work. The novel draws both on London's experiences as a gold prospector in the Canadian wilderness and on his ideas about nature and the struggle for existence. These ideas come from various sources, including Charles Darwin, the English naturalist famous for his theories about biological evolution, and Friedrich Nietzsche, a prominent German philosopher. Although *The Call of the Wild* is first and foremost a story about a dog, its philosophical depth reaches far beyond that of most animal adventure stories.

THE CALL OF THE WILD: KEY FACTS

Time and place written: 1903; California	
Date of first publication: Serialized June 20–July 18, 1903	
Publisher: The Saturday Evening Post	
Type of work: Novel	
Genre: Adventure story	

Language: English

Setting (time): The late 1890s

Setting (place): Alaska and the Klondike region of Canada; California

Tense: Past

Tone: Romantic, heroic, sweeping

Narrator: Third-person, anonymous narrator

Point of View: Buck's; briefly, John Thornton's

Protagonist: Buck

Antagonist: The harsh natural world; the call of Buck's wild instincts; Buck's bad masters

THE CALL OF THE WILD: PLOT OVERVIEW

Buck, a powerful dog who is half St. Bernard and half sheepdog, lives on Judge Miller's estate in California's Santa Clara Valley. His comfortable life comes to an end when gold is discovered in the Klondike region of Canada, causing the demand for sled dogs to skyrocket. One of the judge's gardeners kidnaps Buck and sells him to dog traders, who teach Buck to obey by beating him with a club before shipping him north to the Klondike.

Buck is shocked by the cruelty of the chilly North. Curly, one of the dogs that arrived with Buck, is violently attacked and killed by a pack of huskies as soon as Curly gets off the ship. Buck vows never to let the same fate befall him. Buck is bought by François and Perrault, two Canadian mail drivers. As Buck adjusts to life as a sled dog, he recovers the instincts of his wild ancestors: he learns to fight, scavenge for food, and sleep beneath a layer of snow on cold nights. At the same time, he develops a fierce rivalry with Spitz, the lead dog on his sled team. One of their fights is broken up by the invasion of a pack of wild dogs. Buck begins to undercut Spitz's authority. The tension erupts in a major battle, during which Buck kills Spitz and takes his place as the lead dog.

With Buck at the head of the team, François and Perrault's sled makes record time. Nevertheless, the men turn the dog team over to a different mail driver, who forces the dogs to carry much heavier loads. On a particularly arduous trip, one of the dogs falls ill, and eventually the driver has to shoot him. After the journey, the dogs are too exhausted to go on another trip immediately, so the mail driver sells them to a group of American gold hunters—Hal, his sister Mercedes, and her husband Charles.

Buck's new masters are inexperienced and out of place in the wilderness. They plan poorly, overload the sled, and beat the dogs. Halfway through their journey, they realize they are short on food. While the humans bicker, some of the weaker, starving dogs die. Of an original team of fourteen, only five dogs are still alive when they limp into a camp set up by John Thornton, an experienced gold hunter. Thornton warns the Americans that they are traveling on dangerously thin ice. Hal dismisses these warnings and tries to continue the journey immediately. The other dogs move, but Buck refuses. When Hal beats him, Thornton intervenes, knocking a knife from Hal's hand and cutting Buck loose. Hal curses Thornton and starts the sled again, without Buck. Before the sled has gone a quarter of a mile, the ice breaks open and swallows both the humans and the dogs.

Thornton becomes Buck's master, and Buck is completely devoted to him. He saves Thornton from drowning in a river, attacks a man who tries to start a fight with Thornton in a bar, and wins a $1,600 wager for his new master by pulling a sled carrying a thousand-pound load. But Buck's love for Thornton is mixed with a growing attraction to the wild. He feels that he is being called away from civilization and into the wilderness. This feeling grows stronger when he accompanies Thornton and his friends in search of a lost mine hidden deep in the Canadian forest.

While the men search for gold, Buck ranges far afield, befriending wolves and hunting bears and moose. He always returns to Thornton, until one day he comes back to camp to find that Yeehat Indians have attacked and killed his master. Buck attacks the Indians, killing several and scattering the rest, and then heads off into the wild, where he becomes the leader of a pack of wolves. He becomes a legendary figure, a Ghost Dog, fathering countless cubs and inspiring fear in the Yeehats. Every year he returns to the place where Thornton died to honor his master before returning to his life in the wild.

CHARACTERS IN *THE CALL OF THE WILD*

DOGS

Buck A powerful dog, half St. Bernard and half sheepdog, who feels the "call of the wild" of the title. Buck is stolen from a California estate and sold as a sled dog in the Arctic. Over the course of the novel, Buck evolves from a pampered pet into a fierce, masterful animal, a survivor in the cruel Northern wilderness.

Curly A friend of Buck's on the sea journey to the North. In the North, Curly is killed by a pack of huskies when she incautiously tries to make friends. Her death teaches Buck that the North is harsh and hostile.

Dave A dog on Buck's sled team. Dave falls ill on one of the team's journeys. He wants to die while pulling the sled.

Sol-leks An older, more experienced dog on Buck's team.

Spitz The original leader of François's dog team and Buck's archrival. A fierce "devil-dog" used to winning fights with other dogs, Spitz is finally defeated and killed by Buck, who is as strong as Spitz and more cunning. Amoral and ruthless, Spitz believes in fighting for survival with all of his might.

DOG OWNERS

Charles Mercedes' husband and Hal's brother-in-law. Charles, like Mercedes and Hal, is inexperienced and foolish.

François A French Canadian mail driver who buys Buck and adds him to his team. François is an experienced man, accustomed to life in the North, and he impresses Buck with his fairness and good sense.

Hal An American gold seeker. Together with his sister Mercedes and her husband Charles, Hal buys Buck's dog team. The group's inexperience in the wilderness makes them terrible masters. Hal and his companions represent the weakness of civilized people and embody the worst kind of man-dog relationship.

Manuel A gardener's helper on Judge Miller's estate. Manuel kidnaps Buck and sells him to dog traders in order to pay off his gambling debts.

Judge Miller Buck's original master. Judge Miller is the owner of a large estate in California's Santa Clara Valley. His judgeship symbolizes the proper and civilized lifestyle Buck leads on his estate.

Mercedes Hal's sister and Charles's wife. Spoiled and pampered, Mercedes slows down the journey. Unlike Hal and Charles, she initially feels pity for the exhausted dogs. Her behavior, London suggests, demonstrates how civilized women who are babied by their men are unsuited for life in the wild.

Perrault A French Canadian. Perrault, together with François, turns Buck into a sled dog. Perrault and François speak in heavily accented English.

John Thornton Buck's final master. Thornton is a gold hunter experienced in the ways of the Klondike. Thornton and Buck's relationship is the man-dog ideal: they protect each other and are devoted to each other. Only the strength of their bond prevents Buck from answering the call of the wild.

THEMES IN *THE CALL OF THE WILD*

THE STRUGGLE FOR SURVIVAL AND MASTERY As Buck watches Curly's violent death, he realizes that the Northern wilderness is a cruel, uncaring place where moral considerations are irrelevant and only the strong prosper. London's conception of the struggle for survival owes much to the work of Charles Darwin, a nineteenth-century botanist who proposed the evolutionary model of development of life on Earth and envisioned a natural world defined by fierce competition for scarce resources. Darwin's theory is often referred to as "survival of the fittest," a phrase that also describes Buck's experiences.

Buck strives not only for survival, but also for mastery, especially in his conflict with Spitz and his battles to become the leader of the wolf pack at the end of the novel. London's celebration of the quest for domination is informed by the work of Friedrich Nietzsche, a German philosopher of the late nineteenth century. Nietzsche suggested that there are two types of human beings: "masters," who possess "the will to power," and "slaves," who do not. In his writings, Nietzsche often used animal imagery, comparing masters to "birds of prey" and "blond beasts," and slaves to herd animals. Buck, with his indomitable strength and fierce desire for mastery, is a canine incarnation of the Nietzschean master.

Like Darwin and especially Nietzsche, London rejects the idea that morality is a universal that governs the world. The novel applauds Buck's savage, amoral ferocity.

THE POWER OF ANCESTRAL MEMORY AND PRIMITIVE INSTINCTS The novel suggests that Buck does not actually *learn* the ways of the wild; rather, Buck gradually *recovers* the primitive instincts and memories possessed by his wild ancestors. These instincts have been buried in the canine psyche as dogs have become civilized creatures. The term *atavism* described this phenomenon of the reappearance, in a modern creature, of traits that defined its remote forebears. In lines such as "He was older than the days he had seen and the breaths he had drawn" and "He linked the past with the present, and the eternity behind him throbbed through him in a mighty rhythm to which he swayed as the tides and seasons swayed," London reminds us that Buck is "retrogressing" into a wilder way of life that all dogs once shared. Moreover, Buck's connection to his ancestral identity is mystical as well as instinctual: he occasionally has visions of this older world, of humans dressed in animal skins and living in caves, and wild dogs hunting in primeval forests.

THE INDIVIDUAL AND THE GROUP In the North, Buck learns how to work as part of a group. For example, Dave and Sol-leks, two dogs on his team, teach him how to pull a sled properly. The members of the team take pride in their work. When they make good time on a trip, they congratulate each other.

At the same time, rugged individualism is valued highly in the wilderness. Only an individual who has separated himself from the group, such as John Thornton, can achieve mastery over this unconquered world. For most of the novel, Buck serves either his human master or his pack. John Thornton cuts Buck's harness to release him both from his team and from the pack mentality. Although Buck continues to serve Thornton, he is eventually overcome by his yearnings for a solitary life in the wild.

At the end of the novel, Buck becomes the leader of a pack of wolves. The final section suggests that despite the importance of individualism, survival in the wild requires cooperation with a group.

SYMBOLS IN *THE CALL OF THE WILD*

MERCEDES' POSSESSIONS Mercedes loads the sled up with too many things for the dogs to pull. Later, she sits on the sled, making the load even heavier. Mercedes' body and her heavy possessions are the physical embodiment of the heavy burden she, a hypercivilized woman, places on others in the wilderness. Her insistence on keeping all of her things highlights the difference between the wild, where objects are valued for their immediate utility, and civilization, where otherwise useless objects can bear cultural value or serve as markers of wealth. Mercedes' attitude has no place in the wild, and she dies when the overburdened sled falls through the ice.

BUCK'S TRACES The symbolic significance of Buck's traces (traces are the straps that bind him to the rest of the sled team) evolves with the development of the plot. Initially, the traces represent his subservience to men: Buck is harnessed into a sled and must work against his will. Later, as Buck adapts to the wild and understands the hierarchy of the sled team, his traces embody the force of teamwork that ties the dogs together. After his duel with Spitz, Buck is harnessed at the head of the pack. His traces now represent his leadership over the dogs. Finally, as Hal mistreats the dogs, the traces again represent subservience to humans. In cutting them, John Thornton liberates Buck from servitude forever.

IMPORTANT QUOTATIONS FROM *THE CALL OF THE WILD*

He was beaten (he knew that); but he was not broken. He saw, once for all, that he stood no chance against a man with a club. He had learned the lesson, and in all his after life he never forgot it. That club was a revelation. It was his introduction to the reign of primitive law, and he met the introduction halfway. The facts of life took on a fiercer aspect and, while he faced that aspect uncowed, he faced it with all the latent cunning of his nature aroused.

Location: Late in Chapter I, "Into the Primitive"
Speaker: The narrator
Context: By way of introduction into his new life, Buck is beaten by his kidnappers

As his kidnappers beat him, Buck repeatedly leaps up to attack them until finally they knock him unconscious. This incident is Buck's radical introduction to a new way of life, which is vastly different from the pampered existence that he has led in the Santa Clara Valley. There, civilized law and civilized morality regulated life. The refinement of Buck's life was symbolized by the fact that his California master was a judge—one who enforces society's rules. In the wild, Buck comes to terms with "the reign of primitive law," according to which stronger creatures—a man with a club, a powerful dog—can dominate weaker ones. Buck learns his lesson well and soon dominates others.

A pause seemed to fall. Every animal was motionless as though turned to stone. Only Spitz quivered and bristled as he staggered back and forth, snarling with horrible menace, as though to frighten off impending death. Then Buck sprang in and out; but while he was in, shoulder had at last squarely met shoulder. The dark circle became a dot on the moon-flooded snow as Spitz disappeared from view. Buck stood and looked on, the successful champion, the dominant primordial beast who had made his kill and found it good.

Location: Final paragraph of Chapter III
Speaker: The narrator
Context: Buck wins his decisive fight against Spitz, after which Buck becomes the team's lead dog

This passage marks the moment when Buck comes into his own by vanquishing and killing his great rival Spitz. No longer the pampered pet, Buck is now "the successful champion . . . the dominant primordial beast." The Buck-Spitz duel is the central example of the struggle for mastery that, according to London, defines life in the wild.

During the four years since his puppyhood he had lived the life of a sated aristocrat; he had a fine pride in himself, was even a trifle egotistical, as country gentlemen sometimes become because of their insular situation.

Location: Chapter I, "Into the Primitive"
Speaker: The narrator
Context: The narrator describes Buck's leisurely life before he is kidnapped and dragged into the harsh world of the Klondike

---

And not only did he learn by experience, but instincts long dead became alive again. The domesticated generations fell from him. In vague ways he remembered back to the youth of the breed, to the time the wild dogs ranged in packs through the primeval forest and killed their meat as they ran it down. . . . Thus, as token of what a puppet thing life is the ancient song surged through him and he came into his own again. . . .

Location: Chapter II, "The Law of Club and Fang"
Speaker: The narrator
Context: As Buck fights for survival in the harsh world of the Klondike, he relies increasingly on *atavism*—the instincts of his primitive ancestors' instincts resurfaced

[Each] day mankind and the claims of mankind slipped farther from him. Deep in the forest a call was sounding, and as often as he heard this call, mysteriously thrilling and luring, he felt compelled to turn his back upon the fire, and to plunge into the forest. . . . But as often as he gained the soft unbroken earth and the green shade, the love of John Thornton drew him back to the fire again.

Location: Chapter VI, "For the Love of a Man"
Speaker: The narrator
Context: The narrator describes the tension between Buck's natural instincts to live in the wild and his love for John Thornton, his ideal master

CANDIDE

Voltaire

After suffering many misadventures that contradict the idea that God has a grand plan, a man finds happiness in hard work.

THE LIFE OF VOLTAIRE

François-Marie Arouet, later known as Voltaire, was born in 1694 to a middle-class Parisian family. Louis XIV was king of France, and the vast majority of the French lived in crushing poverty. When Voltaire came of age, the French aristocracy was in control, but the intellectual movement known as the Enlightenment was spreading ideas about equality and basic rights of man and the importance of reason and scientific objectivity.

Voltaire received a Jesuit education at the college of Louis-le-Grand, where his wit impressed and sometimes outraged his teachers. Voltaire became legendary in France for his sharp epigrams. After exercising his bitter, satirical wit at the expense of the French Regent, he was exiled from Paris to Sully. He flattered key people and managed to get his exile reversed. Shortly after returning to Paris, Voltaire was imprisoned in the Bastille for satirizing the government. It was during his stay in prison that the author adopted the pen name Voltaire. He was released in 1718, and soon after, his first play, *Oedipe*, was produced in Paris. Voltaire was only twenty-four years old.

Voltaire moved in rich and powerful circles. In his writing he alternately flattered and lambasted his acquaintances, eventually earning himself another stint in the Bastille in 1726. He was soon released on the condition that he move to England. English literati received him with open arms, and within a few months, Voltaire was fluent in English. After three years, he was allowed to return to France.

Voltaire attacked the church and the state with equal fervor. A lifelong champion of the poor and downtrodden, he excoriated tyranny and religious persecution in his writing. In 1759, Voltaire purchased Ferney, an estate near the border between France and Switzerland, so that he could easily escape French authorities by fleeing to Switzerland. Ferney quickly became a retreat for important European intellectuals.

In his later life, Voltaire was involved in many campaigns for social and political justice. When he returned to Paris at the age of eighty-three, the populace greeted him with a hero's welcome. Voltaire died in May 1778. He was buried in consecrated ground at Romilly-on-Seine, but in 1791 the National Assembly ordered his body entombed alongside René Descartes and other great French thinkers at the Panthéon in Paris. In 1814, religious fundamentalists stole the remains of Voltaire, as well as those of Jean-Jacques Rousseau, and dumped them in a pit full of quicklime, a "burial" reserved for individuals condemned by the church. Voltaire would have appreciated the irony of this act, as he and Rousseau were bitter rivals during their lifetimes.

CANDIDE IN CONTEXT

The Enlightenment was a movement that encompassed a wide variety of ideas in philosophy, science, and medicine. The Enlightenment began in the seventeenth century and peaked in the eighteenth century. Many historians mark the French Revolution as the crowning event of the Enlightenment era. The primary feature of Enlightenment philosophy is faith that the exercise of reason and rational thought can create a better society. Enlightenment philosophers shared a spirit of social reform. The champions of the Enlightenment called for rebellion against superstition, fear, and prejudice. They attacked the aristocracy and the church.

Candide (1759) reflects Voltaire's lifelong aversion to Christian regimes and arrogant aristocrats, but it also criticizes certain characteristics of the Enlightenment. It attacks the optimistic idea that rational thought can abolish evil. It also points out the inability of reason to stop witch-hunts and organized religious persecution.

CANDIDE: KEY FACTS

Full title: Candide, or Optimism

Time and place written: 1758–1759; Schwetzingen, Prussia, and Geneva, Switzerland

Date of first publication: January or February, 1759

Publisher: Gabriel Cramer

Type of work: Novel

Genre: Satire; adventure novel; bildungsroman; picaresque

Language: French

Setting (time): 1750s

Setting (place): Real and fictional locations in Europe and South America

Tense: Past and present

Tone: Ironic, melodramatic

Narrator: Anonymous satirical third-person

Point of view: Candide

Protagonist: Candide

Antagonist: Numerous disasters

CANDIDE: PLOT OVERVIEW

Candide, the illegitimate nephew of a German baron, grows up in the baron's castle. His tutor, Pangloss, teaches him that he lives in "the best of all possible worlds." Candide falls in love with the baron's young daughter, Cunégonde. The baron catches his daughter kissing Candide one day and kicks Candide out of the castle. Candide is soon conscripted into the army of the Bulgars. He wanders away from camp for a brief walk, and gets brutally flogged as a deserter. After witnessing a horrific battle he escapes and travels to Holland.

In Holland, a kindly Anabaptist named Jacques gives Candide shelter. Candide runs into a deformed beggar who turns out to be Pangloss. Pangloss explains that he has contracted syphilis, and Cunégonde and her family have been brutally murdered by the Bulgar army. Nonetheless, he maintains his optimistic outlook. Jacques, Pangloss, and Candide set out for Lisbon, but their ship runs into a storm and Jacques drowns. Candide and Pangloss arrive in Lisbon to find it destroyed by an earthquake and the Inquisition. Pangloss is hanged as a heretic, and Candide is flogged for listening with approval to Pangloss's philosophy. An old woman dresses Candide's wounds and then takes him to Cunégonde, who explains that the Bulgars killed the rest of her family but only raped her. A captain sold her to a man named Don Issachar. She is now a sex slave jointly owned by Don Issachar and the Grand Inquisitor of Lisbon. Cunégonde's owners arrive, and Candide kills them both. Terrified, Candide, the old woman, and Cunégonde board a ship bound for South America. During their journey, the old woman tells her story. She is the pope's daughter, and she has suffered greatly. Rape, enslavement, and cannibalism are among the disasters she has endured.

Candide and Cunégonde plan to marry, but as soon as they arrive in Buenos Aires, the governor, Don Fernando, proposes to Cunégonde. She accepts because of his riches. Authorities arrive from Portugal in pursuit of Candide. Along with a newly acquired valet named Cacambo, Candide flees to Jesuit territory. Candide demands an audience with a Jesuit commander, who turns out to be Cunégonde's brother, the baron. He also managed to escape from the Bulgars. The baron insists that his sister will never marry a commoner like Candide. Enraged, Candide runs the baron through with his sword. Candide and Cacambo escape into the wilderness, where they narrowly avoid being eaten by a native tribe called the Biglugs.

After traveling for days, Candide and Cacambo find themselves in the land of Eldorado, where gold and jewels litter the streets. This utopian country has no religious conflict and no court system. It has advanced scientific knowledge and does not value its riches. Candide longs to return to Cunégonde, and after a month in Eldorado he and Cacambo depart with countless invaluable jewels loaded onto swift pack sheep. Candide sends Cacambo to Buenos Aires, telling him to purchase Cunégonde from Don Fernando and then meet him in Venice. An unscrupulous merchant named Vanderdendur steals much of Candide's fortune, dampening his optimism somewhat. Frustrated, Candide sails off to France with a pessimistic scholar named Martin. A Spanish captain sinks Vanderdendur's ship, and Candide recovers part of his fortune, which Candide takes as proof that there is justice in the world. Martin staunchly disagrees with him.

In Paris, Candide and Martin mingle with the social elite. Candide's fortune attracts a number of hangers-on, several of whom steal jewels from him. Candide and Martin proceed to Venice, but they cannot find Cunégonde and Cacambo. They do meet Paquette, the chambermaid-turned-prostitute who gave Pangloss syphilis, and Count Pococurante, a wealthy, bored Venetian. Eventually, Cacambo, now a slave of a deposed Turkish monarch, surfaces and explains that Cunégonde is enslaved in Constantinople. Martin, Cacambo, and Candide depart for Turkey, where Candide buys Cacambo's freedom.

Candide discovers Pangloss and the baron in a Turkish chain gang. Despite everything, Pangloss remains an optimist. Overjoyed, Candide purchases their freedom. When Candide finds Cunégonde, she is ugly, but he purchases her freedom anyway. He also buys the old woman's freedom and a farm outside Constantinople. He marries Cunégonde. The baron still cannot stand the idea of his sister marrying a commoner, so Candide sends him back to the chain gang. Candide, Cunégonde , Cacambo, Pangloss, and the old woman settle into a comfortable life on the farm but soon find themselves growing bored and quarrelsome. Candide meets a farmer who lives a simple life, works hard, and avoids vice and leisure. Inspired, Candide and his friends decide to work without arguing. They become industrious and start a garden.

CHARACTERS IN *CANDIDE*

The Abbé of Perigord An abbot and Paris socialite who cheats Candide out of his money.

The Baron (the Commander) Cunégonde's brother. After his family's castle is destroyed, the Baron becomes a Jesuit priest. Voltaire often suggests that the Baron has homosexual tendencies. He is arrogant about his family's noble lineage.

Cacambo Candide's valet. A mixed-race native of the Americas, Cacambo is very intelligent and moral. A savvy man, he single-handedly rescues Candide from a number of scrapes. As a practical man of action, he contrasts with ineffectual philosophers such as Pangloss and Martin.

Candide The protagonist of the novel. Candide is a good-hearted but hopelessly naïve young man. His misadventures severely test his faith in Pangloss's doctrine of optimism. Candide is less a realistic character than a conduit for the attitudes and events that surround him.

Cunégonde The daughter of Candide' German uncle. Cunégonde loves Candide but is willing to betray him. Like Candide, she is neither intelligent nor complex.

The Farmer A simple, hardworking man who lives outside Constantinople. The farmer impresses Candide and his friends.

Don Fernando d'Ibaraa y Figueora y Mascarenes y Lampourdos y Souza The governor of Buenos Aires. He makes Cunégonde his mistress.

Brother Giroflée A dissatisfied monk. Giroflée pays to sleep with Paquette. Like her, he is miserable. His spirits do not improve after Candide gives him a large sum of money.

The Grand Inquisitor A powerful figure in the Portuguese Catholic Church who orders heretics burned alive. The Grand Inquisitor uses the threat of religious oppression to force Don Issachar to share Cunégonde with him.

Don Issachar A wealthy Jewish man. Don Issachar purchases Cunégonde and makes her his mistress.

Jacques (the Anabaptist) A humane Dutch Anabaptist. Jacques treats Candide and Pangloss kindly. He is pessimistic about human nature. Jacques drowns in the Bay of Lisbon while trying to save the life of an ungrateful sailor.

The Marquise of Parolignac A cunning, sexually licentious Paris socialite. She seduces Candide and steals some of his jeweled rings.

Martin   A cynical scholar whom Candide befriends. More knowledgeable and intelligent than either Candide or Pangloss, Martin is nonetheless a philosopher of limited talent. Because he always expects the worst, he often has trouble seeing the world as it really is.

The Old Woman   The daughter of a pope. The old woman's misfortunes have made her cynical about human nature, but she does not pity herself. She is wise, practical, and loyal to her mistress. Though she has often been close to suicide, she always finds a reason to live.

Pangloss   A philosopher and Candide's tutor. The primary target of Voltaire's satire is Pangloss's optimistic belief that this world is "the best of all possible worlds." Pangloss's own experiences contradict this belief, but he will not give it up.

Paquette   A chambermaid and later a prostitute. Candide is moved by Paquette's misery and gives her a large sum of money, which she quickly squanders.

Count Pococurante   A wealthy Venetian. The Count has a marvelous collection of art and literature, but everything bores him.

Vanderdendur   A cruel slave owner and unscrupulous merchant. After he steals one of Candide's jewel-laden sheep, his ship sinks in a battle.

THEMES IN *CANDIDE*

THE FOLLY OF OPTIMISM   Pangloss and Candide maintain that "everything is for the best in this best of all possible worlds." Their motto is a simplification of some Enlightenment philosophies. Thinkers such as Gottfried Wilhelm von Leibniz believed that God is perfect, and the existence of evil in the world would prove that God is either partly bad or partly weak. Therefore, these philosophers argued, the world must be perfect, and people perceive imperfections in the world only because they do not understand God's grand plan. Voltaire does not assume that God is perfect, or even that he exists, so he mercilessly satirizes the idea that the world must be completely good. Pangloss and Candide, the stand-ins for von Leibniz and his ilk, suffer and witness a wide variety of horrors—floggings, rapes, robberies, unjust executions, disease, an earthquake, betrayals, and crushing ennui. These horrors are meaningless. They point only to the cruelty and folly of humanity and the indifference of the world. Pangloss must bend over backwards to make these horrors fit into his worldview. He claims, for example, that syphilis needed to be transmitted from the Americas to Europe so that Europeans could enjoy New World delicacies such as chocolate. While Jacques drowns, Pangloss stops Candide from saving him "by proving that the bay of Lisbon had been formed expressly for this Anabaptist to drown in." More intelligent and experienced characters, such as the old woman, Martin, and Cacambo, are pessimistic about humanity and the world. By the novel's end, even Pangloss is forced to admit that he doesn't "believe a word of" his own optimistic arguments.

THE HYPOCRISY OF RELIGION   A parade of corrupt, hypocritical religious leaders underlines Voltaire's skepticism about organized religion. The parade includes a pope who vowed celibacy but fathers a daughter, a hard-line Catholic Inquisitor who keeps a mistress, and a Franciscan friar who took a vow of poverty but steals jewels. Religious leaders in the novel carry out inhumane campaigns, oppressing those who disagree with them on even the smallest theological matter. Voltaire skewers religious leaders but does not condemn the everyday religious believer. Jacques, a member of a radical Protestant sect called the Anabaptists, is arguably the most generous and humane character in the novel.

THE NECESSITY OF DEATH   At various points, Candide believes that Cunégonde, Pangloss, and the baron are dead, only to discover later that they have survived. The function of these "resurrections" in the novel is complicated. At first glance, they suggest a strange optimism that is out of step with the general tone of the novel. But on closer examination we see that the resurrected characters are people who do more harm than good. Each resurrected figure embodies a harmful aspect of human nature: Cunégonde is shallow and fickle, Pangloss silly and dim, and the baron snobbish and narrow-minded. By resurrecting these characters, Voltaire suggests that perhaps death is not always a tragedy.

SYMBOLS IN *CANDIDE*

THE GARDEN At the end of the novel, Candide and his companions find happiness in their garden. As Pangloss points out, the garden is reminiscent of the Garden of Eden, in which Adam and Eve enjoyed perfect bliss. However, in *Candide* the garden marks the end of the characters' trials, while for Adam and Eve the garden marked the beginning of sin. In the Garden of Eden, Adam and Eve enjoyed the fruits of nature without having to work, whereas Candide's garden makes people happy by forcing them to do hard, simple labor. Therefore, the garden represents the only Eden humans can enjoy in a sinful world.

THE LISBON EARTHQUAKE The earthquake in *Candide* was inspired by a real earthquake that leveled the city of Lisbon in 1755. Before writing *Candide*, Voltaire wrote a long poem about that event, which he interpreted as a sign of God's indifference or even cruelty toward humanity. The earthquake represents the devastating, senseless, cruel nature of the world. Voltaire argues that such absurd events are not part of some grand plan, much as thinkers like Pangloss might hope they are.

IMPORTANT QUOTATIONS FROM *CANDIDE*

—A hundred times I wanted to kill myself, but always I loved life more. This ridiculous weakness is perhaps one of our worst instincts; is anything more stupid than choosing to carry a burden that really one wants to cast on the ground? to hold existence in horror, and yet to cling to it? to fondle the serpent which devours us till it has eaten out our heart?

Location: Chapter 12
Speaker: The old woman
Context: The old woman has just told of the rape, slavery, and cannibalism she has experienced

In a calamitous world, it sometimes seems that the rational choice is suicide and that the surprising thing is the low rate of suicide deaths. In Voltaire's time, most people believed that God and Christianity forbid suicide and that those who killed themselves would spend eternity in hell. But organized religion does not matter much in the world of *Candide*, and the old woman does not think about it when wondering why people don't kill themselves. Perhaps she believes that hell cannot possibly be worse than life or that if God and the afterlife don't exist, consciousness is better than the finality of death. But if we do not believe in God and the afterlife and therefore do not have to long for them, we are free to cling to life instead of yearn for heaven. The old woman suggests that people hang on to life because they "love" it. Life may be a serpent, but we "fondle" it nonetheless. Human beings naturally embrace life—a "stupid," nonsensical instinct, perhaps, but one that demonstrates passion, strong will, and heroic endurance.

—Let's work without speculating, said Martin; it's the only way of rendering life bearable. The whole little group entered into this laudable scheme; each one began to exercise his talents. The little plot yielded fine crops. . . and Pangloss sometimes used to say to Candide:—All events are linked together in the best of possible worlds; for, after all, if you had not been driven from a fine castle by being kicked in the backside for love of Miss Cunégonde, if you hadn't been sent before the Inquisition, if you hadn't traveled across America on foot, if you hadn't given a good sword thrust to the baron, if you hadn't lost all your sheep from the good land of Eldorado, you wouldn't be sitting here eating candied citron and pistachios.—That is very well put, said Candide, but we must go and work our garden.

Location: The final passage of the novel
Speaker: The narrator
Context: Candide and his friends have found the cure for crushing boredom

The cure for the crushing boredom of stability turns out to be hard work such as gardening. It is surprising that this fictional parody of optimism should end happily. Given this final passage, we might wonder for the first time whether Pangloss is right in claiming to live in "the best of possible worlds." The secret to happiness, Voltaire suggests, is ceasing all philosophizing and devoting yourself to work. As Candide implies in his final line, gardening leaves no time for philosophical speculation, and everyone is happier and more productive as a result.

Pangloss gave instruction in metaphysico-theologico-cosmolo-nigology. . . —It is clear, said he, that things cannot be otherwise than they are, for since everything is made to serve an end, everything necessarily serves the best end. Observe: noses were made to support spectacles, hence we have spectacles. Legs, as anyone can plainly see, were made to be breeched, and so we have breeches.

Location: Chapter 1
Speaker: Pangloss
Context: Pangloss explains his theories, which parody those of Enlightenment philosopher Leibniz

---

The enormous riches which this rascal had stolen were sunk beside him in the sea, and nothing was saved but a single sheep. —You see, said Candide to Martin, crime is punished sometimes; this scoundrel of a Dutch merchant has met the fate he deserved. —Yes, said Martin; but did the passengers aboard his ship have to perish too? God punished the scoundrel, the devil drowned the others.

Location: Chapter 20
Speaker: The narrator
Context: Vanderdendur's ship has sunk

[W]hen they were not arguing, the boredom was so fierce that one day the old woman ventured to say: — I should like to know which is worse, being raped a hundred times by negro pirates, having a buttock cut off, running the gauntlet in the Bulgar army, being flogged and hanged in an auto-da-fé, being dissected and rowing in the galleys—experiencing, in a word, all the miseries through which we have passed—or else just sitting here and doing nothing? —It's a hard question, said Candide. These words gave rise to new reflections, and Martin in particular concluded that man was bound to live either in convulsions of misery or in the lethargy of boredom.

Location: Chapter 30
Speaker: The narrator
Context: After finding money, peace, and security, Candide and his friends debate whether misery or boredom is better

THE CANTERBURY TALES

Geoffrey Chaucer

A group of travelers making a pilgrimage to Canterbury tell each other stories that are by turns crude, hilarious, creepy, gruesome, and pious.

THE LIFE OF GEOFFREY CHAUCER

Little is known about Geoffrey Chaucer's personal life, and even less about his education, but a number of records document his professional life. Chaucer was born in London in the early 1340s. His father, a wine merchant, became tremendously wealthy when he inherited the property of relatives who died in the Black Death of 1349. He could afford to make his son a page to the Countess of Ulster. Geoffrey Chaucer eventually served the countess's husband, Prince Lionel, son of King Edward III. For most of his life, Chaucer served in the Hundred Years War between England and France as both a soldier and a diplomat. He was fluent in French and Italian and conversant in Latin and other languages.

In the late 1360s, Chaucer married Philippa Roet, who served Edward III's queen. They had at least two sons together. Philippa's sister was the mistress of John of Gaunt, the duke of Lancaster. Chaucer wrote one of his first poems, *The Book of the Duchess*, for John of Gaunt. In a legal document that dates from 1380, a woman named Cecily Chaumpaigne released Chaucer from the accusation of seizing her. It is unclear whether "seizing her" refers to rape, consensual sex, or abduction of her son. Chaucer's wife Philippa apparently died in 1387.

In or around 1378, Chaucer began to develop his vision of an English poetry that would be linguistically accessible to all—obedient neither to the court, whose official language was French, nor to the Church, whose official language was Latin. Instead, Chaucer wrote in vernacular English, just as Petrarch and Boccaccio (both of whom Chaucer might have met in Italy) wrote in vernacular Italian.

Nobles and kings, pleased with Chaucer, rewarded him with money, higher appointments, and property. In 1374, the king gave Chaucer a job working with cloth importers. He held the position for twelve years and then left London for Kent, the county in which Canterbury is located. After retiring in the early 1390s, Chaucer worked on *The Canterbury Tales*, which he began around 1387. He had already written a substantial amount of narrative poetry, including the celebrated romance *Troilus and Criseyde*.

Social tension filled England during Chaucer's life. The Black Death wiped out an estimated thirty to fifty percent of the English population. Consequently, the remaining labor force bargained for better wages, incurring the resentment of nobles and rich men. In 1381, the peasantry, helped by the artisan class, revolted against the nobles. Merchants capitalized on a new demand for luxury items, dominating London during Chaucer's life.

THE CANTERBURY TALES IN CONTEXT

William Caxton, England's first printer, published *The Canterbury Tales* in the 1470s. By the English Renaissance, poetry critic George Puttenham had identified Chaucer as the father of the English literary canon. Chaucer succeeded in his highly ambitious project to create a literature and poetic language for all classes of society. Today, Chaucer is universally considered one of the great masters and innovators of literary narrative and character.

Chaucer originally planned that each character in *The Canterbury Tales* would tell four tales, two on the way to Canterbury and two on the way back. But the text ends after twenty-four tales, and the party is still on its way to Canterbury. We do not know whether Chaucer revised his plan or left the work incomplete when he died on October 25, 1400. Writers and printers soon recognized *The Canterbury Tales* as a masterful and highly original work. The format of *The Canterbury Tales* and the intense realism of its characters were virtually unknown to English readers.

The Canterbury Tales is written in Middle English, which bears a close visual resemblance to the English written and spoken today. In contrast, Old English (the language of Beowulf, for example) can be read only in modern translation or by students of Old English. Students often read *The Canterbury Tales* in its original language, not only because of the similarity between Chaucer's Middle English and our own, but because the beauty and humor of the poetry is largely lost in translation.

CANTERBURY TALES: KEY FACTS

Time and place written: Around 1386–1395; England

Date of first publication: Sometime in the early fifteenth century

Publisher: Originally circulated in hand-copied manuscripts

Type of work: Poetry (two tales are in prose: the Tale of Melibee and the Parson's Tale)

Genre: Poetry; character portraits; parody; estates satire; romance; fabliau

Language: Middle English

Setting (time): Late fourteenth century, after 1381

Setting (place): The Tabard Inn; the road to Canterbury

Tense: Past

Tone: By turns satirical, elevated, pious, earthy, bawdy, comical

Narrator: The primary narrator is an anonymous, naïve member of the pilgrimage, who is not described (and who must not be equated with Geoffrey Chaucer, even though his name is Chaucer). The other pilgrims narrate most of the tales

Point of view: First person in the General Prologue; omniscient third-person in the tales (though narrated by different pilgrims, each tale is told by a third-person narrator who explains the thoughts and actions of the characters)

Protagonists: Each story has protagonists, but all of the storytellers are equally important

Antagonist: Clashes between social classes, tastes, professions, and the sexes

THE CANTERBURY TALES: PLOT OVERVIEW

GENERAL PROLOGUE

At the Tabard Inn near London, the narrator joins a company of twenty-nine pilgrims. The pilgrims, like the narrator, are traveling to the shrine of Saint Thomas Becket in Canterbury. The narrator gives a descriptive account of twenty-seven of these pilgrims. The Host suggests that the group ride together and entertain each other with stories. He decides that each pilgrim will tell two stories on the way to Canterbury and two on the way back. The best storyteller will receive a meal at Bailey's tavern. The pilgrims draw lots and determine that the Knight will tell the first tale.

THE KNIGHT'S TALE

Theseus, duke of Athens, imprisons Arcite and Palamon, two knights from Thebes. From prison, the knights see and fall in love with Theseus's sister-in-law, Emelye. Arcite is freed but then banished from Athens. He returns in disguise and becomes a page in Emelye's chamber. Palamon escapes from prison. He meets Arcite and fights with him over Emelye. Theseus arranges a tournament between the two knights, with Emelye as the prize. Arcite wins, but he is accidentally thrown from his horse and dies. Palamon marries Emelye.

THE MILLER'S PROLOGUE AND TALE

The Host asks the Monk to tell the next tale, but the drunken Miller butts in and insists that his tale should be next. He tells the story of an impoverished student named Nicholas who persuades his landlord's sexy young wife, Alisoun, to spend the night with him. Nicholas convinces his landlord, a carpenter named John, that the second flood is coming, and tricks him into sleeping in a tub hanging from the ceiling of his barn. Absolon, a young parish clerk who is also in love with Alisoun, comes to Alisoun's window at night and begs for a kiss. She sticks her rear end out the window and lets him kiss it. Absolon fetches a red-hot poker, returns to the window, and asks for another kiss. Nicholas sticks his bottom out the window and farts, and Absolon brands him on the buttocks. Nicholas's cries for water make John think the flood has come, so he cuts the rope connecting his tub to the ceiling, falls down, and breaks his arm.

THE REEVE'S PROLOGUE AND TALE

The Reeve takes offense at the Miller's tale of a stupid carpenter and counters with a story about a dishonest miller. In his tale, two students, John and Alayn, go to watch the miller grind their corn to make sure he doesn't steal any of it. The miller unties their horse, and while they chase it, he steals some of the flour he has just ground for them. By the time the students catch the horse, it is dark, so they spend the night in the miller's house. Alayn seduces the miller's daughter, and John seduces the miller's wife. The miller wakes up and tries to beat the students. His wife, thinking that her husband is one of the students, hits him over the head with a staff. The students take back their stolen goods and leave.

THE COOK'S PROLOGUE AND TALE

The Cook tells of an apprentice named Perkyn who drinks and dances so much that he is called "Perkyn Reveler." Perkyn's master decides he would rather send his apprentice away than let him stay home and corrupt the other servants. Perkyn arranges to stay with a friend who loves drinking and gambling, and who is married to a prostitute. The tale breaks off, unfinished, after fifty-eight lines.

THE MAN OF LAW'S INTRODUCTION, PROLOGUE, TALE, AND EPILOGUE

The Host reminds his fellow pilgrims to waste no time. He asks the Man of Law to tell the next tale. The Man of Law says Chaucer has already told all suitable tales. Chaucer may be unskilled as a poet, says the Man of Law, but he has told more stories of lovers than Ovid, and he doesn't print tales of incest as John Gower does (Gower was a contemporary of Chaucer). In the Prologue to his tale, the Man of Law laments the miseries of poverty. He then remarks how fortunate merchants are and says that his tale is one told to him by a merchant.

In the tale, the Muslim sultan of Syria converts his entire sultanate (including himself) to Christianity in order to persuade the emperor of Rome to give him his daughter, Custance, in marriage. The sultan's mother and her attendants remain secretly faithful to Islam. The mother holds a banquet and massacres her son and all the Christians except for Custance, whom she sets adrift in a rudderless ship. After years of floating, Custance runs ashore in Northumberland, where a constable and his wife, Hermengyld, offer her shelter. She converts them to Christianity.

One night, Satan makes a young knight murder Hermengyld. The constable comes in with Alla, the king of Northumberland, and finds his wife dead. The knight who murdered Hermengyld swears that Custance is the true murderer, but as he lies he is struck down and his eyes burst out of his face. The knight is executed, Alla and many others convert to Christianity, and Custance and Alla marry.

While Alla is away in Scotland, Custance gives birth to a boy named Mauricius. Alla's mother, Donegild, contrives to send Custance and her son away on the same ship on which Custance arrived. Alla returns home, finds out what has happened, and kills Donegild. After many adventures at sea, including an attempted rape, Custance ends up back in Rome, where she reunites with Alla. She also reunites with her father, the emperor. Alla dies after a year. Mauricius becomes the next Roman emperor.

The Host asks the Parson to tell the next tale, but the Parson reproaches him for swearing, and they bicker.

THE WIFE OF BATH'S PROLOGUE AND TALE

The Wife of Bath, quoting from the Bible, argues against the belief that it is wrong to marry more than once. She explains how she dominated and controlled each of her five husbands. The Friar butts in to complain that she is taking too long, and the Summoner says friars are like flies, always meddling. The Friar promises to tell a tale about a summoner, and the Summoner promises to tell a tale about a friar. The Host asks everyone to quiet down and allow the Wife to commence her tale.

In her tale, a young knight of King Arthur's court rapes a maiden. As punishment, Arthur's queen sends him on a quest to discover what women want most. An ugly old woman promises the knight she will tell him the secret if he promises to do whatever she wants. He agrees, and she tells him women want control of their husbands and their own lives. Arthur's queen accepts this answer, and the old woman tells the knight that he must marry her. The knight confesses later that he is repulsed by her appearance, and she gives him a choice: she can either be ugly and faithful or beautiful and unfaithful. The knight tells her to make the choice herself, and she rewards him for this answer by becoming both beautiful *and* faithful.

THE FRIAR'S PROLOGUE AND TALE

In the Friar's story, an archdeacon enforces the law without mercy. A summoner works for the archdeacon, employing a network of spies who let him know who has been lecherous. The summoner extorts money from those he's sent to summon. He tries to serve a summons on a yeoman who is actually a devil in disguise. When the summoner unfairly tries to prosecute an old wealthy widow, the widow cries out that the summoner should be taken to hell. The devil follows the woman's instructions and drags the summoner off to hell.

THE SUMMONER'S PROLOGUE AND TALE

The Summoner, furious, tells the company that there is little difference between friars and fiends. He says when an angel took a friar down to hell, the friar asked why there were no friars in hell. In answer, the angel pulled up Satan's tail, and 20,000 friars came out of his ass.

In the Summoner's tale, a friar begs for money from a dying man named Thomas and his wife, who have recently lost their child. The friar shamelessly exploits the couple's misfortunes to extract money from them. Thomas says he is sitting on something he will bequeath to the friars. The friar reaches for the bequest, and Thomas lets out an enormous fart. The friar complains to the lord of the manor, whose squire promises to divide the fart evenly among all the friars.

THE CLERK'S PROLOGUE AND TALE

The Clerk says he will tell a tale by the Italian poet Petrarch. In his tale, Griselde is a hardworking peasant who marries into the aristocracy. Her husband tests her fortitude several ways, pretending to kill her children and divorcing her. He forces her to prepare for his wedding to a new wife. She dutifully does what he says, and her husband tells her that she has always been and will always be his wife (the divorce was a fraud). They live happily ever after.

THE MERCHANT'S PROLOGUE, TALE, AND EPILOGUE

The Merchant reflects on the great difference between the patient Griselde and the horrible shrew he has been married to for the past two months. He tells a story about an old blind knight named January who marries May, a beautiful young woman. Unhappy with his enthusiastic sexual efforts, May plans to cheat on him with his squire, Damien. January takes May into his garden to have sex with her. She tells him she wants to eat a pear, and he helps her up into the pear tree, where she has sex with Damien. Pluto, the king of the faeries, restores January's sight. May, caught in the act, assures him that he must still be blind.

THE SQUIRE'S INTRODUCTION AND TALE

The Squire tells of King Cambyuskan of the Mongol Empire, who receives a birthday visit from a knight bearing gifts from the king of Arabia and India. The gifts include a magic brass horse, a magic mirror, a magic sword, and a magic ring that gives Cambyuskan's daughter, Canacee, the ability to understand the language of birds. Canacee rescues a dying female falcon. The Squire's tale breaks off abruptly, either because Chaucer did not finish it or because he meant for the Franklin to interrupt. The Franklin remarks that he wishes his own son were as eloquent as the Squire. The Host, annoyed at the Franklin's interruption, orders him to begin the next tale.

THE FRANKLIN'S PROLOGUE AND TALE

The Franklin says his tale is a folk ballad of ancient Brittany. Dorigen's husband, Arveragus, has gone to England to win honor. She worries that her husband's ship will run into the coastal rocks. She promises Aurelius, a young man who falls in love with her, that she will sleep with him if he clears the rocks from the coast. Aurelius hires a student of magic to create the illusion that the rocks have disappeared. Arveragus returns home and tells his wife that she must keep her promise to Aurelius. Aurelius is so impressed by Arveragus's honor that he does not make Dorigen sleep with him. The magician, in turn, generously refuses payment for his magic trick.

THE PHYSICIAN'S TALE

In the Physician's story, Appius, a judge, lusts after Virginia, the beautiful daughter of Virginius. Appius persuades a churl named Claudius to says that Virginius stole Virginia from him. Appius says Virginius must return Virginia to Claudius. Virginius tells his daughter she must die rather than suffer dishonor, and she virtuously lets her father cut her head off. Appius sentences Virginius to death, but the Roman people, aware of Appius's hijinks, throw him into prison, where he kills himself.

THE PARDONER'S INTRODUCTION, PROLOGUE, AND TALE

Dismayed by the tragic injustice of the Physician's tale, the Host asks the Pardoner to tell something merry. But the other pilgrims demand a moral tale, which the Pardoner agrees to tell after he eats and drinks. The Pardoner tells the company how he cheats people out of their money by preaching that money is the root of all evil. His tale describes three riotous youths who go looking for Death, thinking that they can kill him. An old man tells them they will find Death under a tree. Under the tree they find eight bushels of gold. The youngest goes into town to fetch food and drink, but brings back poison, hoping to have the gold all to himself. His companions kill him, then drink the poison and die under the tree. His tale complete, the Pardoner offers to sell the pilgrims pardons and singles out the Host to come kiss his relics.

THE SHIPMAN'S TALE

The Shipman's story features a monk who borrows money from a merchant and then gives the money to the merchant's wife, who needs to pay back a debt to her husband. For this favor, the monk demands sexual favors from the wife. The wife realizes she has been duped, but she boldly tells her husband to forgive her debt: she will repay it in bed.

THE PRIORESS'S PROLOGUE AND TALE

The Prioress calls on the Virgin Mary to guide her tale. In her story, a Christian school is located at the edge of a Jewish ghetto in an Asian city. An angelic seven-year-old boy, a widow's son, attends the school. He is a devout Christian and loves to sing *Alma Redemptoris* (Gracious Mother of the Redeemer). Some Jews hire a murderer to slit his throat and throw him into a latrine. The Jews refuse to tell the widow where her son is, but he miraculously begins to sing *Alma Redemptoris*. The Christians recover his body, and the magistrate orders the murdering Jews drawn apart by wild horses and then hanged.

THE PROLOGUE AND TALE OF SIR THOPAS

The Host, after teasing Chaucer, the narrator, about his appearance, asks him to tell a tale. Chaucer says he only knows one tale, then launches into a parody of bad poetry—the Tale of Sir Thopas. Sir Thopas rides about looking for an elf-queen to marry until he is confronted by a giant. The narrator's doggerel continues in this vein until the Host can bear no more. Chaucer asks him why he can't tell his tale, since it is the best he knows, and the Host explains that his rhyme isn't worth a turd. He encourages Chaucer to tell a prose tale.

THE TALE OF MELIBEE

Chaucer tells a long, moral prose story. In it, Melibee's house is raided by his foes, who beat his wife, Prudence, and severely wound his daughter, Sophie. Prudence advises him not to seek rash revenge, and he puts his foes' punishment in her hands. She forgives her attackers.

THE MONK'S PROLOGUE AND TALE

The Host wishes his own wife were as patient as Prudence. He teases the Monk, pointing out that the Monk is clearly no poor cloisterer. The Monk tells a series of tragic tales in which seventeen noble figures—Lucifer, Adam, Sampson, Hercules, Nebuchadnezzar, Belshazzar, Zenobia, Pedro of Castile, and others—are brought low.

THE NUN'S PRIEST'S PROLOGUE, TALE, AND EPILOGUE

The Host calls upon the Nun's Priest to deliver something more lively than the Monk's stories. The Nun's Priest tells of Chanticleer the Rooster. A flattering fox tricks Chanticleer into closing his eyes and displaying his crowing abilities. Then the fox grabs Chanticleer with his mouth. Chanticleer turns the tables on the fox by persuading him to open his mouth and brag to the barnyard about his feat. When he does, Chanticleer escapes. The Host says if the Nun's Priest were not in holy orders, he would be as sexually potent as Chanticleer.

THE SECOND NUN'S PROLOGUE AND TALE

In her Prologue, the Second Nun says she will tell of the life of Saint Cecilia. Before Cecilia's new husband, Valerian, can take her virginity, she sends him on a pilgrimage to Pope Urban, who converts him to Christianity. An angel visits Valerian. Valerian asks his brother Tiburce to be converted to Christianity too. Cecilia, Tiburce, and Valerian are put to death by the Romans.

THE CANON'S YEOMAN'S PROLOGUE AND TALE

A black-clad Canon and his Yeoman come up to the company. They have heard of the pilgrims and their tales and wish to participate. The Yeoman brags that he and the Canon pretend to be alchemists. The Canon departs in shame at having his secrets discovered. The Yeoman tells a tale of a canon who defrauded a priest by creating the illusion of alchemy.

THE MANCIPLE'S PROLOGUE AND TALE

The Host pokes fun at the Cook, who is riding at the back of the company, blind drunk. The Manciple criticizes the Cook for his drunkenness and relates a legend taken from the Roman poet Ovid's *Metamorphoses* and one of the tales in *The Arabian Nights*. In it, Phoebus's talking white crow informs him that his wife is cheating on him. Phoebus kills the wife, pulls out the crow's white feathers, and curses it with blackness.

THE PARSON'S PROLOGUE AND TALE

The company enters a village in the late afternoon. The Parson refuses to tell a fictional story, because it would go against the rule set by St. Paul, and instead delivers a lengthy treatise on the Seven Deadly Sins.

CHAUCER'S RETRACTION

Chaucer asks readers to credit Jesus Christ as the inspiration for anything in his book that they like and to attribute what they don't like to his own ignorance and lack of ability. He retracts and prays for forgiveness for his secular and pagan subjects, asking to be remembered only for what he has written of saints' lives and homilies.

CHARACTERS IN *THE CANTERBURY TALES*

THE PILGRIMS

The Clerk A poor student of philosophy. Spending his money on books and learning left him with no money for clothes or food. He speaks little, but when he does, his words are wise and full of moral virtue.

The Cook An employee of the Guildsmen.

The Franklin A connoisseur of food and wine. In Chaucer's day, a franklin was neither a vassal serving a lord nor a member of the nobility. "Franklin" means "free man."

The Friar A corrupt man who accepts bribes. Roaming priests with no ties to a monastery, friars were common objects of criticism in Chaucer's time.

The Host A large, loud, merry man with a quick temper. He mediates and directs the flow of the tales.

The Guildsmen Five Guildsmen described as a unit. English guilds were a combination of labor unions and social fraternities.

The Knight The ideal of a medieval Christian man-at-arms. He has participated in no less than fifteen of the great crusades of his era. Brave, experienced, and prudent, the knight wins the narrator's deep admiration.

The Man of Law A successful lawyer commissioned by the king.

The Manciple A man in charge of getting provisions for a college or court. Despite his lack of education, this Manciple is smarter than the thirty lawyers he feeds.

The Merchant A trader in furs and other cloths that are mostly from Flanders.

The Miller A stout and brawny man. The Miller has a wart on his nose and a big mouth, both literally and figuratively. He seems to enjoy overturning conventions: he ruins the Host's carefully planned storytelling order, he rips doors off hinges, and he tells a tale that is somewhat blasphemous.

The Monk A man devoted to hunting and eating. He is large, loud, and well dressed in hunting boots and furs. Most monks of the Middle Ages lived in monasteries and were supposed to devote their lives to "work and prayer."

The Narrator The narrator, who is called Chaucer, makes it clear that he is a character. We cannot accept his words and opinions as Chaucer's own. In the General Prologue, the narrator presents himself as gregarious and naïve. Later, the Host accuses him of being silent and sullen.

The Nun's Priest A witty, self-effacing preacher.

The Pardoner A man who is supposed to grant indulgences—forgiveness in exchange for donations to the Church—and, like many pardoners, takes money for himself. The Pardoner carries a bag full of fake relics—for example, he claims to have the veil of the Virgin Mary. He has long, greasy, yellow hair and no beard, characteristics associated with shiftiness and gender ambiguity in Chaucer's time.

The Parson The only devout churchman in the company. The Parson lives in poverty, but is rich in holy thoughts and deeds.

The Physician A pillar of his profession. The Physician rarely consults the Bible and has an unhealthy love of money.

The Plowman The Parson's brother. Like the Parson, the Plowman is very good-hearted. A member of the peasant class, he pays his tithes to the Church and leads a good Christian life.

The Prioress A nun in charge of her convents. The Prioress tries to adopt refined manners, but her efforts betray her as hopelessly middle class. She portrays herself as compassionate and then tells a terrifying, racist story full of blood and feces.

The Reeve A man who shrewdly stewards his lord's manor. The Reeve is excellent at his job, but he steals from his master.

The Second Nun The woman who tells of a saint's life.

The Shipman A sailor who has seen every bay and river in England, and exotic ports in Spain and Carthage as well. He is a bit of a rascal.

The Summoner A lecherous man whose face is scarred by leprosy. He is frequently drunk and grumpy. Summoners brought people accused of violating Church law to ecclesiastical court.

The Squire The Knight's son and apprentice. The Squire is curly-haired and handsome. He loves dancing and courting.

The Wife of Bath A seamstress by trade. The Wife of Bath (Bath is an English town on the Avon River, not the name of this woman's husband) has been married five times and had many other affairs in her youth. She presents herself as someone who loves marriage and sex, but from what we see of her, she also takes pleasure in rich attire, talking, and arguing. She is deaf in one ear and has a gap between her front teeth, which was considered attractive in Chaucer's time.

The Yeoman The servant who accompanies the Knight and the Squire. His dress and weapons suggest he may be a forester.

THEMES IN *THE CANTERBURY TALES*

THE PERVASIVENESS OF COURTLY LOVE The concept of courtly love had an enormous influence on the literature and culture of the Middle Ages. Beginning with the Troubadour poets of southern France in the eleventh century, European poets suggested that true love exists only outside of marriage, may be idealized and spiritual, and can exist without sex. The man in love becomes the servant of his lady and cannot sleep or eat—love ravages him like a disease. Very few people followed the courtly love ideal, but its themes were extremely popular in medieval and Renaissance literature and culture, particularly in royal and noble courts. Courtly love first appears in *The Canterbury Tales* with the description of the Squire in the General Prologue. The Squire is practically a parody of the traditional courtly lover.

THE IMPORTANCE OF COMPANY Many of Chaucer's characters end their stories by wishing the rest of the company well. "Company" derives from two Latin words, *com*, or "with," and *pane*, or "bread." Literally, a company is a group of people with whom one eats, or breaks bread. The word "company" also referred to a group of people engaged in a particular business. In medieval times, workers formed guilds, which were informally known as companies. Guild members ate together in their own dining halls, forming strong social bonds. Guilds gave the working classes power. The pilgrims in *The Canterbury Tales* come from different parts of society—the court, the Church, villages, the feudal manor system. To prevent discord, they create an informal company, making themselves a guild of storytellers.

THE CORRUPTION OF THE CHURCH By the late fourteenth century, the Catholic Church, which governed England, Ireland, and Europe, was extremely wealthy. In a century of disease, plague, and famine, the sight of a church ornamented with gold angered some people. The Church's preaching against greed suddenly seemed hypocritical. People told stories about greedy churchmen who accepted bribes, bribed others, and indulged in sex and fine food while ignoring the poor famished peasants begging at their doors.

Chaucer's religious characters in *The Canterbury Tales* generally confirm common medieval stereotypes. The Monk and the Prioress prefer the aristocratic to the devotional life. The Prioress takes pride in her bejeweled rosary and flaunts dainty mannerisms. The Monk enjoys hunting, a pastime of the nobility, and disdains study and confinement. The Summoner and the Friar quarrel violently because both are competing to extract money from people.

SYMBOLS IN *THE CANTERBURY TALES*

SPRINGTIME *The Canterbury Tales* opens in April, at the height of spring, which symbolizes rebirth. In the spring, people long for pilgrimages, which combine travel, vacation, and spiritual renewal. Springtime also evokes erotic love.

CLOTHING In the General Prologue, the description of garments helps define each character. The clothes symbolize the wearer's personality. The Physician's rich silk and fur stand for his love of wealth, the Squire's floral brocade for his youthful vanity, and the Merchant's forked beard for his duplicity.

IMPORTANT QUOTATIONS FROM *THE CANTERBURY TALES*

Whan that Aprill with his shoures soote
The droghte of March hath perced to the roote,
And bathed every veyne in swich licour
Of which vertu engendred is the flour;
Whan Zephirus eek with his sweete breeth
Inspired hath in every holt and heeth
The tendre croppes, and the yonge sonne
Hath in the Ram his halve cours yronne,
And smale fowles maken melodye,
That slepen al the nyght with open ye
(So priketh hem nature in hir corages),
Thanne longen folk to goon on pilgrimages.

Location: General Prologue, 1–12
Speaker: The narrator
Context: With the onset of spring, the stage is set for a pilgrimage

Imagery of spring fills the opening passage of *The Canterbury Tales*. April's sweet showers have penetrated the dry earth of March, coaxing flowers out of the ground. The constellation Taurus is in the sky, the warm west wind, has breathed life into the fields, and the birds chirp merrily. Sex is also in the air. The verbs used to describe Nature's actions—piercing, engendering, inspiring, and pricking—suggest conception.

After the long sleep of winter, people long to "goon on pilgrimages," to travel and worship a saint's relics as a means of spiritual cleansing. Pilgrimages combined spring vacations with religious purification. The landscape in this passage, with its references to budding flowers, growing crops, and singing birds, clearly situates the story in England.

CATCH-22

Joseph Heller

Near the end of World War II, an army captain struggles to survive by navigating a self-serving and illogical military bureaucracy.

THE LIFE OF JOSEPH HELLER

Joseph Heller was born in Brooklyn in 1923. He served as an Air Force bombardier in World War II, then enjoyed a long career as a writer and a teacher after the war. Heller wrote *Catch-22* (1961), his first novel, while working at a New York City marketing firm producing ad copy. The novel draws heavily on his Air Force experience and presents a war story that is at once hilarious, grotesque, cynical, and stirring. Heller published other best-selling books, including *Something Happened* (1966), *Good as Gold* (1976), *God Knows* (1984), *Picture This* (1988), and a sequel to *Catch-22* called *Closing Time* (1994), but *Catch-22* remains his most famous and acclaimed work. Heller died of a heart attack in 1999.

CATCH-22 IN CONTEXT

Catch-22 paints an utterly unsentimental portrait of war. The story is an absurd nightmare of bureaucracy and violence that wipes away romanticized visions of glory and honor. Bitterly ironic depictions of war are increasingly common in the post–Vietnam War era, but when *Catch-22* was published, World War II was seen as a just and heroic war by most. *Catch-22* shocked American audiences and generated a great deal of controversy upon publication. Critics tended either to adore it or despise it, often for the same reasons.

Earlier novels such as Erich Maria Remarque's *All Quiet on the Western Front* (1928) had suggested that war was psychologically damaging to soldiers. However, *Catch-22* was the first to use humor rather than graphic violence to recreate the absurdity and meaninglessness of day-to-day warfare. Moreover, the novel's ultimate message is hopeful rather than despairing: the desire to live emerges as an unequivocally positive instinct that can save individuals from the dehumanizing machinery of war. *Catch-22* mocks insincerity and hypocrisy, celebrating the individual who is often lost in an impersonal military mass.

Despite its World War II setting, *Catch-22* has often been seen as the signature novel of the 1960s or 70s, an era marked by youth questioning authority, protesting at universities, and supporting the the civil rights movement. Heller seems to support this interpretation. He has said, "I wasn't interested in the war in *Catch-22*. I was interested in the personal relationships in bureaucratic authority."

CATCH-22: KEY FACTS

Time and place written: 1955–1961; New York	
Date of first publication : 1961	
Publisher: Simon & Schuster	
Type of work: Novel	
Genre: War novel; satire	
Language: English	
Setting (time): End of World War II	
Setting (place): Pianosa, a small island off the coast of Italy	
Tense: Past. Most of the plot is presented out of sequence	
Tone: Flatly satirical	
Narrator: Anonymous third-person omniscient	
Point of View: Yossarian; occasionally the chaplain, Hungry Joe, and others	

Protagonist: John Yossarian

Antagonist: An impersonal and irrational military bureaucracy

CATCH-22: PLOT OVERVIEW

During the second half of World War II, John Yossarian is stationed with his Air Force squadron on the island of Pianosa, off the Italian coast in the Mediterranean Sea. Yossarian and his friends endure an absurd, nightmarish existence governed by an irrational bureaucracy and ambitious superiors. The squadron members make risky bombing runs during which they are encouraged to take good aerial photographs rather than destroy their targets. The squadron is bombed by its own mess officer. No one may go home because the authorities continually raise the number of missions that a soldier is required to fly before being discharged.

Unmoved by ideals or abstractions, Yossarian is furious that his life is in constant danger through no fault of his own. He wants to live and spends a great deal of time in the hospital, faking various illnesses in order to escape the war. Throughout the novel, Yossarian is troubled by memories of Snowden, a gunner who died in Yossarian's arms on a mission to Avignon. Since then, Yossarian has lost all desire to participate in the war.

The lives of the characters are governed by a paradoxical law, loosely called Catch-22. (By extension, "catch-22" refers to any similar paradoxical situation). Yossarian discovers that insanity is grounds for discharge from military service. When he claims to be insane, he is told that his claim of insanity proves that he is sane—any sane man would naturally try to pretend to be insane in order to be excused from flying missions.

Yossarian's friend Nately falls in love with a whore from Rome. Nately continues to court her even though her little sister always interferes with their romantic rendezvous. Eventually, the whore falls in love with Nately, but he is killed on his very next mission. When Yossarian tells her that Nately is dead, she blames Yossarian and tries to stab him every time she sees him thereafter.

Over the course of the novel, Milo Minderbinder, the squadron's mess hall officer, builds a black-market empire. Milo borrows military planes and pilots to transport food between various points in Europe, making a massive profit from his sales. Milo's enterprise flourishes, and he is revered by communities throughout Europe.

Troubled by Nately's death, Yossarian refuses to fly any more missions. He wanders the streets of Rome, encountering horrors: rape, disease, murder. Eventually, he is arrested for being in Rome without proper documents. His superior officers, Colonel Cathcart and Colonel Korn, offer him a choice: Yossarian can either face a court-martial or offer public support for Cathcart and Korn's new policy, which requires soldiers to fly eighty missions—an enormous number—before being discharged. If he chooses the latter option, he will be sent home with an honorable discharge. Yossarian is tempted by the offer, but does not want to endanger the lives of his fellow soldiers. He deserts the army and flees to Sweden in a bid to regain control of his own life.

CHARACTERS IN CATCH-22

Aarfy Yossarian's navigator. Aarfy always gets lost. He infuriates Yossarian by pretending that he can't hear orders during bombing runs.

Appleby A handsome, athletic member of Yossarian's squadron. Appleby is a superb ping-pong player.

Captain Black The bitter intelligence officer of Yossarian's squadron. Captain Black wants to be squadron commander. He exults in the men's discomfort and actively tries to increase it.

Colonel Cathcart The ambitious officer in charge of Yossarian's squadron. Cathcart, who wants to be a general, tries to impress his superiors by volunteering his men for as much dangerous combat duty as he can. He calls successful missions "feathers in his cap" and unsuccessful ones "black eyes."

The Chaplain Yossarian's timid and thoughtful friend. Over the course of the novel, the chaplain is haunted by déjà vu and slowly loses his faith in God.

Clevinger An idealistic member of Yossarian's squadron. Clevinger believes in country, loyalty, and duty, and defends his beliefs to Yossarian.

Major — — de Coverley The fierce, intense executive officer of Yossarian's squadron. Although he only has minor bureaucratic duties, De Coverley is revered and feared by the soldiers, who are afraid to ask him about his first name.

Major Danby The timid operations officer of Yossarian's squadron. Danby used to be a college professor.

Doc Daneeka The medical officer of Yossarian's squadron. Doc Daneeka, who first explains Catch-22 to Yossarian, is unhappy that the war has interrupted his lucrative private practice in America.

Dobbs A copilot. Dobbs seized the controls from Huple on the mission to Avignon, during which Snowden died.

General Dreedle The grumpy old general in charge of Yossarian's wing. The ambitious General Peckem hates General Dreedle.

Nurse Duckett The nurse in the Pianosa hospital who becomes Yossarian's lover.

Dunbar Yossarian's friend. Dunbar is one of the only people who understands the danger and the absurdity of the soldiers' situation. Faced with likely death, Dunbar has decided to make time pass as slowly as possible. He treasures boredom and discomfort.

Chief White Halfoat An alcoholic Native American from Oklahoma who has decided to die of pneumonia.

Havermeyer A fearless lead bombardier. Havermeyer never takes evasive action. He shoots field mice at night.

Huple A fifteen-year-old pilot who flew the Avignon mission during which Snowden was killed. Huple is Hungry Joe's roommate. His cat likes to sleep on Hungry Joe's face.

Hungry Joe An unbalanced member of Yossarian's squadron. A former photographer for *Life* magazine, Hungry Joe is obsessed with photographing naked women. He has horrible nightmares unless he is scheduled to fly a combat mission the next morning.

Lieutenant Colonel Korn Colonel Cathcart's wily, cynical sidekick.

Luciana A beautiful Italian girl with whom Yossarian has an affair in Rome.

Major Major Major Major The lonely and awkward squadron commander. Born Major Major Major, he was promoted to the rank of major by a mischievous computer on his first day in the army. Major Major agrees to see people in his office only when he is not there.

McWatt A polite and cheerful pilot who often flies Yossarian's planes.

Milo Minderbinder A fantastically powerful mess officer. Milo controls an international black-market syndicate and is revered all over the world. Ruthlessly money-hungry, he bombs his own soldiers as part of a contract with Germany. Milo takes his official job very seriously, so Yossarian's division eats well.

Mudd ("the dead man in Yossarian's tent") A squadron member who was killed in action before his assignment to the squadron was processed. Mudd is officially listed as never having arrived. His belongings remain in Yossarian's tent.

Nately A good-natured nineteen-year-old boy in Yossarian's squadron. Nately comes from a wealthy home. He tries to keep Yossarian from getting into trouble.

Nately's whore The beautiful prostitute with whom Nately falls in love in Rome.

Orr Yossarian's maddening tent-mate. A handyman, Orr continually makes little improvements to their tent. His plane often crashes, but he always manages to survive.

Lieutenant Scheisskopf (later promoted to colonel and general) The officer who trains Yossarian's squadron in America. Scheisskopf, whose name means "shithead" in German, loves elaborate military parades.

Lieutenant Scheisskopf's Wife The woman who conducts affairs with all the men in Scheisskopf's squadron, including Yossarian.

The Soldier in White A frightening body covered in bandages that stays at the same ward as Yossarian and Dunbar in the Pianosa hospital.

Snowden A young gunner who died on a mission over Avignon. The circumstances of Snowden's death—a shattering experience for Yossarian, who witnessed it—are slowly revealed over the course of the novel.

Corporal Whitcomb (later promoted to sergeant) The chaplain's atheist assistant. Corporal Whitcomb believes that the chaplain has hurt his chances of advancing and implicates the chaplain in the Washington Irving scandal.

Ex-P.F.C. Wintergreen The mail clerk at the 27th Air Force Headquarters. Wintergreen holds enormous power because his position allows him to intercept and forge documents. He often goes AWOL (Absent Without Leave), and is then punished with demotions.

John Yossarian The protagonist and hero of the novel. Yossarian is a captain in the Air Force and a lead bombardier in his squadron. He wants to live and hates the war. He has decided to live forever or die trying. His story forms the core of the novel, and most events are refracted through his point of view.

THEMES IN *CATCH-22*

BUREAUCRACY AS ILLOGICAL AND ABSOLUTE The lives of the men of Yossarian's squadron are governed by the decisions of a remote, impersonal bureaucracy. The soldiers are forced to risk their lives, often without reason. For example, they are sent on combat missions even after the Allies effectively win the war. The bureaucrats are deaf to reason and defy logic at every turn. Major Major agrees to see people in his office only when he is not there. Doc Daneeka refuses to ground Yossarian for reasons of insanity because he believes Yossarian's desire to be grounded proves that Yossarian must be sane. When interrogating Clevinger, Lieutenant Scheisskopf is too busy correcting Clevinger's speech to let him speak. The chaplain is accused of an unnamed crime and interrogated by men who do not know what his crime is. Faced with a bureaucracy wielding absolute power, Yossarian and his companions are forced to learn to use its illogical rules to their own advantage.

LOSS OF RELIGIOUS FAITH Even the chaplain begins to doubt his faith in God by the end of *Catch-22*. The chaplain's disillusionment is partly prompted by Colonel Cathcart's attempts to use religion as a tool for professional advancement. On Thanksgiving, Yossarian discusses religion with Scheisskopf's wife. Both are atheists: Mrs. Scheisskopf rejects a just and loving God, while Yossarian rejects a bumbling and foolish God. Yossarian argues that no truly good, omniscient God would have created such a wide array of human suffering, from tooth pain to the horrors of war. Having lost their faith, the characters are forced to make their moral decisions by themselves, as Yossarian does when he chooses to desert the army rather than betray his squadron.

THE IMPOTENCE OF LANGUAGE The military bureaucracy has sapped language and words of their communicative power. Heller dramatizes the impotence of words when Yossarian, assigned to censor letters home from the front, blacks out words and phrases at random. Language also loses its power when confronted with death and its absurdities. As Snowden dies in the back of the plane, Yossarian can think of nothing to say except "there, there" over and over.

Realizing that words have lost their meaning, Yossarian argues that Catch-22—a clause written with words that circumvent logic—cannot and does not really exist. At the same time, he too is powerless. The military bureaucracy has used words to construct illogical prisons that trap Yossarian and his companions.

SYMBOLS IN *CATCH-22*

CHOCOLATE-COVERED COTTON Aided by Yossarian, Milo comes up with the idea of selling chocolate-covered cotton to the government after he is unable to sell ordinary cotton because there is a glut in the market. Milo's product, which hides its lack of substance beneath an enticing exterior, symbolizes the workings of the bureaucracy, which is easily fooled by appearances and unable to measure real merit.

THE SOLDIER IN WHITE The soldier in white, a bandage-wrapped, faceless, nameless body that lies in the hospital in the first chapter of the novel, represents the way the army treats men as interchangeable objects. When, months after his death, he is replaced by an identical soldier in white, everyone assumes it is the same person.

IMPORTANT QUOTATIONS FROM *CATCH-22*

There was only one catch and that was Catch-22, which specified that a concern for one's own safety in the face of dangers that were real and immediate was the process of a rational mind. Orr was crazy and could be grounded. All he had to do was ask; and as soon as he did, he would no longer be crazy and would have to fly more missions. Orr would be crazy to fly more missions and sane if he didn't, but if he was sane he would have to fly them. If he flew them he was crazy and didn't have to; but if he didn't want to he was sane and had to. Yossarian was moved very deeply by the absolute simplicity of this clause of Catch-22 and let out a respectful whistle. "That's some catch, that Catch-22," he observed. "It's the best there is," Doc Daneeka agreed.

Location: Chapter 5
Speaker: The narrator
Context: The narrator describes the paradoxical law he calls "Catch-22"

Over the course of the novel, the law called Catch-22 is described in a number of different ways. Here, the narrator gives a formulation that applies to Yossarian specifically. To be excused from flying missions, one has to have a medical excuse such as insanity. Clearly, any sane person would want to be excused from flying missions. Almost as clearly, any person who asks to be excused on the basis of insanity cannot be truly insane, since he has enough sense to try to weasel out of missions. Thus Yossarian and others are in an impossible situation. Here Yossarian agrees that this Catch-22 is infallibly logical. Later, he argues that Catch-22 is not real. It is only a trap made of up words, which are inherently flawed and slippery.

These three men who hated [Clevinger] spoke his language and wore his uniform, but he saw their loveless faces set immutably into cramped, mean lines of hostility and understood instantly that nowhere in the world, not in all the fascist tanks or planes or submarines, not in the bunker behind the machine guns or mortars or behind the blowing flame throwers, not even among all the expert gunners of the crack Hermann Goering Antiaircraft Division or among the grisly connivers in all the beer halls in Munich and everywhere else, were there men who hated him more.

Location: Chapter 8
Speaker: The narrator
Context: Clevinger has been unfairly convicted and punished by Lieutenant Scheisskopf and two other officers

---

One of the things [Yossarian] wanted to start screaming about was the surgeon's knife that was almost certain to be waiting for him and everyone else who lived long enough to die. He wondered often how he would ever recognize the first chill, flush, twinge, ache, belch, sneeze, stain, lethargy, vocal slip, loss of balance or lapse of memory that would signal the inevitable beginning of the inevitable end.

Location: Chapter 17
Speaker: The narrator
Context: At the hospital, Yossarian contemplates the many forces that could bring about his death

---

"Haven't you got anything humorous that stays away from waters and valleys and God? I'd like to keep away from the subject of religion altogether if we can."

The chaplain was apologetic. "I'm sorry, sir, but I'm afraid all the prayers I know are rather somber in tone and make at least some passing reference to God."
"Then let's get some new ones."

Location: Chapter 19
Speaker: Colonel Cathcart and the chaplain
Context: Colonel Cathcart wants to institute religion-free group prayers before each mission in order to get a mention in the *Saturday Evening Post*

Yossarian was cold, too, and shivering uncontrollably. He felt goose pimples clacking all over him as he gazed down despondently at the grim secret Snowden had spilled all over the messy floor. It was easy to read the message in his entrails. Man was matter, that was Snowden's secret. Drop him out a window and he'll fall. Set fire to him and he'll burn. Bury him and he'll rot, like other kinds of garbage. That was Snowden's secret. Ripeness was all.

Location: Chapter 41
Speaker: The narrator
Context: As Yossarian watches the dead Snowden's guts spill out of his stomach onto the floor, he realizes that without the human spirit, man is nothing but physical matter

The passage describes a climactic moment in Yossarian's story: the moment when he loses all faith and interest in the war. To Yossarian, Snowden's entrails suggest his own mortality. The only response is to struggle to be truly alive—"ripe"—for a brief period. Yossarian's intense desire to live keeps him alive and leads him to eventually desert the army.

THE CATCHER IN THE RYE

J. D. Salinger

After being expelled from prep school, a sixteen-year-old boy goes to New York City, where he reflects on the phoniness of adults and heads toward a nervous breakdown.

THE LIFE OF J.D. SALINGER

Jerome David Salinger was born in New York City in 1919. The son of a wealthy cheese importer, Salinger grew up in a fashionable neighborhood in Manhattan. He attended various prep schools and graduated from the Valley Forge Military Academy in 1936. He attended a number of colleges, including Columbia University, but did not graduate from any of them. While at Columbia, Salinger took a creative writing class in which he excelled. In 1940, Salinger published a short story. He joined the Army and fought in Europe during World War II, during which time he continued to write. Upon his return to the United States and civilian life in 1946, Salinger wrote more stories, publishing them in many respected magazines. In 1951, Salinger published his only full-length novel, *The Catcher in the Rye*, which brought him to the nation's attention.

Also in 1951, Salinger published a short story in *The New Yorker* magazine called "A Perfect Day for Bananafish," which proved to be the first in a series of stories about the fictional Glass family. Over the next decade, other "Glass" stories appeared in the same magazine: "Franny," "Zooey," and "Raise High the Roof-Beam, Carpenters." These and other stories are available in the only other books Salinger published besides *The Catcher in the Rye*: *Nine Stories* (1953), *Franny and Zooey* (1961), and *Raise High the Roof-Beam, Carpenters and Seymour: An Introduction* (1963). Though *Nine Stories* received some acclaim, critical reception of Salinger's later stories was hostile. Critics generally judged the Glass siblings insufferably precocious and judgmental.

Beginning in the early 1960s, as his critical reputation waned, Salinger began to recede from the public eye. In 1965, after publishing another Glass story ("Hapworth 26, 1924") that was widely reviled by critics, he withdrew almost completely from public life. Salinger's reclusiveness, which has persisted to the present day, has turned him into a cult figure. Many people equate Salinger with his wounded, precocious characters—an oversimplification, but an understandable one.

THE CATCHER IN THE RYE IN CONTEXT

Many events from Salinger's early life appear in *The Catcher in the Rye*, recast in a post–World War II setting. For instance, Holden Caulfield moves from prep school to prep school, faces the prospect of military school, and knows an older Columbia student. Salinger offended many readers by using slang and profanity in *The Catcher in the Rye*. His complex, open discussion of adolescent sexuality also provoked controversy. Some critics argued that the novel was not serious literature, citing its casual and informal tone as evidence. *The Catcher in the Rye* was—and continues to be—banned in some communities. It has been at the center of debates about First Amendment rights, censorship, and obscenity in literature.

Though controversial, the novel appealed to a great number of people. It was a hugely popular bestseller and a critical success. As countercultural revolt began to burgeon during the 1950s and 1960s, *The Catcher in the Rye* was interpreted as a tale of individual alienation in a heartless world. Holden spoke to young people who felt pressured to live their lives according to rules, to do without meaningful human connection, and to conform to a bland cultural norm. Many readers saw Holden Caulfield as a symbol of pure, unfettered individuality in the face of cultural oppression.

KEY FACTS ABOUT THE CATCHER IN THE RYE

Time and place written: Late 1940s–early 1950s, New York

Date of first publication: July 1951

Publisher: Little, Brown and Company

Type of work: Novel

Genre: Bildungsroman

Language: English

Setting (time): A long weekend in the late 1940s or early 1950s

Setting (place): Pencey Prep and New York City

Tense: Past

Tone: Disgusted, cynical, bitter, nostalgic, colloquial

Narrator: Holden Caulfield narrates in first-person

Point of view: Holden Caulfield's

Protagonist: Holden Caulfield

Antagonist: Holden's psyche; the desire to connect with other people conflicts with desire to reject the adult world

THE CATCHER IN THE RYE: PLOT OVERVIEW

It is the 1950s, and Holden Caulfield is undergoing treatment in a mental hospital or sanatorium. The events of his narration happened when he was sixteen years old, on the few days between the end of the fall school term and Christmas.

Holden's story begins at Pencey prep school in Agerstown, Pennsylvania. Holden is being expelled from Pencey, which is his fourth school; he has already failed out of three others. Holden visits his elderly history teacher, Spencer, to say goodbye. Spencer criticizes his poor academic performance, which annoys Holden.

Back in the dormitory, Holden is further irritated by his unhygienic neighbor, Ackley, and by his own roommate, Stradlater. Stradlater goes out on a date with Jane Gallagher, a girl Holden used to date. When Stradlater returns from the date, Holden badgers him about whether he tried to have sex with Jane. They fight, and Stradlater bloodies Holden's nose. Holden decides to go to Manhattan three days early.

On the train to New York, Holden meets the mother of a Pencey student. Although he thinks the woman's son is a complete "bastard," he tells her that her son is shy and well-liked. After arriving at Penn Station, Holden gets in a cab. He asks the cab driver where the ducks in Central Park go when the lagoon freezes, which annoys the driver.

Holden checks in to the Edmont Hotel. From his room, he can see into some of the rooms in the opposite wing. He observes a man putting on elegant women's clothing. In another room, he sees a man and a woman spitting mouthfuls of their drinks at each other and laughing hysterically. This sexual play both upsets and arouses Holden. After smoking a couple of cigarettes, he calls Faith Cavendish, a woman whose number he got from an acquaintance at Princeton. Holden believes he can persuade her to have sex with him. At first Faith is annoyed that a complete stranger is calling her so late at night, but eventually she suggests that they meet the next day. Holden does not want to wait that long, and hangs up without arranging a meeting.

Holden goes downstairs to the Lavender Room, where he flirts with three women in their thirties who seem to be tourists. Holden dances with them and feels "half in love" with the blonde one after seeing how well she dances. After making some wisecracks about his age, they leave him with their tab.

Holden goes out to the lobby. He thinks about Jane Gallagher and remembers meeting her on summer vacation in Maine. One afternoon, Jane's stepfather came onto the porch. When he left, Jane began to cry. Holden kissed her all over her face, but she wouldn't let him kiss her on the mouth. That was the closest they came to "necking."

Holden leaves the Edmont and takes a cab to Ernie's jazz club in Greenwich Village. Again he asks his cab driver where the ducks in Central Park go in the winter, and this cabbie is even more irritated than the first one. Holden sits alone at a table in Ernie's and observes the other patrons with distaste. He runs into Lillian Simmons, one of his older brother's ex-girlfriends. Lillian invites him to sit with her and her date. Holden says he has to meet someone, leaves, and walks back to the Edmont.

Maurice, the elevator operator at the Edmont, offers to send a prostitute to Holden's room for five dollars. Holden agrees, and soon a young woman calling herself Sunny comes to his room. When she pulls off her dress, Holden starts to feel "peculiar" and says he recently underwent a spinal operation and can't have sex. Sunny sits on his lap and talks dirty to him, but he pays her five dollars and shows her the door. Sunny returns with Maurice, who demands another five dollars from Holden. When Holden refuses to pay, Maurice punches him in the stomach while Sunny takes five dollars from his wallet. Holden goes to bed.

He wakes up at ten o'clock on Sunday and calls Sally Hayes, an attractive girl he once dated. They arrange to meet. Holden eats breakfast at a sandwich bar, where he talks to two nuns about Romeo and Juliet. He gives them ten dollars. He tries to telephone Jane Gallagher, but hangs up when her mother answers the phone. He goes to Central Park to look for his younger sister, Phoebe, but she isn't there. He briefly looks for her at the Museum of Natural History.

Holden and Sally go to a Broadway matinee. Holden is annoyed afterward when Sally talks with a boy she knows from Andover. At Sally's suggestion, they go to Radio City to ice skate. Holden tries to explain why he is unhappy at school, and urges her to run away with him to Massachusetts or Vermont and live in a cabin. When she refuses, he calls her a "pain in the ass." Sally gets angry, and Holden laughs at her. She leaves.

Holden calls Jane again, but there is no answer. He calls Carl Luce, a young man who was his student advisor at the Whooton School and now attends Columbia University. Holden and Luce meet at the Wicker Bar in the Seton Hotel. Holden tries to draw Luce into a conversation about sex. Luce grows irritated by Holden's juvenile remarks about homosexuals and Luce's Chinese girlfriend, and makes an excuse to leave early. Holden continues to drink Scotch.

Quite drunk, Holden telephones Sally Hayes and babbles about their Christmas Eve plans. Then he goes to the lagoon in Central Park, where he used to watch the ducks as a child. He sneaks into his own apartment building and wakes Phoebe. He admits that he was kicked out of school, which makes her angry. Holden tries to explain why he hates school, and Phoebe says he does not like anything. He explains his fantasy of being "the catcher in the rye," a person who catches little children as they are about to fall off of a cliff. Phoebe knows this image comes from a Robert Burns poem, and she points out he has gotten the line wrong. It is "if a body meet a body, coming through the rye," not "if a body catch a body."

Holden calls his former English teacher, Mr. Antolini, who tells Holden he can come to his apartment. Holden falls asleep on the couch and wakes to find Mr. Antolini stroking his forehead. Thinking that Mr. Antolini is making a sexual overture, Holden hastily excuses himself and leaves, sleeping for a few hours on a bench at Grand Central Station.

Holden goes to Phoebe's school and leaves her a note saying he is leaving home for good and she should meet him at lunchtime at the museum. Phoebe arrives carrying a suitcase full of clothes and asks Holden to take her with him. He refuses angrily, and Phoebe cries and then refuses to speak to him. Knowing she will follow him, Holden walks to the zoo. He buys her a ticket to the carousel and watches her ride it. It starts to rain hard. Holden is so happy watching his sister ride the carousel that he is close to tears.

Holden ends his narrative here, saying he is not going to tell the story of how he went home and got "sick." He plans to go to a new school in the fall.

CHARACTERS IN *THE CATCHER IN THE RYE*

Ackley The boy who lives next to Holden at Pencey Prep. Ackley is a pimply, insecure boy with terrible dental hygiene. Holden believes Ackley lies about his sexual experience.

Mr. Antolini Holden's former English teacher from the Elkton Hills School. Mr. Antolini now teaches at New York University. He is young, clever, and likable. Like many characters in the novel, Mr. Antolini drinks heavily.

Allie Caulfield Holden's younger brother. Allie died of leukemia three years before the start of the novel. He was a brilliant, friendly, red-headed boy. Allie's death torments Holden. He carries around a baseball glove on which Allie used to write poems in green ink.

D. B. Caulfield Holden's older brother. Holden admires D. B.'s volume of short stories but thinks he prostitutes his talents by writing for Hollywood.

Holden Caulfield   The protagonist and narrator of the novel. Holden is a sixteen-year-old junior in high school. An intelligent and sensitive boy, Holden finds the hypocrisy and ugliness of the world almost unbearable. He tries to be cynical in order to protect himself from disappointment.

Phoebe Caulfield   Holden's ten-year-old sister. Phoebe understands Holden better than most people do. Her innocence and intelligence are one of Holden's only consistent sources of happiness. At times, she exhibits great maturity.

Jane Gallagher   A girl Holden dated one summer in Maine. Jane never actually appears in *The Catcher in the Rye*. She is one of the few girls Holden both respects and finds attractive.

Sally Hayes   An attractive girl Holden has dated for a long time. Sally is well read, but Holden claims she is "stupid." Sally is more conventional than Holden in her tastes and manners.

Carl Luce   A student at Columbia and Holden's former student advisor at the Whooton School. At Whooton, Luce was a font of sexual knowledge for the younger boys.

Maurice   The elevator operator at the Edmont Hotel. Maurice sends a prostitute to Holden's room.

Mr. Spencer   Holden's history teacher at Pencey Prep. Mr. Spencer tries unsuccessfully to shake Holden out of his academic apathy.

Stradlater   Holden's roommate at Pencey Prep. Stradlater is handsome, self-satisfied, and popular. Holden calls him a "secret slob" because although he appears well-groomed, his toiletries are disgustingly dirty. Stradlater is sexually experienced.

Sunny   The prostitute Holden hires.

THEMES IN *THE CATCHER IN THE RYE*

ALIENATION AS A FORM OF SELF-PROTECTION   Holden thinks the world excludes him and victimizes him. He tells Mr. Spencer he feels trapped on "the other side" of life. He uses his isolation to advertise his superiority, but the truth is that interactions with other people usually confuse and overwhelm him, and he uses cynicism and superiority to protect himself. Holden's alienation is the source of what little stability he has in his life. It is also the source of his pain. Holden never examines his own emotions or thinks about the cause of his unhappiness. His desperate need for love conflicts with his fear and alienation. His loneliness makes him seek out Sally Hayes, but his need for isolation makes him drive her away. He longs for the meaningful connection he once had with Jane Gallagher, but he is too frightened to make any real effort to contact her.

THE PAIN OF GROWING UP   *The Catcher in the Rye* is a bildungsroman, a novel about a young character's growth into maturity. Holden Caulfield is an unusual protagonist for a bildungsroman because he longs to resist maturation. He fears change and complexity. It frightens him that he shares the qualities he criticizes in others, but he refuses to acknowledge this fear, expressing it only in a few instances—for example, when he admits that "[s]ex is something I just don't understand. I swear to God I don't." Instead of acknowledging that adulthood scares him, Holden insists that adults live in a world of "phoniness," and children live in a world of innocence and honesty. His theory about these two worlds crystallizes in his fantasy about being catcher in the rye. He imagines childhood as an idyllic field of rye in which children romp and play, and adulthood as death—a fatal fall over the edge of a cliff.

THE PHONINESS OF THE ADULT WORLD   "Phoniness," probably the most famous word from *The Catcher in the Rye*, is one of Holden's favorite concepts. He uses it as a catch-all to describe the superficiality, hypocrisy, pretension, and shallowness he sees. In Chapter 22, Holden explains that adults are phonies who can't see their own phoniness. Holden uses phoniness to justify withdrawing into his cynical isolation. Though oversimplified, Holden's observations are partly accurate. He encounters many affected, pretentious, or superficial people. But although Holden energetically looks for phoniness in others, he never observes his own phoniness. The world is not the black and white place he wants it to be, and even he can't conform to the rigid standards he sets for honesty and kindness.

SYMBOLS IN *THE CATCHER IN THE RYE*

HOLDEN'S RED HUNTING HAT   Holden consciously uses his red hunting hat to symbolize his individuality. Thus, the hat ultimately symbolizes Holden's self-aware, stage-managed uniqueness. Wearing such an unfashionable hat proves Holden's willingness to be different from everyone around him. At the same time, he is very self-conscious about the hat, often deciding not to wear it if he is going to be around people he knows.

THE MUSEUM OF NATURAL HISTORY   The museum represents the world Holden wishes he could live in: the world of his "catcher in the rye" fantasy, a world where nothing ever changes, where everything is understandable. Holden is terrified by the unpredictable nature of the world. He hates conflict and is confused by Allie's senseless death.

IMPORTANT QUOTATIONS FROM *THE CATCHER IN THE RYE*

The best thing, though, in that museum was that everything always stayed right where it was. Nobody'd move. . . . Nobody'd be different. The only thing that would be different would be you.

Location: Chapter 16
Speaker: Holden
Context: Holden walks around the Museum of Natural History and remembers school trips to the museum

Holden fears conflict, confusion, and change, and the museum comforts him with its sameness. He would like to stay the same, as the museum's displays do. In the final sentence of this quotation, Holden says "you" will be different, not "I" will be different, as if trying to pretend that change is something that happens to other people, not to himself. Holden also likes the museum because it does not require human interaction. At the museum, he can be the impassive observer he tries to be in life, thinking about and judging the contents of the display case without being judged himself.

"I have a feeling that you're riding for some kind of terrible, terrible fall. . . . The whole arrangement's designed for men who, at some time or other in their lives, were looking for something their own environment couldn't supply them with. . . . So they gave up looking."

Location: Chapter 24
Speaker: Mr. Antolini
Context: Holden has left his apartment and gone to stay with Mr. Antolini

Holden is unstable after leaving his parents' apartment and goes to Mr. Antolini's seeking help. But Holden's interaction with Mr. Antolini is the event that precipitates his breakdown. Holden blames his confusion on what he interprets as a come-on from Mr. Antolini, but some of it stems from the conversation they have. Like the catcher in the rye that Holden envisions, Mr. Antolini wants to catch Holden before he falls. But the fall Mr. Antolini describes is very different from the one Holden imagines. Holden thinks children fall from innocence into a dangerous world; Mr. Antolini thinks Holden is falling into apathy by giving up and isolating himself. Although Holden envisions himself as a protector, he is the one who needs protection.

"Life is a game, boy. Life is a game that one plays according to the rules."
    "Yes, sir. I know it is. I know it."

Game, my ass. Some game. If you get on the side where all the hot-shots are, then it's a game, all right—I'll admit that. But if you get on the other side, where there aren't any hot-shots, then what's a game about it? Nothing. No game.

Location: Chapter 2
Speaker: Mr. Spencer and Holden
Context: Holden reflects on his alienation

[Ackley] took another look at my hat. . . ."Up home we wear a hat like that to shoot deer in, for Chrissake," he said. "That's a deer shooting hat."
"Like hell it is." I took it off and looked at it. I sort of closed one eye, like I was taking aim at it. "This is a people shooting hat," I said. "I shoot people in this hat."

Location: Chapter 3
Speaker: Ackley and Holden
Context: Holden reveals his desire for independence, his bitterness, and his scorn for convention

---

. . .I'm standing on the edge of some crazy cliff. What I have to do, I have to catch everybody if they start to go over the cliff—I mean if they're running and they don't look where they're going I have to come out from somewhere and catch them. That's all I'd do all day. I'd just be the catcher in the rye and all.

Location: Chapter 22
Speaker: Holden
Context: Holden has snuck into his family's apartment and talks to Phoebe about his fantasy

THE CHOSEN

Chaim Potok

Two boys from Brooklyn learn about themselves and their relationship to Judaism through the conflicting views of their fathers.

THE LIFE OF CHAIM POTOK
Chaim Potok, an American rabbi and scholar, was born into an Orthodox Jewish family in 1929. The eldest son of Polish immigrants, Potok grew up in New York City. He received a rigorous religious and secular education at Yeshiva University, a school the fictional Hirsch Seminary and College in *The Chosen* strongly resembles. He received his rabbinic ordination from the Jewish Theological Seminary and a Ph.D. in philosophy from the University of Pennsylvania.

Potok wrote numerous novels, plays, and short stories. He was also a painter. As an author, he is best known for exploring the interaction between religious Judaism and the broader secular world, a fundamental tension in his own life. *The Chosen* focuses on Jewish communities' attempts to strike a balance between tradition and modernity.

Potok died in 2002 at his home in Pennsylvania.

THE CHOSEN IN CONTEXT
The Chosen, Potok's first novel, is part of a larger tradition of twentieth-century Jewish-American literature, which includes the work of authors Abraham Cahan, Henry Roth, Bernard Malamud, Saul Bellow, Philip Roth, and Cynthia Ozick. One of *The Chosen*'s central characters is a Hasid. The Hasidim are known for their mystical interpretation of Judaism and for their devotion to their leaders. The other central character is a traditional Orthodox Jew. Orthodoxy emphasizes a rational, intellectual approach to Judaism. These two characters are similar enough to become best friends, yet different enough to change each other's view of the world.

The first third of the novel unfolds during the Allied offensive in World War II, the middle third is about the American Jewish community's response to the Holocaust, and the final third explores the Zionist movement to create a Jewish state in Palestine. With his narrative, Potok offers insights on the challenges of faith facing the American Jewish community in the wake of the Holocaust. One of the novel's central conflicts is the clash between tradition and modernity. Characters are constantly forced to choose between isolating themselves from the outside world and retreating into tradition or actively participating in communities other than their own.

KEY FACTS ABOUT *THE CHOSEN*

Time and place written: 1960–1967; Philadelphia, Israel, and Brooklyn
Date of first publication: 1967
Publisher: Simon and Schuster
Type of work: Novel
Genre: Bildungsroman
Language: English
Setting (time): Early summer, 1944 to fall, 1950
Setting (place): The neighborhood of Williamsburg in Brooklyn, New York
Tense: Past
Tone: Thoughtful, intellectual
Narrator: Reuven Malter narrates in the first person

Point of view: Reuven Malter's

Protagonist: Reuven Malter and Danny Saunders

Major conflict: The struggle between family and religious obligations

THE CHOSEN: PLOT OVERVIEW

The Chosen traces a friendship between two Jewish boys growing up in Brooklyn at the end of World War II. Reuven Malter, the narrator and one of the novel's two protagonists, is a traditional Orthodox Jew. He is the son of David Malter, a dedicated scholar and humanitarian. Danny Saunders, the other protagonist, is a brilliant Hasid with a photographic memory and a passion for psychoanalysis. Danny is the son of Reb Saunders, the pious and revered head of a great Hasidic dynasty.

In Book One, Reuven's high school softball team plays against Danny's yeshiva team in a Sunday game. Tension mounts as the Hasidic team insults the faith of Reuven and his teammates. In the final inning, Reuven is pitching. Danny smacks a line drive that hits Reuven in the eye, shattering his glasses and nearly blinding him. While recuperating for a week in the hospital, he becomes friendly with two fellow patients: Tony Savo, an ex-boxer, and Billy Merrit, a young blind boy.

Danny visits Reuven in the hospital to ask his forgiveness. The two boys talk about their intellectual interests and their hopes for the future. Danny has an astounding intellect, including a photographic memory, and a prodigious knowledge of the Talmud. Danny confides that he secretly reads every day in the public library, studying books of which his father would disapprove. He says a nice older man often recommends books to him. Both boys are surprised to discover that David Malter—Reuven's father—is this man.

In Book Two, Reuven and Danny are in high school. Reuven begins spending Shabbat afternoons at Danny's house. On their first Sabbath together, Danny introduces Reuven to his father, Rabbi Isaac Saunders. During the congregation's Sabbath meal, Reb Saunders quizzes Danny in public. Reb Saunders asks Reuven a question about the speech Reb Saunders gave. Reuven answers correctly.

Danny and Reuven spend most afternoons together in the library. On Saturdays, they study Talmud with Reb Saunders. Reb Saunders believes in raising Danny in silence. Except for discussions of Talmud, he never speaks to Danny directly, although he begins to use Reuven as an indirect means of talking to his son.

World War II is being fought. President Roosevelt's death in April 1945 saddens the entire country. In May, Reuven and his father celebrate the end of the war in Europe, but are shocked by the discovery of concentration camps behind enemy lines. Everyone is disturbed by the reports of Jewish suffering and death at the hands of the Nazis.

In the spring, Reuven's father has a heart attack, and Reuven goes to live with the Saunders family for the summer. Danny tells Reuven that he plans to study Freudian psychoanalysis instead of inheriting his father's position in the Hasidic community. Danny hopes his younger brother Levi will take over his father's position. In the fall, both boys start classes at Samson Raphael Hirsch Seminary and College in Brooklyn.

Book Three chronicles Reuven's and Danny's experiences at Hirsch College. Danny immediately becomes a leader of the Hasidic student body. Reuven decides that he wants to become a rabbi. Reuven's father's health is rapidly deteriorating in part due to his frenetic Zionist activity. Under Reuven's tutelage in mathematics, Danny comes to appreciate the value of the experimental method of psychology.

As the conflicts over a Jewish state intensify, tensions swell among the various student factions at the college. After David Malter gives a pro-Zionist speech at Madison Square Garden, Reb Saunders, who is staunchly anti-Zionist, forbids Danny from speaking to Reuven. In their second year at college, the boys both take Rav Gershenson's Talmud class, which allows them to interact indirectly. David Malter has a second heart attack. Reuven dazzles his entire class with a particularly brilliant classroom display of Talmudic knowledge. The college learns that an alumnus of Hirsch died in the fighting in Israel. During Reuven and Danny's third year of college, after the United Nations officially declares the creation of the State of Israel, Reb Saunders relents and allows the two boys to speak to each other again. Reuven holds a grudge against Reb Saunders.

Danny secretly applies to graduate programs in psychology. One night, Reb Saunders, speaking to Danny through Reuven, finally explains why he raised Danny in silence. He says he always knew his son had a great mind, but he worried that his soul was empty. Silence was a way to make Danny explore his own soul and feel the suffering of the world. Reb Saunders reveals that he is aware of Danny's plan to become a psychologist. He apologizes to Reuven for separating him from Danny, and he apologizes to Danny for raising him in silence. He saw no other way to raise Danny to become a true tzaddik (righteous Hasidic leader)—a tzaddik for the world, not only a tzaddik for his congregation. Later, in front of his congregation, Reb Saunders gives his blessing to Danny and the life Danny has chosen. Danny shaves his beard and earlocks and enrolls in a graduate program at Columbia University.

CHARACTERS IN *THE CHOSEN*

Professor Nathan Appleman The chairman of the psychology department at the Hirsch Seminary and College.

Davey Cantor A timid friend of Reuven's.

Mrs. Carpenter A kindly but strict nurse at Brooklyn Memorial Hospital.

Mr. Galanter The gym instructor at Reuven's yeshiva. Mr. Galanter tells Reuven that he "couldn't make it as a soldier."

Rav Gershenson Danny and Reuven's teacher in the highest level Talmud class at the Hirsch Seminary and College. Rav Gershenson, an Orthodox rabbi, considers David Malter a great scholar.

Sidney Goldberg Reuven's friend and softball teammate.

Solomon Maimon An eighteenth century Polish Jew who reminds David Malter of Danny Saunders. Solomon Maimon was a ravenously intelligent student who studied non-Jewish literature after the Talmud could not satisfy his hunger for knowledge. As a result of his heresy, he died rootless and alone.

David Malter Reuven's father. David Malter is a traditional Orthodox Jew and a teacher, scholar, writer, and humanitarian. He is notorious in the Hasidic community for his controversial Biblical scholarship and his outspoken support of Zionism.

Reuven Malter The narrator of the novel and one of its two protagonists. Reuven is intelligent, conscientious, and popular, skilled in softball, math, and Talmud study.

Manya The loving Russian housekeeper who cooks and cleans for the Malters.

Billy Merrit A young blind boy Reuven meets in the hospital.

Roger Merrit Billy Merrit's father. He was the driver in the car accident that resulted in his wife's death and Billy's blindness.

Mickey A sickly six-year-old boy Reuven meets while in the hospital.

Danny Saunders One of the novel's two protagonists. Danny is a brilliant scholar with a photographic memory and a deep interest in Freud and psychoanalysis. He is torn between his duty to his father and his own ideas about how to live his life.

Levi Saunders Danny's sickly younger brother. Unlike Danny, Levi is not raised in silence.

Reb Isaac Saunders Danny's father. Reb Saunders is the pious and zealous patriarch of a Hasidic dynasty. He is a wise, learned, and deeply religious sage who raises Danny in silence. He imposes his strict Hasidic worldview on everyone around him.

Tony Savo A patient Reuven befriends while in the hospital. Tony Savo is a former boxer. He warns Reuven to watch out for religious fanatics like Danny.

Dov Shlomowitz Danny's burly Hasidic classmate and softball teammate.

Dr. Snydman The doctor who operates on Reuven's eye at Brooklyn Memorial Hospital.

THEMES IN *THE CHOSEN*

THE BENEFITS AND DANGERS OF SILENCE Chaim Potok's working title for *The Chosen* was *A Time For Silence*. In the novel, silence, like communication, can help people understand each other. Reb Saunders deprives Danny of a certain physical stimulus so that he will be forced to cultivate other senses of perception. Danny's experience with silence parallels Reuven's experience with blind-

ness. In theory, sound deprivation will force Danny to turn inward and thus develop knowledge of his soul and empathy for others. Potok does not fully endorse Reb Saunder's treatment of Danny. Although we do see moments when silence is warm and comfortable, Reuven considers silence strange, dark, and empty, and Reb Saunders's silence toward Danny strikes him as inexplicable and cruel. Potok suggests that the benefits of silence might not outweigh the drawbacks.

THE CONFLICT BETWEEN TRADITION AND MODERNITY   The novel does not address the world beyond Danny and Reuven's Jewish community in Brooklyn. Its source of tension is the conflict between two philosophies in the Jewish community: Reb Saunders's isolationist fanaticism and David Malter's more open-minded awareness of the world. For most of the novel, Reb Saunders is unwilling to engage with the outside world or listen to views of Judaism that differ from his own. David Malter is tolerant of other points of view and is willing to adapt his religious beliefs to modernity. With his activism and scientific approach to Talmudic study, David Malter represents Potok's ideal of the modern American Jew.

THE PROBLEMS OF BEING CHOSEN   The characters in the novel do not actively choose their faith. Judaism has been chosen for them. Though each character loves his religion, each struggles with what it means to be chosen. For Reb Saunders, being Jewish means accepting a special set of obligations to study Torah and serve God. For David Malter, being Jewish means obeying an intellectual and spiritual obligation to fill your life with meaning. For Reuven, being Jewish means making a joyful commitment to religious tradition and intellectual engagement. For Danny, being Jewish means carrying a difficult burden and respecting a proud intellectual tradition.

As a first-born male, Danny is chosen to inherit his father's position. But as Reb Saunders himself acknowledges in *The Chosen*'s final chapter, modern America is a land of opportunity and choices, and Danny wants to actively choose his own path. As both Reb Saunders and David Malter emphasize, we can choose our friends, but we cannot choose our fathers. Neither can fathers choose their sons.

SYMBOLS IN *THE CHOSEN*

EYES AND EYEGLASSES   Eyes and eyeglasses represent vision, not only in the literal sense, but also in a figurative sense. After injuring his eye, Reuven develops a better appreciation of his eyesight. Danny works to make Reuven more willing to see the world. As Danny develops an increased awareness of the world beyond his Hasidic community, his eyes grow weary and he begins to wear glasses.

THE TALMUD   Potok places an unusual emphasis on the Talmud, which contains a series of commentaries by rabbis. He devotes little discussion to the Torah (the Jewish Bible) or the Kabbalah, the mystic key to Hasidic tradition. Study of the Talmud involves actively engaging with its commentaries, challenging the text and resolving conflicting points. Potok emphasizes Talmudic study to suggest the importance of actively engaging tradition in order to understand Judaism and the world in general.

IMPORTANT QUOTATIONS FROM *THE CHOSEN*

"We are commanded to study His Torah! We are commanded to sit in the light of the Presence! It is for this that we were created!. . . Not the world, but the people of Israel!"

Location: Chapter 7
Speaker: Reb Saunders
Context: Reb Saunders makes an inflammatory speech about what it means to be the "Chosen People"

Reb Saunders compares the duties of Jews, the Chosen People, to the duties of non-Jews. Jews, he argues, are handed at birth a destiny and a set of responsibilities. By dismissing the non-Jewish world around him, Reb Saunders implies that a truly faithful Jew should retreat to an exclusively Jewish community, immerse himself in Jewish study, and pay little attention to anything in the outside world. For Reb Saunders, "the world"—anything beyond the boundaries of his community, any literature beyond the boundaries of conservative Jewish tradition—is unacceptable. Even in response to those world events related to his community, such as the Holocaust, Reb Saunders focuses inward, on his own community and his own suffering. By the end of the novel, Reb Saunders's understanding of the obligations of Jews has shifted. He accepts Danny's decision to become a professional psychologist, which suggests a new belief that one can maintain ties with the outside world and still observe one's faith.

"What does it mean to have to suffer so much if our lives are nothing more than the blink of an eye?. . . I learned a long time ago, Reuven, that a blink of an eye in itself is nothing. But the eye that blinks, that is something. A span of life is nothing. But the man who lives that span, he is something.. . . ."

Location: Chapter 13
Speaker: David Malter
Context: David Malter tells Reuven about the importance of suffering

Explaining his relentless Zionist activism, David Malter emphasizes the pervasiveness of suffering and says that awareness of the world's suffering makes people empathize with others and appreciate every detail of God's creation. His description of observing the eye implies that perception is a reciprocal, two-way process. In David Malter's opinion, deeper appreciation of life leads to an understanding of the obligation to fill one's life with meaning and make the world a better place. David Malter's words contrast with Reb Saunders's diatribe in Chapter 7. Unlike Reb Saunders, David Malter speaks in a gentle tone, explaining rather than proclaiming. His tone is that of a sympathetic teacher rather than a harsh leader. He does not believe that life is given meaning at birth, but that people fill life with meaning as they mature. This contrasts with Reb Saunders's belief that Jews are passively chosen for duty.

I stood in that room for a long time, watching the sunlight and listening to the sounds on the street outside. I stood there, tasting the room and the sunlight and the sounds, and thinking of the long hospital ward.. . . . I wondered if little Mickey had ever seen sunlight come though the windows of a front room apartment. . . . Somehow everything had changed. I had spent five days in a hospital and the world around seemed sharpened now and pulsing with life.

Location: Chapter 5
Speaker: Reuven
Context: Reuven has returned home from the hospital

"[My father] taught me with silence. . . to look into myself, to find my own strength, to walk around inside myself in company with my soul. . . One learns of the pain of others by suffering one's own pain . . . by turning inside oneself. . . It makes us aware of how frail and tiny we are and of how much we must depend upon the Master of the Universe."

Location: Chapter 18
Speaker: Reb Saunders
Context: Reb Saunders finally explains why he raised Danny in silence

"We shook hands and I watched him walk quickly away, tall, lean, bent forward with eagerness and hungry for the future, his metal capped shoes tapping against the sidewalk. Then he turned into Lee Avenue and was gone."

Location: Chapter 18
Speaker: Reuven
Context: Danny prepares to leave the neighborhood and head to Columbia

A CHRISTMAS CAROL

Charles Dickens

A crotchety, selfish old man learns to be generous and love life.

THE LIFE OF CHARLES DICKENS

Charles Dickens was born on February 7, 1812. He spent the first ten years of his life in Kent, a marshy region by the sea in the east of England. Dickens was the second of eight children. His father, John Dickens, was kind and likable, but fiscally irresponsible. His huge debts caused tremendous strain on his family.

When Dickens was ten, his family moved to London. Two years later, his father was arrested and thrown in debtors' prison. Dickens's mother moved into the prison with seven of her children. Throughout this time, Charles tried to earn money for the struggling family. For three months, he worked with other children pasting labels on bottles in a blacking warehouse. Dickens found the months he spent apart from his family highly traumatic. Not only was the job itself miserable, but he considered himself too good for it, earning the contempt of the other children. His experiences at this warehouse inspired passages of *David Copperfield*.

An inheritance gave John Dickens enough money to free himself from his debt and from prison. Dickens attended Wellington House Academy for two years. He became a law clerk, then a newspaper reporter, and finally a novelist. His first novel, *The Pickwick Papers* (1837), met with huge popular success. Dickens was a literary celebrity in England for the rest of his life.

Dickens's work includes *Oliver Twist* (1837–1839), *Nicholas Nickelby* (1838–1839), *A Christmas Carol* (1843), and *Great Expectations* (1860–1861). Dickens died in Kent in 1870, at the age of fifty-eight.

A CHRISTMAS CAROL IN CONTEXT

Dickens's novella *A Christmas Carol* was written in 1843 with the intention of drawing readers' attention to the plight of England's poor. In the tale, Dickens combines a somewhat indirect description of poverty and its hardships with a heart-rending, sentimental celebration of the Christmas season. The calloused character of the coldhearted, penny-pinching Ebenezer Scrooge, who opens his heart after being confronted by three Spirits, remains one of Dickens's most widely recognized and popular creations.

A Christmas Carol, a relatively simplistic allegory, is seldom considered one of Dickens's important literary contributions. But the novella's emotional depth, compelling story, and memorable cast of characters has made it a favorite among readers.

A CHRISTMAS CAROL: KEY FACTS

Full title: A Christmas Carol in Prose: Being A Ghost Story of Christmas	
Time and place written: 1843; England	
Date of first publication: 1843	
Publisher: Chapman and Hall	
Type of work: Novella	
Genre: Gothic fiction; ghost story; holiday story	
Language: English	
Setting (time): Mid-nineteenth century	

Setting (place): London, England	
Tense: Past	
Tone: Sentimental, ironic, wry, humorous	
Narrator: Anonymous, limited omniscient in the third and occasionally the first person	
Point of view: The narrator's	
Protagonist: Ebenezer Scrooge	
Antagonist: Scrooge's own crabbed nature	

A CHRISTMAS CAROL: PLOT OVERVIEW

A mean-spirited, miserly old man named Ebenezer Scrooge sits in his counting-house on a frigid Christmas Eve. His clerk, Bob Cratchit, works in the anteroom. Scrooge refuses to buy enough coal, so the office is freezing. Fred, Scrooge's nephew, visits the counting-house to invite Scrooge to his annual Christmas party. Two portly gentlemen come by to ask Scrooge for a contribution to their charity. Scrooge reacts to the holiday visitors with bitterness and venom, spitting out an angry "Bah! Humbug!" when Fred wishes him a merry Christmas, and rudely turning away the two gentlemen.

Later that evening, after returning to his dark, cold apartment, Scrooge receives a chilling visitation from the ghost of his dead partner, Jacob Marley. Marley, haggard and pallid, explains that because he lived a greedy, self-serving life, his spirit has been condemned to wander the Earth weighted down with heavy chains. Each selfish or cruel deed added another link to the chain. Marley says it tortures him to see the poor and neglected people he could have helped during his life and to know that he is now powerless to help them. Marley hopes to save Scrooge from sharing the same fate. He tells Scrooge that three Spirits will visit him over the course of the next three nights. After the wraith disappears, Scrooge collapses into a deep sleep.

He wakes moments before the arrival of the Ghost of Christmas Past, a phantom with a brightly glowing head. The Spirit takes Scrooge into the past, where he watches his younger self on previous Christmases. Invisible to those he watches, Scrooge revisits his lonely childhood school days. He sees his neglectful father and his loving sister, the now-deceased mother of Fred, Scrooge's nephew. He sees himself working as an apprentice to a jolly merchant named Fezziwig. He sees Belle, his ex-fiancée, and watches her break their engagement, saying Scrooge loves money more than he loves her. Scrooge, deeply moved, weeps with regret before the phantom returns him to his bed.

Scrooge wakes to find the Ghost of Christmas Present enjoying a feast in his apartment. A majestic giant clad in a green fur robe, the Ghost of Christmas Present takes Scrooge through London, showing him Christmas as it will happen that year. Scrooge watches the large, bustling Cratchit family prepare a poor meal in their meager home. He sees Bob Cratchit's crippled son, Tiny Tim, a courageous boy whose kindness and humility warms Scrooge's heart. The specter then shows Scrooge his nephew's Christmas party. Scrooge finds the jovial gathering delightful and begs the Spirit to let him stay until the very end of the festivities. As the day passes, the Spirit ages, becoming noticeably older. Toward the end of the day, he shows Scrooge two starved children, Ignorance and Want, living under his coat. He vanishes, and Scrooge notices a dark, hooded figure coming toward him.

This figure, the Ghost of Christmas Yet to Come, leads Scrooge through a sequence of mysterious scenes, each one relating to someone's recent death. Scrooge sees businessmen reluctantly agreeing to go to the dead man's funeral, vagabonds trading his personal belongings for cash, and a poor couple expressing relief at the death of their unforgiving creditor. He begs the Spirit to show him a tender response to death, to counteract these callous ones, and the Spirit shows him the Cratchit family mourning the death of Tiny Tim. Scrooge pleads with the ghost to tell him the name of the dead man. He finds himself in a churchyard, where the Spirit points to a grave. Scrooge looks at the headstone and is shocked to read his own name. Desperate, he asks the Spirit if his fate can be changed. He promises to renounce his bad ways and to honor Christmas with all his heart. The Spirit gives no answer. As Scrooge sobs, he sees the Spirit shrink and turn into his own bedpost.

Overwhelmed with joy by the chance to redeem himself, and grateful that he has been returned on Christmas Day, Scrooge rushes out onto the street, hoping to share his newfound Christmas spirit. He sends a giant Christmas turkey to the Cratchit house and attends Fred's party, to the surprise of the other guests. The next day, he raises Bob Cratchit's salary and promises to help his family. As the years go by,

Scrooge keeps his promise and honors Christmas all year round. He treats Tiny Tim like his own son and becomes "as good a man, as the good old city knew."

CHARACTERS IN *A CHRISTMAS CAROL*

Belle Scrooge's onetime fiancée. Belle had no dowry and realized that her poverty made her undesirable in Scrooge's eyes. While traveling with the Ghost of Christmas Past, Scrooge sees that Belle has married a kind man and has many loving children.

Bob Cratchit Scrooge's clerk. Cratchit struggles to support his large family on the absurdly small salary Scrooge pays him. Despite his worries, he is a loving, patient, cheerful man.

Mrs. Cratchit Bob Cratchit's wife. Mrs. Cratchit is a spirited woman who makes her dislike for Scrooge plain. She scoffs when her husband calls Scrooge "the Founder of the Feast."

Fanny Scrooge's sister, and Fred's mother. As a young man, Scrooge adored Fanny, and she adored him, urging their cold father to treat him kindly. She died young.

Fred Scrooge's nephew. Fred enjoys Christmas, which he considers "a kind, forgiving, charitable, pleasant time." Despite constant rejection, he doggedly continues making friendly overtures to his uncle.

Fred's Wife A jolly, pretty woman.

The Ghost of Christmas Past A figure that looks both like a child and like an old man. It wears a white tunic decorated with summer flowers and carries a holly branch. Bright light shines from its head.

The Ghost of Christmas Present A hearty, robust figure that grows older as the day goes by. It wears a green garment and a wreath of holly.

The Ghost of Christmas Yet to Come A mysterious Spirit whose black robe conceals it entirely, except for one hand. It never speaks.

Jacob Marley Scrooge's former business partner, now deceased. When Marley was alive, he was just as self-absorbed and greedy as Scrooge. In his death, he is doomed to eternally regret his misspent life.

Ebenezer Scrooge The protagonist of the novel. Scrooge is a mean, greedy, unkind old man. After seeing himself as an objective observer would, he changes his ways.

Tiny Tim Bob Cratchit's youngest son. Tiny Tim, a cripple, is patient, kind, and pious.

THEMES IN *A CHRISTMAS CAROL*

THE INADEQUACIES OF GOVERNMENT During the Industrial Age, an enormous number of workers from rural areas flooded London in search of jobs. The influx resulted in squalid poverty, overcrowding, and crime. Characterizing poverty as a personal failure rather than a public issue, many social critics of the era argued that charity only promotes idleness. Dickens uses Scrooge, who shares the views of these social critics, to reveal the hypocrisy of blaming the victims of poverty for their plight, and the cruelty of refusing to help them. At the beginning of the novel, Scrooge sees the poor as a faceless mass, not as a collection of individuals. When representatives from a charity organization ask him for a donation, he says his tax dollars do enough, asking, "Are there no prisons? . . . And the Union workhouses? . . . The Treadmill and the Poor Law are in full vigour, then? . . . I help to support the establishments I have mentioned: they cost enough: and those who are badly off must go there." When one of the men points out that many people would choose death over life in a poorhouse, Scrooge cheerily welcomes the idea, saying, "If they would rather die. . . they had better do it, and decrease the surplus population."

Scrooge seems shockingly callous, but he is only voicing what many people believe. By including this blunt, truthful expression of commonly held ideas about the poor, Dickens points out how outrageous they are. He argues that the law has not done enough to serve its people and that taxpayer dollars do little to help the poor. He specifically implicates governments at the end of stave one, writing, "Every one of [the phantoms] wore chains like Marley's Ghost; some few (they might be guilty governments) were linked together; none were free." Dickens believes that one generous individual can help the people in his life far more than government programs can, writing of the good Scrooge does after his transformation.

THE IMPORTANCE OF FAMILY TO HAPPINESS A *Christmas Carol* suggests that no amount of money can make you happy in the way that a loving family can. Despite his riches, Scrooge does not enjoy life—something he does not even realize until the Ghost of Christmas Present contrasts Scrooge's solitary existence to the affectionate, happy lives of the impoverished Cratchits. After losing his fiancée and his sister, the two women he loved most in life, Scrooge has decided not to believe in love or family life. When his nephew says he got married because he fell in love, Scrooge says, "Because you fell in love! . . . as if that were the only one thing in the world more ridiculous than a merry Christmas." But Scrooge's contempt for family life does not run very deep. As soon as the Spirits show him scenes from his childhood and from Belle's happy family life, Scrooge breaks down. He can hardly stand to watch Belle's children playing happily, and when Belle and her husband remark on Scrooge's loneliness, he tells the Spirit he can't stand any more.

THE POWER OF FREE WILL Dickens emphasizes that people have control over their own lives, whether they know it or not. Jacob Marley has realized, to his horror, that he sabotaged himself every time he sinned. He says, "I wear the chain I forged in life. . . . I made it link by link, and yard by yard; I girded it on of my own free will, and of my own free will I wore it." The scenes chosen by the Spirits make it clear that Scrooge has not been buffeted by unkind fate, but has built up his miserable existence himself by making a series of bad choices. He chooses to let Belle leave him without protest, he chooses to be friendless, he chooses to underpay his clerk.

After Scrooge realizes that his own behavior makes his own life worthless and others miserable, and that his stinginess will eventually result, indirectly, in the death of Tiny Tim, he worries about the power of free will to change fate. He asks the Spirit, "Are these the shadows of the things that Will be, or are they shadows of things that May be, only? . . . Men's courses will foreshadow certain ends, to which, if persevered in, they must lead. . . . But if the courses be departed from, the ends will change. Say it is thus with what you show me." The ghost refuses to answer him, but the events that follow make it clear that free will can change the future. Tiny Tim does not die, and Scrooge lives a useful life and earns the love of many. Dickens suggests that if a horrible old man like Scrooge can change, so can anyone. He also suggests that it is never too late to find redemption, for even an elderly miser like Scrooge has time to use his life wisely.

SYMBOLS IN *A CHRISTMAS CAROL*

CHAINS The chain that Jacob Marley wears represents the damning power of greed. Marley's chain is made "of cash-boxes, keys, padlocks, ledgers, deeds, and heavy purses wrought in steel." Scrooge's own chain is far longer than Marley's, Marley explains. Only through repentance and good deeds can Scrooge unfetter himself.

TINY TIM Tiny Tim symbolizes the result of the injustices of English society in the industrial age. Dickens's portrayal of him as a model of courage, hope, and charity has sometimes been criticized as overly idealized and sentimental.

IMPORTANT QUOTATIONS FROM *A CHRISTMAS CAROL*

'There are many things from which I might have derived good, by which I have not profited, I dare say,' returned the nephew. 'Christmas among the rest. But I am sure I have always thought of Christmas time, when it has come round—apart from the veneration due to its sacred name and origin, if anything belonging to it can be apart from that—as a good time: a kind, forgiving, charitable, pleasant time: the only time I know of, in the long calendar of the year, when men and women seem by one consent to open their shut-up hearts freely, and to think of people below them as if they really were fellow-passengers to the grave, and not another race of creatures bound on other journeys. And therefore, uncle, though it has *never put a scrap of gold or silver in my pocket, I believe that it has done me good, and will do me good; and I say, God bless it!'*

Location: Stave 1
Speaker: Fred
Context: Fred defends Christmas

In his defense of Christmas, Fred mentions its religious origins only briefly, saying "apart from the veneration due to its sacred name and origin . . ." and then going on to discuss the secular reasons to bless Christmas. *A Christmas Carol*, while it is deeply informed by Christian notions of sin, redemption, forgiveness, and charity, never really argues that Christmas should be loved because it celebrates the birth of Christ. Instead it argues, as Fred does here, that Christmas is valuable because it provokes people to behave kindly and lovingly. Christmas encourages the kind of behavior that Scrooge never indulges in. It is a "kind, forgiving, charitable, pleasant time"—all of the things that Scrooge must become if he is to avoid an unpleasant fate.

'I don't know what day of the month it is.' said Scrooge. 'I don't know how long I've been among the Spirits. I don't know anything. I'm quite a baby. Never mind. I don't care. I'd rather be a baby. Hallo. Whoop. Hallo here.'
  He was checked in his transports by the churches ringing out the lustiest peals he had ever heard. Clash, clang, hammer; ding, dong, bell. Bell, dong, ding; hammer, clang, clash. Oh, glorious, glorious.
  Running to the window, he opened it, and put out his head. No fog, no mist; clear, bright, jovial, stirring, cold; cold, piping for the blood to dance to; Golden sunlight; Heavenly sky; sweet fresh air; merry bells. Oh, glorious. Glorious.

Location: The beginning of Stave 5
Speaker: The narrator
Context: Scrooge wakes up after the final visitation

When Scrooge wakes up after his ordeal, he does not know what month it is. His confusion, and the fact that he doesn't care about his confusion, shows how much he has changed. Before the visitations, he was obsessed with the clock and the hour. Scrooge happily proclaims himself "quite a baby," a phrase that signifies a spiritual rebirth. He feels confident that his slate has been wiped clean, and he can start over. His delight at the church bells suggests his new willingness to embrace morality and Christian charity. The changes in the manner of Scrooge's speech reflect his changed attitude. The joyful "Hallo! Whoop!" replaces the curmudgeonly "Bah! Humbug!" The weather also echoes Scrooge's change, as the cold cloudiness gives way to sun and color.

'Spirit!' he cried, tight clutching at its robe, 'hear me. I am not the man I was. I will not be the man I must have been but for this intercourse. Why show me this, if I am past all hope.... I will honour Christmas in my heart, and try to keep it all the year. I will live in the Past, the Present, and the Future. The Spirits of all Three shall strive within me. I will not shut out the lessons that they teach.'

Location: The end of Stave 4
Speaker: Scrooge
Context: Scrooge promises to redeem himself

In this quotation, which appears at the end of stave four, and at the end of the last of the Spirits' visitations on Scrooge, Scrooge declares what he has learned. While the reader has witnessed his transformation through his actions in the last staves, at this point Scrooge has yet to declare explicitly that he is a changed man. This statement is aptly placed at the end of this particular stave, as here the Ghost of Christmas Yet to Come visits Scrooge, and the fear of death compels him to fully execute his transformation. It is also significant that he promises to live in all three tenses of time, rather than exclusively in the "capitalist" present. This moment represents an official vow and a sealing of commitment to his new perspective on life.

'What right have you to be merry? What reason have you to be merry? You're poor enough.'
　'Come, then,' returned the nephew gaily. 'What right have you to be dismal? What reason have you to be morose? You're rich enough.'

Location: Stave 1
Speaker: Scrooge and Fred
Context: Uncle and nephew quarrel

When this strain of music sounded, all the things that Ghost had shown him, came upon his mind; he softened more and more; and thought that if he could have listened to it often, years ago, he might have cultivated the kindnesses of life for his own happiness with his own hands, without resorting to the sexton's spade that buried Jacob Marley.

Location: Stave 3
Speaker: The narrator
Context: Scrooge finds himself moved by the music at his nephew's party

A CLOCKWORK ORANGE

Anthony Burgess

A violent young boy is imprisoned and undergoes conditioning treatment which is eventually reversed.

THE LIFE OF ANTHONY BURGESS

Anthony Burgess was born John Anthony Burgess Wilson in Manchester, England, in 1917. He was brought up Catholic but rebelled against the church as an adolescent. Nevertheless, his religious upbringing later had a profound influence on his novels, which concern free will and original sin. Burgess began writing as a hobby when he was stationed in Malaya (then a British colony, now part of Malaysia) as an education officer for the British Colonial Service in the 1950s. His first three novels, which formed a trilogy, were about life in Malaya and the conflict between eastern and western values.

In 1960, doctors told Burgess he had a cancerous brain tumor. Burgess didn't want the tumor surgically removed, lest "they hit my talent instead of my tumor." The doctors decided an operation would be impossible anyway. Told he would only live for one more year, Burgess began to write at a furious pace, hoping royalties from his work would support his wife after his death. He wrote five novels and began to think of writing as his true profession. It turned out the doctors were mistaken: Burgess did not have cancer.

A Clockwork Orange (1962) and Stanley Kubrick's film based on the novel achieved great success. The popularity of *A Clockwork Orange* annoyed Burgess, who did not consider the novel his best work. Asked about *A Clockwork Orange* in an interview, he dismissed it as "gimmicky" and "didactic." Burgess continued writing prolifically and composing music until his death in 1993.

A CLOCKWORK ORANGE IN CONTEXT

A Clockwork Orange is primarily concerned with threats to individual freedom. In 1961, Burgess visited Leningrad, now St. Petersburg, in what was then the Soviet Union. His impression of Soviet life under the repressive Communist government heavily influenced the totalitarian world of *A Clockwork Orange*. Burgess objected to the brutality and repression of existing Communist governments, as epitomized by the Soviet Union. He also faulted Communist governments for shifting moral responsibility from individuals to the state. Even if the state made good choices for the people, Burgess believed, it erred gravely by robbing its citizens of their free will. Burgess also objected to the usurpation of individual freedom in non-Communist states. After World War II, Britain's government began providing its citizens with necessities such as medical care, child support, and housing. Burgess disliked this government interference because it forced people to consider the good of society over their own freedom and individuality.

Burgess interpreted America's mass popular culture as a brainwashing force that produced passive, conformist people. He saw the same kind of mindless conformity in Anglo-American youths, who thought they were rebelling but were actually conforming, dressing and speaking exactly like the other members of their group did.

In *A Clockwork Orange*, Burgess also attacks the theories of B. F. Skinner, a behavioral psychologist who believed that individual freedoms were an illusion. Skinner was interested in modifying people's behavior by rewarding them for certain behavior and punishing them for other kinds of behavior. Like other psychologists before him, he believed people would eventually associate the behavior desired with the pleasure of the reward they received for it. Burgess parodies Skinner's techniques with his fictional Ludovico's Technique, which scientists use to brainwash young Alex. Burgess considered behaviorism revolting and its popularity threatening. In an interview, he called one of Skinner's works, *Beyond Freedom and Dignity*, "one of the most dangerous books ever written."

A Clockwork Orange was published in 1962 to mixed reviews. The American version of the novel was published without the last chapter of the novel, which publishers considered too sentimental. Burgess strenuously objected to this truncated version, but his publisher overrode his concerns. The novel became a cult hit among American college students, but it achieved widespread popularity only after Kubrick's film adaptation of the novel, which was a huge scandal and a major success.

A CLOCKWORK ORANGE: KEY FACTS

Time and place written: 1959–1961; England

Date of first publication : 1962

Publisher: W. W. Norton

Type of work: Novel

Genre: Dystopian novel

Language: English

Setting (time): The not-too-distant future

Setting (place): Unspecified city, perhaps London

Tense: Past

Tone: Casual, inclusive

Narrator: Alex in the first person

Point of View: Alex's

Protagonist: Alex

Antagonist: Alex's society

A CLOCKWORK ORANGE: PLOT OVERVIEW

Alex, a happy fifteen-year-old hoodlum who delights in rape and violence, is the leader of a gang of teen-age criminals—Dim, Pete, and Georgie. He narrates his story in language peppered with "nadsat," the slang of teenage hooligans. One night, in search of amusement, Alex and his "droogs" break in to a cottage in the country, beating up the man who lives there and brutally raping his wife. The boys go to their favorite bar. A woman sings a bit of opera, and Dim makes an obscene gesture at her. Alex, a great lover of classical music, punches Dim. Dim and the others begin to think that Alex is abusing his powers of leadership, and they plan to betray him. The next time they go out, they break into the house of an old woman and beat her. Dim whips Alex across the eyes with his chain, and the gang runs away, leaving Alex blinded and helpless. The police arrive and take Alex to the station. He learns that the old woman died at the hospital.

Alex is sentenced to fourteen years in prison. After two years, he is chosen as the first candidate for a new treatment called Ludovico's Technique, a brain-washing method. Alex is injected with a substance that makes him feel extremely ill and then shown violent films. Thus, violence and sickness become linked in his mind. After two weeks of the treatment, Alex is so thoroughly conditioned that the injection is no longer necessary: if he so much as thinks a violent thought, he becomes extremely ill. As an unforeseen side effect, classical music also makes Alex ill because classical music was on the soundtrack of many of the films he was shown. After his treatment, Alex is released. The government boasts of Alex's treatment as a great victory for law and order and plans to implement it on a wide scale.

When Alex is released, he has no idea what to do. The people he wronged in the past have an easy time revenging themselves on him, because when they hit him, he cannot strike back. Dim, his old friend, and Billyboy, an old enemy, now both policemen, take Alex into a field, beat him, and leave him there. Alex goes in search of help and knocks at the door of a cottage. The man who comes to the door gives him dinner and a room for the night. Alex recognizes the man as the writer he beat up long ago, but initially the man does not recognize Alex. This writer, F. Alexander, is a political dissident.

He and his friends decide to use Alex to make the government look bad. They lock him in a room and play classical music for him, trying to drive him to suicide. Alex does throw himself out of the window, but he does not die. Nevertheless, the incident makes the government look bad. Government psychologists reverse Ludovico's Technique on Alex, returning him to his former happy, violent self. For a while he returns to his old ways with a new gang, but he begins to tire of his thug's life. He starts to think about settling down, marrying, and having a son.

CHARACTERS IN *A CLOCKWORK ORANGE*

Alex The protagonist and narrator of the novel. Alex's narration is witty and agile. An aesthete of violence, he commits acts of cruelty for their own sake and insists on imbuing them with style. The source of his malignity is a mystery. As Alex's state-appointed guidance councilor says, "You've got a good home here, good loving parents, you've got not too bad of a brain. Is it some devil that crawls inside you?" Alex is passionate about classical music.

Alex's parents A meek, kind couple. Alex's parents are frightened of their son and do not want to know too much about his activities.

F. Alexander A young, subversive writer enraged by governmental repression. Alexander is the author of a book called *A Clockwork Orange*, a pompous work about "[t]he attempt to impose upon man, a creature of growth and capable of sweetness . . . laws and conditions appropriate to a mechanical creation." Alexander and his dissident friends are guilty of the same dehumanization they criticize the government for, treating Alex as a political weapon instead of a person. Despite their bad treatment of each other, Alexander and Alex have a sometime father-son relationship and are doubles for each other.

Billyboy The leader of a teenage gang that rivals Alex's. Alex's posse and Billyboy's often fight each other with knives, razors, and chains. Alex abhors Billyboy for his ugliness. Eventually Billyboy joins the police force.

Dr. Branom Dr. Brodsky's smarmy assistant. He puts on a show of insincere friendliness toward Alex.

Dr. Brodsky The psychologist in charge of conditioning Alex using Ludovico's Technique. Brodsky knows nothing about music, using it only as an "emotional heightener." He often laughs at Alex's misery.

P. R. Deltoid Alex's state-appointed "Post-Corrective Advisor." Deltoid cannot understand why Alex, who comes from a good family, is so vicious.

Dim The biggest, strongest, and stupidest member of Alex's gang. Dim's sloppiness and vulgarity constantly annoy Alex. In Part III, Dim has become a police officer.

Georgie The most ambitious member of Alex's gang. He capitalizes on his friends' resentment when Alex punches Dim. He leads the mutiny that results in Alex's arrest at the end of Part I. A year later, he dies during a robbery. Unlike Alex, an exponent of violence for violence's sake, Georgie is mostly interested in stealing money.

Joe The lodger Alex's parents take in after Alex is sent to jail. Joe is extremely rude to Alex when he is released from jail.

Marty and Sonietta Two girls not older than ten. Alex, who considers Marty and Sonietta annoying and empty-headed, rapes them when they are drunk. They feebly punch him and call him a "[b]east and hateful animal."

Minister of the Interior The man who orders doctors to use Ludovico's Technique on Alex. The Minister of the Interior (or "Minisiter of the Interior," as Alex calls him) sees Ludovico's Technique as a way of controlling the citizenry. After Alex's suicide attempt makes the government look bad, the minister tries to buy Alex's cooperation with a new stereo and a position at the National Gramodisc Archives.

Pete A mild-mannered member of Alex's gang. Pete eventually becomes an office worker. When Alex runs into Pete and his pretty young wife in a cafe, it makes him think about growing up and finding a girl to settle down with.

Prison Chaplain A kind man who lets Alex choose the music for services. The chaplain is no hero—he is an alcoholic and a careerist who does not speak out against Ludovico's Technique until it is too late—but he voices many of the novel's themes. He strongly opposes Ludovico's Technique because he believes people must choose to do good. He asks, "What does God want? Does God want goodness or the choice of goodness? Is a man who chooses the bad perhaps in some way better than a man who has the good imposed upon him?"

THEMES IN *A CLOCKWORK ORANGE*

THE IMPORTANCE OF FREE WILL Burgess admits that free will can have horrific conse-quences. In the first third of the novel, Alex's ability to exercise free will allows him to rape, steal, and kill. He takes great pleasure in the pain he inflicts. When he thinks about raping two ten-year-old girls, he says, "Then an idea hit me and made me near fall over with the anguish and ecstasy of it, O my brothers, so I could not breathe for near ten seconds." But, Burgess argues, the sometimes dreadful consequences of free will are a price we should pay cheerfully. The alternative, as embodied by the methods of the state, is unbearable. The prison chaplain articulates the importance of free will, repeatedly voicing his horror of the so-called scientific method which leaves Alex unable to act on his own desires. When the reformed Alex is shown off to grandees of the government and the jail, the chaplain complains that Alex "ceases to be a creature capable of moral choice." To remove a man's ability to choose is to defy God, who gave man free will.

THE NATURE OF CAPITALISM Burgess's opinion of capitalism is a matter of debate. The first third of the novel can be interpreted as a criticism of capitalism. Burgess describes Alex's economic inno-cence with approval, suggesting that it makes him a better person than his greedy friends. Alex does not understand why George and Dim are interested in going after "the big big big money," asking, "Have you not every vesch you need? If you need an auto you pluck it from the trees. If you need pretty polly you take it. Yes? Why this sudden shilarny for being the big bloated capitalist?" Alex spends money on classi-cal music and a fancy stereo system only because he is passionate about music. He attaches little value to money, emptying his pockets to buy drinks for a group of old women and giving whatever cash he has to his father. He leans toward socialism, lamenting that the woman he kills hoards a huge apartment for herself, when the space could fit many people. However, the end of the novel can be interpreted as an admission that adulthood requires the acceptance of capitalism. When Alex gets accustomed to a good job with a good salary, he grows reluctant to treat the group of old women to drinks as he usually does, complaining that he doesn't "like just throwing away [his] hard-earned pretty polly." In the last chapter, Alex begins to long for a conventional capitalist family such as the one Pete has.

THE INNATENESS OF GOOD AND BAD Burgess argues that both good and bad behavior are instinctual and have nothing to do with environment. As Alex says, "If lewdies are good that's because they like it, and I wouldn't ever interfere with their pleasures." This argument contradicts the conven-tional interpretation of goodness. If good and bad are both mere instincts, good people are no more praiseworthy than bad people. They, like bad people, are simply acting in the way that gives them plea-sure. Alex goes on to identify badness as something God made on purpose, saying, "badness is of the self, the one, the you or me on our oddy knockies, and that self is made by old Bog or God and is his great pride and radosty." If God made badness just as he made goodness, we must respect it as part of his plan for the world.

SYMBOLS IN *A CLOCKWORK ORANGE*

CLOCKWORK ORANGE In his 1986 introduction to the novel, Burgess explains the meaning of the clockwork orange. The term comes from an English idiom meaning "queer." Burgess uses it to repre-sent "the application of a mechanistic morality to a living organism oozing with juice and sweetness." Like F. Alexander, the author of the fictive tract *A Clockwork Orange*, and like Alex, Burgess is horrified by the idea of a beautiful organic object being forcibly transformed into a mechanical object.

LUNA The moon, or Luna, signifies dreams and fantasy. An old drunk tells Alex and his droogs that he does not wish to live in a world in which men casually land on the moon, saying no attention is paid "to earthly law or order no more." For this old man, the landing of men on the moon symbolizes society's dis-dain for fantasies. However, in the closing chapter, the moon again takes on a romantic function. When Alex thinks of his future, he dwells on Luna as a symbol of the sweetness of the unknown.

IMPORTANT QUOTATIONS FROM *A CLOCKWORK ORANGE*

> *Delimitation is always difficult. The world is one, life is one. The sweetest and most heavenly of activities partake in some measure of violence — the act of love, for instance; music, for instance. You must take your chance, boy. The choice has been all yours.*

Location: Part Two, Chapter 5
Speaker: Dr. Brodsky
Context: Dr. Brodsky responds to Alex's complaint that the treatment is robbing him of his ability to listen to beautiful music

In this passage, Dr. Brodsky explains that violence is a part of everything in life, including such pleasures as sex and music. For that reason, Alex's treatment robs him of the ability to take pleasure in the music he loves so much. The revelation that Ludovico's Technique prevents all passion, not just violent passion, is a disturbing one. If the technique once seemed justifiable on the grounds that society would benefit if Alex stopped raping ten-year-olds and beating up defenseless old men, it seems far less justifiable once we learn that it prevents "sweetest and most heavenly of activities."

> *But where I itty now, O my brothers, is all on my oddy knocky, where you cannot go. Tomorrow is all like sweet flowers and the turning vonny earth and the stars and the old Luna up there and your old droog Alex all on his oddy knocky seeking like a mate. And all that cal. A terrible grahzny vonny world, really, O my brothers. And so farewell from your little droog.*

Location: Part Three, Chapter 7
Speaker: Alex
Context: A maturing Alex closes the novel with a farewell

The final chapter of the novel marks a drastic change in Alex. He begins dreaming of making money, marrying, having a baby, and generally creating a life for himself like the one lived by upright Pete. Burgess presents this maturation in a positive light, contradicting the novel's previous implication that youthfulness and reliance on instincts are the most freeing aspects of life. To the contrary, Alex finds individuality by embracing a life that most consider conventional. Burgess also undermines his previous assertions that Alex's youthful urges were organic. Earlier in the final chapter, Alex compared himself as a boy to a windup toy — a comparison that suggests he did not, as we believed, behave antisocially on purpose, but in innocent foolishness, like a toy that "itties in a straight line and bangs straight into things bang bang and it cannot help what it is doing."

> *But, brothers, this biting of their toe-nails over what is the cause of badness is what turns me into a fine laughing malchick. They don't go into what is the cause of goodness, so why of the other shop? If lewdies are good that's because they like it and I wouldn't ever interfere with their pleasures, and so of the other shop. And I was patronizing the other shop. More, badness is of the self, the one, the you or me on our oddy knockies, and that self is made by old Bog or God and is his great pride and radosty. But the not-self cannot have the bad, meaning they of the government and the judges and the schools cannot allow the bad because they cannot allow the self. And is not our modern history, my brothers, the story of brave malenky selves fighting these big machines?*

Location: Part One, Chapter 4
Speaker: Alex
Context: After receiving a visit from his Post-Corrective Adviser, Alex considers why the state should be so concerned with badness

It may be horrible to be good. I know I shall have many sleepless nights about this. What does God want? Does God want goodness or the choice of goodness? Is a man who chooses the bad perhaps in some way better than a man who has the good imposed upon him?. . . You are passing now to a region where you will be beyond the reach of the power of prayer.

Location: Part Two, Chapter 3
Speaker: Prison Chaplain
Context: The prison chaplain, who has learned that Alex is about to undergo the new reformation treatment, voices his concerns

O most beautiful and beauteous of devotchkas, I throw like my heart at your feet for you to like trample all over. If I had a rose I would give it to you. If it was all rainy and cally now on the ground you could have my platties to walk on so as not to cover your dainty nogas with filth and cal.. . . Let me . . . worship you and be like your helper and protector from the wicked like world.. . . Let me be like your true knight.

Location: Part Two, Chapter 7
Speaker: Alex
Context: Alex, at the meeting called to show off the success of his treatment, is forced to throw himself at the feet of a beautiful girl

THE COLOR PURPLE

Alice Walker

A meek, abused, impoverished young black woman eventually finds independence with the help of her women friends.

THE LIFE OF ALICE WALKER

Alice Walker was born on February 9, 1944, in the small rural town of Eatonton, Georgia. She was the eighth and last child of Willie Lee Walker and Minnie Tallulah Grant, both sharecroppers. When Walker was eight, one of her brothers accidentally shot her, permanently blinding her in one eye. Ashamed of her disfigurement, Walker isolated herself from other children and sought refuge in reading and writing.

In 1961, Walker enrolled in Spelman College in Atlanta on a scholarship for disabled students. There she became active in the Civil Rights movement. After two years at Spelman, Walker transferred to Sarah Lawrence College in New York. During her junior year, she traveled to Uganda as an exchange student. As a senior in college, Walker was shocked to learn that she was pregnant. Afraid of her parents' reaction, she considered suicide. However, a classmate helped Walker obtain a safe abortion, and she graduated from Sarah Lawrence in 1965. She also published her first short story, "To Hell with Dying," and her first volume of poetry, *Once: Poems*.

Walker's involvement with the Civil Rights movement continued. In 1965 and 1966, she worked as a volunteer on black voter registration drives in Georgia and Mississippi. In 1967, Walker married Melvyn Leventhal, a Jewish civil rights lawyer, with whom she had one daughter. The couple divorced in the mid-1970s.

THE COLOR PURPLE IN CONTEXT

In 1982, Walker published her most famous novel, *The Color Purple*. The novel chronicles the struggles of several black women in rural Georgia in the first half of the twentieth century. *The Color Purple* won the Pulitzer Prize and the American Book Award. In 1985, a Steven Spielberg film based on the novel was released to wide acclaim.

The Color Purple prompted a storm of controversy, instigating heated debates about black cultural representation. A number of male African-American critics complained that the novel reaffirmed old racist stereotypes about black communities and black men. Critics also charged Walker with focusing on sexism at the expense of addressing racism in America. Nonetheless, *The Color Purple* also had ardent supporters, especially among black women and others who praised the novel as a feminist fable. The heated disputes surrounding *The Color Purple* testify to its important place in cultural and racial discourse.

THE COLOR PURPLE: KEY FACTS

Time and place written: 1982; California	
Date of first publication : 1982	
Publisher: Simon & Schuster	
Type of work: Historical fiction	
Genre: Epistolary novel	
Language: English	
Setting (time): 1910–1940	
Setting (place): Rural Georgia	
Tense: Present	
Tone: Confessional, uninhibited	

| *Narrator:* First person, limited |
| *Point of view:* Celie's |
| *Protagonist:* Celie |
| *Antagonist:* Men |

THE COLOR PURPLE: PLOT OVERVIEW

Celie, the protagonist and narrator of *The Color Purple*, is a poor, uneducated, fourteen-year-old black girl living in rural Georgia. Her narrative takes the form of letters to God, who Celie writes to because her father, Alphonso, beats and rapes her. Celie gives birth to two children by her father, a girl and a boy. Alphonso steals the babies and disposes of them somehow. After Celie's mother dies, Alphonso remarries but continues to abuse Celie.

Celie and her bright, pretty younger sister, Nettie, learn that a man known only as Mr. _____ wants to marry Nettie. Mr. _____ has a lover named Shug Avery, a sultry lounge singer whose photograph fascinates Celie. Alphonso refuses to let Nettie marry and offers Mr. _____ the "ugly" Celie as a bride. Mr. _____ eventually accepts the offer. Celie's married life is difficult and joyless. Nettie runs away from Alphonso and takes refuge at Celie's house. Mr. _____ makes advances to Nettie, and she flees. Celie does not hear from Nettie and assumes she is dead.

Harpo, Mr. _____'s son, falls in love with a large, spunky girl named Sofia. Shug Avery comes to town to sing at a local bar, but Celie is not allowed to go see her. Sofia gets pregnant and marries Harpo. Harpo and Mr. _____ try to treat Sofia as an inferior, but she will not knuckle under. She is stronger than Harpo and refuses to let him beat her.

Shug falls ill and Mr. _____ takes her into his house. Celie nurses Shug and is sexually attracted to her. Sofia leaves Harpo, taking her children with her. Several months later, Harpo opens a juke joint where Shug sings nightly.

Shug stays with Celie after learning that Mr. _____ beats Celie when Shug is away. Shug and Celie grow increasingly intimate. Sofia returns for a visit and gets in a fight with Harpo's new girlfriend, Squeak. One day in town, the mayor's wife, Miss Millie, asks Sofia to work as her maid. Sofia answers "Hell no." When the mayor slaps Sofia for her insubordination, she knocks the mayor down. Sofia is sent to jail. Squeak tries and fails to get Sofia out of jail. Sofia is sentenced to work for twelve years as the mayor's maid.

Shug returns with a new husband, Grady. She and Celie begin a sexual relationship, frequently sharing the same bed. One night, Shug says she has seen Mr. _____ hide many letters. Shug gets her hands on one of these letters, and they find it is from Nettie. Celie and Shug find dozens of letters from Nettie in Mr. _____'s trunk. Celie reads the letters in order, wondering how to keep herself from killing Mr. _____.

In her letters, Nettie says she has befriended a missionary couple, Samuel and Corrine, and traveled with them to Africa to do ministry work. Samuel and Corrine have two adopted children, Olivia and Adam. Corrine notices that her adopted children resemble Nettie and wonders if Samuel and Nettie had a secret affair. After talking to Samuel, Nettie realizes Olivia and Adam are actually Celie's biological children. She also learns that Alphonso is stepfather, not father, to Nettie and Celie. Their biological father was lynched by white men who resented his success. Alphonso lied to Celie and Nettie because he wanted to inherit their mother's house and property. Nettie tells Samuel and Corrine that she is their children's biological aunt. Corrine dies soon after.

Celie visits Alphonso, who admits he is her stepfather. Celie doubts her faith in God, but Shug encourages her to imagine God in her own way, rather than as the old, bearded white man.

The mayor releases Sofia from her servitude six months early. At dinner one night, Celie angrily curses Mr. _____ for his years of abuse. Shug announces that she and Celie are moving to Tennessee, and Squeak decides to go with them. In Tennessee, Celie designs and sews pants, eventually turning her hobby into a business. Celie returns to Georgia for a visit and finds that Mr. _____ has reformed and Alphonso has died. She moves into Alphonso's house, which is now hers.

Nettie and Samuel marry and prepare to return to America. Before they leave, Samuel's son, Adam, marries Tashi, a native African girl. Following African tradition, Tashi undergoes the painful rituals of female circumcision and facial scarring. In solidarity with Tashi, Adam undergoes the same facial scarring ritual.

Celie and Mr. _____ reconcile and begin to enjoy each other's company. Now that she is financially, spiritually, and emotionally independent, Celie no longer worries about Shug's passing flings with younger men. Sofia remarries Harpo and works in Celie's clothing store. Nettie returns to America with Samuel and the children. Emotionally drained but exhilarated by the reunion with her sister, Celie realizes that although she and Nettie are old, she has never felt younger.

CHARACTERS IN *THE COLOR PURPLE*

Adam Celie and Alphonso's biological son. Adam is adopted by Samuel and Corrine. By marrying Tashi, Adam symbolically links Africa and America. His respect for his wife subverts patriarchal insistence on women's inferiority.

Alphonso Celie and Nettie's stepfather. Alphonso rapes and abuses Celie.

Shug Avery A sultry blues singer. Shug, Celie's friend and lover, mentors Celie and helps her become independent and assertive.

Celie The protagonist and narrator. Celie is a poor, uneducated black woman with little self-confidence, but by the end of the novel, she has become a happy, independent woman.

Corrine Samuel's first wife. She dies of a fever in Africa.

Eleanor Jane The mayor's daughter. Eleanor Jane relies on Sofia for emotional support. Toward the end of the novel, she begins to understand the injustices Sofia has suffered because of her race.

Grady Shug's husband. Grady is loving and sweet, but he is also a womanizer, a profligate spender, and a frequent pot smoker. Eventually he has an affair with Squeak, which does not bother Shug.

Harpo Mr. _____'s eldest son. Harpo is not stereotypically masculine. He cries in Celie's arms, enjoys cooking and housework, kisses his children, and marries Sofia, an independent woman.

Kate One of Mr. _____'s sisters. Kate urges Celie to stand up for herself and defy Mr. _____'s abuses.

Miss Millie The mayor's wife. Miss Millie is racist and condescending.

Mr. _____ Celie's husband. Mr. _____, whose first name is Albert, abuses Celie for years. After Celie finally defies Mr. _____, he changes profoundly.

Nettie Celie's younger sister. Nettie's experiences in Africa broaden the novel's scope, introducing issues of imperialism and pan-African struggles.

Olivia Celie and Alphonso's biological daughter. Olivia is adopted by Samuel and Corrine. Crossing cultural boundaries, she develops a sisterly relationship with Tashi, an Olinka village girl.

Samuel A minister and, eventually, Nettie's husband. Samuel, a wise, spiritually mature black intellectual committed to "the uplift of black people everywhere," does missionary work in Africa.

Sofia A large, fiercely independent woman who befriends Celie and marries Harpo. Sofia refuses to submit to whites, men, or anyone else who tries to dominate her, even when defiance leads to hardship.

Squeak Harpo's lover after Sofia leaves him. Squeak has mixed racial ancestry.

Tashi An Olinka village girl who befriends Olivia and marries Adam. Tashi, who defies white imperialist culture, stands for the struggle of traditional cultures against colonization.

THEMES IN *THE COLOR PURPLE*

THE POWER OF NARRATIVE AND VOICE Walker suggests that the ability to express thoughts and feelings is crucial to developing a sense of self. When the novel opens, Celie is defenseless against those who abuse her, in part because she cannot express herself. After Alphonso warns her that she "better not never tell nobody but God" that he rapes her, Celie feels she must remain silent and invisible if she wants to survive. But when she takes him at his word and writes letters to God, she finds an outlet. Similarly, Nettie finds an outlet in her letters to Celie. Walker suggests that the presence of a willing audience is almost as important as the act of writing. Celie imagines that God is listening, which comforts her, and when Nettie receives no response to her letters, she feels lost.

THE IMPORTANCE OF STRONG FEMALE RELATIONSHIPS   In *The Color Purple*, female friendships give women the courage to tell stories. In turn, these stories allow women to resist oppression and dominance. A refuge from male violence, relationships among women are variously motherly, sisterly, sexual, or simply friendly. Sofia says her ability to fight comes from her strong relationships with her sisters. Nettie's relationship with Celie anchors her in Africa. Samuel notes that the strong relationships among Olinka women are the only thing that make polygamy bearable for them. Celie's relationship with Shug results in Celie's redemption and independence.

THE CYCLICAL NATURE OF ABUSE   Almost none of the abusers in Walker's novel are stereotypical, one-dimensional monsters whom we can dismiss as purely evil. Those who perpetuate violence are themselves victims, often of sexism, racism, or paternalism. Harpo beats Sofia only after his father implies that Sofia's resistance unmans Harpo. Mr. _____ violently mistreats his family just as his own father mistreated him. Some of the characters understand the cyclical nature of violence. For example, Sofia tells Eleanor Jane that her baby boy will inevitably grow up to be a racist because of the society in which he lives.

THE SIGNIFICANCE OF COLOR   Walker uses color to signal spiritual mood. When Kate takes Celie shopping for a new dress, the dresses come in drab colors like brown, maroon, and dark blue. Later, Celie and Sofia use bright yellow fabric from Shug's dress to make a quilt. Bright colors appear in honor of a character's liberation. When Celie describes her religious awakening, she marvels that she never noticed the wonders God created, such as "the color purple." When Mr. _____ undergoes his spiritual transformation, he paints the interior of his house "fresh and white."

SYMBOLS IN *THE COLOR PURPLE*

SEWING AND QUILTS   Quilting symbolizes peacemaking. After Sofia and Celie argue, Sofia offers a truce by suggesting they make a quilt. The quilt, composed of diverse patterns sewn together, also symbolizes unity. The community of love that surrounds Celie at the end of the novel is a patchwork quilt of people with different gender roles, sexual orientations, and talents. Sewing symbolizes the power that comes from channeling creative energy. Celie's business disproves the idea that sewing is marginal women's labor.

GOD   Celie's shifting conception of God symbolizes her growth. At first, Celie has a vague conception of God as a white male patriarch, which she says "don't seem quite right," but is all she has. Shug prompts Celie to imagine God not as a white man but as a genderless, raceless "it" that delights in creation and wants human beings to love what it has created. In her last letter, Celie writes, "Dear God. Dear stars, dear trees, dear sky, dear peoples. Dear Everything. Dear God." She has rejected white male ideas and come up with her own idea of God, just as she has rejected male conceptions of women and come up with her own selfhood.

IMPORTANT QUOTATIONS FROM *THE COLOR PURPLE*

> *Harpo say, I love you, Squeak. He kneel down and try to put his arms round her waist. She stand up. My name Mary Agnes, she say.*

Location: The forty-first letter
Speaker: Celie
Context: Squeak has returned from an unsuccessful attempt to release Sofia from prison

At the prison, the warden rapes Squeak. She returns home battered and torn, but not defeated. She performs an important act of resistance by rejecting the belittling nickname, Squeak, that Harpo has given her, and insisting that he call her by her given name, Mary Agnes. By renaming herself, Mary Agnes reclaims ownership of herself, refusing to be the small, cute, harmlessly feminine figure idealized by patriarchal societies. Walker repeatedly stresses that storytelling and naming are controlling devices, and that reclaiming them means liberation. Just as Shug renames Celie a virgin, and Celie reverses Mr. _____'s accusations and says, "I'm pore, I'm black, I may be ugly and can't cook. . . . But I'm here," Mary Agnes renames herself to show that her boyfriend does not have interpretive control over her. That Squeak performs this act of resistance in the face of affection, not violence or anger, shows that even repression that seems sweet or well meant must be rejected.

Shug act more manly than most men . . . he say. You know Shug will fight, he say. Just like Sofia. She bound to live her life and be herself no matter what.

Mr. _____ think all this is stuff men do. But Harpo not like this, I tell him. You not like this. What Shug got is womanly it seem like to me. Specially since she and Sofia the ones got it.

Location: The eighty-seventh letter
Speaker: Mr. _____ and Celie
Context: Celie expresses her ideas about gender

In *The Color Purple*, traditionally masculine traits such as assertiveness, lust, and physical strength are present in female as well as male characters. Sofia surpasses all the men in assertiveness and strength, for example, and Harpo is nurturing and nesting in a traditionally feminine way. Even those characters who initially act according to rigid definitions of gender eventually take on traits of the opposite sex. Shug picks up Celie's gentleness and care, while Celie picks up Shug's sexual and financial assertiveness. Mr. _____ learns to sew and to listen, and Harpo cooks, changes his baby's diaper, and kisses his children. Walker condones the blurring of gender roles and condemns traditional ideas about men and women.

Us sleep like sisters, me and Shug.

Location: The sixtieth letter
Speaker: Celie
Context: Celie has just learned that Mr. _____ has been hiding Nettie's letters

---

It must have been a pathetic exchange. Our chief never learned English beyond an occasional odd phrase he picked up from Joseph, who pronounces "English" "Yanglush."

Location: The sixty-fifth letter
Speaker: Nettie
Context: Nettie complains about the lack of communication with the Olinka villagers

---

Well, us talk and talk about God, but I'm still adrift. Trying to chase that old white man out of my head. I been so busy thinking bout him I never truly notice nothing God make. Not a blade of corn (how it do that?) not the color purple (where it come from?).. . .

Location: The seventy-third letter
Speaker: Celie
Context: Celie has told Shug that she stopped writing to God

CRIME AND PUNISHMENT

Fyodor Dostoevsky

In an attempt to prove a theory, a student murders two women, after which he suffers greatly from guilt and worry.

THE LIFE OF FYODOR DOSTOEVSKY

Fyodor Dostoevsky, one of the world's greatest novelists and literary psychologists, was born in Moscow in 1821. Dostoevsky was educated first at home and then at a boarding school. When he was a young boy, his father, a doctor, sent him to the St. Petersburg Academy of Military Engineering, from which he graduated in 1843. Dostoevsky's father was murdered—or so the traditionally belief goes—at the hands of his ill-treated servants.

In St. Petersburg, Dostoevsky fell victim to a compulsive gambling habit that would dog him for most of his life. Eventually he resigned his military commission and set to work on a novel, *Poor Folk* (1843), which received mostly harsh reviews. In April 1849, Dostoevsky was arrested and imprisoned in part because of his involvement with the Petrashevsky circle, a Socialist group that belligerently criticized Tsar Nicholas I (1796-1855). Dostoevsky was sentenced to death for his transgressions. At the last minute, as he stood in front of a firing squad, Tsar Nicholas commuted the sentence to four years of working in Siberian prison camps.

Dostoevsky's years in Siberia affected him profoundly. He lived in squalid conditions among petty thieves and murderers. For his entire sentence, his only reading material was the New Testament. In prison, Dostoevsky developed the first symptoms of the epilepsy from which he would suffer for the rest of his life. He became fascinated with the psychology of his fellow prisoners, who afforded him a first-hand glimpse into the inner workings of the criminal mind. He drew on these observations when writing Crime and Punishment and his other great post-exile works. The brutalities of his imprisonment made him shed much of the idealism of his youth, including his strong belief in radical Socialism. In its place, he developed a more conservative, reactionary, religious outlook.

Dostoevsky married Marya Isaeva (c. 1824–1864) and moved back to St. Petersburg. In the early months of 1864, Marya died of tuberculosis. Weeks later, Dostoevsky's brother Mikhail died unexpectedly. Dostoevsky began work on the first sections of *Crime and Punishment* (1866). A few months later, he finished *The Gambler* (1865). With his deadline looming, he hired a young woman, Anna Snitkina, to transcribe the manuscript. Anna and Dostoevsky married in 1867. Dostoevsky, enjoying a new stability, entered into the most prolific period of his career, completing five novels, including *The Brothers Karamazov* (1879).

Dostoevsky's fame expanded throughout Russia in the 1870s. He died in 1881. His funeral was attended by thousands of mourners, and he was buried with high religious honors in St. Petersburg's venerated Tikhvinsky cemetery.

CRIME AND PUNISHMENT IN CONTEXT

Crime and Punishment is perhaps the greatest crime story ever written. It is certainly the first to examine the psychology of the criminal mind in such detail. The novel is a cautionary tale about alienation and the destructive results of zealous theorizing. A story of profound moral and psychological depth, it reflects Dostoevsky's belief that suffering is the true path to happiness, redemption, and salvation.

Dostoevsky drew on his personal experiences in writing *Crime and Punishment*. His time in Siberian prison, for example, informs the description of Raskolnikov's sentence. Dostoevsky's dismissal of leftist political thought is evident in *Crime and Punishment*. Raskolnikov's crime is partly motivated by his theories about society. Lebezyatnikov, whose name derives from the Russian word for "fawning," is obsessed with the so-called new philosophies that raged through St. Petersburg during the time that Dostoevsky was writing the novel. Luzhin, a mid-level government official, is continually afraid of being "exposed" by "nihilists."

The 1866 publication of *Crime and Punishment* improved Dostoevsky's fortunes. The novel's popular and critical success allowed him to keep ahead, just barely, of daunting debts and the burden of supporting a number of children left in his care after the deaths of his brother and sister.

CRIME AND PUNISHMENT: KEY FACTS

Time and place written: 1865–1866; St. Petersburg, Russia

Date of first publication: 1866 in serial form in *The Russian Messenger*; 1867 in book form

Publisher: Bazanov

Type of work: Novel

Genre: Psychological drama; novel of ideas

Language: Russian

Setting (time): 1860s

Setting (place): St. Petersburg; a prison in Siberia

Tense: Past

Tone: Tragic, emotional, melodramatic, critical, despairing, fatalistic, confessional

Narrator: Third-person omniscient narrator

Point of view: Raskolnikov's

Protagonist: Raskolnikov

Antagonist: Luzhin, Porfiry Petrovich, Svidrigailov, Raskolnikov's conscience

CRIME AND PUNISHMENT: PLOT OVERVIEW

Rodion Romanovich Raskolnikov, a former student, lives in a tiny garret on the top floor of a run-down apartment building in St. Petersburg. He is sickly, dressed in rags, and short on money, but he is also handsome, proud, and intelligent. He contemplates committing an awful crime, the nature of which is not yet clear. Raskolnikov goes to the apartment of an old pawnbroker, Alyona Ivanovna, to get money for a watch and to plan the crime. Afterward, he stops for a drink at a tavern, where he meets a man named Marmeladov who abandoned his job in a fit of drunkenness and is now in the midst of a five-day drinking binge. Marmeladov's daughter, Sonya, has been forced into prostitution to support the family. At Marmeladov's squalid apartment, Raskolnikov meets Katerina Ivanovna, Marmeladov's sickly wife.

The next day, Raskolnikov receives a letter from his mother, Pulcheria Alexandrovna, informing him that his sister, Dunya, is engaged to be married to a government official named Luzhin and that they are all moving to St. Petersburg. At a tavern, Raskolnikov overhears a student saying that society would be better off if the old pawnbroker Alyona Ivanovna were dead. The next night Raskolnikov goes to Alyonya's apartment and kills her with an ax. Alyonya's sister Lizaveta walks in, and Raskolnikov kills her too. In a state of shock, Raskolnikov dawdles and barely escapes from the apartment undetected.

The next day, the police summon Raskolnikov on an unrelated matter. During a conversation about the murders, Raskolnikov faints, and the police begin to suspect him. Raskolnikov falls into fever and delirium that last for four days. He wakes up to find out that his housekeeper, Nastasya, and Razumikhin have been taking care of him. Zossimov, a doctor, and Zamyotov, a young police detective, have also been visiting him.

Luzhin, Dunya's fiancé, visits Raskolnikov. Marmeladov is run over by a carriage and dies. Raskolnikov meets Sonya and gives the family twenty rubles that he received from his mother. Raskolnikov's sister and mother visit him. Raskolnikov commands Dunya to break her engagement with Luzhin.

Under the pretense of trying to recover a watch he pawned, Raskolnikov visits the magistrate in charge of the murder investigation, Porfiry Petrovich, a relative of Razumikhin's. Raskolnikov and Porfiry have a tense conversation about the murders. Raskolnikov starts to believe that Porfiry suspects him.

Svidrigailov comes to Raskolnikov's apartment and explains that he would like Dunya to break her engagement with Luzhin. He offers to give Dunya the enormous sum of ten thousand rubles. He also tells Raskolnikov that his late wife, Marfa Petrovna, left Dunya three thousand rubles in her will. Raskolnikov rejects Svidrigailov's offer of money. After hearing Svidrigailov talk about seeing the ghost of Marfa, Raskolnikov suspects that he is insane.

Raskolnikov and Razumikhin walk to a restaurant to meet Dunya, Pulcheria Alexandrovna, and Luzhin. Luzhin and Raskolnikov argue. Luzhin offends everyone in the room, including his fiancée and prospective mother-in-law. Dunya breaks off the engagement and Luzhin leaves, humiliated. Raskolnikov ruins the mood of relief by saying he does not want to see his family anymore. Razumikhin looks Raskolnikov in the eye and realizes, even though not a word is spoken, that Raskolnikov is guilty of the murders.

Raskolnikov goes to Sonya's apartment. He learns that Sonya was a friend of Lizaveta, one of the women he killed. He forces Sonya to read to him the biblical story of Lazarus. Svidrigailov eavesdrops from the apartment next door. The following morning, a workman named Nikolai confesses to the murders.

Katerina has a memorial dinner for her husband. The gathering goes poorly. Few guests show up, and, except for Raskolnikov, those that do are drunk and crude. Luzhin comes in and accuses Sonya of stealing a one-hundred-ruble bill. Lebezyatnikov, Luzhin's roommate, enters and tells everyone that he saw Luzhin slip the bill into Sonya's pocket.

After the dinner, Raskolnikov goes to Sonya's room and confesses that he is the murderer. Sonya urges him to tell to the authorities. Lebezyatnikov enters and informs them that Katerina Ivanovna seems to have gone mad—she is parading her children in the streets and begging for money. Katerina collapses after a confrontation with a policeman and soon dies. Svidrigailov appears and offers to pay for the funeral and the care of the children. He reveals to Raskolnikov that he knows of his crimes.

Razumikhin confronts Raskolnikov, asking him whether he has gone mad and telling him of the pain that he has caused his mother and sister. Porfiry Petrovich appears and says he does not believe Nikolai's confession, but he does not have enough evidence to arrest Raskolnikov. Raskolnikov goes out and finds Svidrigailov in a café. Svidrigailov tells him that although he is still attracted to Dunya, he has gotten engaged to a sixteen-year-old girl.

Svidrigailov manages to bring Dunya to his room, where he threatens to rape her after she refuses to marry him. She fires several shots at him with a revolver and misses. He allows her to leave. Taking the revolver, Svidrigailov wanders aimlessly around St. Petersburg. He gives three thousand rubles to Dunya and fifteen thousand rubles to the family of his fiancée. He checks into a hotel, where he sleeps fitfully and dreams of a flood and a seductive five-year-old girl. In the morning, he kills himself.

Raskolnikov visits his mother, tells her that he will always love her, and then goes to Dunya and tells her he is planning to confess. He goes to visit Sonya, who gives him a cross to wear. Raskolnikov almost refrains from confessing when he learns of Svidrigailov's suicide, but the sight of Sonya convinces him to go through with it.

A year and a half later, Raskolnikov is in prison in Siberia, where he has been for nine months. Sonya has moved to the town outside the prison. She visits Raskolnikov regularly and tries to ease his burden. Because of his confession, his mental confusion, and testimony about his past good deeds, Raskolnikov has received a sentence of eight years of hard labor instead of a death sentence. Raskolnikov's mother has died. Razumikhin and Dunya have married. For a short while, Raskolnikov remains as proud and alienated from humanity as he was before his confession, but he eventually realizes that he truly loves Sonya and expresses remorse for his crime.

CHARACTERS IN *CRIME AND PUNISHMENT*

A NOTE ON RUSSIAN NAMES

Russians have three names: a first name, a patronymic, and a surname. The patronymic is the father's first name with a suffix meaning "son of" or "daughter of": for example, Sofya Semyonovna (daughter of Semyon). In formal address, people are called by both their first names and their patronymics. In informal address, people are sometimes called by nicknames, or diminutives. For instance, Polina Mikhailovna Marmeladov is sometimes called Polya, Polenka, and Polechka, and Rodion Romanovich Raskolnikov is sometimes called Rodya, Rodka. Surnames reflect gender.

Nikolai (Mikolka) Dementiev   A painter. Nikolai was working in an empty apartment next to Alyona Ivanovna's on the day of the murders. He makes a false confession because his religion teaches that redemption is reached through suffering.

Alyona Ivanovna   An old, withered pawnbroker. She cheats the poor out of their money and mistreats her sister, Lizaveta. Raskolnikov kills Alyona.

Lizaveta Ivanovna   Alyona Ivanovna's sister. Lizaveta is simple-minded, and Alyona treats her like a servant.

Andrei Semyonovich Lebezyatnikov   Luzhin's grudging roommate. Lebezyatnikov believes in the "new philosophies," such as nihilism, that are raging through St. Petersburg. Although he is self-centered, confused, and immature, he has a few basic scruples.

Pyotr Petrovich Luzhin   Dunya's fiancé. Luzhin is stingy, narrow-minded, and self-absorbed. He longs to marry a beautiful, intelligent, but desperately poor girl like Dunya so that she will be indebted to him forever.

Katerina Ivanovna Marmeladov   Marmeladov's wife. Katerina Ivanovna has consumption, which gives her a persistent, bloody cough. She is very proud and repeatedly speaks of her aristocratic heritage.

Polina (Polya, Polenka,Polechka) Mikhailovna Marmeladov   Katerina Ivanovna's daughter from her former marriage.

Semyon Zakharovich Marmeladov   An alcoholic public official. Marmeladov understands that his drinking is ruining himself and his family, but he cannot change. He dies after falling under the wheels of a carriage, perhaps in a drunken accident or perhaps in a suicide.

Sofya (Sonya, Sonechka) Semyonovna Marmeladov   Raskolnikov's love and Marmeladov's daughter. Sonya is forced to prostitute herself to support her family. She is meek and easily embarrassed, but her strong religious faith supports her. She is the only person with whom Raskolnikov has a meaningful relationship.

Ilya (Gunpowder) Petrovich   A police official. Raskolnikov encounters Petrovich after committing the murder and confesses to him at the end of the novel. Ilya Petrovich gets his nickname, Gunpowder, from his obliviousness and sudden bouts of temper.

Nastasya (Nastenka, Nastasyushka) Petrovna   A servant in the house where Raskolnikov rents his room.

Porfiry Petrovich   The magistrate in charge of investigating the murders. Porfiry Petrovich has a shrewd understanding of criminal psychology and perfectly understands Raskolnikov's mental state at every moment.

Avdotya (Dunya, Dunechka) Romanovna Raskolnikov   Raskolnikov's sister. Dunya is as intelligent, proud, and good-looking as her brother, but unlike him she is consistently moral and compassionate. She is decisive and brave, ending her engagement with Luzhin when he insults her family and fending off Svidrigailov with a gun.

Pulcheria Alexandrovna Raskolnikov   Raskolnikov's mother. Pulcheria Alexandrovna is deeply devoted to her son and willing to sacrifice everything, even her own and her daughter's happiness, to give him a chance at success.

Rodion (Rodya, Rodka) Romanovich Raskolnikov   The protagonist of the novel. A former student, Raskolnikov is now destitute. He believes that, as Utilitarian theory suggests, an evil action is justified if it leads to an ultimate good. He also believes that certain extraordinary men can commit such evil actions without qualms. Raskolnikov murders the pawnbroker in an attempt to prove to himself that he is such an extraordinary man.

Dmitri Prokofych Razumikhin   Raskolnikov's friend. Razumikhin, Raskolnikov's foil, is kind and amicable where Raskolnikov is selfish and alienated. His name comes from the Russian word razum, which means "reason" or "intelligence."

Arkady Ivanovich Svidrigailov   Dunya's depraved former employer. Svidrigailov longs for Dunya's love.

Alexander Grigorievich Zamyotov A junior official in the police station. Zamyotov suspects Raskolnikov of the murders.

Zossimov Raskolnikov's doctor and a friend of Razumikhin's. Zossimov is a young, self-congratulating man who has little insight into his patient's condition. He suspects that Raskolnikov is mentally ill.

THEMES IN *CRIME AND PUNISHMENT*

ALIENATION FROM SOCIETY Alienation is the primary theme of *Crime and Punishment*. At first, Raskolnikov's pride separates him from society. He sees himself as superior to all other people and so cannot relate to anyone. His personal philosophy is that other people are tools he must use for his own ends. After murdering Alyona and Lizaveta, his isolation grows because of his intense guilt and the delirium into which his guilt throws him. With oppressive regularity, Raskolnikov pushes away the people who are trying to help him, including Sonya, Dunya, Pulcheria Alexandrovna, Razumikhin, and even Porfiry Petrovich. He always suffers because of this unwillingness to accept help. In the end, Raskolnikov cannot tolerate the total alienation that he has brought upon himself. In the Epilogue, when he finally realizes that he loves Sonya, Raskolnikov breaks through the wall of pride and self-centeredness that has separated him from society.

THE MISGUIDED IDEA OF THE SUPERMAN At the beginning of the novel, Raskolnikov sees himself as a "superman," an extraordinary person who understands events in a broad context and stands above the moral rules that govern the rest of humanity. He murders the pawnbroker partly to establish the truth of his superiority. Raskolnikov's inability to quell his subsequent feelings of guilt, however, proves to him that he is not a "superman." In part because he is embarrassed by this realization, he lashes out at his friends and family, refusing to accept their help. He cannot quite let go of the conviction that he is extraordinary in some way, and resists the idea that he is just as mediocre as the rest of humanity by telling himself that the murder was justified. Only in his final surrender to his love for Sonya and his realization that the surrender is joyful does he finally escape his oppressive conception of himself as a superman.

THE PSYCHOLOGY OF CRIME AND PUNISHMENT Dostoevsky addresses crime and punishment in an unexpected fashion. The crime is committed in Part I and the punishment comes hundreds of pages later, in the Epilogue. The real focus of the novel is not on those two endpoints but on what lies between them: the psychology of a criminal. The inner world of Raskolnikov, with its doubts, deliria, second-guessing, fear, and despair, is the heart of the story. Dostoevsky concerns himself not with the actual repercussions of the murder but with the philosophy that causes Raskolnikov to murder and the tormenting guilt that follows the murder. Dostoevsky suggests that actual punishment is much less terrible than the stress and anxiety of trying to avoid punishment. In fact, it is over the course of his punishment that Raskolnikov finds peace. Porfiry Petrovich succeeds at his job by studying criminal psychology. He shows genuine interest, as one theorist to another, in Raskolnikov's ideas about the criminal tendencies of the extraordinary man. Petrovich understands that a guilt-ridden criminal will experience mental torture, and feels certain that Raskolnikov will eventually confess or go mad.

SYMBOLS IN *CRIME AND PUNISHMENT*

THE CITY St. Petersburg, which Dostoevsky portrays as dirty and crowded, represents Raskolnikov's mental state. In the city, drunks sprawl on the street in broad daylight, consumptive women beat their children and beg for money, and everyone lives in tiny, noisy apartments. The city causes, and then represents, Raskolnikov's delirious, agitated state. St. Petersburg's heat, odor, crowds, and disorder rattle Raskolnikov. Only when he is forcefully removed from the city to a prison in a small town in Siberia does he find calm.

THE CROSS Sonya's cross, which once belonged to Lizaveta, symbolizes the burden Raskolnikov must bear. This symbolism comes from the Bible, in which Christ bears his cross as he bore his own and the world's suffering. When Sonya tells him they will bear the cross together, she is taking part of Raskolnikov's burden onto herself. She also connects herself to Lizaveta, as does Raskolnikov when he realizes that Sonya's frightened face reminds him of Lizaveta's face. The cross now connects all three of them, creating a holy trinity of sorts.

IMPORTANT QUOTATIONS FROM *CRIME AND PUNISHMENT*

I've known Rodion [Raskolnikov] for a year and a half: sullen, gloomy, arrogant, proud; recently (and maybe much earlier) insecure and hypochondriac. Magnanimous and kind. Doesn't like voicing his feelings, and would rather do something cruel than speak his heart out in words. At times, however, he's not hypochondriac at all, but just inhumanly cold and callous, as if there really were two opposite characters in him, changing places with each other. At times he's terribly taciturn! He's always in a hurry, always too busy, yet he lies there doing nothing. Not given to mockery, and not because he lacks sharpness but as if he had no time for such trifles. Never hears people out to the end. Is never interested in what interests everyone else at a given moment. Sets a terribly high value on himself and, it seems, not without a certain justification.

Location: Part III, Chapter II
Speaker: Razumikhin
Context: Razumikhin describes Raskolnikov to Sonya and Pulcheria Alexandrovna

Razumikhin emphasizes Raskolnikov's key character traits: self-centeredness, intelligence, and alternating cruelty and kindness. He describes Raskolnikov as possessing "two opposite characters," one dark and depressed, the other proud and confident. Dostoevsky's use of the phrase "two opposite characters" seems clairvoyant, or at least eerily ahead of his time. Austrian psychoanalyst Sigmund Freud theorized about split personalities at the turn of the century, and psychological illnesses known as multiple personality disorder and dissociative personality disorder became well-known in the latter half of the twentieth century. With his distinct personalities, Raskolnikov could be a case study in these sorts of disorders. The idea that he is one man with two characters also points to the unrelenting tension that Raskolnikov experiences as a result of his conflicting desires.

The old woman was a mistake perhaps, but she's not the point! The old woman was merely a sickness . . . I was in a hurry to step over . . . it wasn't a human being I killed, it was a principle! So I killed the principle, but I didn't step over, I stayed on this side.. . . All I managed to do was kill. And I didn't even manage that, as it turns out.

Location: Part III, Chapter VI
Speaker: Raskolnikov
Context: Lying in bed, Raskolnikov thinks about his crime

The abrupt phrases and frequent use of ellipses in this passage reflects Raskolnikov's fractured state of mind. After his meeting with Porfiry, his rational justification for the murder is deteriorating rapidly as his conscience takes over. Raskolnikov is shaken by Porfiry's suspicions and intellectual appraisal of the extraordinary man theory. Raskolnikov no longer sees himself as an extraordinary man and is ashamed to recall that he compared himself to Napoleon. Reexamining his motives for the crime, he concludes that the murder is just one effort of the many he could have made to help his family. He realizes that he is not extraordinary enough to see the theory through to the end and that he could not have benefited humanity with his one puny act. He understands that he did not succeed in proving his theory correct and that he is currently failing to act as a superman would.

What was taking place in him was totally unfamiliar, new, sudden, never before experienced. Not that he understood it, but he sensed clearly, with all the power of sensation, that it was no longer possible for him to address these people in the police station, not only with heartfelt effusions, as he had just done, but in any way at all, and had they been his own brothers and sisters, and not police lieutenants, there would still have been no point in this addressing them, in whatever circumstances of life.

Location: Part II, Chapter I
Speaker: The narrator
Context: Raskolnikov realizes that the murders have isolated him from society

---

What is it, to run away! A mere formality; that's not the main thing; no, he won't run away on me by a law of nature, even if he has somewhere to run to. Have you ever seen a moth near a candle? Well, so he'll keep circling around me, circling around me, as around a candle; freedom will no longer be dear to him, he'll fall to thinking, get entangled, he'll tangle himself all up as in a net, he'll worry himself to death!. . . he'll keep on making circles around me, narrowing the radius more and more, and—whop! He'll fly right into my mouth, and I'll swallow him, sir, and that will be most agreeable, heh, heh, heh!

Location: Part IV, Chapter V
Speaker: Porfiry Petrovich
Context: Petrovich predicts Raskolnikov's behavior

How it happened he himself did not know, but suddenly it was as if something lifted him and flung him down at her feet. He wept and embraced her knees. For the first moment she was terribly frightened, and her whole face went numb. She jumped up and looked at him, trembling. But all at once, in that same moment, she understood everything. Infinite happiness lit up in her eyes; she understood, and for her there was no longer any doubt that he loved her, loved her infinitely, and that at last the moment had come.

Location: The Epilogue
Speaker: The narrator
Context: Sonya realizes that Raskolnikov truly loves her

THE CRUCIBLE

Arthur Miller

Hysteria grips the residents of Salem, Massachusetts, who try their neighbors as witches and execute nineteen people.

THE LIFE OF ARTHUR MILLER

Arthur Miller was born in New York City on October 17, 1915. His career as a playwright began while he was a student at the University of Michigan. Several of his early works won prizes, and during his senior year, the Federal Theatre Project in Detroit performed one of his works. He produced his first great success, *All My Sons*, in 1947. Two years later, in 1949, Miller wrote *Death of a Salesman*, which won the Pulitzer Prize and made Miller a national sensation. Many critics described *Death of a Salesman* as the first great American tragedy, and Miller was hailed as an artist who understood the essence of the United States. He has won the New York Drama Critics Circle Award twice, and his *Broken Glass* (1993) won the Olivier Award for Best Play of the London Season.

THE CRUCIBLE IN CONTEXT

Miller composed *The Crucible* in the early 1950s. From research he had done as an undergraduate, he knew that in 1692, in the small Massachusetts village of Salem, girls began having hallucinations and seizures. At that time, New England was intensely Puritan, and frightening or surprising occurrences were often attributed to the devil or his cohorts. It was not long before the sick girls, followed by other Salem residents, accused people of consorting with devils and casting spells. Hysteria took hold, and people vented old grudges and jealousies by making accusations of witchcraft. The Massachusetts government and judicial system stepped in, and within a few weeks, dozens of people were jailed on charges of witchcraft. By the time the fever had run its course, in late August 1692, nineteen people (and two dogs) had been convicted and hanged for witchcraft.

The general outline of events in *The Crucible* corresponds to what happened in Salem in 1692, but Miller's characters are often composites. Furthermore, his central plot device—the affair between Abigail Williams and John Proctor—has no grounding in fact. The historical Proctor was over sixty at the time of the trials, while Abigail was only eleven.

The Crucible, while most obviously about the Salem witch trials, was also influenced by the Communist hunt conducted by Senator Joseph McCarthy. During the first years of the Cold War, McCarthy's frenzied anti-Communism propelled the United States into a dramatic anti-Communist fervor. Led by McCarthy, special congressional committees conducted highly controversial investigations intended to root out Communist sympathizers in the United States. As with the alleged witches of Salem, suspected Communists were encouraged to confess and to identify other Red sympathizers as means of escaping punishment. The policy resulted in a whirlwind of accusations. As people realized that they might be condemned as Communists regardless of their true political affiliations, many attempted to save themselves by making false confessions. These confessions perpetuated the hysteria by creating the impression that the United States was overrun with Communists.

The liberal entertainment industry, in which Miller worked, was one of the chief targets of these Communist "witch hunts," as their opponents termed them. Some members of the entertainment industry cooperated. Others, like Miller, refused to give in to questioning. Those who were revealed, falsely or legitimately, as Communists, and those who refused to incriminate their friends, were blacklisted from potential jobs for many years afterward.

At the time of its first performance, in January 1953, critics and cast alike perceived *The Crucible* as a direct attack on McCarthyism. Its comparatively short run, compared with those of Miller's other works, was blamed on anti-Communist fervor. But the play is less a direct allegory of the McCarthy era than a lasting commentary on the way mass hysteria, power hunger, and unwavering moral convictions can combine and result in tragedy. *The Crucible* is best read outside its historical context—not as a perfect allegory for anti-Communism, or as a faithful account of the Salem trials, but as a timeless play about universal themes.

THE CRUCIBLE: KEY FACTS

Time and place written: Early 1950s; America

Date of first publication: 1953

Publisher: Viking Press

Type of work: Play

Genre: Tragedy; allegory; courtroom drama

Language: English

Setting (time): 1692

Setting (place): Salem, Massachusetts

Tense: Present

Tone: Serious, tragic, almost Biblical

Narrator: The play is occasionally interrupted by an omniscient, third-person narrator

Point of view: Generally John Proctor's

Protagonist: John Proctor

Antagonist: Abigail Williams

THE CRUCIBLE: PLOT OVERVIEW

In the Puritan New England town of Salem, Massachusetts, a group of girls dances in the forest with a black slave named Tituba. The local minister, Reverend Parris, catches them dancing. Parris's daughter Betty falls into a coma-like state. A crowd gathers in the Parris home, and rumors of witchcraft fill the town. After sending for Reverend Hale, an expert on witchcraft, Parris questions Abigail Williams, the girls' ringleader, about what happened in the forest. Abigail, who is Parris's niece and ward, says nothing happened beyond "dancing."

While Parris tries to calm the crowd that has gathered in his home, Abigail tells the other girls not to admit anything. John Proctor, a local farmer, enters and talks to Abigail alone. Abigail worked in Proctor's home the previous year. She and Proctor had an affair. Elizabeth, Proctor's wife, found out and fired Abigail. No one else knows of the affair. Abigail still wants Proctor, but he fends her off and tells her to end her foolishness with the girls.

Betty wakes up and screams. The crowd rushes upstairs and gathers in her bedroom, arguing about whether she is bewitched. Proctor, Parris, the argumentative Giles Corey, and the wealthy Thomas Putnam argue about money and land deeds. Their quarrel suggests that old controversies are festering in the Salem community.

Reverend Hale arrives and examines Betty. Proctor leaves. Hale quizzes Abigail about the girls' activities in the forest. Suspicious of her behavior, he demands to speak to Tituba. Tituba confesses to communing with the devil and hysterically accuses various townspeople of consorting with the devil. Abigail joins in, saying she saw the devil conspiring with other townspeople. Betty joins them in naming witches. The crowd is thrown into an uproar.

A week later, alone in their farmhouse outside of town, John and Elizabeth Proctor discuss the witch trials and the increasing number of townsfolk accused of being witches. Elizabeth urges her husband to denounce Abigail as a fraud. He refuses, and she accuses him of harboring feelings for Abigail. Mary Warren, their servant and one of Abigail's friends, returns from Salem with news that Elizabeth has been accused of witchcraft but the court did not pursue the accusation. Mary is sent up to bed, and John and Elizabeth continue their argument. Reverend Hale arrives at their house. Giles Corey and Francis Nurse arrive soon after and announce that their wives have been arrested. Officers of the court appear and arrest Elizabeth. Proctor browbeats Mary, insisting that she go to Salem and expose Abigail and the other girls as frauds.

The next day, Proctor brings Mary to court and tells Judge Danforth that she will testify to the girls' fraudulence. Danforth is suspicious of Proctor's motives. He tells Proctor, truthfully, that Elizabeth is pregnant and will be spared for a time. Danforth allows Mary to testify. She tells the court that the girls are lying, but the girls are brought in and accuse Mary of bewitching them. Furious, Proctor confesses to his affair with Abigail and says jealousy of Elizabeth is driving her. To test Proctor's claim, Danforth summons Elizabeth and asks her if Proctor has been unfaithful to her. Despite her natural honesty, she lies to protect Proctor's honor. Danforth denounces Proctor as a liar. Abigail and the girls again pretend that Mary is bewitching them, and Mary breaks down and accuses Proctor of being a witch. Proctor rages against her and against the court. He is arrested.

The summer passes and autumn arrives. The witch trials have caused unrest in neighboring towns, and Danforth grows nervous. Abigail has run away, taking all of Parris's money with her. Hale, who has lost faith in the court, begs the accused witches to confess falsely in order to save their lives, but they refuse. Danforth persuades Elizabeth to talk John into confessing. Conflicted, but desperate to live, John agrees to confess, and the officers of the court rejoice. But when the court insists that he incriminate others and make his confession public, Proctor grows angry, tears up his confession, and retracts his admission of guilt. Despite Hale's desperate pleas, Proctor goes to the gallows with the others, and the witch trials reach their awful conclusion.

CHARACTERS IN *THE CRUCIBLE*

Ezekiel Cheever A man who acts as clerk of the court during the witch trials. He is upright and determined to do his duty.

Giles Corey An elderly but feisty farmer, famous for his tendency to file lawsuits. Giles is held in contempt of court and pressed to death with large stones. With his last breath, he defiantly calls for "more weight."

Martha Corey Giles Corey's third wife. Martha's reading habits lead to her arrest and conviction for witchcraft.

Judge Danforth The Deputy Governor of Massachusetts and the presiding judge at the witch trials. Honest and scrupulous, at least in his own mind, Danforth is convinced that he is right to root out witchcraft.

Reverend John Hale A young minister reputed to be an expert on witchcraft. Hale is a committed Christian and hater of witchcraft, but his intelligence saves him from blind fervor. His arrival in Salem sets the hysteria in motion. He later regrets his actions and attempts to save the lives of those accused.

Judge Hathorne A judge who presides, along with Danforth, over the witch trials.

Herrick The marshal of Salem.

Mercy Lewis The servant in Thomas Putnam's household. Mercy is friends with Abigail.

Francis Nurse A wealthy, influential man in Salem. Most people respect Nurse, but Thomas Putnam and his wife dislike him.

Rebecca Nurse Francis Nurse's wife. Rebecca is a wise, sensible, and upright woman held in tremendous regard by most of the Salem community. The Putnams accuse her of witchcraft and she refuses to confess.

Betty Parris Reverend Parris's ten-year-old daughter. Betty's strange stupor fuels the first rumors of witchcraft.

Reverend Parris The minister of Salem's church. Reverend Parris is a paranoid, power-hungry, yet oddly self-pitying figure. Many of the townsfolk, especially John Proctor, dislike him, and Parris is very concerned with building his position in the community.

Elizabeth Proctor John Proctor's wife. Elizabeth is supremely virtuous, but often cold.

John Proctor A local farmer. Stern and principled, John hates hypocrisy. His affair with Abigail is his downfall. At first he hesitates to expose Abigail as a fraud because he worries that his secret will be revealed and his good name ruined.

Ann Putnam   Thomas Putnam's wife. Ann Putnam has given birth to eight children, only one of whom survived. The other seven died before they were a day old, which Ann attributes to supernatural forces.

Ruth Putnam   The Putnams' lone surviving child. Like Betty Parris, Ruth falls into a strange stupor.

Thomas Putnam   A wealthy, influential citizen of Salem. Putnam holds a grudge against Francis Nurse. He increases his own wealth by accusing people of witchcraft and then buying up their land.

Tituba   Reverend Parris's black slave from Barbados. Tituba agrees to perform voodoo at Abigail's request.

Mary Warren   The servant in John Proctor's household and a friend of Abigail's. Mary is a timid girl, easily influenced by others.

Abigail Williams   Reverend Parris's niece. Abigail is smart, wily, sexual, and vindictive when crossed.

THEMES IN *THE CRUCIBLE*

INTOLERANCE   *The Crucible* is set in a theocratic society, which means church and the state are one, and there is no difference between moral law and state law. In a theocracy, private sinning is a matter of public concern. There is no room for deviation from social norms, since any individual who doesn't follow established moral laws is a threat not only to the public good but also to the rule of God. In Salem, everyone belongs either to God or to the Devil, and dissenters are not just unlawful, but satanic. As Danforth says in Act III, "a person is either with this court or he must be counted against it." The witch trials are the ultimate expression of intolerance, and hanging witches is the ultimate restoration of the community's purity. The trials brand all social deviants—those who have sex too much, those who sue too much, those who read too much—with the taint of devil worship and thus justify their murders.

HYSTERIA   Hysteria can tear apart a community, replacing logic and convincing people that their little grudges are sanctioned by God himself. In the grip of hysteria, people believe that their neighbors are committing absurd and unbelievable crimes—communing with the devil, killing babies, and so on. The townsfolk accept the witch hunt not only out of genuine religious piety but also out of a desire to express repressed sentiments and act on long-held grudges. Claiming to be motivated by piety and righteousness, Abigail revenges herself on her sexual rival, Reverend Parris solidifies his power, and Thomas Putnam satisfies his grudge against Francis Nurse.

EMPOWERMENT   The witch trials empower the young women who set them in motion. In general, women occupy the lowest rung of male-dominated Salem society and have few options in life. They work as servants for townsmen until they are old enough to be married off and have children of their own. Their sexual rights are virtually nonexistent. Abigail, for example, is slave to John Proctor's sexual whims. He strips away her innocence and reputation by deflowering her, terminates the affair against her wishes, and refuses to listen to her expressions of pain and longing. Among the hundreds of theories that exist to explain the Salem witch trials, one suggests that the girls in Salem were reacting against their oppression, sexual repression, and near-invisibility.

SYMBOLS IN *THE CRUCIBLE*

THE WITCH TRIALS   There is little symbolism in *The Crucible*, but the play itself can be seen as symbolic of the McCarthy trials.

IMPORTANT QUOTATIONS FROM *THE CRUCIBLE*

I look for John Proctor that took me from my sleep and put knowledge in my heart! I never knew what pretense Salem was, I never knew the lying lessons I was taught by all these Christian women and their covenanted men! And now you bid me tear the light out of my eyes? I will not, I cannot! You loved me, John Proctor, and whatever sin it is, you love me yet!

Location: Act I
Speaker: Abigail Williams
Context: Abigail confronts Proctor about their affair

Abigail treats Elizabeth cruelly, and deals in death without flinching, but the anger that motivates her is understandable. Proctor stole her innocence and "put knowledge in [her] heart," and now he turns away from her in anger. He is partly responsible for her emotional state, no matter how desperately he wants to forget their affair. Proctor gave her not only carnal knowledge, but knowledge of Salem. He provided her with the motive and the justification for tearing down prominent citizens. When Abigail says, "I never knew what pretense Salem was, I never knew the lying lessons I was taught," she means she never knew until he enlightened her.

You must understand, sir, that a person is either with this court or he must be counted against it, there be no road between. This is a sharp time, now, a precise time—we live no longer in the dusky afternoon when evil mixed itself with good and befuddled the world. Now, by God's grace, the shining sun is up, and them that fear not light will surely praise it.

Location: Act III
Speaker: Judge Danforth
Context: Danforth expresses his simplistic views of good and evil

In a theocracy, one cannot have honest disagreements, because God is infallible, and that which is called godly is automatically placed above criticism. Danforth's words show the terrible danger of deep religious conviction. When you believe that God is on your side, as Danforth does, you believe that your actions are holy and that anyone who thinks differently than you do is evil or ignorant. Danforth is an honorable man, but the strength of his self-confidence is terrifying. In his mind, the court and government of Massachusetts, and their servants, are sanctioned by God. Since the court is conducting the witch trials, anyone who questions the trials is the court's enemy and the Devil's friend.

I want to open myself!. . . I want the light of God, I want the sweet love of Jesus! I danced for the Devil; I saw him, I wrote in his book; I go back to Jesus; I kiss His hand. I saw Sarah Good with the Devil! I saw Goody Osburn with the Devil! I saw Bridget Bishop with the Devil!

Speaker: Abigail Williams
Location: The end of Act I
Context: Tituba has confessed to witchcraft, and Abigail joins in

---

A man may think God sleeps, but God sees everything, I know it now. I beg you, sir, I beg you—see her what she is.... She thinks to dance with me on my wife's grave! And well she might, for I thought of her softly. God help me, I lusted, and there is a promise in such sweat. But it is a whore's vengeance. . . .

Location: Act III
Speaker: John Proctor
Context: Proctor has tried and failed to expose Abigail as a fraud without revealing their affair

Because it is my name! Because I cannot have another in my life! Because I lie and sign myself to lies! Because I am not worth the dust on the feet of them that hang! How may I live without my name? I have given you my soul; leave me my name!

Location: Act IV
Speaker: John Proctor
Context: The court has asked Proctor to make his confession public

CRY, THE BELOVED COUNTRY

Alan Paton

A black South African discovers that his son has murdered a man after leaving his home village for Johannesburg.

THE LIFE OF ALAN PATON

Alan Paton was born in the South African city of Pietermaritzburg on January 11, 1903, to a Scottish father and a South African mother of English heritage. Paton attended Natal University, where, among other activities, he wrote poetry and served as student body president. At age twenty-two, he became a teacher at two of South Africa's elite, all-white schools, first in the village of Ixopo, then in Pietermaritzburg. Ten years later, he left teaching to pursue a career as a reformatory worker. He was appointed principal of the Diepkloof Reformatory, a prison school for black youths. At the reformatory, Paton attempted to loosen the restrictions placed on the youths and emphasized preparation for life outside the reformatory walls. He also traveled extensively to study reformatory schools worldwide. It was on one such trip, shortly after World War II, that he wrote *Cry, the Beloved Country*, the novel that earned him his fame as an author.

Cry, the Beloved Country was published in 1948 to overwhelming international acclaim. At the time of Paton's death in 1988, more than fifteen million copies of the novel had been sold, and it had been published in twenty different languages. In Paton's native South Africa, however, praise for *Cry, the Beloved Country* was muted. The novel's objective take on racial inequality in South Africa created great controversy. Paton's subsequent novels, *Too Late the Phalarope* (1953) and *Ah, But Your Land Is Beautiful* (1981), failed to generate the same excitement as *Cry, the Beloved Country*. Nevertheless, he is considered one of South Africa's greatest writers.

CRY, THE BELOVED COUNTRY IN CONTEXT

Cry, the Beloved Country is set in South Africa in the 1940s. Its story unfolds against a backdrop of economic and political tensions that have a lengthy, complicated history. Thousands of years before the first Europeans arrived there, southern Africa was populated by various African tribal groups, including the San, the Khoikhoi, and, later on, Bantu-speaking peoples who were ancestors of the modern Zulus. The first European settlers in South Africa, the Dutch, arrived in the mid-1600s. By the mid-1700s, the Dutch, who had come to be known as the Boers and who had developed their own language, Afrikaans, had become entrenched in the country. They forced African tribes off their traditional lands, decimated them with disease, and defeated them in battles.

English settlers arrived in 1795. By the early 1800s, they decided to make South Africa a colony. The Boers fought a number of bloody battles with the Zulus and ultimately defeated them. The Boers created several independent republics. When diamonds and gold were discovered in the Boer territories, the British moved to annex them, leading to the first Anglo-Boer war in 1881. The second Anglo-Boer war, also fought over gold, lasted from 1899 to 1902. The British were victorious. In 1910, they officially established the Union of South Africa.

Cry, the Beloved Country takes place after these upheavals and immediately before the 1948 implementation of apartheid, South Africa's infamous system of racial segregation. During the time in which the novel is set, black workers could hold only unskilled jobs and could not travel freely. In 1913, the Natives Land Act radically limited the amount of land that black South Africans were permitted to own. As the character Arthur Jarvis states in the novel, just one-tenth of the land was set aside for four-fifths of the country's people. The resultant overcrowding led many black South Africans to migrate to Johannesburg to work in the mines, where they were exploited.

In 1948, the National Party (representing Afrikaner and conservative interests) came to power and introduced apartheid. Under apartheid, every South African was classified according to race, and blacks were segregated from whites. Under the leadership of Nelson Mandela, the African National Congress (ANC) began protesting against the new laws. After decades of struggle and bloodshed, the ANC prevailed, and South Africa held its first free election in 1994. Mandela was elected president, apartheid was dismantled, and the country ratified one of the most liberal constitutions in the world.

CRY, THE BELOVED COUNTRY: KEY FACTS

Time and place written: 1946; various parts of Europe and the United States

Date of first publication: 1948

Publisher: Charles Scribner

Type of work: Novel

Genre: Quest; courtroom drama; social criticism

Language: English

Setting (time): Mid-1940s, just after World War II

Setting (place): Ndotsheni and Johannesburg, South Africa

Tense: Past

Tone: Lyrical, grieving, elegiac, occasionally bitter

Narrator: Third-person omniscient

Point of view: Books I and III are told largely from Kumalo's point of view; Book II is told largely from Jarvis's point of view

Protagonist: Stephen Kumalo; James Jarvis

Antagonist: White oppression, the corrupting influences of city life

CRY, THE BELOVED COUNTRY: PLOT OVERVIEW

In the remote village of Ndotsheni, in the Natal province of eastern South Africa, the Reverend Stephen Kumalo receives a letter from a fellow minister summoning him to Johannesburg, a city in South Africa. He is needed there, the letter says, to help his sister, Gertrude, who has fallen ill. Kumalo undertakes the difficult and expensive journey to the city in the hopes of aiding Gertrude and of finding his son, Absalom, who traveled to Johannesburg from Ndotsheni and never returned. In Johannesburg, Kumalo is warmly welcomed by Msimangu, the priest who sent him the letter, and given comfortable lodging by Mrs. Lithebe, a Christian woman who feels that helping others is her duty. Kumalo visits Gertrude, who is now a prostitute and liquor-seller, and persuades her to come back to Ndotsheni with her young son.

A more difficult quest follows when Kumalo and Msimangu begin searching the labyrinthine metropolis of Johannesburg for Absalom. They visit Kumalo's brother, John, who has become a successful businessman and politician. He directs them to the factory where his son and Absalom once worked together. As Kumalo travels from place to place, trying to find his son, he begins to see the racial and economic divisions that are threatening to split apart his country. Eventually, Kumalo discovers that his son has spent time in a reformatory and impregnated a girl.

The newspapers announce that Arthur Jarvis, a prominent white crusader for racial justice, has been murdered in his home by a gang of burglars. Absalom is arrested for Jarvis's murder. Absalom has confessed to the crime, but he claims that two others, including his cousin Matthew (John Kumalo's son), aided him, and that he did not intend to murder Jarvis. Kumalo obtains a lawyer for Absalom. John makes separate arrangements for his own son's defense, even though this split will weaken Absalom's case. When Kumalo tells Absalom's pregnant girlfriend what has happened, she is upset. She joyfully agrees when Kumalo suggests that she marry Absalom and return to Ndotsheni.

Arthur Jarvis's father, James Jarvis, tends his bountiful land, which overlooks Ndotsheni. When he learns of his son's death, he and his wife leave immediately for Johannesburg. In an attempt to come to terms with what has happened, Jarvis reads his son's articles and speeches on social inequality, which make him reconsider his own prejudices. He and Kumalo meet by accident. Kumalo expresses sadness and regret for Jarvis's loss. Both men attend Absalom's trial. Absalom testifies that he and his friends broke into Arthur Jarvis's house in order to steal. When Arthur burst in on them, Absalom fired his gun because he was frightened. Absalom is convicted and sentenced to death, and his co-conspirators are acquitted. Kumalo arranges for Absalom to marry his girlfriend. As Kumalo prepares to return to Ndotsheni, Gertrude returns to prostitution.

Kumalo is now deeply aware of how his people have lost the tribal structure that once held them together. James Jarvis has similar thoughts. His grandson, Arthur's son, befriends Kumalo. As the young boy and the old man get acquainted, James Jarvis starts helping the struggling village. He donates milk, then makes plans for a dam and hires an agricultural expert to demonstrate new farming techniques. When Jarvis's wife dies, Kumalo and his congregation send a wreath to Jarvis. The diocese's bishop is on the verge of transferring Kumalo, but Jarvis sends a note offering to build the congregation a new church. Kumalo is permitted to stay in his parish.

On the evening before his son's execution, Kumalo goes into the mountains. On the way, he encounters Jarvis. They speak of the village, of lost sons, and of Jarvis's bright young grandson, whose innocence and honesty have impressed both men. When Kumalo is alone, he weeps for his son's death and clasps his hands in prayer.

CHARACTERS IN *CRY, THE BELOVED COUNTRY*

Absalom's Girlfriend A kindhearted, quiet sixteen-year-old girl. She is sexually experienced but essentially innocent, obedient, and grateful for adult protection.

Arthur's son A boy similar to his father. Arthur's son is curious, intelligent, and generous. He pleases Kumalo by visiting him and practicing Zulu.

Mr. Carmichael Absalom's lawyer. Mr. Carmichael is a tall, serious man. He takes Absalom's case pro deo ("for God").

Dubula One of a trio of powerful black politicians in Johannesburg.

John Harrison The brother of Mary Jarvis, Arthur Jarvis's wife. John is young and quick-witted. Like Arthur, he believes the black people of South Africa should have rights.

Mr. Harrison Mary Jarvis's father. Mr. Harrison has conservative political views and blames black South Africans for the country's problems. Though he disagrees with Arthur, he admires Arthur's courage.

Arthur Jarvis The man Absalom Kumalo murders during a botched robbery. He was an engineer and fierce advocate for justice for black South Africans.

James Jarvis One of the novel's protagonists. Jarvis is a white landowner whose farm overlooks Ndotsheni. He rethinks his views after the death of his son.

Margaret Jarvis James Jarvis's wife. A physically fragile and loving woman, Margaret Jarvis takes the death of her son very hard.

Mary Jarvis Arthur Jarvis's wife. Mary shares her husband's commitment to justice.

The Judge A fair-minded man. The Judge is constrained by unjust laws which he must apply strictly.

Absalom Kumalo Stephen Kumalo's son. Absalom goes astray after fleeing home for Johannesburg, but even after committing murder, he is able to reclaim his fundamental decency. Absalom's story is a cautionary tale about what happens when you abandon your village.

John Kumalo Stephen Kumalo's brother. Once a humble Christian carpenter, John Kumalo becomes one of the three most powerful black politicians in Johannesburg. He speaks out for the rights of black South Africans, but fear prevents him from pushing for radical change.

Gertrude Kumalo Stephen Kumalo's sister. Gertrude, who is twenty-five years younger than Kumalo, is easily influenced and lacks real determination. Eventually she returns to a life of crime.

Gertrude's son Kumalo's nephew. Gertrude's son comforts Kumalo during his troubles. He returns to Ndotsheni with Kumalo.

Matthew Kumalo John Kumalo's son. Matthew lies, denying that he was present at the robbery.

Mrs. Kumalo Stephen Kumalo's strong-minded, supportive, and loving wife. Mrs. Kumalo and her husband make decisions as equals. Mrs. Kumalo rouses her husband to action and bears hardship bravely.

Stephen Kumalo One of the novel's two protagonists. Kumalo is an elderly Zulu priest who has always lived in the village of Ndotsheni. He is a quiet, humble, and gentle man. He accepts suffering with dignity and devotes himself to helping his people.

Napoleon Letsitsi The agricultural expert James Jarvis hires to teach better farming techniques to the people of Ndotsheni. A well-educated middle-class black man, Letsitsi earns a good salary and is eager to help his people.

Mrs. Lithebe The woman with whom Kumalo stays in Johannesburg. Mrs. Lithebe is an Msutu woman and a generous Christian who believes that helping others is her duty.

Theophilus Msimangu Stephen Kumalo's host and guide in Johannesburg. A tall young minister, Msimangu has an acute understanding of the problems that face South Africa. He dedicates himself to Kumalo's search. Msimangu's eventual decision to enter a monastery is a testament to his faith and generosity.

Johannes Pafuri One of the three young men who tried to rob Arthur Jarvis. Absalom testifies that Pafuri was the ringleader of the group.

Tomlinson One of a trio of powerful black politicians in Johannesburg. Tomlinson is considered the smartest of the three men.

Father Vincent An Anglican English priest who offers to help Kumalo. Father Vincent presides over the wedding between Absalom and Absalom's girlfriend. Warm and understanding, he possesses deep faith.

The Young Man A young white man who works at the reformatory and attempts to reform Absalom. He cares deeply for his students.

THEMES IN *CRY, THE BELOVED COUNTRY*

RECONCILIATION BETWEEN FATHERS AND SONS *Cry, the Beloved Country* chronicles the story of two fathers in search of their sons. For Kumalo, the search begins as a physical one as he combs Johannesburg in search of Absalom. As he follows leads, he traces the development of his son, who went from factory worker to burglar to promising reformatory pupil to killer. Kumalo's search turns spiritual after the guilty verdict, when he begins to understand Absalom by reading letters from him, letters that express true repentance. Jarvis's search for his son is never physical, but emotional. After Arthur's death, he seeks to understand a son he hardly knew. By reading his son's writings, Jarvis learns what kind of man Arthur had become.

THE CYCLE OF INEQUALITY AND INJUSTICE The novel's story is set in motion by massive social inequalities. Black South Africans, allowed by law to own only limited quantities of land, are forced to overwork the land. The soil of Ndotsheni, exhausted by over-planting and over-grazing, turns hostile. For this reason, most young people leave the villages to seek work in the cities. In Johannesburg, limited opportunities and disconnection from family and tribal traditions leads young people astray. Both Gertrude and Absalom turn to crime. Absalom's story is a microcosm of race relations in Johannesburg. In search of quick riches, poor people like Absalom burglarize white homes and terrorize their occupants. The white population, which created the poverty in the first place, loses all sympathy for the people they have oppressed. They subject blacks to even more injustice, and the cycle spirals downward. Both sides explain their actions as responses to violence from the other side.

CHRISTIANITY AND INJUSTICE Paton suggests that Christianity can be used as a comfort, a tool for resisting oppression, and a way of explaining away injustice. In the midst of great hardship, Kumalo finds solace in God. He spends a great deal of time praying, both for the souls lost in Johannesburg and for the fractured society of his village. Arthur Jarvis uses Christianity to argue against oppression, calling South Africa's mining policies un-Christian. Paton alludes to priests who have made social justice in South Africa their leading cause. But Christianity can also be used in the service of unjust causes. John Kumalo reminds his brother that black priests are paid less than white ones, and argues that the church works against social change by portraying suffering as normal. Arthur Jarvis points out that people justify mining policies with faulty Christian reasoning. Some people argue that God meant for blacks to be unskilled laborers and that to provide them with opportunities for improvement and education would be flouting God's will.

SYMBOLS IN *CRY, THE BELOVED COUNTRY*

THE CHURCH The church in Ndotsheni represents humble, unpretentious faith. The church is also closely linked to Kumalo, who guides it. Jarvis's offer to build a new church for the community symbolizes not only his commitment to Ndotsheni but also his new friendship with Kumalo.

BRIGHTNESS Both Arthur and his son are notable for their "brightness"—their eager intellects and generous hearts. The quality of brightness, shininess, symbolizes internal brilliance. Paton describes Arthur and his son in mystical language, almost casting them as angels.

IMPORTANT QUOTATIONS FROM *CRY, THE BELOVED COUNTRY*

I see only one hope for our country, and that is when white men and black men . . . desiring only the good of their country, come together to work for it.. . . I have one great fear in my heart, that one day when they are turned to loving, they will find we are turned to hating.

Location: Chapter 7
Speaker: Msimangu
Context: Kumalo and Msimangu have met with John, and Msimangu expresses doubts about John's convictions

Instead of calling John a champion of justice, Msimangu calls him an example of power's corrupting influence. Msimangu warns that power can corrupts blacks and white equally, and it is this corruption that perpetuates conflict in South Africa. In this passage, Msimangu explains his dream of a selfless Christian faith that will bind all people—black and white—together. Msimangu fears that by the time "they"(the whites) turn to loving, "we"(the blacks) will have turned to hating. Like Kumalo, Msimangu understands that black attitudes toward whites are shifting. Members of the older generation like Kumalo and Msimangu do not wish to cause strife, but younger men such as Napoleon Letsitsi are less willing to tolerate white oppression. Through Msimangu's speech, Paton suggests that bad timing, not bad intentions, can stymie quests for peace. Both blacks and whites want reconciliation, but they never want it at the same time.

And now for all the people of Africa, the beloved country. Nkosi Sikelel' iAfrika, God save Africa. But he would not see that salvation. It lay afar off, because men were afraid of it. Because, to tell the truth, they were afraid of him, and his wife, and Msimangu, and the young demonstrator. And what was there evil in their desires, in their hunger? That man should walk upright in the land where they were born, and be free to use the fruits of the earth, what was there evil in it?. . . They were afraid because they were so few. And such fear could not be cast out, but by love.

Location: Chapter 36
Speaker: The narrator
Context: As Absalom hangs, Kumalo thinks about his country

As Kumalo keeps his vigil on the mountain, he prays for Africa. He understands that fear is the root of injustice: whites fear blacks because there are so few whites and so many blacks. Kumalo observes that he and his people simply want their due as humans—to "walk upright" and "use the fruits of the earth." They are not motivated by hatred and revenge, but by a simple desire for dignity. Kumalo's rumination ends with the reflection that fear must be banished with love. He could mean either that blacks' love for whites could make peace, or that whites must love blacks before peace is possible.

The white man has broken the tribe. And it is my belief—and again I ask your pardon—that it cannot be mended again. But the house that is broken, and the man that falls apart when the house is broken, these are the tragic things. That is why children break the law, and old white people are robbed and beaten.

Location: Chapter 5
Speaker: Msimangu
Context: Kumalo has arrived in Johannesburg, and Msimangu explains to him what he believes is ailing the country

---

This is no time to talk of hedges and fields, or the beauties of any country.... Cry for the broken tribe, for the law and the custom that is gone. Aye, and cry aloud for the man who is dead, for the woman and children bereaved. Cry, the beloved country, these things are not yet at an end.

Location: Chapter 11
Speaker: The narrator
Context: The narrator addresses the reader with urgency

The truth is that our civilization is not Christian; it is a tragic compound of great ideal and fearful practice, of high assurance and desperate anxiety, of loving charity and fearful clutching of possessions. Allow me a minute. . . .

Location: Chapter 21
Speaker: Arthur Jarvis
Context: James Jarvis reads the last words written by Arthur Jarvis before his death

THE COUNT OF MONTE CRISTO

Alexandre Dumas

After escaping from unjust imprisonment, a man disguises himself as a count, avenges his downfall, and tries to exact divine retribution before acknowledging that only God has that power.

THE LIFE OF ALEXANDRE DUMAS

Alexandre Dumas was born in 1802 into an impoverished aristocratic family. His father, a former general, had fallen into disfavor with Napoleon three years earlier. Nevertheless, Dumas became a lifelong admirer of Napoleon and his democratic ideals. In 1823 Dumas moved to Paris, where he spent six years as a clerk, a job he obtained because of his admirable handwriting. During this time, Dumas wrote plays and conducted torrid love affairs, living well beyond his means. His first dramatic success, *Henry III and His Court* (1829), thrust him into the limelight as one of the forerunners of the French romantic movement, which emerged as a reaction to the conservative climate of the period following the French Revolution.

Committed to the principles of social equality and individual rights in his actions as much as in his works, Dumas took at active role in the Revolution of 1830. In the late 1830s, Dumas began writing melodramatic *romans feuilletons*, novels for serial publication in cheap newspapers—an enormously lucrative undertaking. His writings soon made him the most famous Frenchman of his day. In 1844, the same year he published *The Three Musketeers*, Dumas began the serialization of *The Count of Monte Cristo*. He continued writing prolifically for most of his life, though his self-indulgent lifestyle and excessive generosity eventually took a toll on his finances. He died after a stroke in 1870 at the home of his son, the novelist Alexandre Dumas *fils*.

In his writings, Dumas relied heavily on outside sources—so much so that he has been accused of plagiarism. The inspiration for *The Count of Monte Cristo* was an anecdote related in the memoirs of police archivist Jacques Peuchet. Though the real-life narrative contains all the essential plot elements of Dumas's novel, it lacks the fantastical, larger-than-life scope of great melodrama. Granting epic proportions to his own life and to his stories was Dumas's greatest gift.

THE COUNT OF MONTE CRISTO IN CONTEXT

The key figure in French politics during the beginning of the nineteenth century—the setting for *The Count of Monte Cristo*—was Napoleon Bonaparte, a general who rose to prominence during the French Revolution (1789). After guiding the French army to victories over Austria, Italy, and Egypt, Napoleon led a coup against the existing French government. In 1799 he installed himself as dictatorial leader, and five years later the French senate voted Napoleon emperor of all the vast lands he had conquered.

Napoleon's popularity was largely due to the social reforms he implemented in the conquered lands. He abolished serfdom and feudalism. He also simplified the court system, took steps toward universal public education, and standardized national codes of law to ensure that the rights and liberties won during the French Revolution—equality before the law and freedom of religion—could not be taken away.

In 1814, threatened by many enemies and a looming military defeat, Napoleon was forced to abdicate his throne. He was exiled to the Mediterranean island of Elba, where Edmond Dantès finds him at the beginning of *The Count of Monte Cristo*. In March 1815, Napoleon escaped from Elba and marched on Paris, defeating the royal troops. It is information about this upcoming return to power that is contained in the letter Dantès is caught conveying to Paris.

Soon after his return to power, a reign known as the Hundred Days, Napoleon was forced to make a preemptive strike against encroaching enemies. He was defeated at the Battle of Waterloo, and eventually surrendered. Napoleon was exiled to the South Atlantic island of Saint Helena, where he remained until his death in 1821. Napoleon's absence from France only intensified his mythic status. Dumas's idealization of Napoleon is not surprising. Since Dumas's lifetime, France has considered Napoleon a great popular hero.

THE COUNT OF MONTE CRISTO: KEY FACTS

Time and place written: 1844; France

Date of first publication : Published serially from August 1844 until January 1846

Publisher: Le Journal des débats

Type of work: Novel

Genre: Adventure story; romance

Language: French

Original Title: Le Comte de Monte-Cristo

Setting (time): 1815–1844, the years following the fall of Napoleon's empire

Setting (place): Paris; also Marseilles, Rome, Monte Cristo, Greece, Constantinople

Tense: Present

Tone: Objective, detached

Narrator: Anonymous third-person narrator

Point of view: The narrator's

Protagonist: Edmond Dantès, alias the Count of Monte Cristo

Antagonist: Danglars; corrupt government officials, especially Caderousse, Fernand, Villefort, and Danglars; the lack of justice in the world

THE COUNT OF MONTE CRISTO: PLOT OVERVIEW

At nineteen, Edmond Dantès is about to become the captain of a ship. He is well-liked by most people and is engaged to a beautiful and kind young woman, Mercédès. His good fortune stirs up dangerous jealousy among some of Dantès's so-called friends. Danglars, the treasurer of Dantès's ship, envies Dantès's career success; Fernand Mondego is in love with Dantès's fiancée; his neighbor Caderousse is simply jealous of Dantès's good luck. Together, these three men draft a letter accusing Dantès of treason. Their accusations are based in truth: as a favor to his recently deceased captain, Dantès has carried a letter from Napoleon to a group of Bonapartist sympathizers in Paris. Though Dantès himself has no political leanings, the presence of the letter is enough to implicate him for treason. On the day of his wedding, Dantès is arrested for his alleged crimes.

The deputy public prosecutor, Villefort, realizes that Dantès has been framed. Villefort is prepared to set Dantès free when he discovers that the man to whom Dantès planned to deliver Napoleon's letter is Villefort's own father. Terrified that public knowledge of his father's treasonous activities will thwart his own ambitions, Villefort sentences Dantès to life in prison at the infamous Château d'If, where the most dangerous political prisoners are kept.

In prison, Dantès meets Abbé Faria, an Italian priest and intellectual who has been jailed for his political views. Faria teaches Dantès history, science, philosophy, and languages, turning him into a well-educated man. Faria also tells Dantès how to find a large treasure hidden on the island of Monte Cristo, should he ever escape. When Faria dies, Dantès hides himself in the abbé's shroud. The shroud, with Dantès inside it instead of Faria, is thrown into the sea—the usual means of burial at Château d'If. Dantès cuts himself loose and swims to freedom.

Dantès travels to Monte Cristo and finds Faria's enormous treasure. He considers his fortune a gift from God, given to him for the sole purpose of rewarding those who have tried to help him and punishing those who have hurt him. Disguising himself as an Italian priest, he travels back to Marseilles and visits the impoverished Caderousse, from whom Dantès learns the details of the plot to frame him. Dantès also discovers that his father has died of grief in his absence and that Mercédès has married Fernand Mondego. Finally, he learns that both Danglars and Mondego have become rich and powerful in Paris. As a reward for this information, and for Caderousse's apparent regret over the part he played in Dantès's downfall, Dantès gives Caderousse a valuable diamond. Before leaving Marseilles, Dantès anonymously saves his kind, former boss Morrel from financial ruin.

Ten years later, Dantès emerges in Rome, calling himself the Count of Monte Cristo. He ingratiates himself with Albert de Morcerf, son of Mercédès and Fernand Mondego (now the Count de Morcerf) by saving him from bandits. In return for the favor, Albert introduces Dantès to Parisian society. No one except Mercédès recognizes the mysterious count, and Dantès is able to insinuate himself into the lives of Danglars, Mondego, and Villefort. Armed with damning information about each of them that he has gathered over the past decade, Dantès sets an elaborate scheme of revenge into motion.

To punish Morcerf, Dantès exposes his darkest secret: Morcerf made his fortune by betraying his former patron, the Greek vizier Ali Pacha, and then selling Ali Pacha's wife and daughter into slavery. Ali Pacha's daughter Haydée, Dantès's ward since he bought her freedom seven years earlier, testifies against Morcerf. Ashamed by Morcerf's treachery, Albert and Mercédès flee, leaving their tainted fortune behind. Morcerf commits suicide.

To punish Villefort, Dantès first subtly tutors the murderous Madame de Villefort in the uses of poison. As Madame de Villefort wreaks havoc by killing off members of the Villefort household, Dantès arranges another public exposé. In court it is revealed that Villefort has tried to bury alive his illegitimate baby. Faced with turmoil both at home and in public, Villefort goes insane.

For revenge on Danglars, Dantès first drains Danglars's fortune with false credit accounts. He then manipulates Danglars's unfaithful wife, costing Danglars more money, and helps Danglars's daughter Eugénie run away from home. Finally, Dantès has the Italian bandit Luigi Vampa kidnap Danglars and rob him of his entire fortune, though Danglars's life is spared.

Meanwhile, Dantès also helps Morrel's son Maximilian by secretly saving Maximilian's beloved, Valentine Villefort, from her murderous stepmother. After a month during which Maximilian thinks that Valentine is dead, Dantès reveals that Valentine is in fact alive. Maximilian's joy is all the more acute after his month of despair. Dantès too finds happiness when he allows himself to fall in love with his beautiful and adoring ward, Haydée.

CHARACTERS IN *THE COUNT OF MONTE CRISTO*

EDMOND DANTÈS'S PSEUDONYMS

Edmond Dantès The novel's protagonist. Dantès is an intelligent, honest, and loving man who turns bitter and vengeful after he is framed for a crime he does not commit.

The Count of Monte Cristo A rich, embittered, vengeful, and cruel count. "The Count of Monte Cristo" is Dantès pseudonym after he escapes from prison and acquires his vast fortune.

Abbé Busoni An Italian priest. Dantès takes on this identity to gain the trust of people in order to manipulate them.

Sinbad the Sailor Dantès's identity in Italy. He also uses this identity for the gift to Morrel.

Lord Wilmore An English eccentric. Under this pseudonym, Dantès commits acts of generosity. Monte Cristo cites Lord Wilmore as one of his enemies.

OTHER MAJOR CHARACTERS

Caderousse A lazy, drunk, and greedy petty criminal. A witness to the plot to frame Dantès, Caderousse does not take active part in the crime.

Danglars A greedy cohort of Mondego's who hatches the plot to frame Dantès for treason. He becomes a wealthy and powerful baron but loses everything when Monte Cristo takes his revenge.

Madame Danglars Danglars's wife. Greedy, conniving, and unfaithful, Madame Danglars conducts a series of love affairs that help ruin her husband financially.

Eugénie Danglars The Danglars' daughter. Eugénie, a musician, despises men and longs for independence. On the eve of her wedding, she escapes to Italy with her companion, Louise d'Armilly.

Abbé Faria A priest and scholar whom Dantès meets in prison. Abbé Faria becomes Dantès's intellectual father and bequeaths to Dantès his vast hidden fortune.

Haydée Ali Pacha's daughter. Haydée is sold into slavery after her father is betrayed and murdered by Mondego. Dantès purchases Haydée's freedom and raises her as his ward, eventually falling in love with her.

Mercédès Dantès's beautiful and good fiancée. Though she marries Fernand Mondego while Dantès is in prison, she never stops loving Dantès. Mercédès is one of the few whom Dantès both punishes (for her disloyalty) and rewards (for her enduring love and goodness).

Fernand Mondego (later Count de Morcerf) Dantès's rival for Mercédès's affections. Mondego helps frame Dantès for treason and then marries Mercédès. Through acts of treachery, Mondego becomes a wealthy and powerful man. He is the first victim of Dantès's vengeance.

Albert de Morcerf The son of Fernand Mondego and Mercédès. Albert is brave, honest, and kind. Mercédès is devoted to him.

Monsieur Morrel Dantès's former boss. Morrel, a kind, honest ship owner, tries to free Dantès from prison and later to save Dantès's father from death. Monte Cristo rewards him accordingly.

Maximilian Morrel Morrel's brave and honorable son. Protected by Dantès, Maximilian and his beloved Valentine remain uncorrupted by power or wealth.

Gérard de Villefort The corrupt and ambitious public prosecutor who sentences Dantès to life in prison. Villefort is eventually punished by Monte Cristo.

Madame d'Villefort Villefort's murderous wife. Devoted wholly to her son Edward, Madame d'Villefort turns to crime in order to secure his fortune.

Valentine Villefort Villefort's saintly and beautiful daughter. Valentine is engaged to Maximilian Morrel and protected by Dantès.

MINOR CHARACTERS

Ali Dantès's mute Nubian slave. Ali is adept with all weapons.

Beauchamp and Franz d'Epinay Good friends of Albert de Morcerf. Beauchamp is a well-known journalist. D'Epinay is Valenine Villefort's unwanted fiancé.

Louise d'Armilly Eugénie Danglars's music teacher and companion.

Benedetto The illegitimate son of Villefort and Madame Danglars. Handsome, charming, and a wonderful liar, Benedetto plays a part in one of Dantès's elaborate revenge schemes.

Signor Bertuccio Dantès's steward. Bertuccio has his own vendetta against Villefort.

Major Cavalcanti A poor and crooked man whom Dantès casts as a phony Italian nobleman.

Baron of Château-Renaud An aristocrat whom Maximilian saves from death at the battle of Constantinople. By way of thanks, Château-Renaud introduces Maximilian into Parisian society.

Louis Dantès Dantès's father. Grief-stricken, Louis Dantès starves himself to death after Dantès is imprisoned.

Lucien Debray A government official who has an affair with Madame Danglars and helps her steal her husband's money.

Julie and Emmanuel Herbaut Morrel's daughter and son-in-law. Julie and Emmanuel are satisfied with their life despite its difficulties.

Countess G— A beautiful Italian aristocrat.

Jacopo A smuggler who helps Dantès win his freedom, for which he is rewarded by Dantès.

Noirtier Villefort's father. Noirtier is a brilliant and willful former French revolutionary.

Ali Pacha A Greek nationalist leader betrayed by Mondego. Ali Pacha is killed by the Turks, and his wife and daughter, Haydée, are sold into slavery.

Peppino An Italian shepherd whom Dantès saves from wrongful execution.

Marquis and Marquise de Saint-Méran The parents of Villefort's first wife.

Luigi Vampa A famous Roman bandit. Set free by Dantès, Vampa aids Dantès with his vengeful schemes.

Edward d'Villefort The Villeforts' spoiled son. Edward is an innocent victim of Dantès's revenge on Villefort.

THEMES IN *THE COUNT OF MONTE CRISTO*

THE LIMITATIONS OF JUSTICE EFFECTED BY HUMANS Dismayed by the failure of the criminal justice system, Edmond Dantès takes justice into his own hands. He reasons that even if his enemies' crimes had been uncovered, the most severe punishment possible is death—which Dantès considers inadequate retribution for the years of emotional anguish he has endured. Instead, Dantès sets out to punish his enemies by destroying all that is dear to them, as they have done to him. In his self-righteous quest, Dantès sees himself as an agent of Providence. Yet as he wreaks havoc on the lives of the innocent as well as the guilty, Dantès learns that justice carried out by human beings is necessarily limited—as limited in comparison to divine justice as men and women are limited in comparison to God, who is omniscient and omnipotent. The moral of Dumas's epic of crime and punishment is that we must be patient and allow God to reward and punish when and how he sees fit.

HAPPINESS AS A RELATIVE, NOT ABSOLUTE, CONDITION The novel's "good," or sympathetic, characters are able to appreciate the good things they have, however small. The "bad," or unsympathetic, characters focus instead on what they lack. Dantès voices his discovery of this universal truth in his letter to Maximilian, in which he claims that "[t]here is neither happiness nor misery in the world; there is only the comparison of one state with another, nothing more."

Caderousse and the Herbauts represent two extremes on this spectrum of appreciating life. Though healthy, clever, and well off, Caderousse finds fault in all the positive aspects of his life. Julie and Emmanuel Herbaut, on the other hand, are happy despite poverty and other hardships. As a more complex example, the happy Dantès of the early chapters contrasts with the Dantès of the later chapters, who emerges from prison dissatisfied and driven to exact his complicated revenge.

THE SIGNIFICANCE OF PSEUDONYMS The constant changing of characters' names in *The Count of Monte Cristo* signifies deeper changes within the characters themselves. Like the God of the Old Testament, Dantès assumes many different names, each associated with a different role in his schemes: Abbé Busoni when standing in judgment, Lord Wilmore when performing extravagantly generous deeds, and Monte Cristo when assuming the role of avenging angel.

Other characters also change their names. Villefort takes a new name to sever his association with his politically disfavored father, a name change that signifies both political opportunism and Villefort's willingness to sacrifice those close to him for personal gain. Fernand Mondego's purchase of the name Count de Morcerf is both a mark of his ascent to power and prestige, and, because he pretends that Morcerf is an old family name, a symbol of his fundamental dishonesty.

SYMBOLS IN *THE COUNT OF MONTE CRISTO*

THE SEA In escaping from prison, Dantès plunges into the ocean, experiencing a symbolic second baptism and a renewed dedication of his soul to God. His imprisonment has represented the death of his innocence and good will; he emerges from the sea reborn (and renamed) a bitter man. Later in the novel, the sea figures as his only real home: Dantès, a skilled sailor, considers himself a citizen of no land and spends a great deal of time traveling on the ocean in his yacht.

THE ELIXIR Dantès's potent potion, which appears to have the power both to kill and to give life, represents Dantès's power as avenger. His overestimation of the elixir's power reflects his overestimation of his own powers. He is wrongly convinced that he has the right and capacity to act as the agent of Providence. This hubris is evident when, faced with Edward's corpse, Dantès initially thinks to use his elixir to bring the dead boy to life. It is when Dantès acknowledges the limits of his elixir that he realizes his own limitations as a human being. The novel suggests that power to grant life, like the power to exact ultimate retribution, rests solely in God's province.

IMPORTANT QUOTATIONS FROM *THE COUNT OF MONTE CRISTO*

"I . . . have been taken by Satan into the highest mountain in the earth, and when there he . . . said he to me, 'Child of earth, what wouldst thou have to make thee adore me?' . . . I replied, 'Listen . . . I wish to be Providence myself, for I feel that the most beautiful, noblest, most sublime thing in the world, is to recompense and punish.'"

Location: Chapter 49
Speaker: The Count of Monte Cristo
Context: Monte Cristo confesses to Villefort his obsession with reward and punishment

This striking passage reveals that Monte Cristo associates his mission of vengeance not only with God but also with the devil, and foreshadows his later realization that his mission indeed has both evil and holy aspects. Ultimately, Monte Cristo acknowledges that only God has the right to act in the name of Providence. Like the devil, Monte Cristo has overstepped his bounds by trying to act in God's domain.

"[U]ntil the day when God will deign to reveal the future to man, all human wisdom is contained in these two words,—'Wait and hope.'"

Location: Chapter 117
Speaker: Monte Cristo, in a letter to Maximilian
Context: Monte Cristo concludes that it is not man's place to tinker with God's designs

Until now, Monte Cristo has considered himself God's agent on earth, carrying out the retribution that he believes God has appointed him to oversee. However, since Edward's unintended death, doubt over both Monte Cristo's capacity and his right to carry out God's justice has been building steadily. With these words, Monte Cristo renounces his just-completed project of vengeance. Rather than taking God's task into their own hands, humans ought to simply "[w]ait and hope" that God will eventually reward the good and punish the bad.

"I regret now," said he, "having helped you in your late inquiries, or having given you the information I did."
"Why so?" inquired Dantès.
"Because it has instilled a new passion in your heart—that of vengeance."

Location: Chapter 17
Speaker: Abbé Faria and Dantès
Context: Abbé Faria has deduced the true circumstances of Dantès's imprisonment and, in this speech, foreshadows Dantès's transformation into the vengeful Monte Cristo

[H]e felt he had passed beyond the bounds of vengeance, and that he could no longer say, "God is for and with me."

Location: Chapter 111
Speaker: The narrator, speaking about Monte Cristo
Context: Monte Cristo has just discovered that Edward de Villefort is dead, an innocent victim of Monte Cristo's machinations

---

"There is neither happiness nor misery in the world; there is only the comparison of one state with another, nothing more. He who has felt the deepest grief is best able to experience supreme happiness."

Location: Chapter 117
Speaker: Monte Cristo, in a letter to Maximilian
Context: In his parting letter, Monte Cristo attempts to explain why he has allowed Maximilian to believe for a whole month that his beloved Valentine is dead

CYRANO DE BERGERAC

Edmond Rostand

In seventeenth-century France, an eloquent poet who is a brilliant swordsman and has a grotesque nose woos his beloved on behalf of the handsome but inarticulate Christian.

THE LIFE OF EDMOND ROSTAND

Edmond Rostand was born in 1868 in Marseilles. As a student in Paris, Rostand developed a passion for literature and theater, much to the dismay of his father, a part-time poet who wanted his son to practice law. After the publication of his first collection of poetry, Rostand gave up his law studies. His early career featured a string of accomplishments: his first play was produced when he was only twenty years old, and his next two plays followed shortly after. His first great success was *Les Romanesques* (1894), which premiered at the Comédie-Française, the most respected theater in Paris. By that time, productions of Rostand's plays had begun to lure prominent actors.

In 1897, Rostand achieved his greatest triumph with his sensationally popular *Cyrano de Bergerac*. The famous actor Benoît Constant Coquelin, to whom the play is dedicated, performed the lead role. The play became a tremendous success.

After *Cyrano de Bergerac*, Rostand's career slowly declined. He died in 1918, but his creations continue to live on in hundreds of productions. *Les Romanesques* became the inspiration for the long-running Broadway musical *The Fantasticks* (1960). More recently, *Cyrano* spawned two popular films: the French *Cyrano de Bergerac* (1990), with Gerard Depardieu in the title role, and the modernized American adaptation, *Roxanne* (1987), starring Steve Martin.

CYRANO DE BERGERAC IN CONTEXT

Late nineteenth-century theater was dominated by grim, realistic stories and unsentimental characters. With its seventeenth-century setting and its swashbuckling hero, *Cyrano de Bergerac* boldly broke with the dreary realist tradition and recalled the historical romances of the early nineteenth century. Audiences enjoyed the play's passionate love story, witty repartee, fast-paced action, and tragic ending. Above all, they responded powerfully to the larger-than-life character of Cyrano, the courageous genius with a ridiculously long nose.

Cyrano de Bergerac evokes a historical era that was romantically seen as France's golden age—a time when men were musketeers, women were beautiful heiresses, and wit flashed as brightly as swordplay. Rostand's play both parodied and paid homage to Alexandre Dumas' famous novel *The Three Musketeers* (1844), a popular historical romance published a full half-century earlier. In the popular imagination, Cyrano's honesty, courage, wit, passion, and extraordinary willpower all represented trappings of this lost golden age. The play sounded a clarion call, reminding France of what it believed it had lost.

Cyrano de Bergerac was a historical figure—a novelist and playwright who lived from 1619 to 1655, around the same time as the fictional Cyrano. There is no evidence that suggests that the historical Cyrano had an unusually long nose. Both the play's events and its other characters are solely the product of Rostand's imagination.

CYRANO DE BERGERAC: KEY FACTS

Full Title: Cyrano de Bergerac: An Heroic Comedy in Five Acts

Time and place written: 1897; Paris, France

Date of first performance: December 28, 1897

Publisher: Charpentier et Fasquelle

Type of work: Play	

Type of work: Play

Genre: Heroic comedy; verse play; historical romance

Language: French

Setting (time): 1640 (Acts I–IV) and 1655 (Act V)

Setting (place): Paris and Arras

Tone: Grandiose, heroic

Protagonist: Cyrano de Bergerac

Antagonist: Cyrano's shame and self-doubts stemming from his long nose; the Comte de Guiche

CYRANO DE BERGERAC: PLOT OVERVIEW

ACT I

In seventeenth-century Paris, a brilliant poet and swordsman named Cyrano de Bergerac is deeply in love with his beautiful, intellectual cousin Roxane. Cyrano is afflicted with a grotesquely large nose, and he considers himself too ugly even to risk telling Roxane about his feelings. The play opens at the playhouse of the Hôtel de Bourgogne. Roxane is in the audience, and Cyrano arrives to make trouble: he has forbidden the actor Montfleury to take the stage for one month, but Montfleury plans to perform in the night's production of *La Clorise*. Also in the audience is a handsome young nobleman named Christian, who confides in his poet friend Lignière that he too loves Roxane.

When Montfleury takes the stage, Cyrano bullies him off and challenges the group of aristocrats who try to send Cyrano away. Cyrano fights the Vicomte de Valvert, who insults Cyrano's nose. During the fight, Cyrano improvises a poem about the duel. As he delivers his last line, Cyrano thrusts his sword and wounds Valvert. Cyrano's performance causes a sensation. Roxane's duenna brings Cyrano a message from her mistress, asking him to meet her in the morning. As he agrees, he learns that Lignière has offended a powerful nobleman with his latest satire and that a hundred men are waiting to ambush him on his way home. Cyrano boldly proclaims that he will see Lignière safely home and, if necessary, fight all one hundred men in the process.

ACT II

The next morning, Cyrano meets Roxane at Ragueneau's pastry shop. He comes close to confessing his feelings, but she confides in him that she loves Christian, who will soon join Cyrano's company of guards, the Cadets of Gascoyne. She asks Cyrano to watch out for Christian, and Cyrano agrees. Outside, a crowd has gathered, buzzing with the news of Cyrano's triumphs the previous night. Upset by his meeting with Roxane, Cyrano angrily ignores them. When the cadets arrive, Christian tries to prove his courage by insulting Cyrano's nose—a notoriously rash act. Cyrano controls his anger. He embraces Christian and tells him about Roxane's feelings. Christian is initially delighted, but then becomes distraught. He worries that Roxane, who expects poetry and eloquence, could never love a man as simple and inarticulate as he is. Cyrano has a bright idea: Cyrano can write to Roxane pretending to be Christian. Christian eagerly agrees. Now, Cyrano can express all his thoughts and feelings secretly.

ACT III

One night soon after, Roxane confides in Cyrano that she thinks Christian is the most ravishing poet in the world. Cyrano's disguised letters have moved her inexpressibly. Christian tells Cyrano he no longer wants Cyrano's help, but then makes a fool of himself trying to speak seductively to Roxane. Roxane cannot understand why Christian has changed, and angrily storms back into her house. Thinking quickly, Cyrano makes Christian stand in front of Roxane's balcony and speak to her while Cyrano stands under the balcony whispering to Christian what to say. Eventually, Cyrano shoves Christian aside and, under cover of darkness, pretends to be Christian, wooing Roxane himself. In the process, he wins a kiss for Christian. That night, Roxane and Christian are secretly married by a Capuchin, but their happiness is short-lived: the Comte de Guiche, who is angry to lose his influence over Roxane, declares that he is sending the Cadets of Gascoyne to the front lines of the war with Spain.

ACT IV

At the siege of Arras, the cadets languish and suffer from hunger. Cyrano writes to Roxane every single day, using Christian's name. He risks his life each morning by sneaking through the Spanish lines to send the letters. De Guiche reveals that the Spaniards will attack within the hour. Suddenly, a coach arrives and Roxane climbs out. She has longed to see Christian again and brings a feast to the soldiers. But Christian has guessed Cyrano's secret feelings for Roxane, and he forces Cyrano to tell her the truth and make her choose between them. On the cusp of revealing his feelings, Cyrano is interrupted by a sudden gunshot that kills Christian. Cyrano knows that he can never tell Roxane the truth. She faints, and de Guiche redeems himself by taking her to safety while Cyrano charges into battle.

ACT V

Fifteen years have passed. Roxane lives in a convent, and Cyrano visits her every week. Cyrano's friend Le Bret informs Roxane that Cyrano is doing very poorly—he has made many powerful enemies, and his life is constantly in danger. Ragueneau rushes in and privately tells Le Bret that Cyrano has been ambushed and hit with a heavy log pushed out of a high window. Le Bret and Ragueneau rush off to their friend's side. As soon as they leave, Cyrano appears at the convent, walking slowly and with a pained expression on his face, but sounding as cheerful as ever. As usual, he gives Roxane her weekly gossip update.

As night falls, Cyrano asks to read Christian's last letter to her. She gives it to him, and he reads it aloud, continuing to recite it after it is too dark to see. Roxane realizes that it was Cyrano who wrote the letters—and that it is his soul she has loved all these years. Ragueneau and Le Bret rush in, proclaiming that Cyrano has killed himself by not resting. Cyrano removes his hat, revealing his heavily bandaged head. Roxane exclaims that she loves him and that he cannot die. But Cyrano draws his sword and engages in one last fight with his "old enemies"—falsehood, prejudice, and compromise—slashing at the air. Then he collapses and dies, smiling as Roxane bends over him and kisses his face.

CHARACTERS IN *CYRANO DE BERGERAC*

Le Bret Cyrano's friend, closest confidant, and fellow guardsman. Le Bret worries that Cyrano's stubbornness—Cyrano's life-long struggle against "Lies . . . Compromise . . . Prejudice . . . Cowardice . . . Stupidity . . ." (V)—will ruin Cyrano's career.

The Capuchin A modest and well-meaning monk. Employed by de Guiche to carry a message to Roxane, the Capuchin is diverted by Cyrano outside Roxane's residence. He presides over Roxane and Christian's hasty wedding.

Carbon de Castel-Jaloux The captain of Cyrano's company. A friend of Cyrano's, Castel-Jaloux is a strong-willed and successful leader.

Cyrano de Bergerac The play's protagonist. Cyrano is a talented poet and swordsman, and a member of the Cadets of Gascoyne, a company of royal guards. He sports a ridiculously long nose that makes him insecure and prevents him from revealing his love for Roxane.

The Duenna Roxane's companion and chaperone, who tries to keep Roxane out of trouble. Her role is reminiscent of that of Juliet's nurse in Shakespeare's *Romeo and Juliet*.

Comte de Guiche A powerful married nobleman in love with Roxane and not fond of Cyrano. Deceitful and always angry, he makes several attempts to have Cyrano killed.

Lignière Christian's friend. Lignière is a satirist and drunkard with many powerful enemies. Cyrano protects Lignière from the hundred men hired by de Guiche to ambush him.

Lise Ragueneau's sharp-tongued wife. She does not approve of her husband's patronage of the local poets. Unhappy and frustrated, she leaves Ragueneau for a musketeer after Act II.

Mother Marguerite de Jesus, Sister Claire, and Sister Marthe Nuns of Roxane's convent in Act V. They admire and respect Cyrano and therefore allow him to visit whenever he wishes.

Montfleury A fat, incompetent actor whom Cyrano bans from the stage.

Baron Christian de Neuvillette A young cadet in love with Roxane. Christian is handsome but lacks wit and intelligence, and becomes a foil for Cyrano. He is an uncomplicated, honorable officer.

Ragueneau A pastry chef with a deep love for poetry. Ragueneau gives away pastries in return for poems. He embodies the theme of poetry as food for the soul, and highlights the division between the physical and spiritual aspects of the world. After his business fails, he becomes Roxane's porter.

Cardinal Richelieu A historical figure referenced as de Guiche's uncle; he does not appear in the play. The advisor to the king, the historical Richelieu was a skilled political manipulator and the most powerful man in France.

Roxane Cyrano's cousin, a beautiful and intellectual heiress. Roxane appreciates Cyrano's wit and courage and has a soft spot for romantic poetry. Though she initially falls in love with Christian for his good looks, she later comes to love him because of the soul expressed in his letters—which she thinks is Christian's, but is actually Cyrano's.

Vicomte de Valvert De Guiche's protégé, an insolent young nobleman. De Guiche wants to marry Valvert and Roxane, a scheme that would give de Guiche access to Roxane. In Act I, Cyrano defeats Valvert in a duel after Valvert insults Cyrano's nose.

THEMES IN *CYRANO DE BERGERAC*

INNER AND OUTER BEAUTY   *Cyrano de Bergerac* can be read as an allegory for the triumph of inner beauty over outer beauty, even though the triumph is incomplete. Cyrano, representing inner beauty, passively battles Christian, who represents outer beauty, for Roxane's love. Roxane becomes the arbiter of these values, and by the end inner beauty has triumphed: in Act IV, Roxane says she loves Christian's letters (written by Cyrano) much more than his looks. At the same time, it is Cyrano's honor and integrity—components of his inner beauty—that prevent him from declaring his love and getting the girl.

HONOR AND VIRTUE   Throughout, *Cyrano de Bergerac* places strong emphasis on honor and virtuous ideals. Cyrano is the play's eloquent and ardent defender of integrity, bravery, glory, and the pursuit of love and women. The main conflict in Acts IV and V—Cyrano's inability to tell Roxane how much he loves her out of respect for Roxane's memory of Christian—results from Cyrano's unwavering adherence to his principles. Cyrano protects his secret nearly to his death. His death itself, though tragic, is also transcendent. The play suggests that by holding fast to his strict morals at the expense of personal desire, Cyrano achieves an ideal untarnished moral standing.

SYMBOLS IN *CYRANO DE BERGERAC*

THE LETTERS   Cyrano is constantly composing, whether ballads on a duel, poetry in the dark, or love letters for Roxane. His compositions are a physical manifestation of his talents and inner beauty. Over the course of the play, Cyrano's epistolary identity takes on a life of its own, especially in Roxane's mind, and begins to replace Cyrano himself. However, the letters also reveal Cyrano's weakness: just as Christian cannot express his love in words, Cyrano cannot express his love in action.

CYRANO'S NOSE   Cyrano's nose, the play's most obvious symbol, both generates and embodies Cyrano's main flaw: his lack of self-confidence in love. His most noticeable feature, his nose becomes a physical barrier to love: every time he opens his eyes, the nose is there, stretching out into his field of vision. Within the more general thematic structure of the play, Cyrano's nose represents society's inability to look past outer beauty to see beauty within.

CYRANO'S TEARS AND CHRISTIAN'S BLOOD   In Act V, when Roxane realizes that Christian's last letter—in fact, all of Christian's letters—were written by Cyrano, she guesses that its tear stains are from Cyrano's tears. In response, Cyrano deflects her comment and observes that the blood is Christian's. This mixture of blood and tears on the page of the final letter she has treasured symbolizes the melding of Cyrano and Christian into one ideal romantic hero, particularly in the eyes of Roxane, their joint conquest.

IMPORTANT QUOTATIONS FROM *CYRANO DE BERGERAC*

ROXANE: *He is a soldier too,*
   In your own regiment—
CYRANO: *Ah!...*
ROXANE: *Yes, in the Guards,*
   Your company, too.
CYRANO: *Ah!...*
ROXANE: *And such a man!—*
   He is proud—noble—young—brave—beautiful—
CYRANO (Turns pale; rises.):   *Beautiful!!*
ROXANE: *What's the matter?*
CYRANO (Smiling):   *Nothing—this—*
   My sore hand!

Location: Early in Act II at Ragueneau's shop
Speakers: Roxane and Cyrano
Context: Roxane describes the man she loves; until this exchange, Cyrano thought Roxane may have
   loved him

As Roxane lists the characteristics of the man she loves, saying he is in the Guards, "proud," and "noble," Cyrano thinks that she might be referring to him. Not until she says that this man is "beautiful" does Cyrano realize that she is talking about somebody else. Cyrano cringes in pain, but manages to cover up for his heartbreak by pretending that he winced because of his hand wound. This sequence of dramatic irony (we understand Cyrano's remarks better than Roxane does) heightens the play's suspense. The sequence also develops Cyrano as a character, demonstrating both his presence of mind and his stoicism. Finally, this sequence drives the plot: it marks the moment when Cyrano explicitly realizes that beauty is important to Roxane, and begins to believe that she will never love him. This realization frees him to resolve to help Christian win her love later in the act.

ROXANE: *...—forgive me*
   For being light and vain and loving you
   Only because you were beautiful.
CHRISTIAN (Astonished):   *Roxane!*
ROXANE: *Afterwards I knew better. Afterwards*
   ...I loved you
   For yourself too—...
   ...And now—
CHRISTIAN: *Now?*
ROXANE: *It is yourself*
   I love now: your own self.
CHRISTIAN (Taken aback):   *Roxane!*
   ...
ROXANE: *...If you were less*
   Lovable—
CHRISTIAN: *No!*
ROXANE: *—Less charming—ugly even—*
   I should love you still.
CHRISTIAN: *You mean that?*
ROXANE: *I do*
   Mean that!
CHRISTIAN: *Ugly?...*

ROXANE: *Yes. Even then!*

Location: Act IV
Speakers: Roxane and Christian
Context: Roxane has made a surprise visit to the Arras battlefield

To encourage Christian before he goes off to battle, Roxane tells him that she loves him for his soul, and no longer for his beauty. Roxane rejects the romantic hero's typical mixture of inner and outer beauty in favor of inner beauty alone. Her line "It is yourself / I love now: your own self" is ironic: she is mistaken, and the "self" she loves is Cyrano's. This excerpt is another instance of dramatic irony, as we understand Christian's anguish better than Roxane does. He knows that without his looks, he has nothing to offer her. His pain and his subsequent encouragement of Cyrano to reveal their secret to Roxane mark Christian as a man of honor. Dramatically, Roxane's words that she would love Christian's soul even if he were "ugly" create the pathos of the final act, in which Cyrano is bound by honor and love to be so near to and so far from Roxane.

VALVERT: *Your nose is. . . rather large!*
CYRANO (gravely):   *Rather.*
VALVERT (simpering):   *Oh well—*
CYRANO (coolly):   *Is that all?*
VALVERT (Turns away with a shrug):   *Well, of course—*
CYRANO: *Ah, no, young sir!*
  You are too simple. Why you might have said—
  Oh, a great many things! Mon dieu, why waste
  Your opportunity? For example, thus:—
  Aggressive: *I, sir, if that nose were mine,*
  I'd have it amputated—on the spot!
  Friendly: *How do you drink with such a nose?*
  You ought to have a cup made specially.
  Descriptive: *'Tis a rock—a crag—a cape—*
  A cape? say, rather, a peninsula!
  Inquisitive: *What is that receptacle—*
  A razor-case or a portfolio?
  Kindly: *Ah do you love the little birds*
  So much that when they come and sing to you,
  You give them this to perch on?. . .

Location: Act I
Speakers: Cyrano and Valvert
Context: At the theatre, after Cyrano banishes Montfleury from the stage, Valvert insults Cyrano's nose

---

CHRISTIAN: *Oh, if I had words*
  To say what I have here!
CYRANO: *If I could be*
  A handsome little Musketeer with eyes!—
CHRISTIAN: *Besides—you know Roxane—how sensitive—*
  One rough word, and the sweet illusion—gone!
CYRANO: *I wish you might be my interpreter.*
CHRISTIAN: *I wish I had your wit—*
CYRANO: *Borrow it, then!—*
  Your beautiful young manhood—lend me that,
  And we two make one hero of romance!
CHRISTIAN: *What?*

CYRANO: *Would you dare to repeat to her the words*
    I gave you, day by day?
CHRISTIAN: *You mean?*
CYRANO: *I mean*
    Roxane shall have no disillusionment!
    Come, shall we win her both together? Take
    The soul within this leathern jack of mine,
    And breathe it into you?

Location: The end of Act II
Speakers: Christian and Cyrano
Context: Cyrano, who knows that Roxane is in love with Christian, meets Christian for the first time and encourages him to woo her

---

ROXANE: *And all these fourteen years,*
    He has been the old friend, who came to me
    To be amusing.
CYRANO: *Roxane!—*
ROXANE: *It was you.*
CYRANO: *No, no, Roxane, no!*

Location: Act V
Speakers: Roxane and Cyrano
Context: Cyrano asks to read "Christian's" last letter to Roxane, and continues reciting it after it is too dark to see

DEATH OF A SALESMAN

Arthur Miller

A salesman, depressed about his failure to achieve financial success, grows increasingly unhinged and finally kills himself.

THE LIFE OF ARTHUR MILLER

Arthur Miller was born in New York City on October 17, 1915. His career as a playwright began while he was a student at the University of Michigan. Several of his early works won prizes, and during his senior year, the Federal Theatre Project in Detroit performed one of his works. He produced his first great success, *All My Sons*, in 1947. In 1953, he published *The Crucible*, a searing indictment of the anti-Communist hysteria that pervaded 1950s America. He has won the New York Drama Critics Circle Award twice, and his *Broken Glass* (1993) won the Olivier Award for Best Play of the London Season.

DEATH OF A SALESMAN IN CONTEXT

After World War II, the United States faced profound domestic tensions. The war had made Americans confident and secure, but the United States became embroiled in a tense cold war with the Soviet Union. Some saw the United States as peaceful and homogenous, but underneath the happy veneer, the country was plagued by anxiety about Communism, bitter racial conflict, and economic and social stratification.

Uneasy with the denial and discord they saw in their country, a new generation of American artists and writers influenced by existentialist philosophy took up arms in a battle for individuality and self-expression. Such discontented individuals railed against the idea that financial success and social approval should go hand in hand. It disturbed them that so many American families centered their lives around material possessions (cars, appliances, and televisions, a new innovation)—often in an attempt to keep up with their equally materialistic neighbors.

Postwar artists and writers found new inspiration in the theories of Sigmund Freud and Carl Jung on the human subconscious. They also responded to existentialist ideas about the individual's responsibility for understanding his or her existence. Perhaps the most famous and widely read dramatic work associated with existentialist philosophy is Samuel Beckett's *Waiting for Godot*.

In *Death of a Salesman* (1949), Miller fashioned a particularly American version of existentialism. The play won the Pulitzer Prize and transformed Miller into a national sensation. Many critics described *Death of a Salesman* as the first great American tragedy, and Miller was hailed as an artist who understood the deep essence of the United States.

Death of a Salesman addresses the painful conflicts in one family, and American values in general. The play, which examines the cost of blind faith in the American Dream, is a postwar, American version of personal tragedy in the tradition of Sophocles' *Oedipus Cycle*. Miller charges America with selling a false myth by telling its people that money is more important than truth and moral vision.

The central conflict in *Death of a Salesman* is inspired by Miller's own life. He had a conflicted relationship with his uncle, Manny Newman. Newman, a salesman, imagined a continuous competition between his son and Miller. In his youth, Miller wrote a short story about an unsuccessful salesman. His relationship with Manny revived his interest in the abandoned manuscript, and he transformed the story into one of the most successful dramas in the history of the American stage.

DEATH OF A SALESMAN: KEY FACTS

Full title: Death of a Salesman: Certain Private Conversations in Two Acts and a Requiem

Time and place written: Six weeks in 1948; Connecticut

Date of first publication: 1949

Publisher: The Viking Press	

Publisher: The Viking Press

Type of work: Play

Genre: Tragedy, social protest drama

Language: English

Setting (time): The late 1940s or the time period in which the play is being produced. Nearly all of the action takes place during a twenty-four-hour period interspersed with flashbacks

Setting (place): Brooklyn, New York, and Boston

Tense: Present

Tone: Sincere, mocking, tender

Protagonist: Willy Loman, Biff Loman

Antagonists: Biff Loman, Willy Loman, the American Dream

DEATH OF A SALESMAN: PLOT OVERVIEW

Willy Loman returns to his home in Brooklyn one night, exhausted from a failed sales trip. His wife, Linda, urges him to ask his boss, Howard Wagner, to let him work in New York so that he won't have to travel. The Lomans' thirty-four-year-old son, Biff, has come home to visit, and Willy complains that Biff hasn't made anything of himself. Linda scolds Willy for being so critical.

As Willy talks to himself in the kitchen, Biff and his younger brother, Happy, who is also visiting, reminisce about their adolescence and fantasize about buying a ranch out West. Willy daydreams about his sons' childhood: Biff, a high-school football star, and Happy interact affectionately with their father as they polish the car. Willy tells his sons that one day he is going to open his own business—one bigger than the business his neighbor, Charley, owns. Willy points out that Charley's son, Bernard, is doomed to failure because although he is smart, he is not "well-liked," as Biff and Happy are.

A younger Linda enters, and the boys leave. Willy boasts of a phenomenally successful sales trip, but Linda figures out that it was actually only a slight success. Willy worries that soon he won't be able to make all of the payments on their appliances and car. He complains that people don't like him and that he's not good at his job. As Linda consoles him, he hears the laughter of his mistress, The Woman. Willy's memory takes him back to a hotel room, where The Woman is just finishing getting dressed. She thanks him for giving her stockings.

The Woman disappears, and Willy returns to his prior reverie: Linda is mending her stockings, and Willy angrily orders her to throw them out. Bernard rushes in and whines that Biff should be studying for a test. Linda says that Biff must return a football that he stole. She adds that Biff is too rough with the neighborhood girls. The Woman laughs in the background. Willy explodes at Linda and Bernard. The daydream ends, but Willy continues to mutter to himself.

Happy comes downstairs and tries to quiet Willy. Agitated, Willy shouts his regret about not going to Alaska with his brother, Ben, who eventually found a diamond mine in Africa and got rich. Charley comes in, Happy goes off to bed, and Willy and Charley play cards. Charley offers Willy a job, but Willy, insulted, refuses it. Willy talks to Ben, who he thinks has come in. Charley, seeing no one there, gets confused and questions Willy. Willy yells at Charley, who leaves. Willy continues to daydream about Ben.

Back in the present, Biff and Happy come downstairs and discuss Willy's condition with their mother. Linda scolds Biff for judging Willy harshly. Biff says he knows Willy is a fake, but he refuses to elaborate. Linda tells her sons that Willy has tried to commit suicide. Willy enters and yells at Biff. Happy intervenes and proposes that he and Biff go into the sporting goods business together. Willy immediately brightens and gives Biff a host of tips about asking for a loan from Bill Oliver, one of Biff's old employers. After more arguing and reconciliation, everyone goes to bed.

Act II opens with Willy enjoying the breakfast that Linda has made for him. Linda tells Willy that Biff and Happy are taking him out to dinner that night. Excited, Willy says he will make Howard Wagner give him a New York job. Linda reminds Biff to be nice to his father at the restaurant that night.

The lights fade on Linda and come up on Howard, who treats Willy rudely and then denies his request to work in New York. Willy launches into a long story about how a legendary salesman named Dave Singleman inspired him to go into sales. Howard tells Willy to take some time off, and then leaves.

Ben enters and invites Willy to join him in Alaska. The younger Linda enters and reminds Willy of his sons and job. The young Biff enters, and Willy praises Biff's prospects and popularity.

Ben leaves and Bernard rushes in, excited about Biff's big football game. The lights rise on a different part of the stage, and present time resumes. Willy continues yelling from offstage, and Jenny, Charley's secretary, asks Bernard to quiet him down. Willy enters and prattles about a "very big deal" that Biff is working on. Bernard mentions that he is going to Washington to fight a case. Daunted by Bernard's success, Willy asks him why Biff turned out to be such a failure. Bernard asks Willy what happened in Boston that made Biff decide not to go to summer school. Willy defensively tells Bernard not to blame him.

Charley enters and sees off Bernard. Willy asks for more money than Charley usually loans him, and Charley again offers Willy a job. Willy refuses and eventually confesses that he was fired. Charley scolds Willy for always needing to be liked and angrily gives him the money. Calling Charley his only friend, Willy exits on the verge of tears.

At Frank's Chop House, Happy helps Stanley, a waiter, prepare a table. They flirt with Miss Forsythe, a call girl. Biff enters and says he waited six hours for Bill Oliver, who didn't even recognize him. Willy is mistakenly convinced that Biff was a salesman for Oliver, a misconception Biff plans to correct. Willy enters, and Biff tries, gently at first, to tell him what happened at Oliver's office. Willy blurts out that he was fired. Stunned, Biff again tries to let Willy down easily.

Willy's daydreams overlap with reality as he argues with his sons and imagines the young Bernard running in and shouting for Linda. As Biff explains what happened, their conversation recedes into the background, and Willy's daydream comes to the foreground. The young Bernard tells Linda that Biff failed math. Then the restaurant conversation comes back into focus, and Willy criticizes Biff for failing math. Willy hears the voice of a hotel operator in Boston and shouts that he is not in his room. Biff and Willy continue arguing. Willy hears The Woman laugh and shouts back at Biff, hitting him and staggering. Miss Forsythe enters with another call girl, Letta. Biff helps Willy to the washroom and then argues with Happy about Willy. Biff storms out, and Happy follows with the girls.

Willy and The Woman enter, dressing themselves and flirting. A knock sounds at the door, and Willy hurries The Woman into the bathroom. The young Biff enters and tells Willy he failed math. Willy tries to usher him out of the room, but Biff imitates his math teacher's lisp, which elicits laughter from Willy and The Woman. Willy tries to cover up his indiscretion, but Biff refuses to believe his stories and storms out, dejected, calling Willy a "phony little fake."

Back in the restaurant, Stanley helps Willy up. Willy asks him where he can find a seed store. Stanley gives him directions to one, and Willy hurries off.

Biff and Happy go home. Linda yells at them for abandoning Willy. Biff goes in search of Willy and finds him planting seeds in the garden with a flashlight. Willy is consulting Ben about a $20,000 proposition. Willy moves into the house at Biff's urging, growing angry again about Biff's failure. Again they erupt in fury at each other. Biff starts to sob, which touches Willy. Everyone goes to bed except Willy, who renews his conversation with Ben. He is elated to think that Biff will flourish with $20,000 of insurance money. Linda calls out for Willy but gets no response. Biff and Happy hear Willy's car speed away.

In the requiem, Linda and Happy stand in shock after Willy's poorly attended funeral. Biff says Willy had the wrong dreams. Charley defends Willy as a victim of his profession. Biff invites Happy to go back out West with him, but Happy says he will stick it out in New York to validate Willy's death. Linda sobs, repeating, "We're free." All exit, and a flute melody is heard as the curtain falls.

CHARACTERS IN *DEATH OF A SALESMAN*

Bernard Charley's son. Bernard is an important, successful lawyer. Willy used to mock Bernard for studying hard, but Bernard always loved Willy's sons.

Charley Willy's next-door neighbor. Charley owns a successful business. He gives Willy money and repeatedly offers him a job. Willy is jealous of Charley, but considers him his only friend.

Miss Forsythe and Letta Two young women who Happy and Biff meet at Frank's Chop House. Miss Forsythe and Letta seem to be prostitutes, judging from Happy's repeated comments about their moral character and the fact that they are "on call."

Jenny Charley's secretary.

Ben Loman Willy's wealthy older brother. Ben, who recently died, appears only in Willy's daydreams. Willy regards Ben as a symbol of the success he so desperately craves for himself and his sons.

Biff Loman Willy's thirty-four-year-old son. Biff led a charmed life in high school, where he was a football star with scholarship prospects, many friends, and fawning female admirers. Because he failed math, he did not graduate. Since then, his kleptomania has gotten him fired from every job he has held. Bill's instincts tell him to abandon Willy's paralyzing dreams and move out West to work with his hands. Biff represents Willy's vulnerable, poetic, tragic side.

Happy Loman Willy's thirty-two-year-old son. Happy has lived in Biff's shadow all of his life, but he compensates with his relentless sex drive and professional ambition. Although he works as an assistant to an assistant buyer in a department store, Happy presents himself as supremely important. He has bad business ethics and sleeps with the girlfriends of his superiors. Happy represents Willy's self-importance, ambition, and acceptance of societal expectations.

Linda Loman Willy's loyal, loving wife. Occasionally, Linda is taken in by Willy's self-deluded dreams of success, but most of the time she seems more realistic and hardy than her husband. Linda's emotional strength supports Willy until his collapse.

Willy Loman An insecure, self-deluded traveling salesman. Willy believes in the American Dream of easy success and wealth, but he never achieves it. In vain, he hopes that his sons will succeed where he has failed. As reality increasingly contradicts Willy's illusions, his mental health unravels.

Stanley A waiter at Frank's Chop House. Stanley and Happy seem to be friends.

Howard Wagner Willy's boss. Howard inherited the company from his father, whom Willy regarded as "a masterful man" and "a prince." Though much younger than Willy, Howard treats Willy with condescension and eventually fires him, despite Willy's wounded assertions that he named Howard.

The Woman Willy's mistress when Happy and Biff were in high school. The Woman's attention and admiration boost Willy's fragile ego. When Biff catches Willy in his hotel room with The Woman, he loses faith in his father, and his dream of going to college dies.

THEMES IN *DEATH OF A SALESMAN*

THE AMERICAN DREAM Willy believes in the American Dream, which he understands as the promise that a "well liked" and "personally attractive" man in business will find financial success. His fixation on the superficial qualities of attractiveness and likeability is at odds with a more gritty and rewarding understanding of the American Dream that identifies uncomplaining hard work as the key to success. Willy does not understand how important intelligence is to success. He thinks that because Bernard is a nerd, he will never thrive. Bernard's achievements astonish him. Willy's inability to accept the gulf between his own life and the American Dream leads to his rapid psychological decline.

THE PAIN OF BETRAYAL Willy believes that Biff betrayed him by failing to succeed. Willy thinks he has every right to demand that Biff lives up to Willy's expectations. When Biff rejects Willy's ambitions for him, Willy feels he has been personally affronted, calling the rejection an "insult" born of "spite." Biff's crushing rebuff reflects Willy's ineptness at his profession, for Willy failed to sell his son on the American Dream—the product in which Willy believes most fervently. The feelings of betrayal and anger are mutual: Biff thinks that his father, a "phony little fake," has betrayed him with his unending stream of ego-stroking lies.

THE DANGER OF MYTHOLOGIZING Willy's tendency to mythologize people worsens his deluded understanding of the world. He speaks of Dave Singleman as a legend and imagines that his death must have been beautifully noble. He believes that his sons are pinnacles of "personal attractiveness" and power, and compares them to the mythic Greek figures Adonis and Hercules. By mythologizing those he knows, Willy sets impossibly high standards for himself and his sons. He does not grasp the hopelessness of Singleman's life or the sadness of his on-the-job, on-the-road death. It never crosses his mind that Biff and Happy might not live the lives of gods.

SYMBOLS IN *DEATH OF A SALESMAN*

SEEDS For Willy, seeds represent the opportunity to prove his worth as a salesman and a father. His desperate nocturnal attempt to grow vegetables shows that he is ashamed that he must struggle to put food on the table. The slim chance that the seeds will flourish reflects Willy's failure to thrive.

STOCKINGS Stockings symbolize betrayal and sexual infidelity. The teenage Biff accuses Willy of giving Linda's stockings to The Woman. New stockings suggest spending money, so the fact that Willy gives stockings to his mistress instead of to his wife reveals his general failure to provide for his family first.

IMPORTANT QUOTATIONS FROM *DEATH OF A SALESMAN*

And when I saw that, I realized that selling was the greatest career a man could want. 'Cause what could be more satisfying than to be able to go, at the age of eighty-four, into twenty or thirty different cities, and pick up a phone, and be remembered and loved and helped by so many different people?

Location: Act II
Speaker: Willy
Context: In Howard's office, Willy explains how his meeting with Dave Singleman inspired him to become a salesman

Willy idealizes Dave Singleman, who died the noble "death of a salesman" that Willy himself covets. In these lines, he reveals his obsession with being well liked. For Willy, the warmth and love of business contacts would be far more satisfying than the devotion of his family, because it would prove that he had been successful at his job. Willy glorifies Singleman's on-the-job death as dignified and graceful. He never considers the sadness of the fact that Singleman was still working at age eighty-four. He never imagines that Singleman might have experienced the same financial difficulties and consequent pressures and misery that he himself experiences.

A diamond is hard and rough to the touch.

Location: Act II
Speaker: Ben
Context: Ben tells Willy that his suicide will be like a diamond

Ben's mantra, "The jungle is dark, but full of diamonds," turns Willy's suicide into a moral struggle and a matter of commerce. Willy's suicide, according to Ben, will be "not like an appointment at all" but like a "diamond . . . rough and hard to the touch." The diamond Ben speaks of is a tangible reminder of Willy's failure to achieve financial success and of the missed opportunity to get rich with Ben. Ben suggests that suicide, as opposed to the fruitless, emotionally ruinous meetings Willy has had with Howard Wagner and Charley, will yield something concrete for Willy and his family. It will lead to money, the thing Willy has always craved. Willy latches onto this appealing idea, convinced that suicide will allow him to prove himself, at last, to be a successful businessman. He is certain that with the $20,000 from his life insurance policy, Biff will finally live up to his potential in business. In selling himself for the metaphorical diamond of $20,000, Willy bears out his earlier assertion to Charley that "after all the highways, and the trains, and the appointments, and the years, you end up worth more dead than alive."

I saw the things that I love in this world. The work and the food and the time to sit and smoke. And I looked at the pen and I thought, what the hell am I grabbing this for? Why am I trying to become what I don't want to be . . . when all I want is out there, waiting for me the minute I say I know who I am.

Location: Act II
Speaker: Biff
Context: During a climactic, final confrontation, Biff explains why he considers material success unimportant

---

Nothing's planted. I don't have a thing in the ground.

Location: Act II
Speaker: Willy
Context: After eating at Frank's Chop House, Willy comes home and decides he must plant seeds

---

He's a man way out there in the blue, riding on a smile and a shoeshine.. . . A salesman is got to dream, boy.

Location: Act II
Speaker: Charley
Context: In a eulogy, Charley identifies Willy as a victim of his profession

DAVID COPPERFIELD

Charles Dickens

After surviving a poverty-stricken childhood, the death of his mother, a cruel stepfather, and an unfortunate first marriage, a boy finds success as a writer.

THE LIFE OF CHARLES DICKENS

Charles Dickens was born on February 7, 1812. He spent the first ten years of his life in Kent, a marshy region by the sea in the east of England. Dickens was the second of eight children. His father, John Dickens, was kind and likable, but fiscally irresponsible. His huge debts caused tremendous strain on his family.

When Dickens was ten, his family moved to London. Two years later, his father was arrested and thrown in debtors' prison. Dickens's mother moved into the prison with seven of her children. Charles tried to earn money for the struggling family. For three months, he worked with other children pasting labels on bottles in a blacking warehouse. Dickens found the three months he spent apart from his family highly traumatic. Not only was the job itself miserable, but he considered himself too good for it, earning the contempt of the other children. His experiences at this warehouse inspired passages of *David Copperfield*.

An inheritance gave John Dickens enough money to free himself from his debt and from prison. Dickens attended Wellington House Academy for two years. He became a law clerk, then a newspaper reporter, and finally a novelist. His first novel, *The Pickwick Papers* (1837), met with huge popular success. Dickens was a literary celebrity in England for the rest of his life.

Dickens's work includes *Oliver Twist* (1837–1839), *Nicholas Nickelby* (1838–1839), and *A Christmas Carol* (1843). Perhaps his best known novel, *Great Expectations* (1860–1861) shares many thematic similarities with *David Copperfield*. Dickens died in Kent in 1870, at the age of fifty-eight.

DAVID COPPERFIELD IN CONTEXT

In 1849, Dickens began to write *David Copperfield*, a novel based on his early life experiences. Like Dickens, David Copperfield works as a child, pasting labels onto bottles. Also like Dickens, David becomes first a law clerk, then a reporter, and finally a successful novelist. Mr. Micawber is a satirical version of Dickens's father, a likable man who can never scrape together the money he needs. Many of the secondary characters in *David Copperfield* spring from Dickens's experiences as a young man in financial distress in London. In later years, Dickens called *David Copperfield* his "favourite child," and many critics consider the novel to be one of his best depictions of childhood.

David Copperfield is set in early Victorian England, against a backdrop of great social change. The Industrial Revolution of the late eighteenth and early nineteenth centuries had enabled capitalists and manufacturers to amass huge fortunes. Although the Industrial Revolution increased social mobility, the gap between rich and poor was wide. London, a teeming mass of people lit by gas lamps at night and darkened by sooty clouds during the day, contrasted with Britain's sparsely populated rural areas. More and more people moved from the country to the city in search of the opportunities that technological innovation promised. This migration overpopulated the already crowded cities of England. Poverty, disease, hazardous factory conditions, and ramshackle housing became widespread. *David Copperfield* takes place in the rapidly changing London of the industrial era.

DAVID COPPERFIELD: KEY FACTS

Full Title: The Personal History and Experience of David Copperfield the Younger

Time and place written: May 1849–November 1850; England

Date of first publication: May 1849–November 1850 (serial publication)

Publisher: Bradbury and Evans

Type of work: Novel

Genre: Bildungsroman (coming-of-age novel)	
Language: English	
Setting (time): 1800s	
Setting (place): England	
Tense: Past	
Tone: Fond, wistful	
Narrator: David Copperfield, who looks back on his youth	
Point of View: First-person limited	
Protagonist: David Copperfield	
Antagonist: Poverty, the cruelty of the world	

DAVID COPPERFIELD: PLOT OVERVIEW

David Copperfield, now an adult, tells the story of his youth. As a young boy, David lives happily with his mother and his nurse, Peggotty. His father died before he was born. His mother marries the violent Mr. Murdstone, who moves into the Copperfield house along with his strict sister, Miss Murdstone. The Murdstones treat David cruelly, beating and berating him. The Murdstones send David away to school.

Peggotty takes David to visit her brother, Mr. Peggotty, in Yarmouth. Mr. Peggotty has two adopted children, Ham and Little Em'ly. They all live in an upside-down boat—a space they share with Mrs. Gummidge, the widowed wife of Mr. Peggotty's brother.

David goes to Salem House, a school run by a man named Mr. Creakle. At Salem House, David befriends and idolizes an egotistical young man named James Steerforth. He also befriends Tommy Traddles, an unfortunate, fat young boy. David's mother dies, and David returns home, where the Murdstones neglect him. He works at Mr. Murdstone's wine-bottling business and moves in with Mr. Micawber, who mismanages his finances. When Mr. Micawber leaves London to escape his creditors, David decides to search for Miss Betsey Trotwood, his father's sister and David's only living relative. He walks a long distance to Miss Betsey's home, and she takes him in on the advice of her mentally unstable friend, Mr. Dick.

Miss Betsey sends David to a school run by Doctor Strong. David moves in with Mr. Wickfield and his daughter, Agnes, while he attends school. Agnes and David become best friends. One of Mr. Wickfield's boarders is a snakelike young man named Uriah Heep, who often pokes his nose in other people's business.

David graduates and heads for Yarmouth to visit Peggotty, who is now married to a carrier named Mr. Barkis. David reflects on what profession he should pursue. On his way to Yarmouth, he encounters James Steerforth. After a detour to visit Steerforth's mother, David and Steerforth arrive in Yarmouth, where Steerforth and the Peggottys become fond of one another.

Miss Betsey persuades David to pursue a career as a proctor, a kind of lawyer. David works as an apprentice at the London firm of Spenlow and Jorkins and takes up lodgings with a woman named Mrs. Crupp. Mr. Spenlow invites David to his house for a weekend. There, David meets Spenlow's daughter, Dora, and quickly falls in love with her. In London, David is reunited with Tommy Traddles and Mr. Micawber. Word reaches David that Mr. Barkis is terminally ill. David goes to Yarmouth to visit Peggotty in her hour of need.

Little Em'ly and Ham plan to marry upon Mr. Barkis's death, but Little Em'ly is unhappy about the engagement. When Mr. Barkis dies, she runs off with Steerforth, who she believes will make her a lady. Mr. Peggotty vows to find Little Em'ly and bring her home. Miss Betsey visits London to inform David that Mr. Wickfield has partnered with Uriah Heep, ruining her financial security. David, who has grown increasingly infatuated with Dora, vows to work as hard as he can to make their life together possible. But Mr. Spenlow forbids Dora to marry David.

Mr. Spenlow dies in a carriage accident, and Dora goes to live with her two aunts. Meanwhile, Uriah Heep informs Doctor Strong that he suspects the doctor's wife, Annie, of having an affair with her young cousin, Jack Maldon. Dora and David marry. Dora is a terrible housewife, incompetent at her chores, but David loves her regardless. Mr. Dick facilitates a reconciliation between Doctor Strong and Annie, who was not cheating. Miss Dartle, Mrs. Steerforth's ward, tells David that Steerforth has left Little Em'ly. David and Mr. Peggotty enlist the help of Little Em'ly's childhood friend, Martha, who locates Little Em'ly and brings Mr. Peggotty to her.

Little Em'ly and Mr. Peggotty decide to move to Australia, as do the Micawbers, who expose Uriah Heep's fraud against Mr. Wickfield. A powerful storm hits Yarmouth and kills Ham as he is attempting to rescue a shipwrecked sailor. The sailor turns out to be Steerforth. Meanwhile, Dora falls ill and dies. David leaves the country to travel abroad. His love for Agnes grows. When David returns, he and Agnes, who has long harbored a secret love for him, get married and have several children. David pursues his writing career and finds commercial success.

CHARACTERS IN *DAVID COPPERFIELD*

Clara Copperfield David's mother. The kind, generous, and goodhearted Clara embodies maternal devotion until her death, which occurs early in the novel. David remembers his mother as an angel whose independent spirit was destroyed by Mr. Murdstone's cruelty.

David Copperfield The protagonist and narrator of the novel. David is innocent, trusting, and naïve, despite the abuse he suffers as a child. At times, David can be chauvinistic toward the lower classes, and occasionally he makes foolhardy decisions that undermine his good intentions.

Rosa Dartle The ward of Mrs. Steerforth. Rosa, the orphan child of Mr. Steerforth's cousin, is bitter and proud. Like Mrs. Steerforth, she loves James Steerforth and dislikes David.

Uriah Heep A two-faced, conniving villain who puts on a false show of meekness to disguise his evil intentions. Uriah believes the world owes him something for all the humiliations he suffered as a young man.

Little Em'ly Peggotty's unfaithful niece. Little Em'ly is sweet but also coy and vain. Her desire to be a lady causes her to disgrace herself by running away from her family.

Clara Peggotty David's nanny and caretaker. Peggotty is gentle and selfless, helping David whenever he is in need. She is faithful to David and his family all her life.

Mr. Peggotty, Ham, and Mrs. Gummidge The simple relatives of Clara Peggotty. Mr. Peggotty, Ham, and Mrs. Gummidge represent the virtues of simple people. Mr. Peggotty and Ham are sailors, and Mrs. Gummidge is a sailor's widow. They are devoted and loving to each other and to David.

Mr. and Mrs. Wilkins Micawber An unlucky couple crippled by precarious finances. Although Mr. Micawber can't support his own family, he generously and industriously serves others. Mrs. Micawber stands by her husband despite his flaws.

Mr. Edward Murdstone and Miss Jane Murdstone The cruel second husband of David's mother, and Murdstone's sister. The Murdstones are brutal to both David and his mother.

Dora Spenlow David's first wife and first real love. Dora is foolish and giddy, more interested in playing with her dog, Jip, than in keeping house with David. She behaves like a spoiled child, but David cannot bear to displease her.

James Steerforth A condescending, self-centered villain. Steerforth has a restless energy he can neither satisfy nor divert. He charms both women and men because he enjoys the feeling of power it gives him. He also abuses David, although David is too enraptured with him and too grateful for his patronage to notice.

Mrs. Steerforth Steerforth's mother. Mrs. Steerforth is a cruel, haughty woman. She loves her son and disdains David.

Doctor Strong and Annie Strong A couple who exemplify the best of married life. Doctor Strong and Annie are faithful and selfless. Their deep love for each other enables them to survive Uriah's scheming.

Tommy Traddles Young David's simple, goodhearted schoolmate. Traddles works hard but faces great obstacles because he lacks money and connections. He eventually succeeds in making a name and a career for himself.

Miss Betsey Trotwood David's eccentric, kindhearted aunt. Although Miss Betsey's intentions are mysterious at the beginning of the novel, her generosity is soon clear. She becomes a mother figure for David.

Agnes Wickfield David's true love and second wife. Agnes, the daughter of Mr. Wickfield, is calm and gentle. She patiently endures David's other romances, hiding her love for him. Agnes always comforts David with kind words or advice.

THEMES IN *DAVID COPPERFIELD*

THE PLIGHT OF THE WEAK Throughout *David Copperfield*, the powerful abuse the weak and helpless. Dickens shows that exploitation—not pity or compassion—is the rule in an industrial society. Rich men readily take advantage of orphans, women, and the mentally disabled. Dickens draws on his own childhood experiences to describe the inhumanity of child labor and debtors' prison. In *David Copperfield*, David starves and suffers in a wine-bottling factory as a child. Mr. Murdstone can exploit David as factory labor because the boy is too small and dependent on him to disobey. Likewise, the boys at Salem House have no recourse against the cruel Mr. Creakle. In both situations, men abuse their role as protectors, harming the children in their care.

Dickens suggests that the weak cannot escape the domination of the powerful by challenging it. Instead, the weak must ally themselves with other, more sympathetic powerful people. For example, David doesn't stand up to Mr. Murdstone and challenge his authority. Instead, he flees to the wealthy Miss Betsey, whose financial stability allows her to shelter David from Mr. Murdstone.

THE IMPORTANCE OF EQUALITY IN MARRIAGE In the world of the novel, marriages succeed best when husband and wife have an equal partnership. Dickens uses the Strongs' marriage as proof that marriages are happy when neither spouse is subjugated to the other. He criticizes characters who think themselves superior to their spouses. Mr. Murdstone is one such character. He forces Clara into submission in the name of improving her, leaving her meek and voiceless. In contrast, although Doctor Strong does attempt to improve Annie's character, he does so not out of a desire to show his moral superiority but out of love and respect for Annie.

Despite his praise for kind men, Dickens does not challenge his society's constrictive views about the roles of women. Although Doctor Strong's marriage is based at least partially on an ideal of equality, he still assumes that his wife, as a woman, depends on him and needs him for moral guidance.

THE DANGERS OF WEALTH AND CLASS Dickens criticizes his society for equating wealth and class with human worth. Many people in Dickens's time, as in our own, believed that poverty was a symptom of moral degeneracy and that people who were poor deserved to suffer because of inherent deficiencies. But Dickens sympathizes with the poor and implies that their woes result from society's unfairness, not their own failings. His character Steerforth, who is wealthy, powerful, and noble, is treacherous and self-absorbed. His characters Mr. Peggotty and Ham, both poor, are generous and sympathetic.

Dickens does not suggest that all poor people are absolutely noble and that all rich people are utterly evil. Poor people frequently swindle David when he is young, poor, and helpless. Doctor Strong and Agnes, both wealthy, middle-class citizens, are morally upstanding people. Dickens's broad point is that wealth and class are unreliable indicators of character and morality.

SYMBOLS IN *DAVID COPPERFIELD*

THE SEA The sea represents an unknown and powerful force in the lives of the characters. It is almost always connected with death. Like death, the force of the sea is beyond human control. The sea took Little Em'ly's father in an unfortunate accident. It also takes the lives of Ham and Steerforth. The storm in the concluding chapters of the novel suggests the danger of ignoring the sea's power and indicates that the novel's conflicts have reached their apex.

MR. DICK'S KITE Mr. Dick's enormous kite represents his separation from society. Just as the kite soars above the other characters, Mr. Dick, whom the characters believe to be insane, stands apart from the rest of society. The kite's carefree movement suggests Mr. Dick's childish innocence. The pleasure the kite gives him resembles the honest, unpretentious joy Mr. Dick brings to those around him.

IMPORTANT QUOTATIONS FROM *DAVID COPPERFIELD*

If anyone had told me, then, that all this was a brilliant game, played for the excitement of the moment . . . in the thoughtless love of superiority, in a mere wasteful careless course of winning what was worthless to him, and next minute thrown away . . . I wonder in what manner of receiving it my indignation would have found a vent!

Location: Chapter XXI
Speaker: David Copperfield
Context: David remembers Steerforth's deceptively convincing kindness to the Peggottys

David comments on Steerforth's ability to seduce the Peggottys upon meeting them for the first time. The sentiment reflects three crucial elements of the novel. First, it shows how artless and naïve David is, trusting Steerforth completely until Steerforth's ultimate crime is revealed. David's willingness to trust comes across in all his interactions with Steerforth, including this one. Second, the quotation exemplifies the foreshadowing Dickens uses throughout the novel. When the adult David comments that Steerforth was playing a dangerous game, we realize that Steerforth is not what he seems. This foreshadowing ratchets up the suspense about Steerforth's intentions. Third, David, as an adult narrator, reveals in this quotation more than the young David himself knew at the time—a disparity that creates dramatic irony by giving us more knowledge than the characters themselves have. The adult perspective of the narrative voice also highlights how much David matures before the end of the novel, demonstrating that he recognizes the errors of his youthful perceptions.

My meaning simply is that whatever I have tried to do in life, I have tried with all my heart to do well . . . I have always been thoroughly in earnest.

Location: Chapter XLII
Speaker: David Copperfield
Context: David reflects on the importance of being earnest

The later chapters of *David Copperfield* are filled with these kinds of musing asides. As David matures, his narration focuses more on his life and emotions and less on the action swirling around him. In this remark, David mentions his efforts to be earnest. Throughout the novel, Dickens portrays earnestness as a desirable characteristic that usually wins out over scheming and sophistication. The characters who reveal their true feelings prevail at the conclusion of the novel, while those who plot, contrive, and conceal their true intentions suffer. Dickens uses both plot elements and these kinds of narrative asides to emphasize the importance of this kind of moral ordering. He implies that we, like David, should try to live our lives in earnest.

I was fond of wandering about the Adelphi, because it was a mysterious place, with those dark arches. I see myself emerging one evening from some of these arches, on a little public-house close to the river, with an open space before it, where some coal-heavers were dancing; to look at whom I sat down upon a bench. I wonder what they thought of me!

Location: Chapter XI
Speaker: David Copperfield
Context: David remembers eating alone in the public house as a young boy

"*The sun sets every day, and people die every minute, and we mustn't be scared by the common lot. If we failed to hold our own, because that equal foot at all men's doors was heard knocking somewhere, every* object in this world would slip from us. No! Ride on! Rough-shod if need be, smooth-shod if that will do, but ride on! Ride on over all obstacles, and win the race!"

Location: Chapter XXVIII
Speaker: James Steerforth
Context: Steerforth ostensibly comforts David in the face of Mr. Barkis's impending death and secretly encourages himself to seduce Little Em'ly

---

"There can be no disparity in marriage like unsuitability of mind and purpose."

Location: Chapter XLV
Speaker: Annie Strong
Context: In words that will haunt David after his marriage to Dora, Annie expresses the importance of unity in a marriage

THE DIARY OF A YOUNG GIRL

Anne Frank

While hiding from the Nazis with her family, a young girl keeps a diary detailing her daily life and thoughts.

THE LIFE OF ANNE FRANK

On June 12, 1929, Anne Frank was born in Frankfurt, Germany. Her father, Otto, came from a wealthy background, but his family's banking fortune was lost during the German economic depression that followed World War I. After the Nazis came to power in Germany, Otto moved his family to Amsterdam in 1933 to protect them from persecution. There he made a living selling chemical products and provisions. They lived in relative peace until 1940, when Germany occupied the Netherlands and imposed stringent anti-Semitic laws. These new measures prohibited Jews from riding streetcars, forced them to attend separate schools, required them to wear yellow stars to identify themselves as Jewish, and imposed boycotts of the businesses they owned.

Within two years of the imposition of these anti-Semitic laws, many Jews in the Netherlands were harassed, arrested, and sent to concentration camps where they were killed. The Franks and other well-connected families were able to go into hiding, often at mortal risk to themselves and to those who helped them.

On her thirteenth birthday, Anne received a diary. She was thrilled and hoped the diary would become her one trusted confidant. She immediately began filling it with details of her life, including descriptions of her friends, boys she liked, and events at school. In 1942, less than one month after she began documenting her relatively carefree childhood, Anne and her family were suddenly forced into hiding.

Margot, Anne's sixteen-year-old sister, had been "called up" by the Gestapo, Germany's brutal secret-police force. It was common knowledge among Jews that those who were called up would eventually be sent to one of the notorious concentration camps. The Franks were relatively prepared to go into hiding, since they had been sending furniture and provisions to a secret annex in Otto's office building in anticipation of the Gestapo's demands. The Franks had arranged to share the annex with another family, the van Daans. Some of Otto's non-Jewish colleagues had agreed to help them hide. The Franks later invited one more person, Mr. Dussel, to share their annex.

While they were in hiding, the Franks used a radio to keep up with news from the war, and Anne frequently wrote in her diary about events that caught her attention. The mention of these events provides a vivid historical context for Anne's personal thoughts and feelings.

The Gestapo finally arrested Anne and her family on August 4, 1944, almost two years after they had gone into hiding. Later, two secretaries who worked in the building found Anne's diary entries strewn over the floor of the annex. The secretaries gave the diaries to Miep Gies, an assistant in Otto's office. Miep kept the diary, unread, in a desk drawer. When the war ended in 1945, Miep delivered the diary to Otto Frank, who had survived the Auschwitz concentration camp. Anne and Margot died of typhus at the Bergen-Belsen concentration camp in February or March of 1945. Their mother died of hunger and exhaustion in Auschwitz in January 1945. The van Daans and Mr. Dussel also perished in the camps.

THE DIARY OF A YOUNG GIRL IN CONTEXT

Anne originally kept her diary only as a private memoir. In 1944, she heard a broadcast by Gerrit Boklestein, a member of the Dutch government in exile. When Anne heard Boklestein speak of his desire to publish Dutch people's accounts of the war, Anne began to consider writing for posterity. In addition to her diary, Anne wrote several fables and short stories, planning to publish them someday. She also had thoughts of becoming a journalist.

Otto Frank knew of his daughter's wish to become a published writer. After Miep gave him the diary, he read it and selected passages for publication, keeping in mind constraints on length and appropriateness for a young-adult audience. He also left out certain passages that he considered unflattering to his late wife and the other residents of the annex. When Mr. Frank died in 1980, the Anne Frank Foundation in Basel, Switzerland, inherited the copyright to the diary. A new edition, which restored the passages Mr. Frank originally left out, was published in 1991. Since its first publication in 1947, *The Diary of a Young Girl* has sold over 25 million copies.

THE DIARY OF A YOUNG GIRL: KEY FACTS

Full Title: Anne Frank: The Diary of a Young Girl

Time and place written: Amsterdam; 1942–1945

Date of First Publication: 1947

Publisher: Doubleday

Type of Work: Diary

Genre: Diary; autobiographical literature

Language: Dutch

Setting (time): June 12, 1942–August 1, 1944

Setting (place): Amsterdam, the Netherlands

Tense: Present

Tone: Emotional, insecure, personal, philosophical

Narrator: Anne Frank in the first person

Point of view: Anne Frank's

Protagonist: Anne Frank

Antagonist: The Nazis

THE DIARY OF A YOUNG GIRL: PLOT OVERVIEW

Anne's diary begins on her thirteenth birthday, June 12, 1942, and ends shortly after her fifteenth birthday. Anne, addressing her diary as "Kitty," describes fairly typical girlhood experiences, writing about her friendships with other girls, her crushes on boys, and her academic performance at school. Because anti-Semitic laws forced Jews into separate schools, Anne and her older sister, Margot, attended the Jewish Lyceum in Amsterdam.

After the Germans invade the Netherlands in 1940, the Franks go into hiding. Along with another family, the van Daans, and an acquaintance, Mr. Dussel, they move into a small, secret annex above Otto Frank's office, where they had already stockpiled food and supplies. The employees from Otto's firm help hide the Franks and keep them supplied with food, medicine, and information about the outside world.

The residents of the annex pay close attention to the war by listening to the radio. The adults make optimistic bets about when the war will end. Their mood depends on the war's progress. Allied setbacks or German advances depress them. As the Franks hide, Amsterdam is devastated by the war. Food becomes scarce in the city, and robberies more frequent.

Anne often writes about her feelings of isolation and loneliness. She has a tumultuous relationship with the adults in the annex, particularly her mother, whom she considers lacking in love and affection. She adores her father. Mr. and Mrs. van Daan and Mr. Dussel frequently scold her and criticize her. Anne thinks her sister, Margot, is smart, pretty, and agreeable, but she does not feel close to her and does not write much about her. Anne eventually develops a close friendship with Peter van Daan, the teenage boy in the annex. Mr. Frank does not approve of their closeness, and the intensity of Anne's infatuation begins to lessen.

The progress of Anne's diary entries show her maturation. She moves from detailed accounts of basic activities to deeper, more profound thoughts about humanity and her own nature. She does not understand why the Jews are being singled out and persecuted. Anne also confronts her own identity. She considers herself German, but her German citizenship has been revoked. She calls Holland her home, but many of the Dutch have turned against the Jews. Anne feels solidarity with her people, but she wants to be seen as an individual rather than a member of a persecuted group.

During the two years in which Anne writes in her diary, she discusses confinement and deprivation. Her diary describes the struggle to define herself within a climate of oppression. Anne's diary ends without comment on August 1, 1944. The abruptness of the ending reflects the sudden capture of the Franks, who were betrayed to the Nazis and arrested on August 4, 1944. Anne's diary—the observations of an imaginative, friendly, sometimes petty, and rather normal teenage girl—comes to a sudden, silent end.

CHARACTERS IN *THE DIARY OF A YOUNG GIRL*

Mr. van Daan The father of the family that hides in the annex along with the Franks. Mr. van Daan had worked with Otto Frank as an herbal specialist in Amsterdam. His actual name is Hermann van Pels, but Anne gives him a new name in the diary, as she does all the van Daans. According to Anne, he is intelligent, opinionated, pragmatic, and somewhat egotistical. He dies in the gas chambers at Auschwitz in October or November of 1944.

Peter van Daan The teenage son of the van Daans. His real name is Peter van Pels. Anne first sees Peter as obnoxious, lazy, and hypersensitive, but later she becomes friends with him. Peter is sweet to Anne, but he does not share her strong convictions. Peter is Anne's first kiss and her one confidant in the annex. Peter dies at the concentration camp at Mauthausen only three days before the camp is liberated.

Petronella van Daan Mr. van Daan's wife. Her real name is Auguste van Pels. Anne initially describes Mrs. van Daan as a friendly, teasing woman, but later calls her an instigator. She is a fatalist and can be petty, flirtatious, and stingy. Mrs. van Daan frequently complains about the family's situation—criticism that Anne does not respect. Mrs. van Daan does not survive the war. The exact date of her death is unknown.

Albert Dussel A dentist and an acquaintance of the Franks who hides with them in the annex. His real name is Fritz Pfeffer. Anne must share a room with Mr. Dussel, so she bears the brunt of his odd personal hygiene, pedantic lectures, and controlling tendencies. Mr. Dussel's wife is a Christian, so she does not go into hiding. Mr. Dussel dies on December 20, 1944, at the Neuengamme concentration camp.

Anne Frank The author of the diary. Anne is very intelligent and perceptive, and she wants to become a writer. Over the course of the diary, she grows from an innocent, precocious, and somewhat petty teenager to an empathetic and sensitive thinker. Anne dies of typhus in the concentration camp at Bergen-Belsen in late February or early March of 1945.

Edith Frank Anne's mother. Anne has a tumultuous relationship with her mother, for whom she feels little sympathy. Anne thinks her mother is sentimental, critical, and cold. Edith dies of hunger and exhaustion in the concentration camp at Auschwitz in January 1945.

Margot Frank Anne's older sister. Anne devotes little space to Margot in her diary and does not provide a real sense of her character. Anne thinks that Margot is pretty, smart, emotional, and everyone's favorite. Margot appears in the diary largely when she makes Anne jealous or angry. She dies of typhus in the concentration camp at Bergen-Belsen a few days before Anne does.

Otto Frank Anne's father. Otto is practical and kind, and Anne feels a particular kinship to him. Otto is the only member of the family to survive the war.

Jan Gies Miep's husband. He dies in 1993.

Miep Gies A secretary at Otto's office who helps the Franks hide. After the Franks are arrested, she stows the diary away in a desk drawer and keeps it there, unread, until Otto's return in 1945.

Hanneli Anne's school friend. The Nazis arrest her early in the war.

Mr. Kleiman A man who helps the Franks hide. Johannes Kleiman is arrested in 1944 but released because of poor health. Mr. Kleiman is also referred to as Mr. Koophuis.

Mr. Kugler A man who helps hide the Franks in the annex. Victor Kugler is arrested along with Kleiman in 1944 but escapes in 1945. Mr. Kugler is also referred to as Mr. Kraler.

Peter Schiff The love of Anne's sixth-grade year. Peter Schiff is one year older than Anne. She dreams about him in the annex.

Hello Silberberg A boy with whom Anne has an innocent, though romantic, relationship before she goes into hiding. Hello is also referred to as Harry Goldberg.

Bep Voskuijl A worker in Otto Frank's office. Elizabeth (Bep) Voskuijl serves as a liaison between the Franks and the outside world.

Mr. Voskuijl Bep's father.

THEMES IN *THE DIARY OF A YOUNG GIRL*

THE LONELINESS OF ADOLESCENCE Anne Frank's perpetual loneliness and her feeling of being misunderstood provide the impetus for her writing. Even in her early diary entries, in which she writes about her many friends and her lively social life, Anne expresses gratitude that she can share her innermost thoughts with her diary. Later, we learn that neither Mrs. Frank nor Margot gives Anne emotional support. Though Anne has a close relationship with her father, he is not a fitting confidant for a thirteen-year-old girl. Near the end of her diary, Anne shares a quotation she once read with which she strongly agrees: "Deep down, the young are lonelier than the old." Anne's embattled religion, and her cramped and deprived circumstances, heighten her isolation. Occasionally, Anne turns to the cats that live in the annex for affection. Her eventual friendship with Peter also fends off loneliness.

THE INWARD VERSUS THE OUTWARD SELF Anne frequently expresses her conviction that there are "two Annes": the lively, jovial public Anne whom people find amusing or exasperating, and the private, sentimental Anne whom only she herself truly knows. Anne expresses regret that she does not share her true self with her friends or family. Her inner split aggravates her, and she struggles with her two selves, trying to be honest and genuine while still fitting in with the rest of the group. On January 22, 1944, Anne asks, "Can you tell me why people go to such lengths to hide their real selves?" The question suggests she realizes she is not alone in seeing a difference between her public and her private selves. In her final diary entry, on August 1, 1944, Anne continues to grapple with this difference and finally resolves to be true to herself and not to fold her heart inside out so that only the bad parts show.

GENEROSITY AND GREED IN WARTIME Anne's diary demonstrates that war brings out both the best and the worst in people. In particular, generosity and greed define characters in the annex. The Dutch people who care for Anne and her family exhibit great generosity, bringing food, money, and other resources to the annex, at great risk to themselves. In an act of generosity, the Franks and van Daans invite Mr. Dussel to live with them in the annex and share their scanty resources. Mr. Dussel never makes any attempt to acknowledge or reciprocate their generosity. The two people Anne most reviles, Mr. Dussel and Mrs. van Daan, share the tendency to look out for themselves first. Generosity and greed also come to bear on Anne's guilt about being in hiding. She struggles with the idea that perhaps she and her family could have been more generous and helped more people, even though by the end of their time in the annex the residents have practically run out of food.

SYMBOLS IN *THE DIARY OF A YOUNG GIRL*

HANNELI Hanneli, one of Anne's close friends, frequently appears in Anne's dreams as a symbol of guilt. In the dreams, Hanneli is wearing rags and looks sad. She wishes Anne could stop her suffering. For Anne, Hanneli represents the fate of her friends and of the millions of Jews, many of them children, who were tortured and murdered by the Nazis. Anne wonders why her friend has to suffer while she survives in hiding.

ANNE'S GRANDMOTHER Anne's grandmother appears to Anne in her dreams. She symbolizes unconditional love and support, as well as longing for the life Anne lived before being forced into hiding. Anne wishes she could tell her grandmother how much they all love her, just as she wishes she had appreciated her own life before she was confined to the annex. Anne imagines that her grandmother is her guardian angel and will protect her. She looks to this image for sustenance when she feels particularly afraid or insecure.

IMPORTANT QUOTATIONS FROM *THE DIARY OF A YOUNG GIRL*

I sometimes wonder if anyone will ever understand what I mean, if anyone will ever overlook my ingratitude and not worry about whether or not I'm Jewish and merely see me as a teenager badly in need of some good, plain fun.

Location: December 24, 1943
Speaker: Anne Frank
Context: Anne expresses her frustration

This passage reminds us that Anne is just a normal young girl who has been forced into extraordinary circumstances. She willingly makes sacrifices and uncomplainingly deals with the restrictions of the annex because she knows that she is more fortunate than her friends who have already been arrested and sent to concentration camps. This attitude demonstrates Anne's remarkable maturity, but it clearly takes its toll on her spirit. Aside from wanting to return to the freedoms and comforts she had before the war, Anne simply wants to experience a normal childhood. She wants to be in a place where she does not have to measure her life in days and months and worry about whether her friends are suffering. She does not want to live in a world that places such significance on her nationality and religion. Anne Frank's diary has such emotional impact because we see Anne not as a saint but as a normal girl with real human feelings and imperfections.

It's difficult in times like these: ideals, dreams and cherished hopes rise within us, only to be crushed by grim reality. It's a wonder I haven't abandoned all my ideals, they seem so absurd and impractical. Yet I cling to them because I still believe, in spite of everything, that people are truly good at heart.

Location: July 15, 1944
Speaker: Anne Frank
Context: Less than one month before the Nazis sends the Franks to concentration camps, Anne writes of her hopefulness

This is perhaps the best-known passage from Anne's diary. It is a brave expression of optimism in the face of imminent and incomprehensible cruelty. It also provides a brief glimpse into Anne's mind during her last days in the annex and demonstrates how much she has changed from the days when her family first went into hiding. When she began her diary, Anne did not have the insight to make such a philosophical statement. After two years of mental and psychological growth while living in extremely difficult circumstances, however, she can draw on a core of hope, optimism, and thoughtfulness.

I hope I will be able to confide everything to you, as I have never been able to confide in anyone, and I hope you will be a great source of comfort and support.

Location: The inside cover of the diary
Speaker: Anne Frank
Context: After receiving the diary for her thirteenth birthday, Anne expresses her hopes for it

I see the eight of us in the Annex as if we were a patch of blue sky surrounded by menacing black clouds. . . . [They loom] before us like an impenetrable wall, trying to crush us, but not yet able to. I can only cry out and implore, "Oh ring, ring, open wide and let us out!"

Location: November 8, 1943
Speaker: Anne Frank
Context: As the war rages on, Anne becomes increasingly frightened

I get cross, then sad, and finally end up turning my heart inside out, the bad part on the outside and the good part on the inside, and keep trying to find a way to become what I'd like to be and what I could be if . . . if only there were no other people in the world.

Location: August 1, 1944
Speaker: Anne Frank
Context: Anne's last diary entry

DOCTOR FAUSTUS

Christopher Marlowe

A sixteenth-century German scholar sells his soul to the devil in exchange for knowledge, wealth, and supernatural powers.

THE LIFE OF CHRISTOPHER MARLOWE

Born in Canterbury, England, in 1564—the same year as William Shakespeare—Christopher Marlowe became an actor, poet, and playwright during the reign of Queen Elizabeth I (1558–1603). In his twenties Marlowe studied religion. Cambridge University initially tried to withhold his degree, apparently because it suspected him of practicing Catholicism, a religion forbidden in Elizabethan England, where the monarch was the official head of the Church. Queen Elizabeth's Privy Council intervened on Marlowe's behalf, saying that he had "done her majesty good service" in "matters touching the benefit of the country." This peculiar sequence of events has invited conjectures that Marlowe worked as a spy for England, possibly by infiltrating Catholic communities in France.

After leaving Cambridge, Marlowe moved to London, where he became a playwright and led a turbulent life punctuated by public scandals. He wrote seven immensely popular plays, including *Tamburlaine the Great* (c. 1587), *The Jew of Malta* (c. 1589), and *Doctor Faustus* (c.1592). In his works, Marlowe pioneered the use of blank verse—nonrhyming lines of iambic pentameter—which many of his contemporaries, most notably Shakespeare, later adopted. In 1593, Marlowe's career was cut short. He was arrested on charges of heresy—endorsement of beliefs that dissent from the established religion. In 1593, shortly after his release, Marlowe was killed by a blow to the head in a tavern brawl. After his death, rumors flew that he was treasonous, atheistic, and homosexual. Some people speculated that the tavern brawl might have been the work of government agents. Little evidence to support these allegations has come to light.

DOCTOR FAUSTUS IN CONTEXT

Doctor Faustus was likely written in 1592, though it was not published until a decade later. The story of the man who sells his soul to the devil in exchange for knowledge is an old trope in Christian folklore, beginning with the story of Adam and Eve. By Marlowe's time, the story had become attached to Johannes Faustus, a disreputable astrologer who lived in Germany in the early 1500s. Marlowe seems to have lifted the bulk of the plot for his play from the *Historia von D. Iohan Fausten*, an anonymous 1587 German work translated into English in 1592. Although not the first telling of the story, Marlowe's *Doctor Faustus* is the first renowned literary incarnation of Faustus. Later versions include the famous epic poem *Faust* by the nineteenth-century Romantic writer Johann Wolfgang von Goethe, as well as operas by Charles Gounod and Arrigo Boito, and a symphony by Hector Berlioz. Meanwhile, the phrase "Faustian bargain" has entered the English lexicon, referring to any deal made for short-term gain with great long-term costs.

DOCTOR FAUSTUS: KEY FACTS

Full Title: Initially published as *The Tragicall History of D. Faustus*; then as *The Tragicall History of the Life and Death of Doctor Faustus*	
Time and place written: Early 1590s; England	
Date of publication: Two editions were published in Marlowe's lifetime, one in 1604, the other in 1616	
Publisher: Unknown; possibly the theatrical entrepreneur Philip Henslowe	
Type of work: Play	
Genre: Tragedy	
Language: English	

Setting (time): The 1580s

Setting (place): Europe, especially Germany and Italy

Tone: Grandiose and tragic, leavened by occasional moments of low comedy

Protagonist: Doctor Faustus

Antagonist: Lucifer

DOCTOR FAUSTUS: PLOT OVERVIEW

Doctor Faustus, a well-respected German scholar, grows dissatisfied with the limitations of traditional forms of knowledge and decides he wants to learn magic. His friends Valdes and Cornelius instruct him in the black arts, and he begins his new career as a magician by summoning the devil Mephastophilis. Despite Mephastophilis's warnings about the horrors of hell, Faustus sends Mephastophilis back to his master Lucifer to offer to exchange Faustus's soul for twenty-four years of service from Mephastophilis. Meanwhile, Faustus's servant Wagner uses magic that he has picked up to compel a clown to become his servant.

Mephastophilis returns with news that Lucifer has accepted Faustus's offer. Faustus hesitates, wondering whether he should repent and save his soul. Finally, he commits to selling his soul. As soon as Faustus signs the deed in blood, the words "Homo fuge," Latin for "O man, fly," appear branded on his arm. Faustus is unsettled, but Mephastophilis gives him rich gifts and a book of new spells. Later, Mephastophilis answers all of Faustus's questions about the world, though he refuses to reveal who created the universe. Faustus experiences more misgivings, but the personifications of the Seven Deadly Sins summoned by Mephastophilis and Lucifer impress Faustus enough to soothe his doubts.

Armed with his new powers and attended by Mephastophilis, Faustus sets out to travel. In Rome, at the pope's court, Faust plays a series of tricks. Making himself invisible, he disrupts the pope's banquet by stealing food and boxing the pope's ears. As his fame spreads, Faustus travels through the courts of Europe. Eventually, he is invited to the court of the pope's enemy, the German Emperor Charles V. At Charles's request, Faustus conjures up an image of Alexander the Great—the renowned Macedonian conqueror-king from the fourth century B.C. Although Charles is impressed, one of his knights scoffs at Faustus's powers. Faustus punishes the knight by making antlers sprout from his head. Furious, the knight vows revenge.

Meanwhile, Robin has picked up some magic on his own. Robin and his fellow stablehand Rafe (called Dick in some editions) experience a number of comic misadventures. Robin manages to summon Mephastophilis, who threatens to turn Robin and Rafe into animals (or perhaps actually transforms them; the text isn't clear) to punish them for their foolishness.

Continuing on his travels, Faustus plays a trick on a horse-courser by selling him a horse that turns into a heap of straw as he rides through a river. Eventually, Faustus is invited to visit the duke of Vanholt, at whose court Faustus performs various feats. At the court, many people gather who have fallen victim to Faust's trickery, including the horse-courser, Robin, and Rafe. Faustus casts spells on them and sends them away, to the amusement of the duke and duchess.

As the twenty-four years of his deal with Lucifer come to a close, Faustus begins to dread his impending death. He asks Mephastophilis to call up Helen of Troy—the famous beauty from the ancient world whose abduction caused the Trojan War—to impress a group of scholars. An old man urges Faustus to repent, but Faustus drives him away. Faustus summons Helen again to admire her beauty. Time is growing short. On his last night, Faustus tells the scholars about his pact. Horror-stricken, they promise to pray for him. Overcome by fear and remorse, Faustus begs for mercy, but it is too late. At midnight, a host of devils carry his soul off to hell. In the morning, the scholars find Faustus's limbs and resolve to hold a funeral for him.

CHARACTERS IN *DOCTOR FAUSTUS*

MAJOR CHARACTERS

Chorus A character outside the story who provides narration and commentary. Greek tragedies usually included a Chorus character.

Clown A clown who becomes Wagner's servant. The clown's ridiculous antics provide comic relief and contrast with Faustus's initial grandeur. As the play goes on, Faustus begins to resemble the clown in some ways.

Faustus The play's protagonist. Faustus is a brilliant sixteenth-century scholar from Wittenberg, Germany. Hungry for knowledge, wealth, and fame, Faustus pays Lucifer the ultimate price—his soul—in exchange for supernatural powers. Ambitious and plagued by doubts, Faustus is able neither to repent nor to embrace his dark path.

Lucifer Mephastophilis's master. Lucifer is the prince of the devils and the ruler of hell.

Mephastophilis A devil who becomes Faustus's servant. Mephastophilis delivers moving descriptions of what the devils have lost in their eternal separation from God and repeatedly reflects on the torment of eternal damnation, emerging as a tragic figure in his own right.

Rafe (Known as Dick *in some editions)* An ostler friend of Robin's. Like Robin and the clown, Rafe provides contrast to Faustus.

Robin An ostler who provides comic contrast to Faustus. The fact that Robin and Rafe can perform magic and like silly tricks highlights Faustus's degradation.

Wagner Faustus's servant. Wagner uses his master's books to learn how to summon devils and work magic.

MINOR CHARACTERS

Emperor Charles V The most powerful European monarch. Faustus visits Charles's court.

Cornelius and Valdes Faustus's magician friends, who teach him black magic.

The Good Angel and the Evil Angel Spirits who embody aspects of Faustus's conscience and will. The good angel urges Faustus to repent and return to God. The bad angel helps Faustus justify his unholy actions.

The Horse-courser A trader of horses and victim of Faustus's tricks. The horse that the horse-courser buys from Faustus vanishes when the horse-courser rides it into water.

The Knight A German nobleman at Charles's court who vows to avenge himself for Faustus's trickery. See also *Benvolio*, below.

The Pope The head of the Roman Catholic Church and a powerful political figure in Faustus's Europe. The pope serves as both a source of amusement for the play's Protestant audience and a symbol of the religious faith that Faustus has rejected.

The Old Man An enigmatic figure who, in the final scene, urges Faustus to repent and to ask God for mercy.

The Scholars Faustus's colleagues at the University of Wittenberg. The scholars bookend the play, appearing in the beginning to express dismay at the direction of Faustus's studies, and at the end to marvel at his achievements and to hear his agonized confession of his pact with Lucifer.

Duke of Vanholt A German nobleman whom Faustus visits.

CHARACTERS WHO APPEAR ONLY IN EDITIONS BASED ON THE 1614 TEXT

Benvolio The same character as the *knight* above. Benvolio plans to revenge himself by murdering Faustus.

Bruno Charles's pick for the papacy. Bruno is imprisoned by the pope and freed by Faustus.

Dick The same character referred to as *Rafe* here.

Martino and Frederick Friends of Benvolio who reluctantly join his scheme to kill Faustus.

THEMES IN *DOCTOR FAUSTUS*

SIN, REDEMPTION, AND DAMNATION   *Doctor Faustus* is firmly grounded in the Christian tradition. In making a pact with Lucifer, Faustus commits the ultimate sin. He not only disobeys God's will, but also consciously renounces God and swears allegiance to the devil. Even though he is troubled by his conscience, which is personified as the good angel, Faustus fails to seek redemption and refuses to ask God's forgiveness. Turning away from God, Faustus is sentenced to damnation—an eternity in hell.

During the last moments of his life, Faustus does ask God for forgiveness. But it is too late, and he is doomed to hell. In a Christian framework, Faustus would have been allowed to repent at any time before his death. Marlowe steps outside the Christian paradigm in order to maximize the dramatic power and pathos of the last scene: Faustus is still alive but condemned to eternal suffering in hell.

THE CONFLICT BETWEEN MEDIEVAL AND RENAISSANCE VALUES   The scholar R. M. Dawkins struck at the heart of one of the play's central themes when he famously remarked that *Doctor Faustus* tells "the story of a Renaissance man who had to pay the medieval price for being one." The medieval ideology placed God at the center of existence, shunting both man and nature aside. The Renaissance—a revival of classical art and learning that began in Italy in the fifteenth century—placed a new emphasis on the individual and on scientific inquiry into the nature of the world. Faustus explicitly rejects the medieval model of living. In his opening monologue, he quotes and rejects an authority for each field of scholarship—Aristotle on logic, the Greek physician Galen on medicine, the Byzantine emperor Justinian on law, and the Bible on religion. This rejection of authority in favor of individual inquiry exemplifies the Renaissance spirit. But however much his beliefs clash with it, Faustus must live in the medieval world, where eternal damnation is the price for committing the sin of pride.

The play's attitude toward this conflict of values is ambiguous. Marlowe disapproves of Faustus's behavior, especially as Faustus descends from grand ambitions to petty conjuring tricks. On the other hand, many readers have seen Faustus as a hero of the new modern world—a world free of God, religion, and the limitations that these imposed on human development.

POWER AS A CORRUPTING INFLUENCE   At the beginning of the play, Faustus eloquently shares his grandiose ideas: he yearns for power and wealth in order to plumb the mysteries of the universe and remake the map of Europe. This ambition is sapped once Faustus actually obtains supernatural powers. He contents himself with becoming a petty celebrity by performing conjuring tricks for aristocrats and playing practical jokes on commoners. Absolute power has corrupted Faustus, making him not evil, but mediocre.

According to Christian ideology, true greatness can be achieved only with God's blessing. By cutting himself off from God, Faustus has cut himself off from the possibility of grandeur.

SYMBOLS IN *DOCTOR FAUSTUS*

BLOOD   Blood plays several symbolic roles in the play. When Faustus signs away his soul, he signs in blood, symbolizing the permanent and visceral nature of this pact. His blood congeals on the page, which suggests that his own body revolts against what he intends to do. Later, during his last night, Faustus sees Jesus' blood running across the sky. According to Christian belief, Jesus' sacrifice on the cross, which involved bloodshed, opened the way for all people to repent their sins and be saved. Jesus' blood in the sky evokes Faustus's missed opportunity for salvation.

THE GOOD ANGEL AND THE EVIL ANGEL   The two angels that appear at Faustus's shoulders early on in the play embody Faustus's divided will, part of which wants to do good and part of which is mired in sin. The internal struggle continues throughout the play.

IMPORTANT QUOTATIONS FROM *DOCTOR FAUSTUS*

The reward of sin is death? That's hard.
Si peccasse negamus, fallimur, et nulla est in nobis veritas.

If we say that we have no sin,
We deceive ourselves, and there's no truth in us.
Why then belike we must sin,
And so consequently die.
Ay, we must die an everlasting death.
What doctrine call you this? Che sarà, sarà:
What will be, shall be! Divinity, adieu!
These metaphysics of magicians,
And necromantic books are heavenly!

Location: Scene 1, lines 40–50
Speaker: Doctor Faustus
Context: In his opening soliloquy, Faustus quotes and rejects authorities on all disciplines of study; here
   he quotes the Bible

The message of the quotations Faustus has chosen—"The reward of sin is death" (Romans 6:23) and "If
we say that we have no sin, / We deceive ourselves, and there's no truth in us" (1 John 1:8)—is pessimistic: everyone sins, and sin leads to death. Faustus rejects this gloomy view and decides not to worry,
exclaiming, "What will be, shall be! Divinity, adieu!" Faustus chooses not to address Christianity's more
optimistic messages that open up the possibility of redemption, such as the next line in 1 John: "If we
confess our sins, [God] is faithful and just to forgive us our sins, and to cleanse us from all unrighteous-
ness" (1 John 1:9).

   In his next line, "These metaphysics of magicians, / And necromantic books are heavenly," Faustus
makes black magic "heavenly" and religion the source of "everlasting death," inverting the traditional
worldview by inverting the traditional meanings of words. At the same time, he is firmly rooted in the
Christian tradition. He rejects Christian morality with a Christian term, "heavenly."

The clock strikes eleven
Ah Faustus,
Now hast thou but one bare hour to live,
And then thou must be damned perpetually.
   . . .
The stars move still, time runs, the clock will strike,
The devil will come, and Faustus must be damned.
O I'll leap up to my God! Who pulls me down?
See, see where Christ's blood streams in the firmament!
One drop would save my soul, half a drop: ah my Christ—
Ah, rend not my heart for naming of my Christ;
Yet will I call on him—O spare me, Lucifer!
   . . .
Earth, gape! O no, it will not harbor me.
You stars that reigned at my nativity,
Whose influence hath allotted death and hell,
Now draw up Faustus like a foggy mist
Into the entrails of yon laboring cloud,
That when you vomit forth into the air
My limbs may issue from your smoky mouths,
So that my soul may but ascend to heaven.
   . . .
O God, if thou wilt not have mercy on my soul,
   . . .
Let Faustus live in hell a thousand years,
A hundred thousand, and at last be saved.
   . . .

Cursed be the parents that engendered me:
No, Faustus, curse thy self, curse Lucifer,
That hath deprived thee of the joys of heaven.
The clock striketh twelve
It strikes, it strikes! Now body turn to air,
Or Lucifer will bear thee quick to hell.
Thunder and lightning
O soul, be changèd into little water drops,
And fall into the ocean, ne'er be found
Enter the devils
My God, my God, look not so fierce on me!
Adders, and serpents, let me breathe awhile!
Ugly hell gape not! Come not, Lucifer!
I'll burn my books—ah, Mephastophilis!
Exeunt with him

Location: Scene 13, lines 57–113

Speaker: Faustus

Context: Faustus delivers his last soliloquy during his last hour of life on earth, just before the devils take him away to hell

After searching in vain for a way to escape his fate, Faustus ends by understanding his own guilt: "No, Faustus, curse thy self, curse Lucifer, / That hath deprived thee of the joys of heaven." Marlowe's play proves itself more classical tragedy, in which great figures end in great suffering, than Christian morality play, in which redemption is possible until the end. Here, Faustus's desperate cries to God are not heard; there is a point beyond which redemption is no longer possible, and Faustus is damned while still alive.

Faustus's last line, "I'll burn my books," returns to the play's thematic clash of Renaissance values with medieval values. For the first time since the beginning of the play, Faustus suggests that he formed his pact with Lucifer to gain knowledge—an ambition celebrated by the Renaissance spirit but denounced by medieval Christianity as an expression of sinful human pride. As he is carried off to hell, Faustus repents and re-embraces Christian ideals, denouncing the humanistic quest for knowledge that has defined most of his life.

FAUSTUS: *How comes it then that thou art out of hell?*
MEPHASTOPHILIS: *Why this is hell, nor am I out of it.*
   Think'st thou that I, who saw the face of God,
   And tasted the eternal joys of heaven,
   Am not tormented with ten thousand hells
   In being deprived of everlasting bliss?
   O Faustus, leave these frivolous demands,
   Which strike a terror to my fainting soul.
FAUSTUS: *What, is great Mephastophilis so passionate*
   For being deprivèd of the joys of heaven?
   Learn thou of Faustus manly fortitude,
   And scorn those joys thou never shalt possess.

Location: Scene 3, lines 75–86

Speaker: Faustus and Mephastophilis

Context: Mephastophilis described the torment of hell and tries to dissuade Faustus from striking a deal with Lucifer

---

MEPHASTOPHILIS: *Hell hath no limits, nor is circumscribed*
   In one self-place; for where we are is hell,

> *And where hell is, there must we ever be.*
> *. . .*
> *All places shall be hell that is not heaven.*
> FAUSTUS: *Come, I think hell's a fable.*
> MEPHASTOPHILIS: *Ay, think so still, till experience change thy mind.*
>
> *. . .*
> FAUSTUS: *Think'st thou that Faustus is so fond to imagine*
> *That after this life there is any pain?*
> *Tush, these are trifles and mere old wives' tales.*

Location: Scene 5, lines 12–135
Speaker: Mephastophilis and Faustus
Context: Mephastophilis again warns Faustus about the horrors of hell; Faustus, a Renaissance man, dismisses his observations

---

> *Was this the face that launched a thousand ships,*
> *And burnt the topless towers of Ilium?*
> *Sweet Helen, make me immortal with a kiss:*
> *Her lips suck forth my soul, see where it flies!*
> *Come Helen, come, give me my soul again.*
> *Here will I dwell, for heaven be in these lips,*
> *And all is dross that is not Helena!*

Location: Scene 12, lines 81–87
Speaker: Faustus
Context: Nearing the end of his life, Faustus has summoned Helen of Troy and contemplates her beauty. "The face that launched a thousand ships" has become an epithet for Helen

A DOLL'S HOUSE

Henrik Ibsen

A late-nineteenth-century bourgeois wife and mother leaves her family after coming to the realization that she has led a sheltered, childlike existence that her father and her husband enabled and encouraged.

THE LIFE OF HENRIK IBSEN

Henrik Ibsen, "the father of modern drama," was born in Skien, Norway, in 1828, the second of six children. Ibsen's merchant father went bankrupt when Ibsen was eight years old, and Ibsen spent much of his early life in poverty. He wrote his first play, the five-act verse tragedy *Catiline*, at the age of twenty-one, and spent much of his twenties and thirties working in theaters in Bergen and Christiana (present-day Oslo).

In 1858, Ibsen married Suzannah Thoreson. Eventually the couple had one son. Ibsen believed strongly that marriage should leave a husband and wife free to become their own human beings—a belief that became the focus of *A Doll's House*. Critics attacked him for this belief, which they perceived as a lack of respect for marriage. Ibsen's writings stirred up other sensitive social issues. Criticized for both his work and his private life, Ibsen traveled to Italy in 1864 on a grant. He spent the next twenty-seven years abroad, mostly in Italy and Germany.

Ibsen's early years as a playwright were not particularly lucrative, but in 1866 and 1867, he published two successful verse plays, *Brand* and *Peer Gynt*, which solidified his reputation as a premier Norwegian dramatist. In 1877, he wrote the drama *The Pillars of Society*, the first of a series of his last twelve plays written in an innovative realist style. But it was *A Doll's House* (1879) that marked a true breakthrough for modern drama. *A Doll's House* was followed by *Ghosts* (1881) and *An Enemy of the People* (1882), both successful. Ibsen began to gain international recognition, and his works were produced across Europe and translated into many languages.

In his later work, Ibsen began to tackle questions of a psychological and subconscious nature. His best known works from this symbolist period are *The Wild Duck* (1884), *Hedda Gabler* (1890), and *A Doll's House*. These three works are also his most frequently produced plays. In 1891, Ibsen returned to Oslo. His later dramas include *The Master Builder* (1892) and his last play, *When We Dead Awaken* (1899). In 1900, he suffered a stroke and was eventually overcome by a crippling sickness. He died in 1906.

A DOLL'S HOUSE IN CONTEXT

Nineteenth-century theater had been dominated by romanticism. After *Brand* (1866), Ibsen rejected romanticism, focusing on more realistic situations and characters.

A Doll's House was a landmark in the development of modern drama. Contemporary audiences were shocked by Nora's decision to abandon her family, so much so that original German productions of the play changed the ending. The slamming door that ends the play has been compared to the "shot heard around the world" that began the American Revolution. Although Ibsen condemned neither marriage nor motherhood—his message is about knowledge of self—the play became a rallying point for the emerging feminist movement.

A DOLL'S HOUSE: KEY FACTS

Time and place written: 1879; Italy (Rome and Amalfi)	
Date of first publication: 1879	
Type of work: Play	
Genre: Modern drama; drama of ideas; social protest drama	
Language: Norwegian	
Setting (time): Late 1870s	

Setting (place): Norway; the Helmers' living-room

Tone: Serious, intense, somber

Protagonist: Nora Helmer

Antagonist: Nora's sheltered lifestyle; the society and the people (Nora's father and husband) that have enabled and encouraged this lifestyle; Krogstad

A DOLL'S HOUSE: PLOT OVERVIEW

ACT ONE

On Christmas Eve morning, Nora Helmer returns home with packages. Her husband Torvald comes out of his study to their well-furnished living-room. He greets her playfully and affectionately, but chides her for spending so much money on Christmas gifts. The Helmers have had to be careful with money for many years, but Torvald has recently been promoted at the bank where he works.

The Helmers' maid Helene announces that an unknown female visitor has arrived at the same time as Dr. Rank, a close family friend. Torvald leaves to join Dr. Rank in the study. Nora recognizes the female visitor as Kristine—now Mrs. Linde—a former school friend. The two have not seen each other for years, but Nora remembers reading that Mrs. Linde's husband died three years earlier. Mrs. Linde tells Nora that after her husband's death, she was left childless and penniless. Nora tells Mrs. Linde about her first year of marriage to Torvald, when they were very poor and both worked long hours. Torvald became sick, Nora adds, and the couple had to travel to Italy so that Torvald could recover.

Mrs. Linde tells Nora that after her husband's death, she took care of her sick mother and two younger brothers. Now that her mother is dead and her brothers have grown up, Mrs. Linde says, she feels empty because she has nothing to do. Nora promises to speak to Torvald about helping Mrs. Linde find a job. Then Nora reveals a great secret: without Torvald's knowledge, she borrowed money for their trip to Italy. She told Torvald that the money came from her father. She has been saving her allowance and working in secret to repay the loan, and soon it will be fully repaid.

Krogstad, a low-level lawyer at Torvald's bank, arrives and goes into Torvald's study. Nora reacts uneasily to Krogstad's presence. Dr. Rank, coming out of the study, says that Krogstad is "morally sick." After meeting with Krogstad, Torvald returns to the living room and says he may be able to hire Mrs. Linde at the bank. Dr. Rank, Torvald, and Mrs. Linde depart, leaving Nora by herself. The nanny, Anne-Marie, returns with Nora's three children, and Nora plays with them until Krogstad enters the room.

As Nora and Krogstad talk, we discover that he was the one who loaned her money. Krogstad reveals that Torvald wants to fire him and says he made a "bad mistake" (committing forgery, we later find out) that has ruined his reputation. After Nora refuses to persuade Torvald to let Krogstad keep his job, Krogstad reveals that he knows she forged her father's signature on the promissory note backing her loan. He threatens to ruin her and her family if Torvald fires him, and leaves.

When Torvald returns, Nora tries to convince him not to fire Krogstad, but Torvald will not listen to her. He says that Krogstad is an immoral man in whose presence he feels physically ill.

ACT TWO

On Christmas morning, Mrs. Linde comes to visit and agrees to help mend Nora's costume for a party the following evening. Nora tells Mrs. Linde that Dr. Rank has a fatal illness inherited from his promiscuous father (her implication is that the illness is syphilis). Faced with Nora's anxiety, Mrs. Linde guesses that Dr. Rank was the one who loaned Nora money. Nora denies the charge. Torvald arrives, and Nora again begs him to keep Krogstad employed at the bank. Pressed, he admits that he dislikes Krogstad more for Krogstad's overly familiar manner than for his immoral character. Torvald and Nora argue until Torvald sends the maid to deliver Krogstad's letter of dismissal. Torvald leaves.

Dr. Rank arrives and tells Nora that his death is imminent. She flirtatiously attempts to cheer him up. She is about to ask him for help when, suddenly, he tells Nora that he loves her. Disturbed by the revelation, she refuses to tell him what is troubling her. Dr. Rank leaves.

Krogstad arrives and demands that Nora explain his dismissal. He puts a letter exposing Nora's loan and forgery into Torvald's letterbox, announcing that he now wants Torvald to rehire him for a better position. In a panic, Nora confides in Mrs. Linde, who instructs Nora to keep Torvald from opening the letter while she herself goes to speak with Krogstad. Nora manages to make Torvald promise not to open his mail until after her dance performance at the party the following evening. In order to distract Torvald from the letterbox, she practices her tarantella dance. In her agitated emotional state, she dances wildly and violently, displeasing Torvald. Mrs. Linde returns for dinner with news that Krogstad is out of town until the next evening.

ACT THREE

The next night, during the party at the upstairs neighbors', Krogstad meets Mrs. Linde in the Helmers' living room. Their conversation reveals that they were in love once, but she left him for Linde, a wealthier man who would enable her to support her mother and brothers. She says that now that her family no longer needs her, she wants to be with Krogstad and take care of his children. Overjoyed, Krogstad offers to take back his letter incriminating Nora before Torvald can read it. But Mrs. Linde insists that it will be better for both Helmers if the truth comes out. Krogstad leaves.

Nora and Torvald return from the party. After Mrs. Linde leaves, Torvald tells Nora how desirable she looked as she danced. Dr. Rank stops by to say goodnight, interrupting Torvald's advances. Torvald opens his letterbox and finds two of Dr. Rank's visiting cards, each with a black cross above the name, which Nora knows is his announcement that he will stop visiting them because he is dying.

Torvald reads Krogstad's letter and is outraged. He calls Nora a liar and a hypocrite, and declares that she will not be allowed to raise their children. Helene brings in a letter from Krogstad, which includes the forged promissory note. Relieved, Torvald says that life can now return to normal, but Nora says that Torvald has treated her like a "doll" to be played with and admired, just as her father used to treat her. She decides to leave Torvald and her children, declaring that she must "make sense of [her]self and everything around her." Ignoring Torvald's pleas, she walks out. The door slams behind her.

CHARACTERS IN *A DOLL'S HOUSE*

Anne-Marie The Helmers' kindly, elderly nanny. Anne-Marie is also Nora's former nanny. Like Mrs. Linde, Anne-Marie has made emotional sacrifices for money: she gave up her illegitimate daughter in order to take a nursing job.

Helene The Helmers' maid.

Nora Helmer Torvald's wife and the play's protagonist. At the start of the play, Nora behaves like a playful, naïve child, although her small acts of rebellion—the loan and forgery, for example—indicate that she is both stronger and less happy than she appears. Over the course of the play, she comes to see her role in her marriage with increasing clarity, finally resolving to leave her family to find out what she can become on her own.

Torvald Helmer Nora's husband. Patronizing but not unkind, Torvald calls Nora his "squirrel" and treats her as he would a capricious child. He takes pleasure in positions of authority, both at home and at his bank. He dislikes ugliness of any kind, in everything from sewing, to death, to disease, and is deeply concerned about his reputation and his place in society.

Bob, Ivan, and Emmy Helmer Nora and Torvald's young children. In her brief interactions with them, Nora plays with them as if she is playing a game. At the end of the play, she decides that she knows too little about the world to be a good mother.

Nils Krogstad Torvald's coworker and former classmate, and Mrs. Linde's former beau. Krogstad is a widower with many children, largely ostracized from polite society because he once committed a forgery. He has loaned Nora money and resorts to blackmail to protect his job and his family. His behavior is ironic, given that respectability is something he desperately seeks.

Mrs. Linde (Kristine) Nora's childhood friend. Practical, sensible, and motherly, Mrs. Linde is a foil for the childlike and romantic Nora. Unlike Nora, who abandoned her father when he was ill, Mrs. Linde has made many sacrifices to help her mother and her brothers. Her sympathetically portrayed betrothal to Krogstad shows that Ibsen does not attack marriage as an institution. Unlike Nora, Mrs. Linde has led a difficult life and makes an informed decision. At the same time, Mrs. Linde feels empty when she has no one to mother, and has not learned about herself as Nora intends to do at the end.

Dr. Rank A close friend of the Helmers'. A doctor and a pillar of the community, Dr. Rank is in love with Nora and is dying of syphilis, which his father contracted from his mistresses. He represents a society tainted by moral weakness (love for Nora, his father's adultery) and physical weakness (syphilis).

THEMES IN *A DOLL'S HOUSE*

THE SACRIFICES WOMEN MAKE   The women of *A Doll's House*, regardless of their economic status, have all had to sacrifice their integrity—as men refuse to do, and as "hundreds of thousands of women have" (Nora, Act III). Mrs. Linde left the penniless Krogstad, whom she loved, in order to marry a richer man. Anne-Marie abandoned her daughter so that she could work as Nora's (and then as Nora's children's) nanny. Nora lies about her loan because Torvald could never bear to know that she had saved his life. Because it is illegal for a woman to take out a loan without her husband's permission, Nora's sacrifice has left her vulnerable to blackmail.

OBLIGATIONS BETWEEN PARENTS AND CHILDREN   Nora, Torvald, and Dr. Rank all believe that a parent's immorality is passed on to their children like a disease. Indeed, Dr. Rank's father passed a venereal disease to his son, meaning that Dr. Rank pays with his life for his father's moral depravity. "Nearly all young criminals had lying mothers," declares Torvald. Later, after discovering that Nora lied and committed forgery, he forbids her to interact with their children for fear that she will corrupt them.

At the same time, the play explored the duties of adults to their aging parents. Mrs. Linde marries into money and spends years taking care of her sick mother. Nora, on the other hand, chooses to take care of her sick husband instead of her sick father. Ibsen does not pass harsh judgment on these decisions, but he does suggest that our first obligation is to ourselves. He thinks it is the human project to become fully realized human beings through knowledge and introspection.

UNRELIABLE APPEARANCES   Over the course of the play, several characters are radically transformed. Nora initially seems to be a silly, childish woman, but as the play progresses, we see that she is intelligent, motivated, and, by the play's conclusion, independent and strong-willed. Torvald, who plays the part of the strong, benevolent husband, reveals himself to be petty, cowardly, and selfish when faced with the threat of scandal. Krogstad emerges as merciful and sympathetic by the end of the play. Dr. Rank turns out to be a syphilitic lover. The kindhearted Mrs. Linde forces Torvald's discovery of Nora's secret against her wishes. These misleading exteriors suggest that Torvald's emphasis on image and reputation are misguided. By the end of the play, Torvald's willingness to suppress the truth in favor of appearance has damaged his family irreparably.

SYMBOLS IN *A DOLL'S HOUSE*

THE CHRISTMAS TREE   The play draws parallels between Nora and the Christmas tree, whose decorative role in the living room symbolizes Nora's role as a charming plaything in the household. Just as the children are not allowed to see the tree until it has been decorated, Torvald cannot see Nora in her costume until the party. At the beginning of Act Two, the Christmas tree's "disheveled" appearance mirrors Nora's anxiety and psychological turmoil. Like Christmas, the tree has been stripped of spiritual significance in this secular bourgeois household. Similarly, Nora has been denied the chance to explore herself by society and by the men in her life.

THE NEW YEAR   Both Nora and Torvald look forward to New Year's Day, hoping it will mark the start of a new, happier phase in their lives. They expect that Torvald will be promoted to a more lucrative job, and Nora will finally repay her debt to Krogstad. By the end of the play, the new start has changed dramatically: both must become new people and face new challenges in life.

IMPORTANT QUOTATIONS FROM *A DOLL'S HOUSE*

Free. To be free, absolutely free. To spend time playing with the children. To have a clean, beautiful house, the way Torvald likes it.

Location: Act One
Speaker: Nora
Context: Nora exults to Mrs. Linde about paying off her debt to Krogstad after the New Year

In describing her anticipated freedom, Nora highlights the very factors that constrain her. Freedom will give her time to be a wife and mother who maintains a beautiful home as her husband likes it. Over the course of the play, however, Nora realizes that she must change her life to find true freedom, and her understanding of the word "free" evolves accordingly. By the end of the play, she relieves herself of her obligations to her family in order to explore her new ambitions and beliefs.

From now on, forget happiness. Now it's just about saving the remains, the wreckage, the appearance.

Location: Act Three
Speaker: Torvald
Context: Torvald laments to Nora after finding out about Nora's forgery and Krogstad's power over their family

Torvald, deeply concerned with what his colleagues think of him, has already made it clear that he is attracted to Nora for her beauty and its flattering reflection on himself. Here, he explicitly states that the appearance of happiness is more important to him than happiness itself. Torvald's reaction contrasts dramatically with Nora's expectations: rather than gallantly sacrificing his reputation, Torvald seeks to protect it, proving himself to be the opposite of the strong, noble man that he would like to appear to be.

One day I might, yes. Many years from now, when I've lost my looks a little. Don't laugh. I mean, of course, a time will come when Torvald is not as devoted to me, not quite so happy when I dance for him, and dress for him, and play with him.

Location: Act One
Speaker: Nora
Context: Nora, talking to Mrs. Linde, describes the circumstances under which she would consider telling Torvald that she had secretly taken out a loan to save his life

---

Something glorious is going to happen.

Location: Act Two
Speaker: Nora
Context: Nora predicts to Mrs. Linde that after Torvald finds out about Nora's forgery and secret loan, he will take the blame on himself and sacrifice his reputation to save hers. At the end of the play, the phrase refers to how profoundly Torvald would have to change for Nora to consider living with him again

I have been performing tricks for you, Torvald. That's how I've survived. You wanted it like that. You and Papa have done me a great wrong. It's because of you I've made nothing of my life.

Location: Act Three
Speaker: Nora
Context: At the end of the play, Nora explains to Torvald why she must leave him to find herself

DON QUIXOTE

Miguel de Cervantes

A seventeenth-century middle-aged gentleman who wants to be a knight-errant sets off with his peasant squire on a series of quixotic adventures in a world no longer governed by chivalric values.

THE LIFE OF MIGUEL DE CERVANTES

Miguel de Cervantes Saavedra was born in 1547 to a poor Spanish doctor. He joined the army at age twenty-one and fought against Turkey at sea and Italy on land. In 1575, pirates kidnapped Cervantes and his brother and sold them as slaves to the Moors, the longtime Muslim enemies of Catholic Spain. Cervantes ended up in Algiers. He attempted to escape his enslavement three times and was eventually ransomed in 1580 and returned to Spain.

In 1585, Cervantes published his first novel, but he did not achieve either financial success or popular renown until the publication of the first volume of *Don Quixote* in 1604. *Don Quixote* was so popular that a writer using the pseudonym Avellaneda published an unauthorized sequel several years after the original. The sequel inspired Cervantes to hurry up with his own second volume, which he published in 1614. Cervantes died the following year.

DON QUIXOTE IN CONTEXT

Many of the elements of *Don Quixote* are drawn from Cervantes's life: Algerian pirates on the Spanish coast, Moors exiled from Spain, prisoners frustrated by the consequences of their failed escape attempts, and Spanish courage in the face of defeat in battle, for example. The tale of the captive details many of the historical battles in which Cervantes participated. The novel also reflects Cervantes's biases, most notably his mistrust of foreigners.

With gold and silver pouring in from American colonies, the Spanish empire reached the height of its power during Cervantes's life. At the same time, the late sixteenth century saw some of Spain's most crippling defeats, including the destruction of the seemingly invincible 1588 Armada expedition by bad weather and English forces. With his country caught in the tumult of a new age, Cervantes attempted, with *Don Quixote*, to create a forum to investigate human identity, shifting morality, and the role of art and literature in life.

Through the beginning of the Renaissance, popular literature was dominated by romances—highly stylized stories about wandering knights, or knight-errants, who traveled around and performed good deeds by subduing giants, battling evil enchanters, and rescuing court ladies in distress. Under chivalry, a medieval honor code of noble conduct that knights were supposed to follow, good knights protected weak and idealized women.

On one hand, the first volume of *Don Quixote* is a parody of the romances of Cervantes's time: Don Quixote is an absurd knight-errant, his squire and his lady are peasants, his horse pathetic, his quests imaginary, and his chivalry ridiculous and outdated. At the same time, Cervantes suggests that this code of honor of earlier times could guide a Spain troubled by war and bewildered by its own technological and colonial successes.

Don Quixote bitterly criticizes the Spanish class hierarchy in which the arrogant aristocracy retained its traditional hold on power and property even as common people were becoming more educated and capable. The novel's moral victory rests with Sancho and Tereza Panza, peasants who embrace old-fashioned values and folk wisdom faced with a world of petty pragmatism.

DON QUIXOTE: KEY FACTS

Full title: The Adventures of Don Quixote

Time and place written: Turn of the seventeenth century; Spain

Date of publication: 1604 (First Part), 1614 (Second Part)

Type of work: Novel	
Genre: Parody; romance; picaresque	
Language: Spanish	
Setting (time): 1614	
Setting (place): Spain	
Tense: Past; occasionally present	
Tone: Ironically detached, mock serious	
Narrator: Cervantes (who claims to be translating the work of Cide Hamete Benengeli)	
Point of view: Third-person limited when narrating Don Quixote's adventures; first-person when discussing Benengeli's "original" manuscript	
Protagonist: Don Quixote de la Mancha's	
Antagonist: A mean and petty world no longer governed by honor and idealism	

DON QUIXOTE: PLOT OVERVIEW

FIRST PART

Don Quixote, a middle-aged gentleman from the central Spanish region of La Mancha, is inspired by chivalric ideals in books to take up his lance and sword to defend the helpless and destroy the wicked. He needs a lady in whose name to perform his deeds, so he chooses a peasant girl, naming her Dulcinea del Toboso and imagining that she is as a princess. Searching for glory and grand adventure, Don Quixote rides the roads of Spain on his barn nag Rocinante. After a failed first adventure, he sets out on a second one with a befuddled laborer named Sancho Panza. Don Quixote has persuaded Sancho to accompany him as his faithful squire. He promises Sancho a wealthy isle to govern in return.

On the first day of their expedition, Don Quixote charges a windmill that he mistakes for a giant. The next day, Don Quixote and Sancho attack monks that Don Quixote thinks are evil enchanters and try to steal their clothes. Don Quixote steals a barber's basin, believing that it is the legendary Mambrino's helmet. He becomes convinced of the healing powers of something he calls the Balsam of Fierbras, an elixir that makes him so ill that after he stops taking it, he feels healed. Sancho Panza tries to mitigate the scrapes that Don Quixote gets them into, often bearing the brunt of the consequences.

Along the way, Don Quixote witnesses the funeral of a student who has died because of his love for a disdainful lady turned shepherdess. He frees the wicked and devious galley slave Gines de Pasamonte. He unwittingly reunites two separated couples, Cardenio and Lucinda, and Ferdinand and Dorothea. Torn apart by Ferdinand's treachery, the four lovers finally come together at the inn where Don Quixote sleeps, dreaming that he is battling a giant.

Eventually two of Don Quixote's friends, the priest and the barber, hatch a plan to drag Don Quixote home. Don Quixote accompanies them back, believing that he is being influenced by an enchantment.

SECOND PART

Cervantes begins the second part of his story with a passionate invective against a phony sequel to the first part of *Don Quixote*.

Even though his niece and his housekeeper implore him to stay home, Don Quixote sets off on another adventure with Sancho Panza. Don Quixote's reputation—gleaned from both the original story and the phony sequel—precedes them everywhere they go. As they begin their travels, Sancho tells Don Quixote that an evil enchanter has transformed Dulcinea into a peasant girl. This is a lie, but even Sancho himself eventually believes it. Rescuing Dulcinea from this spell becomes Don Quixote's main quest.

Don Quixote meets a duke and duchess who conspire to play tricks on him. They make a servant dress up as Merlin (a magician from medieval romances) and tell Don Quixote that Dulcinea's enchantment—which they know to be a hoax—can be undone only if Sancho whips his own naked backside 3,300 times. Under the watch of the duke and duchess, Don Quixote and Sancho undertake several adventures. They set out on a flying wooden horse, hoping to slay a giant who has turned a princess and her lover into metal figurines. For ten days, Sancho rules a fictitious isle, until he is wounded in an onslaught sponsored by the duke and duchess. Sancho decides that it is better to be a happy laborer than a miserable governor. A young court maid falls in love with Don Quixote, but he remains faithful to Dulcinea. Don Quixote's never-consummated affair amuses the court to no end.

Eventually Don Quixote sets out to continue his journey but is vanquished by the Knight of the White Moon—an old friend in disguise—shortly after arriving in Barcelona. In the end, the beaten and battered Don Quixote abandons all the chivalric truths he followed so fervently. He dies from a fever.

Cervantes relates the story of Don Quixote as a historical narrative, which he claims to have translated from a manuscript by Cide Hamete Benengeli, a (fictitious) Moor historian. The novel concludes with a note from Benengeli saying that his main purpose in chronicling Don Quixote's story was to illustrate the demise of chivalry.

CHARACTERS IN *DON QUIXOTE*

THE AUTHORS (REAL AND FICTIONAL)

Cide Hamete Benengeli The fictional Moor historian whose history of Don Quixote Cervantes has supposedly translated. Benengeli's history is rife with contempt for authors who warp or embellish stories of chivalry. Cervantes creates this construct of a lost first author to comment on authorship and literature.

Cervantes The narrator and translator of Benengeli's supposed historical novel. Cervantes interjects commentary into his narrative at key times.

THE ADVENTURERS

Don Quixote de la Mancha The novel's tragicomic hero and protagonist. Obsessed with medieval romances, Don Quixote seeks to revive knight-errantry in a world where chivalry has become obsolete. Idealistic and dignified, willful and self-delusional, Don Quixote changes from an absurd and isolated figure to a pitiable, sympathetic old man over the course of the novel.

Sancho Panza The peasant laborer who joins Don Quixote on his adventures as his squire. Greedy but generous, cowardly but loyal, Sancho is a a common man of "old Christian" values and a foil to Don Quixote. Sancho dispenses wisdom in loopy proverbs. By the end of the novel, his moral system emerges as the most compelling one.

Dulcinea del Toboso A peasant woman whom Don Quixote casts as his princess lady love and muse. Though Don Quixote's vision of Dulcinea drives the action, she never appears in the novel.

THE FRIENDS

The Barber Don Quixote's friend. The barber realizes that Don Quixote is delusional and strenuously disapproves of his antics .

Teresa Panza Sancho's goodhearted wife. Teresa speaks in wise proverbs and endures Sancho's exploits.

The Priest Don Quixote's friend. Tales of chivalry are a guilty pleasure for the priest. He enjoys Don Quixote's madness but tricks him into going home in the First Part.

Sampson Carrasco A sarcastic and self-important student from Don Quixote's village. After losing to Don Quixote in combat, Sampson dedicates himself to revenge.

Gines de Pasamonte An ungrateful galley slave freed by Don Quixote. Gines provides some comic relief.

THE FOUR-LEGGED FRIENDS

Dapple Sancho's donkey. Dapple's disappearance and reappearance stirs much controversy in the novel—and among literary critics.

Rocinante Don Quixote's worn-out barn horse. Slow and faithful, Rocinante evokes his master.

THE COUPLES

Cardenio The quintessential romantic lover. Cardenio is an honorable man driven mad by his wife Lucinda's infidelities with the treacherous Duke Ferdinand.

Dorothea Ferdinand's faithful and persistent lover. Cunning and aggressive, Dorothea tracks down Ferdinand after he sleeps with her and refuses to marry her.

Ferdinand An arrogant young duke who steals Lucinda from her husband Cardenio.

Lucinda Cardenio's wife and a model courtly woman. Docile and beautiful, Lucinda obliges her parents and her lover, Ferdinand.

THE DUKE AND DUCHESS'S COURT

Altisidora The Duchess's bratty maid. Altisidora pretends to be in love with Don Quixote, mocking his romantic ideals.

The Duke & Duchess A cruel and haughty couple who, in the Second Part, contrive adventures for Don Quixote for their own amusement.

Roque Guinart A chivalrous bandit. Roque believes in justice and kindness but kills an underling who criticizes his generosity.

The Duke's Steward (a.k.a. Countess Trifaldi) The duke's henchman. The steward pretends to be a maidservant in distress to exploit Don Quixote's sympathy for the duke's amusement. His name, *Trifaldi*, means "three-skirt."

THEMES IN *DON QUIXOTE*

NARRATIVE STYLE Cervantes employs three different types of narration over the course of *Don Quixote*. The first section of the First Part (through Chapter VIII) is a parody of contemporary romance tales, narrated straightforwardly by Cervantes. The rest of the First Part plods along under the guise of a historical narrative, devoting a chapter to each episode and carefully documenting each day's events. At the same time, Cervantes informs us that Don Quixote is not his invention, claiming that this text is a translation of the manuscript of one Cide Hamete Benengeli. He often interrupts the narrative to point out inconsistencies in Benengeli's account. The Second Part, which features a third style of narration, is organized by emotional and thematic content and takes time to develop character. Cervantes enters the novel as a character and allows Don Quixote and Sancho to modify their stories and criticize false accounts of their adventures.

This convoluted, self-referential narrative structure leaves us disoriented as we try to figure out exactly what has happened in Don Quixote's world. This disorientation both engrosses us and calls into question what it means to be lucid and sane—a theme the novel explores by debating Don Quixote's sanity. As soon as he introduces Benengeli, Cervantes becomes an unreliable narrator and loses our trust. But in the Second Part, as Cervantes, Don Quixote, and Sancho Panza combine forces to challenge alternative "false" histories, we lose all footing and realize that we must let go of traditional ideas about plot. Cervantes manipulates our preconceptions in order to force us to examine them more closely. Just as Don Quixote forces his compatriots to question their principles, so Cervantes forces us to question the principles of narration. The form of the novel mirrors its function.

INCOMPATIBLE VALUE SYSTEMS The conflict between Don Quixote's chivalric morality and everyone else's less genteel values results in an impasse: Sancho Panza is the only one who can mediate between Don Quixote and the rest of the world. Toward the end of the Second Part, however, Cervantes allows Don Quixote's imaginary world and the duke and duchess's "reality" to infiltrate and influence each other, allowing us to see the advantages and disadvantages of each. Sancho Panza's commonsense middle ground prevails. His is a mix of timeless aphorisms, ascetic discipline, and reasoning skills.

SYMBOLS IN *DON QUIXOTE*

BOOKS AND MANUSCRIPTS Books and manuscripts, so often mentioned in *Don Quixote*, symbolize the importance and influence of fiction and literature in everyday life. The books both teach and provide an imaginative outlet for otherwise dull lives. Don Quixote's actions are deeply influenced by the books he has read. Characters often contemplate writing their personal histories. On several occasions, characters debate the relative merits of different types of texts. Most characters, notably the priest, conclude that literature should tell the truth. Several even propose government censorship against books that could corrupt the populace, as medieval romances have corrupted Don Quixote. But the novel itself presents a complicated relationship between history and fiction. Cervantes maintains that Don Quixote is an account of historical events, as recorded in the La Mancha archives and by Benengeli. Since both the archives and Benengeli's manuscript are his inventions, Cervantes implies that the line between history and fiction is blurry, no matter how earnest the intention to tell only the truth.

INNS The novel's many inns represent democratic institutions. The inns are the only places where people ordinarily segregated by class meet and exchange stories. Associated with rest and food, money and greed, inns represent realistic, flawed human society. The tension between Sancho's desire to stay at an inn and Don Quixote's romantic preference to sleep under the stars suggests the tension between messy everyday life and lofty ideals. Even at an inn, Don Quixote is removed from the thrumming life of a socially mixed place: as the four lovers are reunited at the inn where he sleeps, Don Quixote dreams of quixotic battles.

HORSES Horses symbolize movement, and the condition of the horses often reflects characters' status. For example, the pilgrims outside Barcelona walk to the city, the noblemen ride in carriages, and Don Quixote and the robbers ride on horseback. To Don Quixote, the appearance of horses on the horizon signals a new adventure. Rocinante and Dapple are not only means of transport and symbols of status but also companions.

IMPORTANT QUOTATIONS FROM *DON QUIXOTE*

I shall never be fool enough to turn knight[-]errant. For I see quite well that it's not the fashion now to do as they did in the olden days when they say those famous knights roamed the world.

Location: First Part, Chapter XXXII
Speaker: The innkeeper to the priest
Context: The priest has tried to convince the innkeeper that the books of chivalry are not true; the innkeeper does not believe him but nevertheless says he realizes that knight-errantry is outdated

The innkeeper's remark inspires Sancho, who overhears him, to resolve once again to return to his wife and children, since knight-errantry has fallen out of fashion. Sancho's subsequent decision to remain with Don Quixote is poignant given Sancho's temptation to leave. Additionally, comparing the innkeeper's sincere attitude with the priest's exposes the priest's hypocrisy: despite condemning Don Quixote's expeditions, the priest has furtively encouraged Don Quixote's madness in order to live vicariously through Don Quixote's adventures.

For me alone Don Quixote was born and I for him. His was the power of action, mine of writing.

Location: Second Part, Chapter LXXIV
Speaker: Cide Hamete Benengeli
Context: This is the concluding note of the fictional author of Don Quixote's adventures

Benengeli's parting words echo Cervantes's opening statement that Don Quixote is only his stepson and thus he cannot be fully responsible for him. Benengeli, the Moorish historian whose manuscript Cervantes has translated, is Don Quixote's real "father." These constructs—the faux-historical novel, the fictitious translator—endow the text with a mythic, unreal tone, leaving us unsure of exactly what has transpired, whether in Don Quixote's narrative or in the story of its composition.

[F]or what I want of Dulcinea del Toboso she is as good as the greatest princess in the land. For not all those poets who praise ladies under names which they choose so freely, really have such mistresses.. . . I am quite satisfied. . . to imagine and believe that the good Aldonza Lorenzo is so lovely and virtuous. . .

Location: First Part, Chapter XXV
Speaker: Don Quixote
Context: Don Quixote explains to Sancho Panza that Aldonza Lorenzo's actual behavior does not matter so long as he is free to imagine her as his Princess Dulcinea del Toboso

---

Now that I've to be sitting on a bare board, does your worship want me to flay my bum?

Location: Second Part, Chapter XLI
Speaker: Sancho Panza
Context: Don Quixote has suggested that Sancho whip himself to free Dulcinea from her alleged enchantment, and Sancho refuses with sarcastic wit

---

Great hearts, my dear master, should be patient in misfortune as well as joyful in prosperity. And this I judge from myself. For if I was merry when I was Governor now that I'm a squire on foot I'm not sad, for I've heard tell that Fortune, as they call her, is a drunken and capricious woman and, worse still, blind; and so she doesn't see what she's doing, and doesn't know whom she is casting down or raising up.

Location: Second Part, Chapter LXVI
Speaker: Sancho Panza
Context: In his parting words, Sancho for once takes the dominant role of teacher and cautions Don Quixote to be patient in his retirement

DR. JEKYLL AND MR. HYDE

Robert Louis Stevenson

A respectable doctor concocts a potion that enables him to become an evil and violent man.

THE LIFE OF ROBERT LOUIS STEVENSON

Robert Louis Stevenson, one of the masters of the Victorian adventure story, was born in Edinburgh, Scotland, on November 13, 1850. He was a sickly child, and respiratory troubles plagued him throughout his life. As a young man he traveled through Europe, leading a bohemian lifestyle and penning two travel narratives. In 1876, he fell in love with a married woman, Fanny Van de Grift Osbourne. Mrs. Osbourne eventually divorced her husband and married Stevenson.

Stevenson and Fanny returned to London. In spite of his terrible health, Stevenson wrote prolifically over the next decade. In 1883, he wrote the widely acclaimed *Treasure Island*, an adventure story set on the high seas. In 1886, Stevenson published *Kidnapped*, an adventure story and historical novel set in Stevenson's native Scotland. *Dr. Jekyll and Mr. Hyde*, which Stevenson described as a "fine bogey tale," was also published in 1886. The novel met with tremendous success, selling 40,000 copies in six months and solidifying Stevenson's fame as a writer.

By the late 1880s, Stevenson was considered one of the leading lights of English literature. He traveled often, seeking a climate that would not aggravate his tuberculosis. Eventually he settled in Samoa. In 1894, at the age of forty-four, he died suddenly.

DR. JEKYLL AND MR. HYDE IN CONTEXT

Dr. Jekyll and Mr. Hyde, a tale of a respectable doctor who transforms himself into a savage murderer, tapped directly into the anxieties of Stevenson's age. The Victorian era, named for Queen Victoria, who ruled England for most of the nineteenth century, was a time of unprecedented technological progress and European power. By the end of the century, however, many people were beginning to question the ideals of progress and civilization that had defined the era. A growing sense of pessimism and decline pervaded artistic circles. Many felt that as the century came to a close, Western culture was on the wane.

With the notion of a single body containing both the upstanding Dr. Jekyll and the depraved Mr. Hyde, Stevenson's novel imagines an inextricable link between civilization and savagery, good and evil. When Dr. Jekyll finds Mr. Hyde in himself, he learns that freedom, cruelty, and lust lurk underneath his respectable surface. Dr. Jekyll's discovery suggests that Victorian England, by coming into contact with other cultures and ways of life, realized that aspects of these cultures existed within England itself and both desired and feared to indulge them. These aspects included open sensuality, physicality, and other so-called "irrational" tendencies. Victorian England sought to assert its civilization over and against these instinctual sides of life, but it found them fascinating—just as Jekyll tries to squelch his rebellious side but finds it too alluring to resist. Indeed, for Victorian England as for Jekyll, repression of the darker side only increased its fascination.

DR. JEKYLL AND MR. HYDE: KEY FACTS

Full title: The Strange Case of Dr. Jekyll and Mr. Hyde
Time and place written: 1885; Bournemouth, England
Date of first publication: January 1886
Publisher: Longmans, Green and Co.
Type of work: Novel

Genre: Gothic novel; science fiction

Language: English

Setting (time): The late nineteenth century

Setting (place): London

Tense: Past

Tone: Mysterious, serious

Narrator: Anonymous third person; Dr. Lanyon and Dr. Jekyll each narrate one chapter of the novel via confessional letters

Point of view: Mainly Utterson's; in the last two chapters, Lanyon's and Jekyll's

Protagonist: Henry Jekyll

Antagonist: Edward Hyde

DR. JEKYLL AND MR. HYDE: PLOT OVERVIEW

Mr. Utterson, a sensible, trustworthy lawyer, listens as his friend Enfield tells a gruesome tale of assault. Enfield explains that a sinister figure named Mr. Hyde trampled a young girl, disappeared into a door on the street, and reemerged to pay off her relatives with a check signed by a respectable gentleman. Since both Utterson and Enfield disapprove of gossip, they agree to speak no further of the matter. It happens, however, that Dr. Jekyll, one of Utterson's clients and close friends, has written a will transferring all of his property to this same Mr. Hyde. Soon Utterson begins having dreams in which a faceless figure stalks through a nightmarish version of London.

Puzzled, Utterson visits Dr. Lanyon, a friend of his and Jekyll's, to try to learn more. Lanyon says he no longer sees much of Jekyll because they had quarreled over the course of Jekyll's research, which Lanyon calls "unscientific balderdash." Curious, Utterson stakes out a building that Hyde visits—which, it turns out, is a laboratory attached to the back of Jekyll's home. Utterson encounters Hyde and is amazed by how ugly he is. It is as if Hyde is somehow deformed. Much to Utterson's surprise, Hyde willingly offers Utterson his address. Jekyll tells Utterson not to concern himself with the matter of Hyde.

A year passes uneventfully. Then one night a servant girl witnesses Hyde brutally beat to death an old man named Sir Danvers Carew, a member of Parliament and one of Utterson's clients. The police contact Utterson. He suspects Hyde committed the murder, so he leads the officers to Hyde's apartment. The weather is eerie and foreboding. Although it is morning, it is dark and foggy. When they arrive at the apartment, Hyde has vanished.

On his own, Utterson visits Jekyll, who claims he has ended all relations with Hyde. He shows Utterson a note Hyde wrote him, apologizing for the trouble he has caused and saying goodbye. That night, Utterson's clerk points out that Hyde's handwriting bears a remarkable similarity to Jekyll's own.

For a few months, Jekyll acts especially friendly and sociable, as if a weight has been lifted from his shoulders. Then he suddenly begins to refuse visitors. Lanyon receives some kind of shock associated with Jekyll. He gives Utterson a letter, instructing him to open it only after Jekyll's death. After giving Utterson the letter, Lanyon dies.

While out for a walk, Utterson and Enfield see Jekyll at a window of his laboratory. They stop and talk to him, but soon a look of horror comes over Jekyll's face and he slams the window and disappears. Soon afterward, Jekyll's butler, Mr. Poole, visits Utterson in a state of desperation. Jekyll has secluded himself in his laboratory for several weeks, and now the voice that comes from the room sounds nothing like the doctor's. Utterson and Poole travel to Jekyll's house through empty, windswept, sinister streets. After arguing for a time, they break into Jekyll's laboratory. Inside they find the body of Hyde in Jekyll's clothes. It seems he has committed suicide. They find a letter from Jekyll to Utterson promising to explain everything.

At home Utterson first reads Lanyon's letter, which reveals that Lanyon's deterioration and eventual death were caused by the shock of seeing Mr. Hyde take a potion and metamorphose into Dr. Jekyll. Then Utterson reads the letter from Jekyll. In it, Jekyll explains that in seeking a way to separate his good side from his dark side, he discovered a way to transform himself periodically into a deformed monster free of conscience—Mr. Hyde. At first he delighted in becoming Hyde and rejoiced in Hyde's moral freedom. But he started turning into Hyde involuntarily in his sleep, even without taking the potion. At this point Jekyll resolved to cease becoming Hyde. One night, however, the urge gripped him too strongly, and after the transformation he rushed out and violently killed Sir Danvers Carew. Horrified, Jekyll adamantly tried to stop the transformations, and for a time he proved successful. One day while sitting in a park, he suddenly turned into Hyde—the first time an involuntary metamorphosis had happened while he was awake.

Far from his laboratory and hunted by the police as a murderer, Hyde asked Lanyon to get his potions and help him become Jekyll again. When he transformed in Lanyon's presence, the shock of the sight indirectly killed Lanyon. Jekyll returned home. His transformations increased in frequency, and reversing them required ever-larger doses of potion. It was the onset of one of these spontaneous metamorphoses that caused Jekyll to slam his laboratory window shut in the middle of his conversation with Enfield and Utterson. Eventually the potion ran out, and Jekyll was unable to find a key ingredient to make more. His ability to change from Hyde into Jekyll slowly vanished. Jekyll writes that even as he composes his letter he knows that he will soon become Hyde permanently. He wonders if Hyde will face execution for his crimes or choose to kill himself. Jekyll notes that, in any case, the end of his letter marks the end of the life of Dr. Jekyll. With these words, both the letter and the novel come to a close.

CHARACTERS IN *DR. JEKYLL AND MR. HYDE*

Sir Danvers Carew Hyde's murder victim. Carew was a well-liked old nobleman, a member of Parliament, and a client of Utterson's.

Mr. Enfield A distant cousin and lifelong friend of Mr. Utterson. Like Utterson, Enfield is reserved, formal, and scornful of gossip.

Mr. Guest Utterson's clerk and confidant. Guest, an expert in handwriting, notices that Hyde's script is nearly the same as Jekyll's.

Mr. Edward Hyde Dr. Jekyll's dark side. Hyde is a violent, repugnant man who looks almost pre-human. Everyone who sees him describes him as ugly and deformed, but no one can explain why. Language itself seems to fail around Hyde. He does not belong in the rational world.

Dr. Henry Jekyll A respected doctor. Jekyll is a prosperous man known for his decency and charitable works. Since his youth, he has secretly engaged in unspecified corrupt behavior. Because Jekyll finds this dark side a burden, he undertakes experiments intended to separate his good and evil selves.

Dr. Hastie Lanyon A reputable London doctor. Lanyon, along with Utterson, is one of Jekyll's closest friends. An embodiment of rationalism, materialism, and skepticism, Lanyon is a foil for Jekyll, who embraces mysticism. Lanyon's death represents the general dominance of supernaturalism over materialism in *Dr. Jekyll and Mr. Hyde*.

Mr. Poole Jekyll's butler.

Mr. Gabriel John Utterson A prominent lawyer. Utterson is reserved and dignified, but he has a furtive curiosity about the sordid side of life. While not a man of science, Utterson resembles his friend Dr. Lanyon in his devotion to reasonable explanations and his denial of the supernatural.

THEMES IN *DR. JEKYLL AND MR. HYDE*

THE DUALITY OF HUMAN NATURE Jekyll asserts that "man is not truly one, but truly two." He imagines the human soul as the battleground for an "angel" and a "fiend," each struggling for mastery. Events seem to prove him wrong, however. His potion, which he hoped would separate and purify each element, succeeds only in bringing the dark side into being. Hyde emerges, but he has no angelic counterpart. Jekyll, Hyde's counterpart, is no angel.

Stevenson posits many theories of human behavior. One of them suggests that perhaps man is not "truly two," but one primitive creature brought under tentative control by civilization, law, and conscience. According to this theory, the potion simply strips away the civilized veneer, exposing man's essential nature. Another theory suggests that civilization itself creates evil. In many ways, Hyde is an animalistic, primitive creature. But unlike an animal, Hyde takes delight in violence. He is happily *im*moral rather than *a*moral. He knows the moral law and revels in flouting it. So perhaps man is not animalistic under his appearance of civilization. Perhaps civilization creates beings who understand morality and still lust for evil.

THE IMPORTANCE OF REPUTATION For the characters in *Dr. Jekyll and Mr. Hyde*, the preservation of reputation is all-important. Upright men such as Utterson and Enfield avoid gossip at all costs because they consider it a great destroyer of reputation. When Utterson suspects that Jekyll is being blackmailed, and then suspects that he is sheltering Hyde from the police, he does not make his suspicions known for fear of harming Jekyll's reputation. The importance of reputation in the novel reflects the importance of appearances, facades, and surfaces—which often hide a sordid core. In many instances in the novel, Utterson adamantly tries not only to preserve Jekyll's reputation, but to preserve the appearance of order and decorum, even when he senses a vile truth lurking underneath.

THE MEANING OF SILENCE Characters repeatedly fail or refuse to articulate themselves. One kind of silence is a refusal to discuss sordid things. For example, neither Jekyll nor the third-person narrator provide any details about Hyde's odious behavior. This disdain for the sordid is a product of Victorian society, which prizes decorum above all and prefers to repress or even deny the truth if the truth might upset the conventional worldview. Another kind of silence is involuntary speechlessness. This variety of silence has to do with the interaction of the rational and the irrational. By its nature, language is rational and logical, a system of mapping the world. When confronted with the irrational and the mystical—Hyde's appearance, for example—language breaks down. The cataloguing, explanatory nature of verbal expression is at odds with the supernatural. Silence can heighten the power of the supernatural: Stevenson's reticence on the topic of Jekyll's and Hyde's crimes makes them more terrifying.

SYMBOLS IN *DR. JEKYLL AND MR. HYDE*

JEKYLL'S HOUSE AND LABORATORY Jekyll's house, with its "great air of wealth and comfort," symbolizes his civilized side. His laboratory, "a certain sinister block of building . . . [which] bore in every feature the marks of profound and sordid negligence," symbolizes his corrupt side. The buildings are adjoined, but look out on different streets, just as Jekyll and Hyde are connected but opposite. Because of the convoluted layout of the streets in the area, the casual observer cannot tell that the structures are two parts of a whole, just as he or she cannot readily detect the relationship between Jekyll and Hyde.

HYDE'S PHYSICAL APPEARANCE According to the indefinite remarks made by his overwhelmed observers, Hyde is small, shrunken, and hairy. His physical ugliness and deformity symbolize the warped repulsiveness of his character. For readers in Stevenson's time, the connection between ugliness and wickedness might have been seen as more than symbolic. Many people believed in the science of physiognomy, which held that criminals could be identified by their physical appearance. Hyde's small stature suggests that Jekyll has been repressing him for years.

IMPORTANT QUOTATIONS FROM *DR. JEKYLL AND MR. HYDE*

> *Mr. Utterson the lawyer was a man of a rugged countenance, that was never lighted by a smile; cold, scanty and embarrassed in discourse; backward in sentiment; lean, long, dusty, dreary, and yet somehow lovable.. . . . He was austere with himself; drank gin when he was alone, to mortify a taste for vintages; and though he enjoyed the theater, had not crossed the doors of one for twenty years. But he had an approved tolerance for others; sometimes wondering, almost with envy, at the high pressure of spirits involved in their misdeeds; and in any extremity inclined to help rather than to reprove.. . . . [I]t was frequently his fortune to be the last reputable acquaintance and the last good influence in the lives of down-going men.*

Location: The first paragraph of the novel
Speaker: The narrator
Context: Stevenson sketches Utterson's character

In one way, Utterson comes across as an uninteresting character—unsmiling, "scanty" in speech, "lean, long, dusty, dreary" in person. But Stevenson's first description of Utterson reveals cracks in his rigid, civilized facade—cracks that make Utterson the ideal person to pursue the bizarre case of Jekyll and Hyde.

The passage calls Utterson "lovable" and remarks on his tendency to "help rather than to reprove." This geniality and approachability puts Utterson at the center of the novel's social web. All of the other characters confide in him and turn to him for help, allowing him glimpses of the mystery from every point of view. Lanyon and Jekyll confide in him, Enfield gives him salient information, Poole comes to him for help, and Sir Danvers Carew employs him. The passage also notes Utterson's keen interest in individuals with dark secrets, in those who suffer from scandal. Far from judging sinners, Utterson feels something close to "envy" for them.

He put the glass to his lips, and drank at one gulp. A cry followed; he reeled, staggered, clutched at the table and held on, staring with injected eyes, gasping with open mouth; and as I looked there came, I thought, a change—he seemed to swell—his face became suddenly black and the features seemed to melt and alter—and at the next moment, I had sprung to my feet and leaped back against the wall, my arm raised to shield me from that prodigy, my mind submerged in terror.

"O God!" I screamed, and "O God!" again and again; for there before my eyes—pale and shaken, and half fainting, and groping before him with his hands, like a man restored from death—there stood Henry Jekyll!

Location: Chapter 9, "Dr. Lanyon's Narrative"
Speaker: Lanyon
Context: Lanyon describes seeing Hyde become Jekyll

Lanyon, who once ridiculed Jekyll's experiments as "unscientific balderdash," sees the proof of Jekyll's success firsthand. The transformation he witnesses is the climactic moment in the novel, the moment when all the questions about Jekyll's relationship to Hyde are answered. As this passage emphasizes, the true horror of Jekyll and Hyde's secret is not that they are two sides of the same person, each one able to assert itself at will, but that each is trapped in the other, fighting for dominance. The transformation process is fittingly violent and ravaging, causing the metamorphosing body to "reel," "stagger," and "gasp." By this point in the novel, Jekyll is losing ground to Hyde, so he emerges "half fainting," as if "restored from death."

"He is not easy to describe. There is something wrong with his appearance; something displeasing, something downright detestable. I never saw a man I so disliked, and yet I scarce know why. He must be deformed somewhere; he gives a strong feeling of deformity, although I couldn't specify the point. He's an extraordinary-looking man, and yet I really can name nothing out of the way. No, sir; I can make no hand of it; I can't describe him. And it's not want of memory; for I declare I can see him this moment."

Location: Chapter 1, "Story of the Door"
Speaker: Enfield
Context: After seeing Hyde trample a little girl, Enfield struggles to describe him to Utterson

---

It was on the moral side, and in my own person, that I learned to recognise the thorough and primitive duality of man; I saw that, of the two natures that contended in the field of my consciousness, even if I could rightly be said to be either, it was only because I was radically both; and from an early date . . . I had learned to dwell with pleasure, as a beloved daydream, on the thought of the separation of these elements.

Location: Chapter 10, "Henry Jekyll's Full Statement of the Case"
Speaker: Jekyll
Context: In a letter to Utterson, Jekyll describes the years leading up to his discovery of the potion

---

[T]his brief condescension to my evil finally destroyed the balance of my soul. And yet I was not alarmed; the fall seemed natural, like a return to the old days before I had made discovery.. . . I sat in the sun on a

bench; the animal within me licking the chops of memory; the spiritual side a little drowsed, promising subsequent penitence, but not yet moved to begin. After all, I reflected, I was like my neighbours; and then I smiled, comparing myself with other men, comparing my active goodwill with the lazy cruelty of their neglect. And at the very moment of that vainglorious thought, a qualm came over me, a horrid nausea and the most deadly shuddering.. . . I began to be aware of a change in the temper of my thoughts, a greater boldness, a contempt of danger, a solution of the bonds of obligation. I looked down; my clothes hung formlessly on my shrunken limbs; the hand that lay on my knee was corded and hairy. I was once more Edward Hyde.

Location: Chapter 10, "Henry Jekyll's Full Statement of the Case"
Speaker: Jekyll
Context: Lanyon describes seeing Hyde become Jekyll

DRACULA

Bram Stoker

Using folk remedies and Christian symbols, a band of men succeeds in killing a powerful, centuries-old vampire.

THE LIFE OF BRAM STOKER

Bram Stoker was born in Dublin, Ireland, in 1847. His father was a civil servant, and his mother was a writer and a charity worker. Stoker was a sickly child, and his mother often entertained him with fantastic tales. Stoker studied math at Trinity College. Upon graduating in 1867, he joined the Irish civil service. He also worked as a freelance journalist and drama critic, work that allowed him to meet the legendary stage actor Henry Irving. Stoker and Irving became lifelong friends. Stoker married an aspiring actress, Florence Balcombe, and in 1879 the couple had a son, Noel. Stoker moved to London to oversee Irving's theater, which he did from 1878 until Irving's death in 1905. Stoker took part in London's literary scene, socializing with men such as Oscar Wilde, Arthur Conan Doyle, and Alfred Lord Tennyson.

Stoker's early fiction is not of particularly high quality. His first novel, *The Snake's Pass* (1890), was unsuccessful. But Stoker's fortune changed in 1897, when *Dracula* was published. Although the novel was not an immediate popular success, it has been in print continuously since its first publication and has inspired countless films and other literary works. Stoker continued to write until his death in 1912, producing several adventure novels, including *The Jewel of Seven Stars* (1904) and *The Lair of the White Worm* (1911).

DRACULA IN CONTEXT

In many parts of the world, vampire legends have been part of popular folklore since ancient times. Throughout the Middle Ages and even into the modern era, reports of corpses rising from the dead with supernatural powers were widely believed. Stoker bases his Dracula family on a real fifteenth-century family. Its most famous member, Vlad Dracula—or Vlad the Impaler, as he was commonly known—had a bloody career that rivaled that of his fictional counterpart. Vlad, the Prince of Wallachia, was a brilliant and notoriously savage general who impaled his enemies on long spikes. He had a reputation for murdering beggars, forcing women to eat their babies, and nailing the turbans of disrespectful ambassadors to their heads. While Stoker's Count Dracula is supposed to be a descendant of Vlad, and not the prince himself, Stoker's count closely resembles Vlad. Its basis in historical truth makes *Dracula* convincing. With his Author's Note and coda, Stoker bolsters the impression that the documents assembled in the novel are real.

Stoker relies heavily on the conventions of Gothic fiction, a genre that was extremely popular in the early nineteenth century. Gothic fiction traditionally includes elements such as gloomy castles, sublime landscapes, and innocent maidens threatened by evil. In *Dracula*, Stoker modernizes the Gothic tradition, setting the story not only in Dracula's ruined castle, but in bustling modern England. As Stoker portrays the collision of two disparate worlds—the count's ancient Transylvania and the protagonist's modern London—he reveals many of the anxieties that characterized his age: the repercussions of scientific advancement, the consequences of abandoning traditional beliefs, and the dangers of female sexuality.

DRACULA: KEY FACTS

Time and place written: 1891–1897; London, England	
Date of first publication: 1897	
Publisher: Constable	
Type of work: Novel	
Genre: Gothic, horror	

Language: English

Setting (time): End of the nineteenth century

Setting (place): England and Eastern Europe

Tense: Past

Tone: Dark, melodramatic, righteous

Narrator: Dracula is told primarily through a collection of journal entries, letters, and telegrams written by its main characters

Point of view: Shifts among the first-person perspectives of several characters

Protagonist: The members of Van Helsing's gang—Van Helsing, Jonathan Harker, John Seward, Arthur Holmwood, Mina Murray, and Quincey Morris

Antagonist: Dracula

DRACULA: PLOT OVERVIEW

Jonathan Harker, a young English lawyer, travels to Castle Dracula in the Eastern European country of Transylvania to conclude a real estate transaction on behalf of his firm with a nobleman named Count Dracula. As Harker makes his way through the picturesque countryside, the local peasants warn him about his destination, giving him crucifixes and other charms against evil and uttering strange words that Harker later translates into "vampire."

Frightened but no less determined, Harker meets the count's carriage as planned. The journey to the castle is harrowing, and the carriage is nearly attacked by angry wolves along the way. Upon arriving at the crumbling old castle, Harker finds that the elderly Dracula is a well educated and hospitable gentleman. After only a few days, however, Harker realizes that he is a prisoner in the castle.

The more Harker investigates the nature of his confinement, the more uneasy he becomes. He realizes that the count possesses supernatural powers and diabolical ambitions. One evening, Harker is nearly attacked by three beautiful and seductive vampires, but the count staves them off, telling them that Harker belongs to him. Fearing for his life, Harker attempts to escape from the castle by climbing down the walls.

Meanwhile, in England, Harker's fiancée, Mina Murray, corresponds with her friend Lucy Westenra. Lucy has received marriage proposals from three men—Dr. John Seward, Arthur Holmwood, and an American named Quincey Morris. Though saddened that she must reject two of these suitors, Lucy accepts Holmwood's proposal.

Mina visits Lucy at the seaside town of Whitby. A Russian ship is wrecked on the shore near the town. Its crew is missing and its captain is dead. The only sign of life aboard is a large dog that bounds ashore and disappears into the countryside; the only cargo is a set of fifty boxes of earth shipped from Castle Dracula. During Mina's visit, Lucy begins sleepwalking. One night, Mina finds Lucy in the town cemetery and believes she sees a dark form with glowing red eyes bending over Lucy. Lucy becomes pale and ill. She has two tiny red marks on her throat. Unable to arrive at a satisfactory diagnosis, Dr. Seward sends for his old mentor, Professor Van Helsing.

Harker, suffering from brain fever, reappears in the city of Buda-Pest. Mina joins him. Van Helsing arrives in Whitby, examines Lucy, and orders that her chambers be covered with garlic—a traditional charm against vampires. For a time, this effort seems to stave off Lucy's illness. She begins to recover, but her mother, unaware of the garlic's power, unwittingly removes the odiferous plants from the room, leaving Lucy vulnerable to further attack.

Seward and Van Helsing spend several days trying to revive Lucy, performing four blood transfusions. Their efforts come to nothing. One night, the men momentarily let down their guard, and a wolf breaks into the Westenra house. The shock gives Lucy's mother a fatal heart attack. Lucy dies soon after. After a rash of injuries to children in the area where Lucy was buried, Van Helsing leads Holmwood, Seward, and Quincey Morris to her tomb, saying Lucy belongs to the "Un-Dead"—in other words, she has become a vampire. The men remain unconvinced until they see Lucy preying on a defenseless child. They agree to follow the ritual of vampire slaying to ensure that Lucy's soul will return to eternal rest. While the undead Lucy sleeps, Holmwood plunges a stake through her heart. The men then cut off her head and stuff her mouth with garlic. After this deed is done, they pledge to destroy Dracula himself.

Mina and Jonathan, now married, return to England and join forces with the others. Mina helps Van Helsing collect the various diary and journal entries that Harker, Seward, and the others have written, attempting to piece together a narrative that will lead them to the count. Van Helsing and his band track down the boxes of earth from his castle that the count uses as a sanctuary during the night. One of Dr. Seward's mental patients, Renfield, lets Dracula into the asylum where the others are staying, and Dracula preys on Mina.

As Mina begins the slow change into a vampire, the men sterilize the boxes of earth, forcing Dracula to flee to the safety of his native Transylvania. The men pursue the count, dividing their forces and tracking him across land and sea. Van Helsing takes Mina with him, and they cleanse Castle Dracula by killing the three female vampires and sealing the entrances with sacred objects. The others catch up with the count just before he reaches his castle. Jonathan and Quincey kill him with knives. Mina makes a full recovery.

CHARACTERS IN *DRACULA*

Count Dracula   A centuries-old vampire and Transylvanian nobleman. Beneath a veneer of aristocratic charm, the count has a dark, evil soul. He can assume the form of an animal and control the weather. His powers are limited, however—he cannot enter a victim's home uninvited, cross water unless carried, or use his powers during the day.

Jonathan Harker   A solicitor, or lawyer. Initially naive, Harker eventually becomes a brave and fearless fighter.

Arthur Holmwood   Lucy's fiancé. In the course of his fight against Dracula's dark powers, Holmwood does whatever circumstances demand: he is the first to offer Lucy a blood transfusion, and he agrees to kill her demonic form.

Quincey Morris   A plainspoken American from Texas. Quincey, a brave and good-hearted man, never begrudges Holmwood his success in winning Lucy's hand. Quincey sacrifices his life in order to rid the world of Dracula's influence.

Mina Murray   Jonathan Harker's fiancé. Mina is a practical young woman who works as a schoolmistress. Mina, the heroine of the novel, embodies purity, innocence, and Christian faith even when suffering at the vampire's hands. She is intelligent and resourceful, and her research leads Van Helsing's men to Castle Dracula.

Renfield   A patient at Seward's mental asylum. A behemoth and a refined gentleman, Renfield consumes living creatures—flies, spiders, birds, and so on—which he believes provide him with strength and vitality.

John Seward   A talented young doctor. Seward, a former pupil of Van Helsing's, is the administrator of an insane asylum not far from Dracula's English home. Even after Lucy turns down his proposal of marriage, Seward devotes himself to her safety.

Van Helsing   A Dutch professor and "one of the most advanced scientists of his day." Unlike his comrades, Van Helsing is not blinded by the limitations of Western medicine: he knows that traditional science and reason will not defeat Dracula. Van Helsing becomes Dracula's chief antagonist.

Lucy Westenra   Mina's best friend. Lucy is an attractive, vivacious young woman. Her much-praised chastity and virtue are sullied when she becomes a vampire.

Mrs. Westenra   Lucy's mother. A brittle woman of failing health, Mrs. Westenra inadvertently sabotages her daughter's safety by interfering with Van Helsing's folk remedies.

THEMES IN *DRACULA*

THE CONSEQUENCES OF MODERNITY   Harker voices one of the central concerns of the Victorian era when he says, "unless my senses deceive me, the old centuries had, and have, powers of their own which mere 'modernity' cannot kill." The end of the nineteenth century brought drastic developments that forced English society to question the systems of belief that had governed it for centuries. Darwin's theory of evolution, for instance, called the validity of long-held religious doctrines into question. The Industrial Revolution brought profound economic and social change to the previously agrarian England.

Though Stoker begins his novel in a ruined castle—a traditional Gothic setting—he soon moves the action to Victorian London, where modern advancements allow the count to prey on English society. When Lucy falls victim to Dracula's spell, modern science is useless. Only Van Helsing, whose facility with modern medical techniques is tempered with open-mindedness about ancient legends and non-Western folk remedies, can understand Lucy's affliction.

THE THREAT OF FEMALE SEXUAL EXPRESSION   Most critics agree that *Dracula* indulges the Victorian male imagination, particularly regarding the topic of female sexuality. In Victorian England, acceptable sexual behavior in women was extremely limited. A Victorian woman was expected to be either a virgin or a wife and mother. If she was neither of these, she was considered a whore and thus of no consequence to society.

In *Dracula*, the battle between good and evil hinges on female sexuality. Lucy and Mina are less like real people than two-dimensional embodiments of female virtues. Both women are chaste, pure, and devoted to their men. Dracula threatens to corrupt the women, making them voluptuous—a word Stoker uses again and again—and unapologetically open about their sexual desire.

He succeeds in transforming Lucy, and once she becomes a sexualized and seductive vampire, Van Helsing's men decide they must destroy her in order to return her to a purer, more socially respectable state. After Lucy's transformation, the men keep a careful eye on Mina, worried they will lose yet another model of Victorian womanhood to the dark side. The men believe that sexual women will compromise their safety. Late in the novel, Dracula mocks Van Helsing's crew, saying, "Your girls that you all love are mine already; and through them, you and others shall yet be mine." Here, in addition to the homoerotic suggestion, the count voices a male fantasy that has existed since Adam and Eve were turned out of Eden: namely, that women's ungovernable desires will make men fall from grace.

THE PROMISE OF CHRISTIAN SALVATION   Van Helsing's methods suggest that the most effective weapons in combating supernatural evil are icons of Christian faith, such as the crucifix. The novel is so invested in the strength and power of these Christian symbols that at times it reads like a propagandistic Christian promise of salvation. Dracula, who is practically as old as religion itself, is a satanic figure, most obviously in his appearance—pointed ears, fangs, and flaming eyes—but also in his consumption of blood. Dracula's bloodthirstiness is a perversion of Christian ritual, as it extends his physical life but cuts off his spiritual existence. In an inverted version of Christian belief in the eternal life of the soul, vampires are cursed with eternal physical life.

SYMBOLS IN *DRACULA*

THE WEIRD SISTERS   The three beautiful vampires Harker encounters in Dracula's castle symbolize both the dream and the nightmare of the Victorian male. The sisters are just what the ideal Victorian woman should not be—voluptuous and sexually aggressive. They are the more sexy because they are forbidden, and they offer Harker more sexual gratification in two paragraphs than his fiancée Mina does in an entire novel. In the moral world of the novel, sexual women must be destroyed because they threaten to undermine the foundations of a male-dominated society by compromising men's ability to reason and maintain control.

THE STAKE DRIVEN THROUGH LUCY'S HEART   Arthur Holmwood buries a stake deep in Lucy's heart in order to return her to a state of purity and innocence. The language with which Stoker describes this violent act is unmistakably sexual, and the stake is an unambiguous symbol for the penis. It is fitting that the blow comes from Lucy's fiancé. Lucy is being punished not only for being a vampire, but also for being available to the vampire's seduction—Dracula can attack only willing victims. The stabbing also suggests that sex with the appropriate man—in this case Holmwood, who would have been Lucy's husband—will maintain, rather than destroy, feminine virtue.

IMPORTANT QUOTATIONS FROM *DRACULA*

The castle is on the very edge of a terrible precipice. A stone falling from the window would fall a thousand feet without touching anything! As far as the eye can reach is a sea of green tree tops, with occasionally a deep rift where there is a chasm. Here and there are silver threads where the rivers wind in deep gorges through the forests.

But I am not in heart to describe beauty, for when I had seen the view I explored further; doors, doors, doors everywhere, and all locked and bolted. In no place save from the windows in the castle walls is there an available exit.

The castle is a veritable prison, and I am a prisoner!

Location: Chapter II
Speaker: Harker
Context: In his journal, Harker describes Dracula's castle

This passage exemplifies the dark, ominous tone Stoker creates in the novel. The tone of Harker's journal changes with amazing rapidity as his stay in Castle Dracula progresses. In the course of a single chapter, Harker stops feeling like an honored houseguest and starts thinking of himself as a prisoner. Here, Stoker demonstrates his mastery of the conventions of the Gothic novel, evoking the ruined castle, the beautiful but overpowering landscape, and the mounting sense of dread. Though Stoker did not invent Dracula or vampire lore, he did more to solidify it in the imaginations of English-speaking audiences than any author has since. Passages such as this have spawned countless imitators, and scores of horror films owe a debt to the simple but powerful repetition of Stoker's "doors, doors, doors everywhere."

Thus are we ministers of God's own wish: that the world, and men for whom His Son die, will not be given over to monsters, whose very existence would defame Him. He has allowed us to redeem one soul already, and we go out as the old knights of the Cross to redeem more. Like them we shall travel toward sunrise; and like them, if we fall, we fall in good cause.

Location: Chapter XXIV
Speaker: Van Helsing
Context: As the men chase Dracula across Europe, Van Helsing summarizes the nature of their quest

To modern readers, the professor's words sound like an exercise in hyperbole, as he draws bold lines between good and evil. However, Stoker does intend *Dracula* to be as much a cautionary moral tale as a novel of horror and suspense. Deeply informed by the anxieties of the Victorian age—the threat that scientific advancement posed to centuries of religious tradition, and the threat that broadening liberties for women posed to patriarchal society—*Dracula* makes bold distinctions between socially acceptable and socially unacceptable; between right and wrong; between holy and unholy. When Van Helsing likens his mission to one of "the old knights of the Cross," we should understand him not as a bombastic windbag, but as a product of genuine Victorian fear and righteousness.

I was afraid to raise my eyelids, but looked out and saw perfectly under the lashes. The girl went on her knees, and bent over me, simply gloating. There was a deliberate voluptuousness which was both thrilling and repulsive, and as she arched her neck, she actually licked her lips like an animal.. . . Lower and lower went her head as the lips went below the range of my mouth and chin and seemed about to fasten on my throat.. . . I closed my eyes in a languorous ecstasy and waited—waited with beating heart.

Location: Chapter III
Speaker: Harker
Context: Three beautiful vampires seduce Harker

You are a clever man, friend John; you reason well, and your wit is bold; but you are too prejudiced.. . . Ah, it is the fault of our science that it wants to explain all; and if it explain not, then it says there is nothing to explain. But yet we see around us every day the growth of new beliefs, which think themselves new; and which are yet but the old, which pretend to be young. . . .

Location: Chapter XIV
Speaker: Van Helsing
Context: Van Helsing criticizes Seward for relying on reason

She still advanced, however, and with a languorous, voluptuous grace, said:—"Come to me, Arthur. Leave these others and come to me. My arms are hungry for you. Come, and we can rest together. Come, my husband, come!"

There was something diabolically sweet in her tones—something of the tingling of glass when struck—which rang through the brains even of us who heard the words addressed to another. As for Arthur, he seemed under a spell; moving his hands from his face, he opened wide his arms.

Location: Chapter XVI
Speaker: Seward
Context: When the men go to Lucy's tomb, she attempts to seduce her fiancé

DUBLINERS

James Joyce

Dubliners of all stripes live their lives.

THE LIFE OF JAMES JOYCE

James Joyce was born on February 2, 1882, in Dublin, Ireland, into a Catholic middle-class family that soon became poverty-stricken because of its patriarch's financial irresponsibility. Despite this impoverishment, Joyce received the best education available to someone of his station. He attended Jesuit schools, followed by University College in Dublin, where he began publishing essays and writing lyric poetry. After graduating in 1902, Joyce went to Paris, where he devoted all of his time to writing poetry, stories, and theories of aesthetics. Joyce returned to Dublin the following year upon learning that his mother was seriously ill. After his mother's death, Joyce stayed in Dublin, where eventually he met his future wife, Nora Barnacle, a chambermaid at Finn's Hotel.

Nora and Joyce left Dublin in1904. They spent most of the next eleven years living in Rome and Trieste, Italy, where Joyce taught English. He and Nora had two children, Giorgio and Lucia. Joyce's first book of poems, *Chamber Music*, was published in 1907. In 1914, he published both a book of short stories, *Dubliners*, and a serialized autobiographical novel, *A Portrait of the Artist as a Young Man*.

Joyce began writing *Ulysses* in 1914. When World War I broke out, he moved his family to Zurich, Switzerland, where his fortunes improved. His talent attracted several wealthy patrons, including Harriet Shaw Weaver. He published *Portrait* in book form (1916), a play, *Exiles* (1918), and the first episodes of *Ulysses* in *The Little Review* (1918). In 1919, the Joyces moved back to Trieste, but in 1920, at Ezra Pound's urging, they moved to Paris. *Ulysses* was published in Paris in book form in 1922, causing an international scandal with its frank sexual content and revolutionary prose style. In 1923, with his eyesight quickly diminishing, Joyce began working on what became *Finnegans Wake* (1939). Joyce died in 1941.

DUBLINERS IN CONTEXT

James Joyce is usually considered a modernist writer, one of a group of post–World War I poets and novelists who shared a disillusionment with traditional religious and moral values, a pessimistic view of society, and an unconventional use of language. Modernist authors include T. S. Eliot, Virginia Woolf, W. B. Yeats, Ezra Pound, and Gertrude Stein. Even *Dubliners*, one of Joyce's earliest works, contains evidence of his modernist sensibilities.

Joyce wanted *Dubliners* to capture the different facets of life in Dublin, to be "a chapter of the moral history of [his] country." Joyce felt that Ireland in general, and Dublin in particular, was paralyzed. No longer a significant center of arts and culture nor a burgeoning, modern European city, turn-of-the-century Dublin was plagued by poverty, rigid class systems, oppressive moral codes, and conflicting allegiances to the Catholic Church, to England (which still controlled Ireland), and to the dream of Irish independence.

When Joyce wrote *Dubliners*, political turmoil was agitating Ireland following the death of Charles Stuart Parnell, the Nationalist political leader who had rallied the country in support of Irish independence from Britain. After Parnell's disgrace—he was caught having an affair with a married woman—and death, the country was left reeling, sharply divided between Protestants and Catholics, Conservatives and Nationalists. Joyce captures this division in *Dubliners*, in which the Irish sense of enslavement and paralysis goes deeper than politics, seeping into everyday life and making it impossible for individuals to change their plights.

Joyce had a deep yet qualified affection for "dear, dirty Dublin," which is the setting for all of his major works. Like many of Joyce's works, *Dubliners* provoked controversy. Publishers were nervous about the collection's frank depiction of the Irish lower classes, its satirical assault on living people, and its mention of real citizens and locations. Because of these worries, the collection was not printed until 1914. Today, the stories in *Dubliners* are recognized as masterpieces of the short story genre. "The Dead," one of the stories in the collection, is widely considered one of the finest short stories of the twentieth century. The stories' controlled style contains no hint of the stream-of-consciousness style that Joyce began to develop with his next work, *Portrait of the Artist as a Young Man*. Instead, they demonstrate Joyce's total mastery of conventional prose styles.

DUBLINERS: KEY FACTS

Time and place written: 1904–1907; Dublin

Date of first publication: 1914

Publisher: Grant Richards

Type of work: Short-story collection

Genre: Short stories

Language: English

Setting (time): Around the beginning of the twentieth century

Setting (place): Dublin, Ireland

Tense: Past

Tone: Objective, detached

Narrator: Most stories are narrated by an anonymous, third-person narrator; "The Sisters," "An Encounter," and "Araby" are narrated by the protagonists of the stories

Point of View: Varies

Protagonist: It can be argued that the people of Dublin, or even the city itself, are the protagonists of the collection

Antagonist: Varies

DUBLINERS: PLOT OVERVIEW

On the surface, many of the characters in *Dubliners* seem to have nothing in common beyond their Irishness and their presence in Dublin. Joyce writes about men and women of all ages, occupations, and social classes. But a number of common themes and concerns emerge. Many of the stories concern the way people attempt to escape numbness and inertia, and the painful realizations they reach after making those attempts. *Dubliners* is also about religion, art, politics, the relationships between generations, the awakenings of love in the young, the vague confusion of the old, and the effects of alcohol abuse on Dubliners. Disappointment, weariness, and shame color many of the stories, but *Dubliners* never feels cynical.

"The Sisters": A young boy encounters death for the first time when his friend, a much older priest named Father Flynn, has a stroke and dies.

"An Encounter": Two school-aged boys skip classes and lark around Dublin. They meet an unnerving old man who talks about punishing young boys.

"Araby": A young boy is, for the first time, intensely attracted to a girl. He tries to buy her a present at the bazaar and feels deep shame when he fails.

"Eveline": A young woman has a horrible life with her alcoholic father. She tries to elope to Argentina with a sailor named Frank but cannot bring herself to leave.

"After the Race": A rich young man named Jimmy Doyle spends a decadent night gambling with a group of wealthy young men and realizes he is not sophisticated enough to keep up with them.

"Two Gallants": A pair of seedy men, Lenehan and Corley, scheme to coax some money out of a woman with whom one of them is involved.

"The Boarding House": A complicated web of motivations and manipulations surrounds Mrs. Mooney's attempt to wed her daughter, Polly, to Mr. Doran, a young man staying at her boarding house.

"A Little Cloud": A timid man called Little Chandler enjoys a reunion with his rakish friend Gallagher, now a successful journalist in London.

"Counterparts": A bloated, impoverished, alcoholic clerk named Farrington pawns his watch for a night of drunkenness, then goes home and beats his son with a walking stick.

"Clay": An old woman, Maria, pays a visit to the family of Joe, a man whom she nursed when he was a little boy.

"A Painful Case": Mr. James Duffy, an intellectual bank clerk, nearly falls in love with the wife of a ship captain, but rejects her in the end. Four years later, he reads a newspaper account of her suicide.

"Ivy Day in the Committee Room": A group of stuffy, pompous Dublin politicos assemble to discuss the current election and the state of Ireland in the aftermath of Parnell's death.

"A Mother": Mrs. Kearney contracts her daughter to play in a series of Irish Revival concerts, then makes a dreadful scene when the committee officials attempt to lower her daughter's fee.

"Grace": Mr. Kernan is sliding toward alcohol abuse, so his wife and friends conspire to send him to a religious retreat.

"The Dead": Gabriel Conroy and his wife, Gretta, attend a festive Christmas party. Gretta hears a song that reminds her of a young man, now dead, whom she loved once.

CHARACTERS IN *DUBLINERS*

"THE SISTERS"

Eliza Nannie and Father Flynn's sister.

Father Flynn An old priest. Father Flynn, who dies during "The Sisters," was a friend to the little boy who narrates the story.

Nannie Eliza and Father Flynn's sister.

Old Cotter An old man. Old Cotter disapproves of the boy's relationship with Father Flynn.

"AN ENCOUNTER"

Mahony The narrator's friend.

"ARABY"

Mangan's sister A young girl. The narrator of the story yearns for Mangan's sister with an intensity he has never felt before.

"EVELINE"

Eveline A young girl. Eveline dreams of escaping Dublin and her alcoholic father but somehow cannot bring herself to leave.

Frank A sailor. Frank tries to convince Eveline to elope with him to Buenos Aires.

"AFTER THE RACE"

Jimmy Doyle A wealthy, directionless young man.

"THE BOARDING HOUSE"

Mr. Doran A young man. Mr. Doran has an affair with Polly and finds himself manipulated by Mrs. Mooney into marrying Polly.

Mrs. Mooney Polly's mother and the proprietress of the boarding house. Mrs. Mooney's guests call her "the Madam."

Polly Mrs. Mooney's daughter. Polly has an affair with Mr. Doran.

"THE TWO GALLANTS"

Corley The repugnant son of a police inspector. Corley uses women for sex and money.

Lenehan The main character of the story. Lenehan is a dissipated leech who uses his friends for money.

"A LITTLE CLOUD"

Gallagher Little Chandler's rakish, successful friend. Gallagher was once an irresponsible rogue, but has made a success of himself on the London newspaper scene.

Little Chandler A modest, shy clerk. Little Chandler once dreamed of poetry but now finds himself stifled by routine.

"COUNTERPARTS"

Farrington An impoverished alcoholic.

"CLAY"

Joe The boy (now grown) whom Maria nursed when he was a child.

Maria An old woman who pays a holiday visit to the home of a man she nursed many years ago.

"A PAINFUL CASE"

Mr. James Duffy A prim, intellectual bank clerk. Mr. Duffy leads a solitary, well-ordered life before nearly falling in love with Mrs. Sinico.

Mrs. Sinico The neglected wife of a ship captain. Mrs. Sinico falls in love with Mr. James Duffy and starts drinking when he rejects her. Eventually, she commits suicide.

"A MOTHER"

Hoppy Holohan The assistant secretary in the *Eire Abu* society that is putting on a concert. He is nicknamed "Hoppy" because one of his legs is shorter than the other. Mrs. Kearney hates Hoppy.

Kathleen Mrs. Kearney's daughter. Kathleen has been coaxed into Irish Revivalism by her mother.

Mrs. Kearney Kathleen's waspish, sharp-tongued mother. Mrs. Kearney arranges for her daughter to play in a concert series, then almost ruins the final concert by insisting on being paid up front.

"GRACE"

Martin Cunningham A well-respected, unhappily married man. Cunningham orchestrates the attempt to bring Mr. Kernan to the religious revival. His friends think that his face resembles Shakespeare's.

Mr. Kernan A once-successful man on the brink of alcoholism. Mr. Kernan is manipulated into attending a religious revival by his wife and by Martin Cunningham and a group of well-meaning friends.

Father Purdon A priest. Father Purdon delivers a sermon urging his listeners to perform the businesslike moral action of "squaring their accounts."

"THE DEAD"

Gabriel Conroy A moderately successful writer and teacher. When Gabriel realizes that his wife has been thinking of a young man, Michael Furey, at the very moment when he was thinking of her alone, he experiences an agonizing moment of shame followed by the realization that no human being can ever truly know another.

Gretta Conroy Gabriel's wife. When Gretta hears the song "The Lass of Aughrim," she remembers her old lover, Michael Furey, who used to sing the same song.

Michael Furey A young boy who died at seventeen. Before Gretta left him to attend a convent school, Michael Furey snuck out to see her on a rainy night. The rain exacerbated his illness, and he died a week later.

Miss Ivors A young woman. Miss Ivors is an ardent nationalist, and she accuses Gabriel of being a West Briton.

THEMES IN *DUBLINERS*

THE NEAR-IMPOSSIBILITY OF CHANGE   Each of the stories in *Dubliners* is suffused with a sense of paralysis. The characters live predictable, unchanging lives. They are unhappy with their families, their marriages, their jobs, or themselves, but various factors—religion, poverty, middle-class morality, force of habit, terror of the unfamiliar—prevent them from changing anything. Despite the inability of the characters to escape the monotony of their lives, almost all of them have a violent desire to do so. Many of them have lofty dreams of artistic glory, political triumph, or ideal love. Often, they try to make these dreams come true in unrealistic, ineffective, even laughable ways. The boy in "Araby" convinces himself that a trinket from the bazaar will win the love of Mangan's sister; Little Chandler believes that a visit from his friend Gallagher will give him access to Gallagher's exciting literary lifestyle. Just as frequently, characters substitute meaningless diversions and addictions for actual change or escape. The two gallants find amusement in their search for money and women, and Farrington drinks to escape his miserable life. But the fruitlessness of these efforts is not entirely devastating. Even though their desires go unfulfilled, the characters continue to desire—proof that they are living, optimistic beings.

THE DANGEROUS INFLUENCE OF RELIGION   The Catholic Church, an extremely influential force in Irish society, makes its presence felt in *Dubliners*. Priests, nuns, and churches crop up constantly, and the Church influences everything from politics to the treatment of alcoholism. However, Joyce does not portray religion as a redemptive or useful force. Instead, he associates it with paralysis and ruin. Religious iconography surrounds the priest's death in "The Sisters" and dominates the ludicrous retreat in "Grace." The stories suggest that the Catholicism that dominates Ireland does very little to help, and may actually harm, the Irish people.

THE PAIN OF ISOLATION   Many of the characters in *Dubliners* are isolated—emotionally, physically, or both—from the people in their lives. They find it extremely difficult, almost impossible, to communicate their feelings and desires to others, no matter how much they want to. Joyce emphasizes the loneliness of this failure to connect. Several of the stories end with the main character standing or sitting alone, thinking about the emptiness of his or her life. Even when companionship or romantic love seems possible, the characters willfully return themselves to a state of isolation. In "A Painful Case," Mr. Duffy ends his relationship with Mrs. Sinico because she is too passionate about him. In "Eveline," Eveline refuses to leave with the man she loves, looking at him with eyes that give him "no sign of love or farewell or recognition."

SYMBOLS IN *DUBLINERS*

SNOW   The snow that falls in "The Dead" symbolizes paralysis, helplessness, and isolation. It falls over all of Ireland at the end of the story, concealing the countryside in the same way that Gabriel feels his wife's true feelings have been concealed from him. Snow also symbolizes the universality of isolation and paralysis, which are, like the snow, "general all over Ireland."

MONEY   The characters in *Dubliners* often think of money as something that will magically transform their ordinary lives, but money rarely effects any change. Money represents false hope, as in "Araby," in which the little boy believes money will indirectly buy him the love of the Mangan girl, since he can use money to buy a trinket with which to woo her. It also represents an inadequate substitute for real spiritual fulfillment, as in "Two Gallants," in which men equate spending money with finding happiness.

IMPORTANT QUOTATIONS FROM *DUBLINERS*

No! No! No! It was impossible. Her hands clutched the iron in frenzy. Amid the seas she sent a cry of anguish!

"Eveline! Evvy!"

He rushed beyond the barrier and called to her to follow. He was shouted at to go on but still he called to her. She set her white face to him, passive, like a helpless animal. Her eyes gave him no sign of love or farewell or recognition.

Location: The end of "Eveline"
Speaker: The narrator
Context: Frank begs Eveline to join him

At the last minute, Eveline refuses to follow her fiance to Buenos Aires. Eveline's sudden inability to leave her life in Dublin, even though she longs to escape, exemplifies the paralysis that overcomes many of the characters in *Dubliners*. Eveline is almost literally paralyzed: she thinks it is "impossible" for her to leave, and her hands grip the iron railing almost of their own accord. She is "helpless." Joyce suggests that fear, habit, and loyalty weigh so heavily on Eveline that she is like an animal stuck in a cage.

There were so many different moods and impressions that he wished to express in verse. He felt them within him. He tried to weigh his soul to see if it was a poet's soul.. . . The English critics, perhaps, would recognise him as one of the Celtic school by reason of the melancholy tone of his poems; besides that, he would put in allusions. He began to invent sentences and phrases from the notice which his book would get.. . . It was a pity his name was not more Irish-looking. Perhaps it would be better to insert his mother's name before the surname: Thomas Malone Chandler, or better still: T. Malone Chandler. He would speak to Gallagher about it.

Location: "A Little Cloud"
Speaker: The narrator
Context: Little Chandler waits to meet Gallagher

In this passage, Little Chandler dreams of changing his life and achieving glory and respect. The passage shows how people like Little Chandler make their lives more bearable by deluding themselves. Little Chandler's grandiose dreams are at once poignant and ridiculous. His excitement about meeting with Gallagher, an old friend who has become a successful London journalist, inspires him to dream of achieving literary greatness himself, but Joyce makes it clear that Little Chandler cares less about creating great art than about getting good reviews and winning fame. Even as Little Chandler plans to "speak to Gallagher about it," we know that his dreams will be dashed.

Little Chandler hopes to be recognized as one of the "Celtic school," and considers making his name more "Irish-looking." However, although Little Chandler is eager to be associated with Irish nationalist poetry, he is also eager to win approval from the English critics. These conflicting desires suggest the inability of the Irish to truly free themselves of England's influence, despite all of their nationalist ideals.

Gazing up into the darkness I saw myself as a creature driven and derided by vanity; and my eyes burned with anguish and anger.

Location: The last lines of "Araby"
Speaker: The protagonist
Context: The protagonist, now a man looking back on a boyhood experience, remembers a painful epiphany

[A]nd, as he attached the fervent nature of his companion more and more closely to him, he heard the strange impersonal voice which he recognised as his own, insisting on the soul's incurable loneliness. We cannot give ourselves, it said: we are our own.

Location: The middle of "A Painful Case"
Speaker: The narrator
Context: Mr. Duffy tells Mrs. Sinico his theories about isolation

The time had come for him to set out on his journey westward. Yes, the newspapers were right, snow was general all over Ireland. It was falling on every part of the dark central plain, on the treeless hills, falling softly upon the Bog of Allen and, farther westward, softly falling into the dark mutinous Shannon waves. It was falling, too, upon every part of the lonely churchyard on the hill where Michael Furey lay buried. It lay thickly drifted on the crooked crosses and headstones, on the spears of the little gate, on the barren thorns. His soul swooned slightly as he heard the snow falling faintly through the universe and faintly falling, like the descent of their last end, upon all the living and the dead.

Location: The end of "The Dead"
Speaker: The narrator
Context: Snow falls on Ireland

EMMA

Jane Austen

After meddling unsuccessfully in the love life of her friend, a woman marries a man as intelligent and spirited as she.

THE LIFE OF JANE AUSTEN

Jane Austen, whom some critics consider England's best novelist, was born in 1775 in Steventon, England. The seventh of eight children, she lived with her parents for her entire life, first in Steventon and later in Bath, Southampton, and Chawton. Her father was a parish rector. Although not wealthy, her family was well connected and well educated. Austen briefly attended boarding school in Reading but received the majority of her education at home. According to rumor, she had a brief love affair when she was twenty-five, but it did not lead to a marriage proposal. Two years later she accepted and then quickly rejected a proposal. She never married. In 1817, Austen died of Addison's disease, at age forty-one.

Austen began writing stories at a very young age and completed her first novel in her early twenties. However, she did not publish until 1811, when *Sense and Sensibility* appeared anonymously, followed by *Pride and Prejudice* (1813) and *Mansfield Park* (1814). *Emma*, published in 1816, was the last novel published during Austen's lifetime. (*Northanger Abbey* and *Persuasion* appeared posthumously.)

Austen's novels received little critical or popular recognition during her lifetime, and her identity as a novelist was not revealed until after her death. She wrote during the Romantic period, but her satirical novels have little to do with the passionate intensity and individuality that interested the Romantics. Critics have pointed out that the Romantics were almost exclusively male, and women with literary ambitions were excluded from the movement. While male writers such as Percy Bysshe Shelley and Lord Byron were free to promote their own individuality through wide travel and sexual and military adventurism, women were largely denied these freedoms. For women, the penalty for excessive freedom was social ostracism and poverty.

In this social context, Austen's commitment to reason and moderation can be seen as feminist and progressive rather than conservative. With intelligence and resourcefulness, her heroines push the limits of their constricted world of courtship and marriage.

EMMA IN CONTEXT

Some consider *Emma* Austen's best and most representative novel. It is also her longest novel, and by many accounts, her most difficult. Long praised for its rich domestic realism, *Emma* also presents puzzling questions: how can a character as intelligent as Emma be wrongheaded so often? When does Austen expect us to sympathize with Emma, and when does she expect us to criticize her? Is the ending a genuinely happy one, or does Austen inject it with a note of subversive irony?

EMMA: KEY FACTS

Time and place written: 1814–1815; Chawton, England	
Date of first publication: 1816	
Publisher: John Murray	
Type of work: Novel	
Genre: Satire	
Language: English	
Setting (time): Early nineteenth century	
Setting (place): Highbury, England	
Tense: Immediate past	

Tone: Ironic, satirical, sympathetic

Narrator: Anonymous third-person narrator who often uses free indirect discourse

Point of view: Mainly Emma's; occasionally other characters, such as Mr. Knightley

Protagonist: Emma

Antagonist: Emma's vanity and fear of confronting her own feelings

EMMA: PLOT OVERVIEW

Although convinced that she herself will never marry, Emma Woodhouse, a precocious twenty-year-old resident of the village of Highbury, thinks she has a natural gift for matching up other people. Emma takes it upon herself to find an eligible match for her new friend, Harriet Smith. Though Harriet's parentage is unknown, Emma is convinced that Harriet deserves to be a gentleman's wife. She decides Mr. Elton, the village vicar, would make an ideal husband for Harriet. Meanwhile, Emma persuades Harriet to reject the proposal of Robert Martin, a well-to-do farmer for whom Harriet clearly has feelings.

With Emma's encouragement, Harriet becomes infatuated with Mr. Elton, but Emma's plans go awry when Elton makes it clear that his affection is for Emma, not Harriet. Mr. Knightley, the brother of Emma's sister's husband, and Emma's treasured friend, watches Emma's matchmaking efforts with a critical eye. He believes that Mr. Martin is a worthy young man whom Harriet would be lucky to marry. He and Emma quarrel over Emma's meddling, and as usual, Mr. Knightley gets the better of Emma. Elton, spurned by Emma and offended by the idea that Harriet is his equal, leaves for the town of Bath, where he marries a girl almost immediately.

Emma is left to comfort Harriet and to wonder about the character of Frank Churchill, a new visitor expected in Highbury. Frank is the son of Mr. Weston, a widower who recently remarried Emma's governess, thanks to Emma's machinations. Frank has been raised by his aunt and uncle in London. Mr. Knightley is immediately suspicious of the young man, especially after Frank rushes back to London merely to have his hair cut. Emma, however, finds Frank delightful and notices that his charms are directed mainly toward her. Though she plans to discourage him, she finds herself flattered and flirts with the young man. Emma greets Jane Fairfax, another addition to the Highbury set, with less enthusiasm. Jane is beautiful and accomplished, but Emma dislikes her because of her reserve and, the narrator insinuates, because she is jealous of Jane.

Suspicion, intrigue, and misunderstandings ensue. Mr. Knightley says Jane deserves compassion because, unlike Emma, she has no independent fortune and must soon leave home to work as a governess. Mrs. Weston suspects that Mr. Knightley defends Jane because he has romantic feelings for her, an implication Emma resists. Everyone assumes that Frank and Emma are forming an attachment, although Emma dismisses Frank as a potential suitor and imagines him as a match for Harriet. At a village ball, Knightley earns Emma's approval by offering to dance with Harriet after Mr. Elton and his new wife humiliate her. The next day, Frank saves Harriet from Gypsy beggars. When Harriet tells Emma that she has fallen in love with a man above her social station, Emma believes she means Frank. Knightley begins to suspect that Frank and Jane have a secret understanding, and he attempts to warn Emma about it. Emma laughs off the suggestion. She loses Knightley's approval when she flirts with Frank and insults Miss Bates, a kindhearted spinster and Jane's aunt, at a picnic. When Knightley reprimands Emma, she weeps.

News comes that Frank's aunt has died, an event that leads to the solution of mysteries. Frank and Jane have been secretly engaged, and Frank has flirted with Emma so that no one would suspect his engagement. His aunt would have disapproved of the match, but with her death and his uncle's approval, Frank is free to marry Jane. Emma worries that Harriet will be crushed, but she soon discovers that it is Knightley, not Frank, who is the object of Harriet's affection. Harriet believes that Knightley returns Harriet's feelings. Upset by Harriet's revelation, Emma realizes she is in love with Knightley. Emma expects Knightley to tell her he loves Harriet, but to her delight, he declares his love for Emma. Harriet is soon comforted by a second proposal from Robert Martin, which she accepts. The novel ends with the marriage of Harriet and Mr. Martin and the marriage of Emma and Mr. Knightley.

CHARACTERS IN *EMMA*

Miss Bates Jane Fairfax's aunt and Mr. Woodhouse's friend. Miss Bates is a middle-aged spinster without beauty or cleverness but with universal goodwill and a gentle temperament. Emma treats her with unattractive impatience.

Mrs. Bates Miss Bates's mother. An elderly woman, Mrs. Bates is quiet, amiable, and somewhat deaf.

Colonel Campbell A friend of Jane Fairfax's father. Colonel Campbell took charge of orphaned Jane when she was eight years old. He loves Jane but is unable to provide her with an inheritance.

Frank Churchill Mr. Weston's son. Frank lives at Enscombe with his aunt and uncle, Mr. and Mrs. Churchill. Although Frank is attractive and charming, he is also irresponsible, deceitful, and rash.

Mrs. Churchill Mr. Weston's ailing former sister-in-law and Frank Churchill's aunt and guardian. Mrs. Churchill is capricious, ill-tempered, and extremely possessive of Frank.

Mr. and Mrs. Cole Tradespeople and longtime residents of Highbury whose good fortune of the past several years has led them to adopt a luxurious lifestyle that is only a notch below that of the Woodhouses'. Their social ambitions irritate Emma.

Mr. Dixon Husband to the Campbells' daughter. Emma suspects that Mr. Dixon had a romance with Jane Fairfax before his marriage.

Mrs. Dixon The Campbells' daughter and Jane's friend.

Mr. Elton The village vicar. Mr. Elton is a handsome and agreeable man. When he marries a woman in Bath only a short time after proposing to Emma, he seems proud and superficial.

Mrs. Elton The woman Mr. Elton meets and marries in Bath. Although somewhat attractive and accomplished, she is also vain, superficial, and vulgar.

Jane Fairfax Miss Bates's niece. Jane's arrival in Highbury irritates Emma, because Jane rivals her in accomplishment, beauty, and kindness. Jane's lack of money means she must consider working as a governess, but her marriage to Frank Churchill saves her from that fate.

Mrs. Goddard Mistress of the local boarding school, where Harriet lives.

George Knightley Mr. John Knightley's brother and the Woodhouses' trusted friend and advisor. Knightley is a respected landowner in his late thirties. He is the only character to criticize Emma openly. Because he genuinely cares for her, he frankly points out her flaws and foibles.

Isabella Knightley Emma's older sister. Isabella lives in London with her husband, Mr. John Knightley, and their five children. She is pretty, amiable, and devoted to her family, but slow and diffident compared to Emma.

John Knightley Mr. George Knightley's brother and Isabella's husband. John Knightley, a lawyer, is clear-minded but somewhat sharp-tempered.

Elizabeth Martin Mr. Martin's kind sister.

Robert Martin A twenty-four-year-old farmer. Mr. Martin is industrious and good-hearted, though he lacks the refinements of a gentleman. He lives at Abbey-Mill Farm, a property owned by Knightley, with his mother and sisters.

Mr. Perry An apothecary and associate of Emma's father.

Harriet Smith A pretty but unremarkable seventeen-year-old woman of uncertain parentage. Harriet becomes Emma's protégé and the object of her matchmaking schemes.

Mr. Weston The widower and proprietor of Randalls. When the novel begins, Mr. Weston has just married Miss Taylor. Mr. Weston has a son, Frank, from his first marriage to Miss Churchill. Mr. Weston is warm, sociable, and perpetually optimistic.

Mrs. Weston Mr. Weston's wife. Before she married, Mrs. Weston was Miss Taylor, Emma's beloved governess and companion. She is devoted to Emma.

Emma Woodhouse The protagonist of the novel. In the famous first sentence of the novel, the narrator describes twenty-year-old Emma as "handsome, clever, and rich, with a comfortable home and happy disposition." Because her mother is dead and her older sister married, Emma is the head of her father's household. Emma's misplaced matchmaking attempts and her prudish fear of love constitute the central focus of the novel, which traces Emma's mistakes and growing self-understanding.

Mr. Woodhouse Emma's father and the patriarch of Hartfield, the Woodhouse estate. Mr. Woodhouse is nervous, frail, and prone to hypochondria. He is also known for his friendliness and his attachment to his daughter. His horror of change makes him unhappy to see his daughters or Emma's governess marry. He is not Emma's intellectual equal, but she entertains him with insight and affection.

THEMES IN *EMMA*

THE IMPORTANCE OF APPROPRIATE MARRIAGES
Emma is structured around a number of marriages recently consummated or anticipated. Each marrying couple solidifies its social status. In Austen's time, social status was determined by a combination of family background, reputation, and wealth. A fortuitous marriage could raise an individual's social status. This method of social advancement was especially important to women, who could not improve their status through hard work or personal achievement.

Austen suggests that marrying too far above oneself leads to strife. Mr. Weston's first wife, Miss Churchill, came from a wealthy and well-connected family, and the inequality of the relationship (Mr. Weston is a tradesman) caused hardship to both. His marriage to Mrs. Weston is happier because their social statuses are more equal. Emma's attempt to match Harriet with Mr. Elton is dismissed by the other characters as inappropriate because of Harriet's unknown parentage. When it is revealed that Harriet is the daughter of a tradesman, Emma's critics are vindicated. However, Austen does sanction the seeming mismatch between Frank Churchill, who is rich, and Jane Fairfax, who is not. In their case, Jane's gentility and refinement adequately compensate for her poverty.

THE CONFINED NATURE OF WOMEN'S EXISTENCE
The novel's limited, almost claustrophobic scope of action gives us a strong sense of the confined nature of a woman's existence in early nineteenth-century rural England. Emma possesses a great deal of intelligence and energy, but she has no real outlet for these qualities, which is why she turns to matchmaking. Austen depicts the pastimes available to women—social visits, charity visits, music, artistic endeavors—as relatively trivial, at times even monotonous. Through her portrait of Isabella, Austen suggests that a mother's life is not an intellectually stimulating one. And Jane Fairfax's comparison of the governess profession and the slave trade suggests that the life of a working woman is in no way preferable to the idleness of a woman of fortune. The novel focuses on marriage because marriage offers women a chance to exert their power, if only for a brief time, and to affect their own destinies.

THE OBSTACLES TO OPEN EXPRESSION
The misunderstandings that permeate the novel are created, in part, by the conventions of social propriety. Convention prohibits characters from expressing their feelings directly and openly, and confusion results. While Austen never suggests that the manners and rituals of social interaction should be eliminated, she censures the overly clever, complex speech of Mr. Elton, Frank Churchill, and Emma. She presents Mr. Martin's natural, warm, and direct manner of expressing himself as preferable to Mr. Elton's ostentatious and insincere compliments. The cleverness of Frank's and Emma's banter upsets Jane, and their flirting at the Box Hill party hurts both Knightley and Jane.

SYMBOLS IN *EMMA*

RIDDLES
Also known as charades, riddles in the novel take the form of elaborate wordplay. They symbolize the subtexts of conversation that need decoding. In Chapter 9, for example, Mr. Elton presents a riddle to Emma and Harriet. Emma decodes it immediately as "courtship," but she believes, incorrectly, that it is meant for Harriet rather than herself.

TOKENS OF AFFECTION
The characters in *Emma* turn objects into symbols of affection. Mr. Elton frames Emma's portrait of Harriet as a symbol of affection for her. Harriet keeps court plaster and a

pencil stub as souvenirs of Mr. Elton. When quarreling with Frank, Jane returns his letters to symbolize her relinquishment of his love.

IMPORTANT QUOTATIONS FROM *EMMA*

She was vexed beyond what could have been expressed—almost beyond what she could conceal. Never had she felt so agitated, so mortified, grieved, at any circumstance in her life. She was most forcibly struck. The truth of his representation there was no denying. She felt it at her heart. How could she have been so brutal, so cruel to Miss Bates! How could she have exposed herself to such ill opinion in any one she valued! And how suffer him to leave her without saying one word of gratitude, of concurrence, of common kindness!

Location: Chapter 43
Speaker: The narrator
Context: Mr. Knightley has reprimanded Emma for insulting Miss Bates, and Emma is flooded with remorse

This quotation marks the point at which Emma's growing self-understanding, which helps her understand how cruelly she has treated Miss Bates, coincides with her growing attachment to Knightley. This moment is also Emma's most emotional in the novel. It is narrated directly, unlike Mr. Elton's proposal and Emma's response to Mr. Knightley's proposal, which underscores the seriousness of Emma's emotions.

Seldom, very seldom does complete truth belong to any human disclosure; seldom can it happen that something is not a little disguised, or a little mistaken; but where, as in this case, though the conduct is mistaken, the feelings are not, it may not be very material.

Location: Chapter 49
Speaker: The narrator
Context: Emma and Mr. Knightley have just gotten engaged

This quotation could be taken as the novel's motto. In it, Austen says that everything we say holds something back, or misrepresents the truth, or is misinterpreted by our listener. But as long as the speech is loyal to the speaker's feelings, it does not matter that language will never connote the whole truth. *Emma* is filled with disguises and mistakes, some reprehensible, some unnecessary, and some innocent. Though Austen is critical of Elton's insincerity, Frank's conscious deception, and Emma's mistakes, we are left with the sense that social conventions and the limitations of language make misunderstandings inevitable. The remedy for such imperfect communication, according to Austen, is the genuine emotion of the human heart.

The real evils, indeed, of Emma's situation were the power of having rather too much her own way, and a disposition to think a little too well of herself: these were the disadvantages which threatened alloy to her many enjoyments. The danger, however, was at present so unperceived, that they did not by any means rank as misfortunes with her.

Location: Chapter 1
Speaker: The narrator
Context: The narrator outlines the major flaws in Emma's character

The first error, and the worst, lay at her door. It was foolish, it was wrong, to take so active a part in bringing any two people together. It was adventuring too far, assuming too much, making light of what ought to be serious—a trick of what ought to be simple. She was quite concerned and ashamed, and resolved to do such things no more.

Location: Chapter 16
Speaker: The narrator
Context: Mr. Elton has proposed to Emma, and she realizes that she was wrong to assume he loved Harriet

---

Emma's eyes were instantly withdrawn; and she sat silently meditating, in a fixed attitude, for a few minutes. A few minutes were sufficient for making her acquainted with her own heart. A mind like hers, once opening to suspicion, made rapid progress; she touched, she admitted, she acknowledged the whole truth. Why was it so much worse that Harriet should be in love with Mr. Knightley than with Frank Churchill? Why was the evil so dreadfully increased by Harriet's having some hope of a return? It darted through her with the speed of an arrow that Mr. Knightley must marry no one but herself!

Location: Chapter 47
Speaker: The narrator
Context: Harriet has confessed her feelings for Mr. Knightley

ETHAN FROME

Edith Wharton

A man longs to flee from his wretched wife and run off with her vivacious cousin but finds he lacks the courage.

THE LIFE OF EDITH WHARTON

Edith Wharton, nee Edith Jones, was born into an upper-class New York City family in 1862. As was typical for members of her class at that time, Edith had a distant relationship with her parents. At a young age, she accepted a marriage proposal, but the wedding was thwarted by her prospective in-laws, who found her family incredibly snobbish. In 1885, at the age of twenty-three, Edith married Edward Wharton, an older man whom the Jones family found to be of suitably lofty social rank. The marriage soon soured, but Wharton stayed with her husband for well over twenty years. She finally divorced him in 1913.

Much of Wharton's fiction concerns the temptations of illicit passion, and many have pointed to Wharton's unhappy marriage as her inspiration. Wharton's doctor advised her to devote herself to her writing more seriously in order to relieve tension and stress. Eventually, Wharton found temporary solace in her surreptitious affair with the journalist Morton Fullerton, which coincided with the disintegration of her marriage. It was in the wake of this affair and her ensuing divorce that Wharton wrote many of her most successful and enduring works.

Criticized as an immoral radical in her early years and as a moralizing conservative in her later years, Wharton has been difficult for the critics to pin down. She was undoubtedly concerned with the moral universe, but her fiction shows the clash between conformity and rebelliousness. She can perhaps best be described as a critic of moral recklessness. Wharton wanted individuals to consider each moral decision on its own terms.

After producing a great quantity of little-read short stories and novels, Wharton enjoyed her first true critical and popular success with the publication of *The House of Mirth* in 1905. In the early 1910s, she settled in Paris, where she remained for the rest of her days. One of her close associates there was the novelist Henry James, a fellow American expatriate of similarly intense and complex moral sensibility.

In 1921, Wharton won the Pulitzer Prize for her highly esteemed novel *The Age of Innocence*. She continued to write novels throughout the 1920s. In 1934, she wrote her autobiography, *A Backward Glance*. In 1937, Edith Wharton died in her villa near Paris at the age of seventy-five.

ETHAN FROME IN CONTEXT

Ethan Frome, a curious and slender volume first published in 1911, is one of the few pieces of Wharton's fiction that does not take place in an urban, upper-class setting. The novel is remarkable for its austere and penetrating portrait of rural working-class New England, especially given that its author was a woman of leisure, writing from the comfort of her Paris salon. Wharton based the narrative of *Ethan Frome* on an accident that had occurred in Lenox, Massachusetts, where she had traveled extensively and had come into contact with one of the victims of the accident. Wharton found the notion of the tragic sledding crash irresistible as an extended metaphor for the complexities of a secret love affair.

ETHAN FROME: KEY FACTS

Time and place written: 1910; Paris	
Date of first publication: 1911	
Publisher: Scribner's	
Type of work: Novel	
Genre: Tragic romance	

Language: English

Setting (time): The late nineteenth–early twentieth century

Setting (place): Starkfield, Massachusetts

Tense: Past

Tone: Foreboding, bleak, ironic, tragic, spare

Narrator: An anonymous visitor narrates the introduction and conclusion in the first person; a limited third person narrator tells the story of Ethan Frome's youth

Point of view: Ethan Frome's in the bulk of the novel; anonymous visitor's in the introduction and conclusion

Protagonist: Ethan Frome

Antagonist: Ethan's conscience, home, and surroundings; Zeena

ETHAN FROME: **PLOT OVERVIEW**

Finding himself in the small New England town of Starkfield for the winter, the narrator decides to learn about the life of a mysterious local named Ethan Frome, who had a tragic accident twenty years earlier. After questioning various locals with little success, the narrator finally learns the details of Ethan's "smash-up" (as the locals call it) when a violent snowstorm forces him to stay overnight at the Frome household.

The narrative switches to the year of Ethan's accident. Ethan walks through snowy Starkfield at midnight and arrives at the village church, where a dance is going on in the basement. Ethan loiters by the window, transfixed by the sight of a young girl in a cherry-colored scarf. He has come to the church to fetch his wife's cousin, Mattie Silver, who has been living with the Fromes for over a year, helping around the house. Eventually, we learn that Mattie is the girl in the red scarf—and the object of Ethan's affection.

When the dance ends, Ethan hangs back. Mattie refuses the offer of a ride from a young man named Denis Eady and begins to walk home alone. Ethan catches up with her. As they continue on their way together, tension crackles between them. The tension dissipates when they arrive home and see Zeena, Ethan's sickly, shrewish wife, who has stayed up late in anticipation of their return. She is clearly suspicious of the relationship between Mattie and Ethan.

Ethan spends the next morning cutting wood and returns home to find his wife prepared for a journey. She has decided to seek treatment for her illness in a neighboring town, where she will spend the night with some distant relatives. Excited by the prospect of an evening alone with Mattie, Ethan quickly assents to his wife's plan. He goes into town to make a lumber sale, hurrying so he will make it home to Mattie in time for supper.

That evening, tensions run high between Ethan and Mattie. They never verbalize their longing, but their mutual feelings are palpable. The cat shatters Zeena's favorite pickle dish, potentially ruining the mood, but Ethan quickly pieces the shards together and tucks the broken dish back in its place. After supper, with Mattie busy at her sewing, Ethan contemplates an outright demonstration of his affections, but stops himself. Just after eleven, the two turn in for the night without so much as touching.

The next morning, Ethan is eager to reveal his feelings to Mattie, but the presence of his hired man, Jotham Powell, coupled with his own inhibitions, silence him. Ethan goes into town to pick up some glue for the pickle dish. When he arrives back at the farm, Mattie tells him that Zeena has returned already. Quickly collecting himself, Ethan goes to the bedroom to greet his wife. Zeena bitterly informs Ethan that her health is failing rapidly. In light of this fact, Zeena announces, she plans to replace Mattie with a more efficient hired girl. Ethan hides his anger at this decision.

In the kitchen, Ethan's passions spill over, and he kisses Mattie. He tells her about Zeena's plan to dismiss her. Zeena interrupts them by unexpectedly coming down for dinner. After the meal, Zeena discovers the broken pickle dish. Enraged, she grows all the more determined to chase out Mattie.

That evening, Ethan retreats to his makeshift study, where he contemplates the decision that lies before him. Unable to tolerate Mattie's dismissal, but effectively unable to prevent it, Ethan briefly considers eloping with Mattie, and even begins to draft a letter of farewell to Zeena. After a sober evaluation of his financial situation, Ethan understands the impossibility of running away and falls asleep in a state of hopelessness.

At breakfast the next morning, Zeena announces that Mattie must leave that day. At midmorning, Ethan steals into town. His plan, hatched on the fly, is to make a second attempt to collect an advance from Andrew Hale on a recently delivered lumber load, in hopes of financing his elopement with Mattie. On his way down the hill Ethan encounters the Hale sleigh. In passing, Hale's wife praises him for his patience in caring for the ailing Zeena. Her kind words halt his plan, and he returns to the farm with a guilty conscience.

Against Zeena's wishes, Ethan decides to bring Mattie to the station himself. In a fit of nostalgia, they stop to take a sledding adventure they once proposed but never undertook. They have a successful first run. Then Mattie asks Ethan if, on the second trip, he will run the sled into the elm tree at the foot of the hill, allowing them to spend their last moments together. Ethan initially rejects her proposal but is slowly won over, and they take their positions on the sled, locking themselves in a final embrace. In the wake of the collision, Ethan regains consciousness and reaches out to feel the face of the softly moaning Mattie, who opens her eyes and weakly says his name.

The narrative jumps forward twenty years. The narrator enters the squalid Frome house and sees two frail and aging women. Frome apologizes for the lack of heat in the house and introduces the narrator to his wife, Zeena, and the seated, crippled woman in the chair by the fire—Miss Mattie Silver. Both women complain and bicker with each other. The next day, the narrator returns to town, where he lodges with Mrs. Ned Hale and her mother, Mrs. Varnum. Sensing their curiosity, he gives a brief account of his evening in the Frome household. After supper, he and Mrs. Hale mourn the tragic plight of the silent, cursed man and the two women fated to keep him company during the long New England winter nights.

CHARACTERS IN *ETHAN FROME*

Denis Eady The son of Starkfield's rich Irish grocer, Michael Eady. Denis shows interest in Mattie, which makes Ethan jealous until he understands Mattie's true feelings.

Ethan Frome The protagonist of the novel. Ethan is a farmer whose family has lived and died on the same Massachusetts farm for generations. A sensitive figure, Ethan has a deep, almost mystical appreciation of nature. He lacks the strength to escape the oppressive forces of convention, climate, and his sickly wife.

Zenobia (Zeena) Frome Ethan's sickly wife. Zeena is prematurely aged, caustic, prone to alternating fits of silence and rage, and utterly unattractive. Despite Zeena's apparent physical weakness, she dominates Ethan and cares for everyone after the accident.

Harmon Gow A former stage-driver and town gossip. Gow provides the narrator with a few details about Ethan Frome's life.

Andrew Hale Ned's father. Andrew Hale is an amiable builder involved in regular business dealings with the young Ethan. Ethan mistakenly regards him as a possible source of a loan.

Mrs. Andrew Hale Ned's mother and Andrew's wife. Mrs. Hale warmly praises Ethan's kindness to Zeena, causing him to reevaluate his plans to elope.

Mrs. Ned Hale (Ruth Varnum) The widow of Ned Hale and the narrator's landlady. The narrator describes Mrs. Hale as more refined and educated than most of her neighbors.

Ned Hale Ruth Varnum's husband. Ned and Ruth's romance contrasts with the fruitless love of Ethan and Mattie. Ned has died by the time the narrator comes to Starkfield.

Mattie Silver Zeena's cousin. Because the reader sees Mattie only through Ethan's lovesick eyes, she never emerges as a well-rounded character. Attractive, young, and energetic, she often seems more a focus for Ethan's rebellion against Zeena and Starkfield than an actual person.

The Narrator An engineer. He plays no part in the main story of the novel. As a stranger to Starkfield, he is the connection between the closely guarded story of Frome's tragedy and the reader.

Jotham Powell The hired man on the Frome farm.

THEMES IN *ETHAN FROME*

SOCIETY AND MORALITY AS OBSTACLES TO THE FULFILLMENT OF DESIRE   By denying Zeena a single positive attribute while presenting Mattie as the epitome of glowing, youthful attractiveness, Wharton makes Ethan's desire to cheat on his wife perfectly understandable. The conflict does not stem from within Ethan's own heart—his feelings for Mattie never waver. Instead, the conflict is between his passions and the constraints placed on him by society. Wharton shows how tenaciously social conventions cling to Ethan. Although he has one night alone with Mattie, sitting in the kitchen with her reminds him of his domestic duties and his wife. Although he longs to elope with Mattie, he cannot bring himself to lie to his neighbors in order to procure the necessary money. In the end, Ethan opts out of the battle between his desires and social order. Lacking the courage to ignore convention, he tries to abandon life's burdens by abandoning life itself. The disaster that follows shows what Wharton thinks of Ethan's choice.

WINTER AS A STIFLING FORCE   An old man says that Ethan has "been in Starkfield too many winters." As the story progresses, the narrator begins to understand the deep meaning of this statement. Although a wintry mood grips *Ethan Frome* from the beginning—even the name Starkfield conjures images of northern winters—at first the narrator appreciates the winter's spare loveliness. But as time goes on, eventually he realizes that Starkfield and its inhabitants spend much of each year under siege by the elements. Wharton suggests that winter crushes sensitive souls like Ethan, breaking their resolve and very sense of self. Ethan yearns to escape Starkfield. As a young man, he hoped to leave his family farm and work as an engineer in a larger town. Though Zeena and poverty keep Ethan from fulfilling his dream, the major impediment is the climate. Wharton suggests that physical environment is destiny.

ILLNESS AS A SIGN OF INNER DECAY   In *Ethan Frome*, physical appearance reflects personality. Most of the characters in the novel are ill or crippled, which points to their inward states of destitution and decline. Ethan and everyone close to him suffer from sickness or disability. Caring for the sick and the lame defines Ethan's life. He spends the years before the novel begins tending to his ailing mother, and then he has to care for his hypochondriac wife. Finally, the attempted suicides leave Mattie and Ethan himself crippled.

SYMBOLS IN *ETHAN FROME*

MATTIE'S RED SCARF AND RED RIBBON   At the dance, Mattie wears a red scarf, and for her evening alone with Ethan, she puts a red ribbon in her hair. Red is the color of blood, ruddiness, good health, and vitality, all of which Mattie has in abundance, and all of which Zeena lacks. In the oppressive white landscape of Starkfield, red stands out, just as Mattie stands out in the oppressive landscape of Ethan's life. Red is also the color of transgression and sin—the trademark color of the devil—especially in New England, where in Puritan times adulterers were forced to wear red A's on their clothes (a punishment immortalized in Nathaniel Hawthorne's *The Scarlet Letter*). Thus, Mattie's scarlet adornments also symbolize her role as Ethan's temptress.

THE FINAL SLED RUN   The momentous sled ride symbolizes Ethan's life. Normally, although a sled rider forfeits a considerable amount of control, he maintains an ability to steer the sled. Ethan forfeits this ability on the final sled run. Just as he decides not to steer on the sled, he decides not to steer in his life. He lets Zeena dominate him and he lets Mattie pressure him into the suicide attempt. Unable to face the consequences of any decision, he lets external circumstances—other individuals, society, convention, financial constraints—make his decisions for him.

IMPORTANT QUOTATIONS FROM *ETHAN FROME*

All the long misery of his baffled past, of his youth of failure, hardship and vain effort, rose up in his soul in bitterness and seemed to take shape before him in the woman who at every turn had barred his way. She had taken everything else from him; and now she meant to take the one thing that made up for all the others. For a moment such a flame of hate rose in him that it ran down his arm and clenched his fist against her. He took a wild step forward and then stopped.

"You're—you're not coming down?" he said in a bewildered voice.

Location: Chapter VII
Speaker: The third person narrator
Context: Zeena has announced her intention to expel Mattie from the house

As this passage makes clear, Ethan is physically strong, but he lacks force of personality. When Zeena announces that Mattie must go, Ethan's fury suggests that he will confront his wife at last. His clenched fist even hints at potential physical violence. Yet even after Zeena's brazen provocation, Ethan's fury dissipates into a "bewildered voice." Ethan may hate his wife, but he is much weaker than she is. Zeena imposes her will as she likes, and Ethan cannot oppose her. Because of Ethan's weakness, *Ethan Frome* is in many ways a story of inaction, of an affair that doesn't happen. Ethan's only proactive move is his attempted suicide, which is more an expression of cowardice than of true courage. Ethan blames Zeena for his thwarted dreams and recurring failures. As he looks at her, his failures "take shape before him" in the figure of his wife. Zeena is responsible for much of Ethan's suffering: shrewd, calculating, manipulative, and domineering, she makes her husband's life a misery. But as Wharton points out in this passage, Ethan is wrong to place the blame entirely on his wife. Zeena had nothing to do with Ethan's "baffled past" or "youth of failure." She is horrible, but she is also a convenient lightning rod for Ethan's general anger and disappointment.

There was one day, about a week after the accident, when they all thought Mattie couldn't live. Well, I say it's a pity she did . . . if [Mattie] ha' died, Ethan might ha' lived; and the way they are now, I don't see's there's much difference between the Fromes up at the farm and the Fromes down in the graveyard; 'cept that down there they're all quiet, and the women have got to hold their tongues.

Location: The last lines of the novel
Speaker: Mrs. Hale
Context: In discussion with the first-person narrator, Mrs. Hale speaks of Ethan's plight

Mrs. Hale's words seal the brutal despair that permeates the conclusion of the novel. They point to the horror of Ethan's life: he is trapped in a dilapidated farmhouse, buried under a perpetual winter, and forced to live not only with Zeena, but with Mattie, who has been transformed into a crippled copy of his wife. The comparison between the living Fromes and their ancestors in the graveyard underlines the permanence of Ethan's situation. Although Mrs. Hale speaks of Ethan as if he had died ("if [Mattie] ha' died, Ethan might ha' lived"), her implication is that Ethan's fate is worse than death—that he is the living dead. With bitter irony, Mrs. Hale points out that at least the women in the graveyard hold their tongues, implicitly contrasting this silence to the whining that fills the Frome household. In this regard, corporeal death seems preferable to spiritual death, for at least when the body dies, peace and rest are attained. A living death—Ethan's tragic fate—continues to torment the soul for years.

When I had been there a little longer, and had seen this phase of crystal clearness followed by long stretches of sunless cold; when the storms of February had pitched their white tents about the devoted village and the wild cavalry of March winds had charged down to their support; I began to understand why Starkfield emerged from its six months' siege like a starved garrison capitulating without quarter.

Location: The introduction
Speaker: The first-person narrator
Context: The narrator attempts to understand the influence of winter on Starkfield's inhabitants

Against the dark background of the kitchen she stood up tall and angular, one hand drawing a quilted counterpane to her flat breast, while the other held a lamp. The light . . . drew out of the darkness her puckered throat and the projecting wrist of the hand that clutched the quilt, and deepened fantastically the hollows and prominences of her high-boned face under its rings of crimping-pins.

Location: Chapter II
Speaker: The third person narrator
Context: The narrator describes Zeena

He knew that most young men made nothing at all of giving a pretty girl a kiss, and he remembered that the night before, when he had put his arm about Mattie, she had not resisted. But that had been out-of-doors, under the open irresponsible night. Now, in the warm lamplit room, with all its ancient implications of conformity and order, she seemed infinitely farther away from him and more unapproachable.

Location: Chapter V
Speaker: The third person narrator
Context: Alone with Mattie, Ethan feels shy

FAR FROM THE MADDING CROWD

Thomas Hardy

After her admirer shoots her husband, a woman marries the steady man who has long loved her.

THE LIFE OF THOMAS HARDY

Thomas Hardy was born on June 2, 1840, in Higher Brockhampton, Dorset, England. At age nine, he began studying Latin, French, and German at a nearby school. The son of a builder, Hardy was apprenticed at the age of sixteen to John Hicks, an architect who lived in the city of Dorchester, which would later serve as the model for Hardy's fictional Casterbridge. Hicks's office was next door to that of Reverand William Barnes, a poet and scholar. During these years, Hardy read the Greek playwrights under the tutelage of Horace Moule, a scholar. By the early 1860s, Hardy was reading the work of Charles Darwin, who popularized the theory of biological evolution, and writing his first poems.

From 1862 to 1867, Hardy lived in London and worked as an assistant to an architect. He absorbed the city's culture ravenously, attending operas and theatre performances, and going to museums and galleries. He read widely and lost his religious faith. In 1867, Hardy published an architectural article, "How I Built Myself a House." By this time he had begun submitting poems to magazines and receiving rejections.

Hardy's return to Higher Brockhampton coincided with his first attempt to write a novel. *The Poor Man*, which is lost to us, was finished in 1868. Although the publisher Chapman and Hall accepted the novel, one of the publisher's readers advised Hardy not to publish it. While continuing to work as an architect, Hardy completed three novels between 1871 and 1873. Their publication earned Hardy a reputation as a young writer of promise in literary circles, but not until the publication of *Far From the Madding Crowd* in 1874 did Hardy attain any measure of popularity. In 1874, Hardy married Emma Gifford, the sister-in-law of the rector of a church whose restoration he had supervised. Emma soon convinced her husband to give up architecture entirely in favor of literary pursuits.

Between 1876 and 1896, Hardy traveled extensively with his wife and published eleven novels and three collections of stories. *The Return of the Native* (1878), *The Mayor of Casterbridge* (1886), *Tess of the D'Urbervilles* (1891), and *Jude the Obscure* (1896) are his best-known works. After the publication of *Jude*, Hardy gave up the writing of fiction and devoted himself to the composition of poetry. He published eight volumes of verse, comprising more than 900 poems written over the course of six decades. Although his poetry never garnered as much praise during his lifetime as did his novels, Hardy is now considered one of the great English poets.

From the mid-1890s until his wife's death in 1912, Hardy's family life was troubled, but this strain and the loss of his wife inspired some of his most acclaimed poetry. In 1914, Hardy married his secretary, Florence Dugdale, who lived with him and helped him cope with the attentions of an admiring public until his death on January 11, 1828.

FAR FROM THE MADDING CROWD IN CONTEXT

Despite the mostly good reviews they won, Hardy's first two novels did not enjoy public success. However, Hardy's publisher believed in him and encouraged him to continue writing. The publication of *Far From the Madding Crowd* marked a turning point in Hardy's career. Due to the novel's success, Hardy was able to give up architecture and devote himself to writing fiction full time.

Among Hardy's supporters was Leslie Stephen, one of the preeminent figures of British literature at the time and the father of Virginia Woolf. After reading *Under the Greenwood Tree*, a short story that Hardy published anonymously, Stephen obtained Hardy's identity from his publishers and wrote to him, saying "If you are, as I hope, writing anything more, I should be very glad to have the offer of it for our pages." By "our pages," he meant *Cornhill Magazine*, a publication edited by William Thackeray, author of *Vanity Fair*.

Stephen liked what he called Hardy's "prose idyl"—his description of farmers and the rural life. Hardy told Stephen that he would be happy to supply him with another story of country life featuring a young woman farmer, a shepherd, and a sergeant of cavalry under the title *Far from the Madding Crowd*.

The title, characters, and storyline of what would become Hardy's first successful novel suggest an escape from city life and from the industrialization that was rapidly overtaking much of Britain. While Hardy's focus on the pastoral can and has been interpreted as a political statement against industrialization and urbanization, it can also be understood as a commercial decision. Leslie Stephen believed Hardy's pastoral work would sell, particularly to those numerous readers who lived in urban or academic settings and viewed country life as a novelty or an occasion for nostalgia.

Hardy was interested in portraying pastoral life as it actually existed, not as a symbolic opposition to industrialization. Although Hardy had spent time in the city, he had grown up in the country and lived there at the time he was composing the novel. He endeavored to create three-dimensional farmers, shepherds, and farmhands with identities more nuanced than Londoners' ideas about rural rubes. Hardy reinterpreted the folklore of his childhood in writing the novel, basing the character of Bathsheba on a woman featured in stories told to him by his mother.

George Eliot (the pseudonym of Mary Ann Evans), one of the foremost figures of British literature at the time Hardy was starting out, mined the pastoral tradition in her greatest work, *Middlemarch* (subtitled *A study of Provincial Life*), which was published serially in 1871–1872. As Hardy had feared, most reviews of Hardy's novel compared him to Eliot, and while it was being published anonymously in serial form, *Far From the Madding Crowd* was often mistaken for Eliot's work. But the reviews were also overwhelmingly positive. The *Times* of London said of the novel, "There is not a lady or a gentleman in this book in the ordinary sense of the words. They are all working people, and ever so much more interesting than the idle lords and ladies, with the story of whose loves and sorrows the [bookstore's] shelves are always crammed."

FAR FROM THE MADDING CROWD: KEY FACTS

Time and place written: 1873–1874; Weymouth, England	
Date of publication: Serially in Cornhill Magazine, 1874; as a novel in 1874	
Publisher: Cornhill Magazine (serial); Smith Elder and Co. (novel in two volumes)	
Type of work: Novel	
Genre: Pastoral; Victorian novel	
Language: English	
Setting (time): 1840s	
Setting (place): Most of the action takes place in Weatherbury, a town in Wessex, an imaginary county in the south of England	
Tense: Past	
Tone: Somber	
Narrator: Omniscient narrator in the third person	
Point of View: The narrator's	
Protagonist: Bathsheba Everdene, Gabriel Oak	
Antagonist: Sergeant Francis Troy, William Boldwood	

FAR FROM THE MADDING CROWD: PLOT OVERVIEW

Gabriel Oak, a farmer in the south of England, briefly meets Bathsheba Everdene, a beautiful, fortuneless young woman who is living near his farm and working as a milkmaid. One day, soon after their first meeting, Bathsheba notices that Oak has shut himself up in his hut, risking suffocation. She comes to his rescue and saves his life. Oak visits Bathsheba and asks her to marry him, but she refuses, saying she feels no love for him. Soon she disappears from the area. Oak's two hundred sheep escape their fenced shelter and fall from a cliff to their deaths, ruining his business. He sells his farm to pay his debts and takes to the road as a shepherd for hire.

Months later, Oak goes to Weatherbury looking for work. A fire breaks out at a local farm, and he puts it out almost single-handedly. When he asks the mistress of the farm if she could use his help as a shepherd, she reveals herself to be Bathsheba. Her uncle has bequeathed her the farm, which she now runs.

Bathsheba meets her neighbor, a farmer named William Boldwood. Boldwood is a mature, wealthy, and much desired member of the community. On a whim, Bathsheba sends him a Valentine inscribed with the words "MARRY ME." This message stirs a love in Boldwood's heart that quickly turns to obsession. He tries to court Bathsheba, but she refuses his advances, saying she does not love him. Boldwood prods her, and she agrees to reconsider her decision. That night, Bathsheba meets Sergeant Francis Troy, a handsome swordsman. Unbeknownst to Bathsheba, Troy has impregnated Fanny Robin, a poor local girl. Troy and Fanny planned to marry, but there was a miscommunication about the church they were to meet at, after which Troy angrily refused to marry her. Troy makes advances on Bathsheba and she responds, enraging Boldwood and hurting Oak. Bathsheba travels by night to meet Troy in Bath and warn him of Boldwood's potentially violent anger. Troy convinces her to marry him.

Back in Weatherbury, Boldwood accosts Troy and demands that he stop courting Bathsheba. When Bathsheba approaches, Boldwood hides and sees her greet Troy familiarly and invite him into her house. Boldwood tells Troy he must marry Bathsheba to preserve her honor, and Troy humiliates him by showing him a newspaper announcement of his marriage to Bathsheba.

Bathsheba and Troy begin an uneasy married life together. The income from her farm accounts for all of their wealth. One day they come upon the pregnant Fanny Robin. Troy stops to talk to her, which makes Bathsheba suspicious. Fanny dies in labor, and Bathsheba learns that Troy was the father of Fanny's child. In a fit of shame and grief, Troy runs away. He stops at a cove for a swim and is swept away by a current. A passing ship picks him up, but Bathsheba and the other townspeople believe he is dead.

Boldwood resumes his efforts to win Bathsheba's hand. Months pass, and Troy, who has traveled as far as America, returns to the area and spots Bathsheba at a fair. He decides to reveal himself to her at Boldwood's Christmas party. At the party, Boldwood again asks Bathsheba to marry him, and she gives in. Suddenly, Troy arrives to claim Bathsheba as his wife. As Bathsheba screams, Boldwood shoots Troy dead. Boldwood is threatened with the gallows, but Oak's pleading on his behalf results in a sentence of life imprisonment. A few months later, Bathsheba marries Oak, who is now a prosperous bailiff.

CHARACTERS IN *FAR FROM THE MADDING CROWD*

Cainy Ball A young boy who works as Gabriel Oak's assistant shepherd on the Everdene farm.

William Boldwood Bathsheba's second suitor and the owner of a nearby farm. Boldwood is a somewhat wooden, reserved man. He seems uninterested in romance until Bathsheba sends him a valentine, after which he becomes irrationally, and eventually violently, obsessed with her.

Jan Coggan A farm laborer and friend of Gabriel Oak's.

Bathsheba Everdene The young woman at the center of the novel. Bathsheba is vain, beautiful, and impulsive. Her financial independence makes marriage a neutral prospect.

Gabriel Oak With Bathsheba, one of the novel's protagonists. Gabriel Oak is a farmer, shepherd, and bailiff. He is humble, honest, loyal, and exceptionally skilled with animals and farming. He has an extraordinary ability to read the natural world and control it without fighting it.

Pennyways The bailiff on Bathsheba's farm. Pennyways is caught stealing grain and dismissed. Later, he recognizes Troy at Greenhill Fair.

Joseph Poorgrass A shy, timid farm laborer. Poorgrass carries Fanny's coffin back to the farm for burial.

Fanny Robin A young orphaned servant girl at the farm. Fanny dies giving birth to Sergeant Troy's child at the poor house in Casterbridge.

Liddy Smallbury Bathsheba's maid and confidante.

Sergeant Francis (Frank) Troy The novel's antagonist. Troy is handsome, vain, young, and irresponsible. He has the capacity for strong emotion and cannot forgive himself when Fanny dies.

THEMES IN *FAR FROM THE MADDING CROWD*

MARRIAGE, COURTING, AND ROMANTIC RIVALRY The central plot of *Far From the Madding Crowd* concerns the marital status of Bathsheba Everdene. Although the notion of a wedding pleases Bathsheba, the prospect of being forever tied to a husband threatens her sense of individuality. Because of this threat, she reacts to the various men in her life with capriciousness and an unwillingness to consider serious commitment. She cannot resign herself to the kind of life Gabriel Oak envisions. She takes an interest in William Boldwood only because he ignores her, sending a marriage proposal to him on a whim, not because she actually wants to marry him. She succumbs to Sergeant Troy precisely because he lacks seriousness or steadiness. In complete contrast to Oak and Boldwood, Troy is a dazzling swordsman and a romantic who meets Bathsheba in secret at night.

Each of these men react to Bathsheba according to their own limitations. Boldwood succumbs to a foolish obsession, killing a man because he refuses to give up his courtship of Bathsheba after she proves herself both unwilling and unsuitable to be his wife. Troy undoes himself with his erratic and unreliable behavior, breaking down after his affair with Fanny Robin and receiving punishment at the hands of the jealous Christian Boldwood. Oak succeeds in winning Bathsheba because of his consistency of character, and because Bathsheba eventually learns the value of being able to trust in and rely on another person. That Oak has not allowed his love for Bathsheba to compromise his own character makes him all the more attractive to her. Their union may not represent the height of a romantic ideal, but it restores order to Bathsheba's life and brings her in line with her society.

THE MAIDEN FARMER By assuming the ownership of her uncle's farm, Bathsheba disrupts the social structure of her community which consists entirely of men who control and share it at their discretion with the women they marry. The farmhand Henry Fray thinks that Bathsheba's financial and spiritual independence disqualifies her from the normal fate of women: "I don't see why a maid should take a husband when she's bold enough to fight her own battles, and don't want a home; for 'tis keeping another woman out." Fray describes marriage as a purely economic agreement that Bathsheba does not need. Whereas most women depend utterly on their husbands for financial support, Bathsheba's husband, Troy, depends on *her* for money.

NATURE AS THE SUBLIME In *Far From the Madding Crowd*, Hardy depicts natural landscapes in lofty, lyrical language. In Chapter 2, Oak stops on a hill by himself to behold the night's sky, and Hardy's narration turns discursive and philosophical: "To persons standing alone on a hill during a clear midnight such as this, the roll of the world eastward is almost a palpable movement. . .it is hard to believe that the consciousness of such majestic speeding is derived from a tiny human frame." This scene paints Oak as an ideal pastoral figure, less an individual man or a member of a society than another element in a natural landscape. Hardy describes crops in bloom as divinely infused: "Every green was young, every pore was open, and every stalk was swollen with racing currents of juice. God was present in the country, and the devil had gone with the world to town." Hardy associates the divine with natural settings, and the devil with urban locations, emphasizing the corrupting influence of the city by making the primary agent of moral transgression, Sergeant Troy, an intruder on the rural scene. Troy's seduction of and marriage to Bathsheba occurs in the town of Bath, not in the country, which underlines the dangerously immoral atmosphere of urban centers.

SYMBOLS IN *FAR FROM THE MADDING CROWD*

BOLDWOOD'S HOME Hardy describes the gloomy interior of Boldwood's farmhouse as a place with "the atmosphere of a Puritan Sunday lasting all week." This description reveals as much about Boldwood's character as it does about the ambiance of his dreary residence. His Christian morality and aesthetic have paralyzed him in a lonely and joyless life. This critical depiction of Boldwood's dour house also suggests Hardy's bias against rural Christianity and his preference for the more pagan beliefs represented by the shepherd Oak.

TROY'S SWORD Troy's sword, which he wields to impress Bathsheba, symbolizes his sexuality. Hardy describes the exercises he does with it in overtly sexual language. The vigorous way Troy whips the sword around, "like electricity," simulates the sexual act. Bathsheba responds with excitement to the blade, which looks to her "like a living thing." As Troy "cuts" and "thrusts," she trembles, trying not to flinch and continually expecting to see blood. Troy's exercises involve her entire body, as Hardy writes: "had it been possible for the edge of the sword to leave in the air a permanent substance wherever it flew past, the space left untouched would have been almost a mould of Bathsheba's figure."

IMPORTANT QUOTATIONS FROM *FAR FROM THE MADDING CROWD*

---

marry me

Location: Chapter XIII
Speaker: Bathsheba
Context: Bathsheba writes a valentine to William Boldwood

Bathsheba's message to Boldwood springs from vanity and narcissism. Unlike all of the other farmers, Boldwood ignored her as she strode through the farmer's market, so Bathsheba insists on attracting his attention by boldly commanding him to marry her in writing. She is preoccupied with the way Weatherbury perceives her, and she wants not Boldwood in particular, but everyone in general, to take notice of her. Her valentine to Boldwood does not express interest in him, but a refusal to let anyone ignore her. Also, Bathsheba imagines Boldwood as an impenetrable emotional fortress, and the idea of breaking down his wall strikes her as an amusing game. She never considers Boldwood's possible reaction, and Boldwood never considers the possibility that Bathsheba's valentine was not seriously meant. He misreads the whimsical, impulsive proposal as a carefully considered one—a misreading that sparks his obsession and sets the events of the rest of the novel in motion. Bathsheba neither intends nor imagines the dramatic results of her two-word note, because she has no understanding of Boldwood's character. Hardy writes: "Bathsheba was far from dreaming that the dark and silent shape on which she had so carelessly thrown a seed was a hotbed of tropical intensity."

This woman is more to me, dead as she is, than ever you were, or are, or can be. If Satan had not tempted me with that face of yours, and those cursed coquetries, I should have married her.

Location: Chapter XLIII
Speaker: Troy
Context: Standing over the coffin of Fanny Robin, Troy tells Bathsheba how he really feels

Before uttering these harsh, scornful words, Troy collapses in front of Fanny Robin's corpse and kisses Fanny's face with a combination of grief and reverence, inciting hysterical jealous rage in Bathsheba. Blaming his betrayal of Fanny on the devil, Troy bluntly reveals his true feelings to his wife with an emotional honesty we have not seen in him before. Fanny's death makes Troy seem more human, for it produces genuine grief in him. His outburst here confirms his earlier confession to Boldwood that he prefers Fanny to Bathsheba and was only briefly enflamed by his new wife's beauty. But despite its humanizing effects, this scene also emphasizes Troy's cynicism and cruelty. He claims to see the devil in Bathsheba's face and flirtations, but the real devil is Troy's poverty. He loved Fanny, but he chose to abandon her in favor of a richer, more established woman. Hardy criticizes Troy for his self-interest, but he shows a surprising lack of sympathy for the deceased Fanny. Later in this scene, he explains that she probably never suffered as badly as Bathsheba does as she watches her husband kiss his dead lover's corpse.

But a husband . . . why he'd always be there, whenever I looked up, there he'd be.

Location: Chapter III
Speaker: Bathsheba
Context: Gabriel Oak has asked Bathsheba to marry him, and she has refused

Thank you for the sight of such a beautiful face.

Location: Chapter XXIV
Speaker: Troy
Context: Troy says these words to Bathsheba at their first meeting

This may be called fort meeting feeble, hey Boldwood?

Location: Chapter XXXIV
Speaker: Troy
Context: Troy mocks Boldwood, comparing himself to the strong part of a fencing foil (the "fort") and Boldwood to the weak part (the "feeble," or "foible")

FAHRENHEIT 451

Ray Bradbury

In a futuristic America, a firefighter decides to buck society, stop burning books, and start seeking knowledge.

THE LIFE OF RAY BRADBURY

Ray Bradbury was born in Waukegan, Illinois, on August 22, 1920. By age eleven, he had begun writing stories on butcher paper. His family moved fairly frequently. He graduated from a Los Angeles high school in 1938. Bradbury had no further formal education, but he studied on his own at the library and continued to write. For several years, he earned money by selling newspapers on street corners. His first published story was "Hollerbochen's Dilemma," which appeared in 1938 in *Imagination!*, a magazine for amateur writers. In 1942, he was published in *Weird Tales*, the legendary pulp science-fiction magazine that launched such luminaries of the genre as H. P. Lovecraft. Bradbury honed his sci-fi sensibility writing for popular television shows, including *Alfred Hitchcock Presents* and *The Twilight Zone*. He also ventured into screenplay writing, composing the screenplay for John Huston's 1956 film *Moby Dick*. His novel *The Martian Chronicles*, published in 1950, established his reputation as a leading American writer of science fiction.

Bradbury has received many awards and honors for his writing. Most notably, Apollo astronauts named the Dandelion Crater on the moon after his novel *Dandelion Wine*. In addition to his novels, screenplays, and television scripts, Bradbury has written two musicals, co-authored two "space-age cantatas," collaborated on an Academy Award–nominated animation short called *Icarus Montgolfier Wright*, and started his own television series, *The Ray Bradbury Theatre*. Bradbury lives in California, where he continues to write. Although recognized primarily for his ideas and sometimes denigrated for his writing style, which some find alternately dry and maudlin, Bradbury is acknowledged as one of the masters of the science-fiction genre. He has a place among important literary science-fiction talents and visionaries like Jules Verne, H. P. Lovecraft, George Orwell, Arthur C. Clarke, and Philip K. Dick.

FAHRENHEIT 451 IN CONTEXT

In the spring of 1950, while living with his family in a humble home in Venice, California, Bradbury began writing what was to become *Fahrenheit 451*. He used a pay-by-the-hour typewriter in the library basement of the University of California at Los Angeles. He finished the first draft, a shorter version called "The Fireman," in just nine days. *Fahrenheit 451*, which follows in the futuristic-dustpan tradition of George Orwell's *1984*, was published in 1953 and became Bradbury's most popular and widely read work of fiction. He produced a stage version of the novel at the Studio Theatre Playhouse in Los Angeles. The seminal French New Wave director François Truffaut made a critically acclaimed film adaptation of the novel in 1967.

FAHRENHEIT 451: KEY FACTS

Time and place written: 1950–1953; Los Angeles, California

Date of first publication: 1953 (a shorter version entitled "The Fireman" was published in 1951 in *Galaxy Science Fiction*)

Publisher: Ballantine Books

Type of work: Novel

Genre: Science fiction

Language: English

Setting (time): Sometime in the twenty-first century

Setting (place): In and around an unspecified city in the United States

Tense: Past, with occasional transitions into present

Tone: Foreboding, menacing, disoriented, poetic, bitterly satirical

Narrator: Third-person, limited omniscient

Point of view: Montag's

Protagonist: Montag

Antagonist: Beatty, society in general

FAHRENHEIT 451: PLOT OVERVIEW

Guy Montag is a fireman who burns books in a futuristic American city. In Montag's world, firemen start fires rather than put them out. The people in this society do not read books, enjoy nature, spend time alone, think independently, or have meaningful conversations. Instead, they drive fast, watch excessive amounts of television on wall-sized sets, and listen to the radio on "Seashell Radio" sets attached to their ears.

Montag encounters a gentle seventeen-year-old girl named Clarisse McClellan who opens his eyes to the emptiness of his life with her innocently penetrating questions and her unusual love of people and nature. Over the next few days, Montag experiences a series of disturbing events. First, his wife, Mildred, attempts suicide by overdosing on sleeping pills. Then, when Montag responds to an alarm that an old woman has a stash of hidden literature, the woman shocks him by choosing to be burned alive with her books. A few days later, he hears that Clarisse has been killed by a speeding car. Montag's dissatisfaction with his life increases, and he searches for comfort in a stash of books that he has stolen from his own fires and hidden inside an air-conditioning vent.

When Montag fails to show up for work, his fire chief, Beatty, pays a visit to his house. Beatty explains that it is normal for a fireman to go through a phase of wondering what books have to offer. He delivers a dizzying monologue explaining how books came to be banned in the first place. According to Beatty, special-interest groups and other "minorities" objected to books that offended them. Soon, all books began to look the same, as writers tried to avoid offending anybody. This was not enough, however, and society decided to burn books rather than permit conflicting opinions. Beatty tells Montag to take twenty-four hours or so to see if his stolen books contain anything worthwhile and then to turn them in for incineration. Montag begins a long and frenzied night of reading.

Overwhelmed by the task, Montag looks to his wife for help and support, but she prefers television to her husband's company and cannot understand why he would want to take the terrible risk of reading books. He remembers that he once met a retired English professor named Faber sitting in a park. He wonders if Faber could help him understand what he reads. Montag visits Faber, who tells him that the value of books lies in the detailed awareness of life that they contain. Faber says that Montag needs not only books but also the leisure to read them and the freedom to act upon their ideas.

Faber agrees to help Montag with his reading, and they concoct a risky scheme to overthrow the status quo. Faber will contact a printer and begin producing books, and Montag will plant books in the homes of firemen to discredit the profession and to destroy the machinery of censorship. Faber gives him a two-way radio earpiece (the "green bullet") so that he can hear what Montag hears and talk to him secretly.

Montag goes home. Two of his wife's friends arrive to watch television. The women frivolously discuss their families and the war that is about to be declared. Their superficiality angers Montag, and he takes out a book of poetry and reads aloud "Dover Beach" by Matthew Arnold. Faber buzzes in his ear for him to be quiet, and Mildred tries to explain that the poetry reading is a standard way for firemen to demonstrate the uselessness of literature. But Mildred's friends are extremely disturbed by the poem and leave to file a complaint against Montag.

Montag goes to the fire station, where Beatty barrages him with contradictory quotations from great books. Beatty exploits these contradictions to show that literature is morbid and dangerously complex, and that it deserves incineration. Suddenly, the alarm sounds, and they rush off to answer the call. It turns out that the alarm is at Montag's own house. Mildred gets into a cab with her suitcase, and Montag realizes that his own wife has betrayed him.

Beatty forces Montag to burn his own house. Then Beatty arrests him. When Beatty continues to berate Montag, Montag turns the flamethrower on him and burns him to ashes. Montag knocks the other firemen unconscious and runs. The Mechanical Hound, a monstrous machine that Beatty has set to attack Montag, pounces and injects Montag's leg with a large dose of anesthetic. Montag destroys it with his flamethrower. Then he walks off the numbness in his leg and escapes with some books that were hidden in his backyard. He hides these in another fireman's house and calls in an alarm from a pay phone.

Montag goes to Faber's house, where he learns that a new Hound has been put on his trail, along with several helicopters and a television crew. Faber tells Montag that he is leaving for St. Louis to see a retired printer who may be able to help them. Montag gives Faber some money and tells him how to remove Montag's scent from his house so the Hound will not enter it. Montag then takes some of Faber's old clothes and runs off toward the river. The whole city watches as the chase unfolds on television. Montag escapes into the river and changes into Faber's clothes to disguise his scent. He drifts downstream into the country and follows a set of abandoned railroad tracks until he finds a group of renegade intellectuals ("the Book People"), led by a man named Granger, who welcome him. They are a part of a nationwide network of book lovers who have memorized many great works of literature and philosophy. They hope to be of help to mankind in the aftermath of the war that has just been declared. Montag's role is to memorize the Book of Ecclesiastes. Enemy jets appear in the sky and completely obliterate the city with bombs. Montag and his new friends move on to search for survivors and rebuild civilization.

CHARACTERS IN *FAHRENHEIT 451*

Captain Beatty The captain of Montag's fire department. Beatty is extremely well-read, but he hates books and people who insist on reading them. He is cunning, devious, and so perceptive that he appears to read Montag's thoughts.

Mrs. Bowles One of Mildred's friends. Mrs. Bowles does not seem to care about her own miserable life, which includes one divorce, one husband killed in an accident, one husband killed by his own hand, and two children who hate her. She is a typical member of society.

Professor Faber A retired English professor. Faber, who longs for books, admits that the current state of society is due to the cowardice of people like himself, who would not speak out against book-burning when it was still possible to stop it.

Granger The leader of the "Book People," the group of hobo intellectuals Montag finds in the country. Granger is intelligent, patient, and confident in the strength of the human spirit. He is committed to preserving literature through the current Dark Age.

Clarisse McClellan A beautiful seventeen-year-old who introduces Montag to the world's potential for beauty and meaning. Clarisse is an outcast from society because of her odd habits, which include hiking, playing with flowers, and asking questions.

Guy Montag The protagonist of the novel. A third-generation fireman, Montag is sometimes rash and has a hard time thinking for himself, but he is determined to break free from the oppression of his own ignorance.

Mildred Montag Montag's brittle, sickly wife. Mildred is obsessed with watching television and refuses to engage in frank conversation with her husband about their marriage or her feelings. She refuses to acknowledge her own suicide attempt.

Mrs. Phelps One of Mildred's vapid friends. Mrs. Phelps is emotionally disconnected from her life. She seems unconcerned when her third husband is sent off to war, but she breaks down crying when Montag reads a poem, which suggests that her feelings are deeply repressed.

Stoneman and Black Two firemen who work with Montag. They go about their jobs unquestioningly.

THEMES IN *FAHRENHEIT 451*

CENSORSHIP Bradbury suggests that many different factors combined to create a society that encourages book-burning. People gradually lost interest in reading because of competing forms of entertainment such as television and radio. More broadly, Bradbury suggests, fast cars, loud music, and advertisements overstimulated people, leaving them with no time to concentrate. Also, the huge mass of published material was too overwhelming to think about, leading to a society that preferred condensed books (which were very popular at the time Bradbury wrote *Fahrenheit 451*) to the real thing. Active hostility to books developed because people disliked feeling inferior to those who had read more than they had. But the most important factor leading to censorship, Bradbury suggests, were the objections of special-interest groups and "minorities" to certain published material that offended them. Bradbury carefully refrains from referring to racial minorities—Beatty mentions dog lovers and cat lovers, for instance. The reader can only guess at which special-interest groups he really has in mind.

KNOWLEDGE VERSUS IGNORANCE The plot centers around the tension between knowledge and ignorance. The fireman's duty is to destroy knowledge and promote ignorance in order to create a homogenized population. Montag's encounters with Clarisse, the old woman, and Faber—unique non-homogenized individuals—ignite in him a spark of doubt about this approach. His resultant search for knowledge destroys the unquestioning ignorance he used to share with nearly everyone else in his society.

RELIGION AS KNOWLEDGE-GIVER Bradbury uses religious imagery in *Fahrenheit 451* to suggest the unholy quality of Montag's society. Those who oppose ignorance and book-burning do so in the language of Christianity. Faber invokes the Christian value of forgiveness, telling Montag that he should pity his society instead of hating it. In a reference to the biblical story of the miracle at Cana, where Christ transformed water into wine, Faber describes himself as water and Montag as fire, asserting that the merging of the two will produce wine. In the Bible, fire symbolizes both heresy and divinity. Fire in *Fahrenheit 451* is similarly contradictory. At the beginning of the novel, it is the weapon of a restrictive society, but Montag reverses its meaning, using it to burn Beatty and win his freedom. In the last pages of the novel, as Montag and Granger's group set out to find survivors after the bombing of the city, Montag tries to remember appropriate passages from the Bible. He brings to mind Ecclesiastes 3:1, "To everything there is a season," and also Revelations 22:2, "And on either side of the river was there a tree of life . . . and the leaves of the tree were for the healing of the nations."

SYMBOLS IN *FAHRENHEIT 451*

"THE SIEVE AND THE SAND" The title of the second part of *Fahrenheit 451*, "The Sieve and the Sand," is taken from Montag's childhood memory of trying to fill a sieve with sand on the beach and crying at the futility of the task. The sand symbolizes the tangible truth Montag seeks, and the sieve the human mind that seeks elusive knowledge. Montag compares his childhood memory to his attempt to read the whole Bible as quickly as possible in the hope that he would retain some of the material.

THE PHOENIX After the bombing of the city, Granger thinks of the phoenix, which repeatedly burns itself up and then rises out of its ashes. He says that humankind has an advantage over the phoenix, because unlike the phoenix, it can recognize when it has made a mistake and eventually learn not to repeat it. Remembering the mistakes of the past is the task Granger and his group have set for themselves. The phoenix symbolizes the human ability to rise up out of the ashes, but it also suggests the human ability to transcend the endless cycle of the phoenix and stop the fire from burning in the first place.

IMPORTANT QUOTATIONS FROM *FAHRENHEIT 451*

So it was the hand that started it all . . . His hands had been infected, and soon it would be his arms . . . His hands were ravenous.

Location: "The Hearth and the Salamander"
Speaker: The narrator
Context: Montag steals books from the old woman's house

Montag guiltily portrays his theft of the old woman's books as an involuntary bodily reflex. As the novel unfolds, he blames his hands for several other crimes. Montag's hands become a symbol of his rebelliousness and will. When he steals books, almost unconsciously, he reveals a hidden, unspoken dissatisfaction bubbling to the surface, just as when Mildred attempts suicide, she reveals the silent pain she can't acknowledge.

We must all be alike. Not everyone born free and equal, as the constitution says, but everyone made equal . . . A book is a loaded gun in the house next door. Burn it. Take the shot from the weapon. Breach man's mind.

Location: "The Hearth and the Salamander"
Speaker: Captain Beatty
Context: Beatty justifies the destruction of books

Captain Beatty's speech in defense of book-burning is suffused with irony. He defends the disintegration of authenticity in a passionate but almost regretful tone. He defends the "equalization" of society, but he himself is an educated man. He denounces the use of books as weapons, but he himself uses them as weapons to manipulate Montag. Because of these contradictions, Beatty is the most complex character in the novel. One wonders, as Faber does, if Beatty really chose his job after losing his faith in books, as he claims, or if he chose it in order to gain legal access to books.

Do you know why books such as this are so important? Because they have quality. And what does the word quality mean? To me it means texture. This book has pores.

Location: "The Sieve and the Sand"
Speaker: Faber
Context: Faber explains the importance of books

It's perpetual motion; the thing man wanted to invent but never did. . . . It's a mystery. . . . Its real beauty is that it destroys responsibility and consequences . . . clean, quick, sure; nothing to rot later. Antibiotic, aesthetic, practical.

Location: "Burning Bright"
Speaker: Beatty
Context: Right before Montag burns him to death, Beatty muses about fire

---

The sun burnt every day. It burnt Time . . . Time was busy burning the years and the people anyway, without any help from him. So if he burnt things with the firemen and the sun burnt Time, that meant that everything burnt!

Location: "Burning Bright"
Speaker: The narrator
Context: As he escapes the city and floats down the river, Montag thinks about the sun

A FAREWELL TO ARMS

Ernest Hemingway

A disaffected young soldier falls in love with a nurse and flees the war to be with her; she dies in childbirth.

THE LIFE OF ERNEST HEMINGWAY

Ernest Hemingway was born in Oak Park, Illinois, in the summer of 1899. He later described his middle-class parents in harsh terms, condemning them for their conventional morality and values. As a young man, he left home to become a newspaper writer in Kansas City. Early in 1918, he joined the Italian Red Cross. He served as an ambulance driver in Italy during World War I, in which the Italians allied with the British, French, and Americans against Germany and Austria-Hungary. During his time abroad, Hemingway had two experiences that affected him profoundly and that would later inspire one of his most celebrated novels, *A Farewell to Arms*. The first occurred on July 8, 1918, when a trench mortar shell struck him as he crouched beyond the front lines with three Italian soldiers. Hemingway embellished the story over the years, so the actual facts are difficult to ascertain, but it is certain that he was transferred to a hospital in Milan, where he fell in love with a Red Cross nurse named Agnes von Kurowsky. Scholars are divided over Agnes's role in Hemingway's life and writing, but there is little doubt that his relationship with her informed the relationship between Lieutenant Henry and Catherine Barkley in *A Farewell to Arms*.

After his recovery, Hemingway spent several years as a reporter, during which time he honed the clear, concise, and emotionally evocative writing style that generations of authors after him would imitate. In September 1921, he married and settled in Paris, where he made valuable connections with American expatriate writers like Gertrude Stein and Ezra Pound. Hemingway's landmark collection of stories, *In Our Time*, introduced Nick Adams, one of the author's favorite protagonists, whose difficult road from youth into maturity he chronicled. Hemingway's reputation as a writer was most firmly established by the publication of *The Sun Also Rises* in 1926 and *A Farewell to Arms* in 1929.

Most critics maintain that Hemingway's writing fizzled after World War II, when his physical and mental health declined. Despite fantastic bouts of depression, Hemingway did muster enough energy to write *The Old Man and the Sea*, one of his most beloved stories, in 1952. This novella earned him a Pulitzer Prize, and three years later Hemingway was awarded the Nobel Prize in Literature. Still, not even these accolades could soothe the devastating effects of a lifetime of debilitating depression. On July 2, 1961, Hemingway killed himself in his home in Ketchum, Idaho.

A FAREWELL TO ARMS IN CONTEXT

Critics generally agree that *A Farewell to Arms* is Hemingway's most accomplished novel. It offers powerful descriptions of life during and immediately following World War I and brilliantly maps the psychological complexities of its characters. Its pared-down prose style was revolutionary in a way that is difficult to comprehend today, since so many writers have modeled their own styles on Hemingway's. The novel helped to establish the author's myth of himself as a master of many trades: writing, soldiering, boxing, bullfighting, big-game hunting.

A FAREWELL TO ARMS: KEY FACTS

Time and place written: 1926–1928; America and abroad

Date of first publication: 1929

Publisher: Charles Scribner's Sons

Type of work: Novel	
Genre: War novel	
Language: English	
Setting (time): 1916–1918, in the middle of World War I	
Setting (place): Italy and Switzerland	
Tense: Past	
Tone: Straightforward, unemotional, masculine	
Narrator: Lieutenant Frederic Henry in the first person	
Point of view: Henry's	
Protagonist: Henry	
Antagonist: Henry's innate restlessness	

A FAREWELL TO ARMS: PLOT OVERVIEW

Lieutenant Frederic Henry is a young American ambulance driver serving in the Italian army during World War I. As the novel begins, winter is coming on and the war is winding down. Henry arranges to tour Italy. The following spring, upon his return to the front, Henry meets Catherine Barkley, an English nurse's aide at the nearby British hospital and the love interest of Henry's friend Rinaldi. Rinaldi quickly fades from the picture as Catherine and Henry begin an elaborate game of seduction. Grieving the recent death of her fiancé, Catherine longs for love so deeply that she will settle for the illusion of it. Even though her passion is pretended, it wakens a desire for emotional interaction in Henry, whom the war has left detached and numb.

Henry is wounded on the battlefield and brought to a hospital in Milan to recover. Several doctors recommend that he stay in bed for six months and then undergo a necessary operation on his knee. Unable to accept such a long recovery period, Henry finds a bold, garrulous surgeon named Dr. Valentini who agrees to operate immediately. Catherine has been transferred to Milan, and Henry begins his recuperation under her care. During the following months, his relationship with Catherine intensifies. No longer simply a game in which they exchange empty promises and playful kisses, their love becomes powerful and real. As the lines between scripted and genuine emotions blur, Henry and Catherine fall in love.

Once Henry's damaged leg has healed, the army grants him three weeks convalescence leave, after which he is scheduled to return to the front. Catherine reveals that she is pregnant, and Henry plans a trip with her. The following day, Henry is diagnosed with jaundice. Miss Van Campen, the hospital superintendent, accuses him of bringing the disease on himself through excessive drinking. Miss Van Campen, convinced that Henry's illness is an attempt to shirk his duty, has his leave revoked. Once the jaundice is cleared, Henry is sent to the front. As they part, Catherine and Henry pledge their mutual devotion.

On the front, Italian forces are losing ground and manpower daily. Soon after Henry's arrival, a bombardment begins. When word comes that German troops are breaking through the Italian lines, the Allied forces prepare to retreat. Henry leads his team of ambulance drivers into the great column of evacuating troops. The men pick up two engineering sergeants and two frightened young girls on their way. Henry and his drivers decide to leave the column and take secondary roads, which they assume will be faster. When one of their vehicles bogs down in the mud, Henry orders the two engineers to help in the effort to free the vehicle. When they refuse, he shoots one of them. The drivers continue in the other trucks until they get stuck again. They send off the young girls and continue on foot toward Udine. As they march, one of the drivers is shot dead by the easily frightened rear guard of the Italian army. Another driver marches off to surrender, while Henry and the remaining driver seek refuge at a farmhouse. When they rejoin the retreat the following day, chaos has broken out: soldiers, angered by the Italian defeat, pull commanding officers from the melee and execute them on sight. The battle police seize Henry, who manages to break away and dive into the river. After swimming a safe distance downstream, Henry boards a train bound for Milan. He hides beneath a tarp that covers stockpiled artillery, thinking that his obligations to the war effort are over and dreaming of his return to Catherine.

Henry reunites with Catherine in the town of Stresa. From there, the two escape to safety in Switzerland, rowing all night in a tiny borrowed boat. They settle happily in a lovely alpine town called Montreux and agree to put the war behind them forever. Although Henry is sometimes plagued by guilt for abandoning the men on the front, he has a beautiful, peaceful life with Catherine. When spring arrives, the couple moves to Lausanne so they can be closer to the hospital. Early one morning, Catherine goes into labor. The delivery is exceptionally painful and complicated. Catherine delivers a stillborn baby boy and, later that night, dies of a hemorrhage. Henry stays at her side until she is gone. He attempts to say goodbye but cannot. He walks back to his hotel in the rain.

CHARACTERS IN *A FAREWELL TO ARMS*

Bonello An ambulance driver under Henry's command. Bonello displays his ruthlessness when he brutally unloads a pistol round into the head of an uncooperative engineer whom Henry has already shot.

Catherine Barkley An English nurse's aide who falls in love with Henry. Catherine is exceptionally beautiful. Eventually she swears lifelong fidelity to Henry.

Emilio A bartender in the town of Stresa. Emilio frequently aids Henry and Catherine, helping them reunite, saving them from arrest, and ushering them off to safety.

Helen Ferguson A nurse's aide who works at the American hospital. Helen is a dear friend of Catherine's, but eventually she has a hysterical outburst over Henry and Catherine's "immoral" affair.

Miss Gage An American nurse who helps Henry through his recovery at the hospital in Milan. Easygoing and accepting, Miss Gage becomes a friend to Henry, someone with whom he can share a drink and gossip.

Gino A young Italian whom Henry meets at a decimated village. Gino's patriotic belief that his fatherland is sacred and should be protected at all costs contrasts sharply to Henry's attitude toward war.

Count Greffi A spry, ninety-four-year-old nobleman. The count represents a more mature version of Henry, and is Hemingway's masculine ideal. Count Greffi lives life with exuberance and thinks for himself. Henry sees him as a father figure.

Lieutenant Frederic Henry The novel's narrator and protagonist. Henry meets his military duties with quiet stoicism and displays courage in battle, but his selfishness undermines all sense of glory and heroism, abstract ideas for which Henry has little patience. His life lacks real passion until he meets Catherine Barkley.

Ettore Moretti An American soldier from San Francisco. Ettore, like Henry, fights for the Italian army. He is an obnoxious braggart who pursues the glory and honor that Henry finds absurd.

The Priest A sweet young man who provides spiritual guidance to the few soldiers interested in it. Often the butt of the officers' jokes, the priest responds with good-natured understanding.

Rinaldi A surgeon in the Italian army. Mischievous, wry, and oversexed, Rinaldi is Henry's closest friend.

Ralph Simmons An opera student of dubious talent. Simmons is a generous friend, giving Henry civilian clothes so that he can travel to Switzerland without drawing suspicion.

Dr. Valentini An Italian surgeon. Dr. Valentini comes to the American hospital and agrees to perform surgery on Henry immediately. This decision, which contradicts the opinion of many doctors, displays the kind of self-assurance and confidence that Henry (and the novel) celebrates.

Miss Van Campen The superintendent of nurses at the American hospital in which Catherine works. Miss Van Campen is strict, cold, and unpleasant.

THEMES IN *A FAREWELL TO ARMS*

THE GRIM REALITY OF WAR As the title of the novel makes clear, *A Farewell to Arms* is concerned primarily with war, namely the process by which Frederic Henry removes himself from it and leaves it behind. The majority of the characters are ambivalent about the war. The few characters in the novel who actually support it—Ettore Moretti and Gino—are a dull braggart and a naïve youth, respectively. The novel offers masterful descriptions of the senseless brutality of war. Hemingway's depiction of the Italian army's retreat remains one of the most profound evocations of war in American literature. As the neat columns of men begin to crumble, so do the soldiers' nerves and minds. When Henry shoots the engineer, the murder seems justifiable because it is a byproduct of the spiraling violence and disorder of war. Nevertheless, the novel cannot be said to condemn the war; *A Farewell to Arms* is hardly the work of a pacifist. Hemingway suggests that although war is regrettable, it is the inevitable condition of a cruel, senseless world.

THE RELATIONSHIP BETWEEN LOVE AND PAIN Against the backdrop of war, Hemingway offers a deep, mournful meditation on the nature of love. In the beginning of their relationship, Henry and Catherine turn to each other for temporary solace from the things that plague them. No sooner does Catherine tell Henry that she is in mourning for her dead fiancé than she begins a game meant to seduce Henry. Her reason for doing so is clear: she wants to distance herself from the pain of her loss. Likewise, Henry intends to get as far away from talk of the war as possible. The couple's feelings for each other quickly pass from an amusement that distracts them to a fuel that sustains them. Henry does not believe in glory on the battlefield, but he does believe in true love. His moral compass permits him to flee the war in order to seek her out. Reunited, they plan an idyllic life together that will heal the damage that the war has inflicted. The tragedy of the novel rests in the fact that their love, though it is genuine, can never be more than temporary in this world.

THE IMPORTANCE OF GAMES In *A Farewell to Arms*, games are dignified because one can depend on their simple pleasures. They may not match up to the nobility of pursuits such as love, but their quiet consistency is a comfort. The count says that he unwisely values love most in life. But he hedges against the transitory nature of love by taking pleasure in games, birthday parties, and the taking of "a little stimulant." Flirting with Catherine, which Henry compares to bridge, allows Henry to "drop the war." For Catherine, flirting is a way to forget the death of her fiancé. Going to the horse races lets Catherine and Henry block out the thought of Henry's return to the front. Ironically, Henry and Catherine's relationship becomes the source of suffering from which Henry needs diversion. Henry cannot stand to be away from Catherine. Although playing pool with Count Greffi takes his mind off of her, the best diversion turns out to be the war itself. When Catherine instructs him not to think about her when they are apart, Henry replies, "That's how I worked it at the front. But there was something to do then." The transformations of the war from fatal threat into distraction and love from distraction into pain signal not only Henry's attachment to Catherine but also the transitory nature of happiness.

SYMBOLS IN *A FAREWELL TO ARMS*

RAIN Rain is a potent symbol of the inevitable evaporation of happiness. As Catherine and Henry lie in bed listening to a storm outside, Catherine admits that the rain scares her. She says it has a tendency to ruin things for lovers. Catherine imbues the rain with a symbolism that proves prophetic. After Catherine's death, Henry walks home from the hospital in the rain. Here, the falling rain validates Catherine's anxiety and confirms one of the novel's main contentions: great love, like anything else in the world— good or bad—cannot last.

CATHERINE'S HAIR In the early, easy days of their relationship, as Henry and Catherine lie in bed, Catherine takes down her hair and lets it cascade around Henry's head. The tumble of hair reminds Henry of being enclosed inside a tent or behind a waterfall. Catherine's hair symbolizes the couple's love, and Henry's description suggests their isolation from the world, which they effect through love.

IMPORTANT QUOTATIONS FROM *A FAREWELL TO ARMS*

When we were out past the tanneries onto the main road the troops, the motor trucks, the horse-drawn carts and the guns were in one wide slow-moving column. We moved slowly but steadily in the rain, the radiator cap of our car almost against the tailboard of a truck that was loaded high, the load covered with wet canvas. Then the truck stopped. The whole column was stopped. It started again and we went a little farther, then stopped. I got out and walked ahead, going between the trucks and carts and under the wet necks of the horses.

Location: Chapter XXVIII
Speaker: Henry
Context: The Italian army is retreating

This passage begins the description of the Italian army's retreat. The prose is indicative of Hemingway's style: bold, declarative sentences; sharply observed details; and a rhythm that underscores the physical and emotional movement being described. Here, the rhythm of the two long opening sentences, which fluidly describe the great convergence and crawling pace of the retreating troops, is interrupted by short bursts that detail the action. The repetition of "stopped" in "Then the truck stopped. The whole column stopped" jars the reader, as does the jerky motion of the subsequent "It started again . . . then stopped," brilliantly mimicking the stop-and-go action of the troops.

But we were never lonely and never afraid when we were together. I know that the night is not the same as the day: that all things are different, that the things of the night cannot be explained in the day, because they do not then exist, and the night can be a dreadful time for lonely people once their loneliness has started. But with Catherine there was almost no difference in the night except that it was an even better time. If people bring so much courage to this world the world has to kill them to break them, so of course it kills them. The world breaks every one and afterward many are strong at the broken places. But those that will not break it kills. It kills the very good and the very gentle and the very brave impartially. If you are none of these you can be sure it will kill you too but there will be no special hurry.

Location: Chapter XXXIV
Speaker: Henry
Context: Henry and Catherine are lying in bed after their reunion in Stresa

These musings cast a long shadow from which the couple cannot escape. Henry's thoughts here are initially positive, focusing on how Catherine's presence alleviates his feelings of loneliness. He stresses an important aspect of their relationship: together, they manage to overcome the great sense of fear and loneliness that they feel in the presence of other people. Henry's rapturous thinking about Catherine, however, disconcertingly switches to dark philosophizing about a world designed to kill the good, the gentle, and the brave—all terms that Henry has used or will use to describe Catherine. This unforced glide from contentedness into pessimism reflects the inability of positive forces such as love to triumph over the grimness of life. As if talking about malevolence out loud brings it on, from this point Henry and Catherine seem to be running from a force that wants to harm them and that, soon enough, catches up with them.

"There, darling. Now you're all clean inside and out. Tell me. How many people have you ever loved?"
"Nobody."
"Not even me?"
"Yes, you."
"How many others really?"
"None."
"How many have you—how do you say it?—stayed with?"
"None."
"You're lying to me."
"Yes."

"It's all right. Keep right on lying to me. That's what I want you to do. Were they pretty?"

Location: Chapter XVI
Speaker: Catherine and Henry
Context: Henry has arrived at the American hospital in Milan, and Catherine is preparing him for an operation

---

I had seen nothing sacred, and the things that were glorious had no glory and the sacrifices were like the stockyards at Chicago if nothing was done with the meat except to bury it. There were many words that you could not stand to hear and finally only the names of places had dignity. Certain numbers were the same way and certain dates and these with the names of the places were all you could say and have them mean anything. Abstract words such as glory, honor, courage, or hallow were obscene beside the concrete names of villages, the numbers of roads, the names of rivers, the numbers of regiments and the dates.

Location: Chapter XXVII
Speaker: Henry
Context: Henry has met Gino, a patriot

Poor, poor dear Cat. And this was the price you paid for sleeping together. This was the end of the trap. This was what people got for loving each other. Thank God for gas, anyway. What must it have been like before there were anesthetics?

Location: The final chapter
Speaker: Henry
Context: Henry is watching Catherine suffering through the agony of childbirth

THE FOUNTAINHEAD

Ayn Rand

A brilliant, uncompromising architect representing the excellence of individualism clashes with and triumphs over mediocre American society.

THE LIFE OF AYN RAND

Ayn Rand was born in 1905 to an upper-middle-class Jewish family in St. Petersburg, Russia. As a teenager she became a committed atheist and was passionately interested in politics. In particular, Rand opposed the ideals of the Bolshevik Party, which was struggling for power during the Russian Revolution, and the party's ideals of communism, socialism, and collectivization. In 1917, the Bolsheviks nationalized Rand's father's business, diminishing the family's fortunes considerably.

Rand graduated from the University of Petrograd with highest honors in philosophy and history. In 1925, she obtained a temporary visa to visit relatives in Chicago and left Russia with no intention of returning. She moved to Hollywood to pursue a career as a screenwriter and took a job as an extra on the set of *King of Kings*, a film directed by the legendary Cecil B. DeMille. In California, Rand met Frank O'Connor, whom she married in 1929. In 1932, she sold her first screenplay, *Red Pawn*, to Universal Studios and saw her first stage play, *Night of January 16th*, produced on Broadway. Her first novel, *We the Living*, was completed in 1933 and published by Macmillan in 1936. The novel was based on Rand's life in Russia and drew strong criticism from leftist members of the American intelligentsia.

Rand began work on *The Fountainhead* in 1938. Over the next two years, *The Fountainhead*'s reputation grew by word of mouth, and the novel became a bestseller when it came out in 1943. By the time she published *Atlas Shrugged* (1957), Rand's work had found a devoted following. She made numerous public appearances to lecture and explain the ideas behind her work. Her philosophy—called Objectivism—advocates rational self-interest and denounces altruism as the hobgoblin of mediocrity. Rand disliked being associated with either the conservative or the libertarian political movements in the United States. During the 1950s and 1960s, Rand promoted her ideas with the help of two young protégés, Nathaniel and Barbara Branden—an alliance that ended when Rand and Nathaniel had an affair.

At the time of Rand's death in 1982, more than twenty million copies of her books had been sold. Rand's work continues to draw heated reactions from critics. She has been called a fascist, and Objectivism has been called a cult. Nonetheless, the Ayn Rand Institute and the Objectivist Center continue their work in America, and Rand's novels still attract a global following.

THE FOUNTAINHEAD IN CONTEXT

The Fountainhead is an Objectivist parable. It suggests that egoism that leads to excellence is an absolute moral good, and therefore any person, institution, or system that blocks individual freedom and talent is evil. Each character in the novel represents a different place on the spectrum of good and evil. Like other authors of satirical or allegorical works, Rand designs personalities to prove a point, and as a result the characters are not fully realized human beings—nor or they meant to be.

THE FOUNTAINHEAD: KEY FACTS

Time and place written: New York; 1938–1942	
Date of publication: May, 1943	
Publisher: Bobbs-Merrill	
Type of work: Novel	
Genre: Allegory; novel of ideas	

Language: English	

Language: English

Setting (time): 1922–1939

Setting (place): New York City, Connecticut, Monadnock Valley, Massachusetts, and Ohio

Tense: Present; occasional past to provide background information

Tone: Formal, moralizing, didactic

Narrator: Third-person omniscient narrator

Point of view: Howard Roark's and others; the narration provides psychological analyses of most characters, with a heavy bias toward Roark

Protagonist: Howard Roark

Antagonist: Ellsworth Toohey, compromise, collectivism, mediocrity

THE FOUNTAINHEAD: PLOT OVERVIEW

Howard Roark, a brilliant young architect, is expelled from his architecture school for refusing to follow the school's outdated traditions. He goes to New York to work for Henry Cameron, a disgraced architect whom Roark admires. Roark's schoolmate, Peter Keating, moves to New York and goes to work for the prestigious architectural firm Francon & Heyer, run by the famous Guy Francon. Roark and Cameron create beautiful work, but their projects rarely receive recognition, whereas Keating's ability to flatter and please brings him quick success. In just a few years, he becomes a partner at the firm after causing Francon's previous partner to have a stroke. Henry Cameron retires, financially ruined, and Roark opens his own small office. His unwillingness to compromise his designs in order to satisfy clients eventually forces him to close down the office and take a job at a granite quarry in Connecticut. The quarry happens to belong to Guy Francon.

Dominique Francon, Guy Francon's temperamental and beautiful daughter, is disgusted by society and has retreated to her family's Connecticut estate to escape the mediocre architecture of New York City. Roark feels an immediate, passionate attraction to Dominique. One night, he enters her house and rapes her. Dominique discovers that this humiliation is what she needed, but by the time she goes to look for her rapist, he has left the quarry to design a building for a prominent New York businessman. Dominique returns to New York and finds out who Roark is. She realizes that he designed a building she admires. Dominique and Roark begin meeting in secret at night, but in public she tries to sabotage his career and destroy him.

Ellsworth Toohey, an architectural critic and socialist, seeks to become more powerful. He encourages mediocrity by teaching that talent and ability are of no great consequence, and that the greatest virtue is humility. Toohey sees Roark as a great threat and tries to destroy him. Toohey convinces Hopton Stoddard, a weak-minded businessman, first to hire Roark as the designer for a temple dedicated to the human spirit, then to sue Roark once the building is completed. At Roark's trial, every prominent architect in New York testifies that Roark's style is unorthodox and not legitimate, but Dominique declares that the world does not deserve the gift Roark has given it. Stoddard wins the case and Roark loses his business again. To punish herself for desiring Roark, Dominique marries Peter Keating.

Enter Gail Wynand, a brilliant publisher who has lost his early idealism and made his fortune by printing newspapers that say exactly what the public wants to hear. Wynand meets Dominique and falls in love with her, so he buys her from Keating by offering him money and a prestigious contract in exchange for his wife. Dominique agrees to marry Wynand because she thinks that he is an even worse person than Keating. She is surprised to find that Wynand is a man of principle. Wynand and Roark meet and become fast friends. Wynand does not know about Roark and Dominique's affair. Meanwhile, Keating, who has fallen from grace, asks Roark for help with the Cortlandt Homes, a public housing project. Intrigued by the idea of building economical housing, Roark agrees to design the project and let Keating take the credit on condition that the buildings are built exactly as he designs them.

When Roark returns from a summer-long yacht trip with Wynand, he finds that, despite the agreement, the Cortlandt Homes plans have been altered. Roark asks Dominique to distract the night watchman one night and then dynamites the building. When the police arrive, he submits without resistance. The entire country condemns Roark, but Wynand finally finds the courage to follow his convictions and orders his newspapers to defend him. The *Banner*'s circulation drops and the workers go on strike, but

Wynand keeps printing with Dominique's help. Eventually, Wynand gives in and denounces Roark. At the trial, Roark rouses the courtroom with a statement about the value of selfishness and the need to remain true to oneself. Roark describes the triumphant role of creators and the price they pay at the hands of corrupt societies. The jury finds him not guilty. Roark marries Dominique. Wynand asks Roark to design one last building, a skyscraper that will testify to the supremacy of man.

CHARACTERS IN *THE FOUNTAINHEAD*

Henry Cameron　Roark's mentor. Cameron is an intractable and aggressive architect. Like Roark, Cameron has a difficult time because he values his buildings more than people. Because he lacks Roark's strength, Cameron lives a frustrated and anguished life. He dies fighting, ruined physically and financially.

The Dean　The dean of Roark's architecture school is a staunch traditionalist. He believes that everything worthy has already been designed and finds Roark dangerous.

Dominique Francon　Guy Francon's beautiful daughter. Capable, dispassionate, and cold, Dominique nurses a masochistic streak and surrounds herself with everything she despises in order to avoid watching the world destroy everything she loves. She loves Roark and recognizes his greatness, but wants to destroy him before the world does.

Guy Francon　The owner of the architectural firm Francon & Heyer. Francon is also Keating's employer and business partner and Dominique's father. A fundamentally honest and decent man, Francon has no architectural talent of his own. Eventually he finds salvation through his love for his daughter.

Catherine (Katie) Halsey　Toohey's niece and Keating's sometime fiancée. Innocent and sincere if not beautiful, Katie provides Keating with a refuge from himself. Keating loves Katie but abandons her, and Toohey slowly destroys her spirit.

Peter Keating　An architect who lives only for fame and approval. Good-looking and successful, Keating steals his ideas from Roark, who is his classmate. To rise to the top, Keating flatters, lies, steals, kills, and even trades his wife Dominique for the opportunity to work on a promising project. After a rapid fall, he recognizes his mistakes and lives the rest of his life in frightened misery.

Mrs. Keating　Keating's forceful and manipulative mother. Preoccupied with money and success, Mrs. Keating pushes her son to compromise.

Stephen Mallory　A gifted but disillusioned sculptor who feels alone and misunderstood until Roark rescues him from his drunken doldrums. The world rejects Mallory's statues of men in heroic and triumphant poses. Mallory blames Toohey for the world's mediocrity and tries to kill him. Eventually Mallory regains his self-confidence through his work on Roark's buildings.

Mike　A tough, ugly electrician who admires talent. He recognizes Roark's ability instantly and helps construct buildings Roark designs.

Howard Roark　The novel's protagonist and hero. Roark is a brilliant architect of absolute integrity. Gaunt and angular, Roark has gray eyes and distinctive orange hair. Though not without friends and colleagues, Roark relies on himself alone. Born poor, Roark supported himself throughout high school and college by working odd jobs on construction sites. He brings fiery intensity to all his work and loves Dominique with violent passion. Roark is the novel's idealized man—unwilling to compromise and committed to excellency.

Alvah Scarret　The *Banner*'s editor-in-chief. Scarret embodies the mediocrity of the masses. Scarret believes every word his newspaper publishes, and Wynand uses him to gauge public opinion.

John Erik Snyte　A supposedly progressive architect who is in fact the ultimate plagiarizer. Snyte's designs are a composite of the designs of five architects.

Ellsworth Toohey　The novel's villain and Roark's antithesis. Toohey is a man with a lust for power but no talent. He has always despised others' achievements and has dedicated himself to squelching talent and ambition by encouraging selflessness and altruism. Small and fragile in appearance, Toohey has a persuasive voice and a knack for manipulation that make him a formidable opponent. His philosophy is a blend of religion, fascism and socialism. At times he resembles the Russian dictator Joseph Stalin.

Gail Wynand Owner of the *Banner* and a ruthless media tycoon who compromises his principles to gain power. Born in the slums of New York, Wynand is entirely self-taught and self-made. He initially sought power to rule the incompetent and corrupt, but has become like them in acquiring wealth. His faith in humanity is restored when he meets the incorruptible Roark. Wynand becomes Roark's great ally and friend but ultimately betrays him.

THEMES IN *THE FOUNTAINHEAD*

INDIVIDUALISM The main idea of *The Fountainhead* is that individuals must act selfishly in order to be free from society's mediocrity and herd mentality. Roark is Rand's paradigm of the perfect man — talented and courageous, he resists society's sway and remains true to himself. His struggle to retain his individuality in the face of forces bent on bringing him to heel forms the core of the plot. The novel's other sympathetic characters also struggle for independence from society. In Rand's novel, the desire to assert one's self becomes the single greatest virtue a character can possess. At his second trial, Roark passionately and lyrically argues that individuals, not societies, propel history: individual creators are "the fountainhead" of civilization.

REASON AND SCIENCE In the world of *The Fountainhead*, everything worth thinking and feeling is the product of reason and logic. Those who work with scientific facts — mathematicians, engineers, builders, and businessmen — are inevitably more intelligent than sentimental writers and journalists. Roark, Dominique and Wynand support their position on the supremacy of the individual with logical arguments rather than emotional appeals. In contrast, the arch-villain Toohey controls the weak by advocating selflessness and altruism. Rand condemns sentimentality and compassion because they confuse the mind by manipulating the heart, compromising individualism. She argues that even the most well-intentioned emotionalism leads to imprisonment, while cold, unflinching reason sets man free.

In the novel, technical progress — rather than art or philosophy — is the measure of society's development. Rand glorifies the New York skyline, which represents human conquest over nature and symbolizes modernity. The novel scoffs at other forms of art: every new play or work of literature is portrayed as ridiculous and self-indulgent.

THE COLD FEROCITY OF LOVE Love, like integrity and invention, is a *Fountainhead* principle worth fighting for. To square love with the novel's faith in reason, the characters demand perfect relationships and approach them with levelheaded logic. Roark stands by while Dominique marries first Keating and then Wynand, calculating that she will emerge from the marriages more suited to him. Roark and Dominique make love with violent and calculating fury, described in prose that is more technical than romantic. As long as relationships help people maximize their potential, love is blessed by logic and becomes a virtue.

SYMBOLS IN *THE FOUNTAINHEAD*

GRANITE AND ICE Granite evokes Howard Roark — his face, body, and mind are hard, rare, unchanging, and beautiful. But Roark is even stronger than the rock, Rand suggests: in several scenes, he breaks granite or uses it in his designs. Convinced of the absolute supremacy of man, the novel rejoices when man triumphs over nature.

Similarly, ice is associated with Dominique. Her body is fragile and angular, and her clothes glitter like ice, shine like glass, or are the color of water. The necklace that Wynand gives her looks like loose pieces of ice scattered on her cool skin. Ice suggests her blank and frigid attitude, especially before she becomes involved with Roark.

THE BANNER The *Banner* symbolizes the worst instincts of the masses. Rand suggests that any medium that relies on the public is doomed to mediocrity. At the end of the novel, Wynand realizes that, try as he might, he cannot ennoble the masses, even if he uses the *Banner* as a tool. Indeed, the novel suggests that journalism represents all that is banal and corrupt, in contrast to architecture, which represents human potential. The villainous Toohey works his ill will as a manipulative journalist, and Wynand makes his fortune on a chain of exploitative and sensationalist papers that cater to the public's most depraved emotions. The results of Wynand's fundraising contest—in which the public donates much more money to the pregnant girlfriend of a convicted murderer than to a brilliant scientist—bring the idiocy of the masses into sharp relief.

IMPORTANT QUOTATIONS FROM *THE FOUNTAINHEAD*

When they lay in bed together it was—as it had to be . . . an act of violence.. . . . it was the moment made of hatred, tension, pain.

Location: Part Two, Chapter 8
Speaker: The narrator
Context: The narrator describes Dominique and Roark's relationship in New York

Dominique and Roark are both lovers and enemies: by night they sleep together, and by day Dominique tries to destroy Roark in order to determine whether he is truly principled. The violence of their relationship turns the tenderness of love into something hard and tough, and therefore (for Rand) admirable. This quotation recalls the violence of their first sexual encounter—a highly idealized rape that Rand endorses for its cold brutality. Rand contrasts this hard love between two strong people with the whiny and comfortable love between Katie and Keating, which leads only to mediocre and painful codependence.

Tell man that he must live for others.. . . Not a single one of them has ever achieved it and not a single one ever will. His every living impulse screams against it. But don't you see what you accomplish?. . . He'll obey.. . . Use big vague words. 'Universal Harmony'—'Eternal Spirit'— 'Divine Purpose'— 'Nirvana'—'Paradise'—'Racial Supremacy'—'The Dictatorship of the Proletariat.'

Location: Part Four, Chapter 14
Speaker: Ellsworth Toohey
Context: Toohey visits Keating, who has been hiding from the media after the destruction of the Cortlandt buildings, and explains how he manipulates the masses by appealing to their emotions

In this speech, Toohey reveals his sinister and manipulative true nature. The "big vague words" that Toohey thinks will control people come from the lexicons of real-world religions and ideologies. The villain Toohey's endorsement of religious phrases such as "Eternal Spirit," "Divine Purpose," "Paradise," "Nirvana," and "Universal Harmony" signal that Rand disapproves of organized religions such as Christianity and Buddhism. "Racial Supremacy" and "The Dictatorship of the Proletariat" refer to and condemn Nazism and communism, respectively. Rand believed that social engineering restricted individual liberty and so hampered individual achievement. This quotation is unusual for its directness; most of the time, Rand delivers her critique through allegory.

[Y]ou've gone beyond the probable and made us see the possible, but possible only through you. Because your figures are more devoid of contempt of humanity than any work I've ever seen.. . . I came for a simple, selfish reason . . . to seek the best.

Location: Part Two, Chapter 11
Speaker: Howard Roark
Context: Roark summarizes his philosophy as he asks Mallory to work with him on the Stoddard Temple

He was not the corrupt publisher of a popular empire. He was an aristocrat aboard a yacht. He looked, she thought, like what one believes an aristocrat to be when one is young: a brilliant kind of gaiety without guilt.

Location: Part Three, Chapter 9
Speaker: The narrator
Context: Looking at her husband Wynand on his yacht, Dominique thinks that his physical bearing reveals his true self

---

Howard, I'm a parasite. I've been a parasite all my life.. . . . I have fed on you and all the men like you who lived before we were born.. . . if they hadn't existed I wouldn't have known how to put stone to stone.. . . I have taken that which was not mine and given nothing in return.

Location: Part Four, Chapter 8
Speaker: Peter Keating
Context: Keating admits that he is a failure and asks Roark for help on the Cortlandt housing project

FRANKENSTEIN

Mary Shelley

A scientist creates a monster, and then abandons it in horror, a decision that leads to disaster and the deaths of nearly everyone he loves.

THE LIFE OF MARY SHELLEY

Mary Wollstonecraft Godwin was born on August 30, 1797, in London. Her mother, Mary Wollstonecraft, was the author of *A Vindication of the Rights of Woman*, a feminist tract urging women to think and act for themselves. Wollstonecraft died giving birth to Mary, who was brought up by her father, William Godwin, a member of a circle of radical thinkers in England that counted Thomas Paine and William Blake among its ranks. Mary grew up in a rarefied atmosphere, exposed to cutting-edge ideas and introduced to such notables as Lord Byron.

Another of the literary types that Mary met as a teenager was Percy Bysshe Shelley, a dashing young poet. Shelley was married to a woman named Harriet, but in 1814 he ran off with Mary. They toured France, Switzerland, and Germany. At first blissful, their affair soon came under strain. Shelley's relationship with Mary waxed and waned with the demands of Harriet. Mary busied herself with another man. Despite these distractions, the relationship endured and was eventually formalized under scandalous circumstances: Harriet, pregnant with Percy's child, drowned herself in London in November 1816, and Shelley married Mary just weeks later.

The fantastic success of *Frankenstein* was a bright spot in Mary Shelley's grim life. From 1815 to 1819, three of her four children died in infancy. In 1822, Shelley drowned off the shore of Tuscany, leaving Mary a widow and single mother. She turned to her husband's poetry and prose, editing and publishing his *Posthumous Poems* in 1824 and his *Poetical Works and Letters* in 1839. She also pursued her own writing, publishing *Valperga* in 1823, *The Last Man* in 1826, *The Fortunes of Perkin Warbeck* in 1830, Lodore in 1835, and *Falkner* in 1837. Serious illness plagued Mary Shelley, and she died in London in February 1851.

FRANKENSTEIN IN CONTEXT

In the summer of 1816, Mary traveled with Shelley, then her lover, to the Swiss Alps. Unseasonable rain kept them trapped inside, where they entertained themselves by reading ghost stories. At the urging of renowned poet Lord Byron, they decided to have a competition to see who could write the best ghost story. Mary took the prize with her story, *Frankenstein*. In 1818, her tale was published and became an immediate bestseller. Now considered a classic text, *Frankenstein* still resonates with readers almost two centuries later. Its characters are indelibly imprinted on Western culture.

FRANKENSTEIN: KEY FACTS

Full title: Frankenstein: or, The Modern Prometheus	
Time and place written: 1816–1817; Switzerland and London	
Date of first publication: January 1, 1818	
Publisher: Lackington, Hughes, Harding, Mavor, & Jones	
Type of work: Novel	
Genre: Gothic; science fiction; epistolary novel	
Language: English	
Setting (time): Eighteenth century	
Setting (place): Geneva; the Swiss Alps; Ingolstadt; England and Scotland; the northern ice	
Tense: Past	

Tone: Gothic, romantic, emotional, tragic, fatalistic

Narrator: The primary narrator is Robert Walton, who, in his letters, quotes Victor Frankenstein's first-person narrative; Victor, in turn, quotes the monster's first-person narrative; Elizabeth Lavenza and Alphonse Frankenstein narrate parts of the story through their letters to Victor

Point of view: Shifts from Robert Walton to Victor Frankenstein to Frankenstein's monster

Protagonist: Victor Frankenstein

Antagonist: Frankenstein's monster

FRANKENSTEIN: PLOT OVERVIEW

Robert Walton, the captain of a ship bound for the North Pole, writes a series of letters to his sister back in England, telling her about the progress of his dangerous mission. Impassable ice soon interrupts the mission. Walton encounters a man named Victor Frankenstein, who has been traveling by dog-drawn sledge across the ice. Victor is weakened by the cold, and Walton takes him aboard ship and helps nurse him back to health. Victor tells him a fantastic tale about a monster he created.

Victor first describes his early life in Geneva. At the end of a blissful childhood spent in the company of Elizabeth Lavenza (his cousin in the 1818 edition, his adopted sister in the 1831 edition) and friend Henry Clerval, Victor enters the university of Ingolstadt to study natural philosophy and chemistry. He is consumed by the desire to discover the secret of life and, after several years of research, believes he has found it.

For months, Victor feverishly fashions a creature out of old body parts. One climactic night, in the secrecy of his apartment, he brings his creation to life. When he looks at the monster that he has created, however, the sight horrifies him. After a fitful night of sleep interrupted by the specter of the monster looming over him, he runs into the streets. Victor bumps into Henry, who has come to study at the university. Back at his apartment, the monster is gone. Victor falls into a feverish illness.

Sickened by his horrific deed, Victor prepares to return to Geneva, to his family, and to health. Just before leaving Ingolstadt, he receives a letter from his father informing him that his youngest brother, William, has been murdered. Grief-stricken, Victor hurries home. While passing through the woods where William was strangled, he catches sight of the monster and becomes convinced that the monster killed his brother. Arriving in Geneva, Victor finds that Justine Moritz, a kind, gentle girl who had been adopted by the Frankensteins, has been accused. She is tried, condemned, and executed, despite her assertions of innocence. Victor grows despondent, guilty at the thought that the monster he created is responsible for the death of two innocent loved ones.

Hoping to ease his grief, Victor takes a vacation to the mountains. One day as he crosses an enormous glacier, the monster approaches him. The monster speaks, admitting that he murdered William and begging for understanding. Lonely, shunned, and forlorn, he says that he struck out at William in a desperate attempt to injure Victor, his cruel creator. The monster begs Victor to create a mate for him, a monster equally grotesque that will keep him company.

Victor refuses at first, horrified by the prospect of creating a second monster. The monster is eloquent and persuasive, however, and eventually Victor agrees to what he asks. After returning to Geneva, Victor heads for England, accompanied by Henry, to plan the creation of a female monster. Leaving Henry in Scotland, he secludes himself on a desolate island in the Orkneys and reluctantly works at repeating his first success. One night, struck by doubts about the morality of his actions, Victor glances out the window to see the monster glaring in at him with a frightening grin. Horrified by the possible consequences of his work, Victor destroys his new creation. The monster, enraged, vows revenge, swearing that he will be with Victor on Victor's wedding night.

Later that night, Victor dumps the remains of the second creature in the lake. The wind picks up and prevents him from rowing back to the island. In the morning, he finds himself ashore near an unknown town. He is arrested and informed that he will be tried for a murder discovered the previous night. Victor denies any knowledge of the murder, but when shown the body, he is shocked to behold his friend Henry Clerval, with the mark of the monster's fingers on his neck. Victor begins raving. He is kept in prison until his recovery, after which he is acquitted of the crime.

Shortly after returning to Geneva with his father, Victor marries Elizabeth. He recalls the monster's words and suspects that he will be murdered on his wedding night. To be safe, he sends Elizabeth away to wait for him. While he awaits the monster, he hears Elizabeth scream and realizes that the monster meant he would kill Elizabeth, not Victor. A short time after Elizabeth's murder, Victor's father dies of grief. Victor vows to devote the rest of his life to finding the monster and exacting his revenge. He soon departs to begin his quest.

Victor tracks the monster northward into the ice. In a dogsled chase, Victor almost catches up with him, but the sea beneath them swells and the ice breaks, making an unbridgeable gap. It was then that Walton encountered Victor.

Walton tells the remainder of the story in another series of letters to his sister. Victor, already ill when the two men meet, dies shortly thereafter. When Walton returns, several days later, to the room in which the body lies, he is startled to see the monster weeping over Victor. The monster tells Walton of his immense solitude, suffering, hatred, and remorse. He says that because his creator has died, he too can end his suffering. The monster then departs for the northernmost ice to die.

CHARACTERS IN *FRANKENSTEIN*

Beaufort A merchant and friend of Victor's father. Beaufort is Caroline's father.

Caroline Beaufort Beaufort's daughter. After her father's death, Caroline marries Alphonse Frankenstein. She dies of scarlet fever, which she contracts from Elizabeth.

Henry Clerval Victor's boyhood friend. Clerval nurses Victor back to health in Ingolstadt. He is a cheerful, loyal man.

The De Laceys A family of peasants. De Lacey, a blind old man who has lost his fortune, has a son, Felix, and a daughter, Agatha. The monster learns how to speak and interact by observing them. When he reveals himself to them, hoping for friendship, they flee in terror.

Alphonse Frankenstein Victor's father. Alphonse consoles Victor in times of pain and encourages him to remember the importance of family.

Victor Frankenstein The doomed protagonist and narrator of the main portion of the story. Victor lets his ambitions overtake his morals, and then can't find the courage to solve the problems he has created. His cowardice and revulsion for his monster result in the deaths of everyone he loves.

William Frankenstein Victor's youngest brother and the darling of the Frankenstein family. The monster strangles William in the woods outside Geneva.

Mr. Kirwin The Scottish magistrate who accuses Victor of murdering Clerval.

M. Krempe A professor of natural philosophy at Ingolstadt. Krempe dismisses Victor's study of the alchemists as a waste of time and encourages him to begin his studies anew.

Elizabeth Lavenza An orphan whom the Frankensteins adopt. In the 1818 edition of the novel, Elizabeth is Victor's cousin. In the 1831 edition, Victor's mother rescues Elizabeth from a destitute peasant cottage in Italy. Elizabeth passively and patiently waits for Victor's attention.

The Monster The eight-foot-tall, hideously ugly creation of Victor Frankenstein. Intelligent and sensitive, the monster longs to interact with people, but all who see him shun him.

Justine Moritz A young girl adopted into the Frankenstein household. Justine is wrongfully convicted and executed for William's murder.

Safie The Turkish woman with whom Felix is in love.

Margaret Saville Walton's sister. Saville is the recipient of letters from her seafaring brother.

M. Waldman The professor of chemistry who sparks Victor's interest in science. Waldman dismisses the alchemists' conclusions as unfounded but sympathizes with Victor's interest in a science that can explain the "big questions," such as the origin of life.

Robert Walton The Arctic seafarer whose letters bookend *Frankenstein*.

THEMES IN *FRANKENSTEIN*

THE SUBTLETIES OF MONSTROSITY Although Victor's monster is the most obvious exemplar of monstrosity, he is perhaps less monstrous than his creator. The monster's hideousness is physical only.

He starts life unformed, and given the chance to mold himself, he becomes a literate, compassionate creature. He kills, but only out of desperation. His total lack of companionship makes him frantic: "I, the miserable and the abandoned, am an abortion, to be spurned at, and kicked, and trampled on." Victor's monstrosity is less noticeable because it is internal. His ambition, secrecy, and selfishness alienate him from human society. His fear and instinct for self-preservation lead to the murder of his family members. Like a mother who abandons her baby, he strands his creation, running away from it without devoting a thought to its well-being. Of the monster, he says, "When I thought of him, I gnashed my teeth, my eyes became inflamed, and I ardently wished to extinguish that life which I had so thoughtlessly made."

THE MEANING OF TEXTS *Frankenstein* overflows with texts: letters, notes, journals, inscriptions, and books fill the novel, sometimes nestled inside each other, sometimes alluded to or quoted. Walton's letters envelop the entire tale; Victor's story fits inside Walton's letters; the monster's story fits inside Victor's; and the love story of Felix and Safie, and references to *Paradise Lost*, fit inside the monster's story. This profusion of texts suggests the monstrosity of the novel itself, which, like the monster, is stitched together from disparate parts.

THE PASSIVITY OF WOMEN *Frankenstein* is strikingly devoid of strong female characters. The women who populate it are passive creatures who suffer calmly and then expire. Caroline Beaufort is a self-sacrificing mother who dies taking care of her adopted daughter. Justine calmly submits to her sentence and execution, despite her innocence. The female monster is aborted by Victor partly because he fears he will not be able to control her actions once she is animated. Elizabeth waits, helpless and quiet, for Victor to return to her. The novel lacks strong women because the obsessive relationship of Victor and his monster leaves no room for them. Victor and the monster are mother and child, almost husband and wife. They chase each other over the frozen tundra in a perverse version of courtship. On Victor's wedding night, thoughts of the monster consume him. Elizabeth, his new wife, is little more than a distraction. It never occurs to him that the monster could be coming for her, not him. In order to stress the singlemindedness with which Victor and his monster think of each other, Shelley does not distract them with compelling women.

SYMBOLS IN *FRANKENSTEIN*

LIGHT AND FIRE In *Frankenstein*, light symbolizes knowledge, discovery, and enlightenment. The natural world is a place of dark secrets, hidden passages, and unknown mechanisms which science must illumine with the light of knowledge. The dangerous and more powerful cousin of light is fire, which symbolizes dangerous knowledge such as the secret of creating life. The monster's first experience with flame reveals the dual nature of fire: he discovers excitedly that it creates light, but also that it hurts him when he touches it. Fire relates to the full title of Shelley's novel, *Frankenstein: or, The Modern Prometheus*. The Greek god Prometheus gave the knowledge of fire to humanity and was severely punished for it. Victor attempts to become a modern Prometheus, for which he is punished. He seeks the dangerous knowledge symbolized by fire, not the desirable knowledge symbolized by light.

IMPORTANT QUOTATIONS FROM *FRANKENSTEIN*

> *Did I request thee, Maker, from my clay*
> *To mould me Man, did I solicit thee*
> *From darkness to promote me?*

Location: The title page of *Frankenstein*
Speaker: Adam
Context: Shelley prefaces her novel with lines from John Milton's *Paradise Lost*

In these lines from Milton's epic poem, Adam bemoans his fallen condition (Book X, 743–745) and complains that he did not ask to be born. The monster, who reads *Paradise Lost*, conceives of himself as a tragic figure. He sees shades of himself in both Adam and Satan, each creations of God. Like Adam, the monster is punished by his creator, though he strives to be good. Like Satan, he is scorned by his creator. Milton does not make his God a particularly likable character. We are much more likely to feel sympathetic to Satan, whom Milton makes a passionate, brilliant character. Similarly, Shelley does not make Victor Frankenstein the hero of her novel. The monster is much braver, kinder, and even smarter than his creator. Adam and the monster have a point: they did not ask to be born. They were created against their will, and it seems unfair that the man who created them brushes them aside and punishes them instead of helping the beings he gave life.

What may not be expected in a country of eternal light?

Location: Walton's first letter to his sister
Speaker: Walton
Context: Walton writes of his high hopes

Walton's question encapsulates one of the main themes of *Frankenstein*—that appropriate knowledge and discovery bring light to the darkness. Walton's quest to reach the northernmost part of the earth is similar in spirit to Victor's quest for the secret of life: both seek ultimate knowledge. The beauty and simplicity of Walton's phrasing epitomize the eighteenth-century scientific rationalists' optimism about, and trust in, knowledge as a pure good. But Shelley does not see knowledge as a pure good, which the novel's answer to Walton's question proves. It turns out that Walton's implication—that we can expect nothing but good from a place of eternal light—is wrong. Men who seek the eternal, as Walton and Victor do, go too far. They trespass on God's territory, and only evil will come of it. Walton's trip ends in defeat. He writes to his sister, "I have lost my hopes of utility and glory." Victor's experimenting ends in disaster. He loses all those he loves, including his monster. Walton's question, which seems so cheerful and sunny at first glance, is chilling in light of the events that come after it.

I saw—with shut eyes, but acute mental vision—I saw the pale student of unhallowed arts kneeling beside the thing he had put together. I saw the hideous phantasm of a man stretched out, and then, on the working of some powerful engine, show signs of life and stir with an uneasy, half-vital motion. Frightful must it be, for supremely frightful would be the effect of any human endeavor to mock the stupendous mechanism of the Creator of the world.

Location: Author's Introduction to the 1831 edition of *Frankenstein*
Speaker: Shelley
Context: Shelley describes the germ of her idea

So much has been done, exclaimed the soul of Frankenstein—more, far more, will I achieve; treading in the steps already marked, I will pioneer a new way, explore unknown powers, and unfold to the world the deepest mysteries of creation.

Location: Chapter 3
Speaker: Victor
Context: Victor tells Walton how his chemistry teacher inspired him to seek knowledge of the secret of life

---

I, the miserable and the abandoned, am an abortion, to be spurned at, and kicked, and trampled on.

Location: Walton's final letter
Speaker: Frankenstein's monster
Context: Walton recounts what the monster said as he looked at Victor's corpse

THE EPIC OF GILGAMESH

Unknown

A man matures from a powerful person into a good king, but fails to achieve immortality.

THE EPIC OF GILGAMESH IN CONTEXT

Many centuries before Homer lived and before the Old Testament scriptures were written, ancient Mesopotamian poets and scribes composed and transcribed the epic of Gilgamesh, a king at the dawn of civilization coming to terms with the meaning of his life and death.

The earliest known human civilizations were established by the inhabitants of the fertile Tigris and Euphrates river plains around 3000 B.C. The historical record indicates that a king named Gilgamesh ruled Uruk, one of these early city-states, in the twenty-eighth century B.C. By the twenty-sixth century B.C., Gilgamesh was worshipped as the ruler-judge of the underworld, and his reign as a king on earth was reputed to have lasted 126 years. The earliest Mesopotamian writing, cuneiform (wedge-shaped) characters on clay tablets, appeared around 3000 B.C. The two principal languages of the day were Sumerian, which predominated in the urban south, and Akkadian, more common in the rural north. The earliest surviving fragment of a Gilgamesh story has been dated to the twentieth century B.C.. Scholars hypothesize that oral poems about Gilgamesh's life began appearing several hundred years earlier. Sometime between 1300 and 1000 B.C., the Babylonian poet Sin-liqe-unninni redacted the tales of Gilgamesh into a single coherent narrative, a 3000-line, eleven-tablet poetic epic. In later transcribings Sin-liqe-unninni's version may have been altered, but fragments of what is substantially the same text have been found throughout the region and, most importantly, in the libraries of the Assyrian King Ashurbanipal of Nineveh (ruled 668–627 B.C.). Ashurbanipal's version of Sin-liqe-unninni's manuscript—known, from its first line, as "He who saw the Deep"—has become accepted as the standard version of the Gilgamesh epic. Because it is incomplete—more than 575 lines are missing—it has been supplemented by fragments from other versions, composed in different languages over thousands of years.

The tablets were discovered after an Englishman named Austen Henry Layard, stopping in Mesopotamia in 1839, began exploring what turned out to be a buried library in the ancient palace of Nineveh. The tablets were excavated and transported to the British Museum. Early interest in the epic arose out of its links with the Bible, in particular with its surprisingly corroborative account of a great deluge. Excavation work continues, and the record may never be complete, but our picture of the origins of Western culture has been radically altered because of Layard's discovery.

THE EPIC OF GILGAMESH: KEY FACTS

Author: Largely Sin-liqe-unninni, who arranged the best-preserved version out of many earlier accounts

Time and place written: Near East; Sin-liqe-unninni's version composed between 1300 and 1000 B.C.; earliest fragments date from the third millennium B.C.

Publisher: Sin-liqe-unninni's tablets discovered in the library of the Assyrian King Ashurbanipal

Type of work: Poem

Genre: Epic

Language: Sin-liqe-unninni's tablets are in Babylonian cuneiform

Setting (time): The great heroic past

Setting (place): City of Uruk; otherworldly environs

Tense: Past

Tone: Adulatory	
Narrator: Limited omniscient third-person narrator	
Point of View: Gilgamesh's	
Protagonist: Gilgamesh	
Antagonist: Mortality	

THE EPIC OF GILGAMESH: PLOT OVERVIEW

TABLETS I–XI

King Gilgamesh of Uruk, is a powerful man and a tyrannical king. He exhausts his men in contests of strength and claims *droit de seigneur*—the right to sleep with any bride on her wedding night. To alleviate the suffering of the populace, the god Anu and the mother god Aruru create Enkidu, a rival for Gilgamesh. Enkidu is a wild creature who lives among beasts outside Uruk. He is lured away from the herd by the prostitute Shamhat, who beds him. Coupling with a woman makes Enkidu more man than beast. Shamhat takes Enkidu to Uruk to meet the lonely Gilgamesh, who has been having dreams about a new comrade and counselor. Enkidu and Gilgamesh meet in combat. Matched in strength, they cease fighting and seal their friendship with a kiss.

Gilgamesh resolves to travel to the Forest of Cedar to challenge its superhuman guardian Humbaba. Enkidu advises against the expedition, but his warnings are in vain. Gilgamesh and Enkidu set off after consulting with the Uruk elders and seeking the blessing of Gilgamesh's divine mother Ninsun, who implores the sun god Shamash to protect Gilgamesh and adopts Enkidu as Gilgamesh's brother. On the way to the Forest of Cedars, Gilgamesh is repeatedly frightened by dreams, but Enkidu finds ways of reinterpreting the bad omens favorably. Each bolstering the other's morale, Gilgamesh and Enkidu reach the forest. With Shamash's supernatural help, they manage to destroy Humbaba.

On his triumphant return, Gilgamesh is propositioned by the goddess Ishtar. Mindful of the misfortunes that have befallen Ishtar's previous lovers, Gilgamesh scornfully rejects her. Furious, she unleashes the ferocious supernatural Bull of Heaven on Uruk. Gilgamesh and Enkidu defeat the bull and throw it at Ishtar. That night, Enkidu dreams that the gods have determined that he must die as punishment for the deaths of Humbaba and the Bull of Heaven. Despondent, Enkidu curses his past, but realizes that past events that have led to the present are irreversible. He has a detailed vision of the underworld, which heralds his eventual death.

Enkidu's death leaves Gilgamesh both devastated and fearful of his own death. He wanders the wilderness, searching for the immortal Uta-napishti who knows the secret to eternal life. Eventually, Gilgamesh arrives at the edge of the world, where he meets the goddess Shiduri and the ferryman Ur-Shanabi. He tells them about Enkidu's death and his own quest for immortality. Ur-Shanabi takes him across the ocean to Uta-napishti's home, where Gilgamesh again relates his story. Uta-napishti counsels Gilgamesh to be satisfied with his good fortune and not to pursue the unattainable.

Pressed by Gilgamesh, Uta-napishti tells the story of how he became immortal. He was chosen by the god Ea to survive the catastrophic deluge decreed by the god Enlil. Uta-napishti built a boat and loaded it with all kinds of beasts and people with many different skills. They were saved while the rest of the world was destroyed. After the deluge, Enlil granted Uta-napishti immortality.

To prove that Gilgamesh must succumb to death, Uta-napishti challenges Gilgamesh to go without sleep for six days and seven nights. Uta-napishti fails to complete this challenge. Uta-napishti sends Ur-shanabi to accompany Gilgamesh, freshly bathed and clothed, back to Uruk. Before Gilgamesh leaves, Uta-napishti tells him about a plant that restores the youth of its possessor. Gilgamesh dives into the "Ocean Below"—the freshwater ocean under the earth—and finds this plant. Through his carelessness, the plant is soon stolen by a snake. Gilgamesh is left with nothing to show for his quest but wisdom. He returns to Uruk, whose walls mark his greatest claim to immortality.

CHARACTERS IN *THE EPIC OF GILGAMESH*

MORTALS

Enkidu A creature created by the gods as a rival and companion for Gilgamesh. Enkidu grows up outside civilization, but is tamed and socialized by Shamhat. Enkidu's wisdom contrasts with and tempers Gilgamesh's impetuosity. Enkidu's death from an illness sent by Enlil triggers Gilgamesh's quest for immortality.

Gilgamesh The king of Uruk and the epic's protagonist. *Gilgamesh* traces Gilgamesh's growth to full maturity. A strong and handsome man but a callow and tyrannical ruler, Gilgamesh possesses a potential for greatness that is realized through his friendship with Enkidu and his quests for renown and immortality. According to Babylonian mythology, Gilgamesh is posthumously deified and becomes the judge and ruler of the dead.

Humbaba The tusked ogre set by Enlil to guard the sacred Forest of Cedar. Humbaba is killed by Gilgamesh and Enkidu, aided by Shamash.

Shamhat The prostitute who seduces and socializes the wild Enkidu.

Ur-Shanabi The ferryman who carries people to Uta-napishti's dwelling. At the end, Uta-napishti dismisses Ur-Shanabi from service to accompany Gilgamesh to Uruk. Ur-shanabi bears witness to the grandeur of Uruk's walls, which are Gilgamesh's bid for immortality.

MAJOR GODS

Anu The god of the sky and the father of the gods, including Ishtar. Anu conceives of Enkidu and later suggests punishing Gilgamesh or Enkidu for slaughtering Humbaba and the Bull of Heaven.

Belet-ili (Aruru) The mother goddess who gives birth to all humans. With Anu's assistance, Aruru creates Enkidu.

Ea The clever god of the ocean depths. Ea saves Uta-napishti from the deluge and sends the Seven Sages to civilize humans.

Enlil The chief god and a harsh ruler over earth and humans. "Enlil" means "Lord Wind." Enlil sends the deluge to destroy all humans, and decrees that Enkidu should die.

Shamash The sun god and the ancient patron of travelers. Shamash protects Gilgamesh and Enkidu in their quests for glory. He sends the "thirteen winds" to blind Humbaba, and intercedes in vain on Enkidu's behalf when Enlil decrees his death.

LESSER IMMORTALS

Ishtar Uruk's patron goddess. Ishtar is the goddess of sexual love and war and is Anu's daughter. Furious when Gilgamesh rejects her advances, Ishtar sends the Bull of Heaven to destroy him.

Lugalbanda A former king of Uruk, later deified. Depending on the tradition, Lugalbanda is either Gilgamesh's father or his guardian deity.

Ninsun (Lady Wild Cow) Gilgamesh's mother and a minor goddess. Ninsun offers Gilgamesh counsel and appeals to the gods on his behalf.

Shiduri A goddess who inhabits a tavern at the edge of the world. "Shiduri" means "She is my Rampart." Shiiduri eventually tells Gilgamesh how to find Ur-Shanabi.

Uta-napishti (Atra-Hasis) A human who has achieved immortality. "Uta-napishti" means "I Found Life"; "Atra-Hasis" means "Surpassing Wise." Uta-napishti plays the role of Noah in the Babylonian version of the story of the Flood. Counseled by Ea, Uta-napishti builds a boat and survives the deluge, after which he is made immortal by a council of gods. Uta-napishti counsels Gilgamesh to accept the inevitability of death and appreciate his good fortune.

THEMES IN *THE EPIC OF GILGAMESH*

THE INEVITABILITY OF DEATH In the first half of *Gilgamesh*, the inevitability of death spurs Gilgamesh to action: he wants do so something extraordinary that will live on after his death, to be recorded on clay tablets. He undertakes a journey to kill Humbaba and later rebuffs Ishtar, remembering the difficulties of other mortals who have tangled with her. Gilgamesh's perspective changes after Enkidu dies not in battle but of a sickness—a shameful death that further underscores human mortality. Prompted by grief and fear of death, Gilgamesh leaves the fold of civilization, dresses in animals skins, and sets off on a rambling new journey. When at last he reaches Uta-napishti, Gilgamesh is taught by experience that his death is indeed inevitable when the magical rejuvenating plant is stolen away by a snake. Finally convinced of his fate, Gilgamesh returns to Uruk with nothing to show for his journey but wisdom and a keener awareness of the delicate balance between the struggles of man and the inevitability of death.

NEGOTIATING THE HUMAN BETWEEN THE DIVINE AND THE BESTIAL Gilgamesh is only one-third human. His restlessness and ambition are attributed to his divine part. Other creatures too have godlike aspects: Enkidu is told that he is handsome like a god. After sleeping with Shamhat, Enkidu acquires human reason and understanding. This wisdom, which includes the desire for human companionship, marks him as different from beasts and similar to humans. The bread and fermented alcohol that initiate Enkidu into civilization are symbols of human cultivation and are often used in religious rites to this day. As human beings, we have aspects that are not only bestial (the mortal body) and divine (wisdom and restlessness), but also essentially human, such as the tendency to join society and the need for communion with others.

KNOWLEDGE AS SUFFERING Both paradigms for gaining knowledge in *Gilgamesh* liken knowledge to suffering. Enkidu falls from animal innocence after encountering a harlot who introduces him to sexual pleasure and, more broadly, to the pleasure of interpersonal relationships. He suffers both when his former herd rejects him and when, with his newfound wisdom, he fully realizes that he is mortal and will die. Later in the story, Gilgamesh gains similarly painful knowledge. He returns after his journey beyond the bounds of the world certain that he too will die, and that his past has irrevocably marked him. He earns his epithet from the epic's first line, becoming "he who saw the Deep."

SYMBOLS IN *GILGAMESH*

HUMBABA Humbaba, the guardian of the Forest of Cedar, symbolizes the power—both the riches and the danger—of wild nature, that chaos out of which primordial man cut out his orderly universe. As a trope, Humbaba resurfaces throughout world literature, from the Green Knight of the medieval English poem *Sir Gawain and the Green Knight* to the Ents from J. R. R. Tolkien's *Lord of the Rings* saga.

BREAD Bread symbolizes civilization and communion between humans, as well as transformation. Enkidu is inducted into society through eating bread and coupling with Shamhat. Later, Uta-napishti's wife uses fresh bread loaves to number the days that Gilgamesh has slept. Gilgamesh's sleep mimics death, and the moldy decaying loaves by his side foreshadow the decay of the human body in death. Like ale, bread undergoes a radical transformative process as it is created—a process that the more optimistic medieval theologians frequently compared to the resurrection of the body after death.

IMPORTANT QUOTATIONS FROM *THE EPIC OF GILGAMESH*

For six days and seven nights Enkidu was erect, as he coupled with Shamhat.
*   When with her delights he was fully sated, he turned his gaze to his herd. The gazelles saw Enkidu,*
they started to run, the beasts of the field shied away from his presence.

Enkidu had defiled his body so pure, his legs stood still, though his herd was in motion. Enkidu was weakened, could not run as before, but now he had reason, and wide understanding.

Location: Tablet I, lines 193–202
Speaker: The narrator
Context: Enkidu couples with the harlot Shamhat and loses his wild innocence

Enkidu starts out as an innocent creature of nature, happy to run and eat with the wild animals. His fall from grace is similar to that of the Judæo-Christian Adam: both have an interaction with a woman that strips them of innocence, and both leave an Edenic state of happiness endowed with new, painful wisdom. Enkidu has lost his former strength, and his herd rejects him as foreign. In exchange, he has "reason" and "wide understanding." To cement Enkidu's transformation, Shamhat lures Enkidu away to the city with the persuasive argument that there he will find an equal. Enkidu follows her because he now feels the need for a friend—Shamhat has awakened not only sexual desire but also the human need for companionship. Later, on his deathbed, Enkidu both curses Shamhat for forcing him to leave the wilderness and blesses her for all that he has gained in exchange.

Gilgamesh found a pool whose water was cool, down he went into it, to bathe in the water. Of the plant's fragrance a snake caught scent, came up [in silence], and bore the plant off.
As it turned away it sloughed its skin. Then Gilgamesh sat down and wept, down his cheeks the tears were coursing . . . . [he spoke] to Ur-shanabi the boatman:
"[For whom], Ur-shanabi, toiled my arms so hard, for whom ran dry the blood of my heart? Not for myself did I find a bounty, [for] the "Lion of the Earth" I have done a favour!
Now far and wide the tide is rising.. . . . Had I only turned back, and left the boat on the shore!"

Location: Tablet XI, lines 303–315
Speaker: The narrator
Context: Gilgamesh mourns the loss of the youth-restoring plant Old Man Grown Young to a snake (the Lion of the Earth)

Having lost the magic plant, Gilgamesh will not be able to become immortal or rescue the elders of Uruk from old age and death. His disillusioned return home is representative of the human experience: the toils of men win only the miserable knowledge that their travails are fruitless and that death is inevitable. In this passage, Gilgamesh completes the arc of what would come to be the traditional hero story, observed in works from the *Odyssey* to *The Wizard of Oz*. Scholars have been displeased with this "unsatisfying" ending to the *Gilgamesh* epic, but its smallness mimics the smallness of the new knowledge that Gilgamesh has gained. All he has is a deeper awareness of his life and all lives. On Gilgamesh's sudden return home, the otherworldly land of his travels blurs into the familiar, and his large, epic physical journey becomes a small, local spiritual one.

In Uruk-the-Sheepfold he walks [back and forth] like a wild bull lording it, head held aloft. He has no equal when his weapons are brandished, his companions are kept on their feet by his contests.
The young men of Uruk he harries without warrant, Gilgamesh lets no son go free to his father. By day and by night his tyranny grows harsher, Gilgamesh, [the guide of the teeming people!]

Location: Tablet I, lines 63–70
Speaker: The narrator
Context: The narrator describes Gilgamesh as a powerful man and a tyrannical king

---

[Gilgamesh] *opened his mouth to speak,* [saying] *to the Lady Ishtar:* "[And if indeed I] *take you in marriage,. . .*
[Would you feed me] *bread that is fit for a god,* [and pour me ale] *that is fit for a king?. . .*

What bridegroom of yours did endure for ever? What brave warrior of yours went up [to the heavens?]"

Location: Tablet VI, lines 22–24, 27–28, 42–43
Speaker: The narrator
Context: Gilgamesh rudely rebuffs the amorous advances of the goddess Ishtar

---

[Then I was afraid that I too would die,] [I grew fearful of death, and so wander the wild.] *What became of my friend* [was too much to bear] …

How can I keep silent? How can I stay quiet? [My friend, whom I loved, has turned] *to clay, my friend Enkidu, whom I loved, has* [turned to clay.] [Shall I not be like] *him, and also lie down,* [never] *to rise again, through all eternity?*

Location: Tablet X, lines 61–63, 67–71
Speaker: Gilgamesh
Context: Gilgamesh tells Shiduri aobut his experiences after Enkidu's death

THE GLASS MENAGERIE

Tennessee Williams

A young man, fed up with his responsibilities to his nostalgic mother and crippled sister, flees family life.

THE LIFE OF TENNESSEE WILLIAMS

Tennessee Williams was born in Columbus, Mississippi, in 1911. His given name was Thomas Lanier Williams III. In college, his classmates nicknamed him "Tennessee" because of his Southern accent and his father's home state. The Williams family produced several illustrious Tennessee politicians, but Williams's grandfather squandered the family fortune. Williams's father, C. C. Williams, was a traveling salesman and a heavy drinker. Williams's mother, Edwina, was the daughter of a Mississippi clergyman and prone to hysterical attacks. The young Williams, always shy and fragile, was ostracized at school. During his school years, he became extremely close to Rose, his older sister.

In high school, Williams turned to the movies and writing for solace. When he was sixteen, he won five dollars in a national competition for his answer to the question "Can a good wife be a good sport?" The next year, he published a horror story in a magazine called *Weird Tales*, and the year after that he entered the University of Missouri as a journalism major. While there, he wrote his first plays. When Williams failed a required ROTC program course, his father forced him to withdraw from school and go to work at the same shoe company where he himself worked.

After working at the shoe factory for three years, Williams suffered a minor nervous breakdown. When he recovered, he returned to college, this time at Washington University in St. Louis. While he was studying there, a St. Louis theater group produced his plays *The Fugitive Kind* and *Candles to the Sun*. Personal problems led Williams to drop out of Washington University and enroll in the University of Iowa. While he was in Iowa, his sister, Rose, had a prefrontal lobotomy (an intensive brain surgery). Despite this trauma, Williams finally graduated in 1938. In the years that followed, he lived a bohemian life, working menial jobs, wandering from city to city, and writing. During the early years of World War II, Williams worked in Hollywood as a scriptwriter.

The Glass Menagerie (1944), a highly personal, explicitly autobiographical play, earned Williams fame, fortune, critical respect, and a Drama Critics' Circle Award. He won another Drama Critics' Circle Award and a Pulitzer Prize for *A Streetcar Named Desire*. In 1955, he won the same two prizes again, for *Cat on a Hot Tin Roof*.

The impact of success on Williams's life was colossal and detrimental. Alcoholism, depression, thwarted desire, loneliness in search of purpose, and insanity plagued Williams. He was gay, and homosexuality was not accepted in his era and culture. He referred to the 1960s as his "stoned age." He suffered a period of intense depression after the death of his longtime partner in 1961 and, six years later, entered a psychiatric hospital in St. Louis. He continued to write, but most critics agree that the quality of his work diminished in his later life. His life's work adds up to twenty-five full-length plays, five screenplays, over seventy one-act plays, hundreds of short stories, two novels, poetry, and a memoir. Five of his plays were made into movies. Williams died from choking in a drug-related incident in 1983.

THE GLASS MENAGERIE IN CONTEXT

Around 1941, Williams began the work that would become *The Glass Menagerie*. The play evolved from a short story entitled "Portrait of a Girl in Glass." In December of 1944, *The Glass Menagerie* was staged in Chicago with the collaboration of a number of well-known theatrical figures. Initially, attendance was sparse. The financial backer was on the verge of closing the play, but Chicago's theater critics mounted an all-out campaign to save it, begging readers of their daily columns not to miss the play. Within another couple of weeks, *The Glass Menagerie* was playing to full houses. In March of 1945, the play moved to Broadway, where it won the prestigious New York Drama Critics' Circle Award.

THE GLASS MENAGERIE: KEY FACTS

Time and place written: 1941–1943; a number of American cities, including New York, St. Louis, and Los Angeles

Date of first publication: 1945

Publisher: Random House

Type of work: Play

Genre: Southern play

Language: English

Setting (time): The winter and spring of 1937

Setting (place): An apartment in St. Louis

Tense: Present and past

Tone: Tragic, sarcastic, bleak

Narrator: Tom Wingfield

Point of view: Tom's; he both narrates and participates in the play

Protagonist: Tom Wingfield

Antagonist: Hopelessness, disappointment, and fear

THE GLASS MENAGERIE: PLOT OVERVIEW

The Glass Menagerie is a memory play. Its action is drawn from the memories of the narrator, Tom Wingfield, who looks back on the events of his life in St. Louis in 1937. In 1937, Tom is an aspiring poet who toils in a shoe warehouse to support his mother, Amanda, and sister, Laura. Mr. Wingfield, Tom and Laura's father, ran off years ago and, except for one postcard, has not been heard from since.

Amanda, originally from a genteel Southern family, often regales her children with tales of her idyllic youth and many suitors. She is disappointed that Laura, who wears a brace on her leg and is painfully shy, does not attract any gentleman callers. She enrolls Laura in a business college, hoping that she will make her own and the family's fortune through a business career. Weeks later, however, Amanda discovers that Laura's crippling shyness has led her to secretly drop out of the class and spend her days wandering the city alone. Amanda then decides that Laura's last hope lies in marriage. She begins selling newspaper subscriptions, hoping that the extra money she earns will help to attract suitors for Laura. Meanwhile, Tom, who loathes his warehouse job, finds escape in liquor, movies, and literature, much to his mother's chagrin. During one of his frequent arguments with his mother, Tom accidentally breaks several of the glass animal figurines that are Laura's most prized possessions.

Amanda and Tom discuss Laura's prospects, and Amanda asks Tom to keep an eye out for potential suitors at the warehouse. Tom selects Jim O'Connor, a casual friend, and invites him to dinner. Amanda quizzes Tom about Jim and is delighted to learn that he is an ambitious young man. She prepares an elaborate dinner and insists that Laura wear a new dress. At the last minute, Laura learns the name of her caller and realizes that it is the boy she had a devastating crush on in high school. When Jim arrives, Laura answers the door, on Amanda's orders, and then disappears, leaving Tom and Jim alone. Tom confides to Jim that he has used the money for his family's electric bill to join the merchant marine and plans to leave in search of adventure. Laura refuses to eat dinner with the others, feigning illness. Amanda, wearing an ostentatious dress from her glamorous youth, talks vivaciously with Jim throughout the meal.

As dinner is ending, the lights go out because of the unpaid electric bill. The characters light candles, and Amanda encourages Jim to entertain Laura in the living room while she and Tom clean up. At first Laura is paralyzed by Jim's presence, but his warm manner soon draws her out of her shell. She confesses that she knew and liked him in high school but was too shy to approach him. Laura reminds him of the nickname he gave her: "Blue Roses," an accidental corruption of the name of Laura's medical condition, pleurosis. Jim reproaches her for her shyness and low self-esteem but praises her uniqueness. Laura shows him her favorite glass animal, a unicorn. Jim dances with her, but in the process, he accidentally knocks over the unicorn, breaking off its horn. Laura is not angry. She notes that now the unicorn is a normal horse. Jim kisses her, but quickly draws back and apologizes, explaining that he was carried away by the moment and that he has a serious girlfriend. Resigned, Laura offers him the broken unicorn as a souvenir.

Amanda enters the living room, full of good cheer. Jim hastily explains that he must leave because of an appointment with his fiancée. Amanda sees him off warmly and then turns on Tom, who did not know Jim was engaged. Amanda calls Tom an inattentive, selfish dreamer and then turns to comfort Laura.

From the fire escape outside of their apartment, the older Tom watches the two women and explains that, not long after Jim's visit, he got fired from his job and left Amanda and Laura behind. Years have passed and he has traveled great distances, but he cannot leave behind guilty memories of Laura.

CHARACTERS IN *THE GLASS MENAGERIE*

Jim O'Connor An old acquaintance of Tom and Laura. Jim, a popular athlete in high school, now works as a shipping clerk at the shoe warehouse. He is devoted to professional achievement.

Amanda Wingfield Laura and Tom's mother. A proud, vivacious woman, Amanda clings to memories of a vanished, genteel past. She is simultaneously admirable, charming, pitiable, and laughable.

Laura Wingfield Amanda's daughter and Tom's older sister. Laura wears a brace on her leg and walks with a limp. Twenty-three years old and painfully shy, she has largely withdrawn from the outside world. She devotes herself to old records and her collection of glass figurines.

Mr. Wingfield Amanda's husband and Laura and Tom's father. Mr. Wingfield, a handsome man who worked for a telephone company, abandoned his family years before the action of the play and never appears onstage.

Tom Wingfield Amanda's son and Laura's younger brother. An aspiring poet, Tom works at a shoe warehouse to support his family. He is frustrated by the numbing routine of his job.

THEMES IN *THE GLASS MENAGERIE*

THE DIFFICULTY OF ACCEPTING REALITY None of the Wingfields can accept reality, and each, as a result, withdraws into a private world of illusion. Of the three Wingfields, Laura is most removed from reality. Unlike his sister, Tom can function in the real world, holding down a job and talking to strangers. But he has no more motivation than Laura does to pursue professional success, romantic relationships, or even ordinary friendships. Just as Laura retreats into a world of glass figurines, he retreats into literature, movies, and drunkenness. Amanda's relationship to reality is the most complicated in the play. Unlike her children, she longs for social and financial success. Yet her attachment to these values is exactly what prevents her from perceiving the truth about her life. She cannot accept Laura's peculiarities, Tom's ineptitude at business, or her own partial responsibility for the sorrows and flaws of her children. She refuses to admit that she is not the pampered Southern belle she was brought up to be. Amanda's retreat into illusion is in many ways more pathetic than her children's. She does not retreat from reality, she distorts it.

Williams suggests that the Wingfields's fantasies, though extreme, are part of the modern human condition. The young people at the Paradise Dance Hall waltz under an illusion created by a glass ball. Tom thinks that all moviegoers substitute on-screen adventure for real-life adventure. Jim, who represents the "world of reality," is banking his future on public speaking and the television and radio industries—all of which center around the creation of illusions.

THE IMPOSSIBILITY OF TRUE ESCAPE At the beginning of Scene Four, Tom tells Laura about a magician who managed to escape from a nailed-up coffin. Tom sees the magician as a stand-in for himself. He views his life with his family and at the warehouse as a kind of coffin—cramped, suffocating, and morbid. The promise of escape, represented by Tom's fleeing father, the Merchant Marine Service, and the fire escape outside the apartment, haunts Tom from the beginning of the play. Williams takes an ambiguous attitude toward the moral implications and even the effectiveness of Tom's escape. What traps Tom is his loyalty to Laura and Amanda. To escape, Tom must suppress his affection for

Laura and Amanda and do great harm to them. One cannot say for certain that leaving home even means true escape for Tom. No matter how far he wanders, guilt and memories still "pursue" him.

THE UNRELENTING POWER OF MEMORY   According to Tom, *The Glass Menagerie* is a memory play. Because its style and content are shaped by memory, it is unrealistic and highly dramatic. It uses overblown and too-perfect symbolism. A play drawn from memory can cloak itself in layers of melodrama and unlikely metaphor, chalking it up to the exaggeration and distortion of memory. Memory motivates Tom, urging him to tell his story. Williams writes in the Production Notes that "nostalgia . . . is the first condition of the play." Amanda lives in thrall to memories of her youth. Laura treasures old records from her childhood. For these characters, memory is a crippling force that prevents them from finding happiness in the present or thinking optimistically about the future. But it is also the vital force for Tom, prompting him to the act of creation that culminates in the telling of his story.

SYMBOLS IN *THE GLASS MENAGERIE*

LAURA'S GLASS MENAGERIE   As the title of the play informs us, the glass menagerie, or collection of animals, is the play's central symbol. Laura's menagerie represents a number of facets of her personality. Like the figurines, Laura is delicate, fanciful, and old-fashioned. Like glass, which is transparent but also capable of refracting light and creating a rainbow, Laura, though quiet and bland around strangers, is a source of strange, multifaceted delight to those who look at her in the right light. The menagerie also represents the imaginative world to which Laura devotes herself—a world that is colorful and enticing but based on fragile illusions.

THE GLASS UNICORN   The glass unicorn in Laura's collection—her favorite figure—represents her peculiarity. As Jim points out, unicorns are "extinct" in modern times and are lonesome because of their difference. Laura too is unusual, lonely, and ill-adapted to the world in which she lives. The fate of the unicorn symbolizes Laura's fate. When Jim dances with and then kisses Laura, the unicorn's horn breaks off and it becomes just another horse. Jim's advances endow Laura with a new normalcy, making her seem like just another girl, but Laura cannot become normal without shattering. Eventually, Laura gives Jim the unicorn as a "souvenir." Now normal, the unicorn is more appropriate for him than for her, and the broken figurine represents what he has taken from her and destroyed in her.

IMPORTANT QUOTATIONS FROM *THE GLASS MENAGERIE*

Well, in the South we had so many servants. Gone, gone, gone. All vestige of gracious living! Gone completely! I wasn't prepared for what the future brought me. All of my gentlemen callers were sons of planters and so of course I assumed that I would be married to one and raise my family on a large piece of land with plenty of servants. But man proposes—and woman accepts the proposal! To vary that old, old saying a bit—I married no planter! I married a man who worked for the telephone company! . . . A telephone man who—fell in love with long-distance!

Location: Scene Six
Speaker: Amanda
Context: Jim comes to the Wingfield apartment for dinner, and Amanda tells him of her past

Moments after Jim arrives for dinner, Amanda turns on her girlish Southern charm with full force, explaining the central story of her life: her fall from pampered belle to deserted wife. As she does throughout the play, in these lines Amanda equates her own downfall with the end of the "gracious living" associated with the Old South. Her genteel girlhood lifestyle contrasts starkly with the vulgarity and squalor of 1930s St. Louis. Amanda's memories of her many "gentlemen callers" prompt her to wangle a visit from Jim, whom she imagines as a comparable gentleman caller for Laura. That Amanda immediately tells Jim about her gentlemen callers reveals the high hopes she has for his visit. Rather tactlessly, she puts herself and her story at the center of attention rather than encouraging her daughter to shine.

I descended the steps of this fire escape for a last time and followed, from then on, in my father's footsteps, attempting to find in motion what was lost in space.. . . I would have stopped, but I was pursued by something.. . . I pass the lighted window of a shop where perfume is sold. The window is filled with pieces of colored glass, tiny transparent bottles in delicate colors, like bits of a shattered rainbow. Then all at once my sister touches my shoulder. I turn around and look into her eyes. Oh, Laura, Laura, I tried to leave you behind me, but I am more faithful than I intended to be!

Location: Scene Seven
Speaker: Tom
Context: After the action of the play ends, Tom talks about his escape

In Scenes Four and Six, Tom speaks of pursuing "adventure." From these lines, which offer only a vague description of his fate after leaving home, it is unclear whether Tom has found adventure or not. What is clear is that his escape was an imperfect, incomplete one. Memories of Laura chase him wherever he goes, confining him just as the Wingfield apartment did. Tom's cry, "I am more faithful than I intended to be!" indicates that he considers the desertion of his family a faithless and morally reprehensible act, and admits that he wanted to forget his family. The guilt associated with his desertion may have something to do with his inability to leave Laura fully behind. But the word "faithful" also has strong sexual connotations. A number of critics have suggested that Tom's feelings for Laura have incestuous undertones.

But the wonderfullest trick of all was the coffin trick. We nailed him into a coffin and he got out of the coffin without removing one nail.. . . There is a trick that would come in handy for me—get me out of this two-by-four situation! . . . You know it don't take much intelligence to get yourself into a nailed-up coffin, Laura. But who in hell ever got himself out of one without removing one nail?

Location: Scene Four
Speaker: Tom
Context: After returning from a movie, Tom tells Laura about a magic trick

---

LAURA: *Little articles of [glass], they're ornaments mostly! Most of them are little animals made out of glass, the tiniest little animals in the world. Mother calls them a glass menagerie! Here's an example of one, if you'd like to see it! . . . Oh, be careful—if you breathe, it breaks! . . . You see how the light shines through him?*
JIM: *It sure does shine!*
LAURA: *I shouldn't be partial, but he is my favorite one.*
JIM: *What kind of a thing is this one supposed to be?*
LAURA: *Haven't you noticed the single horn on his forehead?*
JIM: *A unicorn, huh? —aren't they extinct in the modern world?*
LAURA: *I know!*
JIM: *Poor little fellow, he must feel sort of lonesome.*

Location: Scene Seven
Speaker: Laura and Jim
Context: Laura overcomes her shyness and shows her collection to Jim

---

JIM: *Aw, aw, aw. Is it broken?*
LAURA: *Now it is just like all the other horses.*
JIM: *It's lost its—*

LAURA: *Horn! It doesn't matter.. . . [smiling] I'll just imagine he had an operation. The horn was removed to make him feel less—freakish!*

Location: Scene Seven
Speaker: Laura and Jim
Context: Jim persuades Laura to dance with him and accidentally breaks her unicorn

THE GOOD EARTH

Pearl S. Buck

A poor Chinese farmer lives a long life of difficulties and successes, struggling with the tension between his desire for wealth and his traditional Chinese values.

THE LIFE OF PEARL SYDENSTRICKER BUCK

Pearl S. Buck was born in 1892 in Hillsboro, West Virginia, to Christian missionaries Absalom and Carie Sydenstricker. When Buck was three months old, her family moved to China on a mission; her parents stayed there for forty years. In 1910, Buck returned to the United States to attend Randolph-Macon Woman's College in Lynchburg, Virginia. Though she was a good student and achieved some measure of popularity, she felt like a foreigner in her unfamiliar native country. After graduating, she returned to China to take care of her ailing mother. In 1917, she married John Lossing Buck, an agricultural economist and graduate of Cornell. Her first and only biological child, Carol, was born in 1921. Due to a uterine tumor discovered during the delivery, Buck had to undergo a hysterectomy. Soon after, Buck discovered that her daughter was severely retarded. Almost at the same time, Buck's mother died after her long illness. These misfortunes placed a great deal of strain on Buck's marriage. She divorced her husband in 1935 and married a man named Richard J. Walsh later the same year.

In 1931, Buck published *The Good Earth*, her second and best-known book. The novel, a complex moral parable that draws heavily on Buck's firsthand knowledge of Chinese culture, quickly gained an international reputation and won the Pulitzer Prize in 1932. Over the next few years, Buck wrote two sequels, *Sons* (1932) and *A House Divided* (1935), but neither was as popular as *The Good Earth*. Buck also wrote biographies of her parents. Buck was awarded the Nobel Prize for literature in 1938, mainly in recognition of these biographies and *The Good Earth*.

Throughout her life, Buck devoted herself to humanitarian causes. She fought constantly on behalf of women's rights. With her husband, Richard Walsh, she founded an adoption agency for children of mixed Asian and American parentage. These children were frequently outcasts in Asian countries, both because of their mixed blood and because they were often the illegitimate children of American servicemen. Buck also took an active interest in other social issues, from the difficult lives of immigrants in New York City to the independence movement in India. She was also a staunch supporter of free speech and civil liberties. Buck died in 1973.

THE GOOD EARTH IN CONTEXT

Buck drew on her knowledge of and experiences in China for *The Good Earth* and other novels. She grew up playing with Chinese children, who referred to her as a "foreign devil." Although contempt for the Chinese was common among families of missionaries from the West, Buck never developed that sense of superiority. Her objective perspective of Western missionaries and the absurdities of their lives is evident in *The Good Earth*.

THE GOOD EARTH: KEY FACTS

Time and place written: 1930–1931; China	
Date of publication: 1931	
Publisher: The John Day Company	
Type of work: Novel	
Genre: Parable; American literature about China	
Language: English	
Setting (time): ca. 1890–1930	

Setting (place): China: Ahwei, Wang Lung's nearby farm, and Nanking (a far-off southern city)

Tense: Past

Tone: Solemn, detached, grave, biblical

Narrator: Third-person limited narrator

Point of view: Wang Lung's

Protagonist: Wang Lung

Antagonist: Difficult life of poverty and famine; cultural conflicts stemming from the modernization of China

THE GOOD EARTH: PLOT OVERVIEW

Wang Lung is a poor young farmer in rural, turn-of-the-century China. His society beginning to modernize while remaining deeply connected to ancient traditions and customs. When Wang Lung reaches marriageable age, his father arranges for him to purchase a twenty-year-old slave named O-lan from the powerful local Hwang family. Wang is disappointed that O-lan does not have bound feet. Although they exchange few words, they are generally pleased with each other. Together, Wang Lung and O-lan cultivate a bountiful and profitable harvest from their land. Wang Lung is overjoyed when their first baby is a son. Meanwhile, the Hwang family has been leading a decadent lifestyle. The husband is a womanizer and the wife is an opium addict. Because of their costly habits, the Hwangs fall on hard times, and Wang Lung is able to purchase a piece of their fertile rice land. He enjoys another profitable harvest, and O-lan gives birth to another son.

Wang Lung's new wealth catches the attention of his greedy, lazy uncle. Custom dictates that Wang Lung must show the utmost respect to members of the older generation, especially relatives, so he loans his uncle money even though he knows that his uncle will waste the money on drinking and gambling. The Hwang family's finances continue to falter and they must sell another tract of land to Wang Lung. O-lan gives birth to a daughter.

In the midst of a terrible famine, O-lan gives birth to another daughter. She strangles the baby because there is not enough food to feed her and the rest of the family. Wang Lung is forced to take his family to a southern city for the winter, where he earns money by transporting people in a rented rickshaw while O-lan and the children beg. They make just enough money to eat. Wang Lung begins to worry that he may never make enough money to return to his land, and he and O-lan briefly consider selling their surviving daughter as a slave. Eventually, Wang Lung and O-lan join a group of poor and desperate people who are ransacking a rich man's home. Wang Lung ends up with a pile of gold coins. With this new money, he moves the family back home and purchases a new ox and some seeds. O-lan has stolen some jewels during the looting. Wang Lung allows her to keep two small pearls and uses the rest to buy three hundred acres of Old Master Hwang's land. O-lan gives birth to twins shortly thereafter. The couple realizes that their oldest daughter is severely retarded, but Wang Lung loves the child dearly.

Wang Lung hires laborers to plant and harvest his land. He enjoys several years of profitable harvests and becomes a rich man. When a flood forces him to be idle, he begins to feel restless and bored. He finds fault with O-lan's appearance and cruelly criticizes her for having big feet. He develops an obsession with Lotus, a beautiful, delicate prostitute with bound feet. Eventually, he purchases Lotus to be his concubine. When O-lan falls terminally ill, Wang Lung regrets his cruel words and comes to appreciate everything his wife has done for him. Meanwhile, to reduce the demands of his uncle and his uncle's wife, who have moved their family into his house and continued to exploit his wealth, Wang tricks them into becoming opium addicts. Eventually, Wang Lung buys the Hwangs' house and moves into it with his family, leaving his own house to his uncle's family.

After O-lan's death, Wang Lung's sons begin to rebel against his plans for their lives. They do not want to work as farmers and do not share his devotion to the land. Furthermore, Wang Lung's first and second sons often argue over money, and their wives develop an intense animosity toward each other. In his old age, Wang Lung takes a concubine, a young slave named Pear Blossom who promises to care for his retarded daughter after his death. He is surrounded by grandchildren, but also by petty family disagreements. By the end of the novel, despite Wang's passionate dissent, his sons plan to sell the family land and divide the money among themselves, marking their final break with the land that made them wealthy.

CHARACTERS IN *THE GOOD EARTH*

THE WANG LUNG CLAN

Wang Lung The novel's protagonist. A poor farmer by birth, Wang Lung maintains a fierce attachment to the land. At the same time, he is ambitious and envies the wealth and decadent lifestyle of the Hwangs. By the end of the novel, his piety and love of the land only partially maintain his good character and moral standing.

O-lan Wang Lung's wife. Sold to the Hwang family as a slave at the age of ten and then bought by Wang Lung, O-lan achieves respectability as the mother of three sons. Strong and hardworking, O-lan is a resourceful woman and a devoted wife. She is often marginalized by Wang Lung and is eventually replaced in his affections.

Wang Lung's First Son Extravagant, arrogant, and obsessed with appearances, Wang Lung's first son grows up spoiled and rejects his father's values.

Wang Lung's First Son's Wife The daughter of Liu, a wealthy local grain merchant. Spoiled and reckless, she urges her husband to spend money on luxury items. She has bound feet.

Wang Lung's Second Son Crafty, enterprising, and miserly. More responsible than his older brother, he also rejects his father's traditional values as outmoded.

Wang Lung's Second Son's Wife The daughter of a modest landowning village family. She and Wang Lung's first son's wife become enemies.

Wang Lung's Third Son The twin brother of Wang Lung's second daughter. He dreams of glory and becomes a soldier against his father's wishes.

Wang Lung's First Daughter Because she suffers from severe malnutrition as an infant during a famine year, she grows up retarded and never learns to speak. Wang Lung is very attached to her and makes arrangements for her care after his death.

Wang Lung's Second Daughter The twin sister of Wang Lung's third son. After Wang Lung begins to criticize O-lan's big feet, O-lan binds the second daughter's feet. The second daughter is promised in marriage to Liu's son.

Wang Lung's Father A traditional and morally severe man.

Wang Lung's Uncle Wang's father's younger brother; a cunning scoundrel and thief. Out of filial piety, Wang Lung shows his uncle respect and supports him in difficult times despite the uncle's despicable nature.

Wang Lung's Uncle's Son A prodigal scoundrel and a sexual predator.

Wang Lung's Uncle's Wife The village gossip. Like her husband and son, she is lazy and manipulative.

ADDITIONAL CHARACTERS

Cuckoo A slave in the Hwang household at the same time as O-lan. In her youth, Cuckoo was beautiful and became the Old Master's concubine. She insulted and berated O-lan, who worked in the kitchen.

Ching Wang Lung's neighbor in the village; later, Wang Lung's capable, faithful, and valued servant.

Old Master Hwang The patriarch of the great Hwang family. Extravagant with his money, he drains his coffers by taking a succession of concubines.

Liu A town grain merchant. Liu is Wang Lung's relative by marriage, first as Wang's first son's father-in-law, then also as Wang's second daughter's father-in-law.

Old Mistress Hwang The opium-addicted matriarch of the great Hwang family.

Lotus A beautiful, delicate prostitute with bound feet and a bad temper. Lotus becomes Wang Lung's concubine.

Pear Blossom A slave purchased by Wang Lung during the famine years, when she is a young girl. She becomes Lotus's personal servant.

THEMES IN *THE GOOD EARTH*

MAN'S RELATIONSHIP TO THE EARTH In the novel, a strong connection to the land is associated with moral piety, good sense, and a strong work ethic; alienation from the land is associated with decadence and corruption. Buck's novel situates this universal theme within the context of traditional Chinese culture. Wang Lung, a farmer, has an intimate, reverent relationship with the earth because he produces his harvest through his own labor. In contrast, the Hwang family is estranged from the earth because their wealth and harvests are produced by hired labor. The novel draws a parallel between people's moral qualities and their relationship with the earth. For example, Wang Lung's inner goodness parallels his good relationship with the land, and the Hwangs' depravity parallels their bad one. Buck also suggests that human success is transitory, but the nourishing earth endures forever.

WEALTH AS DESTROYER OF TRADITIONAL VALUES As Wang Lung's fortunes rise, he begins to resemble the amoral Hwang family, whose fall parallels Wang Lung's rise. The Old Master's debauchery and the Old Mistress's opium addiction are funded by their wealth. Because they hire laborers to work their land, they become idle and estranged from the earth. As Wang Lung grows wealthier, his habits mirror the Hwangs': he hires laborers, funds his uncle's opium addiction, becomes obsessed with Lotus and other women, and, finally, moves into the Hwang house. His well-to-do household also spoils his children: they grow up with little respect for the land, little reverence for their father, and little regard for the religious customs that have given structure to Wang Lung's and his father's lives.

Wang Lung's life story shows how traditional values erode under the influence of wealth—though not necessarily individual wealth. Wang Lung's sons' new values and ideas are manifestations of greater changes in Chinese culture. Buck argues that the modernization of China, closely tied to higher standards of living and increased wealth, creates cultural conflict.

THE OPPRESSION OF WOMEN IN CHINESE CULTURE Although a lifelong feminist, Buck takes a cool, neutral tone toward the oppression of women in China, focusing on individual experience rather than large-scale critique. Without ever endorsing the acts themselves, Buck draws attention to the circumstances that would impel women or families to bind girls' feet, sell daughters into slavery, or kill female infants. She also suggests that husbands who work their wives like slaves or take concubines may only be responding to the pressures of their culture.

Buck uses the character of O-lan to explore the position of women in traditional Chinese culture, demonstrating the crucial economic contributions women make to their families. She also uses O-lan to suggest that, ironically, as women do more to help the household, men value them less romantically and sexually.

SYMBOLS IN *THE GOOD EARTH*

FOOT-BINDING For thousands of years, traditional, wealthy Chinese girls grew up with painfully tightly bound feet to ensure that the feet remained small, which was considered very attractive. Foot-binding made girls desirable to men, but it also immobilized them. Throughout *The Good Earth*, Buck uses foot-binding as a symbol for the moral depravity of wealth. Because foot-binding had become a marker of status, Wang Lung's disappointment upon discovering that O-lan's feet are not bound signals his ambitions. Ironically, it is O-lan's unbound feet that enable her to work in the fields and contribute to the family fortune. Although Buck openly criticized the practice of foot-binding, she takes a neutral tone in the novel, drawing attention to the cultural influences that compel a woman to do such a thing to her daughter. For example, O-lan binds her second daughter's feet after Wang Lung mocks her own "large" unbound feet because she wants her daughter to have a happy marriage.

O-LAN'S PEARLS The pearls that O-lan steals during the revolt in Chapter 14, and which Wang Lung allows her to keep, become a symbol of Wang Lung's love and respect for his wife. The moment when Wang Lung gives O-lan's pearls to Lotus represents the transfer of his affections from O-lan to

Lotus. O-lan is inwardly devastated, and the incident symbolized the extent to which wealth and idleness have corrupted the once admirable Wang Lung.

IMPORTANT QUOTATIONS FROM *THE GOOD EARTH*

There was only this perfect sympathy of movement, of turning this earth of theirs over and over to the sun, this earth which formed their home and fed their bodies and made their gods.. . . Some time, in some age, bodies of men and women had been buried there, houses had stood there, had fallen, and gone back into the earth. So would also their house, some time, return into the earth, their bodies also. Each had his turn at this earth. They worked on, moving together—together—producing the fruit of this earth.

Location: Chapter 2
Speaker: The narrator
Context: The narrator describes Wang Lung and O-lan's connection to the earth during the first year of their marriage

This passage highlights the spherical nature of the earth and the periodic cycle of life. The repeated motions of "turning this earth of theirs over and over" parallel the image of people, homes, and fortunes rising up and falling back into the earth over and over again. The excerpt explains Wang Lung's ethical and spiritual connection to the land and emphasizes the image of a permanent earth silently witnessing the rise and fall of fleeting lives and fickle fortunes of human beings.

Hunger makes thief of any man.

Location: Chapter 15
Speaker: A villager, on the looting of Wang Lung's house
Context: Wang Lung returns back to his land and discovers that his house has been ransacked

The moral relativism of this line's forgiving sentiment characterizes Buck's attitude toward her characters' actions. Although Wang is angry that his house has been looted, he has learned firsthand that poverty and its desperations can compel anyone to compromise moral beliefs in the interest survival. He himself has paid for his journey home with money stolen from the house of a wealthy man. Eventually, Wang forgives Ching his part in the looting of Wang's house during the famine, and the two become enduring friends. Wang's willingness to understand what compels reprehensible behavior echoes Buck's attitude toward practices such as slavery, infanticide, and foot-binding in the novel.

But Wang Lung thought of his land and pondered this way and that, with the sickened heart of deferred hope, how he could get back to it. He belonged, not to this scum which clung to the walls of a rich man's house; nor did he belong to the rich man's house. He belonged to the land and he could not live with any fullness until he felt the land under his feet and followed a plow in the springtime and bore a scythe in his hand at harvest.

Location: Chapter 14
Speaker: The narrator
Context: In Nanking, a remote southern city, Wang Lung looks back on his land with longing

---

Then slowly she thrust her wet wrinkled hand into her bosom and she drew forth the small package and she gave it to him and watched him as he unwrapped it; and the pearls lay in his hand and they caught softly and fully the light of the sun, and he laughed. But O-lan returned to the beating of his clothes and when tears dropped slowly and heavily from her eyes she did not put up her hand to wipe them away; only she beat the more steadily with her wooden stick upon the clothes spread over the stone.

Location: Chapter 19
Speaker: The narrator
Context: On Wang Lung's demand, O-lan gives Wang Lung her pearls—which he previously allowed her to keep after she stole them during the sacking of a rich man's house in Nanking—so that he can give them to Lotus

---

Now, evil, idle sons—sell the land!. . . It is the end of a family—when they begin to sell the land.. . . Out of the land we came and into it we must go—and if you will hold your land you can live—no one can rob you of land.. . . If you sell the land, it is the end.

Location: Chapter 34
Speaker: Wang Lung to his sons
Context: At the end of the novel, Wang Lung, in vain, pleads with his sons not to sell their land

THE GRAPES OF WRATH

John Steinbeck

A terrible drought forces thousands of farming families, the Joads among them, to move to California in search of work.

THE LIFE OF JOHN STEINBECK

John Steinbeck was born in Salinas, California, on February 27, 1902. He attended Stanford University but did not graduate. Steinbeck began writing novels in 1929, but he garnered little commercial or critical success until the publication of *Tortilla Flat* in 1935. In his fiction, Steinbeck frequently delved into the lives of the downtrodden. A trio of novels in the late 1930s focus on the lives of migrant workers in California: *In Dubious Battle* (1936), *Of Mice and Men* (1937), and Steinbeck's masterpiece, *The Grapes of Wrath* (1939), which soared to the top of the bestseller lists and sold half a million copies. In 1940, the novel was awarded the Pulitzer Prize and adapted to the screen. Steinbeck won the Novel Prize for Literature in 1962.

Critical opinions of Steinbeck's work have always been mixed. Both stylistically and in his emphasis on manhood and male relationships, Steinbeck was strongly influenced by his contemporary, Ernest Hemingway. Even though Steinbeck was hailed as a great author in the 1930s and '40s, many critics have called his work superficial, sentimental, and overly moralistic.

Steinbeck continued writing throughout the 1940s and 1950s. He went to Europe during World War II, then worked in Hollywood both as a filmmaker and a scriptwriter. His important later works include *East of Eden* (1952) and *Travels with Charley* (1962). He died in New York City in 1968.

THE GRAPES OF WRATH IN CONTEXT

The Grapes of Wrath tells the story of migrant farm workers, a group that came into being after the early 1930s when a severe drought led to massive agricultural failure in parts of the southern Great Plains, particularly in western Oklahoma and the Texas panhandle. In the absence of rain, crops withered and died. Wind picked up the topsoil and carried it in billowing clouds across the region. Huge dust storms occasionally blocked out the sun and suffocated those caught unprepared. The afflicted region came to be known as the "Dust Bowl."

By the mid-1930s, the drought had crippled countless farm families, and America had fallen into the Great Depression. Unable to pay their mortgages or buy necessary industrial equipment, many Dust Bowl farmers were forced to leave their land. Thousands of families flooded California, hoping to find work. Jobs and food were scarce, and the migrants faced prejudice and hostility from Californians, who gave them the derisive epithet "Okie." These workers and their families lived in impoverished camps called "Hoovervilles," named after President Hoover, who was blamed for the problems that led to the Great Depression. Many camp residents starved to death.

When Steinbeck decided to write a novel about the plight of migrant farm workers, he journeyed to California with an Oklahoma farm family. Although many Oklahomans and Californians reviled *The Grapes of Wrath*, calling Steinbeck's characters unflattering representations of their states' people, the large majority of readers and scholars praised the novel highly. The story of the Joad family, in the words of critic Robert DeMott, "entered both the American consciousness and conscience."

THE GRAPES OF WRATH: KEY FACTS

Time and place written: 1938; Los Gatos, CA	
Date of first publication: April 14, 1939	
Publisher: The Viking Press	

Type of work: Novel	
Genre: Social protest novel	
Language: English	
Setting (time): Late 1930s	
Setting (place): Oklahoma, California, and points along the way	
Tense: Mainly past	
Tone: Mournful, awed, enraged, sympathetic	
Narrator: Anonymous, omniscient, historically aware third person	
Point of view: Shifts dramatically	
Protagonist: Tom Joad	
Antagonist: The disastrous drought of the 1930s; locals and property owners	

THE GRAPES OF WRATH: PLOT OVERVIEW

Tom Joad has been released from an Oklahoma state prison after serving four years for a manslaughter conviction. On his way back to his family's farm in Oklahoma, he meets Jim Casy, a former preacher who now believes that all life is holy—even those aspects that are usually considered sinful—and that sacredness is the endeavor to be equal among your fellow man. Jim accompanies Tom to his farm, only to find it—and all the surrounding farms—deserted. Muley Graves, an old neighbor, wanders by and tells the men that everyone has been "tractored" off the land. Most families, he says, including his own, have headed to California to look for work. The next morning, Tom and Jim set out to see Tom's uncle John, where Muley assures them they will find the Joad clan. Upon arrival, Tom finds Ma and Pa Joad packing up the family's few possessions. They have seen handbills advertising fruit-picking jobs in California.

The family makes the long journey to California in a rickety used truck. Grampa Joad, a feisty old man who objects to leaving his land, dies on the road shortly after the family's departure. Dilapidated cars and trucks, loaded down with scrappy possessions, clog Highway 66. It seems the entire country is fleeing to the Promised Land of California. The Joads meet Ivy and Sairy Wilson, a couple who are having car trouble, and invite them to travel with the family. Sairy Wilson falls ill and cannot continue the journey.

As the Joads near California, they hear rumors of a depleted job market. One migrant tells Pa that 20,000 people show up for every 800 jobs and that his own children have starved to death. Soon after the Joads arrive in California, Granma Joad dies. The remaining family members move from one squalid camp to the next, looking for work without success and struggling to find food. Noah, the oldest of the Joad children, soon abandons the family, as does Connie, a young dreamer who is married to Tom's pregnant sister, Rose of Sharon.

The Joads meet great hostility in California. The camps are overcrowded and full of starving migrants, who are often nasty to each other. The locals fear and dislike the flood of newcomers. Work, on those rare occasions when it is available, pays such a meager wage that a family cannot buy a decent meal with a day's wages. Fearing an uprising, the large landowners do everything in their power to keep the migrants poor and dependent. While staying in a ramshackle camp known as a "Hooverville," Tom and several men get into a heated argument with a deputy sheriff. When the argument turns violent, Jim Casy knocks the sheriff unconscious and is arrested. Police officers arrive and announce their intention to burn the Hooverville to the ground.

A government-run camp proves much more hospitable to the Joads. The family makes many friends and finds a bit of work. One day, Tom learns that the police are planning to stage a riot in the camp, which will allow them to shut down the facilities. By alerting and organizing the men in the camp, Tom helps to defuse the danger. The Joads cannot find steady work and must leave the government camp. They find employment picking fruit, but soon learn that they are earning a decent wage only because they have been hired to break a workers' strike. Tom runs into Jim Casy who has been released from jail and has begun organizing workers, making many enemies among the landowners in the process. When the police hunt down Jim and kill him in Tom's presence, Tom retaliates by killing a police officer.

Tom goes into hiding while the family moves into a boxcar on a cotton farm. One day, Ruthie, the youngest Joad daughter, tells a girl in the camp that her brother has killed two men and is hiding nearby. Fearing for his safety, Ma Joad finds Tom and sends him away. Tom heads off to organize the migrant workers, as Jim was doing before his murder. The end of the cotton season means the end of work. Rain floods the land. Rose of Sharon gives birth to a stillborn child. Ma, desperate to keep her family safe from the floods, leads them to a dry barn not far away. Here, they find a young boy kneeling over his father, who is slowly starving to death. For days, he has been giving all his food to his son. Ma sends the others outside so that Rose of Sharon can nurse the dying man.

CHARACTERS IN *THE GRAPES OF WRATH*

Jim Casy   A former preacher who gave up his ministry out of a belief that all human experience is holy. Often the moral voice of the novel, Casy articulates many of its most important themes, among them the sanctity of the people and the essential unity of humankind.

Connie   Rose of Sharon's husband. Connie is an unrealistic dreamer who abandons the Joads after they reach California. His selfishness and immaturity surprise no one but his naïve wife.

Muley Graves   One of the Joads' neighbors in Oklahoma. When the bank evicts his family, Muley's wife and children move to California, but he stays behind and lives outdoors.

Al Joad   Tom's sixteen-year-old brother. Al, a vain boy, is obsessed with cars and girls. He idolizes Tom, but by the end of the novel he has become his own man.

Granma Joad   Tom Joad's grandmother. A pious Christian, Granma loves casting hellfire and damnation in her husband's direction.

Grampa Joad   Tom Joad's grandfather. The founder of the Joad farm, Grampa used to have a cruel and violent temper, but his advanced age now restricts him to sinful talk. He is mainly a comic character, but he also exhibits a poignant connection to the land.

Ma Joad   The mother of the Joad family. Steinbeck describes Ma as a woman who gladly fulfills her role as "the citadel of the family." She heals the family's ills and arbitrates its arguments. She grows stronger as the family's situation worsens.

Noah Joad   Tom's older brother. Slow and quiet, Noah has been slightly deformed since his birth. He leaves his family behind at a stream near the California border, telling Tom that he feels his parents do not love him as much as they love the other children.

Pa Joad   Ma Joad's husband and Tom's father. Pa, a plainspoken, good-hearted man, must take his family to California after being evicted from his Oklahoma farm. Once there, unable to find work and increasingly desperate, Pa finds himself looking to Ma Joad for strength and leadership.

Ruthie Joad   The second Joad daughter. Ruthie has a fiery relationship with her brother Winfield. Despite their fierce competition, they depend on each other.

Tom Joad   The novel's protagonist. Tom, Ma and Pa Joad's favorite son, is good-natured and thoughtful. He lives fully for the present moment without regretting the past. A wise guide and a fierce protector, Tom earns the awed respect of his family and the workers he organizes into unions.

Winfield Joad   The youngest of the Joad children. Ma worries that without a proper home, Winfield will grow up to be wild and rootless.

Uncle John   Tom's uncle. Years ago, John refused to fetch a doctor for his pregnant wife when she complained of stomach pains. She died as a result, and John has never forgiven himself.

Floyd Knowles   The migrant worker who first inspires Tom and Casy to aspire to labor organization. Floyd's outspokenness sparks a scuffle with the police.

Rose of Sharon   The oldest of Ma and Pa Joad's daughters, and Connie's wife. An impractical, petulant, and romantic young woman, Rose of Sharon has grand notions of making a life for herself in a city until Connie abandons her, and her child is born dead. By the end of the novel, Rose of Sharon has matured considerably.

Agnes Wainwright   The daughter of the couple that shares the Joads' boxcar toward the end of the novel. Agnes and Al Joad get engaged, and Al leaves his family in order to stay with her.

Ivy and Sairy Wilson   A couple traveling to California. The Joads meet them on Highway 66. The Wilsons lend the Joads their tent so that Grampa can have a comfortable place to die, and in return, the Joads fix the couple's broken-down car.

THEMES IN *THE GRAPES OF WRATH*

MAN'S INHUMANITY   Steinbeck points out that people, not bad weather or bad luck, cause the migrants' suffering. He suggests that the division between the privileged from the poor is the primary source of evil and suffering in the world. Historical, social, and economic circumstances separate people into opposing groups: rich and poor, landowner and tenant. Those in power struggle viciously to preserve their positions. In his brief history of California in Chapter Nineteen, Steinbeck portrays the state as the product of land-hungry squatters who took the land from Mexicans. Now, generations later, California's landowners see this historical example as a threat. They believe the influx of migrant farmers might cause history to repeat itself, so they squash the newcomers by treating them like animals, shuffling them from one filthy roadside camp to the next, denying them livable wages, and forcing them to turn against their brethren simply to survive.

THE SAVING POWER OF FAMILY AND FELLOWSHIP   *The Grapes of Wrath* suggests that the migrant workers as a whole are just as much a family as the Joads are. The Joads are joined by blood, but Steinbeck suggests that it is their loyalty and commitment to one another that makes them a family. For migrants, family boundaries must be malleable. For example, when the Joads meet the Wilsons, the two families merge into one unit almost immediately, sharing each other's hardships and committing to each other's survival. In the migrant community, "twenty families became one family, the children were the children of all. The loss of home became one loss, and the golden time in the West was one dream." The unity of the migrant community contrasts with the selfishness of the landowners.

THE DIGNITY OF WRATH   Steinbeck makes a clear connection between dignity and rage. As long as people maintain a sense of injustice and stay angry at those who seek to undercut their pride, he suggests, they will never lose their dignity or compassion. In Chapter Twenty-Nine, the worker women watch their husbands and brothers and sons, reflecting that these men will remain strong "as long as fear [can] turn to wrath." The Joads refuse to be broken by the circumstances that conspire against them. At every turn, they show dignity and honor, especially at the end of the novel, which is a triumph of human kindness over unthinkable circumstances. The Joads have suffered greatly. Noah, Connie, and Tom are gone, Rose of Sharon has given birth to a stillborn baby, and the family has neither food nor promise of work. Yet despite their many troubles, the family manages to perform an act of kindness and generosity for a starving man. They have maintained a belief that all human life, including their own, is valuable.

SYMBOLS IN *THE GRAPES OF WRATH*

ROSE OF SHARON'S PREGNANCY   Rose of Sharon's pregnancy symbolizes the Joads' ability to fend off despair. When Rose of Sharon delivers a stillborn baby, the family moves forward boldly and gracefully, just as they have done in the face of starvation and displacement.

THE DEATH OF THE JOADS' DOG   When the Joads stop for gas, a fancy roadster runs down their dog and leaves it dead in the middle of the road. The gruesome death is the first of many symbols foreshadowing the tragedies that await the family.

IMPORTANT QUOTATIONS FROM *THE GRAPES OF WRATH*

The last clear definite function of man—muscles aching to work, minds aching to create beyond the single need—this is man. To build a wall, to build a house, a dam, and in the wall and house and dam to put something of Manself, and to Manself take back something of the wall, the house, the dam; to take hard muscles from the lifting, to take the clear lines and form from conceiving. For man, unlike any other thing organic or inorganic in the universe, grows beyond his work, walks up the stairs of his concepts, emerges ahead of his accomplishments.

Location: Chapter 14
Speaker: The narrator
Context: Steinbeck emphasizes the need to restore dignity to hard work

Steinbeck does not demonize hard work in *The Grapes of Wrath*—in fact, he thinks hard work is a spiritual necessity. The real evil is not asking people to do hard work, but stripping them of their dignity. In demanding higher wages and fairer treatment, the workers' rights movement seeks to restore dignity to hard work. Only when the workers are respected, when expectations are high and achievement acknowledged, can they find transcendence in labor. This passage is also important because it exemplifies the exalted, highly stylized tone of the brief expository chapters that punctuate the story of the Joads. Linguistically, the passage has an almost biblical tenor: "To build a wall, to build a house, a dam, and in the wall and house and dam to put something of Manself."

Says one time he went out in the wilderness to find his own soul, an' he foun' he didn't have no soul that was his'n. Says he foun' he jus' got a little piece of a great big soul. Says a wilderness ain't no good, 'cause his little piece of a soul wasn't no good 'less it was with the rest, an' was whole.

Location: Chapter Twenty-Eight
Speaker: Tom Joad
Context: As Tom says goodbye to his mother, he tells her about Jim Casy's self-discovery

Tom's words testify to the transformation of his character and echo Casy's definition of holiness. Enlightened by his friend's teaching and his own experiences, Tom no longer focuses his energies only on the present moment. He realizes he has a responsibility to his fellow human beings and looks toward bettering the future and helping future generations of workers. By thinking of the future of his brethren, Tom becomes more than just "a little piece of a great big soul"; he joins with a universal spirit and becomes "whole."

This passage articulates Casy's controversial idea that human connections always takes precedence over an individual's connection to the land. Casy acknowledged the spiritual value of nature by going out into "the wilderness" to find his soul, but he found that the wilderness offered no spiritual sustenance unless he felt joined to other people. Other characters in the novel contest this view: Grampa refuses to leave the Oklahoma farm, and his family drugs him to force him into submission; the Joads' neighbor, Muley Graves, refuses to leave for California with his family, preferring to stay behind and linger on the land that used to be his. Both men resist leaving the land that has shaped their identities. But the Joads, like Casy, believe human connections can sustain life and spirit better than land can.

I got thinkin' how we was holy when we was one thing, an' mankin' was holy when it was one thing. An' it on'y got unholy when one mis'able little fella got the bit in his teeth an' run off his own way, kickin' an' draggin' an' fightin'. Fella like that bust the holi-ness. But when they're all workin' together, not one fella for another fella, but one fella kind of harnessed to the whole shebang—that's right, that's holy.

Location: Chapter Eight
Speaker: Jim Casy
Context: As he says grace over breakfast, Casy explains his definition of holiness

---

"We're Joads. We don't look up to nobody. Grampa's grampa, he fit in the Revolution. We was farm people till the debt. And then—them people. They done somepin to us. Ever' time they come seemed like they was a-whippin' me—all of us. An' in Needles, that police. He done somepin to me, made me feel

mean. *Made me feel ashamed. An' now I ain't ashamed. These folks is our folks—is our folks. An' that manager, he come an' set an' drank coffee, an' he says, 'Mrs. Joad' this, an' 'Mrs. Joad' that—an' 'How you gettin' on, Mrs. Joad?'" She stopped and sighed. "Why, I feel like people again."*

Location: Chapter Twenty-Two
Speaker: Ma Joad
Context: Ma Joad explains how the camp manager's kindness makes her feel human again

---

Wherever they's a fight so hungry people can eat, I'll be there. Wherever they's a cop beatin' up a guy, I'll be there. If Casy knowed, why, I'll be in the way guys yell when they're mad an'—I'll be in the way kids laugh when they're hungry n' they know supper's ready. An' when our folks eat the stuff they raise an' live in the houses they build—why, I'll be there. See? God, I'm talkin' like Casy. Comes of thinkin' about him so much. Seems like I can see him sometimes.

Location: Chapter Twenty-Eight
Speaker: Tom Joad
Context: After the death of Jim Casy, Tom reassures his mother that he will not lose his life in the worker's movement

GREAT EXPECTATIONS

Charles Dickens

After a kindly criminal makes him rich, a boy learns that wealth and class do not determine worth.

THE LIFE OF CHARLES DICKENS

Charles Dickens was born on February 7, 1812. He spent the first ten years of his life in Kent, a marshy region by the sea in the east of England. Dickens was the second of eight children. His father, John Dickens, was kind and likable, but fiscally irresponsible. His huge debts caused tremendous strain on his family.

When Dickens was ten, his family moved to London. Two years later, his father was arrested and thrown in debtors' prison. Dickens's mother moved into the prison with seven of her children. Charles tried to earn money for the struggling family. For three months, he worked with other children pasting labels on bottles in a blacking warehouse. Dickens found the three months he spent apart from his family highly traumatic. Not only was the job itself miserable, but he considered himself too good for it, earning the contempt of the other children. His experiences at this warehouse inspired passages of *David Copperfield*.

An inheritance gave John Dickens enough money to free himself from his debt and from prison. Dickens attended Wellington House Academy for two years. He became a law clerk, then a newspaper reporter, and finally a novelist. His first novel, *The Pickwick Papers* (1837), met with huge popular success. Dickens was a literary celebrity in England for the rest of his life.

Dickens's work includes *Oliver Twist* (1837–1839), *Nicholas Nickelby* (1838–1839), and *A Christmas Carol* (1843). Perhaps his best known novel, *Great Expectations* (1860–1861) shares many thematic similarities with *David Copperfield*. Dickens died in Kent on June 9, 1870, at the age of fifty-eight.

GREAT EXPECTATIONS IN CONTEXT

In *Great Expectations*, Dickens mines his early life for material. Aside from *David Copperfield*, *Great Expectations* is his most autobiographical novel. Pip, the novel's protagonist, lives in the marsh country, works at a job he hates, considers himself too good for his surroundings, and experiences material success in London at a very early age, exactly as Dickens did. In addition, one of the novel's most appealing characters, Wemmick, is a law clerk.

Great Expectations is set in early Victorian England, a time when great social changes were sweeping the nation. The Industrial Revolution of the late eighteenth and early nineteenth centuries had transformed the social landscape, enabling capitalists and manufacturers to amass huge fortunes. Although birth was no longer the sole factor in determining social class, the divisions between rich and poor remained nearly as wide as ever. London teemed with people as job-seekers moved from the country to the city. These conditions inform Pip's progress in *Great Expectations*. He goes from country laborer to city gentleman, moving from one social extreme to another while dealing with the strict rules that governed Victorian England society.

GREAT EXPECTATIONS: KEY FACTS

Time and place written: 1860–1861; London,

Date of first publication: Published serially in England from December 1860 to August 1861; published in book form in England and America in 1861

Publisher: Serialized in *All the Year Round*; published in England by Chapman & Hall; published in America by Harper & Brothers

Type of work: Novel	

Type of work: Novel

Genre: Bildungsroman, social protest novel, autobiographical novel

Language: English

Setting (time): Mid-nineteenth century

Settings (place): Kent and London, England

Tense: Past

Tone: Comic, satirical, wry, critical, sentimental, dark

Narrator: Pip in the first person

Point of view: Pip's

Protagonist: Pip

Antagonist: Magwitch, Mrs. Joe, Miss Havisham, Estella, Orlick, Bentley Drummle, and Compeyson

GREAT EXPECTATIONS: PLOT OVERVIEW

Pip, a young orphan who lives with his sister and her husband in the marshes of Kent, is sitting in a cemetery one evening looking at his parents' tombstones. Suddenly, an escaped convict springs up from behind a tombstone, grabs Pip, and orders him to bring him food and a file for his leg irons. Pip obeys. The fearsome convict is soon captured, but he protects Pip by claiming to have stolen the items himself.

One day Pip's wealthy Uncle Pumblechook takes him to Satis House, the home of the wealthy, eccentric dowager Miss Havisham, who wears an old wedding dress and keeps all the clocks in her house stopped at the same time. At Miss Havisham's, Pip meets a beautiful young girl named Estella. She treats him contemptuously, but he falls in love with her and dreams of becoming a wealthy gentleman so that he might be worthy of her.

With Miss Havisham's guidance, Pip is apprenticed to his brother-in-law, Joe, who is the village blacksmith. Pip, unhappy in the forge, struggles to better his education with the help of Biddy, his plain, kind friend. One night, Pip has an altercation with Orlick, a vicious employee of Joe's. Pip's sister, known as Mrs. Joe, is viciously attacked and becomes a mute invalid. From her signals, Pip suspects that Orlick was responsible for the attack.

One day a lawyer named Jaggers appears with strange news: a secret benefactor has given Pip a large fortune, and Pip must come to London immediately to begin his education as a gentleman. Pip assumes that Miss Havisham is his secret benefactor. In London, Pip befriends a young gentleman named Herbert Pocket and Jaggers's law clerk, Wemmick. He disdains his former friends and loved ones, especially his brother-in-law, but he continues to pine for Estella. He studies with Matthew Pocket, Herbert's father. Herbert helps Pip learn how to act like a gentleman. Pip plans to help Herbert in business once he turns twenty-one and begins to receive an income from his fortune. For now, Herbert and Pip lead a fairly undisciplined life in London, enjoying themselves and running up debts. Orlick reappears in Pip's life, employed as Miss Havisham's porter, but Jaggers fires him after Pip reveals Orlick's unsavory past. Mrs. Joe dies, and Pip goes home for the funeral, feeling tremendous grief and remorse.

Several years go by. One night a familiar figure barges into Pip's room—the convict, Magwitch, who stuns Pip by announcing that he, not Miss Havisham, is the source of Pip's fortune. He was so moved by Pip's boyhood kindness that he dedicated his life to making Pip a gentleman, and he made a fortune in Australia for that very purpose.

Pip is appalled, but he feels morally bound to help Magwitch escape London. The convict is being pursued both by the police and by Compeyson, his former partner in crime. Pip discovers that Compeyson is the gentleman who abandoned Miss Havisham at the altar. He also realizes that Estella is Magwitch's daughter. Estella's mother is Molly, Jaggers's housekeeper. Miss Havisham has raised Estella to break men's hearts as revenge for the pain her own broken heart caused her. Miss Havisham saw Pip as a boy for Estella to practice on.

As the weeks pass, Pip sees the good in Magwitch and begins to care for him deeply. Estella marries an upper-class lout named Bentley Drummle. Pip makes a visit to Satis House, where Miss Havisham begs and receives his forgiveness for the way she has treated him in the past. Later that day, she bends over the fireplace and her clothing catches fire. She survives but becomes an invalid. In her final days, she will continue to repent for her misdeeds and to plead for Pip's forgiveness.

The time comes for Pip and his friends to spirit Magwitch away from London. Just before the escape attempt, Pip is called to a shadowy meeting in the marshes, where he encounters the vengeful Orlick. Orlick is on the verge of killing Pip when Herbert arrives with a group of friends and saves Pip's life. Pip and Herbert hurry back to effect Magwitch's escape. They try to sneak Magwitch down the river on a rowboat, but Compeyson tipped off the police and the plot is discovered. Magwitch and Compeyson fight in the river, and Compeyson drowns. Magwitch is sentenced to death, and Pip loses his fortune. Magwitch feels that his sentence is God's forgiveness and dies at peace.

Pip falls ill. Joe comes to London to care for him, and they reconcile. Joe gives him the news: Orlick has robbed Pumblechook and is in jail; Miss Havisham has died and left most of her fortune to the Pockets; and Biddy has taught Joe how to read and write. Pip decides to rush home after him and marry Biddy, but when he arrives he discovers that she and Joe have already married.

Pip decides to go abroad with Herbert to work in the mercantile trade. Many years later, he returns and encounters Estella in the ruined garden at Satis House. Drummle, Estella's husband, treated her badly, but he is now dead. Pip finds that Estella's coldness and cruelty have been replaced by a sad kindness. The two leave the garden hand in hand. Pip believes they will never part again. (Note: In Dickens's original ending to *Great Expectations*, Pip hears that Estella has remarried. One day he runs into Estella. They have a very brief meeting and shake hands.)

CHARACTERS IN *GREAT EXPECTATIONS*

Biddy A simple, kindhearted country girl. Biddy befriends Pip at school. After Mrs. Joe is attacked, Biddy cares for her. Biddy is Estella's opposite—plain, kind, moral, and of Pip's own social class.

Compeyson A criminal and the former partner of Magwitch. Compeyson is an educated, gentlemanly outlaw who left Miss Havisham at the altar.

Bentley Drummle An unpleasant young man. Drummle feels superior because he is a minor member of the nobility. Eventually he marries Estella.

Estella Miss Havisham's beautiful young ward. Estella sometimes seems to consider Pip a friend, but she is usually cold and cruel to him. She repeatedly warns him that she has no heart.

Joe Gargery Pip's brother-in-law. Joe stays with Mrs. Joe, his overbearing, abusive wife, solely out of love for Pip. Joe's quiet goodness makes him one of the few completely sympathetic characters in *Great Expectations*. Although he is uneducated and unrefined, he is deeply good to those he loves.

Miss Havisham A wealthy, eccentric old woman. Miss Havisham often seems insane, flitting around her house in a faded wedding dress and keeping a decaying feast on her table. As a young woman, Miss Havisham was jilted by her fiancé minutes before her wedding, and now she has a vendetta against all men. She deliberately raises Estella to be the tool of her revenge, training her to break men's hearts.

Jaggers A powerful, foreboding lawyer. Despite his worldliness and impenetrability, Jaggers often seems to care for Pip. He also helps Miss Havisham adopt the orphaned Estella. Jaggers washes his hands obsessively in an attempt to keep criminals from corrupting him.

Mrs. Joe Pip's sister and Joe's wife, known only as "Mrs. Joe." A stern and overbearing woman, Mrs. Joe keeps her house spotless and frequently menaces her husband and her brother with her cane, which she calls "Tickler." She also forces them to drink a foul-tasting concoction called tar-water. Mrs. Joe is petty and ambitious.

Abel Magwitch ("The Convict") A fearsome criminal. After Pip shows him kindness, Magwitch becomes Pip's secret benefactor.

Molly Jaggers's housekeeper and Estella's mother.

Dolge Orlick The day laborer in Joe's forge. Orlick is a slouching, oafish embodiment of evil. He attacks Mrs. Joe and almost murders Pip.

Pip The protagonist and narrator of the novel. Pip is passionate, romantic, and somewhat unrealistic. He has unreasonably high expectations for his life. Pip also has a powerful conscience and real commitment to improving himself, both morally and socially.

Herbert Pocket Pip's best friend after Pip becomes a gentleman. Herbert nicknames Pip "Handel." He is the son of Matthew Pocket, Miss Havisham's cousin, and he hopes to become a merchant so that he can afford to marry Clara Barley.

Uncle Pumblechook Joe's pompous, arrogant uncle. A merchant obsessed with money, Pumblechook shamelessly takes credit for Pip's rise in social status.

Miss Skiffins Wemmick's wife.

Startop A friend of Pip's and Herbert's. Startop is a delicate young man who helps with Magwitch's escape.

Wemmick Jaggers's clerk and Pip's friend. At work, Wemmick is cynical and sarcastic, but at home in Walworth, he is jovial, wry, and tender to his "Aged Parent."

Mr. Wopsle The church clerk in Pip's country town. Sometime after Pip becomes a gentleman, Mr. Wopsle moves to London and becomes an actor.

THEMES IN *GREAT EXPECTATIONS*

THE AMBIGUOUS VALUE OF AMBITION Pip's desire for self-improvement gives the novel its title: because he believes in the possibility of advancement in life, he has "great expectations" about his future. Ambition and self-improvement take three forms in *Great Expectations*—moral, social, and educational. These motivate Pip's best and worst behavior. Pip wants to improve his morals. He is extremely hard on himself when he acts immorally and his powerful guilt makes him act better in the future. Second, Pip wants to improve his social standing. He longs to become a member of Estella's social class and entertains fantasies of becoming a gentleman. Dickens makes it clear that Pip's life as a gentleman is no more satisfying—and certainly no more moral—than his life as a blacksmith's apprentice. Third, Pip wants to improve his education. This desire is connected to his social ambition: gentleman must be educated. Ultimately, through the examples of Joe, Biddy, and Magwitch, Pip learns that only moral improvement is relevant to real worth. The moral theme of *Great Expectations* is a simple one: affection, loyalty, and conscience are more important than social advancement, wealth, and class.

THE UNIMPORTANCE OF SOCIAL CLASS IN JUDGING CHARACTER In *Great Expectations*, Dickens explores the range of the class system of Victorian England, from wretched criminals (Magwitch) to poor peasants (Joe and Biddy) to the middle class (Pumblechook) to the very rich (Miss Havisham). Dickens suggests that wealth and class are not accurate indicators of inner worth. Drummle, for instance, is an upper-class lout, while Magwitch is a persecuted convict with deep worth. Perhaps because the class system Dickens portrays is post-Industrial Revolution, he generally ignores the nobility and the hereditary aristocracy and focuses on characters whose fortunes have been earned through commerce. Even Miss Havisham's family fortune was made through the brewery that is still connected to her manor.

THE UNRELIABILITY OF THE JUSTICE SYSTEM From the handcuffs Joe mends at the smithy to the gallows at the prison in London, the imagery of crime pervades the book. In general, just as social class is an unreliable barometer of worth, the criminal justice system is an untrustworthy judge of character. Initially, Pip does not understand that those people society calls criminals are not necessarily evil. At first Magwitch frightens Pip simply because he is a convict, and Pip feels guilty for helping him for the same reason. By the end of the novel, however, Pip has discovered Magwitch's inner nobility and learned to disregard his criminal status.

SYMBOLS IN *GREAT EXPECTATIONS*

SATIS HOUSE In *Great Expectations*, settings are almost always symbolic. In Satis House, Dickens creates a magnificent Gothic setting whose various elements symbolize Pip's romantic perception of the upper class. On her decaying body, Miss Havisham's wedding dress becomes an ironic symbol of death and degeneration. The wedding dress and the wedding feast symbolize Miss Havisham's past, and the stopped clocks symbolize her determined attempt to freeze time. The brewery next to the house symbolizes the connection between commerce and wealth: Miss Havisham's fortune is the product of recent success in industrial capitalism.

THE MISTS ON THE MARSHES The misty marshes near Pip's childhood home in Kent symbolize danger and uncertainty. As a child, Pip brings Magwitch a file and food in these mists; later, he is kidnapped by Orlick and nearly murdered in them. Pip must go through the mists when he travels to London shortly after receiving his fortune, alerting the reader that this apparently positive development in his life may have dangerous consequences.

IMPORTANT QUOTATIONS FROM *GREAT EXPECTATIONS*

My convict looked round him for the first time, and saw me.... I looked at him eagerly when he looked at me, and slightly moved my hands and shook my head. I had been waiting for him to see me, that I might try to assure him of my innocence. It was not at all expressed to me that he even comprehended my intention, for he gave me a look that I did not understand, and it all passed in a moment. But if he had looked at me for an hour or for a day, I could not have remembered his face ever afterwards as having been more attentive.

Location: Chapter 5
Speaker: Pip
Context: Silently, Pip tries to tell Magwitch that it was not he who turned Magwitch in to the police

Pip, who is always concerned with other people's impressions of his behavior, is anxious for Magwitch to know that he did not betray him. But when Magwitch looks at Pip, he has feelings that have nothing to do with Pip's innocence or guilt. He gives Pip an inscrutable look that is the most "attentive" Pip has ever received. This is an important moment of foreshadowing in the novel, our first impression that Pip's kindness has moved Magwitch to strong feelings of loyalty and love. It is also an important moment of character development. For the first time, we glimpse something in Magwitch's character beyond the menace and bluster of his early scenes.

"Pip, dear old chap, life is made of ever so many partings welded together, as I may say, and one man's a blacksmith, and one's a whitesmith, and one's a goldsmith, and one's a coppersmith. Divisions among such must come, and must be met as they come."

Location: Chapter 27
Speaker: Joe
Context: Pip and Joe have an uncomfortable meeting in London

Pip, now a gentleman, is embarrassed by both Joe's commonness and his own opulent lifestyle. Unpretentious Joe feels like a fish out of water in Pip's sumptuous apartment. He tells Pip that he does not blame him for the awkwardness of their meeting, but instead chalks it up to the natural divisions of life. Joe concocts a metaphor of metalsmithing to describe these natural divisions: some men are blacksmiths, such as Joe, and some men are goldsmiths, such as Pip. In these simple terms, Joe arrives at a wise and resigned position toward the changes in Pip's social class that have driven them apart. He shows his essential goodness and loyalty by blaming the division not on Pip but on the unalterable nature of the human condition.

"[I]f you had taught [your adopted daughter], from the dawn of her intelligence, with your utmost energy and might, that there was such a thing as daylight, but that it was made to be her enemy and destroyer, and she must always turn against it, for it had blighted you and would else blight her—if you had done this, and then, for a purpose, had wanted her to take naturally to the daylight and she could not do it, you would have been disappointed and angry?. . ."

"So," said Estella, "I must be taken as I have been made. The success is not mine, the failure is not mine, but the two together make me."

Location: Chapter 38
Speaker: Estella
Context: Miss Havisham complains that Estella treats her coldly, and Estella explains that Miss Havisham expects her to know love even though she has taught her to hate love

---

"Look'ee here, Pip. I'm your second father. You're my son—more to me nor any son. I've put away money, only for you to spend. When I was a hired-out shepherd in a solitary hut, not seeing no faces but faces of sheep till I half-forgot wot men's and women's faces wos like, I see yourn.. . . I see you there a many times plain as ever I see you on them misty marshes. 'Lord strike me dead!' I says each time—and I goes out in the open air to say it under the open heavens—'but wot, if I gets liberty and money, I'll make that boy a gentleman!' And I done it. Why, look at you, dear boy! Look at these here lodgings of yourn, fit for a lord! A lord? Ah! You shall show money with lords for wagers, and beat 'em!"

Location: Chapter 39
Speaker: Magwitch
Context: Magwitch reveals that he is Pip's benefactor

"Dear Magwitch, I must tell you, now at last. You understand what I say?"
    A gentle pressure on my hand.
    "You had a child once, whom you loved and lost."
    A stronger pressure on my hand.
    "She lived and found powerful friends. She is living now. She is a lady and very beautiful. And I love her!"

Location: Chapter 56
Speaker: Pip
Context: Pip tells the dying Magwitch about his daughter, Estella

THE GREAT GATSBY

F. Scott Fitzgerald

A self-made man woos and loses the aristocratic woman he loves.

THE LIFE OF F. SCOTT FITZGERALD

Francis Scott Key Fitzgerald was born in St. Paul, Minnesota, in 1896. He was named after Francis Scott Key, Fitzgerald's ancestor and the composer of "The Star-Spangled Banner." Although he was a bad student, Fitzgerald managed to get into Princeton in 1913. Plagued by apathy and academic troubles, he dropped out in 1917, at the tail end of World War I, and joined the army. As a second lieutenant, Fitzgerald was stationed at Camp Sheridan in Montgomery, Alabama, where he met and fell in love with Zelda Sayre, the beautiful and wild seventeen-year-old daughter of an Alabama Supreme Court judge. Zelda finally agreed to marry Fitzgerald after his first novel, *This Side of Paradise*, propelled him into literary stardom in 1920.

As a celebrity, Fitzgerald fell into a wild, reckless lifestyle of parties and decadence. Simultaneously, he desperately tried to please Zelda by writing to earn money. As the giddiness of the Roaring Twenties dissolved into the bleakness of the Great Depression, Zelda suffered a nervous breakdown and Fitzgerald battled alcoholism, which hampered his writing. He published *The Great Gatsby* in 1925, *Tender Is the Night* in 1934, and short stories in *The Saturday Evening Post*. In 1937, he went to Hollywood to write screenplays. He died of a heart attack at the age of forty-four while working on his novel *The Love of the Last Tycoon*.

THE GREAT GATSBY IN CONTEXT

Fitzgerald is the most famous chronicler of 1920s America, an era that he dubbed "the Jazz Age." *The Great Gatsby* is one of the greatest literary documents of this period. During the 1920s, the American economy soared, bringing unprecedented prosperity to the nation. Prohibition, the ban on the sale and consumption of alcohol mandated by the Eighteenth Amendment to the Constitution (1919), made millionaires out of bootleggers and fostered an underground culture of revelry. Sprawling private parties tried to elude police notice, and speakeasies—secret clubs that sold liquor—thrived. The chaos and violence of World War I left America in a state of shock, and the generation that fought the war turned to wild and extravagant living in response. The staid conservatism and values of the previous decade were turned on their ear as money, opulence, and exuberance became the order of the day.

Like Nick in *The Great Gatsby*, Fitzgerald found this new lifestyle seductive and exciting. Also like Nick, he had always idolized the very rich. Like Gatsby, he was driven by his love for a woman who symbolized everything he wanted, even as she led him toward everything he despised. He found fame in an era in which unrestrained materialism set the tone of society, particularly in the large cities of the East. Even so, Fitzgerald, like Nick, saw through the glitter of the Jazz Age to the moral emptiness and hypocrisy beneath, and part of him longed for a moral center. In many ways, *The Great Gatsby* represents Fitzgerald's attempt to confront his conflicting feelings about the Jazz Age.

THE GREAT GATSBY: KEY FACTS

Time and place written: 1923–1924; America and France

Date of publication: 1925

Publisher: Charles Scribner's Sons

Type of work: Novel

Genre: Modernist novel

Language: English

Setting (time): Summer of 1922

Setting (place): Long Island and New York City

Tense: Past

Tone: Disapproving, nostalgic, elegiac

Narrator: Nick Carraway in the first and third person

Point of view: Nick Carraway's

Protagonist: Gatsby; Nick Carraway

Antagonist: The heady New York lifestyle and America, which encourages and then crushes self-invention and grand dreams

THE GREAT GATSBY: PLOT OVERVIEW

Nick Carraway, a young Minnesotan, moves to New York in the summer of 1922 to learn about the bond business. He rents a house in the West Egg district of Long Island, a wealthy but unfashionable area populated by the *nouveaux riches*—those who have made their fortunes too recently to have established social connections and who are prone to garish displays of wealth. Nick's next-door neighbor in West Egg is a mysterious man named Jay Gatsby, who lives in a gigantic Gothic mansion and throws extravagant parties every Saturday night.

Nick is unlike the other inhabitants of West Egg. He was educated at Yale and has social connections in East Egg, a fashionable area of Long Island populated by the established upper class. Nick drives out to East Egg one evening for dinner with his cousin Daisy Buchanan and her husband Tom, a fellow Yalie. Daisy and Tom introduce Nick to Jordan Baker, a beautiful, cynical young woman with whom Nick begins a romantic relationship. Nick also learns a little about Daisy and Tom's marriage. Jordan tells him that Tom is having an affair with a woman named Myrtle Wilson, who lives in the valley of ashes, a gray industrial wasteland between West Egg and New York City. Nick soon travels to New York City with Tom and Myrtle. At a vulgar, gaudy party in the apartment that Tom keeps for the affair, Myrtle begins to taunt Tom about Daisy. Tom breaks her nose.

Later in the summer, Nick is invited to one of Gatsby's legendary parties. At the party, he encounters Jordan Baker, and the two of them meet Gatsby himself, a surprisingly young man who affects an English accent, has a remarkable smile, and calls everyone "old sport." Gatsby asks to speak to Jordan alone. Through Jordan, Nick later learns more about his mysterious neighbor. Gatsby met Daisy in Louisville in 1917. He spends many nights staring across the bay to the green light at the end of her dock. Gatsby's extravagant lifestyle and wild parties are only attempts to impress Daisy. Gatsby wants Nick to arrange a reunion between himself and Daisy, but he is afraid that Daisy will refuse to see him if she knows that he still loves her. Nick invites Daisy to have tea at his house without telling her that Gatsby will also be there. After an initially awkward reunion, Gatsby and Daisy reestablish their connection. Their love rekindles and they begin an affair.

As the summer progresses, Tom grows increasingly suspicious of his wife's relationship with Gatsby. At a luncheon at the Buchanans' house, Gatsby stares at Daisy with such undisguised passion that Tom realizes Gatsby is in love with her. Tom is outraged by the possibility that his wife could be unfaithful. He forces everyone to drive into New York City, where he confronts Gatsby in a suite at the Plaza Hotel. Tom says he and Daisy have a history that Gatsby could never understand and tells Daisy that Gatsby is a criminal because his fortune has come from bootlegging alcohol and other illegal activities. Daisy realizes that her allegiance is to Tom, and Tom contemptuously sends her back to East Egg alone with Gatsby to prove that Gatsby cannot hurt him.

As Nick, Jordan, and Tom drive back through the valley of ashes in another car, they discover that Gatsby's car has struck and killed Tom's lover Myrtle. Back in Long Island, Nick learns from Gatsby that Daisy was behind the wheel, but that Gatsby intends to take the blame for Myrtle's death. The next day, Tom tells Myrtle's husband, George, that Gatsby was the driver of the car. George has leaped to the conclusion that the driver of the car that killed Myrtle must have been her lover. He finds Gatsby in the pool at his mansion and shoots him dead. He then fatally shoots himself.

Nick stages a small funeral for Gatsby, ends his relationship with Jordan, and moves back to the Midwest to escape the disgust he feels at the emptiness and moral decay of life among the wealthy on the East Coast. Nick reflects that just as Gatsby's dream of Daisy was corrupted by money and dishonesty, the American dream of happiness and individualism has disintegrated into a pursuit of wealth. Though

Gatsby's power to transform his dreams into reality is what makes him great, Nick thinks the era of dreaming—both Gatsby's dream and the American dream—is over.

CHARACTERS IN *THE GREAT GATSBY*

Jordan Baker Daisy's beautiful friend and Nick's sometime lover. A competitive golfer, Jordan is one of the "new women" of the 1920s—cynical, boyish, and self-centered. She cheated to win her first golf tournament and often bends the truth.

Daisy Buchanan Nick's cousin and Gatsby's object of adoration. Daisy and Gatsby met in Louisville, Daisy's hometown, and got engaged, or something close to it. During the war, Daisy broke her promise to wait for Gatsby and married powerful, wealthy Tom Buchanan. Now a beautiful socialite, Daisy lives with Tom in fashionable, upper-class East Egg and feigns sardonic flippancy to mask her pain at her husband's infidelity.

Tom Buchanan Daisy's husband. Tom, who is a former member of Nick's social club at Yale, comes from old money. An arrogant, bigoted, powerful-built bully, Tom cheats on Daisy but is outraged at the thought that Daisy and Gatsby may be having an affair.

Nick Carraway The novel's narrator. Nick is a young Yale graduate from Minnesota and a veteran of World War I. He moves to New York to learn about bonds and settles in *nouveau riche* West Egg, next door to Gatsby's mansion. Nick reunites Daisy, his cousin, and Gatsby, his friend. Nick becomes a confidant for those with troubling secrets. He proclaims himself honest, tolerant, and inclined to reserve judgment, but he is not a reliable narrator.

Jay Gatsby The title character and, with Nick, one of the novel's protagonists. After working for a millionaire, Gatsby decided to dedicate his life to getting rich, and made a fortune through criminal activity. Gatsby lives in a Gothic mansion in West Egg and throws lavish parties every Saturday night in an attempt to impress Daisy, the woman he loves. Nick views Gatsby as a deeply flawed man, dishonest and vulgar, but also a great one because of his extraordinary optimism and power to transform his dreams into reality.

Klipspringer A shallow freeloader who essentially lives in Gatsby's mansion. After Gatsby's death, Klipspringer disappears without attending the funeral, but later calls Nick about a pair of tennis shoes he left behind at Gatsby's house.

Owl Eyes An eccentric, bespectacled drunk. Nick meets Owl Eyes at one of Gatsby's parties. Owl Eyes claims to be surprised that the books in Gatsby's library are real.

George Wilson Myrtle's husband. George Wilson is the lifeless, exhausted owner of a run-down auto shop at the edge of the valley of ashes. George loves and idealizes Myrtle, and is devastated by her affair with Tom and her death. George is a dreamer ruined by unrequited love.

Myrtle Wilson Tom's lover and George's wife. Myrtle is fiercely vital and desperate to improve her lot in life. Tom treats her as a mere object of desire.

THEMES IN *THE GREAT GATSBY*

THE POSTWAR DECLINE OF THE AMERICAN DREAM Fitzgerald portrays the 1920s as an era of decayed social and moral values, a time of cynicism, greed, and the empty pursuit of pleasure. He suggests that the reckless jubilance that led to decadent parties and wild jazz music—epitomized in *The Great Gatsby* by the opulent parties that Gatsby throws every Saturday night—lead not to happiness, but to the corruption of the American dream, as the unrestrained desire for money and pleasure surpass more noble goals.

NOUVEAU RICHE VERSUS OLD MONEY *The Great Gatsby* examines the sociology of wealth. Specifically, it investigates how the newly minted millionaires of the 1920s differ from and relate to the old aristocracy of the country's richest families. In the novel, West Egg and its inhabitants represent the newly rich, while East Egg and its inhabitants, especially Daisy and Tom, represent the old aristocracy. Fitzgerald portrays the newly rich as vulgar, gaudy, ostentatious, and lacking in social graces and taste. Gatsby, for example, lives in a monstrously ornate mansion, wears a pink suit, drives a Rolls-Royce, and does not pick up on subtle social signals, such as the insincerity of the Sloanes' invitation to lunch. In contrast, he portrays the old aristocracy as graceful, tasteful, subtle, and elegant, epitomized by the Buchanans' tasteful home and the flowing white dresses of Daisy and Jordan Baker.

SYMBOLS IN *THE GREAT GATSBY*

THE GREEN LIGHT Situated at the end of Daisy's East Egg dock and barely visible from Gatsby's West Egg lawn, the green light represents Gatsby's hopes and dreams. Gatsby associates it with Daisy, and in Chapter I he reaches toward it in the darkness as if reaching toward Daisy or beseeching the light to guide him. The green light also symbolizes the American dream, with which Gatsby's quest for Daisy is broadly associated. In Chapter IX, Nick compares the green light to America, saying it looks like America must have looked to early settlers of the new nation.

THE EYES OF DOCTOR T. J. ECKLEBURG The eyes of Doctor T. J. Eckleburg are a painted pair of fading, bespectacled eyes on an old advertising billboard overlooking the valley of ashes. Fitzgerald does not give them a specific meaning. Instead, he uses them to suggest that objects only have symbolic meaning because characters imagine that they do. George Wilson, for example, imagines that the eyes represent God staring down on and judging American society as a moral wasteland, but Fitzgerald does not confirm this interpretation. This lack of concrete significance makes the image an unsettling one. In the eyes' lack of definite symbolism, they represent the essential meaninglessness of the world and the arbitrariness of the mental process by which people invest objects with meaning. Nick explores these ideas in Chapter VIII, when he imagines that in his final moments, Gatsby thought about the emptiness of symbols and dreams.

THE VALLEY OF ASHES, EAST EGG, WEST EGG, AND NEW YORK CITY Each of the novel's four key settings symbolize a lifestyle or character. West Egg, like Gatsby, is full of garish extravagance, symbolizing the emergence of the *nouveau riche* alongside the established aristocracy. East Egg is like the Buchanans: wealthy, possessed of high social status, and powerful. It symbolizes the old upper class that continued to dominate the American social landscape despite the emergence of the newly rich. The valley of ashes is like George Wilson: desolate, desperate, and utterly without hope, symbolizing the moral decay of American society hidden by the glittering surface of upper-class extravagance. New York City symbolizes chaos, an abundant swell of variety and life associated with the "quality of distortion" that Nick perceives in the East in general.

IMPORTANT QUOTATIONS EXPLAINED

He had one of those rare smiles with a quality of eternal reassurance in it, that you may come across four or five times in life. It faced, or seemed to face, the whole external world for an instant and then concentrated on you with an irresistible prejudice in your favor. It understood you just as far as you wanted to be understood, believed in you as you would like to believe in yourself.

Location: Chapter III
Speaker: Nick Carraway
Context: Nick describes Gatsby soon after meeting him

This passage is part of Nick's first close examination of Gatsby's character and appearance. His description of Gatsby's smile captures both Gatsby's charisma and the theatrical quality of his character. Nick's description also encapsulates how Gatsby appears to the outside world, an image Fitzgerald slowly deconstructs as the novel progresses toward Gatsby's death in Chapter VIII. A crucial fact about Gatsby's persona is that he is acting out a role he defined for himself when he was seventeen years old. His smile seems to be both an important part of that role and a result of the singular combination of hope and imagination that enables him to play it so effectively. Here, Nick describes Gatsby's rare focus. Gatsby has the ability to make the recipient of his smile feel that he or she has been chosen out of "the whole external world." Gatsby's attention bathes people in a happy, friendly light and makes them feel understood and satisfied with themselves.

That's my Middle West . . . the street lamps and sleigh bells in the frosty dark.. . . I see now that this has been a story of the West, after all—Tom and Gatsby, Daisy and Jordan and I, were all Westerners, and perhaps we possessed some deficiency in common which made us subtly unadaptable to Eastern life.

Location: Chapter IX
Speaker: Nick Carraway as narrator
Context: Two years after Gatsby's death, Nick muses on his and Gatsby's story

This quotation from Nick's lengthy meditation in Chapter IX concludes the motif of geography in *The Great Gatsby*. Throughout the novel, Fitzgerald associates places with certain themes, characters, and ideas. He associates the East with a fast-paced lifestyle, decadent parties, crumbling moral values, and the pursuit of wealth, while he associates the West and the Midwest with more traditional moral values. In this passage, Nick realizes for the first time that though his story is set on the East Coast, the western character of his acquaintances ("some deficiency in common") is the source of the story's tensions and attitudes. He believes each character's behavior and choices are a reaction to the wealth-obsessed culture of New York. This perspective contributes powerfully to Nick's decision to leave the East Coast and return to Minnesota. The clash of Nick's Midwestern values with New York society parallels the impracticality of Gatsby's dream.

I hope she'll be a fool—that's the best thing a girl can be in this world, a beautiful little fool.

Location: Chapter I
Speaker: Daisy to Nick and Jordan
Context: Daisy describes her hopes for her infant daughter

The truth was that Jay Gatsby, of West Egg, Long Island, sprang from his Platonic conception of himself. He was a son of God—a phrase which, if it means anything, means just that—and he must be about His Father's business, the service of a vast, vulgar, and meretricious beauty. So he invented just the sort of Jay Gatsby that a seventeen-year-old boy would be likely to invent, and to this conception he was faithful to the end.

Location: Chapter IV
Speaker: Nick Carraway
Context: Nick describes Gatsby's background, comparing Gatsby to Jesus—who, according to a nineteenth-century theory of Ernest Renan's, decided to make himself the son of God and then brought himself to ruin by refusing to acknowledge his self-deception

---

Gatsby believed in the green light, the orgastic future that year by year recedes before us. It eluded us then, but that's no matter—tomorrow we will run faster, stretch out our arms farther.. . . And then one fine morning—
  So we beat on, boats against the current, borne back ceaselessly into the past.

Location: Chapter IX, the novel's concluding words
Speaker: Nick Carraway
Context: Nick concludes his narrative with a melancholy metaphor summarizing both Gatsby's struggle and the American dream

GRENDEL

John Gardner

The monster of Beowulf longs to take part in human communities and struggles to reconcile his intellectual knowledge that the world is meaningless with his emotional desire to believe art's promise that life has meaning.

THE LIFE OF JOHN GARDNER

John Champlin Gardner was born in Batavia, New York, on July 21, 1933, to John Champlin, a dairy farmer and lay Presbyterian preacher, and Priscilla Gardner, an English teacher. When he was eleven years old, Gardner accidentally killed his younger brother Gilbert in a gruesome accident, running him over with a heavy farm machine. The incident haunted Gardner for the rest of his life and informed much of his work, particularly the posthumously published novel *Stillness* (1986).

Gardner graduated Phi Beta Kappa from Washington University in St. Louis in 1955 and then studied medieval literature and creative writing at the University of Iowa. His doctoral dissertation was a novel called *The Old Men*. After earning his Ph.D., Gardner gained prominence as a teacher of creative writing.

Gardner, a prolific and mercurial writer, produced a remarkable thirty-five volumes in just twenty-five years. Though most noted for his novels, Gardner also published poetry, plays, short stories, opera librettos, scholarly texts, and children's picture books. Critical response to Gardner's work has been divided. *Grendel* (1971) was the first and only Gardner volume to receive near-unanimous critical acclaim, though three of his novels—*The Sunlight Dialogues* (1972), *Nickel Mountain*, and *October Light* (1976)—were popular best-sellers.

Though Gardner and his contemporaries wrote highly inventive, genre-bending works of literature in the 1970s, Gardner was never a career postmodernist. Critics could never agree on whether Gardner was a traditionalist masquerading as an innovator or vice versa. Gardner himself rejected the postmodern label. In the literary manifesto *On Moral Fiction* (1978), Gardner calls for art that uplifts, decrying contemporary literature as too cynical and fatalistic. The book's moralizing enraged the literary community and sparked a nationwide debate. Reviewers attacked not only Gardner's smugness but also what they perceived as shoddy reasoning.

Gardner published several more works after the publicity disaster of *On Moral Fiction*, but, with the possible exception of *Freddy's Book* (1980), none were particularly well received. Gardner died in a motorcycle accident near Susquehanna, Pennsylvania, on September 14, 1982, just days before he was to wed his third wife, Susan Thornton.

GRENDEL IN CONTEXT

Grendel, one of Gardner's more postmodern novels, is metafiction—fiction about fiction. The plot and characters of the novel come from the sixth-century Anglo-Saxon poem *Beowulf*, a text that Gardner had been teaching at the university level for some time. *Beowulf* is a heroic epic chronicling the illustrious deeds of the great Geatish warrior Beowulf, who voyages across the sea to rid the Danes of a horrible monster, Grendel, who has been terrorizing their kingdom. In his novel, Gardner narrates the story from the monster's point of view, depicting Grendel not as a fearsome beast but as a lonely but intelligent outsider who bears a striking resemblance to his human adversaries.

Gardner's boyhood interest in cartoons and comics informs his fiction. He often uses grotesque, cartoonish imagery to distance readers emotionally from his characters, forcing them to avoid overly sentimental interpretations. An avid cartoonist and illustrator himself, Gardner insisted that Knopf publish illustrations to accompany his novels. *Grendel* features the nearly abstract woodcuts of Emil Antonucci.

GRENDEL: KEY FACTS

Time and place written: 1969–1970; San Francisco

Date of first publication: 1971	

Date of first publication: 1971

Publisher: Knopf

Type of work: Novel

Genre: Postmodern novel; prose poem

Language: English

Setting (time): The fourth century A.D.

Setting (place): Denmark

Tense: Present, but with substantial flashbacks

Tone: Grendel attempts to maintain a satirical, mocking tone, but often slips into impassioned earnest-ness

Narrator: Grendel

Point of view: Grendel in the first person

Protagonist: Grendel

Antagonist: A potentially meaningless world

GRENDEL: PLOT OVERVIEW

Grendel, a large, bearlike monster, has spent the last twelve years warring against a band of humans. As a young monster, Grendel lives with his mother in a cave on the outskirts of human civilization. Grendel's mother, a foul, wretched creature who long ago abandoned language, is Grendel's only companion. One day, young Grendel discovers a lake full of firesnakes, swims through it, and reaches the human world on the other side. On one of his early explorations of the human world, he gets caught in a tree. A bull and then a band of humans attack Grendel before his mother rescues him.

Fascinated, Grendel watches from a safe distance as mankind evolves from a nomadic, tribal culture into a feudal system with roads, governments, and militaries. He is alternately befuddled by their actions and disgusted by their wasteful violence. Grendel watches as Hrothgar of the Danes (also known as the Scyldings, after an illustrious ancestor) becomes the most powerful king in the area.

Eventually, Hrothgar's power and fortune attract the services of the Shaper, a court bard who sings glorious tales of Danish kings and heroes. The Shaper's songs, which are only partially based on fact, invigorate listeners with their visions of a supremely ordered moral world. Inspired by the Shaper's words, Hrothgar builds a magnificent meadhall and names it Hart. Even Grendel, who has witnessed the true, savage progress of the Danes, finds the Shaper's rewrite of history extremely seductive and becomes ashamed of his own brute, bestial nature.

Grendel, increasingly upset by his split feelings about the Shaper, visits a dragon to ask for advice. The dragon belittles the Shaper and declares all moral and philosophical systems pointless. Grendel gradually adopts the dragon's worldview and becomes enraged at the humans. He begins to raid Hart, initiating the twelve-year war. In his first battle, Grendel handily defeats Unferth, one of Hrothgar's mightiest thanes (or soldiers), and adds insult to injury by scoffing at Unferth's romantic ideas of heroism.

Other kings increasingly threaten Hrothgar, including Hygmod, king of the Helmings. Hrothgar plans a preemptive strike on Hygmod, but Hygmod, anxious to avoid a war, offers Hrothgar the hand of his sis-ter, Wealtheow, in marriage. Hrothgar accepts, and Wealtheow becomes the much beloved queen of the Scyldings. She brings a new sense of peace and harmony to the vulgar, masculine world of Hart. The lovely queen briefly enraptures Grendel, and only a nighttime attack on Hart and a look at her genitals, which repulse him, rids him of her spell.

Some years later, Hrothgar's brother Halga is killed, and Halga's orphaned son, Hrothulf, comes to live at Hart. Hrothgar and Wealtheow already have two sons of their own, and the presence of so many possible heirs to the Scylding throne makes Wealtheow nervous. Hrothulf, disgusted by the split between the laboring class and the aristocracy, plans a revolutionary overthrow of the government. Hrothulf's counselor, a peasant named Red Horse, tries to convince Hrothulf that all governments are inherently evil and that a revolution merely replaces one corrupt system with another.

In the winter of the final year of the war, Grendel meets an old, blind priest and pretends to be the supreme Scylding deity known as the Destroyer. Grendel asks the old priest, Ork, to say what he knows about the Destroyer, and Ork explains a complex metaphysical system he has spent years working out. Ork is almost moved to a state of ecstasy by the experience. A puzzled Grendel withdraws as three younger priests come to chastise Ork for his strange behavior. A fourth priest meets them and is overjoyed at the news of Ork's vision.

Later the same winter, the Shaper dies. Grendel feels increasingly fearful, but does not know why. His mother also feels dread. She tries to warn Grendel, but she can only produce the gibberish phrase "Warrovish," which Grendel later deciphers to mean "Beware the fish." Fifteen strangers arrive from over the sea. They are Geats, and their leader is Beowulf, who has come to rid the Scyldings of Grendel. Grendel knows that the Geats are what he has been waiting for, and he is both frightened and excited. The Scyldings are none too pleased about Beowulf's arrival. At dinner, Unferth taunts Beowulf about his notorious loss in a swimming contest. Beowulf responds that Unferth has been misled, and calmly declares that Unferth is doomed to hell because he killed his own brothers.

At night, Grendel attacks Hart. Beowulf manages to surprise Grendel and grabs his arm. As they struggle, Grendel slips on a pool of blood, and Beowulf gets the upper hand. Beowulf begins whispering madly in Grendel's ear. Grendel hallucinates, seeing Beowulf sprout an enormous pair of wings. Beowulf smashes Grendel against a wall, cracking his head open and demanding that he "sing of walls." Beowulf manages to rip Grendel's arm off at the shoulder, and Grendel runs off into the night. He finds himself at the edge of a cliff, staring down into its dark, murky depths. A host of animals gather around Grendel, seeming to condemn him. The novel closes as Grendel whispers to them, "Poor Grendel's had an accident.. . . *So may you all.*"

CHARACTERS IN *GRENDEL*

Beowulf A Geatish hero who comes across the sea to rid the Scyldings of Grendel. Beowulf is hugely strong, cold, and mechanical, showing little emotion or personality. In the climactic battle with Grendel, Beowulf appears to sprout dragonlike wings and speak fire.

The Bull A bull that discovers Grendel hanging in a tree and attacks him.

The dragon A cranky beast that rules over a vast hoard of treasure. The dragon believes the world is meaningless. Grendel frequently weighs the fatalistic words of the dragon against the beautiful words of the Shaper. Some critics argue that the dragon is actually a personification of one aspect of Grendel's mind.

Ecgtheow Beowulf's father.

The Fourth Priest A younger priest who is overjoyed to hear that Ork encountered the Destroyer.

Freawaru Hrothgar's teenage daughter. Hrothgar plans to marry Freawaru to Ingeld in order to avoid a war with the Heathobards.

The Goat A goat that climbs a cliff despite Grendel's screaming. Grendel tries to bludgeon the goat to death with stones, but it continues to climb.

Grendel The protagonist and narrator of the novel. A great, bearlike monster, Grendel is the first of three monsters defeated by the Geatish hero Beowulf in the sixth-century poem *Beowulf*. In *Grendel*, he is a lonely creature who wants to understand the seemingly meaningless world around him.

Grendel's mother A foul, wretched being. Grendel's mother desperately tries to protect Grendel from the humans and his fate. She has either forgotten or never known how to speak, though at times her gibberish approaches coherent language.

Halga Hrothgar's brother and Hrothulf's father. He is murdered.

Hrothgar King of the Danes. Hrothgar's kingdom is highly powerful and prosperous until Grendel begins terrorizing it. In *Beowulf*, Hrothgar is an exemplary model of kingship, but in *Grendel* he is flawed. Grendel often describes his war with the humans as a personal battle between Hrothgar and himself.

Hrothulf Hrothgar's nephew. In *Beowulf*, Hrothulf usurps Hrothgar's son's role as ruler of the Scyldings. In *Grendel*, he forms ideas of revolution after seeing the aristocratic thanes subjugate the Danish peasants.

Hygilac King of the Geats and Beowulf's lord.

Hygmod King of the Helmings and Wealtheow's brother. Hygmod, a young king who is gaining power, is a military threat to Hrothgar.

Ingeld King of the Heathobards and an enemy of the Scyldings.

Ork An old, blind, Scylding priest. Ork is a theologian—one who studies the theories behind religion. He believes ultimate wisdom as the perception that the universe wastes nothing. Ork is one of the few priests in the novel for whom religion is more than an empty show.

The Ram The first creature Grendel encounters in the novel, other than his mother. The ram stands stupidly at the edge of a cliff and will not budge despite Grendel's repeated protests.

Red Horse Hrothulf's mentor and advisor. A crotchety old man, Red Horse believes that all governments are inherently evil.

The Shaper A harpist and storyteller in Hrothgar's court. The Shaper depicts the world as connected and purposeful—a vision that Grendel finds incredibly seductive, even though he knows it is built on lies. The Shaper represents the power of art to create meaning in a meaningless world.

The Shaper's Assistant A young man who apprentices to the Shaper and then takes over his duties upon his death.

Scyld Shefing The legendary king from whom Hrothgar is descended. In Scyld Shefing's honor, the Danes are sometimes referred to as the Scyldings.

Unferth A Scylding hero whom Grendel defeats. Unferth believes wholeheartedly in the heroic ideals of his warrior culture.

Wealtheow Hrothgar's wife and Queen of the Danes. Wealtheow represents love, altruism, and idealized womanhood. She brings balance and harmony to her adopted community.

THEMES IN *GRENDEL*

THE LIES OF ART Grendel is stranded painfully between what he knows to be true and what he wishes were true. Intellectually, Grendel understands the world to be a brutish, mechanical place that has no meaningful pattern or universal laws. He knows that all the beautiful concepts of which the Shaper sings—heroism, religion, love, beauty—are merely human projections, attempts to pretend that our world has meaning. The Shaper gives history meaning where none exists, cleaning up its messy ambiguities and producing explicit, rigid moral systems. This clear, knowable vision of the world comforts the Danes. With made-up stories, the Shaper makes the Danes see themselves as inheritors of a proud tradition who must adhere to the strict moral and ethical code that the Shaper has established.

Even though Grendel knows that the version of history the epics set forth is a lie, he yearns for the emotional and spiritual fulfillment that the Shaper's beautiful fictions provide. When Grendel first hears the Shaper's song, he is so overcome that he bursts into tears and momentarily loses the ability to speak. Time and again, Grendel's emotional response to art overcomes his intellect. At times, Grendel is even willing to accept the role of the evil adversary in order to be granted a place in the Shaper's world.

THE POWER OF STORIES The Shaper's stories have power over Grendel's self-expression. It alternately pleases and frustrates Grendel that he must use the language of the humans to tell his tale. Taking a page from the Shaper's book, and from the original Anglo-Saxon poet of *Beowulf*, he proudly refers to himself as "Grendel, Ruiner of Meadhalls, Wrecker of Kings!" But in less confident moods, Grendel is frustrated by human language. When he is chased out of Hart after attempting to join the humans, he expresses his frustration in a stream of human swearwords and then bitterly observes, "We, the accursed, [do not] even have words for swearing in!"

One story has total power over both the novel and Grendel himself: *Beowulf*, the plotline of which operates like the hand of fate in *Grendel*. Before we read the first page of Gardner's novel, we know that Grendel will die at Beowulf's hands.

THE PAIN OF ISOLATION Grendel has no community, no one to talk to. The animals that surround him are dumb and undignified. His mother lacks the capacity for language, but even if she could speak, she would likely be an unworthy conversational partner for her intelligent, inquisitive son. Grendel often finds himself talking to the sky or the air. He is trapped in a lonely, extended interior monologue. It is deeply painful when humans, who resemble Grendel in many ways, rebuff him. Grendel and humankind share a common heritage—Cain is Grendel's ancestor, and Abel, humankind's—but this heritage keeps them forever locked in battle instead of bringing them together.

SYMBOLS IN *GRENDEL*

THE BULL Grendel condemns animals because they, like machines, pursue tedious routines determined by outside forces. The bull that repeatedly attacks Grendel in the same ineffective way symbolizes the world, which acts in a similarly uncalculated manner.

HART For Hrothgar, the meadhall symbolizes his own political power and altruism. For the Danish community at large, Hart symbolizes their persistence: every time Grendel knocks down the door, the Danes repair it. This constant reparation suggests their obstinate desire to hold onto meaning despite the cruel, chaotic nature of the world.

IMPORTANT QUOTATIONS FROM *GRENDEL*

I had become something, as if born again. I had hung between possibilities before, between the cold truths I knew and the heart-sucking conjuring tricks of the Shaper; now that was passed: I was Grendel, Ruiner of Meadhalls, Wrecker of Kings!
   But also, as never before, I was alone.

Location: Chapter 6
Speaker: Grendel
Context: Grendel bites off the head of a Scylding guard, accepting the role the Shaper created for him in his song

When Grendel accepts the role the Shaper imagined for him, he shows the power of stories to shape identity. Grendel never thought of himself as a monster, but he will play a monster if it will allow him to take part in the beautiful charade of meaning the Shaper creates. But agreeing to play the villain in the Shaper's play comes with a heavy price. By nature, Grendel sympathizes with humans and longs to find acceptance among them. By agreeing to accept his role as the son of Cain, he brings himself into the world of men but ensures that they will hate him. Grendel knows this and says, "as never before, I was alone." The Shaper is not the only factor in Grendel's decision, however. A monstrous streak, or at least a cruel streak, prompts Grendel to kill; he wants to teach humans a lesson, just as a bitter parent might teach his children a lesson. He wants to punish humans for their infuriatingly naïve belief in the righteousness of their moral systems—systems that Grendel knows have no foundation in universal moral law, because universal moral law does not exist.

As you see it is, while the seeing lasts, dark nightmare-history, time-as-coffin; but where the water was rigid there will be fish, and men will survive on their flesh till spring. It's coming, my brother.. . . .
Though you murder the world, transmogrify life into I and it, strong searching roots will crack your cave and rain will cleanse it: The world will burn green, sperm build again.

Location: Chapter 12
Speaker: Beowulf
Context: Beowulf talks to Grendel as they engage in their final battle

Beowulf denounces the nihilism the dragon espouses while accepting the dragon's basic premise that time is essentially a "coffin," a promise of death and destruction for all. However, Beowulf also talks of spring emerging from winter, stressing the role of rebirth in the grand scheme of life. This imagery echoes the song sung at the Shaper's funeral. This conception of the seasons as a natural cycle full of meaning directly contradicts Grendel's earliest conception of the seasons as a pointless and mechanical routine.

The imagery in this passage describes rigid, hard objects being burst open with violent but cleansing force. This image is soon replicated, gruesomely, with Grendel's own head, which Beowulf is about to smash against the walls of the meadhall. In this passage, the forces that break through barriers are natural and life-giving in their violence, which suggests that Beowulf's merciless treatment of Grendel is a project of salvation. Beowulf calls Grendel "brother," a reference to the Cain and Abel story, but also a compassionate remark that brings Grendel much closer to humankind than he has ever been before. Beowulf's reference to the fish in the frozen river reminds us of the Christian elements of Beowulf's character, and the fact that he can be interpreted as a kind of avenging Christ figure.

I understood that the world was nothing: a mechanical chaos of casual, brute enmity on which we stupidly impose our hopes and fears. I understood that, finally and absolutely, I alone exist. All the rest, I saw, is merely what pushes me, or what I push against, blindly—as blindly as all that is not myself pushes back.

Location: Chapter 2
Speaker: Grendel
Context: As the bull attacks him, Grendel thinks about philosophy for the first time

---

Thus I fled, ridiculous hairy creature torn apart by poetry—crawling, whimpering, streaming tears, across the world like a two-headed beast, like mixed-up lamb and kid at the tail of a baffled, indifferent ewe—and I gnashed my teeth and clutched the sides of my head as if to heal the split, but I couldn't.

Location: Chapter 3
Speaker: Grendel
Context: Grendel reacts to hearing the Shaper's song for the first time

---

"Nevertheless, something will come of all this," I said.
  "Nothing," he said. "A brief pulsation in the black hole of eternity. My advice to you—"
"Wait and see," I said.
  He shook his head. "My advice to you, my violent friend, is to seek out gold and sit on it."

Location: Chapter 5
Speaker: Grendel and the dragon
Context: The dragon, who can see the past and the future, advises Grendel

GULLIVER'S TRAVELS

Jonathan Swift

A seventeenth-century English doctor chronicles his travels to four fantastical lands, whose inhabitants Swift uses to satirize and critique English society.

THE LIFE OF JONATHAN SWIFT

Jonathan Swift, posthumous son of English lawyer Jonathan Swift the elder, was born in 1667 in Dublin, Ireland. After graduating from Dublin's Trinity College, Swift went to England to work as a secretary to Sir William Temple, a Whig-party politician. In 1694 Swift was ordained a priest in the (Anglican) Church of Ireland. After a yearlong stint in Ireland as a country parson, he returned to England to work for Temple.

Swift began to write satires on political and religious corruption while in Temple's service. In *The Battle of the Books* (1697), Swift argued, in support of Temple, for the supremacy of the classics against contemporary literature. Swift's 1704 religious satire *A Tale of a Tub* defended the Anglican Church from both conservative and liberal critics. Swift also wrote pamphlets for the Whigs, although he later severed his relationship with the party, largely because of conflicts over his strong allegiance to the church. He became a member of the more conservative Tory party in 1710.

After the Tory government lost control of government in 1714, Swift returned to Dublin. Together with writer friends such as Alexander Pope, Swift established the famous Martinus Scriblerus Club dedicated to satirizing pretentious scholarship. During this time, Swift began working on *Gulliver's Travels*, a work he did not complete until 1726. He also became a staunch national supporter of Ireland against the encroaching power of England, and composed the bitterly satirical *A Modest Proposal* (1729), which suggests that both famine and overpopulation could be resolved by feeding babies of poor Irish families to the rich.

In his last years, Swift seemed to become increasingly caustic and bitter. He suffered a paralytic stroke, and was declared insane in 1742, three years before his death.

GULLIVER'S TRAVELS IN CONTEXT

Gulliver's Travels caused much controversy after its initial publication in 1726. In fact, the work did not appear in Swift's intended form until 1736. Editors since that time have excised many passages, particularly the more caustic ones concerned with bodily functions. Nevertheless, *Gulliver's Travels* has remained a biting satire, both humorous and critical, relentlessly attacking England and European society through descriptions of imaginary countries.

Over time, *Gulliver's Travels* has lost some of its immediacy, but it remains a classic work of English literature. It owes its staying power to its depiction of the human condition and its despairing exploration of the ability of humans to rein in their baser instincts.

GULLIVER'S TRAVELS: KEY FACTS

Full title: Gulliver's Travels, or Travels into Several Remote Nations of the World

Time and place written: ca. 1712–1726; London and Dublin

Date of publication: 1726 (unabridged edition published in 1735)

Publisher: George Faulkner (1735 unabridged edition)

Type of work: Novel

Genre: Satire

Language: English

Setting (time): Early eighteenth century

Setting (place): England and the imaginary lands of Lilliput, Brobdingnag, Laputa, and the land of the Houyhnhnms

Tense: Past

Tone: Satirical, naïve, embittered

Narrator: Lemuel Gulliver in the first person

Point of view: Lemuel Gulliver's

Protagonist: Lemuel Gulliver

Antagonist: Parts I–III: Fickleness of fortune and character flaws of the inhabitants of the lands Gulliver visits that prevent Gulliver from returning home; Part IV: base human nature; throughout: the moral defects and corruption of English society

GULLIVER'S TRAVELS: PLOT OVERVIEW

PART I: A VOYAGE TO LILLIPUT

Lemuel Gulliver, a practical-minded English surgeon, takes to the seas when his business fails. In a deadpan tone evincing little self-reflection or deep emotional response, Gulliver narrates the adventures that befall him on these travels.

Shipwrecked in the South Pacific, Gulliver wakes to find himself bound by innumerable tiny threads and addressed by tiny six-inch captors. Awestruck but fiercely protective of their kingdom, the Lilliputians shoot Gulliver with arrows that hurt little more than pinpricks. Overall, his captors are hospitable. They risk famine to feed Gulliver, who consumes enough food for a thousand Lilliputians. They build an enormous wagon to take him into the capital city and present him to the emperor. The emperor finds Gulliver entertaining, and Gulliver is flattered by royal attention. Eventually Gulliver becomes a national resource for the army in the war against the people of Blefuscu, whom the Lilliputians hate for doctrinal differences about the proper way to crack eggs. Gulliver's good standing with the government evaporates when he is convicted of treason for putting out a fire in the royal palace with his urine. He is condemned to being blinded by poisoned arrows. Gulliver flees to Blefuscu, finds a shipwrecked boat, repairs it, and sets sail for England.

PART II: A VOYAGE TO BROBDINGNAG

After two months in England with his wife and family, Gulliver departs on another sea voyage. He finds himself stranded in Brobdingnag, a land inhabited by giants. He is discovered by a farmer who treats him like an animal and takes him on the road to exhibit him for money as a freak. Eventually the farmer sells him to the queen. Gulliver becomes a court curiosity and entertains the queen with his musical talents. Life at the court is easy, but not particularly enjoyable. Gulliver is often repulsed by the Brobdingnagians' bodies, whose ordinary flaws are magnified by their huge size. Playing on the naked bodies of two ladies of the court, he is disgusted by their enormous skin pores, their pungent stench, and the sound of their torrential urination. He is surprised by the ignorance of the populace—even the king knows nothing about politics. Animals endanger his life; insects leave slimy trails on his food. He longs to escape. One day as he accompanies the royal couple on a trip to the frontier, an eagle plucks him up in his cage and then drops it in the sea. Human sailors discover the cage and take him back to England.

PART III: A VOYAGE TO LAPUTA, BALNIBARBI, LUGGNAGG, GLUBBDUBDRIB, AND JAPAN

After a pirate attack on his next sea voyage, Gulliver ends up in Laputa, a floating island populated by theoreticians and academics who oppress the land of Balnibarbi, over which Laputa hovers. The scientific research in Laputa seems inane and impractical, and its residents too are out of touch with reality. Gulliver takes a short side trip to Glubbdubdrib, the island of magicians, where he speaks to conjurings of historical figures—Julius Caesar, Aristotle, and other military leaders and philosophers—who are less impressive in person than in books. He then visits the island of Luggnagg, where he meets Struldbrugs, senile immortals who prove that age does not bring wisdom. Finally, Gulliver manages to sail to Japan and from there back to England.

PART IV: A VOYAGE TO THE COUNTRY OF THE HOUYHNHNMS

Gulliver starts his fourth journey as the captain of his own ship, but his crew mutinies and abandons him on an unknown shore. This land is populated by Houyhnhnms, rational, thinking horses, and Yahoos, brutish anthropomorphic creatures who serve the Houyhnhnms. Gulliver learns the Houyhnhnms' language and tells them about his voyages and explains the English constitution. The Houyhnhnms treat him with great courtesy and kindness, and Gulliver is enlightened by his exposure to their noble culture. He wants to stay with the Houyhnhnms, but they banish him after they see his naked body and realize that he is similar to the Yahoos. Grief-stricken, Gulliver agrees to leave. He constructs a canoe and makes his way to a nearby island, where he is picked up by a Portuguese ship. The ship's captain treats him well, but Gulliver is dismayed by how Yahoolike the captain and all humans appear to him now. At the end of his narrative, Gulliver claims the lands that he has visited as English colonies, even as he questions the practice of colonialism.

CHARACTERS IN *GULLIVER'S TRAVELS*

HUMANS

James Bates Young Gulliver's surgeon mentor.

Lemuel Gulliver The story's protagonist and narrator. Well-educated but naïve, Gulliver is easily impressed with royalty and never acknowledges the absurdities of the fantastical societies he meets on his voyages. The contrast between what Gulliver consciously relates and what we glean from his narration makes Swift's work a satire. Gulliver's narration is detached, fact-oriented, and unemotional. He describes the creatures on his voyages much more carefully than his fellow humans—indicating that humans, including his wife, hold little interest for him.

Mary Gulliver, née Burton Gulliver's wife. He mentions her only perfunctorily at the beginning of each voyage, and shows no sentimental attachment to her or to any other human being. He goes on his travels against her wishes.

Don Pedro de Mendez The Portuguese captain who takes Gulliver back to Europe after the voyage to the land of the Houyhnhnms. Despite his kindness and generosity, Don Pedro repulses Gulliver because he, like all humans, looks like the loathsome Yahoos.

Abraham Pannell The captain of the *Swallow*, Gulliver's first ship.

William Prichard The captain of the *Antelope*, the ship whose 1699 wreck washes Gulliver up on the Lilliput shore.

Richard Sympson Gulliver's cousin, who (within Gulliver's world) publishes Gulliver's account of his travels. Sympson's fictional prefatory note, "The Publisher to the Readers," warns that half of Gulliver's original manuscript has been excised as irrelevant prior to publication. Swift's device throws into question Gulliver's judgment; it may have also lent authenticity to his narrative for contemporary readers.

FIRST VOYAGE: LILLIPUT

Lilliputians and Blefuscudians Two races of miniature, six-inch-tall people. Lilliputians and Blefuscudians have been engaged in longstanding war with each other over the proper way to break eggs. Prone to conspiracies and jealousies, they are quick to take advantage of Gulliver. Despite having helped the Lilliputians defeat the Blefuscudian navy, Gulliver is nevertheless warmly received by the Blefuscudian court.

Skyresh Bolgolam High Admiral of Lilliput. Bolgolam is the sole member of the administration to oppose allowing Gulliver to roam free in Lilliput.

The Emperor of Lilliput The ruler of Lilliputians. He impresses Gulliver with his power and majesty, but his small stature renders his delusions of grandeur—such as the ability to control Gulliver—laughable. With his sinister tendency to execute subjects for minor political or moral infractions, the emperor is both a satire of the autocratic ruler and a portrait of a serious politician.

Flimnap Lord High Treasurer of Lilliput. Flimnap's jealous hatred of Gulliver arises from the absurd suspicion that Gulliver is having an affair with Flimnap's wife.

Reldresal Principal Secretary of Private Affairs of Lilliput. Friendly to Gulliver, Reldresal explains to him the intricacies of Lilliputian politics.

Slamecksan ("Low-Heels") A Lilliputian political party that symbolizes the British Whigs. Though Low-Heels have fewer members than their rivals, the High-Heels, all government officials must be Low-Heels, per order of the emperor, who wears low heels in sympathy with the party.

Tramecksan ("High-Heels") A Lilliputian political party that represents the British Tories. High-Heels policies are influenced by the ancient constitution of Lilliput. More numerous than Low-Heels, High-Heels are underrepresented in government. The crown prince limps because he wears one high heel, in sympathy with the High-Heels, and one low heel, in deference to the emperor's preference.

SECOND VOYAGE: BROBDINGNAG

Brobdingnagians A race of giants. Polite, gentle, and fair, they contrast with the petty, quarrelling Lilliputians. Brobdingnagians are kind to Gulliver, but do not take him seriously, treating him as a curious plaything.

The Farmer Gulliver's first owner. The farmer owns the land on which Gulliver first lands. He treats Gulliver with gentleness and initially respects his intelligence, but later puts him on display as a freakshow attraction. Less cruel than simpleminded, he exploits Gulliver and inadvertently almost starves him.

Glumdalclitch The farmer's forty-foot, nine-year-old daughter. She treats Gulliver as a living doll and becomes his babysitter, both at home and later at the court. She teaches him her language and delights in clothing him.

The King of Brobdingnag The ruler of Brobdingnag. Unlike the emperor of Lilliput, this king is an intellectual who is particularly versed in political science. He engages in serious discussion about English history and political institutions with Gulliver, ultimately dismissing Englishmen as "odious vermin."

The Queen of Brogdingnag She purchases Gulliver from the farmer for a thousand gold pieces and brings him to the court. Pleasant and genuinely considerate, the queen possesses "infinite" wit and humor, according to Gulliver.

THIRD VOYAGE: LAPUTA

Laputans Absentminded intellectuals. The Laputans are Swift's parody of useless, self-indulgent, purely academic pursuits. Laputans inhabit an island that hovers over Balnibarbi, the land that produces their supplies, by virtue of a magnetic field. Laputans focus on abstract, impractical theorizing and neglect practical matters such as their dilapidated houses. Their servants ("flappers") must shake rattles in their ears to break their meditative trances. They dismiss Gulliver as intellectually deficient.

Lord Munodi An aristocrat of Lagado, the capital of Balnibarbi, the land that supports the Laputans. Munodi hosts Gulliver on Gulliver's third voyage. Unlike the other Laputians, Munodi is practical-minded. He fell from grace with the ruling Laputian elite when he proposed implementing a commonsense, proven method of agriculture.

FOURTH VOYAGE: THE LAND OF THE HOUYHNHNMS

Houyhnhnms Wise and rational-thinking horse creatures. The Houyhnhnms maintain a peaceful socialist society governed by reason and truthfulness. Gulliver becomes deeply attached to the Houyhnhnms, but they ask him to leave when they realize how much he physically resembles the brutish

Yahoos. The encounter with the Houyhnhnms causes Gulliver to reevaluate the differences between humans and beasts and to question humans' claim to rational thought.

Gulliver's Houyhnhnm Master The Houyhnhnm who discovers and hosts Gulliver. His good hygiene, tranquil temperament, and cogent approach to life make a deep impression on Gulliver, who eventually feels more at home in this Houyhnhnm household than with his human family.

Yahoos Filthy anthropomorphic beasts who live in servitude to the Houyhnhnms and perform manual labor. They live naked, the men covered by hair, the women with low-hanging breasts. Their lasciviousness and primitive eating habits repel Gulliver. By the end of his journey, Gulliver, full of bitterness and self-loathing, refers to himself—and later to any human—as a Yahoo.

THEMES IN *GULLIVER'S TRAVELS*

THE INDIVIDUAL IN SOCIETY *Gulliver's Travels* has been called the first novel of modern alienation: it focuses on an individual's repeated failures to integrate into societies to which he does not belong. With his surgeon's business unprofitable and his father's estate insufficiently large to support him, Gulliver feels out of place even in England. Although he never complains of loneliness, Gulliver is a profoundly isolated individual who is embittered and misanthropic by the end of the novel. If Swift's satire mocks the inadequacies of communal life—the bickering Lilliputians who raise their children communally or the faceless utopian Houyhnhnms—it also mocks the excesses of individualism with a miserably and lonely Gulliver who talks to his horses at home in England.

SYMBOLS IN *GULLIVER'S TRAVELS*

EXCREMENT Frequently mentioned on Gulliver's journey, excrement represents all that is visceral and ignoble about the human body. Swift's emphasis on the everyday filth of human life, especially in the comparison of humans to the beastly Yahoos, was a slap in the face of the Enlightenment philosophers of his day. Enlightenment thinkers preferred to see humans as spiritual creatures who, through reason and contemplation, could transcend the instincts and needs of their bodies. Swift's images—Gulliver up to his waist in cow dung in Lilliput, Brobdingnagian flies defecating on Gulliver's food, the Lagado experiments to transform excrement into food—remind us that the human condition is inextricably linked to the base, unexalted needs of the body.

CLOTHING Gulliver pays close attention to clothes throughout his journeys: his pants have rips in the crotch as the Lilliputian army marches between his legs, he wears a mouse skin because the finest Brobdingnagian silks are as thick as blankets to him. His ragged clothes and his strange new wardrobe symbolize his distance from the comforts and conventions of England. At the end of the fourth voyage, Gulliver's refusal of Don Pedro's offer of a new set of clothes suggests that Gulliver may never fully reintegrate into European society.

Gulliver describes two instances of nudity, both troubling and humiliating experiences: in Brobdingnag, he cavorts nude on the mountainous breasts of women, and later an eleven-year-old Yahoo girl assaults him as he bathes. Gulliver associates nudity with extreme vulnerability to such an extent that critics have suggested that Gulliver needs clothes to affirm his otherwise empty, unreflective identity.

LANDS AND POPULATIONS AS SYMBOLS IN *GULLIVER'S TRAVELS*

LILLIPUTIANS The Lilliputians symbolize humankind's megalomaniac pride in its own puny existence. The Lilliputians are tiny creatures with tiny minds who imagine themselves to be grand. They proudly parade their armies between Gulliver's legs, which serve as a makeshift Arc de Triomphe. Their war with Blefuscu is an absurdity, springing from arguments over interpretations of scripture on egg-cracking technique. They smugly and pompously condemn Gulliver for treason, and he naïvely cowers before their threats, forgetting that he is a giant among them.

BROBDINGNAGIANS The Brobdingnagians symbolize the private, personal, and physical side of humans when examined up close and in great detail. Enlightenment philosophy tended to overlook the routines of everyday life and the sordid or tedious little facts of existence, but in Brobdingnag such facts become very important for Gulliver, sometimes matters of life and death. As the Brobdingnagians' plaything, Gulliver is also allowed to see into their private lives: he hears housemaids urinate and learns about women's sexual lives.

LAPUTANS The Laputans represent the folly of theoretical knowledge that has no relation to human life and no use in the actual world. A cultural conservative, Swift was a critic of newfangled seventeenth-century ideas, preferring traditional, tested knowledge. Gulliver's experience in Laputa highlights the ludicrous side of Enlightenment intellectualism. Theoretical knowledge in Balnarbi has resulted in the ruin of agriculture and architecture and the impoverishment of the population. Inhabitants of Laputa have few material worries, but are tormented by practically useless astronomical speculations.

HOUYHNHNMS The Houyhnhnms represent an ideal of rational existence, a life governed by sense and moderation as advocated by philosophers since ancient times. As endorsed in Plato's *The Republic*, the Houyhnhnms reject superficial entertainment and luxury, appeal to reason rather than scripture to make decisions, plan their families communally, refrain from using force, and always tell the truth.

At the same time, by making the Houyhnhnms horses, Swift may be implying that the ideal that they represent is not a human ideal. Nameless and virtually interchangeable, the Houyhnhnms have little individual identity. Their lives, harmonious and happy, lack challenges and excitement.

IMPORTANT QUOTATIONS FROM *GULLIVER'S TRAVELS*

My Father had a small Estate in Nottinghamshire; I was the Third of five Sons.. . . . I was bound Apprentice to Mr. James Bates, an eminent Surgeon in London . . . my Father now and then sending me small Sums of Money.. . . When I left Mr. Bates, I went down to my Father; where, by the Assistance of him and my Uncle John . . . I got Forty Pounds, and a Promise of Thirty Pounds a Year.

Location: Part I, Chapter I
Speaker: Gulliver
Context: Gulliver introduces himself

At the beginning of the novel, we learn that Gulliver is primarily interested in money, property, and achievement. He sets out to sea in part because as the third-born son, he is not due to inherit his father's estate. The tone of this passage is starkly impersonal, and continues to characterize Gulliver's narrative until his nervous breakdown at the end of the novel.

[T]hey go on Shore to rob and plunder; they see an harmless People, are entertained with Kindness, they give the Country a new Name, they take formal Possession of it for the King, they set up a rotten Plank or a Stone for a Memorial, they murder two or three Dozen of the Natives, bring away a Couple more by Force for a Sample, return home, and get their Pardon. Here commences a New Dominion acquired with a Title by Divine Right . . . the Earth reeking with the Blood of its Inhabitants.

Location: Part IV, Chapter XII
Speaker: Gulliver
Context: By way of apology and explanation for why he did not claim the land he has visited for the English crown, Gulliver criticizes colonialist practices

Gulliver's portrays colonialism as criminal enterprise—a perspective familiar by the end of the twentieth century, but revolutionary in the seventeenth. In Swift's time, even those who condemned using violence against indigenous populations usually agreed that colonialism would bring the blessing of western civilization to ignorant barbarians.

He said, he knew no Reason, why those who entertain Opinions prejudicial to the Publick, should be obliged to change, or should not be obliged to conceal them. And, as it was Tyranny in any Government to require the first, so it was Weakness not to enforce the second.

Location: Part II, Chapter VI
Speaker: Gulliver reports the King of Brobdingnag's speech
Context: The king, in conversation with Gulliver, insists that people have the right to their own beliefs but not the right to express them at will, echoing an opinion that Swift himself has expressed elsewhere

My little Friend Grildrig.. . . . I cannot but conclude the Bulk of your Natives, to be the most pernicious Race of little odious Vermin that Nature ever suffered to crawl upon the Surface of the Earth.

Location: Part II, Chapter VI
Speaker: The king of Brobdingnag
Context: After Gulliver tells him about England, the king passes this famous judgment of the English

My Reconcilement to the Yahoo-kind in general might not be so difficult, if they would be content with those Vices and Follies only which Nature hath entitled them to. I am not in the least provoked at the Sight of a Lawyer, a Pick-pocket, a Colonel.. . . . This is all according to the due Course of Things: But, when I behold a Lump of Deformity, and Diseases both in Body and Mind, smitten with Pride, it immediately breaks all the Measures of my Patience; neither shall I ever be able to comprehend how such an Animal and such a Vice could tally together.

Location: Part IV, Chapter XII
Speaker: Gulliver
Context: After all of his travels, Gulliver describes his difficulties in readjusting to human culture, which he now associates with the Yahoos

HAMLET

William Shakespeare

Ordered by his father's ghost to kill his uncle, the new king, a young prince struggles with doubt and alienation in Denmark's corrupt court.

THE LIFE OF WILLIAM SHAKESPEARE

William Shakespeare, the most influential writer in all of English literature, was born in 1564 to a successful middle-class glove-maker in Stratford-upon-Avon, England. Shakespeare's formal education did not progress beyond grammar school. In 1582, he married an older woman, Anne Hathaway. His union with Anne produced three children. Around 1590, Shakespeare left his family behind and traveled to London to work as an actor and playwright. He quickly earned public and critical acclaim, and eventually became the most popular playwright in England and a part-owner of the Globe Theater. Shakespeare's career bridged the reigns of Elizabeth I (ruled 1558–1603) and James I (ruled 1603–1625), and he was a favorite of both monarchs. James paid Shakespeare's company a great compliment by giving its members the title of King's Men. Shakespeare retired to Stratford a wealthy and renowned man and died in 1616 at the age of fifty-two. At the time of Shakespeare's death, literary luminaries such as Ben Jonson hailed his works as timeless.

Shakespeare's works were collected and printed in various editions in the century following his death, and by the early eighteenth century his reputation as the greatest poet ever to write in English was well established. The unprecedented regard in which Shakespeare's works were held led to a fierce curiosity about his life, but many details of Shakespeare's personal history are unknown or shrouded in mystery. Some people have concluded from this lack of information and from Shakespeare's modest education that Shakespeare's plays were actually written by someone else—Francis Bacon and the Earl of Oxford are the two most popular candidates—but the support for this claim is overwhelmingly circumstantial, and the theory is not taken seriously by many scholars.

Shakespeare is generally thought to be the author of the thirty-eight plays (two of them possibly collaborations) and 154 sonnets that bear his name. The legacy of this body of work is immense. A number of Shakespeare's plays seem to have transcended even the category of brilliance, influencing the course of Western literature and culture.

HAMLET IN CONTEXT

Written in the first years of the seventeenth century, *Hamlet* was probably first performed in July 1602. It was first published in printed form in 1603 and appeared in an enlarged edition in 1604. As was common practice during the sixteenth and seventeenth centuries, Shakespeare often borrowed ideas and stories from earlier literary works. The story of Hamlet probably came from several sources, possibly including a twelfth-century Latin history of Denmark compiled by Saxo Grammaticus and a prose work by the French writer François de Belleforest entitled *Histoires Tragiques*.

The raw material that Shakespeare appropriated in writing *Hamlet* is the story of a Danish prince whose uncle murders the prince's father, marries his mother, and claims the throne. The prince pretends to be feeble-minded to throw his uncle off guard, then manages to kill his uncle in revenge. Shakespeare altered the emphasis of this story: his Hamlet struggles with existential questions and delays taking action. Many of the play's questions are never answered: did Gertrude help Claudius murder her husband? Does Hamlet love Ophelia? Is the ghost telling the truth? At the same time, the stakes are enormous—the actions of these characters could bring disaster upon an entire kingdom.

By changing the focus of his story, Shakespeare transformed an unremarkable revenge story into a play whose problems resonate with the most fundamental concerns of the Renaissance, a cultural phenomenon marked by a new interest in the human experience and an enormous optimism about the potential scope of human understanding. Hamlet's famous speech in Act II, "What a piece of work is a man! How noble in reason, how infinite in faculty, in form and moving how express and admirable, in action how like an angel, in apprehension how like a god—the beauty of the world, the paragon of animals!" (II.ii.293–297) is directly based on one of the major texts of the Italian humanists, Pico della Mirandola's *Oration on the Dignity of Man*. Humanists initially sought to cultivate reason in order to understand how to act in a way that would benefit society as a whole. As the Renaissance spread throughout Europe during the sixteenth and seventeenth centuries, some humanists turned to studying the limitations of human understanding. For example, Michel de Montaigne maintained that human beings could never hope to understand the realities hiding behind the masks of the world. This is the world of *Hamlet*: Hamlet is responsible for correcting an injustice that he can never understand completely. The play as a whole demonstrates how difficult it is to know other people—their guilt or innocence, their motivations, their feelings, their mental states. *Hamlet* is, fundamentally, a play about the difficulty of living in an unknowable world.

HAMLET: KEY FACTS

Full Title: The Tragedy of Hamlet, Prince of Denmark

Date of first publication: 1603 (a pirated quarto edition)

Genre: Tragedy

Setting (time): Late middle ages

Setting (place): Denmark

Protagonist: Hamlet

Antagonist: Claudius

Major conflict: Hamlet struggles with doubts and difficulties as he considers killing his uncle Claudius to avenge his father's death

HAMLET: PLOT OVERVIEW

On a dark winter night, a ghost walks the ramparts of Elsinore Castle in Denmark. He is discovered first by a pair of watchmen, and then by the scholar Horatio. The ghost resembles the recently deceased King Hamlet, whose brother, Claudius, has inherited the throne and married the king's widow, Queen Gertrude. Horatio and the watchmen bring Prince Hamlet, the son of Gertrude and the dead king, to see the ghost. The ghost speaks to Hamlet, ominously declaring himself to be King Hamlet's spirit and saying he was murdered by Claudius. After ordering Hamlet to seek revenge on Claudius, who usurped his throne and married his wife, the ghost disappears with the dawn.

Hamlet devotes himself to avenging his father's death, but because he is contemplative and thoughtful by nature, he delays taking action, falling into deep melancholy and even apparent madness. Claudius and Gertrude worry about the prince's erratic behavior and attempt to discover its cause. They employ a pair of Hamlet's friends, Rosencrantz and Guildenstern, to watch him. When Polonius, the pompous Lord Chamberlain, suggests that Hamlet may be mad with love for Polonius's daughter, Ophelia, Claudius agrees to spy on Hamlet in conversation with the girl. Hamlet certainly seems mad, and he says cruel things to Ophelia, ordering her to enter a nunnery and declaring that he wishes to ban marriages.

A group of traveling actors comes to Elsinore, and Hamlet has an idea about how to test his uncle's guilt: he will have the actors, or players, perform a scene that resembles the way Hamlet thinks his uncle murdered his father. If Claudius is guilty, he will surely react. In the theater, when the moment of the staged murder arrives, Claudius leaps up and leaves the room. Hamlet and Horatio agree that this proves his guilt. Hamlet goes to kill Claudius but finds him praying. He believes that killing Claudius while he is praying would send Claudius's soul to heaven, which would be inadequate revenge. Claudius, now frightened of Hamlet's madness and fearing for his own safety, orders Hamlet sent to England at once.

Hamlet goes to confront his mother, in whose bedchamber Polonius has hidden behind a tapestry. Hearing a noise from behind the tapestry, Hamlet believes the king is hiding there. He draws his sword and stabs through the fabric, killing Polonius. For this crime, he is immediately dispatched to England with Rosencrantz and Guildenstern. Claudius has secretly given Rosencrantz and Guildenstern sealed orders for the King of England demanding that Hamlet be put to death.

In the aftermath of her father's death, Ophelia goes mad with grief and drowns in the river. Polonius's son, Laertes, who has been staying in France, returns to Denmark in a rage. Claudius convinces him that

Hamlet is to blame for his father's and sister's deaths. When Horatio and the king receive letters from Hamlet saying he has returned to Denmark after pirates attacked his ship en route to England, Claudius decides to use Laertes' desire for revenge to kill Hamlet. Laertes will fence with Hamlet in innocent sport, but Claudius will poison Laertes' blade so that if he draws blood, Hamlet will die. As a backup plan, the king decides to poison a goblet, which he will give Hamlet to drink should Hamlet score the first or second hits of the match. Hamlet returns to the vicinity of Elsinore just as Ophelia's funeral is taking place. Stricken with grief, he attacks Laertes and declares that he always loved Ophelia. Back at the castle, he tells Horatio that he believes one must be prepared to die, since death can come at any moment. A foolish courtier named Osric arrives on Claudius's orders to arrange the fencing match between Hamlet and Laertes.

The sword-fighting begins. Hamlet scores the first hit, but declines to drink when Claudius offers him the goblet. Instead, Gertrude takes a drink from it and is swiftly killed by the poison. Laertes succeeds in wounding Hamlet, but before Hamlet dies, Laertes is cut by his own sword's blade. After revealing to Hamlet that Claudius is responsible for the queen's death, Laertes dies from the blade's poison. Hamlet stabs Claudius through with the poisoned sword and forces him to drink down the rest of the poisoned wine. Claudius dies, and Hamlet dies immediately after achieving this revenge.

At this moment, a Norwegian prince named Fortinbras, who has led an army to Denmark and attacked Poland earlier in the play, enters with ambassadors from England, who report that Rosencrantz and Guildenstern are dead. Fortinbras is stunned by the gruesome sight of the entire royal family lying dead on the floor. He moves to take power of the kingdom. Horatio, fulfilling Hamlet's last request, tells him Hamlet's tragic story. Fortinbras orders that Hamlet be carried away in a manner befitting a fallen soldier.

CHARACTERS IN *HAMLET*

Bernardo and Marcellus Officers. It is Bernardo and Marcellus who first see the ghost walking the ramparts of Elsinore.

Claudius The King of Denmark, Hamlet's uncle, King Hamlet's brother, and the play's antagonist. Claudius is a calculating, ambitious politician driven by his sexual appetites and his lust for power. He sincerely loves Gertrude.

Fortinbras The young Prince of Norway. Fortinbras's father, King Fortinbras of Norway, was killed by Hamlet's father, King Hamlet of Denmark. A foil for Hamlet, Fortinbras seeks to avenge his father's honor by conquering Denmark.

Francisco A soldier and guardsman at Elsinore.

Queen Gertrude Hamlet's mother. After the death of King Hamlet, Gertrude marries Claudius. Gertrude loves Hamlet, but she seeks the good life more energetically than she does truth. Hamlet feels that Gertrude has betrayed his father—and, by extension, him.

The Ghost The spirit of King Hamlet, Hamlet's recently deceased father. The ghost claims to have been murdered by Claudius, and calls upon Hamlet for revenge. The question of what the ghost is or where it comes from is never definitively resolved.

Hamlet, Prince of Denmark The play's protagonist. Hamlet is the son of Gertrude and the late King Hamlet and the nephew of Claudius. Thirty years old at the start of the play, Hamlet is melancholy, bitter, and cynical, full of hatred for Claudius's scheming and disgust for Gertrude's sexuality. A reflective young man who has studied at the University of Wittenberg, Hamlet is often indecisive and hesitant, but at other times prone to rash and impulsive acts.

Horatio Hamlet's close friend. Horatio, who is a classmate of Hamlet's at the University in Wittenberg, is loyal and helpful to Hamlet throughout the play. He is the only major character to survive past the last act.

Laertes Polonius's son and Ophelia's brother. Passionate and quick to act, Laertes is a foil for the reflective Hamlet. Laertes spends much of the play in France.

Ophelia Polonius's daughter, Laertes's sister, and Hamlet's sometime love. A sweet and innocent young girl, Ophelia obeys both Polonius and Laertes. Ophelia is smart and loving, but madness and death overtake her.

Osric The foolish courtier who summons Hamlet to his duel with Laertes.

Polonius The Lord Chamberlain of Claudius's court, and the father of Laertes and Ophelia. Polonius is a pompous, conniving old man.

Reynaldo Polonius's servant. Reynaldo is sent to France to spy on Laertes.

Rosencrantz and Guildenstern Bumbling courtiers and former friends of Hamlet's from Wittenberg. They are summoned by Claudius and Gertrude to discover the cause of Hamlet's strange behavior.

Voltimand and Cornelius Courtiers sent to Norway to prevent Fortinbras's attack.

THEMES IN *HAMLET*

THE IMPOSSIBILITY OF CERTAINTY What separates *Hamlet* from other revenge plays is that the action we expect to see, particularly from Hamlet himself, is continually postponed while Hamlet tries to obtain more certain knowledge about what he is doing. He questions that which the people around him take for granted: that ghosts exist, that the ghost of Hamlet's father is what it appears to be and not a lying fiend, that the ghost has reliable knowledge about its own death. Hamlet also wonders how we can know the facts about a crime that has no witnesses. He wonders if he can know the state of Claudius's soul by watching his behavior or know the facts about what Claudius did by observing the state of his soul. He wonders if our actions will have their intended consequences, and if we can know anything about the afterlife. His refusal to leap to conclusions about these questions paralyzes him.

THE COMPLEXITY OF ACTION In *Hamlet*, the difficulty of taking reasonable, effective action is complicated by rational considerations, such as the need for certainty. It is also complicated by emotional, ethical, and psychological factors. Hamlet seems to question whether it is even possible to act in a controlled, purposeful way. When he does act, he does so blindly, recklessly, and violently. The other characters think little about the philosophy of action: they act without first wondering whether it is possible to act effectively. But the fact that all of their actions go awry might mean that Hamlet is right to worry. By taking bold action, Claudius gets a queen and a crown, but his conscience torments him, and he is beset by threats to his authority. In the end, his power grab results in his death. Laertes resolves that nothing will distract him from acting out his revenge, but he is easily influenced and manipulated into serving Claudius's ends, and his poisoned rapier is turned upon himself.

DEATH In the aftermath of his father's murder, Hamlet is obsessed with the idea of death, and over the course of the play he considers death from many perspectives. He ponders both the spiritual aftermath of death and the physical remainders of the dead, such as Yorick's skull and the decaying corpses in the cemetery. Hamlet often thinks about his own death, wondering whether or not suicide is a morally legitimate action in an unbearably painful world. Hamlet's grief and misery pain him so much that he frequently longs for death to end his suffering, but he fears that if he commits suicide, he will be consigned to eternal suffering in hell (Christianity prohibits suicide). In his famous "To be or not to be" soliloquy (III.i), Hamlet concludes that no one would choose to endure the pain of life if he or she were not afraid of what will come after death, and that it is this fear of what happens after we die that makes us worry about complex moral considerations and prevents us from taking action.

SYMBOLS IN *HAMLET*

YORICK'S SKULL In *Hamlet*, physical objects are rarely used to represent thematic ideas. One important exception is Yorick's skull, which Hamlet discovers in the graveyard in the first scene of Act V. The skull makes Hamlet think about the inevitability of death and bodily disintegration. He reveals his fascination with the physical consequences of death, tracing the skull's mouth and saying, "Here hung those lips that I have kissed I know not how oft" (V.i.174–75). Physical decomposition after death is an image that recurs throughout the play. Hamlet frequently alludes to the eventual decay of every human body: Polonius will be eaten by worms, even kings are eaten by worms, and dust from the decayed body of Alexander the Great might be used to plug a hole in a beer barrel.

ROT In *Hamlet*, the welfare of the royal family affects the health of the state as a whole. The play's early scenes explore the general anxiety and dread that surround the transfer of power from one ruler to the next. Throughout the play, characters draw explicit connections between the moral legitimacy of a ruler and the health of the nation. Denmark is frequently described as a physical body made ill by the moral corruption of Claudius and Gertrude, and many observers interpret the presence of the ghost as a supernatural omen indicating that "[s]omething is rotten in the state of Denmark" (I.iv.67). The dead King Hamlet is portrayed as a strong, forthright ruler under whose guard the state was in good health, while Claudius, a wicked politician, is portrayed as a power-hungry man who has corrupted and compromised Denmark. At the end of the play, the upright Fortinbras's rise to power suggests that Denmark will be strengthened once again.

IMPORTANT QUOTATIONS FROM *HAMLET*

O that this too too solid flesh would melt,
Thaw, and resolve itself into a dew!
Or that the Everlasting had not fixed
His canon 'gainst self-slaughter! O God! O God!
How weary, stale, flat, and unprofitable
Seem to me all the uses of this world!
Fie on 't! O fie! 'tis an unweeded garden,
That grows to seed; things rank and gross in nature
Possess it merely. That it should come to this!
But two months dead!—nay, not so much, not two:
So excellent a king; that was, to this,
Hyperion to a satyr; so loving to my mother,
That he might not beteem the winds of heaven
Visit her face too roughly. Heaven and earth!
Must I remember? Why, she would hang on him
As if increase of appetite had grown
By what it fed on: and yet, within a month,—
Let me not think on 't,—Frailty, thy name is woman!—
A little month; or ere those shoes were old
With which she followed my poor father's body
Like Niobe, all tears;—why she, even she,—
O God! a beast that wants discourse of reason,
Would have mourned longer,—married with mine uncle,
My father's brother; but no more like my father
Than I to Hercules: within a month;
Ere yet the salt of most unrighteous tears
Had left the flushing in her galled eyes,
She married:— O, most wicked speed, to post
With such dexterity to incestuous sheets!
It is not, nor it cannot come to good;
But break my heart,—for I must hold my tongue.

Location: I.ii.129–158
Speaker: Hamlet
Context: Hamlet has agreed to remain in Denmark instead of continuing his studies at Wittenberg; angst-ridden, he contemplates his father's death and his mother's swift remarriage

In this soliloquy, Hamlet considers suicide: the world is "weary, stale, flat, and unprofitable," so he desires his flesh to "melt" and wishes that God had not made "self-slaughter" a sin. In other words, suicide seems like a desirable alternative to life in a painful world, but is unfortunately forbidden by religion. Hamlet then goes on to describe the causes of his pain, specifically his intense disgust at his mother's marriage to Claudius. He describes the haste of their marriage, noting that the shoes his mother wore to his father's funeral were not worn out before her marriage to Claudius. He compares Claudius and his father—his father was "so excellent a king" while Claudius is a bestial "satyr." He blames his mother for remarrying so quickly (she moved "with such dexterity to incestuous sheets") and blames all women for being fickle and unfaithful ("Frailty, thy name is woman!"). The marriage, he thinks, is a bad omen for Denmark.

To be, or not to be: that is the question:
Whether 'tis nobler in the mind to suffer
The slings and arrows of outrageous fortune
Or to take arms against a sea of troubles,
And by opposing end them?—To die,—to sleep,—
No more; and by a sleep to say we end
The heartache, and the thousand natural shocks
That flesh is heir to,—'tis a consummation
Devoutly to be wished. To die,—to sleep;—
To sleep: perchance to dream:—ay, there's the rub;
For in that sleep of death what dreams may come,
When we have shuffled off this mortal coil,
Must give us pause: there's the respect
That makes calamity of so long life;
For who would bear the whips and scorns of time,
The oppressor's wrong, the proud man's contumely,
The pangs of despised love, the law's delay,
The insolence of office, and the spurns
That patient merit of the unworthy takes,
When he himself might his quietus make
With a bare bodkin? Who would these fardels bear,
To grunt and sweat under a weary life,
But that the dread of something after death,—
The undiscovered country, from whose bourn
No traveler returns,—puzzles the will,
And makes us rather bear those ills we have
Than fly to others that we know not of?
Thus conscience does make cowards of us all;
And thus the native hue of resolution
Is sicklied o'er with the pale cast of thought;
And enterprises of great pith and moment,
With this regard, their currents turn awry,
And lose the name of action.

Location: III.i.58–90
Speaker: Hamlet
Context: Tormented by his sense of his responsibility to avenge his father's death, Hamlet contemplates
    why people do not commit suicide

In the most famous speech of the English language, Hamlet examines the moral legitimacy of suicide in an unbearably painful world. He first debates the possibility of committing suicide as a logical problem: "To be, or not to be"—that is, to live or not to live. He then weighs the moral ramifications of living and dying. Is it nobler to suffer life—"[t]he slings and arrows of outrageous fortune"—or to try to put an end to suffering? He compares death to sleep and thinks of death as an end to suffering, pain, and uncertainty, "[t]he heartache, and the thousand natural shocks / That flesh is heir to." He decides that suicide is a desirable course of action, "a consummation / Devoutly to be wished." But, as signaled by the religious word "devoutly," there is more to the question—namely, what will happen in the afterlife. Hamlet reconfigures his metaphor of death as sleep to include the possibility of dreaming. He says that the dreams that may come in the sleep of death are daunting, that they "must give us pause"—the possibility of nightmares leads us to hesitate before committing suicide, as does the possibility that dreams will not exist at all, because consciousness will not exist after death.

Hamlet decides that it is the impossibility of knowing what happens after death that prevents humans from killing themselves to end the pain of life. He outlines a long list of the miseries of experience, ranging from lovesickness to hard work to political oppression, and asks who would choose to bear those miseries if he could bring himself peace with a knife. He answers his own question, saying no one would choose to live if not for "the dread of something after death," which makes people submit to the suffering of their lives rather than choose another state of existence which might be even more miserable. The dread of the afterlife that our consciousnesses allow, Hamlet concludes, makes action impossible.

Hamlet's speech connects many of the play's main themes, including Hamlet's obsession with death and suicide, the impossibility of knowledge in a spiritually ambiguous universe, and the tension between thought and action. The speech also illuminates Hamlet's thought processes: his relentless intellect works furiously to find a logical solution to his misery. Religion has proved inadequate to spur him on to action. Here, Hamlet turns to a logical philosophical inquiry and finds it equally frustrating.

Give thy thoughts no tongue,
Nor any unproportioned thought his act.
Be thou familiar, but by no means vulgar.
Those friends thou hast, and their adoption tried,
Grapple them unto thy soul with hoops of steel;
But do not dull thy palm with entertainment
Of each new-hatched, unfledged comrade. Beware
Of entrance to a quarrel; but, being in,
Bear 't that the opposed may beware of thee.
Give every man thine ear, but few thy voice:
Take each man's censure, but reserve thy judgment.
Costly thy habit as thy purse can buy,
But not expressed in fancy; rich, not gaudy:
For the apparel oft proclaims the man;
And they in France of the best rank and station
Are most select and generous chief in that.
Neither a borrower nor a lender be:
For loan oft loses both itself and friend;
And borrowing dulls the edge of husbandry.
This above all: to thine own self be true;
And it must follow, as the night the day,
Thou canst not then be false to any man.

Location: I.iii.59–1880
Speaker: Polonius to Laertes
Context: Polonius gives his son Laertes trite advice about how to live before Laertes leaves for France

Something is rotten in the state of Denmark.

Location: I.iv.67
Speaker: Marcellus
Context: Marcellus and Horatio debate whether or not to follow Hamlet and the ghost into the dark night

I have of late, — but wherefore I know not, — lost all my mirth, forgone all custom of exercises; and indeed, it goes so heavily with my disposition that this goodly frame, the earth, seems to me a sterile promontory; this most excellent canopy, the air, look you, this brave o'erhanging firmament, this majestical roof fretted with golden fire, — why, it appears no other thing to me than a foul and pestilent congregation of vapors. What a piece of work is man! How noble in reason! how infinite in faculties! in form and moving, how express and admirable! in action how like an angel! in apprehension, how like a god! the beauty of the world! the paragon of animals! And yet, to me, what is this quintessence of dust?

Location: II.ii.287–298
Speaker: Hamlet
Context: Hamlet explains to Rosencrantz and Guildenstern why Gertrude and Claudius have sent for them to cheer him up

THE HANDMAID'S TALE

Margaret Atwood

A woman tells the story of her severely restricted life as a state-sanctioned babymaker in a totalitarian society in the imagined near future.

THE LIFE OF MARGARET ATWOOD

Margaret Atwood was born in 1939 in Ottawa, Ontario. She published her first book of poetry in 1961 while attending the University of Toronto. She later received degrees from both Radcliffe College and Harvard University, and pursued a career in teaching at the university level. Her first novel, *The Edible Woman*, was published in 1969 to wide acclaim. As her literary career has blossomed, Atwood has continued teaching. She gives lectures and has served as a writer-in-residence at many colleges and universities, from the University of Toronto to Macquarie University in Australia.

The Handmaid's Tale, Atwood's sixth novel, was published in 1985 and quickly became a best-seller. Atwood lives in Toronto with novelist Graeme Gibson and their daughter Jess. She won Great Britain's Booker Prize for her 2000 novel, *The Blind Assassin*. Her most recent novel, *Oryx and Crake* (2003), like *The Handmaid's Tale*, takes place in a dystopic future.

THE HANDMAID'S TALE IN CONTEXT

Along with classics such as Aldous Huxley's *Brave New World* and George Orwell's *1984*, *The Handmaid's Tale* is a dystopian novel, a genre that portrays imagined societies that are in some way terrifying or restrictive. Atwood wrote her novel shortly after Ronald Reagan became president of the United States and Margaret Thatcher became prime minister of Great Britain, during a period of conservative revival in the West partly fueled by a strong, well-organized movement of religious conservatives who criticized what they perceived as the excesses of the sexual revolution of the 1960s and 1970s. Feminists feared that the growing power of the religious right would cause women to lose the gains they had made in previous decades. At the same time, the 1980s were a time of concern about declining birthrates, the dangers of nuclear power, and environmental degradation. Atwood's novel addresses the fears of the times, exploring an extreme case of a male-dominated society in a world undone by nuclear pollution.

Some of the novel's concerns seem dated today, and its implicit condemnation of the political goals of American religious conservatives has been criticized as unfair and overly paranoid. Nonetheless, *The Handmaid's Tale* remains a powerful portrayal of a totalitarian society, and one of the few dystopian novels to examine the intersection of politics and sexuality in detail. In particular, the exploration of the controversial politics of reproduction will likely guarantee the novel a readership well into the twenty-first century.

THE HANDMAID'S TALE: KEY FACTS

Time and place written: Early 1980s, West Berlin and Alabama

Date of first publication: 1985

Publisher: McClelland & Stewart in Canada; Houghton Mifflin in the United States

Type of work: Novel

Genre: Dystopian novel

Language: English

Setting (time): The not-too-distant future

Setting (place): The fictional Republic of Gilead, in present-day Cambridge, Massachusetts

Tense: Present; past for flashbacks of the Red Center and life before Gilead

Tone: Dark, paranoid, fearful, nostalgic

Narrator: Offred in the first person

Point of View: Offred's

Protagonist: Offred

Antagonist: The restrictions imposed by the totalitarian Republic of Gilead regime

THE HANDMAID'S TALE: PLOT OVERVIEW

Offred is a Handmaid in the Republic of Gilead, assigned to a Commander and his wife Serena Joy. The narrator is called Offred because she is the Handmaid "of Fred," her Commander. Once a month, at the most fertile point of her menstrual cycle, Offred must take part in the Ceremony to try to conceive a baby. Offred's freedom, like that of all women, is extremely restricted. She may leave the house only on shopping trips, the door to her room may never be shut, and the Eyes of Gilead's secret police force watch her every public move.

We reconstruct the recent past from frequent flashbacks. Offred was raised by a single mother who was a feminist activist. In the old world, before Gilead, Offred had an affair with a married man named Luke. He divorced his wife and married Offred, and they had a child together. The architects of Gilead began their rise to power in an age of prostitution, readily available pornography, and frequent violence against women, as fertility rates declined because of pollution and chemical spills. Backed by the military, they assassinated the president and members of Congress and launched a coup, claiming that they were taking power temporarily. They gradually restricted women's rights until women could no longer work or own property. Offred, Luke, and their daughter were arrested as they attempted to flee into Canada, and Offred has seen neither her husband nor her daughter since.

Her marriage annulled because Luke had been married before, Offred was sent to the Red Center to be indoctrinated into Gilead ideology and prepared to become a handmaid. According to Gilead ideology, women should be subservient to men and concerned solely with childbearing. Aunt Lydia, one of the Aunts who ran the Center, argued that the Gilead social order ultimately offers women more respect than the old order did. Offred's fiercely independent best friend Moira was also brought to the Red Center, but she managed to escape, and Offred does not know what happened to her.

At the Commander's house, Offred's life has settled into a restrictive routine. She takes shopping trips with Ofglen, another Handmaid, and they visit the Wall around what used to be Harvard University, where the bodies of rebels hang. She must visit the doctor frequently to be checked for diseases and other complications, and she must endure the monthly sexual Ceremony with the Commander and his Wife.

On a routine visit to the doctor, the doctor suggests to Offred that the Commander may be infertile and offers to impregnate her himself. She judges his proposition too risky and refuses. After a Ceremony, the Commander sends Nick, his gardener and chauffeur, to ask Offred to come see him in his study the following night. She begins visiting the Commander regularly. They play Scrabble (which is forbidden, since women are not allowed to read), and he lets her look at old magazines such as *Vogue*. At the end of these meetings, he asks her to kiss him.

On a shopping trip, Ofglen reveals to Offred that she is a member of Mayday. Meanwhile, Offred finds the Ceremony less impersonal now that she knows the Commander better. Their nighttime conversations begin to touch on the Gilead regime, which the Commander helped establish. When Offred admits how unhappy she is, the Commander replies, "you can't make an omelette without breaking eggs."

Because Offred has not been able to conceive with the Commander, Serena suggests that Offred secretly have sex with Nick and pass the child off as the Commander's. In exchange, Serena promises to bring Offred a picture of her daughter. On the same night that Serena has arranged for Offred to visit Nick, the Commander secretly takes Offred out to a club named Jezebel's, where Commanders mingle with prostitutes. Offred sees Moira working there. In the club's bathroom, Moira tells Offred that after she was recaptured, she chose Jezebel's over the Colonies. Offred tells us that after that night in Jezebel's, she never sees Moira again. After a few hours, the Commander takes Offred upstairs, and they have sex in what used to be a hotel room. She tries to feign passion.

Late at night after Offred returns home, Serena takes her to Nick's room. Offred and Nick have sex. Soon they begin to sleep together frequently, without anyone's knowledge. Caught up in the affair, Offred ignores Ofglen's requests to gather information from the Commander for Mayday. One day, all the Handmaids take part in a Particution of a supposed rapist, supervised by Aunt Lydia. Ofglen strikes the first blow, later telling Offred that the so-called rapist was actually a member of Mayday and that she hit him to put him out of his misery.

Shortly thereafter, Ofglen is replaced by a new Handmaid, who tells Offred that the old Ofglen hanged herself when she saw the secret police coming for her. At home, Serena has found out about Offred's trip to Jezebel's, and promises punishment. As Offred waits in her room, she sees a black van from the Eyes approach. Nick comes in and tells her that the Eyes are really Mayday members who have come to save her. Offred leaves with them over the Commander's futile objections, on her way either to prison or to freedom—she does not know which.

The novel closes with an epilogue from 2195, after Gilead has fallen, written in the form of a lecture given by Professor Pieixoto. He explains the formation and customs of Gilead in objective, analytical language. He discusses the significance of Offred's story, which has turned up on cassette tapes in Bangor, Maine. He suggests that Nick arranged Offred's escape and says her fate after that is unknown.

GLOSSARY

SOCIAL ROLES IN GILEAD SOCIETY

Angels Officers in the Gilead military.

Aunts Older, unmarried women. The Aunts work as disciplinarians and midwives, and train Handmaids-to-be.

Commandesr of the Faithful Male members of the Gilead elite.

Econowives The wives of poor Gileadeans.

Eyes of God The Gilead secret police.

Handmaids Fertile women assigned to bear the children of elite, barren couples.

Marthas Infertile females who work as a domestic servant.

Guardians of the Faith Male Gileadeans too young, too old, or too weak for the army. Guardians staff the police force and often work for Commanders as servants.

Wives The wives of Commanders.

OTHER TERMS

Birth Day The day a Handmaid gives birth to a child.

The Ceremony A ritual during which a Commander reads from the Bible and then has sexual intercourse with a Handmaid while his Wife sits behind her and holds her hands.

Children of Ham African Americans.

The Colonies Forced-labor toxic cleanup camps for the most dangerous enemies of the state.

Gender Traitors Homosexuals.

Republic of Gilead The totalitarian, theocratic political regime that has replaced the United States of America.

Mayday An underground organization dedicated to overthrowing Gilead. *M'aidez* is French for "help me."

Particution A capital punishment ceremony during which a large group of Handmaids release their aggressions by tearing apart the condemned with bare hands.

Prayvaganza A public same-sex gathering. Women's prayvaganzas usually celebrate a Wife's daughter's wedding; men's prayvaganzas celebrate military victories.

The Red Center The Rachel and Leah Re-education Center, a training center for future Handmaids that is staffed by Aunts.

Sons of Jacob Jews.

Salvaging A public execution.

Unbaby A malformed or otherwise "defective" baby, discarded at birth.

Unwoman Any female enemy of the state (for example, a feminist).

CHARACTERS IN *THE HANDMAID'S TALE*

The Commander The head of the household where Offred lives. Although he was involved in establishing the Gilead regime, the Commander is a sympathetic figure. He is kind to Offred and recognizes that Gilead has problems.

Cora A Martha at the Commander's household. Cora hopes that Offred will have a baby so that she will be able to help raise a child.

Aunt Elizabeth A Red Center Aunt. Moira attacks Aunt Elizabeth and steals her Aunt uniform to escape from the Red Center.

Janine A Handmaid who stayed at the Red Center at the same time as Offred. Janine, who takes the name Ofwarren, is the envy of the other Handmaids when she becomes pregnant, possibly by her doctor. However, her baby turns out to be malformed—an "Unbaby." A well-indoctrinated conformist, Janine endears herself to the Aunts and earns Offred's contempt.

Moira Offred's best friend from college. A lesbian and a staunch feminist, Moira embodies everything the architects of Gilead want to stamp out. She is also one of the few to repeatedly defy the system, making several escape attempts from the Red Center. Later, as a prostitute at Jezebel's, she seems resigned to her fate, suggesting that totalitarian society crushes even the most resourceful and independent people.

Aunt Lydia A Red Center Aunt whose slogans continue to echo in Offred's head. Aunt Lydia argues that despite all the restrictions, women are treated with more respect under the Gilead regime than they were previously.

Luke Offred's pre-Gilead husband. Because Luke was married once before (he got a divorce while having an affair with Offred), their marriage is void under Gilead law. Offred's loving memories of Luke contrast with the regimented, passionless male-female relations in the new society.

Nick A Guardian who is the Commander's gardener and chauffeur and possibly a member of Mayday, the Eyes, or both. After Serena Joy arranges for them to meet so that Offred can conceive, Nick and Offred begin a covert sexual affair. At the end of the novel, Nick orchestrates Offred's escape from the Commander's house, but we do not know whether he delivers her to the Eyes or the resistance.

Offred The novel's narrator and protagonist. Offred is a Handmaid in the fictional future Republic of Gilead. She remembers but never reveals her real name, which has been discarded in favor of "of Fred," a name that announces Fred as her Commander. In her former life she was married to Luke and had a young daughter.

Offred's Mother A single mother and a feminist activist. At the Red Center, Offred sees a video of her mother as a young woman protesting violence against women in a Take Back the Night march.

Ofglen A Handmaid and Offred's shopping partner. Ofglen is a member of Mayday, the underground resistance. Soon after the Particution, Ofglen hangs herself before the Eyes can arrest her.

Professor Pieixoto One of the transcribers of Offred's audio diary. Pieixoto is the keynote speaker at the year 2195 symposium portrayed in the epilogue. Through his lecture, Atwood situates the Republic of Gilead within a (fictional) historical context and pokes gentle fun at academia.

Rita A Martha at the Commander's household. Rita is less content with her lot than Cora.

Serena Joy The Commander's cruel and unhappy Wife. Before Gilead, Serena was a gospel singer and later an anti-feminist activist. Through her we see that Gilead's restrictive, male-dominated society cannot bring happiness even to its most pampered and powerful women.

THEMES IN *THE HANDMAID'S TALE*

LANGUAGE AS A TOOL OF POWER   Like other novels of totalitarian dystopia, *The Handmaid's Tale* explores the connection between repression and perversion of language. Gilead's official lexicon serves the needs of the elite, maintaining control over women's bodies by maintaining control over their names. Women are stripped of their identities and defined solely by their social roles—Wives, Handmaids, Aunts, Marthas. Feminists and deformed babies—Unwomen and Unbabies—are denied humanity. Gilead rituals are designated either by newly coined words (Prayvaganza, Particution) or by words co-opted from the old language (Salvaging, the Ceremony).

Gilead is a theocracy, and many of its terms come from the Bible, particularly the New Testament. "Martha" is the name of a biblical woman who focuses on housekeeping when Jesus comes to visit. The military ranks range from Angels to Commanders of the Faithful. Store names refer to biblical stories: Loaves and Fishes, All Flesh, Milk and Honey. Religious terminology whitewashes political skullduggery with pious language, turning repression into a holy deed.

COMPLACENCY   Atwood implicitly agrees with Offred's mother's sentiment that it is "truly amazing, what people can get used to, as long as there are a few compensations." Offred and Nick's physical relationship and companionship makes Offred's restricted life bearable: she becomes complacent and does not respond to Ofglen's request that she help Mayday by gathering information from the Commander. Excluded from the world of men, Serena Joy wields tyrannical power over her own household. While Atwood does not condone Offred's, Serena's, or Moira's complacency, she also suggests that their resistance would probably fail to make a difference.

SIMILARITIES BETWEEN REACTIONARY AND FEMINIST IDEOLOGIES   In a few instances, Atwood draws similarities between the architects of Gilead and radical feminists such as Offred's mother. Both groups claim to protect women from sexual violence, sometimes resorting to censorship to accomplish that goal. (Offred recalls her mother burning pornographic magazines.) Both also use the rhetoric of female solidarity and "sisterhood" to their advantage. In her critique of the religious right, Atwood implies that feminism too has a dark side.

SYMBOLS IN *THE HANDMAID'S TALE*

CAMBRIDGE, MASSACHUSETTS, AND HARVARD UNIVERSITY   Though never explicitly named, the area where Offred lives, near the center of Gilead's power, can be identified as Cambridge, Massachusetts. In particular, we can identify several buildings around Harvard University. Atwood's choice of setting emphasizes the link between Gilead and seventeenth-century Puritan Boston, which was America's first restrictive, theocratic society.

Under Gilead, a Harvard building has become a secret police detention center, bodies of executed dissidents hang from the wall around Harvard Yard, and Salvagings take place on the steps of Harvard's Widener library. Harvard University becomes a symbol of the inverted world that Gilead has created: a place that was founded to pursue knowledge and truth has become the seat of oppression and torture.

THE HANDMAIDS' RED HABITS   The red costumes symbolize fertility, which is the Handmaids' primary value. The color red is associated both with the blood of menstruation and the of childbirth, and with sexual transgression, recalling the scarlet A (as in *adultery*) worn by Hester Prynne, the heroine of Nathaniel Hawthorne's *The Scarlet Letter*. The Handmaids' adultery may be sanctioned by the state and justified with the Bible, but it nevertheless pains the Commanders' Wives, who call the Handmaids sluts.

IMPORTANT QUOTATIONS FROM *THE HANDMAID'S TALE*

I would like to believe this is a story I'm telling. I need to believe it. I must believe it. Those who can believe that such stories are only stories have a better chance.
If it's a story I'm telling, then I have control over the ending. Then there will be an ending, to the story, and real life will come after it. I can pick up where I left off.

Location: Chapter 7
Speaker: Offred
Context: Offred stands back from her narrative and thinks that her real-life story is beginning to resemble a fictional story because she is telling it

Throughout the novel, Offred steps away from her narrative to contemplate the storytelling process, which makes a fiction—a bedtime story—out of historical events. If it were truly only a fictional story, she says, she would not be forced to tell such a horrible one. These ruminations are complicated by the fact that Offred's narrative is presented, by the historians of the epilogue, as an artifact whose authenticity must necessarily be questioned, and by the fact that the whole novel, including the epilogue, is Atwood's invention.

I used to think of my body as an instrument, of pleasure, or a means of transportation, or an implement for the accomplishment of my will.. . . Now the flesh arranges itself differently. I'm a cloud, congealed around a central object, the shape of a pear, which is hard and more real than I am and glows red within its translucent wrapping.

Location: Chapter 13
Speaker: Offred
Context: Offred sits in the bath, naked, and thinks about how the way she views her body has changed

Before Gilead, Offred's body was her own; now her body is significant only for its "central object," her womb. This passage crystallizes one of the ideas Atwood explores, that of the way women's bodies are used as instruments of power and policy. Formed partially in response to a decreasing birthrate crisis, Gilead is structured to control reproduction. The state assumes complete control of women's bodies: women are not permitted to read, vote, own property, or pursue careers for fear they might subvert their husbands or the state. Women's bodies become a "national resource."

Ordinary, said Aunt Lydia, is what you are used to. This may not seem ordinary to you now, but after a time it will. It will become ordinary.

Location: End of Chapter 6
Speaker: Aunt Lydia (as remembered by Offred)
Context: Looking at bodies of people hanged by Gilead, Offred remembers Aunt Lydia's prediction that their restrictive lifestyle will "become ordinary" once they are used to it

He was not a monster, to her. Probably he had some endearing trait: he whistled, offkey, in the shower, he had a yen for truffles, he called his dog Liebchen and made it sit up for little pieces of raw steak. How easy it is to invent a humanity, for anyone at all. What an available temptation.

Location: Chapter 24
Speaker: Offred
Context: Offred compares her new almost-warm feelings toward the Commander to something she once saw in a documentary: a Nazi death-camp guard's mistress insisting that her lover was not a monster

---

The problem wasn't only with the women, he says. The main problem was with the men. There was nothing for them anymore.. . . I'm not talking about sex, he says. That was part of it, the sex was too easy.. . . You know what they were complaining about the most? Inability to feel. Men were turning off on sex, even. They were turning off on marriage. Do they feel now? I say. Yes, he says, looking at me. They do.

Location: End of Chapter 32
Speaker: Offred and the Commander (as recounted by Offred)
Context: The Commander attempts to explain to Offred the reasons behind the formation of Gilead: feminism and the sexual revolution left men without a purpose in life—a void now filled by their new roles as providers and caretakers of society

HARD TIMES

Charles Dickens

A wealthy merchant raises his children using principles of rational self-interest, which leaves them emotionally crippled; a morally upright factory worker suffers and dies because of his goodness.

THE LIFE OF CHARLES DICKENS

Charles Dickens was born on February 7, 1812. He spent the first ten years of his life in Kent, a marshy region by the sea in the east of England. Dickens was the second of eight children. His father, John Dickens, was kind and likable, but fiscally irresponsible. His huge debts caused tremendous strain on his family.

When Dickens was ten, his family moved to London. Two years later, his father was arrested and thrown in debtors' prison. Dickens's mother moved into the prison with seven of her children. Charles tried to earn money for the struggling family. For three months, he worked with other children pasting labels on bottles in a blacking warehouse. Dickens found the three months he spent apart from his family highly traumatic. Not only was the job itself miserable, but he considered himself too good for it, earning the contempt of the other children. His experiences at this warehouse inspired passages of *David Copperfield*.

An inheritance gave John Dickens enough money to free himself from his debt and from prison. Dickens attended Wellington House Academy for two years. He became a law clerk, then a newspaper reporter, and finally a novelist. His first novel, *The Pickwick Papers* (1837), met with huge popular success. Dickens was a literary celebrity in England for the rest of his life.

Dickens's work includes *Oliver Twist* (1837–1839), *Nicholas Nickelby* (1838–1839), and *A Christmas Carol* (1843). Perhaps his best known novel, *Great Expectations* (1860–1861) shares many thematic similarities with *David Copperfield*. Dickens died in Kent on June 9, 1870, at the age of fifty-eight.

HARD TIMES IN CONTEXT

Dickens was deeply concerned with the plight of the poor, particularly poor children. The Victorian England in which Dickens lived was fraught with massive economic turmoil, as the Industrial Revolution sent shockwaves through the established order. Factory owners exploited their employees, referred to as "the Hands" in *Hard Times* (1854), forcing them to work long hours for low pay in cramped, sooty, loud, and dangerous factories. Dickens was involved with a number of organizations that worked to better the horrible living conditions of the London poor. He was a speaker for the Metropolitan Sanitary Organization, and he organized projects to clear up the slums and build clean, safe, cheap housing for the poor.

Dickens often used his art to focus attention on the plight of the poor and to awaken the conscience of the reader. *Hard Times*, set amid the industrial smokestacks and factories of Coketown, England, exposes the massive gulf between the nation's rich and poor and criticizes what Dickens perceived as the self-interest of the middle and upper classes. *Hard Times* suggests that England itself is turning into a factory machine: the middle class is concerned only with making a profit in the most efficient and practical way possible. *Hard Times* is not a subtle novel: Dickens hammers home his point with vicious, often hilarious, satire and sentimental melodrama. Neither is it a difficult novel: Dickens wanted all his readers to catch his point, and he repeatedly and explicitly articulates the moral theme of the novel. While not Dickens's most popular novel, *Hard Times* is an important expression of the values he considered fundamental.

HARD TIMES: KEY FACTS

Original title: Hard Times for These Times

Time and place written: 1854; London

Date of first publication: Published in serial installments in Dickens's magazine between April 1 and August 12, 1854

Publisher: Household Words

Type of work: Novel

Genre: Satire; social protest novel

Language: English

Setting (time): The middle of the nineteenth century

Setting (place): Coketown, a manufacturing town in the south of England

Tense: Past

Tone: Ironic, mocking, satirical, empathetic

Narrator: Anonymous, limited omniscient, third person

Point of view: The narrator's

Protagonist: Louisa Gradgrind

Antagonist: Louisa's upbringing and loveless marriage

HARD TIMES: PLOT OVERVIEW

Thomas Gradgrind, a wealthy, retired merchant in the industrial city of Coketown, England, believes in rationalism and self-interest. He raises his oldest children, Louisa and Tom, according to his precepts and never allows them to engage in imaginative pursuits. He founds a school and takes in one of the students, the kindly and imaginative Sissy Jupe, after her father, a circus entertainer, disappears.

Tom becomes a dissipated, self-interested hedonist, and Louisa struggles with deep inner confusion. She feels she is missing something important in her life. Eventually she marries her father's friend Josiah Bounderby, a wealthy factory owner and banker more than twice her age. Bounderby continually trumpets his role as a self-made man who succeeded even though his mother abandoned him in the gutter when he was an infant. Tom is apprenticed at the Bounderby bank, and Sissy remains at the Gradgrind home to care for the younger children.

In the meantime, an impoverished "Hand"—Dickens's term for the lowest laborers in Coketown's factories—named Stephen Blackpool is in love with Rachael, another poor factory worker. He is already married to a horrible, drunken woman who disappears for months and even years at a time. Stephen visits Bounderby to ask about a divorce and learns that only the wealthy can obtain them. Outside Bounderby's home, Stephen meets Mrs. Pegler, a strange old woman with an inexplicable devotion to Bounderby.

James Harthouse, a wealthy young sophisticate from London, arrives in Coketown to begin a political career as a disciple of Gradgrind, who is now a Member of Parliament. He immediately takes an interest in Louisa. With the unspoken aid of Mrs. Sparsit, a former aristocrat who has fallen on hard times and now works for Bounderby, he sets about trying to seduce Louisa.

The Hands, at the urging of a crooked union spokesman named Slackbridge, try to form a union. Only Stephen refuses to join. He feels that a union strike would only increase tensions between employers and employees. The other Hands cast him out, and Bounderby fires him when he refuses to spy on the Hands. Louisa, impressed with Stephen's integrity, visits him before he leaves Coketown and gives him some money. Tom tells Stephen that if he waits outside the bank for several consecutive nights, help will come to him. Stephen does so, but no help arrives. Eventually, he leaves Coketown, hoping to find agricultural work in the country. Not long after that, the bank is robbed, and the lone suspect is Stephen, the Hand who was seen loitering outside the bank for several nights just before disappearing from the city.

Harthouse declares his love for Louisa. Louisa agrees to meet him in Coketown later that night, but actually flees to her father's house and tells Gradgrind that her upbringing has left her married to a man she does not love, disconnected from her feelings, deeply unhappy, and possibly in love with Harthouse. She collapses. Gradgrind, struck dumb with self-reproach, begins to question his philosophy of rational self-interest.

Sissy, who loves Louisa deeply, convinces Harthouse to leave Coketown forever. Bounderby, furious that his wife has left him, redoubles his efforts to capture Stephen. When Stephen tries to return to clear his good name, he falls into a mining pit called Old Hell Shaft. Rachael and Louisa discover him, but he dies soon after bidding an emotional farewell to Rachael. Gradgrind and Louisa realize that Tom robbed the bank, and they arrange to sneak him out of England with the help of the circus performers. They are thwarted by Bitzer, a young man who went to Gradgrind's school and who embodies all the qualities of the detached rationalism that Gradgrind once espoused, but who now sees its limits. Sleary, the lisping circus proprietor, helps Tom escape from England after all.

It is revealed that Mrs. Pegler, a known associate of the late Stephen Blackpool, is Bounderby's loving mother. She never abandoned him—he forbid her to visit him. Bounderby fires Mrs. Sparsit and sends her away to her hostile relatives. Five years later, he dies alone in the streets of Coketown. Gradgrind gives up his old philosophy and devotes his political power to helping the poor. Tom realizes the error of his ways but dies without ever seeing his family again. Sissy marries and has a large and loving family. Louisa never remarries and never has children, but Sissy's family loves her and she learns how to feel sympathy for her fellow human beings.

CHARACTERS IN *HARD TIMES*

Bitzer One of the successes of Gradgrind's rationalistic system of education. Initially a bully at Gradgrind's school, Bitzer later becomes an employee and a spy at Bounderby's bank. He tries to stop Tom from fleeing.

Stephen Blackpool A Hand in Bounderby's factory. Stephen, who is married to a wretched woman, loves Rachael. A man of great honesty and compassion, Stephen maintains his moral standards even in the face of ruin. The narrator endorses his values.

Josiah Bounderby Gradgrind's friend and later Louisa's husband. Although he was actually raised by loving parents, Bounderby claims to be a self-made man whose mother abandoned him.

Jane Gradgrind Gradgrind's younger daughter. Because Sissy largely raises her, Jane is happier than her sister, Louisa.

Louisa Gradgrind Gradgrind's daughter. Louisa eventually recognizes that her father's system of education has deprived her of joy and the ability to empathize with others.

Mrs. Gradgrind Gradgrind's whiny, anemic wife. Although Mrs. Gradgrind does not share her husband's interest in facts, she lacks the energy and the imagination to oppose his system of education.

Thomas Gradgrind A wealthy, retired merchant who becomes a Member of Parliament. Mr. Gradgrind espouses a philosophy of rationalism and self-interest. He raises his six children to be practical by stunting the development of their imaginations and emotions.

Thomas (Tom) Gradgrind, Jr. Gradgrind's eldest son and an apprentice at Bounderby's bank. Because of his upbringing, Tom is hedonistic and hypocritical. He loves money and gambling even more than he loves Louisa.

James Harthouse A sophisticated, manipulative young London gentleman who enters Coketown politics out of boredom. Harthouse resolves to seduce Louisa because he thinks it would amuse him.

Cecelia Jupe The daughter of a clown in Sleary's circus. Gradgrind takes in Sissy when her father disappears. She is a foil for Louisa, imaginative and compassionate where Louisa is rational and unfeeling. Sissy embodies the Victorian ideal of femininity.

Mr. McChoakumchild The unpleasant teacher at Gradgrind's school. As his name suggests, McChoakumchild stifles children's imaginations and feelings.

Mrs. Pegler Bounderby's mother. Mrs. Pegler makes an annual visit to Coketown in order to admire her son's prosperity from a safe distance.

Rachael A simple, honest Hand who loves Stephen Blackpool. To Stephen, Rachael represents domestic happiness and moral purity.

Slackbridge A crooked orator who convinces the Hands to unionize and turns them against Stephen Blackpool.

Mr. Sleary The lisping proprietor of the circus where Sissy's father was an entertainer. Mr. Sleary and his troop of entertainers value laughter and fantasy, in contrast to Mr. Gradgrind, who values rationality and fact.

Mrs. Sparsit Bounderby's housekeeper. Once a member of the aristocratic elite, Mrs. Sparsit fell on hard times when her marriage collapsed. A selfish, manipulative, dishonest woman, Mrs. Sparsit hopes to sabotage Bounderby's marriage so she can marry him herself.

THEMES IN *HARD TIMES*

THE MECHANIZATION OF HUMAN BEINGS *Hard Times* suggests that nineteenth-century England's overzealous embrace of industrialization threatens to turn human beings into machines by thwarting the development of their emotions and imaginations. The narrator draws a parallel between the factory Hands and the Gradgrind children—both lead monotonous, uniform existences, untouched by pleasure. Consequently, their fantasies and feelings are dulled, and they become almost mechanical themselves. Dickens's primary goal in *Hard Times* is to point out the dangers of Gradgrind's philosophy, suggesting that without compassion and imagination, life would be unbearable. Louisa's unhappiness and Tom's immorality point to the foolishness of their father's methods.

THE IMPORTANCE OF FEMININITY During the Victorian era, compassion, moral purity, and emotional sensitivity were identified as feminine traits. *Hard Times* suggests that because they possess these traits, women can counteract the mechanizing effects of industrialization. When Stephen feels depressed about the monotony of his life as a factory worker, Rachael's gentle fortitude inspires him to keep going. Sissy introduces love into the Gradgrind household, ultimately teaching Louisa how to feel emotion. Dickens suggests that Mr. Gradgrind's philosophy of self-interest and calculating rationality has prevented Louisa from developing her natural feminine traits. He also suggests that dangerous imbalance results when married couples lack the right dose of femininity. Mrs. Gradgrind's laziness and unwillingness to be properly feminine leads to Gradgrind's overemphasis of fact. Bounderby marries Louisa, a cold, emotionless product of Mr. and Mrs. Gradgrind's marriage who can do nothing to counter her husband's rigidity.

THE UNLIKELIHOOD OF UPWARD SOCIAL MOBILITY By exposing Bounderby's real origins, Dickens suggests that social mobility is a myth. The poor, he says, cannot overcome poverty through sheer determination. Only the charity and compassion of the wealthy can help them. Bounderby's fake history—which, coincidentally, could also be held up as an example of the American Dream—holds that he was born in a ditch, abandoned by his mother, raised by his alcoholic grandmother, and kept alive by his own labor. From these ignominious beginnings, the story goes, he became the wealthy owner of both a factory and a bank. This story, and others like it, is the keystone of the myth that any individual can overcome all obstacles to success—including poverty and lack of education—through hard work. The fact that Dickens slashes this story to ribbons shows that he thinks the idea of social mobility is a pretty lie.

SYMBOLS IN *HARD TIMES*

PEGASUS Mr. Sleary's circus entertainers stay at an inn called the Pegasus Arms. Inside this inn is a pegasus, a model of a flying horse with "golden stars stuck on all over him." The pegasus represents a world of fantasy and beauty from which the young Gradgrind children are excluded.

SMOKE SERPENTS The streams of smoke that fill the skies above Coketown—the literal effects of industrialization—symbolize the moral blindness of factory owners like Bounderby. Because he is so concerned with making money, Bounderby interprets the serpents of smoke as proof that the factories are producing goods and profit. He fails to see that they also signify pollution and the abuse of the Hands in his factories. The smoke becomes a moral smokescreen that prevents him from noticing his workers' miserable poverty.

IMPORTANT QUOTATIONS FROM *HARD TIMES*

Thou art an Angel. Bless thee, bless thee!

Location: Book the First, Chapter 13
Speaker: Stephen
Context: Stephen expresses his gratitude to Rachael

More a symbol than a fully developed character, Rachael is often referred to as an angel by Stephen. Like Sissy Jupe, whom she later befriends, Rachael represents the feminine qualities Dickens considers necessary to counteract the dehumanizing, morally corrupting effects of industrialization. She is compassionate, honest, generous, and faithful to Stephen, even when everyone else shuns him and believes him a thief. Rachael also draws out Stephen's good qualities, making him realize that joy can be found even in the moral darkness of Coketown. Rachael and Sissy are both socially marginal characters—the former is a Hand, and the latter is the daughter of a circus entertainer. They are also relatively minor characters in the novel. By giving them marginal status, Dickens suggests that the self-serving rationalism of Coketown threatens to exclude morally pure people.

Look how we live, an' wheer we live, an' in what numbers, an' by what chances, an' wi' what sameness; and look how the mills is awlus a-goin', and how they never works us no nigher to onny distant object— 'ceptin awlus Death. Look how you considers of us, and writes of us, and talks of us, and goes up wi' your deputations to Secretaries o' State 'bout us, and how yo are awlus right, and how we are awlus wrong, and never had'n no reason in us sin ever we were born. Look how this ha' growen an' growen sir, bigger an' bigger, broader an' broader, harder an' harder, fro year to year, fro generation unto generation. Who can look on't sir, and fairly tell a man 'tis not a muddle?

Location: Book the Second, Chapter 5
Speaker: Stephen Blackpool
Context: Stephen talks to Bounderby

This speech is one of the few glimpses that we receive into the lives of the Hands. Stephen's long sentences and repetition of words such as "an'" and "look" mimic the monotony of the workers' lives. His dialect reveals his lack of education and contrasts with the proper English spoken by the middle-class characters and by the narrator. In spite of his lack of formal education, however, Stephen possesses greater insight about the relationship between employer and employee than does Bounderby. Stephen notes that the factory owners and employers and the Hands are thrown into constant opposition, and the Hands stand no chance in the contest because the employers possess all the wealth and power. However, he does not blame the employers alone for the suffering of the poor, concluding that the situation is a "muddle" and that it is difficult to determine who is responsible for society's ills. Stephen also suggests that the monotony of factory labor seems futile to the Hands, who need to strive for some larger goal in order to make the endless round of production seem worthwhile. The "distant object" that he mentions here is later symbolized by the bright star he gazes at while trapped at the bottom of the mine shaft.

Now, what I want is Facts. Teach these boys and girls nothing but Facts. Facts alone are wanted in life. Plant nothing else, and root out everything else. You can only form the mind of reasoning animals upon Facts: nothing else will ever be of any service to them.

Location: The novel's opening lines
Speaker: Mr. Gradgrind
Context: Mr. Gradgrind explains his philosophy

It is known, to the force of a single pound weight, what the engine will do; but not all the calculators of the National debt can tell me the capacity for good or evil, for love or hatred, for patriotism or discontent, for the decomposition of virtue into vice, or the reverse, at any single moment in the soul of one of these quiet servants, with the composed faces and the regulated actions.

Location: Book the First, Chapter 11
Speaker: The narrator
Context: The narrator points out the mysteries of the human mind

---

Coketown lay shrouded in a haze of its own, which appeared impervious to the sun's rays. You only knew the town was there because you knew there could have been no such sulky blotch upon the prospect without a town. A blur of soot and smoke, now confusedly tending this way, now that way, now aspiring to the vault of Heaven, now murkily creeping along the earth, as the wind rose and fell, or changed its quarter: a dense formless jumble, with sheets of cross light in it, that showed nothing but masses of darkness—Coketown in the distance was suggestive of itself, though not a brick of it could be seen.

Location: Book the Second, Chapter 1
Speaker: The narrator
Context: The narrator says that Coketown is just what it appears to be—a dark, dirty "blotch"

HEART OF DARKNESS

Joseph Conrad

A sailor tells the story of his journey through the Congo, where he met an enigmatic, powerful, insane imperialist who had abandoned the rules of English civilization.

THE LIFE OF JOSEPH CONRAD
Joseph Conrad was born Jozef Teodor Konrad Korzeniowski on December 3, 1857, in the Polish Ukraine. When Conrad was quite young, his father was exiled to Siberia on suspicion of plotting against the Russian government. Conrad's mother died, and he was sent to live with his maternal uncle in Krak to be educated. Conrad never saw his father again. He traveled to Marseilles when he was seventeen, and spent the next twenty years as a sailor. He began to learn English when he was twenty-one years old. In 1878, Conrad signed on to an English ship. Eight years later, he became a British subject. In 1889, he began his first novel, *Almayer's Folly*, and started actively searching for a way to fulfill his boyhood dream of traveling to the Congo. In 1890, he took command of a steamship in the Belgian Congo. Conrad's time in Africa wreaked havoc on his health, and he went to England to recover. He returned to sea twice before finishing *Almayer's Folly* in 1894. In 1898, he began his masterpiece, *Heart of Darkness*, a novel inspired by his experiences in the Congo. Over the next two decades, he wrote many of his most important works, including *Lord Jim*, *Nostromo*, and *The Secret Agent*. Conrad died in 1924.

HEART OF DARKNESS IN CONTEXT
Conrad's works, *Heart of Darkness* in particular, provide a bridge between Victorianism and modernism. His novels feature traditional ideas of heroism, but these ideas come under constant attack. His female characters occupy traditional roles as arbiters of domesticity and morality, but they are almost never present in the narrative, and the concepts of "home" and "civilization" are merely hypocritical ideals. The threats his characters face are concrete, but they have a philosophical character. Like much of the best modernist literature produced in the early decades of the twentieth century, *Heart of Darkness* is about alienation, confusion, and profound doubt.

Imperialism is also at the center of *Heart of Darkness*. By the 1890s, most of the world's "dark places" were at least nominally under European control, and the major European powers were stretched thin, trying to administer massive empires. Cracks were beginning to appear in the system: riots and wars threatened white men living in the distant corners of empires. *Heart of Darkness* suggests that things inevitably fall apart when men are allowed to wield power unchecked, especially power over other human beings. Conrad asks whether we can call a man insane or wrong when he is part of a system that is corrupted and corrupting. *Heart of Darkness*, at its most abstract level, is about how far one man can judge another.

Although *Heart of Darkness* was one of the first novels to criticize European imperialism, no one found it controversial at first. It was usually interpreted either as a condemnation of adventurers who take advantage of imperialism's opportunities, or as a sentimental novel reinforcing domestic values. Conrad's decision to set the novel in a Belgian colony made it even easier for British readers to avoid seeing themselves reflected in *Heart of Darkness*.

HEART OF DARKNESS: KEY FACTS

Time and place written: England, 1898–1899

Date of first publication: Serialized in *Blackwood's Magazine* in 1899; published in 1902 in the volume *Youth: A Narrative; and Two Other Stories*

Publisher: J. M. Dent & Sons, Ltd.

Type of work: Novella

Genre: Adventure tale, frame story

Language: English

Setting (time): Probably sometime between 1876 and 1892

Setting (place): The Thames River outside London; Brussels; the Congo

Tense: Past

Tone: Ambivalent, matter-of-fact, poetic

Narrator: An anonymous passenger on a pleasure ship, who listens to Marlow's story and speaks in the first person plural, and Marlow himself, a middle-aged ship's captain who speaks in the first person

Point of view: The passengers who listen to Marlow's tale, and Marlow

Protagonist: Marlow

Antagonist: The conflict between civilization and the temptation to abandon morality completely

HEART OF DARKNESS: PLOT OVERVIEW

Marlow, an introspective sailor, takes a job as a riverboat captain with the Company, a Belgian concern organized to trade in the Congo. He sets off, going to Africa and then up the Congo River to meet Kurtz, reputed to be an idealistic man of great abilities. He encounters widespread inefficiency and brutality in the Company's stations. The native inhabitants of the region have been forced into the Company's service, and they suffer terribly from overwork and ill treatment at the hands of the Company's agents. The impassive, majestic jungle contrasts sharply with the cruel, squalid white man's settlements, making them look like tiny islands amidst a vast darkness.

Marlow arrives at the Central Station, which is run by an unwholesome general manager. He finds that his steamship has been sunk. Over several months, as he waits for parts to repair it, his interest in Kurtz grows. The manager and his favorite, the brickmaker, seem to fear Kurtz as a threat to their position. Kurtz is rumored to be ill. Marlow eventually gets the parts he needs to repair his ship, and he and the manager set out with a few agents (whom Marlow calls pilgrims because they carry long, wooden staves wherever they go) and a crew of cannibals on a long, difficult voyage up the river. The dense jungle and the oppressive silence make everyone a little jumpy, and the occasional glimpse of a native village or the sound of drums work the pilgrims into a frenzy.

Marlow and his crew come across a hut with stacked firewood. A note says the wood is for them but they should approach cautiously. A dense fog surrounds the steamer. When the fog clears, an unseen band of natives fire arrows at the ship from the safety of the forest. The African helmsman is killed before Marlow frightens the natives away with the ship's steam whistle. Marlow and his companions soon arrive at Kurtz's Inner Station, expecting to find him dead. A half-crazed Russian trader meets them as they come ashore and assures them that everything is fine. He tells them he is the one who left the wood. The Russian claims that Kurtz has enlarged his mind and cannot be subjected to the same moral judgments as normal people. Apparently, Kurtz has convinced the natives that he is a god and has gone on brutal raids in search of ivory. The collection of severed heads adorning the fence posts around the station attests to his "methods."

The pilgrims bring Kurtz out of the station house on a stretcher, and a large group of native warriors pours out of the forest and surrounds them. Kurtz speaks to them, and the natives disappear into the woods. The manager brings Kurtz, who is quite ill, aboard the steamer. A beautiful native woman, apparently Kurtz's mistress, appears on the shore and stares out at the ship. The Russian implies that she is involved with Kurtz and has caused trouble before through her influence over him. The Russian swears Marlow to secrecy and then tells him that Kurtz had ordered the attack on the steamer. He wanted Marlow and his crew to believe he was dead so they would turn back and leave him to his plans. The Russian leaves by canoe. Kurtz disappears in the night. Marlow goes out in search of him and finds him crawling on all fours toward the native camp. Marlow convinces him to return to the ship. They set off down the river the next morning. Kurtz's health is failing fast.

Marlow listens to Kurtz talk while he pilots the ship. Kurtz entrusts Marlow with a packet of personal documents, including an eloquent pamphlet on civilizing the savages which ends with a scrawled message that says, "Exterminate all the brutes!" The steamer breaks down, and they have to stop for repairs. Kurtz dies, uttering his last words—"The horror! The horror!"—in the presence of the confused Marlow. Marlow falls ill soon after and barely survives. Eventually he returns to Europe and goes to see Kurtz's Intended (his fiancée). She is still in mourning even though it has been over a year since Kurtz's death. She praises him as a paragon of virtue and achievement. She asks Marlow what his last words were, but Marlow cannot bring himself to shatter her illusions with the truth. Instead, he tells her that Kurtz's last word was her name.

CHARACTERS IN *HEART OF DARKNESS*

Aunt Marlow's doting relative. She secures him a position with the Company and believes that imperialism is a charitable activity that brings civilization and religion to suffering, simple savages.

Brickmaker A petty, conniving employee at the Central Station. The Brickmaker is a favorite of the manager and seems to be a corporate spy. He never actually produces any bricks, supposedly because he is waiting for some essential element that is never delivered.

Cannibals Natives hired as the crew of the steamer. Marlow respects the cannibals' restraint and calm acceptance of adversity. The leader of the group is particularly intelligent, and has a healthy sense of irony.

Chief Accountant An efficient worker who dresses in spotless whites and keeps himself absolutely tidy despite the squalor and heat of the Outer Station, where he lives and works.

Fresleven Marlow's predecessor as captain of the steamer. Fresleven, by all accounts a good-tempered, nonviolent man, was killed in a dispute over some hens, apparently after striking a village chief.

General Manager The chief agent of the Company in its African territory. The General Manager owes his success to a hardy constitution that allowed him to outlive all his competitors. Although average in appearance and ability, he makes those around him uneasy.

Helmsman A young man from the coast. He is killed when natives attack the steamer.

Kurtz The chief of the Inner Station and the object of Marlow's quest. Kurtz is a gifted musician, a fine painter, and a charismatic leader. The eloquence of his writing obscures its horrifying message. He fraternizes with the natives, a taboo among imperialists, becoming wildly successful and incurring the wrath of his fellow white men.

Kurtz's Intended Kurtz's naïve and long-suffering fiancée. Her unshakable faith in Kurtz's love for her reinforces Marlow's belief that women live in a dream world.

Kurtz's Mistress A fiercely beautiful African woman loaded with jewelry who exerts a strong influence over both Kurtz and the natives around the station. The Russian trader points her out as someone to fear. Like Kurtz, she is an enigma.

Marlow The protagonist of the novel. Marlow is philosophical, independent-minded, and skeptical. He is also a master storyteller. Although Marlow shares many of his fellow Europeans' prejudices, he questions imperialism.

The Men Aboard the Nellie Marlow's friends aboard a ship on the Thames at the story's opening. They are the audience for the central story of *Heart of Darkness*, which Marlow narrates. All have been sailors at one time or another and now have important jobs ashore and middle-class lives. They represent the kind of man Marlow would have likely become had he not gone to Africa: well-meaning and moral but ignorant about the world beyond England.

Pilgrims The bumbling, greedy agents of the Central Station. They all want to be appointed to a station so that they can trade for ivory and earn a commission. They are obsessed with keeping up the appearance of civilization and proper conduct. They hate the natives and treat them like animals.

Russian Trader A Russian sailor employed as the trading representative of a Dutch company. He is boyish, glamorous, and adventurous. His brightly patched clothes remind Marlow of a harlequin. He is a devoted disciple of Kurtz's.

THEMES IN *HEART OF DARKNESS*

THE HYPOCRISY OF IMPERIALISM Conrad paints a harsh picture of colonial enterprise. As Marlow travels, he encounters scenes of torture, cruelty, and near-slavery. Hypocrisy sets Marlow's adventures in motion. The men who work for the Company describe their work as "trade," and their treatment of Africans as a benevolent project of "civilization." Kurtz, who does not feel the need to talk politely, openly admits that he is not trading, but stealing ivory, and that he is not "civilizing" the natives, but suppressing and exterminating them.

Despite Conrad's condemnatory treatment of imperialism, it can be argued that *Heart of Darkness* participates in the oppression of nonwhites. For Marlow as much as for Kurtz or for the Company, Africans are objects. Marlow refers to his helmsman as a piece of machinery, and Kurtz's African mistress is at best a piece of statuary. He considers Africans a mere backdrop, a human screen against which he can play out his philosophical and existential struggles. This kind of dehumanization is more dangerous than colonial violence or open racism, because it is not as obvious. Critics argue about whether Conrad shared Marlow's views or viewed them as repugnant.

MADNESS AS A RESULT OF IMPERIALISM Conrad has a contradictory view of madness. On one hand, he suggests that the definition of madness is a flexible one that bends to fit different societies. Marlow is told that Kurtz is mad, but as he forms a more complete picture of Kurtz, he learns that Kurtz's madness is only relative. Compared to the insanity of the Company, which the English consider normal, Kurtz is not insane. On the other hand, Conrad suggests that madness is not always relative. In some sense, Kurtz is insane in a universal way that everyone must acknowledge. Kurtz goes mad because he is removed from his social context and allowed to determine morality in a vacuum. He answers to no authority but himself, which is more than anyone could bear.

THE ABSURDITY OF EVIL *Heart of Darkness* argues that idealism is always misplaced. Marlow must align himself either with the hypocritical and malicious colonial bureaucracy or with the violent, rule-defying Kurtz—an impossible choice. Conventional morality is of no use to Marlow, who must choose between two evils. Conrad suggests that in the mundane as well as in the life-or-death, absurdity reigns. Men carry water in buckets filled with holes. Laborers blast away at a hillside for no reason. Kurtz is a homicidal megalomaniac. Terrifyingly but sensibly, Marlow reacts in the same way to a leaky bucket as he does to Kurtz's insanity.

SYMBOLS IN *HEART OF DARKNESS*

WOMEN Both Kurtz's Intended and his African mistress function as blank slates upon which their cultures' values and wealth can be displayed. Marlow frequently claims that women are the keepers of naïve illusions. This is a belittling but crucial role, because naïve illusions justify colonial expansion.

THE RIVER The Congo River is the key to Africa for Europeans. It allows them access to the center of the continent without having to physically cross it. In other words, it allows them to stay separate. The river also symbolizes Africa's wish to expel its invaders. It makes upriver travel slow and difficult, but it makes downriver travel easy, as if eager to flush out the whites. Marlow's struggles as he travels upstream reflect his struggles to understand his situation. The ease with which he journeys back downstream, on the other hand, reflects his acquiescence to Kurtz and his "choice of nightmares."

IMPORTANT QUOTATIONS FROM *HEART OF DARKNESS*

"The word 'ivory' rang in the air, was whispered, was sighed. You would think they were praying to it. A taint of imbecile rapacity blew through it all, like a whiff from some corpse. By Jove! I've never seen anything so unreal in my life. And outside, the silent wilderness surrounding this cleared speck on the

earth struck me as something great and invincible, like evil or truth, waiting patiently for the passing away of this fantastic invasion."

Location: The fourth section of Part I
Speaker: Marlow
Context: Marlow gives his initial impression of Central Station and its employees

The word "ivory" takes on a life of its own for the men who work for the Company. To them, ivory is far more than the tusk of an elephant; it represents economic freedom, social advancement, an escape from the life of an employee. The word has lost all connection to physical reality and has itself become an object of worship. Marlow's reference to a decaying corpse is both literal and figurative: elephants and Africans both die as a result of the white man's pursuit of ivory, and the entire enterprise is rotten at the core. The cruelties and the greed are part of a greater, timeless evil, even though they are petty in the greater scheme of the natural world.

"It was unearthly, and the men were—No, they were not inhuman. Well, you know, that was the worst of it—the suspicion of their not being inhuman. It would come slowly to one. They howled and leaped, and spun, and made horrid faces; but what thrilled you was just the thought of their humanity—like yours— the thought of your remote kinship with this wild and passionate uproar. Ugly. Yes, it was ugly enough; but if you were man enough you would admit to yourself that there was in you just the faintest trace of a response to the terrible frankness of that noise, a dim suspicion of there being a meaning in it which you—you so remote from the night of first ages—could comprehend. And why not?"

Location: The first section of Part II
Speaker: Marlow
Context: Marlow describes catching occasional glimpses of native villages

Marlow's glimpses of native villages along the riverbanks and the drums, chants, and howls he hears engage his imagination. It troubles him that he feels "kinship" with these men, whom he has so far been able to classify as "inhuman." This moment is one of several in the text in which Conrad seems to point out the limits of Marlow's perception. These moments mean *Heart of Darkness* can be interpreted as highly critical of colonialism and ironic about the stereotypes it engenders.

"In a few days the Eldorado Expedition went into the patient wilderness, that closed upon it as the sea closes over a diver. Long afterwards the news came that all the donkeys were dead. I know nothing as to the fate of the less valuable animals. They, no doubt, like the rest of us, found what they deserved. I did not inquire."

Location: The first section of Part II
Speaker: Marlow
Context: Marlow reports the fate of the Eldorado Exploring Expedition, a band of freelance bandits

---

"The brown current ran swiftly out of the heart of darkness, bearing us down towards the sea with twice the speed of our upward progress; and Kurtz's life was running swiftly, too, ebbing, ebbing out of his heart into the sea of inexorable time.... I saw the time approaching when I would be left alone of the party of 'unsound method.'"

Location: The third section of Part III
Speaker: Marlow
Context: Marlow and Kurtz journey back

"I was within a hair's-breadth of the last opportunity for pronouncement, and I found with humiliation that probably I would have nothing to say. This is the reason why I affirm that Kurtz was a remarkable man. He had something to say. He said it.... He had summed up—he had judged. 'The horror!' He was a remarkable man."

Location: The final section of Part III
Speaker: Marlow
Context: Marlow recovers from his near-fatal illness and finds he has nothing to say

HEDDA GABLER

Henrik Ibsen

Constrained by a dull husband and a fear of scandal, a woman turns her energy and thirst for power to destruction, ultimately killing herself.

THE LIFE OF HENRIK IBSEN

Henrik Ibsen, "the father of modern drama," was born in Skien, Norway, in 1828, the second of six children. Ibsen's merchant father went bankrupt when Ibsen was eight years old, and Ibsen spent much of his early life in poverty. He wrote his first play, the five-act verse tragedy *Catiline*, at the age of twenty-one, and spent much of his twenties and thirties working in theaters in Bergen and Christiana (present-day Oslo).

In 1858, Ibsen married Suzannah Thoreson. Eventually the couple had one son. Ibsen believed strongly that marriage should leave a husband and wife free to become their own human beings—a belief that became the focus of *A Doll's House*. Critics attacked him for what this belief, which they perceived as a lack of respect for marriage. Ibsen's writings also stirred up sensitive social issues. Criticized for both his work and his private life, Ibsen traveled to Italy in 1864 on a grant. He spent the next twenty-seven years abroad, mostly in Italy and Germany.

Ibsen's early years as a playwright were not particularly lucrative, but in 1866 and 1867, he published two successful verse plays, *Brand* and *Peer Gynt*, which solidified his reputation as a premier Norwegian dramatist. In 1877, he wrote the drama *The Pillars of Society*, the first of a series of his last twelve plays written in an innovative realist style. But it was *A Doll's House* (1879) that marked a true breakthrough for modern drama. *A Doll's House* was followed by *Ghosts* (1881) and *An Enemy of the People* (1882), both successful. Ibsen began to gain international recognition, and his works were produced across Europe and translated into many languages.

In his later work, Ibsen began to tackle questions of a psychological and subconscious nature. His best known works from this symbolist period are *The Wild Duck* (1884), *Hedda Gabler* (1890), and *A Doll's House*. These three works are also his most frequently produced plays. In 1891, Ibsen returned to Oslo. His later dramas include *The Master Builder* (1892) and his last play, *When We Dead Awaken* (1899). In 1900, he suffered a stroke and was eventually overcome by a crippling sickness. He died in 1906.

HEDDA GABLER IN CONTEXT

Ibsen's work marked a decisive shift in the development of modern prose drama. Nineteenth century theater had been dominated by romanticism. Leaving that behind, Ibsen wrote in a realistic style and demystified the romantic hero. His later work is explicitly psychological, and explores character conflicts, specifically the tension between the individual and an antiquated or oppressive, or nostalgic bourgeoisie. The Irish playwright George Bernard Shaw, whose own work was heavily influenced by Ibsen, gave a series of lectures which were ultimately published as "The Quintessence of Ibsenism," which praised Ibsen for facing the bleak realities of life and openly criticizing societal conventions.

Between 1879 and 1880, Ibsen's interest shifted from controversial social dilemmas to psychological drama. In his work, Ibsen was likely influenced by Friedrich Nietzsche, who published *The Birth of Tragedy* in 1872 and *Thus Spake Zarathustra* in 1883. Ibsen's focus on the psychological side of his characters coincided with Freud's preparation of his seminal work on psychoanalysis: *The Interpretation of Dreams* (1900).

Ibsen's earlier plays, many of which are written in verse, are epic and sweeping in scope. Many of them deal with mystical or supernatural elements. From the late 1870s through the end of his career, Ibsen forced himself to reign in his epic tendencies. His characters and situations became grounded in reality. *Hedda Gabler*, for example, takes place in the drawing room of a middle-class Oslo family. Its main characters are members of the intelligentsia: academics hoping to be professors and the women and friends who love them. By using easily recognizable situations and frank, understandable dialogue,

Ibsen tapped into the psychological underpinnings of his dramas. The simple, occasionally stilted dialogue is full of symbolism and subtext.

Hedda Gabler was heavily criticized during its first staging in 1890, but has become one of Ibsen's most-produced plays. Its eponymous heroine is one of the strongest and most complex female characters in dramatic history.

HEDDA GABLER: KEY FACTS

Time and place written: Norway; late 1880s

Date of publication: December 1890

Publisher: Gyldendalske Boghandels Forlag

Type of work: Play

Genre: Drama of ideas; social protest play

Language: Norwegian

Setting (time): Two days in an unspecified time period

Setting (place): Oslo, the Tesmans' living room

Tone: Critical

Protagonist: Hedda Tesman, née Gabler

Antagonist: Hedda's oppressive society; Hedda's boring husband; Hedda's thirst for power and beauty; Hedda's fear of scandal

HEDDA GABLER: PLOT OVERVIEW

ACT I

George and Hedda (née Gabler) Tesman have recently returned from a nearly six-month-long honeymoon. Tesman wakes in the morning to find that his Aunt Julle, who raised him and still supports him financially, has come for a visit. Hedda enters and is somewhat rude to Aunt Julle. Hedda dismisses Tesman's requests that she treat Aunt Julle with more kindness. Unexpectedly, Mrs. Elvsted, Hedda's former classmate, comes to visit. She brings news that Ejlert Lövborg, a recently reformed alcoholic and Tesman's professional rival, has come back to town. Hedda manages to persuade Tesman to leave, then convinces Mrs. Elvsted to confide in her. Mrs. Elvsted has grown close to Ejlert, who has been tutoring her stepchildren, and she has come to town without her husband's permission because she is afraid that Ejlert will start drinking again. In fact, she admits to Hedda that she means to leave her husband for good. Mrs. Elvsted also mentions that although she would like to be closer to Ejlert, an old flame of his stands in the way. This other woman threatened Ejlert with a pistol when their relationship ended, Mrs. Elvsted tells Hedda. Mrs. Elvsted leaves, and Tesman returns. Judge Brack, the Tesmans' close friend, arrives. He brings gossip: Ejlert has made quite a splash with his new book and may give Tesman some competition for the professorship that Tesman has been counting on to provide for Hedda financially. Tesman tells Hedda that they will have to cut back on their expenses.

ACT II

Later that day, Brack finds Hedda playing with her pistols out of boredom. They speak and agree that they should become close friends. Hedda tells Brack how bored she was with Tesman on her honeymoon and says she is not particularly attached to this house, which Tesman has gone to great lengths to buy because of a flippant comment she once made. Tesman arrives, and they discuss Brack's stag party that evening. Ejlert Lövborg comes to call. While Tesman and Brack drink in another room, Hedda and Ejlert speak intimately of their former close friendship, which Hedda broke off when it started becoming too serious. Mrs. Elvsted arrives. Hedda plays with Mrs. Elvsted's fears about Ejlert's alcoholism and provokes Ejlert into taking a drink and agreeing to go to Brack's party. Mrs. Elvsted is very upset, but Ejlert promises to return in a few hours to escort her home. Hedda, too, is sure that he will triumph over his weakness and return "with vine leaves in his hair."

ACT III

It is just before dawn. Mrs. Elvsted has been waiting for Ejlert. Hedda is asleep on the couch. Hedda awakes and send Mrs. Elvsted to rest on her bed. Tesman arrives and tells his wife that Ejlert got completely drunk and dropped his manuscript on his way home. Tesman picked it up. He plans to return the manuscript, but is called away to see his dying Aunt Rina. Brack arrives and tells Hedda that Ejlert was arrested after Tesman. Brack leaves, and Ejlert arrives. He tells Mrs. Elvsted that he has destroyed his manuscript, with which she had been helping him. Crushed, she leaves immediately. Ejlert confesses to Hedda that he has, in fact, lost the manuscript and that he wants to kill himself. Hedda gives him one of her pistols and wishes him a beautiful death. After he leaves, Hedda throws his manuscript into the fire.

ACT IV

The living room is dark. Aunt Julle arrives, in mourning for Aunt Rina, and says she must find someone else to care for now. She leaves. Tesman is anxious about a rumor that Ejlert told Mrs. Elvsted that he tore up the manuscript. Tesman worries about what Ejlert may do. Tesman is horrified when Hedda tells him that she burned the manuscript, but is almost overjoyed when he learns that she did it out of love for him. Mrs. Elvsted arrives. She has heard that Ejlert is in the hospital. Brack arrives and reports that Ejlert has died at the hospital, having wounded himself in the chest. The chest wound pleases Hedda—there was some beauty in his death after all. Tesman and Mrs. Elvsted decide to try to reconstruct Ejlert's manuscript, based on notes Mrs. Elvsted has kept. In private, Brack tells Hedda that Ejlert's death was quite ugly: the pistol went off accidentally. Moreover, Brack has recognized the pistol as one of General Gabler's, and if it is traced to Hedda, there may be a scandal. Hedda leaves the room. Wild piano playing is heard, and then a pistol shot rings out. Hedda has shot herself.

CHARACTERS IN *HEDDA GABLER*

Berta The Tesman's maid. Berta used to work for Aunt Julle. She tries hard to please Hedda, but her efforts are in vain.

Judge Brack A well-connected local judge. A friend of both Tesmans, Brack visits the Tesman home regularly. Worldly and cynical, he enjoys meddling in other people's affairs.

Mrs. Elvsted (née Thea Rysing) Hedda's weak but passionate classmate. Mrs. Elvsted is a former maid who married the widow for whom she worked. Secluded in the country, she has grown very attached to Ejlert Lövborg, Mr. Elvsted's children's tutor, and has been aiding him in his research and writing. Mrs. Elvsted leaves her husband to follow and watch out for the unstable Ejlert. She remembers being tormented by Hedda during their school days.

Ejlert Lövborg A genius academic, Tesman's professional rival, and Hedda's former beau. After a series of scandals related to his alcoholism, Ejlert left the city and tutored the Elvsted children. He became close to Mrs. Elvsted. After returning to the city and publishing an important sociological work, he has begun work on another, even more promising manuscript.

Hedda Tesman (née Gabler) Daughter of the famous General Gabler and George Tesman's wife. Intelligent, bored, and unpredictable, Hedda is not afraid to manipulate the people around her. Used to a life of daring and luxury, she is depressed by her more financially and spiritually modest lifestyle with Tesman.

George Tesman An amiable, if naïve, young scholar; Hedda's husband. Raised by his Aunt Julle, Tesman has always been in awe of Hedda, and can hardly believe that she consented to marry him. Tesman is meticulous in his work, but he has no vision. As the play opens, he hopes for a professorship and a steady income and knows that only Ejlert Lövborg could stand in his way.

Miss Juliane Tesman (Aunt Julle) Tesman's aunt, who raised Tesman after the death of his parents. Aunt Julle is happy to see Tesman settled and hopes he and Hedda will have a baby. She comes from a lower class background than Hedda, and does not get along with Hedda, despite her best efforts. Aunt Julle lives with the ailing Aunt Rina.

Aunt Rina Tesman's sick aunt. Rina helped Aunt Julle raise Tesman. She never appears onstage and dies during the play.

THEMES IN *HEDDA GABLER*

SOCIETY AS A STIFLING FORCE   Ibsen's drama was a tool of social criticism. He portrays Oslo society as one that oppresses individual freedom. Weaker characters such as Tesman are less troubled by its force, while corrupt characters such as Brack have learned to exploit the general fear of scandal. It is the characters with potential for true greatness, like Hedda and Ejlert, who suffer under society's constraints. Ejlert's greatness rests in his intellect, but society has no tolerance for his weaknesses, which are alcoholism and adulterous admiration for Hedda. As a woman, Hedda is constrained by her loveless marriage. Despite her great strength, she too fears scandal. She never considers leaving her husband, as Mrs. Elvsted does, or using her tremendous energy to create rather than destroy. Ultimately, she chooses to kill herself rather than rely on Brack to cover up her role in Ejlert's death. By committing suicide, she conquers her fear of scandal.

THE AESTHETICS OF STRONG ACTIONS   Hedda sees beauty in strong actions such as suicide. She tries to provoke Ejlert into a beautiful suicide and is bitterly disappointed to find out that instead of killing himself cleanly with a shot to the chest or the head, he shot himself in the belly by accident and died in a hospital. Her own suicide is in part an attempt to create something beautiful in her dreary life.

THE SPECTER OF THE PAST   Hedda Gabler is, as Ibsen himself wrote, her father's daughter much more than she is her husband's wife. General Gabler is dead, but his presence lingers: his portrait hangs ominously in the living room, and Hedda plays with his pistols.

   As in all of Ibsen's social realist plays, the characters have complicated past relationships that heavily inform the present. Hedda and Ejlert are former companions; Hedda and Mrs. Elvsted are former classmates. Tesman knows that Hedda is accustomed to a life of privilege, and he wants to recreate such a life for her. Ejlert's past of self-destructive behavior is the stuff of scandal and an obstacle to his future. Mrs. Elvsted tells a complicated story about how she married the aloof elderly widow whose children she cared for, how they hired Ejlert to tutor these children, and how she and Ejlert grew closer as she reformed him and they collaborated on his research. Fittingly, Tesman and Ejlert are both scholars of history.

SYMBOLS IN *HEDDA GABLER*

EJLERT'S MANUSCRIPT   Ejlert's ambitious work-in-progress, created with his genius and Mrs. Elvsted's perseverance, addresses the future of humanity. It is referred to as Mrs. Elvsted's and Ejlert's child. Its destruction—Ejlert loses it and Hedda burns it—represents the end of Ejlert's future.

VINE LEAVES   After provoking Ejlert to begin drinking again, Hedda reassures Mrs. Elvsted that he will return "with vine leaves in his hair." Vine leaves were used to crown Greek heroes, and represent a glorious, classical heroism. At the same time, they recall alcohol, which Hedda uses to test Ejlert's strength, and which brings about his downfall. In the play, they symbolize Hedda's cruel and destructive pursuit of beauty.

IMPORTANT QUOTATIONS FROM *HEDDA GABLER*

Yes, Hedda; and when I used to confess to you! Told you things about myself that no one else knew in those days. Sat there and owned up to going about days and nights blind drunk. Days and nights on end. Oh, Hedda, what sort of power in you was it—that forced me to confess things like that?

Location: Act II
Speaker: Ejlert Lövborg
Context: Meeting Hedda for the first time in a long time, Ejlert recalls the power dynamic of their former
   close friendship

Ejlert recalls how, during their former "hidden intimacy," Hedda would question him, both "frankly" and "indirectly," about his bad his drinking and his sexual exploits. Each was impressed with the other's boldness—Ejlert that Hedda would dare ask such a question, and Hedda that Ejlert would dare answer openly. For Hedda, these conversations were a glimpse into a world into which she, as a woman, had no access. She satisfied her thirst for recklessness and freedom by living vicariously through Ejlert. Moreover, in forcing him to open up about his depravities, she exercised her enigmatic and greatly-desired "power" over people.

I want, for once in my life, to have power over a human being's fate.

Location: End of Act II
Speaker: Hedda Gabler
Context: Hedda explains to Mrs. Elvsted why she just provoked the recovering alcoholic Ejlert to attend a drinking party

This sentence lucidly encapsulates what Hedda desires; freedom and power. Hedda has been emerging as cruel and manipulative, but now she has extended her scope and announces that she wants complete control over another. She chooses Ejlert in part because she knows she can. If Ejlert conquers himself and resists the alcohol, Hedda will have provoked a beautiful manifestation of heroic human strength. If Ejlert succumbs to weakness, she will have complete control over him. Either way, she wins.

You can understand that, can't you, with General Gabler's daughter? Think what she was accustomed to in the General's day.

Location: Act I
Speaker: Aunt Julle
Context: Aunt Julle soothes Berta, who worries that she will never be able to please her new mistress, Hedda

---

That kind of thing comes over me, just like that. And then I can't stop myself. I don't know, myself, how to explain it.

Location: Act II
Speaker: Hedda
Context: Hedda tries to explain to Brack why she was intentionally rude to Aunt Julle earlier

---

In your power, all the same. At the mercy of your will and demands. And so a slave! A slave! No! That thought I cannot tolerate. Never!

Location: Act IV
Speaker: Hedda
Context: Brack has offered his help in concealing Hedda's role in Ejlert's death; Hedda refuses it

THE HOBBIT

J. R. R. Tolkien

A complacent hobbit discovers hidden heroism in himself when a wizard recruits him to undertake a dangerous mission.

THE LIFE OF J. R. R. TOLKIEN

John Ronald Reuel Tolkien was born on January 3, 1892, in Bloemfontain, South Africa. His parents had moved there from England so that his father, Arthur, could work for the Bank of Africa. Tolkien lost both parents early in life—his father died in Africa in 1896 after the rest of the family had returned to England, and his mother, Mabel, died in 1904 near Birmingham, England. After Mabel's death, Tolkien and his younger brother, Hilary, were entrusted to the care of Father Francis Morgan, a friend of the family's. Soon after, Tolkien went to King Edward's School and then to Oxford.

At Oxford, Tolkien pursued a degree in English language and literature. He developed a particular passion for philology, the study of languages. While studying Old English, Anglo-Saxon, and Welsh poetry, he continued experimenting with a language he had started to develop in his youth. This language would form the basis of Middle-Earth, his imagined world.

By 1916, Tolkien had received his degree and married his childhood sweetheart, Edith Bratt. He eventually took a teaching position at Oxford. By 1929, he had had his fourth child with Edith. He served on the front lines in World War I.

Tolkien developed a friendship with another well-known Oxford professor and writer, C. S. Lewis, author of *The Chronicles of Narnia*. Their friendship lasted for many years. Tolkien helped convert Lewis to Christianity, and the two critiqued each other's work as part of an informal group of writers known as the Inklings.

From 1945 to 1959, Tolkien continued to teach at Oxford and wrote *The Lord of the Rings* trilogy. The trilogy brought Tolkien fame in England and America, but he was never comfortable being a public figure. He most enjoyed middle-class surroundings and having peace in which to write and think. Tolkien died on September 2, 1973. *The Silmarillion*, Tolkien's mythology of Middle-Earth, was edited and published posthumously by his son Christopher in 1977.

THE HOBBIT IN CONTEXT

The Hobbit (1936), Tolkien's first published work, is a simple children's story about a small person who takes part in great adventures. The novel's playful tone and imagery made it a hit with both children and adults. *The Hobbit* fans, huge in number, were anxious to learn more about the meticulously developed world that Tolkien had created around his invented language and mythology, only a small part of which was detailed in *The Hobbit*.

The Hobbit's plot and characters combine the ancient heroic Anglo-Saxon and Scandinavian epics Tolkien studied with the middle-class rural England in which he lived. In many ways, the novel's charm and humor lie in transplanting a simple, pastoral Englishman of the 1930s into a heroic medieval setting.

THE HOBBIT: KEY FACTS

Full title: The Hobbit, or There and Back Again	
Time and place written: Roughly between 1929 and 1936 in Oxford, England	
Date of first publication: 1937	
Publisher: Houghton Mifflin	
Type of work: Novel	
Genre: Fantasy; quest; satire; social protest novel	
Language: English	

Setting (time): The Third Age of Middle-Earth, 2941–2942

Settings (place): Various locales in the imaginary world of Middle-Earth

Tense: Past

Tone: Light, joking, periodically dark

Narrator: Anonymous, omniscient third person

Point of view: Bilbo Baggins's

Protagonist: Bilbo

Antagonist: Sauron

THE HOBBIT: PLOT OVERVIEW

Bilbo Baggins lives a quiet, peaceful life in his comfortable hole at Bag End near the bustling hobbit village of Hobbiton. Bilbo lives in a hole because he is a hobbit—one of a race of small, plump people about half the size of humans, with furry toes and a love of good food and drink. One day the old wizard Gandalf arrives and persuades Bilbo to set out on an adventure with a group of thirteen militant dwarves. The dwarves are embarking on a great quest to reclaim their treasure from the marauding dragon Smaug, and Bilbo is to act as their "burglar." The dwarves are very skeptical about Bilbo's capabilities, and Bilbo is terrified to leave his comfortable life to seek adventure. But Gandalf assures both Bilbo and the dwarves that there is more to the little hobbit than meets the eye.

Shortly after the group sets out, three hungry trolls capture everyone except Gandalf. Gandalf tricks the trolls into remaining outside until dawn, and the sunlight turns the nocturnal trolls to stone. The group finds a great cache of weapons in the trolls' camp. Gandalf and the dwarf lord Thorin take magic swords, and Bilbo takes a small sword of his own.

The group rests at the elfish stronghold of Rivendell, where they receive advice from the great elf lord Elrond. Then they set out to cross the Misty Mountains. During a snowstorm, they take shelter in a cave. A group of goblins who live in the caverns beneath the mountain take them prisoner. Gandalf leads the dwarves to a passage out of the mountain, but they accidentally leave Bilbo behind.

Wandering through the tunnels, Bilbo finds a golden ring lying on the ground. He puts it in his pocket. Soon he encounters Gollum, a hissing, whining creature who lives in a pool in the caverns and hunts fish and goblins. Gollum wants to eat Bilbo, and the two have a contest of riddles to determine Bilbo's fate. Bilbo wins by asking the dubious riddle, "What have I got in my pocket?"

Gollum wants to eat Bilbo anyway, and disappears to fetch his magic ring, which turns its wearer invisible. But Gollum's ring is the same one Bilbo found, and Bilbo uses it to escape from Gollum and flee the goblins. He finds a tunnel leading out of the mountain and discovers that the dwarves and Gandalf have already escaped. Evil wolves known as Wargs pursue them, but a group of great eagles helps Bilbo and his comrades to safety. Beorn, a creature who can change shape from a man into a bear, also helps them.

The company enters the dark forest of Mirkwood. Gandalf abandons them to see to some other urgent business. In the forest, the dwarves are caught in the webs of some giant spiders, and Bilbo must rescue them with his sword and magic ring. After slaying a spider, Bilbo names his sword Sting. Shortly after escaping the spiders, the unlucky dwarves are captured by a group of wood elves who live near the river that runs through Mirkwood. Bilbo uses his ring to help the company escape. He spirits away the dwarves by hiding them inside barrels, which he then floats down the river. The dwarves arrive at Lake Town, a human settlement near the Lonely Mountain, under which the great dragon sleeps with Thorin's treasure.

After sneaking into the mountain, Bilbo talks to the sly dragon Smaug, who unwittingly reveals that his armorlike scales have a weak spot near his heart. Bilbo steals a golden cup from the dragon's hoard. Smaug discovers the theft and, furious, flies out of the mountain to burn Lake Town. Bard, a heroic archer, has learned the secret of Smaug's weakness and fires an arrow into the dragon's heart, killing him. Before Smaug dies, he burns Lake Town to the ground.

The humans of Lake Town and the elves of Mirkwood march to the Lonely Mountain to seek a share of the treasure, but Thorin greedily refuses. The humans and elves besiege the mountain, trapping the dwarves and the hobbit inside. Bilbo sneaks out to join the humans in an attempt to make peace. When

Thorin learns what Bilbo has done, he is livid, but Gandalf suddenly reappears and saves Bilbo from the dwarf lord's wrath.

At this moment, an army of goblins and Wargs marches on the mountain, and the humans, elves, and dwarves are forced to band together to defeat them. The goblins nearly win, but the arrival of Beorn and the eagles tips the scale, and the good armies win the battle.

After the battle, Bilbo and Gandalf return to Hobbiton. Bilbo's adventurousness means he is no longer accepted by respectable hobbit society, but he does not care. He now prefers to talk to elves and wizards, and he is happy to be back among the familiar comforts of home after his grand adventures.

CHARACTERS IN *THE HOBBIT*

INDIVIDUAL CHARACTERS

Bard A grim human. Bard is the honorable captain of the guard in Lake Town, a human city. He kills Smaug.

Beorn A man who can turn into a bear. Beorn helps Bilbo and the dwarves.

Bilbo Baggins The hero of the story. Bilbo is a hobbit, "a short, human-like person." Commonsensical, quiet, and fastidious, Bilbo also has an untapped streak of strength. His adventures awaken his courage and initiative.

Dark Lord Sauron An evil sorcerer. Sauron, also called the Necromancer, created the magic ring. He is mentioned in The Hobbit, but he never actually appears.

Elrond The great leader of the elves at Rivendell. Elrond gives Bilbo's group helpful advice. He is "as strong as a warrior, as wise as a wizard, as venerable as a king of dwarves, and as kind as summer."

Gandalf A wise old wizard. Gandalf has a vast command of magic and always seems to know more than he reveals. He tends to show up at just the moment he is needed most.

Gollum A strange, small, slimy creature who lives deep in the caves of Moria beneath the Misty Mountains. Gollum broods over his "precious," a magic ring, until he accidentally loses it and Bilbo finds it.

Thorin Oakenshield A dwarf. Thorin leads his fellow dwarves in a quest to reclaim their treasure from Smaug, who stole it from Thorin's grandfather. He is a proud, sturdy, and stubborn warrior. As the novel progresses, his inability to formulate successful plans, his greed, and his reliance on Bilbo make him somewhat unappealing, but he is partly redeemed by the remorse he shows before he dies.

Smaug The great dragon who lives in the Lonely Mountain. His flaming breath can scorch a city, his huge wings can carry him great distances, and his armorlike hide is almost impenetrable. Smaug can speak and has a dark, sardonic sense of humor.

Thror Thorin's grandfather. Thror mined Moria, a series of caves under the Mountain, and discovered a wealth of gold and jewels. He was King under the Mountain until the dragon Smaug killed or scattered all of his people.

RACES

Dwarves A greedy, tricky race. Some are "decent enough people ... if you don't expect too much." Thorin's group of dwarves consists of Fili, Kili, Dwalin, Balin, Oin, Gloin, Ori, Dori, Nori, Bifur, Bofur, and Bombur.

Elves The first creatures in Middle-Earth. Immortal unless killed in battle, they have fair faces, beautiful voices, and a close communion with nature. There are two varieties of elves: wood elves and high elves. The wood elves reside in Mirkwood and, as a result, are more suspicious and less wise than their high relatives.

Goblins Evil creatures. Goblins are infamous for their ability to make cruel weapons and torture devices.

Humans   A race who live in Lake Town near the Lonely Mountain. Tolkien emphasizes their mortality, their lack of wisdom, their discordance with nature, and their rampant feuding.

Trolls   Short-tempered and dull-witted creatures who will eat just about anything. The trolls are based on mythological creatures from Old English and Anglo-Saxon poems and on figures from popular fairy tales and folklore. In Tolkien's novels, they speak with a cockney accent, the dialect of lower-class Londoners.

Wargs   Evil wolves. The Wargs pursue Bilbo and the dwarves soon after Bilbo acquires the ring.

THEMES IN *THE HOBBIT*

THE HEROISM INHERENT IN ALL MEN   *The Hobbit*'s main theme is the ability of a common person to become a hero when circumstances demand it. At the beginning of the story, Bilbo is timid, comfortable, and complacent. When Gandalf tells him about the quest of Thorin's dwarves, Bilbo is so frightened that he faints. But Bilbo possesses reserves of inner strength that are hidden even to him as the quest begins. He manages to confront the trolls, outwit Gollum, slay the spider, rescue the dwarves in Mirkwood, and speak face-to-face with the great dragon Smaug. As he builds confidence, Bilbo emerges as a true hero.

Because Tolkien acknowledged that his hobbits were inspired by rural Englishmen of his own time, Bilbo's development might represent the heroism of England in World War I or the heroism latent in every man. But given Tolkien's stated distaste for allegory—he wrote to tell stories, not to explore themes—it is debatable whether Bilbo's story refers to anyone except Bilbo himself.

THE IMPORTANCE OF RACE AND LINEAGE   Major and simplistic differences exist among Tolkien's imaginary races. Elves, dwarves, trolls, and goblins differ from one another physically, psychologically, and morally. These inherent racial differences drastically limit the possibility of individual choice but make moral distinctions easy to maintain. All goblins are evil, for example, and all elves are good. Family lineage also shapes identity in *The Hobbit*. Throughout Middle-Earth, lineage determines prospects, character, and social position. For instance, Tolkien portrays Bilbo's conflicting feelings of fear and courage as a struggle between his Baggins side and his Took side. Bard is heroic because he descended from the lords of Dale. Whereas race dictates morals, family dictates specific personality: Bilbo is good because he is a hobbit, but he is adventurous because he is a Took.

CONTRASTING WORLDVIEWS   Tolkien was a scholar of ancient languages at Oxford. A major source of inspiration for *The Hobbit*'s plot was the ancient epic literature that Tolkien studied, particularly Scandinavian and Anglo-Saxon epics like *Beowulf*. The influence of these epics can be seen in the heroic quest, the dragon's treasure hoard, the importance of named swords, the elves' mysterious magic, and the focus on birthright and family lineage. But if Tolkien's inspiration is ancient, his tone is modern. *The Hobbit* revisits ancient conventions with a playful, comic tone. Bilbo himself, with his common sense, love of peace, and self-doubt, is in many ways a rural Englishman of the 1930s transplanted into a medieval adventure. Tolkien's exploration of the contrast between his world and the worlds he studied is one source of the novel's comedy.

SYMBOLS IN *THE HOBBIT*

NAMED SWORDS   In epic literature, swords with names and lineages are the marks of great heroes. One of the most famous examples is King Arthur's sword, Excalibur. The swords that Thorin and Gandalf win from the trolls symbolize their heroic deeds. Bilbo's decision to name his short sword Sting is a major turning point in his quest that symbolizes his bravery and confidence.

HOBBITS   Though the thematic importance of hobbits is highly debatable, Tolkien himself acknowledged that he based his hobbits on the rural, middle-class English people among whom he lived.

IMPORTANT QUOTATIONS FROM *THE HOBBIT*

"Let's have no more argument. I have chosen Mr. Baggins and that ought to be enough for all of you. If I say he is a Burglar, a Burglar he is, or will be when the time comes. There is a lot more in him than you guess, and a deal more than he has any idea of himself. You may (possibly) all live to thank me yet."

Location: Chapter 1
Speaker: Gandalf
Context: Bilbo faints from terror, but Gandalf defends him

After Bilbo's display of fear, the dwarves are skeptical that Bilbo will make a good addition to the party, and Gandalf gives this speech to ease their doubts. The speech is important both because it exemplifies Gandalf's habit of insisting that his own authority is definitive proof and because it foreshadows Bilbo's transformation into a hero. The trajectory of the novel from this point forward involves Bilbo's discovery of the "lot more in him."

"It's got to ask uss a question, my preciouss, yes, yess, yess. Jusst one more question to guess, yes, yess."

Location: Chapter 5
Speaker: Gollum
Context: Gollum and Bilbo play a riddle game, and Gollum speaks directly to the ring

These sentences perfectly capture Gollum's corrupt, sibilant, hissing form of speech. He never addresses Bilbo directly but speaks only to his mysterious "precious," calling Bilbo "It." Gollum's infatuation with his precious also acts as a bit of foreshadowing. Precious turns out to be the magic ring that Bilbo had discovered and placed in his pocket. Gollum's devotion to the ring foreshadows its extreme, seductive powers, which only become clear in the *Lord of the Rings* trilogy.

Somehow the killing of this giant spider, all alone by himself in the dark . . . made a great difference to Mr. Baggins. He felt a different person, and much fiercer and bolder in spite of an empty stomach, as he wiped his sword on the grass and put it back into its sheath. "I will give you a name," he said to it, "and I shall call you Sting."

Location: Chapter 8
Speaker: The narrator
Context: Bilbo kills a spider and names his sword

The most that can be said for the dwarves is this: they intended to pay Bilbo really handsomely for his services; they had brought him to do a nasty job for them, and they did not mind the poor little fellow doing it if he would; but they would all have done their best to get him out of trouble, if he got into it.. . . There it is: dwarves are not heroes, but calculating folk with a great idea of the value of money; some are tricky and treacherous and pretty bad lots; some are not, but are decent enough people like Thorin and Company, if you don't expect too much.

Location: Chapter 12
Speaker: The narrator
Context: The narrator apologizes for the bad behavior of the dwarves, who have sent Bilbo into the dragon's lair all alone

"There is more in you of good than you know, child of the kindly West. Some courage and some wisdom, blended in measure. If more of us valued food and cheer and song above hoarded gold, it would be a merrier world."

Location: Chapter 18
Speaker: Thorin
Context: Before dying, Thorin asks Bilbo's forgiveness

THE HOUSE OF THE SEVEN GABLES

Nathaniel Hawthorne

A family finally breaks a curse brought down on it by an ancestor.

THE LIFE OF NATHANIEL HAWTHORNE

Nathaniel Hawthorne was born in Salem, Massachusetts, in 1804. His family descended from the earliest settlers of the Massachusetts Bay Colony. Among his forebears was John Hathorne (Hawthorne added the "w" to his name when he began to write), one of the judges at the 1692 Salem witch trials. Throughout his life, Hawthorne was both fascinated and disturbed by his kinship with John Hathorne. Hawthorne's father died when Hawthorne was two. His widowed mother raised him on a lonely farm in Maine. Hawthorne attended Bowdoin College, where he met two people who were to have great impact upon his life: Henry Wadsworth Longfellow, who would later become a famous poet, and Franklin Pierce, who would later become president of the United States.

After college, Hawthorne tried his hand at writing, producing historical sketches and an anonymous novel, *Fanshawe*, that detailed his college days rather embarrassingly. He also held positions as an editor and as a customs surveyor. He was part of the intellectual circle that included Ralph Waldo Emerson and Margaret Fuller, an association that led him to abandon his customs post for the utopian experiment at Brook Farm, a commune designed to promote economic self-sufficiency and transcendentalist principles.

After marrying fellow transcendentalist Sophia Peabody in 1842, Hawthorne left Brook Farm and moved into the Old Manse, a home in Concord where Emerson had once lived. In 1846, he published *Mosses from an Old Manse*, a collection of essays and stories that earned Hawthorne the attention of the literary establishment. America was trying to establish a cultural independence to complement its political independence, and Hawthorne's collection of stories displayed both a stylistic freshness and an interest in American subject matter. Herman Melville, among others, hailed Hawthorne as the "American Shakespeare."

In 1845, Hawthorne again went to work as a customs surveyor, this time, like the narrator of *The Scarlet Letter*, at a post in Salem. In 1850, after having lost the job, he published *The Scarlet Letter* to enthusiastic, if not widespread, acclaim. His other major novels include *The House of the Seven Gables* (1851), *The Blithedale Romance* (1852), and *The Marble Faun* (1860). In 1853, Hawthorne's college friend Franklin Pierce, now president, appointed Hawthorne a United States consul. Hawthorne spent the next six years in Europe. He died in 1864, a few years after returning to America.

THE HOUSE OF THE SEVEN GABLES IN CONTEXT

Hawthorne was not a devoted follower of transcendentalism, and he had difficulties with the movement's optimism and idealism. Compared with Melville's *Moby-Dick* and Henry David Thoreau's *Walden*, Hawthorne's work seems closer to the American Gothic movement of the late eighteenth and early nineteenth century than it is to transcendentalism. Novels in the Gothic genre are typified by dark, brooding themes of romance, passion, and human fallibility.

A mildly cynical view of human nature pervades Hawthorne's novels. He frequently explores human flaws like hypocrisy and immorality. *The Scarlet Letter*, for example, has an adulterous preacher as one of its main characters, and the Pyncheon family at the center of *The House of the Seven Gables* has many dark, deadly secrets, despite its social prominence. *The House of the Seven Gables* boldly blends realism and fantasy. Hawthorne himself called *The House of the Seven Gables* a romance, arguing that romances were not bound by the ordinary course of human experience.

The House of the Seven Gables also reflects the changing America of Hawthorne's day. The novel is filled with predictions of sweeping change, particularly of a world made more mobile by trains and the telegraph. A few of the characters explicitly state that they see their world shifting toward a more connected, mobile age.

THE HOUSE OF THE SEVEN GABLES: KEY FACTS

Time and place written: 1850–1851; Lenox, Massachusetts

Date of first publication: 1851

Publisher: James T. Fields

Type of work: Novel, romance

Genre: Satire, moral fable

Language: English

Setting (time): 1850s

Setting (place): A town like those in the county of Essex, Massachusetts

Tense: Immediate past

Tone: Straightforward, gloomy, sarcastic

Narrator: Third-person omniscient

Point of view: Mostly the narrator's

Protagonist: Hepzibah Pyncheon, Phoebe Pyncheon, Clifford Pyncheon, Holgrave

Antagonist: Judge Pyncheon

PLOT OVERVIEW: *THE HOUSE OF THE SEVEN GABLES*

The House of the Seven Gables begins with a preface that identifies the work as a romance, not a novel. Hawthorne prepares readers for the fluid mixture of realism and fantasy that the romance genre allows. The preface also conveys the major theme of the book, which Hawthorne refers to as a moral: "the wrong-doing of one generation lives into the successive ones, and . . . becomes a pure and uncontrollable mischief."

A battered house with seven gables stands in a small New England town. (Gables are the triangular structures formed by two intersecting points of a roof.) The house, which belongs to the Pyncheon family, has a long and controversial history.

In the mid-1600s, a local farmer named Matthew Maule builds a house on fertile land near a pleasant spring. In the late-1600s, the surrounding neighborhood has become fashionable, and the wealthy Colonel Pyncheon covets Maule's land. Several years later, Maule is hanged for witchcraft, and rumors abound that Pyncheon was behind Maule's conviction. Maule curses Colonel Pyncheon from the scaffold, but the Colonel is unfazed. He even hires Maule's own son to build him a new mansion with seven gables on the property. At a party held to inaugurate his new house, the Colonel is found dead in his study, his beard covered in blood. One of the Colonel's important documents—the deed for a giant land claim in Maine—is missing. The deed is never found, even though generations of Pyncheons search for it in vain. From then on, the Pyncheon house continues to bring bad luck, culminating with young Clifford Pyncheon's alleged murder of his uncle.

Many years later, the old maid who resides in the Pyncheon mansion, a nearsighted, scowling woman named Hepzibah, is forced to open a small store in her home to keep from starving. Hepzibah considers the store a source of great shame despite the comforting words of Uncle Venner, a neighborhood character, and of Holgrave, Hepzibah's rebellious young lodger, who practices an early form of photography known as daguerreotype. The very day Hepzibah opens her shop, she receives a visit from Phoebe, a young girl who is Hepzibah's distant cousin. At first, Hepzibah worries that Phoebe's presence will upset Hepzibah's brother, Clifford, who is returning home from prison, but Phoebe uses her charm and convinces Hepzibah to let her stay. When Clifford returns, battered and almost imbecilic from his time in prison, he is impressed by Phoebe. Their poverty bothers him more than the fact that his sister has opened a store.

Clifford and Hepzibah anticipate with terror a visit from their cousin, Judge Pyncheon. The Judge has a very charismatic smile. He greets Hepzibah warmly and offers her financial support, but in response she tries to prevent him from entering the house. From inside, Clifford begs him to go away. Even the normally unflappable Phoebe experiences a moment of revulsion when the Judge greets her.

Phoebe spends a lot of time with Holgrave, the house's lodger. Together they tend the garden and feed the house chickens. Holgrave explains his radical politics. He believes that each generation should tear down the work of those before it. He constantly asks Phoebe about Clifford's past. He tells Phoebe the story of Alice Pyncheon. A hundred years before, Alice's father, Gervayse Pyncheon, summoned Matthew Maule, the young grandson of a man also named Matthew Maule. Gervayse believed that since the younger Maule's father built the Pyncheon house, the young man might know where to find the missing deed. The younger Maule, although bitter at the Pyncheons' mistreatment of his family, agreed to help in exchange for the house of the seven gables and the land on which it stands. He summoned the spirits of his father, grandfather, and Colonel Pyncheon by hypnotizing Gervayse's young daughter, Alice. The two Maule spirits prevented Colonel Pyncheon's ghost from revealing where the deed is. The young Maule was elated to find that Alice remained under his spell, and tormented her in cruel and petty ways. On his wedding night, the young Maule forced Alice to serve his new bride. When Alice awakened from her trance, she rushed home through the snow, caught pneumonia, and died. Maule was devastated by what he had done.

As Holgrave finishes his story, he realizes he has hypnotized Phoebe, but his integrity prevents him from abusing his power, and he breaks her trance. While Phoebe is making a visit to her home in the country, Judge Pyncheon returns to the house of the seven gables and forces Hepzibah to fetch Clifford, saying he will put Clifford in an asylum if she refuses. The Judge explains that Clifford knows where the deed is. Hepzibah cannot find Clifford in his room, but when she comes back downstairs she finds her brother pointing gleefully to the slumped figure of Judge Pyncheon.

Worried that Clifford will be blamed for the murder, the brother and sister flee. When Phoebe returns, only Holgrave is home. Excitedly, he shows her a daguerreotype of the dead Judge and tells her that the curse has been lifted. He confesses his love to Phoebe, and she admits she loves him. Hepzibah and Clifford return before the body is discovered. Clifford is not suspected in the Judge's death, and it is rumored (correctly) that the Judge himself framed Clifford for the crime for which he served thirty years in prison. News arrives that the Judge's estranged son has died in Europe, so the Judge's inheritance—which was hidden behind the portrait—goes to Clifford. Clifford, Hepzibah, Phoebe, Holgrave, and Uncle Venner move to the Judge's country estate, leaving the house of the seven gables to rot.

CHARACTERS IN *THE HOUSE OF THE SEVEN GABLES*

CHARACTERS IN THE BACK STORY

Matthew Maule (the elder) A simple farmer in the 1600s. Maule was hanged for witchcraft, most likely at the instigation of Colonel Pyncheon, who then stole his land and built the house of the seven gables on it. Maule's curse still haunts the Pyncheons.

Matthew Maule (the younger) The grandson of the first Matthew Maule and the son of Thomas Maule. Matthew nursed a powerful grudge against the Pyncheon family. His misuse of his hypnotic powers caused the death of young Alice Pyncheon.

Thomas Maule The carpenter forced to build a new house on land stolen from his own family. People believe he stole the Pyncheons' deed to the Maine land and hid it somewhere in the house.

Alice Pyncheon The daughter of Gervayse Pyncheon. Alice's life was destroyed after she fell under the hypnotic spell of the younger Matthew Maule. It is said that the sounds of her harpsichord still haunt the house of the seven gables.

Colonel Pyncheon A bastion of the town's Puritan community. Colonel Pyncheon's greed and heartlessness were responsible for the Pyncheon curse.

Gervayse Pyncheon The grandson of Colonel Pyncheon and the father of Alice. Gervayse's attempts to retrieve his family's deed cost Alice her life.

CHARACTERS IN THE MAIN STORY

Holgrave A young lodger in Hepzibah's home. Holgrave earns his living by making an early kind of photograph known as a daguerreotype. He is a kind man with revolutionary politics. No one knows that Holgrave is actually a descendant of the first Matthew Maule. This link has given him hypnotic powers.

The Organ-Grinder A traveling musician whose act includes a monkey and a moving diorama.

Clifford Pyncheon Hepzibah's brother. Once a beautiful young man, Clifford was broken by the thirty years he spent in prison for allegedly murdering his uncle, old Jaffrey Pyncheon, a crime the Judge committed and framed him for. Clifford returns home more idiot than man, but Hepzibah and Phoebe gradually bring him back to his wits.

Hepzibah Pyncheon The current occupant of the house. Hepzibah is Clifford's sister and a cousin to Judge Pyncheon and Phoebe. Nearsightedness locks Hepzibah's face in a permanent scowl, which scares customers away from her small store, but she has a kind heart and takes good care of her brother.

Judge Jaffrey Pyncheon The wealthy, popular cousin of Hepzibah and Clifford. With his brilliant smile, Judge Jaffrey is viewed, by himself and by others, as a pillar of the community, but truly he has a dark and greedy nature. The true culprit in the death of old Jaffrey Pyncheon, the Judge covets the rest of the dead man's missing property.

Old Jaffrey Pyncheon The uncle of Clifford, Hepzibah, and the Judge. Old Jaffrey Pyncheon dies of an apoplectic fit after finding young Jaffrey rummaging through his notes.

Judge Pyncheon's son Judge Pyncheon's estranged son. He dies from cholera.

Phoebe Pyncheon Hepzibah's and Clifford's cousin. Although she lacks the aristocratic upbringing of her cousins, Phoebe is a vibrant, beautiful, wise young woman who brings cheer to the gloomy Pyncheon house.

Uncle Venner A colorful figure in the village. Despite his poverty, Uncle Venner preaches a philosophy of optimism.

THEMES IN *THE HOUSE OF THE SEVEN GABLES*

THE PERSISTENCE OF SINS As Hawthorne states in the Preface, the sins of one generation dog the lives of their descendents. The misdeeds of Colonel Pyncheon lead to the subsequent misfortunes of the Pyncheon family. The apoplectic deaths of three Pyncheons fulfill Matthew Maule's curse on the Colonel: "God will give him blood to drink." Old Jaffrey Pyncheon and his nephew, Judge Jaffrey Pyncheon, are both found dead with blood coating their shirts and beards. Two hundred years after their ancestor's crime, the Pyncheons suffer for it.

Paradoxically, however, Hawthorne suggests that we can choose our own fates regardless of what outrages our ancestors perpetrated. The Pyncheons' misery is brought about not because they are cursed but because they are greedy and overly ambitious. Only when a Pyncheon grasps for excessive wealth or power is he or she brought down. Maule's curse may be no more than a self-fulfilling prophecy.

THE IMPORTANCE OF CLASS Hawthorne satirizes nineteenth-century New England's preoccupation with class in *The House of the Seven Gables*. The feud between the Maules and the Pyncheons is a class conflict of its own—a modest farming family pitted against elite Puritan followers of the church, the law, and the army. Matthew Maule is a poor farmer sent to the gallows by Colonel Pyncheon, a wealthy landowner and one-time army man. The interaction between the younger Matthew Maule and Gervayse Pyncheon makes this class distinction even more evident. The young Maule first refuses to enter the house of the seven gables from the back, as would befit a member of the working class, and then is disturbed by Alice Pyncheon's apparent disdain for his workman's status. Even lineage fails to prevent class discrimination. Hepzibah knows that the Judge would not hesitate to send Clifford to an asylum.

THE DECEPTIVENESS OF APPEARANCES *The House of the Seven Gables* frequently uses the Judge's infectious smile to demonstrate that appearances can mask the truth. Even as his cruelty becomes apparent, Judge Pyncheon's brilliant smile continues to dazzle almost everyone. Hepzibah's scowl has the opposite effect but proves the same point. It keeps customers away from her store and even repulses her beloved brother, Clifford. Her scowl, which is caused by her nearsightedness, hides a kind heart.

SYMBOLS IN *THE HOUSE OF THE SEVEN GABLES*

THE PORTRAIT OF COLONEL PYNCHEON The portrait of the Colonel, permanently affixed to the wall, watches generation after generation of Pyncheons fall prey to the same ambitions that brought him down. It symbolizes the persistence of previous generations. Judge Pyncheon strongly resembles the portrait, which hints at his corruption. Clifford recoils at the sight of the portrait, evidence of his upstanding character.

THE CHICKENS The Pyncheon chickens, a scraggly bunch, symbolize the waning fortunes of the family that breeds them. Once the size of turkeys, the chickens have shrunk and now look weak. Still, they persevere. The selection of the ungraceful chicken to represent the Pyncheon family is a satirical touch in the novel.

IMPORTANT QUOTATIONS FROM *THE HOUSE OF THE SEVEN GABLES*

This being, made only for happiness, and heretofore so miserably failing to be happy . . . this poor, forlorn voyager from the Islands of the Blest, in a frail bark, on a tempestuous sea, had been flung, by the last mountain-wave of his shipwreck, into a quiet harbor. There, as he lay more than half-lifeless on the strand, the fragrance of an earthly rosebud had come to his nostrils, and, as odors will, had summoned up reminiscences or visions of all the living and breathing beauty, amid which he should have had his home.

Location: Chapter 9
Speaker: The narrator
Context: We learn how prison has brutalized Clifford's mind

Throughout the novel, Clifford is a difficult, sometimes unpleasant character. Here, Hawthorne's poetic portrayal of Clifford's degeneration helps us sympathize with Clifford. This passage explains how his once-beautiful mind has so thoroughly gone to waste. The image of Clifford "half-lifeless" on the sand, captivated by the scent of a rose, illustrates the terrible suffering that accompanies his return and the sense that he has missed his youth. The tone is one of exhaustion, but it is also one of recovery, for the image does not end with Clifford's drowning but with his slow recovery of consciousness. Throughout the novel, Hawthorne links decay and renewal.

[A]n individual of this class builds up, as it were, a tall and stately edifice, which, in the view of other people, and ultimately in his own view, is no other than the man's character, or the man himself. Behold, therefore, a palace!. . . [I]n some low and obscure nook . . . may lie a corpse, half-decayed, and still decaying, and diffusing its death-scent all through the palace! The inhabitant will not be conscious of it; for it has long been his daily breath!. . . Here, then, we are to seek the true emblem of the man's character, and of the deed that gives whatever reality it possesses, to his life.

Location: Chapter 15
Speaker: The narrator
Context: The narrator speaks of the Judge's character

This passage addresses the complex character of the Judge, who is charming and self-assured on the outside but thoroughly rotten on the inside. Hawthorne stresses the power of the Judge's station and charisma, likening them to a "palace," a building of opulence and splendor. The secret is not that this palace is a sham, but that it has been poisoned by a rotting corpse locked deep inside. The corpse—the Judge's avarice—has been hidden so completely that even the Judge has forgotten its existence. This gloomy Gothic image helps to establish the theme that the current generation inherits the flaws of past generations. The rotting corpse becomes a physical symbol of dangerous legacies. The palace that is the Pyncheon family is infested with the smell of a rotting ancestor, and no one even notices or thinks to root out the problem.

[T]hey . . . hinted that he was about to build his house over an unquiet grave.. . . The terror and ugliness of Maule's crime, and the wretchedness of his punishment, would darken the freshly plastered walls, and infect them early with the scent of an old and melancholy house.

Location: Chapter 1
Speaker: The narrator
Context: The narrator points out that Colonel Pyncheon cursed himself by building on the land he stole from Matthew Maule

---

"[I]t will startle you to see what slaves we are to by-gone times—to Death, if we give the matter the right word!. . . We read in Dead Men's books! We laugh at Dead Men's jokes, and cry at Dead Men's pathos!. . . Whatever we seek to do, of our own free motion, a Dead Man's icy hand obstructs us!"

Location: Chapter 12
Speaker: Holgrave
Context: Holgrave advocates beginning anew instead of enslaving ourselves to the past

---

"A man will commit almost any wrong—he will heap up an immense pile of wickedness, as hard as granite, and which will weigh heavily upon his soul, to eternal ages—only to build a great, gloomy, dark-chambered mansion, for himself to die in, and for his posterity to be miserable in. He lays his own dead corpse beneath the underpinning, as one may say, and hangs his frowning picture on the wall, and, after thus converting himself into an Evil Destiny, expects his remotest great-grandchildren to be happy there!"

Location: Chapter 17
Speaker: Clifford
Context: Clifford articulates the novel's main theme

THE HOUSE ON MANGO STREET

Sandra Cisneros

A woman growing up in poverty in 1960s Chicago is determined to find her own path in life without forgetting her past.

THE LIFE OF SANDRA CISNEROS

Sandra Cisneros was born in Chicago in 1954 to a Mexican father and a Chicana (Mexican-American) mother. During her childhood, Cisneros's family frequently moved between Chicago and Mexico City. Cisneros found these relocations very painful, especially given her family's poverty. She was the sole daughter in a family of seven children. Cisneros read voraciously. In high school, she edited the school literary magazine and dabbled in poetry. However, it was not until her first creative writing class at Chicago's Loyola University that Cisneros began devoting significant time and energy to writing. After graduation, she worked toward an M.F.A. at the University of Iowa Writers' Workshop. Her writing focused on the lives of working class Mexican-American women struggling for an independent sense of self and sexuality.

After earning her M.F.A., Cisneros returned to Chicago, where she worked with Chicano high-school dropouts at the Latino Youth Alternative High School. She became a college recruiter and minority student counselor at her alma mater, Loyola. In 1984, she published *The House on Mango Street* to critical acclaim and became one of the first Hispanic-American writers to achieve commercial success. In 1985, *The House on Mango Street* won the Before Columbus American Book Award. In the 1980s, Cisneros received several fellowships and lectureships to support her work, including two fellowships from the National Endowment for the Arts in 1982 and 1987. In 1987, she published the poetry collection *My Wicked Wicked Ways*. In 1991, she won several prestigious awards for *Woman Hollering Creek*, a collection of short stories. Sandra Cisneros lives in San Antonio, Texas, where she continues to be involved in the local Hispanic community.

THE HOUSE ON MANGO STREET IN CONTEXT

Like Sandra Cisneros herself, the fictional Esperanza is a Chicana growing up in 1960s Chicago. Chicano literature evolved as an independent genre in the aftermath of the Mexican War of 1846–1848. It has incorporated many Mexican-American values and traditions. It explores themes of homesickness and nostalgia, and deals in legends and superstitions. Poetry also plays a strong role in Chicano literature.

After World War II, as whites increasingly moved to the suburbs, large numbers of Mexican immigrants and Mexican-Americans who had worked as agricultural laborers moved to American urban areas hoping to find work doing manual labor. They often lived difficult lives plagued by poverty and discrimination such as Esperanza describes in *The House on Mango Street*. In her novel, Cisneros also examines the role of women in Mexican-American culture.

THE HOUSE ON MANGO STREET: KEY FACTS

Time and place written: Early 1980s; United States	
Date of publication: 1984	
Publisher: Arte Público Press	
Type of work: Novella	
Genre: Autobiographical novella; bildungsroman; künstlerroman	
Language: English	
Setting (time): Mid-twentieth century (most likely 1960s)	

Setting (place): Chicago

Tense: Past and present

Tone: Lyrical, sad, childlike, carefree, angry

Narrator: Esperanza Cordero in the first person

Point of View: Esperanza Cordero's

Protagonist: Esperanza Cordero

Antagonist: Esperanza's shame about her family's poverty and her Mango Street neighborhood; encroaching adulthood and sexuality

HOUSE ON MANGO STREET: PLOT OVERVIEW

The House on Mango Street is a collection of forty-four vignettes from a year in the life of Esperanza, a twelve-year-old Mexican-American girl who moves with her family into a new house on Mango Street, which is in a poor Hispanic neighborhood of Chicago. Esperanza, a shy and highly observant girl, is disappointed in the house and neighborhood. Through dialogue and poetic monologue, she captures the details of her community—such as the fact that boys are close with girls only when other boys aren't around.

Esperanza does not like her name (which means "hope" in Spanish) because her classmates cannot pronounce it properly. She was named after her grandmother, from whose difficult life Esperanza would like to separate herself.

As the new kid on the block, Esperanza yearns for a best friend. She tries to befriend a snobby and obnoxious girl named Cathy, but Cathy's family soon moves to a more affluent neighborhood. Lucy and Rachel become Esperanza's best friends. The three girls buy a bicycle together and ride through the streets, having fun and getting to know the neighborhood.

Esperanza is close to her younger sister Nenny. Despite their connection, Esperanza often feels that they have different priorities and are affected by different experiences.

Esperanza gets to know the neighborhood kids. A boy named Meme Ortiz moves into Cathy's old house. Marin, an older girl who has a boyfriend in Puerto Rico, tells Esperanza and her friends how to attract men with makeup, clothes, and nylons. When Marin discusses sex, Esperanza does not know how to react. Esperanza says that outsiders "who don't know any better" are scared when they wander into her neighborhood. At the same time, she realizes that her friends and neighbors know little about other communities. Esperanza talks about the Vargas family, whose many children make trouble in the neighborhood.

Esperanza's vignettes continue:

A neighbor named Alicia struggles to attend college while also caring for her family. Esperanza notices how much Alicia's father expects her to contribute to the household.

Esperanza's mother lends her and her friends high-heeled shoes, which, they soon realize, highlight their sexuality.

Esperanza wants to eat lunch in the school canteen with the popular kids. Her mother gives her permission, but the school nun does not allow her to eat there. The nun forces Esperanza to point out her house from the school window. Esperanza weeps.

Esperanza attends her cousin's baptism party. She initially feels that her shoes and feet are large and clumsy, but ends up dancing well with her uncle.

The girls discuss the mysteries of hips and womanhood.

Esperanza takes a job at a photo-processing lab. She feels lonely at work. An older man makes her feel welcome and then shocks her with a forceful kiss.

Esperanza's grandfather dies, and she comforts her father. She thinks about how he, too, will die.

Esperanza, Rachel, and Lucy mock Esperanza's sick aunt and then pray for redemption.

Marin's sometime dance partner, a man named Geraldo, is hit by a car. He dies because he does not receive prompt treatment.

Ruthie, Edna's daughter, entertains Esperanza and her friends with her childish antics.

Earl claims to be married, but Esperanza and others observe many women visiting him at his apartment.

A neighborhood boy named Sire piques Esperanza's curiosity. She wonders what it would be like to have a boyfriend, but her parents say that she should not date.

Esperanza feels an affinity for four skinny trees, which plant their roots and grow their branches simultaneously.

Mamacita resents the dominance of English over Spanish in her daily life. Rafaela must stay indoors because her husband thinks that she is "too beautiful" to be permitted outdoors. Minerva's husband repeatedly leaves her, but Minerva always takes him back. Sally's father beats her.

Esperanza imagines that if she had a great big house, she would invite all the vagabonds to stay with her. She wants to have control over her life, unlike her peers and neighbors, whose fathers and husbands control them. Esperanza's mother advises her not to feel ashamed about her background or her poverty.

A group of boys force Esperanza and her friends to kiss them, incurring Esperanza's anger. Later, Sally leaves Esperanza alone at a carnival, and Esperanza is sexually assaulted. Sally gets married and moves to a nice house, but her controlling husband does not allow her to see her friends. Esperanza decides to leave Mango Street, but to come back to help those who are not strong enough to leave.

CHARACTERS IN *THE HOUSE ON MANGO STREET*

FAMILY

Esperanza The novel's perceptive, poetic narrator. Twelve-year-old Esperanza is a Mexican-American girl . Esperanza is ashamed of her family's poverty, their house, and their neighborhood. The novel chronicles a year in Esperanza's life, as she matures emotionally, sexually, and artistically.

Magdalena (Nenny) Esperanza's younger sister and closest companion. While Nenny is old enough to be Esperanza's playmate, she is too young to share in the changes Esperanza is experiencing.

Carlos and Kiki Esperanza's younger brothers.

NEIGHBORS

Marin A Puerto Rican girl. Flirtatious, lively, and older than Esperanza and her friends, Marin shares her knowledge about makeup and boys. She lives with her aunt and uncle for a time, but is soon sent back to Puerto Rico.

Rachel and Lucy Esperanza's neighbors and best friends. Rachel and Lucy, Hispanic girls from Texas, share Esperanza's love of words.

Sally Esperanza's neighbor. Sally, who is Esperanza's age, is sexually bold and seems glamorous to Esperanza. Sally's father beats her because he is convinced that all women are immoral. Before eighth grade, Sally elopes with an older man who does not allow her to see friends or leave the house.

THEMES IN *THE HOUSE ON MANGO STREET*

THE TENSION BETWEEN CHILDHOOD AND MATURITY On the brink of puberty, Esperanza finds herself caught between childhood and womanhood. She feels alternately intrigued, intimidated, and angry about her blossoming sexuality. In the vignette "Hips," she says of hips, "[o]ne day you wake up and they are there. Ready and waiting like a new Buick with the keys in the ignition. Ready to take you where?" At her first job, Esperanza is unpleasantly surprised when an older coworker forcefully kisses her. The people around her begin to regard her as a sexual being, and she must change her behavior accordingly. Esperanza grows up in other ways, too: when her grandfather dies, she finds that the usual roles have been reversed, and she must comfort her father. At the same time, Esperanza still takes a child's comfort in her mother's hair—"sweet to put your nose into when she is holding you, holding you and you feel safe."

THE AMERICAN DREAM AND THE IMMIGRANT IDENTITY The novel opens with Esperanza's disappointment in her new house on Mango Street, which falls far short of her dream of a "a real house that would be ours for always. . . white with trees around it, a great big yard and grass growing without a fence." The American Dream proves an empty one for the people in Esperanza's life, who do not profit from their hard work. Without proper medical care, Geraldo dies, leaving nothing behind: "No address. No name. Nothing in his pockets." As an immigrant, Esperanza feels torn between two worlds.

She dislikes the prejudice she encounters from the students at school, but at the same time she longs to escape her stifling community, whose members share her heritage but not her aspirations.

DISILLUSIONMENT WITH ROMANTIC LOVE   The experiences of Esperanza's neighbors and friends shape her attitudes toward sexual relationships. She is torn between her desire for a romantic relationship and her desire to avoid the humiliations that she has watched other women suffer. Many of the female characters, including Sally, Marin, Minerva, are profoundly saddened by their experiences with men, a sadness that is signaled by the image of a woman sitting by the window all day. Esperanza both envies women she finds beautiful and understands the difficulties their beauty creates. Nenny gets things she wants because she has "pretty eyes," but Rafaela must stay indoors because her husband is afraid that she is too beautiful and will run away. After her first sexual encounter, which is an assault, Esperanza confronts Sally, asking her, "Why did you leave me all alone? I waited my whole life. You're a liar. They all lied. All the books and magazines, everything that told it wrong. Only his dirty fingernails against my skin, only his sour smell again." This incident marks a loss of innocence and the onset of a new weariness for Esperanza.

SYMBOLS IN *THE HOUSE ON MANGO STREET*

SHOES AND FEET   Esperanza's shoes are closely connected to her sense of her own beauty, ugliness, and sexual maturity. Esperanza's mother gives the girls high-heeled shoes to play with, and the shoes transform them into sexual beings who are half girls, half women. The grocer, Mr. Benny, warns them that the shoes are "dangerous." By the end of the chapter, the girls understand the burden of being grown up, and Esperanza remarks, "We are tired of being beautiful." In "Chanclas," Esperanza feels ugly because of her shoes and feet. Her discomfort with her appearance is part of the awkwardness and self-consciousness that often accompany puberty.

RED BALLOON   In "Boys & Girls," Esperanza thinks about the social division between boys and girls and wishes for a friend. She says, "Until then I am a red balloon, a balloon tied to an anchor." The red balloon represents Esperanza as she sees herself. Like the balloon, she imagines that she is marked as different from everyone else. The anchor represents the forces that bind her to her house, family, and neighborhood.

IMPORTANT QUOTATIONS FROM *THE HOUSE ON MANGO STREET*

I don't tell them I am ashamed—all of us staring out the window like the hungry. I am tired of looking at what we can't have. When we win the lottery . . . Mama begins, and then I stop listening.

    People who live on hills sleep so close to the stars they forget those of us who live too much on earth. They don't look down at all except to be content to live on hills. They have nothing to do with last week's garbage or fear of rats. Night comes. Nothing wakes them but the wind.

    One day I'll own my own house, but I won't forget who I am or where I came from. Passing bums will ask, Can I come in? I'll offer them the attic, ask them to stay, because I know how it is to be without a house. Some days after dinner, guests and I will sit in front of a fire. Floorboards will squeak upstairs. The attic grumbles.

    Rats? they'll ask.

    Bums, I'll say, and I'll be happy.

Location: "Bums in the Attic"
Speaker: Esperanza
Context: Esperanza speaks about her shame about her family's poverty, and describes her dream house

Esperanza is frequently ashamed of her background—of her ethnicity, her language, her race, and her economic status. Tired and disillusioned, she has stopped listening to her mother's unrealistic hopes for their future. Esperanza imagines that if she lived in the house of her dreams, she would provide shelter for homeless bums. Cisneros implicitly criticizes the willful obliviousness of the rich to the suffering of the poor by showing us that Esperanza will be happy not because she has a big house, but because she is able to help others.

When I am too sad and too skinny to keep keeping, when I am a tiny thing against so many bricks, then it is I look at trees. When there is nothing left to look at on this street. Four who grew despite concrete. Four who reach and do not forget to reach. Four whose only reason is to be and be."

Location: "Four Skinny Trees"
Speaker: Esperanza
Context: Esperanza explains her sense of connection to four trees near her house

The trees mentioned in this passage resemble Esperanza physically. When she feels weak, sorrowful, and small, they still reach for the sky, reminding her of her dreams and aspirations. The trees' roots run deep, and their branches grow high. Inspired by the trees and their symbolism, Esperanza wants to seek out opportunities to fulfill her potential while maintaining the solid foundation of her heritage.

Just another brazer who didn't speak English. Just another wetback. You know the kind. The ones who always look ashamed. . . .

What does it matter?

They never saw the kitchenettes. They never knew about the two-room flats and sleeping rooms he rented, the weekly money orders sent home, the currency exchange. How could they?

His name was Geraldo. And his home is in another country. The ones he left behind are far away, will wonder, shrug, remember. Geraldo—he went north . . . we never heard from him again.

Location: "Geraldo No Last Name"
Speaker: Esperanza
Context: Esperanza talks about Geraldo, who dies because he doesn't get immediate medical attention after he was hit by a car.

In the movies there is always one with red red lips who is beautiful and cruel. She is the one who drives the men crazy and laughs them all away. Her power is her own. She will not give it away.

I have begun my own quiet war. Simple. Sure. I am one who leaves the table like a man, without putting back the chair or picking up the plate.

Location: "Beautiful & Cruel"
Speaker: Esperanza
Context: Esperanza expresses her desire to be a woman with power

---

When you leave you must remember to come back for the others. A circle, understand? You will always be Esperanza. You will always be Mango Street. You can't erase what you know. You can't forget who you are. . . . You must remember to come back. For the ones who cannot leave as easily as you.

Location: "The Three Sisters,"
Speaker: The *comadre* with the "porcelain hands"
Context: Esperanza realizes that, in important ways, she will never be able to escape her past

THE ADVENTURES OF HUCKLEBERRY FINN

Mark Twain

An intelligent thirteen-year-old boy flees with an escaped slave and slowly recognizes the hypocrisy of his society.

THE LIFE OF MARK TWAIN

Mark Twain was born Samuel Langhorne Clemens in Florida, Missouri, in 1835. At the age of four he moved with his family to Hannibal, a town on the Mississippi River. Twain's father was a prosperous man who owned a number of household slaves. He died when Twain was twelve. Twain left school and worked as a printer, finding work in numerous American cities, including New York and Philadelphia. In his early twenties, Twain found work on the Mississippi riverboats. Eventually, he became a riverboat pilot. The river inspired his pen name; "Mark Twain" means a river depth of two fathoms. Life on the river also gave Twain material for several of his novels, including the raft scenes of *The Adventures of Huckleberry Finn*.

During the Civil War, Twain joined a Confederate cavalry division. His division deserted en masse, and Twain made his way west with his brother, working first as a silver miner in Nevada and then as a journalist. In 1863, he began signing articles with the name Mark Twain. Twain's writing—articles, stories, memoirs, and novels characterized by unique humor and a deft ear for language—made Twain incredibly famous. In 1876, *The Adventures of Tom Sawyer* was published to wild national acclaim, cementing Twain's position as a behemoth of American literature. Book sales made him wealthy enough to build a large house in Hartford, Connecticut, for himself and his wife Olivia, whom he had married in 1870.

In the early 1880s, the hopefulness of the post-Civil War years began to fade. Reconstruction, the political program designed to reintegrate the defeated South into the Union, was failing. Southern states and individuals oppressed the black men and women that the war had freed.

Meanwhile, Twain's personal life began to collapse. His wife was sickly, and the couple's first son died when he was nineteen months old. Because of an investment gone wrong, Twain found himself mired in debilitating debt. As his fortune dwindled, he continued to write. Drawing on his personal plight and troubles of the nation, he finished a draft of his masterpiece, *The Adventures of Huckleberry Finn*, in 1883. In 1884, when it was published, the novel met with great public and critical acclaim.

Over the next ten years, Twain continued to write. He published two more popular novels, *A Connecticut Yankee in King Arthur's Court* (1889) and *Pudd'nhead Wilson* (1894). After that, he went into an artistic decline and never again published work up to the standards of *Huck Finn* or even *Pudd'nhead*. His finances burdened him, and his wife and two daughters died over the course of a few years. Twain's writing from this period until the end of his life reflects depression and righteous rage at the injustices of the world. Despite his feelings of alienation, Twain's literary reputation was stellar, and he was in continual demand as a public speaker until his death in 1910.

THE ADVENTURES OF HUCKLEBERRY FINN IN CONTEXT

Huck Finn has become famous not just as a crown jewel in American literature, but also as a subject of intense controversy. The novel has been banned by some Southerners because of its steadfastly critical take on the South and its scorn for the hypocrisies of slavery. It has also been banned by those who consider it vulgar or racist because it uses the word "nigger," a word whose connotations can obscure the novel's antislavery stance. That the word was not particularly charged in Twain's day, and that he used it because he wanted to replicate the way people actually spoke, does not comfort some modern readers. Despite the controversy surrounding the novel, *Huck Finn* is considered a masterpiece.

THE ADVENTURES OF HUCKLEBERRY FINN: KEY FACTS

Time and place written: 1876–1883 (not continuously); mostly in Hartford, Connecticut, and Elmira, New York

Date of publication: 1885

Publisher: Charles L. Webster & Co.

Type of work: Novel

Genre: Picaresque; satire; bildungsroman

Language: English

Setting (time): Before the Civil War; roughly 1835–1845

Setting (place): St. Petersburg, Missouri; Arkansas

Tense: Immediate past

Tone: Ironic, mocking, contemplative, boyish, exuberant

Narrator: Huckleberry Finn in the first person

Point of view: Huck's

Protagonist: Huck, Jim

Antagonist: Society

PLOT OVERVIEW: *THE ADVENTURES OF HUCKLEBERRY FINN*

Huckleberry Finn begins his narrative by explaining what happened in *Tom Sawyer*, the story that precedes this one and stars Huck himself and his friend Tom. In the town of St. Petersburg, which lies along the Mississippi River, Huck, a poor boy with a drunken bum for a father, and Tom, a middle-class boy with an overactive imagination, found a robber's stash of gold and got rich. Huck was adopted by the Widow Douglas, a kind but stifling woman who lives with her sister, the self-righteous Miss Watson. Huck dislikes his new life of cleanliness, manners, church, and school, but he sticks it out for Tom, who tells him that he must stay "respectable" if he wants to belong to his new "robbers' gang."

Huck's brutish father, Pap, reappears and demands Huck's money, which is saved at the bank. Judge Thatcher and the Widow try to get legal custody of Huck, but a well-intentioned new judge in town believes in the rights of Huck's natural father and even takes the old drunk into his own home in an attempt to reform him. This effort fails miserably, and Pap soon returns to his old ways. Outraged when the Widow Douglas warns him to stay away from her house, Pap kidnaps Huck, holding him in a cabin across the river from St. Petersburg.

Pap locks Huck in the cabin when he goes out and beats him when he gets drunk. Tired of his confinement, and fearing the beatings will worsen, Huck escapes from Pap by faking his own death. Hiding on Jackson's Island in the middle of the Mississippi River, he watches the townspeople search the river for his body. After a few days on the island, he encounters Jim, one of Miss Watson's slaves. Jim has run away from Miss Watson after hearing her talk about selling him to a plantation down the river, where he would be treated horribly and separated from his wife and children. Huck and Jim team up, despite Huck's uncertainty about the legality or morality of helping a runaway slave. While they camp out on the island, a great storm causes the Mississippi to flood. Huck and Jim spot a log raft and an uprooted house floating past the island. They capture the raft and loot the house, which contains the body of a man who has been shot. Jim won't let Huck see the man's face. Although the island is blissful, they are forced to leave after Huck learns from a woman onshore that her husband thinks Jim is hiding out there. Huck also learns that a reward has been offered for Jim's capture.

Huck and Jim start downriver on the raft, intending to leave it at the mouth of the Ohio River and proceed by steamboat to the free states, where slavery is prohibited. They have an encounter with a gang of robbers on a wrecked steamboat and manage to escape with the robbers' loot. One foggy night, Huck and Jim encounter a group of men looking for escaped slaves. Huck has a brief moral crisis over concealing stolen "property," but lies to the men and tells them that his father is on the raft suffering from small-pox. Terrified of the disease, the men give Huck money and hurry away. The next night the raft is rammed by a steamboat and Huck and Jim are separated.

Huck ends up in the home of the kindly Grangerfords, Southern aristocrats locked in a bitter and silly feud with the Shepherdsons. A Grangerford daughter elopes with a Shepherdson son, leading to a gun battle in which everyone is killed. Jim shows up with the repaired raft. Huck hurries to Jim's hiding place and they take off down the river.

A few days later, they rescue a pair of men being pursued by armed bandits. The men, who are clearly con artists, claim to be a displaced English duke and the long-lost heir to the French throne. Powerless to tell two white adults to leave, Huck and Jim continue down the river with the pair of "aristocrats." The Duke and Dauphin pull several scams in the small towns along the river. They hear that a man named Peter Wilks has recently died and left everything to his two brothers, who should be arriving from England any day. The duke and dauphin enter the town claiming to be Wilks's brothers. Wilks's three nieces welcome them and quickly set about liquidating the estate. A few townspeople are skeptical, and Huck, who admires the Wilks sisters, decides to thwart the con. He steals the dead man's gold from the Duke and Dauphin and reveals the truth to the eldest Wilks sister. Then Wilks's real brothers arrive from England. The duke and dauphin barely escape in the melee.

The duke and dauphin sell Jim to a local farmer. Huck finds out where Jim is being held and resolves to free him. At the house where Jim is a prisoner, a woman greets Huck excitedly and calls him "Tom." Huck realizes that the people holding Jim are Tom Sawyer's aunt and uncle, Silas and Sally Phelps. The Phelpses have mistaken him for Tom, who is due to arrive for a visit, and Huck does not correct them. He intercepts Tom on his way to the Phelpses, and Tom pretends to be his own younger brother, Sid.

Tom hatches a wild plan to free Jim, adding all sorts of unnecessary obstacles. Huck is sure Tom's plan will get them all killed, but he complies. After an eternity of preparation, they put the plan into action. Jim is freed, but Tom is shot in the leg by a pursuer. Jim sacrifices his freedom to care for Tom and ends up in chains. When he wakes the next morning, Tom reveals that Jim has actually been a free man all along. Miss Watson, who made a provision in her will to free him, died two months earlier. Tom planned the escape attempt as a game and intended to pay Jim for his troubles. Tom's Aunt Polly shows up and reveals who Huck and Tom actually are. Jim tells Huck that the body they found on the floating house was Pap's. Aunt Sally offers to adopt Huck, but Huck, who has had enough "sivilizing," announces his plan to set out for the West.

CHARACTERS IN *THE ADVENTURES OF HUCKLEBERRY FINN*

The Duke and Dauphin A pair of con men. The older man, who appears to be about seventy, claims to be the "Dauphin," the son of Louis XVI and heir to the French throne. The younger man, who is about thirty, claims to be the usurped Duke of Bridgewater.

Huckleberry Finn The thirteen-year-old protagonist and narrator of the novel. Always a bit of an outcast, Huck is thoughtful, intelligent, and willing to ignore society's norms if his conscience tells him to.

The Grangerfords A kindhearted family that lives in a tacky country home. The Grangerfords are locked in a longstanding feud with another family, the Shepherdsons.

Jim One of Miss Watson's household slaves. Jim is superstitious and occasionally sentimental. He is also intelligent, practical, and more of an adult than anyone else in the novel. Because he is a black man and a runaway slave, Jim is at the mercy of almost all the other characters in the book and is often forced into ridiculous and degrading situations.

Pap Huck's father. Pap, the town drunk, has disgusting white skin and hopelessly tattered clothes. An illiterate man, he disapproves of his son's education.

The Phelps family Tom Sawyer's aunt and uncle. Sally is the sister of Tom's aunt Polly.

Aunt Polly Tom Sawyer's aunt and guardian, and Sally Phelps's sister.

Tom Sawyer Huck's friend. In this novel, he serves as a foil to Huck. Tom is imaginative, dominating, and given to wild plans inspired by adventure novels. Tom's stubborn reliance on the "authorities" of romance novels leads him to acts of incredible stupidity and startling cruelty. His rigid adherence to convention aligns him with the "sivilizing" forces that Huck learns to view skeptically.

Sherburn A repulsive figure who nonetheless gives a notable speech when a mob of townspeople comes to lynch him, lambasting them for their cowardice and twisted sense of justice.

Judge Thatcher The man who shares responsibility for Huck with the Widow Douglas. Judge Thatcher safeguards the money that Huck and Tom found at the end of *Tom Sawyer*. His daughter, Becky (or "Bessie," as Huck calls her), was Tom's girlfriend in the earlier novel.

Widow Douglas and Miss Watson Two wealthy sisters who live together in a large house in St. Petersburg. Miss Watson, gaunt and severe-looking, represents society's hypocrisy. The Widow Douglas is somewhat gentler in her beliefs and has more patience with the mischievous Huck.

The Wilks family A family conned by the Duke and Dauphin. Peter Wilks has died, leaving a substantial inheritance, and the con men pretend to be Peter Wilks's two brothers from England, the preacher Harvey and the deaf-mute William. They fool the good-hearted and vulnerable Wilks sisters.

THEMES IN *THE ADVENTURES OF HUCKLEBERRY FINN*

RACISM AND SLAVERY Although the Civil War had officially ended slavery twenty years before Mark Twain wrote *Huck Finn*, an antislavery novel, racial problems still tormented the nation. By the early 1880s, Reconstruction, the plan to put the United States back together after the war and integrate freed slaves into society, was floundering. Three years after the publication of *Huck Finn*, it failed entirely. As Twain wrote *Huck Finn*, the South imposed Jim Crow laws designed to oppress black people.

It is possible to interpret the slavery in *Huck Finn* as an allegory of post-slavery conditions. Jim Crow, Twain suggests, is little better than slavery. In fact, the new racism of the South, less institutionalized and monolithic, is dangerous because it is harder to identify and rage against. Many people believed that slavery was a hateful, immoral practice, but not as many were equally repulsed when white Southerners enacted racist laws or policies and justified them as self-defense against newly freed blacks.

INTELLECTUAL AND MORAL EDUCATION *Huck Finn* is a bildungsroman, a coming-of-age story. Huck Finn, an outcast, distrusts the morals of the society that labels him a pariah and fails to protect him from abuse. This apprehension about society, and his friendship with Jim, lead Huck to question conventional wisdom about race. Time and again, he says he would rather "go to hell" than go along with what he's been taught. When some commonly accepted rule strikes Huck as fishy, he consults his experiences, instincts, and developing conscience. On the raft, away from civilization, Huck represents natural man untainted by society. Early in the novel, Huck learns to read books. By the novel's end, Huck has learned to "read" the world around him, to distinguish good, bad, right, wrong, menace, friend, and so on.

CIVILIZED SOCIETY Twain depicts society as degraded and illogical. In defiance of logic, the new judge gives Pap custody of Huck because his rights as a father demand it. Huck repeatedly encounters individuals who seem good, like Sally Phelps, but who are deeply prejudiced. Terrible acts go unpunished. Frivolous crimes lead to executions. At the end of the novel, when Huck rejects further "sivilizing," he is not simply avoiding school and regular baths. He is avoiding corrupt society.

SYMBOLS IN *THE ADVENTURES OF HUCKLEBERRY FINN*

THE MISSISSIPPI RIVER For Huck and Jim, the Mississippi River symbolizes freedom. Alone on their raft, they don't have to answer to anyone. The river carries Jim toward the free states and Huck away from his abusive father and the restrictive "sivilizing" of St. Petersburg. The fluid, fast-moving river reflects the characters at this point: free from society, Huck and Jim are in flux, willing to change their attitudes about each other.

But the river is not entirely benevolent. It floods, bringing Huck and Jim into contact with criminals, wrecks, and stolen goods. It fogs over, making them miss the mouth of the Ohio River, which was to be their route to freedom. It takes them continually southward, toward the deep South and entrenched racism. Eventually the river suggests the complicated state of the South itself.

IMPORTANT QUOTATIONS FROM *THE ADVENTURES OF HUCKLEBERRY FINN*

The Widow Douglas she took me for her son, and allowed she would sivilize me; but it was rough living in the house all the time, considering how dismal regular and decent the widow was in all her ways; and so when I couldn't stand it no longer I lit out. I got into my old rags and my sugar-hogshead again, and was free and satisfied. But Tom Sawyer he hunted me up and said he was going to start a band of robbers, and I might join if I would go back to the widow and be respectable. So I went back.

Location: The first page of the novel
Speaker: Huck
Context: Huck brings us up to speed

In these lines, Huck establishes his opposition to "sivilizing," which seems natural for a thirteen-year-old boy. Our initial inclination is to laugh and dismiss Huck's longing for freedom. However, Huck's opposition to civilization is based on mature observations about the worth of society. In this quotation, he associates civilization and respectability with a childish game—a game in which the participants are to play criminals.

It was a close place. I took . . . up [the letter I'd written to Miss Watson], and held it in my hand. I was a-trembling, because I'd got to decide, forever, betwixt two things, and I knowed it. I studied a minute, sort of holding my breath, and then says to myself: "All right then, I'll go to hell"—and tore it up. It was awful thoughts and awful words, but they was said. And I let them stay said; and never thought no more about reforming.

Location: Chapter XXXI
Speaker: Huck
Context: Jim has been sold by the Duke and Dauphin

These lines mark the moral climax of the novel. Jim is being held by the Phelpses pending his return to his owner. Huck thinks it might be better for Jim to be home in St. Petersburg than in his current state of peril, so he starts to write a letter to Miss Watson revealing Jim's location. But when Huck thinks of his friendship with Jim, and realizes that Jim will be sold down the river anyway, he decides to tear up the letter. This is a rebellious gesture, since everyone Huck knows would tell him that revealing Jim's whereabouts is the moral thing to do. Huck decides that he would rather go to hell than follow rules he considers cruel. This decision is Huck's true break with society. He realizes that he cannot reenter the civilized world; he has moved beyond it.

I hadn't had a bite to eat since yesterday, so Jim he got out some corn-dodgers and buttermilk, and pork and cabbage and greens—there ain't nothing in the world so good when it's cooked right—and whilst I eat my supper we talked and had a good time. . . . We said there warn't no home like a raft, after all. Other places do seem so cramped up and smothery, but a raft don't. You feel mighty free and easy and comfortable on a raft.

Location: Chapter XVIII
Speaker: Huck
Context: Huck describes the raft as a place of simple pleasures and good company

Tom told me what his plan was, and I see in a minute it was worth fifteen of mine for style, and would make Jim just as free a man as mine would, and maybe get us all killed besides. So I was satisfied, and said we would waltz in on it.

Location: Chapter XXXIV
Speaker: Huck
Context: Tom convinces Huck to carry out a needlessly complicated escape plan for Jim

---

But I reckon I got to light out for the territory ahead of the rest, because Aunt Sally she's going to adopt me and sivilize me, and I can't stand it. I been there before.

Location: The last lines of the novel
Speaker: Huck
Context: Huck decides not to stay in the society he has come to question

I KNOW WHY THE CAGED BIRD SINGS

Maya Angelou

A black girl growing up in the South struggles against racism, sexism, and lack of power.

THE LIFE OF MAYA ANGELOU

Maya Angelou was born Marguerite Anne Johnson on April 4, 1928, in St. Louis, Missouri. Her older brother, Bailey Johnson, Jr., could not pronounce her name when he was little, so he called her Mya Sister, then My, which eventually became Maya. When Angelou was three years old, her parents divorced and sent their children to live in the rural, segregated town of Stamps, Arkansas, with their paternal grandmother, Annie Henderson. During their teens, they lived with their mother, Vivian Baxter, in California. Angelou battled racism with dogged persistence. She became the first African American streetcar conductor in San Francisco.

In New York, Angelou won a role in the Gershwin opera *Porgy and Bess*. The show was on the road from 1954 to 1955, and Angelou and the cast toured nearly two dozen countries in Europe and Africa. After marrying a South African freedom fighter, Angelou lived in Cairo, Egypt, for several years, where she edited an English-language newspaper. Later, she taught at the University of Ghana and edited the *African Review*.

Angelou often shared stories about her childhood, and her friends and associates encouraged her to write an autobiography. In 1969, Angelou published *I Know Why the Caged Bird Sings*, the first in a series of autobiographical works. It quickly became a best-seller and was nominated for the National Book Award. Angelou's *Georgia, Georgia* became the first original screenplay by a black woman to be produced and filmed. *Just Give Me a Cool Drink of Water 'fore I Die*, a collection of poetry, was nominated for the Pulitzer Prize. Angelou was also nominated for an Emmy award for her performance in the film adaptation of Alex Haley's *Roots*. By 1995, she had spent two years on *The New York Times* Paperback Nonfiction Bestseller list, becoming the first African American author to do so.

Angelou's civil rights activism is a key part of her life. At Dr. Martin Luther King, Jr.'s request, Angelou became the northern coordinator for the Southern Christian Leadership Conference in the 1960s. President Gerald Ford appointed her to the American Revolutionary Bicentennial Advisory Commission, and President Jimmy Carter appointed her to the National Commission on the Observance of the International Woman's Year. At President Bill Clinton's request, she wrote and delivered a poem, "On the Pulse of Morning," for his 1993 presidential inauguration. She was only the second poet in American history to receive such an honor.

I KNOW WHY THE CAGED BIRD SINGS IN CONTEXT

Of her five autobiographies, *I Know Why the Caged Bird Sings* is Angelou's most popular and critically acclaimed. It is frequently read as a complement to fictional works that address racism, such as Harper Lee's *To Kill a Mockingbird* and Ralph Ellison's *Invisible Man*. It has also been banned from some classrooms because of its honest depictions of sexuality and its account of Angelo's rape. Angelou's book conveys the racial and gender discrimination a southern black girl endures. It also speaks to universal issues, among them the relationships between parents and children, child abuse, and the search for direction.

I KNOW WHY THE CAGED BIRD SINGS: KEY FACTS

Time and place written: New York City; late 1960s

Date of first publication: 1969

Publisher: Random House

Type of work: Autobiographical novel

Genre: Autobiography

Language: English

Setting (time): 1930s–1950s

Setting (place): Stamps, Arkansas; St. Louis, Missouri; Oakland, California; San Francisco, California

Tone: Personal, comical, woeful, philosophical

Tense: Past

Narrator: Maya Angelou in the first person

Point of View: Maya Angelou's

Protagonist: Maya Angelou

Antagonist: Racism, sexism, violence, and loneliness

I KNOW WHY THE CAGED BIRD SINGS: PLOT OVERVIEW

In *I Know Why the Caged Bird Sings*, Maya Angelou describes her coming of age as a precocious but insecure black girl in the American South during the 1930s and in California during the 1940s. Maya's parents divorce when she is only three years old and send Maya and her older brother, Bailey, to live with their paternal grandmother, Annie Henderson, in rural Stamps, Arkansas. Annie, whom they call Momma, runs the only store in the black section of Stamps and becomes the central moral figure in Maya's childhood.

As young children, Maya and Bailey struggle with the pain of having been rejected and abandoned by their parents. Maya is tormented by the belief that she is an ugly child who will never measure up to genteel white girls. She does not feel equal to other black children. One Easter Sunday, Maya is unable to finish reciting a poem in church. Feeling ridiculed, she races from the church, crying, laughing, and wetting herself. Bailey sticks up for Maya when people make fun of her to her face.

Deep-seated racism pervades Stamps. Blacks are subjected to wearying daily indignities and terrifying lynch mobs. Maya spends time at Momma's store, observing the cotton-pickers as they journey to and from work in the fields. When Maya is eight, her father arrives in Stamps unexpectedly and takes her and Bailey to live with their mother, Vivian, in St. Louis, Missouri. Vivian, a beautiful, wild woman, works in gambling parlors. One morning her live-in boyfriend, Mr. Freeman, sexually molests Maya. Later he rapes her. Vivian takes Maya to the police. Mr. Freeman is convicted, but before he begins serving his one-year sentence he is violently murdered, probably by some criminal associates of Maya's family.

Maya feels guilty about the rape. She also believes she is responsible for Mr. Freeman's death because she lied in court, saying he had not molested her prior to the rape. Believing that she has become a mouthpiece for the devil, Maya stops speaking to everyone except Bailey. At first her mother's family accepts her silence as temporary post-rape trauma, but they later perceive it as disrespect, and it makes them angry.

To Maya's relief, but Bailey's regret, Maya and Bailey return to Stamps to live with Momma. Momma manages to break through Maya's silence by introducing her to Mrs. Bertha Flowers, a kind, educated woman who tells Maya to read works of literature out loud, giving her books of poetry that help her to regain her voice.

Maya becomes aware of both the fragility and the strength of her community in Stamps. She attends a church revival at which a pastor implicitly preaches against white hypocrisy with a sermon on charity. The spiritual strength whipped up by the sermon soon dissipates as the revival crowd walks home. Maya observes the entire community listening to the Joe Louis heavyweight championship boxing match and longing for him to defend his title against his white opponent.

Maya endures several appalling incidents that teach her about the insidious nature of racism. At age ten, she takes a job for a white woman who decides to call Maya "Mary." In an effort to get fired, Maya breaks the woman's fine china. At Maya's eighth-grade graduation, a white speaker says black students are expected to become athletes or servants. Momma takes Maya to the only dentist in Stamps, a white man who says he'd rather place his hand in a dog's mouth than in hers. The last straw comes when Bailey encounters the rotting corpse of a black man and witnesses a white man's satisfaction at seeing the body.

Momma begins to fear for the children's well-being and saves money to bring them to Vivian, who now lives in California.

When Maya is thirteen, the family goes to live with Vivian in Los Angeles and then in Oakland, California. When Vivian marries Daddy Clidell, a positive father figure, they move with him to San Francisco, the first city where Maya feels at home. She spends one summer with her father, Big Bailey, in Los Angeles and has to put up with his cruel indifference and his hostile girlfriend, Dolores. After Dolores cuts her in a fight, Maya runs away and lives for a month with a group of homeless teenagers in a junkyard. She returns to San Francisco strong and self-assured. She defies racist hiring policies in wartime San Francisco, becoming the first black streetcar conductor at age fifteen. At sixteen, she gets pregnant. For eight months, she hides her condition from her mother and stepfather. She graduates from high school. As the story ends, Maya begins to feel confident about being a mother to her newborn son.

CHARACTERS IN *I KNOW WHY THE CAGED BIRD SINGS*

Maya Angelou   The writer and narrator of the autobiography. As a girl, Maya is very curious and perceptive. Haunted by her displacement from her biological parents and her sense that she is ugly, Maya often isolates herself, escaping into her reading.

Vivian Baxter   Bailey and Maya's mother. Although she has a nursing degree, Vivian supports herself by working in gambling parlors. A somewhat inattentive mother, Vivian nevertheless treats her children with love and respect.

Daddy Clidell   Vivian's second husband. Daddy Clidell becomes the only real father figure in Maya's life. He combines strength and tenderness and enjoys thinking of himself as Maya's father. Daddy Clidell is a successful businessman despite his lack of education.

Mrs. Viola Cullinan   A Southern white woman in Stamps. Perhaps unwittingly, she hides her racism under a veneer of gentility. Mrs. Cullinan employs Maya as a maid.

Mr. Edward Donleavy   A white speaker at Maya's eighth-grade graduation ceremony. He insults the black community by talking about their limited potential in a racist society.

Mr. Freeman   Vivian's live-in boyfriend in St. Louis. Mr. Freeman rapes Maya. Guilt about Mr. Freeman's murder haunts Maya throughout her childhood.

Mrs. Bertha Flowers   A black aristocrat living in Stamps, Arkansas. One of Maya's idols, Mrs. Flowers takes an interest in Maya, encouraging her love of literature.

Glory   Mrs. Cullinan's cook. A descendent of the slaves once owned by the Cullinan family, she accepts Mrs. Cullinan's condescension and racism.

Annie Henderson (Momma)   Maya and Bailey's paternal grandmother. Momma largely raises her grandchildren. Her store, the only one in the black section of Stamps, Arkansas, serves as the central gathering place for the black community. She raises the children according to stern Christian values and strict rules.

Bailey Johnson, Jr.   Maya's older brother. Like Maya, Bailey is intelligent and mature. He excels in sports and conversation, and shows deep compassion for Maya.

Big Bailey Johnson   Maya and Bailey's father. Big Bailey is handsome, vain, and selfish. He stands out for his proper English and flashy possessions. Big Bailey does not respect or care for Maya.

Willy Johnson   Momma's son and Maya's and Bailey's uncle. Uncle Willy, who is in his thirties, was crippled in a childhood accident and has always lived with Momma. He suffers insults and jokes because of his disability. Like Momma, he is a devout Christian. He is disciplinarian and protector to the children.

Joyce   Bailey's first love. Four years older than Bailey, Joyce turns his innocent displays of sexual curiosity into sex and eventually runs away with a railroad porter, leaving Bailey heartbroken.

Louise Kendricks   Maya's first friend outside her family.

Miss Kirwin   Maya's teacher in San Francisco.

Dr. Lincoln A white dentist in Stamps. Momma lent him money during the Great Depression. She insists that he look at Maya's tooth.

Henry Reed The valedictorian of Maya's eighth-grade class. Henry leads the class in "Lift Ev'ry Voice and Sing," popularly known as the Black National Anthem, renewing his community's pride following Mr. Donleavy's speech. This moment catalyzes Maya's great pride in her heritage and inspires her passion for black poets and orators.

Dolores Stockland Big Bailey's prim live-in girlfriend in Los Angeles. Maya's presence drives Dolores into a jealous rage.

Stonewall Jimmy, Spots, Just Black, Cool Clyde, Tight Coat, and Red Leg Daddy Clidell's con-men friends. They teach Maya that it is possible to gain advantage over whites by using their own prejudice against them.

Mr. Taylor An acquaintance of Maya's family. Mr. Taylor is devastated by the loss of his wife, Florida.

Mrs. Florida Taylor Mr. Taylor's wife of forty years. At Florida's funeral, Maya confronts her own mortality for the first time.

Tommy Valdon An eighth-grader who writes Maya a valentine.

THEMES IN *I KNOW WHY THE CAGED BIRD SINGS*

RACISM In a racist society, the black people Maya knows struggle to maintain dignity. Stamps, Arkansas, is so segregated that as a child, Maya does not quite believe that white people exist. As Maya gets older, she is confronted by overt, personal incidents of racism. The white speaker at her graduation condescendingly dismisses the idea that black people can succeed; her white boss casually changes Maya's name; a white dentist refuses to treat her. Maya learns that living in a racist society has profoundly shaped the character of her family members. Their resistance to racism takes many forms. Momma tries to see things objectively and keep to herself. Big Bailey buys flashy clothes and drives a fancy car to prove his worth and runs around with women to assert his masculinity. Daddy Clidell's friends practice elaborate and lucrative cons against white people. Vivian's family cultivates toughness. Blacks also use the church as a venue of subversive resistance.

DISPLACEMENT Maya is shuttled around to seven different homes between the ages of three and sixteen, a personal displacement that echoes the displacement of blacks all across the country. "I didn't come to stay," a line from the poem Maya tries to recite, suggests that Maya defends herself against the pain of rootlessness by pretending she never wanted to stay in the first place. Part of the reason Maya finally feels at home in San Francisco is that she thinks the city is full of displaced people like herself. Maya realizes that thousands of terrified black children make journeys like the ones she and Bailey make, traveling on their own to newly affluent parents in northern cities or back to southern towns when the North failed to live up to its promise of economic prosperity.

NAMES Angelou suggests that names are strongly connected to identity. Maya, born Marguerite, chooses to go by the name her brother gave her, which indicates her love for him. When Maya reunites with her mother and her mother's family, one of her uncles tells her the story of how she got this name. Maya notes that for African Americans in general, naming provides proof of identity in a hostile world that aims to stereotype blacks and erase their individuality. Mrs. Cullinan shows her contempt for Maya by refusing to learn her name, and then insisting that Maya go by Mary. Her disrespect for Maya's name betrays her disrespect for Maya.

SYMBOLS IN *I KNOW WHY THE CAGED BIRD SINGS*

THE STORE Momma's store, the central gathering place in Stamps, symbolizes the rewards of hard work and the importance of community. At the store, Maya witnesses the cycles of nature and labor. She notes that until she left Arkansas for good at age thirteen, the Store was her favorite place to be.

MAYA'S EASTER DRESS The lavender taffeta dress that Momma alters for Maya symbolizes Maya's lack of self-respect. She believes that the only kind of beauty is *white* beauty and imagines that the dress will transform her into a paragon of white beauty. But on Easter morning, she realizes that the dress is only a white woman's throwaway that cannot change her.

IMPORTANT QUOTATIONS FROM *I KNOW WHY THE CAGED BIRD SINGS*

My race groaned. It was our people falling. It was another lynching, yet another Black man hanging on a tree. One more woman ambushed and raped. . . This might be the end of the world. If Joe lost we were back in slavery and beyond help. It would all be true, the accusations that we were lower types of human beings. Only a little higher than the apes.

Location: Chapter 19
Speaker: Maya
Context: A group of people congregate at the Store to listen to Joe Louis defend his world heavyweight boxing title

Maya suggests that the entire black community of Stamps pins its hopes and psychological salvation on Louis, "the Brown Bomber." This passage describes the precarious nature of black pride, which in Stamps depends largely on the outcome of a boxing match. The black community imbues the match with deep symbolism. Louis's fistfight with a white man becomes the ultimate clash of the races, the symbol of blacks' stand against centuries of enslavement, rape, and torture perpetrated by whites. Louis's loss would mean the "fall" of the race and a return to the idea that whites had a right to denigrate black people. Louis must shoulder the burden of this symbolism partly because in Maya's time, so few blacks were allowed to achieve public prominence. Cynics might say that Louis's win does little more than stave off the black community's despair. It does not turn the tables on whites because it is a symbolic victory only. But his public victory does inject the community with a shot of energy and pride.

Bailey was talking so fast he forgot to stutter, he forgot to scratch his head and clean his fingernails with his teeth. He was away in a mystery, locked in the enigma that young Southern Black boys start to unravel, start to try to unravel, from seven years old to death. The humorless puzzle of inequality and hate.

Location: Chapter 25
Speaker: Maya
Context: Bailey encounters the rotting corpse of a black man and sees a white man gloating over the sight

When Bailey sees a white man's satisfaction at the grisly death of a black man, he must confront a degree of hatred that he cannot comprehend. Bailey asks Uncle Willy to explain how colored people offended whites originally, an unanswerable question that reveals the total illogic of racism. Bailey's experience here precipitates Momma's decision to remove the children from both the physical and psychological dangers associated with growing up in the South.

If growing up is painful for the Southern Black girl, being aware of her displacement is the rust on the razor that threatens the throat. It is an unnecessary insult.

Location: The end of the opening section
Speaker: Maya
Context: From an adult perspective, Angelou looks back on her childhood

A light shade had been pulled down between the Black community and all things white, but one could see through it enough to develop a fear-admiration-contempt for the white "things"—white folks' cars and white glistening houses and their children and their women. But above all, their wealth that allowed them to waste was the most enviable.

Location: Chapter 8
Speaker: Maya
Context: Maya thinks about her perceptions of whites

The Black female is assaulted in her tender years by all those common forces of nature at the same time that she is caught in the tripartite crossfire of masculine prejudice, white illogical hate and Black lack of power. The fact that the adult American Negro female emerges a formidable character is often met with amazement, distaste and even belligerence.

Location: Chapter 34
Speaker: Maya
Context: Maya thinks about why black women develop strong characters

THE ILIAD

Homer

During the Trojan War, a great Trojan warrior dies at the hands of a great Greek warrior.

THE LIFE OF HOMER

Nearly three thousand years after they were composed, the *Iliad* and the *Odyssey* remain two of the most celebrated and widely read stories ever told, yet next to nothing is known about their author. He was certainly an accomplished Greek bard, and he probably lived in the late-eighth and early-seventh centuries B.C. Most believe that he was a blind poet named Homer. But mystery surrounds the works. As early as the third and second centuries B.C., Greeks were questioning whether Homer existed and whether the two epics were written by a single individual.

THE *ILIAD* IN CONTEXT

The writer of *The Iliad* owes a debt to the tradition of oral poetry. Stories of a glorious expedition to the East and back had been circulating in Greece for hundreds of years before the *Iliad* and *Odyssey* were composed, passed down through the generations by casual storytellers and minstrels.

The epics are set in Mycenaean Greece in about the twelfth century B.C., during the Bronze Age. The Greeks believed that this historical period was a sublime age, when gods still frequented the earth and heroic mortals lived in Greece. Although Homer uses a high style appropriate for the Bronze Age, he incorporates details from eighth- and seventh-century B.C. Greece (the Iron Age), the time when he was writing.

For centuries, many scholars believed that the Trojan War was a story dreamed up by the Greeks, not a real war. But in the late nineteenth century, an archaeologist named Heinrich Schliemann declared that he had discovered the remnants of Troy off of the Aegean coast in northwestern Turkey. Most scholars believe that Schliemann discovered Troy, but some still say that the Trojan War never took place.

THE *ILIAD*: KEY FACTS

Time and place written: Unknown, but probably around 750 B.C. in mainland Greece,

Date of first publication: Unknown

Publisher: Unknown

Type of work: Poem

Genre: Epic

Language: Ancient Greek

Setting (time): Bronze Age (around the twelfth- or thirteenth-century B.C.)

Setting (place): Troy

Tense: Past

Tone: Awe-inspired, ironic, lamenting, pitying

Narrator: The omniscient poet in the third person

Point of view: The poet's

Protagonist: Achilles

Antagonist: Achilles' wounded pride

THE *ILIAD*: PLOT OVERVIEW

Nine years after the start of the Trojan War, the Greek ("Achaean") army sacks Chryse, a town allied with Troy. During the battle, the Achaeans capture a pair of beautiful maidens, Chryseis and Briseis. Agamemnon, the leader of the Achaean forces, takes Chryseis as his prize, and Achilles, the Achaeans' greatest warrior, claims Briseis. Chryseis's father, Chryses, a priest of the god Apollo, offers an enormous ransom in return for his daughter, but Agamemnon refuses to give Chryseis back. Chryses prays to Apollo, who sends a plague upon the Achaean camp.

After many Achaeans die, Agamemnon consults the prophet Calchas to determine the cause of the plague. When he learns that Chryseis is the cause, he reluctantly gives her up but then demands Briseis from Achilles as compensation. Furious at this insult, Achilles returns to his tent in the army camp and refuses to fight in the war any longer. He yearns to see the Achaeans destroyed and asks his mother, the sea-nymph Thetis, to work with Zeus, king of the gods, to thwart the Achaeans. The Trojans breach a cease-fire treaty, and Zeus comes to their aid.

Several days of fierce conflict ensue, including duels between Paris and Menelaus and between Hector and Ajax. The Achaeans make no progress, despite the heroism of the great Achaean warrior Diomedes. A nighttime reconnaissance mission by Diomedes and Odysseus yields information about the Trojans' plans, but the next day brings disaster. The Trojans advance to the boundary of the Achaean camp and set fire to one of the ships. Without the ships, the army will be stranded at Troy and almost certainly destroyed.

Concerned for his comrades but still too proud to help them himself, Achilles agrees to let his beloved friend Patroclus take his place in battle, wearing his armor. Patroclus's presence on the battlefield helps the Achaeans push the Trojans away from the ships and back to the city walls. But the counterattack soon falters. Apollo knocks Patroclus's armor to the ground, and Hector slays him. Hector ends up with Patroclus's armor, but the Achaeans manage to bring his body back to their camp. The death of Patroclus fills Achilles with such grief and rage that he agrees to reconcile with Agamemnon and rejoin the battle. Thetis goes to Mount Olympus and persuades the god Hephaestus to forge Achilles a new suit of armor. Achilles rides out to battle at the head of the Achaean army.

Hector has ordered his men to camp outside the walls of Troy. When the Trojan army glimpses Achilles, it flees in terror. Achilles cuts down every Trojan he sees. He even fights the god of the river Xanthus, who is angry that Achilles has caused so many corpses to fall into his streams. Finally, Achilles chases Hector around the city's periphery. The goddess Athena finally tricks Hector into turning around and fighting Achilles. In a dramatic duel, Achilles kills Hector. He lashes the body to the back of his chariot and drags it across the battlefield to the Achaean camp. The triumphant Achaeans celebrate Patroclus's funeral with a long series of athletic games in his honor. Each day for the next nine days, Achilles drags Hector's body in circles around Patroclus's funeral bier.

The gods agree that Hector deserves a proper burial. Zeus sends the god Hermes to escort King Priam, Hector's father and the ruler of Troy, into the Achaean camp. Priam tearfully pleads with Achilles to take pity on him and return Hector's body. Deeply moved, Achilles relents and returns Hector's corpse to the Trojans. Both sides agree to a temporary truce, and Hector receives a hero's funeral.

EVENTS THAT TAKE PLACE AFTER THE *ILIAD*

Although the Trojan War is still being fought at the end of the *Iliad*, Homer's audience knew what happened after the war ended. The potency of the *Iliad* depends on familiarity with postwar events. After the end of the poem, Achilles sights the beautiful Polyxena, a princess of Troy, at Hector's funeral feast. Hoping to marry her, Achilles agrees to use his influence with the Achaean army to end the war. But when he travels to the temple of Apollo to negotiate the peace, Paris shoots him in the heel—the only vulnerable part of his body—with a poisoned arrow, killing him. In other versions of the story, the wound occurs in the midst of battle.

Ajax and Odysseus recover Achilles' body. Thetis instructs the Achaeans to bequeath Achilles' armor to the most worthy hero. When it is awarded to Odysseus, Ajax commits suicide out of humiliation. Troy's defenses have been bolstered. The Achaean commanders are nearly ready to give up, but Odysseus concocts a plan. The Achaeans build a massive, hollow, wooden horse large enough to hold a contingent of warriors. Odysseus and a group of soldiers hide in the horse.

The next morning, the Trojans discover the mysterious horse and wheel it into the city as a tribute to Athena. That night, Odysseus and his men slip out of the horse, kill the Trojan guards, and fling open the gates of Troy to the Achaean army. The Achaeans massacre the citizens of Troy, plunder the city's riches, and burn the buildings to the ground. All of the Trojan men are killed except for a small group led by Aeneas.

After the war, Odysseus spends ten years trying to return to Ithaca. These years are the subject of Homer's other great epic, the *Odyssey*. Helen and Menelaus voyage back to their home in Sparta. Agamemnon, who has taken Priam's daughter Cassandra as a slave, returns home to his wife, Clytemnestra, and his kingdom, Mycenae. Clytemnestra has taken a man named Aegisthus as her lover, and with him she kills Agamemnon and Cassandra. Aeneas wanders for many years, searching for a new home for his surviving fellow citizens. His adventures are recounted in Virgil's epic *Aeneid*.

CHARACTERS IN THE *ILIAD*

THE ACHAEANS (ALSO CALLED THE "ARGIVES" OR "DANAANS")

Achilles   The son of the military man Peleus and the sea-nymph Thetis. The most powerful warrior in the *Iliad*, Achilles is proud and headstrong.

Agamemnon (also called "Atrides")   King of Mycenae and leader of the Achaean army; brother of King Menelaus of Sparta. Arrogant and often selfish, Agamemnon is a strong but sometimes reckless and self-serving leader.

Calchas   An important soothsayer.

Diomedes (also called "Tydides")   The youngest of the Achaean commanders. Diomedes is bold and sometimes impetuous. Inspired by Athena, he wounds two gods, Aphrodite and Ares.

Great Ajax (also called "Telamonian Ajax" or "Ajax")   An Achaean commander. After Achilles, Great Ajax is the mightiest Achaean warrior. His extraordinary size and strength help him wound Hector.

Idomeneus   King of Crete and a respected commander. Idomeneus leads a charge against the Trojans in Book 13.

Little Ajax   An Achaean commander. Little Ajax is the son of Oileus. He often fights alongside Great Ajax, whose stature and strength complement Little Ajax's speed and small size. The two together are sometimes called the "Aeantes."

Machaon   A healer. Machaon is wounded by Paris in Book 11.

Menelaus   King of Sparta; the younger brother of Agamemnon. The Trojan War begins because Menelaus's wife, Helen, is abducted by the Trojan prince Paris. Menelaus is quieter, less imposing, and more modest than Agamemnon.

The Myrmidons   The soldiers under Achilles' command. They hail from Achilles' homeland, Phthia.

Nestor   King of Pylos and the oldest Achaean commander. Nestor is very wise. He and Odysseus are the Achaeans' most deft and persuasive orators.

Odysseus   A fine warrior, speaker, and Achaean commander. Odysseus is the protagonist of Homer's other great epic, the *Odyssey*.

Patroclus   Achilles' beloved friend and advisor. Patroclus is devoted to both Achilles and the Achaean cause.

Peleus   Achilles' father and Zeus's grandson. Although his name often appears in the epic, Peleus never appears in person. Priam powerfully invokes the memory of Peleus when he convinces Achilles to return Hector's corpse.

Phoenix   A kindly old warrior. Phoenix helped raise Achilles.

THE TROJANS

Aeneas   A Trojan nobleman and mighty warrior. Aeneas is the son of Aphrodite. The Romans believed that Aeneas founded their city. He is the protagonist of Virgil's masterpiece, the *Aeneid*.

Agenor   A Trojan warrior who attempts to fight Achilles in Book 21.

Andromache   Hector's loving wife.

Antenor   A Trojan nobleman. Antenor is advisor to King Priam and father of many Trojan warriors. He thinks Helen should be returned to Menelaus.

Astyanax   Hector and Andromache's infant son.

Briseis   A woman Achilles claims as a war prize. When Agamemnon is forced to return Chryseis to her father, he takes Briseis as compensation, infuriating Achilles.

Chryseis   Chryses's daughter.

Chryses   A priest of Apollo in a Trojan-allied town. Chryses is Chryseis's father.

Dolon   A Trojan sent to spy on the Achaean camp in Book 10.

Glaucus   A powerful Trojan warrior.

Hector   Son of King Priam and Queen Hecuba. Hector is the mightiest warrior in the Trojan army. He is devoted to his wife, Andromache, and son, Astyanax. He resents his brother Paris for bringing war on their city.

Hecuba   Queen of Troy, wife of Priam, and mother of Hector and Paris.

Helen   The most beautiful woman in the ancient world. Helen left her husband, Menelaus, for Paris. She loathes herself for the misery caused by her betrayal. She is contemptuous of Paris, but she stays with him.

Pandarus   A Trojan archer.

Paris (also known as "Alexander")   Son of Priam and Hecuba and brother of Hector. Paris's abduction of the beautiful Helen, wife of Menelaus, sparked the Trojan War. Paris is self-centered and often unmanly. He fights effectively but prefers to sit in his room making love to Helen while others fight for him.

Polydamas   A young Trojan commander. Polydamas is calm and prudent. He gives the Trojans sound advice, but Hector seldom acts on it.

Priam   King of Troy, husband of Hecuba, and father of fifty Trojan warriors, including Hector and Paris. Though too old to fight, he is level-headed, wise, and benevolent.

Sarpedon   One of Zeus's sons.

THE GODS AND IMMORTALS

Aphrodite   Goddess of love and daughter of Zeus. Aphrodite is married to Hephaestus. Ares is her lover. She supports the Trojans in the war, although she is somewhat ineffectual in battle.

Apollo   A son of Zeus and the twin brother of the goddess Artemis. Apollo is god of the arts and archery. He supports the Trojans.

Ares   God of war and lover of Aphrodite. Ares generally supports the Trojans.

Artemis   Goddess of the hunt, daughter of Zeus, and twin sister of Apollo. Artemis supports the Trojans.

Athena   The goddess of wisdom, purposeful battle, and the womanly arts. Athena is Zeus's daughter. She hates the Trojans.

Hephaestus   God of fire and husband of Aphrodite. Hephaestus is the gods' metalsmith and is known as the lame or crippled god. He forges a new set of armor for Achilles and saves him from the river god.

Hera   Queen of the gods and Zeus's wife. Hera is a conniving and headstrong woman. She works with Athena to crush the Trojans, whom she passionately hates.

Hermes   The messenger of the gods.

Iris   Zeus's messenger.

Poseidon God of the sea. Poseidon, Zeus's brother, holds a grudge against the Trojans and supports the Achaeans in the war.

Thetis A sea-nymph. Thetis is the devoted mother of Achilles.

Zeus King of the gods and husband of Hera. Zeus claims neutrality in the mortals' conflict but throws his weight behind the Trojan side at Thetis's request.

THEMES IN THE *ILIAD*

THE GLORY OF WAR The *Iliad* celebrates war. Competence in battle and willingness to fight determine worth. For example, Paris doesn't like to fight, a shortcoming that earns him the scorn of his family and his lover. Achilles wins eternal glory by explicitly rejecting a long, comfortable life at home. Homer holds up warlike deities such as Athena for the reader's admiration and makes fun of timid gods such as Aphrodite and Artemis. The *Iliad* doesn't ignore the realities of war. Men die gruesome deaths; women become slaves and concubines; a plague decimates the Achaean army. Homer tells us that both armies regret that the war ever began. But despite his objective examination of war, Homer never questions the legitimacy of the ongoing struggle. In his portrayal, each side has a justifiable reason to fight, and warfare is a respectable and even glorious way to settle the dispute.

MILITARY GLORY OVER FAMILY LIFE Homer admires the bonds of deference and obligation that bind families together, but he reserves his highest esteem for the pursuit of *kleos*, the glory people win by performing great deeds. He constantly forces his characters to choose between their loved ones and the quest for kleos. The most heroic characters invariably choose kleos. Andromache pleads with Hector not to risk orphaning his son, but Hector knows that fighting among the front ranks is the only means of "winning [his] father great glory." Achilles debates returning home to live in ease with his aging father, but he remains at Troy to win glory. Paris, on the other hand, spends time with Helen rather than fighting. The noblest characters prize honor, bravery, and glory, willingly choosing them over a long life with those they love.

THE BRIEF SPAN OF HUMAN LIFE AND ITS CREATIONS Although the *Iliad* chronicles a brief period in a long war, it is acutely conscious of the specific ends awaiting its characters. Priam and all of his children will die. Achilles will meet an early end. Homer makes it clear that even great men cannot escape death. Indeed, the very greatest may yield to death sooner than their peers. Similarly, the *Iliad* repeatedly reminds us that the creations of mortals have a mortality of their own. The glory of men does not live on in their constructions, institutions, or cities. Troy will fall. The Greek fortifications will crumble. The impermanence of human life and creation makes it even more important to achieve glory. Only by living honorably can people find immortality after death, living on in the memories of those who survive them. Even if physical bodies and material creations cannot survive, reputations can.

SYMBOLS IN THE *ILIAD*

THE ACHAEAN SHIPS The Achaean ships symbolize the future of the Greek race. They are the army's only means of getting home. The ships' destruction would mean the annihilation—or automatic exile—of every soldier, and the decimation of a civilization.

THE SHIELD OF ACHILLES Achilles' shield, which depicts normal life in peacetime, symbolizes the world beyond the battlefield—feasts, dances, marketplaces, and crops. It reminds us that war is only one part of life.

IMPORTANT QUOTATIONS FROM THE *ILIAD*

We everlasting gods.. . . Ah what chilling blows
we suffer—thanks to our own conflicting wills—
whenever we show these mortal men some kindness.

Location: Book 5
Speaker: Ares
Context: Diomedes wounds Ares, who complains about his ill treatment

Ares's complaint concisely captures the Homeric relationship between gods and men and, perhaps, Homer's attitude toward that relationship. Homeric gods frequently intervene in the mortal world because they are emotionally attached to some human or cause. Ares describes this emotion as a desire to do "kindness," but kindness toward one mortal often translates into unkindness toward another. Also, each god favors different men, and when these men are at war, divine wars are often the result. This is why Ares attributes the gods' "chilling blows" to their "own conflicting wills."

Ares's whining is fairly typical of the gods. Homer's immortals expect to govern just as they wish, and they complain when they do not get their way. Ares' melodramatic and self-pitying lament, which Zeus scorns a few lines later, suggests Homer's critical view of the gods. He often portrays the gods as temperamental, sulky, vengeful, and petty—a collection of characteristics that may explain the inequities and absurdities in life on earth.

There is nothing alive more agonized than man
of all that breathe and crawl across the earth.

Location: Book 17
Speaker: Zeus
Context: Zeus talks to the horses pulling Achilles' chariot

Zeus speaks these grim words to the horses of Achilles' chariot, who weep over the death of Patroclus. The lines reflect the Homeric view of humans as frantic little ants. Throughout the *Iliad* and the *Odyssey*, mortals are often little more than the playthings of the gods, who can whisk them away from danger as easily as they can put them in the thick of it. Unlike other animals that "breathe and crawl across the earth," humanity understands the arbitrariness of their treatment at the hands of the gods, an awareness that increases their agony. They see the gods' interventions but are powerless to contradict them. They also have a fruitless knowledge of their fates. Achilles and Hector both know that they are doomed to die early deaths. Hector knows that his city will fall, his brothers and family will die, and his wife will be reduced to slavery. These men are agonized because they know their fates but cannot change them.

Rage—Goddess, sing the rage of Peleus' son Achilles,
murderous, doomed, that cost the Achaeans countless losses,
hurling down to the House of Death so many sturdy souls,
great fighters' souls, but made their bodies carrion,
feasts for the dogs and birds,
and the will of Zeus was moving toward its end.
Begin, Muse, when the two first broke and clashed,
Agamemnon lord of men and brilliant Achilles.

Location: The first lines of the poem
Speaker: The poet
Context: Homer summarizes his poem

Cattle and fat sheep can all be had for the raiding,
tripods all for the trading, and tawny-headed stallions.
But a man's life breath cannot come back again —
. . .
Mother tells me,
the immortal goddess Thetis with her glistening feet,
that two fates bear me on to the day of death.
If I hold out here and I lay siege to Troy,
my journey home is gone, but my glory never dies.
If I voyage back to the fatherland I love,
my pride, my glory dies.. . .

Location: Book 9
Speaker: Achilles
Context: The Achaean commanders ask Achilles to come back to their side, but he still prizes life over
glory

Remember your own father, great godlike Achilles —
as old as I am, past the threshold of deadly old age!
No doubt the countrymen round about him plague him now,
with no one there to defend him, beat away disaster.
No one — but at least he hears you're still alive
and his old heart rejoices, hopes rising, day by day,
to see his beloved son come sailing home from Troy.

Location: Book 24
Speaker: Priam
Context: Priam appeals to Achilles' filial piety, begging him to return Hector's corpse for proper burial

THE IMPORTANCE OF BEING EARNEST

Oscar Wilde

Two young men court two young women, winning their hearts by pretending to be named Ernest.

THE LIFE OF OSCAR WILDE

Oscar Wilde was born on October 16, 1854, in Dublin, Ireland. He was educated at Trinity College in Dublin and at Magdalen College, Oxford. He settled in London, where he married Constance Lloyd in 1884. In the literary world of Victorian London, Wilde fell in with an exalted artistic crowd that included W. B. Yeats, the great Irish poet, and Lillie Langtry, mistress of the Prince of Wales. A remarkable conversationalist and a famous wit, Wilde began his writing career by publishing mediocre poetry, but soon achieved fame and critical success with his comic plays: *Vera; or, The Nihilists* (1880), *Lady Windermere's Fan* (1892), *A Woman of No Importance* (1893), *An Ideal Husband* (1895), and his most famous play, *The Importance of Being Earnest* (1895). These plays are successful not because of their plots, which are relatively uncomplicated and familiar, but because of their brilliant dialogue and biting satire.

In 1891, the year that the second edition of *The Picture of Dorian Gray* was published, Wilde began a homosexual relationship with Lord Alfred Douglas, an ambitious but rather untalented poet. The affair caused a scandal. Douglas's father, the Marquess of Queensberry, eventually criticized it publicly. When Wilde sued the marquess for libel, he himself was convicted under English sodomy laws for acts of "gross indecency." In 1895, Wilde was sentenced to two years of hard labor. While serving his sentence, Wilde wrote a long, heartbreaking letter to Lord Alfred titled *De Profundis* (Latin for "Out of the Depths"). After his release, Wilde left England and divided his time between France and Italy, living in poverty. He never published under his own name again. Wilde died in Paris on November 30, 1900.

THE IMPORTANCE OF BEING EARNEST IN CONTEXT

In *The Importance of Being Earnest*, Oscar Wilde satirizes the English aristocracy, a class with which he was personally familiar. His characters are stereotypical Victorian snobs: arrogant, formal, prim, and status conscious. None of the characters need to work for a living, which leaves them free to focus on marriage to the exclusion of all else. Wilde pokes fun at marriage as an institution, pointing out its various hypocrisies and absurdities. *The Importance of Being Earnest* achieved immediate and enduring popularity and today is frequently performed at theaters around the world.

THE IMPORTANCE OF BEING EARNEST: KEY FACTS

Full title: The Importance of Being Earnest: A Trivial Comedy for Serious People	
Time and place written: 1894–95, Worthing and Brighton	
Date of first publication: 1899 (first performed in 1895)	
Publisher: Leonard Smithers	
Type of work: Play	
Genre: Comedy	
Language: English	
Setting (time): Late nineteenth century	
Setting (place): London (Act I) and Hertfordshire (Acts II and III), a rural county not far from London	
Tone: Witty, superficial, satirical	

Protagonist: Jack Worthing and Algernon Moncrieff

Antagonist: The impediments preventing Jack and Algernon from marrying Gwendolen and Cecily, respectively

THE IMPORTANCE OF BEING EARNEST: PLOT OVERVIEW

The play begins in the apartment of Algernon Moncrieff, an upper-class English bachelor. He is visited by his friend Jack Worthing, whom everyone knows as "Ernest." Jack announces he has come to town to propose to Gwendolen Fairfax, who is Lady Bracknell's daughter and Algernon's first cousin. Algernon says that as Gwendolen's first cousin, he refuses to allow Jack to marry Gwendolen until Jack can explain why the name Cecily is inscribed in Jack's cigarette case. After making up a story about an old aunt, Jack finally admits that Cecily is his ward and she lives in the country. Jack also admits that his name is Jack, not Ernest. Algernon jokingly accuses Jack of "Bunburying," the practice of giving yourself an excuse to leave by pretending to have a friend in some other part of the world. Algernon explains that he himself has an imaginary friend called Bunbury who frequently gets sick, giving Algernon an excuse to get out of London social obligations.

Gwendolen and Lady Bracknell arrive at Algernon's flat for tea. Algernon tells Lady Bracknell that due to the illness of his friend Bunbury, he must leave London and will not be able to attend her dinner that night. He distracts her for a while so that Jack can propose to Gwendolen. Jack tells Gwendolen that he loves her, and she replies that she loves him too, particularly because he is named Ernest, a name that "inspires absolute confidence." Jack privately resolves to get baptized and change his name. Gwendolen accepts his proposal. Algernon and Gwendolen exit while Lady Bracknell interrogates Jack to see if he will make a suitable husband for Gwendolen. All goes well until Jack admits that he was abandoned by his parents and found in a handbag by a Mr. Thomas Cardew in Victoria Station. Lady Bracknell, horrified, refuses to let her daughter marry a man with no knowledge of his own parentage, and suggests to Jack that he "acquire some relations."

Gwendolen returns and agrees to write to Jack at his country estate to figure out what to do. He gives her the address, which Algernon overhears and copies down.

Act II begins in Jack's country estate, where his ward, Cecily, is learning German and geography from Miss Prism, a tutor who once wrote a long novel that mysteriously disappeared. Miss Prism enjoys flirting with the house Rector, Dr. Chasuble. Algernon, pretending to be Jack's brother Ernest, arrives to meet Cecily. They click right away and go into the house to get food. Prism and Chasuble meet Jack as he arrives home. He is dressed in mourning in order to keep up the ruse that his brother, who does not actually exist, has died. Cecily comes out of the house and tells Jack that his brother has returned. Jack is shocked and angry when his "brother" Algernon comes out of the house. As the others exit, Jack tells Algernon that he must leave the house at once. Algernon agrees, provided Jack change out of his morbid mourning clothes. As Jack exits to do so, Cecily returns. Algernon proposes to her, and she says yes, noting that she particularly loves him because he is named Ernest, a name that "seems to inspire absolute confidence." Algernon secretly resolves to get rechristened.

Algernon exits. Gwendolen arrives to see Jack and chats with Cecily, whom she has never met before. Gwendolen mentions that she is engaged to Ernest, and things get heated as the women realize that they may be engaged to the same man. After arguing, they lapse into hostile pleasantries until Algernon and Jack re-enter. The men confess that they have lied about their names and that neither of them is named Ernest. The two women are shocked. Jack begins to panic. Algernon sits back and eats muffins.

Act III is set inside the Manor House. Algernon tells Cecily that he lied to her only so that he could meet her, and Jack tells Gwendolen that he lied to her about having a brother so that he could spend more time in the city with her. They also say that they are scheduled to be christened that afternoon. All seems well until Lady Bracknell arrives. When she learns that Cecily is extremely wealthy, she consents to let Ernest marry her. However, as Cecily's legal guardian, Jack will not consent to the marriage unless Lady Bracknell approves of his engagement to Gwendolen. Lady Bracknell again refuses and prepares to leave with Gwendolen. Dr. Chasuble enters and learns that a christening will no longer be necessary, so he resolves to return to Miss Prism.

Lady Bracknell, remembering that she once employed a Miss Prism to take care of her sister's baby, asks to see Miss Prism. When she appears, Lady Bracknell demands to know what happened to the baby, which disappeared twenty-eight years previously when Miss Prism was taking it for a stroll in the perambulator. Miss Prism confesses that she accidentally put her three-volume novel in the perambulator and the baby in her handbag, which she then left in the cloakroom at Victoria Station. Jack, suddenly realizing that he was that baby, fetches the briefcase in which he was found, which Miss Prism confirms was hers. Lady Bracknell tells Jack that he is her nephew and Algernon's older brother. Their father's first name was Ernest, and because first sons are always named after the father, they realize that Jack's name has been Ernest all along. Overjoyed, Jack realizes that he has been telling the truth his whole life. In the end, he gets together with Gwendolen, and Algernon gets together with Cecily. When Lady Bracknell accuses Jack of triviality, he retorts that he has only just discovered "the vital Importance of Being Earnest."

CHARACTERS IN *THE IMPORTANCE OF BEING EARNEST*

Lady Bracknell Algernon's aunt and Gwendolen's mother. A member of the English aristocracy, Lady Bracknell forbids her daughter to marry Jack because of his obscure background.

Cecily Cardew Jack's niece and ward. Cecily falls in love with Algernon.

Dr. Chasuble The Rector of the Manor House. Chasuble and Miss Prism flirt throughout Acts II and III.

Gwendolen Fairfax Lady Bracknell's daughter. Gwendolen is in love with Jack.

Lane Algernon's butler in the city.

Merriman The butler at the Manor House.

Algernon Moncrieff A good friend of Jack's. Algernon lives in a nice flat in a prestigious part of London. He is Lady Bracknell's nephew and, it turns out, Jack's younger brother. Algernon falls in love with Cecily.

Miss Prism Cecily's tutor. Miss Prism lost Jack when he was a baby, accidentally putting him in her handbag instead of in his stroller.

Jack Worthing The central figure of the play. He loves Lady Gwendolen and wishes to marry her. When he is in the city, he goes by Ernest; when he is in the country, he goes by Jack. Jack is the legal guardian of Cecily Cardew. In the end, it is revealed that Jack is Algernon's older brother.

THEMES IN *THE IMPORTANCE OF BEING EARNEST*

THE MEANINGLESSNESS OF SOCIAL CONVENTION All of the characters in the play are concerned with appearance more than they are with substance. For example, when Lady Bracknell interviews Jack to determine his suitability as a potential husband for Gwendolen, she is concerned not with whether Jack will be a loving husband or a kind father, but whether he has the kind of lifestyle that meets her social standards. She worries that his house in Belgrave Square is on the "unfashionable" side of the street—a more important matter to her than the question of whether Jack and Gwendolen actually like each other.

Wilde satirizes this Victorian emphasis on the minutest details of social behavior, suggesting that correct behavior is totally meaningless. But instead of condemning it outright, he undermines it subversively. His characters embrace social conventions with such gusto and thoughtlessness that the stupidity of those conventions becomes clear. Lady Bracknell embraces the idea that men should have an occupation, for example. When Jack admits that he smokes, Lady Bracknell approves, saying, "[a] man should always have an occupation of some kind. There are far too many idle men in London as it is."

THE UNIMPORTANCE OF TRUTH Truth and honesty are generally considered admirable qualities, but in *The Importance of Being Earnest*, truth is considered embarrassingly impolite. In Act I, when Algernon suggests that Jack simply tell Gwendolen the truth about his double life, Jack replies, "[m]y dear fellow, the truth isn't quite the sort of thing one tells to a nice, sweet, refined girl." In Act II, when Gwendolen and Cecily confront Jack about his deceptions, he explains, "it is very painful for me to be forced to speak the truth. It is the first time in my life that I have ever been reduced to such a painful position, and I am really quite inexperienced in doing anything of the kind."

Jack speaks of telling the truth the way others might speak of lying: as an unfortunate and embarrassing consequence of being caught in a bind where no other alternative presents itself.

In high society, Wilde suggests, charm and beauty are of paramount importance. Truth often detracts from charm and beauty, so it must be shunted aside. The characters in *The Importance of Being Earnest* care nothing for the pleasures of moral virtue; they care only for the pleasures of good taste. It is not in good taste to tell the girl you love about your real private life, so Jack cannot imagine confessing the truth to Gwendolen. In fact, it is not in good taste to speak the truth at all, since lies or half-truths can be made much more charming than the real thing. Lying is so widespread in high society that truth-telling seems gimmicky and pretentious. As Lady Bracknell says, "Indeed, no woman should ever be quite accurate about her age. It looks so calculating."

THE RITUALS OF MATURATION For the aristocrats of late Victorian England, family determined position in life. The social standing and wealth of a man's parents dictated his position in the world, and the birth order of his siblings determined his inheritance. In one way, *The Importance of Being Earnest* is a coming-of-age story about two bachelors growing out of youthful immaturity and taking their rightful places in their families. At the beginning of the play, Algernon and Jack have wriggled free of family bonds. Both men invent friends and family members, even imagining a brother, in order to escape family responsibilities. Both value their bachelor freedom and worry about the duties of family life. Jack, in particular, is living a life unnaturally free of family standing. He does not know his parentage, a fact that appalls Lady Bracknell because it means his place in the world is undefined.

Wilde's play is far too tongue-in-cheek to represent any kind of sober maturation, but Jack and Algernon do take up their rightful family roles by the end of the play. Algernon "kills" his imaginary friend Bunbury, and Jack tries to "kill" his imaginary brother Ernest, the two inventions who had kept them from fulfilling family duties. Most significantly, Jack discovers his parentage, a discovery that gives him a ready-made and extensive family structure. Not only is he born of good parents, he is an older brother — a traditional position of responsibility in a family, and also traditionally the most lucrative place in the birth order.

SYMBOLS IN *THE IMPORTANCE OF BEING EARNEST*

BUNBURY Bunbury symbolizes the freedom and irresponsibility of the bachelor's life. Whenever Algernon wishes to skip an appointment, he pretends that his friend Bunbury is dangerously ill and needs his help. Jack has a similar ruse with his imaginary brother Ernest, whose dissolute ways provide Jack with an excuse to escape the tedium of country life and go to the city. Algernon has named this kind of ruse "Bunburyism." On learning of Jack's imaginary brother, Algernon remarks: "I was quite right in saying you were a Bunburyist. You are one of the most advanced Bunburyists I know." When Jack and Algernon decide to settle into married life, they get rid of their imaginary associates, an act that symbolizes their acceptance of family responsibilities.

FOOD The way in which characters eat or serve food symbolizes their emotional state. Algernon provides cucumber sandwiches for his aunt, but he selfishly eats them all himself before she arrives, which suggests a subtle rebellion against his aunt's authority. Cecily shows her antipathy for Gwendolen by giving her cake when she asks for bread and butter and dumping sugar in her tea against her expressed wish.

IMPORTANT QUOTATIONS FROM *THE IMPORTANCE OF BEING EARNEST*

JACK: *Oh, that's nonsense, Algy. You never talk anything but nonsense.*
ALGERNON: *Nobody ever does.*

Location: Act I
Speaker: Jack and Algernon
Context: Anticipating his visit to the country, Algernon tells Jack how he enjoys getting himself into trouble

Jack and Algernon do not take anything seriously. Every word they utter is nonsense; nothing they say has any serious implications. But Algernon implies that his refusal to talk seriously is in fact more honest and serious than other people's earnest attempts to tell the truth. Everyone talks nonsense, but not everyone admits it. By cheerfully owning up to his own frivolity, Algernon saves himself from the sin of hypocrisy, something those who purport to tell the truth cannot claim to do.

GWENDOLEN: *In matters of grave importance, style, not sincerity, is the vital thing.*

Location: Act III
Speaker: Gwendolen
Context: Cecily admires Algernon's excuses even if she does not believe them

This quotation, like so many of Wilde's famous witticisms, reverses a piece of conventional wisdom. Gwendolen challenges the assumption that important matters require sincerity. We might like to believe that we can ferret out true sincerity, but really we cannot see beyond style. Sincerity is nothing more than one style of behavior, and those who are sincere are playing a role just as much as those who are frivolous.

JACK: *[Very seriously.] Yes, Lady Bracknell. I was in a hand-bag—a somewhat large, black leather hand-bag, with handles to it—an ordinary hand-bag in fact.*
LADY BRACKNELL: *In what locality did this Mr. James, or Thomas, Cardew come across this ordinary hand-bag?*
JACK: *In the cloak-room at Victoria Station. It was given to him in mistake for his own.*
LADY BRACKNELL: *The cloak-room at Victoria Station?*
JACK: *Yes. The Brighton line.*
LADY BRACKNELL: *The line is immaterial. Mr. Worthing, I confess I feel somewhat bewildered by what you have just told me. To be born, or at any rate bred, in a hand-bag, whether it had handles or not, seems to me to display a contempt for the ordinary decencies of family life that reminds one of the worst excesses of the French Revolution.*

Location: Act I
Speaker: Jack and Lady Bracknell
Context: Lady Bracknell is shocked to learn of Jack's origins

ALGERNON: *What on earth you are serious about I haven't got the remotest idea. About everything, I should fancy. You have such an absolutely trivial nature.*

Location: Act II
Speaker: Algernon
Context: To Jack's astonishment, Algernon expresses his serious commitment to Bunburyism

GWENDOLEN: *Mr. Worthing, what explanation can you offer to me for pretending to have a brother? Was it in order that you might have an opportunity of coming up to town to see me as often as possible?*
JACK: *Can you doubt it, Miss Fairfax?*
GWENDOLEN: *I have the gravest doubts upon the subject. But I intend to crush them.*

Location: Act III
Speaker: Gwendolen and Jack
Context: After learning of Jack's deception, Gwendolen forgives him

INFERNO

Dante Alighieri

Fearful, confused, and lost, a man is taken on a tour of Hell and led toward salvation by a classical poet.

THE LIFE OF DANTE ALIGHIERI

Dante Alighieri was born in 1265 in Florence, Italy, to a political family of moderate wealth. As a child, he met and was profoundly struck by a girl named Beatrice. Although eventually he married and had several children, he remained in love with Beatrice long after her sudden death in 1290. In 1293, Dante published *Vita Nuova* ("New Life"), a poetic chronicle of Beatrice's role as the muse and inspiration in his life.

Around the same time, Dante began a serious study of philosophy and intensified his involvement in the government of Florence, which was in a period of great political turmoil. After serving in a number of significant public offices, Dante was exiled from Florence by the leaders of the Black Guelphs, the political faction in power at the time.

As an exile, Dante traveled around the Northern Italian courts and began work on his *Comedy*, a three-part allegorical journey, in poem form, through Hell (*Inferno*), Purgatory (*Purgatorio*), and Heaven (*Paradiso*). Dante continued writing and occasionally lecturing until his death from a sudden illness in 1321.

THE *INFERNO* IN CONTEXT

The *Inferno* bears the scars of late-thirteenth-century Florentine politics, in which the struggle for power reflected a larger struggle between church (represented by the pope) and state (represented by the Holy Roman Emperor), both of which wanted secular authority. This crisis afflicted Italy and much of Europe between the twelfth and the fourteenth centuries. In Florence, the Guelph party supported the pope, and the Ghibelline party supported the emperor. By Dante's time, imperial power was weak, and the Guelphs, who controlled Florence, had split into the White Guelphs, who supported a Florence independent of papal authority, and the Black Guelphs, who were more closely allied with the pope. In 1301, with the aid of Pope Boniface VIII, the Black Guelphs gained control of Florence. Dante, an influential White Guelph party leader, was exiled within the year. Dante reserves a place in his fictional Hell for Pope Boniface, as well as for a number of other Florentine political figures. Because Dante set his work about a decade before he wrote it, he was also able to voice political criticism by having his damned sinners "prophecy" future political events, emphasizing the corruption and turmoil of the so-called future Florence.

As the first influential medieval work written in the vernacular (the dialect of the common people), the *Inferno* marked a crucial transition in the development of European languages and literature. Prior to Dante, most major literary works had been written in Latin, the dying language of the Roman Empire and the Catholic Church. Many scholars believed that the everyday language of the common people was incapable of true poetic expression. Dante's use of the Tuscan dialect—one of hundreds in medieval Italy—helped unify the language, made literature less elitist, and determined the shape of contemporary Italian.

By naming his work the *Comedy*, Dante placed his poetry in the tradition of classical works, which were divided into tragedies and comedies. (Dante's work only came to be called the *Divine Comedy* centuries later.) Tragedy, the high style of epics, told stories of heroic promise and destructive ends, whereas comedy was the low style that encompassed grotesque characters and happy endings.

POETIC FORM IN THE *INFERNO*: TERZA RIMA

The *Divine Comedy* is the first known poem written in terza rima, a poetic form in which the middle line of each tercet (three-line stanza) rhymes with the first and last lines of the next: *aba, bcb, cdc, ede*, and so on. Though many English-language translators of the *Inferno* have dropped the terza rima form—in part because writing in terza rima is notoriously difficult in English—terza rima underscores the *Divine Comedy*'s intricate connections between plot, form, and theme. The interlaced rhyme scheme creates a feeling of effortless forward motion, a dynamic that matches the endless advance of Dante and Virgil as they descend into Hell.

Additionally, the terza rima's tercet structure echoes sets of threes found throughout Dante's poem. In the Catholic tradition, God is composed of three beings: the Father, the Son, and the Holy Spirit. Dante encounters three beasts, and three holy women send Virgil to guide Dante; Satan has three heads and chews on three sinners. Moreover, the complete *Divine Comedy* has three parts—*Inferno*, *Purgatorio*, and *Paradiso*—each of which is thirty-three cantos long (*Inferno* Canto I is a prologue to the whole work). *Inferno*'s Hell is divided into three sections—Fore-Hell, Upper Hell, and Lower Hell—and nine Circles. Terza rima links the poem's smaller formal structure to both its thematic elements and its larger geometry.

THE *INFERNO*: KEY FACTS

Time and place written: ca. 1308–1314; Italy

Date of publication: 1314 (publisher unknown)

Type of work: Narrative poem

Genre: Epic poem; religious allegory; fantasy

Language: Italian (medieval vernacular)

Poetic Form: Terza rima

Rhyme Scheme: aba, bcb, cdc, etc.

Setting (time): 1300, Maundy Thursday night (the eve of Good Friday) through Easter Sunday morning

Setting (place): Hell

Tense: Past

Tone: Righteously moralistic; at times sardonic or ironic

Narrator: Dante (the character) in the first person

Point of View: Dante's (the character)

Protagonist: Literally, Dante the narrator; allegorically, Everyman—humankind

Antagonist: Dante's/humankind's fear, emotional turmoil, and lack of faith

THE *INFERNO*: PLOT OVERVIEW

On the eve of Good Friday in the year 1300, Dante has lost his path traveling through dark woods. He attempts to climb a mountain whose summit is lit by the sun, but his way is blocked by three beasts—a leopard, a lion, and a she-wolf. Frightened and helpless, Dante returns to the dark woods, where he encounters the ghost of the ancient Roman poet Virgil. Virgil says that he will guide Dante through Hell and Purgatory, and that Dante will eventually reach Heaven, where Dante's beloved Beatrice awaits. Virgil tells Dante that it was Beatrice and two other holy women who, seeing Dante lost in the woods, sent Virgil to guide him.

III: FORE-HELL: THE NEUTRALS (III)

Virgil leads Dante through the gates of Hell, which are marked by the haunting inscription "abandon all hope, you who enter here" (III.7). They enter Fore-Hell, where Dante looks on with repugnance and pity as souls who, in life, committed to neither good nor evil are bitten by hornets and sucked by worms as they chase a blank banner. The ferryman Charon takes Dante and Virgil across the river Acheron into Hell.

IV: FIRST CIRCLE / LIMBO: THE UNBAPTIZED

In the First Circle live pagans, including Virgil and many other great figures of antiquity, who died without knowing Jesus. In the First Circle, Dante meets Horace, Ovid, and Lucan.

V: SECOND CIRCLE: THE LUSTFUL

At the border of the Second Circle, the monster Minos assigns condemned souls to their punishments by curling his tail around himself. The number of times his tail curls signals the circle of hell to which the soul is consigned. Inside the Second Circle, the souls of the Lustful swirl around in a terrible storm. Dante meets Francesca, who tells him the story of her doomed adulterous affair with Paolo da Rimini, her husband's brother.

VI: THIRD CIRCLE: THE GLUTTONOUS

In the Third Circle, Gluttons lie in mud and endure a rain of filth and excrement.

VII: FOURTH CIRCLE: SPENDERS AND HOARDERS

In the Fourth Circle, Spenders and Hoarders charge at one another with giant boulders.

VIII–IX: FIFTH CIRCLE OF HELL: THE WRATHFUL AND THE SULLEN

In the Fifth Circle, the Wrathful spend eternity struggling with each other in the river Styx, a swampy, fetid cesspool. The Sullen lie bound beneath the Styx's waters, choking on the mud. Dante glimpses Filippo Argenti, a political opponent, and watches in delight as other souls tear him to pieces. At the gates to Dis, Hell's city, demons refuse to let Virgil and Dante pass. A messenger from Heaven arrives and opens the gates for Virgil and Dante.

X–XI: SIXTH CIRCLE / DIS: HERETICS

Inside the gates of Dis, Dante talks to Farinata, a rival Florentine politician.

XII–XVII SEVENTH CIRCLE: THE VIOLENT

A deep valley leads into the First Ring, where those who committed violence against others spend eternity in a river of boiling blood. A Centaur takes Dante and Virgil into the Second Ring, where souls who committed suicide (which is violence against the self) have been turned into trees. Dante speaks with Pier della Vigna, a twelfth-century political advisor. They progress to the Third Ring, in the First Zone of which they meet the Blasphemers (those who do verbal violence to God). In the Second Zone, Dante meets his old patron, Brunetto Latini, walking on a desert of burning sand among the Sodomites (those who are violent against nature). In the Third Zone, they encounter the Usurers (those who are violent against art).

XVIII–XXX: EIGHTH CIRCLE: THE FRAUDULENT

The monster Geryon transports Virgil and Dante across a wide abyss to the Malebroge, the "evil pouches" of the earth into which the Eighth Circle is divided. In the First Pouch, the Panderers and the Seducers receive lashings from whips. In the Second Pouch, the Flatterers lie in a river of human feces. In the Third Pouch, the Simoniacs hang upside down in baptismal fonts while their feet burn with fire. In the Fourth Pouch, the Diviners walk with their heads on backward—a sight that moves Dante to great pity. In the Fifth Pouch, the Barrators (those who accepted bribes) steep in pitch while demons tear them apart. In the Sixth Pouch, the Hypocrites forever walk in circles, wearing heavy robes made of lead. Caiphas, the priest who confirmed Jesus' death sentence, lies crucified on the ground, and the other sinners tread on him as they walk. In the Seventh Pouch, the Thieves sit trapped in a pit of vipers, becoming vipers themselves when bitten. To regain their form, they must bite another thief.

In the Eighth Pouch of the Eighth Circle of Hell, Dante speaks to Ulysses, the wandering hero of Homer's epics, now doomed as a False Counselors (one guilty of spiritual theft) for his role in executing the ruse of the Trojan Horse. In the Ninth Pouch, the Schismatics walk in a circle, afflicted by wounds that open and close repeatedly. In the Tenth Pouch, the Falsifiers suffer from horrible plagues and diseases.

XXXI–XXXIV: NINTH CIRCLE: THE BETRAYERS

The giant Antaeus deposits Virgil and Dante at the bottom of the Giants' Well, which leads to a massive drop to Cocytus, a great frozen lake. In Caina, the first section of the Ninth Circle, Betrayers of their families stand frozen up to their necks in the lake's ice. In Antenora, the second section, Betrayers of country and party stand frozen up to their heads. In this section Dante meets Count Ugolino, who is doomed to gnaw on the head of the man responsible for his imprisonment. In Ptolomea, the third section, Betrayers of guests spend eternity lying on their backs in the frozen lake, their tears making blocks of ice over their eyes. Dante follows Virgil into Judecca, the fourth section and the lowest depth of Hell, where Betrayers of benefactors spend eternity in complete icy submersion.

Dante approaches a huge, mist-shrouded form of the three-headed giant Lucifer, who is plunged waist-deep into the ice. Lucifer's body lies where it fell when God hurled him down from Heaven, piercing the center of the Earth. Each of Lucifer's mouths chews one famous sinner: Judas, who betrayed Jesus, and Cassius and Brutus, both of whom betrayed Julius Caesar. Virgil and Dante climb down Lucifer's massive form, holding on to tufts of his frozen hair. They reach the Lethe, the river of forgetfulness, and emerge on the other side of the earth on Easter morning, just before sunrise.

CHARACTERS IN THE *INFERNO*

VISITORS AND VISIONS

Beatrice Dante's dead beloved, now one of the blessed in Heaven. The historical Beatrice was Dante's childhood friend and lifelong muse. Dante's fictional Beatrice sends Virgil to guide Dante on his journey, which is a journey toward Beatrice herself, especially because she embodies divine grace and love.

Dante The narrator and protagonist. While the narrator of the *Inferno* is named Dante, he should not be equated with Dante the author of the *Inferno*. Sympathetic and fearful of danger, Dante the narrator is confused, both morally and intellectually, by his experiences in Hell. As the poem progresses, Dante adopts a more pitiless attitude toward the punishment of sinners, which he views as perfect divine justice.

Virgil An ancient Roman poet and Dante's guide through Hell. The historical Virgil lived in the first century B.C. and is widely considered the greatest of the Latin poets. Dante's fictional Virgil is wise and resourceful but unable to protect Dante from Hell's dangers. Virgil is an allegorical representation of human reason, both as immensely powerful and as inferior to faith in God.

DEMONS AND HELL STAFF

Antaeus Location: Canto VIII: Eighth Circle, Tenth Pouch. The giant who lowers Dante and Virgil into the Ninth Circle.

Charon Location: Canto III: Between Fore-Hell and the First Circle. An old man who ferries the dead across the river Acheron to Hell. Dante appropriates Charon from Greek mythology.

Geryon Location: Canto VIII: Seventh Circle, Third Ring. The massive serpentine monster who flies Dante and Virgil down to the Eighth Circle.

Lucifer Location: Canto XXXIV: Ninth Circle, Judecca (Fourth Ring). The three-headed prince of Hell, also known as Satan and Dis. According to Christian legend, Lucifer, God's favorite angel, was thrown out of Heaven after rebelling against God. Dante imagines that in his fall, Lucifer plunged into the center of the earth.

Malacoda Location: Canto XXI: Eighth Circle, Fifth Pouch. The leader of the Malabranche, the demons who guard the Fifth Pouch. Malacoda ("evil tail") intentionally gives Virgil and Dante bad directions.

Minos Location: Canto V: Second Circle. A giant beast who judges the sinners in Hell. The number of times Minos curls his tail around himself corresponds to the Circle of Hell appropriate for each sinner. In Greek mythology, Minos was the wise and just king of Crete.

Nessus Location: Canto XII: Seventh Circle, First Ring. A Centaur (a mythological half-man, half-horse creature) who carries Dante through a ring of boiling blood.

Phlegyas Location: Canto VIII: Fifth Circle. The boatman who rows the dead across the river Styx.

SINNERS

Fra Alberigo and Branca d'Oria Location: Canto XXXIII: Ninth Circle, Ptolemea (Third Ring). Sinners suffering among the Betrayers of Guests. Technically, Alberigo and d'Oria are not dead: their crimes were so grave that devils now occupy their bodies while their souls are tormented in Hell.

Filippo Argenti Location: Canto VIII: Fifth Circle. A political enemy of Dante's who was a member of the Black Guelphs.

Pope Boniface VIII A notoriously corrupt pope. Boniface, who tried to increase the political power of the Catholic Church, and Dante, who advocated church-state separation, were political enemies.

Farinata Location: Canto X: Sixth Circle. A Florentine political leader from the Ghibelline party, which Dante opposed.

Francesca and Paolo da Rimini Location: Canto V: Second Circle. Lovers condemned for an adulterous affair that began as they read about Lancelot and Guinevere. Paolo is Francesca's husband's brother.

Pier della Vigna Location: Canto XIII, Seventh Circle, Second Ring. A former advisor to the Holy Roman Emperor Frederick II, della Vigna committed suicide after falling into disfavor at court. He must spend eternity as a tree.

Count Ugolino Location: Canto XXXIII: Ninth Circle, Antenora (Second Ring). A traitor condemned to gnawing the head of another traitor, Archbishop Ruggieri. Count Ugolino is condemned because he ate the corpses of his dead children when dying of hunger.

Ulysses Location: Canto XXVI: Eighth Circle, Eighth Pouch. The great hero of the Homeric epics *The Iliad* and *The Odyssey*. Ulysses is imprisoned among the False Counselors for his participation in the Trojan horse ruse.

THEMES IN *INFERNO*

PERFECT DIVINE JUSTICE The punishment of the *Inferno* sinners always corresponds, allegorically, to their worldly sins. The Wrathful attack one another; the Gluttonous eat excrement; the Lustful, who were blown about by passion in life, are blown about by a ferocious storm in death. The blank banner chased by the Neutrals symbolizes the meaninglessness of their activity in life. Punishments that fit the crime—called the *contrapasso*—not only provide vivid imagery and symbolic power, but also illuminate a major theme: the perfection of divine justice. The inscription over the gates of Hell explicitly states that God has created Hell to exact justice. The poem shows that God's justice is balanced and carried out mechanically and impersonally.

Over the course of the *Inferno*, Dante the narrator stops sympathizing with the tormented souls he meets, learning that to pity their suffering is to fail to understand perfect justice.

IMMORTALITY THROUGH STORYTELLING Several shades in Hell ask Dante the narrator to tell their stories upon his return to the earth. If he does, they will live on in memory, if not in flesh. Dante the narrator does not always promise to oblige, but Dante the author has indeed written their stories: however moralistic the framework, he has enabled these characters, many of whom are historical figures, to live on by casting them in his narrative. Dante may have been motivated by vainglory—indeed, he states that he has outdone both Ovid (Roman author of *Metamorphoses*, an account of fantastical transformations) and Lucan (first-century B.C. Roman political chronicler) in his descriptions in Canto

XXIV—but ultimately he has presented storytelling as a vehicle for the legacy of the story, the subjects, and the storyteller.

THE DEBT TO CLASSICAL LITERATURE AND MYTHOLOGY Although the *Inferno*'s moral values are Christian, the poem owes much to Greek and Roman traditions. Dante's Christian Hell features myriad mythological and legendary figures (the fantastical creatures Centaurs, King Minos, and the Trojan War hero Ulysses) and places (the Underworld rivers Acheron and Styx). Dante often references and imitates great writers of antiquity such as Homer, Ovid, Lucan, and Virgil himself, thereby situating himself within the classical epic tradition. By bringing many elements under one umbrella, and implying that Christianity has subsumed all these stories, Dante heightens the urgency and relevance of his narrative of the human quest.

SYMBOLS IN *INFERNO*

The *Inferno* is an allegory on many levels, and Dante uses hundreds of symbols, both minutely specific and overarching. A few examples follow.

THE *DIVINE COMEDY* Dante's hundred-canto work—of which Inferno is the first third—symbolizes the human spiritual quest.

VIRGIL Virgil represents reason.

BEATRICE Beatrice represents divine grace and spiritual love.

THE DARK FOREST The forest embodies Dante's confusion and fear.

THE LEOPARD, THE LION, AND THE SHE-WOLF The symbolism of these three animals has long been debated, but most agree that they represent three categories of sins—betrayal, violence (or pride), and incontinence (or debauchery).

GERYON With the head of an innocent man and the body of a foul serpent, Geryon represents dishonesty and fraud.

IMPORTANT QUOTATIONS FROM *INFERNO*

Midway on our life's journey, I found myself
In dark woods, the right road lost.

Location: Canto I, lines 1–2
Speaker: Dante the narrator
Context: Dante establishes the literal and allegorical setups for his journey

On the allegorical level, the words "journey" and "right road," as well as the image of being lost in "dark woods," signal the religious message to come. The juxtaposition of the "dark woods," which embody Dante's fear and inner turmoil, and the lost "right road," which embodies Dante's flagging faith in God, makes his challenge clear: he must look for God in a difficult world. The phrase "our life's journey" suggests that the journey is a universal one undertaken by every human being to understand his or her sins and find peace with his or her world.

. . . One day, for pleasure,
We read of Lancelot, by love constrained:
Alone, suspecting nothing, at our leisure.
Sometimes at what we read our glances joined,
Looking from the book each to the other's eyes,

And then the color in our faces drained.
But one particular moment alone it was
Defeated us: the longed-for smile, it said,
Was kissed by that most noble love: at this
This one, who now will never leave my side,
Kissed my mouth, trembling. A Galeotto, that book!
And so was he who wrote it; that day we read
No further.

Location: Canto V, lines 112–124; Second Circle (the Lustful)
Speaker: Francesca
Context: Francesca tells Dante how reading a romance impelled her and Paolo to consummate their
   adulterous affair, for which they are now in Hell

Overcome by emotion while reading about Lancelot and Guinevere—legendary adulterous lovers in
King Arthur's court—Francesca and Paolo consummated their own adulterous affair, condemning themselves to Hell. This passage, one of *Inferno*'s most famous, illuminates the power of literature to excite the
emotions, a power that Dante sought to harness. These lines imitate romantic poetry. The passage also
allows Dante and us to experience compassion for the suffering of souls in Hell—compassion that grows
more scarce as the narrative progresses.

Through me you enter into the city of woes
Through me you enter into eternal pain,
Through me you enter the population of loss
Justice moved my high maker, in power divine
Wisdom supreme, love primal. No things were
Before me not eternal; eternal I remain.
Abandon all hope, you who enter here.

Location: Canto III, lines 1–7
Speaker: Inscription on the Gate of Hell
Context: Dante reads these lines as he and Virgil enter Fore-Hell and prepare to cross the river Acheron

---

I did not open them—for to be rude
To such a one as him was courtesy.

Location: Canto XXXIII, lines 146–47; Ninth Circle, Ptolomea (Betrayers of Guests)
Speaker: Dante the narrator
Context: Dante refuses to remove the frozen tears covering Fra Alberigo's eyes, despising Fra Alberigo for
   his sins

To get back up to the shining world from there
My guide and I went into that hidden tunnel;
. . .
Through a round aperture I saw appear
Some of the beautiful things that heaven bears,

Where we came forth, and once more saw the stars.

Location: Canto XXXIV, lines 134–140
Speaker: Dante the narrator
Context: In these closing lines, Dante describes the climb out of Hell to the earth's surface to see the divine grace of the stars (Each of the three parts of the *Divine Comedy* ends with the word *stele* — stars)

INVISIBLE MAN

Ralph Ellison

A young black man grows disillusioned with the stereotypes propagated by whites and blacks alike.

THE LIFE OF RALPH ELLISON

Ralph Ellison was born in 1914 in Oklahoma City, Oklahoma. His father was a construction worker, and his mother was a domestic servant who also volunteered for the local Socialist Party. His grandparents had been slaves. As a young man, Ellison developed an interest in jazz music and befriended a group of musicians, many of whom later played with Count Basie's legendary big band in the late 1930s. Ellison studied the cornet and trumpet, and planned a career as a jazz musician. In 1933, he left Oklahoma to study music at the Tuskegee Institute in Tuskegee, Alabama. The Institute, which is now called Tuskegee University, was founded in 1881 by Booker T. Washington, one of the foremost black educators in American history. It later served as the model for the black college attended by the narrator in *Invisible Man* (1952).

Ellison left the Tuskegee Institute in 1936 and moved to New York City, where he settled in Harlem. As an employee of the Federal Writers' Project, Ellison befriended many of the most important African American writers of the era, including Langston Hughes and Richard Wright. Ellison also befriended the eminent jazz writer and sociologist Albert Murray, with whom he carried on a lengthy and important literary correspondence, later collected in the book *Trading Twelves*. After a year editing the *Negro Quarterly*, Ellison left for the Merchant Marines, in which he served during World War II. After the war, Ellison won a Rosenwald Fellowship, which he used to write *Invisible Man*.

INVISIBLE MAN IN CONTEXT

Employing a shifting, improvisational style directly based on Ellison's experience of jazz performance, *Invisible Man* ranges in tone from realism to surrealism, and in genre from tragedy to vicious satire to near-slapstick comedy. The novel spent sixteen weeks on the bestseller list and won the National Book Award in 1953. Writers like Saul Bellow and critics like Irving Howe hailed *Invisible Man* as a landmark publication. Some critics called it the most important American novel to appear after World War II.

Invisible Man was heavily influenced by the work of twentieth-century French writers known as the existentialists. Existentialism, whose foremost proponents included Albert Camus and Jean-Paul Sartre, explored individuality and meaning in a seemingly meaningless universe. Ellison adapted the existentialists' universal themes to the black experience of oppression and prejudice in America. He also incorporated the tradition of African-American social debate. In the character of Dr. Bledsoe, the novel vehemently rejects the philosophy of Booker T. Washington, who said blacks should work toward economic success before demanding racial equality. It also critiques, through the character of Ras the Exhorter, Marcus Garvey's philosophy of black nationalism.

Despite—or possibly because of—the overwhelming success of *Invisible Man*, Ellison never published another novel in his lifetime. He published two books of essays—*Shadow Act* in the 1960s and *Going to the Territory* in the 1980s—and spent his later decades laboring on a vast novel, which he never finished. Upon his death in 1994, Ellison left behind more than 2,000 pages of unedited, incomplete manuscript. In heavily abridged and edited form, this manuscript was published five years after his death under the title *Juneteenth*, to generally unfavorable reviews.

INVISIBLE MAN: KEY FACTS

Time and place written: Late 1940s–1952; New York City	
Date of first publication: 1952	
Publisher: Random House	
Type of work: Novel	

Genre: Bildungsroman; existentialist novel; social protest novel

Language: English

Setting (time): The 1930s

Setting (place): A black college in the South; New York City, especially Harlem

Tense: Past, with present-tense sections in the Prologue and Epilogue

Tone: Bitterly cynical, optimistic, anguished, respectful

Narrator: An unnamed black man in the first person

Point of view: The narrator's

Protagonist: The narrator

Antagonist: The narrator's difficulty understanding his own identity

INVISIBLE MAN: PLOT OVERVIEW

The narrator begins by calling himself an "invisible man." He is not literally invisible, but people refuse to see him. Because of his invisibility, he has been hiding from the world, living underground and stealing electricity from the Monopolated Light & Power Company. He has gone underground in order to write the story of his life.

As a young man, in the late 1920s or early 1930s, the narrator lives in the South. A group of important white men give him a scholarship to a prestigious black college, but only after humiliating him by forcing him to fight in a "battle royal" in which he is pitted against other young black men, all blindfolded, in a boxing ring. The white men also force the youths to scramble over an electrified rug in order to snatch at fake gold coins.

Three years later, the narrator is a student at the college. He is hired to drive a wealthy white trustee of the college, Mr. Norton, around the campus. Norton talks incessantly about his daughter. He is strangely interested in the narrator's story of Jim Trueblood, a poor, uneducated black man who impregnated his own daughter. The narrator takes Norton to the Golden Day, a saloon and brothel that normally serves black men. Norton passes out and a veteran tends him, taunting Norton and the narrator about their blindness to race relations.

Back at the college, the narrator listens to a long, impassioned sermon by the Reverend Homer A. Barbee, who glorifies the college's Founder. After the sermon, the college president, Dr. Bledsoe, chastises the narrator, telling him he should have shown Norton an idealized version of black life. He expels the narrator, giving him seven letters of recommendation.

The narrator travels to Harlem, where he looks for work without success. At last, he goes to the office of a trustee named Mr. Emerson. Emerson's son opens the letter and tells the narrator that he has been betrayed: the letters from Bledsoe actually portray the narrator as dishonorable and unreliable. The young Emerson helps the narrator get a low-paying job at the Liberty Paints plant, whose trademark color is "Optic White."

An on-the-job accident lands the narrator in the paint factory's hospital. The white doctors seize upon the arrival of this unidentified black patient as an opportunity to conduct electric shock experiments. After the narrator recovers his memory and leaves the hospital, he collapses on the street. Some black community members take him to a woman named Mary, who lets him live with her for free in Harlem and nurtures his awareness of black heritage.

A man named Brother Jack offers the narrator a position as a spokesman for the Brotherhood, a political organization that allegedly works to help the socially oppressed. After being trained in rhetoric by a white member of the group, the narrator goes to his assigned branch in Harlem, where he meets the black nationalist leader Ras the Exhorter, who opposes the interracial Brotherhood and believes that black Americans should fight for their rights against all whites. The narrator becomes a high-profile figure in the Brotherhood. One night he is seduced by a white women at a women's rights gathering. She wants to play out her sexual fantasies about black men.

Many black members have left the Brotherhood because much of the Harlem community feels that the Brotherhood has betrayed their interests. The narrator finds Clifton on the street selling dancing "Sambo" dolls. Clifton does not have a permit to sell his wares on the street. White policemen accost him and shoot him dead as the narrator and others look on. The narrator holds a funeral for Clifton and gives a speech in which he portrays his dead friend as a hero, galvanizing public sentiment in Clifton's favor. The Brotherhood is furious with him for staging the funeral without permission. As Jack rants, a glass eye falls from one of his eye sockets.

The narrator leaves, longing to take revenge on Jack and the Brotherhood. In Harlem, he finds the neighborhood agitated over race relations. Ras sends his men to beat up the narrator, and the narrator is forced to disguise himself in dark glasses and a hat. Many people on the streets mistake the disguised narrator for someone named Rinehart, who seems to be a pimp, bookie, lover, and reverend.

At last, the narrator goes to Brother Hambro's apartment. Hambro cynically declares that people are tools and that the larger interests of the Brotherhood are more important than individuals. The narrator decides to flatter and seduce a woman close to one of the party leaders in order to obtain secret information about the group. The woman he chooses, Sybil, knows nothing about the Brotherhood and attempts to use the narrator to fulfill her fantasy of being raped by a black man.

Ras incites a riot in Harlem. The narrator and others set fire to a tenement building. Running from the scene of the crime, the narrator encounters Ras dressed as an African chieftain. Ras calls for the lynching of the narrator. The narrator flees, only to encounter two policemen, who suspect that his briefcase contains loot from the riots. In his attempt to evade them, the narrator falls down a manhole. The police mock him and draw the cover over the manhole.

The narrator says he has stayed underground ever since. He has realized that he must honor his individuality without sacrificing his responsibility to the community. He finally feels ready to emerge from underground.

CHARACTERS IN *INVISIBLE MAN*

Reverend Homer A. Barbee A preacher from Chicago. Ellison uses Barbee to satirize the college's desire to transform the Founder into a mythic hero.

Dr. Bledsoe The president of the narrator's college. Dr. Bledsoe, a black man, is selfish, ambitious, and treacherous. He acts servile to the white community.

Brother Jack The white, blindly loyal leader of the Brotherhood. Although Brother Jack initially seems compassionate, intelligent, and kind, he is actually racist and cold. His glass eye and his red hair symbolize his blindness and his communist views, respectively.

Tod Clifton A black member of the Brotherhood and a resident of Harlem. Tod Clifton is passionate, handsome, articulate, and intelligent.

Emerson The son of one of the wealthy white trustees of the narrator's college. The younger Emerson expresses sympathy for the narrator and helps him get a job, but he is too preoccupied with his own problems to help the narrator in any meaningful way.

Mary A serene and motherly black woman with whom the narrator stays after the Men's House bans him.

The Narrator The nameless protagonist of the novel. The narrator is the "invisible man" of the title. A black man in 1930s America, the narrator considers himself invisible because people see a projection of their stereotypes and prejudices when they look at him. The narrator is intelligent, introspective, and gifted with language.

Mr. Norton One of the wealthy white trustees at the narrator's college. Mr. Norton is a narcissistic man who thinks his relationship with the narrator proves that he is liberal-minded and philanthropic. Norton takes an incestuous, voyeuristic pleasure in the story of Jim Trueblood.

Ras the Exhorter A stout, charismatic, angry man. Ras represents the black nationalist movement, which advocates the violent overthrow of white supremacy. He is likely inspired by black nationalist leader Marcus Garvey.

Rinehart A surreal figure who never appears in the novel. Rinehart possesses a seemingly infinite number of identities, among them pimp, bookie, and a preacher who speaks on the subject of "invisibility." His shape-shifting represents both freedom and inauthenticity.

Sybil A white woman. She uses the narrator to act out her fantasy of being raped by a "savage" black man.

Jim Trueblood   An uneducated black man who lives on the outskirts of the narrator's college campus. Whites have shown an increased interest in him since the story of his incest spread.

The Veteran   An institutionalized black man who claims he graduated from the narrator's college. The veteran exposes the blindness and hypocrisy of the narrator and Mr. Norton. Although society has deemed him "shell-shocked" and insane, the veteran is the only character who speaks the truth in the first part of the novel.

THEMES IN *INVISIBLE MAN*

RACISM AS AN OBSTACLE TO INDIVIDUAL IDENTITY   As the narrator of *Invisible Man* struggles to understand his own identity, he is hindered by the fact that he is a black man living in a racist American society. All of the communities he encounters, from the Liberty Paints plant to the Brotherhood, have a different idea of how blacks should behave in society. Each idea limits the narrator's complexity and forces him to play an inauthentic part.

Eventually, the narrator realizes that people see him only as they want to see him, not as he actually is. Symbolically, people are blind, which makes him invisible. Although the narrator initially embraces his invisibility because he thinks it will help him defy stereotype, in the end he finds this tactic too passive. He decides to emerge from his underground "hibernation" and contribute to society, thereby forcing others to acknowledge that his behavior contradicts their racist ideas.

THE LIMITATIONS OF IDEOLOGY   Over the course of the novel, the narrator realizes that the ideologies advanced by institutions are too simplistic to describe or change something as complex as human identity. The novel contains many examples of ideology, from the tame, ingratiating ideology of Booker T. Washington to the violent, separatist ideology of Ras the Exhorter. The novel criticizes ideology most strongly in its depiction of the Brotherhood, which promises to save "the people," but actually limits individual freedom. Ellison implies that life is too rich and unpredictable to be bound up neatly in an ideology.

THE DANGER OF FIGHTING STEREOTYPE WITH STEREOTYPE   Even when they are well meant, racism and stereotypes are dangerous. The narrator encounters many blacks who think there is one right way to be black in America and that anyone who does not act in this one way betrays the race. The narrator's grandfather believes that in order to undermine racism, blacks should exaggerate their servility to whites. Dr. Bledsoe thinks that blacks should work industriously and adopt the manners and speech of whites if they want to succeed. Ras the Exhorter thinks that blacks should seize freedom by destroying whites. These ideas come from the black community, which makes them seem less dangerous than whites' stereotypes, but Ellison argues that they are just as dangerous. Instead of admitting that human identity is complex and indefinable, as the narrator does, Bledsoe and Ras try to cram themselves and everyone else into one-dimensional roles. By trying to restrict and choreograph the behavior of the black American community as a whole, they betray their people.

SYMBOLS IN *INVISIBLE MAN*

THE SAMBO DOLL AND THE COIN BANK   The coin bank in the shape of a grinning black man (Chapter Fifteen) and Tod Clifton's dancing Sambo doll (Chapter Twenty) serve similar purposes in the novel. Both symbolize degrading stereotypes and the damaging power of prejudice. The coin bank depicts the stereotypical good slave who fawns over whites for trivial rewards. The Sambo doll is made in the image of the Sambo slave, who, according to white stereotype, is lazy and obsequious. The Sambo doll illustrates a stereotype's power to control, as the doll is literally controlled by invisible strings.

THE LIBERTY PAINTS PLANT   The Liberty Paints plant is a complex metaphor for racism in American society. Like America, the plant calls itself free, but racism is deeply ingrained at its roots. The factory authorities boast of the superiority of their white paint, a parody of those who believe in white supremacy. With the plant's claim that its trademark "Optic White" can cover up any tint or stain, Ellison points out that America wants to cover up black identity with white culture, to ignore difference, and to treat black people as "stains" on white "purity."

IMPORTANT QUOTATIONS FROM *INVISIBLE MAN*

"I's big and black and I say 'Yes, suh' as loudly as any burrhead when it's convenient, but I'm still the king down here.. . . . The only ones I even pretend to please are big white folk, and even those I control more than they control me.. . . . That's my life, telling white folk how to think about the things I know about.. . . It's a nasty deal and I don't always like it myself.. . . . But I've made my place in it and I'll have every Negro in the country hanging on tree limbs by morning if it means staying where I am."

Location: Chapter Six
Speaker: Dr. Bledsoe
Context: Bledsoe rebukes the narrator for showing Mr. Norton less desirable black communities

Dr. Bledsoe explains that playing the subservient, fawning black to powerful whites has enabled him to maintain his position of power and authority. He mockingly lapses into the dialect of uneducated Southern blacks, saying "I's" instead of "I am" to show the narrator how he does it. Bledsoe claims that by making himself unthreatening to whites and telling them what they want to hear, he is able to control them. But his desire to control whites has nothing to do with combating injustice and everything to do with selfishness. Bledsoe is only interested in his own power, as evidenced by his statement that he would rather see every black man in America lynched than give up his place of authority.

This speech prompts the first of the narrator's many moments of sudden disenchantment. As a naïvely loyal adherent of the college's philosophy, the narrator has always considered Bledsoe an admirable exponent of black advancement. It devastates him to realize that Bledsoe is actually a power-hungry, cynical hypocrite.

And my problem was that I always tried to go in everyone's way but my own. I have also been called one thing and then another while no one really wished to hear what I called myself. So after years of trying to adopt the opinions of others I finally rebelled. I am an invisible man.

Location: The Epilogue
Speaker: The narrator
Context: The narrator realizes that his own identity is the key to freedom

In this passage, the narrator neatly encapsulates the main source of his difficulties. He has not been himself and has not lived his own life. Instead, he has allowed his complex identity to be smoothed over by the expectations and prejudices of others. He has followed the ideology of the college and the ideology of the Brotherhood without trusting or developing his own identity. Now, however, he has realized that his own identity, both in its flexibility and authenticity, is the key to freedom. Rinehart, a master of many identities, first suggested to the narrator the limitless capacity for individual variation. However, Rinehart ultimately proves an unsatisfactory model for the narrator because Rinehart's life lacks authenticity. The narrator strives for authenticity. At the beginning of the novel, the narrator called himself "an invisible man." He says the same thing at the end, but he means something different by it. At the outset, he meant that others could not see him. Now he knows that his identity, his inner self, is real, even if others cannot see it.

"Our white is so white you can paint a chunka coal and you'd have to crack it open with a sledge hammer to prove it wasn't white clear through."

Location: Chapter Ten
Speaker: Lucius Brockway
Context: The narrator has taken a job at the Liberty Paints plant, and Brockway brags about the masking qualities of their white paint

[T]he cast-iron figure of a very black, red-lipped and wide-mouthed Negro . . . stared up at me from the floor, his face an enormous grin, his single large black hand held palm up before his chest. It was a bank, a piece of early Americana, the kind of bank which, if a coin is placed in the hand and a lever pressed upon the back, will raise its arm and flip the coin into the grinning mouth.

Location: Chapter Fifteen
Speaker: The narrator
Context: The narrator finds a coin bank at Mary's just before leaving to join the Brotherhood

I looked at Ras on his horse and at their handful of guns and recognized the absurdity of the whole night and of the simple yet confoundingly complex arrangement of hope and desire, fear and hate, that had brought me here still running, and knowing now who I was and where I was and knowing too that I had no longer to run for or from the Jacks and the Emersons and the Bledsoes and Nortons, but only from their confusion, impatience, and refusal to recognize the beautiful absurdity of their American identity and mine.. . . . And I knew that it was better to live out one's own absurdity than to die for that of others, whether for Ras's or Jack's.

Location: Chapter 25 Twenty-Five
Speaker: The narrator
Context: The narrator realizes that his own absurd opinions are more important to him than the absurd opinions of others

JANE EYRE

Charlotte Brontë

An impoverished young woman struggles to maintain her autonomy in the face of oppression, prejudice, and love.

THE LIFE OF CHARLOTTE BRONTË

Charlotte Brontë was born in Yorkshire, England on April 21, 1816, to Maria Branwell and Patrick Brontë. When Brontë was five, her mother died. In 1824, Brontë and three of her sisters—Maria, Elizabeth, and Emily—were sent to Cowan Bridge, a school for clergymen's daughters. Maria and Elizabeth died of tuberculosis, and Charlotte and Emily were brought home. Several years later, Brontë went to school in Roe Head, England. In 1835, she became a teacher at the school. After several years of teaching, she went to live with and tutor the children of the wealthy Sidgewick family in 1839. She hated working as a governess and recruited her sisters to establish a school with her.

Although the Brontës' school was unsuccessful, their literary projects flourished. Charlotte, Anne, and Emily collaborated on a book of poems, publishing under male pseudonyms: Charlotte was Currer Bell, Emily was Ellis Bell, and Anne was Acton Bell. When the poetry volume received little public notice, the sisters decided to work on separate novels, still using their pseudonyms. Anne and Emily produced their novels in 1847 (*Agnes Grey* and *Wuthering Heights*, respectively), but Charlotte never found a publisher for her first novel, *The Professor*. She wrote *Jane Eyre* later that year. The novel became one of the most successful of its era, both critically and commercially.

After the success of *Jane Eyre*, Charlotte Brontë revealed her identity to her publisher. She went on to write several other novels, most notably *Shirley* in 1849. She became a respected member of London's literary set. The deaths of her sister Emily and brother Branwell in 1848, and of her sister Anne in 1849, left Charlotte dejected and isolated. In 1854, she wed the Reverend Arthur Nicholls, whom she did not love. The following year, while pregnant, she died of pneumonia.

JANE EYRE IN CONTEXT

Charlotte Brontë drew on her own life in writing *Jane Eyre*. Jane's dearest school friend dies of tuberculosis, just as Brontë's sisters died at Cowan Bridge. The hypocritical religious fervor of the fictional headmaster, Mr. Brocklehurst, is based in part on the fervor of the Reverend Carus Wilson, the Evangelical minister who ran Cowan Bridge. John Reed's decline into alcoholism and dissolution is most likely modeled on the life of Brontë's brother Branwell, who was addicted to opium and alcohol in the years preceding his death. Finally, Jane, like Charlotte, is a governess.

JANE EYRE: KEY FACTS

Time and place written: 1847; London

Date of first publication: 1847 (originally published under the pseudonym Currier Bell)

Publisher: Smith, Elder, and Co., Cornhill

Type of Work: Novel

Genre: Gothic novel; bildungsroman; social protest novel

Language: English

Setting (time): Early decades of the 19th century

Setting (place): Northern England

Tense: Past

Tone: Mysterious, affectionate, confessional, philosophical, political

Narrator: Jane Eyre in the first person

Point of view: Jane's point of view

Protagonist: Jane Eyre

Antagonist: Aunt Reed, Mr. Brocklehurst, Bertha Mason, Mr. Rochester, St. John Rivers

JANE EYRE: PLOT OVERVIEW

Jane Eyre, a young orphan, is in the care of Mrs. Reed, her cruel, wealthy aunt. Only a servant named Bessie treats Jane with kindness. One day, as punishment for fighting with her bullying cousin John Reed, Jane is imprisoned in the "red-room," where Jane's Uncle Reed died. Jane thinks she sees her uncle's ghost and faints. She wakes to find herself in the care of Bessie and the kindly apothecary Mr. Lloyd, who suggests that Jane be sent away to school. To Jane's delight, Mrs. Reed agrees.

Jane's life at the Lowood School is hard. The headmaster, Mr. Brocklehurst, is a cruel, hypocritical, and abusive man. He preaches a doctrine of poverty and privation to his students while using the school's funds to provide an opulent lifestyle for his own family. Jane befriends a girl named Helen Burns, whose strong, martyred attitude toward the school's miseries both helps and annoys Jane. A typhus epidemic sweeps Lowood. Helen dies of consumption, and Mr. Brocklehurst leaves after being publicly exposed and discredited. After a group of more sympathetic gentlemen takes Brocklehurst's place, Jane's life improves dramatically. After six more years of studying at Lowood, she spends two teaching there.

Jane accepts a governess position at a manor called Thornfield, where she teaches a lively French girl named Adéle. The distinguished housekeeper, Mrs. Fairfax, presides over the estate. Jane's employer is a dark, passionate man named Rochester. Jane finds herself falling in love with him. One night, Jane saves Rochester from a fire, which he claims was started by a drunken servant named Grace Poole. Jane sinks into despondency when Rochester brings home a beautiful but vicious woman named Blanche Ingram. Jane expects Rochester to propose to Blanche, but instead he proposes to Jane. She accepts almost disbelievingly.

The wedding day arrives. As Jane and Mr. Rochester prepare to exchange their vows, a man cries out that Rochester already has a wife. The man, Mr. Mason, introduces himself as the brother of that wife—a woman named Bertha. He says Bertha, whom Rochester married when he was a young man in Jamaica, is still alive. Rochester says Bertha has gone mad. The wedding party goes back to Thornfield, where they witness the insane Bertha Mason scurrying around on all fours and growling like an animal. Rochester keeps Bertha hidden on the third story of Thornfield and pays Grace Poole to keep his wife under control. Bertha was the real cause of the mysterious fire earlier in the story. Jane flees Thornfield.

Penniless and hungry, Jane must sleep outdoors and beg for food. Three siblings take her in. Their names are Mary, Diana, and St. John (pronounced "Sinjin") Rivers. St. John, a clergyman, finds Jane a job teaching at a charity school. He surprises her one day by declaring that her uncle, John Eyre, has died and left her a large fortune: 20,000 pounds. He shocks her further by declaring that her uncle was also his uncle: Jane and the Riverses are cousins. Jane immediately decides to split her inheritance with her three newfound relatives.

St. John decides to travel to India as a missionary, and he urges Jane to accompany him—as his wife. Jane agrees to go but refuses to marry him because she does not love him. St. John pressures her to reconsider, and she nearly gives in. But one night she hears Rochester's voice calling her name over the moors. Jane immediately hurries back to Thornfield and finds that it has been burned to the ground by Bertha Mason, who lost her life in the fire. Rochester saved the servants but lost his eyesight and one of his hands. Jane travels on to Rochester's new residence, Ferndean, where he lives with two servants named John and Mary.

Rochester and Jane marry. Jane writes that she has been married for ten blissful years and that she and Rochester enjoy perfect equality. After two years of blindness, Rochester regained sight in one eye and was able to behold their first son at his birth.

CHARACTERS IN JANE EYRE

Mr. Briggs John Eyre's attorney. Mr. Briggs helps Richard Mason prevent Jane's wedding to Rochester and eventually tells Jane about her inheritance.

Mr. Brocklehurst The cruel, hypocritical master of the Lowood School. Mr. Brocklehurst preaches privation, while stealing from the school.

Helen Burns Jane's close friend at the Lowood School. Helen endures her miserable life with passive dignity. She dies of consumption in Jane's arms.

Jane Eyre The protagonist and narrator of the novel. Jane is an intelligent, honest, plain-featured girl. Her strong belief in gender and social equality challenges Victorian ideas about women and the poor.

John Eyre Jane's uncle. John Eyre leaves Jane his vast fortune of 20,000 pounds.

Alice Fairfax The housekeeper at Thornfield Hall. Alice is the first to tell Jane that the mysterious laughter often heard echoing through the halls is the laughter of Grace Poole—a lie that Rochester often repeats.

Blanche Ingram A beautiful socialite who despises Jane and hopes to marry Rochester for his money.

Bessie Lee The maid at Gateshead. Bessie treats Jane kindly. She later marries Robert Leaven, the Reeds' coachman.

Mr. Lloyd The Reeds' apothecary. A kind man, Mr. Lloyd suggests that Jane be sent away to school. He writes a letter to Miss Temple denying Mrs. Reed's charge that Jane is a liar.

Bertha Mason Rochester's secret wife. Bertha Mason is a formerly beautiful, wealthy Creole woman who has become insane, violent, and bestial.

Richard Mason Bertha's brother. He thwarts Rochester and Jane's wedding.

Grace Poole Bertha Mason's keeper at Thornfield. Grace's drunken carelessness frequently allows Bertha to escape.

Eliza Reed One of Mrs. Reed's two daughters. Eliza, who is not as beautiful as her sister, devotes herself—somewhat self-righteously—to the church.

Georgiana Reed One of Mrs. Reed's two daughters. The beautiful Georgiana treats Jane cruelly when they are children, but later befriends her.

John Reed Mrs. Reed's son. John treats Jane with appalling cruelty during their childhood. As an adult, he drinks and gambles. John commits suicide when his mother stops paying his debts for him.

Mrs. Reed Jane's cruel aunt. Mrs. Reed raises Jane and sends her to school at age ten.

Uncle Reed Mrs. Reed's late husband. Uncle Reed always preferred Jane to his own children.

Diana Rivers Jane's cousin. Diana, a kind and intelligent woman, urges Jane not to go to India with St. John.

Mary Rivers Jane's cousin. Mary must work as a governess after her father loses his fortune. Like her sister, she is a model of an independent, loving, intelligent woman.

St. John Rivers Jane's cousin. With his sisters, St. John shelters and feeds Jane after she runs away from Rochester. St. John is cold, reserved, and often controlling. A foil to Rochester, he is ambitious and entirely alienated from his feelings.

Edward Rochester Jane's employer. Rochester is a wealthy, passionate man with a dark secret. He is unconventional, willing to set aside propriety to interact with Jane frankly. He committed many rash indiscretions in his youth, but he is a sympathetic figure.

Miss Scatcherd Jane's sour and vicious teacher at Lowood.

Sophie Adéle's French nurse at Thornfield.

Adéle Varens Jane's pupil at Thornfield. Adéle Varens is a lively, somewhat spoiled child from France. Rochester brought her to Thornfield after her mother, Celine, abandoned her. Although Celine was once Rochester's mistress, he does not think he is Adéle's father.

Celine Varens A French opera dancer with whom Rochester once had an affair. Rochester broke off the relationship after learning that Celine was unfaithful to him and only interested in his money.

THEMES IN *JANE EYRE*

INDEPENDENCE Jane longs for love without subservience. This is a difficult project, because most of the men in her life believe women are inferior to men. Mr. Brocklehurst, Edward Rochester, and St. John Rivers are misogynists eager to keep Jane in a submissive position. Taking a radically feminist position for her day, Jane refuses to be submissive. Fear of losing her autonomy makes Jane refuse to stay with Rochester while he remains legally tied to Bertha. Jane does not want to become a mistress and sacrifice her integrity for the sake of emotional gratification. With her stay at Moor House, Jane proves to herself that she is self-sufficient and financially independent. She can return to Rochester and feel that she is returning to an equal, not a master. In fact, because of Rochester's blindness, Jane is her husband's "prop and guide," not his servant.

RELIGION Jane struggles to find the right balance between moral duty and earthly pleasure. Mr. Brocklehurst, Helen Burns, and St. John Rivers each represent different models of religion, all of which Jane ultimately rejects. Mr. Brocklehurst illustrates the cruelties and hypocrisies that Charlotte Brontë perceived in the nineteenth-century Evangelical movement. He treats his students cruelly and robs the school, calling his misdeeds holy. Helen Burns practices a meek version of Christianity. Her religion is too passive for Jane's taste. St. John Rivers practices a Christianity of ambition and extreme self-importance. He urges Jane to sacrifice her emotional needs for the fulfillment of her moral duty. Jane rejects all three models of religion in favor of her own brand of spirituality. She relies on God for help, strongly objects to Rochester's lustful ways, and refuses to live with him while church and state say he is married to another woman. Jane's middle-ground spirituality is not hateful and oppressive like Brocklehurst's, nor does it require retreat from the everyday world as Helen's and St. John's do. For Jane, religion helps curb immoderate passions and spurs one on to worldly achievements.

SOCIAL CLASS In *Jane Eyre*, Brontë criticizes Victorian England's strict social hierarchy. Like Heathcliff in *Wuthering Heights*, Jane has ambiguous class standing, which makes the people she encounters nervous. Her manners, sophistication, and education are those of an aristocrat, but her poverty keeps her out of high society. This muddle makes her the ideal governess. Victorian governesses were expected to possess the "culture" of the aristocracy. But as paid employees, they were treated as servants. Jane's uncertain position becomes painful when she falls in love with Rochester, who is her intellectual equal but her social better. Even before she finds out about Bertha Mason, Jane is hesitant to marry Rochester because she worries that she would feel indebted to him for "condescending" to marry her. Jane does not hide her distress at class prejudice. In Chapter 23, she asks Rochester, "Do you think, because I am poor, obscure, plain, and little, I am soulless and heartless? You think wrong!—I have as much soul as you—and full as much heart! And if God had gifted me with some beauty and much wealth, I should have made it as hard for you to leave me, as it is now for me to leave you." Despite her fire and brains, Jane can only marry Rochester as his equal once she comes into her own inheritance.

SYMBOLS IN *JANE EYRE*

BERTHA MASON Some critics have read Bertha Mason as a symbol of non-British cultures, which Britain feared and psychologically locked away. Other critics interpret Bertha as symbolic of the trapped Victorian wife, who cannot travel or work outside the house and so becomes frenzied. Bertha's insanity could be interpreted as a warning to Jane of what results from complete surrender to Rochester. Bertha's actions can also be interpreted as a manifestation of Jane's subconscious rage against oppressive social and gender norms.

THE RED-ROOM The red-room symbolizes the obstacles that Jane must overcome in her struggles to find freedom, happiness, and belonging. In the red-room, it becomes clear that Jane is socially ostracized, financially helpless, and excluded from love.

IMPORTANT QUOTATIONS FROM *JANE EYRE*

I could not help it; the restlessness was in my nature; it agitated me to pain sometimes. Then my sole relief was to walk along the corridor of the third story . . . and allow my mind's eye to dwell on whatever bright visions rose before it. . . . and, best of all, to open my inward ear to a tale that was never ended—a tale my imagination created, and narrated continuously; quickened with all of incident, life, fire, feeling, that I desired and had not in my actual existence. It is in vain to say human beings ought to be satisfied with tranquility: they must have action; and they will make it if they cannot find it. Millions are condemned to a stiller doom than mine, and millions are in silent revolt against their lot. Nobody knows how many rebellions besides political rebellions ferment in the masses of life which people earth. Women are supposed to be very calm generally: but women feel just as men feel; they need exercise for their faculties, and a field for their efforts as much as their brothers do; they suffer from too rigid a restraint, too absolute a stagnation, precisely as men would suffer; and it is narrow-minded in their more privileged fellow-creatures to say that they ought to confine themselves to making puddings and knitting stockings, to playing on the piano and embroidering bags.

Location: Chapter 12
Speaker: Jane
Context: Jane describes her first few weeks at Thornfield

In this passage, Brontë's feminist manifesto, Jane rails against the fetters of patriarchy. Brontë criticizes stifling Victorian notions of the woman's role, describing the "doom" to which "millions in silent revolt against their lot" "are condemned." The diction of this passage highlights Jane's feelings of imprisonment. The images of restlessness and pacing, of "stagnation" and "too rigid a restraint," exemplify the novel's central theme of imprisonment, both physical and spiritual. Bertha Mason can be interpreted as Brontë's symbol of the female condition. Bertha is made a wife and then imprisoned, driven mad when her suppressed feelings turn to madness and fury.

Jane's description of the way she copes with her imprisonment could be a description of the artistic process. She describes retreating into her mind as a writer would, finding solace in "a tale that was never ended—a tale my imagination created, and narrated continuously." Perhaps Brontë used writing to cope with the kind of rage Jane feels.

Feeling . . . clamoured wildly. "Oh, comply!" it said. ". . . soothe him; save him; love him; tell him you love him and will be his. Who in the world cares for you? or who will be injured by what you do?" Still indomitable was the reply: "I care for myself. The more solitary, the more friendless, the more unsustained I am, the more I will respect myself. I will keep the law given by God; sanctioned by man."

Location: Chapter 27
Speaker: Jane
Context: Rochester tries to convince Jane to stay with him despite his marriage to Bertha

In a display of grit, Jane relies on her own morals to save her from her intense feelings. Rochester's argument almost persuades Jane: he is the first person who has ever truly loved her. Yet she knows that staying with him would mean compromising herself. She refuses to lose her self-respect. She asserts her worth and her ability to love herself even if no one else does. The passage also sheds light on Jane's understanding of religion. She sees God as the giver of the laws by which she must live. When she can no longer trust herself to exercise good judgment, she relies on these laws as demands she must follow.

"I will never call you aunt again as long as I live. I will never come to visit you when I am grown up; and if any one asks me how I liked you, and how you treated me, I will say the very thought of you makes me sick, and that you treated me with miserable cruelty . . . I shall remember. . . that punishment you made

me suffer because your wicked boy struck me—knocked me down for nothing. I will tell anybody who asks me questions this exact tale."

'Ere I had finished this reply, my soul began to expand, to exult, with the strangest sense of freedom, of triumph, I ever felt.

Location: Chapter 4
Speaker: Jane
Context: Jane, about to leave for Lowood School, berates her aunt

---

I. . . . fancied myself in idea his wife. Oh! it would never do! As his curate, his comrade, all would be right: I would cross oceans with him in that capacity; toil under Eastern suns, in Asian deserts with him in that office.. . . . I should suffer often, no doubt, attached to him only in this capacity: my body would be under a rather stringent yoke, but my heart and mind would be free. I should still have my unblighted self to turn to: my natural unenslaved feelings with which to communicate in moments of loneliness . . . . but as his wife—at his side always, and always restrained, and always checked—forced to keep the fire of my nature continually low, to compel it to burn inwardly and never utter a cry, though the imprisoned flame consumed vital after vital—this would be unendurable.

Location: Chapter 34
Speaker: Jane
Context: St. John Rivers asks Jane to marry him and go on a missionary trip to India with him, and Jane contemplates the request

---

I have now been married ten years. I know what it is to live entirely for and with what I love best on earth. I hold myself supremely blest—blest beyond what language can express; because I am my husband's life as fully as he is mine. No woman was ever nearer to her mate than I am: ever more absolutely bone of his bone, and flesh of his flesh.

Location: One of the final passages of the novel
Speaker: Jane
Context: Jane discusses her marriage

THE JOY LUCK CLUB

Amy Tan

A group of Chinese mothers and their American-born daughters struggle to communicate and understand each other.

THE LIFE OF AMY TAN

Amy Tan was born in Oakland, California, in 1952. Her parents were Chinese immigrants. When Tan was in her early teens, her father and one of her brothers both died of brain tumors within months of each other. Tan learned that her mother had been married to an abusive man in China. She divorced him and fled China just before the Communist takeover in 1949. She left behind three daughters.

Tan's mother moved her family to Switzerland, where Tan finished high school. During these years, she argued with her mother about college and career plans. Tan eventually followed her boyfriend to San Jose City College, where she earned a bachelor's and a master's degree in English and linguistics, despite her mother's wish that she study medicine. Tan married her boyfriend, Louis DeMattei, and began to pursue a Ph.D. in linguistics. She eventually abandoned the program in order to work with developmentally disabled children. She developed a successful career as a freelance business writer, but she found the work unfulfilling and began to write fiction as a creative release.

Tan's mother suffered from a serious illness, and Tan resolved to take a trip to China with her if she recovered. In 1987, Tan and her mother traveled to China, where Tan's mother was reunited with her daughters.

After the publication of *The Joy Luck Club*, Tan has continued to publish popular works. Many people say that she writes primarily to portray the Chinese American experience, but Tan says she writes first and foremost as an artist, independent of heritage. She argues that her bicultural upbringing inspires her work, but is not its primary subject. In her writing, Tan explores the universal themes of family, memory, and cultural conflict.

THE JOY LUCK CLUB IN CONTEXT

Tan's trip to China with her mother gave her a fresh perspective on her mother, and served as the key inspiration for her first novel, *The Joy Luck Club* (1989). *The Joy Luck Club* garnered enthusiastic reviews and stayed on the *New York Times* bestseller list for many months. It won both the National Book Award and the *L.A. Times* Book Award in 1989.

THE JOY LUCK CLUB: KEY FACTS

Time and place written: 1985–1989; San Francisco

Date of first publication: 1989

Publisher: G. P. Putnam's Sons

Type of work: Novel

Genre: Modern

Language: English with occasional Mandarin and Cantonese words and accents

Setting (time): 1920s–1930s in China; 1940s–1980s in America

Setting (place): China, San Francisco and Oakland California

Tense: Past and present

Tone: Bemused, sorrowful, speculative, respectful

Narrator: Jing-mei Woo, Lena and Ying-ying St. Clair; An-mei Hsu and Rose Hsu Jordan; Lindo and Waverly Jong

Point of view: Each of the seven narrators', all in the first person

Protagonist: Each of the seven narrators

Antagonist: The clash between cultures and generations

THE JOY LUCK CLUB: PLOT OVERVIEW

The Joy Luck Club consists of sixteen interwoven stories about conflicts between Chinese immigrant mothers and their American-raised daughters. The book hinges on Jing-mei's trip to China to meet her twin half-sisters, Chwun Yu and Chwun Hwa. Jing-mei's mother, Suyuan, was forced to leave her twin babies Chwun Yu and Chwun Hwa on the roadside during her desperate flight from Japan's invasion of Kweilin during World War II. Years later, in America, Suyuan remarried. Her second husband is Jing-mei's father.

Suyuan had organized the Joy Luck Club, a weekly mahjong gathering. Now, Jing-mei has taken her mother's place in the club. The club's other members—Lindo, Ying-ying, and An-mei—are three of her mother's fellow immigrants and oldest friends. They tell Jing-mei that just before Suyuan died she had finally located the address of her lost daughters. The three women repeatedly urge Jing-mei to travel to China and tell her sisters about their mother's life. But Jing-mei wonders whether she is capable of telling her mother's story, and the three older women fear that Jing-mei's doubts may be justified. They worry that their own daughters, like Jing-mei, may not know or appreciate the stories of their mothers' lives.

The novel is composed of four sections, each of which contains four separate narratives. In the first four stories of the novel, the mothers, speaking in turn, recall their relationships with their own mothers. In the second section, the daughters—Waverly, Jing-mei, Lena, and Rose—recall their childhood relationships with their mothers. In the third group of stories, the four daughters narrate their adult dilemmas—career and marriage troubles. Although they believe that their mothers' antiquated ideas do not pertain to their own American lifestyles, their search for solutions bring them back to their mothers. In the final group of stories, the mothers examine themselves. Lindo realizes that she has been irrevocably changed by American culture. Ying-ying realizes that Lena has unwittingly followed her passive example in her marriage to Harold Livotny. An-mei realizes that Rose has not completely absorbed the lessons she intended to teach her about faith and hope.

Jing-mei speaks for her mother, telling her story. When Jing-mei finally travels to China and helps her half-sisters to know a mother they cannot remember, she forges two new mother-daughter bonds. Her journey represents a reconciliation between Suyuan's two lives, between two cultures, and between mother and daughter. The journey also makes the other members of the Joy Luck Club optimistic that they too can reconcile past and present, China and America, and old and young.

CHARACTERS IN *THE JOY LUCK CLUB*

WOO FAMILY

Wang Chwun Yu and Wang Chwun Hwa Chwun Suyuan's twin daughters by her first husband, Wang Fuchi. Yu and Chwun Hwa are the half-sisters of Jing-mei. When an officer told Suyuan she should go to Chungking with her daughters, Suyuan knew the Japanese were going to invade Kweilin. Suyuan was forced to leave her daughters by the side of the road.

Canning Woo Suyuan's second husband and father of her daughter, Jing-mei. Canning met Suyuan in the hospital in Chungking, where she was recovering from her flight from Kweilin. After Suyuan's death, he travels to China with Jing-mei to meet Suyuan's children.

Jing-mei (June) Woo The newest member of the Joy Luck Club. Jing-mei worries that she will not be able to tell her mother's story.

Suyuan Woo Jing-mei's mother and the founder of the Joy Luck Club. During her flight from a war-torn area of China, Suyuan lost her twin daughters, Chwun Yu and Chwun Hwa.

JONG FAMILY

Marvin Chen Waverly's first husband and the father of her daughter, Shoshana. Waverly's mother, Lindo, always pointed out Marvin's faults. Soon Waverly could see nothing but his shortcomings, and divorced him. Waverly fears that the same thing will happen when she marries Rich.

Shoshana Chen Waverly's four-year-old daughter. Waverly loves Shoshana unconditionally.

Lindo Jong A member of the Joy Luck Club. Lindo teaches her daughter, Waverly, about the power of invisible strength. She worries that in trying to give Waverly American opportunities, she may have undermined her daughter's Chinese identity. Lindo also worries that she herself may be too assimilated.

Lindo's mother After Lindo was engaged at the age of two, Lindo's mother pretended Lindo was already someone else's daughter. Lindo knows that her mother only wanted to keep herself from feeling too attached to the daughter she loved so dearly.

Tin Jong Lindo's second husband. Tin is the father of her three children: Vincent, Waverly, and Winston.

Vincent Jong Lindo and Tin Jong's second child.

Waverly Jong The youngest of Lindo and Tin Jong's children. Waverly has always been a model of success, winning chess tournaments as a child and eventually building a lucrative career as an attorney. Jing-mei feels a rivalry with her. Waverly worries about her mother's reaction to her white fiancé, Rich.

Winston Jong Lindo and Tin Jong's first child. Winston was killed in a car accident at the age of sixteen.

Rich Schields Waverly's fiancé. Waverly wants to tell her mother about their engagement, but she is afraid that Lindo will attack Rich, who is white.

Huang Taitai Tyan-yu's mother. Taitai trained Lindo to be an obedient wife. Domineering and tyrannical, Taitai made Lindo's life miserable and blamed her for the fact that Lindo and Tyan-yu had no children, even though Tyan-yu was at fault.

Huang Tyan-yu Lindo's first husband, in China. Huang's mother was Huang Taitai. When Tyan-yu and Lindo were one and two, respectively, a matchmaker arranged their marriage. Pampered and self-centered, Tyan-yu made Lindo's life extremely unpleasant. When Lindo was sixteen, they got married. Tyan-yu had no sexual desire for Lindo.

HSU FAMILY

An-mei Hsu A member of the Joy Luck Club and the mother of seven. An-mei has learned the necessity of speaking up for herself, but, she notes with pain, she has not taught her daughter Rose the importance of assertiveness. Although she has lost most of her faith in God, An-mei has faith in the power of will and effort.

An-mei's Mother A strong but sorrowful woman. Her husband died young, and she was tricked into becoming the fourth wife of Wu Tsing. Eventually, An-mei's mother committed suicide so that An-mei would not live a life of shame and unhappiness. An-mei's mother taught her daughter to sacrifice herself for her family, mask her pain, and be wary of people who seem too kind or generous.

Bing Hsu The youngest of An-mei's and George Hsu's seven children. When Bing was four years old, he drowned at the beach. Rose blames herself for the death. An-mei believed that God and nengkan, the power to control her fate, would help her find Bing, but both failed her.

George Hsu An-mei's husband.

Rose Hsu The youngest of An-mei and George Hsu's three daughters. Rose married Ted Jordan over the protests of An-mei and Mrs. Jordan. She has always allowed Ted to make all the decisions, and when Ted asks her to take on some responsibility, their marriage disintegrates.

Ted Jordan Rose's estranged husband.

Popo An-mei's maternal grandmother. When An-mei's mother married Wu Tsing and became a third concubine, Popo disowned her. When Popo fell terminally ill, An-mei returned and, following superstitious healing methods, sliced off a piece of her flesh to put in a broth for Popo.

Second Wife Wu Tsing's first concubine. Second Wife entirely dominated the household in Tientsin by deceiving and manipulating. After her mother's death, An-mei stands up to Second Wife.

Syaudi The son of An-mei's mother and Wu-Tsing. Second Wife stole Syaudi and raised him as her own.

Wu Tsing A wealthy Chinese merchant who took An-mei's mother as his third concubine, or "Fourth Wife." Wu Tsing, a coward, was manipulated by Second Wife. After An-mei's mother killed herself, he feared the vengeance of her ghost and promised to raise An-mei in wealth and status.

ST. CLAIR FAMILY

Harold Livotny Lena's husband. He insists on splitting the cost of everything they share, saying this makes their love purer. In fact, the practice renders Lena powerless.

Clifford St. Clair Ying-ying's second husband. He never learned to speak Chinese fluently, and Ying-ying never learned to speak English fluently. Clifford often puts words into his wife's mouth.

Lena St. Clair The only child of Ying-ying and Clifford St. Clair. When she married Harold Livotny, Lena unwittingly began to follow her mother's passive example, believing herself incapable of control in her marriage and her career.

Ying-ying St. Clair A member of the Joy Luck Club. As a child, Ying-ying was headstrong and independent, but as she matured she grew passive, allowing her American husband, Clifford, to translate incorrectly her feelings and thoughts.

Ying-ying's Amah Ying-ying's childhood nursemaid. She loved Ying-ying as if she were her own child and tried to instill traditional Chinese feminine values in her.

THEMES IN *THE JOY LUCK CLUB*

THE CHALLENGES OF CULTURAL TRANSLATION The various narrators of *The Joy Luck Club* meditate on their inability to translate concepts from one culture to another. The mothers don't know English fully, and the daughters don't know Chinese fully, which results in sketchy cultural understanding. Often when the mothers and daughters speak, the intended meaning of the words they use differs from the accepted meaning, leading to subtle misunderstandings. Jing-mei points out that the daughters think their mothers are stupid because of their fractured English, while the mothers are impatient with their daughters because they don't understand the cultural nuances of their language and don't intend to pass along their Chinese heritage to their own children.

STORYTELLING AS A MEANS OF SELF-ASSERTION AND COMMUNICATION The mothers tell stories to circumvent language and cultural barriers. Their stories warn against certain mistakes, hold up past successes for emulation, communicate love and pride, and reveal the storyteller's secret self. The mothers also tell stories because they want their histories to be remembered. They want their daughters to respect their Chinese ancestors and their Chinese pasts. When Jing-mei sets out to tell her half-sisters Suyuan's story, she wants to assure them of Suyuan's love and tell them who their mother was and what she was like so that she will live on in their minds. Storytelling is also a way of controlling one's fate. In many ways, the Joy Luck Club was formed as a place to exchange stories. Faced with pain and hardship, Suyuan took control of the plot of her life by forming the club. The Joy Luck Club was not just a distraction. It enabled transformation—of community, of love and support, of circumstance.

THE INESCAPABLE DUALITY OF IMMIGRANT IDENTITY Each of the major characters expresses anxiety over her inability to reconcile her Chinese heritage with her American surroundings. While the daughters in the novel are born to Chinese parents and raised in mostly Chinese households, they are Americans who feel at home in modern American culture. Waverly, Rose, and Lena have white boyfriends or husbands. They regard many of their mothers' customs and tastes as old-fashioned or even ridiculous. Most of them have spent their childhoods trying to escape their Chinese identities. As a child, Lena opened her eyes as far as she could to make them look European. As an adolescent, Jing-mei denied that she had any internal Chinese aspects, insisting that her Chinese identity was limited to her external features. Lindo knows that Waverly would have clapped her hands for joy during her teen years if her mother had told her she did not look Chinese. But as they mature, the daughters become interested in their Chinese heritage. Waverly hopes that she will blend in well in China and is angry when Lindo says she will be recognized instantly as a tourist. Jing-mei worries that when she goes to China, she will fail to recognize any Chinese elements within herself.

Of the four mothers, Lindo expresses the most anxiety about her cultural identity. After being identified as a tourist during a trip to China, she wonders how America has changed her. Even as a young girl in China, Lindo chafed against Chinese custom, longing to extricate herself from a miserable marriage without dishonoring her parents, and secretly promising herself to remain true to her own desires. This promise shows the value she places on autonomy and happiness—two qualities Lindo associates with American culture.

SYMBOLS IN *THE JOY LUCK CLUB*

SUYUAN'S PENDANT Suyuan gives Jing-mei a jade pendant, calling it her "life's importance." At first, Jing-mei finds the pendant garish and symbolic of the cultural differences between herself and her mother. After Suyuan's death, however, Jing-mei comes to see it as a symbol of her mother's love and concern.

LENA'S VASE A vase in Lena's home symbolizes her marriage. Lena places the vase on a wobbly table, knowing that the vase might fall and break. Like the vase, Lena's marriage is in danger of falling and shattering. It was Lena's husband, Harold, who built the wobbly table. The table comes to symbolize Harold, who jeopardizes his marriage because he is not solid enough in his commitment to it.

IMPORTANT QUOTATIONS FROM *THE JOY LUCK CLUB*

"A mother is best. A mother knows what is inside you," she said.. . . . "A psyche-atricks will only make you hulihudu, make you see heimongmong."

Back home, I thought about what she said.. . . . [These] were words I had never thought about in English terms. I suppose the closest in meaning would be "confused" and "dark fog." But really, the words mean much more than that. Maybe they can't be easily translated because they refer to a sensation that only Chinese people have.

Location: "Without Wood"
Speaker: Rose Hsu Jordan
Context: Rose and her mother, An-mei, sit in church and talk about Rose's visit to a psychiatrist

Challenging her daughter's adherence to what she thinks is an odd Western convention, An-mei asks Rose why she tells a psychiatrist—a complete stranger—about her marital woes, when she refuses to tell her mother about them. This passage highlights linguistic barriers. An-mei seems unable to pronounce "psychiatrist." Yet her mispronunciation may be deliberate: her reinvention of the word as "psyche-atricks," suggests someone who plays tricks on the psyche—a quack not to be trusted. Rose thinks about the Chinese words her mother has used, struggling to explain them and wondering whether they can be translated into English at all. She thinks maybe the sensation they connote can be felt only by Chinese people.

I wanted my children to have the best combination: American circumstances and Chinese character. How could I know these two things do not mix? I taught [my daughter] how American circumstances work. If you are born poor here, it's no lasting shame.. . . . In America, nobody says you have to keep the circumstances somebody else gives you. She learned these things, but I couldn't teach her about Chinese character . . . How not to show your own thoughts, to put your feelings behind your face so you can take advantage of hidden opportunities.. . . .Why Chinese thinking is best.

Location: "Double Face"
Speaker: Lindo Jong
Context: Lindo worries about her daughter's character

Lindo Jong questions the feasibility of the mixed cultural identity she once wished for her daughter. She fears that Waverly is mostly American. But from Waverly's narrative, we know that Lindo's fears are not entirely justified: Waverly exhibits a deep respect and concern for her Chinese identity. She attributes much of her early talent in chess to her mother's lessons in how "not to show [her] thoughts," a skill she retains in adulthood.

"What will I say? What can I tell them about my mother? I don't know anything.. . . ." The aunties are looking at me as if I had become crazy right before their eyes.. . . . And then it occurs to me. They are frightened. In me, they see their own daughters, just as ignorant.. . . They see daughters who grow impatient when their mothers talk in Chinese . . . who will bear grandchildren born without any connecting hope passed from generation to generation.

Location: The end of the "The Joy Luck Club"
Speaker: Jing-mei Woo
Context: The Joy Luck Club members urge Jing-mei to find her twin sisters and tell them Suyuan's story

---

I . . . looked in the mirror.. . . . I was strong. I was pure. I had genuine thoughts inside that no one could see, that no one could ever take away from me. I was like the wind.. . . . And then I draped the large embroidered red scarf over my face and covered these thoughts up. But underneath the scarf I still knew who I was. I made a promise to myself: I would always remember my parents' wishes, but I would never forget myself.

Location: "The Red Candle"
Speaker: Lindo Jong
Context: Lindo stares into the mirror as she prepares to marry a man she does not love

---

Her wisdom is like a bottomless pond. You throw stones in and they sink into the darkness and dissolve. Her eyes looking back do not reflect anything.
I think this to myself even though I love my daughter. She and I have shared the same body.. . . . But when she was born, she sprang from me like a slippery fish, and has been swimming away ever since. All her life, I have watched her as though from another shore. And now I must tell her everything about my past. It is the only way to . . . pull her to where she can be saved.

Location: "Waiting Between the Trees"
Speaker: Ying-ying St. Clair
Context: Ying-ying thinks about her daughter's painful marriage and inscrutability

JULIUS CAESAR

William Shakespeare

After a statesmen murders Caesar, a Caesar loyalist casts doubt on his motives, drives him out of Rome, and hunts him down.

THE LIFE OF WILLIAM SHAKESPEARE

William Shakespeare, the most influential writer in all of English literature, was born in 1564 to a successful middle-class glove-maker in Stratford-upon-Avon, England. Shakespeare's formal education did not progress beyond grammar school. In 1582, he married an older woman, Anne Hathaway. His union with Anne produced three children. Around 1590, Shakespeare left his family behind and traveled to London to work as an actor and playwright. He quickly earned public and critical acclaim, and eventually became the most popular playwright in England and a part-owner of the Globe Theater. Shakespeare's career bridged the reigns of Elizabeth I (ruled 1558–1603) and James I (ruled 1603–1625), and he was a favorite of both monarchs. James paid Shakespeare's company a great compliment by giving its members the title of King's Men. Shakespeare retired to Stratford a wealthy and renowned man and died in 1616 at the age of fifty-two. At the time of Shakespeare's death, literary luminaries such as Ben Jonson hailed his works as timeless.

Shakespeare's works were collected and printed in various editions in the century following his death, and by the early eighteenth century his reputation as the greatest poet ever to write in English was well established. The unprecedented regard in which Shakespeare's works were held led to a fierce curiosity about his life, but many details of Shakespeare's personal history are unknown or shrouded in mystery. Some people have concluded from this lack of information and from Shakespeare's modest education that Shakespeare's plays were actually written by someone else—Francis Bacon and the Earl of Oxford are the two most popular candidates—but the support for this claim is overwhelmingly circumstantial, and the theory is not taken seriously by many scholars.

Shakespeare is generally thought to be the author of the thirty-eight plays (two of them possibly collaborations) and 154 sonnets that bear his name. The legacy of this body of work is immense. A number of Shakespeare's plays seem to have transcended even the category of brilliance, influencing the course of Western literature and culture.

JULIUS CAESAR IN CONTEXT

Julius Caesar takes place in ancient Rome in 44 B.C., when Rome was the center of an empire stretching from Britain to North Africa and from Persia to Spain. As the empire grew stronger, the dangers threatening its existence increased: Rome suffered from constant infighting between ambitious military leaders and the weak senators to whom they supposedly owed allegiance. The empire also suffered from a sharp division between citizens who were represented in the senate, and plebeian masses who were increasingly underrepresented. A succession of men aspired to rule Rome, Julius Caesar among them. Fearful of Caesar's growing power, a group of conspirators assassinated him. The assassination failed to put an end to Rome's power struggles, and civil war erupted. The plot of *Julius Caesar* includes the events leading up to the assassination of Caesar as well as much of the subsequent war.

Shakespeare's English contemporaries, who were well versed in ancient Greek and Roman history, probably detected parallels between *Julius Caesar*'s portrayal of Rome's shift from republicanism to imperialism and their own country's trend toward consolidated monarchal power. In 1599, when the play was first performed, Queen Elizabeth I had sat on the throne for nearly forty years, consolidating her power at the expense of the aristocracy and the House of Commons. She was sixty-six years old, so her reign seemed likely to end soon, but she had no heirs (neither did Julius Caesar). Many feared that her death would plunge England into the kind of chaos that had plagued England during the fifteenth-century Wars of the Roses. In an age when censorship would have limited direct commentary on these worries, Shakespeare perhaps intended the story of Caesar to imply what he could not say outright.

As his chief source in writing *Julius Caesar*, Shakespeare probably used Thomas North's translation of Plutarch's *Lives of the Noble Greeks and Romans*, written in the first century A.D. Plutarch, who believed that great men propelled history, saw the role of the biographer as inseparable from the role of the historian. Shakespeare followed Plutarch's lead by emphasizing how the actions of Rome's leaders, rather than class conflicts or larger political movements, determined history. However, he also concedes that the leaders' power depends on the fickle favor of the populace.

Contemporary accounts tell us that *Julius Caesar*, Shakespeare's shortest play, was first performed in 1599. It was probably the first play performed in the Globe Theater, the playhouse that was erected around that time in order to accommodate Shakespeare's increasingly successful theater company. The first authoritative text of the play did not appear until the 1623 First Folio edition. The elaborate stage directions suggest that this text was derived from the company's promptbook rather than Shakespeare's manuscript.

JULIUS CAESAR: KEY FACTS

Full Title: The Tragedy of Julius Caesar

Time and place written: 1599; London

Date of first publication: Published in the First Folio of 1623

Genre: Tragedy; historical drama

Setting (time): 44 B.C.

Setting (place): Ancient Rome

Protagonist: Brutus

Antagonist: Antony, Octavius, Cassius

Major conflict: Brutus attempts to think only of the public good, but his actions lead to bloodshed and civil war

JULIUS CAESAR: PLOT OVERVIEW

Two tribunes, Flavius and Murellus, find scores of Roman citizens wandering the streets, neglecting their work in order to watch Julius Caesar's triumphal parade. Caesar has defeated the Roman general Pompey, his archrival, in battle. The tribunes scold the citizens for abandoning their duties and remove decorations from Caesar's statues. Caesar enters with his entourage, including the military and political figures Brutus, Cassius, and Antony. A Soothsayer calls out to Caesar to "beware the Ides of March," but Caesar ignores him and proceeds with his victory celebration (I.ii.19, I.ii.25).

Cassius and Brutus, both longtime intimates of Caesar and each other, converse. Cassius tells Brutus that he has seemed distant lately; Brutus replies that he has been at war with himself. Cassius states that he wishes Brutus could see himself as others see him, for then Brutus would realize how honored and respected he is. Brutus says that he fears that the people want Caesar to become king, which would overturn the republic. Cassius concurs that Caesar is treated like a god though he is merely a man, no better than Brutus or Cassius. Cassius recalls incidents of Caesar's physical weakness and marvels that this fallible man has become so powerful. He blames his and Brutus's lack of will for allowing Caesar's rise to power: surely the rise of such a man cannot be the work of fate. Brutus considers Cassius's words as Caesar returns. Upon seeing Cassius, Caesar tells Antony that he deeply distrusts Cassius.

Caesar departs, and another politician, Casca, tells Brutus and Cassius that, during the celebration, Antony offered the crown to Caesar three times and the people cheered, but Caesar refused it each time. He reports that Caesar then fell to the ground and had some kind of seizure before the crowd; his demonstration of weakness, however, did not alter the plebeians' devotion to him. Brutus goes home to consider Cassius's words regarding Caesar's poor qualifications to rule, while Cassius hatches a plot to draw Brutus into a conspiracy against Caesar.

That night, Rome is plagued with violent weather and a variety of bad omens and portents. Brutus finds letters in his house apparently written by Roman citizens worried that Caesar has become too powerful. The letters have in fact been forged and planted by Cassius, who knows that if Brutus believes it is the people's will, he will support a plot to remove Caesar from power. A committed supporter of the republic, Brutus fears the possibility of a dictator-led empire, worrying that the populace would lose its voice. Cassius arrives at Brutus's home with his conspirators, and Brutus, who has already been won over by the letters, takes control of the meeting. The men agree to lure Caesar from his house and kill him. Cassius wants to kill Antony too, for Antony will surely try to hinder their plans, but Brutus disagrees, believing that too many deaths will render their plot too bloody and dishonor them. Having agreed to spare Antony, the conspirators depart. Portia, Brutus's wife, observes that Brutus appears preoccupied. She pleads with him to confide in her, but he rebuffs her.

Caesar prepares to go to the Senate. His wife, Calpurnia, begs him not to go, describing recent night-mares she has had in which a statue of Caesar streamed with blood and smiling men bathed their hands in the blood. Caesar refuses to yield to fear and insists on going about his daily business. Finally, Calpur-nia convinces him to stay home—if not out of caution, then as a favor to her. But Decius, one of the con-spirators, then arrives and convinces Caesar that Calpurnia has misinterpreted her dreams and the recent omens. Caesar departs for the Senate in the company of the conspirators.

As Caesar proceeds through the streets toward the Senate, the Soothsayer again tries but fails to get his attention. The citizen Artemidorus hands him a letter warning him about the conspirators, but Caesar refuses to read it, saying that his closest personal concerns are his last priority. At the Senate, the conspir-ators speak to Caesar, bowing at his feet and encircling him. One by one, they stab him to death. When Caesar sees his dear friend Brutus among his murderers, he gives up his struggle and dies.

The murderers bathe their hands and swords in Caesar's blood, thus bringing Calpurnia's premoni-tion to fruition. Antony, having been led away on a false pretext, returns and pledges allegiance to Brutus but weeps over Caesar's body. He shakes hands with the conspirators, thus marking them all as guilty while appearing to make a gesture of conciliation. When Antony asks why they killed Caesar, Brutus replies that he will explain their purpose in a funeral oration. Antony asks to be allowed to speak over the body as well; Brutus grants his permission, though Cassius remains suspicious of Antony. The conspira-tors depart, and Antony, alone now, swears that Caesar's death shall be avenged.

Brutus and Cassius go to the Forum to speak to the public. Cassius exits to address another part of the crowd. Brutus declares to the masses that though he loved Caesar, he loves Rome more, and Caesar's ambition posed a danger to Roman liberty. The speech placates the crowd. Antony appears with Caesar's body, and Brutus departs after turning the pulpit over to Antony. Repeatedly referring to Brutus as "an honorable man," Antony's speech becomes increasingly sarcastic; questioning the claims that Brutus made in his speech that Caesar acted only out of ambition, Antony points out that Caesar brought much wealth and glory to Rome, and three times turned down offers of the crown. Antony then produces Cae-sar's will but announces that he will not read it for it would upset the people inordinately. The crowd nevertheless begs him to read the will, so he descends from the pulpit to stand next to Caesar's body. He describes Caesar's horrible death and shows Caesar's wounded body to the crowd. He then reads Caesar's will, which bequeaths a sum of money to every citizen and orders that his private gardens be made pub-lic. The crowd becomes enraged that this generous man lies dead; calling Brutus and Cassius traitors, the masses set off to drive them from the city.

Meanwhile, Caesar's adopted son and appointed successor, Octavius, arrives in Rome and forms a three-person coalition with Antony and Lepidus. They prepare to fight Cassius and Brutus, who have been driven into exile and are raising armies outside the city. At the conspirators' camp, Brutus and Cas-sius have a heated argument regarding matters of money and honor, but they ultimately reconcile. Bru-tus reveals that he is sick with grief, for in his absence Portia has killed herself. The two continue to prepare for battle with Antony and Octavius. That night, the Ghost of Caesar appears to Brutus, announcing that Brutus will meet him again on the battlefield.

Octavius and Antony march their army toward Brutus and Cassius. Antony tells Octavius where to attack, but Octavius says that he will make his own orders; he is already asserting his authority as the heir of Caesar and the next ruler of Rome. The opposing generals meet on the battlefield and exchange insults before beginning combat.

Cassius witnesses his own men fleeing and hears that Brutus's men are not performing effectively. Cassius sends one of his men, Pindarus, to see how matters are progressing. From afar, Pindarus sees one of their leaders, Cassius's best friend, Titinius, being surrounded by cheering troops and concludes that he has been captured. Cassius despairs and orders Pindarus to kill him with his own sword. He dies pro-claiming that Caesar is avenged. Titinius himself then arrives–the men encircling him were actually his comrades, cheering a victory he had earned. Titinius sees Cassius's corpse and, mourning the death of his friend, kills himself.

Brutus learns of the deaths of Cassius and Titinius with a heavy heart, and prepares to take on the Romans again. When his army loses, doom appears imminent. Brutus asks one of his men to hold his sword while he impales himself on it. Finally, Caesar can rest satisfied, he says as he dies. Octavius and Antony arrive. Antony speaks over Brutus's body, calling him the noblest Roman of all. While the other conspirators acted out of envy and ambition, he observes, Brutus genuinely believed that he acted for the benefit of Rome. Octavius orders that Brutus be buried in the most honorable way. The men then depart to celebrate their victory.

CHARACTERS IN *JULIUS CAESAR*

Antony A friend of Caesar's. Antony is a masterful public speaker, taking an audience of fervent Brutus supporters and convincing them to condemn Brutus as a traitor. Antony's desire to exclude Lepidus from power hints at his own ambitious nature.

Brutus A supporter of the republic. Brutus's inflexible sense of honor makes it easy for Caesar's enemies to manipulate him into believing that Caesar must die in order to preserve the republic. While the other conspirators act out of envy and rivalry, Brutus acts because he loves Caesar but truly believes that his death will benefit Rome. Because he puts matters of state above personal loyalties, Brutus epitomizes Roman virtue.

Julius Caesar A great Roman general and senator. Caesar does not exhibit the hunger for tyranny of which his enemies accuse him. Still, he cannot separate his public life from his private life, and he allows himself to be seduced by the populace's adoration.

Calpurnia Caesar's wife. Calpurnia believes in omens and portents.

Casca A public figure opposed to Caesar's rise to power. Casca believes that Caesar's repeated refusals of the crown are an act designed to lull the populace into believing that he has no personal ambition.

Cassius A talented general and longtime acquaintance of Caesar's. Cassius is sly, envious, impulsive, and unscrupulous. He tricks Brutus into believing that Caesar must die for the good of Rome.

Cicero A Roman senator renowned for his oratorical skill.

Decius A member of the conspiracy against Caesar.

Flavius A tribune (an official elected by the people to protect their rights). Flavius condemns the plebeians for their fickleness in cheering Caesar, when once they cheered Caesar's enemy, Pompey.

Lepidus The third member of Antony's and Octavius's coalition. Antony has a low opinion of Lepidus, but Octavius thinks he is loyal.

Murellus A tribune who condemns the plebeians for their fickleness in cheering Caesar.

Octavius Caesar's adopted son and appointed successor. By following Caesar's example, Octavius emerges as a figure of authority.

Portia Brutus's wife. Portia is accustomed to being Brutus's confidante and worries when Brutus will not tell her what is troubling him. When Antony and Octavius gain power, Portia kills herself out of grief.

THEMES IN *JULIUS CAESAR*

FATE VERSUS FREE WILL Cassius refuses to believe that Caesar's rising power is fated, calling a belief in fate nothing more than passivity or cowardice. As he tells Brutus, "The fault, dear Brutus, is not in our stars, / But in ourselves, that we are underlings" (I.ii.140–142). He blames the situation on his own and Brutus's passivity, not on a predestined plan. In contrast, Caesar purports to believe in fate. He wonders why men fear death, since they can do nothing to control the hour of their own deaths. He believes that certain events lie beyond human control, and that to realize this is to free one's self from fear. Both men get to maintain their worldviews to the last. Cassius takes control of his life, assassinating Caesar and feeling he has changed the course of Roman history. Caesar dies after a series of portents, probably feeling that his death was fated.

THE DANGER OF NEGLECTING THE PRIVATE SELF Part of the play's tragedy stems from the characters' neglect of private feelings and loyalties in favor of what they believe to be the public good. Brutus rebuffs his wife, Portia, when she pleads with him to confide in her. Believing himself to be acting on the people's will, he murders Caesar without consulting her. Brutus puts aside his personal loyalty to Caesar and kills him out of loyalty to the public. Cassius also focuses exclusively on his public life. Caesar's neglect of his private life indirectly leads to his death. Although he briefly agrees to stay home in order to please Calpurnia, who has dreamed of his murder, he gives way to ambition after Decius tells him that the senators plan to offer him the crown. When Caesar stops seeing the difference between his omnipotent, immortal public image and his vulnerable human body, he makes himself vulnerable.

MISINTERPRETATIONS AND MISREADINGS Misinterpretation fills the play, often revealing what characters desire or fear. As Cicero says, "Men may construe things after their fashion, / Clean from the purpose of the things themselves" (I.iii.34–35). The night before Caesar's assassination, Cassius misreads the many portents. He believes they signify the danger that Caesar's impending coronation would bring to the state, when really they warn of the destruction that Cassius is about to wreak on Rome. Cassius encourages Brutus to misinterpret, forging letters that Brutus wrongly believes are authentic pleas from the Roman people. Misinterpretation causes Cassius's death. Pindarus's erroneous conclusion that Titinius has been captured by the enemy causes Cassius to kill himself.

SYMBOLS IN *JULIUS CAESAR*

OMENS AND PORTENTS Until Caesar's death, each omen and nightmare seems to signal Caesar's impending demise. These portents may simply announce what is fated to occur, or they may be warnings about what might occur if the characters do not take active steps to change their behavior.

WOMEN AND WIVES Calpurnia and Portia function not as sympathetic personalities or sources of insight or poetry but as symbols of the private, domestic realm. Both women ask their husbands to confide in them, to trust them, to combat danger by paying attention to the home. Caesar and Brutus rebuff their wives, actively turning away from the domestic realm.

IMPORTANT QUOTATIONS FROM *JULIUS CAESAR*

He was my friend, faithful and just to me.
But Brutus says he was ambitious,
And Brutus is an honourable man.
…
When that the poor have cried, Caesar hath wept.
…
Yet Brutus says he was ambitious,
And Brutus is an honourable man.
…
I thrice presented him a kingly crown,
Which he did thrice refuse. Was this ambition?
Yet Brutus says he was ambitious,
And sure he is an honourable man.

Location: III.ii.82–96
Speaker: Antony
Context: Antony gives Caesar's funeral oration to the Romans

Antony's funeral oration is a rhetorical tour de force, damning the conspirators while appearing to praise them. Antony's rhetoric is the verbal equivalent of his action in the previous scene, when he shook hands with each of the murderers in turn, smearing Caesar's blood among all of them and marking them as guilty while appearing to make a gesture of reconciliation. The funeral oration draws power from repetition. Antony alternates memories of Caesar's friendship and kindness with Brutus's claim that Caesar was "ambitious," making Brutus's claim appear increasingly ridiculous. Antony repeatedly declares that Brutus "is an honourable man," layering on sarcasm until the meaning of the sentiment has been turned on its head. Without showing the crowd what he is doing, Antony incites it to bloodthirsty mutiny.

> We at the height are ready to decline.
> There is a tide in the affairs of men
> Which, taken at the flood, leads on to fortune;
> Omitted, all the voyage of their life
> Is bound in shallows and in miseries.
> On such a full sea are we now afloat,
> And we must take the current when it serves,
> Or lose our ventures.

Location: IV.ii.269–276
Speaker: Brutus
Context: Brutus tries to convince Cassius that the time is right to engage Octavius and Antony in battle

Brutus speaks of a metaphorical "tide" in the lives of human beings: by taking advantage of the high tide, one may float out to sea and travel far. If one misses this chance, the "voyage" will be confined to the shallows. Brutus conceives of life as influenced by both fate and free will: we cannot control fate, just as we cannot control the tide, but we can control our reaction to fate, just as we can choose to swim out with the high tide or stay in the shallows. Brutus assumes that we can tell when the tide is high, but characters repeatedly neglect fate's opportunities and warnings.

> I could be well moved if I were as you.
> If I could pray to move, prayers would move me
> But I am constant as the Northern Star,
> Of whose true fixed and resting quality
> There is no fellow in the firmament.
> The skies are painted with unnumbered sparks;
> They are all fire, and every one doth shine;
> But there's but one in all doth hold his place.

Location: III.i.58–65
Speaker: Caesar
Context: Metellus has asked Caesar to pardon his banished brother, Publius Cimber; here, Caesar speaks
to the senators

> [My horse] is a creature that I teach to fight,
> To wind, to stop, to run directly on,
> His corporal motion governed by my spirit;
> And in some taste is Lepidus but so.
> He must be taught, and trained, and bid go forth—
> A barren-spirited fellow, one that feeds
> On objects, arts, and imitations,
> Which, out of use and staled by other men,
> Begin his fashion. Do not talk of him
> But as a property.

Location: IV.i.31–40
Speaker: Antony to Octavius
Context: Antony and Octavius make plans to retake Rome

THE JUNGLE

Upton Sinclair

A turn-of-the-century Lithuanian immigrant and his family struggle to survive in wretched poverty in the meatpacking district of Chicago, oppressed by America's brutal capitalism; at last, the head of the household discovers and embraces socialism.

THE LIFE OF UPTON SINCLAIR

Upton Sinclair was born in Baltimore, in 1878, into a family of impoverished southern aristocrats. At the age of fourteen, Sinclair enrolled at New York's City College, where he became a staunch supporter of the Socialist Party. The following year, he began writing to help with college expenses. After graduation, he pursued graduate studies at Columbia University.

None of the five novels Sinclair published between 1901 and 1906 generated much income. Late in 1904, the editors of the popular socialist newspaper *Appeal to Reason* sent Sinclair to Chicago to examine the lives of stockyard workers. He spent seven weeks in the city's meatpacking plants, learning every detail about the work itself, the home lives of workers, and the structure of the business. *The Jungle*, the fruit of this research, was first published in serial form in *Appeal to Reason*. The text was deemed too shocking by publishers Sinclair initially approached, so he funded the first book printing himself. *The Jungle* caused a sensation—though not for the reason Sinclair intended. Sinclair had sought to elicit sympathy for the working class and build support for the socialist movement, but the public was most outraged by his exposé of the unsanitary meatpacking industry. Sinclair invested the profits from the novel into building a utopian colony in New Jersey, but the settlement burned down within four months.

In 1911, Sinclair divorced his first wife and married the writer Mary Craig Kimbrough. They moved to California, where Sinclair continued to support socialism through writing and activism. In 1934, he ran an unsuccessful campaign to become California's Democratic Party governor. Late in life, he enjoyed a revival in popularity and won a Pulitzer Prize for *Dragon's Teeth* (1942), a novel about the rise of Nazism in Germany. In the 1950s, Sinclair and his wife moved to a small town in Arizona. Kimbrough died in 1961, and Sinclair married again. He died, again a widower, in 1968. Though Sinclair published more than ninety books in his lifetime, *The Jungle* remains his best-known work.

THE JUNGLE IN CONTEXT

The Jungle raised a public outcry against the unhealthy standards in the meatpacking industry. The public pressed less for the socialist reforms that Sinclair advocated than for food handling reform, prompting Sinclair's famous remark: "I aimed at the public's heart, and by accident I hit it in the stomach." In response, the Pure Food and Drug Act was passed in 1906. No novel had made such significant social impact since Harriet Beecher Stowe's 1951 novel *Uncle Tom's Cabin*, which inspired many to back the abolitionist movement.

The Jungle is not a nuanced novel in theme, character development, or form. In it, capitalism is portrayed as pure evil. The characters are not three-dimensional individuals, but stand-ins for social classes and forces. The narrative follows Jurgis's descent into the hellish reality of capitalism, until he is saved by discovering socialism. Sinclair fleshes out capitalistic hell with a lurid style that relies heavily on stomach-churning description.

In the aftermath of the Soviet Union, the Warsaw Pact, and the Berlin Wall, the novel's idealistic glorification of socialism may seem naïve, but the novel remains an important social record of the psychology of American capitalism in the early twentieth century.

THE JUNGLE: KEY FACTS

Time and place written: 1905–1906; Chicago and Princeton, New Jersey

Date of publication: 1906

Publisher: Serialized in *Appeal to Reason*; then published at Sinclair's own expense

Type of work: Novel

Genre: Social protest novel

Language: English

Setting (time): Early 1900s

Setting (place): Packingtown, the meatpacking district of Chicago

Tense: Past

Tone: Incendiary, condemnatory, righteous, outraged, lurid

Narrator: Anonymous, third-person narrator with knowledge of future events; Sinclair's mouthpiece

Point of view: Jurgis Rudkus's

Protagonist: Jurgis Rudkus

Antagonist: Ruthless capitalistic system

THE JUNGLE: PLOT OVERVIEW

Jurgis Rudkus and Ona Lukoszaite, recent emigrants from Lithuania, celebrate their wedding at a Chicago bar. The couple has come with relatives to America in search of a better life, but Packingtown, the center of both the Lithuanian community and Chicago's meatpacking industry, is a dangerous and filthy place where it is difficult to find a job. After the reception, Jurgis and Ona learn that they owe more than a hundred dollars to the saloonkeeper. In Lithuania, wedding guests customarily help pay for the wedding, but in Chicago many of the impoverished immigrant guests have left no money. Jurgis, a great believer in the American Dream, vows to work harder to make more money.

Young and energetic, Jurgis quickly finds work. So do Ona's relatives Marija Berczynskas and Jonas. The family is swindled into signing a bad agreement to buy a house. There are many hidden costs and the house is poorly maintained. As the family's living expenses increase, even Ona and Stanislovas, Ona's young stepbrother, must find jobs. Jobs in Packingtown involve backbreaking labor in unsafe conditions. Furthermore, the immigrant community is plagued by crime and corruption. Jurgis's father, Dede Antanas, agrees to pay a third of his wages to a middleman who helps him find work, but the job is too difficult for the old man, and it quickly kills him.

Winter is the most dangerous season in Packingtown. Jurgis, forced to work in an unheated, poorly lit slaughterhouse, risks his life every day simply by going to work. A likeable violinist named Tamoszius courts Marija, but the couple cannot marry because they cannot afford a wedding. Marija loses her job when her factory closes down. Distressed by the plight of his family, Jurgis joins a union and slowly comes to understand the machine of political corruption and bribery that runs Packingtown. He starts learning English. Marija is rehired but fired after she complains about missing wages. Pregnant, Ona has difficulty working at her factory. Her supervisor, Miss Henderson, oversees a prostitution ring that employs most of the other girls Ona works with. Ona and Jurgis name their new healthy baby Anatanas after Jurgis's late father. Ona is forced to return to work only seven days after she gives birth.

Jurgis injures his ankle on the job and is forced to spend nearly three months recuperating without pay. Unable to face the family's misery, Jonas disappears. Ona's youngest stepbrother, Kristoforas, dies of food poisoning. His ankle healed, Jurgis finds out that he no longer has a job at the factory. After a long, frustrating search for work, he ends up taking a job at the fertilizer plant, the foulest place in all of Packingtown. He starts drinking.

Ona is pregnant again. One night, she doesn't return home from work. Jurgis discovers that her boss, Phil Connor, kept her after work and forced her to sleep with him. Jurgis attacks Connor and is arrested. After an unfair trial, Jurgis is sentenced to a month in prison. Once again, the family must scrape by without his wages. In prison, Jurgis befriends a criminal named Jack Duane. When he is released, Jurgis discovers that his family has been evicted from its home and is living at the rundown boardinghouse where they stayed when they first arrived in Chicago. He arrives at the boardinghouse to find Ona prematurely in labor, screaming. Both she and the baby die in childbirth. Jurgis goes on a drinking binge.

Ona's stepmother, Teta Elzbieta, convinces Jurgis to pull himself together and think of his son Antanas, and he begins searching for a job. With the help of a philanthropic wealthy woman who takes an interest in the family, Jurgis finds a good job at a steel mill. He dedicates himself to Antanas. But his renewed hopes in life are shattered when Antanas drowns in the mud on the street. In despair, Jurgis abandons his surviving family members and wanders the countryside as a tramp.

In the winter, Jurgis returns to Chicago, where he finds a job digging freight tunnels. He spends two weeks in a hospital after injuring his arm at work, and loses his job. Unemployed and penniless, Jurgis begs on the street. One night, a wealthy young man gives him a hundred-dollar bill, but a bartender cheats Jurgis out of the money when Jurgis asks him for change. Jurgis attacks the bartender and is sent to jail, where again he encounters Jack Duane. When they are released from jail, Duane and Jurgis become partner burglars and muggers. Eventually, Jurgis is recruited to work for Mike Scully, the corrupt political boss. During a series of Packingtown strikes, Jurgis makes a lot of money as a strikebreaker.

Jurgis runs into Phil Connor on the street and attacks him. He is again sent to prison. After being released, he lives on charity. One day, he meets an old acquaintance who tells him how to find Marija, who has become a morphine addict and works as a prostitute to help support Teta Elzbieta and the children. Jurgis decides to wait until he finds a good job before seeing Teta Elzbieta.

One night, crushed by the wretchedness of his life, Jurgis wanders into a socialist political rally. The orator's speech advocates that workers—not a few wealthy capitalists—should own factories and plants. The speech inspires Jurgis to join the socialist party. Jurgis finds a job as a porter at a socialist-run hotel and is reunited with Teta Elzbieta. At a socialist rally, Jurgis hears the speaker proclaim that if socialism spreads, "CHICAGO WILL BE OURS!"

CHARACTERS IN *THE JUNGLE*

JURGIS'S FAMILY

Marija Berczynskas Ona's cousin. A large, assertive woman, Marija fights back against the corrupt bosses. She represents the defiant immigrant spirit slowly crushed by capitalism.

Jonas Teta Elzbieta's brother. Jonas encourages the family to emigrate to America, then abandons them after months of miserable poverty.

Teta Elzbieta Lukoszaite Ona's stepmother and a mother of six. A resilient, strong-willed old woman, Teta Elzbieta represents the redemptive power of family, home, and tradition.

Juozapas Lukoszaite Teta Elzbieta's crippled son, injured as a toddler by a wagon that ran over his leg. While foraging for food at a local dump, Juazapas meets a rich lady who later helps the family.

Kotrina Lukoszaite Teta Elzbieta's daughter. Kotrina takes care of the children and the household, and sells newspapers with her brothers when Jurgis is sent to prison.

Ona Lukoszaite Teta Elzbieta's stepdaughter and Jurgis's wife. A lovely, kind, optimistic girl, Ona is ruined by the forces of capitalism. She is raped by her boss, Phil Connor.

Stanislovas Lukoszaite Teta Elzbieta's young teenage son. Terrified of frostbite, Stanislovas often refuses to go to work until Jurgis beats him.

Dede Antanas Rudkus Jurgis's father. A proud old man, Dede Antanas is humiliated when he must pay a middleman to help him find a job.

Antanas Rudkus Jurgis and Ona's son. Antanas, who is Jurgis's last hope, drowns in the mud on the street.

Jurgis Rudkus The novel's protagonist; a young Lithuanian immigrant. Jurgis's determination, health, family, and faith in the American Dream are slowly destroyed by Packingtown's miserable living and working conditions. Sinclair creates this flat character to demonstrate how workers are exploited by capitalism and how they can be redeemed by socialism.

OTHER CHARACTERS

Phil Connor Ona's boss. A bullying, depraved man, Connor harasses and eventually rapes Ona. He has many connections with politicians, criminals, and businessmen, which enable him to ruin Jurgis's life. He represents the moral corruption that comes of too much power.

Jack Duane A polished, charismatic criminal whom Jurgis meets in prison. Jack later introduces Jurgis to a lucrative lifestyle in Chicago's criminal underworld.

Grandmother Majauszkiene The family's Lithuanian immigrant neighbor. A socialist and a concerned old woman, Grandmother Majauszkiene has seen generations of immigrants destroyed by the merciless labor practices of the Packingtown factories.

Miss Henderson The cruel and embittered forelady at Ona's factory. Jilted by one of the factory superintendents, Miss Henderson now runs a brothel on the side. She hates Ona for being a "decent married girl."

Tommy Hinds A well-known socialist and the proprietor of a small Chicago hotel where Jurgis finally finds work as a porter.

Ostrinski A Polish immigrant who inspires Jurgis with a rousing speech at a socialist political meeting and later teaches Jurgis about socialism.

Nicholas Schliemann A socialist who functions as a mouthpiece for Sinclair's political philosophy, explaining socialist philosophy at great length to an antisocialist magazine editor.

Mike Scully A wealthy and corrupt Chicago democrat who owns the dump where children forage for food. Scully rigs elections and profits from the housing scam to which Jurgis's family falls victim. Jurgis briefly works as one of Scully's henchmen.

Jokubas Szedvilas The kind proprietor of a failing Packingtown delicatessen and Jonas's acquaintance from Lithuania. Jokubas introduces the family to the harsh realities of poor immigrant life.

THEMES IN *THE JUNGLE*

SOCIALISM AS A REMEDY FOR THE EVILS OF CAPITALISM

In its first twenty-seven chapters, *The Jungle* relentlessly blames capitalism for the plight of disillusioned immigrants. The novel's stories stand for the stories of millions of immigrants—and more generally, the experience of the working class at the hands of a cruel economic and social system. Sinclair presents socialism as a cure for the problems created by capitalism. As portrayed in the novel, capitalism harms the masses for the benefit of an elite few, whereas socialism benefits everyone. The novel also suggests that a socialist state would naturally uphold Christian moral values. *The Jungle*'s message is not nuanced: its goal is to persuade us to becomes socialists.

THE HOLLOWNESS OF THE AMERICAN DREAM AND THE IMMIGRANT EXPERIENCE

The Jungle explores the plight of immigrants in America. Jurgis's family has come to the New World with idealistic faith in the American Dream—the idea that America is a land where hard work and determination brings material success and happiness. However, the America they encounter is a land of prejudice and exploitation rather than endless opportunity, a land where the poor can achieve success only by taking part in corruption, crime, and graft.

To make sure that his immigrant family does not appear alien to his American readers, Sinclair repeatedly emphasizes that Jurgis's family has the same values the native American public is supposed to have—family togetherness, honesty, hard work, thrift. Sinclair uses the disintegration of Jurgis's family to suggest that capitalism attacks American values, rendering the American Dream hollow.

SYMBOLS IN *THE JUNGLE*

PACKINGTOWN STOCKYARDS AND SLAUGHTERHOUSES

Just as the stockyards are crammed with animals on their way to slaughter, so too are they packed with laborers flailed by economic forces beyond their control. Stripped of human identity, the laborers—like the animals they process--are reduced to a mass of muscles that help run the meatpacking plant to profit the factory owners. The stockyards' crowded animal pens evoke the workers' cramped, dehumanizing living quarters. As waves of slaughtered animals pass through Packingtown slaughterhouses, so generations of expendable immigrants pass through Packingtown factories before being destroyed by backbreaking work.

CANS OF ROTTEN MEAT   The cans of rotten and diseased meat (which provoked a public outcry upon the novel's publication) represent the capitalist system. Like the shiny cans, capitalism presents an attractive face to immigrants, luring them to the so-called land of opportunity; like the putrid meat inside, capitalism reveals itself to be rotten and corrupt.

THE JUNGLE   The title of Sinclair's novel compares Packingtown to a Darwinian jungle in which living creatures, engaged in a brutal, amoral struggle for survival, must prey on the weak. The title casts the novel as Sinclair's response to the social Darwinist, nineteenth-century philosophers who argued that rewarding strength and oppressing weakness ensures that society will stay strong. In *The Jungle*, Sinclair argues that it is the most morally corrupt—not the strongest—who succeed in a capitalistic system.

IMPORTANT QUOTATIONS FROM *THE JUNGLE*

Here was a population, low-class and mostly foreign, hanging always on the verge of starvation, and dependent for its opportunities of life upon the whim of men every bit as brutal and unscrupulous as the old-time slave drivers; under such circumstances immorality was exactly as inevitable, and as prevalent, as it was under the system of chattel slavery. Things that were quite unspeakable went on there in the packing houses all the time, and were taken for granted by everybody; only they did not show, as in the old slavery times, because there was no difference in color between master and slave.

Location: Chapter 10
Speaker: The narrator
Context: Sinclair compares the lot of girls in Ona's factory, who work as prostitutes for Miss Henderson, to slavery

In this passage, Sinclair foreshadows Ona's rape by Phil Connor, suggesting the factory girls are regularly sexually abused by their employers. Additionally, the last sentence raises a Marxist argument against the capitalistic system, suggesting that capitalism is no less exploitative than slavery or feudalism. The only difference is that capitalism, unlike slavery or feudalism, conceals the true nature of the relationship between worker and factory owner under a veneer of propriety.

[T]he meat would be shoveled into carts, and the man who did the shoveling would not trouble to lift out a rat even when he saw one—there were things that went into the sausage in comparison with which a poisoned rat was a tidbit. There was no place for the men to wash their hands before they ate their dinner, and so they made a practice of washing them in the water that was to be ladled into the sausage. There were the butt-ends of smoked meat, and the scraps of corned beef, and all the odds and ends of the waste of the plants, that would be dumped into old barrels in the cellar and left there. Under the system of rigid economy which the packers enforced, there were some jobs that it only paid to do once in a long time, and among these was the cleaning out of the waste barrels. Every spring they did it; and in the barrels would be dirt and rust and old nails and stale water—and cartload after cartload of it would be taken up and dumped into the hoppers with fresh meat, and sent out to the public's breakfast.

Location: Chapter 14
Speaker: The narrator
Context: Sinclair describes the unsanitary conditions at a meatpacking plant

This passage, one of the novel's most famous and influential, demonstrates why the book caused a public furor upon its publication: Sinclair's lurid, pseudo-naturalistic style drew attention to the revolting filth of the stockyards.

They put him in a place where the snow could not beat in, where the cold could not eat through his bones; they brought him food and drink—why, in the name of heaven, if they must punish him, did they not put his family in jail and leave him outside—why could they find no better way to punish him than to leave three weak women and six helpless children to starve and freeze?

Location: Chapter 16
Speaker: The narrator
Context: Imprisoned after attacking Phil Connor, Jurgis reflects that he is better off than his family because he is sheltered and fed

---

All day long the blazing midsummer sun beat down upon that square mile of abominations: upon tens of thousands of cattle crowded into pens whose wooden floors stank and steamed contagion; upon bare, blistering, cinder-strewn railroad tracks, and huge blocks of dingy meat factories, whose labyrinthine passages defied a breath of fresh air to penetrate them; and there were not merely rivers of hot blood, and carloads of moist flesh, and rendering vats and soap caldrons, glue factories and fertilizer tanks, that smelt like the craters of hell—there were also tons of garbage festering in the sun, and the greasy laundry of the workers hung out to dry, and dining rooms littered with food and black with flies, and toilet rooms that were open sewers.

Location: Chapter 26
Speaker: The narrator
Context: In the inflammatory style of the novel, Sinclair describes the live-and-work facilities of the Packingtown laborers

---

To Jurgis the packers had been equivalent to fate; Ostrinski showed him that they were the Beef Trust. They were a gigantic combination of capital, which had crushed all opposition, and overthrown the laws of the land, and was preying upon the people.

Location: Chapter 29
Speaker: The narrator
Context: Jurgis learns about the evils of capitalism from the socialist Ostrinsky

KING LEAR

William Shakespeare

A king divides Britain between his flattering daughters, who bring ruin to the kingdom.

THE LIFE OF WILLIAM SHAKESPEARE

William Shakespeare, the most influential writer in all of English literature, was born in 1564 to a successful middle-class glove-maker in Stratford-upon-Avon, England. Shakespeare's formal education did not progress beyond grammar school. In 1582, he married an older woman, Anne Hathaway. His union with Anne produced three children. Around 1590, Shakespeare left his family behind and traveled to London to work as an actor and playwright. He quickly earned public and critical acclaim, and eventually became the most popular playwright in England and a part-owner of the Globe Theater. Shakespeare's career bridged the reigns of Elizabeth I (ruled 1558–1603) and James I (ruled 1603–1625), and he was a favorite of both monarchs. James paid Shakespeare's company a great compliment by giving its members the title of King's Men. Shakespeare retired to Stratford a wealthy and renowned man and died in 1616 at the age of fifty-two. At the time of Shakespeare's death, literary luminaries such as Ben Jonson hailed his works as timeless.

Shakespeare's works were collected and printed in various editions in the century following his death, and by the early eighteenth century his reputation as the greatest poet ever to write in English was well established. The unprecedented regard in which Shakespeare's works were held led to a fierce curiosity about his life, but many details of Shakespeare's personal history are unknown or shrouded in mystery. Some people have concluded from this lack of information and from Shakespeare's modest education that Shakespeare's plays were actually written by someone else—Francis Bacon and the Earl of Oxford are the two most popular candidates—but the support for this claim is overwhelmingly circumstantial, and the theory is not taken seriously by many scholars.

Shakespeare is generally thought to be the author of the thirty-eight plays (two of them possibly collaborations) and 154 sonnets that bear his name. The legacy of this body of work is immense. A number of Shakespeare's plays seem to have transcended even the category of brilliance, influencing the course of Western literature and culture.

KING LEAR IN CONTEXT

King Lear, which Shakespeare wrote around 1605, is usually ranked with *Hamlet* as one of Shakespeare's greatest plays. *King Lear* dramatizes events from the eighth century B.C., but the parallel stories of Lear's and Gloucester's sufferings at the hands of their own children reflect anxieties that would have resonated with current events of Shakespeare's day. One event that may have influenced this play is a lawsuit that occurred not long before *King Lear* was written, in which the eldest of three sisters tried to have her elderly father, Sir Brian Annesley, declared insane so that she could take control of his property. Annesley's youngest daughter, Cordell, successfully defended her father against her sister. Another relevant story concerned William Allen, a mayor of London, who divided his wealth among his daughters and subsequently suffered poor treatment at their hands. Finally, *King Lear* relates to the 1603 transfer of power from Elizabeth I to James I. Elizabeth had produced no male heir, and people worried that uncertainty over her successor would lead to a dynastic struggle along the lines of the fifteenth-century Wars of the Roses.

KING LEAR: KEY FACTS

Full Title: The Tragedy of King Lear

Time and place written: England; 1604–1605

Date of first publication: 1623 in First Folio

Genre: Tragedy

Setting (time): Eighth century B.C.

Setting (place): England

Protagonist: King Lear

Antagonist: Goneril, Regan, Edmund

Major conflict: Lear unjustly exiles Cordelia and suffers at the hands of his older daughters; Edmund
tricks his father because he wants land and respect

KING LEAR: PLOT OVERVIEW

Lear, the aging king of Britain, decides to step down from the throne and divide his kingdom evenly
among his three daughters. Before doing this, he puts his daughters through a test, asking each to tell
him how much she loves him. Goneril and Regan, Lear's older daughters, give their father flattering
answers. But Cordelia, Lear's youngest and favorite daughter, remains silent, saying that she has no words
to describe how much she loves her father. Lear flies into a rage and disowns Cordelia. The king of
France, who has courted Cordelia, says that he still wants to marry her even without her land, and she
accompanies him to France without her father's blessing.

Lear quickly learns that he made a bad decision. Goneril and Regan swiftly begin to undermine the
little authority that Lear still holds. Unable to believe that his beloved daughters are betraying him, Lear
slowly goes insane. He flees his daughters' houses to wander on a heath during a great thunderstorm,
accompanied by his Fool and by Kent, a loyal nobleman in disguise.

Meanwhile, an elderly nobleman named Gloucester also experiences family problems. His illegitimate son, Edmund, tricks him into believing that his legitimate son, Edgar, is trying to kill him. Fleeing
the manhunt that his father has set for him, Edgar disguises himself as a crazy beggar and calls himself
"Poor Tom." Like Lear, he heads out onto the heath.

When the loyal Gloucester realizes that Lear's daughters have turned against their father, he decides
to help Lear in spite of the danger. Regan and her husband, Cornwall, discover him helping Lear, accuse
him of treason, blind him, and turn him out to wander the countryside. He ends up being led by his disguised son, Edgar, toward the city of Dover, where Lear has also been brought.

In Dover, a French army lands as part of an invasion led by Cordelia in an effort to save her father.
Edmund apparently becomes romantically entangled with both Goneril and Regan, whose husband,
Albany, is increasingly sympathetic to Lear's cause. Goneril and Edmund conspire to kill Albany.

The despairing Gloucester tries to commit suicide, but Edgar saves him by pulling the strange trick of
leading him off an imaginary cliff. Meanwhile, the English troops reach Dover, and the English, led by
Edmund, defeat the Cordelia-led French. Lear and Cordelia are captured. In the climactic scene, Edgar
duels with and kills Edmund; we learn of the death of Gloucester; Goneril poisons Regan out of jealousy
over Edmund and then kills herself when her treachery is revealed to Albany; Edmund's betrayal of
Cordelia leads to her needless execution in prison; and Lear finally dies out of grief at Cordelia's passing.
Albany, Edgar, and the elderly Kent are left to take care of the country under a cloud of sorrow and
regret.

CHARACTERS IN *KING LEAR*

Albany   The husband of Lear's daughter Goneril. Albany is good at heart, and eventually he denounces
the cruelty of Goneril, Regan, and Cornwall. Yet he is indecisive and obtuse.

Cordelia   Lear's youngest daughter. Cordelia remains loyal to Lear despite his cruelty to her, and is
patient with her brutal sisters. Despite her obvious virtues, Cordelia's reticence makes her motivations
difficult to read.

Cornwall   The husband of Lear's daughter Regan. Cornwall is domineering, cruel, and violent. With his
wife and sister-in-law, Goneril, he persecutes Lear and Gloucester.

Edgar   Gloucester's older, legitimate son. Edgar plays many different roles, from a gullible fool easily
tricked by his brother, to a mad beggar, to an armored champion.

Edmund Gloucester's younger, illegitimate son. Edmund resents his status as a bastard and schemes to usurp Gloucester's title and possessions from Edgar. Almost all of his schemes are successful, and he harms almost everyone around him.

Fool Lear's jester. The fool uses double-talk and seemingly frivolous songs to give Lear important advice.

Gloucester A nobleman loyal to King Lear. Gloucester has one legitimate son, Edgar, and one bastard son, Edmund. Like Lear, Gloucester trusts the wrong child. He is weak and ineffectual in the early acts, but he later proves himself capable of great bravery.

Goneril Lear's ruthless oldest daughter and the wife of the duke of Albany. Goneril is jealous, treacherous, and amoral. She challenges Lear's authority, boldly initiates an affair with Edmund, and wrests military power away from her husband.

Kent A nobleman loyal to King Lear. Kent spends most of the play disguised as "Caius," a peasant, so that he can continue to serve Lear even after Lear banishes him. Kent is extremely loyal, but his blunt outspokenness gets him in trouble.

King Lear The protagonist of the play. Lear, the aging king of Britain, is used to absolute power and flattery, and he does not respond well when people contradict him. At the beginning of the play, Lear prioritizes the appearance of love over actual devotion and wishes to maintain the power of a king while casting off a king's responsibilities. Nevertheless, he inspires loyalty in subjects such as Gloucester, Kent, Cordelia, and Edgar, all of whom risk their lives for him.

Oswald The steward, or chief servant, in Goneril's house. Oswald aids Goneril in her conspiracies.

Regan Lear's middle daughter and the wife of the duke of Cornwall. Like Goneril, Regan is ruthless and aggressive. When they are not egging each other on to further acts of cruelty, Regan and Goneril compete for Edmund.

THEMES IN *KING LEAR*

THE UNLIKELIHOOD OF JUSTICE *King Lear* is a brutal play filled with human cruelty and awful, seemingly meaningless disasters. The play's succession of terrible events makes the characters wonder whether there is any possibility of justice or whether the world is fundamentally indifferent or even hostile to humankind. Gloucester believes "As flies to wanton boys are we to the gods; / They kill us for their sport" (IV.i.37–38). He thinks it is foolish to imagine that some benevolent force cares for humans or is even kind enough to be indifferent to them. Rather, he believes the world is governed by malevolent beings who kill us for fun. In contrast, Edgar believes that "the gods are just," and people get what they deserve (V.iii.169). The play suggests that Edgar's opinion is naïve: the wicked may die in the end, but so do the good.

AUTHORITY VERSUS CHAOS *King Lear* is about political authority as much as it is about family strife. Lear is not only a father but also a king, and when he gives away his authority to the unworthy Goneril and Regan, he delivers not only himself and his family but all of Britain into chaos. As the two wicked sisters indulge their appetites for power, and Edmund begins his ascension, the kingdom descends into civil strife and it is clear Lear has destroyed not only his own authority but all authority in Britain. The stable, hierarchal order that Lear initially represents falls apart, and disorder engulfs the realm.

THE POSSIBILITY OF RECONCILIATION Darkness and unhappiness pervade *King Lear*, but the play's central relationship dramatically embodies true, self-sacrificing love. Rather than despising Lear for banishing her, Cordelia remains devoted, even from afar, and eventually brings an army from a foreign country to rescue her father from his tormentors. Lear learns a lesson in humility and eventually reunites with Cordelia and experiences the balm of her forgiving love. He comes to understand the sincerity and depth of Cordelia's love for him, which makes him understand how gravely he wronged her when he accused her of not loving him. Cordelia's reconciliation with Lear suggests that love can flourish, if only briefly.

SYMBOLS IN *KING LEAR*

THE STORM As Lear wanders on a desolate heath in Act III, a terrible storm rages overhead. The storm is partly a physical, turbulent symbol of Lear's inner turmoil and mounting madness. It also symbolizes the awesome power of nature, which forces the powerless king to recognize his own human frailty and to feel humble for the first time. The storm may also symbolize a divine presence, as if nature itself is angry about the events in the play. Finally, the storm symbolizes Britain's political disarray.

BLINDNESS Gloucester's physical blindness symbolizes the metaphorical blindness of Gloucester and Lear. Both men have loyal children and disloyal children, both are blind to the truth, and both end up banishing the loyal children and making the wicked children their heirs. Only when Gloucester has lost the use of his eyes and Lear has gone mad does each understand his error.

IMPORTANT QUOTATIONS FROM *KING LEAR*

> *Thou, nature, art my goddess; to thy law*
> *My services are bound. Wherefore should I*
> *Stand in the plague of custom, and permit*
> *The curiosity of nations to deprive me,*
> *For that I am some twelve or fourteen moonshines*
> *Lag of a brother? Why bastard? wherefore base?*
> *…*
> *Legitimate Edgar, I must have your land.*
> *Our father's love is to the bastard Edmund*
> *As to the legitimate. Fine word—"legitimate"!*
> *Well, my legitimate, if this letter speed,*
> *And my invention thrive, Edmund the base*
> *Shall top the legitimate. I grow; I prosper.*
> *Now, gods, stand up for bastards!*

Location: I.ii.1–22
Speaker: Edmund
Context: Edmund is about to trick his father into believing that Edgar is plotting against him

Deprived by his bastard birth of the respect and rank that he believes are rightfully his, Edmund focuses his entire existence on raising himself up by his bootstraps, forging personal prosperity by betraying and lying to his relatives. The repeated use of the epithet "legitimate" in this passage reveals Edmund's obsession with his brother's enviable status as their father's rightful heir. Edmund characterizes the social order as a "plague of custom" that he refuses to respect, invoking "nature" as an unregulated, anarchic place where a person of low birth could achieve his goals. He wants recognition more than anything else—perhaps, it is suggested later, because of the familial love that has been denied him.

> *As flies to wanton boys are we to the gods;*
> *They kill us for their sport.*

Location: IV.i.37–38
Speaker: Earl of Gloucester
Context: Cornwall and Regan have gouged out Gloucester's eyes

Gloucester wanders on the heath, gripped by profound despair. He voices one of the play's key themes: the question of whether justice exists in the universe. Gloucester believes that it does not. Even a godless universe would be better than what he believes exists: a universe ruled by capricious, cruel beings who reward cruelty and enjoy the sight of suffering humans. In many ways, the events of the play bear out

Gloucester's understanding of the world, as the good die along with the wicked, and no reason is offered for the unbearable suffering of the characters.

Unhappy that I am, I cannot heave
My heart into my mouth. I love your majesty
According to my bond; no more nor less.

Location: I.i.90–92
Speaker: Cordelia
Context: Lear has asked his daughters to tell him how much they love him before he divides his kingdom among them

---

O, reason not the need! Our basest beggars
Are in the poorest thing superfluous.
Allow not nature more than nature needs,
Man's life's as cheap as beast's.. . . .
…
You heavens, give me that patience, patience I need!
…
If it be you that stir these daughters' hearts
Against their father, fool me not so much
To bear it tamely; touch me with noble anger,
And let not women's weapons, water-drops,
Stain my man's cheeks! No, you unnatural hags,
…
No, I'll not weep.
I have full cause of weeping, but this heart
Shall break into a hundred thousand flaws,
Or ere I'll weep. O fool, I shall go mad!

Location: II.iv.259–281
Speaker: King Lear
Context: The cruelties of his daughters have shattered Lear, who rages at Goneril and Regan

---

Howl, howl, howl, howl! O, you are men of stones:
Had I your tongues and eyes, I'd use them so
That heaven's vault should crack. She's gone forever!
I know when one is dead, and when one lives;
She's dead as earth.

Location: V.iii.256–260
Speaker: King Lear
Context: Lear emerges from prison carrying Cordelia's body

THE LAST OF THE MOHICANS

James Fenimore Cooper

During the French and Indian War on the wild frontier, a supremely competent white woodsman joins forces with the last two Mohican Indians to save a group of British colonists from the Huron Indians.

THE LIFE OF JAMES FENIMORE COOPER

James Fenimore Cooper was one of the first popular American novelists. Born in 1789, Cooper grew up in present-day Cooperstown, New York, a frontier settlement that he later dramatized in his novels. Expelled from Yale for playing pranks, Cooper was forced by his father to join the Navy. According to legend, he began writing on a whim: frustrated with a popular English novel that he was reading aloud to his wife, he tossed the book aside, exclaiming, "I could write you a better book myself!" He lived up to his claim: his second novel, *The Spy* (1821), was a popular success.

In 1826, Cooper moved to Europe and published *The Last of the Mohicans*, widely considered his best work. It was in Europe over the next seven years that he wrote many of his most memorable stories—high-spirited, often sentimental adventures that take place on the American frontier. Over the rest of his life, Cooper attracted an enormous readership on both sides of the Atlantic, attaining a popularity rivaled only by that of the Scottish historical novelist Sir Walter Scott. At the time of his death in 1851, Cooper was one of the worlds' most famous writers.

THE LAST OF THE MOHICANS IN CONTEXT

The Last of the Mohicans takes place on the American frontier in 1757 during the French and Indian War, in which France (aided by Native American allies) and England battled for control of the North American colonies. Many of the incidents dramatized in the novel, such as the massacre of British soldiers by Huron Indians, are embellished accounts of historical events. Several characters, General Montcalm in particular, are based on historical figures. In grounding the adventures of *The Last of the Mohicans* in history, Cooper followed the example of many of his contemporaries, including Sir Walter Scott.

For Europeans, the eighteenth-century American frontier was uncharted territory, wild land without government or civilization. In Cooper's romanticized vision, this uncontrolled wilderness inspired unbridled desires, such as Uncas and Cora's liaison, and provided an appropriate backdrop for outbreaks of violence.

Over the last 150 years, Cooper's reputation has fluctuated wildly. He was admired by Victor Hugo and D. H. Lawrence, but Mark Twain considered him a national embarrassment because of his stylistic excesses, inaccuracies, and sentimental scenes. Indeed, *The Last of the Mohicans* tells an implausible story in a style often considered overwrought by modern readers. Whatever its literary merit, Cooper's work remains important as a portrait of frontier life that explores the tensions between two races and cultures poised on opposite sides of a shrinking frontier.

The Last of the Mohicans is the best known of the five "Leatherstocking Tales" that feature Cooper's famous character, the heroic woodsman-scout Natty Bumppo, alias Hawkeye. The others are *The Pioneers* (1823), *The Prairie* (1827), *The Pathfinder* (1840), and *The Deerslayer* (1841).

THE LAST OF THE MOHICANS: KEY FACTS

Full title: The Last of the Mohicans: A Narrative of 1757

Time and place written: 1826; Europe

Date of publication: 1826

Publisher: Carey & Lea of Philadelphia

Type of work: Novel

Genre: Adventure novel; frontier romance

Language: English

Setting (time): Late July to mid-August 1757, during the French and Indian War

Setting (place): The wilds of the American frontier in present-day upstate New York

Tense: Past

Tone: Ornate, solemn, sentimental, occasionally poetic

Narrator: Anonymous, third-person narrator

Point of view: The narrator's

Protagonist: Hawkeye

Antagonist: Magua; the Huron Indians; the French; the wild frontier

THE LAST OF THE MOHICANS: PLOT OVERVIEW

In the late 1750s, the wild forest frontier of western New York is in the grips of the French and Indian War. Fort William Henry, a British outpost commanded by Colonel Munro, has been attacked by the French. Munro's daughters Alice and Cora, escorted by Major Duncan Heyward, set out from nearby Fort Edward to visit their father. The group, soon joined by Calvinist religious singer David Gamut, is guided through the dangerous forest by an Indian named Magua. They encounter Natty Bumppo, a white scout who goes by the name Hawkeye, and his two companions, Chingachgook and his son Uncas, the only surviving members of the once great Mohican tribe. Hawkeye says that Magua is a member of the untrustworthy Huron tribe and has betrayed the group by leading them in the wrong direction. Magua escapes before the Mohicans can capture him.

Hawkeye and the Mohicans lead the group to safety in a cave near a waterfall, but their camp is attacked by Hurons early the next morning. Alice, Cora, Heyward, and Gamut are captured; Hawkeye and the Mohicans manage to escape down the river. When Heyward tries to entice Magua to switch sides and help the British, Magua reveals that he seeks revenge on Colonel Munro for past humiliations and proposes to free Alice if he can marry Cora. Cora, who has developed feelings for Uncas, angrily refuses. Suddenly, Hawkeye and the Mohicans burst onto the scene, rescuing the captives and killing every Huron but Magua, who escapes. After a harrowing journey punctuated by Indian attacks, the group reaches Fort William Henry. They sneak past the French army laying siege to the fort, and Cora and Alice reunite with their father.

A few days later, Munro learns that he will receive no reinforcements for the fort and will have to surrender. He reveals to Heyward that Cora's mother was part "Negro," which explains Cora's dark complexion and raven hair. Munro accuses Heyward of racism because he prefers blond Alice to dark Cora. As the British troops withdraw from Fort William Henry, Indian allies of the French attack the vulnerable retreating soldiers. In the chaos of slaughter, Magua recaptures Cora, Alice, and Gamut, and escapes with them into the forest.

Three days later, Heyward, Hawkeye, Munro, and the Mohicans discover Magua's trail and begin their pursuit. Gamut reappears with news that Alice is with the Hurons, and Cora has been sent to the Delaware Indians. Through trickery and disguises, the group manages to rescue Alice. Heyward confesses his love for her. Magua convinces the Delawares that Hawkeye and his companions are their enemies. Uncas reveals that he is the descendant of the Delaware sage Tamenund and demands the release of all his friends except Cora, whom he concedes to Magua. Magua drags Cora away. In the ensuing chase and battle, Magua and the Hurons suffer painful defeat, but Cora is killed by a rogue Huron. As Uncas attacks Cora's killer, Magua stabs Uncas in the back. To escape, Magua leaps from a precipice but falls short of the other side. As Magua holds on to a shrub for his life, Hawkeye shoots him, and Magua plummets to his death.

The Delawares bury Cora and Uncas with ritual chants. Tamenund sorrowfully declares that he has lived to see the last warrior of the noble Mohicans.

CHARACTERS IN *THE LAST OF THE MOHICANS*

THE BRITISH AND THE AMERICANS

Hawkeye The novel's frontier hero; a woodsman, hunter, and scout. Hawkeye's famed marksmanship and Killdeer, his rifle, have earned him the nickname La Longue Carabine ("Long Rifle"). Born Natty Bumppo, Hawkeye has no Indian blood but has adopted Indian culture and lifestyle. Excluded from the novel's love plots, Hawkeye is a supremely competent lone wanderer.

Major Duncan Heyward A young Southern colonist in the British army. Courageous, noble, and well-intentioned, Heyward is unfamiliar with Indian relations and feels out of place in the forest frontier.

David Gamut A young American Calvinist proselytizing through song on the frontier. Hawkeye initially makes fun of Gamut for being so absurdly unsuited for the wilderness, but Gamut matures into a helpful ally.

Colonel Munro Commander of the British forces at Fort William Henry; Cora and Alice's father. A massive and powerful man, Munro has become withdrawn and ineffectual in the war. Munro met his first wife, Cora's "Negro" mother, in the West Indies. After her death he married his Scottish childhood sweetheart, Alice's mother.

Alice Munro Munro's younger daughter and Cora's half-sister. Fair, girlish, and faint of heart, Alice is a foil for the dark and fiery Cora. Alice and Heyward are in love.

Cora Munro Munro's elder daughter. A solemn, poised girl, Cora inherits her dark complexion from her mother. She cautiously returns Uncas's love, but suffers the tragic fate of the sentimental heroine.

General Webb Commander of the British forces at Fort Edward.

THE INDIANS

Chingachgook Uncas's father and Hawkeye's longtime friend; one of two surviving Mohican Indians. Chingachgook is also known as Le Gros Serpent ("Great Snake") for his crafty intelligence.

Magua The novel's villain; a cunning Huron Indian nicknamed Le Renard Subtil ("Subtle Fox"). A former Huron chief, Magua was exiled from his tribe for alcoholism. He carries a grudge against Colonel Munro, who humiliated him by whipping him for drunkenness.

Tamenund The Delaware Indian sage. Wise and revered, Tamenund has outlived three generations of warriors.

Uncas Chingachgook's son; the last Mohican Indian. A noble, proud, self-possessed young man, Uncas falls in love with Cora Munro, a woman of mixed race. Hawkeye mentors Uncas and teaches him about leadership.

THE FRENCH

General Montcalm Commander of the French forces; also known as Marquis Louis Joseph de Saint-Veran. Montcalm enlists the help of Indian tribes to navigate the unfamiliar forest terrain in the war against their common enemy, the British.

THEMES IN *THE LAST OF THE MOHICANS*

INTERRACIAL RELATIONSHIPS *The Last of the Mohicans* is deeply concerned with race and the difficulty of overcoming racial divides. Cooper admires the longtime, genuine friendship between Hawkeye, a white man, and Chingachgook, a Mohican Indian. Their friendship enables them to help Heyward and other major characters. On the other hand, though, all of the novel's interracial romances are doomed: Cora and Uncas's love ends in tragedy, Cora's West Indian mother dies soon after her marriage to Munro, and the union between Cora and Magua is portrayed as unnatural. Cooper also suggests that Cora inherited her interracial desire from her parents.

THE TREACHERY OF NATURE   In the novel's opening paragraphs, Cooper describes how the unpredictable terrain of the colonies complicates warfare, especially for those used to the flat European battlefields. The forbidding landscape favors the Indians, who know the land, and their allies, the French. European skills are useless in the forest: Gamut's Calvinism appears ridiculous in the wilderness.

The characters' relationships with nature correspond to their other qualities. The heroic Hawkeye respects the land, and Major Heyward establishes his incompetence in misunderstanding the natural world. Magua uses the treacherous features of the landscape to carry out his villainy: he hides women in caves, crouches behind boulders, and jumps over abysses.

RELIGION IN THE WILDERNESS   Cooper uses the character of David Gamut to explore the role of religion in the wild. Untouched by Western civilization, the American frontier appears as a blank slate to Europeans such as Gamut, whose aggressive proselytizing is one of the manifestations of Western encroachment on the New World. Hawkeye's frequent mockery of Gamut's psalmody provides the novel's comic relief. Coming from the novel's hero, this mockery also suggests that institutional religion has no place in the wilderness.

As a Calvinist, Gamut believes in predestination—the idea that a human being's fate is determined at birth by God. This fatalism contrasts with Hawkeye's pragmatism. Hawkeye adapts to his surroundings and carries out improbable rescue missions. Ultimately, Gamut becomes a helpful and committed ally when he starts believing in his ability to shape his future. Cooper's exploration of Calvinism set the stage for later American writers: for example, Herman Melville's tragic hero Ahab believes in predestination.

SYMBOLS IN *THE LAST OF THE MOHICANS*

HAWKEYE   Hawkeye—white by blood, Indian by habit—symbolizes the blending of European and Indian cultures, a combination that enables his success. Through Hawkeye, Cooper challenges the notion that the two cultures are separated by essential differences.

"THE LAST OF THE MOHICANS"   Uncas, "the last of the Mohicans," symbolizes the death of Indian culture at the hands of the encroaching European civilization. The title foreshadows Uncas's tragic death at the end of the novel. The phrase also alludes to a specific historical event: the forced removal of Native Americans from the eastern part of the United States, ordered by President Andrew Jackson in the 1830s.

IMPORTANT QUOTATIONS FROM *THE LAST OF THE MOHICANS*

I am not a prejudiced man, nor one who vaunts himself on his natural privileges, though the worst enemy I have on earth, and he is an Iroquois, daren't deny that I am genuine white.

Location: Chapter III
Speaker: Hawkeye
Context: Hawkeye explains to Chingachgook how a white man like himself knows so much about Indians

Although he has strong friendships with many Indians, Hawkeye reveals his prejudices when he implies that he would injure a man who accused him of having Indian blood. The adjective "genuine" suggests sexual purity, foreshadowing the novel's later exploration of interracial liaisons.

The pale-faces are masters of the earth, and the time of the red-men has not yet come again. My day has been too long.

Location: Chapter XXXIII
Speaker: Tamenund
Context: Tamenund laments Uncas's death

For Tamenund, who has lived through three generations of Delaware warriors and has witnessed the death of the last Mohican, survival has become a burden. Tamenund suggests that tides of history will turn: although white men dominate the land, Indians will eventually rise to power again.

There is reason in an Indian, though nature has made him with a red skin! . . . I am no scholar, and I care not who knows it; but judging from what I have seen, at deer chases and squirrel hunts, of the sparks below, I should think a rifle in the hands of their grandfathers was not so dangerous as a hickory bow and a good flint-head might be, if drawn with Indian judgment, and sent by an Indian eye.

Location: Chapter III
Speaker: Hawkeye
Context: With a mixture of respect and racism, Hawkeye responds to Chingachgook's comment that Indians and white men should be viewed equally

---

A Mingo is a Mingo, and God having made him so, neither the Mohawks nor any other tribe can alter him.

Location: Chapter IV
Speaker: Hawkeye
Context: As soon as Hawkeye learns that Magua is a Huron Indian, he pronounces Magua a bad man

---

The Hurons love their friends the Delawares. . . . . Why should they not? They are colored by the same sun, and their just men will hunt in the same grounds after death. The redskins should be friends, and look with open eyes on the white men.

Location: Chapter XXVIII
Speaker: Magua
Context: Magua tries to incite the Delaware council to help him combat Hawkeye and his friends

LES MISÉRABLES

Victor Hugo

A hardened criminal finds redemption, adopts an orphan, flees a monomaniacal cop, saves lives, encounters misunderstandings and cruelties of all kinds, and finally dies a happy man.

THE LIFE OF VICTOR HUGO

Victor Hugo was born in 1802 in the French town of Besançon. His father was a general in Napoléon's army. At the age of eleven, Hugo went to live with his mother in Paris, where he became infatuated with books and literature.

Hugo wrote prolifically in all genres. He first found critical and commercial successes with his plays. France's 1830 July Revolution inspired Hugo, and he began producing a steady stream of work, most notably the novel *The Hunchback of Notre-Dame* (1831). Hugo also began to cultivate his interest in politics and was elected to France's National Assembly after the revolution of 1848. As Hugo grew older, his politics became increasingly leftist, and he was forced to flee France in 1851 because of his opposition to the monarch Louis Napoléon. Hugo remained in exile until 1870, when he returned to his home country as a national hero. He continued to write until his death in 1885. He was buried with every conceivable honor in one of the grandest funerals in modern French history.

Hugo remains one of the most popular and respected authors in French literature. His writings were cultural fixtures throughout the nineteenth century, and he quickly emerged as one of the leaders of the Romantic movement in literature. Hugo also developed his own brand of imaginative realism, a literary style that combines realistic elements with exaggerated symbolism and allegorical characters. Political concerns dominate much of Hugo's writing. He used his work to champion causes such as universal suffrage and free education. Hugo believed that the modern writer had a mission to defend the less fortunate members of society.

LES MISÉRABLES IN CONTEXT

Hugo began writing *Les Misérables* twenty years before its eventual publication in 1862. The novel is primarily a great humanitarian work that encourages compassion and hope in the face of adversity and injustice. It is also a historical novel of great scope and analysis that provides a detailed picture of nineteenth-century French politics and society. By coupling his story of redemption with a meticulous documentation of the injustices of France's recent past, Hugo hoped *Les Misérables* would encourage a more progressive and democratic future. He wrote *Les Misérables* with nothing less than a literary and political revolution in mind.

Les Misérables emphasizes the three major predicaments of the nineteenth century. Each of the three major characters in the novel symbolizes one of these predicaments: Jean Valjean represents the degradation of men in the proletariat, Fantine represents the subjection of women through hunger, and Cosette represents the destruction of the child by darkness.

LES MISÉRABLES: KEY FACTS

Time and place written: 1845–1862; Paris and the Channel Islands	
Date of first publication: 1862	
Publisher: Pagnerre	
Type of work: Novel	
Genre: Epic novel; historical novel; romance	
Language: French	
Setting (time): 1789–1832	

Setting (place): France; primarily the cities of Arras, Digne, Montreuil-sur-mer, Montfermeil, Paris, and Toulon

Tense: Past

Tone: Empathetic, outspoken

Narrator: Anonymous, omniscient narrator in the third person

Point of view: The narrator's

Protagonist: Jean Valjean

Antagonist: Javert

LES MISÉRABLES: PLOT OVERVIEW

The convict Jean Valjean is released from a French prison after serving nineteen years for stealing a loaf of bread and for subsequent attempts to escape from prison. Valjean arrives at the town of Digne. Desperate to find shelter, he knocks on the door of M. Myriel, the kindly bishop of Digne. Myriel treats Valjean with kindness, but Valjean repays the bishop by stealing his silverware. When the police arrest Valjean, Myriel covers for him, claiming that the silverware was a gift. The authorities release Valjean and Myriel makes him promise to become an honest man. Eager to fulfill his promise, Valjean enters the town of Montreuil-sur-mer under the assumed name Madeleine. There he invents an ingenious manufacturing process that brings the town prosperity. Valjean eventually becomes the town's mayor.

Fantine, a young woman from Montreuil, lives in Paris. She falls in love with Tholomyès, a wealthy student who gets her pregnant and then abandons her. Fantine returns to her home village with her daughter, Cosette. On the way to Montreuil, Fantine realizes that she will never be able to find work if the townspeople know she has an illegitimate child. In the town of Montfermeil, she meets the Thénardiers, the family that runs the local inn. They agree to look after Cosette as long as Fantine sends them a monthly allowance.

In Montreuil, Fantine finds work in Madeleine's factory. Fantine's coworkers find out about Cosette, and Fantine is fired. The Thénardiers demand more money to support Cosette, and Fantine resorts to prostitution to make ends meet. One night, Javert, Montreuil's police chief, arrests Fantine. She is to be sent to prison, but Valjean intervenes. Fantine has fallen ill and longs to see Cosette. Valjean promises to send for her. First he must contend with Javert, who has discovered his criminal past. Javert comes to Fantine's bedside and arrests Valjean. Fantine dies from the shock.

After a few years, Valjean escapes from prison and heads to Montfermeil, where he buys Cosette from the Thénardiers. The Thénardiers turn out to be a family of scoundrels who abuse Cosette and spoil their own two daughters, Eponine and Azelma. Valjean and Cosette move to a run-down part of Paris. Javert discovers their hideout, and they are forced to flee. They find refuge in a convent, where Cosette attends school and Valjean works as a gardener.

Marius Pontmercy is a young man who lives with his wealthy grandfather, M. Gillenormand. Because of political differences within the family, Marius has never met his father, Georges Pontmercy. After his father dies, however, Marius learns more about him and comes to admire his democratic politics. Angry with his grandfather, Marius moves out of Gillenormand's house and lives as a poor law student. He associates with a group of radical students, the Friends of the ABC, who are led by the charismatic Enjolras. One day, Marius sees Cosette at a public park and instantly falls in love with her. The protective Valjean does his utmost to prevent Cosette and Marius from meeting. Their paths cross once again, however, when Valjean makes a charitable visit to Marius's poor neighbors, the Jondrettes. The Jondrettes are in fact the Thénardiers, who have lost their inn and moved to Paris under an assumed name. After Valjean leaves, Thénardier announces a plan to rob Valjean when he returns. Marius alerts the local police inspector, who turns out to be Javert. The ambush is foiled and the Thénardiers are arrested. Valjean escapes before Javert can identify him.

Thénardier's daughter Eponine, who is in love with Marius, helps Marius find Cosette. Marius and Cosette declare their love for each other, but Valjean, worried that he will lose Cosette and unnerved by political unrest in the city, announces that he and Cosette are moving to England. In desperation, Marius runs to his grandfather to ask permission to marry Cosette. Their meeting ends in a bitter argument. Marius goes back and finds that Cosette and Valjean have disappeared. Heartbroken, he decides to join his radical friends, who have started a political uprising. Armed with two pistols, Marius heads for the barricades.

The uprising seems doomed, but Marius and his fellow students stand their ground and vow to fight for freedom and democracy. The students discover Javert among their ranks. Enjolras, realizing that he is a spy, ties him up. As the army attacks against the students, Eponine throws herself in front of a rifle to save Marius's life. As Eponine dies in Marius's arms, she hands him a letter from Cosette. Marius quickly scribbles a reply and orders a boy, Gavroche, to deliver it to Cosette.

Valjean intercepts the note and sets out to save Marius's life. He arrives at the barricade and volunteers to execute Javert. Then Valjean secretly lets Javert go free. As the army storms the barricade, Valjean grabs the wounded Marius and flees through the sewers. When Valjean emerges hours later, Javert immediately arrests him. Valjean begs Javert to let him take the dying Marius to his grandfather. Javert feels torn between his duty to his profession and the debt he owes Valjean for saving his life. Ultimately, he lets Valjean go and throws himself into the river, where he drowns.

Marius makes a full recovery and is reconciled with Gillenormand, who consents to Marius and Cosette's marriage. Their wedding is a happy one, marred only when Valjean confesses his criminal past to Marius. Alarmed by this revelation and unaware that it was Valjean who saved his life at the barricades, Marius tries to prevent Cosette from having contact with Valjean. Lonely and depressed, Valjean takes to his bed and awaits his death. Marius eventually finds out that Valjean saved his life. Marius and Cosette rush to Valjean's side just in time for a final reconciliation. Happy to be reunited with his adopted daughter, Valjean dies in peace.

CHARACTERS IN *LES MISÉRABLES*

Azelma The Thénardiers' younger daughter.

Champmathieu A poor, uneducated man. Champmathieu resembles Valjean so closely that he is identified, tried, and almost convicted as Valjean. Champmathieu is too dim-witted to defend himself successfully, revealing the callousness of the French justice system.

Cosette Fantine's daughter. Despite spending her childhood as a servant for the abusive Thénardiers, Cosette is not hard or cynical. Under the care of Valjean and the nuns of Petit-Picpus, she blossoms into a beautiful, educated young woman. Cosette is innocent and docile, but she is also intelligent and brave, as her participation in Valjean's many escapes from the law proves.

Enjolras A radical student revolutionary. Enjolras leads the Friends of the ABC. A wild and beautiful man, he is one of the leaders of the insurrection at the barricade.

Fantine A working-class girl. Fantine's innocent affair leaves her pregnant and abandoned. Although she is frail, she makes a Herculean effort to feed herself and her daughter, Cosette. Fantine represents the destruction that nineteenth-century French society wreaks on the less fortunate.

Fauchelevent A critic of Valjean's while Valjean is the mayor of Montreuil-sur-mer. Fauchelevent becomes indebted to Valjean when Valjean saves him from a carriage accident, and returns the favor years later by hiding Valjean and Cosette in a convent.

Gavroche The Thénardiers' oldest son. Gavroche is kicked out of the house at an early age and becomes a Parisian street urchin. He is a happy-go-lucky child who enjoys the small pleasures of life and demonstrates unusual generosity. He is also fierce and brave.

M. Gillenormand Marius's ninety-year-old maternal grandfather. A devout monarchist, Gillenormand rejects the French Revolution and Napoléon. Gillenormand truly loves his grandson.

Javert A police inspector. Javert believes in law and order and will stop at nothing to enforce France's harsh penal codes. A pitiless man, he performs his work with such passion that he takes on a nearly animal quality when he is on the chase. Javert sees Valjean's escapes and prosperity as an affront to justice. But in the end, Javert is not sure that Valjean deserves to be punished. This sudden recognition of ambiguity calls Javert's entire life into question.

M. Mabeuf A churchwarden in Paris. Mabeuf tells Marius the truth about his father and later dies a heroic death on the barricade.

M. Myriel The bishop of Digne. M. Myriel's great kindness and charity have made him popular throughout his parish. He passes on these same qualities to Valjean.

Patron-Minette A Parisian crime ring so close-knit that its four members—Montparnasse, Babet, Claquesous, and Gueulemer—are described as four heads of the same violent beast.

Petit-Gervais A small boy whom Valjean robs shortly after leaving Digne.

Colonel Georges Pontmercy An officer in Napoléon's army and Marius's father.

Marius Pontmercy The son of Georges Pontmercy, a colonel in Napoléon's army. An innocent young man, Marius is nonetheless capable of great things and manages both to fight on the barricades and successfully court the love of his life, Cosette.

Eponine Thénardier The Thénardiers' eldest daughter. Eponine is eventually redeemed by her love for Marius. She proves that no one is beyond redemption, and she emerges as one of the novel's most tragic and heroic figures.

M. Thénardier A cruel, money-obsessed man. Thénardier is Cosette's keeper and tormentor. He robs, commits fraud, and murders.

Mme. Thénardier M. Thénardier's wife. Mme. Thénardier is just as evil as her husband and takes special pleasure in abusing Cosette. In later years, she becomes her husband's most devoted accomplice.

Felix Tholomyès Fantine's lover in Paris. Tholomyès is a wealthy student who gets Fantine pregnant and then abandons her as a joke.

Jean Valjean Cosette's adopted father. Valjean is an ex-convict who leaves behind a life of hatred and deceit. He loves his adopted daughter and helps people even when it means risking his own life. Valjean combines a convict's street smarts with idealism and compassion. His life is a quest for redemption.

THEMES IN *LES MISÉRABLES*

THE IMPORTANCE OF LOVE AND COMPASSION In *Les Misérables*, Hugo asserts that love and compassion are the most important qualities in life. Valjean's transformation from a hardened criminal into a heroic philanthropist epitomizes Hugo's opinions about love, for it is only by learning to love others that Valjean improves himself. Hugo makes it clear that loving others, while difficult, is not always a thankless task. Love begets love, and compassion begets compassion. Valjean rescues Fauchelevent, and years later, Fauchelevent rescues Valjean and Cosette. Valjean treats Javert with compassion, sparing his life, and later Javert treats Valjean with compassion. In Hugo's novel, love and compassion are nearly infectious. After M. Myriel transforms Valjean with acts of trust and affection, Valjean treats Cosette compassionately, rescuing her from the cruel Thénardiers.

SOCIAL INJUSTICE IN NINETEENTH-CENTURY FRANCE Hugo condemns the unjust, class-based social system of nineteenth-century France. Over and over, he demonstrates how society's structure turns good people into beggars and criminals. He conveys much of his message through his character Fantine, condemning the hypocrisy of a society that fails to educate girls and ostracizes women like Fantine while winking at the behavior of promiscuous, irresponsible men. After Fantine's aristocratic lover abandons her, her reputation is indelibly soiled by the fact that she has an illegitimate child. Her lack of education dooms her—the scribe to whom Fantine dictates her letters reveals her secret to the whole town. Finally, Fantine must resort to prostitution.

Hugo also condemns the French criminal-justice system, which transforms a simple bread thief like Valjean into a career criminal. Valjean's nineteen years on the chain gang only make him sneaky and vicious—a result that contrasts sharply with the effect of Myriel's kindness, which sets Valjean on the right path almost overnight. The justice system is not only ineffective, it is irrational. Bread thieves receive heavy sentences. Real criminals like Patron-Minette rob and murder on a grand scale, but they receive only short sentences.

THE FUTILITY OF VIOLENT REVOLUTION In *Les Misérables*, Hugo traces the social impact of the revolutions and executions that took place in late eighteenth- and early nineteenth-century

France. Though Hugo's sympathies are with republican movements rather than with the monarchy, he criticizes all of the regimes since the French Revolution of 1789 for their inability to make a just society and eliminate France's rigid class system. Hugo describes the battle at the barricade as both heroic and futile—a few soldiers are killed, but the insurgents are slaughtered without achieving anything. The revolution that Hugo champions is an intangible, moral one, in which the old system of greed and corruption is replaced by one of compassion. Although both Napoléon and the students at the barricade come closer to espousing these values than the French monarchs do, no amount of violence, however well meant, can enforce compassion.

SYMBOLS IN *LES MISÉRABLES*

MYRIEL'S SILVER CANDLESTICKS M. Myriel's candlesticks symbolize compassion. At the beginning of the novel, Hugo uses the contrast between light and darkness to underscore the differences between Myriel, an upstanding citizen, and Valjean, a dark, brooding man. When Myriel gives Valjean his silver candlesticks, he is literally passing on this light as he tells Valjean he must promise to become an honest man. Subsequently, the candlesticks reappear frequently to remind Valjean of his duty. When Valjean dies, the candlesticks shine brightly across his face, a symbolic affirmation that he has attained his goal of love and compassion.

SNAKES, INSECTS, AND BIRDS Hugo uses animal imagery to accentuate qualities of good and evil. He refers to Cosette as a lark, Gavroche as a fly, and the Thénardiers as snakes and beetles.

IMPORTANT QUOTATIONS FROM *LES MISÉRABLES*

[T]*he poor little despairing thing could not help crying: "Oh my God! Oh God!"*
   At that moment she suddenly felt that the weight of the bucket was gone. A hand, which seemed enormous to her, had just caught the handle, and was carrying it easily.. . . .

. . .
   The child was not afraid.

Location: Book III of "Cosette"
Speaker: The narrator
Context: Mme. Thénardier tells Cosette to fetch a pail of water from the forest

In describing Cosette's plight, Hugo foregoes realism in favor of prose that could come from a ghost story. The melodramatic language and imagery underscores the nightmarish quality of Cosette's life with the Thénardiers. The forest is dark, frightening, and seemingly never-ending—a metaphor for Cosette's life as a near-slave at the inn. This haunted setting also sets the stage for Valjean's entrance, which Hugo describes as if it is the descent of God. Immediately after Cosette prays to God, Valjean appears, as if he is God or a saint. He has been a decent man since his conversion at Digne, but now he appears almost angelic. Hugo emphasizes Valjean's Christlike aspect by setting this scene on Christmas Eve.

To owe life to a malefactor . . . to be, in spite of himself, on a level with a fugitive from justice . . . to betray society in order to be true to his own conscience; that all these absurdities . . . should accumulate on himself—this is what prostrated him.

Location: Book IV of "Jean Valjean"
Speaker: The narrator
Context: Javert struggles with the knowledge that a criminal has saved him

Valjean's compassion shatters Javert's worldview. Torn between his inflexible commitment to enforce the letter of the law and his personal debt to Valjean, Javert becomes profoundly confused. He is completely disarmed by Valjean's unconditional love and finds it impossible to continue carrying out his duty with honor. Javert has always believed that the letter of the law is infallible, but now he finds that a literal interpretation of the law contradicts the spirit of the law. By the letter of the law, Valjean is a criminal, but by the spirit of the law, he is a saint. Javert kills himself—but not because he feels guilty or remorseful about the way he has lived his life. He kills himself because to be true to his conscience and spare Valjean would be "to betray society"—an option Javert cannot accept.

[Valjean] strained his eyes in the distance and called out . . . "Petit Gervais! . . ." His cries died away into the mist, without even awaking an echo.. . . [H]is knees suddenly bent under him, as if an invisible power suddenly overwhelmed him with the weight of his bad conscience; he fell exhausted . . . and cried out, "I'm such a miserable man!"

Location: Book II of "Fantine"
Speaker: The narrator
Context: Valjean leaves Myriel's house and realizes how wretched he is

---

"Here, I am going to write something to show you."
. . . [S]he wrote on a sheet of blank paper.. . . ."The cops are here."

Location: Book VIII of "Marius"
Speaker: The narrator
Context: Eponine tries to impress Marius by showing him she can write, choosing to jot down a phrase that is familiar in her household

---

[Valjean] had fallen back, the light from the candlesticks fell across him; his white face looked up toward heaven, he let Cosette and Marius cover his hands with kisses; he was dead.

Location: Book IX of "Jean Valjean"
Speaker: The narrator
Context: Valjean dies a happy death

LIGHT IN AUGUST

William Faulkner

A half-black man kills his white lover, a crime for which he is eventually killed and castrated.

THE LIFE OF WILLIAM FAULKNER

William Faulkner was born in New Albany, Mississippi, on September 25, 1897, the oldest of four sons in a southern family descended from the great Civil War soldier, statesman, and railroad builder Colonel William Clark Falkner. A number of his ancestors were involved in the Mexican-American War, the Civil War, and the Reconstruction, and were part of the local railroad industry and political scene. Faulkner showed signs of artistic talent from a young age, but became bored with his classes and never finished high school.

Faulkner grew up in the town of Oxford, Mississippi, and eventually returned there in his later years and purchased his famous estate, Rowan Oak. Oxford and the surrounding area were Faulkner's inspiration for the fictional Yoknapatawpha County, Mississippi, and its town of Jefferson. These locales became the setting for a number of his works. Faulkner's "Yoknapatawpha novels" include *The Sound and the Fury* (1929), *As I Lay Dying* (1930), *Light in August* (1932), *Absalom, Absalom!* (1936), *The Hamlet* (1940), and *Go Down, Moses* (1942), and they feature some of the same characters and locations.

Faulkner was particularly interested in the decline of the Deep South after the Civil War. Many of his novels explore the deterioration of the Southern aristocracy after the destruction of its wealth and way of life during the Civil War and Reconstruction. Faulkner populates Yoknapatawpha County with the skeletons of old mansions and the ghosts of great men, patriarchs and generals from the past whose aristocratic families fail to live up to their family legacies. These families try to cling to old Southern values, codes, and myths that are corrupted and out of place in the reality of the modern world. The families in Faulkner's novels are populated by failed sons, disgraced daughters, and smoldering resentments between whites and blacks.

Faulkner's reputation as one of the greatest novelists of the twentieth century is largely due to his highly experimental style. Faulkner was a pioneer in literary modernism, dramatically diverging from the forms and structures traditionally used in novels before his time. Faulkner often employs stream-of-consciousness narrative, nonchronological order, multiple narrators, shifts between the present and past tense, and impossibly long and complex sentences. Not surprisingly, these stylistic innovations make some of Faulkner's novels challenging to the reader. However, these bold innovations had a deep impact on literature.

Although eventually he found critical success, Faulkner did not fare well financially. He was forced to work as a screenwriter in Hollywood to supplement his dwindling income. His fortunes were revived with the 1946 publication of *The Portable Faulkner*, which featured a large and varied selection of his writings. He was awarded the Nobel Prize in Literature in 1950. A pair of Pulitzer Prizes followed in 1955 and 1962. Faulkner continued to write until his death in 1962.

LIGHT IN AUGUST IN CONTEXT

Stylistically speaking, *Light in August* (1932) is one of Faulkner's least demanding novels. The prose is easily comprehensible on a first reading. But thematically, the novel is one of Faulkner's richest and most complicated. The story of Joe Christmas, Lena Grove, and Gail Hightower takes up a wide range of thematic concerns centered on the conflict between the individual and the community. Propelled by illicit sex, racial hatred, religious fanaticism, and brutal violence, the novel is a large-scale attempt to capture an entire community in crisis. *Light in August* is one of Faulkner's most thorough examinations of human psychology and of the forces that threaten and disrupt the cohesion of communities.

LIGHT IN AUGUST: KEY FACTS

Time and place written: 1932; Oxford, Mississippi

Date of first publication: 1932

Publisher: Harrison Smith and Robert Haas, Inc.

Type of work: Novel

Genre: Southern literature; bildungsroman

Language: English

Setting (time): The Great Depression

Setting (place): Mississippi, Alabama, and Tennessee

Tense: Past and present

Tone: Lyrical, free-flowing

Narrator: Anonymous, omniscient, third-person narrator

Point of view: The narrator's

Protagonist: Joe Christmas

Antagonist: Joe Christmas's struggle to come to terms with his ancestry and identity

LIGHT IN AUGUST: PLOT OVERVIEW

A young, pregnant girl named Lena Grove comes to Jefferson, Mississippi, in search of Lucas Burch, the father of her unborn child. On the day of her arrival, Jefferson is shaken by a tragedy: the home of Joanna Burden, the heiress of a Northern abolitionist family, burns to the ground. Miss Burden is found dead, her head almost completely severed from her body. A man named Joe Brown comes forward to claim the thousand-dollar reward for information regarding the murder. He says that Joe Christmas, a half-black mill worker who used to be his bootlegging partner, murdered Joanna. He also says that Joe Christmas and Joanna were lovers. (We later learn that both claims are true; Joe and Joanna were lovers, and Joe murdered Joanna after she held him at gunpoint and demanded that he undergo a religious conversion.)

A man named Byron Bunch helps Lena find a place to stay in Jefferson. He realizes that Joe Brown is the same person as Lucas Burch, and that he is using "Joe Brown" as an alias. Against the advice of his friend, the outcast Reverend Hightower, Byron installs Lena in the old cabin where Joe Brown and Joe Christmas lived before the murder. He does not tell her about Joe Brown's role in the recent tragic events.

As a boy, Christmas was adopted by a strict, almost inhuman Presbyterian man named Mr. McEachern and his kind wife, Mrs. McEachern. Now he lives in the wilderness, trying to evade capture and thinking of his past. After he killed Mr. McEachern and separated from his first lover, the prostitute Bobbie Allen, he turned to fighting and whoring. At last, fed up with trying to elude capture, Christmas goes to Mottstown, where he is captured. The townspeople are outraged that Christmas, a "nigger," would dare to lay hands on a white woman. Christmas only escapes lynching because a local man stands to collect a reward if Christmas is transported safely to Jefferson. Christmas's white grandparents, whom he has never seen, happen to live in Mottstown and hear of his capture. His grandfather, a fanatic religionist and racist named Uncle Doc Hines, wants to kill him or have him lynched, but his grandmother, Mrs. Hines, protects him.

The Hineses follow him to Jefferson, where they meet Byron Bunch. Byron takes them to see Reverend Hightower and asks Hightower to provide an alibi for Joe Christmas by claiming that he and Christmas were together on the night of the murder. The alibi is tantamount to acknowledging a homosexual relationship with Christmas, and Hightower, who has been accused of such a relationship in the past, angrily declines. Shortly thereafter, Lena's baby is born. Byron cannot find a doctor, so Hightower is forced to deliver it himself. Through this act, he begins to feel triumphantly reconnected to the world from which he has been isolated for so long.

Christmas escapes from his captors in Jefferson and runs to Hightower's house, where he is killed and castrated by Percy Grimm, a racist army captain. Before Grimm kills Christmas, Hightower claims that Christmas was with him the night of the murder. The claim fails, but the attempt completes Hightower's redemption. He soon dies, but before he expires he sees a giant, luminous wheel made of faces from his life, his own face among them. Lena and Byron leave Jefferson with the baby and go in pursuit of Lucas Burch, who fled when he saw Lena. Byron hopes that Lena will give up the search for Burch and marry him, but Lena insists on continuing the journey—possibly just because she enjoys traveling.

CHARACTERS IN *LIGHT IN AUGUST*

Bobbie Allen   A waitress and prostitute. Bobbie was Joe Christmas's first lover.

Miss Atkins   The dietitian in Joe Christmas's childhood orphanage. When Joe overhears her having sex with a doctor, she believes he will turn her in and have her fired, so she takes steps to have him sent away from the institution.

Byron Bunch   A quiet, diminutive man. Byron works at the Jefferson planing mill six days a week because he believes working will keep him from doing any harm. His only friend is Gail Hightower. He falls in love with Lena Grove the instant he sees her.

Lucas Burch (a.k.a. Joe Brown)   A shiftless, cowardly man who loves to hear himself talk. In Jefferson, Lucas Burch uses the alias "Joe Brown." He starts the fire at Miss Burden's house after he discovers her body, then tries to turn in his bootlegging partner, Joe Christmas, and collect the thousand-dollar reward. Lucas is the father of Lena Grove's child.

Joanna Burden   The daughter of a family of Northern abolitionists who moved to Jefferson during Reconstruction. She helps and advises black students and colleges. When she holds her lover, Joe Christmas, at gunpoint and demands that he undergo a religious conversion, he murders her.

Joe Christmas   A sullen, contemptuous man. Joe's father was black, but Joe looks white. He lives in Jefferson, Mississippi, where he works in a planing mill and brews illegal whiskey on the side. He murders his lover, Joanna Burden, shortly before the action of the novel begins.

Percy Grimm   A fiercely racist army captain. Grimm organizes a group of American Legion men to keep the townspeople from lynching Joe Christmas, but after Joe Christmas escapes, Grimm tracks him down, kills, and castrates him.

Lena Grove   A young pregnant girl. Lena travels from Alabama to Mississippi in search of Lucas Burch (Joe Brown), the father of her child. She loves seeing new places and maintains a positive attitude despite her scandalous out-of-wedlock pregnancy.

Reverend Gail Hightower   A minister in Jefferson. Hightower fell from grace and was forced out of his church many years ago after his wife died in a Memphis hotel room where she was staying with her lover. Obsessed with the memory of his grandfather, who died in Jefferson during the Civil War, Hightower spends a great deal of time alone, although Byron Bunch visits him occasionally.

Uncle Doc Hines   Joe Christmas's maternal grandfather. Uncle Doc is a white racist who murdered Joe's father, a black circus employee. He places Joe in an orphanage.

Mrs. Hines   Joe Christmas's maternal grandmother. She tries to keep her husband from killing Joe or having him lynched.

Mr. McEachern   Joe Christmas's adoptive father. McEachern is a stern, unfeeling, demanding man, and a pious Presbyterian. Joe kills him by hitting him over the head with a chair at a local dance.

Mrs. McEachern   Joe Christmas's adoptive mother. Mrs. McEachern is a soft, clumsy, loving woman. Joe hates her.

THEMES IN *LIGHT IN AUGUST*

THE ROLE OF RACE IN SHAPING IDENTITY   Many people, even those who are not overtly racist, seem most comfortable believing that fundamental differences exist between black and white. Joe Christmas, who struggles with the ambiguity of his racial identity, finds that in different points in his life he identifies with whites and with blacks, never quite feeling comfortable among either race. This kind of uncertainty angers people, both blacks and whites. Faulkner writes, "He never acted like either a nigger or a white man. That was it. That was what made the folks so mad." Faulkner argues that no intrinsic differences separate the races. When Christmas is moved from a black to a white orphanage, Faulkner writes, "The place where they now were was no different from the one which they had left in the night—the same children, with different names; the same grown people, with different smells."

Because of her upbringing, Joanna Burden assumes that blacks and whites are inherently different. Her father passionately condemns slavery and racism, but in the process he warps Joanna's ability to see blacks as fellow humans. After he tells Joanna that slavery cursed every white child for the sins of the white race, Joanna says she started to see blacks "not as people, but as a thing, a shadow in which I lived, we lived, all white people, all other people." Even though Joanna devotes her life to the advancement of blacks, she maintains the racist idea that blacks and slavery are the "white man's burden," to be carried nobly.

THE LONELINESS OF PEOPLE

Most of the characters in *Light in August* are homeless, rootless, or alienated from their communities. Faulkner writes of Byron Bunch, "there was something definitely rootless about him, as though no town nor city was his, no street, no walls, no square of earth his home. And that he carried this knowledge with him always as though it were a banner, with a quality ruthless, lonely, and almost proud." Like many characters in this novel, Byron Bunch struggles to remain dignified and hopeful despite the sadness and frustration of his life, turning his loneliness into a "banner" because it is the only thing he can cling to.

Christmas feels alone both because of his heritage and because of the hardships of everyday life. Faulkner provides a visual image to describe Christmas's loneliness: "Nothing can look quite as lonely as a big man going along an empty street. Yet though [Christmas] was not large, not tall, he contrived somehow to look more lonely than a lone telephone pole in the middle of a desert. In the wide, empty, shadowbrooded street he looked like a phantom, a spirit, strayed out of its own world, and lost." This mention of a phantom is one of many in the novel, which has constant tension between the living, the flesh and blood, the present, and the dead, memory, and the past.

Joanna Burden also suffers from a sense of isolation. Despite her longtime residence in Jefferson, people regard her as a "foreigner" and ignore her. Hightower is isolated because his preaching style alienates his spiritual and social community. Lena Grove is truly rootless, traveling from state to state during her pregnancy. Still, because she lives in the present and seems satisfied with her lot, she is arguably the most content of the novel's characters.

REAL AND IMAGINED DIFFERENCES BETWEEN MEN AND WOMEN

Joe Christmas is most comfortable with men, even cruel men, because he knows what to expect from them. The softness of women scares him because it forces him to face his own vulnerability. Faulkner writes, "It was the woman: that soft kindness which he believed himself doomed to be forever victim of and which he hated worse than he did the hard and ruthless justice of men. 'She is trying to make me cry,' he thought." While Christmas has difficulty relating to all people, male and female, he feels that he can at least understand the rules by which the male world functions, something he can't say for the female world. Despite his tormented relationship with McEachern, Christmas accepts the terms of his treatment and endures his punishment without protest. But when Joe Christmas starts an affair with Joanna Burden, all of his beliefs about women are called into question. Her hardness throws Christmas off balance and makes him wonder if he knows anything about women. When they have sex, Joanna displays "no feminine vacillation, no coyness of obvious desire and intention to succumb at last," behavior that makes Christmas feels like a woman. In reaction to his struggles with women, Christmas develops a ruthlessness that characterizes many of the novel's male characters. Faulkner does not necessarily portray this ruthlessness as a negative trait. When Lena first meets Hightower, she sees a ruthlessness in his face that she associates with goodness.

SYMBOLS IN *LIGHT IN AUGUST*

BLOOD For Joe Christmas, blood symbolizes women. He is repulsed when he learns about menstruation, and considers himself superior to women because he does not experience this "sickness." He murders Joanna Burden partly because she has reached menopause and stops bleeding, a change that infuriates Christmas and challenges his sense of proper gender roles. Consequently, he kills her in the bloodiest possible manner—by cutting her throat.

WOOD Wood is one of many symbols in *Light in August* linking Joe Christmas to Christ. Faulkner draws several parallels between the story of Christmas and the story of Christ, most obviously by naming Joe "Christmas." Christmas is born in December, the month in which Christ's birth is celebrated, and he dies at age thirty-three, as Christ did. Faulkner makes many references to wood, which suggests the crucifix. Christmas runs through the woods many times and also passes telephone poles and posts.

IMPORTANT QUOTATIONS FROM *LIGHT IN AUGUST*

Nothing can look quite as lonely as a big man going along an empty street. Yet though he was not large, not tall, he contrived somehow to look more lonely than a lone telephone pole in the middle of a desert. In the wide, empty, shadowbrooded street he looked like a phantom, a spirit, strayed out of its own world, and lost.

Then he found himself. Without his being aware the street had begun to slope and before he knew it he was in Freedman Town, surrounded by the summer smell and the summer voices of invisible negroes. They seemed to enclose him like bodiless voices murmuring talking laughing in a language not his.

Location: Chapter 5
Speaker: The narrator
Context: Christmas wanders through Jefferson

This passage suggests the overwhelming solitude that characterizes Christmas. "Like a phantom," he is impermanent, lost, alone, and part of the past. When he passes into Freedman Town, a black neighborhood, his situation seems to improve. Faulkner writes that he "[finds] himself" in this neighborhood. However, because Christmas is neither all white nor all black, he never feels comfortable in communities that are one or the other, and he will soon feel awkward in Freedman Town. The end of this passage foreshadows Christmas's impending discomfort; he hears that the townspeople speak in "a language not his."

It was as if he couldn't get religion and that galloping cavalry and his dead grandfather shot from the galloping horse untangled from each other, even in the pulpit. And he could not untangle them in his private life, at home either, perhaps.

Location: Chapter 3
Speaker: The narrator
Context: Byron Bunch thinks about his friend Hightower

Here Byron Bunch thinks about Hightower and the reasons for his downfall in the community. He astutely observes that Hightower cannot free himself from the past or from his notion of his grandfather as a Civil War hero. To compensate for his difficult relationship with his father, Hightower glorifies his grandfather's death and regards him as a hero. Faulkner makes it clear that Hightower's obsession is both damaging and misplaced, for his grandfather died in a rather absurd and pointless manner. So preoccupied is Hightower with his grandfather that he incorporates him into his sermons, isolating his church community in the process. As Hightower loses touch with the present, he also loses his family life, his position as a minister, and the respect of his townspeople. Faulkner presents Hightower's attitude as a microcosm of the way many postbellum Southerners glamorize Confederate victories long past. Many critics see biographical implications in Faulkner's depiction of Hightower's grandfather, since Faulkner's own grandfather was a great Civil War soldier and statesman.

[H]e was hearing a myriad sounds of no greater volume—voices, murmurs, whispers: of trees, darkness, earth; people: his own voice; other voices evocative of names and times and places—which he had been conscious of all his life without knowing it, which were his life, thinking God perhaps and me not

knowing that too He could see it like a printed sentence, fullborn and already dead God loves me too like the faded and weathered letters on a last year's billboard God loves me too.

Location: Chapter 5
Speaker: The narrator
Context: Christmas smokes a cigarette and contemplates killing Joanna Burden

---

There was no feminine vacillation, no coyness of obvious desire and intention to succumb at last. It was as if he struggled physically with another man for an object of no actual value to either, and for which they struggled on principal alone.... "My God. How little I know about women, when I thought I knew so much ." . . . it was like I was the woman and she was the man.. . . But that was not right, either. Because she had resisted to the very last.

Location: Chapter 11
Speaker: The narrator
Context: Christmas and Joanna have sex

"I had seen and known negroes since I could remember. I just looked at them as I did at rain, or furniture, or food or sleep. But after that I seemed to see [negroes] for the first time not as people, but as a thing, a shadow in which I lived, we lived, all white people, all other people. I thought of all the children coming forever and ever into the world, white, with the black shadow already falling upon them before they drew breath. And I seemed to see the black shadow in the shape of a cross. And it seemed like the white babies were struggling, even before they drew breath, to escape from the shadow that was not only upon them but beneath them too, flung out like their arms were flung out, as if they were nailed to the cross."

Location: Chapter 11
Speaker: Joanna Burden
Context: Joanna tells Christmas about her father and how he made her feel about black people

LITTLE WOMEN

Louisa May Alcott

Four sisters in nineteenth-century New England struggle with poverty, juggle their duties and their desires, and find love.

THE LIFE OF LOUISA MAY ALCOTT

Louisa May Alcott was born on November 29, 1832. She was the second daughter of Amos Bronson and Abigail "Abba" May Alcott. Alcott was raised in Concord, Massachusetts, a small town north of Boston that was home to many great writers of the day. Ralph Waldo Emerson, Nathaniel Hawthorne, and Henry David Thoreau were neighbors to the Alcotts. All of these writers were part of the transcendentalist movement during the New England Renaissance.

Louisa May Alcott had an older sister, Anna, and two younger sisters, Lizzie and Abba May. These names are noticeably similar to the names Alcott gives her characters in *Little Women* (Meg, Beth, and Amy). Her sister Lizzie died at age twenty-two after a bout of scarlet fever. Alcott also had a brother, Dapper, who died in infancy.

Amos Bronson Alcott was not a particularly responsible father or husband, although he was an enthusiastic transcendentalist philosopher, abolitionist, and teacher. His family lived in dire poverty. Alcott was educated at home by her father. She loved to read and write and enjoyed borrowing books from Emerson's large library. As a child, Alcott struggled with the ladylike behavior that was expected of girls in the nineteenth century. Like Jo March in *Little Women*, Alcott could not get over her disappointment about not being a boy, since opportunities for women were limited. When the Civil War broke out in 1861, Alcott had an urge to go and fight in it. Since as a woman she could not join the military, she signed up to be a Union nurse and was stationed in Washington, D.C. Later in life, Alcott became active in the women's suffrage movement in the United States, whose supporters sought to extend the right to vote to women.

Alcott caught pneumonia while working as a nurse in the Civil War. She was treated with calomel, which gave her mercury poisoning. Because of the poisoning, Alcott suffered from hair loss, weakness, intense pain, and hallucinations that could only be controlled with opium. Her right hand hurt her so badly that she had to learn how to write with her left hand. Alcott died on March 6, 1888, and was buried in Sleepy Hollow Cemetery in Concord, alongside her father, Emerson, Hawthorne, and Thoreau.

Alcott is most famous for her domestic tales for children, which brought her fame and fortune during her lifetime. Alcott also wrote sensationalist gothic novels, such as *A Long Fatal Love Chase*, and serious adult novels, such as *Moods* and *Work*, which received middling reviews.

LITTLE WOMEN IN CONTEXT

Alcott did not particularly like *Little Women*, which she wrote at the request of her publisher. When it became a great success, she worried that she was doing nothing more than writing "moral pap" fit for children. *Little Women* possesses many qualities of the didactic genre, a class of works that have a moral lesson. But unlike most didactic fiction of its time, *Little Women* does not preach directly to the reader. The narrator refrains from too much explicit moralizing, allowing us to draw our own lessons from the outcome of the story.

Because Jo becomes a lady at the end of the novel, it is possible that Alcott wants to teach her readers the value of conformity. Interestingly, however, *Little Women* has been championed by feminists for more than a century because Jo in her untamed phase is portrayed so compellingly. Also, Alcott often values rebellion over conformity. So while *Little Women* can be called a didactic novel, the question of what it teaches is an open one.

LITTLE WOMEN: KEY FACTS

Time and place written: 1868–1869; Concord and Boston, Massachusetts

Date of first publication: 1868–1869

Publisher: Roberts Brothers

Type of work: Novel

Genre: Didactic novel; bildungsroman

Language: English

Setting (time): During and after the Civil War, roughly 1861–1876

Setting (place): A small New England town

Tense: Past

Tone: Sympathetic, matter-of-fact, sometimes moralizing

Narrator: Third person omniscient

Point of view: The narrator's

Protagonist: Jo March

Antagonist: Convention and internal flaws

LITTLE WOMEN: PLOT OVERVIEW

The four March girls—Meg, Jo, Beth, and Amy—sit in their living room, lamenting their poverty. The girls decide that they will each buy themselves a present in order to brighten their Christmas. Then they change their minds and decide that instead of buying presents for themselves, they will buy presents for their mother, Marmee. Marmee comes home with a letter from Mr. March, the girls' father, who is serving as a Union chaplain in the Civil War. The letter inspires the girls to bear their burdens more cheerfully and stop complaining about their poverty.

On Christmas morning, the girls wake up to find books under their pillows. Later that day, Marmee encourages them to give away their breakfast to a poor family, the Hummels. Their elderly neighbor, Mr. Laurence, whom the girls have never met, sees their charitable activities and rewards them by sending over a feast. Soon, Meg and Jo are invited to attend a New Year's Party at the home of Meg's wealthy friend, Sally Gardiner. At the party, Jo retreats to an alcove, and there meets Laurie, who lives with Mr. Laurence, his grandfather. While dancing, Meg sprains her ankle. Laurie escorts the sisters home.

Jo visits Laurie when he is sick and meets his grandfather, Mr. Laurence. She inadvertently insults a painting of Mr. Laurence in front of the man himself. Luckily, Laurie's grandfather admires Jo's spunk, and they become friends. Soon, Mr. Laurence meets all the sisters, and Beth becomes his special favorite. Mr. Laurence gives her his deceased granddaughter's piano.

The girls have various adventures. Amy is caught trading limes at school, and the teacher hits her as punishment. As a result, Mrs. March withdraws her daughter from school. Jo refuses to let Amy go with her to the theater. In retaliation, Amy burns Jo's manuscript, and Jo, in her anger, nearly lets Amy drown while ice-skating. Pretty Meg attends her friend Annie Moffat's party and, after allowing the other girls to dress her up in high style, learns that appearances are not everything. While at the party, she hears that people think she intends to marry Laurie for his money.

That year, the Marches form the Pickwick Club. In the spring, Jo smuggles Laurie into one of the club meetings, and he becomes a member. At the beginning of June, the Marches decide to neglect their housework. At the end of a lazy week, Marmee takes a day off too. The girls spoil a dinner, but everyone ends up laughing over it. Laurie has English friends over, and the Marches go on a picnic with them. Jo gets a story published for the first time.

One dark day, the family receives a telegram saying that Mr. March is sick in the hospital in Washington, D.C. Marmee goes to tend to him, and Jo sells her hair to help finance the trip. Chaos ensues in Marmee's wake, for the girls neglect their chores again. Only Beth goes to visit the Hummels, and after one of her visits, she contracts scarlet fever from the Hummel baby. Beth teeters on the brink of death until Marmee returns. Meanwhile, Amy spends time at Aunt March's house in order to escape the disease. Beth recovers, though not completely. Mr. Brooke, Laurie's tutor, falls in love with Meg, much to Jo's dismay. Mr. Brooke and Meg are engaged by the end of Part One.

Part Two opens three years after Part One ended. Mr. March is home from the war, and Laurie is nearly done with school. Meg marries and moves into a new home with Mr. Brooke. Amy decides to have a lunch for her art school classmates, but poor weather ruins the festivities. Jo gets a novel published, but she must cut it down in order to please her publishers. Meg struggles with the duties of keeping house and gives birth to twins, Demi and Daisy. Amy gets to go to Paris instead of Jo because their Aunt Carroll prefers Amy's ladylike behavior.

Jo begins to think that Beth loves Laurie. Jo moves to New York to escape Laurie's affection for her and give Beth a chance to win Laurie's affections. In New York Jo meets Professor Bhaer, a poor German language instructor. Professor Bhaer discourages Jo from writing sensationalistic stories. She takes his advice and finds a simpler writing style. When Jo returns home, Laurie proposes to her, but she turns him down. Beth soon dies.

Amy and Laurie reunite in France and fall in love. They marry and return home. Jo begins to hope that Professor Bhaer will come for her. He does, and they marry a year later. Amy and Laurie have a daughter named Beth, who is sickly. Jo inherits Plumfield, Aunt March's house, and decides to turn it into a boarding school for boys. The novel ends with the family happily gathered together, each sister thankful for her blessings and family.

CHARACTERS IN *LITTLE WOMEN*

Dr. Bangs A doctor who tends to Beth when she is ailing.

Frederick Bhaer A respected professor in Germany who becomes an impoverished language instructor in America. Mr. Bhaer is kind and fatherly. He and Jo marry.

Mr. Brooke Laurie's tutor and eventually Meg's husband. Mr. Brooke is poor and virtuous.

Aunt Carrol One of the March girls' aunts. Aunt Carrol, a ladylike woman, takes Amy with her to Europe.

Daisy and Demi Meg and Mr. Brooke's twins. Their given names are Margaret and John Laurence.

Esther Aunt March's servant. Esther is a French Catholic.

Florence Aunt Carrol's daughter.

Sallie Gardiner Meg's rich friend. Sallie represents the good life to Meg.

Hannah The Marches' loyal servant.

The Hummels A poor, unhealthy family that lives near the Marches.

Mrs. Kirke The woman who runs the New York boarding house where Jo lives.

Laurie Laurence The rich boy who lives next door to the Marches. Laurie, whose real name is Theodore Laurence, is like a son and brother to the Marches. He is charming, clever, and kindhearted.

Mr. Laurence Laurie's grandfather and the Marches' next-door neighbor. Mr. Laurence seems gruff, but he is loving and kind.

Amy March The youngest March sister. Amy is an artist who has a weakness for pretty possessions. She is given to pouting, fits of temper, and vanity, but she does attempt to improve herself.

Aunt March A rich widow and one of the March girls' aunts. Although crotchety and difficult, Aunt March loves her nieces and wants the best for them.

Beth March The third March sister. Beth is very quiet and very virtuous. She adores music and plays the piano very well.

Josephine (Jo) March The protagonist of the novel, and the second-oldest March sister. Jo, who wants to be a writer, is based on Louisa May Alcott herself. Jo has a temper and a quick tongue, although she works hard to control both. She is a tomboy, and reacts with impatience to the many limitations placed on women and girls. She hates romance in her real life, and wants nothing more than to hold her family together.

Marmee March The March girls' mother. Marmee is the moral role model for her daughters. She works hard but happily while her husband is at war.

Meg March   The oldest March sister. Responsible and kind, Meg mothers her younger sisters. She has a small weakness for luxury and leisure, but the greater part of her is gentle, loving, and morally vigorous.

Mr. March   The March girls' father and Marmee's husband. He serves in the Union army as a chaplain. When he returns home, he works as the minister to a nearby parish.

Annie Moffat   A wealthy friend of Meg's. Annie is fashionable and social. She wears stylish clothing that Meg envies.

Ned Moffat   Annie Moffat's older brother.

Frank Vaughn   One of the Vaughn siblings. Frank is sickly.

Fred Vaughn   Laurie's friend. Fred has a romantic interest in Amy.

Grace Vaughn   The youngest sister of the Vaughn family. Grace and Amy become friends on a picnic.

Kate Vaughn   One of the Vaughn siblings. At first Kate turns up her nose at the bluntness and poverty of the Marches, but later she decides she likes them.

THEMES IN *LITTLE WOMEN*

THE STRUGGLE BETWEEN DUTY AND SELF   *Little Women* centers on the conflict between a woman's attention to herself and her attention to her family. At the time when Alcott wrote her novel, progress toward gender equality was inching along. Through the four March sisters, Alcott explores four different ways nineteenth-century women could approach the social constraints that bound them: marry young and create a new family, as Meg does; be subservient and dutiful to one's parents and immediate family, as Beth is; focus on one's art, pleasure, and self, as Amy does at first; or struggle to have both a dutiful family life and a meaningful professional life, as Jo does. While Meg and Beth conform to society's expectations of the role that women should play, Amy and Jo initially attempt to break free from these constraints and nurture their individuality. Eventually, however, both Amy and Jo marry and settle into more customary lives. Alcott presents this development objectively, without decrying society for preventing women from being artists or hailing a society for sanctifying wifedom and motherhood.

THE NECESSITY OF WORK   Over the course of *Little Women*, the March sisters try to find happiness through daily activities, dreams, and each other. But it is work, most of all, that guarantees happiness. When they do not engage in productive work, the sisters feel guilty and remorseful. Various kinds of selfishness—dressing up in finery, hoarding limes, neglecting chores, getting revenge—make them unhappy. The novel demonstrates the importance of the Puritan work ethic, which dictates that to work is holy. This work ethic fit in with the transcendentalist teachings with which Alcott grew up. It thrived in New England, where many Puritans lived and where the novel takes place. Alcott recommends work not as a means to a material end, but as a means to the expression of inner goodness and creativity.

THE UNIMPORTANCE OF MONEY   Many nineteenth-century Americans, transcendentalists in particular, believed that nurturing the inner, spiritual self was far more important than paying attention to temporary, earthly things like wealth and impressive appearances. Unlike their counterparts in Europe, many middle-class Americans were not embarrassed by humble origins and did not crave titles or other trappings of wealth. These Americans wanted only what they deserved and believed that what they deserved depended on how hard they worked. Alcott incorporates this transcendentalist ideal into *Little Women*. She presents the Marches' snug New England home as more desirable than mansions in Paris. She contrasts the March sisters with more well-to-do young women like Amy Moffat and Sally Gardiner, pointing out that what the Marches lack in riches they make up for in kindness and purity. Meg and Amy constantly struggle with vanity and eventually overcome it. Amy turns down Fred Vaughn's offer of marriage even though he is rich because she does not love him. All of the March sisters take pleasure in hard work, supporting themselves or contributing to their family's upkeep. The March sisters all learn to be happy with their respective lots in life and not to yearn for meaningless riches.

SYMBOLS IN *LITTLE WOMEN*

UMBRELLAS   Umbrellas symbolize the protection a man offers a woman. Before Meg and John Brooke get married, Jo gets angry at Mr. Brooke's umbrella, suggesting her anger about the fact that Mr. Brooke is going to take care of her sister. At the end of the novel, Professor Bhaer extends his umbrella over Jo, and her acceptance of its coverage symbolizes her readiness to accept not only his love and protection, but also the idea that men are supposed to offer women love and protection.

FIRE   *Little Women* is filled with images of burning that represent writing, genius, and anger. At a party, Jo wears a dress with a burn mark on the back, which symbolizes her rebellion against conventional, prettified womanhood. In anger, Amy burns Jo's manuscript after Jo will not let her come to a play. Whenever Jo writes, her family describes her inspiration as genius burning. At the end of the novel, Jo burns her sensationalist stories after Professor Bhaer criticizes that style of writing. This fire destroys her earlier self as well, marking the end of fiery Jo and the beginning of docile Jo.

IMPORTANT QUOTATIONS FROM *LITTLE WOMEN*

> *Money is a needful and precious thing,—and, when well used, a noble thing,—but I never want you to think it is the first or only prize to strive for. I'd rather see you poor men's wives, if you were happy, beloved, contented, than queens on thrones, without self- respect and peace.*

Location: Chapter 9
Speaker: Marmee
Context: Meg returns from a stay with the rich Moffats

Marmee tells Meg that she does not want any of her daughters to marry for material comforts, as was suggested by a guest at the Gardiners'. At a moment in history when the quality of women's lives depended solely on their choice of a husband, and when marriage to a rich man could improve the lives of a woman's family, Marmee's statement is very compassionate and unusual. After all, the other guests at the party instantly assume that Meg must intend to marry for money, and do not condemn her for it.

Alcott does not completely sanction Marmee's statement. *Little Women* depicts marrying poor men as a serious burden for nineteenth-century women to bear. One should not marry for money, but at the same time, marriage without money results in quarrels and stress. Alcott does not depict romantic love without mentioning the practical reality of living with little money. The daughter of an irresponsible father, she knew firsthand the worry of having to depend on someone else for a living.

> *I'd have a stable full of Arabian steeds, rooms piled with books, and I'd write out of a magic inkstand, so that my works should be as famous as Laurie's music. I want to do something splendid before I go into my castle—something heroic, or wonderful—that won't be forgotten after I'm dead. I don't know what, but I'm on the watch for it, and mean to astonish you all, some day. I think I shall write books, and get rich and famous; that would suit me, so that is my favorite dream.*

Location: Chapter 13
Speaker: Jo
Context: The March girls and Laurie discuss their dreams

In contrast to the typical dreams of her sisters, Jo's dream is startlingly big and confidently expressed. The horses Jo wants, and with which she is constantly compared, represent the wild freedom for which she yearns. Significantly, Jo does not mention a husband or children in her dream, but says she wants books and ink. This powerful dream reaches well beyond the confines of a woman's small living room and demands lasting fame and independence in a man's world. Jo's sentences are very direct and begin commandingly with the word "I." Jo also mentions the desire to have her work equal Laurie's. The pursuit of an art is represented as an idyllic field in which men's and women's work are considered equal. Also, Jo associates going into a castle—that is, getting married and having a house—with dying. She wants to do something great before she marries or dies.

I'll try and be what he loves to call me, "a little woman," and not be rough and wild; but do my duty here instead of wanting to be somewhere else.

Location: Chapter 1
Speaker: Jo
Context: Jo heeds a letter from her father and voices a desire to be stereotypically female, as he wishes

---

I am angry nearly every day of my life.

Location: Chapter 8
Speaker: Marmee
Context: Marmee confesses that she, like Jo, has a temper

Oh, my girls, however long you may live, I never can wish you a greater happiness than this!

Location: Chapter 47
Speaker: Marmee
Context: Marmee concludes the novel with these words, and sums up its message

LOLITA

Vladimir Nabokov

A man has a love affair with his stepdaughter and kills the man who stole her away from him.

THE LIFE OF VLADIMIR NABOKOV

Vladimir Nabokov was born in St. Petersburg, Russia, on April 22 or 23, 1899, into a very wealthy family. V. D. and Elena Nabokovs' large, pink granite home was a salon for world-famous intellectuals, musicians, poets, and bankers. When Vladimir was sixteen years old, his beloved Uncle Ruka (1874–1916) gave him an astonishing birthday gift: a large estate and the equivalent of two million dollars. One of Vladimir's first extravagances was to pay for the private publication of a book of his poems in a limited, 500-copy edition. A few months later, Tsar Nicholas II abdicated, and life took a bad turn for the Nabokovs. Bolsheviks seized control of the government, and soldiers began confiscating the estates of the rich and politically suspect. The Nabokovs had to flee St. Petersburg, taking only a few handfuls of jewelry with them. The Russian Revolution (1917–1921) had begun.

The Nabokovs found themselves struggling with desperate poverty. They settled in Yalta, traveled to Constantinople, and from there went to England, where Vladimir and his brother Sergi (1900–1945) qualified for émigré scholarships and enrolled in Cambridge in 1919. V. D. and Elena Nabokov then moved to Berlin. Three years later, during a political lecture, V. D. was killed in an outburst of gunfire meant to assassinate the speaker.

After graduating from Cambridge in 1922, Nabokov settled in Berlin and worked at a variety of jobs— movie extra, tennis coach, translator, and tutor. In 1925, when Nabokov was twenty-six, he married Véra Slonim (1902–1991), another Russian émigré. The following year, he published his first novel, *Mashenka* (Mary). During the next twelve years, Nabokov completed several plays and published short stories and eight other novels, all in Russian. He was a highly respected member of Russian publishing circles in Berlin, but money was scarce, especially for writers. Inflation and unemployment ran rampant in Germany, despite the promises of Germany's Führer, Adolph Hitler (1889–1945).

Revolution was in the air, but both Vladimir and his Jewish wife, Véra, did their best to ignore what was happening. Book burnings had begun, and the Nazis had marched into the Rhineland. In 1934, Véra and Nabokov had a son, Dmitri. Nabokov and his family stayed in Berlin until 1937, when Nabokov learned that Hitler had released his father's killer from prison and made him supervisor of emigration. After moving to Paris with Vera, Nabokov began writing his first novel in English, *The Real Life of Sebastian Knight* (1941), in his converted study—a sunny bathroom. He wrote most of the novel there, using a suitcase placed across a bidet as his desk.

By 1940, the German army was threatening Paris with invasion, and the Nabokovs moved to the United States, where Nabokov taught at Stanford University and then at Wellesley College. In 1948, Nabokov began teaching at Cornell University, where he would stay for ten years. In 1961, Nabokov moved to Montreux, Switzerland, where he began translating all of his Russian novels into English. He also produced *Pale Fire* (1962) and *Ada* (1968). Nabokov died on July 2, 1977.

LOLITA IN CONTEXT

Nabokov began writing *Lolita* during World War II. He attempted to sell the manuscript to several U.S. publishers, but they all refused, calling it lewd and scandalous, a "time bomb" waiting to explode. Indeed, *Lolita* stunned the Western world when a Parisian publishing house published it in 1955. In 1958, three years after *Lolita* had met with financial success and critical acclaim in Europe, it was published in the U.S., where it remained on the bestseller list for over six months. Many public libraries banned it, and the *Chicago Tribune* refused to review it.

Lolita is one of a series of twentieth century novels considered obscene by many readers, a relative of such banned books as D. H. Lawrence's *Lady Chatterley's Lover* (1928) and James Joyce's *Ulysses* (1922). But whereas those novels caused a scandal because they depicted adultery and masturbation, respectively, *Lolita* went further, exploring pedophilia and sexual slavery. *Lolita* neither glorifies pedophilia nor excuses the behavior of its protagonist, but the mere exploration of a love affair between a man and a girl infuriated some readers. More than a novel about sex, *Lolita* is a satire of postwar American culture, of the exuberant consumerism and bland, mass-produced entertainment that characterized the conformist culture. Whatever his intentions in writing *Lolita*, Nabokov said the novel should not be interpreted as symbolic of anything, or as an elaborate moral lesson.

LOLITA: KEY FACTS

Time and place written: 1949–1954; the United States	
Date of first publication: 1955	
Publisher: Olympia Press, Paris	
Type of work: Novel	
Genre: Confession; dark comedy	
Language: English	
Setting (time): 1947–1952	
Setting (place): Various small towns in the United States	
Tense: Mainly past, occasionally present	
Tone: Emotional, lyrical, mocking, self-conscious, ironic	
Narrator: Humbert Humbert in the first person	
Point of view: Humbert's	
Protagonist: Humbert Humbert	
Antagonist: The forces that stand in the way of Humbert's desire for nymphets	

LOLITA: PLOT OVERVIEW

In a foreword, a fictional character named John Ray, Jr. explains that Humbert Humbert, the author of this work, died in prison of a heart attack, and that Lolita died in childbirth. Ray marvels that we can love Humbert's lyrical prose while abhorring Humbert's behavior. He hopes that Humbert's manuscript will remind parents, teachers, and social workers to be ever vigilant in protecting their innocent children from such depraved monsters as Humbert.

Humbert Humbert recounts the history of his sexual affair with a young "nymphet" named Dolores "Lolita" Haze. He writes that his lifelong obsession with nymphets began with his boyhood passion for a young girl named Annabel. He and Annabel were always interrupted in the middle of their sexual encounters. Humbert mentions his first marriage to a woman named Valeria. He fell for Valeria because she looked like a child, but eventually he discovered that her youthful looks were an illusion accomplished with makeup. To Humbert's delight, Valeria left him for another man on the eve of their emigration from France to America.

In America, Humbert follows the advice of a friend and takes up residence in the town of Ramsdale, where he rents a room from Charlotte Haze. He immediately becomes obsessed with Charlotte's twelve-year-old Lolita, a nymphet who reminds him of Annabel. Charlotte has a crush on Humbert and resents Lolita for stealing his attention. She sends Lolita off to summer camp and then to boarding school. When Charlotte proposes marriage to Humbert, he readily accepts despite his great dislike for her, thrilled that the marriage will bring him close to Lolita. After they are married, Charlotte discovers Humbert's private journal, which details Humbert's disgust for her and lust for Lolita. Enraged, Charlotte tells Humbert he will never see Lolita again. She runs out into the street to mail a letter, and a car hits and kills her.

Humbert goes to fetch Lolita from camp, telling her that her mother is in the hospital. They go to a hotel and have sex. Lolita confesses that she is not a virgin. She had sex with a boy she met at camp. Humbert eventually tells Lolita that her mother is dead. Humbert and Lolita continue their affair, taking a long road trip across America.

After a year of traveling, they move to Lolita's hometown, Beardsley, where Humbert enrolls Lolita in a private girl's school that stresses social interaction with males above academics. Humbert himself spends time with his friend Gaston Godin, a tidy man who likes young boys. Humbert quickly becomes paranoid and jealous, fighting with Lolita frequently about her allowance and her associations with boys her age. Lolita announces her wish to leave Beardsley and go on another long drive. Humbert readily consents. As they travel, Humbert notices a man following them and worries that it is a detective on his trail. One day, Lolita vanishes. Humbert drives around, searching for her. Later, he has a two-year love affair with a woman in her mid-twenties named Rita.

About three years after Lolita's disappearance, Humbert receives a letter from her. Lolita, who is now eighteen, writes that she is married, pregnant, and in need of money. Humbert goes to her house and tells her that he still loves her immensely. He gives her four thousand dollars and demands to know the name of the man who took her away from him. She tells him that it was Clare Quilty, a writer. He took her to his ranch and asked her to participate in orgies. When she refused, he threw her out. Humbert says goodbye to Lolita and drives to Quilty's house. Quilty is drunk or drugged, and cannot take Humbert's death threats seriously. Humbert shoots Quilty several times, finally succeeding in killing him.

Humbert drives away from the house, runs a red light, and drifts into a field. Eventually, the police arrest him and later charge him with the murder of Quilty. Humbert concludes his narrative, which he began fifty-six days ago. He says, "Had I come before myself, I would have given Humbert at least thirty-five years for rape, and dismissed the rest of the charges."

CHARACTERS IN *LOLITA*

Aunt Sybil Humbert's maternal aunt. After Humbert's mother is killed by lightning while picnicking, Aunt Sybil moves in and becomes Humbert's governess and his father's housekeeper.

Barbara Burke Lolita's friend at Camp Q. Barbara and Lolita take turns having sex with thirteen-year-old Charlie Holmes.

John and Jean Farlow Charlotte Haze's neighbors.

Gaston Godin A French teacher and friend of Humbert's. Godin is a mirror reflection of Humbert. Where Humbert is meticulously neat, Godin is slovenly; where Humbert is slim and manly, Godin is obese; where Humbert dotes on little girls, Godin cherishes young boys.

Harold Haze Charlotte's first husband.

Charlie Holmes The thirteen-year-old son of Camp Q's headmistress. Charlie seduces both Barbara and Lolita when Lolita is twelve.

Charlotte Haze Humbert Lolita's mother and Humbert's second wife. Charlotte, an uncultured woman, is swept away by Humbert's European background, accent, expensive wardrobe, polished manners, and cultured taste in food and perfumes.

Humbert Humbert The narrator of the story. Humbert is self-involved, brilliant, and occasionally genuine.

Annabel Leigh A young girl whom Humbert meets at a seaside resort in France and falls in love with.

Louise Charlotte's maid.

Mr. McCoo The man who was originally supposed to host Humbert in Ramsdale.

Clare Quilty A heavy-drinking playwright. Like Humbert, Quilty lusts for young girls.

Ivor Quilty Clare's uncle. Ivor is an overweight Ramsdale dentist.

John Ray, Jr. The editor of Humbert's confession and author of the foreword to it.

Dolores (Lolita) Haze Schiller To Humbert, Lolita is both the embodiment of the ideal nymphet and the in-flesh reincarnation of his beloved childhood sweetheart, Annabel Leigh. Lolita is by turns coquettish, innocent, and temperamental.

Richard (Dick) Schiller The man Lolita marries after escaping from Quilty. Dick is a war veteran with bad hearing in one ear. Humbert notes Dick's "arctic blue eyes, black hair, ruddy cheeks, and unshaven chin."

Rita The woman with whom Humbert lives after Lolita leaves him.

Valeria Humbert's first wife. Humbert marries Valeria because her skillful makeup makes her look like a little girl and because he hopes that she will cure him of his obsession for little girls. Both hopes are dashed immediately.

THEMES IN *LOLITA*

THE AESTHETICIZING OF SEXUAL DESIRE Although Humbert is ashamed of his desire for nymphets, he also takes a perverse pride in it, because he feels that his rare, exquisitely painful desires and pleasures set him apart from other men whose normal sexual desire for adult women is an unthinking part of their lives, no different than any other bodily function. Humbert considers his appreciation for nymphets a sublime artistic gift as well as a curse. He wants to believe, and wants us to believe, that he is a poetic soul in search of beauty, not a pervert or a "sex fiend" who molests little girls. Aestheticism gives him a way to rationalize his behavior to himself and to his readers. And for many readers, the technique works: Humbert uses incredibly beautiful, poetic language to describe his lust for Lolita and his erotic experiences with her. In this way, Humbert tries to persuade the reader that his feelings for Lolita are the feelings of a poet, not a pervert, and that his affair with her is a sublime poem, not a criminal act. Occasionally, Humbert's mask slips, and we see the horror of what he has done to Lolita, but soon he coaxes us back to his side. Many readers come away from *Lolita* feeling puzzled by the sympathy that they feel for Humbert, and wondering why they don't detest him as a sexual predator. Their confusion testifies to Nabokov's genius.

THE POWER OF LANGUAGE In *Lolita*, language is very powerful and very malleable. Humbert uses language to simultaneously reveal and conceal information. He writes candidly about his actions, revealing his own cruelty, snobbery, statutory rape, and murder. But he conceals the true evil of these acts, manipulating language to make them seem less brutal, perverse, and condemnable than they are. He uses understatement to make tragedies seem casual, sarcasm to make deep emotion seem laughable, and lyricism to make sexual deviancy seem noble and beautiful. Most of this manipulation is directed at the reader, or the jury to whom Humbert is pleading his case, but some of it is directed at Lolita. Humbert very rarely threatens Lolita with physical force or roughly explains his demands. Especially during the period immediately after Charlotte's death, he keeps Lolita near him by manipulating her with persuasive language and gently lying to her about the horrible things the authorities will do to her if she tells anyone about their affair.

Language isn't only used for persuasive purposes, however. Both Humbert and Nabokov himself take enormous delight in verbal games, puns, and riddles (Nabokov once wrote that *Lolita* is about his own love affair with the English language). Humbert's love of puns and wordplay reflects the giddiness of the man who has mastered a new language. Nabokov, himself a non-native English speaker, exhibits a similar kind of delight, peppering the novel with verbal clues and jokes, some of which are not necessarily understandable to Humbert. This joyful, unsubtle manipulation of syllables, rhymes, synonyms, and antonyms is the sunny flipside of the more dangerous manipulation of ideas that Humbert employs in his narrative.

THE TRAGEDY OF RANDOM CHANCE *Lolita* is dominated by freak accidents and chance occurrences, which illustrate the randomness of fate and the fragility of life. Most of the important women in Humbert's life die sudden deaths, including his mother, his first love, his second wife, and even Lolita. Perhaps Humbert loves nymphets in part because their fates, while tragic, are at least not random or unexpected. By Humbert's own definition, nymphets only exist between the ages of nine and fourteen, after which they become women and die to him. In loving them, Humbert chooses predictable suffering over unpredictable fate. Humbert is aware that, at age twelve, Lolita has only "two years of . . . remaining nymphage" before she will cease to be attractive to him. However, fate ends up cheating Humbert of even this much certainty. By the end of the novel, Lolita is seventeen, well past nymphage, and yet Humbert still loves her.

SYMBOLS IN *LOLITA*

THE MIMOSA GROVE The mimosa grove is the site of Humbert's first sexual experience and the start of his lifelong obsession with girls of about Annabel's age. The grove symbolizes sexuality for Humbert. He describes it as if describing the nymphets he loves, writing about its pale, glowing stars, "vibrant" sky, and "nervous and slender" leaves. The delicacy and fragility of the grove suggests the youth and fragility of the nervous, slender nymphets that obsess Humbert.

OUR GLASS LAKE/HOURGLASS LAKE When Humbert first hears the name Hourglass Lake, he thinks that it is called "Our Glass Lake." The discrepancy between Humbert's understanding of the name and the actual name symbolizes Humbert's and Charlotte's vastly different ideas about life, each other, their relationship, and Lolita. "Our Glass" and "Hourglass" both connote fragility and impermanence: glass is delicate, and an hour passes quickly through an hourglass. Therefore, the lake symbolizes not just the misunderstandings between Charlotte and Humbert, but also the changeability of everything in Humbert's life.

IMPORTANT QUOTATIONS FROM *LOLITA*

"Lolita" should make all of us — parents, social workers, educators — apply ourselves with still greater vigilance and vision to the task of bringing up a better generation in a safer world.

Speaker: John Ray, Jr., Ph.D.
Location: The foreword
Context: Ray explains his own opinion of *Lolita*

In his foreword, the fictional John Ray, Jr., Ph.D, a psychiatrist studying Humbert's case, claims that *Lolita* should be read as a cautionary tale. This foreword serves several purposes. First, it allows Nabokov to sidestep accusations that *Lolita* is nothing but gratuitous pornography. Even though Nabokov mocks Dr. Ray's earnest moralizing, at least he gives lip service to the theory that *Lolita* can be interpreted as a cautionary tale. Nabokov reminds the reader that he is aware of the moral objections the novel will provoke, and that he has taken these objections into consideration. Second, the foreword reminds us of the psychological and moral consequences of Humbert's behavior so that we do not surrender completely to the power of Humbert's beautiful prose. Third and most importantly, the foreword discourages all simplistic readings of the novel. After a few pages of *Lolita*, Ray's explanation seems patently absurd. It becomes clear that the novel is not a cautionary tale of any kind, and that there are no simple lessons to take away from it. By including the foreword with its overly simplistic moral message, Nabokov warns his readers not to read the novel as Ray does. By refusing to say whether he endorses Humbert's behavior or reviles it, Nabokov urges us to strive for a more complex reading of Humbert's story. His reticence suggests that *Lolita* should not be read as a sexy thriller any more than it should be read as a morality tale.

"At the hotel we had separate rooms, but in the middle of the night she came sobbing into mine, and we made up very gently. You see, she had absolutely nowhere else to go."

Location: Part One, Chapter 33
Speaker: Humbert Humbert
Context: Humbert has just told Lolita that her mother is dead

This quotation marks an important transition in *Lolita*. Humbert's poetic language and heartfelt arguments have convinced us to sympathize with him for the duration of Part One, but after he actually has sex with Lolita, his offhanded cruelty forces us to confront the discrepancy between Humbert's delusions and the harsh reality of his relationship with Lolita. Until this point, Humbert has spoken of Lolita only in idealized terms. In these two sentences, his essential monstrosity cuts through the veil of lyricism, and we realize that despite Humbert's convincing explanations, his actions damage Lolita just as much as we would expect them to. Humbert protests that he is not a criminal, but here he shows that he lacks humanity. Aware that Lolita has "absolutely nowhere else to go," Humbert unapologetically takes advantage of her vulnerability, using his role as her "father" to control her emotionally, financially, and sexually.

Although we have to rely on Humbert's version of events—as the narrator, his perspective is the only one available—statements like this one allow us to step outside of Humbert's seductive illusions and see the situation for what it really is. Despite Humbert's brilliance, he is a criminal, and despite Lolita's sexy posturing and adolescent whining, she is a victim. She is not the enchanted nymph or cold-hearted beauty that Humbert describes. She is a vulnerable, inexperienced child who cries like a child when her mother dies, and who is too young and afraid to defend herself against Humbert's sexual advances.

My very photogenic mother died in a freak accident (picnic, lightning) when I was three.

Speaker: Humbert Humbert
Location: Part One, Chapter 2
Context: Humbert offhandedly describes his mother's death

Quilty, Clare, American dramatist. Born in Ocean City, N.J. 1911. Educated at Columbia University. Started on a commercial career, but turned to playwriting. Author of The Little Nymph, The Lady Who Loved Lightning *(in collaboration with Vivian Darkbloom),* Dark Age, The Strange Mushroom, Fatherly Love, *and others. His many plays for children are notable.* Little Nymph *(1940) traveled 14,000 miles and played 280 performances on the road during the winter before ending in New York. Hobbies: fast cars, photography, pets.*

Quine, Dolores . . .

Location: Part One, Chapter 8
Speaker: Humbert Humbert
Context: Humbert quotes the 1946 edition of *Who's Who in the Limelight*, a guide to famous figures in show business

---

If I dwell at some length upon the tremors and gropings of that distant night, it is because I insist upon proving that I am not, and never was, and never could have been, a brutal scoundrel. The gentle and dreamy regions through which I crept were the patrimonies of poets, not crime's prowling ground.

Location: Part One, Chapter 29
Speaker: Humbert Humbert
Context: Humbert excuses his behavior, characterizing it as part of a dream that has nothing to do with reality

LORD OF THE FLIES

William Golding

A group of English boys, marooned on an island, rapidly turn lawless and bloodthirsty.

THE LIFE OF WILLIAM GOLDING

William Golding was born on September 19, 1911, in Cornwall, England. After graduating from Oxford, he worked briefly as an actor, then became a schoolteacher. When England entered World War II, Golding joined the Royal Navy. After the war, he resumed teaching and also began writing novels. His first and greatest success came with 1954's *Lord of the Flies*, after which he was able to retire from teaching and devote himself fully to writing. Although he never again attained the kind of popular and artistic success he enjoyed with *Lord of the Flies*, because of that novel he remained a respected and distinguished author for the rest of his life, publishing several novels and a play, *The Brass Butterfly* (1958). He was awarded the Nobel Prize for Literature in 1983. William Golding died in 1993, one of the most acclaimed writers in England.

LORD OF THE FLIES IN CONTEXT

Lord of the Flies, which tells the story of a group of English boys marooned on a tropical island, is fiction. But the novel's exploration of human evil is partially based on Golding's World War II experience with the violence and savagery of which human beings are capable. In observing a group of boys freed from the moral constraints of civilization and society, *Lord of the Flies* dramatizes a fundamental human struggle: the conflict between the impulse to obey rules and the impulse to seek brute power over others. Golding suggests that humans have a civilizing instinct, which encourages us to work together toward common goals and behave peacefully, and a barbarizing instinct, which encourages us to rebel against civilization and seek anarchy, chaos, despotism, and violence.

The novel's structure and style are extremely straightforward. Golding largely excludes poetic language, lengthy description, and philosophical interludes. *Lord of the Flies* is an allegory that can be interpreted in many ways. During the 1950s and 1960s, many critics connected the novel to grand historical, religious, and psychological schemes, claiming it dramatized the history of civilization, the history of religion, or the struggle among the Freudian components of unconscious identity—id, ego, and superego. Since the book does deal with fundamental human tendencies, there is truth in each of these readings. Still, the novel's philosophical register is almost entirely restricted to the two extremes represented by Ralph and Jack, and is not complex or subtle enough to offer a realistic parallel to the history of human endeavors.

LORD OF THE FLIES: KEY FACTS

Time and place written: Early 1950s; Salisbury, England	
Date of first publication: 1954	
Publisher: Faber and Faber	
Type of work: Novel	
Genres: Allegory; castaway novel	
Language: English	
Setting (time): Near future	
Setting (place): A deserted tropical island	
Tense: Past	
Tone: Lush, tragic, pessimistic, dark, unsparing	

Narrator: Third-person omniscient

Point of view: Primarily Ralph's; also Jack's and Simon's

Protagonist: Ralph

Antagonist: Jack

LORD OF THE FLIES: PLOT OVERVIEW

In the midst of a raging war, a plane evacuating a group of English boys from Britain is shot down over a deserted tropical island. Marooned, the boys set about electing a leader and finding a way to be rescued. They choose Ralph as their leader. Ralph appoints Jack leader of the hunters. Ralph, Jack, and Simon set off to explore the island. When they return, Ralph says they must light a signal fire to attract the attention of passing ships. The boys do so using the lens from Piggy's eyeglasses to ignite dead wood, but they are more interested in playing than in paying close attention to their work, and the fire quickly spreads to the forest. A large swath of dead wood burns out of control. One of the youngest boys disappears, presumably burned to death.

At first, the boys enjoy their life without grown-ups. They splash in the lagoon and play games, though Ralph complains that they should be maintaining the signal fire and building huts for shelter. The hunters have trouble catching a pig. Jack becomes increasingly preoccupied with hunting. One day, a ship passes by on the horizon. Ralph and Piggy notice, to their horror, that the signal fire has burned out. It was the hunters' responsibility to maintain it. Furious, Ralph accosts Jack, but the hunter has just returned with his first kill, and all the boys are gripped with a strange frenzy, reenacting the chase in a kind of wild dance. When Piggy criticizes him, Jack hits him across the face.

Ralph summons the boys by blowing the conch shell and reprimands them in a speech intended to restore order. Yet there is a larger, more insidious problem than keeping the signal fire lit and finding enough food: the boys are afraid. The littlest boys (known as "littluns") have been troubled by nightmares from the beginning, and more and more boys now believe that there is some sort of beast or monster lurking on the island. At the meeting, the older boys try to convince the others to think rationally: if there were a monster, where would it hide during the daytime? One of the littluns suggests that it hides in the sea, a proposition that terrifies the whole group.

Not long after the meeting, an aircraft battle takes place high above the island. The boys are sleeping, so they do not notice the flashing lights and explosions in the clouds. A parachutist drifts to earth on the mountain where the boys keep the signal fire. He is dead. Sam and Eric, the twins responsible for watching the fire at night, have fallen asleep and do not see him land. When they wake up, they see the enormous silhouette of the parachute and hear the strange flapping noises it makes. Thinking the beast is at hand, they rush back to the camp in terror and report that the beast has attacked them.

The boys organize a hunting expedition to search for monsters. Jack and Ralph, who are increasingly at odds, travel up the mountain. They see the silhouette of the parachute from a distance and think it looks like a huge, deformed ape. The group holds a meeting, and Jack and Ralph tell the others of the sighting. Jack calls Ralph a coward and says he should be removed from office, but the other boys refuse to vote him out of power. Jack angrily runs away down the beach, calling to all the hunters to join him. Ralph rallies the remaining boys to build a new signal fire, this time on the beach instead of on the "monster's" mountain. They obey, but gradually most of them slip away to join Jack.

Jack declares himself the leader of this new tribe. He organizes a hunt and the violent, ritual slaughter of a sow to solemnize the occasion. They decapitate the sow and place its head on a sharpened stake in the jungle as an offering to the beast. Encountering the bloody, fly-covered head, Simon has a terrible vision. He thinks the head is speaking in the voice of the Lord of the Flies. The voice says Simon will never escape him, for he exists in all men. Simon faints. When he wakes up, he goes to the mountain and sees the dead parachutist. Understanding then that the monster exists not externally, but in each boy, Simon travels to the beach to tell the others what he has seen. But they are in the midst of a chaotic revelry—even Ralph and Piggy have joined Jack's feast—and when they see Simon's shadowy figure emerge from the jungle, they fall upon him and kill him with their bare hands and teeth.

The following morning, Ralph and Piggy discuss what they have done. Jack's hunters attack them and their few followers, stealing Piggy's glasses in the process. Ralph's group travels to Jack's stronghold, called Castle Rock, in an attempt to make Jack see reason. But Jack orders Sam and Eric tied up and fights with Ralph. In the ensuing battle, one boy, Roger, rolls a boulder down from the mountain, killing Piggy and shattering the conch shell. Ralph barely manages to escape a torrent of spears.

Ralph hides all night and into the next day as the other boys hunt him like an animal. Jack has the other boys ignite the forest in order to smoke him out of his hiding place. Ralph discovers and destroys the sow's head in the forest. Eventually, he is forced out onto the beach, where he knows the other boys will soon arrive to kill him. Ralph collapses in exhaustion, but when he looks up, he sees a British naval officer standing over him. From his ship, he saw the blazing fire now raging in the jungle. The other boys reach the beach and stop in their tracks at the sight of the officer. Amazed at the spectacle of this group of bloodthirsty, savage children, the officer asks Ralph to explain. Ralph is overwhelmed by the knowledge that he is saved, but thinking about what has happened on the island, he begins to weep. The other boys begin to sob as well. The officer turns his back so that the boys may regain their composure.

CHARACTERS IN *LORD OF THE FLIES*

Jack   The novel's antagonist. Jack, one of the older boys stranded on the island, is the leader of the hunters, but he longs for total power. He becomes increasingly wild, barbarous, and cruel as the novel progresses and he accrues more power. He is adept at manipulating the other boys. Jack represents the savage instinct in human beings.

The Lord of the Flies   The name given to the sow's head impaled on a stake and erected in the forest as an offering to the "beast." It comes to symbolize the primordial instincts of power and cruelty that lurk in the boys.

Piggy   Ralph's "lieutenant." A whiny, intellectual boy, Piggy's inventiveness frequently leads to innovation such as a makeshift sundial. Piggy represents the scientific, rational side of civilization.

Ralph   The novel's protagonist. Ralph, a twelve-year-old English boy, is elected leader of the marooned group of boys. He attempts to build a miniature civilization on the island. Ralph represents the civilizing instinct in human beings.

Roger   Jack's "lieutenant." A sadistic, cruel boy, Roger brutalizes the littluns and murders Piggy by rolling a boulder onto him.

Sam and Eric   Twins closely allied with Ralph. Sam and Eric are always together. The other boys often treat them as a single entity, referring to them as "Samneric." They are part of the group known as the "bigguns." Excitable boys, they are eventually manipulated by Jack and his cronies.

Simon   The only wholly good boy on the island. Simon is kind to the younger boys and willing to work for the good of the community. Moreover, because his motivation is rooted in his deep feeling of connectedness to nature, Simon is the only boy whose morality is instinctual, not imposed by society. Simon represents natural goodness, as opposed to the imposed morality represented by Ralph and Piggy.

THEMES IN *LORD OF THE FLIES*

CIVILIZATION AND SAVAGERY   The overriding theme of the novel is the conflict between two competing impulses that exist within all human beings: the instinct to live by rules, act peacefully, and follow the moral orders of society and the instinct to gratify every desire, act violently to obtain power over others, and think of personal profit instead of the good of the group. The first instinct promotes ordered society, and the second threatens it. The conflict between the two instincts can be interpreted as a clash of order and chaos, reason and impulse, law and anarchy, and even good and evil.

The conflict between civilization and savagery is represented most directly by the novel's two main characters: Ralph represents order and civic-mindedness, and Jack represents savagery and power hunger. The other characters are civilized and savage in varying degrees. Piggy, for instance, has no savage feelings, Roger seems incapable of comprehending the rules of civilization. In general, Golding suggests that our savage instincts are primal and fundamental, and our civilized instincts are not. When people are not controlled by society, he says, they will become cruel, wild, and barbaric.

LOSS OF INNOCENCE   As the boys change from well-behaved, orderly children into cruel, bloodthirsty hunters who hardly remember civilization, they naturally lose the sense of innocence that characterized them at the beginning of the novel. The painted savages in Chapter 12 who have hunted, tortured, and killed animals and human beings are worlds away from the simple children who swam in the lagoon in Chapter 3. Golding points out that the children lose their innocence not because someone corrupted them, but because they allow their own evil instincts to flourish. Golding shows the transformation of civilized boys into savages, which is quite different from showing the savagery of boys who have never been civilized—it points to the ultimate weakness of civilizing forces. Golding suggests that civilization can control, but never wipe out, the innate evil that exists in all people.

CHRISTIANITY Golding makes subtle use of Christian iconography. The island itself, particularly Simon's glade, suggests a Garden of Eden that is gradually corrupted by the introduction of evil. Simon is killed because he has identified moral truth, making him a Christ figure. His conversation with the Lord of the Flies suggests a confrontation between Christ and the devil. However, the parallels between Simon and Christ are inexact, so the novel should not be read as a pure Christian allegory. Unlike Christ, Simon lacks a reliable supernatural connection to the divine, dies before he can explain his moral truth, and fails to bring salvation to the island with his murder.

SYMBOLS IN *LORD OF THE FLIES*

SYMBOLS OF CIVILIZATION The conch shell, which Piggy and Ralph first use to summon the boys together after they are separated by the crash, becomes a powerful symbol of civilization and order. During meetings, the boy who holds the shell has the right to speak, making the shell an actual vessel of democratic power. As the island civilization erodes, the conch shell loses its power. When Roger kills Piggy with the boulder, the conch shell is crushed, signifying the complete demise of civilization on the island. The signal fire symbolizes the boys' desire for civilization. When they maintain it carefully, it means they want to return to society. When they let it burn low or go out, it means they have lost interest in civilization.

SYMBOLS OF SAVAGERY The imaginary beast stands for the primal instinct of savagery. Only Simon realizes that the boys fear the beast because it exists in each of them. As the boys grow more savage, their belief in the beast grows stronger. By the end of the novel, they are leaving it sacrifices and treating it as a totemic god. The Lord of the Flies, one of the sacrifices to the beast, is the most important symbol in the novel. It is a physical manifestation of the boys' beastly instincts and a Satanic figure who encourages savagery. "Lord of the Flies" is a translation of the name Beelzebub, a biblical demon sometimes thought to be the devil himself.

IMPORTANT QUOTATIONS FROM *LORD OF THE FLIES*

Roger gathered a handful of stones and began to throw them. Yet there was a space round Henry, perhaps six yards in diameter, into which he dare not throw. Here, invisible yet strong, was the taboo of the old life. Round the squatting child was the protection of parents and school and policemen and the law.

Location: Chapter 4
Speaker: The narrator
Context: Roger starts to be cruel to the littluns

Roger's urge to torment the littluns is an important early step in the group's decline into savagery. At this point, the boys are still trying to cobble together a society, and the civilized instinct still quashes the savage instinct. But the cracks are beginning to show. For instance, some of the older boys are tempted to use violence to flaunt their superiority over the smaller boys. This passage describes the psychological workings behind that temptation. Roger wants to torment Henry, a littlun, by pelting him with stones, but vestiges of civilized behavior cling to him, preventing him from giving in completely to his savage urges. He feels constrained by "parents and school and policemen and the law," agencies that enforce society's moral code. Before long, Roger and most of the other boys will lose their respect for those forces, and violence, torture, and murder will result.

His mind was crowded with memories; memories of the knowledge that had come to them when they closed in on the struggling pig, knowledge that they had outwitted a living thing, imposed their will upon it, taken away its life like a long satisfying drink.

Location: Chapter 4
Speaker: The narrator
Context: Jack gloats over the experience of killing his first pig

Jack's first successful hunt marks another milestone in the boys' decline into savage behavior. The quotation emphasizes Jack's exhilaration, which comes from the rush of power and superiority he experienced while killing the pig. The kill excites him not because it helps the group, but because he "outwitted" another creature and "imposed" his will on it. Earlier, Jack claimed that hunting was important to provide meat for the group. Now it becomes clear that Jack's obsession has nothing to do with helping the group.

"What I mean is . . . Maybe it's only us.. . ."

Location: Chapter 5
Speaker: Simon
Context: The boys consider the question of the beast, and Simon suggests perhaps it does not exist

---

"There isn't anyone to help you. Only me. And I'm the Beast . . . Fancy thinking the Beast was something you could hunt and kill! . . . You knew, didn't you? I'm part of you? Close, close, close! I'm the reason why it's no go? Why things are the way they are?"

Location: Chapter 8
Speaker: The Lord of the Flies
Context: The beast talks to Simon

Ralph wept for the end of innocence, the darkness of man's heart, and the fall through the air of a true, wise friend called Piggy

Location: Chapter 12
Speaker: The narrator
Context: A naval officer arrives on the island, and Ralph reflects on his experiences

MACBETH

William Shakespeare

Inspired by a witches' prophecy, a man murders his way to the throne of Scotland, but his conscience plagues him and his fellow lords rise up against him.

THE LIFE OF WILLIAM SHAKESPEARE

William Shakespeare, the most influential writer in all of English literature, was born in 1564 to a successful middle-class glove-maker in Stratford-upon-Avon, England. Shakespeare's formal education did not progress beyond grammar school. In 1582, he married an older woman, Anne Hathaway. His union with Anne produced three children. Around 1590, Shakespeare left his family behind and traveled to London to work as an actor and playwright. He quickly earned public and critical acclaim, and eventually became the most popular playwright in England and a part-owner of the Globe Theater. Shakespeare's career bridged the reigns of Elizabeth I (ruled 1558–1603) and James I (ruled 1603–1625), and he was a favorite of both monarchs. James paid Shakespeare's company a great compliment by giving its members the title of King's Men. Shakespeare retired to Stratford a wealthy and renowned man and died in 1616 at the age of fifty-two. At the time of Shakespeare's death, literary luminaries such as Ben Jonson hailed his works as timeless.

Shakespeare's works were collected and printed in various editions in the century following his death, and by the early eighteenth century his reputation as the greatest poet ever to write in English was well established. The unprecedented regard in which Shakespeare's works were held led to a fierce curiosity about his life, but many details of Shakespeare's personal history are unknown or shrouded in mystery. Some people have concluded from this lack of information and from Shakespeare's modest education that Shakespeare's plays were actually written by someone else—Francis Bacon and the Earl of Oxford are the two most popular candidates—but the support for this claim is overwhelmingly circumstantial, and the theory is not taken seriously by many scholars.

Shakespeare is generally thought to be the author of the thirty-eight plays (two of them possibly collaborations) and 154 sonnets that bear his name. The legacy of this body of work is immense. A number of Shakespeare's plays seem to have transcended even the category of brilliance, influencing the course of Western literature and culture.

MACBETH IN CONTEXT

Shakespeare's shortest and bloodiest tragedy, *Macbeth* tells the story of Macbeth, a brave Scottish general who receives a prophecy from a trio of sinister witches that one day he will become king of Scotland. Consumed with ambitious thoughts and spurred to action by his wife, Macbeth murders King Duncan and seizes the throne for himself. He begins his reign wracked with guilt and fear and soon becomes a tyrannical ruler, as he is forced to commit more and more murders to protect himself from enmity and suspicion. The bloodbath swiftly propels Macbeth and Lady Macbeth to arrogance, madness, and death.

Macbeth was most likely written in 1606, early in the reign of James I, who had been James VI of Scotland before he succeeded to the English throne in 1603. James was a patron of Shakespeare's acting company, and of all the plays Shakespeare wrote under James's reign, *Macbeth* most clearly reflects the playwright's close relationship with the sovereign. In focusing on Macbeth, a figure from Scottish history, Shakespeare paid homage to his king's Scottish lineage. Additionally, the witches' prophecy that Banquo will found a line of kings is a clear nod to James's family's claim to have descended from the historical Banquo. In a larger sense, the theme of bad versus good kingship, embodied by Macbeth and Duncan, respectively, would have resonated at the royal court, where James was busy developing his English version of the theory of divine right.

Macbeth is not Shakespeare's most complex play, but it is certainly one of his most powerful and emotionally intense. Whereas Shakespeare's other major tragedies, such as *Hamlet* and *Othello*, fastidiously explore the intellectual predicaments faced by their subjects, and the fine nuances of their subjects' characters, *Macbeth* tumbles madly from its opening to its conclusion. It is a sharp, jagged sketch of theme and character that has shocked and fascinated audiences for nearly four hundred years.

MACBETH: KEY FACTS

Full Title: Macbeth

Time and place written: 1606; England

Date of first publication: 1623 (First Folio)

Genre: Tragedy

Setting (time): Eleventh century

Setting (place): Scotland and, briefly, England

Protagonist: Macbeth

Antagonist: Macduff; Macbeth's conscience

Major conflict: Ambitious Macbeth struggles with his conscience before and after he murders Duncan; evil (Macbeth and Lady Macbeth) struggles with good (Malcolm and Macduff)

MACBETH: PLOT OVERVIEW

The play begins with the brief appearance of a trio of witches and then moves to a military camp, where the Scottish King Duncan hears the news that his generals, Macbeth and Banquo, have defeated two separate invading armies—one from Ireland, led by the rebel Macdonald, and one from Norway. Following their pitched battle with these enemy forces, Macbeth and Banquo encounter the witches as they cross a moor. The witches prophesy that Macbeth will be made thane (a rank of Scottish nobility) of Cawdor and eventually king of Scotland. They also prophesy that Macbeth's companion, Banquo, will beget a line of Scottish kings, although Banquo will never be king himself. The witches vanish, and Macbeth and Banquo treat their prophecies skeptically until some of King Duncan's men come to thank the two generals for their victories in battle and to tell Macbeth that he has been named thane of Cawdor. The previous thane betrayed Scotland by fighting for the Norwegians and Duncan has condemned him to death. Macbeth is intrigued by the possibility that he will be crowned king, as the witches said, but he does not know what to expect. He visits with King Duncan, and they plan to dine together at Inverness, Macbeth's castle, that night. Macbeth writes ahead to his wife, Lady Macbeth, telling her all that has happened.

Lady Macbeth suffers from none of her husband's uncertainty. She desires the kingship for him and wants him to murder Duncan in order to obtain it. When Macbeth arrives at Inverness, she overrides all of her husband's objections and persuades him to kill the king that very night. He and Lady Macbeth plan to get Duncan's two chamberlains drunk enough that they black out. The next morning they will blame the murder on the chamberlains, who will be defenseless, as they will remember nothing. While Duncan is asleep, Macbeth stabs him, despite his doubts and a number of supernatural portents, including a vision of a bloody dagger. When Duncan's death is discovered the next morning, Macbeth kills the chamberlains—ostensibly out of rage at their crime—and easily assumes the kingship. Duncan's sons Malcolm and Donalbain flee to England and Ireland, respectively, fearing that whoever killed Duncan desires their demise as well.

Fearful of the witches' prophecy that Banquo's heirs will seize the throne, Macbeth hires a group of murderers to kill Banquo and his son, Fleance. They ambush Banquo on his way to a royal feast, but fail to kill Fleance, who escapes into the night. Macbeth is furious. As long as Fleance is alive, he fears that his grip power is insecure. At the feast that night, Banquo's ghost visits Macbeth. When he sees the ghost, Macbeth babbles in fear, startling his guests, who include most of the great Scottish nobility. Lady Macbeth tries to neutralize the damage, but nobles and subjects begin to resist Macbeth's kingship.

Frightened, Macbeth goes to visit the witches in their cavern. They show him a sequence of demons and spirits who present him with further prophecies: he must beware of Macduff, a Scottish nobleman who opposed Macbeth's accession to the throne; he is incapable of being harmed by any man born of woman; and he will be safe until Birnam Wood comes to Dunsinane Castle. Macbeth is relieved and feels secure, because he knows that all men are born of women and that forests cannot move. When he learns that Macduff has fled to England to join Malcolm, Macbeth orders that Macduff's castle be seized and, most cruelly, that Lady Macduff and her children be murdered.

When news of his family's execution reaches Macduff in England, he is stricken with grief and vows revenge. Prince Malcolm, Duncan's son, has succeeded in raising an army in England, and Macduff joins him as he rides to Scotland to challenge Macbeth's forces. The invasion has the support of the Scottish nobles, who are appalled and frightened by Macbeth's tyrannical and murderous behavior. Lady Macbeth, meanwhile, is plagued by fits of sleepwalking during which she thinks she sees bloodstains on her hands.

Before Macbeth's opponents arrive, Macbeth receives news that Lady Macbeth has killed herself. He sinks into a deep despair. He awaits the English and fortifies Dunsinane, to which he seems to have withdrawn in order to defend himself, certain that the witches' prophecies guarantee his invincibility. He is struck numb with fear, however, when he learns that the English army is advancing on Dunsinane shielded with boughs cut from Birnam Wood. Birnam Wood is indeed coming to Dunsinane, fulfilling half of the witches' prophecy.

In the battle, Macbeth struggles violently, but the English forces gradually overwhelm his army and castle. On the battlefield, Macbeth encounters the vengeful Macduff, who declares that he was not "of woman born" but was instead "untimely ripped" from his mother's womb (what we now call birth by cesarean section). Though he realizes that he is doomed, Macbeth continues to fight until Macduff kills and beheads him. Malcolm, now the king of Scotland, declares his benevolent intentions for the country and invites all to see him crowned at Scone.

CHARACTERS IN *MACBETH*

Banquo   The brave, noble general whose children, according to the witches' prophecy, will inherit the Scottish throne. Like Macbeth, Banquo thinks ambitious thoughts, but he does not translate those thoughts into action. In a sense, Banquo's character stands as a rebuke to Macbeth, since he represents the path Macbeth chose not to take: a path in which ambition need not lead to betrayal and murder. Appropriately, it is Banquo's ghost—not Duncan's—that haunts Macbeth. In addition to embodying Macbeth's guilt over killing Banquo, the ghost also reminds Macbeth that he did not react as well as Banquo did to the witches' prophecy.

Donalbain   Duncan's son and Malcolm's younger brother.

King Duncan   The good king of Scotland whom Macbeth murders in order to attain the crown. Duncan is the model of a virtuous, benevolent, and farsighted ruler. His death symbolizes the destruction of an order in Scotland that can be restored only when Duncan's line, in the person of Malcolm, once more occupies the throne.

Fleance   Banquo's son. Fleance survives Macbeth's attempt to murder him, and at the end of the play his whereabouts are unknown. Presumably, he may rule Scotland one day, fulfilling the witches' prophecy that Banquo's sons will sit on the Scottish throne.

Hecate   The goddess of witchcraft. Hecate helps the three witches work their mischief on Macbeth.

Lennox   A Scottish nobleman.

Macbeth   The main character in the play. Macbeth, a Scottish general and the Thane of Glamis, is led to wicked by the prophecies of the three witches. Macbeth is a brave soldier and a powerful man, but he is not a virtuous one. He has ambitions to the throne and is easily tempted into murder in order to fulfill them. Once he commits his first crime and is crowned king of Scotland, he embarks on further atrocities with increasing ease. His response to every problem is violence and murder. Ultimately, Macbeth lacks the skills necessary to rule without being a tyrant, and is better suited to the battlefield than to political intrigue. Unlike Shakespeare's great villains, such as Richard III and *Othello*'s Iago, Macbeth is never truly comfortable in his role as a criminal.

Lady Macbeth   Macbeth's wife. Lady Macbeth is a deeply ambitious woman who lusts for power and position. Early in the play she seems to be the stronger and more ruthless of the two, as she urges her husband to kill Duncan and seize the crown. After the bloodshed begins, however, Lady Macbeth falls victim to guilt and madness to an even greater degree than her husband. Her conscience affects her to such an extent that eventually she commits suicide. Shakespeare suggests that she and Macbeth are deeply in love, and many of Lady Macbeth's speeches imply that her influence over her husband is primarily sexual. Their joint alienation from the world, occasioned by their partnership in crime, strengthens their already strong attachment.

Macduff A Scottish nobleman hostile to Macbeth's kingship from the start. Eventually Macduff becomes a leader of the crusade to unseat Macbeth. The crusade's mission is to place the rightful king, Malcolm, on the throne, but Macduff also desires vengeance for Macbeth's murder of Macduff's wife and young son.

Lady Macduff Macduff's wife. The scene in her castle provides our only glimpse of a domestic realm other than Macbeth and Lady Macbeth's. Lady Macduff and her home serve as contrasts to Lady Macbeth and the hellish world of Inverness.

Malcolm The son of Duncan, whose restoration to the throne signals Scotland's return to order following Macbeth's reign of terror. Initially weak and uncertain of his own power, as when he and Donalbain flee Scotland after their father's murder, Malcolm becomes a serious challenge to Macbeth with Macduff's aid and the support of England.

The Murderers A group of ruffians ordered by Macbeth to murder Banquo, Fleance (whom they fail to kill), and Macduff's wife and children.

Porter The drunken doorman of Macbeth's castle.

Ross A Scottish nobleman.

The Three Witches Three "black and midnight hags" who plot mischief against Macbeth using charms, spells, and prophecies. The witches' predictions prompt Macbeth to murder Duncan, order the deaths of Banquo and his son, and blindly believe in his own immortality. The play leaves the witches' true identity unclear. Aside from the fact that they are servants of Hecate, we know little about their place in the cosmos. In some ways they resemble the mythological Fates, who impersonally weave the threads of human destiny. The witches take a perverse delight in using their knowledge of the future to toy with and destroy human beings.

THEMES IN *MACBETH*

UNCHECKED AMBITION AS A CORRUPTING FORCE The destruction wrought when ambition goes unchecked by moral constraints, which is the main theme of *Macbeth*, finds its most powerful expression in the play's two main characters. Macbeth is a courageous Scottish general who is not naturally inclined to commit evil deeds, yet deeply desires power and advancement. He kills Duncan against his better judgment and afterward stews in guilt and paranoia. Toward the end of the play he descends into a kind of frantic, boastful madness. Lady Macbeth, in contrast, pursues her goals with greater determination than her husband, yet has more difficulty withstanding the repercussions of her immoral acts. One of Shakespeare's most forcefully drawn female characters, she spurs her husband mercilessly to kill Duncan and urges him to be strong in the murder's aftermath, but she is eventually driven to distraction by the very violence she has demanded. In each case, ambition—helped along by the malign prophecies of the witches—is what drives the couple to commit ever more terrible atrocities. The problem, the play suggests, is that once one decides to use violence to further one's quest for power, it is difficult to stop. There are always potential threats to the throne—Banquo, Fleance, Macduff—and it is always tempting to use violent means to dispose of them.

THE RELATIONSHIP BETWEEN CRUELTY AND MASCULINITY Both Macbeth and Lady Macbeth equate masculinity with naked aggression, and whenever they converse about manhood, violence soon follows. Lady Macbeth manipulates her husband by questioning his manhood, wishes that she herself could be "unsexed," and does not contradict Macbeth when he says that a woman like her should give birth only to boys. Using tactics his wife would condone, Macbeth provokes the murderers he hires to kill Banquo by questioning their manhood.

At the same time, women are a clear source of evil in the play. The witches' prophecies spark Macbeth's ambitions and then encourage his violent behavior, and Lady Macbeth provides the brains and the will behind her husband's plotting. *Macbeth* traces the root of chaos and evil to women, which has led some critics to argue that this is Shakespeare's most misogynistic play.

KINGSHIP VERSUS TYRANNY In the play, Duncan is always referred to as a "king," while Macbeth soon becomes known as a "tyrant." The difference between the two types of rulers is expressed in a conversation that occurs in scene IV.iii, when Macduff meets Malcolm in England. In order to test Macduff's loyalty to Scotland, Malcolm pretends that he would make an even worse king than Macbeth. He tells Macduff of his reproachable qualities, such as a thirst for personal power and a violent temperament, both of which characterize Macbeth perfectly. On the other hand, Malcolm says that the right virtues for a king are "justice, verity, temp'rance, stableness, / Bounty, perseverance, mercy, [and] lowliness" (IV.iii.92–93). The model king, then, offers the kingdom an embodiment of order and justice, but also comfort and affection. Under him, subjects are rewarded according to their merits, as when Duncan makes Macbeth Thane of Cawdor after Macbeth's victory over the invaders. Most important, a good king is loyal to Scotland above himself. Macbeth, by contrast, brings only chaos to Scotland, as symbolized by the bad weather and bizarre supernatural events. He offers no real justice, only a habit of capriciously murdering those he sees as a threat. As the embodiment of tyranny, he must be overcome by Malcolm so that Scotland can have a true king once more.

SYMBOLS IN *MACBETH*

BLOOD Blood is everywhere in *Macbeth*, beginning with the opening battle between the Scots and the Norwegian invaders, which is described in harrowing terms by the wounded captain in scene I.ii. Once Macbeth and Lady Macbeth embark upon their murderous journey, blood comes to symbolize their guilt, and they begin to feel that their crimes have stained them and they cannot be washed clean: "Will all great Neptune's ocean wash this blood / Clean from my hand?" (II.ii.58–59). Macbeth cries after he has killed Duncan, even as his wife scolds him and says that a little water will clean up the mess. Later, though, she comes to share his horrified sense of being stained: "Out, damned spot; out, I say . . . who would have thought the old man to have had so much blood in him?" (V.i.30–34) she asks as she wanders through the halls of their castle near the close of the play. Blood symbolizes the guilt that sits like a permanent stain on the consciences of both Macbeth and Lady Macbeth.

WEATHER Macbeth's grotesque murder spree is accompanied by a number of unnatural occurrences in the natural realm. This link between weather and behavior is a common one in Shakespearean tragedies. From the thunder and lightning that accompany the witches' appearances to the terrible storms that rage on the night of Duncan's murder, these violations of the natural order reflect corruption in the moral and political orders.

IMPORTANT QUOTATIONS FROM *MACBETH*

Out, damned spot; out, I say. One, two,—why, then 'tis time to do't. Hell is murky. Fie, my lord, fie, a soldier and afeard? What need we fear who knows it when none can call our power to account? Yet who would have thought the old man to have had so much blood in him?

Location: V.i.30–34
Speaker: Lady Macbeth
Context: On the night of Macbeth's last battle, Lady Macbeth is sleepwalking and thinks she sees Duncan's blood on her hands

Earlier in the play, Lady Macbeth possessed a stronger resolve and sense of purpose than her husband, and was the driving force behind their plot to kill Duncan. When Macbeth believed his hand was irreversibly bloodstained earlier in the play, Lady Macbeth told him, "A little water clears us of this deed" (II.ii.65). Now, however, she too sees blood. She is completely undone by guilt and descends into madness. It may be a reflection of her mental and emotional state that she is not speaking in verse. This is one of the few moments in the play when a major character—save for the witches, who speak in four-foot couplets—strays from iambic pentameter. Lady Macbeth's inability to sleep was foreshadowed in the voice that her husband thought he heard while killing the king. This voice cried out that Macbeth was murdering sleep. Here, Lady Macbeths' delusion that there is a bloodstain on her hand furthers the play's use of blood as a symbol of guilt. "What need we fear who knows it when none can call our power to account?" she asks, asserting that as long as her own and her husband's power is secure, the murders they committed cannot harm them. But her guilty state and her mounting madness show how hollow her words are. So, too, does the army outside her castle. "Hell is murky," she says, implying that she already knows that darkness intimately. The pair, in their destructive power, have created their own hell, where they are tormented by guilt and insanity.

> *She should have died hereafter.*
> *There would have been a time for such a word.*
> *Tomorrow, and tomorrow, and tomorrow*
> *Creeps in this petty pace from day to day*
> *To the last syllable of recorded time.*
> *And all our yesterdays have lighted fools*
> *The way to dusty death. Out, out, brief candle.*
> *Life's but a walking shadow, a poor player*
> *That struts and frets his hour upon the stage,*
> *And then is heard no more. It is a tale*
> *Told by an idiot, full of sound and fury,*
> *Signifying nothing.*

Location: V.v.16–27
Speaker: Macbeth
Context: Macbeth has learned that Lady Macbeth is dead

Macbeth's oddly muted response to his wife's death quickly segues into an expression of pessimism and despair that is one of Shakespeare's most famous speeches. Macbeth insists that there is no meaning or purpose in life. Rather, life "is a tale / Told by an idiot, full of sound and fury, / Signifying nothing." One can easily understand how, with his wife dead and armies marching against him, Macbeth succumbs to such pessimism. But there is also a defensive and self-justifying quality to his words. If everything is meaningless, then Macbeth's crimes are less horrific, because, like everything else, they too "signify nothing."

Macbeth's statement that "[l]ife's but a poor player / That struts and frets his hour upon the stage" can be read as Shakespeare's somewhat deflating reminder of the illusionary nature of the theater. After all, Macbeth is only a "player" himself, an actor strutting on an Elizabethan stage and playing a king. In any play, there is a conspiracy of sorts between the audience and the actors, as both pretend to accept the play's reality. Macbeth's comment calls attention to this conspiracy and partially explodes it. His nihilism embraces not only his own life but the entire play. If we take his words to heart, the play, too, can be seen as an event "full of sound and fury, / Signifying nothing."

> *The raven himself is hoarse*
> *That croaks the fatal entrance of Duncan*
> *Under my battlements. Come, you spirits*
> *That tend on mortal thoughts, unsex me here,*
> *And fill me from the crown to the toe top-full*
> *Of direst cruelty. Make thick my blood,*
> *Stop up th' access and passage to remorse,*
> *That no compunctious visitings of nature*
> *Shake my fell purpose, nor keep peace between*
> *Th' effect and it. Come to my woman's breasts,*
> *And take my milk for gall, you murd'ring ministers,*
> *Wherever in your sightless substances*
> *And pall thee in the dunnest smoke of hell,*
> *That my keen knife see not the wound it makes,*
> *Nor heaven peep through the blanket of the dark,*

To cry 'Hold, hold!'

Location: I.v.36–52
Speaker: Lady Macbeth
Context: Lady Macbeth appeals to evil spirits to give her masculine courage so that she can help Macbeth murder King Duncan

---

If it were done when 'tis done, then 'twere well
It were done quickly. If th' assassination
Could trammel up the consequence, and catch
With his surcease success: that but this blow
Might be the be-all and the end-all, here,
But here upon this bank and shoal of time,
We'd jump the life to come. But in these cases
We still have judgment here, that we but teach
Bloody instructions which, being taught, return
To plague th' inventor. This even-handed justice
Commends th' ingredience of our poisoned chalice
To our own lips. He's here in double trust:
First, as I am his kinsman and his subject,
Strong both against the deed; then, as his host,
Who should against his murderer shut the door,
Not bear the knife myself. Besides, this Duncan
Hath borne his faculties so meek, hath been
So clear in his great office, that his virtues
Will plead like angels, trumpet-tongued against
The deep damnation of his taking-off,
And pity, like a naked new-born babe,
Striding the blast, or heaven's cherubin, horsed
Upon the sightless couriers of the air,
Shall blow the horrid deed in every eye
That tears shall drown the wind. I have no spur
To prick the sides of my intent, but only
Vaulting ambition which o'erleaps itself
And falls on th' other.

Location: I.vii.1–28
Speaker: Macbeth
Context: Macbeth debates whether or not to kill Duncan

Whence is that knocking?—
How is 't with me, when every noise appalls me?
What hands are here! Ha, they pluck out mine eyes.
Will all great Neptune's ocean wash this blood
Clean from my hand? No, this my hand will rather
The multitudinous seas incarnadine,
Making the green one red.

Location: II.ii.55–61
Speaker: Macbeth
Context: Having just murdered Duncan, Macbeth is startled by a knocking on his door

MADAME BOVARY

Gustave Flaubert

A middle-class woman, frustrated by her humdrum life, embarks on a series of careless affairs that lead to her financial ruin and suicide.

THE LIFE OF GUSTAVE FLAUBERT

Gustave Flaubert was born in 1821 in Rouen, France. His father was a respected and wealthy doctor. As an adult, Flaubert moved in the highest literary circles in Paris. He was reclusive and spent most of his time in solitude. At an early age, Flaubert became fixated upon an older, married woman named Elisa Schlessinger. For many years, he fantasized about having a romantic relationship with her.

Flaubert suffered from poor health and may have had epilepsy. He was frequently depressed. His French contemporaries held him in high esteem, but the public did not. Flaubert was deeply hurt when his masterpiece, *Madame Bovary* (1857), was met with outrage. The novel depicted extramarital sex in what Flaubert's society considered graphic terms, and Flaubert and his publisher were put on trial for violation of public morals. They were acquitted, but the experience intensified Flaubert's hatred of middle-class morality.

In Flaubert's lifetime, France was caught in the throes of immense social upheaval. The Revolution of 1789 and the imperial reign of Napoleon were recent memories, and as the aristocracy collapsed, a new middle class—or bourgeoisie, in French—flourished, consisting of merchants and capitalists with commercial, rather than inherited, fortunes. As a member of the educated elite, Flaubert found the moral conservatism, rough manners, and unsophisticated taste of this new class appalling, opinions he vented in *Madame Bovary* and *A Sentimental Education* (1869). Flaubert was impoverished in his later years. He died on May 8, 1880.

MADAME BOVARY IN CONTEXT

Flaubert once remarked, "Madame Bovary, *c'est moi*" ("Madame Bovary is me"). Like Flaubert, Emma Bovary becomes obsessed with an idealized vision of romantic love, suffers from ill health and a nervous condition, and sinks into frequent depressions.

Madame Bovary is, in part, a reaction against romanticism. Romantic writers, who were popular in France between the late eighteenth and mid-nineteenth centuries, wrote emotional, subjective novels that stressed feeling instead of facts and reason. When Flaubert began writing, a new school called realism had started challenging romantic idealism by focusing on the harsh realities of life. This school included other French writers such as Stendhal and Honorè De Balzac as well as English writers such as George Eliot and Thomas Hardy. Unlike his contemporaries, however, Flaubert recognized a strong streak of romanticism in himself. Moments of romanticism punctuate *Madame Bovary*, but Flaubert treats them with irony.

Though it was his first novel, *Madame Bovary* is Flaubert's most accomplished and admired work. Flaubert was a pioneering stylist, matching the style of his prose to the action of his story in a remarkable new way that has become almost universal in twenty-first century fiction. Other realist novels of the mid-nineteenth century use detached, objective narration, but Flaubert's prose conveys the mood of his characters. When Emma is bored and restless, the prose plods dully. When she experiences sensual pleasure, it moves rapturously and swiftly. In many ways, *Madame Bovary* provided the blueprint for the modern novel.

MADAME BOVARY: KEY FACTS

Time and place written: Croisset, France; 1851–1857

Date of first publication: 1857

Publisher: Revue de Paris

Type of work:	Novel
Genre:	Realist fiction
Language:	French
Setting (time):	Mid-1800s
Setting (place):	France, including the towns of Tostes, Yonville, and Rouen
Tense:	Past
Tone:	Sympathetic, contemptuous
Narrator:	Omniscient third person
Point of view:	Charles Bovary's, Emma Bovary's, and, briefly, Charles Bovary's schoolfellows'
Protagonist:	Emma Bovary
Antagonist:	Ambition, desire

MADAME BOVARY: PLOT OVERVIEW

Charles Bovary is a young boy ridiculed by his classmates at his new school. As a child, and later as a young man, Charles is mediocre and dull. He fails his first medical exam and barely manages to become a second-rate country doctor. His mother marries him off to a widow who soon dies, leaving Charles much less money than he expected.

Charles soon falls in love with Emma, the daughter of a patient. After an elaborate wedding, Emma and Charles set up house in Tostes, where Charles has his practice. Emma, who grew up in a convent, always imagined that love and marriage would solve her problems. But marriage doesn't live up to Emma's romantic expectations. After she attends an extravagant ball at the home of a wealthy nobleman, she begins to dream constantly of a more sophisticated life. She grows bored and depressed when she compares her fantasies to the humdrum reality of village life, and eventually her listlessness makes her ill. When Emma becomes pregnant, Charles decides they should move to a different town in hopes of reviving her health.

In the town of Yonville, the Bovarys meet Homais, the town pharmacist, a pompous windbag who loves to hear himself speak. Emma also meets Leon, a law clerk. Like her, Leon is bored with rural life and loves to escape by reading romantic novels. Emma wants a son, but she gives birth to a daughter, Berthe. Motherhood disappoints her, and she continues to be despondent. Romantic feelings blossom between Emma and Leon. However, when Emma realizes that Leon loves her, she feels guilty and throws herself into the role of dutiful wife. Leon grows tired of waiting and goes to study law in Paris. His departure makes Emma miserable.

At an agricultural fair, a wealthy neighbor named Rodolphe tells Emma that he loves her. He seduces her, and they begin having a passionate affair. Emma is often indiscreet, and the townspeople gossip about her, but Charles suspects nothing. His adoration for his wife and his stupidity blind him to her indiscretions. Meanwhile, his professional reputation suffers a severe blow when he and Homais attempt an experimental surgical technique to treat a club-footed man and end up having to call in another doctor to amputate the leg. Disgusted with her husband's incompetence, Emma throws herself even more passionately into her affair with Rodolphe. She borrows money to buy him gifts and suggests that they run off together and take Berthe with them. The jaded, worldly Rodolphe grows bored of Emma's demanding affections and leaves her. Heartbroken, Emma grows desperately ill and nearly dies.

Charles is in financial trouble from having to borrow money to pay off Emma's debts and pay for her treatment. Still, he decides to take Emma to the opera in the nearby city of Rouen. There, they encounter Leon. This time, Emma embarks on a love affair with Leon, sneaking off to Rouen to meet him. The moneylender Lheureux lends her more and more money at inflated interest rates. She grows increasingly careless in conducting her affair with Leon, and on several occasions her acquaintances nearly discover her infidelity.

Over time, Emma grows bored with Leon. Not knowing how to leave him, she becomes increasingly demanding. Her debts pile up, and eventually Lheureux orders the seizure of Emma's property to compensate for the debt she has accumulated. Terrified, Emma frantically tries to raise the money that she needs, appealing to Leon and all the town's businessmen. She even attempts to prostitute herself by offering to get back together with Rodolphe if he will give her the money she needs. He refuses. Driven to despair, Emma commits suicide by eating arsenic. She dies in horrible agony.

For a while, Charles idealizes the memory of his wife. Eventually, though, he finds her letters from Rodolphe and Leon and is forced to confront the truth. He dies alone in his garden, a broken man. Berthe is sent off to work in a cotton mill.

CHARACTERS IN *MADAME BOVARY*

Berthe Charles and Emma's daughter.

Binet A tax collector.

Rodolphe Boulanger A wealthy landowner. Rodolphe is shrewd, selfish, and manipulative. He has had scores of lovers besides Emma.

Abbé Bournisien The Yonville town priest. Bournisien focuses on worldly matters, and although he often argues with Homais about the value of religion, he seems incapable of grasping deep spiritual problems.

Charles Bovary A country doctor. Charles is kind, dull, and terrible at his job. He dotes on his wife, Emma, who can do no wrong in his eyes, but he doesn't understand her. Her looks and dress captivate him, but her personality perplexes him. His innocent love for his wife leads to his financial ruin.

Emma Bovary The novel's protagonist. Emma harbors idealistic romantic illusions and covets sophistication and passion. Her middle-class life depresses her, and her daughter annoys her. Occasionally, guilt or a memory of her simple childhood cause Emma to repent, and for a brief time she becomes devoutly religious and devoted to her family.

The elder Madame Bovary Charles's mother. Madame Bovary is a bitter, conservative woman who spoiled her son and disapproves of Emma. She sees through Emma's lies and tries to get Charles to rein in his wife's excessive spending.

Heloise Dubuc Charles's first wife.

Guillaumin A well-to-do lawyer. When Emma seeks his help, he offers to give her money in return for sexual favors—an offer she angrily declines.

Hippolyte A crippled servant at the inn in Yonville. Under pressure from Emma and Homais, Charles attempts to operate on Hippolyte's club foot. The operation fails, gangrene sets in, and Hippolyte loses his leg.

Monsieur Homais An apothecary. Homais is a pompous, superficial man. He loves to hear himself talk and believes that religion and prayer are useless. Homais embodies the bourgeois values and characteristics that disgust Flaubert and bore Emma.

Justin Homais's assistant. Justin is young, impressionable, and simple. He falls in love with Emma and unwittingly gives her access to arsenic.

Lariviere An esteemed doctor from Rouen. Lariviere is called in after Emma takes arsenic at the end of the novel. He is cold but brilliant.

Leon Emma's friend and eventually her lover. Although Emma believes Leon is cosmopolitan, he is actually awkward and conceited.

Monsieur Lheureux A sly, sinister merchant and moneylender. Lheureux leads Emma into debt, financial ruin, and eventually suicide by playing on her weakness for luxury and extravagance.

Rouault Emma's father. Rouault is a simple, essentially kindly farmer with a weakness for drink. He is devoted to Emma and to the memory of his first wife.

THEMES IN *MADAME BOVARY*

THE INADEQUACY OF LANGUAGE *Madame Bovary* explores the possibility that the written word fails to capture even a small part of the depth of a human life. The characters' frequent inability to communicate with each other is emblematic of the fact that words do not perfectly describe what they signify. Words fail Emma again and again as she tries to make her distress known to the priest or to express her love to Rodolphe. The lies that fill *Madame Bovary* contribute to the sense that words obscure truth more than they convey it. Flaubert describes Emma's life as "a tissue of lies." By pointing out the inadequacy of language, Flaubert argues that no kind of writing, even writing in the school of realism, can claim to capture life. Flaubert, himself a realist in some sense, believes it is wrong to claim that realism provides a more accurate picture of life than romanticism does. In this novel, he shows that ironic romantic descriptions, not realism, best convey the gap between the way people see events and the way events actually happen.

THE POWERLESSNESS OF WOMEN

Flaubert demonstrates an intimate understanding of the plight of women in his time. He sympathizes with Emma, who has no control over her own life. She must depend on her husband for wealth and advancement, and when Charles's laziness and incompetence prevent him from becoming a good doctor and moving into a higher social class, Emma can do nothing to help. When Rodolphe abandons her, she must give up her dreams of escaping her little town, since women cannot flee on their own. When Leon moves to the city, Emma must stay behind, shackled to a husband and child.

Emma makes bad choices, but her life ends in disaster mainly because she is insufficiently cunning, not because she behaves immorally. She correctly realizes that while men have power in the form of wealth and property, women have power only in the form of their bodies, which they must trade in secret. Flaubert does not condemn Emma for using her body to get what she wants. He condemns her because she uses her body as inexpertly as Charles wields a scalpel. With a little cleverness, Emma's financial ruin and suicide could have been avoided easily.

THE FAILURES OF THE BOURGEOISIE

Emma's disappointments stem largely from her dissatisfaction with the world of the French bourgeoisie, which she considers unrefined and unsophisticated. Her frustration reflects a rising social and historical trend of the late nineteenth century. In Flaubert's day, the word "bourgeois" referred to the class of people who lacked the independent wealth and ancestry of the nobility, but who did not perform physical labor to earn their living. A whole set of stereotypes sprung up around the bourgeois. They were said to be gaudy, materialistic people who indulged themselves without discrimination. The mediocrity of the bourgeoisie annoyed Flaubert, and he uses Emma Bovary as a mouthpiece for his disgust with her class. *Madame Bovary* shows how ridiculous, stifling, and potentially harmful the attitudes of the bourgeoisie can be. In Homais's longwinded, know-it-all speeches, Flaubert mocks the bourgeois class's pretensions to knowledge and learning, and its faith in technologies it doesn't understand. But Homais is not just funny; he is also dangerous. When he urges Charles to try a new medical procedure on Hippolyte, the patient loses his leg. When he attempts to treat Emma for her poisoning, he shows off by analyzing the poison and coming up with an antidote. Later, a doctor remarks that he should have simply stuck a finger down Emma's throat to save her life.

SYMBOLS IN *MADAME BOVARY*

THE BLIND BEGGAR

A picture of physical decay, the blind beggar symbolizes Emma's moral corruption. He sings songs about "birds and sunshine and green leaves" in a voice that suggests "some vague despair." This coupling of innocence with disease suggests Emma's combination of beauty and corruption. Her words, appearance, and fantasies are those of an innocent and beautiful wife, but her spirit is foul and corrupt. When Emma dies, we discover that the beggar's song is not about an innocent woman. In fact, it is bawdy and sexual. The song's progression from innocence to degradation parallels the path of Emma's life.

THE LATHE

Binet's habit of making napkin rings on his lathe is a symbol with several meanings. First, it represents the useless, nonproductive, ornamental character of bourgeois tastes. Second, the repetitiveness of the habit represents the monotony of the life that traps Emma. The sound of the lathe calls Emma to suicide. Finally, the lathe represents an artist's labors. Flaubert once compared himself to a craftsman working on a lathe.

IMPORTANT QUOTATIONS FROM *MADAME BOVARY*

But it was above all at mealtimes that she could bear it no longer, in that little room on the ground floor, with the smoking stove, the creaking door, the oozing walls, the damp floor-tiles; all the bitterness of life seemed to be served to her on her plate, and, with the steam from the boiled beef, there rose from the depths of her soul other exhalations as it were of disgust. Charles was a slow eater; she would nibble a few hazel-nuts, or else, leaning on her elbow, would amuse herself making marks on the oilcloth with the point of her table-knife.

Location: Part One, Chapter IX
Speaker: The narrator
Context: The narrator describes Emma's frustration

This passage illustrates Flaubert's combination of realism and emotional subjectivity. In the realistic style, Flaubert pays attention to tiny details, no matter how unpleasant. But he employs these tiny details in a subjective way, using them to make us feel Emma's disgust and frustration. He emphasizes how important the object world is to Emma's thoughts, showing us how she links her soul's exhalations to the steam rising from the beef. By making emotions inseparable from objects, as he does throughout the novel, Flaubert denies Emma her most fervent longing: to escape the physical world she inhabits and live the life she imagines. Because Flaubert does not let us observe Emma's environment from a distance, but forces us down on the level of the "oozing walls" and the "damp floor-tiles," he makes us share Emma's frustration and claustrophobia.

And besides, should [Rodolphe] hesitate to come to her assistance, she would know well enough how one single glance would reawaken their lost love. So she set out towards La Huchette, unaware that she was hastening to offer what had so angered her a while ago, not in the least conscious of her prostitution.

Location: Part Three, Chapter VII
Speaker: The narrator
Context: Emma goes to see Rodolphe

What angered Emma "a while ago" was the idea that she might sell her body for money. She angrily refused Guillaumin's offers of money in exchange for sex. Flaubert points out that her willingness to rekindle her romance with Rodolphe is no better than prostitution. Her unawareness of the equivalence of the two actions demonstrates the degree of her moral corruption. At the same time, her belief that Rodolphe truly loved her enough to help her now is proof of her continued naïveté and self-delusion.

She hoped for a son; he would be strong and dark; she would call him George; and this idea of having a male child was like an expected revenge for all her impotence in the past. A man, at least, is free; he can explore all passions and all countries, overcome obstacles, taste of the most distant pleasures. But a woman is always hampered. Being inert as well as pliable, she has against her the weakness of the flesh and the inequity of the law. Like the veil held to her hat by a ribbon, her will flutters in every breeze; she is always drawn by some desire, restrained by some rule of conduct.

Location: Part Two, Chapter III
Speaker: The narrator
Context: Emma thinks about her unborn child

The whitish light of the window-panes was softly wavering. The pieces of furniture seemed more frozen in their places, about to lose themselves in the shadow as in an ocean of darkness. The fire was out, the clock went on ticking, and Emma vaguely wondered at this calm of all things while within herself there was such a tumult.

Location: Part Two, Chapter VI
Speaker: The narrator
Context: The narrator describes Emma's overriding frustration—that the outside world does not match her inner world

---

[Rodolphe] had heard such stuff so many times that her words meant very little to him. Emma was just like any other mistress; and the charm of novelty, falling down slowly like a dress, exposed only the eternal monotony of passion, always the same forms and the same language. He did not distinguish, this man of such great expertise, the differences of sentiment beneath the sameness of their expressions. Because he had heard such-like phrases murmured to him from the lips of the licentious or the venal, he hardly believed in hers; you must, he thought, beware of turgid speeches masking commonplace passions; as though the soul's abundance does not sometimes spill over in the most decrepit metaphors, since no one can ever give the exact measure of their needs, their ideas, their afflictions, and since human speech is like a cracked cauldron on which we knock out tunes for dancing-bears, when we wish to conjure pity from the stars.

Location: Part Two, Chapter IX
Speaker: The narrator
Context: The narrator comments on the inadequacy of language

A MAN FOR ALL SEASONS

Robert Bolt

A man refuses to swear an oath to the supremacy of King Henry VIII and is beheaded.

THE LIFE OF ROBERT BOLT

Robert Bolt was born in 1924 in Manchester, England. In 1941, he began working at an insurance agency. Later, he attended Manchester University, served in the Royal Air Force, and fought in World War II. After the war, Bolt worked in England as a schoolteacher until 1958, when his play *Flowering Cherry* met with success and critical acclaim. He wrote *A Man for All Seasons* in 1960. The play was mounted on the London stage that same year and in New York in 1961. Bolt went on to write the screenplays for director David Lean's famous films *Lawrence of Arabia* (1962) and *Dr. Zhivago* (1965). He adapted *A Man for All Seasons* for director Fred Zinnemann in 1966, and he won Oscars for both *Zhivago* and *A Man for All Seasons*.

A MAN FOR ALL SEASONS IN CONTEXT

Bolt puts his play in context with a foreword, saying the "bit of English history which is the background to this play is pretty well known" and summarizing that bit of history. In 1509, King Henry VIII married his brother's widow, Catherine of Aragón (Spain), cementing his alliance with Spain. The pope granted Henry a dispensation (an exemption from Catholic law) to allow this illegal union between a man and his brother's widow. The couple tried and failed to produce an heir.

The king became enamored of the lusty and presumably more fertile Anne Boleyn, so he sought to overturn the pope's previous dispensation in order to annul his marriage to Catherine and marry Anne. Citing Leviticus 18—"Thou shalt not uncover the nakedness of thy brother's wife"—Henry requested a second dispensation from the pope, this time for a divorce from Catherine. Henry argued that Catherine's inability to produce a male child proved that their marriage was wrong. When Pope Clement VII refused to allow the divorce, Henry dismissed his adviser, Cardinal Wolsey, who died of heart complications soon after. In 1529, Henry appointed Thomas More (1477–1535) Lord Chancellor of England.

Henry and his associate Thomas Cromwell enacted legislation to undermine the authority of the Catholic Church in England. As soon as the pope assented to Henry's appointment of Thomas Crammer as Archbishop of Canterbury, Crammer authorized Henry's divorce and remarriage. As a result, Henry was excommunicated from the Catholic Church. In 1534, Parliament enacted the Act of Supremacy, which established Henry as the head of the Church in England and eliminated the authority of the pope.

Sir Thomas More, a humanist and friend to Erasmus, was author of *Utopia* (1516), a novel that imagined a society founded solely on reason. He was a true Renaissance man, "a man for all seasons." More was beheaded on July 6, 1535, for failing to swear an oath to Henry's supremacy. For his courage and commitment, More was sainted on May 19, 1935.

Bolt dismisses the modern tendency to analyze texts according to socioeconomic trends—such as from the perspective of progressive economy or conservative religion—because this type of analysis wrongly focuses on the power of social forces rather than on human beings as individual agents. Bolt believes it is important to see conflicts as collisions between human beings, not just between systems or ideas, and he holds the individuals in his play accountable for their actions. Bolt argues that if we see history as the interaction of large-scale, abstract forces, such as religion and economy, we rob ourselves of identity. We begin to use social categories to describe individuals, so the answer to the question "What am I?" becomes a statement of material and social circumstances.

Bolt says he is not interested in how socioeconomic forces and trends influenced More. He is attracted to More's unyielding "sense of his own self." Because Catholicism is something More believes in, Bolt argues, Catholicism is something that More essentially *is*, so he cannot swear an oath against it. Bolt says that modern audiences might view the oath More was asked to swear as a symbolic or ritual exercise, but More saw it as an "invitation to God" to judge More. His own life, his own soul, depended on whether he kept his word.

A MAN FOR ALL SEASONS: KEY FACTS

Time and place written: England; 1960

Date of first publication: 1960

Publisher: William Heinemann Ltd.

Type of work: Play

Genre: Historical drama; satire

Language: English

Setting (time): 1529–1535

Setting (place): More's home in London's Chelsea district and the king's court at Hampton

Tone: Ominous, foreboding

Narrator: The Common Man

Protagonist: Sir Thomas More

Antagonist: King Henry VIII

A MAN FOR ALL SEASONS: PLOT OVERVIEW

The Common Man figures prominently both in the plot of the play and also as a narrator and commentator, but in the plot overview, his presence is indicated only when he interacts directly with the other characters in the play.

Sir Thomas More, a scholar and statesman, objects to King Henry VIII's plan to divorce and remarry in order to father a male heir. But More, ever the diplomat, keeps quiet about his feelings. At a meeting with Cardinal Wolsey, Lord Chancellor of England, More reviews the letter to Rome that requests the pope's approval of Henry's divorce. More points out that the pope had to bend the rules for Henry to marry Catherine, his current wife, because she was his brother's widow. More doubts that the pope will overturn his first dispensation. Wolsey accuses More of being too moralistic.

Sir Thomas More, a scholar and statesman, objects to King Henry VIII's plan to divorce and remarry in order to father a male heir. But More, ever the diplomat, keeps quiet about his feelings. At a meeting with Cardinal Wolsey, Lord Chancellor of England, More reviews the letter to Rome that requests the pope's approval of Henry's divorce. More points out that the pope had to bend the rules for Henry to marry Catherine, his current wife, because she was his brother's widow. More doubts that the pope will overturn his first dispensation. Wolsey accuses More of being too moralistic.

More runs into Thomas Cromwell, the king's confidante. Cromwell, recently promoted to the position of cardinal's secretary, insincerely professes himself a great admirer of More. More also meets Signor Chapuys, the Spanish ambassador to England. Chapuys assumes that More, like him, disapproves of the divorce. Chapuys worries that Henry will insult Catherine, who is also the aunt of the king of Spain.

More's daughter, Margaret, has received a visit from Roper, her Lutheran boyfriend. Roper asks More for Margaret's hand, but More considers Roper a heretic and refuses.

Wolsey dies in disgrace—the king was displeased with Wolsey's failure to secure a papal dispensation to annul his marriage to Catherine. More is appointed as Wolsey's replacement.

Cromwell meets with Richard Rich, a low-level functionary whom More helped establish. Cromwell tempts Rich with an opportunity for advancement. Rich seems eager to accept the job in exchange for information on More. Cromwell tells Rich and Chapuys, who has just come in, that he does whatever the king wants done. He mentions that the king has planned a boat ride down the Thames to visit More. More's manservant, Matthew (played by the Common Man) has entered the room, and Cromwell, Rich, and Chapuys try to bribe him for information. Matthew tells them only commonly known facts about his master, but the trio pays him off anyway.

The king comes to More's home in London's Chelsea district. More flatters the king, but he says he cannot agree to the divorce. The king storms off, telling More he will leave him alone provided More does not speak out against the divorce. Alice, More's wife, thinks her husband should do as Henry wants. Rich arrives to tell More that Cromwell and Chapuys are collecting information about him. He asks for employment, but More turns him away.

At a local pub called the Loyal Subject, Cromwell meets Rich to conspire against More. Rich, though reluctant and guilt-ridden, agrees to tell Cromwell about a bribe More received (More did not know it was a bribe) and passed on to him. In exchange, Cromwell will give Rich a job.

Parliament passes the Act of Supremacy, which establishes the Church in England and appoints King Henry as its head. More decides that if the English bishops decide to go along with the act, he will resign as Lord Chancellor. Both Chapuys and Roper call it a remarkable "gesture," but More thinks of it as a practical necessity.

Cromwell meets with the Duke of Norfolk and tells him of his plan to bring More up on bribery charges. But Norfolk proves that More gave the cup to Rich as soon as he realized it was a bribe, and Cromwell is forced to come up with some other way to entrap More. He tells Norfolk that the king expects him to participate in the persecution of More.

More, now impoverished, refuses to receive a letter of appreciation from the king of Spain and turns down the bishops' sincere offer of charity. Cromwell calls More to his office and accuses him of sympathizing with the Holy Maid of Kent, who was executed for treason. Cromwell also accuses him of writing a book attributed to King Henry. More deconstructs both these charges, but when Cromwell reads a letter from King Henry calling More a villain, More is genuinely shaken. Meeting Norfolk outside, More tells Norfolk to break off their friendship if he wants to remain in the king's favor.

Parliament passes another act, this time requiring subjects to swear an oath to King Henry's supremacy in England over the Church and to the validity of his divorce and remarriage. The next time we see More, he is in jail for having refused to take the oath. Cromwell, Norfolk, and the Archbishop of Canterbury interrogate More in prison, but they cannot trick him into signing the oath or divulging his opinion of the king's behavior. As long as More refuses to talk or sign the oath, Cromwell can keep him locked up but cannot have him executed. He removes More's books but lets his family visit, hoping they will be able to reason with him. Though More's daughter, Margaret, tries to convince her father he has done all he can, More refuses to relent. Alice understands More's predicament. They reconcile just before the jailer (the Common Man) insists that the visit is over.

Cromwell gives Rich the office of attorney general for Wales in exchange for Rich's false testimony at More's trial. Rich lies and says he heard More deny the king's authority over the Church. More is sentenced to death, but not before he can express his disapproval of the Supremacy Act and his disappointment with a government that would kill a man for keeping quiet. More goes to his death with dignity and composure. The play ends with his beheading.

CHARACTERS IN *A MAN FOR ALL SEASONS*

The Common Man The occasional narrator of the play. The Common Man plays the roles of most of the lower-class characters: More's steward Matthew, the boatman, the publican (innkeeper), the jailer, the jury foreman, and the headsman (executioner). Bolt says the Common Man personifies attitudes and actions that are common to everyone, but he is also "common" in that he is contemptible, ignoble.

Chapuys The Spanish ambassador to England. Chapuys is loyal to his country and has an aptitude for hiding his political agenda under the guise of religious fervor.

Thomas Cromwell A crafty lawyer. In contrast to Rich and the Common Man, who are sometimes reluctant to act badly, Cromwell plots against More because he is evil.

Duke of Norfolk More's close friend. A large and rather simpleminded man, he is often too dense to know what's going on.

King Henry VIII The king of England. Henry appears onstage only briefly, but he is a constant presence in the speech and the thoughts of the other characters. Henry wants people to think of him as a moral person and longs to put his conscience at ease by making authorities validate his desires.

Alice More   More's wife. Initially, More's stubbornness angers and confuses Alice, but eventually she understands it.

Sir Thomas More   The protagonist of the play. Bolt does not depict More as a saint, or even as a man who takes a stand and sacrifices himself for a cause. Rather, Bolt's More gives up his life because he cannot sacrifice his own commitment to his conscience.

Richard Rich   A low-level functionary whom More helped establish. Rich's disloyalty and immorality lead to his meteoric rise to wealth and power, which parallels More's fall from favor. Rich conquers and destroys his conscience rather than obeying it.

Margaret Roper   More's well-educated and inquisitive daughter. Margaret understands her father perhaps better than anyone else in the play, although she does question his actions.

William Roper   The man Margaret marries. Roper is an overzealous young man who is a staunch Lutheran at the beginning of the play and a Catholic at the end of it. His high-minded ideals contrast with More's level-headed morality.

Cardinal Wolsey   The Lord Chancellor of England.

THEMES IN *A MAN FOR ALL SEASONS*

THE LAW OF MEN   More believes in the rule of men and society. He considers God's law supreme, but he does not pretend to understand it. As he says to Will Roper, "I find [God] rather too . . . subtle." Because God is too subtle, More thinks, men's law is the best available guide even if occasionally it contradicts God's law. When More decides that men's law prohibits Henry's divorce, he sticks to his decision. More's pragmatic maneuvering contrasts with Roper's "seagoing" principles, as More calls them. Roper follows ideals instead of his conscience or the law, a strategy More compares to being lost at sea. Roper switches willy-nilly from Catholicism to Lutheranism and back again, each time utterly convinced of his own righteousness.

CORRUPTION   *A Man for All Seasons* focuses on the rise of Richard Rich as much as on the fall of Sir Thomas More. As More's steadfast faithfulness to himself brings him ever closer to disaster, Rich's disloyalty to himself and his friend brings him more wealth and status. Although at first Rich bemoans his loss of innocence, by the end of the play he has no qualms about perjuring himself in exchange for a high-ranking position. Act I, scene viii, recalls cautionary stories about the seductive powers of the devil. Rich gives Cromwell information about the silver cup in exchange for a job and then laments that he has lost his innocence, as if he has sold his soul to the devil. But Bolt does not suggest that people like Rich go to hell. Their punishment happens in life. Bolt thinks self-respect and goodness are what make life worth living, and when Rich allows Cromwell to seduce him, he loses both.

THE SELF AND THE OTHER   Bolt asks whether we can be both true to ourselves and good to others. More looks to himself, not to others, for strength and comfort. He relies on his own conscience as his guide, and through tests and through the example he sets, he attempts to teach his friends and relatives to do the same. More's role as teacher rather than lover or friend can make him seem cold, but his desire to teach is also an expression of love. In conversations with Norfolk and Alice, More shows that he truly cares about them. With his friend's welfare in mind, More tells Norfolk to "cease knowing him." He tells his wife that he could not die peacefully if he knew she did not understand his silence. More also tells Matthew that he will miss him.

SYMBOLS IN *A MAN FOR ALL SEASONS*

WATER AND DRY LAND   In his preface, Bolt writes that his play is full of water and seafaring imagery, which symbolizes the uncertain moral territory of the great beyond, the unknowable realm of God and the devil. Characters who live in this enigmatic moral space include King Henry, who sails down the Thames to visit More, and Roper, who has what More calls "seagoing" principles. Unlike Henry and Roper, More roots his actions in his own conscience and in the law, which he compares to a forest filled with protective trees.

THE GILDED CUP   The gilded cup symbolizes corruption. When More realizes it is a bribe, he wants to get rid of it right away, which suggests his attitude toward corruption. When Rich gets the bribed cup, he pawns it for money and new clothes. The cup symbolizes corruption. More's attempt to test Rich with the cup sets in motion the events that lead to More's conviction at the end of the play—a conviction that Rich helps secure by lying under oath in court.

IMPORTANT QUOTATIONS FROM *A MAN FOR ALL SEASONS*

My Master Thomas More would give anything to anyone. Some say that's good and some say that's bad, but I say he can't help it—and that's bad . . . because some day someone's going to ask him for something that he wants to keep; and he'll be out of practice.

Location: Act I, scene i
Speaker: More's servant, Matthew
Context: Matthew predicts More's dilemma

In the beginning of the play, the characters played by the Common Man—Matthew, for example—seem to be insightful, clever members of the lower class. They make astute points and satirize the nobility. Here, when Matthew predicts More's future, he sounds sage. But at the play's close, the Common Man has unraveled and behaved reprehensibly, causing us to rethink our original opinions of him.

Better a live rat than a dead lion.

Location: Act II, scene vii
Speaker: The jailor
Context: The jailor justifies himself

The jailer, played by the Common Man, invokes what he calls an "old adage" to justify the fact that he does not live according to his conscience. The jailer's statement is actually a misquoted version of the biblical saying, "Better a live dog than a dead lion" (Ecclesiastes 9:4), which the jailor interprets to mean that it is better to live a dishonorable life than to die honorably. The play argues that it is always better to be a dead lion, as More is.

Although in the end More gives up his life for the good of his soul, he can go to his death in peace only because he believes God has chosen the time of his departure. He believes that men should outwit death until death is the only course left.

Well . . . I believe, when statesmen forsake their own private conscience for the sake of their public duties. . . they lead their country by a short route to chaos.

Location: Act I, scene ii
Speaker: More
Context: More criticizes Wolsey's approach to politics

(Quietly) I neither could nor would rule my King. (Pleasantly) But there's a little . . . little, area . . . where I must rule myself. It's very little—less to him than a tennis court.

Location: Act I, scene vii
Speaker: More
Context: After King Henry visits their home, More says he will allow the king to rule him except in matters pertaining to his conscience

And when the last law was down, and the Devil turned round on you—where would you hide, Roper, the laws all being flat? (He leaves him) This country's planted thick with laws from coast to coast—man's laws, not God's—and if you cut them down—and you're just the man to do it—d'you really think you could stand upright in the winds that would blow then?

Location: Act I, scene vii
Speaker: More
Context: Roper accuses More of respecting God's law more than man's

THE MAYOR OF CASTERBRIDGE

Thomas Hardy

A man tries and fails to atone for his past mistake—selling his wife and daughter to a sailor.

THE LIFE OF THOMAS HARDY

Thomas Hardy was born on June 2, 1840, in a rural region of southwestern England. The son of a builder, Hardy was apprenticed at the age of sixteen to John Hicks, an architect who lived in the city of Dorchester, which would later serve as the model for Hardy's fictional Casterbridge. Although Hardy gave serious thought to attending university and then entering the church, a struggle he dramatized in his 1895 novel *Jude the Obscure*, his religious skepticism and lack of money led him to pursue a career in writing instead. Hardy spent nearly a dozen years toiling in obscurity and producing unsuccessful novels and poetry. *Far from the Madding Crowd*, published in 1874, was his first critical and financial success. Hardy married Emma Lavinia Gifford later that year.

Hardy considered poetry his calling and novels his way of earning a living. In many respects, he was caught between the nineteenth and twentieth centuries, between Victorian and modern sensibilities, and between tradition and innovation.

Hardy accepted Charles Darwin's theory of evolution. He also studied the works of the German philosopher Arthur Schopenhauer, who described an "Immanent Will," a blind force that drives the universe. Though his novels often end in crushing tragedies that reflect Schopenhauer's philosophy, Hardy described himself as a *meliorist*, one who believes that the world tends to become better and that people aid in this betterment. Hardy died in 1928 at his estate in Dorchester. His heart was buried in his wife's tomb.

THE MAYOR OF CASTERBRIDGE IN CONTEXT

The Mayor of Casterbridge has Victorian and modern elements. It charts one man's development, but it also chronicles the dramatic change of an isolated, rural agricultural community into a modern city. In *The Mayor of Casterbridge*, Hardy explores the effects of cultural and economic development: the decline of Christianity and folk traditions, the rise of industrialization and urbanization, and the unraveling of moral codes.

THE MAYOR OF CASTERBRIDGE: KEY FACTS

Full title: The Life and Death of the Mayor of Casterbridge: A Story of a Man of Character

Time and place written: 1885–1886; Dorchester, England

Date of first publication: 1886

Publisher: Graphic magazine in England and in *Harper's Weekly* in the United States (both published it in serial form); Smith, Elder in England; Henry Holt in America

Type of work: Novel

Genre: Bildungsroman

Language: English

Setting (time): Mid-1800s

Setting (place): Casterbridge, England (a fictional town based on the city of Dorchester)

Tense: Past

Tone: Tragic, melodramatic, naturalistic

Narrator: Anonymous narrator in the third person

Point of view: The narrator's

Protagonist: Michael Henchard

Antagonist: Henchard's guilt

THE MAYOR OF CASTERBRIDGE: PLOT OVERVIEW

Michael Henchard is traveling with his wife, Susan, and baby daughter, Elizabeth-Jane, looking for employment as a hay-trusser. When they stop to eat, Henchard gets drunk. In an auction that begins as a joke but turns serious, he sells his wife and baby to Newson, a sailor, for five guineas. In the morning, Henchard regrets what he has done and searches the town for his wife and daughter. Unable to find them, he goes into a church and swears an oath that he will not drink alcohol for twenty-one years, the same number of years he has been alive.

Eighteen years later, after the sailor's death, Susan and Elizabeth-Jane find Henchard, who is now mayor of Casterbridge. Elizabeth-Jane thinks Henchard is a relative, not her father. Susan and Henchard decide that in order to prevent Elizabeth-Jane from learning the truth, Henchard should court and remarry Susan as if they had met only recently.

Henchard has hired Donald Farfrae, a young Scotchman, as the new manager of his corn business. Elizabeth-Jane and Farfrae begin to spend time together. Farfrae constantly outdoes Henchard in every respect, and Henchard asks Farfrae to leave his business and stop courting Elizabeth-Jane.

Susan falls ill and dies. Henchard learns that Elizabeth-Jane is the sailor's daughter, not hers—his baby, also called Elizabeth-Jane, died soon after he sold her. Henchard becomes increasingly cold to Elizabeth-Jane, who goes to live with a lady who has just arrived in town. This lady turns out to be Lucetta Templeman, a woman with whom Henchard was involved during Susan's absence. Having learned of Susan's death, Lucetta has come to Casterbridge to marry Henchard.

Farfrae goes to Lucetta's house to call on Elizabeth-Jane. He and Lucetta take to each other and eventually marry. Lucetta asks Henchard to return the letters she sent him. Henchard sends them to her via a messenger, Jopp, who stops at an inn and winds up reading the letters aloud. The peasants at the inn decide to hold a "skimmity-ride," a humiliating parade portraying Lucetta and Henchard together. The event takes place one afternoon when Farfrae is away. Lucetta faints upon seeing the spectacle and falls ill. Shortly afterward, she dies.

The morning after Lucetta's death, Newson arrives at Henchard's house. It turns out that he let Susan think he died at sea, because she had grown unhappy with him. Henchard tells Newson that Elizabeth-Jane is dead, and Newson leaves in sorrow. Elizabeth-Jane stays with Henchard and begins to spend more time with Farfrae. One day, Henchard learns that Newson has returned to town, and he decides to leave rather than risk another confrontation. Elizabeth-Jane is reunited with Newson, her father, and learns of Henchard's deceit. Farfrae and Elizabeth-Jane decide to marry.

Henchard comes back to Casterbridge on the night of the wedding to see Elizabeth-Jane, but she snubs him. He leaves again, telling her he will not return. She soon regrets her coldness, and she and Farfrae go looking for Henchard so that she can make her peace with him. They learn that he has died alone in the countryside. In his will, he says his dying wish is to be forgotten.

CHARACTERS IN *THE MAYOR OF CASTERBRIDGE*

Christopher Coney A peasant in Casterbridge. Coney represents the bleak reality of peasant life.

Mother Cuxsom A peasant.

Donald Farfrae The Scotchman who eventually marries Elizabeth-Jane. Farfrae's business efficiency, good humor, and polish make him extremely popular among the town's citizens. Farfrae is fair-minded, patient, and even kind in his dealings with the ruined Henchard.

Benjamin Grower One of Henchard's creditors.

Michael Henchard The novel's protagonist. Henchard tries to atone for the crimes of his youth, but his focus on his past misdeeds sends him on a downward trajectory.

Susan Henchard The wife of Henchard and then Newson. A meek, unassuming woman, Susan is anxious to be respectable. She keeps secrets about Henchard's and Elizabeth-Jane's identities in order to create the appearance of perfect family harmony.

Joshua Jopp The man Henchard intends to hire as his assistant before meeting Farfrae.

Solomon Longways A peasant.

Nance Mockridge A peasant who is instrumental in planning the skimmity-ride.

Elizabeth-Jane Newson The daughter of Susan and Newson. Over the course of the novel, the independent and self-possessed Elizabeth-Jane transforms herself from an unrefined country girl into a cultured young woman. She stays calm in the face of the many hardships that dog her.

Newson The sailor who buys Susan and Elizabeth-Jane from Henchard.

Lucetta Templeman Henchard's ex-lover, and Farfrae's first wife. Like Henchard, Lucetta is guided by her emotions.

Abel Whittle A worker in Henchard's hay-yard.

THEMES IN *THE MAYOR OF CASTERBRIDGE*

THE IMPORTANCE OF CHARACTER A "Story of a Man of Character," *The Mayor of Casterbridge* examines the characteristics that allow Henchard to endure. The word character suggests honor and moral righteousness, but those are not the qualities that help Henchard. He is volatile, insecure, unremarkable, and sometimes cruel. He competes ruthlessly with Farfrae, he loses his pride and property, he deceives Elizabeth-Jane, the one person he truly cares about, he dies an unremarkable death, and he stipulates in his will that no one mourn or remember him. Yet despite all this, Hardy portrays Henchard as a worthy man. What makes him a "Man of Character" is his determination to suffer and his ability to endure great pain. He manages to bear, and bear willingly, the great weight of his own mistakes as he sells his family, mismanages his business, and encounters many unlucky coincidences. In a world that seems guided by the "scheme[s] of some sinister intelligence bent on punishing" human beings, there can be no more honorable or righteous characteristic than Henchard's "defiant endurance."

THE VALUE OF A GOOD NAME In the first few chapters of the novel, Hardy stresses the value of a good name: when Henchard wakes to find that the sale of his wife was not a dream or a drunken hallucination, his most pressing worry is whether he divulged his name to anyone during the course of the previous evening. Susan warns Elizabeth-Jane of the need for discretion at the Three Mariners Inn—their respectability could be jeopardized if anyone discovered that they did chores as payment for lodging. Henchard has little besides his name, so he must protect it. After becoming a civic leader, he attempts to earn, or to believe that he has earned, his position. But a conviction of his own worthlessness plagues him, and he places himself in situations that can only tarnish his name. His long competition with Farfrae results in the loss of Henchard's position, business, loved one, and, most crucially, good name. Once he has lost these essentials, he follows the same course toward death as Lucetta, whose demise is precipitated by the loss of respectability brought about by the skimmity-ride.

THE PERSISTENCE OF THE PAST The past haunts *The Mayor of Casterbridge*. Henchard's careless, drunken decision to sell his wife and child shapes the rest of his life. He spends the novel attempting to right the wrongs of long ago. He succeeds only in making more grievous mistakes, but he never fails to acknowledge that the past cannot be buried or denied. Roman history hangs over Casterbridge, where every farmer who tills a field turns up the remains of long-dead Roman soldiers. The Ring, the ancient Roman amphitheater that dominates Casterbridge and provides a forum for the secret meetings of its citizens, is a potent symbol of the persistence of the past.

SYMBOLS IN *THE MAYOR OF CASTERBRIDGE*

THE CAGED GOLDFINCH The caged goldfinch, which Henchard gives to Elizabeth-Jane as a wedding day present, stands for Henchard. He leaves the bird in a corner while he speaks to his stepdaughter and forgets it when she coolly dismisses him. Days later, a maid discovers the starved bird, which prompts Elizabeth-Jane to search for Henchard, whom she finds dead in Abel Whittle's cottage. When Whittle says Henchard "didn't gain strength, for you see, ma'am, he couldn't eat," he unwittingly ties Henchard's fate to the bird's: both lived and died in a prison. The finch's prison was literal, while Henchard's was metaphorical—an inescapable prison of his personality and his past.

THE BULL   The bull that chases down Lucetta and Elizabeth-Jane symbolizes the brute forces that threaten human life. Malignant, deadly, and bent on destruction, the bulls embodies the unnamed forces that Henchard often bemoans. The bull's rampage provides Henchard with an opportunity to display his strength and courage, thus making him more sympathetic in our eyes.

IMPORTANT QUOTATIONS FROM *THE MAYOR OF CASTERBRIDGE*

He advertised about the town, in long posters of a pink colour, that games of all sorts would take place here; and set to work a little battalion of men under his own eye. They erected greasy-poles for climbing, with smoked hams and local cheeses at the top. They placed hurdles in rows for jumping over; across the river they laid a slippery pole, with a live pig of the neighborhood tied at the other end, to become the property of the man who could walk over and get it. There were also provided wheelbarrows for racing, donkeys for the same, a stage for boxing, wrestling, and drawing blood generally; sacks for jumping in.

Location: Chapter XVI
Speaker: The narrator
Context: The narrator describes a day of celebration

Several times in *The Mayor of Casterbridge*, Hardy details a kind of life that was becoming extinct even as he described it. Casterbridge is a town situated between two times: the age of simple, agricultural England and the age of modern, industrialized England. The drama enacted between Henchard and Farfrae stands for the conflict between tradition and innovation, between the past and the future. Hardy plays the part of the anthropologist, recalling details of rural living eclipsed by the advent of modern technologies. In this passage, he describes the day of celebration that Henchard plans. It is a day of simple pleasures—smoked hams and local cheeses—in a world in which neighbors own livestock together instead of competing against each other as industrial capitalism demands. It is essentially a romantic and nostalgic view of a world that, even during Hardy's time, no longer existed. Yet Hardy does not pretend that the old world wasn't just as murderous and brutal, in its way, as the new one. The day of festivity includes "boxing, wrestling, and drawing blood generally."

Character is Fate, said Novalis, and Farfrae's character was just the reverse of Henchard's, who might not inaptly be described as Faust has been described—as a vehement gloomy being who had quitted the ways of vulgar men without light to guide him on a better way.

Location: Chapter XVII
Speaker: The narrator
Context: Hardy quotes Novalis, an eighteenth-century German novelist and poet

This passage relates to Farfrae's enormous business success after Henchard requests that he leave his employment and stop courting Elizabeth-Jane. The phrase "Character is Fate" offers us a context for understanding much of Henchard's ensuing struggle. Henchard blames much of the suffering he endures on cruel forces that are bent on human destruction. In Chapter XVII, however, Hardy reminds the reader that Henchard has much to do with his own downfall. In the same chapter, we read that "there was still the same unruly volcanic stuff beneath the rind of Michael Henchard as when he had sold his wife at Weydon Fair." This "volcanic stuff" refers to Henchard's passionate disposition. Whatever he feels—be it love, hate, desire, or contempt—he feels it overpoweringly. The same holds true for his guilt over selling Susan, which tracks him from Weydon-Priors to Casterbridge, where it overshadows his life for twenty years. His desire to right these past wrongs and his conviction that he deserves to suffer for them account for his suffering as much as any malignant force of the universe.

The difference between the peacefulness of interior nature and the wilful hostilities of mankind was very apparent at this place. In contrast with the harshness of the act just ended within the tent was the sight of several horses crossing their necks and rubbing each other lovingly as they waited in patience to be harnessed for the homeward journey. Outside the fair, in the valleys and woods, all was quiet. The sun had recently set, and the west heaven was hung with rosy cloud, which seemed permanent, yet slowly changed. To watch it was like looking at some grand feat of stagery from a darkened auditorium. In presence of this scene after the other there was a natural instinct to abjure man as the blot on an otherwise kindly universe; till it was remembered that all terrestrial conditions were intermittent, and that mankind might some night be innocently sleeping when these quiet objects were raging loud.

Location: Chapter I
Speaker: The narrator
Context: Henchard steps out of a tent and looks at his surroundings

---

MICHAEL HENCHARD'S WILL
That Elizabeth-Jane Farfrae be not told of my death, or made to grieve on account of me.
& that I be not bury'd in consecrated ground.
& that no sexton be asked to toll the bell.
& that nobody is wished to see my dead body.
& that no murners walk behind me at my funeral.
& that no flours be planted on my grave.
& that no man remember me.
  To this I put my name.
  Michael Henchard

Location: The final chapter
Speaker: Henchard
Context: Henchard leaves his will

Her experience had been of a kind to teach her, rightly or wrongly, that the doubtful honour of a brief transit through a sorry world hardly called for effusiveness, even when the path was suddenly irradiated at some half-way point by daybeams rich as hers. But her strong sense that neither she nor any human being deserved less than was given, did not blind her to the fact that there were others receiving less who had deserved much more. And in being forced to class herself among the fortunate she did not cease to wonder at the persistence of the unforeseen, when the one to whom such unbroken tranquillity had been accorded in the adult stage was she whose youth had seemed to teach that happiness was but the occasional episode in a general drama of pain.

Location: The final passage of the novel
Speaker: The narrator
Context: Elizabeth-Jane decides to honor Henchard's will, but she pities him and thinks he deserved better from the world

MEDEA

Euripides

A woman, enraged at her husband's betrayal, kills her sons.

THE LIFE OF EURIPIDES

Euripides was born around 484 B.C. He lived during the Golden Age of Athens, the city where he was born and lived most of his years. When Euripides was a baby, Athens repulsed a Persian invasion, a military victory that secured Athens' political independence and eventual dominance over the Mediterranean world. At the time of his death around 406 B.C., Athens was on the wane after suffering a protracted defeat at the hands of Sparta, its main rival, in the Peloponnesian War. Sandwiched between these two wars was a creative period of political, economic, and cultural activity that spawned many of Western civilization's distinctive traits, including tragic drama. The art of tragic drama was mastered by Euripides' older contemporaries, Aeschylus and Sophocles, and Euripides amplified it significantly.

When Euripides wrote, plays had only recently begun to include individual characters played by individual actors in addition to the conventional chorus. Euripides made innovative use of the new opportunities presented by multiple characters. Unlike his distinguished predecessors Aeschylus and Sophocles, he focused on the delicate web of relations between people instead of on the heroism of one particular character. His plays are less eloquent elegies to the mythic dead than realistic examinations of the relationships between characters who remind the audience members of their own lives. He was a dramatic innovator, paving the way for realism by writing pared-down dialogue patterned on natural speech. He created melodrama as we know it with the subtle emotional vacillations of his characters.

Euripides' pioneering realism was not always so popular. While Aristotle heralded him as "the most tragic of poets," he also criticized Euripides' confused handling of plot and his less-than-heroic protagonists. Aristophanes, a comic dramatist, constantly mocked Euripides' weakness for word-play and paradox. But Socrates and other philosophers admired him greatly, perhaps because he distinguished himself as a free thinker. He was the first playwright to express overt skepticism about the gods and anger about the oppression of women and slaves. More than edifying pieces of art, works such as *The Bacchae*, *Trojan Women*, *Iphigenia at Aulis*, *Alcetis*, and *Electra* became basic components of the Athenian citizen's political education. Euripides is said to have written ninety-two plays (critic Harry Thurston Peck puts the figure at 120), of which eighteen survive—more than any other classical playwright.

MEDEA IN CONTEXT

Euripides' audience would have been familiar with the story of Medea, whose infanticide challenged the Athenian moral universe. Although Medea's is no longer a universally familiar story, the ethical problem posed by the play still enchants and horrifies us. As late as the nineteenth century, editions of Euripides' play included apologias, or criticism, of the playwright's disturbing moral universe. Medea has been resurrected endlessly in modern theater and literature. Like Salome and Eve, she is a deep archetype in Western culture.

Medea is meant to be a stereotype, a confirmation of Athenian prejudices about the Persians they fought. To a modern reader, Medea's hometown on the Black Sea does not seem that far away from Greece. Yet for the Athenians of Euripides' time, it was practically at the edge of the world. Greeks were notoriously suspicious of foreigners; our word "barbarian" comes from the name Greeks used for all those who did not speak Greek (to the Greeks, other languages were unintelligible babbling, an idiotic *bar bar* noise).

To Euripides' audience, Medea, as an outsider and therefore a barbarian, represents the forces of chaos and disorder which are fundamentally incompatible with Greek order and law. That she is Asian is meant to make her seem even more dangerous. Asians threatened to overtake Greek cities when the Athenians defeated the invading Persians in a decisive naval battle at Salamis in 480 B.C. In the Athenian cultural imagination, the battle of Salamis was the moment when Greek rationality, order, and measure definitively repulsed the waves of disorder, mysticism, and excess that threatened from Asia.

MEDEA: KEY FACTS

Time and place written: 431 B.C.; Athens

Date of publication: Performed 431 B.C.

Publisher: Unknown

Type of work: Play

Genre: Tragedy

Language: Ancient Greek

Setting (time): The mythological past

Setting (place): Corinth, Greece

Tone: Dramatic, highly stylized

Protagonist: Medea

Antagonist: Medea's willfulness, Jason's infidelity

MEDEA: PLOT OVERVIEW

Euripides' play starts in medias res. His audience would have known about the following events, which precede the action of the play.

Medea's homeland is Colchis, an island in the Black Sea, which the Greeks considered the edge of the earth—a territory of barbarians. Hera, Queen of the Gods, causes Medea, a sorceress and a princess, to fall in love with Jason so that Jason will be protected. Medea helps Jason secure the Golden Fleece, thereby betraying her father, to whom the fleece belongs. She abandons her country and family to go with Jason to Iolcus, his home. As she and Jason flee across the Mediterranean, Medea kills her brother and dumps him overboard, forcing her pursuers to slow down and bury him. In Iolcus, she manipulates the daughters of the local king, Pelias, into murdering their own father. Exiled as murderers, Jason and Medea settled in the Greek city of Corinth, where they have two children and achieve a degree of fame and respectability.

As the play opens, Jason has abandoned his wife, Medea, along with their two children. He hopes to advance his social standing by marrying Glauce, the daughter of Creon, king of Corinth. Outside the royal palace, a nurse laments the events that have led to the present crisis. Jason's recent abandonment of the family has crushed Medea. She curses her own existence and the lives of her two children.

Fearing a possible revenge plot, Creon banishes Medea and her children from the city. After pleading for mercy, Medea is granted one day more in the city. She secretly plans to use this day to wreak "justice" by murdering Creon, Glauce, and Jason. Jason accuses Medea of overreacting. By voicing her grievances so publicly, she has endangered her own life and her children's. He claims that his decision to remarry is in everyone's best interest. Medea thinks him spineless. She refuses to accept his token offers of help.

Aegeus, King of Athens, appears by chance in Corinth and offers Medea sanctuary in his home city in exchange for her knowledge of drugs that can cure his sterility. Now guaranteed an eventual haven in Athens, Medea has cleared all obstacles to completing her revenge. She decides she must murder her children too, telling herself the satisfaction she will get from making Jason suffer will outweigh their loss.

Medea pretends to sympathize with Jason and has her sons offer his new wife a coronet and a dress as gifts. She claims the gifts are meant to soften Glauce, who might then ask her father if he will allow the children to stay in Corinth. But the coronet and dress are poisoned, and when Glauce puts them on, she dies horribly. Seeing his daughter ravaged by the poison, Creon chooses to die by her side by embracing her and absorbing the poison himself.

A messenger recounts the gruesome details of these deaths, which Medea absorbs with cool attentiveness. Her earlier state of anxiety, which intensified as she struggled with the decision to commit infanticide, has given way to assured determination. Against the protests of the chorus, which until now has supported her fully, Medea murders her children and flees the scene in a dragon-pulled chariot provided by her grandfather, the Sun-God.

Jason curses his lot. His hope of advancing his station by abandoning Medea and marrying Glauce has been dashed, and everything he values has been lost.

CHARACTERS IN *MEDEA*

Aegeus The King of Athens. Aegeus passes through Corinth after visiting the Oracle at Delphi, where he sought a cure for his sterility. His appearance marks a turning point in the play. After he promises Medea sanctuary, she changes from a passive victim to an aggressor.

Children The sons of Jason and Medea. Euripides characterizes them as naïvely oblivious to the intrigue that surrounds them.

Chorus The women of Corinth. The chorus comments on the action and occasionally engages directly in the dialogue. The chorus members fully sympathize with Medea's plight, although they draw the line at infanticide.

Creon The King of Corinth. Although he is a minor character, Creon's suicidal embrace of his dying daughter is one of the play's most dramatic moments.

Glauce Creon's beautiful young daughter. She never appears onstage, but she is a constant presence in Medea's mind. Glauce is also referred to as Creusa.

Jason Medea's husband. Jason can be considered the play's villain, although his evil stems from weakness, not strength. His tactless self-interest and whiny rationalizing make him an unsympathetic character.

Medea The protagonist of the play. Over the course of the play, Medea progresses from suicidal despair to sadistic fury. She loves Jason passionately, and her steely will in the face of his betrayal is terrifying.

Messenger The man who relates, in gruesome detail, the deaths of Glauce and Creon, which occur offstage.

Nurse Caretaker of the house and nurse to the children. The nurse witnesses Medea's rage and predicts her violence.

Tutor The man in charge of Medea's children.

THEMES IN *MEDEA*

THE STRUGGLE BETWEEN ORDER AND DISORDER The cultural associations of the conflict between Asia and Greece form the backdrop of *Medea*. Medea is so frightening partly because she threatens to disrupt the order of society. In particular, she represents the "Other," the not-Greek. Medea and Jason are in Corinth in the first place because of a dramatic campaign against order: Medea murdered King Pelias of Iolchus by tricking his daughters into cutting his body into tiny pieces. Throughout the play, characters emphasize Medea's foreignness and wildness with comments such as, "She is a strange woman" and "[h]er heart is violent." They associate her with destructive natural objects or forces like a storm and a "lioness guarding her cubs." They say she has a "wild and bitter nature" that reason can't subdue. Her passionate love, which is excessive and out of proportion, creates a destruction that is similarly excessive and out of proportion.

THE NATURE OF WORDS In a play with so much dramatic action—the gruesome murders of a king and princess, and a double infanticide—the critical events are really linguistic ones. Language is so important in part because the conventions of Greek theater prevented Euripides from showing certain actions to his audience. But Euripides' concern with language goes beyond the limitations of convention. He repeatedly suggests that drama is made entirely of words. The seed of the play's tragedy is that Medea mistakes "a Greek's words" for a reality. When Jason vows his love to her in Colchis, she thinks of his word as steely, unbreakable, physical. When she finds out his word is not a real object, but a flimsy nothing, she reacts as if her most basic assumptions about the world have been shattered. Jason's words, and their ultimate fragility, are what set the action of the play in motion. Words also solidify Medea's plans. She longs to exact revenge, but until King Aegeus pledges to give her sanctuary, she can do nothing.

Besides these two crucial oaths, there are dozens of references to messages, decrees, insults, curses. Euripides also makes a brief mention of lyric poetry and its effect on the reputation of women. People act because of words. Jason says Medea has been exiled because of her "loose talk"; Medea kills her children partly because she cannot bear the idea that people will mock them; King Aegeus winds up in Corinth because of the words of the Delphic oracle. Jason's vow aside, words can almost take on physical being: Jason calls Medea a "living curse."

THE IMPORTANCE OF HOME Euripides suggests that people must cultivate deep-rooted, extended family connections instead of turning inward and relying on spouse and children alone. Jason's misdeeds alone are not solely to blame for Medea's tragic situation. Part of the fault lies with Medea's isolation. She has abandoned her homeland and killed off her brother, forever alienating her family, and she is an outsider in Corinth. Medea herself recognizes that her catastrophe has its roots in the moment she made Jason "everything" and abandoned her home and family. Her adopted city might tolerate her, but it will never embrace her, even though she has made friends and borne children there. Greeks considered Asians like Medea a threat, so they denied them basic rights. As a non-Greek, Medea is not legally recognized as Jason's wife. She was a princess in her homeland, but in this new place she is stripped of her rights, treated like a commoner or a criminal. She must rely on Jason alone to revere her and treat her with respect. When he cuts her off, in part because he is ambitious and her diminished status impedes his advancement, Medea has nowhere to turn. Her solitude increases her desperation and fury. Glauce provokes such rage in her not only because she stole Jason, but because she is what Medea used to be: a princess at the bosom of a loving family in the heart of her hometown.

SYMBOLS IN *MEDEA*

EARTH AND SUN In *Medea*, characters repeatedly invoke the Earth and the Sun, both of which symbolize Medea's ferocity and wildness. When Aegeus pledges sanctuary to Medea, for example, she asks him to swear by the Earth and Sun. These two natural objects discreetly play the part that anthropomorphic gods like Zeus or Athena play in other Greek dramas. Making gods of the Earth and Sun gives *Medea* a curious moral landscape. The Earth and Sun are primal forces. They do not do things like invent lyres, judge beauty contests, or lay down the rules for a fair system of trial by jury, as Greek gods tend to do. They predate manmade notions of language, law, and reason. Like the Sun and the Earth, Medea can be unconscious of her own actions and unfazed by the opinions of others. Like them, Medea has wild, primal power. She is a granddaughter of the Sun and can use his magic at will. The Sun's power poisons the robes that kill Glauce and King Creon, and the Sun's magic dragon chariot effects Medea's miraculous departure.

SYMPLEGADES The Symplegades are the "Clashing Rocks" through which Jason had to pass on the voyage to Colchis. They symbolize Medea's rage. When Jason had to pass through the Symplegades on his boat, a seer told him to send a dove through them first. When the rocks slammed shut, the dove lost only its tail feathers. Emulating the dove's path, the Argo sailed through and lost only the end of its stern. Jason does not ask a seer to help him navigate Medea's power, so her rage destroys him. The Symplegades's power, like Medea's, does not reason and cannot be reasoned with. Cross them, or cross Medea, and the trap snaps shut. The Symplegades kill automatically, which suggests that perhaps Medea's actions are beyond her control.

IMPORTANT QUOTATIONS FROM *MEDEA*

Great people's tempers are terrible, always
Having their own way, seldom checked,
Dangerous they shift from mood to mood.
How much better to have been accustomed
To live on equal terms with one's neighbors.
I would like to be safe and grow old in a
Humble way. What is moderate sounds best,

Also in practice is best for everyone.
Greatness brings no profit to people.
God indeed, when in anger, brings
Greater ruin to great men's houses.

Location: Lines 119–130
Speaker: Nurse
Context: The Nurse tells the Chorus her fear that something horrible will come of Medea's anger at
Jason

In this passage, Euripides gives us a clear picture of the past and present events of the drama. He also
introduces the Nurse, who has an uncanny insight into Medea's nature and what she is capable of performing. The Nurse stands in for the audience. She is an ordinary person who seems to know what will
happen, and although she is only indirectly involved with the great tragedy to come, she cares about the
people involved. In this passage, she stresses the value of moderation. Moderation (*sophrosyne*) was a
principle cherished in the Greek philosophy of Euripides' time. The Nurse asserts that greatness is an
inherently unstable position and that she herself would rather be without it. Unlike the Nurse, Medea is
a woman without moderation of emotion or action. Her wild fury and extreme behavior contrast completely with what the Nurse advocates here. Yet the Nurse is fatalistic, and her praise of moderation is less
than totally convincing, which suggests that Euripides wants us to question the real virtue of moderation.

So it must happen. What profit have I in life?
I have no land, no home, no refuge from my pain.
My mistake was made the time I left behind me
My father's house, and trusted the words of a Greek,
Who, with heaven's help, will pay me the price for that.
For those children he had from me he will never
See alive again, nor will he on his new bride
Beget another child . . .
Let no one think me a weak one, feeble-spirited,
A stay-at-home, but rather just the opposite,
One who can hurt my enemies and help my friends,
For the lives of such persons are most remembered.

Location: Lines 798–810
Speaker: Medea
Context: Medea speaks of the cause of her bad position and the revenge she plans to take for it

After securing the promise of sanctuary from Aegeus of Athens, Medea is free to take her revenge. She
has already told the Chorus of her intention to kill Jason, Glauce, and Creon, and now she announces
her decision to murder her children. In these lines, Medea admits that her troubles began when she cut
herself off from her family and home, trading her secure world for "the words of a Greek." For the first
time in these lines, self-interested calculation creeps into Medea's diction. She speaks of profit,
exchange, and price, and admits that a desire for fame partly fuels her murderous longings. Medea
believes there are two kinds of people: the weak and the strong. She can see no middle ground between a
despicable "feeble-spirited" woman and a woman who would murder to hurt her husband. A moderate
response does not occur to her. In these lines, Medea displays a fatalism that she makes even more
explicit a few lines later, when she declares, "So it must be. No compromise is possible." She believes that her
future actions are beyond her control. Instead of considering multiple alternatives, Medea identifies the one
action she thinks she is fated to perform and clings to it. Questions of right or wrong would strike her as irrelevant. She thinks fate has shown her the path, and she must follow it, even if it is unpleasant.

There is nothing tyrannical about my nature,

And by showing mercy I have often been the loser.
Even now I know that I am making a mistake.
All the same you shall have your will. But this I tell you,
That if the light of heaven tomorrow shall see you,
You and your children in the confines of my land,
You die. This word I have spoken is firmly fixed.
But now, if you must stay, stay for this day alone.
For in it you can do none of the things I fear.

Location: Lines 348–356
Speaker: Creon
Context: Creon allows Medea and her children to delay their exile for one day

---

In so far as you helped me, you did well enough.
But on this question of saving me, I can prove
You have certainly got from me more than you gave.
Firstly, instead of living among barbarians,
You inhabit a Greek land and understand our ways,
How to live by law instead of the sweet will of force.
And all the Greeks considered you a clever woman.
You were honored for it; while, if you were living at
The ends of the earth, nobody would have heard of you.
For my part, rather than stores of gold in my house
Or power to sing even sweeter songs than Orpheus,
I'd choose the fate that made me a distinguished man.

Location: Lines 533–544
Speaker: Jason
Context: Jason defends himself against Medea's angry accusations by describing what he has already
given her in recompense for her help

Long would be the answer which I might have made to
Those words of yours, if Zeus the father did not know
How I have treated you and what you did to me.
No, it was not to be that you should scorn my love,
And pleasantly live your life through, laughing at me;
Nor would the princess, nor he who offered the match,
Creon, drive me away without paying for it.
So now you may call me a monster, if you wish,
A Scylla housed in the caves of the Tuscan sea.
I too, as I had to, have taken hold of your heart.

Location: Lines 1351–1360
Speaker: Medea
Context: Before leaving Corinth, Medea responds to Jason's scathing words

THE MERCHANT OF VENICE

William Shakespeare

A man tries to use the law to butcher a merchant, but a resourceful woman disguises herself as a legal scholar and saves the threatened man.

THE LIFE OF WILLIAM SHAKESPEARE

William Shakespeare, the most influential writer in all of English literature, was born in 1564 to a successful middle-class glove-maker in Stratford-upon-Avon, England. Shakespeare's formal education did not progress beyond grammar school. In 1582, he married an older woman, Anne Hathaway. His union with Anne produced three children. Around 1590, Shakespeare left his family behind and traveled to London to work as an actor and playwright. He quickly earned public and critical acclaim, and eventually became the most popular playwright in England and a part-owner of the Globe Theater. Shakespeare's career bridged the reigns of Elizabeth I (ruled 1558–1603) and James I (ruled 1603–1625), and he was a favorite of both monarchs. James paid Shakespeare's company a great compliment by giving its members the title of King's Men. Shakespeare retired to Stratford a wealthy and renowned man and died in 1616 at the age of fifty-two. At the time of Shakespeare's death, literary luminaries such as Ben Jonson hailed his works as timeless.

Shakespeare's works were collected and printed in various editions in the century following his death, and by the early eighteenth century his reputation as the greatest poet ever to write in English was well established. The unprecedented regard in which Shakespeare's works were held led to a fierce curiosity about his life, but many details of Shakespeare's personal history are unknown or shrouded in mystery. Some people have concluded from this lack of information and from Shakespeare's modest education that Shakespeare's plays were actually written by someone else—Francis Bacon and the Earl of Oxford are the two most popular candidates—but the support for this claim is overwhelmingly circumstantial, and the theory is not taken seriously by many scholars.

Shakespeare is generally thought to be the author of the thirty-eight plays (two of them possibly collaborations) and 154 sonnets that bear his name. The legacy of this body of work is immense. A number of Shakespeare's plays seem to have transcended even the category of brilliance, influencing the course of Western literature and culture.

THE MERCHANT OF VENICE IN CONTEXT

The Merchant of Venice was probably written in either 1596 or 1597, after Shakespeare had written such plays as *Romeo and Juliet* and *Richard III*, but before he penned the great tragedies of his later years. Its basic plot outline, which features a merchant, a poor suitor, a fair lady, and a villainous Jew, is found in a number of contemporary Italian story collections. Shakespeare borrowed several details, such the choice of chests that Portia inflicts on all her suitors, from preexisting sources. *The Merchant of Venice*'s Italian setting and marriage plot are typical of Shakespeare's earlier comedies, but the characters of Portia, Shakespeare's first great heroine, and Shylock, an unforgettable villain, mark a new level of achievement for Shakespeare.

Shylock is one of literature's most memorable villains, but many readers and playgoers have also found him a compelling and sympathetic figure. The question of whether or not Shakespeare endorses the anti-Semitism of the Christian characters in the play has been much debated. Jews in Shakespeare's England were a marginalized group, and portrayals of Jews as villains and fools were common. For example, Christopher Marlowe's *The Jew of Malta*, a bloody farce about a murderous Jewish villain, was a great popular success. Shakespeare certainly draws on this anti-Semitic tradition in portraying Shylock, exploiting Jewish stereotypes for comic effect. But Shylock is a more complex character than the Jew in

Marlowe's play, and Shakespeare makes it clear that his hatred is born of the mistreatment he has suffered in a Christian society.

THE MERCHANT OF VENICE: KEY FACTS

Full title: The Comical History of the Merchant of Venice, or Otherwise Called the Jew of Venice

Time and place written: 1598; London, England

Date of first publication: 1600 (in quarto)

Genre: Comedy

Setting (time): Sixteenth century

Setting (place): Venice and Belmont, Italy

Protagonist: Bassanio

Antagonist: Shylock

Major conflict: Antonio defaults on a loan from Shylock

THE MERCHANT OF VENICE: PLOT OVERVIEW

Antonio, a Venetian merchant, complains to his friends of a melancholy that he cannot explain. His friend Bassanio is desperately in need of money to court Portia, a wealthy heiress who lives in the city of Belmont. Bassanio asks Antonio for a loan in order to travel in style to Portia's estate. Antonio agrees, but is unable to make the loan himself because his own money is all invested in a number of trade ships that are still at sea. Antonio suggests that Bassanio secure the loan from one of the city's moneylenders and name Antonio as the loan's guarantor. In Belmont, Portia expresses sadness over the terms of her father's will, which stipulates that she must marry the man who correctly chooses one of three caskets. None of Portia's current suitors are to her liking, and she and her lady-in-waiting, Nerissa, fondly remember a visit paid some time before by Bassanio.

In Venice, Antonio and Bassanio approach Shylock, a Jewish moneylender, for a loan. Shylock nurses a long-standing grudge against Antonio, who has made a habit of berating Shylock and other Jews for their usury, the practice of loaning money at exorbitant rates of interest, and who undermines their business by offering interest-free loans. Although Antonio refuses to apologize for his behavior, Shylock acts agreeably and offers to lend Bassanio three thousand ducats with no interest. Shylock adds, however, that should the loan go unpaid, Shylock will be entitled to a pound of Antonio's own flesh. Despite Bassanio's warnings, Antonio agrees. In Shylock's own household, his servant Lancelot decides to leave Shylock's service to work for Bassanio, and Shylock's daughter Jessica schemes to elope with Antonio's friend Lorenzo. That night, the streets of Venice fill up with revelers, and Jessica escapes with Lorenzo by dressing as his page. After a night of celebration, Bassanio and his friend Graziano leave for Belmont, where Bassanio intends to win Portia's hand.

In Belmont, Portia welcomes the prince of Morocco, who has come in an attempt to choose the right casket to marry her. The prince studies the inscriptions on the three caskets and chooses the gold one, which proves to be an incorrect choice. In Venice, Shylock is furious to find that his daughter has run away, but rejoices in the fact that Antonio's ships are rumored to have been wrecked and that he will soon be able to claim his debt. In Belmont, the prince of Aragon also visits Portia. He, too, studies the caskets carefully, but he picks the silver one, which is also incorrect. Bassanio arrives at Portia's estate, and they declare their love for one another. Despite Portia's request that he wait before choosing, Bassanio immediately picks the correct casket, which is made of lead. He and Portia rejoice, and Graziano confesses that he has fallen in love with Nerissa. The couples decide on a double wedding. Portia gives Bassanio a ring as a token of love, and makes him swear that under no circumstances will he part with it. They are joined, unexpectedly, by Lorenzo and Jessica. The celebration, however, is cut short by the news that Antonio has indeed lost his ships, and that he has forfeited his bond to Shylock. Bassanio and Graziano immediately travel to Venice to try and save Antonio's life. After they leave, Portia tells Nerissa that they will go to Venice disguised as men.

Shylock ignores the many pleas to spare Antonio's life, and a trial is called to decide the matter. The duke of Venice, who presides over the trial, announces that he has sent for a legal expert, who turns out to be Portia disguised as a young man of law. Portia asks Shylock to show mercy, but he remains inflexible and insists the pound of flesh is rightfully his. Bassanio offers Shylock twice the money due him, but Shylock insists on collecting the bond as it is written. Portia examines the contract and, finding it legally binding, declares that Shylock is entitled to the merchant's flesh. Shylock ecstatically praises her wisdom, but as he is on the verge of collecting his due, Portia reminds him that he must do so without causing Antonio to bleed, as the contract does not entitle him to any blood. Trapped by this logic, Shylock hastily agrees to take Bassanio's money instead, but Portia insists that Shylock take his bond as written, or nothing at all. Portia informs Shylock that he is guilty of conspiring against the life of a Venetian citizen, which means he must turn over half of his property to the state and the other half to Antonio. The duke spares Shylock's life and takes a fine instead of Shylock's property. Antonio also forgoes his half of Shylock's wealth on two conditions: first, Shylock must convert to Christianity, and second, he must will the entirety of his estate to Lorenzo and Jessica upon his death. Shylock agrees and takes his leave.

Bassanio, who does not see through Portia's disguise, showers the young law clerk with thanks, and is eventually pressured into giving Portia the ring with which he promised never to part. Graziano gives Nerissa, who is disguised as Portia's clerk, his ring. The two women return to Belmont, where they find Lorenzo and Jessica declaring their love to each other under the moonlight. When Bassanio and Graziano arrive the next day, their wives accuse them of faithlessly giving their rings to other women. Before the deception goes too far, however, Portia reveals that she was, in fact, the law clerk, and both she and Nerissa reconcile with their husbands. Lorenzo and Jessica are pleased to learn of their inheritance from Shylock, and the joyful news arrives that Antonio's ships have in fact made it back safely. The group celebrates its good fortune.

CHARACTERS IN *THE MERCHANT OF VENICE*

Antonio A merchant. Antonio's love for his friend Bassanio prompts him to sign a contract with Shylock and almost lose his life. Antonio is often inexplicably melancholy. As Shylock points out, he dislikes all Jews. However, Antonio's friends love him, and he does show mercy to Shylock.

Bassanio A kinsmen and dear friend of Antonio's. Bassanio's love for the wealthy Portia leads him to borrow money from Shylock with Antonio as his guarantor. Bassanio is an ineffectual businessman but a worthy suitor.

Balthasar Portia's servant.

Doctor Bellario A wealthy Paduan lawyer and Portia's cousin. Doctor Bellario never appears in the play, but he sends Portia the letters of introduction she needs to make her appearance in court.

The Duke of Venice The ruler of Venice. The duke presides over Antonio's trial.

Graziano A friend of Bassanio's. A coarse young man, Graziano is Shylock's most vocal and insulting critic during the trial. Graziano falls in love with and eventually weds Portia's lady-in-waiting, Nerissa.

Jessica Shylock's daughter. Jessica hates life in her father's house and elopes with a young Christian gentleman, Lorenzo. The play's characters question the fate of her soul, wondering if her marriage can overcome the fact that she was born a Jew.

Lancelot Gobbo Bassanio's servant. A comical, clownish, punning figure, Lancelot leaves Shylock's service in order to work for Bassanio.

Lorenzo A friend of Bassanio's and Antonio's. Lorenzo is in love with Shylock's daughter, Jessica, with whom he elopes to Belmont.

Nerissa Portia's lady-in-waiting and confidante. Nerissa marries Graziano and escorts Portia to Venice by disguising herself as a law clerk.

Old Gobbo Lancelot's father. Old Gobbo is a servant in Venice.

Portia A wealthy heiress from Belmont. Portia's beauty is matched only by her intelligence. Bound by a clause in her father's will that forces her to marry whichever suitor chooses correctly from among three chests, Portia is nonetheless able to marry her true love, Bassanio. Portia, in the disguise of a young law clerk, saves Antonio from Shylock.

The Prince of Aragon An arrogant Spanish nobleman. The prince attempts to win Portia's hand, but makes an unwise choice of chests.

The Prince of Morocco   A Moorish prince. The prince seeks Portia's hand in marriage, asking her to ignore his dark countenance. He picks the wrong chest.

Salerio   A Venetian gentleman and friend to Antonio, Bassanio, and Lorenzo. Salerio escorts the newly-weds Jessica and Lorenzo to Belmont, and returns with Bassanio and Graziano for Antonio's trial. He is often almost indistinguishable from his companion Solanio.

Solanio   A Venetian gentleman. Solanio is a frequent companion of Salerio.

Shylock   A Jewish moneylender. Angered by his mistreatment at the hands of Venice's Christians, particularly Antonio, Shylock schemes to take revenge by demanding a pound of Antonio's flesh in payment for a debt.

Tubal   One of Shylock's friends.

THEMES IN *THE MERCHANT OF VENICE*

SELF-INTEREST VERSUS LOVE   On the surface, the main difference between the Christian characters and Shylock appears to be that the Christians value human relationships over business ones, whereas Shylock is only interested in money. The Christian characters certainly view the difference this way. Merchants like Antonio lend money free of interest and put themselves at risk for those they love, whereas Shylock agonizes over the loss of his money and is reported to run through the streets crying, "O, my ducats! O, my daughter!" (II.viii.15), words that suggest he values his money at least as much as his daughter. However, upon closer inspection, this supposed difference between Christian and Jew breaks down. In Act III, scene i, Shylock seems more hurt by the fact that his daughter sold a ring that his dead wife gave to him than distraught over the loss of the ring's monetary value. In a different way, his relationship with his persecutors also matters to him more than money. He insists on a pound of flesh rather than any amount of money, because vengeance is more important to him than wealth.

Neither are the Christian characters always more interested in love than they are in money. Though Portia and Bassanio come to love one another, Bassanio seeks her hand in the first place because he is monstrously in debt and needs her money. Bassanio is anxious to view his relationship with Antonio as a matter of business rather than of love, which is why he asks Antonio to look at the loan as an investment, though Antonio insists that he lends him the money solely out of love. And while the Christian characters may talk more about mercy, love, and charity, they show none of those virtues in their dealings with Jews, whom they hate for no reason other than their religion.

THE DIVINE QUALITY OF MERCY   The conflict between Shylock and the Christian characters comes to a head over the issue of mercy. The other characters acknowledge that the law is on Shylock's side, but they expect him to show mercy, which he refuses to do. When, during the trial, Shylock asks Portia what could possibly compel him to be merciful, Portia's long reply, beginning with the words "The quality of mercy is not strained," clarifies what is at stake in the argument (IV.i.179). She says human beings should be merciful because God is merciful: mercy is an attribute of God himself and therefore greater than power, majesty, or law. Portia's understanding of mercy is based on the way Christians in Shakespeare's time understood the difference between the Old and New Testaments. The Old Testament depicts a God who requires strict adherence to rules and harshly punishes those who stray. The New Testament, in contrast, emphasizes adherence to the spirit rather than the letter of the law, portraying a God who forgives and offers salvation to those who forgive others. When Portia warns Shylock against pursuing the law without regard for mercy, she is promoting what Elizabethan Christians would have seen as a pro-Christian, anti-Jewish agenda.

Once she has turned Shylock's greatest weapon—the law—against him, Portia has the opportunity to practice the mercy she advocates. Instead, she backs Shylock into a corner, stripping him of his bond, his estate, and his dignity, and forcing him to kneel and beg for mercy. Antonio decides not to seize Shylock's goods as punishment for conspiring against him, an action that could be interpreted as merciful. But it may not be merciful to return half of Shylock's goods to him only to take away his religion and his profession. By forcing Shylock to convert, Antonio prevents him from practicing usury, which, according to Shylock's reports, was Antonio's primary reason for berating him and spitting on him in public. Antonio's compassion seems to stem as much from self-interest as from concern for his fellow man. Mercy, as delivered in *The Merchant of Venice*, is never as sweet, selfless, or full of grace as Portia suggests.

HATRED AS A CYCLICAL PHENOMENON   Throughout the play, Shylock claims that he is simply applying the lessons taught to him by his Christian neighbors. This claim becomes an integral part of his character and his argument in court. In Shylock's first appearance, as he conspires to harm Antonio, he seems motivated by the insults and injuries Antonio has inflicted on him in the past. As the play continues and Shylock unveils more of his reasoning, he continues to blame his behavior on years of conditioning. Responding to Salerio's query of what good the pound of flesh will do him, Shylock responds, "The villainy you teach me I will execute, and it shall go hard but I will better the instruction" (III.i.60–61). Not all of Shylock's actions can be blamed on his poor treatment at the hands of the Christians. Also, it is possible that Antonio understands that he is partly to blame for his own near execution.

SYMBOLS IN *THE MERCHANT OF VENICE*

THE THREE CASKETS   The contest for Portia's hand, in which suitors from various countries choose among a gold, a silver, and a lead chest, resembles the cultural and legal system of Venice in some respects. Like the Venice of the play, the chest contest presents the same opportunities and the same rules to men of various nations, ethnicities, and religions. Also like Venice, the hidden bias of the chest test is fundamentally Christian. To win Portia, Bassanio must ignore the gold chest, which bears the inscription, "Who chooseth me shall gain what many men desire" (II.vii.5), and the silver chest, which says, "Who chooseth me shall get as much as he deserves" (II.vii.7). The correct chest is lead and warns that the person who chooses it must give and risk everything he has. The contest combines a number of Christian teachings, such as the idea that desire is an unreliable guide and should be resisted, and the idea that human beings do not deserve God's grace but receive it in spite of themselves. Christianity teaches that appearances are often deceiving, and that people should not trust the evidence of their senses—hence the humble appearance of the lead chest. Faith and charity are the central values of Christianity, and these values are evoked by the lead chest's injunction to give all and risk all, as one does in making a leap of faith. Portia's father conceives of marriage as a union between people who risk and give everything for each other. The contest suits Bassanio, who knows he does not deserve his good fortune but is willing to risk everything on a gamble.

THE POUND OF FLESH   The pound of flesh that Shylock seeks lends itself to multiple interpretations. It is a metaphor for two of the play's closest relationships, and also a symbol of Shylock's inflexible adherence to the law. The fact that Bassanio's debt is to be paid with Antonio's flesh shows that their friendship is so binding it has made them almost one. Shylock's determination is strengthened by Jessica's departure, as if he were seeking recompense for the loss of his own flesh and blood by collecting it from his enemy. Lastly, the pound of flesh is a constant reminder of the rigidity of Shylock's world, in which numerical calculations are used to evaluate even the most serious of situations. Shylock never explicitly demands that Antonio die, but instead, and more chillingly, asks for a pound in exchange for his three thousand ducats.

IMPORTANT QUOTATIONS FROM *THE MERCHANT OF VENICE*

What if my house be troubled with a rat,
And I be pleased to give ten thousand ducats
To have it baned? What, are you answered yet?
Some men there are love not a gaping pig,
Some that are mad if they behold a cat,
And others when the bagpipe sings i'th' nose
Cannot contain their urine; for affection,
Mistress of passion, sways it to the mood
Of what it likes or loathes.. . .
. . .
So can I give no reason, nor I will not,
More than a lodged hate and a certain loathing
I bear Antonio, that I follow thus

A losing suit against him. Are you answered?

Location: IV.i.43–61
Speaker: Shylock
Context: Antonio and Shylock have been summoned before the court; Shylock responds to the duke

When the duke asks Shylock to show his adversary some mercy, Shylock responds by reasoning that he has no reason. He blames his hatred of Antonio on "affection, / Mistress of passion," who affects men's moods and actions in ways they cannot explain (IV.i.49–50). Just as certain people have inexplicable aversions to cats or certain strains of music or eating meat, Shylock has an illogical dislike for Antonio.

Shylock's language patterns in this speech reinforce our impression of his character. He frequently repeats himself, returning to the same imagery—the "gaping pig" (IV.i.53) and the "woolen bagpipe" (IV.i.55)—and bookending his speech with the simple question, "Are you answered?" (IV.i.61). Shylock's tightly controlled speech reflects the narrow and determined focus of his quest to satisfy his hatred.

The speech's prosaic imagery is typical of Shylock. Other characters speak in dreamily poetic language, evoking images of angels and waters scented with spice, but Shylock draws on the most mundane examples to prove his point. He suggests that Antonio is a rat, and that his dislike of Antonio is similar to the dislike some men feel toward pigs or cats. Shylock uses bodily functions to drive home his point, likening rage to urination. Also, Shylock's suggestion that a mere whim has made him hate Antonio makes him seem unpredictable, and fuels the perception that his actions are careless and cruel.

The quality of mercy is not strained.
It droppeth as the gentle rain from heaven
Upon the place beneath.. . . .
. . .
It is enthronèd in the hearts of kings;
It is an attribute to God himself,
And earthly power doth then show likest God's
When mercy seasons justice. Therefore, Jew,
Though justice be thy plea, consider this:
That in the course of justice none of us
Should see salvation. We do pray for mercy,
And that same prayer doth teach us all to render
The deeds of mercy.

Location: IV.i.179–197
Speaker: Portia
Context: During Shylock's trial, Portia, disguised as a lawyer, tells Shylock why he must be merciful

Portia appeals to Shylock's methodical mind, making a reasonable rather than an emotional case for mercy. She states that forgiving the bond would benefit Shylock and elevate him to a godlike status. She also warns him that his quest for justice without mercy may result in his own damnation. Although well-measured and well-reasoned, Portia's speech also makes mercy a polarizing issue dividing Jews from Christians. Her frequent references to the divine are appeals to a Christian God, and mercy emerges as a marker of Christianity. Although it seems as if Portia is offering an appeal, in retrospect it is clear that her speech is an ultimatum, a final chance for Shylock to save himself before Portia crushes his legal arguments.

I am a Jew. Hath not a Jew eyes? Hath not a Jew hands, organs, dimensions, senses, affections, passions;
fed with the same food, hurt with the same weapons, subject to the same diseases, healed by the same
means, warmed and cooled by the same winter and summer as a Christian is? If you prick us do we not
bleed? If you tickle us do we not laugh? If you poison us do we not die? And if you wrong us shall we not
revenge? If we are like you in the rest, we will resemble you in that. If a Jew wrong a Christian, what is
his humility? Revenge. If a Christian wrong a Jew, what should his sufferance be by Christian example?

Why, revenge. The villainy you teach me I will execute, and it shall go hard but I will better the instruction.

Location: III.i.49–61
Speaker: Shylock
Context: Shylock has blamed Antonio for persecuting him because he is a Jew; here he speaks to Salanio and Salerio about his own humanity

---

You have among you many a purchased slave
Which, like your asses and your dogs and mules,
You use in abject and in slavish parts
Because you bought them. Shall I say to you
'Let them be free, marry them to your heirs.
Why sweat they under burdens?' . . .

. . .

You will answer
'The slaves are ours.' So do I answer you.
The pound of flesh which I demand of him
Is dearly bought. 'Tis mine, and I will have it.

Location: IV.i.89–99
Speaker: Shylock
Context: Shylock defends himself to the duke during his trial

---

The man that hath no music in himself,
Nor is not moved with concord of sweet sounds,
Is fit for treasons, stategems, and spoils.
The motions of his spirit are dull as night,
And his affections dark as Erebus.

Location: V.i.82–86
Speaker: Lorenzo
Context: Lorenzo and Jessica sit outside, looking at the stars

THE METAMORPHOSIS

Franz Kafka

After turning into an insect, a man falls out of favor with his family and eventually dies.

THE LIFE OF FRANZ KAFKA

Franz Kafka (1883–1924) was born in Prague to middle-class Jewish parents. His father, the son of a village butcher, was a man of little education but strong entrepreneurial ambition. He became a successful retailer and wholesaler, making a good marriage to the daughter of a wealthy brewery owner. Kafka was the firstborn, followed by two boys who died before the age of two, and then three girls. As an adult, Kafka held on to bitter memories of his childhood, particularly of his upwardly mobile, harsh father. As Kafka admitted in the never-sent *Letter to His Father* (1919): "My writing was all about you; all I did there, after all, was to bemoan what I could not bemoan upon your breast. It was an intentionally long-drawn-out leave-taking from you."

After being educated at a typically draconian gymnasium, Kafka entered law school and earned a doctorate degree while clerking for a Prague law office. He briefly held a job with a private insurance company before obtaining an entry-level position with the Workmen's Accident Insurance Institute for the Kingdom of Bohemia in 1908. There he was a diligent and respected functionary until his premature retirement in 1922. He treasured this job for its unexacting hours, which allowed him plenty of time to write.

Only a few of Kafka's works were published in his lifetime, *The Metamorphosis* (1915) among them. They didn't sell well, and Kafka remained fairly obscure, but his stories and novellas were highly praised within a small but respected circle of German-speaking intellectuals. It was only after Kafka's premature death from tuberculosis in 1924, when the bulk of his production—including the unfinished novels *Amerika*, *The Trial* and *The Castle*—was published that his fame began to grow. Kafka's work narrowly escaped obliteration. He had ordered his devoted friend Max Brod to destroy his manuscripts after his death, but Brod disobeyed.

The developments of the twentieth century made Kafka's work seem eerily prescient. Many of the nightmares described in his novels took shape in Europe's new totalitarian states, great bureaucratic enterprises that dehumanized individuals. The world took note of Kafka's foresight, and the word *Kafkaesque* sprung up in hundreds of languages to describe the banal, illogical nightmares in life.

THE METAMORPHOSIS IN CONTEXT

Since Franz Kafka has come to stand for twentieth-century alienation, his work is often introduced in the context of his own alienating experiences. Kafka did not quite fit in anywhere. He was a Czech in the Austro-Hungarian empire, a German-speaker among Czechs, a Jew among German-speakers, and a disbeliever among Jews. He was alienated from his pragmatic and overbearing father, from his bureaucratic job, and from the opposite sex. He was caught between a desire to live the life of an artist and a desire to live a normal, bourgeois life. *The Metamorphosis* has become famous as part of Kafka's account of the struggle to understand humanity in an arbitrary, unjust, or even meaningless world.

The Metamorphosis has inspired a staggering torrent of criticism. Every school of criticism, including the psychoanalytic, the Marxist, the Symbolist, the New Critic, and the New Historicist, has set forth a wide variety of interpretations—many of which *The Metamorphosis* supports. Some argue that Gregor's transformation is symbolic, not literal. It may symbolize the emptiness and insignificance of Gregor's life as a traveling salesman. Or perhaps it symbolizes the degraded nature of modern existence in general, or bourgeois life in particular. Or perhaps it symbolizes Kafka's low opinion of himself as imagined through his father's eyes. Others read the novella as an allegory for, say, the isolation and disappointment of the act of writing.

Despite the reams of analysis, one aspect of *The Metamorphosis* that is often overlooked is its humor. When Kafka read the story to his circle of companions in Prague, they laughed out loud—as did he.

THE METAMORPHOSIS: KEY FACTS

Time and place written: ca. 1915; Prague

Date of first publication: 1915

Publisher: Kurt Wolff Verlag

Type of Work: Novella

Genre: Surrealist novel; tragicomedy

Language: German

Setting (time): Unspecified, but probably the mid-teens of the twentieth century

Setting (place): Almost entirely inside the Samsa house in an unspecified city

Tense: Past

Tone: Matter-of-fact, calm, comic, sympathetic

Narrator: Anonymous narrator in the third person

Point of view: Gregor's

Protagonist: Gregor Samsa

Antagonist: Gregor's life

THE METAMORPHOSIS: PLOT OVERVIEW

Gregor Samsa awakes one morning to find that he has been inexplicably transformed into a giant insect. He has also overslept. Gregor's parents and his sister Grete depend on the money Gregor makes as a traveling salesman, but he cannot go to work in his current state. When Gregor's manager comes to demand an explanation for Gregor's absence, Gregor opens the bedroom door and shows himself. His appearance sends the terrified clerk tearing down the stairwell and shocks his family.

Of all the family members, Grete handles the situation most practically, making sure that Gregor is fed and his room is cleaned. Before long, however, everyone must find work to compensate for the loss of Gregor's income, and they stop paying attention to Gregor—except when he gets out of his room. No one in the family can fully accept Gregor's new appearance, and Gregor cannot express himself to his family. The fear and disgust his presence inspires injures his mother's health and incites his father to brief fits of violence. During one such fit, he bombards Gregor with fruit, wounding Gregor deeply.

Hobbled and neglected, Gregor begins to waste away in his room. The family takes in three complaining lodgers and uses Gregor's room to store excess furniture and other miscellanies. The family does leave Gregor's door ajar in the evenings so that he may take part in the household in a small way. One evening, Grete plays her violin in the parlor, and the music so moves Gregor that he creeps out into the parlor toward her, wanting to convey that he understands her gift and will help it blossom. When the family sees Gregor, they snap. Grete says they must abandon the notion that this hideous bug is their dear Gregor. All sadly agree. Gregor slinks back into his room and dies that night.

A great weight lifts from the family. After a moment of mourning, the father demands that the lodgers leave immediately. The family takes a trolley out of the city and into the countryside. It is a beautiful, sunny day, and as Grete stretches out her limbs in the trolley car, her parents' thoughts turn to finding her a husband.

CHARACTERS IN *THE METAMORPHOSIS*

The Manager Gregor's manager. A suspicious, threatening, man, he suggests that Gregor's absence from work is connected with the theft of funds from the company.

The Roomers Three unnamed and unified tenants. The roomers take up residence in the Samsa home at the end of the novella. They are greatly preoccupied with food.

Gregor's Father A slouching, defeated man. Gregor's father failed at business, but once Gregor's misfortune compels him to find work again, he finds new confidence and better posture. His fruit-flinging fit of rage leads to Gregor's declining health and eventual demise.

Gregor's Mother A physically weak woman. Gregor's mother suffers the most because of her son's metamorphosis. Despite her love for Gregor, she gets sick whenever she catches sight of his bug form. Gregor's father and sister feel protective of her and resent Gregor for endangering her health.

Gregor Samsa A young traveling salesman. Gregor goes into the business to help his father, who has a large debt. As much as he hates the petty and degrading concern for which he works, Gregor is proud of providing his mother, father, and sister with a nice apartment and a fairly comfortable life. He secretly dreams of sending Grete to the conservatory to study violin.

Grete Samsa Gregor's younger sister. Before Gregor's transformation, Grete is devoted to him. After it, she takes on sole responsibility for his care. Gregor thinks a mixture of youthfulness and devotion to his memory motivates Grete. It is Grete who finally voices the family's impatience with Gregor's situation.

THEMES IN *THE METAMORPHOSIS*

THE FAMILY ROMANCE The story of Gregor Samsa lends itself well to a Freudian analysis. Freud posited that like Oedipus, the man in the ancient Greek story who killed his father and married his mother, all sons secretly long to kill their fathers and have sex with their mothers. This universal scenario, which Freud called the "Oedipal complex," has many parallels in Gregor's story. Gregor transforms in his bed, a place that symbolizes the place of sexual perversion. This symbolism is heightened by the highly erotic picture on Gregor's wall—a picture on which he dwells extensively when he wakes. Furthermore, Gregor's bedroom is situated between his sister's room and his parents' room. The three bedrooms blur together, made one by the exchange of noises and lack of privacy from room to room. This proximity suggests that Gregor's guilty sexual energy is directed toward members of his family. Gregor experiences certain unsettling urges, such as the desire to kiss his sister on the neck, which corroborate the implication of incestuous longings. However, in the end, Gregor's story reverses the Oedipal complex. Most sons symbolically kill their fathers in order to become adult men themselves. In a nightmarish reversal of the normal order of human development, Gregor regresses, changing from the head of his household into a prehuman, parasitic beast—while at the same time, his father transforms from a senile, impotent old geezer into a thriving, virile family king.

THE DEHUMANIZING EFFECT OF CAPITALISM When Gregor provides for his family, he is the most important member of it. His father whiles away his days eating and reading newspapers; his mother, an asthmatic, lies in bed; and his sister studies music in a minor way but for the most part enjoys a life of leisure. Gregor's ability to work and earn money has given him an exalted position in his family. He is their focal point.

Yet while Gregor's labor has secured his importance in the family, it has also robbed him of his humanity. Kafka implies this in dozens of tiny ways; the effect is subtle and cumulative. Early on, we learn that Gregor dislikes his work and only continues it to help pay off his parents' debts. He loathes his boss, but fears his boss's disapproval. The narrator contrasts Gregor's current nervous state to an image of Gregor in the old days, wearing an army uniform, "a carefree smile," and a posture that demands respect. Gradually, it becomes clear that Gregor's job turned him into a groveling insect even before he physically became one. Besides alienating him from his own life, Gregor's office work has also estranged him from his family. He has heard accounts of his family's daily domestic routine, but has never experienced it firsthand. His long experience with business trips have put him in the habit of locking his bedroom doors, even at home.

THE LINE BETWEEN THE HUMAN AND THE BESTIAL Kafka forces us to question our assumptions about what distinguishes human from beast. Although Gregor takes on an insect form, he is the least animalistic character in the novella. His metamorphosis brings out not his own bestiality, but the bestiality of everyone around him. Many of the characteristics typically associated with a wild animal—greed, violence, lack of psychological empathy—belong not to Gregor but to his family members.

When Gregor wakes up and discovers that he has become an insect, all he can think about is not disappointing his family or leaving them in the lurch. No one else demonstrates this kind of unselfish goodness except Grete—and she only for a short time. When Grete plays the violin, Gregor is moved by the beautiful music in a way that none of the humans are. Kafka emphasizes this contrast between physical and emotional bestiality by ending the novel with a rumination on it. When Grete gets up to stretch "her young body," her parents gleefully delight in her sexual readiness. The moment has the uncanny echo of a bestial metamorphosis, a nubile emergence from the chrysalis more animalistic than anything Gregor experienced.

SYMBOLS IN *THE METAMORPHOSIS*

THE PICTURE At the beginning of the novella, Kafka devotes a lengthy passage to describing a picture Gregor has clipped from a glossy magazine. This picture depicts "a lady done up in a fur hat and a fur boa, sitting upright and raising against the viewer a heavy fur muff in which her whole forearm had disappeared." Some scholars argue that fur always symbolizes genitalia in Kafka's work, which it certainly does here. The woman's forearm is a phallic symbol penetrating the vaginal "fur muff." In another interpretation, the alluring picture from a magazine represents media and capitalism, and the fur represents the bestiality that capitalism forces on people. The woman is practically swallowed up in this fur as if it is turning her into a beast.

THE APPLE The apple thrown by Gregor's father symbolizes original sin. When Gregor's sister and mother decide he would be more comfortable without any furniture in his room, Gregor panics and attaches himself to his framed erotic picture. His father mistakes Gregor's intentions and throws apples at him, one of which breaks his carapace and sticks. The sequence suggests the story of Adam and Eve, the father and mother of the human race, who sinned by eating an apple, thus condemning humankind to a lifetime of work and suffering. Gregor's parents are the Adam and Eve of his life. Just as humankind must labor to earn its bread because of the sins of its first parents, Gregor must labor to support his family because of the sins of his parents. Gregor's father makes Gregor's burden literal by injuring him with the apple.

IMPORTANT QUOTATIONS FROM *THE METAMORPHOSIS*

He was already beginning to feel winded, just as in the old days he had not had very reliable lungs . . . . a lightly flung object hit the floor right near him. . . . It was an apple; a second one came flying right after it . . . . his father was determined to bombard him. . . . One apple, thrown weakly, grazed Gregor's back. . . . But the very next one that came flying after it literally forced its way into Gregor's back. . . . With his last glance he saw the door of his room burst open as his mother rushed out . . . saw his mother run up to his father and on the way her unfastened petticoats slide to the floor one by one; and saw as . . . . . she forced herself onto his father and embracing him, in complete union with him—but now Gregor's sight went dim—her hands clasping his father's neck, begged for Gregor's life.

Location: The end of Part II
Speaker: The narrator
Context: After accidentally frightening his mother into a faint, Gregor is chased back to his room by his hostile father

This dense, hallucinatory passage features one after another of Kafka's major themes as well as elements from his own life. With the symbolic hurled apple, Kafka emphasizes the parallels between Gregor's relationship with his parents and humankind's relationship with Adam and Eve. He underlines the trauma of the scene by including an archetypal parent-child encounter—the moment when a child accidentally comes upon his parents having sex, which psychologists call the *primal scene.* Gregor's mother's undergarments fall off "one by one," as she forces herself on her husband, forming "complete union" with him.

A number of personal elements in this passage suggest the extent to which Kafka identified with Gregor. Kafka had a notoriously troubled relationship with his own father. His "Letter to His Father," written seven years after *The Metamorphosis*, reveals Kafka's conviction that his father saw him as a parasitic vermin incapable of asserting himself in a fair, manly way. Also like Gregor, Kafka resented being trapped in dull, bureaucratic work that prevented him from writing. These autobiographical elements bubble throughout the story, surfacing most noticeably when Gregor and his father struggle.

> *The roomers rose as one man and mumbled something into their beards. When they were alone again, they ate in almost complete silence. It seemed strange to Gregor that among all the different noises of eating he kept picking up the sound of their chewing teeth, as if this were a sign to Gregor that you needed teeth to eat with and that even with the best make of toothless jaws you couldn't do a thing. "I'm hungry enough," Gregor said to himself, full of grief, "but not for these things. Look how these roomers are gorging themselves, and I'm dying!"*

Location: Part III
Speaker: The narrator
Context: The abused Gregor, displaced and ignored partially because of his family's new tenants, eavesdrops

After his family takes on roomers to help defray their expenses, Gregor's quality of life decays even further than it already has. Although everyone in the family suffers, Gregor suffers most. All kinds of useless objects from the house are shoved into his room, which is rarely cleaned and usually left closed in order to hide his strange, unsettling existence. The filthy and neglected Gregor becomes morose and even resentful toward the rest of his family. He all but stops eating, either refusing to touch his food or toying with it and then spitting it out.

Kafka confines his discussion of the mysterious, ghostly roomers almost exclusively to their eating habits, blending them together into one featureless, hungry creature. Their gluttony contrasts with Gregor's near-starvation. In this novella about desire and the attraction and revulsion of animal appetite, Gregor's obsessive interest in the roomers' chewing has a whiff of sexual frustration about it. When Grete is sent out to entertain the hungry roomers, Gregor gets a bit hysterical and fantasizes about locking her in the room with him, as if he longs for the sexual rapaciousness of the boarders.

> *When Gregor Samsa woke up one morning from unsettling dreams, he found himself changed in his bed into a monstrous vermin. He was lying on his back as hard as armor plate, and when he lifted his head a little, he saw his vaulted brown belly, sectioned by arch-shaped ribs, to whose dome the cover, about to slide off completely, could barely cling.*

Location: The opening lines of Part I
Speaker: The narrator
Context: Gregor discovers his metamorphosis

> *Why didn't his sister go in to the others? She had probably just got out of bed and not even started to get dressed. Then what was she crying about? Because he didn't get up and didn't let the manager in, because he was in danger of losing his job, and because then the boss would start hounding his parents about the old debts? For the time being, certainly, her worries were unnecessary. Gregor was still here and hadn't the slightest intention of letting the family down.*

Location: Part I
Speaker: The narrator
Context: Gregor lies helpless on the carpet in his bedroom while his manager waits for him to open the door

And so he broke out . . . changed his course four times, he really didn't know what to salvage first, then he saw hanging conspicuously on the wall, which was otherwise bare already the picture of the lady all dressed in furs, hurriedly crawled on up it and pressed himself against the glass which gave a good surface to stick to and soothed his hot belly. At least no one would take away this picture, while Gregor completely covered it up. He turned his head toward the living-room door to watch the women when they returned.

Location: Part II
Speaker: The narrator
Context: Gregor's mother and sister decide to remove his furniture, thinking it will make him more comfortable

A MIDSUMMER NIGHT'S DREAM

William Shakespeare

After a bewildering night in a fairy-haunted forest, three couples are united in marriage.

THE LIFE OF WILLIAM SHAKESPEARE

William Shakespeare, the most influential writer in all of English literature, was born in 1564 to a successful middle-class glove-maker in Stratford-upon-Avon, England. Shakespeare's formal education did not progress beyond grammar school. In 1582, he married an older woman, Anne Hathaway. His union with Anne produced three children. Around 1590, Shakespeare left his family behind and traveled to London to work as an actor and playwright. He quickly earned public and critical acclaim, and eventually became the most popular playwright in England and a part-owner of the Globe Theater. Shakespeare's career bridged the reigns of Elizabeth I (ruled 1558–1603) and James I (ruled 1603–1625), and he was a favorite of both monarchs. James paid Shakespeare's company a great compliment by giving its members the title of King's Men. Shakespeare retired to Stratford a wealthy and renowned man and died in 1616 at the age of fifty-two. At the time of Shakespeare's death, literary luminaries such as Ben Jonson hailed his works as timeless.

Shakespeare's works were collected and printed in various editions in the century following his death, and by the early eighteenth century his reputation as the greatest poet ever to write in English was well established. The unprecedented regard in which Shakespeare's works were held led to a fierce curiosity about his life, but many details of Shakespeare's personal history are unknown or shrouded in mystery. Some people have concluded from this lack of information and from Shakespeare's modest education that Shakespeare's plays were actually written by someone else—Francis Bacon and the Earl of Oxford are the two most popular candidates—but the support for this claim is overwhelmingly circumstantial, and the theory is not taken seriously by many scholars.

Shakespeare is generally thought to be the author of the thirty-eight plays (two of them possibly collaborations) and 154 sonnets that bear his name. The legacy of this body of work is immense. A number of Shakespeare's plays seem to have transcended even the category of brilliance, influencing the course of Western literature and culture.

A MIDSUMMER NIGHT'S DREAM IN CONTEXT

Written in the mid-1590s, probably shortly before Shakespeare began *Romeo and Juliet*, *A Midsummer Night's Dream* is one of Shakespeare's strangest and most delightful plays. The range of references in the play is among its most extraordinary attributes: Shakespeare draws on sources as various as Greek mythology (Theseus, for instance, is loosely based on the Greek hero of the same name, and the play is peppered with references to Greek gods and goddesses); English country fairy lore (the character of Puck, or Robin Goodfellow, was a popular figure in sixteenth-century stories); and the theatrical practices of Shakespeare's London (the craftsmen's play refers to and parodies many conventions of English Renaissance theater, such as men playing the roles of women). The characters are inspired by diverse texts: Titania comes from Ovid's *Metamorphoses*, and Oberon may have been taken from the medieval romance *Huan of Bordeaux*, translated into English by Lord Berners in the mid-1530s. Unlike the plots of many of Shakespeare's plays, however, the story in *A Midsummer Night's Dream* seems to be the original product of the playwright's imagination, not a variation on a story already in existence.

A MIDSUMMER NIGHT'S DREAM: KEY FACTS

Full Title: A Midsummer Night's Dream

Time and place written: London; 1594 or 1595

Date of first publication: 1600

Genre: Comedy

Setting (time): Combines elements of Ancient Greece with elements of Renaissance England

Setting (place): Athens and the forest outside its walls

Protagonist: Puck

Major conflict: Six people struggle to satisfy their romantic desires

A MIDSUMMER NIGHT'S DREAM: PLOT OVERVIEW

Theseus, Duke of Athens, is preparing for his marriage to Hippolyta, Queen of the Amazons, with a four-day festival of pomp and entertainment. He commissions his Master of the Revels, Philostrate, to find suitable amusements for the occasion. Egeus, an Athenian nobleman, marches into Theseus's court with his daughter, Hermia, and two young men, Demetrius and Lysander. Egeus wishes Hermia to marry Demetrius (who loves Hermia), but Hermia is in love with Lysander and refuses to comply. Egeus asks for the full penalty of law to fall on Hermia's head if she flouts her father's will. Theseus gives Hermia until his wedding to consider her options, warning her that disobeying her father's wishes could result in her being sent to a convent or even executed. Nonetheless, Hermia and Lysander plan to escape Athens the following night and marry in the house of Lysander's aunt, some seven leagues distant from the city. They make their intentions known to Hermia's friend Helena, who was once engaged to Demetrius and still loves him even though he jilted her after meeting Hermia. Hoping to regain his love, Helena tells Demetrius of the elopement that Hermia and Lysander have planned. At the appointed time, Demetrius stalks into the woods after his intended bride and her lover; Helena follows behind him.

In these same woods are two very different groups of characters. The first is a band of fairies, including Oberon, the fairy king, and Titania, his queen, who has recently returned from India to bless the marriage of Theseus and Hippolyta. The second is a band of Athenian craftsmen rehearsing a play that they hope to perform for the duke and his bride. Oberon and Titania are at odds over a young Indian prince given to Titania by the prince's mother; the boy is so beautiful that Oberon wishes to make him a knight, but Titania refuses. Seeking revenge, Oberon sends his merry servant, Puck, to acquire a magical flower, the juice of which can be spread over a sleeping person's eyelids to make that person fall in love with the first thing he or she sees upon waking. Puck obtains the flower, and Oberon tells him of his plan to spread its juice on the sleeping Titania's eyelids. Having seen Demetrius act cruelly toward Helena, he orders Puck to spread some of the juice on the eyelids of the young Athenian man. Puck encounters Lysander and Hermia; thinking that Lysander is the Athenian of whom Oberon spoke, Puck afflicts him with the love potion. Lysander happens to see Helena upon awaking and falls deeply in love with her, abandoning Hermia. As the night progresses and Puck attempts to undo his mistake, both Lysander and Demetrius end up in love with Helena, who believes that they are mocking her. Hermia becomes so jealous that she tries to challenge Helena to a fight. Demetrius and Lysander nearly do fight over Helena's love, but Puck confuses them by mimicking their voices, leading them apart until they are lost separately in the forest.

When Titania wakes, the first creature she sees is Bottom, the most ridiculous of the Athenian craftsmen, whose head Puck has mockingly transformed into that of an ass. Titania passes a ludicrous interlude doting on the ass-headed weaver. Eventually, Oberon obtains the Indian boy, Puck spreads the love potion on Lysander's eyelids, and by morning all is well. Theseus and Hippolyta discover the sleeping lovers in the forest and take them back to Athens to be married—Demetrius now loves Helena, and Lysander now loves Hermia. After the group wedding, the lovers watch Bottom and his fellow craftsmen perform their play, a fumbling, hilarious version of the story of Pyramus and Thisbe. When the play is completed, the lovers go to bed; the fairies briefly emerge to bless the sleeping couples with a protective charm and then disappear. Only Puck remains, to ask the audience for its forgiveness and approval and to urge it to remember the play as though it had all been a dream.

CHARACTERS IN *A MIDSUMMER NIGHT'S DREAM*

ATHENIANS

Demetrius A young man of Athens. Demetrius is initially in love with Hermia and ultimately in love with Helena. His obstinate pursuit of Hermia throws love out of balance among the quartet of Athenian youths.

Egeus Hermia's father. Egeus has given Demetrius permission to marry Hermia, but Hermia refuses to marry him because she is in love with Lysander. Egeus insists that Hermia either respect his wishes or be held accountable to Athenian law.

Helena A young woman of Athens. Helena is in love with Demetrius, who abandoned her for her friend Hermia. Helena lacks confidence in her looks.

Hermia Egeus's daughter. Hermia, a young woman of Athens, is in love with Lysander. Self-conscious about her short stature, Hermia suspects that Helena has attracted Lysander and Demetrius with her height.

Hippolyta The legendary queen of the Amazons. Hippolyta is engaged to Theseus. Like him, she symbolizes order.

Lysander A young man of Athens. Lysander is in love with Hermia, but Hermia's father wants her to marry Demetrius. In the forest, Lysander becomes the victim of misapplied magic and wakes up in love with Helena.

Philostrate Theseus's Master of the Revels. Philostrate is responsible for organizing the entertainment for the duke's marriage celebration.

Theseus The heroic duke of Athens. Theseus, who is engaged to Hippolyta, represents power and order. He appears only at the beginning and end of the story.

FAIRIES AND THEIR COMPANIONS

Oberon The king of the fairies. Oberon wants to revenge himself on Titania, his wife, because she refuses to relinquish control of a young Indian prince whom he wants for a knight. His vengefulness leads him to send Puck to obtain the love-potion flower that creates so much confusion.

Peaseblossom, Cobweb, Mote, and Mustardseed Fairies. Titania orders them to attend to Bottom after she falls in love with him.

Puck Oberon's jester. Puck, also known as Robin Goodfellow, is a mischievous fairy who delights in playing pranks on mortals. His antics propel the plot.

Titania The beautiful queen of the fairies. Titania is married to Oberon.

PARTICIPANTS IN THE CRAFTSMEN'S PLAY

Nick Bottom An overconfident weaver. Bottom is chosen to play Pyramus in the craftsmen's play for Theseus's marriage celebration. He is full of advice and confidence but frequently makes silly mistakes and misuses language. He is nonchalant about the beautiful Titania's love for him and unaware that Puck has transformed his head into an ass's head.

Francis Flute A bellows-mender. Francis Flute is chosen to play Thisbe, a young girl in love, in the craftsmen's play for Theseus's marriage celebration.

Tom Snout A tinker. Tom Snout is chosen to play Pyramus's father in the craftsmen's play. He ends up playing the part of Wall, dividing the two lovers.

Snug A joiner. Snug is chosen to play the lion in the craftsmen's play. He worries that his roaring will frighten the ladies in the audience.

Robin Starveling A tailor. Robin Starveling is chosen to play Thisbe's mother in the craftsmen's play. He ends up playing the part of Moonshine.

Peter Quince A carpenter and the nominal leader of the craftsmen's play. The abundantly confident Bottom often shoves Quince aside.

THEMES IN *A MIDSUMMER NIGHT'S DREAM*

IMBALANCE IN RELATIONSHIPS "The course of true love never did run smooth," comments Lysander, articulating one of *A Midsummer Night's Dream*'s most important themes: the difficulty of love (I.i.134). Love is almost always out of balance in the play. Disparity or inequality interferes with the harmony of nearly every relationship. The prime instance of this imbalance is the uneven love among the four young Athenians: Hermia loves Lysander, Lysander loves Hermia, Helena loves Demetrius, and Demetrius loves Hermia. In a numeric imbalance, two men love the same woman, leaving one woman with too many suitors and one with too few. As the audience knows, the happy outcome will be achieved when the lovers' tangle resolves itself into symmetrical pairings. In the relationship between Titania and Oberon, an imbalance arises because Oberon's desire for Titania's Indian boy eclipses his love for her. Later, Titania's passion for the ass-headed Bottom is an imbalance of appearance and nature: Titania is beautiful and graceful, Bottom is clumsy and grotesque.

THE USE OF MAGIC The fairies' magic, which brings about many of the most bizarre and hilarious situations in the play, enhances the play's fantastical atmosphere. Shakespeare uses magic both to suggest the almost supernatural power of love, as symbolized by the love potion, and to create a surreal world. Although the misuse of magic causes chaos, as when Puck mistakenly applies the love potion to Lysander's eyelids, magic ultimately resolves the play's tensions by balancing the love among the quartet of Athenian youths.

THE ILLOGICAL, COMFORTING QUALITY OF DREAMS Shakespeare is interested in the illogical quality of dreams, in the way events in dreams occur without explanation, time loses its normal flow, and the impossible occurs as a matter of course. He recreates the effect of dreams with the nonsensical, illogical intervention of the fairies in the magical forest. Shakespeare also examines the way we look at our lives through the filter of dreams. Characters in the play often attempt to explain the bizarre events that take place in the forest by blaming them on dreams. When Bottom cannot fathom the magic that has transpired, he says, "I have had a dream, past the wit of man to say what / dream it was. Man is but an ass if he go about t'expound this dream." At the end of the play, Puck tells the audience that if they have been offended by the play, they should remember it as nothing more than a dream.

SYMBOLS IN *A MIDSUMMER NIGHT'S DREAM*

THESEUS AND HIPPOLYTA Theseus and Hippolyta bookend *A Midsummer Night's Dream*, appearing in the daylight at the beginning and the end of the play's main action. They disappear for the duration of the action, leaving in the middle of Act I, scene i and not reappearing until Act IV, as the sun is coming up to end the magical night in the forest. Shakespeare uses Theseus and Hippolyta, the ruler of Athens and his warrior bride, to represent order and stability. They contrast with the uncertainty, instability, and darkness that characterize most of the play. Whereas an important element of the dream realm is that one is not in control of one's environment, Theseus and Hippolyta are always entirely in control of theirs. Their reappearance in the daylight signifies the end of the dream state of the previous night and a return to rationality.

THE CRAFTSMEN'S PLAY The play-within-a-play that takes up most of Act V, scene i represents, in condensed form, many of the important ideas and themes of the main plot. With their bumbling performance, the actors accidentally satirize the melodramatic Athenian lovers and give the play a purely joyful, comedic ending. Pyramus and Thisbe face parental disapproval in the play-within-a-play, just as Hermia and Lysander do. The theme of romantic confusion enhanced by the darkness of night comes up in the play, just as the Athenian lovers experience intense misery because of the mix-ups caused by the fairies' meddling. The craftsmen's play is a kind of symbol for A *Midsummer Night's Dream* itself: it is a story involving powerful emotions that is made hilarious by its comical presentation.

IMPORTANT QUOTATIONS FROM *A MIDSUMMER NIGHT'S DREAM*

Through Athens I am thought as fair as she.
But what of that? Demetrius thinks not so.
He will not know what all but he do know.
And as he errs, doting on Hermia's eyes,
So I, admiring of his qualities.
Things base and vile, holding no quantity,
Love can transpose to form and dignity.
Love looks not with the eyes, but with the mind,
And therefore is winged Cupid painted blind.

Location: I.i.227–235
Speaker: Helena
Context: Helena thinks about her merits compared to Hermia's

In these lines, Helena articulates the play's general presentation of love as an erratic, inexplicable, and exceptionally powerful force. Distressed by the fact that her beloved Demetrius loves Hermia and not her, Helena says that although she is as beautiful as Hermia, Demetrius cannot see her beauty. Helena says she dotes on Demetrius, even though not all of his qualities are admirable, in the same way that Demetrius dotes on Hermia. She believes that love has the power to transform "base and vile" qualities into "form and dignity"—that is, even ugliness and bad behavior can seem attractive to someone in love. This is the case, Helena argues, because "love looks not with the eyes, but with the mind." That is, love depends not on an objective assessment of appearance but rather on an individual perception of the beloved. These lines prefigure aspects of the play's examination of love, such as Titania's passion for the ass-headed Bottom, which epitomizes the transformation of the "base and vile" into "form and dignity."

I have had a most rare vision. I have had a dream past the wit of man to say what dream it was. Man is but an ass if he go about t'expound this dream. Methought I was—there is no man can tell what. Methought I was, and methought I had—but man is but a patched fool if he will offer to say what methought I had. The eye of man hath not heard, the ear of man hath not seen, man's hand is not able to taste, his tongue to conceive, nor his heart to report what my dream was. I will get Peter Quince to write a ballad of this dream. It shall be called 'Bottom's Dream,' because it hath no bottom.

Location: IV.i.199–209
Speaker: Bottom
Context: Bottom has had an adventure with Titania

Bottom makes this bombastic speech after waking up after his adventure with Titania. His human head restored, he believes that his experience as an ass-headed monster beloved by the beautiful fairy queen was merely a bizarre dream. He says dramatically that his dream is beyond human comprehension. Then, contradicting himself, he says that he will ask Quince to write a ballad about his dream. These lines offer humorous commentary on dreams; they also exemplify much of what is so lovable and amusing about Bottom. His overabundant self-confidence makes him think that no one could possibly understand his dream, but his tremendous self-regard makes him want his dream, which no mortal can understand, to be immortalized in a poem written by his friend. He makes many melodramatic rhetorical mistakes, suggesting that eyes hear, ears see, hands taste, tongues think, and hearts speak.

Ay me, for aught that I could ever read,

Could ever hear by tale or history,
The course of true love never did run smooth.

Location: I.i.132–134
Speaker: Lysander
Context: Hermia despairs about the difficulties facing their relationship; Lysander responds

---

Lord, what fools these mortals be!

Location: III.ii.115
Speaker: Puck
Context: The four Athenians have been behaving outlandishly

If we shadows have offended,
Think but this, and all is mended:
That you have but slumbered here,
While these visions did appear;
And this weak and idle theme,
No more yielding but a dream,
Gentles, do not reprehend.
If you pardon, we will mend.

Location: V.epilogue.1–8
Speaker: Puck
Context: Puck, speaking to the audience, concludes the play

MOBY-DICK

Herman Melville

A monomaniacal captain tries and fails to kill a monstrous white whale.

THE LIFE OF HERMAN MELVILLE

Herman Melville, the third of eight children, was born in New York City in 1819. His parents were Maria Gansevoort Melville and Allan Melvill, a prosperous importer of foreign goods. When the family business failed at the end of the 1820s, the Melvills relocated to Albany in an attempt to revive their fortunes. Overwork drove Allan to an early grave, and Melville (the name was changed after his father's death) was forced to start working in a bank at age thirteen.

Before the age of nineteen, Melville worked as an elementary school teacher and a newspaper reporter. At nineteen, he made his first sea voyage, working as a merchant sailor on a ship bound for Liverpool, England. He returned to America the next summer to seek his fortune in the West. After briefly settling in Illinois, he went back East in the face of continuing financial difficulties. Twenty-one and desperate, Melville committed to going on a whaling voyage on board the *Acushnet*. In the summer of 1842, eighteen months after setting out from New York, Melville and another sailor abandoned ship in the South Seas. The two men found themselves in the Marquesas Islands, where they accidentally stumbled upon a tribe of cannibals. Lamed by an injury to his leg, Melville got separated from his companion and spent a month alone with the natives. This experience provided material for his first novel, *Typee: A Peep at Polynesian Life*, published in 1846. An indeterminate mixture of fact and fiction, the fanciful travel narrative was, during his lifetime, Melville's most popular and successful work.

Melville set out to write a series of novels detailing his adventures and his philosophy of life. *Typee* was the first in this series, followed by *Omoo* (1847), and *Mardi and a Voyage Thither* (1849). Melville went on to publish *Redburn* (1849), and *White-Jacket; or The World in a Man-of-War*. Today, Melville's first five novels are considered a prologue to his masterpiece, *Moby-Dick; or The Whale*, first published in 1851. His next novel, *Pierre; or The Ambiguities* (1852), provoked critical outrage. The sole pastoral romance among Melville's works, *Pierre* features conflicted writing, incestuous themes, and dicey morals. After the disastrous reception of *Pierre*, Melville turned to short story writing. In the following five years, he published numerous fictional sketches in several prominent periodicals of the day. Most notable among these works are "Bartelby, The Scrivener" and "Benito Cereno." He also published *Israel Potter; or Fifty Years of Exile* (1855), and a bleak satire of trust titled *The Confidence Man: His Masquerade*, in 1857.

In the remaining thirty-five years of his life, Melville's literary production ground nearly to a halt. After a brief national lecture tour, he worked for almost twenty years as a customshouse inspector, finally retiring in the late 1880s. A volume of war poetry, *Battle-Pieces and Aspects of the War*, appeared in 1866, and Melville published the lengthy poem *Clarel: A Poem and Pilgrimage in the Holy Land* in 1876. Toward the end of his life, Melville produced two more volumes of verse, *John Marr and Other Sailors* (1888) and *Timoleon* (1891). He died in 1891.

MOBY-DICK IN CONTEXT

In writing *Moby-Dick*, Melville was influenced by the work of Nathaniel Hawthorne, author of *The Scarlet Letter*, whom he met in 1850 and to whom he dedicated *Moby-Dick*. Melville admired Hawthorne's psychological depth and gothic grimness and associated him with a new, distinctively American literature. *Moby-Dick* draws on Shakespeare, Milton, and the Old Testament, but also on popular culture such as Thomas Beale's encyclopedic *Natural History of the Sperm Whale* and J. Ross Browne's narrative *Etchings of a Whaling Cruise*.

A story set on a whaling ship, *Moby-Dick* is both a documentary of life at sea and a vast philosophical allegory of life in general. It satirizes religion, moral values, and the literary and political figures of the day. *Moby-Dick* got lukewarm reviews at first, which did not bother Melville. He defied his critics by writing in an increasingly experimental style.

Moby-Dick remained largely ignored until the 1920s, when it was rediscovered and promoted by literary historians. These critics considered Moby-Dick both a seminal work on classic American themes, such as religion, fate, and economic expansion, and a radically experimental novel that anticipated modernism in its outsized scope and pastiche of forms. Now firmly ensconced in the canon, Moby-Dick stands alongside James Joyce's Ulysses and Laurence Sterne's Tristram Shandy as a novel open to almost infinite interpretation and discovery.

MOBY-DICK: KEY FACTS

Full title: Moby-Dick; or The Whale

Time and place written: 1850–1851; Pittsfield, Massachusetts, and New York City

Date of first publication: 1851

Publisher: Harper & Brothers in America (simultaneously published by Richard Bentley in England as The Whale)

Type of work: Novel

Genre: Epic; adventure story; quest tale; allegory

Language: English

Setting (time): 1830s or 1840s

Setting (place): The whaling ship the Pequod, in the Pacific, Atlantic, and Indian Oceans

Tense: Past

Tone: Ironic, celebratory, philosophical, dramatic, hyperbolic

Narrator: Ishmael in the first and third person

Point of view: Ishmael's

Protagonist: Ishmael, Ahab

Antagonist: Ahab, Moby Dick

MOBY-DICK: PLOT OVERVIEW

Ishmael, the narrator, plans to work on a whaling vessel. He travels to New Bedford, Massachusetts, where he stays in a whalers' inn. Since the inn is rather full, he has to share a bed with a harpooner from the South Pacific named Queequeg. At first repulsed by Queequeg's strange habits and shocking appearance (Queequeg is covered with tattoos), Ishmael eventually appreciates the man's generosity and kind spirit. The two decide to seek work on a whaling vessel together. They take a ferry to Nantucket, the capital of the whaling industry, where they secure berths on the Pequod, a savage-looking ship adorned with the bones and teeth of sperm whales. Peleg and Bildad, the Pequod's Quaker owners, mention the ship's mysterious captain, Ahab, who recently lost his leg in an encounter with a sperm whale.

The Pequod leaves Nantucket on a cold Christmas Day with crew members from many different countries. Ahab makes his first appearance on deck, balancing gingerly on his false leg, which is made from a sperm whale's jaw. He announces his desire to pursue and kill Moby Dick, the legendary great white whale who took his leg. He thinks this whale is the embodiment of evil. Ahab nails a gold doubloon to the mast and says the doubloon will go to the first man who sights the whale. As the Pequod sails toward the southern tip of Africa, the crew sights whales and hunts them without success. A group of men emerges from the hold for the first time. The group's leader is an exotic-looking man named Fedallah. These men are Ahab's private harpoon crew, smuggled aboard in defiance of Bildad and Peleg. Ahab hopes that their skills and Fedallah's prophetic abilities will help him in his hunt for Moby Dick.

The Pequod rounds Africa and enters the Indian Ocean. The crew catches a few whales and processes them for their oil. When the ship encounters other whaling vessels, Ahab always demands information about Moby Dick. One of the ships, the Jeroboam, carries Gabriel, a crazed prophet who predicts doom for anyone who threatens Moby Dick. Those aboard his ship who have hunted Moby Dick have met with disaster. Tashtego, one of the Pequod's harpooners, falls into a whale's head while trying to drain oil from it. The head rips free of the ship and begins to sink. Queequeg saves Tashtego by diving into the ocean and cutting into the slowly sinking head.

During another whale hunt, Pip, the *Pequod*'s black cabin boy, jumps from a whaleboat and for a time is left behind in the middle of the ocean. He goes insane as the result of the experience and becomes a crazy but prophetic jester for the ship. The *Pequod* meets the *Samuel Enderby*, a whaling ship whose skipper, Captain Boomer, lost an arm in an encounter with Moby Dick. The two captains discuss the whale. Boomer is simply happy to have survived his encounter and cannot understand Ahab's lust for vengeance. Soon Queequeg falls ill and has the ship's carpenter make him a coffin. He recovers, however, and the coffin becomes the *Pequod*'s replacement life buoy.

Ahab orders a harpoon forged in the expectation that he will soon encounter Moby Dick. He baptizes the harpoon with the blood of the *Pequod*'s three harpooners. The *Pequod* kills several more whales. Fedallah prophecies that Ahab will see two hearses, the second of which will be made from American wood, and that he will be killed by hemp rope. Ahab believes this prophecy means he will not die at sea, where there are no hearses and no hangings. A typhoon hits the *Pequod*, illuminating it with electrical fire. Ahab thinks this is a sign of imminent confrontation and success, but Starbuck, the ship's first mate, takes it as a bad omen and considers killing Ahab to end the mad quest. After the storm ends, one of the sailors falls from the ship's masthead and drowns.

Ahab's obsession with Moby Dick intensifies. Pip is now his constant companion. The *Pequod* approaches the equator. Ahab finally sights Moby Dick. The harpoon boats are launched, and Moby Dick attacks Ahab's harpoon boat, destroying it. The next day, Moby Dick is sighted again, and the boats are lowered once more. Moby Dick is harpooned, but again attacks Ahab's boat. Fedallah, trapped in the harpoon line, is dragged overboard to his death. Starbuck must maneuver the *Pequod* between Ahab and the angry whale.

On the third day, the boats are once again sent after Moby Dick, who once again attacks them. Ishmael is thrown from a boat at the beginning of the chase. The men can see Fedallah's corpse lashed to the whale by the harpoon line. Moby Dick rams the *Pequod* and sinks it. Ahab is caught in a harpoon line and hurled out of his harpoon boat to his death. All of the remaining whaleboats and men, save Ishmael, are caught in the vortex created by the sinking *Pequod* and pulled under to their deaths. Ishmael floats atop Queequeg's coffin until he is picked up by the *Rachel*, which is still searching for the crewmen lost in her earlier encounter with Moby Dick.

CHARACTERS IN *MOBY-DICK*

Ahab The egomaniacal captain of the *Pequod*. Ahab uses a mixture of charisma and terror to persuade his crew to join him in a crazed pursuit of Moby Dick. As a captain, he is dictatorial but not unfair. At moments he shows a compassionate side, caring for the insane Pip and thinking about his wife and child back in Nantucket.

Bildad A well-to-do retired whaleman from Nantucket. Bildad is one of the owners of the *Pequod*.

Captain Boomer The jovial captain of the English whaling ship the *Samuel Enderby*.

Daggoo Flask's harpooner. Daggoo is an enormous, imperious-looking African.

Fedallah A strange, "oriental" old Parsee (Persian fire-worshipper). Fedallah wears a turban made from his own hair. He is an almost supernaturally skilled hunter.

Flask The third mate of the *Pequod*. A native of Tisbury on Martha's Vineyard, Flask has a confrontational attitude and no reverence for anything. He is short and squat.

Gabriel A sailor aboard the *Jeroboam*. Part of a Shaker sect, Gabriel prophesies that Moby Dick is the incarnation of the Shaker god and that any attempts to harm him will result in disaster.

Ishmael The narrator. Ishmael is a junior member of the *Pequod*'s crew. He doesn't play a major role in the events of the novel, but he dominates the narrative with his eloquent and extravagant discourse on whales and whaling.

Father Mapple A former whaleman. Mapple's trials have led him toward God rather than toward bitterness or vengefulness.

Moby Dick The great white sperm whale. Moby Dick, also referred to as the White Whale, is an infamous threat to seamen.

Peleg A well-to-do retired whaleman of Nantucket. Peleg is one of the principal owners of the *Pequod*.

Pip A young black boy on the *Pequod*. Like the fools in Shakespeare's plays, he is half idiot and half prophet.

Starbuck The first mate of the *Pequod*. Starbuck questions Ahab's judgment, first in private and then in public. He is a Christian man, but not dogmatic or pushy about his beliefs.

Stubb The second mate of the *Pequod*. Stubb is mischievous, easygoing, and popular. He is a bit of a nihilist.

Tashtego Stubb's harpooner. Tashtego is a Gay Head Indian from Martha's Vineyard, one of the last of a tribe about to disappear. Like Queequeg, Tashtego is meant to defy racial stereotypes. He is more practical and less intellectual than Queequeg.

Queequeg Starbuck's skilled harpooner and Ishmael's best friend. Queequeg, a prince from a South Sea island, stowed away on a whaling ship in search of adventure. He is brave and generous.

THEMES IN *MOBY-DICK*

THE LIMITS OF KNOWLEDGE Melville suggests that human knowledge is always limited and insufficient. In the opening pages of *Moby-Dick*, Ishmael tries to offer a simple collection of literary excerpts mentioning whales. During this exercise, he discovers that the whale has an incredible multiplicity of meanings. As the novel progresses, Ishmael makes use of a huge range of disciplines in an attempt to understand the essential nature of the whale. But none of these systems of knowledge, including art, taxonomy, and phrenology, can capture the whale. Moby Dick stands for God, among other things, and the impossibility of knowing him stands for the impossibility of knowing God. The ways of Moby Dick, like the ways of the Christian God, are unknowable to man, and trying to interpret them, as Ahab does, is inevitably futile and often fatal.

THE DUBIOUS EXISTENCE OF FATE Ishmael's narrative highlights many ominous events and references to fate, creating the impression that the *Pequod*'s doom is inevitable. Many of the sailors believe in prophecies, and some even claim they have the ability to foretell the future. A number of events suggest, however, that characters are deluding themselves when they insist they see the hand of fate. Melville suggests that fate either does not exist or is one of the many unknowable forces that guide human life. Ahab clearly exploits the sailors' belief in fate, using it to make them think that the quest for Moby Dick is their common destiny. The prophesies of Fedallah and others are undercut in Chapter 99, when different people interpret the doubloon's meaning in different ways. This episode suggests that when people interpret signs and portents, they are actually only projecting what they want to see, or choosing one of many possible interpretations.

THE EXPLOITATIVE NATURE OF WHALING At first glance, the *Pequod* seems like an island of equality and fellowship in the midst of a racist world. The ship's racially diverse crew comes from all corners of the globe and seems to get along well. Ishmael is initially uneasy upon meeting Queequeg, but he quickly decides it is better to have a "sober cannibal than a drunken Christian" for a shipmate. Additionally, the conditions of work aboard the *Pequod* seem egalitarian since men are promoted and paid according to their skill. However, whaling turns out to be similar to the other exploitative activities—buffalo hunting, gold mining, trading with indigenous peoples—that characterize American and European territorial expansion. The *Pequod*'s mates, all of whom are white, are entirely dependent on nonwhite harpooners, and nonwhites perform most of the dirty or dangerous jobs aboard the ship. Flask literally stands on Daggoo, his African harpooner, in order to beat the other mates to a prize whale. Ahab walks above the black youth Pip, who listens to Ahab's pacing from below deck and is reminded that his value as a slave is less than the value of a whale.

SYMBOLS IN *MOBY-DICK*

MOBY DICK Moby Dick has different symbolic meanings to different men. To the *Pequod*'s crew, Moby Dick symbolizes all that is dangerous and frightening about their jobs. To Ahab, Moby Dick symbolizes the evil in the world. Moby Dick also supports interpretations not tied to specific characters. In his inscrutable silence and mysterious habits, for example, he can be read as an allegorical representation of an unknowable God. As a profitable commodity, he represents the environment, which white men try to destroy in their quest for economic expansion.

QUEEQUEG'S COFFIN Queequeg's coffin symbolizes both life and death. When Queequeg recovers from illness and no longer needs the coffin he had built, it becomes an emblem of his will to live. The coffin also symbolizes life for the crew in general when it replaces the *Pequod*'s life buoy. When the *Pequod* sinks, the coffin saves Ishmael.

IMPORTANT QUOTATIONS FROM *MOBY-DICK*

All that most maddens and torments; all that stirs up the lees of things; all truth with malice in it; all that cracks the sinews and cakes the brain; all the subtle demonisms of life and thought; all evil, to crazy Ahab, were visibly personified, and made practically assailable in Moby Dick. He piled upon the whale's white hump the sum of all the general rage and hate felt by his whole race from Adam down; and then, as if his chest had been a mortar, he burst his hot heart's shell upon it.

Location: Chapter 41
Speaker: Ishmael
Context: Ishmael describes Ahab's feelings about Moby Dick

This passage is the existential heart of the book. While many sailors aboard the Pequod use legends about particularly large and malevolent whales as a way of managing the fear and danger inherent in whaling, they do not take these legends literally. Ahab, on the other hand, believes that Moby Dick is evil incarnate, and imagines himself and humanity struggling against the White Whale in an epic, timeless fight. His belief that killing Moby Dick will eradicate evil shows his inability to understand things symbolically. Ahab reads the world around him too literally. Instead of interpreting the loss of his leg as an unsurprising consequence of his occupation and perhaps as a punishment for taking excessive risks, he sees it as evidence of evil cosmic forces persecuting him.

There is a wisdom that is woe; but there is a woe that is madness. And there is a Catskill eagle in some souls that can alike dive down into the blackest gorges, and soar out of them again and become invisible in the sunny spaces. And even if he for ever flies within the gorge, that gorge is in the mountains; so that even in his lowest swoop the mountain eagle is still higher than other birds upon the plain, even though they soar.

Location: Chapter 96
Speaker: Ishmael
Context: Ishmael snaps out of a hypnotic state brought on by staring into the fires of the tryworks

Ishmael's language in this passage is typical of his philosophical speculation and his habit of quickly turning from a literal subject to its metaphorical implications. This passage suggests that woe and madness can be profitable states for someone with a great soul. For an intelligent, perceptive man whose soul is "in the mountains," even the greatest depths of despair surpass the contentedness of a common man. In other words, Ahab may be insane and "for ever . . . within the gorge," but his inherent greatness makes even his destruction more important than the happy existences of other, more banal men.

How it is I know not; but there is no place like a bed for confidential disclosures between friends. Man and wife, they say, there open the very bottom of their souls to each other; and some old couples often lie and chat over old times till nearly morning. Thus, then, in our hearts' honeymoon, lay I and Queequeg—a cosy, loving pair.

Location: Chapter 10
Speaker: Ishmael
Context: Ishmael shares a bed with Queequeg

Come, Ahab's compliments to ye; come and see if ye can swerve me. Swerve me? ye cannot swerve me, else ye swerve yourselves! man has ye there. Swerve me? The path to my fixed purpose is laid with iron rails, whereon my soul is grooved to run. Over unsounded gorges, through the rifled hearts of mountains, under torrents' beds, unerringly I rush! Naught's an obstacle, naught's an angle to the iron way!

Location: Chapter 37
Speaker: Ahab
Context: Ahab urges his crew to help him kill Moby Dick

Towards thee I roll, thou all-destroying but unconquering whale; to the last I grapple with thee; from hell's heart I stab at thee; for hate's sake I spit my last breath at thee. Sink all coffins and all hearses to one common pool! and since neither can be mine, let me then tow to pieces, while still chasing thee, though tied to thee, thou damned whale! Thus, I give up the spear!

Location: Chapter 135
Speaker: Ahab
Context: Ahab utters his last words after Moby Dick destroys the *Pequod*

MRS. DALLOWAY

Virginia Woolf

A middle-aged woman throws a party, and a young veteran commits suicide.

THE LIFE OF VIRGINIA WOOLF

Virginia Woolf was born on January 25, 1882, to Leslie Stephen and Julia Duckworth Stephen. She was one of four children. Woolf's mother died in 1895, triggering Woolf's first mental breakdown. For weeks after Julia's death, Sir Leslie groaned, threw tantrums, wept, and refused to eat. George Duckworth, Woolf's twenty-seven-year-old half brother, began sexually abusing the grieving thirteen-year-old Woolf, secretly fondling her. Woolf took refuge from harassment and depression in her father's vast library. Sir Leslie remarked that he had never seen anyone "gobble up" books like Woolf did.

Woolf's stepsister, Stella Duckworth, died during emergency surgery when Woolf was fifteen. Seven years after Stella's death, Sir Leslie died after a long bout with cancer. Woolf suffered a breakdown and attempted to commit suicide by jumping out of a window. The Stephen children moved to Bloomsbury, a seedy but still elegant neighborhood in London. A group of intellectual, liberal young men and women met regularly in their house. They called their circle "Bloomsbury," and are known historically as the Bloomsbury Group.

After a trip to Greece, Woolf's brother Thoby died of typhoid fever. Woolf was devastated. She never truly recovered from the loss of her older brother, whom she adored. She memorialized him in her novel *Jacob's Room* (1922) and as Percival in *The Waves* (1931).

In 1912, Woolf married Leonard Woolf. It was a fortunate match. Leonard was a nurturing caretaker, which was a blessing for Woolf. The possibility of professional failure so terrified Woolf that she had to be hospitalized before the publication of her first novel, *The Voyage Out*. After returning home, she attempted suicide with sleeping pills. Her fears proved unfounded, however. Critics greeted *The Voyage Out* with enthusiasm, praising it for being "recklessly feminine" and for exhibiting "something startlingly like genius."

World War I (1914–1918) erupted. Although air warfare was in its infancy, raids over London sometimes occurred. In 1917, a year before the end of the war, Leonard and Woolf moved to a home in the suburbs, bought a printing press, and launched their own printing company, Hogarth Press. The company soon became profitable, publishing works by T. S. Eliot, Maxim Gorky, Katherine Mansfield, and Sigmund Freud.

Woolf succumbed to another bout of depression after finishing *Jacob's Room* in 1922. She began thinking about Clarissa Dalloway, the heroine of her next novel. Three years later, *Mrs. Dalloway* was published to ecstatic reviews. Critical, popular, and financial success followed. Still, Woolf lapsed into months of depression and illness. Woolf's health eventually improved because of her deep friendship and love affair with Vita Sackville-West (1892–1962). Vita was an author, outstanding gardener, and figurehead for feminists—although she abhorred labels like "feminist."

Woolf entered a particularly productive period, completing *To the Lighthouse* (1927) and beginning *The Waves*. Critics began to consider her a novelist of the first rank, a major British writer who had dusted off old forms and established new novelistic conventions. In 1927, happy with life and grateful for Vita's love, Woolf began *Orlando* (1928), a tongue-in-cheek fantasy about a boy who becomes a woman.

During World War II, bombs destroyed the Woolfs' home while they were at their residence in Sussex. Desperate to sustain her mental health, Virginia Woolf continued writing. By early March 1941, she feared she was slipping into a deep mental illness from which she would never recover. She began hearing voices. On March 28, Woolf wrote farewell notes to Leonard and Vanessa, expressing her certainty that she would not recover, and set out across a meadow toward the River Ouse. There, she placed a large stone in her coat pocket and walked or jumped into the river, where she drowned.

MRS. DALLOWAY IN CONTEXT

Mrs. Dalloway is considered Woolf's first great novel. The novel's stream-of-consciousness style is an exercise in technical mastery, capturing the subjective reality of a single day in post-WWI London. Woolf was clearly influenced by James Joyce's *Ulysses*, which portrays a single day in Dublin in somewhat the same manner. One critic even accused Woolf of stealing scenes from *Ulysses* for use in her novel. However, Woolf had no desire to imitate Joyce. She clearly appreciated the potential in the stream-of-consciousness technique, but she thought Joyce was showing off with his endless verbal tricks and obscure references, and she considered the raw sexuality in *Ulysses* to be vulgar. Woolf also saw Joyce as an extremely masculine writer, and she sought to break new ground for female writers by developing a uniquely feminine style. In a sense, *Mrs. Dalloway* can be seen as the female answer to *Ulysses*.

Beyond the individual stories of Clarissa and Septimus, Mrs. Dalloway creates a portrait of London at a time of significant change. Many English citizens were disillusioned after the long and bloody First World War. The British Empire, which had sacrificed the lives of so many of its men in order to preserve itself, was already in decline, as were many of the social structures and conventions that symbolized the Empire's power. Woolf, like Clarissa Dalloway, was raised in the Victorian era, when women were expected to let go of their own desires in order to be good wives. But by the 1920s, women had begun to agitate for social and political equality. Sexual mores also changed. Women walked around London wearing makeup and short skirts, publicly showing affection for their boyfriends and lovers.

Shades of Woolf's own life can be seen in *Mrs. Dalloway*. Like Clarissa, Woolf enjoyed attending parties and entertaining her friends. Although Woolf's bohemian literary circle seems like a far cry from the Prime Ministers and other political figures who come to Clarissa's party, the Bloomsbury group was exclusive, upper-middle class, and considerably snobbish. Many of Woolf's contemporaries regarded the circle with the same contempt that characters like Miss Kilman and Peter Walsh feel towards Clarissa's social circle.

Woolf also had a history of mental breakdowns. The insensitive doctors in *Mrs. Dalloway* are based on her own experiences with the medical profession. In Woolf's day, most mental health problems were considered nonexistent, embarrassing, or a product of moral weakness.

MRS. DALLOWAY: KEY FACTS

Time and place written: 1923; England	
Date of first publication: 1925	
Publisher: The Hogarth Press	
Type of work: Novel	
Genre: Modern novel	
Language: English	
Setting (time): One day in June, after the end of World War I	
Setting (place): London, England	
Tense: Past	
Tone: Objective, lyric, reflective	
Narrator: Anonymous, omniscient narrator in the third person	
Point of view: Shifts constantly	
Protagonist: Clarissa Dalloway	
Antagonist: The inevitability of death	

MRS. DALLOWAY: PLOT OVERVIEW

Mrs. Dalloway portrays the events of one June day in 1920s London. Clarissa Dalloway, the title character, prepares for a party that she will host later that evening. She thinks about her past and about Peter Walsh, an old love that she spurned many years ago, choosing her husband, Richard Dalloway, over him. Woolf introduces the parallel story of a day in the life of Septimus Warren Smith, a veteran of World War

I suffering from shell shock. Septimus walks down the street with his Italian wife, Lucrezia. He hears voices and speaks aloud with his friend Evans, who died during the war.

Peter Walsh unexpectedly drops by Clarissa's house as she mends her dress. They work hard to banter, talking about current matters while privately thinking about the other and their intertwined past. Elizabeth, Clarissa's daughter, arrives. Peter takes his leave and goes to a park. Peter thinks about the past, and the events leading up to Clarissa's decision to marry Richard. He thinks about how he went to India and made an unsuccessful marriage there after Clarissa rejected him.

Meanwhile, Septimus and Lucrezia wander through the park. As they walk, Septimus reasonably argues the benefits of suicide. Lucrezia has made an appointment for Septimus with Sir William Bradshaw, a famous doctor. Peter sees them arguing and imagines they are having a lover's quarrel. Septimus remembers his past. Before the war, he was a sensitive man who wanted to be a poet and loved Shakespeare. When the war broke out, he quickly enlisted for romantic patriotic reasons. When his friend Evans died in the war, Septimus felt little sadness, which he took as proof of his manliness. Now, in the aftermath of the war, he believes his romantic notions were idiotic and his lack of feeling was a great crime. Bradshaw treats Septimus in an offhand manner, calling his problems a lack of proportion. He says Septimus should spend time alone in a rural area.

Richard Dalloway returns home from a lunch with flowers for Clarissa. He intends to tell her he loves her, but it has been a long time since he last said it, and he finds the words won't come out. They part. Clarissa thinks no man can understand her. She goes to see her daughter, who is studying with Miss Kilman, a history teacher. Clarissa and Miss Kilman are jealous of each other. In their apartment, Septimus and Lucrezia wait for the men who will bring Septimus to his retreat. Septimus and Lucrezia share a happy moment, and Septimus does not want to leave. The men arrive, and rather than go with them, Septimus jumps from the window to his death.

Peter hears the ambulance carrying Septimus go by and marvels at the "triumphs of civilisation." He decides to go to Clarissa's party. Clarissa worries that the party will fail, but she is not satisfied when it turns out to be a success. Sir William Bradshaw arrives late. His wife explains that one of his patients, a young veteran (Septimus), has committed suicide. Clarissa privately concludes that the veteran killed himself because he realized that men like Bradshaw made life intolerable. The party ends, and the guests leave. Clarissa approaches Richard, who feels great excitement.

CHARACTERS IN *MRS. DALLOWAY*

Sir William Bradshaw A specialist in "nerve cases." Sir William treats Septimus, prescribing isolation and rest.

Lady Bruton A sixty-two-year-old socialite. Lady Bruton is known for her "extraordinarily amusing" lunch parties. She invites Richard to one of these parties, which makes Clarissa feel left out.

Daisy Peter Walsh's married lover. Daisy is twenty-four years old and has two small children.

Clarissa Dalloway The title character. Clarissa, a middle-aged, upper-class British woman, is alternately extremely sensitive and hopelessly shallow.

Elizabeth Dalloway Clarissa and Richard's only child. Elizabeth, a hauntingly beautiful young woman, is nothing like Clarissa. She disdains parties, dresses, and social niceties. She may have a romantic interest in Miss Kilman, her tutor.

Richard Dalloway Clarissa's husband. Richard is a member of Parliament, but he has failed to accomplish his ambition of getting into the Cabinet. Richard sometimes worries about his success as a husband and father.

Evans Septimus's commanding officer and close friend. Evans was killed during the war.

Mrs. Filmer Septimus and Lucrezia's cook. Mrs. Filmer, a kind woman, does not understand why the doctors want to separate Septimus and Lucrezia.

Ellie Henderson Clarissa's poor, distant cousin. Ellie desperately wants Clarissa to invite her to the party.

Dr. Holmes A general practitioner. He examined Septimus and said there was "nothing wrong" with him.

Miss Kilman Elizabeth's middle-aged tutor. Miss Kilman is poor and ugly. She is devoted to socialism and religion and resents wealthy, privileged women like Clarissa Dalloway. Miss Kilman has strong romantic feelings for Elizabeth and tries to influence her protégée in religious as well as social issues.

Sally Seton A close friend of Clarissa's in their youth. Sally was a wild, rambunctious girl who smoked cigars. Clarissa now realizes she was in love with Sally, who had the kind of personality Clarissa admired but could never match. Sally is now married to the wealthy Lord Rosseter and has five sons.

Lucrezia Smith (Rezia) Septimus's young wife. She loves Septimus, but it is difficult for her to bear the burden of his mental illness alone. She does not understand his illness and cannot help him.

Septimus Warren Smith A young English veteran. Septimus seems to be suffering from posttraumatic stress syndrome and schizophrenia. He fears there is no meaning in the world.

Peter Walsh An old friend of Clarissa's. Peter used to be an impetuous young man who disdained English snobbery. When Clarissa rejected him, he went to India. Now he has a new young lover, Daisy.

Hugh Whitbread An acquaintance from Peter's and Clarissa's youth. Hugh is arrogant, condescending, and generally unpopular. Peter especially dislikes him. Associates of Hugh sardonically dub him "the admirable Hugh."

THEMES IN *MRS. DALLOWAY*

THE COMPLEXITIES OF CONFRONTING MORTALITY Clarissa Dalloway's and Septimus Smith's preoccupations with their own mortality structures the novel. Septimus's preoccupation is more obvious, since he constantly talks about suicide, speculates for hours about the nature of life and death, and sees the ghost of his dead friend Evans. Although Clarissa is not as vocal about her feelings, she is no less preoccupied with death than Septimus is. She constantly thinks about the fact that the life she loves must end. Both Clarissa and Septimus struggle to come to terms with mortality: Septimus by listening for clues about the meanings of life and death, and Clarissa by throwing a party to celebrate life. Both deal with death by trying to find more meaning in life, or at least by appreciating the richness and beauty of life. This explains the seeming paradox that the two characters most obsessed with death are also more in love with life than anyone else in the novel. In the end, Septimus's struggle ends in suicide, and Clarissa's ends in a party. Although it might seem obvious that Septimus has lost the struggle against mortality, while Clarissa has survived, the significance of his suicide and Clarissa's party is ambiguous. As Clarissa notes at the end of the novel, Septimus's death preserves the energy and rapture of his youth. It is also a refusal to submit to the cruel authority of men like Bradshaw. Both Clarissa's party and Septimus's suicide can be thought of as a triumph over death, or both can be thought of as a defeat.

THE INABILITY TO COMMUNICATE None of the characters in *Mrs. Dalloway* really understand each other, or feel that anyone understands them. Clarissa and Peter misunderstand each other when they talk. Richard can't bring himself to speak his love to Clarissa. When Septimus tries to communicate his real feelings to Rezia, she hears only mad ramblings. Woolf suggests that this lack of communication stems partly from what she considers the oppressive nature of English society. The characters are so used to restraining their emotions and feelings, or else they are so skilled in making small talk, that they have no way of actually communicating their real feelings to each other. Societal conditioning is not the only factor, however. Characters frequently fail to understand or even listen to what other characters are saying because they want to maintain their own illusions about them. It is easier to cling to musty old assumptions about someone than to recognize her as a complicated being. This lack of communication makes the characters feel alone and misunderstood, even though they are surrounded by other people.

The only character who does make a real effort to express his feelings is Septimus Warren Smith — and his willingness to explain himself is part of the reason society considers him insane. Partly because of his mental imbalance, but also partly because his society does not encourage the expression of pain and grief, Septimus's attempts to explain his feelings are often incomprehensible and painful for others to hear. Only in death does he manages to communicate with someone — Clarissa — and move her.

THE MISLEADING NATURE OF APPEARANCES The characters in *Mrs. Dalloway* often underestimate each other, assuming that other people are more simple and easier to classify than they actually are. Peter Walsh and Sally Seton believe that Clarissa has become a banal society wife and that Dalloway is nothing but a boring, earnest political figure. Many of the Dalloways' friends think of Peter as a common kind of failure. The world considers Septimus a lunatic. And onlookers often view Mrs. Dalloway's daughter, Elizabeth, as nothing more than a beautiful young girl. Using stream-of-consciousness narration, Woolf delves into the minds of each of these characters to demonstrate their complexity and surprising individuality, which contradict the easy assumptions of the other characters. She shows that by asking moral and intellectual questions, and by harboring desires and resentments that no one would guess they possess from looking at them, most people transcend the predictable roles everyone assumes they are playing. By showing the similarities shared by Clarissa and Septimus, Woolf suggests that most assumptions are entirely wrong. No one guesses that Clarissa, a society wife, has anything in common with Septimus, a deranged veteran, but in fact Clarissa's thoughts and actions parallel Septimus's. They look at the same book in a bookshop, they both fret about mortality, and they both affirm the beauty of life.

SYMBOLS IN *MRS. DALLOWAY*

THE MOTOR CAR The motor car that backfires near the flower shop symbolizes the British Empire. Like the car, the empire is in disrepair, and like the car's passenger (people on the street speculate about whether the car contains the Prime Minister, the Prince of Wales, or the queen) the value and meaning of the empire are not clear. Despite the decline of the empire, the English people still worship its leaders and get unreasonably excited about seeing them, just as the appearance of the motor car provokes a fuss. Woolf implies that the English populace's excitement about the royal family or the Prime Minister is as empty and absurd as the crowd's excitement over a backfiring car.

CLARISSA'S PARTY To many of the characters, Clarissa's party seems like a frivolous venture, a mindless social event that provides momentary and meaningless distraction from real life. For Peter Walsh and even for Richard Dalloway, the party symbolizes meaningless social convention. However, Clarissa thinks of the party as her great offering to the world, a symbol of the beauty and richness of life. By the end of the novel, the characters have retreated from their original positions. Peter Walsh believes that parties suggest the "infinite richness" of life, while Clarissa finds herself unhappy at her party. The party results in revelations: Peter and Sally see Richard with his daughter and revise their dismissive opinion of him, and the news of Septimus's death makes Clarissa search her own soul.

IMPORTANT QUOTATIONS FROM *MRS. DALLOWAY*

He hadn't blamed her for minding the fact, since in those days a girl brought up as she was, knew nothing, but it was her manner that annoyed him: timid; hard; something arrogant; unimaginative; prudish. "The death of the soul." He had said that instinctively, ticketing the moment as he used to do— the death of her soul.

Location: Early in the novel
Speaker: The narrator
Context: Peter thinks about Clarissa as she was when she was young

Peter remembers that when he and Clarissa were young, Clarissa reacted heartlessly to the news that an acquaintance had a baby before she was married, declaring that she could never speak to the woman again. Her reaction was not surprising coming from a young woman raised in the Victorian era, when talking or thinking about sex was taboo, and sexual misconduct or mistakes would likely ruin a woman's life. Peter had understood that Clarissa was a product of her society and could not help the values her upbringing instilled in her. Still, her "unimaginative" reaction bothered him. She was horrified by the news and incapable of feeling sympathy for the woman. Because of Clarissa's reaction, Peter wondered for the first time whether Clarissa's rigid adherence to her society's value system might overshadow the lovable qualities that made her so appealing. He saw her rigidity, arrogance, and prudishness as the very "death of the soul." After meeting with Clarissa again and seeing the conventional, upper-class lifestyle she lives, he is reminded of the phrase "the death of the soul," which seems to apply to her new life. Still, the fact that he is thinking about Clarissa's soul at all shows that he still feels something for her and that it pains him to see her living a seemingly meaningless, soulless life.

But he would wait till the very last moment. He did not want to die. Life was good. The sun hot. Only human beings—what did they want? Coming down the staircase opposite an old man stopped and stared at him. Holmes was at the door. "I'll give it to you!" he cried, and flung himself vigorously, violently down on to Mrs. Filmer's area railings.
"The coward!" cried Dr. Holmes.

Location: Late in the novel
Speaker: The narrator
Context: Septimus kills himself

Even when Septimus knows he will kill himself, he longs to postpone his death—to "wait till the very last moment." Like Clarissa, Septimus loves life, especially its small details. Also like Clarissa, Septimus wants to wring the most pleasure from his life as he can before it ends. For both Clarissa and Septimus, life is finite and valuable, and death is tragic and inevitable.

Septimus dies defiantly, crying out "I'll give it to you!" as if his suicide were an act of physical violence against Holmes. This defiance supports Clarissa's belief that suicide is an attempt to communicate. Although suicide is often thought of as an act of despair and cowardice, as Dr. Holmes suggests, Septimus's can be interpreted as an act of courage or of protest. He says that he does not want to die, but he needs to in order to prove something to Holmes, or to get revenge against Holmes and the social forces that Holmes represents. If Septimus's suicide is a protest, or some other attempt at communication, it is a successful one. Septimus intends to communicate to Holmes, but he actually communicates with Clarissa, making her aware of the destructive nature of the society she belongs to, and provoking feelings and sympathies in her that have been buried for a long time.

For he would say it in so many words, when he came into the room. Because it is a thousand pities never to say what one feels . . .

Location: About midway through the novel
Speaker: The narrator
Context: Richard decides to tell Clarissa that he loves her

And it was an offering; to combine, to create; but to whom? An offering for the sake of offering, perhaps. Anyhow, it was her gift. Nothing else had she of the slightest importance: could not think, write, even play the piano.

Location: Near the end of the novel
Speaker: The narrator
Context: Clarissa thinks about her parties, which she imagines as an offering

---

"What does the brain matter," said Lady Rosseter, getting up, "compared with the heart?"

Location: The end of the novel
Speaker: The narrator
Context: Lady Rosseter, nee Sally Seton, tells Peter that Richard's dullness may be less important than his love

MUCH ADO ABOUT NOTHING

William Shakespeare

Believing that his fiancé is unfaithful, a man publicly shames her before recognizing his mistake and marrying her; two longtime rivals are tricked into admitting that they love each other.

THE LIFE OF WILLIAM SHAKESPEARE

William Shakespeare, the most influential writer in all of English literature, was born in 1564 to a successful middle-class glove-maker in Stratford-upon-Avon, England. Shakespeare's formal education did not progress beyond grammar school. In 1582, he married an older woman, Anne Hathaway. His union with Anne produced three children. Around 1590, Shakespeare left his family behind and traveled to London to work as an actor and playwright. He quickly earned public and critical acclaim, and eventually became the most popular playwright in England and a part-owner of the Globe Theater. Shakespeare's career bridged the reigns of Elizabeth I (ruled 1558–1603) and James I (ruled 1603–1625), and he was a favorite of both monarchs. James paid Shakespeare's company a great compliment by giving its members the title of King's Men. Shakespeare retired to Stratford a wealthy and renowned man and died in 1616 at the age of fifty-two. At the time of Shakespeare's death, literary luminaries such as Ben Jonson hailed his works as timeless.

Shakespeare's works were collected and printed in various editions in the century following his death, and by the early eighteenth century his reputation as the greatest poet ever to write in English was well established. The unprecedented regard in which Shakespeare's works were held led to a fierce curiosity about his life, but many details of Shakespeare's personal history are unknown or shrouded in mystery. Some people have concluded from this lack of information and from Shakespeare's modest education that Shakespeare's plays were actually written by someone else—Francis Bacon and the Earl of Oxford are the two most popular candidates—but the support for this claim is overwhelmingly circumstantial, and the theory is not taken seriously by many scholars.

Shakespeare is generally thought to be the author of the thirty-eight plays (two of them possibly collaborations) and 154 sonnets that bear his name. The legacy of this body of work is immense. A number of Shakespeare's plays seem to have transcended even the category of brilliance, influencing the course of Western literature and culture.

MUCH ADO ABOUT NOTHING IN CONTEXT

One of Shakespeare's best comedies, *Much Ado About Nothing* combines elements of robust humor with more serious meditations on honor, shame, and court politics. It was likely written in 1598–99, as Shakespeare approached the middle of his career. Like *As You Like It* and *Twelfth Night*, *Much Ado* touches upon darker concerns but ends joyfully with multiple marriages and no deaths.

Although characters do not die in Shakespearean comedies, *Much Ado* treats death as part of the natural cycle of life. Indeed, death is vividly present here: for several scenes, many characters believe that Hero has died. The play's central crisis has troubled many readers and audience members. The play deals with anger, betrayal, grief, and despair, and ties up these strong emotions quickly and, some have thought, flippantly.

Many critics have noted that the plot of *Much Ado About Nothing* shares important elements with the plot of *Romeo and Juliet*. *Much Ado* is also similar to a late Shakespearean romance, or "problem play," *The Winter's Tale*. Like Hero, *Winter's Tale*'s Hermione stages a false death only to come back to life once her beloved has repented.

Although the trials of the young lovers Hero and Claudio fuel the main storyline, it is the courtship between the older, wiser Benedick and Beatrice that makes *Much Ado* so memorable. Benedick and Beatrice argue with delightful wit, and Shakespeare develops their journey from antagonism to sincere affection with both rich humor and compassion. Beatrice and Benedick have a back story and are more mature than many of Shakespeare's lovers, but they prove to be childishly competitive amateurs in love.

MUCH ADO ABOUT NOTHING: KEY FACTS

Full Title: Much Ado About Nothing	
Time and place written: 1598; England	
Date of first publication: 1600	
Genre: Comedy	
Setting (time): 1500s	
Setting (place): The Sicilian town of Messina, on and around Governor Leonato's estate	
Protagonist: Claudio, Hero, Beatrice, and Benedick	
Antagonist: Don John	
Major conflict: Don John makes Hero appear to be unfaithful to Claudio; Beatrice and Benedick's rivalry blinds them to the fact that they love each other; Claudio and Benedick fear marriage as an entrapment	

MUCH ADO ABOUT NOTHING: PLOT OVERVIEW

Leonato, a kindly, respectable nobleman, lives in the idyllic Italian town of Messina. He shares his house with his lovely young daughter, Hero, his playful, clever niece, Beatrice, and his elderly brother, Antonio. As the play begins, Leonato prepares to welcome some friends home from a war. The friends include Don Pedro, a prince who is a close friend of Leonato's, and two fellow soldiers: Claudio, a well-respected young nobleman, and Benedick, a clever man who constantly makes witty jokes, often at the expense of his friends. Don John, Don Pedro's illegitimate brother, is part of the crowd as well. Don John is sullen and bitter, and makes trouble for the others.

When the soldiers arrive at Leonato's home, Claudio quickly falls in love with Hero. Meanwhile, Benedick and Beatrice resume the war of witty insults that they have carried on with each other in the past. Claudio and Hero pledge their love to one another and decide to be married. To pass the time in the week before the wedding, the lovers and their friends decide to play a game. They want to get Beatrice and Benedick, who are clearly meant for each other, to stop arguing and fall in love. Their tricks prove successful, and Beatrice and Benedick soon fall secretly in love with each other.

But Don John has decided to disrupt everyone's happiness. He has his companion Borachio make love to Margaret, Hero's serving woman, at Hero's window in the darkness of the night, and brings Don Pedro and Claudio to watch. Believing that he has seen Hero being unfaithful to him, the enraged Claudio humiliates Hero by accusing her of lechery on the day of their wedding and abandoning her at the altar. Hero's stricken family members decide to pretend that she died suddenly of shock and grief and to hide her away while they wait for the truth about her innocence to come to light. In the aftermath of the rejection, Benedick and Beatrice finally confess their love to one another. Fortunately, the night watchmen overhear Borachio bragging about his crime. Dogberry and Verges, the heads of the local police, arrest both Borachio and Conrad, another of Don John's followers. Everyone learns that Hero is really innocent, and Claudio, who believes she is dead, grieves for her.

Leonato tells Claudio that, as punishment, he wants Claudio to tell everybody in the city how innocent Hero was. He also wants Claudio to marry Leonato's "niece"—a girl who, he says, looks much like the dead Hero. Claudio goes to church with the others, preparing to marry the mysterious, masked woman he thinks is Hero's cousin. When Hero reveals herself as the masked woman, Claudio is overwhelmed with joy. Benedick then asks Beatrice if she will marry him, and after some arguing they agree to marry. The joyful lovers all have a merry dance before they celebrate their double wedding.

CHARACTERS IN *MUCH ADO ABOUT NOTHING*

Antonio Leonato's elderly brother, and Hero and Beatrice's uncle.

Balthasar A musician and servant in Leonato's household. Balthasar flirts with Margaret at the masked party and helps Leonato, Claudio, and Don Pedro trick Benedick into falling in love with Beatrice.

Balthasar sings the song, "Sigh no more, ladies, sigh no more," which is about accepting men's infidelity as natural.

Beatrice Leonato's niece and Hero's cousin. Generous and loving, Beatrice has a very sharp tongue and frequently mocks others with elaborately tooled jokes and puns. She has been waging a spirited war of wits with Benedick, but insists that she will never marry.

Benedick An aristocrat soldier who fights under his friend Don Pedro; Claudio's friend. Witty and spirited, Benedick carries on a "merry war" of wits with Beatrice, but swears that he will never fall in love or marry.

Borachio Don John's servant and accomplice; Margaret's lover. Borachio conspires with Don John to trick Claudio and Don Pedro into thinking that Hero is unfaithful to Claudio. *Borachio* means "drunkard" in Italian—perhaps a subtle direction to the actor.

Claudio A young soldier who has won great acclaim fighting under Don Pedro during the recent wars. Claudio falls in love with Hero upon his return to Messina. His suspicious nature makes him quick to believe evil rumors and hasty to despair and seek revenge.

Conrad One of Don John's intimate associates, entirely devoted to Don John. Several recent productions have suggested that Conrad is Don John's male lover, an appealing choice for a director since this relationship would Don John's feelings of being a social outcast and therefore motivates his desire for revenge.

Dogberry The constable in charge of the watchmen of Messina. Dogberry is very sincere and takes his job seriously, but he has a habit of using exactly the wrong word to convey his meaning. Dogberry is one of the few "middling sort," or middle-class characters in the play though his desire to speak formally and elaborately as the noblemen do becomes an occasion for parody.

Hero The beautiful young daughter of Leonato and the cousin of Beatrice. Hero is lovely, gentle, and kind. She falls in love with Claudio, and when Don John slanders her and Claudio rashly takes revenge, she suffers terribly.

Don John (the Bastard) The illegitimate brother of Don Pedro. Don John is melancholy and sullen by nature, and he creates a dark scheme to ruin the happiness of Hero and Claudio. He is the villain of the play. His evil actions are likely motivated by his envy of his brother's social authority.

Leonato A respected, well-to-do, elderly noble at whose home in Messina, Italy, the action is set. Leonato is the father of Hero and the uncle of Beatrice. As governor of Messina, he is second in social power only to Don Pedro.

Margaret Hero's serving woman. Margaret unwittingly helps Borachio and Don John deceive Claudio into thinking that Hero is unfaithful. Unlike Ursula, Hero's other lady-in-waiting, Margaret is lower class. Though she is honest, she does have some dealings with the villainous world of Don John: her lover is the mistrustful and easily bribed Borachio. Also unlike Ursula, Margaret loves to flout decorum, especially with bawdy jokes and teases.

Don Pedro, Prince of Aragon Leonato's longtime friend. Don Pedro is also close to the soldiers who have been fighting under him: the younger Benedick and the very young Claudio. Don Pedro is generous, courteous, intelligent, and loving to his friends, but he is also quick to believe evil of others and hasty to take revenge. He is the most politically and socially powerful character in the play.

Ursula One of Hero's waiting women.

Verges Dogberry's deputy.

THEMES IN *MUCH ADO ABOUT NOTHING*

COURTLY GRACE The dense, metaphor-laden speech of *Much Ado*'s characters in many ways represents the ideal that Renaissance courtiers strove for in their social interactions. Courtiers were expected to speak in highly contrived language but to make their clever performances seem effortless. The most famous model for this kind of behavior is Baldassare Castiglione's sixteenth-century manual *The Courtier*, translated into English from Italian by Thomas Hoby in 1561. According to this work, the ideal courtier masks his effort and appears to project elegance and natural grace by means of what Castiglione calls *sprezzatura*, or the illusion of effortlessness. Benedick, Claudio, and Don Pedro all produce the kind of witty banter that courtiers used to attract attention and approval in noble households.

At the same time, the play pokes fun at the fanciful language of love that courtiers used. When Claudio falls in love, he tries to be the perfect courtier by using intricate language. Benedick notes that Claudio's "words are a very fantastical banquet, just so many strange dishes" (II.iii.18–19), notes Benedick. When Claudio believes that Don Pedro has deceived him and wooed Hero for himself, Claudio, who owes his current popularity to Don Pedro, does not drop his polite civility. Beatrice jokes that Claudio is "civil as an orange" (II.i.256), punning on the Seville orange, a bitter fruit. Claudio remains polite and nearly silent even though he is upset, wishing "[Don Pedro] joy of [Hero]" (II.i.170).

DECEPTION AS A MEANS TO AN END   Several deliberate deceptions, both malevolent and benign, drive the play's plot. Hero is disgraced because Don John dupes Claudio and Don Pedro. Her counterfeited death paves the way for her redemption and reconciliation with Claudio. In the more light-hearted subplot, Beatrice and Benedick are fooled into thinking that each is loved, and the deception helps them fall in love. Deceit in *Much Ado* is not an inherent evil; rather it is a tool to be used for good or bad results.

It is often difficult to distinguish good deception from bad. When Claudio announces his desire to woo Hero, Don Pedro takes it upon himself to woo her for Claudio—a "good" deception that turns sour when, at Don John's instigation, Claudio begins to mistrust Don Pedro's true intentions. The play's characters are caught up in the illusions that they have created for one another, just we, the audience, temporary believe in the illusions of the theater. Benedick and Beatrice flirt caustically at the masked ball, each possibly aware of the other's presence yet pretending not to know the person hiding behind the mask. Likewise, when Claudio has shamed and rejected Hero, Leonato and his household announce that Hero has died in order to punish Claudio for his mistake. When Claudio returns, penitent, to accept the hand of "Leonato's niece" (Hero in disguise), Leonato forces him to wed blindly. The group of masked women, one of whom is the bride, points to the fact that the social institution of marriage has little to do with love. Claudio's confused question, "Which is the lady I must seize upon?" (V.iv.53), highlights his readiness to marry one of a group of unknowns. He marries not only to atone for Hero's death, but also to regain Leonato's favor. Yet again deceit functions as a means to an end.

LOST HONOR   In Shakespeare's time, a woman's honor was based upon her virginity and modest behavior. A woman known to have had sexual relations before marriage lost her good reputation forever. Moreover, her lost honor tainted her whole family. When Leonato believes Claudio's accusations, he initially wants to obliterate Hero entirely: "Hence from her, let her die" (IV.i.153). He speaks of Hero's loss of honor as an indelible stain from which he cannot distance himself: "O she is fallen / Into a pit of ink, that the wide sea / Hath drops too few to wash her clean again" (IV.i.138–140).

SYMBOLS IN *MUCH ADO ABOUT NOTHING*

TAMING WILD ANIMALS   In Beatrice and Benedick's courtship, tamed wild animals represent the two wild souls finally "tamed" and able to submit themselves to the shackles of love and marriage. Beatrice vows to submit to Benedick's love by "[t]aming my wild heart to thy loving hand" (III.i.113). She uses falconry terms to suggest that Benedick will become her master. Similarly, Claudio and Don Pedro compare Benedick to a wild animal in teasing him about his aversion to marriage: "In time the savage bull doth bear the yoke"—that is, in time even the savage Benedick will surrender to being tamed by marriage (I.i.213; see also Quotations 1). At end of the play, Claudio returns to the image on Benedick as a bull:

> Tush, fear not, man, we'll tip thy horns with gold,
> And all Europa shall rejoice at thee
> As once Europa did at lusty Jove
> When he would play the noble beast in love.
> (V.iv.44–47)

Claudio changes Benedick from a laboring farm animal, a bull straining under a yoke, to a wild god, empowered by his bestial form to take sexual possession of his lady. Claudio alludes to the classical myth in which Zeus takes the form of a bull to carry off and seduce the human Europa. This second bull represents the other side of the marriage coin: the bull of bestial male sexuality.

HERO'S DEATH   When Claudio accuses Hero in the church, she faints and collapses, apparently lifeless. Leonato further pushes her into a literal death when he renounces her: "Hence from her, let her die" (IV.i.153). In a symbolic sense, Hero—and Hero's honor—has died. After he realizes his mistake, Claudio performs the rites of mourning and hires a choir to sing a dirge at Hero's tomb. Her honor dead, Hero must be reborn, pure again, in order for Claudio to marry her. Hero's false death functions both as a charade to induce remorse in Claudio and as a social ritual to cleanse her name of infamy.

IMPORTANT QUOTATIONS FROM *MUCH ADO ABOUT NOTHING*

What should I do with him—dress him in my apparel and make him my waiting gentlewoman? He that hath a beard is more than a youth, and he that hath no beard is less than a man; and he that is more than a youth is not for me, and he that is less than a man, I am not for him.

Location: II.i.28–32
Speaker: Beatrice
Context: Beatrice jokingly explains why she can never marry

Beatrice claims that there is no perfect match for her: every man is either too old or too young to satisfy her desires. Beatrice's joke about dressing up a beardless youth as a woman has a secondary meaning for Elizabethan audiences. In Shakespeare's time, the actor playing Beatrice would have been a prepubescent boy doing exactly that. Indeed, beardless adolescents, youths on the cusp of manhood, held special allure for both men and women in Renaissance literature and culture. *Much Ado* toys with Beatrice's desire for a man both with and without a beard: during the course of the play, Benedick shaves off his beard once he falls in love with her.

O Hero! What a Hero hadst thou been
If half thy outward graces had been placed
About thy thoughts and counsels of thy heart!
But fare thee well, most foul, most fair, farewell
Thou pure impiety and impious purity.
For thee I'll lock up all the gates of love,
And on my eyelids shall conjecture hang
To turn all beauty into thoughts of harm,
And never shall it more be gracious.

Location: IV.i.98–106
Speaker: Claudio
Context: Claudio has publicly rebuked Hero at their wedding, believing her to have been unchaste and
    unfaithful to him

Claudio's lines are full of wordplay and double meanings. The word "Hero" appears twice in the first line, denoting first Hero, Leonato's daughter, and then a hero, an idealized conqueror of Claudio's heart. Hero has lost her heroic qualities. "Fare thee well most foul, most fair, farewell" plays with repetition and opposites: the sound of the word "fair" repeats three times in the space of one line, underscoring Claudio's despair at (mistakenly) discovering that Hero's outward beauty, or "fairness," conceals a "foul" spirit.

   Both the combination of "fair" and "foul" in the same line and "pure impiety and impious purity" in the following line are examples of *antithesis*— (the combination of paradoxical opposites for emphasis) a rhetorical technique for which Shakespeare is famous. Shakespeare's characters resort to antithesis usually only at the height of passion. Claudio's use of these particular opposites demonstrate that he is livid with rage and frustration at Hero's seemingly fair exterior and her false and foul interior.

The savage bull may, but if ever the sensible Benedick bear it, pluck off the bull's horns and set them in my forehead, and let me be vilely painted, and in such great letters as they write 'Here is good horse to hire' let them signify under my sign 'Here you may see Benedick, the married man.'

Location: I.i.215–219
Speaker: Benedick
Context: In conversation with Claudio and Don Pedro, Benedick mocks the old adage that even the wildest people eventually settle down and marry

---

They say the lady is fair. 'Tis a truth, I can bear them witness. And virtuous—'tis so, I cannot reprove it. And wise, but for loving me. By my troth, it is no addition to her wit—nor no great argument of her folly, for I will be horribly in love with her.

Location: II.iii.204–208
Speaker: Benedick (soliloquy)
Context: Benedick weighs Beatrice's virtues after overhearing Claudio, Leonato, and Don Pedro discussing Beatrice's (fabricated) love for him

---

Dost thou not suspect my place? Dost thou not suspect my years? O that he were here to write me down an ass! But masters, remember that I am an ass. Though it be not written down, yet forget not that I am an ass. No, thou villain, thou art full of piety, as shall be proved upon thee by good witness. I am a wise fellow, and which is more, an officer, and which is more, a householder, and which is more, as pretty a piece of flesh as any is in Messina, and one that knows the law, go to ... and one that hath two gowns, and everything handsome about him. Bring him away. O that I had been writ down an ass!

Location: IV.ii.67–78
Speaker: Dogberry
Context: Dogberry, who brought Borachio and Conrad before the sexton, responds after Conrad calls him an "ass"

MY ÁNTONIA

Willa Cather

A successful lawyer recalls his childhood in Nebraska.

THE LIFE OF WILLA CATHER
Willa Cather was born on December 7, 1873, in rural Virginia. She spent most of her childhood in Nebraska. After graduating from the University of Nebraska at Lincoln in 1895, she moved to Pittsburgh. For five years, she worked in the Pittsburgh newspaper and magazine trade. Between 1901 and 1906, she taught high school English and Latin, and began to publish her first short stories. These early successes led to a position in New York City with the magazine *McClure's*, where Cather worked as an editor for six years.

In 1912, Cather published her first novel, *Alexander's Bridge*, to lukewarm reviews. The next year, she caught the attention of the literary world with *O Pioneers!*, a novel that celebrates frontier life in the American West. In 1918, she solidified her reputation as one of the most important post-Civil War American authors with the publication of *My Ántonia*. Like many of Cather's novels, *My Ántonia* fictionalizes recollections of a youth spent in rural Nebraska.

Cather was most prolific during the 1920s, when she published many of her finest works. After winning the Pulitzer Prize for *One of Ours* in 1922, she enjoyed continued popular successes with *The Professor's House* (1925), *My Mortal Enemy* (1926), and *Death Comes for the Archbishop* (1927). In 1930, Cather won the Howells Medal for Fiction, and in 1944 she was awarded the gold medal of the National Institute of Arts and Letters.

Willa Cather died in 1947 in New York City, where she had lived for thirty-nine years with her companion, Edith Lewis. Many critics class her with such lauded American authors as William Faulkner and Ernest Hemingway, and some argue that Cather's is the single finest craft of her generation.

MY ÁNTONIA IN CONTEXT
My Ántonia is generally considered a modernist novel. In the early twentieth century, many writers believed that mechanization and industrialization were alienating people. In their fiction, these writers reflected what they perceived as the increased fragmentation of the world by creating fragmented narratives and stories. *My Ántonia* is modernist in form and content. A loosely structured novel, it idealizes a pre-industrial life far from the noise and speed of the city.

Many similarities exist between *My Ántonia* and Cather's life. Like Cather, the fictional Jim Burden moves from Virginia to Nebraska as a child to live with grandparents. Black Hawk, the town to which Jim and his grandparents move, is a fictionalized version of Red Cloud, where Cather grew up. Like Cather, Jim attends the University of Nebraska at Lincoln and eventually moves from Nebraska to New York. *My Ántonia*, which features a nuanced portrait of the prairie landscape and elegantly uncomplicated prose, stands as the most lasting hallmark of Cather's skill.

MY ÁNTONIA: KEY FACTS

Time and place written: 1917; New Hampshire	
Date of first publication: 1918	
Publisher: Houghton Mifflin	
Type of work: Novel	
Genre: Frontier fiction; autobiographical fiction	
Language: English	
Setting (time): 1880s–1910s	

Setting (place): Nebraska

Tense: Past

Tone: Melancholy, nostalgic, optimistic

Narrator: Jim Burden in the first person; briefly one of Jim's childhood acquaintances in the first person

Point of view: Jim's

Protagonist: Jim Burden

Antagonist: Class differences, nostalgia

MY ÁNTONIA: PLOT OVERVIEW

My Ántonia is the fictional memoir of Jim Burden, a successful New York City lawyer. After being orphaned at age ten, Jim takes a train to Nebraska to live with his grandparents. On the train, he gets his first glimpse of the Shimerdas, a Bohemian immigrant family. It turns out the Shimerdas are going to live on the farm neighboring the Burdens'. Jim makes fast friends with the Shimerda children, especially Ántonia, who is close to him in age and eager to learn English. Jim tutors Ántonia, and they explore the land together.

In late January, Mr. Shimerda commits suicide. The Shimerdas despair, and Ántonia and Jim grow apart. A couple of years later, the Burdens move into town. Ántonia takes a job as a housekeeper with the Harlings, a family that lives near the Burdens' new house. Jim begins to see more of Ántonia, especially when a dancing pavilion comes to town.

Jim is accepted to the university in Lincoln. He gives a greatly successful high school commencement speech and spends the summer hard at work in preparation for college. Before leaving, he takes one last trip out to the countryside with Ántonia and her friends, where they reminisce about old times.

In Lincoln, Jim throws himself into his studies. In the spring of his second year, he dates Lena Lingard, a mutual friend of his and Ántonia's. But Jim decides that he needs to make a fresh start and transfers to Harvard University for his final two years of college. While Jim is away, Ántonia gets engaged to a local boy and moves to Denver with him. Days before the wedding, the boy abandons Ántonia. She returns to Nebraska heartbroken and pregnant. She gives birth to a daughter and decides to take care of the baby regardless of her family's disapproval. She continues to work on the farm with her brother.

Jim graduates from college and prepares to start law school. He returns to Nebraska to visit his grandparents. Upon hearing of Ántonia's situation, he drives out to the countryside and visits her. They spend a happy day together reliving old times, and Jim parts with a promise to visit her again very soon. Twenty years pass before Jim visits Ántonia again. In that time, he marries and becomes a prosperous New York City lawyer, and Ántonia marries a man named Cuzak, who is of Bohemian origin. She has many children with him. At last, Jim visits the Cuzak farm. Ántonia and Jim renew their old ties, and Jim resolves to stay in closer contact with the Cuzaks in the coming years.

As he prepares to leave Nebraska and return to New York City, Jim walks along the outskirts of town near the overgrown road that leads to his childhood home. At peace with himself in this familiar landscape, he feels that his life has come full circle. He reflects on all that his past with Ántonia has meant to him.

CHARACTERS IN MY ÁNTONIA

Samson D'Arnault A blind, black pianist. D'Arnault comes to Black Hawk and brings down the house with a concert at the Boys' Home.

Emmaline Burden Jim's grandmother. Emmaline shows great compassion for the Shimerdas and is a loving maternal figure for Jim.

Jim Burden The narrator and protagonist of the novel. Jim is an intelligent, introspective man who responds strongly to the Nebraska land. He is more interested in academics and reflection than in roughhousing.

Josiah Burden Jim's grandfather. Josiah is religious, quiet, and hardworking.

Gaston Cleric Jim's tutor at the university in Lincoln. Cleric gets a teaching position at Harvard University and brings Jim along with him. He dies from pneumonia.

Wick Cutter A shady moneylender in Black Hawk.

Cuzak A Bohemian immigrant who marries Ántonia and raises a large family with her.

Larry Donovan Ántonia's fiancé. Donovan, an arrogant and selfish man, leaves Ántonia on the eve of their wedding.

Otto Fuchs One of the Burdens' hired hands. Otto, an Austrian immigrant, looks like a cowboy to Jim. Otto seeks his fortune in the West after the Burdens move to Black Hawk.

Mrs. Gardener The proprietress of the Boys' Home in Black Hawk.

Frances Harling The oldest of the Harling children. Frances has a sound business mind and skillfully manages her father's accounts.

Charley Harling The only Harling son. Charley has a successful career at the Naval Academy in Annapolis.

Julia Harling The middle Harling daughter. Julia has a penchant for music.

Mr. Harling The patriarch of the Harling family. A businessman of keen ability, Mr. Harling disapproves of Ántonia's lifestyle.

Mrs. Harling The matriarch of the Harling family. A charismatic and active woman, Mrs. Harling develops a strong affection for Ántonia.

Sally Harling The youngest Harling daughter. Sally is a tomboy.

Anton Jelinek A Bohemian homesteader and friend of the Shimerdas. Jelinek moves to Black Hawk and becomes a saloon proprietor.

Peter Krajiek A Bohemian immigrant and neighbor to the Burdens. Krajiek sells the Shimerdas their first farm in America and cheats them out of several comforts.

Lena Lingard A Norwegian immigrant's daughter and a friend of Ántonia's. Lena and Jim date in Lincoln, where she sets up her own dressmaker's shop. Lena, a pretty blonde, craves independence and excitement. Men chase her, but she refuses to marry and give up her freedom.

Jake Marpole One of the Burdens' hired hands. Jake goes out west with Otto. Despite a quick temper, Jake is generally good-natured and innocent.

Russian Pavel A Russian immigrant. Tall, gaunt, and nervous, Pavel left Russia after a frightful incident involving a wolf attack on a wedding party.

Russian Peter Pavel's Russian housemate. Pavel, a fat, happy man, gets into debt and must leave America for a job as a cook in a Russian labor camp.

Ambrosch Shimerda The Shimerdas' oldest son. Mrs. Shimerda and her daughters dote on Ambrosch, citing him as the reason they came to America. Ambrosch shares his mother's curt and presumptuous attitude. He becomes the unquestioned head of the family after Mr. Shimerda's suicide.

Ántonia Shimerda Jim's childhood friend. Intelligent, optimistic, loyal, and kindhearted, Ántonia has a difficult life after her father commits suicide.

Marek Shimerda The younger of the two Shimerda brothers. Marek is physically deformed and mentally unstable.

Mr. Shimerda The patriarch of the Bohemian immigrant family. A melancholy man given to artistic and scholarly pursuits, Mr. Shimerda feels out of place in Nebraska and eventually commits suicide.

Mrs. Shimerda The matriarch of the Bohemian immigrant family. Mrs. Shimerda is a brusque, bossy, and often curt woman.

Yulka Shimerda The youngest of the Shimerda children. Yulka is a pretty young girl who later helps Ántonia raise her baby.

Tiny Soderball One of the hired girls in Black Hawk and a friend to Ántonia and Lena. After working with Mrs. Gardener in the Boys' Home, Tiny travels west and makes a small fortune during the Alaskan gold rush.

Widow Steavens The Burdens' tenant at their old farmhouse.

THEMES IN *MY ÁNTONIA*

THE PAST Jim rarely philosophizes about the past as an idea, but the past suffuses the novel. His memoir comes into existence in the first place becomes he wants to reconnect with his vanished past on the Nebraska prairie. People from Jim's story also look back longingly on their lost pasts. Jim and Ántonia recall their days on the farms, Lena thinks of her life with her family, and the Shimerdas and the Russians remember their home countries. For most of the characters, the past is longed for but unrecoverable. Ántonia misses life in Bohemia just as Jim misses life in Nebraska, but neither of them can ever go back. The impossibility of return gives the novel a nostalgic, emotional tone. But if the past can never be recovered, neither can it be escaped. Jim will always think about Black Hawk. Cather suggests that by revisiting the past, we can incorporate it into the present. When Jim returns to Nebraska twenty years after seeing Ántonia, he decides he will visit Ántonia more frequently. He does not want to make Ántonia a symbol of the past in his own mind; he wants a real relationship with her. The past may be unrecoverable, but the people who shared one's past can be recovered, even after a separation of many years.

THE ENVIRONMENT Jim develops a strong attachment to the Nebraska landscape that never really leaves him, even after two decades spent in New York. As Cather portrays it, environment symbolizes and shapes psychology. It can affect emotional states by giving thoughts and feelings a physical form. The river, for example, makes Jim feel free, so he comes to prize freedom. The setting sun captures his introspective loneliness. The wide-open melancholy of Nebraska's plains helps form his reflective, romantic personality. Because landscape shapes personality, it is particularly painful to leave landscape behind.

THE IMMIGRANT EXPERIENCE *My Ántonia* explores the lives of immigrants on the United States frontier in the second half of the nineteenth century. The Nebraska prairie of the novel is an ethnic hodgepodge of American-born settlers and a wide range of European immigrants, especially eastern and northern Europeans such as the Bohemian Shimerdas, the Russians Peter and Pavel, and the Norwegian Lena. Cather creates a sympathetic portrait of the many hardships immigrants face, including intense homesickness, language difficulties, a bewildering array of cultural and religious differences, and judgmental American settlers. Because of the rigid (and, in Jim's eyes, preposterous) social hierarchy of Black Hawk, simply getting by is difficult for the immigrants. But while Cather sympathizes with the immigrants she describes, she never advocates for them. Jim does not agitate for social change. He shares many of the cultural assumptions of the American-born settlers. Thus, *My Ántonia* has little in common with more socially inflammatory works about the immigrant experience, such as Upton Sinclair's *The Jungle*. *My Ántonia* aims not to bring about social change or awaken moral outrage in its readers, but to recreate the mostly happy experiences of one young man.

SYMBOLS IN *MY ÁNTONIA*

THE NEBRASKA LANDSCAPE Cather's poetic and moving depiction of the Nebraska landscape is perhaps the most famous and highly praised aspect of the novel. The landscape symbolizes the larger idea of a human environment, a setting in which a person lives and moves. Jim's relationship with the Nebraska landscape symbolizes Jim's relationship with himself and with the people and culture of Nebraska. Throughout the novel, the landscape mirrors Jim's feelings—it looks desolate when he is lonely, for instance. Finally, the landscape becomes the novel's most tangible symbol of the vanished past.

THE PLOW The plow symbolizes the connection between human culture and the natural landscape. As the sun sets behind the plow, culture and nature combine in an image of perfect harmony, suggesting that man can coexist harmoniously with his surroundings. But as the sun sinks lower on the horizon, the plow seems to grow smaller and smaller, ultimately symbolizing the dominance of the landscape over those who inhabit it.

IMPORTANT QUOTATIONS FROM *MY ÁNTONIA*

"I never know you was so brave, Jim," she went on comfortingly. "You is just like big mans; you wait for him lift his head and then you go for him. Ain't you feel scared a bit? Now we take that snake home and show everybody. Nobody ain't seen in this kawn-tree so big snake like you kill."

Location: Book I, Chapter VII
Speaker: Ántonia
Context: Ántonia pacifies Jim

In a moment of panic, Ántonia warned Jim about the snake's presence in her native language instead of in English. Jim is angry at her, and in this quotation, she quickly appeases him by gushing about his bravery and manliness. The quotation captures Ántonia's way of speaking in the early part of the novel. It also represents a moment of transition in her relationship with Jim. Ántonia, who is four years older than Jim, has treated him condescendingly, to Jim's increasing frustration. After he proves his strength by killing the rattlesnake, she regards him with a new respect and never talks down to him again. She may never love Jim romantically, but she begins to regard him as an equal.

"Why aren't you always nice like this, Tony?"
  "How nice?"
  "Why, just like this; like yourself. Why do you all the time try to be like Ambrosch?"
  She put her arms under her head and lay back, looking up at the sky. "If I live here, like you, that is different. Things will be easy for you. But they will be hard for us."

Location: Book I, Chapter XIX
Speaker: Jim and Ántonia
Context: Ántonia explains the difference between her life and Jim's

Jim and Ántonia have this conversation as they sit on the roof of the chicken house, watching an electrical storm. They have grown apart after Mr. Shimerda's suicide. Jim now attends school, and Ántonia is forced to work on the farm. Jim is dismayed by Ántonia's increasing coarseness and her pride in her own strength. During this conversation, Jim feels their old intimacy returning, and he brings himself to ask Ántonia why she has changed. Ántonia understands Jim's question. She also understands better than he does why their lives have begun to move in separate directions. Jim has opportunities and a bright future ahead of him, and Ántonia does not. She must help her family get by and cannot think of herself. Ántonia acknowledges these circumstances with her customary wisdom and simplicity: "Things will be easy for you. But they will be hard for us."

During that burning day when we were crossing Iowa, our talk kept returning to a central figure, a Bohemian girl whom we had both known long ago. More than any other person we remembered, this girl seemed to mean to us the country, the conditions, the whole adventure of our childhood.

Location: The introduction
Speaker: Jim's childhood friend
Context: Jim's friend describes a train ride during which he and Jim talked about Ántonia

---

Presently we saw a curious thing: There were no clouds, the sun was going down in a limpid, gold-washed sky. Just as the lower edge of the red disc rested on the high fields against the horizon, a great black figure suddenly appeared on the face of the sun. We sprang to our feet, straining our eyes toward it. In a moment we realized what it was. On some upland farm, a plough had been left standing in the field. The sun was sinking just behind it. Magnified across the distance by the horizontal light, it stood out against the sun, was exactly contained within the circle of the disk; the handles, the tongue, the share — black against the molten red. There it was, heroic in size, a picture writing on the sun.

Even while we whispered about it, our vision disappeared; the ball dropped and dropped until the red tip went beneath the earth. The fields below us were dark, the sky was growing pale, and that forgotten plough had sunk back to its own littleness somewhere on the prairie.

Location: Book II, Chapter XIV
Speaker: Jim
Context: Jim and Ántonia watch the sun set behind a plow

She lent herself to immemorial human attitudes which we recognize by instinct as universal and true. I had not been mistaken. She was a battered woman now, not a lovely girl; but she still had that something which fires the imagination, could still stop one's breath for a moment by a look or gesture that somehow revealed the meaning in common things. She had only to stand in the orchard, to put her hand on a little crab tree and look up at the apples, to make you feel the goodness of planting and tending and harvesting at last. All the strong things of her heart came out in her body, that had been so tireless in serving generous emotions.

It was no wonder that her sons stood tall and straight. She was a rich mine of life, like the founders of early races.

Location: Book V, Chapter I
Speaker: Jim
Context: Jim ruminates on Ántonia's personality

NARRATIVE OF THE LIFE OF FREDERICK DOUGLASS

Frederick Douglass

A freed slave recounts the story of his life.

THE LIFE OF FREDERICK DOUGLASS

Frederick Douglass was born into slavery in Maryland around 1818. Originally named Frederick Bailey, he was enslaved on farms in Maryland and Baltimore throughout his youth. In Baltimore, Douglas learned to read and made contacts with educated free blacks. At around age twenty, he escaped north to New York, where he married his fiancée, a free black woman from Baltimore named Anna Murray. The two settled in New Bedford, Massachusetts, and Frederick changed his last name from Bailey to Douglass. Douglass worked for the next three years as a laborer and continued his self-education.

In the early 1840s, the abolitionist, or antislavery, movement was gaining momentum. In 1841, Douglass attended an abolitionist meeting in Nantucket, Massachusetts, where he met Garrison, editor of an abolitionist newspaper, and was encouraged to tell the crowd about his experiences of slavery. Douglass's account was so well received that Garrison offered to employ him as an abolitionist speaker for the American Anti-Slavery Society. From 1841 to 1845, Douglass traveled extensively in the Northern states, speaking nearly every day on the injustice and brutality of slavery. Douglass encountered hostile opposition. Most people accused him of lying and refused to believe that such an eloquent and intelligent man had so recently been a slave.

Douglass encountered a different brand of opposition from the Anti-Slavery Society. He was one of only a few black men employed by the mostly white society, and the society's leaders, including Garrison, often condescendingly insisted that Douglass merely relate the "facts" of his experience, and leave the philosophy, rhetoric, and persuasive argument to others. Douglass's *Narrative of the Life of Frederick Douglass, An American Slave, Written by Himself* (1845) can be seen as a response to both of these types of opposition.

Because Douglass used real names of people and places in his *Narrative*, he had to flee the United States for a time, as his Maryland "owner" was legally entitled to reclaim him. Douglass spent the next two years traveling in the British Isles, where he was warmly received. He returned to the United States only after two English friends purchased his freedom. His reputation at home had grown during his absence. The *Narrative* was an instant bestseller in 1845 and went through five print runs to accommodate demand. Despite opposition from Garrison, Douglass started his own abolitionist newspaper in 1847 in Rochester, New York, under the name *North Star*.

Douglass continued to write and lecture against slavery and also devoted attention to the women's rights movement. He became involved in politics, to the disapproval of other abolitionists who avoided politics. When the Civil War broke out in 1861, Douglass campaigned to make the war a quest to abolish slavery. He also campaigned to allow black men to fight for the Union.

Beginning in the 1860s, Douglass campaigned for the right of blacks to vote and receive equal treatment in public places. Douglass served in government positions under several administrations in the 1870s and 1880s. He also published the second and third volumes of his autobiography. In 1882, Douglass's wife, Anna, died. Two years later, he married Helen Pitts, a white advocate of the women's movement. Douglass died of a heart attack in 1895.

NARRATIVE OF THE LIFE OF FREDERICK DOUGLASS **IN CONTEXT**

In the *Narrative*, Douglass rejects the arguments of racists and antislavery activists alike, demonstrating his ability not only to tell his story, but to interpret it. The *Narrative* is not only a personal account of Douglass's experiences as a slave, but an eloquent antislavery treatise. The *Narrative* pointedly states that Douglass is its sole author, and it contains two prefaces from Garrison and another abolitionist, Wendell Phillips, to attest to this fact. Douglass's use of the actual names of people and places also silences those detractors who questioned the truthfulness of his story and status as a former slave.

Until the 1960s, Douglass's *Narrative* was largely ignored by critics and historians, who focused instead on the speeches for which Douglass was primarily known. But eventually Douglass's *Narrative* took its place in the canon of slave narratives and slavery fictions that includes Harriet Beecher Stowe's *Uncle Tom's Cabin* and Harriet Jacobs's *Incidents in the Life of a Slave Girl*. Today, Douglass's work is considered one of the finest examples of the slave-narrative genre. Douglass's work expanded the genre, combining spiritual conversion narrative, sentimental novel, oratorical rhetoric, and heroic fiction.

NARRATIVE OF THE LIFE OF FREDERICK DOUGLASS: **KEY FACTS**

Full Title: Narrative of the Life of Frederick Douglass, An American Slave, Written by Himself

Time and place written: 1845; Massachusetts

Date of first publication: 1845

Publisher: American Anti-Slavery Society

Type of work: Autobiography

Genre: Slave narrative; bildungsroman

Language: English

Setting (time): 1818–1841

Setting (place): Maryland, Baltimore, New York City, Massachusetts

Tense: Past

Tone: Straightforward, engaged, ironic, emotional

Narrator: Frederick Douglass in the first person

Point of view: Douglass's

Protagonist: Douglass

Antagonist: Slave owners

NARRATIVE OF THE LIFE OF FREDERICK DOUGLASS: **PLOT OVERVIEW**

Frederick Douglass was born into slavery sometime in 1817 or 1818. Like many slaves, he is unsure of his exact date of birth. Douglass is separated from his mother, Harriet Bailey, soon after his birth. His father is most likely the white master, Captain Anthony. Captain Anthony works for a rich man named Colonel Lloyd who owns several plantations and hundreds of slaves. Life on Lloyd's plantations is brutal. Slaves are overworked, exhausted, and underfed. They have few articles of clothing and no beds. They are beaten, whipped, sometimes even shot by the plantation overseers.

Douglass's life on this plantation is not as hard as that of most of the other slaves. He serves in the house. At the age of seven, he is given to a man named Hugh Auld who lives in Baltimore. Slave owners in Baltimore are more reluctant to appear cruel or neglectful toward their slaves in front of their non-slaveowning neighbors. Sophia Auld, Hugh's wife, has never had slaves before, and at first she treats Douglass with surprising kindness. She begins to teach Douglass to read, but her husband says education makes slaves unmanageable. Eventually, Sophia succumbs to the mentality of slaveowning and loses her natural kindliness. Douglass teaches himself to read with the help of local boys. He becomes conscious of the evils of slavery and of the existence of the abolitionist movement.

Douglass is taken back to serve Thomas Auld, Captain Anthony's son-in-law. Auld, a mean man with false religious piety, considers Douglass unmanageable and rents him for one year to Edward Covey, a man known for "breaking" slaves. Covey works and whips all the spirit out of Douglass, turning him into a brutish man no longer interested in reading or freedom, capable only of resting from his injuries. But one day Douglass fights back. He has a two-hour fight with Covey, after which Covey never touches him again.

Douglass is rented to William Freeland for two years. At Freeland's, he begins educating his fellow slaves at the homes of free blacks. Despite the threat of punishment and violence they face, many slaves from neighboring farms come to Douglass and work diligently to learn. Douglass and three of his fellow slaves form a plan of escape, but someone betrays their plan to Freeland, and Douglass and the others are jailed. Thomas Auld sends Douglass back to Hugh Auld to learn the trade of ship caulking.

In Baltimore's trade industry, white workers have begun to fear that the free black workers will take their jobs. Douglass encounters violent intimidation from his white coworkers and is forced to switch shipyards. He quickly learns the trade of caulking and soon earns the highest wages possible, always turning them over to Hugh Auld. Eventually, Douglass receives permission from Hugh Auld to hire out his extra time. He saves money bit by bit and eventually escapes to New York. Douglass refrains from describing the details of his escape in order to protect the safety of slaves who may attempt the journey. In New York, Douglass fears recapture and changes his name from Bailey to Douglass. Soon after, he marries Anna Murray, a free woman he met in Baltimore. They move north to Massachusetts, where Douglass becomes deeply engaged with the abolitionist movement as a writer and an orator.

CHARACTERS IN *NARRATIVE OF THE LIFE OF FREDERICK DOUGLASS*

Captain Anthony Douglass's first master and probably his father. Anthony manages Colonel Lloyd's plantations and overseers. A cruel man, he takes pleasure in whipping slaves.

Hugh Auld Thomas Auld's brother and Douglass's occasional master. Hugh seems dimly aware that slavery is inhumane, but he does not allow this consciousness to interfere with his treatment of Douglass.

Lucretia Auld Captain Anthony's daughter and Thomas Auld's wife. Lucretia is as cruel an owner as her husband.

Sophia Auld Hugh Auld's wife. Slave ownership transforms Sophia from a sympathetic, kind woman into a vengeful monster.

Captain Thomas Auld Lucretia Auld's husband and Hugh Auld's brother. Thomas Auld uses Christianity to justify his brutality toward his slaves.

Betsy Bailey Douglass's grandmother. Betsy's many children and grandchildren became slaves for the Anthonys. She is put in a hut in the woods instead of being allowed to go free.

Harriet Bailey Douglass's mother. Harriet is taken away from Douglass, but she walks twelve miles to see him at night. She dies when Douglass is young.

Edward Covey A notorious slave "breaker" and Douglass's keeper for one year. Covey creates an atmosphere of surveillance, fear, and violence.

Frederick Douglass The author and narrator of the *Narrative*. Douglass, a rhetorically skilled and spirited man, describes his progress from unenlightened victim of slavery to educated and empowered young man.

William Freeland Douglass's keeper for two years. Freeland is the most fair and straightforward of Douglass's masters.

William Gardner A Baltimore shipbuilder from whom Douglass learns caulking.

William Lloyd Garrison The founder of the American Anti-Slavery Society. Garrison is impressed with Douglass's poise and oratorical skills and hires him for the abolitionist cause.

William Hamilton Thomas Auld's father-in-law. Hamilton arrests Douglass for plotting to escape from Freeland.

Aunt Hester Douglass's aunt. Aunt Hester is exceptionally beautiful. She obsesses Captain Anthony, who constantly whips her.

Sandy Jenkins An acquaintance of Douglass. Sandy represents uneducated, superstitious slaves. She may have informed William Freeland about Douglass's plans to escape.

Nathan Johnson A Massachusetts abolitionist. Johnson is kind and helpful to the Douglasses, loaning them money, helping Douglass find work, and suggesting Douglass's new name.

Colonel Edward Lloyd Captain Anthony's boss and Douglass's first owner. Colonel Lloyd insists on extreme subservience from his slaves and often punishes them unjustly.

Anna Murray Douglass's wife.

Wendell Phillips President of the American Anti-Slavery Society. Phillips considers Douglass a close friend and worries about his safety.

THEMES IN *NARRATIVE OF THE LIFE OF FREDERICK DOUGLASS*

IGNORANCE AS A TOOL OF SLAVERY Douglass shows how white slaveholders bolster slavery by keeping their slaves ignorant. When Douglass wrote his narrative, many people believed that slavery was a natural state of being because blacks were inherently incapable of participating in civil society. Douglass explains that black people have exactly the same inherent capabilities as whites, and slave owners must employ strategies to gain and keep power over blacks. For example, they keep slaves ignorant of basic facts about themselves, such as their birth date or their paternity, thus robbing children of their natural sense of individual identity. They prevent slaves from learning how to read and write, thus preventing them from feeling self-sufficient and from expanding their horizons. Also, keeping slaves illiterate is a way of maintaining control over what the rest of America knows about slavery. If slaves cannot write, their side of the slavery story cannot be told.

SLAVERY'S DAMAGING EFFECT ON SLAVEHOLDERS In his *Narrative*, Douglass suggests that slaveholding is unnatural for all involved in it, slave owner and slave, and should be outlawed for the good of society as a whole. The power that slave owners have over their slaves corrupts them. Many slave-owning men commit adultery and rape, fathering illegitimate children by their slaves and threatening the unity of their own families. Then the father must either sell or perpetually punish his own child, while his wife becomes resentful and treats the slaves even more cruelly. In other instances, slave owners such as Thomas Auld develop a perverted religious sense in order to remain blind to the sins they commit in their own homes. Douglass holds up Sophia Auld as a typical example of the corrupting power of slaveholding. Sophia is an almost ideal woman, but once she becomes a slave owner, she turns into a demon.

SLAVEHOLDING AS A PERVERSION OF CHRISTIANITY Douglass distinguishes between true Christianity, or "the Christianity of Christ," and false Christianity, or "the Christianity of this land." Much as the slaveholders pretend that their Christianity is evidence of their innate goodness, it is really a hypocritical show they use to justify their brutality. Douglass points to the basic incompatibility of Christianity, which demands charity and love, and slaveowning, which is violent and immoral. Thomas Auld illustrates this theme. He is always cruel, but he becomes even more cruel when he finds religion. Bolstered by his own show of Christianity, Auld feels increased confidence in his "God-given" right to own and mistreat slaves. Douglass also demonstrates that the Southern church itself is corrupt. Auld's church benefits from Auld's money, which slaves earned, so it, like many Southern churches, is complicit in the inhuman cruelty of slavery.

SYMBOLS IN *NARRATIVE OF THE LIFE OF FREDERICK DOUGLASS*

WHITE-SAILED SHIPS The white-sailed ships, which Douglass sees on the Chesapeake Bay during the spiritual and physical low point of his first months with Covey, symbolize freedom. To Douglass they seem like a vision, traveling northward from port to port and holding out the hope of freedom.

THE COLUMBIAN ORATOR Douglass first encounters *The Columbian Orator*, a collection of political essays, poems, and dialogues, around the age of twelve, just after he has learned to read. The publication articulates the injustice of slavery and becomes a symbol not only of human rights, but of the power of eloquence and articulation. To some extent, Douglass sees his own life's work as an attempt to replicate the effect of *The Columbian Orator*.

IMPORTANT QUOTATIONS FROM *NARRATIVE OF THE LIFE OF FREDERICK DOUGLASS*

Never having enjoyed, to any considerable extent, her soothing presence, her tender and watchful care, I received the tidings of [my mother's] death with much the same emotions I should have probably felt at the death of a stranger.

Location: Chapter I
Speaker: Douglass
Context: Douglass describes his truncated connection with his mother

Douglass devotes large parts of his *Narrative* to demonstrating how a slave is "made," beginning at birth. Many people in Douglass's day believed it was natural for blacks to be kept as slaves, but Douglass demonstrates the unnaturalness of slavery, showing how slave owners must distort social bonds and the natural processes of life in order to turn men into slaves. This process begins at birth, as Douglass shows here. Slaveholders immediately remove children from their immediate family, destroying the child's support network and sense of personal history.

In this quotation, Douglass uses descriptive adjectives like "soothing" and "tender" to recreate the childhood he would have known if his mother had been with him. Douglass often exercises this imaginative recreation in his *Narrative* in order to contrast normal stages of childhood development with the stunted development of child slaves. This comparative presentation creates a strong sense of the disparity and injustice between the two.

Though Douglass's style in this passage is dry and restrained, his focus on the family structure and the moment of his mother's death is typical of the conventions of nineteenth-century sentimental narratives. Nineteenth-century readers placed great value on the family structure, viewing families as a haven of virtue. They would have interpreted the destruction of family as a signal of the larger moral illnesses of the culture.

I did not, when a slave, understand the deep meaning of those rude and apparently incoherent songs. I was myself within the circle; so that I neither saw nor heard as those without might see and hear.

Location: Chapter II
Speaker: Douglass
Context: Douglass discusses the songs slaves sing

This passage is part of Douglass's long discussion of the songs slaves sing. As he often does in the *Narrative*, here Douglass extrapolates from his personal experience to understand the general experience of slaves. Douglass explains that many Northerners mistakenly believe that slaves sing because they are happy, when actually the songs are evidence of the slaves' deep unhappiness. Douglass explains that the "deep" meaning of the songs was not clear to him until he was no longer part of the group. He could only really understand the songs once he had distance from slavery and could analyze his experience. Douglass must abandon his former slave self in order to become a narrator capable of interpreting the experiences of that former self. Implicit in this passage is the idea that a culture is invisible to those who are raised within it. Everyday practices seem normal to those performing them—they seem to have little meaning and therefore cannot be interpreted. This tension between insider and outsider also gives Douglass a particular position of authority. He has experienced slavery from the inside, and he also has the tools and the distance with which to interpret slavery for outside audiences.

Whilst I was saddened by the thought of losing the aid of my kind mistress, I was gladdened by the invaluable instruction which, by the merest accident, I had gained from my master.

Location: Chapter VI
Speaker: Douglass
Context: Hugh Auld orders his wife to stop Douglass's reading lessons, and Douglass realizes that whites hold blacks in their power through a series of strategies—including depriving blacks of education and literacy

My natural elasticity was crushed, my intellect languished, the disposition to read departed, the cheerful spark that lingered about my eye died; the dark night of slavery closed in upon me; and behold a man transformed into a brute!

Location: Chapter X
Speaker: Douglass
Context: Douglass describes the spirit-crushing results of Covey's treatment

In coming to a fixed determination to run away, we did more than Patrick Henry, when he resolved upon liberty or death.

Location: Chapter X
Speaker: Douglass
Context: Douglass characterizes his escape plan as more noble than the sentiment "Give me liberty or give me death," as expressed by white men during the Revolution

NATIVE SON

Richard Wright

A young black man, terrorized by racism and poverty, kills two women.

THE LIFE OF RICHARD WRIGHT

Richard Wright was born on September 4, 1908, on a farm near the river town of Natchez, Mississippi. He was the first of two sons born to Nathan Wright, an illiterate tenant farmer, and Ella Wilson Wright, a teacher. When Richard was about five years old, his father abandoned the family to live with another woman. Ella soon suffered a stroke that left her physically disabled for the rest of her life. Wright sometimes had to work to support the family, and his attendance at school was sporadic.

Despite his irregular schooling, Wright became an avid reader. When he was sixteen, he published a short story in a local black newspaper and began to dream of writing professionally. But his intensely religious household discouraged "idle" thoughts and creativity, and the dehumanizing Jim Crow South pronounced Wright and all black men unfit for anything but the lowliest work. In the late 1920s, Wright moved with his family to Chicago. As the Great Depression enveloped the country, Wright had to work several stultifying and exhausting jobs to support his family. Nevertheless, he began to write seriously in private.

In 1933, Wright published poetry in several leftist and revolutionary magazines. He joined the Communist Party in 1934. In 1937, Wright moved to New York and became Harlem editor of *The Daily Worker*, a Communist publication. The next eight years were a triumph for Wright. He published important essays such as "The Ethics of Living Jim Crow," acclaimed stories like "Fire and Cloud," and two very successful works: *Native Son* (1940) and the autobiography *Black Boy* (1945).

Wright abandoned the Communist Party in 1942 because he thought it was taking a soft stance on wartime racial discrimination. Wright moved to Paris in 1947, partly to protest the deep flaws he saw in American society. In Paris, he became interested in existentialism, the philosophical movement that attempted to understand individual existence in the context of an unfathomable universe. He often socialized with Jean-Paul Sartre and Simone de Beauvoir, two leading thinkers and writers of the existentialist movement. He also began corresponding with Frantz Fanon, the West Indian social philosopher, in the 1950s. Wright died of a heart attack in 1960. *Native Son* and *Black Boy* have secured Wright a place in the canon. Wright is remembered not merely as an intellectual but as a powerful American artist.

NATIVE SON IN CONTEXT

Wright was disappointed with his short story collection *Uncle Tom's Children* (1938). In the collection, he had tried to capture racism as he saw it, but he felt that "even bankers' daughters could read and feel good about" *Uncle Tom's Children*. He was determined to make his readers understand the reality of race relations by writing something "so hard and deep that they would have to face it without the consolation of tears." He succeeded in this project with *Native Son* (1940), which shocked both black and white America. The protagonist of the novel, Bigger Thomas, stands on the lowest rung of society. Wright does not portray him as heroic or noble, but as a sullen, frightened, violent, hateful, and resentful man—a product of his class.

In his essay "How Bigger Was Born," Wright explains that Bigger is a combination of men Wright himself knew in the South. Confronted by racism and oppression, and given few options in their lives, these men became antisocial and violent. In Chicago, removed from the racism of the South, Wright discovered that Bigger was not an exclusively black phenomenon. Millions of poor whites suffered in the same way. Wright came to believe that American society itself was the direct cause of this suffering. *Native Son* is an urgent warning that if American social and economic realities do not change, the oppressed masses will rise up in fury against those in power.

NATIVE SON: KEY FACTS

Time and place written: 1938–1939; Brooklyn, New York

Date of first publication: 1940

Publisher: Harper and Brothers

Type of work: Novel

Genre: Urban naturalism; novel of social protest

Language: English

Setting (time): 1930s

Setting (place): Chicago

Tense: Past

Tone: Absorbed, direct, objective

Narrator: Limited third person

Point of view: Bigger's

Protagonist: Bigger Thomas

Antagonist: Racism

NATIVE SON: PLOT OVERVIEW

It is the 1930s. Bigger Thomas, a poor, uneducated, twenty-year-old black man, wakes up one morning in his family's cramped apartment on the South Side of Chicago. He sees a huge rat, which he corners and kills with a skillet. Bigger has always been the victim of harsh racial prejudice, so he has a powerful conviction that he has no control over his life and cannot aspire to anything other than menial, low-wage labor. His mother pesters him to take a job with a rich white man named Mr. Dalton, but instead Bigger plans to rob a white man's store with his friends.

Anger, fear, and frustration define Bigger's daily existence. He hides behind a façade of toughness so he won't succumb to despair. Bigger and his gang have robbed many black-owned businesses, but they have never robbed a white man. Bigger sees whites not as individuals, but as a natural, oppressive force — a great looming "whiteness" pressing down on him. Rather than admit that he is afraid to confront this force, Bigger violently attacks a member of his gang to sabotage the robbery of the white-owned store. Left with no other options, Bigger takes a job as a chauffeur for the Daltons.

Mr. Dalton, a wealthy real estate baron, is Bigger's landlord. He is one of the men effectively robbing the poor, black tenants on Chicago's South Side by refusing to allow blacks to rent apartments in pre-dominantly white neighborhoods, thus leading to overpopulation and high rents in the predominantly black South Side. Despite this thievery, Mr. Dalton considers himself a benevolent philanthropist because he donates money to black schools and offers jobs to "poor, timid black boys" like Bigger.

Mary, Mr. Dalton's daughter, frightens and angers Bigger by ignoring the social taboos that govern the relations between white women and black men. On his first day of work, Bigger drives Mary to meet her Communist boyfriend, Jan. Eager to show off their progressive ideals and racial tolerance, Mary and Jan force Bigger to take them to a restaurant in the South Side. To Bigger's embarrassment, they order drinks. All three of them get drunk. Mary is too drunk to make it to her bedroom on her own, so Bigger helps her up the stairs. Drunk and aroused, Bigger kisses Mary.

Just as Bigger puts Mary on her bed, Mary's blind mother, Mrs. Dalton, enters the bedroom. Mrs. Dalton's ghostlike presence terrifies Bigger, and he worries that Mary will reveal his presence. He covers her face with a pillow and accidentally smothers her to death. Unaware that Mary has been killed, Mrs. Dalton prays over her daughter and returns to bed. Bigger tries to conceal his crime by burning Mary's body in the Daltons' furnace. He decides to try to use the Daltons' prejudice against Communists to frame Jan for Mary's disappearance. He plays on the Daltons' racism to avoid suspicion, continuing to play the role of a timid, ignorant black servant who would be unable to harm a white woman.

Mary's murder gives Bigger a sense of power and identity he has never known. The Daltons know only that Mary has vanished, not that she is dead, so Bigger writes a ransom letter, signing it "Red." He urges Bessie, his girlfriend, to take part in the ransom scheme. When Mary's bones are found in the furnace,

Bigger flees with Bessie to an empty building. Bigger rapes Bessie and, frightened that she will give him away, bludgeons her to death with a brick after she falls asleep.

Bigger, now a suspect in Mary's murder, eludes the massive manhunt for as long as he can, but eventually the police capture him after a dramatic shoot-out. The press and the public determine his guilt and punishment before his trial even begins. The furious populace assumes that he raped Mary before killing her and burned her body to hide the evidence of the rape. Whites use Bigger's crime as an excuse to terrorize the entire South Side .

Jan visits Bigger in jail. He says that he understands how he terrified, angered, and shamed Bigger by violating the rules of black and white interaction. Jan enlists his friend, Boris A. Max, to defend Bigger free of charge. Bigger begins to see whites as individuals and himself as their equal. Max tries to save Bigger from the death penalty, arguing that Bigger is a product of a racist society that has given him a fearful, hopeless existence. Max warns that there will be more men like Bigger if America does not put an end to the cycle of hatred and vengeance. Despite Max's arguments, Bigger is sentenced to death.

CHARACTERS IN *NATIVE SON*

Mr. Blum   A white man who owns a delicatessen on the South Side of Chicago. Bigger and his friends plan to rob Mr. Blum, even though they are nervous about robbing a white man.

Britten   A racist, anticommunist private investigator. Britten investigates Mary's disappearance.

Buckley   The incumbent State's Attorney. Buckley is viciously racist and anticommunist.

Mary Dalton   The daughter of Mr. and Mrs. Dalton, Bigger's employers. Mary's transgression of social boundaries indirectly leads to her murder.

Mr. and Mrs. Dalton   A white millionaire couple living in Chicago. Mr. Dalton is Bigger's landlord and eventually his employer. Although Mr. Dalton has earned his fortune by exploiting black people, he thinks himself a generous supporter of them.

Doc   The black owner of a pool hall on the South Side of Chicago. Bigger and his friends hang out at Doc's pool hall.

Jan Erlone   Mary Dalton's boyfriend. Jan is a member of the Communist Party. He sympathizes with Bigger's plight and recognizes his own complicity in the murders.

G. H., Gus, and Jack   Bigger's friends. G. H., Gus, and Jack often rob stores together.

Reverend Hammond   The pastor of Mrs. Thomas's church. Hammond urges Bigger to turn to religion in times of trouble.

Boris A. Max   A Jewish lawyer who works for the Labor Defenders, an organization affiliated with the Communist Party. Boris Max defends Bigger, arguing that institutionalized racism and prejudice — not inherent ethnic qualities — create violence in urban ghettos.

Bessie Mears   Bigger's girlfriend. Bessie and Bigger are not close. Their relationship is one of convenience, not romantic love.

Peggy   An Irish immigrant who has worked as the Daltons' cook for years. Peggy is kind but extremely patronizing to Bigger.

Bigger Thomas   The protagonist of the novel. Bigger is a poor, uneducated black man who has always felt trapped. He hates and fears whites, whom he views as one overwhelming force that controls his life.

Buddy Thomas   Bigger's younger brother. Initially Buddy does not rebel against the forces that oppress him, but as the novel progresses, he begins to take a more antagonistic attitude toward racial prejudice.

Mrs. Thomas   Bigger's devoutly religious mother. Mrs. Thomas has accepted her precarious, impoverished position in life.

Vera Thomas   Bigger's younger sister. Vera lives in constant fear.

THEMES IN *NATIVE SON*

THE EFFECT OF RACISM ON THE OPPRESSED Wright argues that Bigger's psychological damage is the fault of the racist propaganda and racial oppression that constantly barrages him. Media and life scream the same message at him. The movies he sees depict whites as wealthy sophisticates and blacks as jungle savages. He and his family live in cramped and squalid conditions, forced by society to stay poor and uneducated. As a result, Bigger hates and fears whites as an overwhelming force. His accidental killing of Mary Dalton fills him with odd jubilation because it marks the first time he has asserted his own individuality against the white forces that have conspired to destroy it.

Wright emphasizes the vicious cyclical effect of racism: Bigger is violent because it is the only way he can respond to the racist whites who oppress him, but his violence confirms racist whites' basic fears about blacks and worsens the racism in American society. In Wright's portrayal, whites effectively transform blacks into the negative stereotypes they dreamed up in the first place. Wright suggests that only when blacks and whites see each other as individuals, instead of as faceless, stereotyped masses, can they break the cycle.

THE EFFECT OF RACISM ON THE OPPRESSOR Racism hurts racists as well as those they oppress. Many whites in the novel, such as Britten and Peggy, become hypocritical and deluded because of their racism. They cherish an unthinking sense of superiority over black people, believing them to be less than human. Wright shows that this sense of superiority is a weakness. Bigger manipulates whites' superiority complex to cover up Mary's murder. Some white characters in the novel have a self-consciously progressive attitude toward race relations, which makes them racist in their own way. The Daltons, for instance, aggressively present themselves as philanthropists committed to the black American cause in an effort to avoid confronting their guilt about exploiting blacks. They refuse to acknowledge their own deep-seated racial prejudices. Mary and Jan consciously seek to befriend blacks and treat them as equals, but they fail to understand them as individuals. This failure has disastrous results. Mary and Jan's simple assumption that Bigger will welcome their friendship makes them unable to predict that he will react with suspicion and fear—a natural reaction considering that Bigger has never experienced friendly treatment from whites. Wright emphasizes that even well-meaning whites have damaging racial prejudices.

THE HYPOCRISY OF JUSTICE Wright highlights the terrible inequity of the American criminal justice system of his time. Drawing inspiration from actual court cases of the 1930s—especially the 1938–39 case of Robert Nixon, a young black man charged with murdering a white woman during a robbery—Wright portrays the American judiciary as an ineffectual pawn caught between the lurid interests of the media and the driving ambition of politicians. The outcome of Bigger's case is decided before it ever goes to court: in the eyes of the media and the public, a black man who kills a white woman is a monster regardless of the factual circumstances of the killing. Wright never suggests that Bigger is not to blame for Mary's murder. But the justice system bears all of the blame for failing Bigger, giving him neither a fair trial nor an opportunity to defend himself. The motto of the American justice system is "equal justice under law," but Wright depicts a judiciary so compromised by racial prejudice and political corruption that it turns the promise of equality into a farce.

SYMBOLS IN *NATIVE SON*

MRS. DALTON'S BLINDNESS Mrs. Dalton's blindness symbolizes the metaphorical blindness that results when white and black Americans see each other as a mass rather than as a collection of individuals. Mrs. Dalton's blindness to Bigger literally allows him to murder, just as the inability of whites to see blacks as individuals causes blacks to live their lives in fear and violence. Bigger eventually realizes that he has been blind, conceiving of whites as a single oppressive mass.

SNOW The snow that aids in Bigger's capture symbolizes the powerful whiteness that has oppressed Bigger throughout his life. After Mary's bones are found in the furnace, Bigger tries to run, but white snow fills his mouth, ears, and eyes, overwhelming him just as white people have always overwhelmed him.

IMPORTANT QUOTATIONS FROM *NATIVE SON*

The head hung limply on the newspapers, the curly black hair dragging about in blood. He whacked harder, but the head would not come off.. . . . He saw a hatchet. Yes! That would do it.

Location: Book One
Speaker: The narrator
Context: Bigger decapitates Mary so he can fit her in the furnace

Wright intentionally makes this description grisly. He wants us to shudder at Bigger's actions, so he spares no gruesome detail, depicting the excited racing of Bigger's mind and the enthusiasm with which he disposes of Mary's body. Wright does not want to portray Bigger simply as a passive victim of a situation beyond his control or as a heroic fighter of racism. No one forced Bigger to kill Mary. Still, Wright emphasizes that racism is at fault in some way. Racism transformed Bigger into a person capable of furious violence, even capable of craving furious violence. By showing Bigger hacking apart Mary's corpse, Wright reminds us that Bigger has become morally demented.

There was something he knew and something he felt; something the world gave him and something he himself had.. . . . [N]ever in all his life, with this black skin of his, had the two worlds, thought and feeling, will and mind, aspiration and satisfaction, been together; never had he felt a sense of wholeness.

Location: Book Two
Speaker: The narrator
Context: The narrator explains the destructive effect of Bigger's retreat from reality

Early in *Native Son*, Wright describes how Bigger retreats behind a "wall" to keep the reality of his situation from overwhelming him. This passage details the divisive effects of Bigger's retreat. It separates him not only from his friends and family, but from himself. The African-American author W. E. B. DuBois, in *The Souls of Black Folk*, describes the effect of racism on the black psyche: "One ever feels his two-ness—an American, a negro; two souls, two thoughts, two unreconciled strivings; two warring ideals in one dark body whose dogged strength alone keeps it from being torn asunder." Wright describes the similar effect of racism on Bigger. Although Bigger's body is in one piece, his mind is split in two, making him unable to interact with others or understand himself. The quest for wholeness dominates Bigger's life. Only after he has murdered two women does he realize how racism has split him in two.

Was what he had heard about rich white people really true? Was he going to work for people like you saw in the movies . . . ? He looked at Trader Horn unfold and saw pictures of naked black men and women whirling in wild dances.. . . .

Location: Book One
Speaker: The narrator
Context: Bigger goes to the movies and sees white people portrayed as elegant and sophisticated and black people portrayed as savages dancing in a jungle

---

"Listen, Bigger," said Britten. "Did you see this guy [Jan] act in any way out of the ordinary? I mean, sort of nervous, say? Just what did he talk about?"
"He talked about Communists.. . . ."
"Did he ask you to join?"
"He gave me that stuff to read."
"Come on. Tell us some of the things he said."

> *Bigger knew the things that white folks hated to hear Negroes ask for; and he knew that these were the things the Reds were always asking for.*

Location: Book Two
Speaker: The narrator
Context: Britten questions Bigger about Mary's disappearance

> *He had done this. He had brought all this about. In all of his life these two murders were the most meaningful things that had ever happened to him.*

Location: Book Two
Speaker: The narrator
Context: The narrator describes the sensation Bigger has after he commits murder

NIGHT

Elie Wiesel

An eastern European Jewish teenager survives the concentration camps during the Holocaust, having lost his father and his faith in God.

HISTORICAL BACKGROUND AND THE LIFE OF ELIE WIESEL

Elie Wiesel was born in 1928, in Sighet, a small town in Transylvania, a Romanian region under Hungarian control from 1940 to 1945. Wiesel grew up Orthodox Jewish, and his father was very involved with the local Jewish community. As a student, Wiesel distinguished himself in the study of traditional Jewish texts: the Torah (the first five books of the Old Testament), the Talmud (codified oral law), and even the mystical texts of the Kabbalah, an unusual text for someone so young to tackle.

Until 1944, the Jews of Hungary were relatively unaffected by the catastrophe that was destroying the Jewish communities of Europe. The leader of the German National Socialist (Nazi) party, Adolf Hitler, came to power in 1933 on the strength of campaign rhetoric that blamed the Jews for Germany's depression after World War I. Germany embraced Hitler's argument for the superiority of the Nordic peoples, which he (mistakenly) called the Aryan race. The country soon implemented a set of laws, including the infamous Nuremberg Laws of 1935, designed to dehumanize German Jews and subject them to violence and prejudice. As World War II progressed, Hitler and his counselors developed the "Final Solution" to the so-called Jewish Question: systematic extermination. By the end of the war in 1945, six million European Jews had been murdered, along with millions of Gypsies, homosexuals, and "undesirables." A majority of the victims died in concentration camps, where Jews and others were imprisoned, forced into labor, and executed.

In March 1944, the German army occupied Hungary and installed a Nazi-controlled puppet government. That spring, Hungarian Jews—the last large European Jewish community—were deported to concentration camps in Germany and Poland. Most perished. Out of 15,000 Jews in Wiesel's native Sighet, only about fifty families survived the Holocaust. Wiesel's family was deported to Auschwitz, the largest death camp, in May 1944, when he was fifteen. Wiesel's father, mother, and little sister all died. Wiesel survived and emigrated to France.

In 1956, after observing a self-imposed ten-year vow of silence about the Holocaust, Wiesel published *Un di Velt Hot Geshvign* ("and the world remained silent"), an 800-page memoir. Two years later, he published a much shorter French adaptationthat was published in English as *Night* in 1960. Scholars have noted that *Un di Velt Hot Geshvign* expresses more anger and adopts a more vengeful tone than *Night*. *Night* opened the way for other stories and memoirs of the Holocaust published in the second half of the twentieth century. In 1963, Wiesel became an American citizen. He now lives in New York City.

NIGHT: KEY FACTS

Time and place written: Mid-1950s; Paris

Date of publication: 1958 (France); 1960 (US). *Un di Velt Hot Geshvign* was published in Buenos Aires in 1956

Publisher: Argentina: Unión Central Israelita Polaca; France: Les Editions de Minuit; US: Hill & Wang

Type of work: Literary memoir

Genre: World War II and Holocaust autobiography

Language: French. The French manuscript was based on *Un di Velt Hot Geshvign* ("and the world remained silent"), Wiesel's 900-page text in Yiddish

Setting (time): 1941–45, during World War II

Setting (place): Eastern Europe: Sighet, Transylvania (present-day Romania), Auschwitz-Birkenau and its subcamps Buna, Gleiwitz, and Buchenwald (all in present-day Poland and Germany)

Tense: Past

Tone: Intimate

Narrator: Eliezer (a stand-in for Wiesel)

Point of View: Eliezer's

Protagonist: Eliezer

Antagonist: Hitler's Final Solution

NIGHT: PLOT OVERVIEW

Eliezer, a Jewish teenager in Sighet, in Hungarian Transylvania, studies the Torah (Judaism's sacred text, the first five books of the Old Testament) and the Cabbala (Jewish mysticism, which teaches that everything in the world is an "emanation," or reflection, of God). His studies are cut short when his teacher, Moshe the Beadle, is deported. A few months later, Moshe returns with a horrifying tale: the Gestapo (German secret police) took charge of his train, led the passengers into the woods, and systematically butchered them. Moshe's story is dismissed as the ravings of a lunatic.

In the spring of 1944, the Nazis occupy Hungary, passing a series of increasingly repressive measures. Sighet's Jews are first forced into small ghettos in town. Soon, they are herded onto cattle cars for a nightmarish journey. After days and nights crammed into cars, exhausted and near starvation, the passengers arrive at Birkenau, the gateway to Auschwitz.

Eliezer and his father are separated from his mother and sisters. They never see them again. In the first of many "selections," the Jews are evaluated to determine whether they should be killed immediately or put to work. Eliezer and his father pass the evaluation. On the way to the prisoners' barracks, they stumble upon the open-pit furnaces where babies are being burned by the truckload.

The Jewish arrivals are stripped, shaved, and disinfected. They are treated with unimaginable cruelty. Eventually, their captors march them to Auschwitz, the main camp. Later, they arrive in Buna, a work camp where Eliezer is put to work in an electrical-fittings factory. Under slave-labor conditions, severely malnourished and decimated by frequent "selections," the Jews take solace in caring for each other, in religion, and in Zionism. The prisoners are subjected to beatings and repeated humiliations. A vicious foreman forces Eliezer to give him his gold tooth, which is pried out of his mouth with a rusty spoon.

The prisoners are forced to watch as other prisoners are hanged in the camp courtyard. On one occasion, the Gestapo hang a small child associated with a rebellion within Buna. Because of the horrific conditions in the camps and the ever-present danger of death, many of the prisoners themselves begin to slide into cruelty. Sons begin to abandon and abuse their fathers. Eliezer himself begins to lose his humanity and his faith, both in God and in the people around him.

After months in the camp, Eliezer is operated on for a foot injury. While he is in the infirmary, the Nazis decide to evacuate the camp because the Russian advance. In the middle of a snowstorm, the prisoners begin a death march: they are forced to run for more than fifty miles to the Gleiwitz concentration camp. Many die of exhaustion and exposure to the harsh weather. At Gleiwitz, the prisoners are herded into cattle cars for another deadly journey. Only twelve of the hundred Jews who board Eliezer's car are alive when the train reaches the concentration camp Buchenwald. Throughout the ordeal, Eliezer and his father help each other survive. In Buchenwald, Eliezer's father dies of dysentery and physical abuse. Eliezer survives, an empty shell of a man, until the American army liberates the camp on April 11, 1945.

CHARACTERS IN *NIGHT*

Chlomo Eliezer's father. Chlomo is respected by the Jewish community in Sighet. Chlomo and Eliezer desperately try to remain together throughout their ordeal. Chlomo is named only once, at the end of the memoir.

Akiba Drumer A Jewish prisoner who gradually loses his faith in God as a result of his experiences in the concentration camp.

Rabbi Eliahou A devout Jewish prisoner abandoned by his son. Eliezer prays that he will never do a similar thing to his own father.

Eliezer *Night*'s narrator and Elie Wiesel's stand-in. The memoir traces Eliezer's psychological journey as his experiences in concentration camps rob him of his faith in God and expose him to inhumanity at human hands. Throughout his ordeal, Eliezer maintains his devotion to his father. We learn his last name only once, in passing; his intensely personal story is representative of the experiences of hundreds of thousands of Jewish teenagers.

Franek Eliezer's foreman at Buna. Franek gets a camp dentist in the camp to pry out Eliezer's gold tooth with a rusty spoon.

Hilda, Béa, and Tzipora Eliezer's sisters.

Idek Eliezer's Kapo (a Jewish prisoner conscripted to police other Jewish prisoners) at the electrical equipment warehouse in Buna. Idek beats Eliezer during moments of insane rage.

Juliek A young violinist prisoner whom Eliezer meets in Auschwitz. Eliezer hears Juliek playing the violin after the death march to Gleiwitz.

Meir Katz Eliezer's father's friend from Buna. On the train to Buchenwald, Katz saves Eliezer from an unidentified assailant.

Dr. Josef Mengele The historical Nazi physician who presided over the selection of arrivals at Auschwitz and directed horrific experiments on human subjects. He was commonly referred to as the "Angel of Death"—likely after a fearsome angel in Jewish folk tradition who stands at the bedside of the sick and takes their life with his knife.

Moshe the Beadle Eliezer's Cabbala teacher. A poor Sighet Jew, Moshe is deported before the rest of the community. He manages to escape and return to tell his story to the townspeople, but they take him for a lunatic.

Madame Schächter A Sighet Jewish woman deported in the same cattle car as Eliezer. Every night on the journey, Madame Schächter screams that she sees furnaces in the distance—a prophetic vision.

Stein A distant relative from Antwerp, Belgium, whom Eliezer and his father encounter in Auschwitz. Eliezer's father lies to Stein and tells him that his family is alive and well in Antwerp.

Tibi and Yosi Zionist brothers whom Eliezer meets in Buna. Together with Eliezer, they make a plan to move to Palestine after the war.

Zalman A fellow prisoner. Zalman is trampled to death during the run to Gleiwitz.

THEMES IN *NIGHT*

ELIEZER'S STRUGGLE TO MAINTAIN FAITH IN A BENEVOLENT GOD
At the beginning of *Night*, Eliezer's faith in God is absolute. When asked why he prays to God, he answers, "Why did I pray? . . . Why did I live? Why did I breathe?" Informed by the Cabbala, Eliezer believes that the world must be good because God is everywhere in it. This faith is irreparably shaken by his experiences during the Holocaust. He cannot imagine how an omnipotent God could permit such cruelty or how the inhuman concentration camps could possibly reflect a benevolent divinity. Furthermore, he is shaken by the other prisoners: if they united to oppose the Nazis, it would be possible to see the Nazis as an evil aberration and to continue to believe in the essential goodness of the world. Instead, the Holocaust exposes the selfishness and cruelty of which human beings are capable—not only the Nazis, but Eliezer's fellow prisoners, even himself. A world so disgusting and cruel must either reflect a disgusting and cruel God or prove that God cannot exist.

At the same time, the very fact that Eliezer continues to struggle with his faith indicates that he has not abandoned faith entirely. Moshe the Beadle says that he prays "to the God within me that He will give me the strength to ask Him the right questions"; *questioning* is therefore fundamental to faith in God. Wiesel has said of his experiences, "My anger rises up within faith and not outside it"—a sentiment reflected in Eliezer's struggle. Wiesel's religious metaphors undercut Eliezer's claim to have given up on God. In denying his faith, Eliezer refers to scripture. His faith is tested and changed by his experiences, but not abandoned.

SILENCE In one of *Night's* most famous passages, Eliezer states, "Never shall I forget that nocturnal silence which deprived me, for all eternity, of the desire to live." It is the idea of God's silence that he finds most troubling. As the Gestapo hangs a young boy, a man asks, "Where is God?" and the only response is "[t]otal silence throughout the camp." Eliezer and his companions are left to wonder how an all-knowing, all-powerful God can allow such horror and cruelty to occur, especially to such devout worshipers. The existence of this horror and the lack of a divine response forever shakes Eliezer's faith in God.

God's silence during the hanging of the young boy recalls the story of the Akedah—the Binding of Isaac—found in the Hebrew Scriptures (Genesis 22). In the Akedah, God decides to test the faith of Abraham by asking him to sacrifice his only son, Isaac. Abraham does not doubt his God, and he ties Isaac to a sacrificial altar. He raises a knife to kill the boy, but at the last minute God sends an angel to save Isaac. The angel explains that God merely wanted to test Abraham's faith and would never permit him to shed innocent blood. Unlike the God in *Night*, the God in the Akedah is not silent.

Night can be read as a reversal of the Akedah story: at the moment of a horrible sacrifice, God does *not* intervene to save innocent lives. Eliezer and the other prisoners call out for God, and they get only silence in response. During his first night at Birkenau, Eliezer says, "The Eternal... was silent. What had I to thank Him for?" The lesson Eliezer learns is the opposite of the lesson taught in the Bible. The moral of the Akedah is that God demands sacrifice but is ultimately compassionate. During the Holocaust, Eliezer feels that God's silence demonstrates the absence of divine compassion. As a result, he ultimately questions the very existence of God.

There is also a second type of silence operating throughout *Night*: the silence of the victims and the lack of resistance to the Nazi threat. When his father is beaten at the end of his life, Eliezer remembers, "I did not move. I was afraid," and he feels guilty about his inaction. It is implied throughout the text that silence and passivity are what allowed the Holocaust to continue. Wiesel's writing of *Night* is itself an attempt to break the silence, to tell loudly and boldly of the atrocities of the Holocaust.

CRUELTY INSPIRES CRUELTY Eliezer witnesses cruelty breeding cruelty. Faced with inhuman difficulties, prisoners turn against one another. Near the end of the work, a Kapo says to Eliezer, "Here, every man has to fight for himself and not think of anyone else.. . . Here, there are no fathers, no brothers, no friends. Everyone lives and dies for himself alone." Indeed, the task of a Kapo—a prisoner in charge of other prisoners—symbolizes the way the Holocaust's cruelty bred cruelty in its victims. Kapos aided the Nazi mission and often behaved cruelly toward prisoners in their charge. At the beginning of the fifth section, Eliezer refers to them as "functionaries of death."

SYMBOLS IN *NIGHT*

FIRE Fire appears throughout *Night* as a symbol of the Nazis' cruel power. On the way to Auschwitz-Birkenau, Madame Schächter sees visions of fire, a premonition of the horror to come. Eliezer sees the Nazis burning babies in a ditch. Fire is the agent of destruction in the crematoria, where many of the prisoners meet their deaths. The association of fire with Nazi oppression reverses the role fire plays in the Torah and in Jewish tradition, where it is associated with God and divine wrath. God appears to Moses as a burning bush, and vengeful angels wield flaming swords. In postbiblical literature, flame is also a force of divine retribution. But in *Night*, it is the wicked who wield the power of fire to punish the innocent. Such a reversal underscores how deeply his experiences have upset Eliezer's conception of the world.

NIGHT Darkness and night symbolize a world without God's presence. In the Bible, the world begins "without form, and void; and darkness [is] upon the face of the deep" (Genesis 1:2). God's first act is to dispel this darkness by creating light. In *Night*, night brings suffering: "night fell" as Eliezer's father's storytelling is interrupted to announce the deportation of the Jews, Eliezer arrives at Auschwitz-Birkenau at night, and the prisoners begin their death march from Buna in "pitch darkness."

IMPORTANT QUOTATIONS FROM *NIGHT*

Never shall I forget that night, the first night in camp, which has turned my life into one long night, seven times cursed and seven times sealed. Never shall I forget that smoke. Never shall I forget the little faces of the children, whose bodies I saw turned into wreaths of smoke beneath a silent blue sky.
   Never shall I forget those flames which consumed my faith forever.
   Never shall I forget that nocturnal silence which deprived me, for all eternity, of the desire to live.
   Never shall I forget those moments which murdered my God and my soul and turned my dreams to dust.
   Never shall I forget these things, even if I am condemned to live as long as God Himself. Never.

Location: Section Three
Speaker: Eliezer
Context: Eliezer and his father realize that they have survived the first "selection" at Birkenau

In its form, this famous quotation resembles two notable passages: the biblical Psalm 150, and French author Emile Zola's 1898 essay "J'accuse." Psalm 150 is an ecstatic celebration of God. Each line begins with "Hallelujah" ("Praise God"). Wiesel's passage inverts both the language and the meaning of the psalm. Each line of the passage begins with "Never," a negation replacing the psalm's affirmative "Hallelujah." The passage questions God where the psalm praises him. This inversion reflects the perversion that has taken place in Eliezer's moral universe.

Zola's essay "J'accuse" was an open letter written in response to the Dreyfus Affair, an incident in which a Jewish army officer was unjustly convicted of treason at least in part because of his religion. Zola heightened the aggressive tone of his letter by repeating the phrase "J'accuse" ("I accuse"). Like Zola's piece, Wiesel's passage is an impassioned polemic, but its target is God, rather than corrupt officials who have betrayed an innocent Jew. Implicitly, Eliezer's statement depicts God as betraying the Jews—a bold statement that reflects how profoundly his faith has been shaken. Furthermore, Zola's transitive verb (I *accuse*) has been replaced by an objectless adverb (*never*), reflecting the prisoners' complete powerlessness.

In the last line, Eliezer refers to God after claiming that his faith has been "murdered." Just as he is never able to forget the horror of "that night," he is never able to reject his faith completely.

One day I was able to get up, after gathering all my strength. I wanted to see myself in the mirror hanging on the opposite wall. I had not seen myself since the ghetto.
   From the depths of the mirror, a corpse gazed back at me.
   The look in his eyes, as they stared into mine, has never left me.

Location: Section Nine; concluding passage
Speaker: Eliezer
Context: Eliezer survives and reflects that his experiences have changed him forever

This final passage reinforces the book's deliberately limited perspective: *Night* focuses on one person's detailed, personal experiences and ends with that person looking at his own eyes in a mirror. The ending may feel incomplete, but Wiesel cuts the narrative off because the story of what happened to Eliezer after the war would distract from the intensity of his wartime experiences.

The passage implies that although Eliezer has survived the war physically, his soul has been destroyed by what he has witnessed and endured. He is a corpse with haunting eyes. At the same time, by separating Eliezer from his corpse-like reflection in the mirror—both with the physical setup of the scene and through his use of two different pronouns ("*his* eyes stared into *mine*")—Wiesel ends on a note of faint hope. The corpse image will always remind Eliezer how much of himself—his family, his innocence, his faith in God, his faith in mankind—has been killed in the camps. However, he has managed to separate himself from this empty shell and has found a sense of identity beyond the Holocaust.

"Where is God? Where is He?" someone behind me asked.. . . .

For more than half an hour [the child in the noose] stayed there, struggling between life and death, dying in slow agony under our eyes. And we had to look him full in the face. He was still alive when I passed in front of him. His tongue was still red, his eyes were not yet glazed.

Behind me, I heard the same man asking:

"Where is God now?"

And I heard a voice within me answer him:

"Where is He? Here He is—He is hanging here on this gallows.. . ."

Location: Section Four

Speaker: Eliezer

Context: Eliezer witnesses the agonizingly slow death of a young boy hanged for collaborating against the Nazis

---

We were masters of nature, masters of the world. We had forgotten everything—death, fatigue, our natural needs. Stronger than cold or hunger, stronger than the shots and the desire to die, condemned and wandering, mere numbers, we were the only men on earth.

At last, the morning star appeared in the gray sky. A trail of indeterminate light showed on the horizon. We were exhausted. We were without strength, without illusions.

Location: Section Six

Speaker: Eliezer

Context: Eliezer and his fellow prisoners are forced to run from Buna to Gleiwitz; in their worldview, they have replaced God as the master of the world

---

[Rabbi Eliahou's son] had felt that his father was growing weak, he had believed that the end was near and had sought this separation in order to get rid of the burden, to free himself from an encumbrance which could lessen his own chances of survival.

I had done well to forget that. And I was glad that Rabbi Eliahou should continue to look for his beloved son.

And, in spite of myself, a prayer rose in my heart, to that God in whom I no longer believed.

My God, Lord of the Universe, give me strength never to do what Rabbi Eliahou's son has done.

Location: Section Six

Speaker: Eliezer

Context: During a respite on the march from Buna to Gleiwitz, Eliezer prays never to abandon his father as Rabbi Eliahou's son has abandoned his

THE ODYSSEY

Homer

A Greek warrior undertakes an arduous journey back to his homeland and his loyal wife and son, experiencing many fantastical adventures along the way.

THE LIFE OF HOMER

Nearly three thousand years after they were composed, the *Iliad* and the *Odyssey* remain two of the most celebrated and widely read stories ever told, yet next to nothing is known about their author. He was certainly an accomplished Greek bard, and he probably lived in the late eighth and early seventh centuries B.C. Most believe that he was a blind poet named Homer. But mystery surrounds the works. As early as the third and second centuries B.C., Greeks were questioning whether Homer existed and whether the two epics were written by a single individual.

THE ILIAD IN CONTEXT

The writer of the *Odyssey* owes a debt to the tradition of oral poetry. Stories of a glorious expedition to the East and back had circulated in Greece for hundreds of years before the *Iliad* and *Odyssey* were composed, passed down through the generations by casual storytellers and minstrels.

   The epics are set in Mycenaean Greece in about the twelfth century B.C., during the Bronze Age. The Greeks believed that this historical period was a sublime age, when gods still frequented the earth and heroic mortals lived in Greece. Although Homer uses a high style appropriate for the Bronze Age, he incorporates details from eighth- and seventh-century B.C. Greece (the Iron Age), the time when he was writing.

   For centuries, many scholars believed that the Trojan War was a story dreamed up by the Greeks, not a real war. But in the late nineteenth century, an archaeologist named Heinrich Schliemann declared that he had discovered the remnants of Troy off of the Aegean coast in northwestern Turkey. Most scholars believe that Schliemann discovered Troy, but some still say that the Trojan War never took place.

THE ODYSSEY IN CONTEXT

The *Iliad* tells the story of the Greek struggle to rescue Helen, a Greek queen, from her Trojan captors. The *Odyssey* picks up where the *Iliad* ends. It tells the story of Odysseus, a Greek war hero who undertakes a ten-year journey to his home in northwest Greece. A tale of wandering, the *Odyssey* takes place not on the battlefield but on fantastic islands and foreign lands. After the unrelenting tragedy and carnage of the *Iliad*, the *Odyssey* often strikes readers as occasionally comic and surreal. Because of the *Odyssey*'s affable quality, some critics believe that Homer wrote the *Odyssey* at a later time in his life, when he was less interested in war and more interested in the fortunes and misadventures of a single man. Other critics argue that someone other than Homer wrote the *Odyssey*, someone who wanted to provide a companion work to the *Iliad* but had different interests from those of the first epic's author.

THE ODYSSEY: KEY FACTS

Time and place written:	Unknown, but probably around 700 B.C. in mainland Greece
Date of first publication:	Unknown
Publisher:	Unknown
Type of work:	Poem
Genre:	Epic
Language:	Ancient Greek
Setting (time):	The ten years after the fall of Troy (approximately twelfth century B.C.)

Setting (place): The Aegean and surrounding seas, Greece

Tense: Past

Tone: Celebratory, nostalgic

Narrator: Omniscient third person; Odysseus narrates Books 9–12 in the first person

Point of view: The narrator's, Odysseus's

Protagonist: Odysseus

Antagonist: The suitors

THE ODYSSEY: PLOT OVERVIEW

Ten years have passed since the fall of Troy, and the Greek hero Odysseus still has not returned to his kingdom in Ithaca. A large and rowdy mob of suitors has overrun Odysseus's palace, pillaged his land, and unsuccessfully tried to seduce his wife, Penelope. Prince Telemachus, Odysseus's son, desperately wants to banish the suitors but does not have the confidence or experience to do so. One of the suitors, Antinous, plans to assassinate Telemachus. The suitors think that Odysseus is dead and that Telemachus is the only man standing between them and total dominion over the palace.

The beautiful nymph Calypso, possessed by love for Odysseus, has imprisoned him on her island, Ogygia. Odysseus longs to return to his wife and son, but he has no ship or crew to help him escape. While the gods and goddesses on Mount Olympus debate Odysseus's future, Athena, Odysseus's strongest supporter among the gods, resolves to help Telemachus. Disguised as a friend of the prince's grandfather, Laertes, she convinces the prince to call a meeting and reproach the suitors. Telemachus goes to Pylos and Sparta, where Odysseus's companions during the war inform him that Odysseus is trapped on Calypso's island. In Ithaca, Antinous and the other suitors prepare to kill Telemachus when he comes home.

On Zeus's orders, Hermes persuades Calypso to let Odysseus build a ship and leave. The homesick hero sets sail, but Poseidon, god of the sea, sends a storm to wreck Odysseus's ship. Poseidon harbors a bitter grudge against Odysseus, who blinded Poseidon's son, the Cyclops Polyphemus. Athena intervenes to save Odysseus from Poseidon's wrath. Odysseus lands at Scheria, home of the Phaeacians, where he receives a warm welcome from the king and queen. They have heard of his exploits at Troy and beg him to tell the story of his adventures.

Odysseus spends the night describing the fantastic chain of events leading up to his arrival on Calypso's island. He recounts his trip to the Land of the Lotus Eaters, his battle with Polyphemus the Cyclops, his love affair with the witch-goddess Circe, his temptation by the deadly Sirens, his journey into Hades to consult the prophet Tiresias, and his fight with the sea monster Scylla.

The Phaeacians return Odysseus to Ithaca, where he seeks out his faithful swineherd, Eumaeus. Athena has disguised Odysseus as a beggar, and Eumaeus does not recognize him, but he gives Odysseus a warm welcome nevertheless. Odysseus finds his son and with him devises a plan to massacre the suitors and regain control of Ithaca.

When Odysseus arrives at his palace the next day, still disguised as a beggar, the suitors abuse and insult him. The only person who recognizes Odysseus is his old nurse, Eurycleia, but she swears she will not disclose his secret. Penelope suspects this strange beggar might be her long-lost husband. Crafty Penelope organizes an archery contest and promises to marry any man who can string Odysseus's great bow and fire an arrow through a row of twelve axes—a feat that only Odysseus has ever been able to accomplish. Each suitor tries to string the bow and fails. Odysseus steps up to the bow and, with little effort, fires an arrow through all twelve axes. He then turns the bow on the suitors. He and Telemachus, assisted by a few faithful servants, kill every last suitor.

Odysseus reveals himself to the entire palace and reunites with Penelope. He travels to the outskirts of Ithaca to see his aging father, Laertes. They come under attack from the vengeful family members of the dead suitors, but Laertes, reinvigorated by his son's return, kills Antinous's father and puts a stop to the attack. Zeus dispatches Athena to restore peace. With his power secure and his family reunited, Odysseus's long ordeal comes to an end.

CHARACTERS IN *THE ODYSSEY*

PEOPLE

Agamemnon Former king of Mycenae, brother of Menelaus, and commander of the Achaean forces at Troy. Agamemnon was murdered by his wife, Clytemnestra, and her lover, Aegisthus, upon his return from the war. He was later avenged by his son Orestes. Odysseus encounters Agamemnon's spirit in Hades.

Alcinous King of the Phaeacians. Alcinous hears the story of Odysseus's wanderings and provides him with safe passage back to Ithaca.

Amphinomus The only decent suitor. Amphinomus sometimes speaks up for Odysseus and Telemachus.

Antinous The most arrogant and bloodthirsty of Penelope's suitors.

Arete Queen of the Phaeacians. Arete, an intelligent and influential woman, hears Odysseus's appeal for assistance.

Eumaeus A loyal shepherd. Eumaeus treats Odysseus kindly even when he thinks Odysseus is a beggar.

Eurycleia An aged, loyal servant. Eurycleia nursed Odysseus and Telemachus when they were babies. She is well informed about palace intrigues and serves as confidante to her masters.

Helen Wife of Menelaus and queen of Sparta. Helen's abduction by the Trojans sparked the Trojan War.

Laertes Odysseus's aging father. Laertes regains his spirit when Odysseus returns.

Eurymachus A manipulative, deceitful suitor. Eurymachus's charisma and duplicity give him influence over the other suitors.

Melanthius A treacherous, opportunistic goatherd. Melanthius supports the suitors, especially Eurymachus.

Melantho Melanthius's sister. Melantho, a maidservant in Odysseus's palace, abuses Odysseus when he is disguised as a beggar. She is having an affair with Eurymachus.

Menelaus King of Sparta, brother of Agamemnon, and husband of Helen. Menelaus helped lead the Greeks in the Trojan War.

Nausicaa The beautiful daughter of King Alcinous and Queen Arete of the Phaeacians.

Nestor King of Pylos and a warrior in the Trojan War. Nestor is known as a clever speaker.

Odysseus The protagonist of the *Odyssey*. Odysseus is a strong and courageous warrior, but he is most renowned for his cunning.

Penelope Odysseus's wife and Telemachus's mother. Penelope yearns for the husband who left twenty years ago. She is sometimes flighty and excitable, but also clever and loyal.

Telemachus Odysseus's son. An infant when Odysseus left for Troy, Telemachus is about twenty when the *Odyssey* begins. Despite his courage and good heart, initially he lacks the poise and confidence to oppose his mother's suitors.

GODS AND OTHER BEINGS

Athena Daughter of Zeus and goddess of wisdom, purposeful battle, and the womanly arts. Athena assists Odysseus and Telemachus throughout the epic. She often appears in disguise as Mentor, an old friend of Odysseus's.

Calypso A beautiful nymph. Calypso falls in love with Odysseus and holds him prisoner for seven years.

Circe A beautiful witch-goddess. Circe transforms Odysseus's crew into swine. Odysseus resists Circe's transforming powers and becomes her lover, living in luxury at her side for a year.

Polyphemus Poseidon's son and one of the Cyclopes (uncivilized, one-eyed giants). Polyphemus imprisons Odysseus and his crew and tries to eat them, but Odysseus blinds him through a clever ruse and manages to escape.

Poseidon God of the sea and patron of the seafaring Phaeacians. Poseidon despises Odysseus for blinding his son, and constantly complicates his journey home.

Tiresias A Theban prophet who lives in the underworld.

Zeus King of gods and men.

THEMES IN *THE ODYSSEY*

THE SUPERIOR POWER OF CUNNING   If the *Iliad* is about strength, the *Odyssey* is about cunning, a difference that becomes apparent in the first lines of the epic, when the poet announces that Odysseus is a "man of twists and turns" (1.1). Odysseus does have extraordinary strength, as he demonstrates when he wins the archery contest, but he relies on his mind more than on his muscle. For example, he cannot overpower Polyphemus, so he pits his cunning against Polyphemus's stupidity and manages to escape. Similarly, Odysseus knows he is no match for the host of strapping young suitors in his palace, so he rousts them by using his wits. Step by step, employing disguises and deceptions, he engineers a situation in which he alone is armed and the suitors are locked in a room with him. Odysseus's encounter with Achilles in the underworld reminds us that although Achilles won great *kleos*, or glory, during his life, his life was brief and ended violently. Odysseus will live to a ripe old age because he relies on his mind.

THE PITFALLS OF TEMPTATION   Many of the obstacles that Odysseus and his men face arise from their own mortal weakness. This shortcoming has historical roots: before Odysseus's journey, the "lesser" Ajax, an Achaean (Greek) as Odysseus is, raped the Trojan priestess Cassandra while the Greeks were plundering Troy. His impulsive act of impiety and stupidity brought the wrath of Athena upon the Achaean fleet and set in motion the chain of events that turns Odysseus's homecoming into a long nightmare. As Odysseus and his men make their way back to Greece, they give in to the same kind of reckless urges that Ajax did, undermining themselves and angering the gods as a result. They yield to hunger and slaughter the Sun's flocks. They eat the fruit of the lotus and forget about their homes. Odysseus resists the Sirens only by instructing his crew to keep him bound to the ship's mast. Although Odysseus and his men desperately want to complete their *nostos*, or homecoming, their own weaknesses constantly thwart this desire.

THE ENRICHING QUALITY OF STORYTELLING   In the *Odyssey*, storytelling both delivers the plot to the audience and gives the epic cultural context. The meaning of the *Odyssey* itself depends on another story, the *Iliad*. To understand the context of Odysseus's journey, we must also understand the stories of the many other Greek heroes who had to make *nostoi*, or homeward journeys. Many characters in the *Odyssey* tell stories, putting their own lives in context. Menelaus and Nestor tell Telemachus about their wanderings from Troy. Helen tells stories about Odysseus's cunning during the Trojan War. Phemius, a court minstrel in Ithaca, and Demodocus, a Phaeacian bard, sing of the exploits of the Greek heroes at Troy. In the underworld, Agamemnon tells the story of his murder. The more the reader knows about Greek mythology, the richer these stories become, for each touches on and refers to other stories.

SYMBOLS IN *THE ODYSSEY*

EATING   Hunger and eating often have negative associations in the *Odyssey*, symbolizing lack of discipline or submission to temptation. When Odysseus and his men slaughter the Sun's flocks and eat the fruit of the lotus, they reveal their weakness. The suitors' constant eating symbolizes their sloth and greed. Odysseus kills the suitors just as they are starting their dinner, a scene Homer describes graphically. In almost all cases, the monsters of the *Odyssey* show their monstrosity by eating. Scylla swallows six of Odysseus's men, one for each head. The Cyclops eats humans and vomits up wine mixed with pieces of human flesh when he gets drunk. The Laestrygonians seem like nice people—until their queen, who is described as "huge as a mountain crag," tries to eat Odysseus and his men. In these cases, eating represents a total lack of humanity and civility.

THE WEDDING BED   The unmovable wedding bed in Book 23 symbolizes the constancy of Penelope and Odysseus's marriage. Only a single maidservant has ever seen the bed, which is where the happy couple spends their first night together after their twenty-year separation.

IMPORTANT QUOTATIONS FROM *THE ODYSSEY*

Sing to me of the man, Muse, the man of twists and turns
driven time and again off course, once he had plundered
the hallowed heights of Troy.
Many cities of men he saw and learned their minds,
many pains he suffered, heartsick on the open sea,
fighting to save his life and bring his comrades home.
But he could not save them from disaster, hard as he strove—
the recklessness of their own ways destroyed them all,
the blind fools, they devoured the cattle of the Sun
and the Sungod blotted out the day of their return.
Launch out on his story, Muse, daughter of Zeus,
start from where you will—sing for our time too.

Location: The first lines of the epic
Speaker: The poet
Context: The poet invokes the Muse and sums up the subject of his story

Following epic tradition, the poet asks for inspiration from the Muse and imagines her singing through him. He announces the subject of his epic, which will be a "man of twists and turns" rather than a man of strength and war like Achilles. The opening lines also foreshadow the end of the epic, which will see all of Odysseus's men dead except Odysseus himself. The poet blames these deaths on "the recklessness" of the crew. As Knox notes in the introduction to the Fagles translation, in the *Odyssey*, in contrast to the *Iliad*, Homer asks the Muse to choose where to begin. Giving the Muse this freedom prepares us for the more complex narrative structure of the *Odyssey*, which relies on flashbacks as it moves through the many settings of the hero's ten-year journey.

Of all that breathes and crawls across the earth,
our mother earth breeds nothing feebler than a man.
So long as the gods grant him power, spring in his knees,
he thinks he will never suffer affliction down the years.
But then, when the happy gods bring on the long hard times,
bear them he must, against his will, and steel his heart.
Our lives, our mood and mind as we pass across the earth,
turn as the days turn.

Location: 18.150–157
Speaker: Odysseus
Context: Odysseus, disguised as a beggar, talks to the suitor Amphinomus

Odysseus utters these words to Amphinomus shortly after defeating the "Beggar-King" Irus. He tells Amphinomus that he was once a great warrior who plundered faraway lands until one day he was captured. The fatalism and helplessness he expresses here were common to Ancient Greece, but they seem especially natural coming from a onetime king who has become a beggar. The words also foreshadow Amphinomus's death. Much as Odysseus's fictional king once did, Amphinomus is plundering the land of others and living a careless life, and like the fictional king, he is destined for a fall. The words are a prophecy and a warning to Amphinomus, and he does not miss their meaning. He walks away "fraught with grave forebodings" (18.176). Although Odysseus is lying about his identity, the words he speaks here truthfully sum up the lessons he has learned. At the hour of his greatest triumph, after he had sacked Troy and begun to look toward home, his life "turn[ed]" and the gods made him suffer. He endured only by "steel[ing] his heart" and accepting his troubles.

So then,
royal son of Laertes, Odysseus, man of exploits,
still eager to leave at once and hurry back
to your own home, your beloved native land?
Good luck to you, even so. Farewell!
But if you only knew, down deep, what pains
are fated to fill your cup before you reach that shore,
you'd stay right here, preside in our house with me
and be immortal.

Location: 5.223–232
Speaker: Calypso
Context: Begging Odysseus to stay with her, Calypso offers him immortality and warns him of danger

---

"But you, Achilles,
there's not a man in the world more blest than you —
there never has been, never will be one.
Time was, when you were alive, we Argives
honored you as a god, and now down here, I see,
you lord it over the dead in all your power.
So grieve no more at dying, great Achilles."
I reassured the ghost, but he broke out, protesting,
"No winning words about death to me, shining Odysseus!
By god, I'd rather slave on earth for another man —
some dirt-poor tenant farmer who scrapes to keep alive —
than rule down here over all the breathless dead."

Location: 11.547–558
Speaker: Odysseus
Context: In the underworld, Odysseus and Achilles talk about the merits of fame and life

---

Just as I
have come from afar, creating pain for many —
men and women across the good green earth —
so let his name be Odysseus ...
the Son of Pain, a name he'll earn in full.

Location: 19.460–464
Speaker: Autolycus
Context: Odysseus's grandfather explains the origin of Odysseus's name

THE OEDIPUS PLAYS

Sophocles

A king unwittingly kills his father and marries his mother; his sons kill each other; his daughter kills herself after insisting on burying her brother.

THE LIFE OF SOPHOCLES

Sophocles was born in 495 B.C. in Colonus, one mile north of Athens. His father, a wealthy man, provided Sophocles with a well-rounded education. When Sophocles was sixteen, he was chosen to lead, with dance and lyre, the chorus that celebrated the Greek victory at Salamis. At twenty-eight, he wrote a play that won a competition, defeating even the renowned dramatist Aeschylus, who was thirty years his senior. This victory marked the beginning of a dramatic career that produced over one hundred plays, of which only seven have survived intact.

Greek theater was very different from what we call theater today. Theater was part of a religious festival, so to attend a play was an act of worship. The god celebrated by the performances of these plays was Dionysus, a deity who lived in the wild and was known for his subversive revelry, drunkenness, and sexuality. The worship of Dionysus was associated with an ecstasy that bordered on madness. Every citizen attended the plays that celebrated Dionysus. Plays were often performed for as many as 15,000 spectators. At the end of each year's festivals, judges voted on the best play. It is thought that Sophocles won the first prize at the Athenian festival eighteen times.

Sophocles was one of the great innovators of theater, adding to the advancements that Aeschylus had made. Sophocles introduced a third actor to the stage, abbreviated the choral components, and emphasized dialogue. He was the first playwright to abandon the trilogy form, making each tragedy its own entity.

A deeply sensual, religious, and thoughtful dramatist, Sophocles was among the most popular and well-respected men of his day. In addition to his work as a playwright, he was one of ten generals responsible for waging the country's war against Samos. He was also an ordained priest of the god of medicine. For a time, he served as the director of the Treasury. He served on the Board of Generals in administration of the civil and military affairs of Athens. He died in 405 B.C. at the age of ninety.

THE OEDIPUS PLAYS IN CONTEXT

ANTIGONE

Antigone was probably the first of the three Theban plays that Sophocles wrote, although the events dramatized in it happen after the events of the other two plays in the cycle. Antigone is one of the first heroines in literature, a woman who fights against a male power structure, exhibiting greater bravery than any of the men who scorn her. *Antigone* is not only a feminist play but a radical one. It suggests that rebellion against authority is splendid and noble.

OEDIPUS THE KING

The story of Oedipus was well known to Sophocles' audience. Aristotle used this play and its plot as the supreme example of tragedy. Sigmund Freud famously based his theory of the Oedipal complex on this story, claiming that every boy has a latent desire to kill his father and sleep with his mother.

OEDIPUS AT COLONUS

By itself, *Oedipus at Colonus* is not a tragedy. It hardly even has a plot in the normal sense of the word. Critics think Sophocles wrote it toward the end of his life and the conclusion of the Golden Age of Athens. *Oedipus at Colonus* is a quiet and religious play without the dramatic fireworks of the others in the cycle.

THE OEDIPUS PLAYS: KEY FACTS

Time and place written: Antigone is believed to have been written around 441 B.C., *Oedipus the King* around 430 B.C., and *Oedipus at Colonus* around 406 B.C. All were written in Athens, Greece

Date of first publication: Unknown; the plays probably circulated in manuscript in fifth century B.C.

Publisher: Unknown

Type of work: Play

Genre: Tragedy

Language: Ancient Greek

Setting (time): The mythical past of ancient Greece

Setting (place): Antigone and *Oedipus the King* are set in Thebes, *Oedipus at Colonus* in Colonus (near Athens)

Tense: Present

Tone: Tragic

Protagonist: Antigone (*Antigone*), Oedipus (*Oedipus the King* and *Oedipus at Colonus*)

Antagonist: In *Antigone,* Creon; in *Oedipus the King,* Oedipus's fate; in *Oedipus at Colonus,* Oedipus's exile

THE OEDIPUS PLAYS: PLOT OVERVIEW

OEDIPUS THE KING

A plague strikes Thebes. The citizens gather outside the palace of their king, Oedipus, asking him to take action. Oedipus says he has sent his brother-in-law, Creon, to the Oracle at Delphi to learn how to help the city. Creon returns with a message from the Oracle: the plague will end when the murderer of Laius, former king of Thebes, is caught and expelled. Oedipus promises to do as the Oracle says.

Oedipus sends for Tiresias, the blind prophet, and asks him what he knows about the murder. Tiresias responds cryptically, lamenting his ability to see the truth when the truth brings nothing but pain. At last he reveals that Oedipus himself is the murderer. Oedipus refuses to believe this. He accuses Creon and Tiresias of conspiring against his life and charges Tiresias with insanity. He asks why Tiresias did nothing when Thebes suffered under a plague once before. Tiresias defends his skills as a prophet, noting that Oedipus's parents found him trustworthy. At this mention of his parents, Oedipus, who grew up in the distant city of Corinth, asks how Tiresias knew his parents. Tiresias answers enigmatically and puts forth one last riddle, saying that the murderer of Laius is father and brother to his own children and son to his own wife.

After Tiresias leaves, Oedipus threatens Creon with death or exile for conspiring with the prophet. Oedipus's wife, Jocasta (the widow of King Laius), enters and asks why the men are shouting at each other. Oedipus explains the accusation against him. Jocasta says all prophecies are silly, reminding him that the Delphic oracle once told Laius he would be murdered by his son, when in fact his son was cast out of Thebes as a baby, and Laius was murdered by a band of thieves. Her description of Laius's murder sounds familiar to Oedipus, and he asks her to elaborate. Jocasta tells him that Laius was killed at a three-way crossroads just before Oedipus arrived in Thebes. Oedipus, stunned, tells his wife that he may be the one who murdered Laius. Long ago, when he was the prince of Corinth, he overheard someone say that he was not really the son of the King and Queen of Corinth. He therefore traveled to the Oracle of Delphi, who did not answer him but did tell him he would murder his father and sleep with his mother. Oedipus fled, terrified that he would kill his father, Polybus, the King of Corinth. On the journey that would take him to Thebes, Oedipus was confronted and harassed by a group of travelers, whom he killed in self-defense. This skirmish occurred at the very crossroads where Laius was killed.

Oedipus sends for the man who survived the attack, a shepherd. Outside the palace, a messenger tells Jocasta that he has come from Corinth to inform Oedipus that his father, Polybus, is dead, and that Corinth wants Oedipus to rule in his place. Jocasta rejoices, convinced that Polybus's death from natural causes has disproved the prophecy that Oedipus would murder his father. Oedipus rejoices when he hears the news, although he still fears the prophecy that he will sleep with his mother.

The messenger remarks that Oedipus should not worry, because Polybus and his wife, Merope, are not Oedipus's biological parents. The messenger has an intimate knowledge of Oedipus's history, which he explains. One day long ago, he was tending his sheep when another shepherd approached him carrying a baby. The messenger took the baby to the royal family of Corinth, and they raised him as their own. That baby was Oedipus. Oedipus asks who the other shepherd was, and the messenger says he was a servant of Laius.

Jocasta, beginning to suspect the truth, begs her husband not to seek more information. She runs back into the palace. Laius's former servant, the shepherd, enters. He reveals that the baby he gave away was Laius's child. Jocasta gave him the baby, ordering him to kill it because of a prophecy that the baby would grow up to kill his parents. But the shepherd pitied the baby and decided that the prophecy could be avoided if he grew up in a foreign city. That is why he passed the boy on to the shepherd in Corinth.

Realizing who he is and who his parents are, Oedipus screams that he sees the truth and runs back into the palace. The shepherd and the messenger slowly exit. A second messenger enters and describes scenes of suffering. Jocasta has hanged herself, and Oedipus, finding her dead, has pulled the pins from her robe and stabbed out his own eyes. Oedipus now emerges from the palace, bleeding and begging to be exiled. He asks Creon to send him away from Thebes and to look after his daughters, Antigone and Ismene. Creon, covetous of royal power, is all too happy to oblige.

OEDIPUS AT COLONUS

After years of wandering in exile from Thebes, Oedipus arrives in a grove outside Athens. Blind and frail, he walks with the help of his daughter, Antigone. Oedipus and Antigone learn from a citizen that they are standing on holy ground reserved for the Eumenides, goddesses of fate. Oedipus sends the citizen to fetch Theseus, the king of Athens. Oedipus tells Antigone that Apollo once promised Oedipus that he would come to rest on this ground.

Oedipus's second daughter, Ismene, enters. She has returned from consulting Apollo's Oracle at Delphi. She tells her father that, back in Thebes, Oedipus's younger son, Eteocles, has overthrown Polynices, the elder, and that Polynices is now amassing troops for an attack on his brother and Creon, who rules along with Eteocles. The Oracle has predicted that Oedipus's burial place will bring good fortune to the city in which it is located. Creon and Oedipus's sons know of this prophecy and want to claim the right to bury him in their kingdoms. Oedipus swears he will never support either of his sons, for they did nothing to prevent his exile years ago.

King Theseus arrives and asks how he can help Oedipus. Oedipus asks Theseus to harbor him in Athens until his death, warning him that if he does this favor he will incur the wrath of Thebes. Theseus agrees to help Oedipus. When Creon finds he cannot abduct Oedipus, he kidnaps Antigone and Ismene instead. Theseus soon recovers Oedipus's daughters.

Polynices arrives, seeking his father's favor because he wants custody of his eventual burial site. Oedipus asks Theseus to drive Polynices away, but Antigone convinces her father to listen to his son. Polynices tells Oedipus that he never condoned his exile and that Eteocles is the bad son. Oedipus responds with a terrible curse, upbraiding his son for letting him be sent into exile and predicting that Eteocles and Polynices will die at each other's hands. Polynices asks his sisters to provide him with a proper burial should he die in battle. Antigone embraces Polynices, saying that he is condemning himself to death. He prays for the safety of his sisters and then leaves for Thebes.

Terrible thunder sounds, and the Chorus cries out in horror. Oedipus says that his time of death has come and sends for Theseus. Oedipus says he will lead Theseus to the place where he will die. Theseus must reveal that spot only on his own deathbed, passing it on to his son only, who in turn must pass it on to his own son. In this way, Theseus and his heirs will always rule over a safe city. Oedipus strides off with sudden strength, taking his daughters and Theseus to his grave.

A messenger enters to narrate the mysterious death of Oedipus. He seemed to disappear, "the lightless depths of Earth bursting open in kindness to receive him" (1886–1887). Antigone and Ismene enter, chanting a dirge. Antigone wails that they will cry for their father as long as they live. Theseus returns, and the women plead to see their father's tomb, but Theseus refuses. They ask for safe passage back to Thebes so that they may prevent a war between their brothers. Theseus grants them this, and the Chorus tells the women to stop their weeping, for all rests in the hands of the gods. Antigone and Ismene head for Thebes.

ANTIGONE

Antigone and Ismene, the daughters of Oedipus, discuss the disaster that has just befallen them. Their brothers Polynices and Eteocles have killed one another in a battle for control over Thebes, their city. Creon now rules the city, and he has said that because Polynices brought a foreign army against Thebes, he cannot have a proper burial. Creon threatens to kill anyone who tries to bury Polynices and stations sentries over his body. Antigone resolves to give their brother a proper burial.

A nervous sentry tells Creon that someone gave Polynices burial rites while the sentries slept. The sentries dig up Polynices and then catch Antigone in the act of attempting to rebury her brother. Antigone freely admits her guilt to Creon and says that he himself defies the will of the gods by refusing Polynices burial. Creon condemns Antigone and Ismene to death. Haemon, Creon's son and Antigone's fiancé, enters. Gradually, he condemns Creon's stubbornness and petty vindictiveness. Creon curses him and threatens to slay Antigone on the spot. Haemon storms out. Creon decides to pardon Ismene, but vows to kill Antigone by burying her alive in a tomb.

The blind prophet Tiresias arrives, and Creon promises to take whatever advice he gives. Tiresias advises Creon to allow Polynices to be buried. When Creon refuses, Tiresias predicts that the gods will bring down curses upon the city. Creon reluctantly goes to free Antigone from the tomb where she has been imprisoned.

A messenger enters and explains what happened next: Creon and his entourage buried Polynices properly. They heard what sounded like Haemon wailing from Antigone's tomb. They went into the tomb and found Antigone hanging from a noose, and Haemon raving. Creon's son thrust a sword at his father. Missing, he turned the sword against himself and died embracing Antigone's body. Creon's wife, Eurydice, hears this terrible news and rushes away into the palace. Creon enters, carrying Haemon's body and cursing his own tyranny, which he knows has caused his son's death. The messenger tells Creon that Eurydice has stabbed herself. As she died, she cursed her husband's pride. Creon kneels and prays that he too might die. His guards lead him back into the palace.

CHARACTERS IN THE OEDIPUS PLAYS

Antigone Oedipus's daughter and sister. Antigone is the most courageous, clearheaded character in the three Theban plays.

Chorus Sometimes comically obtuse or fickle, sometimes perceptive, sometimes melodramatic, the Chorus reacts to the events onstage.

Creon Oedipus's brother-in-law and Jocasta's brother. Over the course of the cycle, we see the gradual rise and fall of Creon's power. Creon rules Thebes with a stubborn blindness that is similar to Oedipus's rule. Unlike Oedipus, he is bossy and bureaucratic.

Eurydice Creon's wife.

Haemon Creon's son. Haemon is engaged to marry Antigone, whom he loves passionately.

Ismene Oedipus's daughter and sister. Fear prevents her from helping Antigone bury Polynices. Her ordinariness underscores Antigone's grandeur and courage.

Jocasta Oedipus's wife and mother, and Creon's sister. Jocasta is a peacemaker. She comforts Oedipus and calmly urges him to reject Tiresias's terrifying prophecies. Jocasta solves the riddle of Oedipus's identity before Oedipus does, and she shows her love for her son and husband by urging him to remain ignorant of his true origins.

Oedipus King of Thebes, wife and son of Jocasta, son of Laius, and father of Antigone and Ismene. Oedipus is renowned for his intelligence and cleverness—he saved Thebes and became its king by solving the riddle of the Sphinx. Yet Oedipus is stubbornly blind to the truth about himself.

Polynices Oedipus's son and brother. When he seeks his father's blessing, he tries to look loyal but comes off as opportunistic.

Theseus The king of Athens in *Oedipus at Colonus*. A renowned and powerful warrior, Theseus takes pity on Oedipus and defends him against Creon.

Tiresias The blind soothsayer of Thebes. Both Oedipus and Creon claim to trust Tiresias deeply, but they often refuse to believe him. The literal blindness of the soothsayer points to the metaphorical blindness of those who refuse to believe unpleasant truths about themselves.

THEMES IN THE OEDIPUS PLAYS

THE POWER OF UNWRITTEN LAW Creon rigidly insists on following written laws, which leads to disaster. After defeating Polynices and taking the throne of Thebes, Creon commands that Polynices be left to rot unburied, his flesh eaten by dogs and birds, creating an "obscenity" for everyone to see (*Antigone*, 231). Creon thinks that treating Polynices this way is justified because Polynices was a traitor, an enemy of the state. But subsequent events demonstrate that some duties are more fundamental than the duty to obey the state and its laws. Burying the disgraced dead might not be a law of the state, but it is an unwritten law of humanity, an instinct that must be honored. Moral duties make up a body of unwritten law and tradition that is often more important than the written laws of the state.

THE WILLINGNESS TO IGNORE THE TRUTH So desperate are Oedipus and Jocasta to close their eyes to reality that they pin all their hopes on one servant's story. Jocasta says the servant told her Laius was killed by "strangers," whereas Oedipus knows that he acted alone when he killed a man in similar circumstances. Oedipus and Jocasta act as though the servant's story is irrefutable history because they are terrified to consider what it would mean if the servant had gotten that detail wrong. This is perhaps why Jocasta feels she can tell Oedipus of the prophecy that her son would kill his father, and Oedipus can tell her about the similar prophecy given him by an oracle (867–875), and neither feels compelled to remark on the coincidence; or why Oedipus can hear the story of Jocasta binding her child's ankles (780–781) and not think of his own swollen feet. The information in these speeches makes the audience painfully aware of the tragic irony and emphasizes how desperately Oedipus and Jocasta do not want to speak the obvious truth.

THE LIMITS OF FREE WILL Sophocles suggests that people have little power over their own lives. All of the prophecies that fill *Oedipus the King* turn out to be true, a sign of Sophocles' faith in the powers of the gods and prophets, which had recently come under attack in fifth-century B.C. Athens. Sophocles' audience knew the story of Oedipus, which must have intensified the sense of complete inevitability about how the play would end. Fate chases Oedipus with grim intensity. When he is sent away from Thebes to his death, by a remarkable coincidence he is saved and raised as a prince in Corinth. When he hears that he is fated to kill his father, he flees Corinth and, by a still more remarkable coincidence, ends up back in Thebes, becoming king and husband in his father's place. Oedipus knows what his fate should be and struggles mightily against it, but his efforts are useless. Many critics argue that Oedipus brings catastrophe on himself because he has a "tragic flaw," but there is no consensus on what that flaw is. Perhaps his story is meant to show that disaster can happen to anyone, that humans are relatively powerless before fate and the gods, and that cautious humility is the best attitude toward life.

SYMBOLS IN THE OEDIPUS PLAYS

OEDIPUS'S SWOLLEN FOOT "Oedipus" literally means "swollen foot." Oedipus was so named because Laius left him in the mountains with his ankles pinned together, a condition that left a vivid scar. Oedipus's injury symbolizes the way fate has marked him and set him apart. It also symbolizes the confinement of his movements, a confinement that he imposes on himself in an effort to avoid the prophecy.

THE THREE-WAY CROSSROADS Laius was slain at a place where three roads meet. This crossroads, to which characters refer a number of times, symbolizes the crucial moment when Oedipus began to fulfill the prophecy that he would murder his father and marry his mother. They also symbolize the overwhelming power of fate.

IMPORTANT QUOTATIONS FROM THE OEDIPUS PLAYS

My own flesh and blood—dear sister, dear Ismene, how many griefs our father Oedipus handed down! Do you know one, I ask you, one grief that Zeus will not perfect for the two of us while we still live and breathe? There's nothing, no pain—our lives are pain—no private shame, no public disgrace, nothing I haven't seen in your grief and mine.

Location: Antigone, 1–8
Speaker: Antigone
Context: Antigone decries the family fate

Antigone's first words in *Antigone*, "My own flesh and blood," vividly encapsulate the play's concern with familial relationships. *Antigone* is a play about the legacy of incest and about a sister's love for her brother. Family members have been destined to couple unnaturally—in sex, violence, or both—since Oedipus's rash, unwitting slaying of his father. Antigone says that griefs are "handed down" in Oedipus's family, likening grief to an unwanted family heirloom. In these lines, Antigone seems like a dangerous woman capable of desperate behavior. She knows she has nothing to lose, telling Ismene, "Do you know one, I ask you, one grief / that Zeus will not perfect for the two of us / while we still live and breathe?" Before we even have time to imagine what the next grief might be, Antigone reveals it: Creon will not allow her brother Polynices to be buried. Ismene, like the audience, is one step behind Antigone. From the outset, Antigone is the only one who sees what is really going on, the only one willing to speak up and point out the truth.

People of Thebes, my countrymen, look on Oedipus. He solved the famous riddle with his brilliance, he rose to power, a man beyond all power. Who could behold his greatness without envy? Now what a black sea of terror has overwhelmed him. Now as we keep our watch and wait the final day, count no man happy till he dies, free of pain at last.

Location: Oedipus the King, 1678–1684
Speaker: The Chorus
Context: The Chorus ends the play on a cold note

It is an indisputable fact that Oedipus "solved the famous riddle [of the Sphinx] with his brilliance." So is the claim that he "rose to power," to an enviable greatness. In mentioning these facts in the same breath that it mentions his downfall, the Chorus suggests a causal link between Oedipus's rise and his fall—that is, Oedipus fell because he rose too high, because in his pride he inspired others to "envy." But the causal relationship is never explicitly established, and ultimately all the Chorus demonstrates is a progression of time: "he rose to power, a man beyond all power. / . . . / Now what a black sea of terror has overwhelmed him." These lines are objective and terrifying. They have none of the comfort the audience expects, because they refuse to explain the moral of the story. The only moral is, "Remember that even if you're happy now, something terrible might happen to you soon."

Anarchy—show me a greater crime in all the earth! She, she destroys cities, rips up houses, breaks the ranks of spearmen into headlong rout. But the ones who last it out, the great mass of them owe their lives to discipline. Therefore we must defend the men who live by law, never let some woman triumph over us. Better to fall from power, if fall we must, at the hands of a man—never be rated inferior to a woman, never.

Location: Antigone, 751–761
Speaker: Creon
Context: Creon tells the chorus that anarchy, which he equates with women, is the greatest crime on earth

Fear? What should a man fear? It's all chance, chance rules our lives. Not a man on earth can see a day ahead, groping through the dark. Better to live at random, best we can. And as for this marriage with your mother—have no fear. Many a man before you, in his dreams, has shared his mother's bed. Take such things for shadows, nothing at all— Live, Oedipus, as if there's no tomorrow!

Location: Oedipus the King, 1068–1078
Speaker: Jocasta
Context: Jocasta insists that prophecies are silly

Stop, my children, weep no more. Here where the dark forces store up kindness both for living and the dead, there is no room for grieving here—it might bring down the anger of the gods.

Location: Oedipus at Colonus, 1970–1974
Speaker: Theseus
Context: Theseus expresses the unusual sentiment that grief is not always desirable, and insists on making Oedipus's death an end to, rather than the beginning of, more disasters

OF MICE AND MEN

John Steinbeck

Two migrant workers and best friends find tragedy when one of them accidentally kills a woman.

THE LIFE OF JOHN STEINBECK

John Steinbeck was born in Salinas, California, on February 27, 1902. He attended Stanford University but did not graduate. Steinbeck began writing novels in 1929, but he garnered little commercial or critical success until the publication of *Tortilla Flat* in 1935. In his fiction, Steinbeck frequently delved into the lives of the downtrodden. A trio of novels in the late 1930s focus on the lives of migrant workers in California: *In Dubious Battle* (1936), *Of Mice and Men* (1937), and Steinbeck's masterpiece, *The Grapes of Wrath* (1939), which soared to the top of the bestseller lists and sold half a million copies. In 1940, the novel was awarded the Pulitzer Prize and adapted to the screen. Steinbeck won the Novel Prize for Literature in 1962.

Critical opinions of Steinbeck's work have always been mixed. Both stylistically and in his emphasis on manhood and male relationships, Steinbeck was strongly influenced by his contemporary, Ernest Hemingway. Even though Steinbeck was hailed as a great author in the 1930s and 1940s, many critics have called his work superficial, sentimental, and overly moralistic.

Steinbeck continued writing throughout the 1940s and 1950s. He went to Europe during World War II, then worked in Hollywood both as a filmmaker and a scriptwriter. His important later works include *East of Eden* (1952) and *Travels with Charley* (1962). He died in New York City in 1968.

OF MICE AND MEN IN CONTEXT

After World War I, economic and ecological forces brought many rural poor and migrant agricultural workers from the Great Plains states to California. In the early 1930s, a severe drought led to massive agricultural failure in parts of the southern Great Plains, particularly in western Oklahoma and the Texas panhandle. In the absence of rain, crops withered and died. Wind picked up the topsoil and carried it in billowing clouds across the region. Huge dust storms occasionally blocked out the sun and suffocated those caught unprepared. The afflicted region came to be known as the Dust Bowl.

By the mid-1930s, the drought had crippled countless farm families, and America had fallen into the Great Depression. Unable to pay their mortgages or buy necessary industrial equipment, many Dust Bowl farmers were forced to leave their land. Thousands of families flooded California, hoping to find work. Jobs and food were scarce, and the migrants faced prejudice and hostility from Californians, who gave them the derisive epithet "Okie." These workers and their families lived in impoverished camps called Hoovervilles, named after President Hoover, who was blamed for the problems that led to the Great Depression. Many camp residents starved to death.

In several of his novels, including *Of Mice and Men*, Steinbeck illustrates the grueling life of migrant farmers. The economic desperation of the Great Depression victimized workers like George and Lennie, whose quest for land was thwarted by forces beyond their control.

OF MICE AND MEN: KEY FACTS

Time and place written: Mid-1930s; Pacific Grove and Los Gatos ranch, California	
Date of first publication: 1937	
Publisher: Covici, Friede, Inc.	
Type of work: Novel	
Genre: Social protest novel	
Language: English	
Setting (time): 1930s	

Setting (place): South of Soledad, California

Tense: Past

Tone: Sentimental, tragic, doomed, fatalistic, rustic, moralistic, comic

Narrator: Third-person omniscient

Point of view: The narrator's

Protagonist: George and Lennie

Antagonist: Curley, society

OF MICE AND MEN: PLOT OVERVIEW

Two migrant workers, George and Lennie, have been let off a bus miles away from the California farm where they want to seek work. George is a small, dark man with "sharp, strong features." Lennie, is a giant of a man with a "shapeless" face. Overcome with thirst, the two stop in a clearing by a pool and decide to camp for the night. As the men talk, it becomes clear that Lennie has a mild mental disability and is deeply devoted to George and dependent on him for protection and guidance. George finds that Lennie, who loves petting soft things but often accidentally kills them, has been carrying and stroking a dead mouse. He angrily throws it away, fearing that Lennie might catch a disease from the dead animal. George complains loudly that his life would be easier if he didn't have to care for Lennie, but Steinbeck suggests that their friendship and devotion is mutual. George and Lennie share a dream of buying their own piece of land, farming it, and keeping rabbits. George ends the night by treating Lennie to the story he often tells him about what life will be like in such an idyllic place.

The next day, the men report to the ranch. George lies to the boss, saying that he and Lennie are cousins and that Lennie was kicked in the head by a horse when he was a child. They are hired. They meet Candy, an old "swamper," or handyman, with a missing hand and an ancient dog, and Curley, the boss's mean-spirited son. Curley is newly married, possessive of his flirtatious wife, and full of jealous suspicion. Once George and Lennie are alone in the bunkhouse, Curley's wife appears and flirts with them. Lennie thinks she is pretty, but George warns him to stay away from her. George and Lennie meet Slim, a skilled mule driver who has great authority on the ranch. Slim comments on the rarity of the kind of friendship George and Lennie share. Carlson, another ranch-hand, suggests that since Slim's dog has just given birth, they should offer a puppy to Candy and shoot Candy's old, good-for-nothing dog.

The next day, George tells Slim that he and Lennie are not cousins, but have been friends since childhood. Lennie has often gotten them into trouble. They were forced to leave their last job because Lennie tried to touch a woman's dress and was accused of rape. Slim agrees to give Lennie one of his puppies, and Carlson continues to badger Candy to kill his old dog. When Slim agrees with Carlson, saying that death would be a welcome relief to the suffering animal, Candy gives in. Carlson promises to do the job painlessly.

Slim goes to the barn to do some work, and Curley, who is searching for his wife, heads to the barn to accost him. Candy overhears George and Lennie discussing their plans to buy land and offers his life's savings if they will let him live there too. The three make a pact to let no one else know of their plan. Curley, searching for an easy target for his anger, finds Lennie and picks a fight with him. Lennie crushes Curley's hand in the altercation. Slim warns Curley that if he tries to get George and Lennie fired, he will be the laughingstock of the farm.

The next night, most of the men go to the local brothel. Lennie is left with Crooks, the lonely, black stable-hand, and Candy. Curley's wife flirts with them, refusing to leave until the other men come home. She notices the cuts on Lennie's face and suspects that he is the one who hurt her husband. This thought amuses her. The next day, Lennie accidentally kills his puppy in the barn. Curley's wife comes in and consoles him. She admits that life with Curley is a disappointment and that she wishes she had followed her dream of becoming a movie star. Lennie tells her that he loves petting soft things, and she offers to let him feel her hair. When he grabs too tightly, she cries out. In his attempt to silence her, he accidentally breaks her neck.

Lennie goes to a pool of the Salinas River that George designated as a meeting place should either of them get into trouble. As the men back at the ranch discover what has happened and gather together a lynch party, George joins Lennie. Much to Lennie's surprise, George is not mad at him for doing "a bad thing." George begins to tell Lennie the story of the farm they will have together. As he describes the rabbits that Lennie will tend, he hears the lynch party approaching. George shoots Lennie in the back of the head.

When the other men arrive, George lets them believe that George wrestled the gun away from Lennie and shot him. Only Slim understands that George has killed his friend out of mercy. Slim leads him away, and the other men, puzzled, watch them leave.

CHARACTERS IN *OF MICE AND MEN*

The Boss The stocky, well-dressed man in charge of the ranch. The boss is Curley's father. He appears only once in the novel, but he seems to be a fair-minded man. Candy reports that once the boss delivered a gallon of whiskey to the ranch-hands on Christmas Day.

Candy An aging ranch handyman. Candy lost his hand in an accident and worries about his future on the ranch. The fate of Candy's ancient dog, which Carlson shoots in the back of the head in an alleged act of mercy, foreshadows Lennie's death.

Carlson A ranch-hand. Carlson complains bitterly about Candy's old, smelly dog and urges Candy to put the dog out of its misery.

Aunt Clara Lennie's aunt. She appears only at the end of the novel, chastising Lennie for causing trouble for George. She was a kind, patient woman who took good care of Lennie and gave him plenty of mice to pet.

Crooks The black stable-hand. Crooks gets his name from his crooked back. Proud, bitter, and caustically funny, he is isolated from the other men because he is black.

Curley The boss's son. Curley wears high-heeled boots to distinguish himself from the field hands. Rumored to be a champion prizefighter, he is confrontational, mean-spirited, and aggressive. Curley is violently possessive of his flirtatious young wife.

Curley's Wife The only female character in the novel. Curley's wife is never given a name. The men on the farm refer to her as a "tramp," a "tart," and a "looloo." In her fancy, feathered red shoes, she represents the temptation of female sexuality in a male-dominated world. Like the ranch-hands, she is desperately lonely and yearns for a better life.

George A small, wiry, quick-witted man. George is devoted to Lennie, whose childlike faith in their imaginary idyllic farm gives George strength.

Lennie A large, lumbering, childlike man. Due to his mild mental disability, Lennie completely depends on George for guidance and protection. Gentle and kind, Lennie does not understand his own strength.

Slim A highly skilled mule driver and the acknowledged "prince" of the ranch. Slim is the only character who seems to be at peace with himself. The other characters often look to quiet, insightful Slim for advice.

Whit A ranch-hand.

THEMES IN *OF MICE AND MEN*

THE CRUELTY OF THE WEAK *Of Mice and Men* characterizes human existence as essentially lonely and isolated. Nearly all of the characters, including George, Lennie, Candy, Crooks, and Curley's wife, admit to feeling alone. Each longs for the comfort of a friend but will settle for the attentive ear of a stranger. But victimization doesn't make people kind or sympathetic to the problems of others. Even at their weakest, characters seek to destroy those who are even weaker than they. Perhaps the most cruel example of this tendency comes when Crooks explains his own insecurities and then criticizes Lennie's dream of the farm and his dependence on George. In scenes such as this one, Steinbeck records an uncomfortable truth: oppressing others can make the weak feel strong. Crooks puffs himself up by convincing Lennie that something bad has happened to George, just as Curley's wife feels most powerful when she threatens to have Crooks lynched. The novel suggests that the excessive use of strength is motivated by weakness.

THE IDEALIZATION OF MALE FRIENDSHIP Some of the characters in the novel idealize male friendship, which is one of the reasons that the dream of the farm appeals to them so strongly. The farm on which George and Lennie plan to live has a magnetic quality. After hearing a very brief description of the farm, Candy is completely drawn in by its magic. Crooks has witnessed countless men fall under the same silly spell, and even he finds himself asking Lennie if he can have a patch of garden to hoe there. The farm would allow the men to live together like brothers, thinking of each other's best interests, protecting each other, and working together for the good of the group. The tragic end of George and Lennie's friendship is so upsetting partially because it also ends the dream of the farm. Steinbeck suggests that the ideal of male friendship embodied by Lennie and George cannot survive in such a harsh, predatory world.

THE UNREALITY OF THE AMERICAN DREAM Most of the characters in *Of Mice and Men* admit that they dream of a different life. Curley's wife confesses her desire to be a movie star. Crooks allows himself the pleasant fantasy of hoeing a patch of garden on Lennie's farm one day. Candy desperately latches onto George's vision of owning a couple of acres. But even before the action of the novel begins, circumstances have made these dreams impossible. Steinbeck points out that the American Dream is a fiction. George and Lennie's vision of owning a farm is a prototypical American ideal, a plan to find modest success through hard work—but Steinbeck and the characters recognize that even this humble dream is absurd, impossible, almost melodramatic.

SYMBOLS IN *OF MICE AND MEN*

LENNIE'S PUPPY Lennie's puppy symbolizes Lennie. Lennie kills the puppy accidentally, failing to recognize his own strength. The puppy is crushed, as Lennie is, by powerful forces it cannot understand.

CANDY'S DOG Candy's dog symbolizes worthy but undervalued elderly people. Once a fine sheepdog, useful on the ranch, Candy's mutt is now debilitated by age, and only Candy thinks it should be honored simply because it is a beloved being that has lived a useful life. Carlson's insistence that the old animal must die points to the cruel natural law that the strong will dispose of the weak.

IMPORTANT QUOTATIONS FROM *OF MICE AND MEN*

A guy sets alone out here at night, maybe readin' books or thinkin' or stuff like that. Sometimes he gets thinkin', an' he got nothing to tell him what's so an' what ain't so. Maybe if he sees somethin', he don't know whether it's right or not. He can't turn to some other guy and ast him if he sees it too. He can't tell. He got nothing to measure by. I seen things out here. I wasn't drunk. I don't know if I was asleep. If some guy was with me, he could tell me I was asleep, an' then it would be all right. But I jus' don't know.

Location: Section 4
Speaker: Crooks
Context: Crooks tells Lennie about his loneliness

When Lennie visits Crooks in his room, Crooks admits to the same kind of loneliness that George says plagues men without good friends. Both Crooks's race and his physical handicap force him to live on the periphery of ranch life. He is not even allowed to enter the white men's bunkhouse or join them in a game of cards. He usually expresses his resentment in his bitter, caustic wit, but in this passage he displays a rare and touching vulnerability. Crooks's desire for a friend by whom to "measure" things echoes George's earlier description of the life of a migrant worker.

A water snake glided smoothly up the pool, twisting its periscope head from side to side; and it swam the length of the pool and came to the legs of a motionless heron that stood in the shallows. A silent head and beak lanced down and plucked it out by the head, and the beak swallowed the little snake while its tail waved frantically.

Location: The beginning of Section 6
Speaker: The narrator
Context: After killing Curley's wife, Lennie returns to the clearing

The clearing George designates a safe haven is a symbolic Garden of Eden, a beautiful, natural paradise with a shaded pool. But after Lennie kills Curley's wife, the paradise is lost. The snake is a complicated symbol. Traditionally, snakes symbolize sin, for it was a snake that corrupted Eve in the Garden of Eden. In this passage, however, the snake is not the aggressor, but the victim. Like Lennie, the snake seems dangerous at first—and may actually be dangerous—but is easily defeated by an unexpected force. The death of the snake symbolizes Lennie's impending death. He will die, as the snake does, without ever suspecting the nearness of the final blow.

Guys like us, that work on ranches, are the loneliest guys in the world. They got no family. They don't belong no place.. . . . With us it ain't like that. We got a future. We got somebody to talk to that gives a damn about us. We don't have to sit in no bar room blowin' in our jack jus' because we got no place else to go. If them other guys gets in jail they can rot for all anybody gives a damn. But not us.

Location: The end of Section 1
Speaker: George
Context: Before George and Lennie reach the ranch, George articulates the pleasures of their friendship

---

"S'pose they was a carnival or a circus come to town, or a ball game, or any damn thing." Old Candy nodded in appreciation of the idea. "We'd just go to her," George said. "We wouldn't ask nobody if we could. Jus' say, 'We'll go to her,' an' we would. Jus' milk the cow and sling some grain to the chickens an' go to her."

Location: The middle of Section 3
Speaker: The narrator
Context: George enumerates the pleasures of owning a farm

I seen hundreds of men come by on the road an' on the ranches, with their bindles on their back an' that same damn thing in their heads . . . every damn one of 'em's got a little piece of land in his head. An' never a God damn one of 'em ever gets it. Just like heaven. Ever'body wants a little piece of lan'. I read plenty of books out here. Nobody never gets to heaven, and nobody gets no land.

Location: Section 4
Speaker: Crooks
Context: Crooks tries to shoot down Lennie's dreams

THE OLD MAN AND THE SEA

Ernest Hemingway

An old man shows his nobility when he kills a glorious marlin.

THE LIFE OF ERNEST HEMINGWAY

Ernest Hemingway was born in Oak Park, Illinois, in the summer of 1899. He later described his middle-class parents in harsh terms, condemning them for their conventional morality and values. As a young man, he left home to become a newspaper writer in Kansas City. Early in 1918, he joined the Italian Red Cross. He served as an ambulance driver in Italy during World War I, in which the Italians allied with the British, French, and Americans against Germany and Austria-Hungary. During his time abroad, Hemingway had two experiences that affected him profoundly and that would later inspire one of his most celebrated novels, *A Farewell to Arms*. The first occurred on July 8, 1918, when a trench mortar shell struck him as he crouched beyond the front lines with three Italian soldiers. Hemingway embellished the story over the years, so the actual facts are difficult to ascertain, but it is certain that he was transferred to a hospital in Milan, where he fell in love with a Red Cross nurse named Agnes von Kurowsky. Scholars are divided over Agnes's role in Hemingway's life and writing, but there is little doubt that his relationship with her informed the relationship between Lieutenant Henry and Catherine Barkley in *A Farewell to Arms*.

After his recovery, Hemingway spent several years as a reporter, during which time he honed the clear, concise, and emotionally evocative writing style that generations of authors after him would imitate. In September 1921, he married and settled in Paris, where he made valuable connections with American expatriate writers like Gertrude Stein and Ezra Pound. Hemingway's landmark collection of stories, *In Our Time*, introduced Nick Adams, one of the author's favorite protagonists, whose difficult road from youth into maturity he chronicled. Hemingway's reputation as a writer was most firmly established by the publication of *The Sun Also Rises* in 1926 and *A Farewell to Arms* in 1929.

In his writing and in his life, Hemingway embodied a specific kind of masculinity. He was devoted to big-game hunting, fishing, boxing, and bullfighting, endeavors he tried to master as seriously as he did writing. Most critics maintain that Hemingway's writing fizzled after World War II, when his physical and mental health declined. Despite fantastic bouts of depression, Hemingway did muster enough energy to write *The Old Man and the Sea*, one of his most beloved stories, in 1952. This novella earned him a Pulitzer Prize, and three years later Hemingway was awarded the Nobel Prize in Literature. Still, not even these accolades could soothe the devastating effects of a lifetime of debilitating depression. On July 2, 1961, Hemingway killed himself in his home in Ketchum, Idaho.

THE OLD MAN AND THE SEA IN CONTEXT

The Old Man and the Sea was a huge critical and popular success when it was first published. The Nobel Academy cited it for particular recognition. Since then, however, it has been met by divided critical opinion. While some critics have praised *The Old Man and the Sea* as a new classic on par with such established American works as William Faulkner's "The Bear" and Herman Melville's *Moby-Dick*, others have attacked it as "imitation Hemingway" and found fault with Hemingway's departure from the uncompromising realism that once characterized his work.

Because Hemingway always relied heavily on autobiographical sources, some critics interpreted *The Old Man and the Sea* as a thinly veiled assault on them. In this reading, the frenzied fish symbolizes critics on the attack, and the old man symbolizes Hemingway. But this reading is too reductive to be convincing. The more compelling interpretation sees the novella as a parable about life itself, about man's struggle for survival in a world that seems designed to destroy him.

THE OLD MAN AND THE SEA: KEY FACTS

Time and place written: 1951; Cuba

Date of first publication: 1952

Publisher: Scribner's

Type of work: Novella

Genre: Parable; novella

Language: English

Setting (time): Late 1940s

Setting (place): A small fishing village near Havana, Cuba; the waters of the Gulf of Mexico

Tense: Past

Tone: Journalistic, matter-of-fact

Narrator: Limited omniscient narrator in the third person

Point of view: The narrator's and Santiago's

Protagonist: Santiago

Antagonist: A great fish

THE OLD MAN AND THE SEA: PLOT OVERVIEW

For eighty-four days, Santiago, an aged Cuban fisherman, has set out to sea and returned empty-handed. Manolin, his devoted apprentice and friend, has been forced by his parents to leave the old man and fish in a more prosperous boat. Nevertheless, Manolin continues to care for the old man upon his return each night. He helps Santiago tote his gear to his ramshackle hut, secures food for him, and discusses the latest developments in American baseball, especially the trials of Santiago's hero, Joe DiMaggio. Santiago is confident that his streak of bad luck will soon come to an end, and he resolves to sail out farther than usual the following day.

On the eighty-fifth day of his dry spell, Santiago sails his skiff far beyond the island's shallow coastal waters and ventures into the Gulf Stream. He prepares his lines and drops them. At noon, a large marlin takes the bait that Santiago has placed one hundred fathoms deep. The old man expertly hooks the fish, but he cannot pull it in. Instead, the fish begins to pull the boat.

Santiago worries that if he tied the line to the boat, the fish would snap the line, so he bears the strain of the line with his shoulders, back, and hands. The fish pulls the boat for two days and nights, swimming steadily northwest until at last it tires and swims east with the current. Whenever the fish lunges, leaps, or makes a dash for freedom, the cord cuts Santiago badly. The old man feels deep empathy and admiration for the marlin, his brother in suffering, strength, and resolve.

On the third day, the fish tires. Even though Santiago is sleep-deprived, aching, and nearly delirious, he manages to pull the marlin in close enough to kill it with a harpoon thrust. The marlin is the largest Santiago has ever seen. He lashes it to his boat, raises the small mast, and sets sail for home. Santiago is excited by the price that the marlin will bring at market, but he is more concerned that the people who will eat the fish will be unworthy of its greatness.

As Santiago sails on, the marlin's blood leaves a trail in the water and attracts sharks. A great mako shark attacks, and Santiago manages to slay it with the harpoon. In the struggle, the old man loses his harpoon and lengths of valuable rope, which leaves him vulnerable to other shark attacks. Vicious sharks attack in succession, and Santiago fights them off as best he can, stabbing at them with a crude spear he makes by lashing a knife to an oar, and even clubbing them with the boat's tiller. Although he kills several sharks, more and more appear, and by the time night falls, Santiago's fight is useless. Sharks devour the marlin's precious meat, leaving only its skeleton, head, and tail. Santiago chastises himself for going "out too far," and for sacrificing his great and worthy opponent. He arrives home before daybreak, stumbles back to his shack, and falls into a deep sleep.

The next morning, a crowd of amazed fishermen gathers around the skeleton, which is still lashed to the boat. Tourists at a nearby café observe the remains of the giant marlin and mistake it for a shark. Manolin, who has been worried sick about the old man's absence, is moved to tears when he finds Santiago safe in his bed. The boy fetches the old man some coffee and the daily papers with the baseball scores, and watches him sleep. When Santiago wakes, the two agree to fish as partners once more. The old man falls asleep again and dreams his usual dream of lions at play on the beaches of Africa.

CHARACTERS IN *THE OLD MAN AND THE SEA*

Manolin Santiago's young apprentice and devoted attendant. Manolin loves Santiago and takes good care of him.

The Marlin An eighteen-foot fish. Santiago feels a fraternal connection with the fish. Hemingway compares both Santiago and the marlin to Christ.

Martin A café owner in Santiago's village. Martin does not appear in the novella. He is a kind man who often provides Santiago with supper.

Perico The owner of the bodega in Santiago's village. Perico never appears in the novella. He provides Santiago with newspapers that report the baseball scores.

Santiago The old man of the novella's title. Santiago is a Cuban fisherman who is humble but proud of his abilities. His has an unparalleled knowledge of the sea and of his craft, which helps him stay optimistic even during his long spell of bad luck.

THEMES IN *THE OLD MAN AND THE SEA*

THE HONOR IN STRUGGLE, DEFEAT, AND DEATH Santiago believes that "man can be destroyed but not defeated." Hemingway suggests that even though death is inevitable, it only defeats us if we struggle against it with honor and courage. Santiago and the marlin show us how to accomplish this struggle. They fight to the death because they must, not because they enjoy the struggle. As worthy opponents who know they must kill or be killed, they fight with honor and respect for each other. As Santiago reflects when he watches a weary warbler fly toward shore, where it will inevitably meet a hawk, the world is filled with predators, and no living thing can escape the inevitable struggle that will lead to its death. By battling the inevitable, creatures prove themselves. One way man proves himself strong and honorable is by choosing worthy opponents. If a man admires his opponent, his fatal fight with him mixes love and respect with death. At the end of the novella, Santiago has emerged as a hero, destroyed but victorious.

PRIDE AS THE SOURCE OF GREATNESS Santiago worries that he is too proud. After sharks destroy the marlin, he apologizes again and again to his worthy opponent, saying he has ruined them both by sailing beyond the usual boundaries. But even though Santiago's attempt to prove himself a vital fisherman leads to disaster, Hemingway does not condemn his protagonist. On the contrary, he applauds him as proof that pride motivates men to achieve great things. Pride motivates the kill that allows Santiago to transcend defeat. It also allows him to meet each challenge with unwavering determination. When the first shark arrives, Santiago is "full of resolution" even though he has "little hope." He knowingly risks death first to bring in the marlin and then to battle the hungry sharks. Although he returns to Havana without the trophy of his long battle, he returns with the knowledge that he has acquitted himself proudly and manfully—knowledge that, because it will last forever, is more satisfying than the temporary pleasure of the marlin's flesh.

THE HOLINESS OF HONORABLE MEN Hemingway suggests the profundity of Santiago's fight and the glory derived from it by likening him to Christ. When the fishing line cuts Santiago's palms, we are reminded of Christ's stigmata. Later, when the sharks arrive, Hemingway portrays Santiago as a crucified martyr, likening the noise he makes to the noise made by a man whose tormentors are driving nails through his hands. The image of Santiago struggling up the hill with his mast across his shoulders recalls Christ marching toward Calvary with his own cross on his back. Even the position in which Santiago collapses on his bed—face down with his arms out straight and the palms of his hands up—brings to mind the image of Christ suffering on the cross. With these images, Hemingway suggests that Santiago is Christlike because he turns loss into gain, defeat into triumph, and even death into renewed life.

SYMBOLS IN *THE OLD MAN AND THE SEA*

THE MARLIN The marlin symbolizes the ideal opponent. In a world in which "everything kills everything else in some way," Santiago feels genuinely lucky to find himself matched against a creature that brings out the best in him: his strength and courage, his love and respect.

THE SHOVEL-NOSED SHARKS The shovel-nosed sharks symbolize the destructive elements in the universe. Little more than moving appetites, they thoughtlessly and gracelessly attack the marlin. They are unworthy of Santiago's effort and strength.

IMPORTANT QUOTATIONS FROM *THE OLD MAN AND THE SEA* ˙

He no longer dreamed of storms, nor of women, nor of great occurrences, nor of great fish, nor fights, nor contests of strength, nor of his wife. He only dreamed of places now and of the lions on the beach. They played like young cats in the dusk and he loved them as he loved the boy.

Location: The first day
Speaker: The narrator
Context: Santiago dreams of lions on the night before he sets out on his voyage

Critics disagree about the meaning of the lions playing on the African beach, which Hemingway mentions three times in *The Old Man and the Sea*. All agree, however, that the image comforts Santiago. This passage simultaneously confirms and moves beyond Hemingway's usual subject matter. Hemingway made his career telling stories about "great occurrences," "great fish," and "contests of strength." The fact that Santiago no longer dreams of any of these makes him unique among Hemingway's heroes. By dreaming of lions, he places himself in a recognizably Hemingwayesque world, but the lions he dreams of are at play and have nothing to do with hunting or contests. They suggest that in old age, once-virile men take comfort in peaceful memories of youth, not in exciting memories of old battles or torrid affairs.

Then the fish came alive, with his death in him, and rose high out of the water showing all his great length and width and all his power and his beauty. He seemed to hang in the air above the old man in the skiff. Then he fell into the water with a crash that sent spray over the old man and over all of the skiff.

Location: The fourth day
Speaker: The narrator
Context: Santiago kills the marlin

The killing of the marlin marks the climax of the novella. The end of the marlin's life is, paradoxically, the most vital moment of his life. He comes alive "with his death in him" and shows Santiago "all his power and his beauty." The fish seems to transcend his own death. The idea that by dying momentously we can transcend death resonates with Santiago's story. Like the fish, the old man suffers a kind of a death on his way back to the village. He is stripped of his quarry and knows that he will never again have the opportunity to land such a magnificent fish. Nevertheless, he returns to the village with his spirit and his reputation revitalized.

Just then the stern line came taut under his foot, where he had kept the loop of the line, and he dropped his oars and felt the weight of the small tuna's shivering pull as he held the line firm and commenced to haul it in. The shivering increased as he pulled in and he could see the blue back of the fish in the water and the gold of his sides before he swung him over the side and into the boat. He lay in the stern in the sun, compact and bullet shaped, his big, unintelligent eyes staring as he thumped his life out against the planking of the boat with the quick shivering strokes of his neat, fast-moving tail. The old man hit him on the head for kindness and kicked him, his body still shuddering, under the shade of the stern.

Location: The second day
Speaker: The narrator
Context: Santiago kills a tuna

"I have never seen or heard of such a fish. But I must kill him. I am glad we do not have to try to kill the stars." Imagine if each day a man must try to kill the moon, he thought. The moon runs away.. . . Then he was sorry for the great fish that had nothing to eat and his determination to kill him never relaxed in his sorrow for him.. . . There is no one worthy of eating him from the manner of his behavior and his great dignity. I do not understand these things, he thought. But it is good that we do not have to try to kill the sun or the moon or the stars. It is enough to live on the sea and kill our true brothers.

Location: The third day
Speaker: The narrator
Context: Santiago thinks about man's place in the universe

You did not kill the fish only to keep alive and to sell for food, he thought. You killed him for pride and because you are a fisherman. You loved him when he was alive and you loved him after. If you love him, it is not a sin to kill him. Or is it more?

Location: The fourth day
Speaker: The narrator
Context: Santiago sails back to the village

OLIVER TWIST

Charles Dickens

A young pauper endures cruel treatment and persecution before finding benefactors and discovering his inheritance.

THE LIFE OF CHARLES DICKENS

Charles Dickens was born on February 7, 1812. He spent the first ten years of his life in Kent, a marshy region by the sea in the east of England. Dickens was the second of eight children. His father, John Dickens, was kind and likable, but fiscally irresponsible. His huge debts caused tremendous strain on his family.

When Dickens was ten, his family moved to London. Two years later, his father was arrested and thrown in debtors' prison. Dickens's mother moved into the prison with seven of her children. Charles tried to earn money for the struggling family. For three months, he worked with other children pasting labels on bottles in a blacking warehouse. Dickens found the three months he spent apart from his family highly traumatic. Not only was the job itself miserable, but he considered himself too good for it, earning the contempt of the other children. His experiences at this warehouse inspired passages of *David Copperfield*.

An inheritance gave John Dickens enough money to free himself from his debt and from prison. Dickens attended Wellington House Academy for two years. He became a law clerk, then a newspaper reporter, and finally a novelist. His first novel, *The Pickwick Papers* (1837), met with huge popular success. Dickens was a literary celebrity in England for the rest of his life.

Dickens's work includes *Oliver Twist* (1837–1839), *Nicholas Nickelby* (1838–1839), and *A Christmas Carol* (1843). Dickens died in Kent on June 9, 1870, at the age of fifty-eight.

OLIVER TWIST IN CONTEXT

In 1837, the first installment of *Oliver Twist* appeared in the magazine *Bentley's Miscellany*, which Dickens was then editing. George Cruikshank did the illustrations, which still accompany many editions of the novel today. Some critics accused Dickens of writing too quickly and too prolifically, since he was paid by the word for his serialized novels. Yet the passion behind *Oliver Twist*, inspired in part by Dickens's own childhood experiences and in part by his outrage at the living conditions of the poor, touched his contemporary readers, and *Oliver Twist* became a great success.

Oliver Twist is deeply concerned with poverty. In the 1830s, England was rapidly changing from an agricultural, rural economy into an urban, industrial nation. The growing middle class had achieved an economic influence equal to, if not greater than, that of the British aristocracy and had won the right to vote.

In the extremely stratified English class structure, aristocrats who did not have to work for a living were at the top of the heap. Middle-class citizens anxious to distinguish themselves called the lower classes lazy good-for-nothings and held up earned wealth as a sign of moral virtue. Many Victorians believed that God rewarded the virtuous with wealth and punished the lazy or immoral with poverty. This sentiment was reflected in the Poor Law of 1834, which *Oliver Twist* criticizes. The law said the poor could receive public assistance only if they lived and worked in established workhouses. Beggars risked imprisonment. Debtors were sent to prison, often with their entire families, which virtually ensured that they could not repay their debts.

Workhouses were deliberately made as miserable as possible in order to deter the poor from relying on public assistance. On entering a workhouse, husbands were permitted no contact with their wives lest they breed more paupers. Mothers were separated from children lest they pass on their immoral ways to their children. Brothers were separated from their sisters because the middle-class patrons of workhouses feared the lower class's "natural" inclination toward incest.

Because of the great stigma attached to workhouse relief, many poor people chose to die in the streets rather than seek public aid. In *Oliver Twist*, Dickens points out that the Poor Laws punished the defenseless members of the lower class, not the able-bodied. He reveals the hypocrisy of the petty middle-class bureaucrats who abuse a small child while trumpeting the Christian virtue of giving charity to the less fortunate.

OLIVER TWIST: KEY FACTS

Full title: Oliver Twist: The Parish Boy's Progress

Time and place written: 1837–38; London

Date of first publication: Published in serial form between February 1837 and April 1839; published in book form November 1838

Publisher: First published serially in *Bentley's Miscellany*

Type of work: Novel

Genre: Social protest novel

Language: English

Setting (time): 1830s

Setting (place): London and environs

Tense: Past

Tone: Sentimental, ironic, hyperbolic, crusading

Narrator: Anonymous third-person omniscient

Point of view: The narrator's

Protagonist: Oliver Twist

Antagonist: Social injustice

OLIVER TWIST: PLOT OVERVIEW

Oliver Twist is born in a workhouse in 1830s England. His mother dies on the street just after Oliver's birth. Oliver spends the first nine years of his life in a badly-run home for young orphans and then is transferred to a workhouse for adults. After the other boys bully Oliver into asking for more gruel at the end of a meal, Mr. Bumble, the parish beadle (minor church official), offers five pounds to anyone who will take the boy away from the workhouse. Oliver eventually finds an apprenticeship with a local undertaker, Mr. Sowerberry. When the undertaker's other apprentice, Noah Claypole, makes disparaging remarks about Oliver's mother, Oliver attacks him and incurs the Sowerberrys' wrath. Desperate, Oliver runs away at dawn and travels toward London.

Oliver, starved and exhausted, meets Jack Dawkins, a boy his own age. Jack offers him shelter in the London house of his benefactor, Fagin. Fagin is a career criminal who trains orphan boys to pick pockets for him. After a few days of training, Oliver is sent on a pickpocketing mission with two other boys. When he sees them swipe a handkerchief from an elderly gentleman, he is horrified and runs off. He narrowly escapes being convicted of the theft. Mr. Brownlow, the man whose handkerchief was stolen, takes the feverish Oliver to his home and nurses him back to health. Mr. Brownlow is struck by Oliver's resemblance to a portrait of a young woman that hangs in his house. Oliver thrives in Mr. Brownlow's home, but two young adults in Fagin's gang, Bill Sikes and his lover Nancy, capture Oliver and return him to Fagin.

Fagin sends Oliver to assist Sikes in a burglary. Oliver is shot by a servant of the house and taken in by the women who live there, Mrs. Maylie and her beautiful adopted niece Rose. They grow fond of Oliver, and he spends an idyllic summer with them in the countryside. But Fagin and a mysterious man named Monks are bent on recapturing Oliver. We learn that Oliver's mother left behind a gold locket when she died. Monks, in order to keep secret that he is Oliver's half-brother, obtains and destroys the locket. When the Maylies come to London, Nancy meets secretly with Rose and informs her of Fagin's plans. A member of Fagin's gang overhears the conversation, and when word of Nancy's disclosure reaches Sikes, he brutally murders Nancy and flees London. Pursued by his guilty conscience and an angry mob, he inadvertently hangs himself while trying to escape.

Mr. Brownlow, with whom the Maylies have reunited Oliver, confronts Monks and wrings the truth about Oliver's parentage from him. It turns out that Monks is Oliver's half-brother. Their father, Mr. Leeford, was unhappily married to a wealthy woman and had an affair with Oliver's mother, Agnes Fleming. Monks has been pursuing Oliver because he wants to deprive his half-brother of his share of the family inheritance. Mr. Brownlow forces Monks to sign over Oliver's share to Oliver. It also comes out that Rose is Agnes's younger sister and Oliver's aunt. Fagin is hanged for his crimes. Mr. Brownlow adopts Oliver, and they and the Maylies retire to a blissful existence in the countryside.

CHARACTERS IN *OLIVER TWIST*

Charley Bates One of Fagin's pickpockets.

Barney One of Fagin's criminal associates. Like Fagin, Barney is Jewish.

Mrs. Bedwin Mr. Brownlow's kindhearted housekeeper.

Bet One of Fagin's former child pickpockets. Bet is now a prostitute.

Mr. Brittles A handyman for Mrs. Maylie's estate. Mr. Brittles is slightly mentally handicapped.

Mr. Brownlow A wealthy, compassionate gentleman. Mr. Brownlow is Oliver's first benefactor. He owns a portrait of Agnes Fleming and was engaged to Mr. Leeford's sister when she died.

Bull's-eye Bill Sikes's dog. Bull's-eye is as vicious as his master.

Mr. Bumble The pompous, self-important beadle (minor church official) at the workhouse where Oliver is born. Though Mr. Bumble preaches Christian morality, he mistreats the paupers under his care. Dickens mercilessly satirizes his self-righteousness, greed, hypocrisy, and folly.

Charlotte The Sowerberrys' maid. Charlotte becomes romantically involved with Noah Claypole and slavishly follows him around.

Tom Chitling A rather dim member of Fagin's gang.

Noah Claypole Mr. Sowerberry's apprentice. Noah is an overgrown, cowardly bully who mistreats Oliver and eventually joins Fagin's gang.

Mrs. Corney The matron of the workhouse where Oliver is born. Mrs. Corney is hypocritical, callous, and materialistic. After she marries Mr. Bumble, she hounds him mercilessly.

Toby Crackit One of Fagin and Sikes's associates. Toby is crass and not too bright.

Duff and Blathers Two bumbling police officers who investigate the attempted burglary of Mrs. Maylie's home.

Fagin A conniving career criminal. Fagin takes in homeless children and trains them to pick pockets for him. He rarely commits crimes himself. Dickens's portrait of Fagin is tainted by anti-Semitic stereotypes.

Mr. Fang A magistrate. Mr. Fang is harsh, irrational, and power-hungry. He presides over Oliver's trial for pickpocketing.

Agnes Fleming Oliver's mother. A retired naval officer's daughter, she is a beautiful, loving woman. After falling in love with and becoming pregnant by Mr. Leeford, she chooses to die anonymously in a workhouse rather than stain her family's reputation.

The Artful Dodger The cleverest of Fagin's pickpockets. The Dodger's real name is Jack Dawkins. Though no older than Oliver, the Dodger talks and dresses like a grown man.

Mr. Gamfield A brutal chimney sweep. Oliver narrowly escapes becoming Mr. Gamfield's apprentice.

Mr. Giles Mrs. Maylie's loyal and somewhat pompous butler.

Mr. Grimwig Brownlow's pessimistic, curmudgeonly friend. Mr. Grimwig is essentially goodhearted, and his pessimism is mostly just a provocative character quirk.

Mr. Leeford Oliver and Monks's father. He was an intelligent, high-minded man who intended to flee the country with Agnes but died before he could do so.

Mr. Losberne Mrs. Maylie's family physician. A hot-tempered but good-hearted old bachelor, Mr. Losberne is fiercely loyal to the Maylies and, eventually, to Oliver.

Mrs. Mann The superintendent of the juvenile workhouse where Oliver is raised. Mrs. Mann beats and starves the children in her care.

Harry Maylie Mrs. Maylie's son. Harry is a dashing young man with grand political ambitions and career prospects, which he eventually gives up to marry Rose.

Mrs. Maylie A kind, wealthy older woman. Mrs. Maylie is Harry's mother and Rose's adopted aunt.

Rose Maylie Agnes Fleming's sister. Rose, who Mrs. Maylie raises, is beautiful, compassionate, and forgiving.

Monks Oliver's half-brother. Monks is a sickly, vicious young man. With Fagin, he schemes to give Oliver a bad reputation.

Monks's Mother An heiress. Monks's mother lived a decadent life and alienated her husband, Mr. Leeford. She destroyed her husband's will, which left part of his property to Oliver.

Nancy A young prostitute and one of Fagin's former child pickpockets. Nancy is Bill Sikes's lover. Despite her criminal lifestyle, she is among the noblest characters in the novel. She gives her life for Oliver by revealing Monks's plots.

Bill Sikes A brutal, professional burglar brought up in Fagin's gang. Sikes treats Nancy, his lover, and Bull's-eye, his dog, with the same combination of cruelty and familiarity. His murder of Nancy is the most heinous of the many crimes that occur in the novel.

Old Sally An elderly pauper who is the nurse at Oliver's birth. Old Sally steals Agnes's gold locket.

Mr. Sowerberry The undertaker to whom Oliver is apprenticed. Though Mr. Sowerberry makes a grotesque living arranging cut-rate burials for paupers, he is a decent man who is kind to Oliver.

Mrs. Sowerberry Sowerberry's wife. Mrs. Sowerberry is a mean, judgmental woman who henpecks her husband.

Oliver Twist The novel's protagonist. Oliver is between nine and twelve years old when the main action of the novel occurs. Even though he is surrounded by coarse people who treat him cruelly, Oliver is a pious, innocent child whose charms draw the attention of several wealthy benefactors.

THEMES IN *OLIVER TWIST*

THE FOLLY OF INDIVIDUALISM With the rise of capitalism during the Industrial Revolution, the philosophy of individualism came into vogue. Capitalists insisted that society would run most smoothly if individuals looked out for their own interests. Dickens suggests that this philosophy is not restricted to the rich. Fagin, who deals in theft and prostitution, tells Noah Claypole that "a regard for number one holds us all together, and must do so, unless we would all go to pieces in company." In other words, the group will thrive if each member looks out for himself. Dickens points out that individualism results not in the betterment of the group, but in selfishness and cruelty. At the end of the novel, Nancy turns against Monks, Charley Bates turns against Sikes, and Monks turns against Mrs. Corney. Dickens thinks that selflessness, not individualism, is necessary for "perfect happiness." He juxtaposes Fagin's unstable group, held together and eventually done in by self-interest, with the little society formed by Oliver, Brownlow, Rose Maylie, and their many friends. This second group is bound together not by self-interest but by "strong affection and humanity of heart."

THE INCONSEQUENCE OF ENVIRONMENT Dickens concludes that environment does not shape character in predictable ways. The most terrible environments do not necessarily "blacken [the soul]" of those who live in them, and the most luxurious environments do not produce kind, lovely people. Oliver is not corrupted by the abuse and neglect of his early years. Nancy, who considers herself "lost almost beyond redemption," has the moral rigor to sacrifice her life for a child she hardly knows. Even Sikes and Fagin, whose moral sensibilities have been permanently warped, have consciences. After Sikes murders Nancy, he is haunted by her eyes, and Charley Bates has enough decency to try to capture Sikes. In contrast, Monks has had a luxurious life, but he is perhaps the novel's most inhuman villain.

THE IDEALIZATION OF THE COUNTRYSIDE Dickens portrays rural life as an idyllic alternative to urban life. All the injustices and privations suffered by the poor in *Oliver Twist* occur in cities. Dickens asserts that even people who have spent their entire lives in "close and noisy places" are likely, in the last moments of their lives, to find comfort in half-imagined memories "of sky, and hill and plain." He says country scenes have the power to "purify our thoughts" and erase some of the vices that develop in the city. In the country, "the poor people [are] so neat and clean," living a life free of the squalor that torments their urban counterparts. When the Maylies take Oliver to the countryside, he discovers a "new existence." Oliver and his new family settle in a small village at the novel's end, as if a happy ending would not be possible in the city.

SYMBOLS IN *OLIVER TWIST*

BULL'S-EYE Bull's-eye symbolizes Sikes, his owner. Like Bull's-eye, Sikes is a vicious animal. After Sikes murders Nancy, Bull's-eye leaves bloody footprints in the room where the murder was committed, suggesting his owner's guilt.

LONDON BRIDGE London Bridge represents the link between the idyllic world of Brownlow and Rose and the degraded world in which Nancy lives.

IMPORTANT QUOTATIONS FROM *OLIVER TWIST*

Who can describe the pleasure and delight, the peace of mind and soft tranquility, the sickly boy felt in the balmy air and among the green hills and rich woods of an inland village! Who can tell how scenes of peace and quietude sink into the minds of pain-worn dwellers in close and noisy places, and carry their own freshness deep into their jaded hearts! Men who have lived in crowded, pent-up streets, through lives of toil, and who have never wished for change — men to whom custom has indeed been second nature, and who have come almost to love each brick and stone that formed the narrow boundaries of their daily walks — even they, with the hand of death upon them, have been known to yearn at last for one short glimpse of Nature's face, and, carried far from the scenes of their old pains and pleasures, have seemed to pass at once into a new state of being.

Location: Chapter 32
Speaker: The narrator
Context: The narrator idealizes country life

Dickens worries that urban life has a bad influence on the human character. In this passage, he praises the purity and health of the rural environment and claims that even people who love life in the city long for nature when they are dying. He claims that in the country, even "the poor people" are "neat and clean." This claim seems dubious, given the eagerness of England's rural poor to migrate to the city. Dickens's idealized vision of the country marks him as an urban writer — his gritty portraits of city life are accurate and keenly felt, while his blissful portrait of rural life is the clear product of wistful fantasy.

"When ladies as young, and good, and beautiful as you are," replied the girl steadily, "give away your hearts, love will carry you all lengths — even such as you, who have home, friends, other admirers, everything, to fill them. When such as I, who have no certain roof but the coffin-lid, and no friend in sickness or death but the hospital nurse, set our rotten hearts on any man, and let him fill the place that has been a blank through all our wretched lives, who can hope to cure us? Pity us, lady — pity us for having only one feeling of the woman left and for having that turned, by a heavy judgment, from a comfort and a pride into a new means of violence and suffering."

Location: Chapter 40
Speaker: Nancy
Context: Nancy explains her life to Rose

Nancy, a prostitute, is an emblem of the way poverty degrades good people. Rose represents the purity that wealth allows. Nancy is loving and loyal in the same way Rose is, but her poverty makes a mockery of those fine feelings. The only object on which she can practice her love is the wretched Sikes. Nancy's noble attributes put her in an impossible position. She feels she must turn down Rose's offer of help and return to Sikes, even though Sikes is unworthy of this loyalty. Later, she feels she must help Oliver, even though doing so results in her own death.

So they established the rule that all poor people should have the alternative (for they would compel nobody, not they) of being starved by a gradual process in the house, or by a quick one out of it. With this view, they contracted with the waterworks to lay on an unlimited supply of water, and with a corn-factor to supply periodically small quantities of oatmeal, and issued three meals of thin gruel a day, with an onion twice a week and half a roll on Sundays. They made a great many other wise and humane regulations . . . kindly undertook to divorce poor married people . . . instead of compelling a man to support his family.

Location: Chapter 2
Speaker: The narrator
Context: The narrator describes the workhouse where Oliver lives

---

At times he [Sikes] turned with desperate determination, resolved to beat this phantom off, though it should look him dead; but the hair rose on his head and his blood stood still, for it had turned with him and was behind him then. He had kept it before him that morning, but it was behind now—always. He leaned his back against a bank, and felt that it stood above him, visibly out against the cold night sky. He threw himself upon the road—on his back upon the road. At his head it stood, silent, erect, and still—a living grave-stone, with its epitaph in blood. Let no man talk of murderers escaping justice, and hint that Providence must sleep. There were twenty score of violent deaths in one long minute of that agony of fear.

Location: Chapter 48
Speaker: The narrator
Context: Sikes flees London after murdering Nancy

Within the altar of the old village church there stands a white marble tablet which bears as yet but one word: "Agnes".. . . . I believe that the shade of Agnes sometimes hovers round the solemn nook. I believe it none the less because that nook is in a Church, and she was weak and erring.

Location: The final passage of the novel
Speaker: The narrator
Context: The narrator argues that erring people should not be condemned

ON THE ROAD

Jack Kerouac

A man abandons New York and its intellectualism to seek enlightenment through unmediated experience on the American road.

THE LIFE OF JACK KEROUAC

Jack Kerouac was born Jean-Louis Lebris de Kerouac in 1922 in the economically depressed mill-town of Lowell, Massachusetts. His parents were French Canadians, and he grew up attending nearby Catholic and public schools. In 1940, Kerouac earned a football scholarship to New York's Columbia University, but dropped out during sophomore year after a severe knee injury and disagreements with his coach. In New York, he met Allen Ginsberg, Neal Cassady, and William S. Burroughs—fellow beat writers and Kerouac's future companions on the journeys chronicled in *On the Road*. After Columbia, Kerouac joined the Merchant Marines, with whom he traveled throughout the North Atlantic. Afterwards, he took to the road again to see the American West and more exotic regions: Mexico, North Africa and Europe. Throughout his travels he wrote, trying to hone his new experimental prose form.

Kerouac's first novel, *The Town and the City*, was published in 1950. *On the Road*, his second and best-known novel, was completed by 1951 but not published until 1957. According to his friend Ginsberg, Kerouac typed the first draft on a 120-foot-long roll of paper over the course of three weeks. Most of Kerouac's novels are autobiographical. He changed names, but stayed faithful to the events. Other Kerouac novels include *The Dharma Bums*, based on Kerouac's explorations of Buddhism with the poet Gary Snyder, and *The Subterraneans*, written in only three days in Kerouac's "spontaneous prose" style. He also wrote six books of poetry.

In the 1960s, Kerouac advocated U.S. involvement in the Vietnam War and alienated many of his followers, for whom his early work had opened up a new way of life. His image has since been revived in America as a symbol of romantic rebellion. Burroughs remarked that "Kerouac opened a million coffee bars and sold a million pairs of Levi's to both sexes." A nearly lifelong alcoholic, Kerouac died in 1969 at the age of forty-seven.

ON THE ROAD IN CONTEXT

On the Road is considered the representative work of the Beat Generation. The novel chronicles Kerouac's ("Sal Paradise") travels with Neal Cassady ("Dean Moriarty"). Other major characters are based on Kerouac's friends, many of them prominent beat writers such as Ginsberg ("Carlo Marx") and Burroughs ("Old Bull Lee"). With long, stream-of-consciousness sentences and page-long paragraphs, Kerouac sought to revolutionize American prose.

On the Road gave voice to a rising, dissatisfied fringe of young Americans in the late 1940s and 1950s, nicknamed the Beat Generation. Set in the late 1940s, the novel takes place after World War II and more than a decade before the Civil Rights movement and the turmoil of the 1960s—a period of material prosperity and great national confidence in American supremacy. Contemporary mainstream society valued the nuclear family, sobriety, hard work, and material possessions. In describing drugged-out, anti-materialistic young beats (or beatniks), Kerouac brought to light the long-simmering antiestablishment beliefs and practices of New York's bohemians. This counterculture espoused an alternative lifestyle marked by flexible sexual norms, experimentation with mind-altering drugs, and inventive new modes of artistic expression, including jazz music and beat poetry.

ON THE ROAD: KEY FACTS

Time and place written: 1951; America

Date of publication: 1957

Publisher: Viking

Type of work: Novel	
Genre: Picaresque; kunstlerroman	
Language: English	
Setting (time): Late 1940s	
Setting (place): America (New York City, Midwest, San Francisco, Los Angeles, Denver) and Mexico	
Tense: Immediate past—real-time narration	
Tone: Exhilarated, reflective	
Narrator: Sal Paradise	
Point of view: Sal Paradise's	
Protagonist: Sal Paradise	
Antagonist: Bourgeois materialism; intellectualism	

ON THE ROAD: PLOT OVERVIEW

PART I

In the winter of 1947, the reckless and joyous Dean Moriarty, fresh out of another stint in jail and newly married to feisty young blonde Marylou, comes to New York City. Through his friendship with the poet Carlo Marx, he is introduced to the bohemian social circles of Sal Paradise, a young writer who has recently grown weary of his friends' intellectual pretensions. Sal is fascinated by Dean, and this fascination leads to three years of restless journeys back and forth across the country.

Sal leaves the home of his endlessly supportive aunt with only a small sum of money. Over the years he frequently sends requests for more funds. He heads west, sometimes on buses and sometimes by hitchhiking. He lands in Denver, Dean's hometown, and stays with old college friends. He sees Dean only briefly and continues west by himself. He spends several weeks in the outskirts of San Francisco at the unhappy domicile of his old college friend Remi Bonceur and Remi's shrewish girlfriend Lee Ann. He then heads south to Los Angeles, where he conducts a passionate, fifteen-day affair with a young Mexican named Terry and works as a field hand. He returns east.

PART II

A year later, Dean arrives to disrupt Sal's stable life once more, offering heady promises of adventures on the road. Together with their simpleminded sidekick, Ed Dunkel, they drive west. Crazy adventures take place along the way, including a drug-addled stint at their friend Bull Lee's in New Orleans. They end up in San Francisco, where Dean keeps a second wife, Camille, who gives birth to two children over the course of the novel.

PART III

The following spring, Sal goes to see Dean in San Francisco. They blaze across the country together, united as "brothers." For a while, Dean settles in New York, where he marries again, this time a boisterous woman named Inez who bears him another child.

PART IV

In the spring, flush with funds from his recently published first novel, Sal again journeys to Denver. Dean soon joins him. With their naïve young friend Stan Shepard, Dean and Sal head south all the way to Mexico City—their first trip abroad. They indulge in endless hedonistic pleasures, from prostitutes to potent drugs. When Sal contracts a severe case of dysentery, Dean abandons him in Mexico City to head back to Inez in New York.

PART V

Months later, Sal has fallen in love and moved in with a girl named Laura. Dean shows up and wants to hit the road again, but Sal lets him go alone. Sal professes his enduring, yet qualified, admiration for Dean.

CHARACTERS IN *ON THE ROAD*

SAL AND HIS WIVES AND GIRLFRIENDS

Rita Bettencourt A Denver waitress who, according to Dean, has "sex difficulties." Dean sets her up with Sal, who tries and fails to demonstrate that sex is beautiful.

Lucille A New York acquaintance of Sal's. When Sal is attending school in New York, he wants to marry Lucille, who is already married.

Sal Paradise The narrator; a young, penniless New York writer. Sal sets out to travel across America and experience life in order to become a better writer.

Terry A pretty Mexican girl with whom Sal spends fifteen days in California. Terry comes from a family of grape-pickers in Sabinal. She is trying to escape her abusive husband with her son Johnny.

DEAN AND HIS WIVES AND GIRLFRIENDS

Dean Moriarty Sal's friend; a reckless, energetic, womanizing young man from Colorado. Dean has been in and out of jail. While he is deeply flawed, Dean also represents individual freedom. Sal usually considers him a larger-than-life savior figure.

Marylou Dean's first wife. Marylou is a pretty, "dumb" blonde from Colorado.

Camille Dean's second wife. Loyal Camille lives in San Francisco with their children.

Inez Dean's third wife. Inez is a sexy brunette whom Dean meets in New York.

TERRY AND FAMILY

Johnny Terry's seven-year-old son.

Ponzo Terry and Rickey's friend; a smelly seller of manure. Big and eager to please, Ponzo is in love with Terry.

Rickey Terry's wild, alcoholic, happy-go-lucky brother, whom Sal meets in Sabinal.

OTHER CHARACTERS

Remi Boncoeur Sal's prep school friend. Remi, an extravagant and gallant Frenchman, is a gambler and a petty thief who is constantly in debt.

Denver D. Doll Sal's Central City friend. A caricature of an eager official, Denver D. Doll often shakes hands and drops incoherent pleasantries.

Ed Dunkel Sal and Dean's tall, affable, docile, dimwitted friend.

Galatea Dunkel Ed's serious, disapproving new wife.

Sal's Aunt Sal's only relative. Supportive and kind, Sal's aunt sends him money throughout his travels. When not traveling, Sal lives at her house in Paterson, New Jersey, and sometimes on Long Island.

Slim Gaillard A San Francisco friend of Dean's. Slim frequents jazz joints and adds the suffix "orooni" to almost everything he says.

Tim Gray A Denver friend of Sal's.

Elmer Hassel A friend of Sal's and Dean's. Elmer is imprisoned in Riker's Island, but Sal and Dean look for him wherever they go.

Hingham Sal's Tucson friend. Hingham is a shy writer who lives with his wife, mother, and baby.

Chad King Sal's Denver friend. Young, slim, blond, and soft-spoken, Chad is interested in philosophy, anthropology, and prehistoric Indians.

Roy Johnson A friend of Sal's who chauffeurs Dean and Sal in San Francisco.

Old Bull Lee A longtime friend of Sal's and Carlo's. "Long, lean, strange and laconic," Old Bull Lee is a traveler, writer, and junkie.

Jane Lee Bull Lee's sarcastic wife. Jane is a benzedrine junkie.

Lee Ann Remi Boncoeur's sulky girlfriend.

Roland Major Sal's Denver friend, with whom he lives for a while. A Hemingwayesque writer, Roland scorns "arty" types but snobbishly talks about Europe and fine wines.

Carlo Marx Sal's and Dean's close friend. Carlo is a brooding, sensual, and energetic poet.

Babe Rawlins Ray's sister and Tim Gray's girlfriend.

Ray Rawlins Babe's brother and Sal's Denver acquaintance.

Stan Shephard Tim Gray's enthusiastic friend. Stan accompanies Dean and Sal to Mexico, in part to escape his controlling grandfather.

Victor A kind, polite Mexican who serves as Sal, Dean, and Stan's guide in Gregoria.

THEMES IN *ON THE ROAD*

THE REJECTION OF MATERIAL VALUES IN PURSUIT OF SELF-AWARENESS Sal believes that he needs to free himself from his intellectual and social inhibitions in order to write more truthfully about the world. He sees his escape model in Dean Moriarty, the source of a fresh, new intelligence "every bit as formal and shining and complete, without the tedious intellectualness." Sal takes to the road as a hobo, rejecting materialism. Sal emulates Dean's disrespect for personal property. He joins Dean on a night of rampant car-stealing and rides along gleefully as Dean wrecks the Cadillac of a man who has hired them to drive it to Chicago. Sal rejects possessions and materialism as obstacles to unmediated, pure experience.

THE AMERICAN WEST AS LAND OF OPPORTUNITY From earliest colonial times, inhabitants of the American West have embraced the image of the courageous frontiersman striking out on his own in the uncharted hinterlands of the West. Sal heads west to free himself of the shackles of tradition and civilization in the East. In the West he can pick up a Mexican woman on a bus and fall in love with her—an interracial relationship he would not have been able to pursue in the East.

THE BEAT WAY OF LIFE AS MASCULINE IDEAL IN CONFLICT WITH FEMALE DOMESTICITY Dean's rejection of bourgeois values such as marital fidelity and patriarchal leadership are celebrated as markers of his intellectual and spiritual liberation. But in a brief epiphany in Part III, chapter 2, Sal realizes that the wives and girlfriends of the macho beat males "were spending months of loneliness and womanliness together, chattering about the madness of the men." Indeed, throughout the novel, while Sal's cronies travel across the country, their women wait for them to return to their children and responsibilities. Sal's depictions of these women are frequently cruel: Camille is a harsh shrew, Galatea Dunkel is dull and naïve, and Marylou—who mimics the men's promiscuous behavior—is a whore. Ultimately, Sal abandons the beat lifestyle and settles with Laura in New York.

SYMBOLS IN *ON THE ROAD*

THE ROAD Sal seeks new modes of expression via unmediated experiences, and the road represents the path to such enlightenment. The road is the opposite of book learning—its lessons require stamina and physical exertion. The road offers the constant stimulation of motion, speed, jazz, sex, heavy drinking. Sal is excited about his destinations, but he loses interest soon after arriving: it is traveling itself that fuels his excitement.

THE EAST, THE WEST, AND THE SOUTH   The East (New York), rooted in formal traditions, represents both the comforts of home and the intellectualism that Sal seeks to leave behind. The West represents a wild locale of self-determination, a place where anything is possible. Its cities—Denver, San Francisco, and Los Angeles—feel new and fresh, not yet fossilized. Mexico represents a yet wilder way of accessing experience.

IMPORTANT QUOTATIONS FROM *ON THE ROAD*

But then they danced down the streets like dingledodies, and I shambled after as I've been doing all my life after people who interest me, because the only people for me are the mad ones, the ones who are mad to live, mad to talk, mad to be saved, desirous of everything at the same time . . . but burn, burn, burn like fabulous yellow roman candles exploding like spiders across the stars and in the middle you see the blue center light pop and everybody goes "Awww!"

Location: Part I, chapter 1
Speaker: Sal
Context: Sal recalls Dean and Carlo dancing down the street and explains his initial attraction to Dean

Dean and Carlo together—high-brow, philosophical poet and carnal, ever-hungry ex-inmate—embody the edgy new artistic sensibility embraced by the beats. Sal accepts that this new effervescent way of life is as short-lived as it is intense. Sal must constantly chase it, and sets out on the road in hot pursuit. Sal contrasts his own awkwardness and melancholy to Dean's energy: "I shambled after as I've been doing all my life."

I wanted to know what "IT" meant. "Ah well"—Dean laughed—"Now you're asking me impon-de-rables—ahem! Here's a guy and everybody's there, right? Up to him to put down what's on everybody's mind. He starts the first chorus, then lines up his ideas, people, yeah, yeah, but get it, and then he rises to his fate and has to blow equal to it. All of a sudden somewhere in the middle of the chorus he gets it— everybody looks up and knows; they listen; he picks it up and carries. Time stops. He's filling empty space with the substance of our lives, confessions of his bellybottom strain, remembrance of ideas, rehashes of old blowing. He has to blow across bridges and come back and do it with such infinite feeling soul-exploratory for the tune of the moment that everybody knows it's not the tune that counts but IT—" Dean could go no further; he was sweating telling about it.

Location: Part III, chapter 5
Speaker: Sal
Context: Dean and Sal leave San Francisco, remembering jazz musicians they heard perform at a club

Jazz is the musical counterpart to Kerouac's beat literary voice. The diction and amorphous flow of the ideas of this passage, and the novel's prose in general, mimics the improvised, experimental structure and sound of jazz. Dean describes the alto-sax player as possessing "IT"—a bland word that becomes Dean's catchall to describe exhilarating, inexpressible experience.

A western kinsman of the sun, Dean. Although my aunt warned me that he would get me in trouble, I could hear a new call and see a new horizon, and believe it at my young age; and a little bit of trouble or even Dean's eventual rejection of me as a buddy, putting me down, as he would later, on starving sidewalks and sickbeds—what did it matter? I was a young writer and I wanted to take off.

Somewhere along the line I knew there'd be girls, visions, everything; somewhere along the line the pearl would be handed to me.

Location: Part I, chapter 1
Speaker: Sal
Context: Sal explains his decision to hit the road, head west, and escape his increasingly stultifying life among the New York intellectuals

---

Great Chicago glowed red before our eyes. We were suddenly on Madison Street among hordes of hobos, some of them sprawled out on the street with their feet on the curb, hundreds of others milling in the doorways of saloons and alleys. "Wup! wup! look sharp for old Dean Moriarty there, he may be in Chicago by accident this year."

Location: Part III, chapter 10
Speaker: Sal as narrator
Context: Dean and Sal arrive in Chicago

When I got better I realized what a rat he was, but then I had to understand the impossible complexity of his life, how he had to leave me there, sick, to get on with his wives and woes. "Okay, old Dean, I'll say nothing."

Location: Part IV, chapter 6
Speaker: Sal as narrator
Context: After Dean abandons Sal on his sickbed in Mexico, Sal both forgives Dean and condemns him as an irredeemable reincarnation of Dean's father

ONE DAY IN THE LIFE OF IVAN DENISOVICH

Alexander Solzhenitsyn

A man has a comparatively happy day in the Soviet labor camp where he is imprisoned.

THE LIFE OF ALEXANDER SOLZHENITSYN

Alexander Isaevich Solzhenitsyn was born on December 11, 1918, in the Russian town of Kislovodsk, one year after the successful revolt of the working classes against the tsar of Russia, Nicholas II. Solzhenitsyn was a good student and eventually enrolled in the mathematics department of Rostov University. He also took correspondence courses in literature at Moscow State University, the largest and most prestigious university in the Soviet Union. After university, Solzhenitsyn was inducted into the Soviet armed forces and fought in battle as a captain of artillery in World War II. In 1945, his military career was cut short when he was arrested for criticizing the Soviet leader Joseph Stalin in a private letter. Solzhenitsyn was sentenced to eight years in various prisons and labor camps.

In 1956, after the 1953 death of Stalin and the softening of the Soviet regime by Nikita Khrushchev, the first secretary of the Communist party, Solzhenitsyn was released and allowed to settle in Ryazan. There he worked as a math teacher and began to write fiction. He became famous in 1962 with the publication of *One Day in the Life of Ivan Denisovich*. In 1968, Solzhenitsyn published *The First Circle*, a novel about research scientists torn between obeying authority and pursuing truth. In the same year, he wrote *Cancer Ward*, a novel based on his experience as a patient in a Soviet cancer hospital. In 1970, Solzhenitsyn was awarded the Nobel Prize for Literature. He did not travel to Sweden to accept the prize, however, because he was afraid he would not be allowed back into the Soviet Union. He later claimed the prize after his emigration from the U.S.S.R.

Solzhenitsyn began writing what he planned to be a vast, multivolume work about World War I to be called *The Red Wheel*. This series focuses on the German victory in World War I over the Russian tsarist regime and examines the weaknesses of prerevolutionary Russian society. In December 1973, Solzhenitsyn published *The Gulag Archipelago*, a literary study of labor camps. Because of this work, Solzhenitsyn was arrested for treason on February 12, 1974, stripped of Soviet citizenship, and sent into exile. Solzhenitsyn eventually settled in Cavendish, Vermont, in 1975, where he raised his family. In 1980, he published a study of Soviet literature, translated into English as *The Oak and the Calf*.

In 1994, after the demise of the Soviet Union, Solzhenitsyn returned to his homeland, settling in St. Petersburg. There he became a vociferous critic of Western values, including the excessive emphasis on independence. Skeptical of democracy, he began to favor a compassionate authoritarian government based on Christian values. He greeted the presidency of Vladimir Putin with great optimism, but then retracted his support. Solzhenitsyn continues to live in St. Petersburg and to write prolifically.

ONE DAY IN THE LIFE OF IVAN DENISOVICH IN CONTEXT

One Day in the Life of Ivan Denisovich was originally published in the leading Soviet literary journal of the day, *Novy Mir (New World)*. A landmark event in the history of literature and politics in the Soviet Union, *One Day in the Life of Ivan Denisovich* made the first-ever public mention of forced collectivization of farms and of the existence of labor camps. The mere mention of them in print was shocking at the time and would have resulted in a life sentence ten years earlier. Instantaneously, Solzhenitsyn became an international celebrity.

After Khrushchev fell in 1964, Khrushchev's critics came out of hiding and began attacking former critics of Stalinism, including Solzhenitsyn. Eventually, *One Day in the Life of Ivan Denisovich* was denied further publication and forced into underground printings known as *samizdat*—photocopies and hand-written copies distributed from friend to friend.

ONE DAY IN THE LIFE OF IVAN DENISOVICH: KEY FACTS

Time and Place Written: 1959–1962; Russia

Date of First Publication: 1962

Publisher: Novy Mir

Type of Work: Novel

Genre: Prison novel; social protest novel

Language: Russian

Setting (time): Winter, 1951

Setting (place): A Russian labor camp called HQ, which is probably in Siberia

Tense: Past

Tone: Pared-down, uneducated

Narrator: An anonymous narrator in the third person

Point of View: Shukhov's

Protagonist: Ivan Denisovich Shukhov

Antagonist: The unjust Soviet camp system

ONE DAY IN THE LIFE OF IVAN DENISOVICH: PLOT OVERVIEW

One bitterly cold winter morning in 1951, a wake-up call sounds in a Stalinist labor camp. Ivan Denisovich Shukhov, a prisoner in Camp HQ, suffers a fever and aches, and yearns for a little more time in bed. Thinking that a kindly guard is on duty, he stays in bed past the wake-up call. Unfortunately, a different guard is making the rounds, and he punishes Shukhov with three days in the solitary confinement cell, which the characters call "the hole." Shukhov soon realizes that the sentence is just a threat and that he will only have to wash the floors of the officers' headquarters. Shukhov removes his shoes and efficiently completes the job.

Shukhov goes to the mess hall, worrying that he has missed breakfast. He meets the sniveling Fetyukov, who has saved Shukhov's gruel for him. After breakfast, Shukhov heads to sick bay. The medical orderly Kolya tells him he should have been ill the previous night, since the clinic is closed in the morning. Shukhov returns to the hut in time for the usual search in which the prisoners are searched for forbidden articles and counted to make sure none have escaped. Shukhov carefully hides the bread he took at breakfast, sewing it into his mattress. The men undress in the freezing cold for the search. One inmate, Buynovsky, is sentenced to ten days in the hole for wearing a flannel vest. Shukhov has neither food nor letters to his family, which he does not write anymore. He reflects on his wife's recent letter urging him to take up carpet-dyeing when he gets out of prison. But Shukhov is not interested in this, despite the easy money.

After the search, Shukhov's group, Gang 104, is marched off for work at the Power Station, a building site in the open fields. Shukhov looks at his colleague Alyoshka, a devout Baptist who seems happy to slave away. Shukhov is filled with respect for his foreman, Tyurin, a big tough man with a decent soul. Though they are forbidden to do so, the men try to keep the wind out of the windows by covering them with tar paper. The teenage prisoner Gopchik fetches wire for piping and asks Shukhov to show him how to make a spoon. At the noon meal, Shukhov sneaks a second helping of food. On the way back to the work site, Shukhov picks up and hides a bit of scrap metal he finds in the snow, hoping to make a knife out of it later. Tyurin tells a tale of being imprisoned for having a rich peasant father.

The men begin to mortar the wall. Pavlo agrees to be on the mortar team even though, as an officer, he is not required to mortar. Pavlo's friendliness earns him the men's respect. The bricklaying begins. Shukhov works feverishly and well. A camp manager stops by and chides Tyurin for the tar paper in the work site windows. He threatens to punish Tyurin, but Tyurin waves him off. Alyoshka works selflessly. When the meal signal comes, Shukhov continues working. He is late to lunch, but he wants to hide his coveted trowel from the other men. He catches up to the others, who are delayed by preparations for another body count. A man from Moldavia is missing from another gang. It turns out he fell asleep at the site.

At the body search, Shukhov suddenly panics, remembering the bit of steel hidden in his mitten. By a stroke of good luck, the guard does not discover it. At supper, Shukhov finds his comrades, grabs an empty tray, and bring their rations to the table. For his outstanding labor at the Power Station, Shukhov has been awarded 400 grams of bread. He eats in bliss, eyeing his extra rations to make sure no one grabs them. He takes Tsezar's ration to the hut, where Tsezar, in exception to the camp rules, is allowed to eat. Tsezar has received a food package. He displays the contents to everyone and allows Shukhov to keep his (Tsezar's) supper ration. After the body count, Shukhov prepares to sleep, reveling in his abundance of bread. At the second roll call, Tsezar panics, not sure what to do with his parcel. Shukhov helps him guard it from the other prisoners. Tsezar rewards Shukhov with a couple of biscuits and a bit of sausage. Before falling asleep, Shukhov thanks God for getting him through another day. Alyoshka overhears Shukhov's prayer and urges Shukhov to pray properly. He also encourages Shukhov to pursue the goods of the spirit and not, as Tsezar does, those of the flesh. Shukhov reflects on Alyoshka's sentiment. Suddenly, for no reason, he hands Alyoshka one of his biscuits. Shukhov meditates that his day has been almost happy. The narrator comments that this day has been just one of the 3,653 days of Shukhov's sentence.

CHARACTERS IN *ONE DAY IN THE LIFE OF IVAN DENISOVICH*

Alyoshka A prisoner who bunks near Shukhov. Alyoshka is a devout Baptist who reads the New Testament late at night. He does favors for other inmates but never expects or receives rewards for these favors.

Buynovsky A prisoner. People call Buynovsky "the captain" because of his former military rank. Buynovsky's education matters little in the camp.

Eino One of the two Estonians who share a bunk in Shukhov's hut. Eino and the other Estonian chat in their own language, maintaining a private world set apart from the horrors of camp existence.

Fetyukov The scrounger and wheedler of Gang 104. Fetyukov is always nagging the other inmates for a cigarette or an extra bit of bread. Shukhov scorns Fetyukov, but in the end pities him. Fetyukov represents the loss of human dignity the labor camp produces.

Gopchik A sixteen-year-old prisoner. Gopchik, who was jailed for giving milk to nationalist rebels, has not yet been hardened by life in the camp.

Kildigs A Latvian bricklayer. Kildigs is famed for his sense of humor. Shukhov thinks Kildigs's ability to make jokes stems from his regular receipt of food parcels.

Kolya A medical orderly and novice poet. Solzhenitsyn's description of Kolya as an insensitive poet suggests his disdain for old-fashioned literary types who fail to appreciate real-world problems.

Pavlo The deputy foreman of Gang 104. Pavlo, a Ukrainian, is strict but kind. His patience and mercy toward the inmates earn him the devotion of many members of the gang.

Snub Nose A prison warden.

Tsezar A member of Gang 104. Tsezar is a man of uncertain national background and mysterious connections. His food parcels make him the envy of the gang. He is worldly, artistic, and cultivated. By the end of the novel, Shukhov has begun to question the cultural attainment and privilege Tsezar represents.

Ivan Denisovich Shukhov The protagonist of the novel. Shukhov is a working-class, badly educated man. His daily struggle represents that of the average Russian citizen.

Tyurin The foreman of Gang 104. Tyurin is a strict but fair man isolated by his job.

THEMES IN *ONE DAY IN THE LIFE OF IVAN DENISOVICH*

THE STRUGGLE FOR HUMAN DIGNITY The Stalinist labor camp in which Shukhov is imprisoned systematically attacks its prisoners' physical and spiritual dignity. Living conditions are nearly intolerable. Mattresses do not have sheets. Prisoners are given only two hundred grams of bread per meal. Guards force prisoners to undress at temperatures of forty below zero. Spiritual conditions are equally intolerable. By replacing prisoners' names with combinations of letters and numbers, the camp erases all traces of individuality. For example, the camp guards refer to Shukhov as "Shcha-854." Yet despite the totality of this dehumanizing treatment, it is possible for prisoners to maintain their human dignity, as Shukhov proves. Shukhov maintains dignity not through outward rebellion but through a series of small but deeply symbolic gestures. At mealtime, no matter how hungry he is, he removes his cap before eating. This practice, a holdover from his upbringing, gives Shukhov a sense that he is behaving in a civilized manner. No matter how painful his hunger is, Shukhov never stoops to Fetyukov's scrounging and begging for scraps. This high standard of behavior keeps Shukhov from behaving like the animal the camp encourages him to become. Shukhov's quiet insistence on his own dignity amounts to a secret declaration of war against the state that imprisons him.

THE OUTRAGE OF UNJUST PUNISHMENT *One Day in the Life of Ivan Denisovich* is shocking in part because of the harmless nature of the so-called crimes that have landed the inmates in a labor camp. Gopchik gave milk to freedom fighters hiding in the woods; Shukhov was captured by Germans and then accused by the Russians of being a spy; Tyurin was the son of a rich peasant. We do not know much about the other inmates, but none of them appears to be a terrible criminal. Whether the Soviet government has enforced unfair laws or simply made false charges, the inmates' backbreaking labor in subzero temperatures is grossly unjust punishment. The laws that govern the labor camp are as shocking as those that govern Russia. Shukhov is threatened with three days in the hole for being ill. Buynovsky receives ten days in the hole for trying to bundle up against the cold.

THE IMPORTANCE OF FAITH Although Shukhov does not think or talk about religion for the bulk of the novel, his final conversation with Alyoshka, a devout Baptist, suggests that faith can be a means of survival in the oppressive camp system. Shukhov's interest in Alyoshka's discussion of God, faith, and prayer is an expansion beyond Shukhov's usual thoughts of work, warmth, food, and sleep. When Alyoshka urges Shukhov to pursue matters of the spirit rather than matters of the flesh, Shukhov's speechlessness suggests that he is struck by Alyoshka's advice. More important, he actually follows this advice by giving Alyoshka one of his biscuits, voluntarily sacrificing a worldly good in order to treat a fellow human with kindness. Shukhov's inner peace in the novel's last paragraph suggests that religious faith offers strength in the face of adversity.

SYMBOLS IN *ONE DAY IN THE LIFE OF IVAN DENISOVICH*

SHUKHOV'S SPOON The spoon that Shukhov hides in his boot after every meal represents his individuality. The spoon is a useful tool, but it also makes Shukhov feel unique because it is something the other prisoners do not have. The spoon symbolizes the prisoners' need to hide the special and unique part of themselves from the camp's impersonal officialdom and dehumanization. That Shukhov's most prized possession is his spoon, a nurturing tool, rather than his folding knife, a destructive tool, symbolizes his focus on himself. He is committed to taking care of himself and to preserving his identity.

TSEZAR'S PARCEL Tsezar's parcel of fine food symbolizes life's worldly pleasures. Tsezar's mysterious care packages inspire the envy of the starving prisoners and the interest of the guards and officers, who give Tsezar special privileges in exchange for a share of his bounty. But the biblical connotation of Tsezar's name suggests the fleeting nature of his material wealth. "Tsezar" is a Russian version of the name "Caesar." According to the New Testament, Jesus urged his disciples to "render therefore unto Caesar the things which are Caesar's; and unto God the things that are God's," pointing out the difference between worldly and spiritual riches (Matthew 22:21). Similarly, Alyoshka urges Shukhov to look beyond this life—symbolized by Tsezar's parcel of treasures—toward a spiritual existence.

IMPORTANT QUOTATIONS FROM *ONE DAY IN THE LIFE OF IVAN DENISOVICH*

"*Since then it's been decreed that the sun is highest at one o'clock.*"

"Who decreed that?"
"The Soviet government."

Location: Section 5
Speaker: Buynovsky and Shukhov
Context: Buynovsky jokes about a new decree

This exchange between Buynovsky, who jokingly announces the Soviet decree, and Shukhov, who inno-cently half-believes it, shows the absurd pompousness of the Soviet government. Buynovsky's joke sends up the Soviet state's belief in itself as all-powerful, able not only to control the lives of its citizens but to change the very laws of nature. The exchange also demonstrates the disparity of intellect between Buynovsky and Shukhov. Buynovsky is a cultivated Muscovite with artistic interests. His joke satirizing the Soviet state attests to his sophisticated wit. Shukhov, on the other hand, is perhaps not intelligent enough to understand the joke, since his naïve question shows his willingness to believe in such an absurd decree. Still, the fact that Shukhov almost believes Buynovsky also testifies to the incredible hubris of the Soviet government.

His mind and his eyes were studying the wall, the façade of the Power Station, two cinder blocks thick, as it showed from under the ice. Whoever had been laying there before was either a bungler or a slacker. Shukhov would get to know every inch of that wall as if he owned it.

Location: Section 7
Speaker: The narrator
Context: Shukhov examines the wall

The passage reveals Shukhov's passion and intensity. Shukhov is a hard worker whose motivation comes from a deep reserve of energy and concentration—not from external goads or threats. He genuinely cares about doing an excellent job on this wall and scorns the poor job done by the previous worker. This pos-itive portrayal of a Soviet worker was surely one of the reasons that then Soviet prime minister Nikita Khrushchev approved of *One Day in the Life of Ivan Denisovich* in 1962. The phrase "as if he owned it," describing Shukhov's intense relationship with the task at hand, refers to the concept of ownership that is central to both capitalism and communism. While ownership in capitalism refers to the actual posses-sion of items, in communism it refers to something less materialistic. A communist would point to Shukhov's pride in his craftsmanship as evidence that he feels full ownership over the labor he is carrying out and over his existence in general. On one level, Shukhov is a Soviet slave who owns nothing. But on another level, Shukhov's flashes of contentment in the camp and his apparent spiritual contentment at the end of the novel suggest that people who live in a communal society may own their lives as fully as or more than people who live in a capitalist society.

Next, he removed his cap from his shaven head—however cold it was, he wouldn't let himself eat with his cap on—and stirred up his skilly, quickly checking what had found its way into his bowl.

Location: Section 1
Speaker: The narrator
Context: Shukhov prepares to eat breakfast

Writing letters now was like throwing stones into a bottomless pool. They sank without a trace. No point in telling the family which gang you worked in and what your foreman, Andrei Prokofyevich Tyurin, was like. Nowadays you had more to say to Kildigs, the Latvian, than to the folks at home.

Location: Section 4
Speaker: The narrator
Context: Shukhov thinks about the uselessness of writing letters

---

"Come on, boys, don't let it get you down! It's only a Power Station, but we'll make it a home away from home."

Location: Section 7
Speaker: Tyurin
Context: The foreman of Gang 104 calls the men to action

ONE FLEW OVER THE CUCKOO'S NEST

Ken Kesey

A patient in a horrifying mental hospital is invigorated by the presence of a brave, wild, rebellious fellow patient.

THE LIFE OF KEN KESEY

Ken Kesey was born in 1935 in La Junta, Colorado, and grew up in Oregon. In high school, he was voted most likely to succeed. Kesey married in 1956, a year before receiving his bachelor's degree from the University of Oregon. While attending the creative writing program at Stanford University, Kesey volunteered to test the effects of new drugs at the local Veterans Administration hospital. During this time, he discovered LSD and became interested in studying alternative methods of perception. He soon took a job in a mental institution, where he spoke extensively to the patients. His very successful novel *One Flew Over the Cuckoo's Nest* (1962) was largely based on his experiences in the mental institution.

With the proceeds from his novel, Kesey purchased a farm in California, where he and his friends experimented heavily with LSD. He soon became the focus of a growing drug cult. He believed that using LSD to achieve altered states of mind could improve society. Kesey's high profile as an LSD guru attracted the attention of legal authorities. Kesey fled to Mexico after he was caught trying to flush some marijuana down a toilet. When he returned to the United States, he was arrested and sent to jail for several months.

In 1964, Kesey led a group of friends called the Merry Pranksters on a road trip across the United States in a bus named Furthur. The trip involved massive consumption of LSD and numerous subversive adventures. Tom Wolfe detailed the exploits of the Merry Pranksters in *The Electric Kool-Aid Acid Test*, a must-read book for the hippie generation. Kesey died in November 2001.

ONE FLEW OVER THE CUCKOO'S NEST IN CONTEXT

One Flew Over the Cuckoo's Nest is based on Kesey's personal experiences with mental patients. Through the conflict between Nurse Ratched and Randle Patrick McMurphy, the novel explores individuality and rebellion against conformity, ideas that were particularly important to Americans in the 1960s, when the United States was committed to opposing communism and totalitarian regimes around the world. In a move that was revolutionary at the time, Kesey criticized American institutions themselves.

Dale Wasserman adapted *One Flew Over the Cuckoo's Nest* into a play that ran on Broadway in 1963, with Kirk Douglas in the leading role. In 1975, a film version directed by Milos Forman was released without Kesey's permission. It was extremely successful, although it differed significantly from the novel. It was nominated for nine Academy Awards and swept the five major categories. As a result of the film's success, many people associate Randle McMurphy with Jack Nicholson, the famous actor who portrayed him.

ONE FLEW OVER THE CUCKOO'S NEST: KEY FACTS

Time and place written: The late 1950s; Stanford University in California

Date of first publication: 1962

Publisher: Viking Press

Type of work: Novel

Genre: Allegorical novel; social protest novel; protest novel

Language: English

Setting (time): 1950s

Setting (place): A mental hospital in Oregon

Tense: Present

Tone: Critical, psychedelic, paranoid, mischievous, humorous

Narrator: Chief Bromden, also known as Chief Broom, in the first person

Point of view: Chief Bromden's

Protagonist: Randle P. McMurphy

Antagonist: Nurse Ratched, who represents the oppressive force of modern society

ONE FLEW OVER THE CUCKOO'S NEST: PLOT OVERVIEW

Chief Bromden, the half-Indian narrator of *One Flew Over the Cuckoo's Nest*, has been a patient in an Oregon psychiatric hospital for ten years. He is a paranoid man who suffers from hallucinations and delusions. He fears what he calls the Combine, a huge conglomeration that controls society and forces people to conform. Bromden, who is six feet seven inches tall, pretends to be deaf and dumb and tries to go unnoticed.

All of the mental patients are male. They are divided into Acutes, who can be cured, and Chronics, who cannot be cured. Nurse Ratched, a former army nurse, rules the ward with harsh, mechanical precision. During daily Group Meetings, she encourages the Acutes to attack each other's vulnerabilities. If a patient rebels, he is sent to receive electroshock treatments and sometimes a lobotomy, even though both practices have fallen out of favor with the medical community.

A man named Randle McMurphy arrives as a transfer from the Pendleton Work Farm. McMurphy swaggers into the ward and introduces himself as a gambling man with a zest for women and cards. After McMurphy attends his first Group Meeting he tells the patients that Nurse Ratched is a ball-cutter. The other patients view Nurse Ratched as an all-powerful force and say there is no way to defeat her. McMurphy makes a bet that he can make Ratched lose her temper within a week.

At first, the confrontations between Ratched and McMurphy entertain the other patients. But soon McMurphy's insubordination makes them rebellious. To win his bet, McMurphy resists Nurse Ratched's ban on watching the World Series, which is broadcast during chore time. McMurphy protests by sitting in front of the blank television instead of doing his work, and one by one the other patients join him. Nurse Ratched loses control and screams at them. Bromden observes that an outsider would think all of them were crazy, including the nurse.

In Part II, McMurphy, flush with victory, taunts Nurse Ratched and the staff with abandon. McMurphy eventually learns that involuntarily committed patients are stuck in the hospital until the staff decides they are cured, which means he is at Nurse Ratched's mercy. McMurphy begins to submit to her authority, which confuses the other patients. Cheswick, dismayed when McMurphy fails to join him in a stand against Nurse Ratched, drowns in the pool in a possible suicide.

Cheswick's death shows McMurphy that he has unwittingly taken on the responsibility of rehabilitating the other patients. He also witnesses the harsh reality of electroshock therapy and becomes genuinely frightened by the power wielded by the staff. The weight of his obligation to the other patients and his fear for his own life begin to wear down his strength and his sanity. In Part III, he arranges a fishing trip for himself and ten other patients. He shows them how to defuse the hostility of the outside world and enables them to feel powerful and masculine as they catch large fish without his help. He also sets up a date for Billy Bibbit, a virgin, with Candy Starr, a prostitute from Portland.

In Part IV, McMurphy gets into a fistfight with the aides in an attempt to defend George Sorenson. Bromden joins in, and they are both sent to the Disturbed ward for electroshock therapy. McMurphy acts as if the shock treatments do not affect him, and his heroic reputation grows. Nurse Ratched brings him back to the ward so the other patients can see his weakened state. The patients urge McMurphy to escape, but he has arranged Billy's date for that night, and he refuses to let Billy down. McMurphy bribes Mr. Turkle, the night aide, to sneak Candy into the hospital, and they have a party on the ward. Billy has sex with Candy while McMurphy and the other patients smoke marijuana and drink. Harding tries to get McMurphy to escape, but McMurphy is too wasted and falls asleep.

The next morning, when Nurse Ratched finds Billy with Candy, she threatens to tell Billy's mother. Billy becomes hysterical and commits suicide. McMurphy attacks Ratched, ripping open the front of her dress and attempting to strangle her. In retaliation, she has him lobotomized, and he turns into a vegetable. But Ratched has lost her tyrannical power over the ward. The patients transfer to other wards or check themselves out of the hospital. Bromden suffocates McMurphy in his bed, enabling him to die with some dignity rather than live as a symbol of Ratched's power. Bromden, having recovered the immense strength that he thought he had lost during his time in the mental ward, escapes from the hospital by breaking through a window.

CHARACTERS IN *ONE FLEW OVER THE CUCKOO'S NEST*

Pete Bancini   A hospital patient with brain damage. Pete always says he is tired. At one point, he tells the other patients he was born dead.

Billy Bibbit   A shy patient. Billy has a bad stutter and seems much younger than his thirty-one years. He is dominated by his mother, who is one of Nurse Ratched's close friends. Billy chooses to stay in the hospital because he is afraid of the outside world.

Chief Bromden   The narrator of the novel. Chief Bromden suffers from paranoia and hallucinations. He sees the hospital as a place meant to fix people who do not conform.

Charles Cheswick   The first patient to support McMurphy's rebellion against Nurse Ratched. His death, a possible suicide, shows McMurphy the extent of his influence.

Ellis   A patient. Ellis, once an Acute, became a Chronic after excessive electroshock therapy. In the daytime, he is nailed to the wall. He frequently urinates on himself.

Sandy Gilfillian   A prostitute who knows McMurphy.

Dale Harding   An acerbic, college-educated patient and president of the Patients' Council. Harding is a married homosexual who voluntarily stays in the hospital because he has difficulty dealing with society's bigotry. Eventually, he checks himself out of the ward and paves the way for the other cured patients to leave.

The lifeguard   A patient and a former football player. The lifeguard often hallucinates.

Martini   A patient. Martini lives in a world of delusional hallucinations.

Randle McMurphy   The novel's protagonist. Randle McMurphy is a big, redheaded gambler, con man, and backroom boxer. His body is heavily scarred and tattooed. McMurphy was diagnosed as a psychopath for fighting and having sex too much. He is an unlikely Christ figure in the novel.

Chief Tee Ah Millatoona   Chief Bromden's father, also known as The Pine That Stands Tallest on the Mountain. Chief Millatoona, chief of the Columbia Indians, married a Caucasian woman who made him feel small and drove him to alcoholism.

Old Blastic   A patient. Bromden, who is a vegetable, has a prophetic dream about a mechanical slaughterhouse in which Old Blastic is murdered.

Nurse Pilbow   A strict Catholic with a prominent birthmark on her face that she attempts to scrub away. Nurse Pilbow is afraid of the patients' sexuality.

Public Relation   A fat, bald bureaucrat who wears a girdle. Public Relation leads tours of the ward, claiming that it is nice and pleasant.

Nurse Ratched   The head of the hospital ward. Nurse Ratched, the novel's antagonist, is a middle-aged former army nurse who rules her ward with an iron hand. She selects her staff members for their submissiveness and systematically destroys her patients' self-esteem and masculinity.

Rawler   A patient on the Disturbed ward. Rawler commits suicide by cutting off his testicles, a literal castration that symbolizes the psychological emasculation of the patients.

Ruckly   A Chronic patient. Ruckly, like Ellis, was once an Acute but became a Chronic after a botched lobotomy.

Scanlon   The only Acute besides McMurphy who was involuntarily committed to the hospital.

Sefelt and Frederickson Epileptic patients. Sefelt hates to take his medications because they make his teeth fall out, so he gives them to Frederickson.

George Sorenson A patient. Sorenson, a big Swede, is a former seaman nicknamed "Rub-a-Dub George" because he fears dirtiness.

Doctor Spivey A mild-mannered doctor who may be addicted to opiates. Nurse Ratched chose Doctor Spivey as the doctor for her ward because he is as easily cowed and dominated as the patients. When McMurphy arrives, Doctor Spivey begins to assert himself.

Candy Starr A beautiful, carefree prostitute from Portland.

Maxwell Taber A former patient. When Maxwell Taber questioned Nurse Ratched's authority, she punished him with electroshock therapy. After the treatments made him completely docile, he was allowed to leave the hospital. The hospital staff considers him a successful cure.

Mr. Turkle The black nighttime orderly for Nurse Ratched's ward. Mr. Turkle is kind to Bromden.

Warren, Washington, Williams, and Geever Hospital aides. Nurse Ratched hired them because they are filled with hatred and will submit to her wishes completely.

THEMES IN *ONE FLEW OVER THE CUCKOO'S NEST*

WOMEN AS CASTRATORS With the exception of the prostitutes, the women in *One Flew Over the Cuckoo's Nest* are portrayed as terrifying demons. Bromden and McMurphy frequently liken the suffering of the mental patients to emasculation or castration at the hands of Nurse Ratched and the female hospital supervisor. The male characters seem to agree with Harding, who complains, "We are victims of a matriarchy here." Most of the male patients have been damaged by relationships with overpowering women. Bromden's mother is a castrating woman who forced her husband to take her last name, transforming him from a big, strong chief into a small, weak alcoholic. Billy Bibbit's mother treats him like an infant and does not allow him to develop sexually. Images of castration fill the novel. When Rawler commits suicide by cutting off his own testicles, Bromden says "all the guy had to do was wait," implying that the institution itself would have castrated him in the long run. Near the end of the novel, after McMurphy has already received three ineffectual shock treatments, Nurse Ratched suggests taking more drastic measures: "an operation." She means a lobotomy, but McMurphy jokes about castration. Kesey suggests that the two operations are essentially the same—both remove a man's individuality, freedom, and sexual being.

THE IMPORTANCE OF EXPRESSING SEXUALITY Kesey argues that the healthy expression of sexuality is a key component of sanity and that repression of sexuality leads directly to insanity. Most of the patients have warped sexual identities because of damaging relationships with women. In the ward, the patients' sexuality is at the mercy of the aides, who force them to engage in illicit "sex acts" and rape them with Ratched's implicit permission. This sexual abuse turns the patients into "comical little creatures who can't even achieve masculinity in the rabbit world." Missing from the halls of the mental hospital are healthy, natural expressions of sexuality between two people. McMurphy rebels against Nurse Ratched's perverted ideas about sex by flaunting his own sexuality. He has playing cards depicting fifty-two sexual positions, he speaks proudly of a voracious fifteen-year-old lover, and he wears Moby-Dick boxer shorts. In the end, even McMurphy's robust sexuality wilts under pressure from society.

FALSE DIAGNOSES OF INSANITY Sane patients find themselves in an impossible situation: if they question the irrationality of the hospital, the hospital officials will wreak vengeance on them. Nurse Ratched speaks of a former patient, Maxwell Taber, who once asked a nurse what kind of medication he was being given. As punishment for this question, he was subjected to electroshock treatments and possibly brain work, which left him docile and unable to think. The patients constantly seem more sane than their captors. When McMurphy and the patients try to watch the World Series, for example, Nurse Ratched loses control. Harding suggests that Nurse Ratched, like Hitler, is a psychopath who has discovered how to use her insanity to her advantage. Bromden once thinks to himself, "You're making sense, old man, a sense of your own. You're not crazy the way they think." But "crazy the way they think" is all that matters in this hospital, where the authorities decide who is sane and who is insane.

SYMBOLS IN *ONE FLEW OVER THE CUCKOO'S NEST*

MCMURPHY'S BOXER SHORTS A literature major gave McMurphy's whale shorts to him, saying that McMurphy is himself a symbol. The shorts themselves have several symbolic meanings. First, they suggest McMurphy's potent sexuality. The white whales evoke Moby-Dick, a potent figure in literature sometimes interpreted as a phallic symbol. Moby-Dick also represents the evil that inspires Ahab's obsessive, futile pursuit, which suggests that McMurphy is Moby-Dick to Ratched's Ahab. Moby-Dick also stands for the power of nature, signifying McMurphy's refusal to bow down to civilization. Moby-Dick is also associated with God, which resonates with McMurphy's role as a Christ figure. Finally, the whale boxer shorts poke fun at academia and its elaborate interpretations of symbols.

THE ELECTROSHOCK THERAPY TABLE Kesey uses the electroshock therapy table as a symbol for the cross. It is shaped like a cross and performs a function similar to the public crucifixions of Roman times. Ellis, Ruckly, and Taber are "crucified" on the table, made into public examples of what happens to those who rebel against the ruling powers.

IMPORTANT QUOTATIONS FROM *ONE FLEW OVER THE CUCKOO'S NEST*

So you see my friend, it is somewhat as you stated: man has but one truly effective weapon against the juggernaut of modern matriarchy, but it certainly is not laughter. One weapon, and with every passing year in this hip, motivationally researched society, more and more people are discovering how to render that weapon useless and conquer those who have hitherto been conquerors.. . . .

Location: Part I
Speaker: Harding
Context: Harding explains his theory about women

In this passage, Kesey uses Harding as a mouthpiece to introduce his misogynistic theory about modern society. Harding tells McMurphy that the penis is a man's only weapon against women, and that unless men use rape effectively, they have no chance of regaining power in society. Kesey believes that women know how to render men's one weapon useless—in other words, they are all castrators. Kesey fleshes out these crude ideas in the rest of the novel. He equates McMurphy's fearless sexuality with sanity, and lovingly portrays McMurphy's sexual harassment of Ratched. McMurphy wears only a towel, pinches Ratched's rear, remarks on her breasts, and eventually tears open her shirt. Most of the male patients were driven insane by bad relationships with women. Kesey also suggests that only through sex with Candy can Billy briefly regain his confidence and manhood. Kesey's attitude toward women is encapsulated in Harding's claim: "We are victims of a matriarchy here."

Except the sun, on these three strangers, is all of a sudden way the hell brighter than usual and I can see the . . . seams where they're put together. And, almost, see the apparatus inside them take the words I just said and try to fit the words in here and there, this place and that, and when they find the words don't have any place ready-made where they'll fit, the machinery disposes of the words like they weren't even spoken.

Location: Part III
Speaker: Bromden
Context: Bromden remembers an incident that happened when he was ten

Bromden remembers when three government officials came to speak to his father, Chief Tee Ah Millatoona, about buying the tribe's land to build a hydroelectric dam. When Bromden tried to speak to them, he realized that they were dismissing anything they didn't want to hear. He began to see the seams on people, as if they were inhuman machines. Kesey thinks the drones who do the dirty work of an oppressive society are basically machines willing to destroy nature, just as the government officials who visited

Bromden's father wanted to make a profit by destroying the tribe's ancient connection to the land, the river, and the fish. These officials taught Bromden that people who do not have "any place ready-made where they'll fit" will be ignored.

I been silent so long now it's gonna roar out of me like floodwaters and you think the guy telling this is ranting and raving my God; you think this is too horrible to have really happened, this is too awful to be the truth! But, please. It's still hard for me to have a clear mind thinking on it. But it's the truth even if it didn't happen.

Location: Part I
Speaker: Chief Bromden
Context: Bromden, our unreliable narrator, asks us to keep an open mind

---

The flock gets sight of a spot of blood on some chicken and they all go to peckin' at it, see, till they rip the chicken to shreds, blood and bones and feathers. But usually a couple of the flock gets spotted in the fracas, then it's their turn. And a few more gets spots and gets pecked to death, and more and more. Oh, a peckin' party can wipe out the whole flock in a matter of a few hours, buddy, I seen it.

Location: Part I
Speaker: McMurphy
Context: McMurphy likens the Group Meeting to a deadly pecking party

---

While McMurphy laughs. Rocking farther and farther backward against the cabin top, spreading his laugh out across the water — laughing at the girl, the guys, at George, at me sucking my bleeding thumb, at the captain back at the pier and the bicycle rider and the service-station guys and the five thousand houses and the Big Nurse and all of it. Because he knows you have to laugh at the things that hurt you just to keep yourself in balance, just to keep the world from running you plumb crazy.

Location: Part III
Speaker: Bromden
Context: On the fishing expedition, the patients follow McMurphy's example and laugh

ONE HUNDRED YEARS OF SOLITUDE

Gabriel García Márquez

The fortunes of a family wax and wane along with the fortunes of Macondo, the town they founded.

THE LIFE OF GABRIEL GARCÍA MÁRQUEZ

Gabriel García Márquez was born in 1928 in the small town of Aracataca, Colombia. He worked as a journalist for many years. In the mid-1950s, he published short stories and novels for the first time. When *Cien Años de Soledad* (*One Hundred Years of Solitude*) was published in 1967, García Márquez achieved international fame. García Márquez was one of the central figures in *El Boom*, the burst of popular Latin-American writing in the 1960s and 1970s. *One Hundred Years of Solitude* is perhaps the most important and widely read text to emerge from that period. It is also a central work for magical realism, a genre characterized by dreamlike and fantastic elements woven into ordinary events. *One Hundred Years of Solitude* won almost every literary prize awarded in the Western world. In 1982, García Márquez was awarded the Nobel Prize for Literature.

Since the publication of *One Hundred Years of Solitude*, García Márquez has continued to receive accolades for his novels, especially *Chronicle of a Death Foretold* (1981) and *Love in the Time of Cholera* (1985). Today, he lives in Mexico City and, despite being diagnosed with lymphatic cancer, has begun a projected three-volume set of memoirs.

ONE HUNDRED YEARS OF SOLITUDE IN CONTEXT

One Hundred Years of Solitude is a political novel. The progress of the village of Macondo reflects the progress of Latin America, which once had a thriving population of native Aztecs and Incas and changed drastically when European explorers introduced technology and capitalism. *One Hundred Years of Solitude* captures the early days of Latin America as well as the current political status of various Latin American countries. Macondo's frequently fluctuating government suggests the instability of many Latin American nations, which struggle to install stable, organized governments. The various dictatorships that come into power throughout the course of *One Hundred Years of Solitude* mirror dictatorships that have ruled in Nicaragua, Panama, and Cuba. García Márquez's real-life political leanings are decidedly revolutionary, even communist: he is a friend of Fidel Castro. But his depictions of cruel dictatorships show that his communist sympathies do not extend to the cruel governments that communism sometimes produces.

One Hundred Years of Solitude is partly a fictional rendering of García Márquez's own experiences. It is also an ambitious overview of the histories of civil war, plantations, and labor unrest. *One Hundred Years of Solitude* tells a story about Colombian history and, even more broadly, about Latin America's struggles with colonialism and modernity.

ONE HUNDRED YEARS OF SOLITUDE: KEY FACTS

Time and place written: 1965–1967;, Mexico City

Date of first publication: 1967

Publisher: Editorial Sudamericanos, S.A.

Type of work: Novel

Genre: Magical realism

Language: Spanish

Setting (time): Early 1800s–mid 1900s

Setting (place): Macondo, a fictional village in Colombia

Tense: Past	
Tone: Wondering, sympathetic, detached	
Narrator: Omniscient narrator in the third person	
Point of view: The narrator's	
Protagonist: The Buendía family	
Antagonist: The struggle between old and new ways of life	

ONE HUNDRED YEARS OF SOLITUDE: PLOT OVERVIEW

One Hundred Years of Solitude is the history of the isolated town of Macondo and of the Buendía family, which founded the town. For years, Macondo has no contact with the outside world except for gypsies who visit occasionally, peddling technologies like ice and telescopes. The patriarch of the family, José Arcadio Buendía, is impulsive, inquisitive, and deeply solitary—character traits his descendents will inherent. Buendía's oldest child, José Arcadio, is impetuous and vastly strong. His younger child, Aureliano, is intense and enigmatic.

The village loses its innocence and solitude as it gradually establishes contact with other towns in the region. Civil wars begin, bringing violence and death to Macondo for the first time. Aureliano becomes the leader of the Liberal rebels, achieving fame as Colonel Aureliano Buendía. Macondo's government changes hands several times during and after the war. Arcadio, the cruelest of the Buendías, rules as dictator for a time. Eventually, a firing squad shoots him. A mayor rules for a while, but he dies during another civil uprising. After his death, a peace treaty is signed and the civil war ends.

The novel covers more than a century in the lives of the Buendía family. García Márquez describes the major events in the lives of the Buendías: births, deaths, marriages, love affairs. Some of the Buendía men are wild and sexually rapacious, frequenting brothels and taking lovers. Others are quiet and solitary, preferring to shut themselves up in their rooms to make tiny golden fish or to pore over ancient manuscripts. Some of the Buendía women are outrageously outgoing, bringing home seventy-two friends from boarding school and carrying on passionate affairs. Others are prim and proper, like Fernanda del Carpio, who wears a special nightgown with a hole at the crotch when she consummates her marriage with her husband.

Úrsula Iguarán, the family's tenacious matriarch, devotedly works to keep the family together despite its differences. But for the Buendía family, as for the village of Macondo, the forces of modernity are devastating. A banana plantation takes over Macondo, exploiting the land and the workers. The Americans who own the plantation settle in their own gated section of town. Eventually, angry at the inhumane way in which they are treated, the banana workers go on strike. The army, in league with the plantation owners, massacres thousands of the striking workers. Five years of ceaseless rain begins, creating a flood that sends Macondo into its final decline. As the city begins to slip away, so does the Buendía family. As the novel ends, the village is isolated once again. The few remaining Buendía family members turn in upon themselves incestuously, as they have always done. In the final scene of the novel, the last surviving Buendía translates a set of ancient prophecies and finds that they are an accurate prediction of the fate of his family.

CHARACTERS IN *ONE HUNDRED YEARS OF SOLITUDE*

A NOTE ABOUT THE NAMES

García Márquez gives the Buendía family members a very limited selection of names, perhaps to emphasize the idea that each generation of the family is doomed to repeat the mistakes and triumphs of the one that preceded it. In each of the six Buendía generations, the men are named José Arcadio or Aureliano and the women are named Úrsula, Amaranta, or Remedios.

Some characters have the exact same name (José Arcadio Buendía and his son, for example), but García Márquez differentiates between them with nicknames. For example, he always refers to José Arcadio Buendía's son as José Arcadio. We have replicated this practice in the character list. In cases where García Márquez refers to two characters by the exact same name, we have numbered the characters for the sake of clarity.

THE BUENDÍA FAMILY: FIRST GENERATION

José Arcadio Buendía The patriarch of the Buendía clan. José Arcadio Buendía is Macondo's founder and its most charismatic citizen. He is a man of great strength and curiosity. His solitary and obsessive quest for knowledge eventually drives him mad. He spends many years tied to a tree in the Buendía backyard. José Arcadio Buendía is married to Úrsula Iguarán. He is the father of José Arcadio, Colonel Aureliano Buendía, and Amaranta.

Úrsula Iguarán The tenacious matriarch of the Buendía clan. Úrsula lives for well over one hundred years. She revitalizes the family both physically and emotionally. Úrsula is the wife of José Arcadio Buendía and the mother of José Arcadio, Colonel Aureliano Buendía, and Amaranta.

THE BUENDÍA FAMILY: SECOND GENERATION

Amaranta The daughter of Úrsula Iguarán and José Arcadio Buendía. Amaranta fears men. When Pietro Crespi finally falls in love with her, she rejects him, and he kills himself. Aureliano José incestuously lusts after her. Amaranta dies an embittered and lonely virgin. She is the sister of Colonel Aureliano Buendía and José Arcadio.

José Arcadio The first son of Úrsula Iguarán and José Arcadio Buendía. José Arcadio is impulsive and amazingly strong. After running off in pursuit of a gypsy girl, he returns a savage brute of a man and marries Rebeca. He is the father, with Pilar Ternera, of Arcadio. He is brother to Colonel Aureliano Buendía and Amaranta.

Colonel Aureliano Buendía The second son of José Arcadio Buendía and Úrsula Iguarán. Aureliano is solitary and keenly perceptive. Outraged by the corruption of the Conservative government, he joins the Liberal rebellion and becomes Colonel Aureliano Buendía. After years of fighting, he loses his capacity for memory and deep emotion. He withdraws into his workshop, a lonely and hardened man. He is the widower of Remedios Moscote and the father, with Pilar Ternera, of Aureliano José. He also fathers seventeen sons—each named Aureliano—by seventeen different women.

Remedios Moscote The child-bride of Colonel Aureliano Buendía. Remedios Moscote brings joy to the Buendía household for a short while before she dies suddenly, possibly of a miscarriage.

Rebeca An earth-eating orphan girl whom the Buendías adopt. Rebeca infects the town with a plague of memory loss. After the death of her husband, José Arcadio, she becomes a hermit.

THE BUENDÍA FAMILY: THIRD GENERATION

Arcadio The son of José Arcadio and Pilar Ternera. When Colonel Aureliano Buendía places Arcadio in charge of Macondo during the uprising, Arcadio becomes a vicious dictator. Arcadio marries Santa Sofía de la Piedad. He is the father of Remedios the Beauty, Aureliano Segundo, and José Arcadio Segundo.

Aureliano José The son of Colonel Aureliano Buendía and Pilar Ternera. Aureliano José becomes obsessed with his aunt, Amaranta, and joins his father's army when she ends the affair. He deserts the army to return to her, but she rejects him again. He is killed by Conservative soldiers.

Santa Sofía de la Piedad Arcadio's wife. A quiet woman, she continues to live in the Buendía house for many years after her husband's death. She is the mother of Remedios the Beauty, Aureliano Segundo, and José Arcadio Segundo. When she grows old and tired, she simply walks out of the house, never to be heard from again.

THE BUENDÍA FAMILY: FOURTH GENERATION

Fernanda del Carpio The wife of Aureliano Segundo and the mother of Meme, José Arcadio (2), and Amaranta Úrsula. Fernanda del Carpio comes from a family of impoverished aristocrats. She is very haughty and religious.

Remedios the Beauty The daughter of Santa Sofía de la Piedad and Arcadio. Remedios the Beauty is the most beautiful woman in the world, although she does not realize it. One day, she floats to heaven.

Aureliano Segundo The son of Arcadio and Santa Sofía de la Piedad and the twin brother of José Arcadio Segundo. Aureliano Segundo is immense, boisterous, impulsive, and hedonistic. He marries the cold beauty Fernanda del Carpio and has three children with her, but he never ends his affair with his true love, the concubine Petra Cotes.

José Arcadio Segundo The son of Arcadio and Santa Sofía de la Piedad and the twin brother of Aureliano Segundo. José Arcadio Segundo is thin, bony, solitary, and scholarly. He is the lone survivor of the massacre of the strikers, and when he finds that everyone denies that the massacre occurred, he secludes himself in Melquíades' old study, trying to decipher prophecies.

THE BUENDÍA FAMILY: FIFTH GENERATION

José Arcadio (2) The eldest child of Aureliano Segundo and Fernanda del Carpio. Úrsula thinks that José Arcadio (2) is destined to become the Pope, but he slides into dissolution and solitude. José Arcadio (2) leads a life of debauchery with local children who eventually murder him and steal his money.

Gaston The Belgian husband of Amaranta Úrsula. Gaston is loving and cultured but feels isolated in Macondo. He travels to Belgium and, after hearing of the relationship between his wife and Aureliano (2), never returns.

Meme The daughter of Fernanda del Carpio and Aureliano Segundo. Meme's real name is Renata Remedios. A hedonist, she has an illicit affair with Mauricio Babilonia and is imprisoned in a convent forever after. She has Babilonia's son, Aureliano (2).

Amaranta Úrsula The daughter of Aureliano Segundo and Fernanda del Carpio. Amaranta Úrsula marries a Belgian man, Gaston. She falls in love with her nephew, Aureliano (2), and gives birth to his child, Aureliano (3), who is born with a pig's tail and turns out to be the last in the Buendía line. Amaranta dies in childbirth.

THE BUENDÍA FAMILY: SIXTH GENERATION

Aureliano (2) The illegitimate son of Meme and Mauricio Babilonia. Fernanda del Carpio hides Aureliano (2) in the Buendía household, scandalized by his existence. Aureliano (2) becomes a scholar and eventually deciphers the prophecies of Melquíades. With his aunt, Amaranta Úrsula, he fathers the last in the Buendía line, the baby Aureliano (3), who dies soon after birth.

CHARACTERS WHO ARE NOT MEMBERS OF THE BUENDÍA FAMILY

Mauricio Babilonia Meme's lover. A guard shoots the sallow, solemn Mauricio Babilonia, paralyzing him completely. Mauricio Babilonia fathers Meme's child, Aureliano (2).

Petra Cotes Aureliano Segundo's concubine. Petra Cotes and Aureliano Segundo have a supernaturally intense love for each other.

Pietro Crespi A gentle, delicate Italian musician. Both Amaranta and Rebeca love Pietro Crespi, although Rebeca eventually marries the more manly José Arcadio. Pietro commits suicide after Amaranta rejects him.

Colonel Gerineldo Márquez A comrade-in-arms of Colonel Aureliano Buendía. Colonel Gerineldo is the first to tire of the civil war. He falls in love with Amaranta, who spurns him.

Melquíades A gypsy. Melquíades brings technological marvels to Macondo and befriends the Buendía clan. He guides José Arcadio Buendía in his quest for knowledge. Even after dying, Melquíades returns to guide other generations of Buendías. Melquíades writes prophecies about the entire history of Macondo.

Don Apolinar Moscote Father of Remedios Moscote and government-appointed magistrate of Macondo. Don Apolinar Moscote, a Conservative, helps rig the election so that his party will win.

Pilar Ternera A local whore and madam. Pilar has Arcadio by José Arcadio and Aureliano by Colonel Aureliano Buendía. She is also a fortune-teller whose quiet wisdom helps guide the Buendía family.

THEMES IN *ONE HUNDRED YEARS OF SOLITUDE*

THE SUBJECTIVITY OF REALITY *One Hundred Years of Solitude* suggests that overemphasis on logic and reason leads to an inability to see that important and powerful strains of magic run through ordinary lives. By using magical realism, García Márquez reflects reality not as it is experienced by one observer, but as it is experienced by many different individuals. He puts equal emphasis on superstition, religion, and objectivity. He treats biblical narratives and native Latin American mythology as historically credible stories. García Márquez blends reality and fiction partly to suggest that in some cases reality *becomes* fiction. For example, the people of Macondo refuse to admit that thousands were massacred, turning the horrifying reality into a dim dream. Real life becomes a fascinating, scary fantasy, and fantasy becomes a more palatable reality.

THE INSEPARABILITY OF PAST, PRESENT, AND FUTURE *One Hundred Years of Solitude* does not divide neatly into past, present, and future. García Márquez gives his characters the same names and quirks generation after generation, as if the same spirits continually return to the Buendía family in slightly different forms. Time doubles back on itself. Úrsula Iguarán notices that in Macondo, people cannot see the past any more than they can see the future. Other times, the future is as easy to recall as the past. Melquíades sees all of time, noting the fate of the Buendía family as if noting some well-known fact from the past. Melquíades and José Arcadio Buendía wander around after their deaths, suggesting that even mortality does not interfere with the flexibility of time.

THE POWER OF READING AND OF LANGUAGE The language of Macondo residents is in a primitive state at the beginning of *One Hundred Years of Solitude*, but it quickly becomes more complex. Various languages fill the novel, including the Guajiro language that the children learn, the multilingual tattoos that cover José Arcadio's body, the Latin spoken by José Arcadio Buendía, and the Sanskrit translation of Melquíades' prophecies. García Márquez calls attention to his own task as a writer, making the reading of Melquíades' prophecies coincide—or perhaps cause—the final apocalyptic blow that destroys Macondo. This moment of destruction also reminds us that our reading brings *One Hundred Years of Solitude* into being. Like Melquíades' prophecies, which must be translated and interpreted, *One Hundred Years of Solitude* must be read and understood slightly differently by each reader.

SYMBOLS IN *ONE HUNDRED YEARS OF SOLITUDE*

THE GOLD FISHES The thousands of little gold fishes made by Colonel Aureliano Buendía take on different meanings. At first, they symbolize Aureliano's artistic nature. Aureliano gives each of his seventeen sons a little gold fish, which suggests the way Aureliano effects the world through his sons. The messengers for the Liberals use the gold fishes to symbolize their allegiance. Many years later, the fishes become relics of a once-great leader. This disgusts Aureliano, so he stops making new fishes and starts melting down the old ones.

THE RAILROAD The railroad symbolizes the arrival of the destructive modern world in Macondo. It also represents the period when Macondo is most closely connected with the outside world. After the banana plantations close down, the railroad falls into disrepair and the train does not stop in Macondo anymore.

IMPORTANT QUOTATIONS FROM *ONE HUNDRED YEARS OF SOLITUDE*

At that time Macondo was a village of twenty adobe houses, built on the bank of a river of clear water that ran along a bed of polished stones, which were white and enormous, like prehistoric eggs. The world was so recent that many things lacked names, and in order to indicate them it was necessary to point.

Location: The beginning of Chapter 1
Speaker: The narrator
Context: The narrator describes early Macondo

García Márquez likens Macondo both to Eden and to the world we know. He explains the primitive nature of language in Macondo, recalling the biblical story of Adam, who had to dream up names for the animals. He also refers to prehistoric eggs, acknowledging the scientific fact of evolution and suggesting that the story of Eden is metaphorical, not literal. By beginning the book with references to two entirely different accounts of creation, García Márquez suggests that he will invent his own mythology.

It was as if God had decided to put to the test every capacity for surprise and was keeping the inhabitants of Macondo in a permanent alternation between excitement and disappointment, doubt and revelation, to such an extreme that no one knew for certain where the limits of reality lay. It was an intricate stew of truths and mirages that convulsed the ghost of José Arcadio Buendía with impatience and made him wander all through the house even in broad daylight.

Location: Chapter 12
Speaker: The narrator
Context: The railroad arrives in Macondo

After the railroad comes to Macondo, dozens of new inventions flood the town—the phonograph, the telephone, and the electric lightbulb, among others. The citizens of Macondo, who consider flying carpets and miraculous rains of yellow flowers part of the natural way of things, doubt the reality of technological inventions. They find it difficult to accept both science and magic. García Márquez humorously points out that one of the people who cannot believe in the telephone is the ghost of José Arcadio Buendía, a being who probably strikes readers as much more unlikely than any technological invention.

Aureliano José had been destined to find with [Carmelita Montiel] the happiness that Amaranta had denied him, to have seven children, and to die in her arms of old age, but the bullet that entered his back and shattered his chest had been directed by a wrong interpretation of the cards.

Location: Chapter 8
Speaker: The narrator
Context: García Márquez pokes fun at the idea that we can know our destinies

---

[Aureliano (2)] saw the epigraph of the parchments perfectly paced in the order of man's time and space: The first of the line is tied to a tree and the last is being eaten by the ants.. . . . Melquíades had not put events in the order of a man's conventional time, but had concentrated a century of daily episodes in such a way that they coexisted in one instant.

Location: Chapter 20
Speaker: The narrator
Context: Aureliano (2) deciphers the prophecies

[Aureliano (2)] had already understood that he would never leave that room, for it was foreseen that the city of mirrors (or mirages) would be wiped out by the wind and exiled from the memory of men at the precise moment when Aureliano Babilonia would finish deciphering the parchments, and that everything written on them was unrepeatable since time immemorial and forever more, because races condemned to one hundred years of solitude did not have a second opportunity on earth.

Location: Chapter 20
Speaker: The narrator
Context: Aureliano (2) reads Melquíades' prophecies, which he believes absolutely

OTHELLO

William Shakespeare

Wracked by irrational jealousy, a man kills his wife.

THE LIFE OF WILLIAM SHAKESPEARE

William Shakespeare, the most influential writer in all of English literature, was born in 1564 to a successful middle-class glove-maker in Stratford-upon-Avon, England. Shakespeare's formal education did not progress beyond grammar school. In 1582, he married an older woman, Anne Hathaway. His union with Anne produced three children. Around 1590, Shakespeare left his family behind and traveled to London to work as an actor and playwright. He quickly earned public and critical acclaim, and eventually became the most popular playwright in England and a part-owner of the Globe Theater. Shakespeare's career bridged the reigns of Elizabeth I (ruled 1558–1603) and James I (ruled 1603–1625), and he was a favorite of both monarchs. James paid Shakespeare's company a great compliment by giving its members the title of King's Men. Shakespeare retired to Stratford a wealthy and renowned man and died in 1616 at the age of fifty-two. At the time of Shakespeare's death, literary luminaries such as Ben Jonson hailed his works as timeless.

Shakespeare's works were collected and printed in various editions in the century following his death, and by the early eighteenth century, his reputation as the greatest poet ever to write in English was well established. The unprecedented regard in which Shakespeare's works were held led to a fierce curiosity about his life, but many details of Shakespeare's personal history are unknown or shrouded in mystery. Some people have concluded from this lack of information and from Shakespeare's modest education that Shakespeare's plays were actually written by someone else—Francis Bacon and the Earl of Oxford are the two most popular candidates—but the support for this claim is overwhelmingly circumstantial, and the theory is not taken seriously by many scholars.

Shakespeare is generally thought to be the author of the thirty-eight plays (two of them possibly collaborations) and 154 sonnets that bear his name. The legacy of this body of work is immense. A number of Shakespeare's plays seem to have transcended even the category of brilliance, influencing the course of Western literature and culture.

OTHELLO IN CONTEXT

Othello was first performed by the King's Men at the court of King James I on November 1, 1604. Written during Shakespeare's great tragic period, which also included the composition of *Hamlet* (1600), *King Lear* (1604–1605), *Macbeth* (1606), and *Antony and Cleopatra* (1606–1607), *Othello* is set against the backdrop of the wars between Venice and Turkey that raged in the latter part of the sixteenth century. Cyprus, which is the setting for most of the action, was a Venetian outpost attacked by the Turks in 1570 and conquered the following year. Shakespeare's information on the Venetian-Turkish conflict probably derives from *The History of the Turks* by Richard Knolles, which was published in England in the autumn of 1603. The story of *Othello* is also derived from another source—an Italian prose tale written in 1565 by Giovanni Battista Giraldi Cinzio (usually referred to as Cinthio). The original story contains the bare bones of Shakespeare's plot: a Moorish general is deceived by his ensign into believing his wife is unfaithful. To Cinthio's story Shakespeare added supporting characters such as the rich young dupe Roderigo and the outraged and grief-stricken Brabanzio, Desdemona's father. Shakespeare compressed the action into the space of a few days and set it against the backdrop of military conflict. Most memorably, he turned the ensign, a minor villain, into the arch-villain Iago.

The question of Othello's exact race is open to some debate. The word "moor" now refers to the Islamic Arabic inhabitants of North Africa who conquered Spain in the eighth century, but the term was used rather broadly in the period and was sometimes applied to Africans from other regions. George Abbott, for example, in his *A Brief Description of the Whole World* of 1599, made distinctions between "blackish Moors" and "black Negroes"; a 1600 translation of John Leo's *The History and Description of Africa* distinguishes "white or tawny Moors" of the Mediterranean coast of Africa from the "Negroes or black Moors" of the south. Othello's darkness or blackness is alluded to many times in the play, but Shakespeare and other Elizabethans frequently described brunette or darker than average Europeans as black. The opposition of black and white imagery that runs throughout *Othello* is certainly a marker of difference between Othello and his European peers, but the difference is never quite so racially specific as a modern reader might imagine it to be.

While Moor characters abound on the Elizabethan and Jacobean stage, none are given so major or heroic a role as Othello. Perhaps the most vividly stereotypical black character of the period is Aaron, the villain of Shakespeare's early play *Titus Andronicus*. The antithesis of Othello, Aaron is lecherous, cunning, and vicious; his final words are: "If one good deed in all my life I did / I do repent it to my very soul" (*Titus Andronicus*, V.iii.188–189). Othello, by contrast, is a noble figure of great authority, respected and admired by the duke and senate of Venice as well as by those who serve him, such as Cassio, Montano, and Lodovico. Only Iago voices an explicitly stereotypical view of Othello, depicting him from the beginning as an animalistic, barbarous, foolish outsider.

OTHELLO: KEY FACTS

Full Title: The Tragedy of Othello, the Moor of Venice	
Time and place written: Between 1601 and 1604; England	
Date of first publication: 1622	
Genre: Tragedy	
Setting (time): Late sixteenth century, during the wars between Venice and Turkey	
Setting (place): Act I: Venice; Acts II–V: Cyprus	
Protagonist: Othello	
Antagonist: Iago	
Major conflict: Othello and Desdemona marry and attempt to build a life together, despite their differences in age, race, and experience. Their marriage is sabotaged by the envious Iago, who convinces Othello that Desdemona is unfaithful.	

OTHELLO: PLOT OVERVIEW

Othello begins on a street in Venice, in the midst of an argument between Roderigo, a rich man, and Iago. Roderigo has been paying Iago to help him in his suit to Desdemona. But Roderigo has just learned that Desdemona has married Othello, a general whom Iago begrudgingly serves as ensign. Iago says he hates Othello, who recently passed him over for the position of lieutenant in favor of the inexperienced soldier Michael Cassio.

Unseen, Iago and Roderigo cry out to Brabanzio that his daughter Desdemona has been stolen by and married to Othello, the Moor. Brabanzio finds that his daughter is indeed missing, and he gathers some officers to find Othello. Not wanting his hatred of Othello to be known, Iago leaves Roderigo and hurries back to Othello before Brabanzio sees him. At Othello's lodgings, Cassio arrives with an urgent message from the duke: Othello's help is needed in the matter of the imminent Turkish invasion of Cyprus. Not long afterward, Brabanzio arrives with Roderigo and others, and accuses Othello of stealing his daughter by witchcraft. When he finds out that Othello is on his way to speak with the duke, Brabanzio decides to go along and accuse Othello before the assembled senate.

Brabanzio's plan backfires. The duke and senate are very sympathetic toward Othello. Given a chance to speak for himself, Othello explains that he wooed and won Desdemona not by witchcraft but with the stories of his adventures in travel and war. The duke finds Othello's explanation convincing, and Desdemona herself enters at this point to defend her choice in marriage and to announce to her father that her allegiance is now to her husband. Brabanzio is frustrated, but acquiesces and allows the senate meeting to resume. The duke says that Othello must go to Cyprus to aid in the defense against the Turks, who are headed for the island. Desdemona insists that she accompany her husband on his trip, and preparations are made for them to depart that night.

In Cyprus the following day, two gentlemen stand on the shore with Montano, the governor of Cyprus. A third gentleman arrives and reports that the Turkish fleet has been wrecked in a storm at sea. Cassio, whose ship did not suffer the same fate, arrives soon after, followed by a second ship carrying

Iago, Roderigo, Desdemona, and Emilia, Iago's wife. Once they have landed, Othello's ship is sighted, and the group goes to the harbor. As they wait for Othello, Cassio greets Desdemona by clasping her hand. Watching them, Iago tells the audience that he will use "as little a web as this" hand-holding to ensnare Cassio (II.i.169).

Othello arrives, greets his wife, and announces that there will be reveling that evening to celebrate Cyprus's safety from the Turks. Once everyone has left, Roderigo complains to Iago that he has no chance of breaking up Othello's marriage. Iago assures Roderigo that as soon as Desdemona's "blood is made dull with the act of sport," she will lose interest in Othello and seek sexual satisfaction elsewhere (II.i.222). However, Iago warns that "elsewhere" will likely be with Cassio. Iago counsels Roderigo that he should cast Cassio into disgrace by starting a fight with Cassio at the evening's revels. In a soliloquy, Iago explains to the audience that eliminating Cassio is the first crucial step in his plan to ruin Othello. That night, Iago gets Cassio drunk and then sends Roderigo to start a fight with him. Apparently provoked by Roderigo, Cassio chases Roderigo across the stage. Governor Montano attempts to hold Cassio down, and Cassio stabs him. Iago sends Roderigo to raise alarm in the town.

The alarm is rung, and Othello, who had left earlier with plans to consummate his marriage, soon arrives to still the commotion. When Othello demands to know who began the fight, Iago feigns reluctance to implicate his "friend" Cassio, but he ultimately tells the whole story. Othello then strips Cassio of his rank of lieutenant. Cassio is extremely upset, and he laments to Iago, once everyone else has gone, that his reputation has been ruined forever. Iago assures Cassio that he can get back into Othello's good graces by using Desdemona as an intermediary. In a soliloquy, Iago tells us that he will frame Cassio and Desdemona as lovers to make Othello jealous.

In an attempt at reconciliation, Cassio sends some musicians to play beneath Othello's window. Othello, however, sends his clown to tell the musicians to go away. Hoping to arrange a meeting with Desdemona, Cassio asks the clown, a peasant who serves Othello, to send Emilia to him. After the clown departs, Iago passes by and tells Cassio that he will get Othello out of the way so that Cassio can speak privately with Desdemona. Othello, Iago, and a gentleman go to examine some of the town's fortifications.

Desdemona is quite sympathetic to Cassio's request and promises that she will do everything she can to make Othello forgive his former lieutenant. As Cassio is about to leave, Othello and Iago return. Feeling uneasy, Cassio leaves without talking to Othello. Othello inquires whether it was Cassio who just parted from his wife, and Iago, beginning to kindle Othello's fire of jealousy, replies, "No, sure, I cannot think it, / That he would steal away so guilty-like, / Seeing your coming" (III.iii.37–39).

Othello becomes upset and moody, and Iago furthers his goal of removing both Cassio and Othello by suggesting that Cassio and Desdemona are involved in an affair. Desdemona's entreaties to Othello to reinstate Cassio as lieutenant add to Othello's almost immediate conviction that his wife is unfaithful. After Othello's conversation with Iago, Desdemona comes to call Othello to supper and finds him feeling unwell. She offers him her handkerchief to wrap around his head, but he finds it to be "[t]oo little" and lets it drop to the floor (III.iii.291). Desdemona and Othello go to dinner, and Emilia picks up the handkerchief, mentioning to the audience that Iago has always wanted her to steal it for him.

Iago is ecstatic when Emilia gives him the handkerchief, which he plants in Cassio's room as "evidence" of his affair with Desdemona. When Othello demands "ocular proof" (III.iii.365) that his wife is unfaithful, Iago says that he has seen Cassio "wipe his beard" (III.iii.444) with Desdemona's handkerchief—the first gift Othello ever gave her. Othello vows to take vengeance on his wife and on Cassio, and Iago vows that he will help him. When Othello sees Desdemona later that evening, he demands the handkerchief of her, but she tells him that she does not have it with her and attempts to change the subject by continuing her suit on Cassio's behalf. This drives Othello into a further rage, and he storms out. Later, Cassio comes onstage, wondering about the handkerchief he has just found in his chamber. He is greeted by Bianca, a prostitute, whom he asks to take the handkerchief and copy its embroidery for him.

Through Iago's machinations, Othello becomes so consumed by jealousy that he falls into a trance and has a fit of epilepsy. As he writhes on the ground, Cassio comes by, and Iago tells him to come back in a few minutes to talk. Once Othello recovers, Iago tells him of the meeting he has planned with Cassio. He instructs Othello to hide nearby and watch as Iago extracts from Cassio the story of his affair with Desdemona. While Othello stands out of earshot, Iago pumps Cassio for information about Bianca, causing Cassio to laugh and confirm Othello's suspicions. Bianca herself then enters with Desdemona's handkerchief, reprimanding Cassio for making her copy out the embroidery of a love token given to him by another woman. When Desdemona enters with Lodovico, and Lodovico subsequently gives Othello a letter from Venice calling him home and instating Cassio as his replacement, Othello goes over the edge, striking Desdemona and then storming out.

That night, Othello accuses Desdemona of being a whore. He ignores her protestations, seconded by Emilia, that she is innocent. Iago assures Desdemona that Othello is simply upset about matters of state. Later that night, however, Othello ominously tells Desdemona to wait for him in bed and to send Emilia away. Meanwhile, Iago assures the still-complaining Roderigo that everything is going as planned: in order to prevent Desdemona and Othello from leaving, Roderigo must kill Cassio. Then he will have a clear avenue to his love.

Iago instructs Roderigo to ambush Cassio, but Roderigo misses his mark and Cassio wounds him instead. Iago wounds Cassio and runs away. When Othello hears Cassio's cry, he assumes that Iago has killed Cassio as he said he would. Lodovico and Graziano enter to see what the commotion is about. Iago enters shortly thereafter and flies into a pretend rage as he "discovers" Cassio's assailant Roderigo, whom he murders. Cassio is taken to have his wound dressed.

Meanwhile, Othello stands over his sleeping wife in their bedchamber, preparing to kill her. Desdemona wakes and attempts to plead with Othello. She asserts her innocence, but Othello smothers her. Emilia enters with the news that Roderigo is dead. Othello asks if Cassio is dead too and is mortified when Emilia says he is not. After crying out that she has been murdered, Desdemona changes her story before she dies, claiming that she has committed suicide. Emilia asks Othello what happened, and Othello tells her that he has killed Desdemona for her infidelity, which Iago brought to his attention.

Montano, Graziano, and Iago come into the room. Iago attempts to silence Emilia, who realizes what Iago has done. At first, Othello insists that Iago has told the truth, citing the handkerchief as evidence. Once Emilia tells him how she found the handkerchief and gave it to Iago, Othello is crushed and begins to weep. He tries to kill Iago but is restrained. Iago kills Emilia and flees, but he is caught by Lodovico and Montano, who return holding Iago captive. They also bring Cassio, who is now in a chair because of his wound. Othello wounds Iago and is disarmed. Lodovico tells Othello that he must come with them back to Venice to be tried. Othello makes a speech about how he would like to be remembered, then kills himself with a sword he had hidden on his person. The play closes with a speech by Lodovico. He gives Othello's house and goods to Graziano and orders that Iago be executed.

CHARACTERS IN *OTHELLO*

Bianca A courtesan, or prostitute, in Cyprus. Bianca's favorite customer is Cassio, who teases her with promises of marriage.

Brabanzio Desdemona's father, a somewhat blustering and self-important Venetian senator. As a friend of Othello, Brabanzio feels betrayed when the general marries his daughter in secret.

Clown Othello's servant. Although the clown appears only in two short scenes, his appearances reflect and distort the action and words of the main plots: his puns on the word "lie" in Act III, scene iv, for example, anticipate Othello's confusion of two meanings of that word in Act IV, scene i.

Desdemona The daughter of the Venetian senator Brabanzio. Desdemona and Othello are secretly married before the play begins. While in many ways stereotypically pure and meek, Desdemona is also determined and self-possessed. She is equally capable of defending her marriage, jesting bawdily with Iago, and responding with dignity to Othello's incomprehensible jealousy.

Duke of Venice The official authority in Venice, the duke has great respect for Othello as a public and military servant. His primary role within the play is to reconcile Othello and Brabanzio in Act I, scene iii, and then to send Othello to Cyprus.

Emilia Iago's wife and Desdemona's attendant. A cynical, worldly woman, she is deeply attached to her mistress and distrustful of her husband.

Graziano Brabanzio's kinsman who accompanies Lodovico to Cyprus. Amidst the chaos of the final scene, Graziano mentions that Desdemona's father has died.

Iago Othello's ensign (or ancient, or standard-bearer), and the villain of the play. Iago is twenty-eight years old. While his ostensible reason for desiring Othello's demise is that he has been passed over for promotion to lieutenant, Iago's motivations are never clearly expressed and seem to originate in an obsessive, almost aesthetic delight in manipulation and destruction.

Lodovico One of Brabanzio's kinsmen, Lodovico acts as a messenger from Venice to Cyprus. He arrives in Cyprus in Act IV with letters announcing that Othello has been replaced by Cassio as governor.

Michael Cassio Othello's lieutenant. Cassio is a young and inexperienced soldier whose high position is much resented by Iago. Truly devoted to Othello, Cassio is extremely ashamed after being implicated in a drunken brawl on Cyprus and losing his place as lieutenant. Iago uses Cassio's youth, good looks, and friendship with Desdemona to play on Othello's insecurities about Desdemona's fidelity.

Montano The governor of Cyprus before Othello. We see him first in Act II, as he recounts the status of the war and awaits the Venetian ships.

Othello The play's protagonist and hero. A Christian Moor and general of the armies of Venice, Othello is an eloquent and physically powerful figure, respected by all those around him. In spite of his elevated status, he is nevertheless easy prey to insecurities because of his age, his life as a soldier, and his race. He possesses a "free and open nature," which his ensign Iago uses to twist his love for his wife, Desdemona, into a powerful and destructive jealousy (I.iii.381).

Roderigo A jealous suitor of Desdemona. Young, rich, and foolish, Roderigo is convinced that if he gives Iago all of his money, Iago will help him win Desdemona's hand. Repeatedly frustrated as Othello marries Desdemona and then takes her to Cyprus, Roderigo is ultimately desperate enough to agree to help Iago kill Cassio after Iago points out that Cassio is another potential rival for Desdemona.

THEMES IN *OTHELLO*

THE INCOMPATIBILITY OF MILITARY HEROISM & LOVE
Before and above all else, Othello is a soldier. From the earliest moments in the play, his career affects his married life. Asking "fit disposition" for his wife after being ordered to Cyprus (I.iii.234), Othello notes that "the tyrant custom … / Hath made the flinty and steel couch of war / My thrice-driven bed of down" (I.iii.227–229). While Desdemona is used to better "accommodation," she nevertheless accompanies her husband to Cyprus (I.iii.236). Moreover, she is unperturbed by the tempest or Turks that threatened their crossing and genuinely curious rather than irate when she is roused from bed by the drunken brawl in Act II, scene iii. She is, indeed, Othello's "fair warrior," and he is happiest when he has her by his side in the midst of military conflict or business (II.i.179). The military also provides Othello with a means to gain acceptance in Venetian society. While the Venetians in the play are generally fearful of the prospect of Othello's social entrance into white society through his marriage to Desdemona, all Venetians respect and honor him as a soldier. Mercenary Moors were, in fact, commonplace at the time.

Othello predicates his success in love on his success as a soldier, wooing Desdemona with tales of his military travels and battles. Once the Turks are drowned—by natural rather than military might—Othello is left without anything to do: the last act of military administration we see him perform is the viewing of fortifications in the extremely short second scene of Act III. No longer having a means of proving his manhood or honor in a public setting such as the court or the battlefield, Othello begins to feel uneasy with his footing in a private setting, the bedroom. Iago capitalizes on this uneasiness, calling Othello's epileptic fit in Act IV, scene i, "[a] passion most unsuiting such a man." In other words, Iago is calling Othello unsoldierly. Iago also takes care to mention that Cassio, whom Othello believes to be his competitor, saw him in his emasculating trance (IV.i.75).

Desperate to cling to the security of his former identity as a soldier while his current identity as a lover crumbles, Othello begins to confuse the one with the other. His expression of his jealousy quickly devolves from the conventional—"Farewell the tranquil mind"—to the absurd:

> Farewell the plum'd troops and the big wars
> That make ambition virtue! O, farewell,
> Farewell the neighing steed and the shrill trump,
> The spirit-stirring drum, th'ear piercing fife,
> The royal banner, and all quality,
> Pride, pomp, and circumstance of glorious war!"
> *(III.iii.353–359)*

One might well say that Othello is saying farewell to the wrong things—he is entirely preoccupied with his identity as a soldier. But his way of thinking is somewhat justified by its seductiveness to the audience as well. Critics and audiences alike find comfort and nobility in Othello's final speech and the anecdote of the "malignant and … turbaned Turk" (V.ii.362), even though in that speech, as in his speech in Act III, scene iii, Othello depends on his identity as a soldier to glorify himself in the public's memory and to try to make his audience forget his and Desdemona's disastrous marital experiment.

THE DANGER OF ISOLATION The action of *Othello* moves from the metropolis of Venice to the island of Cyprus. Protected by military fortifications as well as by the forces of nature, Cyprus faces little threat from external forces. Once Othello, Iago, Desdemona, Emilia, and Roderigo have come to Cyprus, they have nothing to do but prey upon one another. Isolation enables many of the play's most important effects: Iago frequently speaks in soliloquies; Othello stands apart while Iago talks with Cassio in Act IV, scene i, and is left alone onstage with the bodies of Emilia and Desdemona for a few moments in Act V, scene ii; Roderigo seems attached to no one in the play except Iago. Most prominently, Othello is visibly isolated from the other characters by his physical stature and the color of his skin. Iago is an expert at manipulating the distance between characters, isolating his victims so that they fall prey to their own obsessions. At the same time, Iago, of necessity always standing apart, falls prey to his own obsession with revenge. The characters *cannot* be islands, the play seems to say: self-isolation as an act of self-preservation leads ultimately to self-destruction. Such self-isolation leads to the deaths of Roderigo, Iago, Othello, and even Emilia.

SYMBOLS IN *OTHELLO*

THE HANDKERCHIEF The handkerchief symbolizes different things to different characters. Since the handkerchief was the first gift Desdemona received from Othello, she keeps it about her constantly as a symbol of Othello's love. Iago manipulates the handkerchief so that Othello comes to see it as a symbol of Desdemona herself—her faith and chastity. By taking possession of it, he is able to convert it into evidence of her infidelity. But the handkerchief's importance to Iago and Desdemona derives from its importance to Othello himself. He tells Desdemona that it was woven by a 200-year-old sibyl, or female prophet, using silk from sacred worms and dye extracted from the hearts of mummified virgins. Othello claims that his mother used it to keep his father faithful to her, so, to him, the handkerchief represents marital fidelity. The pattern of strawberries (dyed with virgins' blood) on a white background strongly suggests the bloodstains left on the sheets on a virgin's wedding night, so the handkerchief implicitly suggests a guarantee of virginity as well as fidelity.

THE SONG "WILLOW" As she prepares for bed in Act V, Desdemona sings a song about a woman who is betrayed by her lover. She was taught the song by her mother's maid, Barbary, who suffered a misfortune similar to that of the woman in the song; she even died singing "Willow." The song's lyrics suggest that both men and women are unfaithful to one another. To Desdemona, the song seems to represent a melancholy and resigned acceptance of her alienation from Othello's affections, and singing it leads her to question Emilia about the nature and practice of infidelity.

IMPORTANT QUOTATIONS FROM *OTHELLO*

Were I the Moor I would not be Iago.
In following him I follow but myself;
Heaven is my judge, not I for love and duty,
But seeming so for my peculiar end.
For when my outward action doth demonstrate
The native act and figure of my heart
In compliment extern, 'tis not long after
But I will wear my heart upon my sleeve

For daws to peck at. I am not what I am.

Location: I.i.57–65
Speaker: Iago
Context: Iago explains his tactics to Roderigo

In this early speech, Iago explains his tactics to Roderigo. He follows Othello not out of "love" or "duty," but because he feels he can exploit and dupe his master, thereby revenging himself upon the man he suspects of having slept with his wife. Iago finds that people who are what they seem are foolish. The day he decides to demonstrate outwardly what he feels inwardly, Iago explains, will be the day he makes himself most vulnerable: "I will wear my heart upon my sleeve / For daws to peck at." His implication, of course, is that such a day will never come.

This speech exemplifies Iago's cryptic and elliptical manner of speaking. Phrases such as "Were I the Moor I would not be Iago" and "I am not what I am" hide as much as, if not more than, they reveal. Iago is continually playing a game of deception, even with Roderigo and the audience. The paradox or riddle that the speech creates is emblematic of Iago's power throughout the play: his smallest sentences ("Think, my lord?" in III.iii.109) or gestures (beckoning Othello closer in Act IV, scene i) open up whole worlds of interpretation.

My noble father,
I do perceive here a divided duty.
To you I am bound for life and education.
My life and education both do learn me
How to respect you. You are the lord of my duty,
I am hitherto your daughter. But here's my husband,
And so much duty as my mother showed
To you, preferring you before your father,
So much I challenge that I may profess
Due to the Moor my lord.

Location: I.iii.179–188
Speaker: Desdemona
Context: Desdemona speaks before the Venetian senate

These words, which Desdemona speaks to her father before the Venetian senate, are her first of the play. Her speech shows her thoughtfulness, as she does not insist on her loyalty to Othello at the expense of respect for her father, but rather acknowledges that her duty is "divided." Because Desdemona is brave enough to stand up to her father and even partially reject him in public, these words also establish for the audience her courage and her strength of conviction. Later, this same ability to separate different degrees and kinds of affection will make Desdemona seek, without hesitation, to help Cassio, thereby fueling Othello's jealousy. Again and again, Desdemona speaks clearly and truthfully, but, tragically, Othello is poisoned by Iago's constant manipulation of language and emotions and is therefore blind to Desdemona's honesty.

Haply for I am black,
And have not those soft parts of conversation
That chamberers have; or for I am declined
Into the vale of years—yet that's not much—
She's gone. I am abused, and my relief
Must be to loathe her. O curse of marriage,
That we can call these delicate creatures ours
And not their appetites! I had rather be a toad
And live upon the vapor of a dungeon

Than keep a corner in the thing I love
For others' uses. Yet 'tis the plague of great ones;
Prerogatived are they less than the base.
'Tis destiny unshunnable, like death.

Location: III.iii.267–279
Speaker: Othello
Context: Othello is now convinced of Desdemona's infidelity

When, in Act I, scene iii, Othello says that he is "rude" in speech, he shows that he does not really believe his own claim by going on to deliver a lengthy and very convincing speech about how he won Desdemona over with his wonderful storytelling (I.iii.81). However, after Iago has raised Othello's suspicions about his wife's fidelity, Othello seems to have at least partly begun to believe that he is inarticulate and barbaric, lacking "those soft parts of conversation / That chamberers [those who avoid practical labor and confine their activities to the 'chambers' of ladies] have." This is also the first time that Othello himself, and not Iago, calls negative attention to either his race or his age. His conclusion that Desdemona is "gone" shows how far Iago's insinuations about Cassio and Desdemona have taken Othello: in a matter of a mere 100 lines or so, he has progressed from belief in his conjugal happiness to belief in his abandonment.

The ugly imagery that follows this declaration of abandonment—Othello finds Desdemona to be a mere "creature" of "appetite" and imagines himself as a "toad" in a "dungeon"—anticipates his later speech in Act IV, scene ii, in which he compares Desdemona to a "cistern for foul toads / To knot and gender in," and says that she is as honest "as summer flies are in the shambles [slaughterhouses], / That quicken even with blowing" (IV.ii.63–64, 68–69). Othello's comment, "'tis the plague of great ones," shows that the only potential comfort Othello finds in his moment of hopelessness is his success as a soldier, which proves that he is not "base." He attempts to consider his wife's purported infidelity as an inevitable part of his being a great man, but his comfort is halfhearted and unconvincing, and he concludes by resigning himself to cuckoldry as though it were "death."

I am glad I have found this napkin.
This was her first remembrance from the Moor,
My wayward husband hath a hundred times
Wooed me to steal it, but she so loves the token—
For he conjured her she should ever keep it—
That she reserves it evermore about her
To kiss and talk to. I'll ha' the work ta'en out,
And give't Iago. What he will do with it,
Heaven knows, not I.
I nothing, but to please his fantasy.

Location: III.iii.294–303
Speaker: Emilia
Context: Emilia finds Desdemona's handkerchief

This speech of Emilia's announces the beginning of *Othello*'s "handkerchief plot," a seemingly insignificant event—the dropping of a handkerchief—that becomes the means by which Othello, Desdemona, Cassio, Roderigo, Emilia, and even Iago himself are completely undone. Before Othello lets the handkerchief fall from his brow, we have neither heard of nor seen it. The primary function of Emilia's speech is to explain the prop's importance: as the first gift Othello gave Desdemona, it represents their oldest and purest feelings for one another.

While the fact that Iago "hath a hundred times / Wooed me to steal it" immediately tips off the audience to the handkerchief's imminently prominent place in the tragic sequence of events, Emilia seems entirely unsuspicious. To her, the handkerchief is literally a trifle, "light as air," and this is perhaps why she remains silent about the handkerchief's whereabouts even when Desdemona begins to suffer for its absence. It is as though Emilia cannot, or refuses to, imagine that her husband would want the handkerchief for any devious reason. Many critics have found Emilia's silence about the handkerchief—and in fact the entire handkerchief plot—a great implausibility, and it is hard to disagree with this up to a point. At the same time, however, it serves as yet another instance in which Iago has the extraordinary power to make those around him see only what he wants them to see, and thereby not suspect what is obviously suspicious.

> *Then must you speak*
> *Of one that loved not wisely but too well,*
> *Of one not easily jealous but, being wrought,*
> *Perplexed in the extreme; of one whose hand,*
> *Like the base Indian, threw a pearl away*
> *Richer than all his tribe; of one whose subdued eyes,*
> *Albeit unused to the melting mood,*
> *Drop tears as fast as the Arabian trees*
> *Their medicinable gum. Set you down this,*
> *And say besides that in Aleppo once,*
> *Where a malignant and a turbaned Turk*
> *Beat a Venetian and traduced the state,*
> *I took by th' throat the circumcised dog*
> *And smote him thus.*

Location: V.ii.352–365
Speaker: Othello
Context: Othello accepts ultimate responsibility for the tragic events as he prepares to kill himself

With these final words, Othello stabs himself in the chest. In this farewell speech, Othello reaffirms his position as a figure who is simultaneously a part of and excluded from Venetian society. The smooth eloquence of the speech and its references to "Arabian trees," "Aleppo," and a "malignant and a turbaned Turk" remind us of Othello's long speech in Act I, scene iii, lines 127–168, and of the tales of adventure and war with which he wooed Desdemona. No longer inarticulate with grief as he was when he cried, "O fool! fool! fool!," Othello seems to have calmed himself and regained his dignity and, consequently, our respect (V.ii.332). He reminds us once again of his martial prowess, the quality that made him famous in Venice. At the same time, however, by killing himself as he is describing the killing of a Turk, Othello identifies himself with those who pose a military—and, according to some, a psychological— threat to Venice, acknowledging in the most powerful and awful way the fact that he is and will remain very much an outsider. His suicide is a kind of martyrdom, a last act of service to the state, as he kills the only foe he has left to conquer: himself.

OUR TOWN

Thornton Wilder

In a small town in turn-of-the-century New Hampshire, a girl marries the boy next door and dies in childbirth, realizing how little people appreciate their everyday lives.

THE LIFE OF THORNTON WILDER

Thornton Wilder was born in Madison, Wisconsin, in 1897. He attended Oberlin College in Ohio and then transferred to Yale University, graduating in 1920. After a year in Rome, he took a job teaching French at a New Jersey prep school and began writing on the side. His first novel, *The Cabala*, was published in 1926. In 1927, he was awarded the Pulitzer Prize for *The Bridge of San Luis Rey*. Wilder quit his teaching job and devoted himself to writing. He soon became a literary celebrity, keeping company with writers such as Ernest Hemingway, F. Scott Fitzgerald, and Gertrude Stein.

During the Depression-era 1930s, Wilder came under attack by critics who branded his work as escapist because it did not confront the dark side of people's lives. Frustrated by this criticism and by the failure of his 1934 novel *Heaven's My Destination*, Wilder turned to playwriting. *Our Town*, his most celebrated dramatic effort, opened on Broadway in 1938 to rave reviews. The universal themes enabled audience members to identify with the characters, and the play's structure invited them to participate in the action onstage. *Our Town* won Wilder a second Pulitzer and went on to become one of the most frequently staged American plays of the twentieth century.

The 1920s and 1930s proved to be the heyday of Wilder's career. During World War II, he enlisted and served in Europe. Though he continued writing after returning to the United States, his output decreased during the next two decades. A late novel, *The Eighth Day* (1967), met with mixed reviews. Wilder died in December 1975 at his home in Connecticut.

OUR TOWN IN CONTEXT

Several early-twentieth-century American novels—notably Edgar Lee Masters's *Spoon River Anthology* (1915) and Sherwood Anderson's *Winesburg, Ohio* (1919)—exposed hypocrisy and oppression lurking beneath the surface of American small-town life. In *Our Town*, however, Wilder presents a far more celebratory picture of a small town, the fictional New Hampshire hamlet of Grover's Corners. Wilder neither denies that the town suffers from hypocrisy and social injustice nor idealizes Grover's Corners as a bastion of brotherly love. Instead, he tenderly tracks the residents' day-to-day activities, their triumphs and their sorrows, their casual conversations and their formal traditions, to praise humanity in a world full of both virtue and vice.

The principal message in *Our Town* is that everyday life is fleeting and should be treasured. This message was a source of comfort when the play hit theaters in 1938, as World War II loomed on the horizon of an increasingly troubled Europe. The play directed attention away from fear, uncertainty, and tremendous international tension, focusing instead on the aspects of the human experience that make even the smallest life precious.

OUR TOWN: KEY FACTS

Time and place written: 1934–1938; United States	
Year of first performance and publication: 1938	
Publisher: Coward-McCann, Inc.	
Type of work: Play	
Genre: Elements of tragedy, melodrama, and romance	
Language: English	
Setting (time): 1899–1904	

Setting (place): Grover's Corners, New Hampshire

Tone: Contemplative, sweet, nostalgic, introspective

Narrator: The Stage Manager guides the audience through the action

Protagonist: Emily Webb

Antagonist: Humans' failure to treasure everyday experiences; death

OUR TOWN: PLOT OVERVIEW

ACT I

The Stage Manager welcomes the audience to the fictional town of Grover's Corners, New Hampshire. It is early on a May morning in 1901. The set is sparse, encompassing only tables and chairs that represent the Gibbs and the Webb homes. The actors use no props, instead pantomiming their activities in synch with sound cues. A typical day begins. Howie Newsome, the milkman, and Joe Crowell, Jr., the paperboy, make their delivery rounds. Dr. Gibbs returns from delivering twins in town. Mrs. Gibbs and Mrs. Webb make breakfast, send their children off to school, and meet in their gardens to gossip. The two women also discuss their modest ambitions, and Mrs. Gibbs reveals that she longs to visit Paris.

The Stage Manager interrupts the action and calls Professor Willard and then Mr. Webb out onto the stage to relate some basic facts about Grover's Corners. Mr. Webb also answers questions from planted "audience members."

School lets out in the afternoon, and George Gibbs meets his neighbor Emily Webb outside the gate of her house. In conversation with her mother, Emily asks whether she is pretty. The Stage Manager thanks and dismisses Emily and Mrs. Webb. He says that he would like to put a copy of *Our Town* into the time capsule that is to be placed into the foundation of a new bank building in town.

In the evening, a choir in the orchestra pit sings "Blessed Be the Tie That Binds." The choir, directed by the bitter yet comical choirmaster Simon Stimson, continues to sing as George and Emily talk to each other through their open windows. Mrs. Webb, Mrs. Gibbs, and their gossipy friend Mrs. Soames return home from choir practice and chat about the choirmaster's alcoholism. George and his sister Rebecca sit at a window and look outside. Rebecca muses about the role of Grover's Corners within the vastness of the universe. Night falls.

ACT II

Three years have passed. It is George and Emily's wedding day. George tries to visit his fiancée, but Mr. and Mrs. Webb shoo him away, insisting that it is bad luck for a groom to see his bride before the ceremony. Mrs. Webb goes upstairs, and George and Mr. Webb, left alone, awkwardly discuss weddings and marriage.

The Stage Manager introduces a flashback to the previous year. George, who has become a local baseball star, has just been elected class president. Emily has just been elected secretary and treasurer. On the way home from school Emily tells George that his popularity has made him "conceited and stuck-up." George, hurt, thanks Emily for her honesty, but Emily, embarrassed by her own words, asks George to forget them. The two stop at Mr. Morgan's drugstore, and over ice-cream sodas, confess their affection for each other. George decides to stay in Grover's Corners with Emily instead of attending agriculture school.

Back on their wedding day in 1904, the Webbs and the Gibbses calm their nervous children. The Stage Manager performs the ceremony, and the newlyweds run out through the audience.

ACT III

It is nine years later. The scene is set in a cemetery overlooking the town. Emily has died in childbirth and is about to be buried. The funeral party occupies the back of the stage, and the town's dead souls—including Mrs. Gibbs, Mrs. Soames, Wally Webb, and Simon Stimson—sit in chairs at the front of the stage. As the funeral progresses, the dead make detached remarks. Emily joins the dead, but decides, against the advice of the other dead souls, to go back and relive a part of her life.

With the Stage Manager's help, Emily goes back to 1899, to the morning of her twelfth birthday. Howie Newsome and Joe Crowell, Jr., make their deliveries as usual. Mrs. Webb gives Emily some presents and calls to Mr. Webb. Emily both participates in the scene and observes it, noting her parents' youth and beauty. Agonized by the beauty and transience of everyday life, which passes unappreciated by the living, Emily demands to be taken back to the cemetery. As she returns to the dead, George prostrates himself at her tomb. "They don't understand," Emily says of the living. The stars come out over Grover's Corners. The Stage Manager ends the play.

CHARACTERS IN *OUR TOWN*

Stage Manager The play's host and omniscient narrator. The Stage Manager interacts with both the audience and the characters. He cues and stops scenes, provides background information, and comments on the action of the play. Occasionally, he plays bit parts—an old woman, a druggist, a minister.

THE GIBBSES

George Gibbs The Gibbs's decent, upstanding son. A high-school baseball star, George plans to attend the State Agricultural School after high school. His courtship of and eventual marriage to Emily Webb forms the focus of the play's limited narrative and allows Wilder to ponder questions of love and marriage.

Rebecca Gibbs George's younger sister. Rebecca closes Act I by touching on an important theme: because Grover's Corner is a microcosm representative of the broader human community, the shared human experience of the town lies at the center of a grand structure and is therefore eternal.

Dr. Frank Gibbs George's father and the town doctor. Dr. Gibbs's return home after delivering twins at the start of the play establishes the themes of birth, life, and daily activity. Dr. Gibbs is also a Civil War expert.

Mrs. Julia Gibbs George's mother. Mrs. Gibbs's never-fulfilled desire to visit Paris suggests both how important it is to seize life's opportunities before it is too late and how unnecessary such luxuries are to the ability to appreciate life.

THE WEBBS

Emily Webb The Webbs' daughter; George's schoolmate and next-door neighbor, later his fiancée and wife. Emily is a good student and conscientious daughter. Her realization that human life is precious because it is fleeting is the play's core message.

Wally Webb Emily's younger brother. His untimely death from a burst appendix on a Boy Scout trip underscores the brief and fleeting nature of life.

Mr. Charles Webb Emily's father and the publisher and editor of the Grover's Corners *Sentinel*. In Act I, Mr. Webb draws the audience into the play with an informative report and interactive question-and-answer session.

Mrs. Myrtle Webb Emily's mother. Usually no-nonsense, she worries during Emily's wedding that she has not taught her daughter enough about marriage.

THE TOWNSPEOPLE

Sam Craig Emily Webb's cousin. He has left Grover's Corners to travel west, but returns for Emily's funeral in Act III. Like the audience, he is an outsider who does not know what has happened in town.

Joe Crowell, Jr. The paperboy. Joe's morning delivery establishes the town's comfortable routine.

Si Crowell Joe's younger brother. He takes over Joe's paper route, contributing to the sense of human continuity in Grover's Corners.

Howie Newsome The milkman. Howie's appearance in the morning scene in each act creates a sense of continuity of life in Grover's Corners.

Mrs. Louella Soames A gossipy woman who sings in the church choir with Mrs. Webb and Mrs. Gibbs. She has died by Act III.

Simon Stimson The choirmaster. His alcoholism and other "troubles" have been material for Grover's Corners gossip for a while. By the end of the play, Mr. Stimson has hanged himself in his attic. Through Mr. Stimson's misfortunes, Wilder explores the limitations of small-town life. In Act III, Mr. Stimson bitterly calls human existence nothing but "ignorance and blindness," voicing Emily's own new sentiments.

Joe Stoddard The town undertaker.

Constable Bill Warren A local policeman whose personal knowledge of the town's citizens bespeaks the close-knit nature of the town.

Professor Willard A professor at the State University who gives the audience a report on Grover's Corners.

THEMES IN *OUR TOWN*

THE TRANSIENCE OF HUMAN EXPERIENCE While Wilder explores the reassuring stability of both human traditions and the natural world, he portrays individual human lives as fragile and fleeting, carried off by the relentless passage of time. The Stage Manager, our timekeeper, often remarks that time passes quickly for the play's characters. At one point he even misjudges the time himself.

Act I, subtitled "Daily Life" by the Stage Manager, testifies to the dramatic power of daily routine— eating breakfast, feeding chickens. The flurry of everyday activity is juxtaposed with the characters' casual inattentiveness: the Gibbs and Webb families rush through breakfast, the children run off to school. In light of future events, Wilder suggests that this lack of awareness is the prerogative of human beings who mistakenly assume that their time on earth is infinite. Mrs. Gibbs, for instance, refrains from persuading her husband to take her to Paris, and in the end she never gets to go before her death. In Act III, the dead chastise the living for this "ignorance" and "blindness." Even George's prostration upon Emily's grave is seen as a pitiable waste of human time.

The theatre as a medium is particularly suited to emphasizing the significance of ordinary life. As outsiders, we, like the dead souls, can appreciate Grover's Corner's daily events both because these events are new to us and because seeing them dramatized lends them importance.

THE ARTIFICIALITY OF THE THEATER Wilder intentionally uses devices that emphasize the artificiality of the theater to undermine the impression that we are watching real events. The most obvious such device, the Stage Manager, both takes part in the action and comments on it to the audience. He also manipulates the passage of time, incorporating flashbacks to show certain significant moments. These intentional disruptions in the chronology never allow us to forget that we are watching a play. As no more than a representation of real life, the world onstage is a fair target for Wilder's metaphorical and symbolic manipulation. By acknowledging the distance between the audience and the world of the characters, Wilder partially bridges that gap, forcing us to identify more fully with the characters and their lives.

NATURAL CYCLES OF LIFE *Our Town* is structured like a single cycle of a natural system, such as a single day or a single lifetime. It opens just before dawn with the birth of the Polish twins, peaks at the possibilities of love and marriage, and ends late at night with death and a funeral. Wilder's attention to natural cycles brings into relief the poignant transience of life and the unrelenting passage of time.

SYMBOLS IN *OUR TOWN*

THE TIME CAPSULE In Act I, the Stage Manager mentions a time capsule that will be buried in the foundation of a new bank in town. The townspeople want to put in the works of Shakespeare, the Constitution, and the Bible. The Stage Manager would like to include a copy of *Our Town* as well. The time capsule embodies the human desire to keep a record of the past. Accordingly, it also symbolizes the idea that certain parts of the past deserve to be remembered more than others—a notion that Wilder challenges in his play. The Stage Manager wants to place *Our Town* into the capsule to enable the people of the future to appreciate not only masterpieces of culture, but daily life. He hopes that understanding turn-of-the-century Grover's Corners, will help the people of the future appreciate their own daily lives.

The Stage Manager mentions the play *Our Town* within *Our Town*, thereby acknowledging that the text is an artificial literary creation. This self-reference also illustrates Wilder's willingness to break down the "fourth wall" that divides the play's world from the real world. Moreover, the idea that the play will be saved in a time capsule makes each particular production—its sets, actors, and audience—an important event in history.

THE MILKMAN AND THE PAPERBOY Each of *Our Town*'s three morning scenes features the milkman, Howie Newsome, and a paperboy—either Joe or Si Crowell. Because Grover's Corners is Wilder's microcosm of the human experience, Howie and the Crowells represent stability of life not only in Grover's Corners but in all human communities. The milkman and the paperboys embody the continuity of the human experience from year to year, from generation to generation. As Si replaces his older brother, life's transience itself becomes a stabilizing force: changes in individual lives (Si replacing Joe) are simply a part of larger stable structures.

IMPORTANT QUOTATIONS FROM *OUR TOWN*

[P]*eople are meant to go through life two by two. 'Tain't natural to be lonesome.*

Location: Act II
Speaker: Mrs. Gibbs to Mr. Gibbs
Context: On the morning of George's wedding day, Mrs. Gibbs articulates one of the play's main themes: the sanctity of human interaction

Because both birth and death are inevitable, the most interesting stage of life is the middle one: the quest for companionship, friendship, and love. Wilder suggests that human relationships, particularly love, epitomize human creativity and achievement in the face of the relentless advance of time. In this line, Mrs. Gibbs may be referring to George and Emily's courtship and marriage, which is the most prominent relationship in the play, but her comment applies to all interpersonal relationships. Wilder highlights the value of human connection by portraying many different types of relationships: the milkman chats with family members, children walk to and from school together, housewives meet in their yards, husbands and wives converse in private, the Stage Manager connects to the audience (enabling the audience to connect to the characters). The play features many community groups: the choir, the wedding party, the funeral party, the group of dead souls. The sanctity of human relationships is reiterated in the repeated renditions of "Blessed Be the Tie That Binds." The collective pronoun "our" in the play's title underscores the human desire for community.

Despite Mrs. Gibbs's optimism, some married people remain lonely. Stimson, the solitary drunk who has "seen a peck of trouble," receives very little active compassion from his fellow townspeople Indeed, they never even mention what his "trouble" is. Stimson serves as Wilder's critique of Mrs. Gibbs's small-town idealism.

Do any human beings ever realize life while they live it?—every, every minute?

Location: End of Act III
Speaker: Emily to Stage Manager
Context: Having revisited her twelfth birthday, the dead Emily has a new appreciation for the preciousness of daily life

The play's characters place importance on moments of ceremony and consequence, such as the wedding and the funeral, neglecting to make emotional connections to the daily activities of their rather ordinary lives. Reliving her twelfth birthday, Emily futilely tries to get her mother to genuinely look at her without taking her presence for granted. Emily realizes that she too has failed to pay attention to detail or to fully appreciate her life. Pained by the recognition that human beings waste great opportunities at every moment, with these words she signals her resignation to join the realm of the dead.

So—people a thousand years from now—this is the way we were in the provinces north of New York at the beginning of the twentieth century.—This is the way we were: in our growing up and in our marrying and in our living and in our dying.

Location: Middle of Act I
Speaker: Stage Manager
Context: After discussing how little historical documents reveal about the real lives of ordinary people, the Stage Manager suggests putting a copy of *Our Town* into the time capsule to record something about the lifestyle of the play's characters

---

I think that once you've found a person that you're very fond of . . . I mean a person who's fond of you, too, and likes you enough to be interested in your character. . . . Well, I think that's just as important as college is, and even more so. That's what I think.

Location: Flashback in Act II
Speaker: George to Emily
Context: George and Emily first reveal their feelings to each other at Mr. Morgan's drugstore while drinking ice-cream sodas

---

We all know that something is eternal. And it ain't houses and it ain't names, and it ain't earth, and it ain't even the stars . . . everybody knows in their bones that something is eternal, and that something has to do with human beings. All the greatest people ever lived have been telling us that for five thousand years and yet you'd be surprised how people are always losing hold of it. There's something way down deep that's eternal about every human being.

Location: Beginning of Act III
Speaker: Stage Manager
Context: In suggesting that humans feel that there is something eternal about their lives without ever understanding what it is, the Stage Manager prefigures the sentiments of the dead, who believe that human beings get so caught up in the mundane details of their lives that they "don't understand the true significance of existence"

THE OUTSIDERS

S. E. Hinton

A group of poor kids hold their own against a group of rich kids, losing two of their members in the process.

THE LIFE OF S. E. HINTON

Susan Eloise Hinton was born in the 1950s in Tulsa, Oklahoma, a place that she describes as "a pleasant place to live if you don't want to do anything." She began *The Outsiders* at the age of fifteen, inspired by her frustration with the social divisions in her high school and the lack of realistic fiction for high-school readers. *The Outsiders*, first published in 1967, tells the story of class conflict between the greasers, a group of low-class youths, and the Socs (short for Socials), a group of privileged rich kids who live on the wealthy West Side of town. The novel broke ground in the genre of young adult fiction, transcending established boundaries in its portrayal of violence, class conflict, and prejudice.

Hinton's publishers decided that Hinton should publish her novel under the name S. E. Hinton. They worried that readers would not respect *The Outsiders*, which features male protagonists and violent situations, if they knew a woman wrote it. Hinton has said that she does not mind using a gender-neutral authorial name.

After the publication of her first novel, Hinton felt pressure to turn out a successful sophomore effort. She had difficulty writing under this stress, and her boyfriend (who later become her husband) nudged her along by taking her out only if she completed two pages per day. Hinton successfully finished a second novel, titled *That Was Then, This is Now* (1971). In all, she has written eight novels for young adults. *The Outsiders* is Hinton's best-selling novel. A film version of the novel, starring C. Thomas Howell, Patrick Swayze, Emilio Estevez, Tom Cruise, Matt Dillon, Rob Lowe, and Ralph Macchio, was released in 1983.

THE OUTSIDERS IN CONTEXT

The language and details of *The Outsiders* root the story in the 1960s. Characters call fights "rumbles," and people listen to the Beatles and Elvis Presley. The novel is set in the Southwest, as evidenced by the local rodeos in which many greasers participate. Despite its location in a specific time and place, however, the novel largely transcends location, examining universal urges to form factions, compete, and unite for survival. With only a few minor cosmetic changes, the novel could easily take place in a contemporary setting.

Hinton attempts to humanize the greasers, the outsiders of the story's title, by showing that their exterior toughness masks vulnerability and emotion. She makes both the greasers and the Socs sympathetic and refuses to cast blame on either group. As one character tells another, "Things are rough all over."

THE OUTSIDERS: KEY FACTS

Time and place written: 1960s; Tulsa, Oklahoma	
Date of first publication: 1967	
Publisher: The Viking Press	
Type of work: Novel	
Genre: Bildungsroman	
Language: English	
Setting (time): Mid-1960s	
Setting (place): Tulsa, Oklahoma	
Tense: Past	

Tone: Youthful, melodramatic, slangy, simplistic

Narrator: Ponyboy Curtis

Point of view: Ponyboy in the first person

Protagonist: Ponyboy's

Antagonist: Class differences

THE OUTSIDERS: PLOT OVERVIEW

Ponyboy Curtis belongs to a group of lower-class Oklahoma youths who call themselves greasers because of their greasy, long hair. Walking home from a movie, Ponyboy is attacked by a group of Socs, the greasers' rivals, who are upper-class youths from the West Side of town. The Socs, short for Socials, gang up on Ponyboy and threaten to slit his throat. A group of greasers arrives and chases the bullies away, saving Ponyboy. Ponyboy's rescuers include his brother Sodapop, a charming, handsome high-school dropout, and Darry (Darrell), Ponyboy's oldest brother, who assumed responsibility for his brothers when their parents were killed in a car crash. The rest of the greasers who come to Ponyboy's rescue are Johnny, a sensitive sixteen-year-old; Dally (Dallas), a hardened street hood with a long criminal record; Steve, Sodapop's best friend; and Two-Bit, the oldest and funniest member of the group.

The next night, Ponyboy and Johnny go to a movie with Dally, who soon leaves. They sit near a pair of attractive Soc girls named Cherry and Marcia. Ponyboy and Johnny discover they have a lot in common with the girls. Two-Bit arrives, and the three greasers begin to walk with the Soc girls. They run into Bob and Randy, the girls' drunken boyfriends. The girls leave with their boyfriends in order to prevent a fight between the Socs and the greasers.

Ponyboy is late getting home, and his brother Darry is furious. Sick of Darry's constant scrutiny and criticism, Ponyboy yells at Darry. The brothers fight, and Darry slaps Ponyboy across the face. Ponyboy flees, determined to run away. He finds Johnny, and the two boys heads for the park, where they encounter a group of Soc boys that includes Bob and Randy. The Socs attack Johnny and Ponyboy. One of them holds Ponyboy's head under the frigid water of a fountain until Ponyboy blacks out. When Ponyboy regains consciousness, he is lying on the ground next to Johnny—and next to Bob's corpse. It turns out that Johnny killed Bob because the Socs were going to drown Ponyboy and beat up Johnny.

Desperate and terrified, Ponyboy and Johnny hurry to find Dally Winston, the one person they think might be able to help them. Dally gives them a gun and some money, and sends them to an abandoned church near the neighboring town of Windrixville. They hide out in the church for a week, cutting and dying their hair to disguise themselves, reading *Gone with the Wind* aloud, and discussing poetry. After several days, Dally comes to check on Ponyboy and Johnny. He tells them that since Bob's death, tensions between the greasers and the Socs have escalated. A rumble will take place the next night to settle matters. Dally says that Cherry, who feels partially responsible for Bob's death, has been spying for the greasers. Johnny shocks Dally by declaring his intention to go back and turn himself in.

Dally agrees to drive Ponyboy and Johnny back home. As the boys leave, they notice that the abandoned church has caught fire with a group of schoolchildren inside it. Ponyboy and Johnny rush into the inferno to save the children. Just as they get the last child through the window, the roof caves in, and Ponyboy blacks out. He regains consciousness in an ambulance. At the hospital, he is diagnosed with minor burns and bruises. Dally is not badly hurt either, but Johnny's back was broken by the falling roof, and he is in critical condition. Darry and Sodapop come to get Ponyboy, and Darry and Ponyboy make up. The following morning, the newspapers proclaim Ponyboy and Johnny heroes. They also report that Johnny will be charged with manslaughter and that both Ponyboy and Johnny will have to go to juvenile court so that a judge can decide if they should be sent to a boys' home.

Ponyboy and Two-Bit run into Randy, who says he is sick of all the fighting and does not plan to go to the rumble that night. Ponyboy and Two-Bit visit Johnny in the hospital. Johnny, who seems weak, asks Ponyboy for a new copy of *Gone with the Wind*. Dally asks to borrow Two-Bit's black-handled switchblade. On the way home, Two-Bit and Ponyboy see Cherry. She refuses to visit Johnny because he has killed Bob.

At the rumble, the greasers defeat the Socs. Dally escapes from the hospital and shows up just in time for the fight. After the rumble, Ponyboy and Dally hurry back to see Johnny and find that he is dying. When Johnny dies, Dally loses control and runs from the room in a frenzy. Ponyboy stumbles home late that night, feeling dazed and disoriented. Dally calls to say that he has robbed a grocery store and the cops are looking for him. The greasers hurry to find him, but they are too late. Dally raises a gun to the police and they shoot him. Overwhelmed, Ponyboy passes out.

Ponyboy wakes up in bed at home. He has suffered a concussion from a kick to the head at the rumble and has been delirious in bed for several days. When he is well, he attends his hearing, where the judge treats him kindly and acquits him of responsibility for Bob's death. The court rules that Ponyboy will be allowed to remain at home with Darry. For a time, Ponyboy feels listless and empty. His grades slip, he is hostile to Darry, and he loses his appetite. Sodapop confesses that he is angry because of the tension at home, and tearfully asks that Ponyboy and Darry stop fighting. Finally understanding the value of his family, Ponyboy agrees not to fight with Darry anymore. He finds that for the first time, he can remember Dally's and Johnny's deaths without pain or denial. He decides to tell their story and begins writing a term paper for his English class, which turns out to be the novel itself.

CHARACTERS IN *THE OUTSIDERS*

Randy Adderson Marcia's boyfriend and Bob's best friend. Randy is a handsome Soc who eventually sees the futility of fighting. Randy proves that some of the Socs have redeeming qualities.

Johnny Cade A sixteen-year-old greaser with black hair and large, fearful eyes. The child of alcoholic, abusive parents, Johnny is nervous and sensitive. He sees the greasers as his true family. In turn, the older boys, particularly Dally, are protective of him.

Darrell Curtis Ponyboy's oldest brother. Darrell, known as Darry, is a twenty-year-old greaser who raises his two younger brothers after their parents die in a car crash. Strong, athletic, and intelligent, Darry works two jobs to hold the family together. The other greasers call him "Superman."

Ponyboy Curtis The novel's fourteen-year-old narrator and protagonist. Ponyboy's literary interests and academic accomplishments set him apart from the rest of his gang. He is a reliable and observant narrator who struggles with class division, violence, innocence, and familial love.

Sodapop Curtis Ponyboy's happy-go-lucky, handsome older brother. Sodapop is the middle Curtis boy. He plans to marry Sandy, a greaser girl.

Paul Holden A husky blond Soc. Paul and Darry were friends and football teammates in high school.

Two-Bit Mathews The joker of Ponyboy's group. Two-Bit, whose real name is Keith, is a wisecracking greaser who shoplifts regularly. He instigates the hostilities between the Socs and the greasers by flirting with Marcia.

Marcia Cherry's friend and Randy's girlfriend. Marcia is a pretty, dark-haired Soc who befriends Two-Bit at the drive-in. Marcia and Two-Bit have a similar sense of humor.

Steve Randle Sodapop's best friend since grade school. Steve knows everything about cars and specializes in stealing hubcaps. He is cocky, intelligent, tall, and lean. He is also tough—once he held off four opponents in a fight with a broken soda bottle.

Sandy Sodapop's girlfriend. Sandy gets pregnant with another man's child and moves to Florida to live with her grandmother.

Bob Sheldon Cherry's boyfriend. Bob is a dark-haired Soc who beats up Johnny before the novel begins. His indulgent parents have never disciplined him.

Curly Shepard Tim Shepard's fifteen-year-old brother. Curly is stubborn and rough.

Tim Shepard The leader of another band of greasers and a friend of Dally's. Ponyboy thinks of Tim as an alley cat, hungry and restless. He also thinks that the members of Shepard's gang are real street hoods and criminals, as opposed to his own gang, which is little more than a group of friends fighting to survive.

Mr. Syme Ponyboy's English teacher. Mr. Syme offers to raise Ponyboy's grade if he turns in a well-written autobiographical theme. This assignment inspires Ponyboy to write about the greasers and the Socs.

Cherry Valance Bob's girlfriend. Cherry, whose real name is Sherry, is a Soc cheerleader. She admires Dally's individuality and eventually becomes a spy for the greasers.

Dallas Winston The toughest hood in Ponyboy's group. Dallas, known as Dally, is a hardened teen who used to run with gangs in New York. He has an elfin face and icy blue eyes and, unlike his friends, does not put grease in his white-blond hair.

Jerry Wood The teacher who accompanies Ponyboy to the hospital after Ponyboy saves the children from the fire. Jerry judges the greasers on their merits instead of automatically branding them juvenile delinquents.

THEMES IN *THE OUTSIDERS*

THE BRIDGEABLE GAP BETWEEN RICH AND POOR *The Outsiders* tells the story of two groups of teenagers whose bitter rivalry stems from socioeconomic differences. But Hinton suggests that these differences in social class do not always make the two groups natural enemies. The greasers and Socs share some things in common. Cherry Valance, a Soc, and Ponyboy Curtis, a greaser, discuss their love of literature, popular music, and sunsets. They transcend—if only temporarily—the divisions that feed the feud between their respective groups. Their harmonious conversation suggests that shared passions can fill in the gap between rich and poor. Ponyboy eventually realizes that although greasers and Socs face different hardships, they have the same basic struggles and fears.

HONOR AMONG THE LAWLESS Honor is an important component of the greaser behavioral code. Greasers see it as their duty, Ponyboy says, to stand up for each other in the face of enemies and authorities. Dally Winston constantly carries out this duty. He always behaves honorably, even though most people see him as a man defined by delinquency and lack of refinement. Ponyboy informs us that in a show of group solidarity, Dally once let himself be arrested for a crime that Two-Bit committed. When discussing *Gone with the Wind*, Johnny says that he views Dally as a Southern gentleman—a man with a fixed personal code of behavior. Statements like Johnny's, coupled with acts of honorable sacrifice throughout the narrative, demonstrate that courtesy and propriety can exist even among the most lawless social groups.

THE TREACHEROUSNESS OF MALE-FEMALE INTERACTIONS As hostile and dangerous as the greaser-Soc rivalry becomes, the boys from each group have the comfort of knowing how their male friends will react to their male enemies. When Randy and Bob approach Ponyboy and Johnny, for example, everyone involved knows to expect a fight of some sort. It is only when the female members of the Soc contingent start to act friendly toward the greasers that animosities blur and true trouble starts brewing. Even on the greaser side, Sodapop discovers the perils of female unreliability when he finds out that his girlfriend is pregnant with another man's child. With these plot elements, Hinton conveys the idea that cross-gender interaction creates unpredictable results. She also suggests that male bonding is the only way to create unity and structure.

SYMBOLS IN *THE OUTSIDERS*

CARS Cars represent the Socs' power and the greasers' vulnerability. They also symbolize the way Socs use wealth to hurt their enemies. Because their parents can afford to buy them "tuff" cars, the Socs have increased mobility and protection. The greasers, who move mostly on foot, are physically vulnerable in comparison to the Socs. Greasers like Darry, Sodapop, and Steve have contact with automobiles only when they repair them. Their ability to repair cars could symbolize the greasers' desirable, manly familiarity with the gritty realities of life. But it could also symbolize the power of wealth. When the Socs force the greasers to fix their cars, they are forcing the greasers to work in the service of the very wealth that oppresses them.

GREASER HAIR The greasers' hair symbolizes their outsider identity. They cannot afford rings, cars, or any of the other physical trappings of power that the Socs enjoy. Consequently, they must resort to more affordable markers of identity. By wearing their hair in a specific style, greasers distinguish themselves from other social groups. Conservative cultural values of the 1960s called for men to keep their hair short, and the greaser style is a clear transgression of this social convention.

IMPORTANT QUOTATIONS FROM *THE OUTSIDERS*

Greasers will still be greasers and Socs will still be Socs. Sometimes I think it's the ones in the middle that are really the lucky stiffs.

Location: Chapter 7
Speaker: Randy
Context: Randy tells Ponyboy he will not attend the rumble

Randy says that greasers and Socs will always remain part of their respective groups, suggesting that it is impossible for a greaser or a Soc to change his current status. Randy appears to believe that, despite their youth, the young men in the story will never be able to move on and transcend the narrow limits of their gang identities. It is not painful for Randy to assert a cynical belief in the permanence of social identity. He is a wealthy young man, so the idea that he will probably remain wealthy does not bother him. The greasers have a greater need for optimism. They long to believe that social mobility exists and that they can shed their greaser lifestyles.

We couldn't get along without him. We needed Johnny as much as he needed the gang. And for the same reason.

Location: Chapter 8
Speaker: Ponyboy
Context: Johnny lies dying in the hospital

As Ponyboy watches Johnny dying, he muses on the fragility of group cohesion. It seems obvious that Johnny needs the greasers—he is small, passive, and poor, which makes him an easy target of Soc violence. Less obvious is the gang's need for Johnny. The greasers need a vulnerable friend to give them a sense of purpose. Telling themselves that they exist to protect people like Johnny lets them avoid thinking about the fact that their poverty and vulnerability leave them no choice but to band together. Ponyboy understands Johnny's value only in the moments before Johnny's death, which amplifies the pain of the loss.

Stay gold, Ponyboy. Stay gold.

Location: Chapter 9
Speaker: Johnny
Context: As he dies, Johnny urges Ponyboy to hold onto his innocence

It's okay.. . . . We aren't in the same class. Just don't forget that some of us watch the sunset too.

Location: Chapter 3
Speaker: Ponyboy
Context: Ponyboy tells Marcia that not all greasers are rough

Dally was so real he scared me.

Location: Chapter 5
Speaker: Ponyboy
Context: Johnny likens Dally to a Southern gentleman, and Ponyboy reacts

PARADISE LOST

John Milton

Satan and his followers rebel and go to Hell, God creates the world, and Adam and Eve sin.

THE LIFE OF JOHN MILTON

John Milton was born on December 9, 1608, in London. Milton's father was a prosperous merchant. Milton excelled at the prestigious St. Paul's Cathedral School and then entered college at Christ's College at Cambridge University, where made a name for himself with his prodigious writing. He had an immense, precocious knowledge of languages, including Italian, Greek, Latin, Aramaic, Hebrew, French, Spanish, Anglo-Saxon, and some Dutch. After graduating from Cambridge with a master's degree in 1632, Milton pursued a quiet life of study at the family's estate near Windsor. He spent 1632 to 1638—his mid- to late twenties—reading the classics in Greek and Latin and learning new theories of mathematics and music.

By the age of thirty, Milton had made himself into one of the most brilliant minds of England and one of the most ambitious poets it had ever produced. He began his ascent in his twenties, when he wrote five masterful long poems: "On the Morning of Christ's Nativity," "Comus," "Lycidas," "Il Penseroso," and "L'Allegro." Through these poems, Milton honed his skills at writing narrative, dramatic, elegiac, philosophical, and lyrical poetry. Even in these early poems, Milton's literary output was guided by his faith in God. He believed that poetry should glorify God, enlighten readers, and help people become better Christians.

In 1639, civil war broke out in England. Milton began planning an epic poem, the first ever written in English. These plans were delayed by his marriage to Mary Powell and her subsequent desertion of him. Milton wrote a series of pamphlets, among them *Doctrine of Discipline and Divorce*, calling for the church to relax its position on divorce. Milton's belief in divorce is mainstream today, but it was viewed as shocking and heretical in his own time, when adultery was usually the only grounds for a lawful divorce. Milton believed that any sort of incompatibility—sexual, mental, or otherwise—is justified grounds for a divorce and that the main purpose of marriage is not necessarily procreation, but happy companionship. Milton's position on divorce brought him both greater publicity and angry criticism from the religious establishment in England.

Milton was an activist in his middle years, fighting for human rights and against the rule of Charles I, the king of England during much of Milton's lifetime. He wrote lengthy, rhetorical pamphlets that rigorously argued his point of view. Milton believed that only those men who are better and more fit to rule than their subjects should be leaders and that Charles was not fit to lead his subjects because he did not possess superior faculties or virtues. When the Second Civil War ended in 1648 with the dethronement and execution of King Charles, Milton welcomed the new parliament.

After serving for a few years in a civil position, Milton retired briefly to his house in Westminster because his eyesight was failing. By 1652, he was completely blind. Despite his disability, Milton reentered civil service under the protectorate of Oliver Cromwell, the military general who ruled the British Isles from 1653 to 1658. Two years after Cromwell's death, Milton's worst fears were realized: the Restoration brought Charles II to the throne. Milton had to go into hiding to escape execution. He had already begun work on *Paradise Lost*, the great English epic he had planned so many years ago. Exile gave him the opportunity to work on it in earnest. It was published in 1667, a year after the Great Fire of London. The greatness of Milton's epic was immediately recognized, and the admiring comments of the respected poets John Dryden and Andrew Marvell helped restore Milton to favor. He spent the ensuing years at his residence in Bunhill, continuing to write prolifically. Milton died at home on November 8, 1674.

PARADISE LOST IN CONTEXT

Milton planned to write the great English epic as early as age sixteen. Reading the classical epics in school—Homer's *Odyssey* and *Iliad* and Virgil's *Aeneid*—inspired him to dream of accomplishing similar artistic brilliance in the English language. Milton wanted to write his epic on a distinctly British topic that would inspire nationalist pride in his countrymen. He considered many topics, including King Arthur and the Knights of the Round Table and Oliver Cromwell before settling, in the mid-1650s, on the story of Adam and Eve. When Milton began to write his epic in 1656, he had gone blind. Each morning, he recited verse to one of his two daughters, who transcribed for him. Milton dictated *Paradise Lost* for several years, finishing it in 1667.

Milton's religious views had a great bearing on *Paradise Lost*. Milton, a Presbyterian, thought that the office of priesthood should not exist. He thought that each Christian should be his own church, without any establishment to encumber him. Milton broke with the Presbyterians before 1650 and began advocating the complete abolishment of all church establishments. Milton's highly individual view of Christianity makes *Paradise Lost* simultaneously personal and universal. In his epic, he suggests that Adam and Eve's fall from grace was fortunate, because it gave individuals the opportunity to redeem themselves by true repentance and faith.

Paradise Lost also presents a number of Protestant Christian positions: the union of the Old and New Testaments, the unworthiness of mankind, and the importance of Christ's love in man's salvation. Nonetheless, the poem does not present a unified, cohesive theory of Christian theology, nor does it attempt to identify disbelievers, redefine Christianity, or replace the Bible. Instead, Milton's epic stands as a remarkable presentation of biblical stories meant to engage Christian readers and help them to be better Christians.

Much of Milton's social commentary in *Paradise Lost* focuses on the proper role of women. In Book IV, he makes it clear that he does not think men and women are equals, alluding to biblical passages that identify man as the master of woman. Although Milton believed that wives should be subservient to their husbands, he did not see himself as a woman-hater. In *Paradise Lost*, he distances himself from the brand of misogyny popular in his time—the belief that women are utterly inferior to men, essentially evil, and generally to be avoided. Milton's character Adam voices this harsh view of womankind, but only after the fall, as an expression of anger and frustration. Milton's views in *Paradise Lost* may be misogynistic by today's standards, but they were fairly progressive for his day.

PARADISE LOST: KEY FACTS

Time and place written: 1656–1674; England

Date of first publication: First edition (ten books), 1667; Second edition (twelve books), 1674

Publisher: S. Simmons, England

Type of work: Poem

Genre: Epic

Language: English

Setting (time): Before the beginning of time

Setting (place): Hell, Chaos and Night, Heaven, Earth (Paradise, the Garden of Eden)

Tense: Present

Tone: Lofty, formal, tragic

Narrator: Milton in the third person

Point of view: Milton's

Protagonist: Adam and Eve

Antagonist: Satan

PARADISE LOST: PLOT OVERVIEW

Milton's speaker begins *Paradise Lost* by stating that his subject will be Adam and Eve's disobedience and fall from grace. He invokes a heavenly muse and asks for her help. The action begins with Satan and his fellow rebel angels, who are chained to a lake of fire in Hell. They quickly free themselves and fly to land, where they construct a meeting place called Pandemonium. Inside Pandemonium, the rebel angels, who are now devils, debate beginning another war with God. Beezlebub suggests corrupting

God's beloved new creation, humankind. Satan agrees and volunteers to go himself. As he prepares to leave Hell, he is met at the gates by his children, Sin and Death, who follow him and build a bridge between Hell and Earth.

In Heaven, God orders the angels together for a council. He tells them of Satan's intentions, and the Son volunteers to sacrifice himself for humankind. Meanwhile, Satan travels through Night and Chaos and finds Earth. He disguises himself as a cherub to get past the Archangel Uriel, who stands guard at the sun. He tells Uriel that he wishes to see and praise God's glorious creation, and Uriel assents. Satan then lands on Earth and takes a moment to reflect. Seeing the splendor of Paradise pains him, but he reaffirms his decision to make evil his good and continue to commit crimes against God. Satan leaps over Paradise's wall, takes the form of a cormorant (a large bird), and perches atop the Tree of Life. Looking down at Satan from his post, Uriel notices the volatile emotions reflected in the face of this so-called cherub and warns the other angels that an impostor is in their midst. The other angels agree to search the Garden for intruders.

Adam and Eve tend the Garden, carefully obeying God's order not to eat from the Tree of Knowledge. After a long day of work, they return to their bower and rest. There, Satan takes the form of a toad and whispers into Eve's ear. Gabriel, the angel set to guard Paradise, finds Satan there and orders him to leave. Satan prepares to battle Gabriel, but God makes a sign appear in the sky—the golden scales of justice—and Satan scurries away. Eve awakes and tells Adam that she dreamed an angel tempted her to eat from the forbidden tree. Worried about his creation, God sends Raphael down to Earth to teach Adam and Eve about the dangers they face with Satan.

Raphael arrives on Earth and eats a meal with Adam and Eve. Eve retires, allowing Raphael and Adam to speak alone. Raphael explains that Satan was envious when God appointed the Son his second-in-command. Satan gathered other disgruntled angels together and with them plotted a war against God. One angel, Abdiel, decided not to join Satan's army. The angels battled for two days. Then God sent the Son to end the war and deliver Satan and his rebel angels to Hell.

Raphael warns Adam that Satan wants to corrupt him and Eve. Adam asks Raphael to tell him the story of creation. Raphael explains that God sent the Son into Chaos to create the universe. He created the earth and stars and other planets. Curious, Adam asks Raphael about the movement of the stars and planets. Raphael cautions Adam against searching for knowledge too intently, saying Adam will learn all he needs to know, and anything he does not learn is not meant for humans to comprehend. Adam tells Raphael about his first memories. He woke up and wondered who he was. Then God spoke to him and told him many things. Adam confesses to Raphael his intense physical attraction to Eve. Raphael reminds Adam that he must love Eve more purely and spiritually. With this final bit of advice, Raphael leaves Earth and returns to Heaven.

Eight days after his banishment, Satan returns to Paradise and takes the form of the serpent. Eve suggests to Adam that they work separately for awhile so that they can get more work done. Adam hesitates but then assents. To his delight, Satan finds Eve by herself. Still in the form of a serpent, he compliments Eve on her beauty and godliness. Amazed, Eve asks the serpent how he learned to speak, and he tells her that eating from the Tree of Knowledge gave him the power. He tells Eve that God actually wants her and Adam to eat from the tree, and that his order is merely a test of their courage. Eve is doubtful at first, but she reaches for a fruit from the Tree of Knowledge and eats. Distraught, she searches for Adam, who has been busy making a wreath of flowers for Eve. He drops the wreath, horrified to find that Eve has eaten from the forbidden tree. Knowing that she has fallen, he decides that he would rather fall with her than remain pure and lose her. He eats from the fruit as well. Adam looks at Eve in a new way, and they have lustful sex.

God immediately knows of their disobedience. He tells the angels in Heaven that Adam and Eve must be punished, but with both justice and mercy. He sends the Son to dole out the punishments. The Son first punishes the serpent whose body Satan took, and condemns it to an eternity of slithering on its belly. Then the Son tells Adam and Eve that they must suffer pain and death. Eve and all women will suffer the pain of childbirth and submit to their husbands, and Adam and all men will hunt and grow their own food on a depleted Earth. Satan returns to Hell, where he is greeted with cheers. Everyone believes that he has beaten God, but soon the devils are transformed into snakes.

God tells the angels to transform the Earth, changing its constant climate into seasons of hot and cold. Adam and Eve fear their approaching doom and blame each other for their plight. In a fit of rage, Adam wonders why God ever created Eve. Eve begs Adam not to abandon her. She tells him that they can survive by loving each other. She accepts the blame and ponders suicide. Adam, moved by her speech, forbids her from taking her own life. He believes they can revenge themselves on Satan by remaining obedient to God. Together they pray to God and repent.

God hears their prayers and sends Michael down to Earth. Michael tells them that they must leave Paradise. Before they leave, Michael puts Eve to sleep and takes Adam up onto the highest hill, where he shows him a vision of humankind's future. Adam sees the sins of his children and his children's children, and his first vision of death. Generations sin by lust, greed, envy, and pride. They kill each other selfishly and live only for pleasure. Michael shows Adam a vision of Enoch, who is saved by God as his warring peers attempt to kill him. Adam also sees the story of Noah and his family, whose virtue allows them to survive the flood that kills all other humans. Next is the vision of Nimrod and the Tower of Babel. Adam sees the triumph of Moses and the Israelites, and then glimpses the Son's sacrifice to save humankind. After this vision, it is time for Adam and Eve to leave Paradise. Eve awakes and tells Adam that she had a very interesting and educating dream. Led by Michael, Adam and Eve slowly and woefully leave Paradise hand in hand.

CHARACTERS IN *PARADISE LOST*

MAIN CHARACTERS

Adam The first human and the father of humankind.

Eve The first woman and the mother of mankind. Because Eve was made from one of Adam's ribs, she is subservient to him and weaker than him.

God the Father One part of the Christian Trinity. God the Father creates the world by means of God the Son, creating Adam and Eve last. He foresees the fall of mankind and does not prevent their fall because he wants to preserve their free will.

God the Son Jesus Christ, the second part of the Trinity. The Son offers himself as a sacrifice to pay for the sins of mankind so that God the Father can be both just and merciful.

Satan Head of the rebellious angels who fall from Heaven. The poem's antagonist, Satan is the originator of sin—the first to be ungrateful for God's blessings. Satan often appears to speak rationally and persuasively, but later in the poem we see the inconsistency and irrationality of his thoughts.

DEVILS AND EVIL BEINGS

Beelzebub Satan's second-in-command. At the debate, Beelzebub suggests investigating the newly created Earth. Like Satan, Beelzebub embodies perverted reason. He is eloquent and rational, but he uses these gifts for corrupt ends.

Belial One of the principal devils in Hell. Because he is so lazy, Belial argues against further war with Heaven. His eloquence and learning impress many of the devils.

Death Satan's son by his daughter, Sin. Death rapes his mother, begetting the mass of beasts that torment her middle. Death, Sin, and Satan are a horrible perversion of the Holy Trinity.

Mammon A devil known in the Bible as the epitome of wealth. Mammon always walks hunched over, as if searching the ground for valuables. He argues against war because he doesn't think it will be profitable.

Mulciber The devil who builds Pandemonium, Satan's palace in Hell. Mulciber's character is based on a Greek mythological figure known for being a poor architect, but in Milton's poem he is one of the most productive and skilled devils in Hell.

Moloch A rash, irrational, and murderous devil.

Sin Satan's daughter. When Satan was still in Heaven, Sin sprang from his head fully formed. She is a woman above the waist and a serpent below. Hell Hounds ring her middle, periodically burrowing into her womb and gnawing her entrails. Sin guards the gates of Hell.

ANGELS

Abdiel An angel who considers joining Satan in rebellion but ultimately returns to God. His character demonstrates the power of repentance.

Gabriel One of the archangels of Heaven. Gabriel guards the Garden of Eden.

Michael The chief of the archangels. Michael leads the angelic forces against Satan and his followers in the battle in Heaven and stands guard at the Gate of Heaven. He shows Adam the future of the world in Books XI and XII.

Raphael One of the archangels in Heaven. Raphael is one of God's messengers. He has a long, informative visit with Adam in Eden.

Uriel An angel who guards Earth. Satan disguises himself as a cherub and tricks Uriel.

THEMES IN *PARADISE LOST*

THE IMPORTANCE OF OBEDIENCE TO GOD *Paradise Lost* presents two moral paths that one can take after being disobedient: the downward spiral of increasing sin and degradation, represented by Satan, and the road to redemption, represented by Adam and Eve. While Adam and Eve are the first humans to disobey God, Satan is the first of all God's creation to disobey him. His decision to rebel is worse than Adam and Eve's because it comes only from himself—he was not persuaded or provoked by others. He makes matters worse by continuing to disobey God after his fall into Hell, ensuring that God will not forgive him. Adam and Eve, on the other hand, decide to repent for their sins and seek forgiveness. Unlike Satan, Adam and Eve decide that one instance of disobedience to God should not prevent them from returning to their old obedient ways. This path is obviously the correct one to take: the visions in Books XI and XII demonstrate that obedience to God, even after repeated falls, can lead to humankind's salvation.

THE HIERARCHICAL NATURE OF THE UNIVERSE Hierarchy governs *Paradise Lost*, and when characters ignore or flout that hierarchy, disaster results. The universe itself is a spatial hierarchy, with proximity to God denoting rank—Heaven is above, Hell below, and Earth in the middle. The social hierarchy goes in order of holiness: the Son tops the ranks, followed by angels, men, women, animals, and devils. It is because Satan questions God's hierarchy, refusing to honor the Son as his superior, that he and his followers are banished to Hell. Similarly, Adam and Eve corrupt God's hierarchy. God and Raphael tell Adam that Eve is inferior to him because she was created to serve God and Adam. Eve ignores her inferiority when she persuades Adam to let her work alone, and Adam ignores Eve's inferiority when he follows her lead and eats the fruit, knowingly defying God by obeying Eve and his own instincts. The fall of humankind results from their rebellion.

THE FALL AS PARTLY FORTUNATE After he sees the vision of Christ's redemption of humankind in Book XII, Adam refers to his own sin as a *felix culpa* or "happy fault," suggesting that perhaps the fall of humankind is not the unmitigated catastrophe it seemed to be at first. Adam and Eve's disobedience allows God to show his love and compassion for humankind. People will experience pain and death because of Adam and Eve, but they will also experience the relief of mercy, salvation, and grace in ways made possible by the fall. Also, the Son's sacrifice and resurrection will save humankind from death.

SYMBOLS IN *PARADISE LOST*

THE SCALES IN THE SKY As Satan prepares to fight Gabriel, God makes the image of a pair of golden scales appear in the sky. On one side of the scales, he puts the consequences of running away from Gabriel, and on the other he puts the consequences of fighting him. The side that shows him staying and fighting flies up, signifying its worthlessness. These scales symbolize Satan's defenselessness. He is not a worthy opponent for God. God is all-powerful, and Satan and Gabriel both derive all of their power from him.

ADAM'S WREATH The wreath Adam makes for Eve symbolizes his love for her and his attraction to her. When he sees that she has eaten from the Tree of Knowledge, he drops the wreath in shock, which suggests that his love and attraction to Eve has shattered.

IMPORTANT QUOTATIONS FROM *PARADISE LOST*

Hail holy Light, offspring of Heav'n first-born,
Or of th' Eternal Coeternal beam
May I express thee unblam'd? since God is Light,
And never but in unapproached Light
Dwelt from Eternity, dwelt then in thee,
Bright effluence of bright essence increate.
. . .
thee I revisit safe,
And feel thy Sovran vital Lamp; but thou
Revisit'st not these eyes, that roll in vain
To find thy piercing ray, and find no dawn;
So thick a drop serene hath quencht thir Orbs,
Or dim suffusion veil'd. Yet not the more
Cease I to wander where the Muses haunt
Clear Spring, or shady Grove, or Sunny Hill,
Smit with the love of sacred Song.. . . . .
. . .
So much the rather thou Celestial Light
Shine inward, and the mind through all powers
Irradiate, there plant eyes, all mist from thence
Purge and disperse, that I may see and tell
Of things invisible to mortal sight.

· *Location:* Book III, lines 1–6, 21–29, 51–55
Speaker: Milton
Context: Milton invokes God as light

These passages are part of Milton's second and longest invocation, which is also his most autobiographical and symbolic. Milton refers to light as both divine wisdom and literal light. He begins by praising holy light as the essence of God. He then invokes his heavenly muse, the Holy Spirit, asking his muse to enter his body and fill him with divine knowledge. When Milton writes about his blindness, he means both his inward blindness, or lack of divine wisdom, and his literal blindness, or loss of eyesight. Milton refers to his literal blindness by comparing himself to other famous blind "Prophets old" (III.36) such as Homer (Maeonides) and Tiresias, and asks that he be filled with even more wisdom than they were. He does not seek pity for his blindness, explaining that he is undeterred from his poetic purpose. He hopes to sing beautifully like the darkling bird, which sings at night even though she can't see who or what she is singing to. Milton ends his invocation by asking for his inward blindness to be corrected so that he can properly tell the story of Adam and Eve.

This having learnt, thou hast attained the sum
Of Wisdom; hope no higher, though all the Stars
Thou knew'st by name, and all th' ethereal Powers,
All secrets of the deep, all Nature's works,
Or works of God in Heav'n, Air, Earth, or Sea,
And all riches of this World enjoy'dst,
And all the rule, one Empire: only add
Deeds to thy knowledge answerable, add Faith,

Add Virtue, Patience, Temperance, add Love,
By name to come called Charity, the soul
Of all the rest: then wilt though not be loth
To leave this Paradise, but shalt possess
A paradise within thee, happier far.

Location: Book XII, lines 575–587
Speaker: Michael
Context: Adam and Eve prepare to leave Eden

In these lines, Michael tries to explain to Adam that even though he and Eve have fallen from grace and must leave Paradise, they can still lead a fruitful life. Adam has attained all the wisdom he needs, and he and Eve will by happy if they live their lives by seven tenets: obedience, faith, virtue, patience, temperance, love, and charity. Living by these tenets will allow them to create an inner Paradise. Heaven will become a state of mind rather than a physical place, just as for Satan Hell is a constant presence even when he is not in his physical Hell.

Of Man's First Disobedience, and the Fruit
Of that Forbidden Tree, whose mortal taste
Brought Death into the World, and all our woe,
With loss of Eden, till one greater Man
Restore us, and regain the blissful
Seat, Sing Heav'nly Muse, that on the secret top
Of Oreb, or of Sinai, didst inspire
That Shepherd, who first taught the chosen
Seed, In the Beginning how the Heav'ns and Earth
Rose out of Chaos: Or if Sion Hill
Delight thee more, and Siloa's Brook that flow'd
Fast by the Oracle of God; I thence
Invoke thy aid to my advent'rous Song,
That with no middle flight intends to soar
Above th' Aonian Mount, while it pursues
Things unattempted yet in Prose or Rhyme.

Location: Book I, lines 1–26
Speaker: Milton
Context: Milton presents his purpose, subject, aspirations, and need for heavenly guidance

---

. . .though both
Not equal, as thir sex not equal seem'd;
For contemplation hee and valor form'd,
For softness shee and sweet attractive Grace,
Hee for God only, shee for God in him:
His fair large Front and Eye sublime declar'd
Absolute rule; and Hyacinthine Locks
Round from his parted forelock manly hung
Clust'ring, but not beneath his shoulders broad:
Shee as a veil down to the slender waist
Her unadorned golden tresses wore
Dishevell'd, but in wanton ringlets wav'd
As the Vine curls her tendrils, which impli'd
Subjection, but requir'd with gentle sway,
And by her yielded, by him best receiv'd,

Yielded with coy submission, modest pride,
And sweet reluctant amorous delay.

Location: Book IV, lines 295–311
Speaker: Milton
Context: Adam and Eve prepare for bed

What better can we do, than to place
Repairing where he judg'd us, prostrate fall
Before him reverent, and there confess
Humbly our faults, and pardon beg, with tears
Watering the ground, and with our sighs the
Air Frequenting, sent from hearts contrite, in sigh
Of sorrow unfeign'd, and humiliation meek.
Undoubtedly he will relent and turn
From his displeasure; in whose look serene,
When angry most he seem'd and most severe,
What else but favor, grace, and mercy shone?
So spake our Father penitent, nor Eve
Felt less remorse: they forthwith to the place
Repairing where he judg'd them prostrate fell
Before him reverent, and both confess'd
Humbly their faults, and pardon begg'd, with tears
Watering the ground, and with their sighs the
Air Frequenting, sent from hearts contrite, in sign
Of sorrow unfeign'd, and humiliation meek.

Location: Book X, lines 1086–1104
Speaker: Milton
Context: Adam and Eve decide to ask God for forgiveness

A PASSAGE TO INDIA

E. M. Forster

A sensitive Indian doctor struggles with unjust criminal charges and comes to understand that genuine friendship between Indians and the British is impossible under colonial rule.

THE LIFE OF E. M. FORSTER

Edward Morgan Forster was born in 1879 into a comfortable London family. After his architect father died, the young Forster was raised by his mother and great-aunt. Forster graduated from Cambridge University in 1901 and spent much of the next decade abroad as a writer and journalist. Forster's fiction often draws upon his personal experiences: *A Room with a View* (1908), for example, chronicles the experiences of a group of English vacationers in Italy. In *Howards End* (1910), Forster criticized the class divisions and prejudices of Edwardian England. The novel solidified his reputation as a social critic and a master of incisive observation.

Long before visiting India, Forster learned about Indians and Indian culture from Syed Ross Masood, a young Indian Muslim who became Forster's student and close friend. In 1913, just after his first visit to India, Forster began working on *A Passage to India*. The novel was not completed until three years after Forster's second stay in India, during which he served as secretary to the Maharajah of Dewas State Senior. Upon its publication in 1924, *A Passage to India* was immediately proclaimed Forster's masterpiece. In later years, Forster never again attained the level of craft or the depth of observation that characterized his early work. In his later life, he contented himself primarily with writing lectures and critical essays, most notably *Aspects of the Novel* (1927). In 1946, Forster accepted a fellowship at Cambridge University where he remained until his death in 1970.

A PASSAGE TO INDIA IN CONTEXT

The British government gained official control of India in 1858, after quelling the Sepoy Rebellion against the privately owned British East India Company, which had been gaining financial and political power in India since the seventeenth century. By the time Forster got to know India in the early twentieth century, Britain's control over India was complete: English governors headed each province and reported directly to Parliament. India did not win independence until after World War II, in 1949.

During his time in India, Forster was troubled by the racial oppression and deep cultural misunderstandings that divided the Indian people and the British colonists (the Anglo-Indians). The prevailing attitude among the British in India was that the colonists bore, in novelist Rudyard Kipling's phrase, the "white man's burden" of governing the country because the Indians could not handle the responsibility themselves. Forster, a homosexual living in a world unsympathetic to his lifestyle, had long experienced prejudice and misunderstanding firsthand; *A Passage to India* draws upon his experiences both as a colonialist and a human being. The relationship between Fielding and Aziz echoes aspects of Forster's own relationship with Masood. The novel examines the misunderstandings and cultural hypocrisies that plagued the complex interactions between Indians and English colonialists toward the end of the British occupation.

Much of Forster's writing consists of simple, symbolic tales that neatly epitomize larger-scale problems. He exhibits sympathy for his characters and an ability to see many perspectives of the same story. *A Passage to India* is a traditional social and political novel that, like its contemporaries such as James Joyce's *Ulysses* (1922) and Virginia Woolf's *Mrs. Dalloway* (1925), attempts to represent the chaos of modern human experience through patterns of imagery and form.

A PASSAGE TO INDIA: KEY FACTS

Time and place written: 1912–24; India and England

Date of publication: 1924

Publisher: Edward Arnold

Type of work: Novel

Genre: Modernist novel; psychological novel

Language: English

Setting (time): Early twentieth century

Setting (place): India: Chandrapore and Mau

Tense: Immediate past

Tone: Poetic, ironic, philosophical

Narrator: Anonymous, omniscient third-person narrator

Point of view: Shifts between characters

Protagonist: Dr. Aziz

Antagonist: Adele's accusations; the British colonialists' condescension and injustice toward native Indians

A PASSAGE TO INDIA: PLOT OVERVIEW

Two Englishwomen, the young Adela Quested and the elderly Mrs. Moore, travel to Chandrapore, India, where Ronny Heaslop, Mrs. Moore's son and Adela's future fiancé, serves as a British magistrate. Adela and Mrs. Moore both hope to get to know the real India on their trip.

In Chandrapore, Dr. Aziz, a young Muslim Indian widower, is increasingly frustrated by the English colonialists, particularly by his superior, Major Callendar. Aziz and two well-educated friends, Hamidullah and Mahmoud Ali, discuss whether an Indian and an Englishman can be friends in India. That night, Aziz meets Mrs. Moore at a local mosque, and Aziz is both moved and surprised that she, as an Englishwoman, is so friendly with him.

Mr. Turton, the collector who governs Chandrapore, hosts an awkward party to introduce Adela and Mrs. Moore to the city's prominent and wealthy Indians. During the party, Adela meets Cyril Fielding, the principal of Chandrapore's Government College. Impressed with Adela's open friendliness toward the Indians, Fielding invites Adela and Mrs. Moore to tea with him and the Hindu professor Godbole. At Adela's request, Fielding extends the invitation to Aziz.

At the tea, Aziz and Fielding get to know each other as friends. The otherwise pleasant afternoon sours when Ronny Heaslop arrives and rudely ignores the Indians. That evening, Adela tells Ronny that she has decided not to marry him. However, on the drive home at night, the car they are riding in breaks down. In the emotional tumult, Adela changes her mind about marrying Ronny.

Aziz organizes an expedition to the nearby Marabar Caves. Fielding and Professor Godbole miss the train, so Aziz, Adela, and Mrs. Moore go without them. Inside one of the caves, Mrs. Moore is unnerved by the enclosed space and by the uncanny echo that mutates every sound she makes into *boum*. Aziz, Adela, and a guide go on to the higher caves while Mrs. Moore waits below. Adela, suddenly realizing that she does not love Ronny, unwittingly offends Aziz by asking him whether he has more than one wife. He ducks into a cave to recover. When he returns, Adela is gone. Aziz slaps the guide for losing sight of her. He finds Adela's broken field glasses and heads down the hill. At the picnic site below, Aziz is elated to find Fielding and not perturbed to learn that Adela has hastily taken a car back to Chandrapore. However, upon their return to the city, Aziz is arrested because Adela has accused him of sexually assaulting her in the caves.

Fielding believes that Aziz is innocent and angers all of British India by joining the Indians by defending Aziz. In the weeks before the trial, racial tensions flare up considerably. Mrs. Moore is distracted and miserable, both because of her experience in the cave and because of the upcoming trial. Adela is emotional and ill. Ronny, frustrated by his mother's apathy for Adela's plight, arranges for Mrs. Moore to return to England earlier than planned. On her journey, she realizes that there is no one "real India." Rather, there is a complex coherence of a multitude of Indias. She dies at sea.

On the stand at Aziz's trial, Adela shockingly declares that she has made a mistake: something attacked her in the cave, but it was not Aziz. Aziz is set free. Fielding escorts Adela to his college, where she spends the next several weeks. Fielding begins to recognize Adela's courage in proclaiming Aziz innocent against the colonial British community. Ronny breaks off his engagement to Adela, and she returns to England. Aziz's friendship with Fielding is strained by Fielding's sympathy for Adela. When Fielding leaves for a visit to England, Aziz declares that he intends to avoid all contact with the English from now on.

Two years later, Aziz, now the chief doctor to the Rajah of the Hindu region of Mau, virulently hates the English. He has heard that Fielding has married Adela. One day on a trip though an old temple with his children, Aziz encounters Fielding and his brother-in-law, Ralph Moore, and learns that Fielding married not Adela but Mrs. Moore's daughter Stella. Aziz befriends Ralph, and after accidentally running his rowboat into Fielding's, renews his friendship with Fielding as well. On a final boat ride before Fielding's departure, Aziz tells Fielding that they can be friends only after the English leave India. The sky and the earth seem to agree and say "No, not yet.. . . No, not there."

CHARACTERS IN *A PASSAGE TO INDIA*

INDIANS

Amritrao Aziz's Indian defense lawyer.

Dr. Aziz The novel's protagonist; an intelligent, emotional Muslim Indian doctor in Chandrapore. Through Aziz's experiences with the English, particularly with Fielding, Adela, and Mrs. Moore, Forster explores the possibility of Anglo-Indian interpersonal relationships. A widower, Aziz has three children who live with their grandmother. He enjoys writing and reciting poetry.

Professor Godbole A Brahman Hindu who teaches at Government College. A spiritual man, Godbole is reluctant to involve himself in human affairs.

Hamidullah Aziz's uncle and Fielding's close friend. Educated at Cambridge, Hamidullah thinks that friendship between Englishmen and Indians is possible in England but not in India.

Mahmoud Ali Aziz's friend; a Chandrapore lawyer. Mahmoud Ali is deeply pessimistic about the English in India.

The Nawab Bahadur A wealthy Indian who supports the English. He renounces his role as mediator between the local Indians and the colonial English in protest after Aziz's trial.

Dr. Panna Lal Aziz's professional rival; a lowborn Hindu doctor. Panna Lal intends to testify against Aziz at the trial but regrets this decision after Aziz is exonerated.

BRITISH COLONIALISTS

Major Callendar The Chandrapore civil surgeon; Aziz's boastful, cruel, and ridiculous superior.

Miss Derek A young, easygoing Englishwoman resented by the British community for working as a servant for a wealthy Indian family whose car Miss Derek often "borrows."

Cyril Fielding The principal of Government College. An independent man who believes in educating Indians to be individuals, Fielding befriends Aziz and supports him throughout his trial.

Ronny Heaslop Mrs. Moore's son; the magistrate at Chandrapore; briefly, Adela Quested's fiancé. Like other British colonialist, Ronny treats native Indians with condescension and contempt.

Mr. McBryde The Chandrapore police superintendent and the prosecutor of Aziz's trial. He shows some respect for Indians but elaborately explains why darker-skinned people are inferior. Like his casual friend Fielding, McBryde defies the expectation of the British community, divorcing his wife for his mistress, Miss Derek.

Mrs. Moore An elderly Englishwoman; mother of Ronny Heaslop (first marriage), and Ralph and Stella Moore (second marriage). Mrs. Moore travels to India to visit Ronny, see him married to Adela Quested, and discover the "real India." An unsettling experience in the Marabar caves and its echoes leave Mrs. Moore with a sense of dread, and she slowly withdraws from human relationships. She eventually understands that no one real India exists; India is complex and multifarious. She dies on the journey back to England.

Ralph Moore Mrs. Moore's sensitive son.

Stella Moore Mrs. Moore's daughter; later Fielding's wife.

Adela Quested A young, intellectually minded Englishwoman; briefly Ronny Heaslop's fiancée. Adela travels to India with an academic desire to see the "real India." In the Marabar Caves, Adela's confusion about her feelings for Ronny and about her chaotic experiences in India crystallize into something she perceives as a physical attack, which she blames on Aziz.

Mr. Turton The stern collector (or governor) of Chandrapore.

Mrs. Turton Turton's wife, the epitome of the snobby and prejudiced colonial wife.

THEMES IN *A PASSAGE TO INDIA*

THE DIFFICULTY OF ANGLO-INDIAN FRIENDSHIP In the novel, Forster uses Aziz and Fielding's relationship to explore whether an Englishman and an Indian can be friends within the context of British colonialism. Their relationship provides a framework for exploring, more generally, colonialism in India. As the novel opens, Aziz is content to scornfully ignore the British presence. However, his instant connection with Mrs. Moore in the mosque opens him to the possibility of interracial friendship. In the first half of the novel, Aziz's relationship with Fielding suggests that British colonialism in India could be successful if only all Englishmen and Indians treated each other with frankness, good will, and respect. But their friendship is strained by Adela's accusations and the trial. Aziz and Fielding are driven apart both by their communities and by their respective cultural conditionings: Aziz's overactive imagination is incompatible with Fielding's hyperrationalism. Forster concludes that English-Indian friendships may eventually be possible, but only outside the context of British colonialism, whether in England or in an independent India.

THE "MUDDLE" OF INDIA The novel presents India as a both a "muddle" and a "mystery," and Forster takes care to differentiate these two viewpoints. Fielding—Forster's primary mouthpiece—admits that India is a "muddle," a disorderly mess both disorienting and potentially dangerous. Mrs. Moore and Godbole, who are spiritual characters, see India as a mystery, guided by a spiritual force greater than and unknowable to man. India's muddle is evident in its confused landscape. Plants and animals are unidentified and unidentifiable. The native population is a muddle of different religious, ethnic, linguistic, and geographic groups. Indian architecture is confused and formless: interiors blend into gardens, structures look half-finished or drab. These physical muddles embody a muddle in native culture: Forster portrays Indians as characteristically inattentive to form and logic. The confusion of the Marabar Caves is the culmination of this muddle as it disorients a hyper-organized and -intellectualized Westerner such as Adela. Forster suggests that in the cramped caves of this muddled country, Adela's muddled feelings about Ronny become externalized; she views them as an outside threat, which she blames on the muddle of India, and on Aziz.

Forster's sympathy to India and its people is partially undermined by this portrayal of India as a land of confusion. Forster's is a perspective shared by many contemporary Western writers. The noted critic Edward Said has suggested that by "orientalizing" the East, these authors—whether implicitly or explicitly, deliberately or unconsciously—justified colonialism as bringing desirable Western logic and order to the Eastern muddle.

THE UNITY OF ALL LIVING THINGS Professor Godbole, who stands aside from the novel's narrative conflict, is the novel's mouthpiece for Hinduism, which teaches that all living things are united in love as one. For chaotic India, Hinduism, with its obliteration of social hierarchies, offers redemption.

Over the course of the novel, Mrs. Moore, dissatisfied with what she perceives as the smallness of Christianity, explores some Hindu ideas. She feels connection with all living creatures, even the wasp — the lowest creature incorporated into the Hindu vision of universal unity. For Mrs. Moore, however, the unity of all living things has a terrifying nihilistic undertone: if all creatures are one, the distinction between good and evil is annihilated and no value system is possible. The echo of the Marabar Caves, which obliterate all sounds and noises to *boum*, distills Mrs. Moore's spiritual crisis. She responds by withdrawing from human cares into a paralyzing apathy; her death, Forster implies, is the inevitable result. In Adela's care, such a nihilistic withdrawal is liberating: on the witness stand, she separates herself from the turmoil of her personal situation and clearly sees that Aziz was innocent. Withdrawn from human cares, Adela is able to admit that she has made a terrible mistake.

Forster also suggests that the Hindu vision may be problematic: Professor Godbole is unable to incorporate a stone into a coherent vision of universal unity.

SYMBOLS IN *A PASSAGE TO INDIA*

THE MARABAR CAVES The ancient Marabar Caves, a literal void in the earth, represent all that is alien about nature. Neither Englishmen nor Indians know how to navigate them. Their strange beauty menaces and unsettles visitors; the caves destroy meaning and force visitors to confront previously unexplored aspects of themselves or their world. The obliterating echo of the caves shows Mrs. Moore the darker side of her spirituality: a growing distance from human concerns and an ambivalence about God. Adela realizes with shame that she has no feelings for Ronny and that she may not be attracted to anyone.

THE GREEN BIRD As soon as Adela and Ronny agree not to get married, they notice a green bird in the tree above. Neither of them can identify it. This unidentifiable bird symbolizes the unknowable, muddled India. The incident also points to a cultural tension: Adela and Ronny's impulse to label and name, like Adela's futile desire to see the one real India, is representative of Western obsession with literal knowledge, which is incompatible with the elusive green bird and Indian attentiveness to nuance, undertone, and emotional intent.

IMPORTANT QUOTATIONS FROM *A PASSAGE TO INDIA*

In every remark [Aziz] found a meaning, but not always the true meaning, and his life though vivid was largely a dream.

Location: Chapter VII, before the tea party
Speaker: The narrator
Context: Aziz misinterprets Fielding's comment about post-impressionist art during their first meeting at Fielding's house

Before this comment, a small miscommunication occurs when Aziz decides that Fielding's "silly" remark refers to Aziz's study of Western art rather than to post-impressionism as a movement. This miscommunication foreshadows larger misunderstandings that lead to the breakdown of their friendship. Aziz's intuition and imagination are both a gift and a barrier: they allow Aziz to form genuine bonds with Mrs. Moore and Fielding, but also lead to resentment when Aziz incorrectly suspects that Fielding is courting Adela. Here Forster criticizes Aziz's overactive imagination; elsewhere he presents this character flaw as representative of India. Aziz's dreamy emotionalism damages his relationships; similarly, the land around the Marabar caves is "infected with illusion" and "cut off at its root." Aziz's and India's muddle threatens and upsets Western logic and orderliness.

The quotation is representative of Forster's writing style: he draws comparisons and distinctions, characterizing and categorizing as he narrates. However, the absoluteness of his character judgments are at times belied elsewhere: for example, in many instances throughout the novel, Forster values Aziz's imaginativeness, which he criticizes here.

Were there worlds beyond which they could never touch, or did all that is possible enter their consciousness? They could not tell. . . . Perhaps life is a mystery, not a muddle. . . . Perhaps the hundred Indias which fuss and squabble so tiresomely are one, and the universe they mirror is one. They had not the apparatus for judging.

Location: Chapter XXIX
Speaker: The narrator
Context: Forster describes Fielding's and Adela's reactions to Adela's strange experience at the Marabar Caves, highlighting the inadequacy of English rationalism in evaluating mystical India

As behooves the English, Adela and Fielding conscientiously try to explain Adela's experiences in the caves with logic—hallucination? solitude?—but none of their theories is adequate. The Western logical "apparatus" is insufficient for understanding India. Adela's experience in the cave is a metaphor for the entire bewildering experience of Westerners in India. Like Marabar, India emits a chaos of stimulants, which cannot be incorporated into a single, unified interpretation. The mysteries of Marabar and of India must be ascribed to a mystical, all-encompassing force; the "muddle" is resolved only when the confusion is viewed as a mystery, strangely coherent.

As a plot device, the passage shows Fielding and Adela growing closer as they acknowledge India's strangeness. Aziz, who senses that Fielding and Adela's bonds stem from helplessly classifying India as confusing, resents Fielding for his friendship with Adela.

Fielding did not even want to [correct Aziz]; he had dulled his craving for verbal truth and cared chiefly for truth of mood. As for Miss Quested, she accepted everything Aziz said as true verbally. In her ignorance, she regarded him as "India," and never surmised that his outlook was limited and his method inaccurate, and that no one is India.

Location: Chapter VII, during Fielding's tea party
Speaker: The narrator
Context: Forster highlights a major cultural distinction: unlike the English, Indians privilege the emotional intent of a statement over its literal meaning

---

[Mrs. Moore] felt increasingly (vision or nightmare?) that, though people are important, the relations between them are not, and that in particular too much fuss has been made over marriage.

Location: Chapter XIV, on the train to the Marabar Caves
Speaker: The narrator
Context: Forster foreshadows Mrs. Moore's impending crisis in the caves: since hearing Godbole's song, Mrs. Moore has felt a spiritual presence larger than her Christian God and has become increasingly removed from the world of human cares

---

"Your emotions never seem in proportion to their objects, Aziz."
"Is emotion a sack of potatoes, so much the pound, to be measured out? Am I a machine?"

Location: Chapter XXVII
Speakers: Fielding and Aziz
Context: The relationship between Fielding and Aziz begins to break down in the aftermath of the trial

THE PEARL

John Steinbeck

After finding a hugely valuable pearl, a man becomes greedy and violent.

THE LIFE OF JOHN STEINBECK

John Steinbeck was born in Salinas, California, on February 27, 1902. He attended Stanford University but did not graduate. Steinbeck began writing novels in 1929, but he garnered little commercial or critical success until the publication of *Tortilla Flat* in 1935. In his fiction, Steinbeck frequently delved into the lives of the downtrodden. A trio of novels in the late 1930s focus on the lives of migrant workers in California: *In Dubious Battle* (1936), *Of Mice and Men* (1937), and Steinbeck's masterpiece, *The Grapes of Wrath* (1939), which soared to the top of the bestseller lists and sold half a million copies. In 1940, the novel was awarded the Pulitzer Prize and adapted to the screen. Steinbeck won the Novel Prize for Literature in 1962.

Critical opinions of Steinbeck's work have always been mixed. Both stylistically and in his emphasis on manhood and male relationships, Steinbeck was strongly influenced by his contemporary, Ernest Hemingway. Even though Steinbeck was hailed as a great author in the 1930s and '40s, many critics have called his work superficial, sentimental, and overly moralistic.

Steinbeck continued writing throughout the 1940s and 1950s. He went to Europe during World War II, then worked in Hollywood both as a filmmaker and a scriptwriter. His important later works include *East of Eden* (1952) and *Travels with Charley* (1962). He died in New York City in 1968.

THE PEARL IN CONTEXT

Steinbeck's novella *The Pearl* (1945) explores the destructive effect of colonial capitalism on the simple piety of a traditional native culture. While less complex than Steinbeck's other works, *The Pearl* ranks among his most popular. The novella, which was originally conceived as a film project, features a simple, visually evocative style. Its simple prose style recalls a moral parable, particularly the biblical parables of Jesus. According to the New Testament, Jesus taught his disciples by telling them parables—one of which concerns a man who gives up everything he has to win a great pearl.

Parables are simple, often allegorical stories. For example, in a parable of Jesus', a rich landowner might stand for God. *The Pearl* can be interpreted as a number of different allegories. The pearl might symbolize goodness, which means that Kino's struggle to protect it represents the human struggle to preserve goodness. Kino's desire to use the pearl could stand for the mistaken conviction that hard work will result in wealth. The pearl might symbolize the treasures of native cultures, which colonizers loot or destroy. Finally, the pearl can be interpreted as a sign of the dangers of greed.

THE PEARL: KEY FACTS

Time and place written: 1944–1945; California

Date of first publication: 1945 (in serial form under the title "The Pearl of the World"), 1947 (in book form)

Publisher: The Viking Press

Type of work: Novella

Genre: Parable; allegory

Language: English

Setting (time): Unclear

Setting (place): A Mexican coastal village called La Paz, probably on the Baja Peninsula

Tense: Past

Tone: Respectful, mourning, stylized

Narrator: Anonymous, omniscient narrator in the third person

Point of view: Shifts from character to character

Protagonist: Kino

Antagonist: The human impulse toward greed and violence

THE PEARL: PLOT OVERVIEW

Kino lives in a modest brush house by the sea with his wife, Juana, and their infant son, Coyotito. One morning, calamity strikes when a scorpion stings Coyotito. Kino and Juana rush their son to the doctor in town, but they are turned away because they cannot pay for the doctor's services. Later that morning, Kino and Juana take their family canoe, an heirloom, out to the estuary to go diving for pearls. Juana makes a poultice for Coyotito's wound while Kino searches the sea bottom. Kino surfaces with the largest pearl either of them has ever seen. Kino lets out a triumphant yell at his good fortune, and nearby boats sail over to examine the treasure.

The whole neighborhood gathers at Kino's brush house to celebrate his find. Kino lists things that he will buy, including a church wedding and an education for his son. The neighbors marvel at Kino's boldness and wonder if his ambitions are foolish or wise. The local priest visits Kino to bless him and remind him of his place in the church. The doctor arrives, saying he was out in the morning and now wants to cure Coyotito. He administers a powdered capsule and promises to return in an hour.

Coyotito grows violently ill, and Kino decides to bury the pearl under the floor in a corner of the brush house. The doctor returns and feeds Coyotito a potion. When the doctor inquires about payment, Kino says he will sell his large pearl soon. As he talks, he inadvertently glances toward the corner where he has hidden the pearl. The doctor is intrigued, and Kino feels uneasy. Before going to bed, he reburies the pearl under a stone in his fire hole. That night, he is woken by an intruder digging in the corner. A violent struggle ensues. Terribly upset by this turn of events, Juana proposes that they abandon the pearl, which she considers an agent of evil.

The next morning, Kino and Juana make their way to town to sell the pearl. The dealers conspire to bid low on the pearl. Kino indignantly refuses to accept their offers, resolving to take his pearl to the capital. That evening, as Kino and Juana prepare to leave, Juan Tomás, Kino's brother, cautions Kino against being overly proud, and Juana repeats her wish to be rid of the pearl. Kino silences her, saying he is a man and will take care of things.

In the middle of the night, Juana steals away with the pearl. Kino wakes and pursues her, catching her just as she is poised to throw the pearl into the sea. He tackles her and beats her violently, leaving her in a crumpled heap on the beach. As he returns to the brush house, a group of hostile men confronts him and tries to take the pearl from him. He fights the men off, killing one and causing the rest to flee.

As Juana heads back to the brush house, she finds the pearl lying in the path and Kino on the ground next to the dead man. Kino says he had no intention to kill, but Juana fears he will be labeled a murderer. They decide to flee at once, but Kino discovers his canoe has been destroyed by vandals. When he climbs back up the hill, he sees his house on fire. Kino, Juana, and Coyotito duck into Juan Tomás's house, where they hide out for the day. The neighborhood believes that Kino and his family perished in the blaze. Juan Tomás and his wife, Apolonia, reluctantly agree to hide Kino and Juana.

At night, Kino, Juana, and Coyotito set out for the capital. Kino discovers that three trackers are following them and decides that they must try to elude them by hurrying up the mountain. Kino attempts to mislead the trackers by creating a false trail up the mountain. Kino, Juana, and Coyotito hide in a cave and wait for an opportunity to escape back down the mountain.

The trackers make camp nearby. Two of them sleep while the third stands watch. Kino decides to attack them before the late moon rises. He strips naked to avoid being seen and sneaks up to striking distance. Coyotito lets out a cry, waking the sleepers. When one of them fires his rifle in the direction of the cry, Kino makes his move, killing the trackers in a violent fury. Afterward, Kino realizes that the rifle shot killed his son. The next day, Kino and Juana make their way back to their town. Juana carries her dead son slung over her shoulder. They walk all the way to the sea, as onlookers watch in silent fascination. At the shore, Kino pulls out the pearl and takes one last, hard look at it. Then he flings the pearl back into the sea.

CHARACTERS IN *THE PEARL*

Apolonia Juan Tomás's wife and the mother of four children. Like her husband, Apolonia is sympathetic to Kino and Juana's plight.

Coyotito Kino and Juana's only son.

The Dealers An extremely well-organized and corrupt group. The pearl dealers in La Paz systematically cheat and exploit the Indian pearl divers who sell them their goods.

The Doctor A small-time colonial. The doctor dreams of returning to a bourgeois European lifestyle. He represents the arrogance, condescension, and greed at the heart of colonial society.

Juana Kino's young wife. Juana possesses a simple faith in divine powers, but she also thinks for herself. She submits to her dominant husband, which leads to disaster.

Kino The protagonist of the novella. Kino is a dignified, impoverished native who works as a pearl diver. Ultimately, Kino's material ambition drives him to a state of animalistic violence.

The Priest The local village priest is eager to exploit Kino's wealth.

Juan Tomás Kino's older brother. Deeply loyal to his family, Juan Tomás supports Kino in all of his endeavors but warns him of the danger of possessing such a valuable pearl.

The Trackers A group of violent and corrupt men that follows Kino and Juana when they leave the village, hoping to steal the pearl.

THEMES IN *THE PEARL*

GREED AS A DESTRUCTIVE FORCE As Kino seeks to gain wealth and status through the pearl, he changes from a happy, contented father into a savage criminal. His transformation shows how ambition and greed destroy innocence. Kino's longing for money perverts the pearl's natural beauty and good luck, transforming it from a symbol of hope into a symbol of destruction and death. Kino's greed changes him entirely. Because of it, he beats his wife, indirectly causes his son's death, and ultimately alienates himself from his cultural tradition and society. Steinbeck suggests that Kino's plight is a microcosm of what will happen to his people, whose piety is being corrupted by the materialism of colonial capitalism.

THE ROLES OF FATE AND AGENCY IN SHAPING HUMAN LIFE *The Pearl* depicts a world in which people largely shape their own destinies. They provide for themselves, indulge their desires, and make their own plans. But despite this agency, forces beyond human control—such as chance, accident, and the gods—can sweep in at any moment and change the course of an individual's life. In *The Pearl*, human agency is represented by the village of La Paz, where desires, plans, and motives combine to form civilization. Fate is represented in the novella by the open sea, where the discovery of treasure can ruin a once happy life. Steinbeck does not suggest that fate rules human life, for that would mean that humans have no responsibility for their actions. It is not fate but individual choice that makes Kino ruin his life.

COLONIAL SOCIETY'S OPPRESSION OF NATIVE CULTURES The doctor who refuses to save Coyotito's life because of Kino's poverty stands for colonial arrogance and oppression. Snide and condescending, the doctor displays an appallingly limited and self-centered mindset. He also has an unshakable belief in his own cultural superiority. These qualities become terrifying because the doctor has the power to save or destroy lives. Steinbeck indicts the doctor's entire colonial society for its destructive arrogance, greed, and ambition. The European colonizers that govern Kino and the native people are partly to blame for the destruction of the native society's innocence, piety, and purity.

SYMBOLS IN *THE PEARL*

THE PEARL The pearl's symbolism shifts over the course of the novella. At first, it represents a stroke of divine providence. Kino's people have a prophecy about a great "Pearl That Might Be," and Kino's discovery seems to fulfill this prophecy. It seems like a happy accident, one that counterbalances the tragic accident of Coyotito's scorpion sting. Once the town finds out about the pearl, however, the pearl inspires dangerous greed. The neighbors call it "the Pearl of the World," a name that most obviously refers to the pearl's great size and beauty but also refers to the pearl as a worldly object, one that corrupts innocence. Eventually, the pearl symbolizes the destructive nature of materialism.

KINO'S CANOE   The canoe symbolizes Kino's link to his culture. It is a means of making a living that has been passed down for generations. Kino's possession of the pearl leads directly to the canoe's destruction, which suggests that the pursuit of wealth destroys cultural heritage.

IMPORTANT QUOTATIONS FROM *THE PEARL*

"In the town they tell the story of the great pearl—how it was found and how it was lost again. They tell of Kino, the fisherman, and of his wife, Juana, and of the baby, Coyotito. And because the story has been told so often, it has taken root in every man's mind. And, as with all retold tales that are in people's hearts, there are only good and bad things and black and white things and good and evil things and no in-between anywhere.

If this story is a parable, perhaps everyone takes his own meaning from it and reads his own life into it. In any case, they say in the town that. . . ."

Location: The epigraph
Speaker: The narrator
Context: The narrator introduces his story

By introducing his novella as a legend (he first heard the legend of the Pearl of the World in a Mexican village), Steinbeck sets the tone for the story. He also establishes the parable's moral universe as a place in which there "are only good and bad things … and no in-between." The measured formal language of the epigraph evokes biblical verse, which suggests, even before Steinbeck alludes to the possibility, that *The Pearl* is a parable. Because the epigraph leads directly into Chapter 1 (the first sentence in Chapter 1 effectively concludes the unfinished final sentence of the epigraph), it also creates the sense that Steinbeck is taking us directly to the source of the legend. The quotes that surround the epigraph give us the sense that someone is telling us a story and that the novella that follows is the storyteller's tale.

The ants were busy on the ground, big black ones with shiny bodies and the little dusty quick ants. Kino watched with the detachment of God while a dusty ant frantically tried to escape the sand trap an ant lion had dug for him. (Chapter 1)

He watched the ants moving, a little column of them near to his foot, and he put his foot in their path. Then the column climbed over his instep and continued on its way, and Kino left his foot there and watched them move over it. (Chapter 6)

Location: Chapter 1 and Chapter 6
Speaker: The narrator
Context: Kino observes ants

Kino's two encounters with ants are not important to the novel's plot, but they reveal a great deal about Kino's position and attitude at two key moments in the novel. The quotation from Chapter 1 is part of the description of Kino and Juana's idyllic life. Kino's detached attitude toward the ants suggests that he is part of nature but also above it, like God. The description of the ant caught in the sand trap is subtle foreshadowing. It suggests Kino's eventual imprisonment in his own ambition. The quotation from Chapter 6 describes Kino after the pearl has corrupted him. He is no longer detached from nature, and therefore he is no longer like God. Perhaps the best evidence of his fallen state is that he consciously wants to be like God, like Adam and Eve when they decide they want to have God's knowledge. Kino tries to affect the ants' behavior by placing his foot in their path, but he fails. Nature simply renders him insignificant—the ants ignore him and climb over his shoe.

But the pearls were accidents, and the finding of one was luck, a little pat on the back by God or the gods or both.

Location: Chapter 2
Speaker: The narrator
Context: Kino prepares to dive

In the pearl he saw Coyotito sitting at a little desk in a school, just as Kino had once seen it through an open door. And Coyotito was dressed in a jacket, and he had on a white collar and a broad silken tie. Moreover, Coyotito was writing on a big piece of paper. Kino looked at his neighbors fiercely. "My son will go to school," he said, and the neighbors were hushed.. . .

Kino's face shone with prophecy. "My son will read and open the books, and my son will write and will know writing. And my son will make numbers, and these things will make us free because he will know — he will know and through him we will know.. . . . This is what the pearl will do."

Location: Chapter 3
Speaker: The narrator; Kino
Context: Kino expresses a desire to put his son on a level with his European oppressors

---

And the evils of the night were about them. The coyotes cried and laughed in the brush, and the owls screeched and hissed over their heads. And once some large animal lumbered away, crackling the undergrowth as it went. And Kino gripped the handle of the big working knife and took a sense of protection from it.

Location: Chapter 6
Speaker: The narrator
Context: As Kino deteriorates, his relationship with nature sours

THE PICTURE OF DORIAN GRAY

Oscar Wilde

The portrait of a sinful young man ages while the young man depicted in the portrait remains youthful.

THE LIFE OF OSCAR WILDE

Oscar Wilde was born on October 16, 1854, in Dublin, Ireland. He was educated at Trinity College in Dublin and at Magdalen College, Oxford. He settled in London, where he married Constance Lloyd in 1884. In the literary world of Victorian London, Wilde fell in with an exalted artistic crowd that included W. B. Yeats, the great Irish poet, and Lillie Langtry, mistress of the Prince of Wales. A remarkable conversationalist and a famous wit, Wilde began his writing career by publishing mediocre poetry, but soon achieved fame and critical success with his comic plays: *Vera; or, The Nihilists* (1880), *Lady Windermere's Fan* (1892), *A Woman of No Importance* (1893), *An Ideal Husband* (1895), and his most famous play, *The Importance of Being Earnest* (1895). These plays are successful not because of their plots, which are relatively simple and familiar, but because of their brilliant dialogue and biting satire.

In 1891, the year that the second edition of *The Picture of Dorian Gray* was published, Wilde began a homosexual relationship with Lord Alfred Douglas, an ambitious but rather untalented poet. The affair caused a scandal. Douglas's father, the marquess of Queensberry, eventually criticized it publicly. When Wilde sued the marquess for libel, he himself was convicted under English sodomy laws for acts of "gross indecency." In 1895, Wilde was sentenced to two years of hard labor. While serving his sentence, Wilde wrote a long, heartbreaking letter to Lord Alfred titled *De Profundis* (Latin for "Out of the Depths"). After his release, Wilde left England and divided his time between France and Italy, living in poverty. He never published under his own name again. Wilde died in Paris on November 30, 1900.

THE PICTURE OF DORIAN GRAY IN CONTEXT

The Picture of Dorian Gray, Wilde's only novel, first appeared in the summer of 1890 in *Lippincott's Monthly Magazine*. Critics called it scandalous and immoral. Disappointed with the novel's reception, Wilde revised it in 1891, adding a preface and six new chapters. The preface anticipates some of the criticism that might be leveled at the novel and answers critics who will call *The Picture of Dorian Gray* an immoral tale. It also sets forth the tenets of Wilde's philosophy of art. Wilde, a devotee of aestheticism, believed that art possesses an intrinsic value—that it does not need to serve a moral or a political purpose because its beauty alone makes it worthy. This attitude was revolutionary in Victorian England, where popular belief held that art should encourage morality. In his preface, Wilde also cautions readers against finding meanings "beneath the surface" of art—a caution that has never discouraged readers from setting forth many different interpretations of the novel.

THE PICTURE OF DORIAN GRAY: KEY FACTS

Time and place written: 1890, London	
Date of first publication: 1890 in *Lippincott's Monthly Magazine*, 1891 in book form	
Publisher: Ward, Lock & Company	
Type of work: Novel	
Genre: Gothic	
Language: English	
Setting (time): 1890s	
Setting (place): London, England	

Tense: Past

Tone: Gothic, sardonic, comedic

Narrator: Anonymous, omniscient third-person narrator

Point of view: The narrator's

Protagonist: Dorian Gray

Antagonist: Dorian Gray, Lord Henry Wotton

THE PICTURE OF DORIAN GRAY: PLOT OVERVIEW

A well-known artist, Basil Hallward, is painting a portrait of Dorian Gray, a cultured, wealthy, and impossibly beautiful young man. Basil has painted several portraits of Dorian, usually depicting him as an ancient Greek hero or a mythological figure. This is the first portrait that depicts Dorian as he truly is. Basil tells his friend Lord Henry Wotton that the painting disappoints him because it reveals too much of his own feeling for Dorian. Lord Henry, a famous wit who enjoys scandalizing his friends by championing youth, beauty, and the selfish pursuit of pleasure, disagrees with Basil. He thinks the portrait is Basil's masterpiece. Dorian arrives at the studio, and Basil introduces him to Lord Henry despite his fear that Lord Henry will damage the impressionable young man.

Basil's fears are well founded. Before the end of their first conversation, Lord Henry upsets Dorian with a speech about the transient nature of beauty and youth. Worried that his own youth and beauty are fading day by day, Dorian curses his portrait, which one day will remind him of the beauty he has lost. He says "if it were I who were to be always young and the picture to grow old . . . I would give my soul for it." In an attempt to appease Dorian, Basil gives him the portrait.

Over the next few weeks, Lord Henry's influence over Dorian grows stronger. Dorian becomes a disciple of the "new Hedonism" and decides to devote himself to the pursuit of pleasure. He falls in love with Sibyl Vane, a young actress who performs in a theater in London's slums. He adores her acting, and she adores him, dismissing the advice of her brother, James Vane, who thinks Dorian is no good for her. Sibyl decides that she can no longer act, because after experiencing real love she cannot portray an imitation of it on the stage. Dorian, who loves Sibyl because of her talent for acting, cruelly breaks his engagement with her. He returns home and notices that the face in his portrait has changed: it now sneers. Frightened that his wish has come true, he resolves to make amends with Sibyl. But the following afternoon, he learns that Sibyl has killed herself. At Lord Henry's urging, Dorian decides to consider her death an artistic triumph and put the matter behind him. Dorian hides his portrait in a remote room in his house.

Lord Henry gives Dorian a book about the wicked exploits of a nineteenth-century Frenchman. The book becomes Dorian's bible. He sinks ever deeper into a life of sin and corruption, seeking out new experiences and sensations with no regard for morality or the consequences of his actions. Eighteen years pass. Dorian's reputation suffers in polite London society, where rumors spread about his scandalous exploits. Still, his peers continue to accept him because he remains young and beautiful. The figure in the painting grows increasingly wizened and hideous. One dark, foggy night, Basil Hallward arrives at Dorian's home to confront him about his behavior. They argue, and eventually Dorian offers to show his soul to Basil. He shows Basil the now-hideous portrait. Basil, horrified, begs him to repent. Dorian says it is too late for penance and kills Basil in a fit of rage.

To dispose of the body, Dorian blackmails a doctor. The night after the murder, Dorian makes his way to an opium den, where he encounters James Vane. James attempts to avenge Sibyl's death, but Dorian escapes to his country estate. While entertaining guests, he notices James Vane peering in through a window and feels wracked with fear and guilt. When a hunting party accidentally shoots and kills Vane, Dorian feels safe again. He resolves to change but cannot muster the courage to confess his crimes. The painting now reveals his supposed desire to repent for what it is—hypocrisy. In a fury, Dorian picks up the knife he used to stab Basil Hallward and lunges at the painting. There is a crash, and his servants enter to find the portrait, which now depicts Dorian Gray as a beautiful young man. On the floor lies the body of their master—an old man, horribly wrinkled and disfigured, with a knife plunged into his heart.

CHARACTERS IN THE PICTURE OF DORIAN GRAY

Alan Campbell A friend of Dorian's. Alan is one of many promising young men who severs ties with
  Dorian after hearing word of his exploits.

Dorian Gray The protagonist of the novel. Dorian is a radiantly handsome, impressionable, and wealthy young gentleman who becomes perverse and jaded under the influence of Lord Henry Wotton.

Basil Hallward An artist. Basil claims that Dorian's rare beauty has helped him realize a new kind of art. Basil is a good, kind man.

Lady Agatha Lord Henry's aunt. Lady Agatha does charity work in London slums.

Lord Fermor Lord Henry's testy uncle. Lord Fermor tells Henry the story of Dorian's parentage.

Mrs. Leaf Dorian Gray's housekeeper. Mrs. Leaf is a bustling older woman who takes her work seriously.

Duchess of Monmouth A pretty, bored young noblewoman. The duchess flirts with Dorian at his country estate.

James Vane Sibyl's brother. James, a sailor, cares deeply for his sister and worries about her relationship with Dorian.

Mrs. Vane Sibyl's and James's mother. Mrs. Vane is a faded actress who has consigned herself and her daughter to a tawdry theater company. Because of Dorian's wealth, she welcomes him as a wonderful match for her daughter.

Sibyl Vane A poor, beautiful, and talented actress. Dorian falls in love with her artistry.

Victor Dorian's servant. Although Victor is trustworthy, Dorian worries that he will steal a glance at the portrait.

Lord Henry Wotton A nobleman. Urbane and witty, Lord Henry perpetually fires off well-phrased epigrams criticizing the primness and hypocrisy of Victorian society. His philosophy of "new Hedonism" advocates seeking out stimulating experiences, both moral and immoral.

Victoria Wotton Lord Henry's wife. She is an untidy, foolishly romantic woman with "a perfect mania for going to church."

THEMES IN *THE PICTURE OF DORIAN GRAY*

THE PURPOSE OF ART Wilde's novel seems to contradict his own stated philosophy. In his preface, he says that the purpose of art is to have no purpose. He rejects the Victorian conviction that art should be used as a tool for social education and moral enlightenment. He also implicitly criticizes bourgeois morality. Yet *The Picture of Dorian Gray* does not simply exist for art's sake—it has a moral message, one that utterly contradicts aestheticism: it argues that those who make beauty and experience their first priority will come to a bad end. Wilde uses Basil's painting and Lord Henry's mysterious yellow book to suggest that a compulsive focus on beauty leads to disaster. The portrait is a mirror that makes Dorian's moral sins vividly physical. The French novel is a road map that leads Dorian deeper and deeper into a dark forest of immorality. Perhaps Wilde meant for these breaches of aesthetic philosophy to show readers the danger of art that teaches a moral lesson—the portrait of Dorian, which exists as a moralizing force instead of as a work of beauty alone, leads to the deaths of at least four people. But showing the danger of moralizing art is, in itself, a moral lesson.

THE VALUE OF YOUTH AND BEAUTY *The Picture of Dorian Gray* prizes beauty even while it admits that the price for beauty is high. Characters use beauty to revitalize their wearied senses, as Lord Henry does by looking at Basil's portrait of Dorian. They also use it to escape the brutalities of the world. Dorian distances himself from the horrors of his actions by studying beautiful things—music, jewels, rare tapestries. Physical beauty is a valuable commodity, and the loss of youth and beauty results in a loss of status. Dorian, Lord Henry, and their friends care not about a man's heart, but about his looks. Because Dorian looks pure and fresh, society eventually overlooks his horrifying behavior. Indeed, society equates beauty with morality. As Lady Narborough tells Dorian, "you are made to be good—you look so good."

THE AMBIGUITY OF HOMOEROTICISM In *The Picture of Dorian Gray*, Wilde creates homoerotic relationships that he both enjoys and disdains. Basil creates a masterpiece because Dorian's beauty so inspires him. Lord Henry takes Dorian under his wing, longing to seduce him and mold him. Wilde partially approves of these relationships, linking them to ancient Greece, where it was common and perfectly acceptable for old men to take young men as lovers. But he also condemns them as perverse and dangerous. Basil's homoerotic masterpiece becomes a monstrosity. Lord Henry's influence on Basil supports the assumptions of homophobes—he turns a pure young boy into a corrupt villain. Perhaps because of his mixed guilt and defiance about his own sexuality, Wilde's portrayal of male relationships is a complex one.

SYMBOLS IN *THE PICTURE OF DORIAN GRAY*

THE OPIUM DENS   The opium dens, located in a remote and derelict section of London, represent the sordid state of Dorian's mind. Dorian flees to them after killing Basil, trying to stifle his awareness of his crimes by blunting his consciousness. Although he has a canister of opium in his home, he leaves the safety of his neat and proper parlor to go to a place that better symbolizes the degradation of his soul.

JAMES VANE   James Vane is less a believable character than a symbol of Dorian's tortured conscience. Wilde added James while revising the novel in 1891. As he appears at the dock and later at Dorian's country estate, James has an almost spectral quality. Like the ghost of Jacob Marley in Charles Dickens's *A Christmas Carol*, who warns Scrooge that he will pay for his sins, James reminds Dorian of his crimes.

IMPORTANT QUOTATIONS FROM *THE PICTURE OF DORIAN GRAY*

Yes: there was to be, as Lord Henry had prophesied, a new Hedonism that was to re-create life, and to save it from that harsh, uncomely puritanism that is having, in our own day, its curious revival. It was to have its service of the intellect, certainly; yet it was never to accept any theory or system that would involve the sacrifice of any mode of passionate experience. Its aim, indeed, was to be experience itself, and not the fruits of experience, sweet or bitter as they might be. Of the asceticism that deadens the senses, as of the vulgar profligacy that dulls them, it was to know nothing. But it was to teach man to concentrate himself upon the moments of a life that is itself but a moment.

Location: Chapter Eleven
Speaker: The narrator
Context: Dorian adjusts to constant youth

Dorian devotes himself to the pleasures of all kinds of experience. In order to discover "the true nature of the senses," he studies rare musical instruments, jewelry, embroidery, and the psychological effects of perfume. In addition to these pursuits, he begins to devote his time to more sordid affairs, the nature of which is never perfectly clear. We later learn from Basil that Dorian is connected with the downfall of numerous youths, all of whom have been brought to shame (and some even driven to suicide) by their associations with Dorian. Whether the outcome of these experiences is "sweet or bitter" is not the point of the philosophy by which Dorian lives. Only the experience matters. This "new Hedonism" resists the conventional morality that Lord Henry spends so much of his time criticizing.

"[Y]ou poisoned me with a book once. I should not forgive that. Harry, promise me that you will never lend that book to anyone. It does harm."

"My dear boy, you are really beginning to moralize. You will soon be going about like the converted, and the revivalist, warning people against all the sins of which you have grown tired. You are much too delightful to do that.. . . . As for being poisoned by a book, there is no such thing as that. Art has no

influence upon action. It annihilates the desire to act. It is superbly sterile. The books that the world calls immoral are books that show the world its own shame."

Location: Chapter Nineteen
Speaker: Dorian and Lord Henry
Context: Dorian pledges to reform himself

This exchange between Dorian and Lord Henry takes place in Chapter Nineteen, as Dorian, flayed by his conscience, pledges to live a reformed life. Reflecting on the course of his past twenty years, he confronts Lord Henry, whom he believes is responsible for leading him astray. Dorian criticizes the yellow book that, years before, had such a profound influence over him, claiming that this book did him great harm. This accusation is, of course, alien to Wilde's philosophy of aestheticism, which holds that art cannot be either moral or immoral. Lord Henry says as much, refusing to believe that a book could have such power. While there is something seductive in his observation that "the world calls immoral … books that show the world its own shame," Lord Henry's words here are less convincing than other statements to the same effect that he makes earlier in the novel. In the latter stages of the novel, we know of Dorian's downfall, and we know that he is anything but "delightful." At this point, Lord Henry's praising of Dorian makes Lord Henry seem hopelessly naïve, the victim of a philosophy whose consequences elude him.

We are punished for our refusals. Every impulse that we strive to strangle broods in the mind, and poisons us. The body sins once, and has done with its sin, for action is a mode of purification.. . . Resist it, and your soul grows sick with longing for the things it has forbidden to itself, with desire for what its monstrous laws have made monstrous and unlawful. It has been said that the great events of the world take place in the brain. It is in the brain, and the brain only, that the great sins of the world take place also.

Location: Chapter Two
Speaker: Lord Henry
Context: Lord Henry meets Dorian and explains his theory of sin

---

"To be good is to be in harmony with one's self," he replied, touching the thin stem of his glass with his pale, fine-pointed fingers. "Discord is to be forced to be in harmony with others. One's own life—that is the important thing. As for the lives of one's neighbours, if one wishes to be a prig or a Puritan, one can flaunt one's moral views about them, but they are not one's concern. Besides, Individualism has really the higher aim. Modern morality consists in accepting the standard of one's age. I consider that for any man of culture to accept the standard of his age is a form of the grossest immorality."

Location: Chapter Six
Speaker: Lord Henry
Context: Lord Henry chastises Dorian for dismissing his dangerous theories

---

Society, civilized society at least, is never very ready to believe anything to the detriment of those who are both rich and fascinating. It feels instinctively that manners are of more importance than morals, and, in its opinion, the highest respectability is of much less value than the possession of a good chef. And, after all, it is a very poor consolation to be told that the man who has given one a bad dinner, or poor wine, is irreproachable in his private life. Even the cardinal virtues cannot atone for half-cold entrées, as Lord Henry remarked once, in a discussion on the subject; and there is possibly a good deal to be said for his view. For the canons of good society are, or should be, the same as the canons of art. Form is absolutely essential to it. It should have the dignity of a ceremony, as well as its unreality, and should combine the insincere character of a romantic play with the wit and beauty that make such plays delightful to us. Is insincerity such a terrible thing? I think not. It is merely a method by which we can multiply our personalities.

Location: Chapter Eleven
Speaker: The narrator
Context: The narrator, using the first person for the first and last time, explains the importance of manners

THE PLAGUE

Albert Camus

Quarantined with the Bubonic plague, the citizens of an Algerian town eventually overcome their selfish instincts and battle the epidemic together.

THE LIFE OF ALBERT CAMUS

Albert Camus was born in 1913 in Mondovi, a small town in Algeria, which was then a French colony in Northern Africa. His father was a French-Algerian vineyard worker and his mother was a Spanish char-woman. Less than a year after Camus's birth, his father was killed in World War I. Impoverished, Camus's family relocated to Algiers to live with Camus's grandmother.

As a teenager, Camus lived with an uncle who exposed him to the works of Russian author Fyodor Dostoevsky and French socialist André Gide. In 1930 Camus was diagnosed with tuberculosis, which would plague him for the rest of his life. While convalescing, Camus studied philosophy with Jean Gre-nier, a French émigré who introduced him to the philosophies of Friedrich Nietzsche and Henry Bergson. Camus continued his studies at the University of Algiers and received a degree in philosophy in 1936. Throughout the early thirties he worked odd jobs to support himself and pay his tuition.

A 1934 relapse of tuberculosis conveniently excused the vehemently antiwar Camus from military service. The following year he established the leftist theater troupe Théâtre du Travail, which later became known as Théâtre de l'Equipe. In the mid-thirties, he briefly joined the Communist Party, but left after a heated political dispute. He also began assembling his first book, a collection of essays entitled *The Wrong Side and the Right Side* (1937).

During World War II, Camus relocated to Paris and became a leading writer for the French Resis-tance. As the editor-in-chief of *Combat*, an important underground newspaper, Camus received national recognition. The success of Camus's first novel, *The Stranger* (1942) turned him into an intellectual celebrity. His next novel, *The Plague* (1947), achieved international success both critically and commer-cially. Despite newfound fame, Camus suffered depression and drank heavily.

Camus went on to produce many novels, plays, and essays. In 1949, his lover, the actress Maria Casarès, starred in the first production of his play *The Just Assassins*. *The Rebel* (1951), a philosophical treatise, fomented bitter arguments with longtime friend and intellectual rival Jean-Paul Sartre. In *The Fall* (1956), Camus chronicled his futile attempts to mediate the civil war brewing between Algerian Arabs and the *pieds noirs*, descendants of French colonialists. He won the 1957 Nobel Prize for Litera-ture.

During the 1950s, Camus adapted several works for the stage, notably William Faulkner's *Requiem for a Nun* (1956) and Dostoevsky's *The Possessed* (1959). He began a highly anticipated new novel, *The First Man*, but died a car accident before he could finish. The manuscript for the novel was found in a brief-case near the wreck; Camus's daughter edited and published *The First Man* in 1994.

THE PLAGUE IN CONTEXT

The Plague has often been seen as an allegory for Nazi expansion during World War II. In the years after World War I, a number of European leaders consolidated their power with promises of economic relief, developing their states into brutally repressive totalitarian regimes. In Germany, Adolf Hitler rose to the head of the Nazi Party and took control of government. In Italy, Benito Mussolini solidified his fascist regime. In Spain, Francisco Franco crushed republican resistance and secured his military dictatorship during the Spanish Civil War. In the USSR, Josef Stalin instituted a harshly oppressive form of commu-nist socialism. World War II, begun with Hitler's invasion of neighboring European nations, pitted Nazi Germany, Italy, and Japan against England, France, the USSR, and the United States. France spent most of the war under Nazi occupation, though many, including Camus joined the Resistance efforts.

The 1940s saw the development of existentialism, a philosophical movement that arose amid the rav-ages of the war. Led by the French writer-philosopher Jean-Paul Sartre, who co-founded Camus's anti-totalitarianist newspaper *Combat*, existentialists examined the apparent meaninglessness of a world ravaged by war and threatened by nuclear annihilation, populated by isolated, numbed individuals who had largely lost their faith in God. Some existentialists saw no solution; Sartre argued that atheism liberated individuals to take responsibility for their own actions. Although he borrowed from them, Camus resisted association with the existentialists, preferring to be seen as a humanist who believed in personal morality in the face of life's absurdity.

Algeria, where *The Plague* is set, had been historically populated by Berber-speaking nomads. By the sixteenth century, it was under the control of the Ottoman Turks. The French invaded in the early nineteenth century; Algeria became a French colony in 1848. Racial and religious tensions escalated under French occupation. After World War I, Algerian Muslims began a nationalistic movement that would eventually lead to civil war. As a *pied noir*, Camus was sensitive to Algerian social, religious, and racial stratifications, which are reflected in *The Plague*.

THE PLAGUE: KEY FACTS

Time and place written: Before 1947; France

Date of publication: 1947 (*La Peste*). First publication in English in 1948

Publisher: Librairie Gallimard in France; Alfred A. Knopf in United States

Type of work: Novel

Genre: Existentialism

Language: French

Setting (time): 1940s (from April 16 to the following February)

Setting (place): Oran, a coastal port in French colonial Algeria

Tense: Recent past

Tone: Camus's tone is optimistic and humanistic; Rieux's tone is scientific and objective

Narrator: Third-person narrator, identified as Bernard Rieux in the novel's last section

Point of View: Bernard Rieux; Jean Tarrou

Protagonist: Bernard Rieux

Antagonist: The bubonic plague; selfishness; a meaningless and amoral universe

THE PLAGUE: PLOT OVERVIEW

Over the course of a few days one April in the 1940s, in the large Algerian city of Oran, thousands of rats stagger into the streets and die. The population is gripped by a mild hysteria, and the newspapers begin clamoring for action. The authorities finally arrange to collect and cremate the rats daily. Soon thereafter, M. Michel, the concierge of Dr. Rieux's office building, dies after falling ill with a strange fever. Similar cases of the strange fever begin appearing throughout the city; Rieux's colleague Castel becomes certain that the mysterious illness is the bubonic plague (a contagious epidemic carried by rats). Castel and Rieux urge quick, decisive action to alert the public and quarantine the sick, but face denial and indifference when they approach the authorities as well as other doctors. Finally, after it is impossible to deny that Oran has been crippled by a serious epidemic, the authorities take strict sanitation measures and place the city under quarantine.

Once cut off from the outside world, the people react with sudden and intense longing for absent friends and family. They wallow in their personal distress, each convinced that his or her pain is unique in comparison to common suffering. Father Paneloux, a Jesuit priest, delivers a stern sermon in which he declares that the plague is God's punishment for the sins of Oran's citizens. Raymond Rambert, a Parisian journalist, yearns to return to his wife in Paris, but the Oran bureaucrats refuse to let him leave. Eventually, Rambert makes plans to escape illegally with the help of Cottard, a suspicious man with a shady past.

Meanwhile, Rieux—aided by Grand, an aging civil servant, and Tarrou, an existentialist visiting Frenchman—doggedly battles the plague by caring for patients and organizing volunteers into a sanitation league. Rambert finalizes his escape plan but is shamed when he finds out that Rieux too has been separated from his wife by the quarantine. Rambert decides to stay in Oran and help fight the epidemic.

Cottard accumulates a small fortune through smuggling during the quarantine. He has been living in fear of punishment for a nameless crime for many years. The epidemic has given him a chance to be part a community again, because everyone is afraid now.

Over several months, the citizens of Oran begin to see the plague as their collective problem rather than a personal one. Many citizens embrace social responsibility and join the anti-plague efforts. When little Jacques Othon, the small son of the magistrate, dies after an excruciating battle with the plague, Rieux confronts Paneloux and points out that the plague could not be God's punishment because Jacques was an innocent victim. Deeply shaken, Paneloux delivers a second sermon in which he argues that innocent deaths force us to face a choice: we can either believe in God unconditionally or else lose our faith completely. Paneloux falls ill but refuses to consult a doctor, preferring to leave his life in the hands of providence. He dies clutching his crucifix; because his symptoms are not typical of the plague, Rieux records him as a "doubtful case."

The epidemic runs its course. Cottard snaps and begins firing his gun in the street until he is arrested. Grand narrowly survives a bout of the plague. Tarrou falls ill as the epidemic wanes; he fights for his life with all his strength but ultimately dies. Rambert's wife arrives when the Oran city gates finally open. Rieux's wife, in a sanitarium away from Oran, dies of a prolonged illness before she can be reunited with Rieux. The people resume their routine lives, but Rieux knows that the struggle will never really be over—the bacillus microbe, which causes the bubonic plague, can lie dormant for years. *The Plague* is Rieux's chronicle of human suffering, which is all too easily forgotten.

CHARACTERS IN *THE PLAGUE*

Dr. Castel   An elderly doctor who is the first person to suggest that the rats are dying because of the bubonic plague. Together with Rieux, Castel struggles to convince authorities that sanitation measures must be taken in order to stop the spread of the epidemic.

Cottard   A suspicious and paranoid man guilty of an unnamed crime. For Cottard, the quarantine is a relief from fear and solitude. He does not fear arrest because the authorities are too busy, and he doesn't feel alone in his fear because everyone else is afraid too. During the quarantine, Cottard makes money by smuggling, eschewing responsibility for fighting the plague.

Joseph Grand   An elderly civil servant who never pursued opportunities for promotion. His wife Jeanne eventually left Grand after the marriage settled into a monotonous routine. Crippled by anxiety about finding the perfect "right words" for self-expression, Grand has never managed to write to his wife. Similarly, he has been trying to write a novel, but has never gotten past the first line.

M. Michel   The concierge for the building where Rieux works, and the plague's first victim.

M. Othon   A conservative magistrate whom Tarrou considers "public enemy number one."

Jacques Othon   Othon's small son. The first recipient of Castel's plague serum after he contracts the plague, Jacques dies anyway. He is an innocent victim whose death prompts a religious crisis for Paneloux.

Father Paneloux   A Jesuit priest who gives two public sermons during the novel. Paneloux initially argues that the plague is God's punishment for the people's sins, but then suggests that the plague is the supreme test of faith in God.

Asthma Patient   A patient of Rieux's who serves as mouthpiece for the Oran populace and its changing whims during the epidemic.

The Prefect   An official who resists taking stringent sanitation measures to contain the plague, despite Rieux's and Castel's arguments.

Dr. Richard   The chairman of the Oran medical association. Richard is skeptical in the face of Rieux and Castel's suggestion that the city is in the grips of the plague. He refuses to alarm the public with immediate, decisive action.

Raymond Rambert   A Parisian journalist in Oran to research the sanitary conditions of the Arab population. Trapped in Oran by the quarantine, Rambert struggles to find a way to escape to Paris to rejoin his wife.

Dr. Bernard Rieux The novel's protagonist and narrator. A humanist and atheist, Rieux follows his own code of social ethics. He struggles to convince the authorities to enact sanitation measures to contain the plague, then doggedly battles the plague despite indications that his efforts are fruitless. Separated from his wife during the quarantine, Rieux does not allow his personal distress to distract him from his work to alleviate collective suffering.

Jean Tarrou A visitor vacationing in Oran during the outbreak of the plague. As an outsider, Tarrou is able to observe Oran society more objectively; he is the author of the account that Rieux includes to enhance the texture of his chronicle of the plague epidemic. Like Rieux, Tarrou is an atheist who embraces personal social responsibility and contributes to the anti-plague effort. The voice of Camus's philosophy in the novel, Tarrou believes that life and death have no intrinsic moral meaning; rather, humans create their meaning by voluntarily choosing to participate in the noble, if futile, struggle against death and suffering.

THEMES IN *THE PLAGUE*

LIFE AS ABSURD AND MEANINGLESS Camus sets up a universe where events unfold without rational or moral reason. Oran is an ordinary, capitalistic port city; although Camus may assign some moral social justice to the epidemic, Oran is no better or worse than other cities nearby. The plague kills dispassionately and irrationally. It spreads and then abates spontaneously. It infects and kills people without regard for individual merit: the nobler Othon and Tarrou die, whereas the viler Cottard survives. The epidemic is absurd. It progresses without reason. The citizens can do little to curb the spread of the disease. The efforts of the physicians are futile. Rieux cannot save Tarrou despite months of experience fighting the plague. Othon's small, innocent son dies after an excruciating battle. The only meaning offered by Camus's portrayal of life comes from the doctors' struggle, however futile, against death and suffering.

HUMAN OPTIMISM IN THE FACE OF ADVERSITY In spite of the bleakness of their plight, the citizens of Oran never lose hope. In the face of death and misery, the survivors remain optimistic that their lives will return to normal and they will be reunited with their friends and family. *The Plague* celebrates the characters who never lose hope. Castel's anti-plague serum achieves only modest results at best, especially since improvements become apparent only after the plague has begun to abate on its own. Nonetheless, Castel's diligence is a virtue in itself. Grand continues to rewrite the opening of his novel. By the end, he still has not found the right words, but his efforts are depicted as worthy. Over the course of the novel, several characters overcome their selfishness to help the anti-plague efforts. Rambert abandons his escape plan; Gonzalez, a petty criminal, also becomes a volunteer. Othon stays to help those living under quarantine even after he is allowed to leave. Both Othon and Tarrou die heroes, their lives imbued with meaning because of their compassion for others.

INNER TURMOIL AS UNCONTAINABLE *The Plague* suggests that hidden turmoil and rot will inevitably come to the surface, often exploding spontaneously. The plague itself is emblematic of this process. People who have contracted the plague show no outward symptoms until the disease has already advanced considerably. Patients develop buboes (swollen lymph nodes) that eventually explode in diseased pus.

In the beginning of the epidemic, the Prefect attempts to hide the rat problem behind bureaucratic jargon. He avoids using the word "plague" and focuses on placating the populace. Despite his efforts at hiding and avoiding the problem, the rat situation escalates into a nine-month epidemic. Similarly, the newspapers try but fail to conceal reports of the first human deaths. Rieux himself, as narrator, tries to downplay Paneloux's and Tarrou's symptoms by describing them as a cough. Soon enough, Tarrou contracts full-blown plague; Paneloux dies of mysteriously illness.

Cottard's inner turmoil also explodes to the surface. After the plague subsides, Cottard's fear of arrest returns; he engages in a violent shootout with the police. Camus's characters never succeed in denying or hiding from the buried problems.

SYMBOLS IN *THE PLAGUE*

RATS Unpleasant pests, the rats are a harbinger of the bubonic plague. They usually infest the sewers, but as the plague takes root, they come out into the streets to die. They are a manifestation of hidden rot and ugliness that cannot be contained forever. At the end of the novel, the rats return underground, signaling the end of the epidemic. Like the plague bacillus, they continue to live in hiding, a latent danger.

Within the Nazism allegory, the rats stand for the first signs of the spread of Nazism, ignored by world powers until it was too late to prevent war—just as the Oran authorities ignore the rat problem until it is too late to stop the epidemic.

THE SEA The sea represents health and freedom. In describing Oran, Rieux comments that the town, in its focus on business, "turns its back on the bay, with the result that it's impossible to see the sea." The citizens lead a sickly, capitalistic lifestyle; their avoidance of the sea is a symptom of their unhealthiness. After Rieux realizes that Oran is contaminated with the plague, but before the populace begins to panic, the stormy sea is the only indication of the deadly danger to the city. In the quarantine, Oran is cut off from the healthy sea; it no longer functions as a port, the role that had made it prosperous. In Part Four, Tarrou and Rieux take a break from their efforts combating the plague and go for a swim. The sea is a life-giving force that rejuvenates them before they return to their necessary yet futile work.

IMPORTANT QUOTATIONS IN *THE PLAGUE*

The unusual events described in this chronicle occurred in 194– at Oran. Everyone agreed that considering their somewhat extraordinary character, they were out of place there. For its ordinariness is what strikes one first about the town of Oran, which is merely a large French port on the Algerian coast, headquarters of the prefect of a French department.

The town itself, let us admit, is ugly. It has a smug, placid air and you need time to discover what it is that makes it different from so many business centers in other parts of the world.

Location: Part One, first section
Speaker: The narrator (Rieux)
Context: The narrator opens the novel by describing Oran's as an ordinary Algerian port town

The novel's opening lines emphasize the universality of its story. The town is ordinary, the date is ambiguous. The suggestion is that a similar epidemic could break out anywhere. The novel concludes on a similar, if more sinister tone as Rieux reminds us that "the plague bacillus never dies or disappears for good . . . perhaps the day [will] come when, for the bane and the enlightenment of men, it [will] rouse up its rats again." At the same time, the decade of the 1940s is associated with World War II, a time when ordinary people in Europe and elsewhere experienced extraordinary difficulties and horrors.

Rieux's claim of objectivity as a narrator is belied by his attitude toward Oran, which he describes as "ugly" and "smug." The portrayal of Oran as an unpleasant business center points to Camus's own socialist stance. Preoccupied with making money, the residents neglect to take time to enjoy life and refuse to assume responsibility for resolving the plague crisis. Camus implies that the plight of the citizens is appropriate moral justice for their petty greed.

Cottard and Tarrou, who had merely risen from their seats, gazed down at what was a dramatic picture of their life in those days: plague on the stage in the guise of a disarticulated mummer, and in the auditorium the toys of luxury, so futile now, forgotten fans and lace shawls derelict on the red plush seats.

Location: Part Four, first section
Speaker: The narrator (Rieux)
Context: A performance of *Orpheus and Eurydice* has ended in audience exodus after the lead singer fell
  dead from the plague onstage

At the opera, the audience initially thinks that the lead singer's voice is pained and shaky because he is overwhelmed by strong emotions; when he falls dead, they realize that he has been in the grips of the plague. A prolific theater artist, Camus infuses the opera scene with symbolism. The plague has been disguising itself, just as the actor disguises his identity to play a part onstage. As an allegory for the plague of Nazism, the novel similarly disguises itself, as a chronicle of an epidemic. In the opera scene, the plague bursts out unexpectedly, an instance of the uncontainable buried turmoil that manifests itself throughout the novel. In mentioning the opera accessories abandoned on the plush seats, Camus criticizes greed and materialism. The "toys of luxury" are meaningless to people facing life-and-death dangers.

And then it dawned on him that he and the man with him weren't talking about the same thing. For while he himself spoke from the depths of long days of brooding upon his personal distress, and the image he had tried to impart had been slowly shaped and proved in the fires of passion and regret, this meant nothing to the man to whom he was speaking, who pictured a conventional emotion, a grief that is traded on the marketplace, mass-produced. Whether friendly or hostile, the reply always missed fire, and the attempt to communicate had to be given up.

Location: Part Two, first section
Speaker: The narrator (Rieux)
Context: The narrator describes the experience of any Oran citizen who tries to share his grief with another man

---

They dressed and started back. Neither had said a word, but they were conscious of being perfectly at one, and the memory of this night would be cherished by them both. When they caught sight of the plague watchman, Rieux guessed that Tarrou, like himself, was thinking that the disease had given them a respite, and this was good, but now they must set their shoulders to the wheel again.

Location: Part Four, sixth section
Speaker: The narrator (Rieux)
Context: Tarrou and Rieux return from their swim, a break from attending to plague victims

---

This chronicle is drawing to an end, and this seems to be the moment for Dr. Bernard Rieux to confess that he is the narrator. But before describing the closing scenes, he would wish anyhow to justify his undertaking and to set it down that he expressly made a point of adopting the tone of an impartial observer.. . . . For instance, in a general way he has confined himself to describing only such things as he was enabled to see for himself, and has refrained from attributing to his fellow sufferers thoughts that, when all is said and done, they were not bound to have.

Location: Part Five, fifth section
Speaker: The narrator as Rieux
Context: Rieux confesses that he has narrated the novel, choosing to remain anonymous to preserve objectivity

A PORTRAIT OF THE ARTIST AS A YOUNG MAN

James Joyce

A man concludes that he must be unfettered by family, friends, religion, and nation to be a true artist.

THE LIFE OF JAMES JOYCE

James Joyce was born on February 2, 1882, in Dublin, Ireland, into a Catholic middle-class family that soon became poverty-stricken because of its patriarch's financial irresponsibility. Despite this impoverishment, Joyce received the best education available to someone of his station. He attended Jesuit schools, followed by University College in Dublin, where he began publishing essays and writing lyric poetry. After graduating in 1902, Joyce went to Paris, where he devoted all of his time to writing poetry, stories, and theories of aesthetics. Joyce returned to Dublin the following year upon learning that his mother was seriously ill. After his mother's death, Joyce stayed in Dublin, where eventually he met his future wife, Nora Barnacle, a chambermaid at Finn's Hotel.

Nora and Joyce left Dublin in1904. They spent most of the next eleven years living in Rome and Trieste, Italy, where Joyce taught English. He and Nora had two children, Giorgio and Lucia. Joyce's first book of poems, *Chamber Music*, was published in 1907. In 1914, he published both a book of short stories, *Dubliners*, and a serialized autobiographical novel, *A Portrait of the Artist as a Young Man*.

Joyce began writing *Ulysses* in 1914. When World War I broke out, he moved his family to Zurich, Switzerland, where his fortunes improved. His talent attracted several wealthy patrons, including Harriet Shaw Weaver. He published *Portrait* in book form (1916), a play, *Exiles* (1918), and the first episodes of *Ulysses* in *The Little Review* (1918). In 1919, the Joyces moved back to Trieste, but in 1920, at Ezra Pound's urging, they moved to Paris. *Ulysses* was published in Paris in book form in 1922, causing an international scandal with its frank sexual content and revolutionary prose style. In 1923, with his eyesight quickly diminishing, Joyce began working on what became *Finnegans Wake* (1939). Joyce died in 1941.

A PORTRAIT OF THE ARTIST AS A YOUNG MAN IN CONTEXT

A Portrait of the Artist as a Young Man draws on many details from Joyce's early life. Like Joyce, Stephen grows up with a devoutly Catholic mother and a professionally unsuccessful father; like Joyce, Stephen is educated at Clongowes Wood, Belvedere, and University Colleges; like Joyce, he struggles with his faith and his national identity before leaving Ireland to make his way as an artist. Scenes such as the Christmas dinner and Stephen's first sexual experience with a Dublin prostitute closely resemble events in Joyce's life.

By the nineteenth-century, Ireland had been under British rule for three hundred years. Tensions between the Irish and the British had been exacerbated by the potato blight of 1845. Conflicts often organized around religious lines: the majority of the Irish, especially those who favored Irish independence, were Catholic; the Protestant minority wished to remain united with Britain. Toward the end of the nineteenth century, the Irish nationalism movement was spearheaded by Charles Stewart Parnell. However, in 1890, Parnell's longstanding affair with a married woman, Kitty O'Shea, was exposed. He was condemned by the Catholic Church and lost many of his supporters. Joyce saw Parnell's downfall as a hypocritical betrayal of Ireland by the Irish.

Celebrated today as one of the literary pioneers of the twentieth century, Joyce was one of the first writers to use interior monologue (also known as stream of consciousness), a prose form that seeks to evoke the inner thoughts of and perceptions of the characters in real time. This technique, used in *Por-*

trait during the opening sections and in Chapter 5, may make for difficult reading but crystallizes into a coherent and sophisticated portrayal of a character's experience. Joyce also makes use of the epiphany, a moment of sudden, profound realization that changes a character's perception of the world. The epiphany is a notable device in both *Dubliners* and *Portrait*. The most striking example is Stephen's realization that a secular appreciation of beauty is a true good as he watches a young girl wading on the beach.

A PORTRAIT OF THE ARTIST AS A YOUNG MAN: KEY FACTS

Time and place written: 1907–15; Trieste (Italy), Zurich, and Dublin

Date of publication: 1916

Publisher: B. W. Huebsch, New York

Type of work: Novel

Genre: Bildungsroman, autobiographical novel

Language: English

Setting (time): 1882–1903

Setting (place): Dublin, Ireland

Tense: Past

Tone: Introspective, aware, unironic

Narrator: Anonymous, third-person narrator whose language, cadence, tone, and perspective closely mimics Stephen's

Point of view: Stephen Dedalus's

Protagonist: Stephen Dedalus

Antagonist: The ups and downs of the Dedalus family fortune; Stephen's mixture of pride and sense of inferiority; Stephen's shackles, including family, friends, religion, and country

A PORTRAIT OF THE ARTIST AS A YOUNG MAN: PLOT OVERVIEW

CHAPTER 1

Stephen Dedalus grows up in turn-of-the-century British-controlled Ireland. As a young boy, he is sent to Clongowes Wood College, a strict Catholic boarding school. Stephen is homesick and lonely. He spends time in the infirmary after a bully pushes him into a ditch of cold, dirty water. At home over Christmas dinner, family tensions sparked by the death of the Irish nationalist leader Charles Stewart Parnell erupt in a furious, politically charged argument. Back at school, Stephen finds the courage to tell the rector that one of the teachers, Father Dolan, has unfairly punished him. Stephen is hailed as a hero by his classmates.

CHAPTER 2

Simon Dedalus, Stephen's father, is inept with money, and the family sinks deeper into debt. After a summer spent in the company of his Uncle Charles, Stephen learns that the family can no longer afford Clongowes Wood. The Dedaluses move to Dublin. Stephen attends Belvedere, a prestigious Catholic day school where he excels as a writer and as an actor in student theater. His first sexual experience, with a young Dublin prostitute, unleashes a storm of shame and guilt, as Stephen tries to reconcile his physical desires with his Catholic values.

CHAPTER 3

Stephen throws himself into a life of debauchery and sin, indulging in masturbation, gluttony, and more fornication with prostitutes. Then, on a three-day religious retreat, Stephen hears a trio of fiery sermons about sin, judgment, and hell. Deeply shaken, he confesses his sins and resolves to rededicate himself to a life of piety.

CHAPTER 4

Stephen's religious devotion is so pronounced that the Belvedere director invites him to consider becoming a priest. After considering the offer, Stephen realizes that the austerity of a priest's life is incompatible with his love for sensual beauty. Later that day, Stephen learns from his sister that the family will be moving, once again for financial reasons. Anxiously waiting to hear whether he will be accepted to university, Stephen goes for a walk on the beach. As he watches a nubile young girl wading in the tide, he experiences an epiphany: love of and desire for beauty is good. He sees his life path: a true, free artist-creator.

CHAPTER 5

At the university, Stephen formulates his theories of aesthetics and discusses them with his companions, particularly with his friend Cranly. Determined to free himself from all limiting pressures—family, religion, nation, friends—he resolves to leave Ireland, to fly free like his namesake Dædalus, the mythological Greek artisan.

CHARACTERS IN *A PORTRAIT OF THE ARTIST AS A YOUNG MAN*

THE DEDALUSES

Stephen Dedalus The protagonist and James Joyce's alter ego. The novel chronicles Stephen's childhood and adolescence; over its course, he passes through phases of hedonism and religious asceticism. By the end, Stephen has developed an aesthetic theory that art should rise above the common fray of man.

Simon Dedalus Stephen's father, an impoverished former medical student with a strong sense of Irish patriotism. Sentimental about his past, Simon Dedalus frequently reminisces about his youth.

Mary Dedalus Stephen's mother and Simon Dedalus's wife. Mary is very religious, and argues with her son about attending religious services.

Boody, Katey, Maggie, and Maurice Dedalus Stephen's siblings, who have not had many of the opportunities offered to Stephen.

Uncle Charles Stephen's lively great-uncle.

BRAY: CHAPTER 1

Mr. John Casey Simon Dedalus's friend. At Stephen's first Christmas dinner, he and Simon, both Irish nationalists, argue with Dante and mourn the death of Charles Stuart Parnell.

Dante (Mrs. Riordan) The Dedalus children's governess. Militantly pious, Dante speaks out against Charles Stuart Parnell, whom Mr. Casey and Simon Dedalus support, at Stephen's first Christmas dinner.

Eileen Vance The Dedalus's young neighbor. Stephen's childish wish to marry the Protestant Eileen angers Dante.

CLONGOWES WOOD COLLEGE: CHAPTER 1

Father Arnall A stern Latin teacher. (See also Belvedere: Chapters 2–4)

Athy A fellow student whom Stephen meets at the infirmary.

Father Conmee A rector.

Father Dolan A cruel prefect of studies.

Brother Michael A kindly cleric who takes care of Stephen and Athy at the infirmary.

Fleming Stephen's friend.

Wells A bully who taunts Stephen. He pushes Stephen into a filthy cesspool, which lands him in the infirmary.

BLACKROCK: CHAPTER 2

Mike Flynn Simon Dedalus's friend, who tries (and fails) to train Stephen to be a runner.

Aubrey Mills Stephen's friend. Together they play imaginary adventure games.

DUBLIN: CHAPTERS 2–5

Emma Clery A Dublin girl to whom Stephen is fiercely attracted throughout his adolescence. For Stephen she becomes a symbol of feminine purity and untainted love. His inability to communicate with her is symptomatic of his inability to commune with people, especially women. Accordingly, we know virtually nothing about her until she is revealed as a friendly, ordinary girl in Chapter 5.

BELVEDERE: CHAPTER 2–4

Father Arnall The priest who delivers a series of terrifying lectures on hell at a religious retreat, prompting Stephen to repent for his life of debauchery. Father Arnall was Stephen's Latin teacher at Clongowes Wood.

Boland and Nash Schoolmates who taunt and bully Stephen.

Vincent Heron Stephen's rival.

CORK: CHAPTER 2

Johnny Cashman A friend of Simon Dedalus.

PEERS AT UNIVERSITY COLLEGE: CHAPTER 5

Cranly Stephen's closest friend. Stephen resents Cranly's advice that he try to conform to his family's wishes and try to fit in with his peers.

Davin Stephen's athletic friend; a simple, solid Irish nationalist from the provinces.

Lynch Stephen's poorer friend. Coarse and unpleasantly dry, Lynch listens to Stephen's aesthetic theories.

McCann A fiercely political fellow student.

Temple A student who openly admires and imitates Stephen.

THEMES IN *A PORTRAIT OF THE ARTIST AS A YOUNG MAN*

DEVELOPMENT OF INDIVIDUAL CONSCIOUSNESS   The evolution of the stream of consciousness narrative voice over the course of the novel chronicles the development of Stephen's mind. In Chapter 1, the very young Stephen can describe his world only in simple words and phrases. He relates his sensations in a jumble, without connecting cause and effect. As a teenager, Stephen organizes his thoughts more clearly. Accordingly, the paragraphs and their ideas are more logically ordered. Nevertheless, at times his passionate emotions obscure rational thought. In Chapter 5, at university, Stephen has achieved a measure of emotional, intellectual, and artistic adulthood.

THE ROLE OF THE ARTIST   A *Portrait of the Artist as a Young Man* explores what it means to become an artist. At the end of the novel, Stephen decides to leave his family and friends behind and go into exile in order to become an artist, which suggests that Joyce sees the artist as a necessarily isolated figure. In his decision, Stephen turns his back on his community, refusing to accept the constraints of political involvement, religious devotion, and family commitment that the community places on its members.

However, though the artist is an isolated figure, Stephen's ultimate goal is to give a voice to the very community that he is leaving. In the last few lines of the novel, Stephen expresses his desire to "forge in the smithy of my soul the uncreated conscience of my race." He recognizes that his community will always be a part of him, as it has created and shaped his identity. When he creatively expresses his own ideas, he will also convey the voice of his entire community. Even as Stephen turns his back on the traditional forms of participation and membership in a community, he envisions his writing as a service to the community.

FLIGHT   Stephen's namesake, Dædalus, was a master craftsman in Greek mythology. After Dædalus designs the famous Cretian labyrinth for King Minos, Minos imprisons him and his son Icarus so that Dædalus cannot surpass his creation elsewhere. To escape, Dædalus creates wings out of feathers, twine, and wax for himself and Icarus. Dædalus escapes successfully, but Icarus flies too high. The sun's heat melts the wax, and Icarus plummets into the sea.

In the novel, Stephen plays both Icarus and Dædalus. Like Dædalus, Stephen seeks to create; like Icarus, Stephen is an adolescent son grappling with his pride; like both, he longs to escape the shackles that bind him. Through this mythological allusion, Joyce suggests that Stephen will have to balance his desire to flee Ireland for spiritual freedom, and his desire to be an artist, with his dangerous overconfidence. The flying birds in Chapter 5's third section signal Stephen's imminent flight from Ireland as an artist.

SYMBOLS IN *A PORTRAIT OF THE ARTIST AS A YOUNG MAN*

SONG   Songs combine Stephen's love for language with the vibrancy of the human spirit. He writes his first song as a very young child, turning Dante's threats into a jingle: "Apologize, pull out his eyes, pull out his eyes, apologize." Near the end of the novel, Stephen feels at peace hearing the Irish folk song "Rosie O'Grady" sung by a woman. He resolves to leave Ireland and pursue writing.

THE WADING GIRL   The wading girl from Chapter 4 symbolizes youth, beauty, sensuality, life. When Stephen sees her, he experiences a moment of epiphany and feels called "to live, to err, to fall, to triumph, to recreate life out of life!" Her vibrancy beckons Stephen to live life to the fullest and to create.

IMPORTANT QUOTATIONS FROM *A PORTRAIT OF THE ARTIST AS A YOUNG MAN*

—*The language in which we are speaking is his before it is mine. How different are the words* home, Christ, ale, master, *on his lips and on mine! I cannot speak or write these words without unrest of spirit. His language, so familiar and so foreign, will always be for me an acquired speech. I have not made or accepted its words. My voice holds them at bay. My soul frets in the shadow of his language.*

Location: Chapter 5
Speaker: Stephen (interior monologue)
Context: Stephen considers the ways in which he, as an Irishman, and the English Dean of Studies approach the English language

Stephen is struck by how secure the English Dean of Studies is in his language. For Irishmen such as Stephen, the English that they speak is the language of a conquering nation. Because his words are not Irish, even simple words such as "home" and "ale" can never truly be his own; he must necessarily experience an "unrest of spirit" when using them. The example of the word "Christ" alludes to the fact that Ireland's religion has been inherited from the English occupation; "master" refers to British control over Ireland. Because Stephen wants to write, the potential distance between his Irish identity and his English language is all the more troubling. Nevertheless, Stephen does not study Irish. Instead, by the end of the novel, he seeks to tame and control his borrowed English into a tool for expressing the soul of the imprisoned Irish race.

---

26 April: *I go to encounter for the millionth time the reality of experience and to forge in the smithy of my soul the uncreated conscience of my race.*
27 April: *Old father, old artificer, stand me now and ever in good stead.*

Location: Chapter 5 (novel's last words)
Speaker: Stephen (diary entries)
Context: Stephen leaves Ireland, family, and friends to pursue his artistic calling

Stephen's "smithy of my soul" indicates that he strives to ground his work as an artist in exploring individual consciousness. He will create his art as a blacksmith creates his. Moreover, he seeks to use his voice to speak for his community, "the uncreated conscience of my race"—his Ireland, for which no artist has yet spoken. The final diary entry reinforces Stephen's twofold mission. To acknowledge his debt to his past, he invokes his "old father," Simon Dedalus, his homeland Ireland. To appeal to the artist-father whose heir he hopes to become, he invokes the "old artificer," his namesake, the master craftsman Dædalus.

Once upon a time and a very good time it was there was a moocow coming down along the road and this moocow that was coming along the road met a nicens little boy named baby tuckoo. . . His father told him that story: his father looked at him through a glass: he had a hairy face. He was a baby tuckoo. The moocow came down the road where Betty Byrne lived: she sold lemon platt.
  O, the wild rose blossoms On the little green place.
  He sang that song. That was his song.
  O, the green wothe botheth.
  When you wet the bed first it is warm then it gets cold. His mother put on the oilsheet. That had the queer smell.

Location: Chapter 1 (novel's first words)
Speaker: Stephen (interior monologue)
Context: As a young child, Stephen listens to stories and casts himself in them, making connections and associations as best he can

---

—Corpus Domini nostri. Could it be? He knelt there sinless and timid: and he would hold upon his tongue the host and God would enter his purified body. —In vitam eternam. Amen. Another life! A life of grace and virtue and happiness! It was true. It was not a dream from which he would wake. The past was past. —Corpus Domini nostri. The ciborium had come to him.

Location: End of Chapter 3
Speaker: The narrator
Context: In a moment of epiphany at a religious retreat, Stephen renounces his life of debauchery and resolves to be a pious Catholic

---

His throat ached with a desire to cry aloud, the cry of a hawk or eagle on high, to cry piercingly of his deliverance to the winds. This was the call of life to his soul not the dull gross voice of the world of duties and despair, not the inhuman voice that had called him to the pale service of the altar. An instant of wild flight had delivered him and the cry of triumph which his lips withheld cleft his brain.

Location: Chapter 4
Speaker: The narrator
Context: On the beach awaiting news about his university acceptance, Stephen feels a calling to be an artist

PRIDE AND PREJUDICE

Jane Austen

Five sisters attempt to make happy marriages, and the two eldest succeed.

THE LIFE OF JANE AUSTEN

Jane Austen, whom some critics consider England's best novelist, was born in 1775 in Steventon, England. The seventh of eight children, she lived with her parents for her entire life, first in Steventon and later in Bath, Southampton, and Chawton. Her father was a parish rector. Although not wealthy, her family was well connected and well educated. Austen briefly attended boarding school in Reading but received the majority of her education at home. According to rumor, she had a brief love affair when she was twenty-five, but it did not lead to a marriage proposal. Two years later she accepted and then quickly rejected a proposal. She never married. In 1817, Austen died of Addison's disease, at age forty-one.

Austen began writing stories at a very young age and completed her first novel in her early twenties. However, she did not publish until 1811, when *Sense and Sensibility* appeared anonymously, followed by *Pride and Prejudice* (1813) and *Mansfield Park* (1814). *Emma*, published in 1816, was the last novel published during Austen's lifetime. (*Northanger Abbey* and *Persuasion* appeared posthumously.)

Austen's novels received little critical or popular recognition during her lifetime, and her identity as a novelist was not revealed until after her death. She wrote during the Romantic period, but her satirical novels have little to do with the passionate intensity and individuality that interested the Romantics. Critics have pointed out that the Romantics were almost exclusively male, and women with literary ambitions were excluded from the movement. While male writers such as Percy Bysshe Shelley and Lord Byron were free to promote their own individuality through wide travel and sexual and military adventurism, women were largely denied these freedoms. For women, the penalty for excessive freedom was social ostracism and poverty.

In this social context, Austen's commitment to reason and moderation can be seen as feminist and progressive rather than conservative. With intelligence and resourcefulness, her heroines push the limits of their constricted world of courtship and marriage.

PRIDE AND PREJUDICE IN CONTEXT

Austen completed the original manuscript of *Pride and Prejudice*, originally called *First Impressions*, between 1796 and 1797. A publisher rejected the manuscript, and it was not until 1809 that Austen began the revisions that would bring it to its final form. *Pride and Prejudice* was published two years after *Sense and Sensibility*, Austen's first published novel, and it achieved a popularity that has endured to this day.

PRIDE AND PREJUDICE: KEY FACTS

Time and place written: Between 1796 and 1813; England

Date of first publication: 1813

Publisher: Thomas Egerton of London

Type of work: Novel

Genre: Satire

Language: English

Setting (time): Some point during the Napoleonic Wars (1797–1815)

Setting (place): Longbourn, in rural England

Tense: Past tense

Tone: Comic, satiric

Narrator: Third-person omniscient narrator

Point of view: Elizabeth Bennet's

Protagonist: Elizabeth Bennet

Antagonist: Snobbish class-consciousness (as embodied by Lady Catherine de Bourgh and Miss Bingley)

PRIDE AND PREJUDICE: PLOT OVERVIEW

The news that a wealthy young gentleman named Charles Bingley has rented the manor of Netherfield Park causes a great stir in the nearby village of Longbourn, especially in the Bennet household. The Bennets have five unmarried daughters—from oldest to youngest, Jane, Elizabeth, Mary, Kitty, and Lydia— and Mrs. Bennet is desperate to marry them all off. After Mr. Bennet pays a social visit to Mr. Bingley, the Bennets attend a ball at which Mr. Bingley is present. He is taken with Jane and spends much of the evening dancing with her. His close friend, Mr. Darcy, is less pleased with the evening and haughtily refuses to dance with Elizabeth, which makes everyone decide that he is arrogant and obnoxious.

At social functions over the following weeks, Mr. Darcy finds himself increasingly attracted to Elizabeth's charm and intelligence. Jane's friendship with Mr. Bingley continues to flourish, and Jane pays a visit to the Bingley mansion. On her journey to the house she is caught in a downpour and falls ill. She stays at Netherfield for several days. In order to tend to Jane, Elizabeth hikes through muddy fields and arrives with a spattered dress, much to the disdain of the snobbish Miss Bingley, Charles Bingley's sister. Miss Bingley's spite increases when she notices that Darcy, whom she is pursuing, is interested in Elizabeth.

When Elizabeth and Jane return home, they find Mr. Collins, a young clergyman, visiting their house. Mr. Collins stands to inherit Mr. Bennet's property, which has been entailed, meaning that it can only be passed down to male heirs. Mr. Collins is a pompous fool who is enthralled by the Bennet girls. Shortly after his arrival, he proposes to Elizabeth. She turns him down, wounding his pride. Meanwhile, the Bennet girls have become friendly with militia officers stationed in a nearby town. Among them is Wickham, a handsome young soldier who tells Elizabeth how Darcy cruelly cheated him out of an inheritance.

At the beginning of winter, the Bingleys and Darcy leave Netherfield and return to London, much to Jane's dismay. Mr. Collins becomes engaged to Charlotte Lucas, Elizabeth's best friend and the poor daughter of a local knight. Charlotte tells Elizabeth that she is marrying Collins because she is getting older and needs money. Jane visits the city to see friends in the hopes that she will see Mr. Bingley. Miss Bingley visits her and behaves rudely, while Mr. Bingley fails to visit her at all. The marriage prospects for the Bennet girls appear bleak.

That spring, Elizabeth visits Charlotte, who is married to Mr. Collins and lives near the home of Mr. Collins's patron, Lady Catherine de Bourgh, who is also Darcy's aunt. Darcy calls on Lady Catherine while Elizabeth is there. After visiting Elizabeth several times at the Collins's home, he proposes. Elizabeth quickly refuses, telling him that she considers him arrogant and unpleasant, and scolding him for steering Bingley away from Jane and disinheriting Wickham. Darcy leaves and shortly thereafter delivers a letter to her. In this letter, he admits that he urged Bingley to distance himself from Jane, but claims he did so only because he thought their romance was not serious. As for Wickham, he informs Elizabeth that the young officer is a liar and that the real cause of their disagreement was Wickham's attempt to elope with his younger sister, Georgiana Darcy.

Elizabeth reevaluates her feelings about Darcy. She returns home and acts coldly toward Wickham. The militia is leaving town, which distresses the younger Bennet girls. Lydia manages to obtain permission from her father to spend the summer with an old colonel in Brighton, where Wickham's regiment will be stationed. In June, Elizabeth visits her relatives the Gardiners. The trip takes her to the neighborhood of Pemberley, Darcy's estate. After making sure that Darcy is away, Elizabeth visits Pemberley and delights in the building and grounds. Darcy's servants tell Elizabeth that Darcy is a wonderful, generous master. Darcy arrives and behaves cordially toward her. Making no mention of his proposal, he entertains the Gardiners and invites Elizabeth to meet his sister.

A letter arrives from home, telling Elizabeth that Lydia has run off with Wickham and that the couple is nowhere to be found, which suggests that they may be living together out of wedlock. Fearful of the disgrace such a situation would bring on her entire family, Elizabeth hastens home. At last a letter comes from Mr. Gardiner saying that the couple has been found and that Wickham has agreed to marry Lydia in exchange for an annual income. The Bennets are convinced that Mr. Gardiner has paid off Wickham, but Elizabeth learns that it was really Darcy.

Wickham and Lydia marry and leave for Wickham's new assignment in the North of England. Bingley returns to Netherfield and resumes his courtship of Jane. Darcy goes to stay with him and pays visits to the Bennets but makes no mention of marrying Elizabeth. Bingley proposes to Jane, to the delight of everyone but Bingley's haughty sister. While the family celebrates, Lady Catherine de Bourgh pays a visit to Longbourn. She corners Elizabeth and says she has heard that Darcy, her nephew, is planning to marry her. Since she considers a Bennet an unsuitable match for a Darcy, Lady Catherine demands that Elizabeth promise to refuse him. Elizabeth spiritedly refuses, saying she is not engaged to Darcy, but she will not promise anything that might interfere with her own happiness. A little later, Elizabeth and Darcy go out walking together, and he tells her that his feelings have not altered since the spring. She tenderly accepts his proposal. Both Jane and Elizabeth are married.

CHARACTERS IN *PRIDE AND PREJUDICE*

Catherine Bennet The fourth Bennet sister. Catherine is enthralled with the soldiers.

Elizabeth Bennet The novel's protagonist. The second daughter of Mr. Bennet, Elizabeth is the most intelligent and sensible of the five Bennet sisters. She is well read and quick-witted.

Jane Bennet The eldest and most beautiful Bennet sister. Jane is more reserved and gentler than Elizabeth. The easy pleasantness with which she and Bingley interact contrasts with the sparring that marks the encounters between Elizabeth and Darcy.

Lydia Bennet The youngest Bennet sister. Lydia is gossipy, immature, and self-involved.

Mary Bennet The middle Bennet sister. Mary is bookish and pedantic.

Mr. Bennet The patriarch of the Bennet family. Mr. Bennet is a gentleman of modest income who has a sarcastic, cynical sense of humor that he uses to irritate his wife. Though he loves his daughters, especially Elizabeth, he often withdraws from the marriage concerns of the women rather than offer help.

Mrs. Bennet Mr. Bennet's wife. Mrs. Bennet is a foolish, noisy woman whose only goal in life is to see her daughters married. Because of her low breeding and often unbecoming behavior, Mrs. Bennet often repels the very suitors whom she tries to attract for her daughters.

Charles Bingley Darcy's wealthy best friend. Bingley is a genial, well-intentioned gentleman whose easygoing nature contrasts with Darcy's initially discourteous demeanor. He is blissfully oblivious to class differences.

Miss Bingley Bingley's snobbish sister. Miss Bingley disdains the Bennet's middle-class background. Her vain attempts to attract Darcy's attention make Darcy admire Elizabeth's self-possession even more.

Lady Catherine de Bourgh A rich, bossy noblewoman. Lady Catherine, who is Mr. Collins's patron and Darcy's aunt, is extremely snobbish.

Mr. Collins A pompous, idiotic clergyman who stands to inherit Mr. Bennet's property. Mr. Collins's own social status is unimpressive, but he takes great pains to let everyone know that Lady Catherine de Bourgh is his patroness.

Fitzwilliam Darcy A wealthy gentleman, the master of Pemberley, and the nephew of Lady Catherine de Bourgh. Though Darcy is intelligent and honest, his pride makes him to look down on his social inferiors. Over the course of the novel, he tempers his class-consciousness and learns to admire and love Elizabeth for her strong character.

Georgiana Darcy Darcy's sister. Georgiana is very pretty and very shy.

Mr. and Mrs. Gardiner Mrs. Bennet's brother and sister-in-law. The Gardiners, who are caring, nurturing, and full of common sense, often prove to be better parents to the Bennet daughters than Mr. Bennet and his wife.

Charlotte Lucas Elizabeth's dear friend, and eventually Mr. Collins's wife. Pragmatic where Elizabeth is romantic, Charlotte does not view love as the most vital component of a marriage. She is more interested in having a comfortable home.

George Wickham A handsome, fortune-hunting militia officer. Wickham is a charming scoundrel.

THEMES IN *PRIDE AND PREJUDICE*

IMPEDIMENTS TO LOVE Darcy and Elizabeth face a series of stumbling blocks, most of which they have created themselves. Both are proud, and both are prejudiced. Elizabeth misjudges Darcy on the basis of a poor first impression, while Darcy's prejudice against his social inferiors blinds him, for a time, to Elizabeth's many virtues. Other impediments out of their control also keep them apart, among them Lady Catherine's arrogance, Miss Bingley's snobbery, Mrs. Bennet's idiocy, and Wickham's deceit. In each case, anxieties about social connections, or the desire for better social connections, interfere with the workings of love. Austen frames the realization of Darcy's and Elizabeth's love as a splendid, just outcome, which suggests that she believes love should escape the warping effects of hierarchical society. Despite the optimistic suggestion that love can conquer some class differences, Austen does depict what many would consider a more realistic version of courtship and marriage: Charlotte Lucas marries the buffoon Mr. Collins for his money, and Austen does not condemn her for it. Rather, she portrays Charlotte as a wise, matter-of-fact woman who takes a realistic view of her own romantic prospects.

THE NECESSITY OF GOOD BEHAVIOR *Pride and Prejudice* depicts a society in which a woman's reputation is of the utmost importance. A woman is expected to behave in certain ways, and if she breaks the rules governing behavior, she risks ostracism. When Elizabeth walks to Netherfield and arrives with a muddy skirt, Miss Bingley and her friends are shocked. When Mrs. Bennet behaves ill-manneredly, she gets a bad reputation with the refined Darcys and Bingleys, and jeopardizes her daughters' prospects of marriage. In these incidents, Austen pokes gentle fun at the snobs who sit in judgment and gasp at minor infractions of the rules. But she suggests that although such minor infractions should be ignored, society is right to condemn major infractions such as Lydia's elopement with Wickham. By sleeping with Wickham, Lydia threatens to disgrace the entire Bennet family. The fact that Lydia's behavior could have condemned the other Bennet sisters to spinsterhood might seem grossly unfair, but at the time Austen was writing, premarital sex was a shocking transgression.

THE UNFORTUNATE POWER OF CLASS The lines of class are strictly drawn. The Bennets, who are middle class, may socialize with the upper-class Bingleys and Darcys, but the Bennets are clearly their social inferiors and are treated as such. Austen satirizes this kind of class-consciousness, particularly in the character of Mr. Collins, who spends most of his time flattering his upper-class patron, Lady Catherine de Bourgh. But Mr. Collins is simply frank about the class-consciousness that most of the characters share. Mr. Darcy does not want to sully the purity of his lineage; Miss Bingley dislikes anyone not as socially exalted as she is; Wickham lusts for enough money to vault himself to a higher station. Mr. Collins merely articulates what most of the characters are mannered enough to hide. Austen's satire of him is therefore a subtle satire of the entire social hierarchy.

SYMBOLS IN *PRIDE AND PREJUDICE*

PEMBERLEY Pemberley, Darcy's estate, sits at the center of the novel, literally and figuratively, as a symbol of the man who owns it. Elizabeth is enchanted by its beauty and charm, just as she will be charmed by its owner. Austen makes the connection explicit when she describes the stream that flows beside the mansion: "In front, a stream of some natural importance was swelled into greater, but without any artificial appearance. Its banks were neither formal, nor falsely adorned." Darcy possesses a "natural importance" that is "swelled" by his arrogance, but which coexists with a genuine honesty and lack of "artificial appearance." Like the stream, he is neither "formal, nor falsely adorned." When Elizabeth encounters Darcy on the estate, she is crossing a small bridge, which symbolizes the bridge that their love builds over the gap of their misunderstanding and class prejudice.

IMPORTANT QUOTATIONS FROM *PRIDE AND PREJUDICE*

It is a truth universally acknowledged, that a single man in possession of a good fortune, must be in want of a wife.

Location: The first sentence of the novel
Speaker: The narrator
Context: The narrator sets the plot in motion

This sentence, a famous one, gives a miniature sketch of the entire novel, which concerns itself with the pursuit of "single men in possession of a good fortune" by various female characters. It is also typical of Austen's lightly sarcastic, clever voice. When Austen says "It is a truth universally acknowledged" that every man wants to marry, she means that it is not a universal truth at all, but a desperate hope on the part of parents, especially mothers, who long to marry their daughters to rich men. These parents assume the truth is universal because to admit that some men are not interested in marriage would be to narrow the field of prospective husbands in a terrifying way.

"Which do you mean?" and turning round, he looked for a moment at Elizabeth, till catching her eye, he withdrew his own and coldly said, "She is tolerable; but not handsome enough to tempt me; and I am in no humour at present to give consequence to young ladies who are slighted by other men. You had better return to your partner and enjoy her smiles, for you are wasting your time with me."

Location: Chapter 3
Speaker: Darcy
Context: Bingley has suggested that Darcy dance with Elizabeth

Darcy views the people of Meryton as his social inferiors, so he haughtily refuses to dance with someone "not handsome enough"—and not classy enough—for him. He also makes it clear that he scorns Bingley for enjoying "the smiles" of a woman not worthy of his consideration, for privileging beauty over social standing. Darcy makes these rude remarks in Elizabeth's hearing, thereby establishing a reputation in the community for pride and bad manners. His sense of social superiority later proves his chief difficulty in admitting his love for Elizabeth. Darcy's rudeness also angers Elizabeth, creating a negative impression that will linger for nearly half of the novel.

"In vain have I struggled. It will not do. My feelings will not be repressed. You must allow me to tell you how ardently I admire and love you." Elizabeth's astonishment was beyond expression. She stared, coloured, doubted, and was silent. This he considered sufficient encouragement, and the avowal of all that he felt and had long felt for her, immediately followed. He spoke well, but there were feelings besides those of the heart to be detailed, and he was not more eloquent on the subject of tenderness than of pride. His sense of her inferiority—of its being a degradation—of the family obstacles which judgment had always opposed to inclination, were dwelt on with a warmth which seemed due to the consequence he was wounding, but was very unlikely to recommend his suit.

Location: Chapter 34
Speaker: The narrator
Context: Darcy proposes to Elizabeth, in the process dwelling on her social inferiority

They gradually ascended for half a mile, and then found themselves at the top of a considerable eminence, where the wood ceased, and the eye was instantly caught by Pemberley House, situated on the opposite side of a valley, into which the road with some abruptness wound. It was a large, handsome, stone building, standing well on rising ground, and backed by a ridge of high woody hills;—and in front, a stream of some natural importance was swelled into greater, but without any artificial appearance. Its banks were neither formal, nor falsely adorned. Elizabeth was delighted. She had never seen a place where nature had done more, or where natural beauty had been so little counteracted by an awkward taste. They were all of them warm in her admiration; and at that moment she felt that to be mistress of Pemberley might be something!

Location: Chapter 43
Speaker: The narrator
Context: Elizabeth sees Darcy's estate for the first time

Elizabeth was much too embarrassed to say a word. After a short pause, her companion added, "You are too generous to trifle with me. If your feelings are still what they were last April, tell me so at once. My affections and wishes are unchanged, but one word from you will silence me on this subject forever." Elizabeth feeling all the more than common awkwardness and anxiety of his situation, now forced herself to speak; and immediately, though not very fluently, gave him to understand, that her sentiments had undergone so material a change, since the period to which he alluded, as to make her receive with gratitude and pleasure, his present assurances.

Location: Chapter 58
Speaker: The narrator
Context: Elizabeth accepts Darcy's proposal

THE PRINCE

Niccolò Machiavelli

Machiavelli argues for the separation of politics and ethics in his seminal handbook for rulers.

THE LIFE OF NICCOLÒ MACHIAVELLI

Niccolò Machiavelli was born in Florence, Italy, in 1469. He had a peaceful childhood and received the humanistic education customary for middle-class boys of the Renaissance. He went on to study business math and spent seven years working for a Florentine banker in Rome. In 1494, he returned to Florence and witnessed the expulsion of the Medici family, which had ruled Florence for decades, and the rise to power of Girolamo Savanorola, a Dominican zealot. Three years later, Savanorola lost control of Florence when he was excommunicated by Pope Alexander VI for criticizing Church leadership. The following year, Machiavelli entered Florentine politics as head of the Second Chancery and secretary to the Council of Ten for War.

In 1500, Machiavelli married Marietta di Lodovico Corsini, with whom he had six children. In his official capacity, he helped raise and train a Florentine civil militia in order to reduce Florence's dependence on mercenaries. In 1512, the Medici family regained control of Florence, and Machiavelli was dismissed from office. A year later, he was wrongly accused of participating in a conspiracy to restore the Florentine republic, held in jail for three weeks, and tortured on the rack. He left Florence for the quiet town of Sant'Andrea and decided to pursue a career in writing. In 1513, he began writing his *Discourses on the First Ten Books of Titus Livius*, a book that focused on states controlled by a politically active citizenry. It was not finished until 1521, mainly because he interrupted his work on *Discourses* to write *The Prince* (1514; published 1532).

One of Machiavelli's goals in writing *The Prince* was to win the favor of Lorenzo de' Medici, then governor of Florence and the book's dedicatee. Machiavelli wanted to return to politics and hoped to land an advisory position within the Florentine government. But Medici received the book with indifference, and Machiavelli was not invited to serve in government. The public's initial reaction to *The Prince* was also indifferent, but slowly the book began to be criticized as immoral, evil, and wicked.

Besides the *Discourses*, Machiavelli wrote *The Art of War* (1521) and a comedic play, *The Mandrake* (1520). After Lorenzo's premature death in 1519, his successor, Giulio de' Medici, gave Machiavelli a commission to write *The Florentine History* as well as a few small diplomatic jobs. In 1526, Giulio (now Pope Clement VII), at Machiavelli's urging, created a commission to examine Florence's fortifications and placed Machiavelli on it.

In 1527, the diplomatic errors of Pope Clement led to the sack of Rome by Holy Roman Emperor Charles V's mercenaries. The Florentines expelled their Medici ruler, and Machiavelli, too closely associated with the Medicis, was rejected from politics by the republic. He died several months later.

THE PRINCE IN HISTORICAL CONTEXT

Fifteenth-century Italy was the scene of intense political conflict. The Italian city-states of Florence, Milan, Venice, Naples, and the Papal States fought for control with each other and France, Spain, and the Holy Roman Empire. In 1494, the year that Machiavelli returned to Florence, Italy was invaded by Charles VIII of France. This was the first of several French invasions during Machiavelli's lifetime. The political unrest of the era greatly influenced Machiavelli's attitudes toward government, especially his impassioned pleas for Italian unity.

Machiavelli's political ideas were influenced by the political intrigues of three men: King Louis XII of France, Pope Alexander VI, and his son Cesare Borgia. Machiavelli had traveled to France on a diplomatic mission in 1500 and thereafter met regularly with King Louis XII. In exchange for a marriage annulment, Louis XII helped Pope Alexander establish his son Borgia as the duke of Romagna. Borgia, in particular, greatly shaped Machiavelli's opinions about leadership. Cunning, cruel, and vicious, Borgia was despised by many, but Machiavelli believed that he had the traits necessary for a leader who could unify Italy. In 1503, Pope Alexander VI died of malaria. The new Pope Julius II was Borgia's enemy and later banished him to Spain, where he died in 1526.

THE PRINCE AS A PHILOSOPHICAL WORK

The most revolutionary aspect of *The Prince* is its separation of politics and ethics. Traditional political theory linked political law with a higher, moral law. In contrast, Machiavelli argues that political action must always be considered in light of its practical consequences rather than lofty ideals.

The Prince is also strikingly less theoretical than previous works in political theory. Where earlier thinkers often constructed hypothetical notions of ideal or natural states, Machiavelli pragmatically grounded *The Prince* in historical situations. He dedicated the book to Lorenzo de' Medici, then the ruler of Florence, and intended it as serious advice to the powerful men of his time. *The Prince* is a practical manual rather than an abstract treatise of philosophy.

Medieval and Renaissance thinkers often looked to religion or to classical authors to explain plagues, famines, invasions, and other calamities; they saw preventing such disasters as beyond the scope of human power. In contrast, Machiavelli expresses an extraordinary confidence in human self-determination and affirms his belief in free will over divine destiny.

Machiavelli's ideas have often been oversimplified and vilified in the popular imagination. Indeed, *machiavellian* has come to mean manipulative, deceptive, or ruthless. However, his political stance is usually, and unfairly, defined solely in terms of *The Prince*. Often ignored are Machiavelli's *Discourses*, a considerably longer work that advocates patriotism, civic virtue, and open political participation.

THE PRINCE: KEY FACTS

Time and place written: 1513–14; Florence, Italy	
Date of first publication: 1532 (posthumously); first English translation 1640	
Type of work: Political treatise; letter; practical manual	
Language: Italian	
Tone: Straightforward, practical	
Narrator: Niccolò Machiavelli	

THE PRINCE: AN OVERVIEW

Machiavelli composed *The Prince* as a practical guide for ruling. Accordingly, its prose is simple and its logic straightforward.

DEDICATION

Machiavelli dedicates the book to Lorenzo de' Medici, the ruler of Florence.

CHAPTERS I–III

The first two chapters present the book's scope. *The Prince* discusses autocratic, not republican, regimes, that is, regimes with one ruler—a prince—who has unlimited power. Chapter I defines the various types of principalities and princes, effectively constructing an outline for the rest of the book. Chapter III comprehensively describes how to maintain composite principalities, introducing the book's main concerns: power politics, warcraft, and popular goodwill.

CHAPTERS IV–XIV

In the heart of the book, Machiavelli offers practical advice on various aspects of acquiring and maintaining power. He discusses the advantages and disadvantages of different methods of gaining control of a state, as well as how to acquire and hold new states, how to deal with internal insurrection, how to make alliances, and how to maintain a strong military. Machiavelli's views regarding free will, human nature, and ethics are implicit in these chapters, but he does not discuss these ideas explicitly until later.

CHAPTERS XV–XXIII

Machiavelli addresses the qualities of a prince. Broadly speaking, this discussion is based on his belief that lofty ideals translate into bad government. While certain personal virtues may be admired for their own sake, acting in accordance with virtue is often detrimental to the state. Similarly, while certain vices may be frowned upon, vicious actions are sometimes indispensable to the good of the state. Above all, obtaining the good will of the populace is the best way to maintain power. Thus, the *appearance* of virtue is more important than true virtue, which may be seen as a liability.

CHAPTERS XXIV–XXVI

Machiavelli grounds the discussion in the specific historical context of the disunity of the Italian states. Machiavelli gives his account of the failures of Italy's past rulers. He concludes with an impassioned plea to future rulers, asserting that only Lorenzo de' Medici, the book's dedicatee, can restore Italy's honor and pride.

CHARACTERS AND TERMS IN *THE PRINCE*

HISTORICAL FIGURES TO DO WITH *THE PRINCE*

Agathocles Ruler of Syracuse (317–310 B.C.) who conquered all of Sicily except for territory dominated by Carthage; eventually defeated by the Carthaginian army.

Alexander (the Great) King of Macedonia (336–323 B.C.) who conquered Greece, Persia, and much of Asia.

Pope Alexander VI Elected pope in 1492. Challenged by French invasion of Italy and a war between France and Spain. Father of Cesare Borgia.

Cesare Borgia (Duke Valentino of Romagna) 1476–1507. Made duke of Romagna in 1501 by his father, Pope Alexander II, and lost power after the pope's death. Cesare Borgia is Machiavelli's primary example of a prince of great prowess, as evidenced by success in securing his state and quickly assuming power.

Cyrus Founder of the Persian Empire.

Julius II Pope Julius II (1503–1513) strengthened the power of the Church through vigorous leadership and intelligent diplomacy. He defeated Roman barons and negotiated an alliance against France.

Pope Leo X Elected pope in 1513. Supported the Medici family.

Romulus Founder and first king of Rome.

Septimius Severus Roman emperor (A.D. 193–211).

Theseus King of Athens; hero of Attica. According to Greek myth, he killed the Minotaur in the Cretan labyrinth.

GLOSSARY OF TERMS

Prowess The ability to conquer and govern; opposed to fortune in Machiavelli's work.

TYPES OF ARMIES

Auxiliary troops Troops borrowed from other nations. Organized and effective in battle, they nonetheless retain loyalties to their home state.

Mercenary troops Troops paid to fight. Because they have no loyalty to the prince, they are unreliable as a means of defense. They will be unwilling to die in battle and therefore will not fight vigorously.

Native troops Troops composed of countrymen of a principality, commanded either by a prince or a prince's confidant.

TYPES OF STATES

Principality A localized territory ruled by an autocratic prince; distinguished from a republic. Most of the advice in *The Prince* is geared toward principalities.

Composite principality A principality either newly created or annexed from another power. These principalities pose the most difficulties, since they may differ in culture, language, and attitudes toward the prince.

Ecclesiastical principalities A principality technically ruled by a prince but nonetheless strongly dominated by the Church.

Hereditary principality A principality that has been ruled by the prince's family for several generations. According to Machiavelli, hereditary principalities are easy to rule and maintain.

Republic A state headed not by a monarch or prince, but by elected officials accountable to a larger citizenry. Machiavelli distinguishes a republic from a principality.

THEMES IN *THE PRINCE*

STATESMANSHIP AND WARCRAFT Machiavelli believes that "the presence of sound military forces indicates the presence of sound laws." That is, good laws follow naturally from a good military. He flips the conventional view that war is a necessary but not definitive element in the development of a state, asserting instead that successful war forms the very foundation of every state. Much of *The Prince* is devoted to describing exactly what it means to conduct a good war: how to fortify a city effectively, how to treat subjects in newly acquired territories, and how to prevent distracting domestic insurrections during war. Machiavelli's understanding of warfare comprises aspects other than military strategy: international diplomacy, domestic politics, tactical strategy, geographic mastery, and historical analysis.

GOOD WILL AND HATRED To remain in power, a prince must not be hated by his people. It is not necessary for him to be loved; in fact, it is often better for him to be feared. The people's hatred, however, can cause a prince's downfall. Accordingly, Machiavelli advocates the use of cruelty only insofar as it does not compromise the long-term good will of the populace, which is always the best defense against both domestic insurrection and foreign aggression. To avoid hatred, Machiavelli counsels against extreme measures such as confiscating property or dissolving traditional institutions. The prince is free to cease worrying about incurring the hatred of his subjects only when he is absolutely sure those who hate him will never be able to rise against him. Machiavelli presents the people's good will as a political instrument to ensure the stability of the prince's reign rather than as a natural side effect of a happy populace.

FREE WILL Machiavelli distinguishes princes who come to power through "prowess," or personal talent, from those who do so through "fortune," or good luck. *The Prince* explores how much of a prince's success or failure is determined by his environment and how much can be credited to or blamed on the prince's own actions. Specifically, Machiavelli investigates the failures of past Italian princes. In Chapter XXV, he compromises between free will and determinism by arguing that prowess and fortune each govern half of human actions. At the same time, he suggests that humans can shield themselves against fortune's vicissitudes using foresight. This is a quality championed throughout the book. Thus Machiavelli believes that human beings can shape their destinies to a degree but that human control over events is never absolute.

VIRTUE Machiavelli defines virtues as qualities praised by others—generosity, compassion, piety. A prince should strive to appear virtuous, but acting in accordance with virtue for virtue's sake may prove detrimental to the principality. By the same token, a prince need not avoid vices such as cruelty or dishonesty if resorting to them benefits the state. Neither virtue nor vice should be pursued for its own sake; the effect on the state rather than intrinsic moral value should always be the primary consideration.

HUMAN NATURE Machiavelli sees a number of traits as inherent to human nature. People usually act in their own self-interest. In prosperous times, they may be trustworthy, but they quickly turn selfish and deceitful in times of adversity. People naturally admire honor, generosity, courage, and piety in others, but rarely exhibit such virtues themselves. Most will be content with the status quo so long as they do not fall victims of an atrocity. Ambition is common only among the few who have already achieved some power. People naturally feel a sense of obligation upon receiving a favor or being rendered a service. Though such bonds of obligation are strong, they are never absolute; loyalties may be won and lost. Machiavelli's justifications of some of his political advice with these assumptions about human nature are often less convincing than his justifications with concrete historical evidence elsewhere.

IMPORTANT QUOTATIONS FROM *THE PRINCE*

Only the expenditure of one's own resources is harmful; and, indeed, nothing feeds upon itself as liberality does. The more it is indulged, the fewer are the means to indulge it further. As a consequence, a prince becomes poor and contemptible or, to escape poverty, becomes rapacious and hateful. Of all the things he must guard against, hatred and contempt come first, and liberality leads to both. Therefore it is better to have a name for miserliness, which breeds disgrace without hatred, than, in pursuing a name for liberality, to resort to rapacity, which breeds both disgrace and hatred.

Location: Chapter XVI
Speaker: Machiavelli
Context: Machiavelli advises the prince to disregard the principles of virtue when acting on behalf of his state

While it is desirable for a prince to act virtuously when he can, he should never allow concern for appearing virtuous to interfere with statecraft. Generosity ("liberality") may seem admirable, but it should be avoided because it ultimately hurts the state. A prince will never be hated for lack of virtue; he will be hated only if he fails to maintain the state. Because virtue often promotes self-sacrifice, it often conflicts with that duty.

Here a question arises: whether it is better to be loved than feared, or the reverse. The answer is, of course, that it would be best to be both loved and feared. But since the two rarely come together, anyone compelled to choose will find greater security in being feared than in being loved.. . . . Love endures by a bond which men, being scoundrels, may break whenever it serves their advantage to do so; but fear is supported by the dread of pain, which is ever present.

Location: Chapter XVII
Speaker: Machiavelli
Context: Machiavelli argues that it is often better for a prince to be feared than to be loved

Machiavelli's most infamous argument—that it is better to be feared than loved—is often used to justify the claim that *The Prince* is a handbook for dictators and tyrants. A closer reading reveals that this argument is a logical extension of Machiavelli's assessments of human nature and virtue. Because people will betray the prince if circumstances warrant, cruelty is a more reliable tool than benevolence to keep the people obedient and maintain the state. Machiavelli never advocates cruelty for its own sake, only for the benefit of the state.

At this point one may note that men must be either pampered or annihilated. They avenge light offenses; they cannot avenge severe ones; hence, the harm one does to a man must be such as to obviate any fear of revenge.

Location: Chapter III
Speaker: Machiavelli
Context: Machiavelli uses logical reasoning conspicuously devoid of ethical considerations to explain how a prince should approach his subjects

[P]eople are by nature changeable. It is easy to persuade them about some particular matter, but it is hard to hold them to that persuasion. Hence it is necessary to provide that when they no longer believe, they can be forced to believe.

Location: Chapter VI
Speaker: Machiavelli
Context: Machiavelli uses assumptions about human nature to justify political action

A prince must have no other objective, no other thought, nor take up any profession but that of war, its methods and its discipline, for that is the only art expected of a ruler. And it is of such great value that it not only keeps hereditary princes in power, but often raises men of lowly condition to that rank.

Location: Chapter XIV
Speaker: Machiavelli
Context: Machiavelli highlights warcraft as both a worthy pursuit and an academic discipline to be studied through historical example

PYGMALION

George Bernard Shaw

A man successfully transforms a woman from a Cockney flower girl into a duchess, but her transformation leaves her without a place in society.

THE LIFE OF GEORGE BERNARD SHAW

George Bernard Shaw was born in Dublin in 1856. His father was an impoverished alcoholic grain merchant; his mother eventually abandoned the family to pursue a music career in London. Shaw was raised by servants in near-poverty. His formal education ended when he took a clerical job at age fifteen. In 1876, he moved to London, where he supplemented his education by reading voraciously at the British Museum. Over the course of his life, he rose from poverty and obscurity to become one of the leading literary figures of his day. His is a transformation echoed by Eliza's in *Pygmalion*.

Shaw began his writing career as a music and drama critic. In the 1890s, he started writing plays. His plays were controversial from the outset. One of his earliest plays, *Mrs. Warren's Profession*, which was completed in 1893, was banned until 1925, although it was given a private performance in 1902. Nevertheless, his wit and intellectual force were quickly recognized.

In 1884, Shaw joined the Fabian Society, a group of middle-class socialists who proved a significant force in some of the early twentieth-century liberal reforms in England. Shaw himself publicly advocated equal rights for women, radical reform of the voting system, and abolition of private property. He campaigned for revisions of the English alphabet and spelling simplifications. Famously eccentric, Shaw believed in a Life Force and was rumored to wear only wool. He abstained from alcohol, tobacco, and meat. In 1898, he married Charlotte Payne-Townshend, a union that resulted in a forty-five year marriage that may never have been consummated. He also carried on a number of well-publicized flirtations and nonsexual affairs. Between the wars, he spoke admiringly of Hitler's and Mussolini's fascist regimes. Such unconventional opinions dampened his popularity, but nevertheless he won the 1925 Nobel Prize for Literature. He accepted the prize and donated the prize money to the publication of an English edition of the plays of August Strindberg.

Late in his career, a number of Shaw's plays were made into films. MGM's *Pygmalion* won a 1938 Academy Award for Best Screenplay, making Shaw the only writer ever to have won both an Oscar and a Nobel Prize. Shaw continued writing well into his nineties. He died in 1950 at the age of ninety-four. He left behind him a truly massive corpus of work, including over fifty plays, five novels, and heaps of criticism as well as social commentary and political writings.

PYGMALION IN CONTEXT

In the late nineteenth century, the Norwegian Henrik Ibsen, the Swedish August Strindbeg, and the Russian Anton Chekhov presided over the evolution of a new, highly realistic and socially conscious style of drama. Shaw's plays built on that tradition, but also turned away from strict realism toward sharp intellectualism and philosophy. His characters are far more intelligent, quick-witted, and engaged than the average person. Shaw was often accused of writing too much talk and too little action. His plays carry a clear revolutionary intent, attacking many of the assumptions and social institutions of his day by presenting characters who are intellectually and morally superior to the audience.

Shaw was heavily influenced by Ibsen, who is often hailed as the father of modern drama. Like Shaw, Ibsen used his plays to make his middle-class audience conscious of the social injustices of his time. Shaw was also a great admirer of the philosopher Friedrich Nietzsche and the composer Richard Wagner, both of whom envisioned art as a means of creating a new kind of human who would be free from shackles and limitations of ordinary people.

Pygamalion takes its name and rough storyline from Ovid's *Metamorphoses*. Pygmalion, disgusted by real women, sculpts a statue of Galatea, a perfect woman. He falls in love with his creation, and the goddess Venus takes pity on him and brings Galatea to life. In Shaw's version, Higgins plays Pygmalion to Eliza's Galatea, "creating" an upper-class beauty from a lower-class guttersnipe. Shaw's retelling gives

Eliza-Galatea a distinctive personality of her own, debunking the myth of the male artist-creator and passive female creation. There is a limit to how much Higgins can change Eliza: he can teach her how to speak, but not what to say or how to think. Shaw's Galatea is complicit in creating her own identity.

PYGMALION: KEY FACTS

Time and place written: 1912–1913; London	
Date of first performance: 1913	
Date of publication: 1916	
Publisher: Brentano	
Type of work: Play	
Genre: Comedy; social commentary	
Language: English	
Setting (time): Early twentieth century	
Setting (place): London	
Tone: Realistic, intellectual, satiric	
Protagonist: Henry Higgins; Eliza Doolittle	
Antagonist: Societal conventions; expectations about gender and class	

PYGMALION: PLOT OVERVIEW

Two elderly gentlemen, both linguists, meet in the rain one night at Covent Garden. Professor Higgins is a phonetician (he studies the sounds of language), and Colonel Pickering is a linguist of Indian dialects. Higgins bets Pickering that he can teach a flower girl, the Cockney Eliza Doolittle, to speak as well as a duchess and fool London high society.

The next morning, Eliza appears at Higgins's laboratory on Wimpole Street to ask for speech lessons. She offers to pay him a shilling if he teaches her to speak properly enough to work in a flower shop rather than sell flowers on the street corner. Higgins makes merciless fun of her but is seduced by the idea of putting his knowledge of phonetics into practice. Pickering goads him on by agreeing to cover the costs of the experiment if Higgins can pass Eliza off as a duchess at an ambassador's garden party.

Higgins begins by having his housekeeper bathe and clothe Eliza. Eliza's father, Alfred Doolittle, arrives, ostensibly to demand his daughter back but really to hit Higgins up for some money. Higgins, amused by Doolittle's unusual rhetoric, gives him five pounds. On his way out, Doolittle does not recognize his daughter, now clean and well dressed.

Higgins trains Eliza to speak properly for several months. She faces two trials. For the first, Eliza and Higgins attend an "at home" (a time when a hostess accepts visitors at her house) at Higgins's mother's house. There Eliza meets the Eynsford Hills—mother, daughter, and son Freddy. Freddy is immediately attracted to Eliza and further taken with what he thinks is her affected "small talk" when she slips into cockney. Mrs. Higgins expresses some concern about what will happen to Eliza after the experiment ends, but Higgins and Pickering are too absorbed in their game to take heed. Eliza's second trial—an ambassador's party, not staged—is a resounding success. The wager won, Higgins and Pickering are instantly bored with the project. Upon their return from the party, Higgins and Pickering discuss Eliza's success as if she is not present and give her no credit for the achievement. As usual, Higgins treats her like a servant. Enraged by the situation, Eliza throws Higgins's slippers at him. Confused, he suggests that she marry somebody. She returns his hired jewelry, and he accuses her of ingratitude.

The following morning, Higgins rushes to his mother, panicked because Eliza has run away. Higgins is trailed by Alfred Doolittle, who is unhappy to have inherited a share in the trust of a deceased millionaire who took to heart Higgins's characterization of Doolittle as England's "most original moralist." Mrs. Higgins, who has been hiding Eliza upstairs all along, chides Higgins and Pickering for playing with the girl's affections. When she enters, Eliza thanks Pickering for always treating her like a lady, but threatens Higgins that she will go work with Nepommuck, a rival phonetician, if Higgins does not begin to appreciate all she has to offer. The outraged Higgins cannot help but start to admire her now that she has found her confidence. As Eliza leaves for her father's wedding, Higgins shouts out a few errands for her to run, assuming that she will return to him at Wimpole Street. Eliza, who has a lovelorn sweetheart in Freddy, and the wherewithal to pass as a duchess, never makes it clear whether she will or not.

CHARACTERS IN *PYGMALION*

Alfred Doolittle Eliza's father, an elderly but vigorous dustman. Doolittle "seems equally free from fear and conscience" and claims to have been married at least six times. Unembarrassed and unhypocritical, Doolittle advocates the pursuit of drink and pleasure. When he becomes rich, he becomes miserable; as a poor dustman, he feels freer than as a member of the leisure class.

Eliza Doolittle The Cockney flower girl whom Higgins teaches to speak proper English. Her fairy-tale transformation is less realistic than functional. It is a tool for exploring ideas. Apart from learning a new way of speaking and new manners, she develops from a squawking street urchin into a human being with a sense of dignity and self-worth.

Professor Henry Higgins Phonetician who undertakes to transform Eliza Doolittle. Thoughtless and bullish if not unkind, Higgins values his science, sometimes forgetting that human beings are more than sources of phonetic data. His own public graces leave something to be desired. Higgins thinks the world of his mother.

Mrs. Higgins Henry Higgins' mother. A stately lady in her sixties, Mrs. Higgins is quick to see that Higgins's experiment will lead to problems for Eliza. She treats Higgins and Pickering like children and consoles Eliza when Eliza flees Higgins's house in despair.

Freddy Eynsford Hill A young aristocrat who falls in love with Eliza. Freddy is well-meaning, but weak-willed and not resourceful.

Colonel Pickering Linguist of Indian languages; author of "Spoken Sanscrit." Pickering's gentlemanliness is a foil to Higgins's boorishness. Pickering covers the cost of Higgins's experiment with Eliza, and, through his good manners and kindness, teaches her to respect herself as Higgins teaches her pronunciation.

THEMES IN *PYGMALION*

EXAMINING THE MYTH OF THE EROTICISM OF THE CREATIVE ACT   Ovid's myth presents the male artist-creator and the female passive creation, created by and for man. The myth makes explicit the erotic undertones of the creative act implicit in much Western literature and philosophy— namely, the desire that prompts the creative act and the satisfaction provided by creative expression parallel sexual desire and satisfaction. Indeed, Ovid's Pygmalion creates an artificial woman as a substitute for the imperfect women of the real world, substituting creation for sexual fulfillment.

Shaw sees this eroticization of creation as cheapening to the creative impulse and, in *Pygmalion*, attacks the romanticization of the Pygmalion myth. Higgins and Eliza do not fall in love. Indeed, in an epilogue to the play, Shaw suggests that we expect such a union because we have erroneously eroticized the creative process. He argues that healthy individuals such as Higgins and, more generally, those men with strong mother figures, can separate creativity from sex. The implication is that Shaw, as creator, does not succumb to eroticizing his own creative acts: his plays intentionally carry social or cultural critique. He finds this kind of critique more worthy that the self-indulgent creation of art for art's sake. Building on Shaw's ideas, we can argue that both Higgins and Eliza are masters of, rather than slaves to, their passions. Higgins detaches his creative impulse from sexual desire, and Eliza maintains a sense of her own dignity and refuses to be dependent on Higgins.

THE DRAWBACKS OF SOCIAL MOBILITY   By the early twentieth century, the Industrial Revolution had made it possible for some poor people to become wealthy. However, these *nouveaux riches* were not truly accepted in the upper classes, in part, as Higgins argues, because of their accent. Higgins's experiment with Eliza is an experiment in social mobility. Though Higgins succeeds, Shaw suggests that upward mobility has its drawbacks. Eliza has no money, bristles at the idea of marrying rich, and her new accent and manners will make it impossible for her to work as a flower girl. Similarly, Alfred Doolittle, self-proclaimed member of the "undeserving poor," is displeased with his new obligations and responsibilities once he becomes wealthy. Shaw shows that rising in the social order merely substitutes one set of problems for another.

LANGUAGE AS POWER Higgins can identify where a person comes from "within six miles" based on speech alone; within the rigid hierarchy of British society, background determines class and station in life. Shaw shows that language is a means of political control, not simply because governments necessarily use language in lawmaking or propaganda, but also because how we learn to speak shapes how we learn to think. As an example, the categories "proper" and "improper" English carry an implicit value judgment. Shaw's play encourages a more egalitarian society by making us conscious of the understood connection between dialect and social class.

SYMBOLS IN *PYGMALION*

ELIZA'S FLOWERS At the beginning of the play, Eliza sells her flowers to make a living. As her life becomes more complicated, she can no longer work as a flower girl because her speech and manners are inappropriate for the job. She may have to support herself with a high society marriage by selling herself. The flowers represent the simplicity and innocence of her former life.

MIRROR Looking in mirrors in *Pygmalion*, as elsewhere in literature, symbolizes self-reflection. After taking a bath (Act II), Eliza sees herself in a mirror for the first time and throws her towel over it so that she does not have to see herself. Eliza's life has taken a dramatic turn: for the first time, she is faced with choices and forced to examine who she is. Covering the mirror is deferring this self-examination. At the end of Act IV, Eliza sticks her tongue out at her reflection in the mirror, rejecting the new self that Higgins has created.

IMPORTANT QUOTATIONS FROM *PYGMALION*

Walk! Not bloody likely.. . . I am going in a taxi.

Location: Act III
Speaker: Eliza Doolittle
Context: As Eliza is leaving Mrs. Higgins's dinner party, Freddy asks her if she intends to walk

Eliza's defiant response to Freddy's question (he was hoping to ask if he could walk her home) betrays her humble origins. For her, walking is associated with poverty, because wealthier people take taxis. A girl raised taking taxis for granted would never have responded so violently. The line caused a stir during *Pygmalion*'s first run: it marked the first time the word "bloody" had been used on the British stage.

Would the world ever have been made if its maker had been afraid of making trouble? Making life means making trouble. There's only one way of escaping trouble; and that's killing things. Cowards, you notice, are always shrieking to have troublesome people killed.

Location: Act V
Speaker: Higgins
Context: Eliza has accused Higgins of transforming her without considering what sort of trouble he might be making for her

Higgins's experiment with Eliza reflects his views on society and morality. He does not respect the class system or believe that any person should be treated differently than any other. Because it challenges the existing social order, this attitude (and Higgins's project) is revolutionary, and so, according to Shaw, necessarily troublesome. Revolutions always stir up trouble. Moreover, Higgins suggests that not to undertake such projects is cowardly. Shaw uses his plays as a forum for showcasing his ideas: he is credited with the famous quotation "All great truths begin as blasphemies."

But you have no idea how frightfully interesting it is to take a human being and change her into a quite different human being by creating a new speech for her. It's filling up the deepest gulf that separates class from class and soul from soul.

Location: Act III
Speaker: Higgins
Context: Higgins discusses his project with his mother

I sold flowers. I didn't sell myself. Now you've made a lady of me I'm not fit to sell anything else. I wish you'd left me where you found me.

Location: Act IV
Speaker: Eliza
Context: In response to her question about what she should do after the experiment is over, Higgins has suggested that Eliza should marry

---

The great secret, Eliza, is not having bad manners or good manners or any other particular sort of manners, but having the same manner for all human souls: in short, behaving as if you were in Heaven, where there are no third-class carriages, and one soul is as good as another.

Location: Act V
Speaker: Higgins
Context: When Eliza accuses Higgins of treating her discourteously, he protests that he is careless with everyone, even aristocrats

A RAISIN IN THE SUN

Lorraine Hansberry

An impoverished family dreams of a better life and succeeds in buying a house in a hostile neighborhood.

THE LIFE OF LORRAINE HANSBERRY

Lorraine Hansberry was born in Chicago on May 19, 1930, the youngest of four children. Her parents were well educated and successful. When Hansberry was a child, she and her family lived in a black neighborhood on Chicago's South Side. During this era, segregation—the enforced separation of whites and blacks—was still legal and widespread throughout the South. Northern states, including Illinois, had no official policy of segregation, but they were generally self-segregated along racial and economic lines. Chicago was carved into strictly divided black and white neighborhoods. Hansberry's family became one of the first to move into a white neighborhood, but Hansberry still attended a segregated public school for blacks. When neighbors threatened the Hansberrys with threats of violence and legal action, they defended themselves. Hansberry's father successfully brought his case all the way to the Supreme Court.

Hansberry wrote that she always felt the inclination to record her experiences. At times, her writing—including *A Raisin in the Sun* (1959)—is recognizably autobiographical. She was one of the first playwrights to create realistic portraits of African-American life. When *A Raisin in the Sun* opened in March 1959, it met with great praise from white and black audiences alike. Arguably the first play to portray black characters, themes, and conflicts in a natural and realistic manner, *A Raisin in the Sun* received the New York Drama Critics' Circle Award for Best Play of the Year. Hansberry was the youngest playwright, the fifth woman, and the first black writer to win the award. She used her fame to help bring attention to the American Civil Rights movement and African struggles for independence from colonialism. Her promising career was cut short when she died from cancer in 1965, at the age of thirty-four.

A RAISIN IN THE SUN IN CONTEXT

A Raisin in the Sun addresses many issues important during the 1950s in the United States, a time when the complacency and conformity commonly associated with the 1950s existed alongside roiling domestic and racial tension. *A Raisin in the Sun*, first performed as the conservative 1950s gave way to the radical 1960s, was a revolutionary work for its time. Before this play, African-American theatrical roles were usually small, comedic, and made up of a collection of ethnic stereotypes. Hansberry created a play full of three-dimensional, serious black characters that broaches issues such as poverty, discrimination, and the construction of African-American racial identity.

A Raisin in the Sun explores not only the tension between white and black society but also the tension within the black community itself over the right way to respond to an oppressive white community. Through the character of Joseph Asagai, Hansberry reveals a trend toward celebrating African heritage. His call for a native revolt in his homeland foreshadows the anticolonial struggles in African countries in the decades after the play was first produced, as well as the inevitability and necessity of integration.

Hansberry also addresses feminist questions in *A Raisin in the Sun*. Through the character of Beneatha, she suggests that marriage is not necessary for women and that women can and should have ambitious career goals. She even broaches the topic of abortion, which was illegal at the time.

Hansberry took the title of her play from a line in Langston Hughes's famous 1951 poem "Harlem," which was written twenty years after the Great Depression had crushed the Harlem Renaissance and devastated black communities more terribly than any other group in the United States. The 1950s also heralded the phenomenon of "white flight"—whites fled the cities in favor of the rapidly growing suburbs. Blacks, often unable to afford a move and unwelcome in the suburbs in any case, were left behind in deteriorating cities.

"Harlem" captures the tension between the need for black expression and the impossibility of that expression because of American society's oppression of its black population. In the poem, Hughes asks whether a "dream deferred"—a dream put on hold—withers up "[l]ike a raisin in the sun." His lines confront the racist and dehumanizing attitude prevalent in American society before the Civil Rights movement of the 1960s that African-American desires and ambitions were unimportant or even dangerous. Hughes's closing rhetorical question—"Or does [a dream deferred] explode?"—is incendiary, a bold suggestion that the suppression of black dreams might result in an eruption.

A RAISIN IN THE SUN: KEY FACTS

Time and place written: 1950s; New York

Date of first performance: 1959

Date of first publication: 1959

Publisher: Random House

Type of work: Play

Genre: Realist drama

Language: English

Tone: Realistic

Setting (time): Between 1945 and 1959

Setting (place): The South Side of Chicago

Protagonist: Walter Lee Younger

Antagonist: Poverty and racism

A RAISIN IN THE SUN: PLOT OVERVIEW

A Raisin in the Sun portrays a few weeks in the life of the Youngers, an African-American family living on the South Side of Chicago in the 1950s. When the play opens, the Youngers are about to receive an insurance check for $10,000. Mr. Younger has died, and the money is from his life insurance policy. Each of the adult members of the family has an idea about what to do with this money. The matriarch of the family, Mama, wants to buy a house to fulfill a dream she shared with her husband. Mama's son, Walter Lee, wants to invest in a liquor store with his friends. He believes that the investment will solve the family's financial problems forever. Walter's wife, Ruth, agrees with Mama and hopes that she and Walter can provide more space and opportunity for their son, Travis. Beneatha, Walter's sister and Mama's daughter, wants to use the money for her medical school tuition. She wishes that her family members were not so interested in joining the white world. Beneatha wants to find her identity by looking to the past and to Africa.

Ruth discovers she is pregnant but fears that if she has the child, she will put more financial pressure on the family. Walter says nothing to Ruth's admission that she is considering abortion. Mama puts a down payment on a house for the whole family. She believes that a bigger, brighter dwelling will help them all. This house is in Clybourne Park, an entirely white neighborhood. When the residents of Clybourne Park find out that a black family is moving in, they send a representative to offer the Youngers money in return for staying away. The Youngers refuse the deal, even after Walter loses the rest of the money ($6,500) to his friend Willy Harris, who persuades Walter to invest in the liquor store and then runs off with his cash.

Beneatha rejects her suitor, George Murchison, whom she believes to be shallow and blind to the problems of race. Joseph Asagai, a Nigerian man, proposes to Beneatha. He wants her to get a medical degree and move to Africa with him. The Youngers eventually move out of the apartment. Their future seems uncertain and slightly dangerous, but they are optimistic and determined to live a better life. They believe that they can succeed if they stick together.

CHARACTERS IN *A RAISIN IN THE SUN*

Joseph Asagai A Nigerian student. Asagai is proud of his African heritage. He falls in love with Beneatha.

Bobo One of Walter's partners in the liquor store plan. Bobo appears to be mentally slow.

Willy Harris A friend of Walter's and the coordinator of the liquor store plan. Willy never appears onstage.

Mrs. Johnson The Youngers' neighbor. Mrs. Johnson warns the Youngers about moving into a predominately white neighborhood.

Mr. Karl Lindner A representative from the Clybourne Park Improvement Association.

George Murchison A wealthy African-American man who courts Beneatha. The Youngers approve of George, but Beneatha dislikes his willingness to forget his African heritage. George is arrogant and competitive.

Beneatha (Bennie) Younger Mama's daughter and Walter's sister. Twenty-year-old Beneatha is an intellectual college student who is better educated than the rest of her family. She dreams of being a doctor.

Lena (Mama) Younger The matriarch of the Younger family. Mama is religious, moral, and maternal. She dreams of buying a house with a backyard.

Ruth Younger Walter's wife. Ruth and Walter have a troubled marriage, but she hopes to rekindle their love. The constant struggles with poverty and domestic troubles have made her weary, but her strength and pessimistic pragmatism keep her afloat.

Travis Younger Walter and Ruth's sheltered young son.

Walter Lee Younger The protagonist of the play. Walter is a dreamer who longs for a quick solution to his family's problems.

THEMES IN *A RAISIN IN THE SUN*

THE VALUE AND PURPOSE OF DREAMS   As the members of the Younger family struggle to deal with the oppressive circumstances of their lives, dreams give them hope. Every member of the Younger family has his or her own dream—Beneatha wants to become a doctor, Walter wants to get rich so that he can afford to buy things for his family, and Mama wants a house. The money from the life insurance policy makes these dreams seem tantalizingly possible, and the Youngers devote their energies to attaining them, sometimes with disastrous results. By the end of the play, Mama's dream seems most important, because the house symbolically unites the family.

THE NEED TO FIGHT RACIAL DISCRIMINATION   Although Mr. Lindner is the only white character in the play, his role makes the danger of racial discrimination impossible to ignore. The governing body of the Youngers' new neighborhood, the Clybourne Park Improvement Association, sends Mr. Lindner to bribe the Youngers not to move into the all-white Clybourne Park neighborhood. The offer threatens to tear apart the Younger family, but ultimately they respond to this discrimination with defiance and strength. Their reaction demonstrates that discrimination must be faced down, not ignored or respected.

THE IMPORTANCE OF FAMILY   The Youngers struggle socially and economically throughout the play but unite in the end. Mama strongly believes in the importance of family and tries to pass on this value to her children, struggling to keep everyone together and functioning. Her values do seem to take hold: even after Walter loses the insurance money and Beneatha denies him as a brother, the family comes together to reject Mr. Lindner's racist overtures.

SYMBOLS IN *A RAISIN IN THE SUN*

"EAT YOUR EGGS"   Early in the play, Ruth tells Walter to eat his eggs in an effort to quiet him. Walter uses the phrase as an example of how women keep men from achieving their goals, saying that every time a man gets excited about something, a woman tries to temper his enthusiasm by telling him to eat his eggs. "Eat your eggs" is a symbol of men's perception that women are quashing their dreams. The phrase also symbolizes women's occasionally patronizing attitude toward men. Ruth supports Walter mechanically, providing him with physical nourishment but not with spiritual nourishment.

MAMA'S PLANT   Mama's plant represents both Mama's family and her dream for her family. In Mama's first appearance onstage, she moves directly toward the plant to tend it. She confesses that the plant never gets enough light or water, but she takes pride in how it nevertheless flourishes under her care. Her care for her plant is similar to her care for her children, which is unconditional and successful despite an insufficient environment for growth. Mama practices her gardening skills on her plant in anticipation of the yard she craves.

IMPORTANT QUOTATIONS FROM *A RAISIN IN THE SUN*

MAMA: (Quietly) *Oh*—(very quietly) *So now it's life. Money is life. Once upon a time freedom used to be life—now it's money. I guess the world really do change. . . . . . .*

WALTER: *No—it was always money, Mama. We just didn't know about it.*

MAMA: *No . . . . . . something has changed.* (She looks at him) *You something new, boy. In my time we was worried about not being lynched.. . . . . . . You ain't satisfied or proud of nothing we done. I mean that you had a home; that we kept you out of trouble till you was grown; that you don't have to ride to work on the back of nobody's streetcar—You my children—but how different we done become.*

Location: Act I, scene ii
Speaker: Mama and Walter
Context: Mama has asked Walter why he always talks about money, and Walter has told her that "[m]oney is life"

This exchange demonstrates the ideological differences that separate Mama's generation from Walter's. As in many families, the older generation is outraged that the younger generation cannot appreciate the advances the older generation worked so hard to win. Mama remembers a time when freedom was the most blacks could hope for, and she treasures her family's life because it is a free one in some ways. Walter cannot treasure it as she does, because for him, basic freedom has always been a given. In his eyes, blacks are not truly free because they do not have financial or social freedom. For Walter, who feels enslaved in his job and life, money buys the truest freedom.

MAMA: *There is always something left to love. And if you ain't learned that, you ain't learned nothing.*

Location: Act III, scene i
Speaker: Mama
Context: Beneatha has expressed her disappointment in Walter

Beneatha is angry at Walter for losing the money in the liquor store venture and for apparently deciding to give in to Mr. Lindner. Mama responds to Beneatha's anger with kindness and a reminder that Walter needs support. She also says that instead of constantly crying about herself, Beneatha should cry for Walter and everything that he has been through, and try to understand how badly he wants to make everything better for his family. She suggests to Beneatha that a college education, which Beneatha prizes so highly, is worthless if she cannot love her brother.

WALTER: *You wouldn't understand yet, son, but your daddy's gonna make a transaction . . . a business transaction that's going to change our lives.. . . That's how come one day when you 'bout seventeen years old I'll come home . . . I'll pull the car up on the driveway . . . just a plain black Chrysler, I think, with white walls—no—black tires . . . the gardener will be clipping away at the hedges and he'll say, "Good evening, Mr. Younger." And I'll say, "Hello, Jefferson, how are you this evening?" And I'll go inside and Ruth will come downstairs and meet me at the door and we'll kiss each other and she'll take my arm and we'll go up to your room to see you sitting on the floor with the catalogues of all the great schools in America around you.. . . All the great schools in the world!*

And—and I'll say, all right son—it's your seventeenth birthday, what is it you've decided?... Just tell me, what it is you want to be—and you'll be it.... Whatever you want to be—Yessir! You just name it, son . . . and I hand you the world!

Location: Act II, scene ii
Speaker: Walter
Context: Walter tucks Travis into bed

ASAGAI: *Then isn't there something wrong in a house—in a world—where all dreams, good or bad, must depend on the death of a man?*
BENEATHA: *AND YOU CANNOT ANSWER IT!*
ASAGAI: *(Shouting over her) I LIVE THE ANSWER!*

Location: Act III, scene i
Speaker: Beneatha and Asagai
Context: The Youngers have learned that the money Walter invested is gone

---

WALTER: *[W]e have decided to move into our house because my father—my father—he earned it for us brick by brick.* (MAMA has her eyes closed and is rocking back and forth as though she were in church, with her head nodding the Amen yes) *We don't want to make no trouble for nobody or fight no causes, and we will try to be good neighbors. And that's all we got to say about that.* (He looks the man absolutely in the eyes) *We don't want your money.* (He turns and walks away)

Location: Act III, scene i
Speaker: Walter
Context: Walter tells Mr. Lindner that his family will not accept the bribe

THE RED BADGE OF COURAGE

Stephen Crane

A naïve young man matures as a result of fighting in the Civil War.

THE LIFE OF STEPHEN CRANE

Stephen Crane was born in 1871 in Newark, New Jersey. The fourteenth child of very religious Method-ist parents, Crane planned to be a professional baseball player. After briefly attending Lafayette College and Syracuse University, Crane turned to writing full time. Convinced that he had to invest his work with the authenticity of experience, he often went to outlandish lengths to live through situations that he intended to work into his novels. For his first book, *Maggie, a Girl of the Streets* (1893), Crane lived in poverty in the Bowery slum of New York City. He based his short story *The Open Boat* on his experience as a castaway from a shipwreck. His short novel *The Red Badge of Courage* (1895) made him an interna-tional celebrity. The novel's realistic depictions of war and battle inspired newspapers to give Crane assignments as a foreign correspondent. He worked in many places, including Greece, Cuba, and Puerto Rico.

Crane published volumes of poetry as well as many works of fiction, including the landmark *The Open Boat* (1897). In 1899, Crane moved into a medieval castle in England with his lover, the former madam of a Jacksonville brothel. Here Crane wrote feverishly, hoping to pay off his debts. Crane died of tuberculosis in June 1900, at the age of twenty-eight.

THE RED BADGE OF COURAGE IN CONTEXT

The Red Badge of Courage, a short novel, is Crane's most enduring work. Although Crane was passion-ately committed to living the experiences he wanted to write about, *The Red Badge of Courage* is almost entirely a product of his imagination. Crane had neither fought in war nor witnessed battle. He relied on his powers of invention to create the extraordinarily realistic combat sequences of the novel. His descrip-tions were very convincing; most critics assumed that Crane was an experienced soldier.

Based loosely on the events of the Civil War Battle of Chancellorsville (May 2–6, 1863), *The Red Badge of Courage* broke the mold of the war novel genre. In the decades before Crane's novel, most fic-tion about the Civil War was idealistic or sentimental, portraying the conflict as a great clash of opposing convictions. The universe of Crane's novel is utterly indifferent to human existence and its puny con-flicts. Previous writers took a large, epic view of the war. Crane focuses on the psychology of a single sol-dier, Private Henry Fleming, whose mind is a tangle of illusions, vanity, and romantic naïveté.

Crane's startling innovations drew the world's attention to *The Red Badge of Courage*, as did the novel's vivid and powerful descriptions of battle. With its combination of detailed imagery, moral ambi-guity, and terse psychological focus, *The Red Badge of Courage* exerted an enormous influence on twen-tieth-century American fiction, particularly on the work of the modernists.

THE RED BADGE OF COURAGE: KEY FACTS

Full title: The Red Badge of Courage: An Episode of the American Civil War	
Time and place written: New York; 1893–1895	
Date of publication: October 5, 1895	
Publisher: D. Appleton and Company	
Type of work: Novel	
Genre: War novel	

Language: English

Setting (time): Unspecified, but probably Chancellorsville, Virginia

Setting (place): Unspecified, but probably May 2–6, 1863

Tense: Past

Tone: Detached, journalistic, impressionistic, sardonic, humorous, pathetic, violent

Narrator: Third-person limited omniscient narrator

Point of view: Henry Fleming's

Protagonist: Henry Fleming

Antagonist: The Confederate Army; the Union general who calls the soldiers of the 304th Regiment "mule drivers" and "mud diggers"

THE RED BADGE OF COURAGE: PLOT OVERVIEW

During the Civil War, a Union regiment rests along a riverbank, where it has been camping for weeks. A tall soldier named Jim Conklin spreads a rumor that the army will march soon. Henry Fleming, a recent recruit to this 304th Regiment, worries about his courage. He fears that the sight of battle will cause him to flee. Henry joined the army because he was drawn to the glory of military conflict.

At last the regiment receives orders to march. The soldiers spend several weary days traveling on foot. Eventually, they approach a battlefield and hear the distant roar of conflict. After securing its position, the enemy charges. Henry, boxed in by his fellow soldiers, realizes that he could not run even if he wanted to. He fires mechanically, feeling like a cog in a machine.

The blue (Union) regiment defeats the gray (Confederate) soldiers, and the victors congratulate one another. Henry wakes from a brief nap to find that the enemy is charging his regiment again. Terror overtakes him this time, and he leaps up and runs away from the line. As he runs, he tells himself that he did the right thing, that his regiment could not have won, and that the men who remained to fight were fools. He passes a general on horseback and hears him saying that the regiment has held back the enemy charge. Ashamed of his cowardice, Henry tries to convince himself that he was right to preserve his own life. He wanders through a forest glade where he stumbles across the decaying corpse of a soldier. Shaken, he hurries away.

After a time, Henry joins a column of wounded soldiers winding down the road. He envies these men, who have wounds like "a red badge of courage"—visible proof of valorous behavior. Henry meets a tattered man who has been shot twice and who speaks proudly of the fact that his regiment did not flee. He repeatedly asks Henry where he is wounded. Henry, made uncomfortable by the man's questions, hurries away to a different part of the column. He meets a spectral soldier with a distant, numb look on his face. Henry realizes that the man is Jim Conklin. Jim runs from the line into a small grove of bushes, where he dies.

Henry and the tattered soldier wander through the woods. The tattered soldier continues to ask Henry about his wound. At last, Henry cannot bear the tattered man's questioning and abandons him to die in the forest. Henry gets close to the battlefield. He sees a blue regiment in retreat and attempts to find out what happened. One of the fleeing men hits him on the head with a rifle, opening a bloody gash on Henry's head. Another soldier leads Henry to his regiment's camp, where Henry is reunited with his companions. Henry's friend Wilson, believing that Henry has been shot, cares for him tenderly.

The next day, the regiment proceeds back to the battlefield. Henry fights like a lion. Thinking of Jim Conklin, he vents his rage against the enemy soldiers. His lieutenant says that with ten thousand Henrys, he could win the war in a week. Henry and Wilson overhear an officer say that the soldiers of the 304th fight like "mule drivers." Insulted, they long to prove the man wrong. In an ensuing charge, the regiment's color bearer falls. Henry takes the flag and carries it proudly before the regiment. After the charge fails, the derisive officer tells the regiment's colonel that his men fight like "mud diggers," further infuriating Henry. Another soldier gratifies Henry and Wilson by telling them that the colonel and lieutenant consider them the best fighters in the regiment.

Henry carries the flag into more battles. The regiment charges a group of enemy soldiers fortified behind a fence and wins the fence after a pitched battle. Wilson seizes the enemy flag and the regiment takes four prisoners. As he and the others march back to their position, Henry reflects on his experiences in the war. Although he revels in his recent success in battle, he feels deeply ashamed of his behavior the previous day, especially his abandonment of the tattered man. But after a moment, he puts his guilt behind him and realizes that he has come through "the red sickness" of battle. He looks forward to peace, feeling a quiet, steady manliness in himself.

CHARACTERS IN *THE RED BADGE OF COURAGE*

Jim Conklin A tall soldier in Henry's regiment. Jim dies from wounds received in battle.

Henry Fleming The novel's protagonist. Initially naïve, Henry matures after battle forces him to confront the universe's indifference to his existence and the insignificance of his own life.

Henry's Mother Encountered only in a brief flashback. Henry's mother did not want Henry to enlist in the army.

The Lieutenant Henry's commander. The lieutenant, a youthful officer, swears profusely during battle. As Henry grows braver, he and the lieutenant develop sympathy for each other, often feeling that they must work together to motivate the rest of the men.

The Tattered Soldier A twice-shot soldier whom Henry encounters in the column of wounded men. With his endless speculation about Henry's supposed wound, the tattered soldier acts as Henry's nagging, painful conscience.

Wilson A loud private. Wilson and Henry grow close as they share the experiences of war and gain a reputation as the regiment's best fighters.

THEMES IN *THE RED BADGE OF COURAGE*

THE DEFINITION OF COURAGE In the beginning of the novel, Henry's understanding of courage is traditional and romantic. He believes that the proof of courage is the praise of one's peers, not internal satisfaction. Henry's mother proposes a more mature definition. She cares little whether Henry earns a praiseworthy name, instead instructing him to meet his responsibilities honestly and squarely even if it means sacrificing his own life. The gap between Henry's definition of courage and his mother's fluctuates throughout *The Red Badge of Courage*, sometimes narrowing, as when Henry fights well in his first battle, and sometimes widening, as when he abandons the tattered soldier. At the end of the novel, Henry has revised his definition. He knows that courage is a private matter, but he believes that the opinion of other people and a soldier's regard for his reputation can inspire soldiers to perform courageously.

THE DEFINITION OF MANHOOD Henry's definition and redefinition of manhood parallels his changing understanding of courage. Before experiencing war, Henry laments that education and religion have robbed men of their natural savagery and made them so pale and domestic that they cannot distinguish themselves except on the battlefield. Henry is grateful to be participating in the war because he thinks it will give him a chance to be a real man. As he makes his way from one skirmish to the next, he becomes increasingly convinced that his experiences will earn him the praise of women and the envy of men. Wilson embodies a more humble, realistic kind of manhood. He is self-assured but not arrogant, and his is able to own up to his faults. He begins the novel as an obnoxiously loud soldier, but later he admits to his own fear and vulnerability when he asks Henry to deliver a yellow envelope to his family should he die in battle. By the novel's end, Henry has made a bold step in the same direction, learning that the measure of his manhood lies more in the skill with which he negotiates his stakes and responsibilities than in his conduct on the battlefield.

SELF-PRESERVATION Henry wrestles with his instinct for self-preservation. After fleeing battle and throwing a pinecone at a squirrel, making it scurry away, he believes that he has stumbled upon a universal truth: every being will do whatever it takes, including running from danger, in order to preserve itself. Henry, assuming that his life is worth preserving, uses this revelation to justify his retreat from the battlefield. But soon after his encounter with the squirrel, Henry discovers the corpse of a soldier, which makes him realize that the world is largely indifferent to his life and the questions that preoccupy him.

SYMBOLS IN *THE RED BADGE OF COURAGE*

THE DEAD SOLDIER The dead soldier symbolizes the insignificance of mortal concerns. Decaying and covered by ants, the corpse is anonymous, neither brave nor cowardly.

IMPORTANT QUOTATIONS FROM *THE RED BADGE OF COURAGE*

His self-pride was now entirely restored. In the shade of its flourishing growth he stood with braced and self-confident legs, and since nothing could now be discovered he did not shrink from an encounter with the eyes of judges, and allowed no thoughts of his own to keep him from an attitude of manfulness. He had performed his mistakes in the dark, so he was still a man.

Location: Chapter XV
Speaker: The narrator
Context: Henry prepares for battle a second time

This passage is the most unflattering depiction of Henry's brand of "manfulness" in the novel. After returning to camp with a slight wound, Henry basks in the admiration of the men who believe his concocted tale of heroism. In the midst of this deception, Henry prides himself on managing his retreat with dignity and discretion. He believes that since no one knows of his cowardice, it does not count. This belief shows how little Henry's understanding of himself has to do with his own self-regard. He only exists through the eyes of other people, and if those people do not see his cowardice, his cowardice does not exist. He would experience guilt or unhappiness only if other people knew about his spinelessness. With his mistakes hidden in the dark, Henry feels neither regret nor shame.

The men dropped here and there like bundles. The captain of the youth's company had been killed in an early part of the action. His body lay stretched out in the position of a tired man resting, but upon his face there was an astonished and sorrowful look, as if he thought some friend had done him an ill turn. The babbling man was grazed by a shot that made the blood stream widely down his face. He clapped both hands to his head. "Oh!" he said, and ran. Another grunted suddenly as if a club had struck him in the stomach. He sat down and gazed ruefully. In his eyes there was mute, indefinite reproach. Farther up the line a man, standing behind a tree, had had his knee joint splintered by a ball. Immediately he had dropped his rifle and gripped the tree with both arms. And there he remained, clinging desperately and crying for assistance that he might withdraw his hold upon the tree.

Location: Chapter V
Speaker: The narrator
Context: The 304th Regiment holds off the Confederate charge

This passage is typical of *The Red Badge of Courage*'s graphic and arresting depictions of battle. This description evokes the chaotic violence of war using precise, unemotional, and convincing language. Crane's vivid descriptions of men dropping "like bundles" and a soldier grunting "as if he had been struck by a club in the stomach" make the battle easy to imagine. The image of the soldier with the shattered knee clinging desperately to a tree and calling for help invokes the theme of the universe's fundamental disregard for human suffering. Time and again, Henry realizes that the natural world is deaf to the agonies of human beings, a realization that makes striving for public glory seem petty and foolish.

He felt that in this crisis his laws of life were useless. Whatever he had learned of himself was here of no avail. He was an unknown quantity. He saw that he would again be obliged to experiment as he had in early youth. He must accumulate information of himself, and meanwhile he resolved to remain close upon his guard lest those qualities of which he knew nothing should everlastingly disgrace him.

Location: Chapter I
Speaker: The narrator
Context: Henry worries about his performance in battle

He suddenly lost concern for himself, and forgot to look at a menacing fate. He became not a man but a member. He felt that something of which he was a part—a regiment, an army, a cause, or a country— was in a crisis. He was welded into a common personality which was dominated by a single desire. For some moments he could not flee, no more than a little finger can commit a revolution from a hand.

Location: Chapter V
Speaker: The narrator
Context: Henry engages in battle for the first time

He saw his vivid error, and he was afraid that it would stand before him all his life. He took no share in the chatter of his comrades, nor did he look at them or know them, save when he felt sudden suspicion that they were seeing his thoughts and scrutinizing each detail of the scene with the tattered soldier. Yet gradually he mustered force to put the sin at a distance. And at last his eyes seemed to open to some new ways. He found that he could look back upon the brass and bombast of his earlier gospels and see them truly. He was gleeful when he discovered that he now despised them. With the conviction came a store of assurance. He felt a quiet manhood, nonassertive but of sturdy and strong blood. He knew that he would no more quail before his guides wherever they should point. He had been to touch the great death, and found that, after all, it was but the great death. He was a man.

Location: The last passage of the novel
Speaker: The narrator
Context: Henry finds the ability to analyze himself honestly

THE REPUBLIC

Plato

Plato explores justice and the just society.

THE LIFE OF PLATO

Plato was born in Athens in 428 B.C. to an aristocratic family. His father, Ariston, died during Plato's boyhood, and his mother, Perictione, remarried Pyrilampes, a friend of the Athenian statesman Pericles. Plato's mentor was Socrates, an eccentric philosopher and a cult figure among Athenian youth. In 399 B.C., Socrates was brought to trial on trumped-up charges and sentenced to death. The outrage soured Plato to politics. He devoted himself to continuing the work of Socrates. After years spent traveling around the Mediterranean, he returned to Athens in 387 B.C. and founded the Academy, an institution that became the model for the Western university. The Academy, which counted the philosopher Aristotle among its students, lasted in one form or another until A.D. 527—912 years in total. It is thought that Plato wrote the *Republic* at the Academy around 380 B.C.

From 385 B.C. until his death in 347, Plato left the Academy only twice, both times to visit Sicily. In 367 B.C., Dionysus I, tyrant of Sicily, died. His brother Dion, father of the heir, immediately sent for Plato, his old teacher. Plato answered the call, inspired by the possibility of putting his political theory into practice. Unfortunately, Dionysus II did not believe that the vigorous study of mathematics and philosophy would be the best preparation for his rule, and so the world lost its chance to test the first philosopher-king.

PLATO'S *REPUBLIC* IN CONTEXT

Beginning in 431 B.C., Athens fought Sparta in the Peloponnesian War, finally losing to the Spartans in 404. After the war, the growth of democracies, especially in Athens, called for a new kind of civic virtue. The ability to speak persuasively in the assemblies and law courts became more valuable than the ability to wage war. A new class emerged: the Sophists, itinerant teachers who offered instruction in nearly any subject for a fee. They taught rhetoric and persuasive speech. Many Sophists argued that right and wrong—objective moral standards—do not exist. Some denied any possibility of objective truth and scoffed at the idea of objective knowledge. They claimed that morality is simply a convention imposed by the rulers of societies upon their subjects.

Socrates, Plato's mentor, wanted to combat assaults on morality. He was disturbed by the behavior of Athenian citizens, who struck him as morally complacent, selfish, and unreflective, consolidating their own power and justifying themselves by citing the theories of the Sophists. Socrates' solution was to act as a "gadfly," stinging his fellow citizens into moral self-examination. The unexamined life, he declared, was not worth living. After Socrates was executed, Plato took over his mission.

Plato's dialogues are classed into early, middle, and late periods. The early dialogues, written soon after Socrates' death, focus almost exclusively on ethical questions, using the Socratic method of *elenchus*. In this method, Socrates and a student debate the definition of some virtue. In the middle period, Plato develops a distinct voice and philosophical outlook. Plato uses the figure he calls Socrates as a mouthpiece for his own views, presenting his dialogues as conversation between a teacher and his students. Plato's interests broaden beyond ethics into questions about how to live, the nature and role of love, and the nature of the physical world.

The dialogues from the late period are extremely complex and controversial. In the *Laws*, possibly Plato's last work, he constructs an ideal state that differs vastly from the state portrayed in the *Republic*. Whereas in the *Republic* Plato suggests that law is unnecessary in a city with the right rulers, in *Laws* he emphasizes the value of laws. This late work suggests Plato's willingness to compromise principles in order to find something that might work in practice.

The *Republic* captures the shift from Plato's early to middle periods. Book I has the structure of a typical early dialogue. Socrates uses *elenchus*, philosophical dialectic, in an attempt to define justice, and the result is *aporia*—intellectual gridlock. Over the course of nine more books, Socrates hashes out a detailed theory of justice through lectures, pausing intermittently to respond to objections raised by his students. In Book VII, Socrates declares that *elenchus* is dangerous in the wrong hands and warns that those without proper respect for truth would use the method to argue against everything instead of using it to seek out what is right.

PLATO'S *REPUBLIC*: KEY FACTS

Time and place written: 380 B.C.; Athens

Language: Ancient Greek

Philosophical movement: Platonism

Speaker: Socrates

Areas of philosophy covered: Ethics, political philosophy, epistemology, metaphysics

Philosophical movements opposed: The Sophists

Other works by Plato on similar topics: For more on Plato's political theory see the *Laws*; for more on his theory of Forms see the *Meno*, the *Phaedo*, and the *Symposium*

PLATO'S *REPUBLIC*: OVERVIEW

In the *Republic*, Plato investigates a series of questions. Why do men behave justly? Because they fear societal punishment? Because they worry about divine retribution? Because the stronger elements of society scare the weak into submission? Or because it is good for them to do so? Is justice, regardless of its rewards and punishments, a good thing in and of itself? How do we define justice? Plato wants to define justice and to show that it is worthwhile in and of itself. In Books II, III, and IV, Plato identifies political justice as harmony in a structured political body. An ideal society consists of three main classes of people: producers (craftsmen, farmers, artisans, etc.), auxiliaries (warriors), and guardians (rulers). A society is just when each group performs its appropriate function, and only that function, and has the right amount of power in relation to the others. Rulers must rule, auxiliaries must uphold rulers' mandates, and producers must limit themselves to exercising whatever skills nature granted them.

At the end of Book IV, Plato argues that individual justice mirrors political justice. He claims that the soul of every individual has a three-part structure analogous to the three classes of a society. The rational part of the soul (analogous to the ruler in society) seeks truth and is responsible for our philosophical inclinations; the spirited part (analogous to the warrior) seeks honor and is responsible for our anger; and the appetitive part (analogous to the producer) seeks all sorts of things, money most of all. The just individual, like the just society, has the right balance between the three parts of his soul: the rational part rules, the spirited part supports this rule, and the appetitive part submits to this rule. Books V through VII focus on the rulers as the philosopher kings.

In a series of three analogies—the allegories of the sun, the line, and the cave—Plato explains these individuals and his theory of the Forms. He posits that the world is divided into two realms: the visible (which we grasp with our senses) and the intelligible (which we grasp with our mind). The visible world is the universe we see around us. The intelligible world is Forms—abstract, changeless absolutes such as Goodness, Beauty, Redness, and Sweetness that make the visible realm possible. Only the Forms are objects of knowledge, because only they possess the eternal truth that the mind—not the senses—must grasp.

Only philosophers, whose minds are trained to grasp the Forms, can know anything at all. To become able rulers, philosophers must know the Form of the Good, which is the source of all other Forms, and of knowledge, truth, and beauty. Plato cannot describe this Form directly, but he claims that it is to the intelligible realm what the sun is to the visible realm. The aim of education is not knowledge, but a lust for truth, so that the soul desires to move past the visible world into the intelligible, ultimately to the Form of the Good.

Philosophers, the most just men, are also the only men who possess knowledge. Plato compares the philosopher king to the most unjust kind of man, the tyrant, who is ruled entirely by his nonrational appetites. He claims that justice is worthwhile for its own sake. In Book IX, Plato sketches a psychological portrait of the tyrant, attempting to prove that injustice tortures a man's psyche, whereas a just soul is a healthy, happy one, untroubled and calm. He argues that even though each of the three main character types—money-loving, honor-loving, and truth-loving—has its own conceptions of pleasure, only the philosopher has experienced all three types of pleasure. Therefore, the others should accept the philosopher's judgment and conclude that philosophical pleasures are best. Plato argues that only philosophical pleasure is really pleasure at all and that all other pleasure is nothing more than cessation of pain.

Plato ends the *Republic* on a surprising note. Having defined justice and established it as the greatest good, he banishes poets from his city. Poets, he claims, appeal to the basest part of the soul by imitating unjust inclinations. By encouraging their listeners to sympathize with ignoble characters, poets encourage us to indulge undesirable emotions in life. Poetry makes us unjust. In closing, Plato describes the trajectory of a soul after death. Just souls are rewarded for one thousand lifetimes, while unjust ones are punished for the same amount of time. Each soul must then choose its next life.

IMPORTANT TERMS FROM PLATO'S *REPUBLIC*

Aporia The Greek term for the inability to proceed. In Plato's early dialogues, Socrates uses pointed questioning to show that his interlocutors have no appropriate definition for the topic under consideration. Socrates does not suggest a true definition, and the conversation ends in aporia.

Appetite The largest aspect of our tripartite soul. Appetite is the seat of all our desires for food, drink, sexual gratification, and other such pleasures. It contains both necessary desires (such as the desire to eat enough to stay alive), unnecessary desires (such as the desire to eat a ten pound sirloin steak at every meal), and unlawful desires (such as the desire to eat one's children). In a just man, the appetite is strictly controlled by reason and reason's henchman, spirit.

Auxiliary Society's warriors. Auxiliaries must enforce the convictions of the guardians and ensure the obedience of the producers.

Belief The second-lowest grade of cognitive activity. The object of belief is the visible realm rather than the intelligible realm. A man in a state of belief does not have access to the Forms.

Elenchus The Greek term for Socrates' method of questioning his interlocutors. In an elenchus, Socrates shows that the interlocutors' beliefs are contradictory.

Empirical Question A question that can only be settled by going out into the world and investigating. For example, "What does Idaho look like?" is an empirical question.

Epistemology The branch of philosophy concerned with knowledge, belief, and thought.

Form According to Plato's metaphysical theory, the intelligible realm. Unchanging, eternal, absolute entities called Forms make up this realm, which is more real than the visible world. These absolute entities—such as Goodness, Beauty, Redness, Sourness, and so on—are the cause of all the objects we experience around us in the visible realm. An apple is red and sweet, for instance, because it participates in the Form of Redness and the Form of Sweetness. Only the Forms can be objects of knowledge.

Form of the Good The most important Form. The Form of the Good is the source of intelligibility and of our capacity to know. It brings all of the other Forms into existence. Only when one grasps the Form of the Good can one reach the highest grade of cognitive activity, understanding. When a philosopher-in-training grasps the Form of the Good, he becomes a philosopher-king.

Guardian Society's rulers. The guardians are also known as philosopher-kings.

Imagination The lowest grade of cognitive activity. Someone in the state of imagination believes images and shadows are the most real things.

Instrumental Reason Reason used to attain some end by engaging in means-end analyses.

Intelligible realm The realm that cannot be sensed, only grasped with the intellect. The intelligible realm consists of the Forms.

Kallipolis The Greek term for Plato's just city.

Knowledge Understanding of eternal, unchanging truths. Only the intelligible realm, the realm of the Forms, can be the object of knowledge.

Lover of sights and sounds Socrates' term for the pseudo-intellectuals who claim to be experts in beauty, but who fail to recognize that the Form of the Beautiful exists, which causes all beauty in the visible realm. Lovers of sights and sounds have no knowledge, only opinion.

Metaphysics The branch of philosophy concerned with asking what there is in the world.

Opinion Truths that are not the eternal, unchanging truths of knowledge. Opinion is the highest form of certainty that exists in the visible realm.

Philosopher-king The ruler of the kallipolis. Also called guardians, philosopher-kings are the only people who can grasp the Forms and thus the only people who can claim knowledge.

Pleonexia A Greek term meaning "the desire to have more." Pleonexia refers to the yearning for money and power.

Producers Society's largest class. Producers are of all professions other than warrior and ruler. In a just society, the producers merely obey what the rulers decree and do their designated work.

Reason One aspect of our tripartite soul. Reason lusts after truth and is the source of all of our philosophic desires. In the just man, reason rules the entire soul.

Sensible Particular Physical objects in the visible realm. They are "sensible" because we can perceive them with our senses. They are "particular" because they are particular items that undergo change over time.

Sophist Teachers-for-hire who educated the wealthy men of Athens in the fifth century B.C. Though they were a diverse group with diverse opinions, the Sophists tended to share a disregard for the notion of objective truth and knowledge. Plato believes that objective truth exists.

Specialization The principle that every man must fulfill only the societal role to which nature best suits him. Plato believes that specialization is the source of political justice.

Spirit One aspect of our tripartite soul. Spirit is the source of our desire for honor and victory, and for our anger. In a just soul, spirit ensures that appetite adheres to reason's commands.

Thought The second-highest grade of cognitive activity. The objects of thought are the Forms of the intelligible realm. Unlike understanding, thought can proceed only by relying on unproved assumptions.

Tripartite Soul Plato's conception of the human soul. The tripartite soul has three parts—reason, spirit, appetite—corresponding to the three classes of society in a just city.

Understanding The highest grade of cognitive activity. Understanding involves the use of pure, abstract reason and does not rely on images or unproved assumptions.

Visible Realm The realm that we can grasp with our senses. The visible realm is comprised of the world of sensible particulars. These objects are not as real as those in the intelligible realm. We cannot "know" anything about them, we can only have opinions about them.

THEMES IN PLATO'S *REPUBLIC*

JUSTICE AS THE ADVANTAGE OF THE STRONGER   In Book I of the *Republic*, Thrasymachus, a Sophist, says that justice is nothing but the advantage of the stronger. He does not mean to define justice with this statement, but to debunk the idea that it exists. His claim proceeds from the basic Sophistic view of morality: that what most people consider objective morality is nothing more than conventions which hamper those who adhere to them and benefit those who flout them. Those who behave unjustly gain power and become the rulers. Justice is the advantage of the stronger because stupid, weak people put themselves at a disadvantage by following principles of justice, and the strong put themselves at an advantage by behaving unjustly. C. D. C. Reeve suggests that Thrasymachus is not merely making the usual assertion that the norms of justice are conventions, but is claiming that rulers put these norms in place for the purpose of promoting their own interests.

With Thrasymachus, Socrates gives voice to the opposition. Then he sets about proving that justice is something good and desirable, that it is more than convention, that it is connected to objective standards of morality, and that it is in our interest to adhere to it.

THE SUN, THE LINE, THE CAVE   In the allegory of the cave, Plato asks us to imagine a group of people who have lived in a deep cave since birth. These people are bound in such a way that they can only look straight ahead. Behind them is a fire and statues. The prisoners believe that the shadows cast by the statues are the most real things in the world. When they talk to one another about "men," "women," "trees," "horses," and so on, they refer to these shadows. One of the prisoners is freed. After initial pain and disbelief, he realizes that the fire and the statues he sees are more real than the shadows. Then this prisoner is dragged into the world above, where he sees real objects. He realizes that the statues were only copies of these. Finally, the prisoner looks at the sun and understands that the sun causes everything around him.

The stages the prisoner passes through in the allegory correspond to the process of gaining understanding. The lowest notch on the cognitive line is imagination, symbolized by the prisoner in the cave who can only see shadows. A man stuck in the imagination stage of development takes his truths from fictions like epic poetry or theater. The next notch is belief, symbolized by the prisoner who sees the statues. A believing man mistakes sensible particulars like trees and flowers for the most real things. The next notch is thought, symbolized by the man who ascends into the world above and sees the Forms, of which the sensible particulars are imperfect copies. The final notch is understanding, symbolized by the man who sees the sun, which represents the Form of the Good. After seeing the ultimate Form, the man no longer needs images or unproved assumptions to aid in his reasoning. Only the philosopher can reach understanding, and that is why only he is fit to rule.

THE BENEFIT OF JUSTICE   In Book IX, Plato argues that it pays to be just. He describes the psychological state of a tyrant to prove that injustice takes an unbearable toll on a man's psyche. He says that although money-lovers, honor-lovers, and truth-lovers have their own ideas about pleasure, they must believe the philosopher when he says the just life is best, because only the philosopher has experienced all three kinds of pleasure. Plato also argues that only philosophical pleasure is really pleasure at all.

Yet in all likelihood, Plato did not consider any of these arguments the primary explanation of justice's worth. He believed that justice is worthwhile independent of the advantages it confers, so his arguments that the worth of justice lies in the enormous pleasure it produces is beside his point. To say that we should be just because it will make our lives more pleasant is an argument a Sophist might make. Many philosophers, from Plato's student Aristotle down to modern scholar Richard Kraut, believe that Plato's real argument for the worth of justice takes place long before Book IX. They argue that Plato locates the worth of justice in justice's connection to the Forms, the best things in the world. In this interpretation, justice is worthwhile because it involves grasping the Form of the Good and imitating it.

IMPORTANT QUOTATIONS FROM PLATO'S *REPUBLIC*

They don't understand that a true captain must pay attention to the seasons of the year, the sky, the stars, the winds, and all that pertains to his craft, if he's really to be the ruler of a ship. And they don't believe that there is any craft that would enable him to determine how he should steer the ship, whether the others want him to or not, or any possibility of mastering this alleged craft or of practicing it at the same time as the craft of navigation. Don't you think that the true captain will be called a real stargazer, a babbler, and a good-for-nothing by those who sail in ships governed in that way?

Location: Book VI
Speaker: Socrates
Context: Socrates responds to Adeimantus's objections

After Adeimantus objects to Socrates' notion of the philosopher-king, pointing out that all real-life philosophers are either vicious or useless, Socrates responds with an analogy. He says that modern Athens is like a ship populated by violent sailors ignorant of navigation. These sailors do not believe that a method of steering the ship exists, just as Athenians do not believe that knowledge exists. The sailors react with scorn to the captain who tries to steer, just as Athenians react with scorn to the philosopher who tries to find knowledge.

Once one has seen it, however, one must conclude that it is the cause of all that is correct and beautiful in anything, that it produces both light and its source in the visible realm, and that in the intelligible realm it controls and provides truth and understanding, so that anyone who is to act sensibly in private or public must see it.

Location: Book VI
Speaker: Socrates
Context: Socrates describes the Form of the Good

Socrates describes the Form of the Good, the ultimate object of knowledge and the source of all other Forms—the entire intelligible realm, intelligibility itself, and our cognitive capacity to know. Though Socrates is unable to describe the Form of the Good explicitly, he attempts to give us a sense of it by comparing it to the sun. It is only when a man grasps the Form of the Good that he achieves understanding, the highest level of cognition. When a guardian takes this last step he is finally ready to become a philosopher-king.

The result, then, is that more plentiful and better-quality goods are more easily produced if each person does one thing for which he is naturally suited, does it at the right time, and is released from having to do any of the others.

Location: Book II
Speaker: Socrates
Context: Socrates introduces the principle of specialization

What about someone who believes in beautiful things but doesn't believe in the beautiful itself and isn't able to follow anyone who could lead him to the knowledge of it? Don't you think he is living in a dream rather than a wakened state? Isn't this dreaming: whether asleep or awake, to think that a likeness is not a likeness but rather the thing itself that it is like?

Location: Book V
Speaker: Socrates
Context: Socrates explains what distinguishes the lover of sights and sounds from the true philosopher

---

Under the tyranny of erotic love he has permanently become while awake what he used to become occasionally while asleep.

Location: Book IX
Speaker: Socrates
Context: Socrates describes the tyrant, who acts out what normal people occasionally dream about

ROBINSON CRUSOE

Daniel Defoe

A man is shipwrecked on an island, where he lives for more than twenty years, fending off cannibals and creating a pleasant life for himself.

THE LIFE OF DANIEL DEFOE

Daniel Defoe was born Daniel Foe in 1660, in London. Like his character Robinson Crusoe, Defoe was a third child. His father, James Foe, was a middle-class wax and candle merchant. As a boy, Daniel witnessed two of the greatest disasters of the seventeenth century: a recurrence of the plague, and the Great Fire of London (1666). Defoe attended a respected school in Dorking, where he was an excellent student, but as a Presbyterian, he was forbidden to attend Oxford or Cambridge. He entered Morton's Academy and considered becoming a Presbyterian minister. He abandoned this plan, but his Protestant values endured throughout his life despite discrimination and persecution. In 1683, Defoe became a traveling hosiery salesman. Visiting Holland, France, and Spain on business, he developed a taste for travel that his fiction reflects.

Defoe found successful as a merchant, establishing his headquarters in a high-class neighborhood of London. A year after starting up his business, he married an heiress named Mary Tuffley, whose dowry was a sizeable fortune of 3,700 pounds. A fervent critic of King James II, Defoe affiliated himself with the supporters of the duke of Monmouth, who led a rebellion against the king in 1685. When the rebellion failed, Defoe was essentially forced out of England. He spent three years in Europe writing tracts against James II, returning to England after James II was deposed in the Glorious Revolution of 1688 and replaced by William of Orange.

By 1692, Defoe was bankrupt. Though eventually he paid off most of his 17,000 pounds in debts, he was never again entirely free from debt. When he was about thirty-five, he changed his name to from Foe to Defoe in order to sound more aristocratic. He began to write, partly as a moneymaking venture. One of his first creations was a poem written in 1701 entitled "The True-Born Englishman," which became popular and earned Defoe some celebrity. He also wrote political pamphlets. One of these, *The Shortest Way with Dissenters*, was a satire on persecutors of dissenters and sold well among the ruling Anglican elite until they realized that the pamphlet was mocking their own practices. As punishment for his mockery, Defoe was publicly pilloried—his hands and wrists locked in a wooden device—and jailed in Newgate Prison.

After the intervention of Robert Harley, a Tory minister and Speaker of Parliament, resulted in Defoe's release, Defoe worked as a publicist, political journalist, and pamphleteer for Harley and other politicians. He also worked as a spy, reveling in aliases and disguises.

In his writing, Defoe often used a pseudonym simply because he enjoyed the effect. He was incredibly wide-ranging and productive as a writer, turning out over 500 books and pamphlets in all. He started writing fiction relatively late in life, around the age of sixty. *Robinson Crusoe* (1719) attracted a large middle-class readership. Defoe followed this success in 1722 with *Moll Flanders*. Defoe died in London on April 24, 1731.

ROBINSON CRUSOE IN CONTEXT

Robinson Crusoe straddles the genres of journalism and fiction. It is based on the true story of a shipwrecked seaman named Alexander Selkirk, and Defoe passed it off as history. His focus on the actual conditions of everyday life and avoidance of the courtly and the heroic made Defoe a revolutionary in English literature and helped define the new genre of the novel. Stylistically, Defoe was a great innovator. Dispensing with the ornate style associated with the upper classes, Defoe used the simple, direct, fact-based style of the middle classes, which became the new standard for the English novel. With *Robinson Crusoe*'s theme of solitary human existence, Defoe paved the way for the central modern theme of alienation and isolation.

ROBINSON CRUSOE: KEY FACTS

Full title: The Life and Strange Surprizing Adventures of Robinson Crusoe, of York, Mariner: Who lived Eight and Twenty Years, all alone in an uninhabited Island on the Coast of America, near the Mouth of the Great River of Oroonoque; Having been cast on Shore by Shipwreck, wherein all the Men perished but himself. With An Account how he was at last as strangely deliver'd by Pyrates

Time and place written: 1719; London, England

Date of first publication: 1719

Publisher: William Taylor

Type of work: Novel

Genre: Adventure story; castaway novel

Language: English

Tense: Past

Tone: Detached, meticulous, objective

Setting (time): 1659–1694

Setting (place): England, North Africa, Brazil, a deserted island off Trinidad, Lisbon

Narrator: Robinson Crusoe in the first and third person

Point of view: Crusoe's

Protagonist: Robinson Crusoe

Antagonist: Hardship, privation, loneliness, and cannibals

ROBINSON CRUSOE: PLOT OVERVIEW

Robinson Crusoe is a seventeenth-century Englishman from the town of York. His father, a merchant of German origin, wants him to study law, but Crusoe wants to go to sea. His father says it is good to seek a modest, secure life. Crusoe obeys his father's wishes for a time, but eventually he succumbs to temptation and embarks on a ship bound for London with a friend. When a storm causes the near deaths of Crusoe and his friend, the friend is dissuaded from sea travel, but Crusoe persists, setting himself up as merchant on a ship leaving London. This trip is financially successful, and Crusoe plans another, leaving his profits in the care of a friendly widow. On Crusoe's second voyage, the ship is seized by Moorish pirates, and Crusoe is enslaved to a potentate in the North African town of Sallee. While on a fishing expedition, he and a slave boy break free and sail down the African coast. A kindly Portuguese captain picks them up, buys the slave boy from Crusoe, and takes Crusoe to Brazil. In Brazil, Crusoe establishes himself as a plantation owner and soon finds success. He embarks on a slave-gathering expedition to West Africa but ends up shipwrecked off the coast of Trinidad.

Crusoe, the sole survivor of the expedition, seeks shelter and food. He returns to the wreck's remains twelve times to salvage guns, powder, food, and other items. Onshore, he finds goats he can graze for meat and builds himself a shelter. He erects a cross that he inscribes with the date of his arrival, September 1, 1659, and makes a notch every day to keep track of time. He also keeps a journal of his household activities, noting his attempts to make candles, his lucky discovery of sprouting grain, and his construction of a cellar, among other events. In June 1660, he falls ill and hallucinates that an angel visits him and warns him to repent. Drinking tobacco-steeped rum, Crusoe realizes that God has delivered him from his earlier sins.

After recovering, Crusoe discovers he is on an island. He finds a pleasant valley filled with grapes and builds a shady retreat there. Crusoe begins to feel more optimistic about being on the island, describing himself as its "king." He trains a parrot, takes a goat as a pet, and teaches himself basket weaving, bread making, and pottery. He cuts down an enormous cedar tree and builds a canoe from its trunk, but discovers that he cannot move it to the sea. After building a smaller boat, he rows around the island, nearly dying when a powerful current sweeps him away. Reaching shore, he hears his parrot calling his name and is thankful for being saved once again. He spends several years in peace.

One day Crusoe is shocked to discover a man's footprint on the beach. He first assumes the footprint is the devil's, then decides it must belong to one of the cannibals said to live in the region. Terrified, he arms himself and builds an underground cellar that he herds his goats into at night. One evening he hears gunshots, and the next day he sees a ship wrecked on his coast. It is empty when he arrives on the scene to investigate. Soon afterward, Crusoe discovers that the shore is strewn with human remains, apparently the remnants of a cannibal feast. Later, Crusoe catches sight of thirty cannibals heading for shore with their victims. One of the victims is killed. Another, waiting to be slaughtered, suddenly breaks free and runs toward Crusoe's dwelling. Crusoe protects him, killing one of the pursuers and injuring the other, whom the victim kills. Well-armed, Crusoe defeats most of the cannibals onshore. The victim vows total submission to Crusoe. Crusoe names the man Friday to commemorate the day on which his life was saved, and takes him as his servant.

Finding Friday cheerful and intelligent, Crusoe teaches him some English words and some elementary Christian concepts. Friday explains that the cannibals are divided into distinct nations and only eat their enemies. The cannibals saved the men from the shipwreck Crusoe witnessed earlier. Those shipwrecked men, Spaniards, are living nearby. Friday expresses a longing to return to his people, but Crusoe is upset at the prospect of losing him. Friday admits that he would rather die than lose Crusoe. The two build a boat to visit the cannibals' land together. Twenty-one cannibals arrive in canoes. They are holding three victims, one of whom is in European dress. Friday and Crusoe kill most of the cannibals and release the European, a Spaniard. Friday is overjoyed to discover that another of the rescued victims is his father. The four men return to Crusoe's dwelling to eat and rest. Crusoe sends Friday's father and the Spaniard out in a canoe to explore the nearby land.

Eight days later, an English ship approaches. Friday is alarmed, and Crusoe is suspicious. They watch as eleven men take three captives onshore in a boat. Nine of the men explore the land, leaving two to guard the captives. Friday and Crusoe overpower these two and release the captives, one of whom is the captain of the ship, which has been taken in a mutiny. Friday and Crusoe confront the mutineers, telling them that all but the ringleader may escape with their lives. The men surrender. Crusoe and the captain pretend that the island is an imperial territory and that the governor has spared their lives in order to send them all to England to face justice. Keeping five men as hostages, Crusoe sends the other men out to seize the ship. When the ship is brought in, Crusoe nearly faints.

On December 19, 1686, after twenty-eight years on the island, Crusoe boards the ship to return to England. At home, he finds that his family members are deceased except for two sisters. Crusoe's widow friend has kept his money safe, and after traveling to Lisbon, Crusoe learns from the Portuguese captain that his plantations in Brazil have been highly profitable. He arranges to sell his Brazilian lands. Wary of sea travel, Crusoe attempts to return to England by land but is threatened by bad weather and wild animals in northern Spain. Finally arriving back in England, Crusoe receives word that the sale of his plantations is complete and he now has a considerable fortune. After donating a portion to the widow and his sisters, Crusoe is restless and considers returning to Brazil, but he decides against it because he does not want to convert to Catholicism. He marries, and his wife dies. In 1694, Crusoe departs for the East Indies as a trader. He revisits his island and finds that the Spaniards are governing it well and that it has become a prosperous colony.

CHARACTERS IN *ROBINSON CRUSOE*

Robinson Crusoe The novel's protagonist and narrator. Crusoe's vague, recurring feelings of guilt over his disobedience to his father color the first part of the first half of the story. Crusoe, a man of deep religious faith, is steady and plodding in everything he does, qualities that ensure his survival during his twenty-eight-year isolation on a desert island.

Friday A twenty-six-year-old Caribbean native and cannibal. Under Crusoe's direction, Friday converts to Protestantism. Friday never appears to resent his servitude to Crusoe, perhaps because he sincerely views it as appropriate compensation for the man who saved his life. But whatever Friday's response, his servitude has become a symbol of imperialist oppression throughout the modern world.

The Portuguese Captain A sea captain. The Portuguese captain picks up Crusoe and the slave boy Xury from their boat after they escape from their Moorish captors. He is polite, personable, and extremely generous to Crusoe. He is also very loyal, taking care of Crusoe's Brazilian investments after he vanishes.

The Spaniard One of the men from the Spanish ship that is wrecked off Crusoe's island. After Crusoe saves the Spaniard from the cannibals, he becomes a new "subject" in Crusoe's "kingdom," at least according to Crusoe.

The Widow A friend of Crusoe's. The widow keeps 200 pounds safe for Crusoe during his thirty-five years of journeying.

Xury A nonwhite (Arab or black) slave boy. Crusoe sells Xury to the Portuguese captain.

THEMES IN *ROBINSON CRUSOE*

THE DUBIOUS VALUE OF MASTERY   In the beginning of the novel, Defoe applauds Crusoe's mastery of his situation. Like Adam in Eden, Crusoe finds himself in an unknown environment and makes it his home, taming animals and figuring out how to survive. He stops incessantly blaming himself for disobeying his father and raging at the destiny that drove him to sea and starts thinking of himself as the worthy, competent captain of his life. But after Friday's arrival, Defoe's depiction of the value of mastery become more complex. In Chapter XXIII, Crusoe teaches Friday the word "[m]aster" even before teaching him "yes" and "no," making it clear that "master" was to be [Crusoe's] name. Crusoe never considers treating Friday as a friend or an equal. The racism that was standard in Crusoe's day does not entirely explain his imperiousness: he refers to himself as "king" over not only the natives, but the Europeans on the island. So while Defoe praises Crusoe for mastering his environment and his fate, he stops short of praising his attempts to master other people.

THE NECESSITY OF REPENTANCE   *Robinson Crusoe* is a moral tale as much as it is an adventure story. In the Preface, Defoe states that Crusoe's story should instruct readers in God's wisdom, one vital part of which is the importance of repenting one's sins. While it is important to be grateful for God's miracles, as Crusoe is when his grain sprouts, for example, gratitude is not enough. Neither is prayer. Crusoe needs repentance most, as he learns from the fiery angelic figure that comes to him during a feverish hallucination and says, "Seeing all these things have not brought thee to repentance, now thou shalt die." Crusoe believes that his major sin is his rebellious behavior toward his father, which he refers to as his "original sin," akin to Adam and Eve's first disobedience of God. It is possible to interpret Crusoe's exile from civilization as symbolic of Adam and Eve's expulsion from Eden. For Crusoe, repentance consists of acknowledging his wretchedness and his absolute dependence on the Lord. This admission marks a turning point in Crusoe's spiritual consciousness. After repenting, he stops complaining so much about his sad fate and starts viewing the island more positively. Later, when Crusoe is rescued and his fortune restored, he compares himself to Job, who regained divine favor after God put him through severe trials.

THE IMPORTANCE OF SELF-AWARENESS   The idea that the individual must keep careful tabs on the state of his own soul is a key point in the Presbyterian doctrine that Defoe always took seriously. Instead of reverting to an instinctual, unconscious kind of existence on the island, Crusoe becomes more self-aware as he withdraws from the external social world and turns inward. In his everyday activities, Crusoe keeps accounts of himself enthusiastically and in a variety of ways. His makeshift calendar is not about marking the passing of days, but about marking the number of days he has spent on the island: it is an autobiographical calendar with Crusoe at its center. He also keeps a meticulous journal of his daily activities, even when they amount to nothing more than finding a few pieces of wood on the beach or waiting inside while it rains.

SYMBOLS IN *ROBINSON CRUSOE*

THE FOOTPRINT   Crusoe's shocking discovery of a single footprint on the sand in Chapter XVIII is one of literature's famous moments. The footprint, and Crusoe's reaction to it, symbolizes Crusoe's conflicted feelings about human companionship. Crusoe has said that he misses companionship, yet the evidence of a man on his island sends him into a panic. He interprets the footprint negatively, assuming it is the print of the devil or of an aggressor. This instinctively fearful attitude toward others suggests the possibility that Crusoe does not want to return to human society after all.

THE CROSS   Crusoe marks the passing of days "with [his] knife upon a large post, in capital letters, and making it into a great cross . . . set[s] it up on the shore where [he] first landed." The cross symbolizes Crusoe's longing for civilization, with its records and calendars. It also symbolizes his new life on the island, just as the Christian cross symbolizes Christians' new life in Christ after baptism, an immersion in water like Crusoe's shipwreck. Yet Crusoe does not consciously reference Christ with his cross. Instead, the cross is a memorial to Crusoe himself, a subtle blasphemy that emphasizes how completely Crusoe becomes the center of his own life.

IMPORTANT QUOTATIONS FROM *ROBINSON CRUSOE*

But no sooner were my eyes open, but I saw my Poll sitting on top of the hedge; and immediately knew that it was he that spoke to me; for just in such bemoaning language I had used to talk to him, and teach him; and he learned it so perfectly that he would sit upon my finger and lay his bill close to my face, and cry, "Poor Robin Crusoe! Where are you? Where have you been? How come you here?" and such things as I had taught him.

Location: Chapter XVI
Speaker: Crusoe
Context: Crusoe has returned from a nearly fatal canoe trip

This passage suggests the pathos of Crusoe's solitude. He has escaped death and has no one to tell except his bird. Crusoe domesticates the bird in an attempt to provide himself with a substitute family member, as we learn later when he refers to his pets in Chapter XVII as his "family." Crusoe's solitude may not be as satisfying as he lets on. Poll's words show a self-pitying side of Crusoe that he never reveals in his narration. Teaching the bird to call him "poor" in a "bemoaning" tone suggests that he may feel more like complaining than he admits in his story and that his Christian patience might be wearing thin.

I might well say now indeed, that the latter end of Job was better than the beginning. It is impossible to express here the flutterings of my very heart when I looked over these letters, and especially when I found all my wealth about me; for as the Brazil ships come all in fleets, the same ships which brought my letters brought my goods.

Location: Chapter XXIX
Speaker: Crusoe
Context: Crusoe has returned to England

Crusoe's comparison of himself to the biblical character Job shows that he gives his ordeal religious meaning. He considers his shipwreck and solitude not random events but planned pieces of an elaborate plan to teach him Christian patience. This passage showcases Crusoe's characteristic neutral tone—the detached, deadpan style in which he narrates even thrilling events. Although he reports that the emotional effects make his heart flutter, he displays very little emotion in the passage. The biblical grandeur of the original Job is lost in Crusoe's ordinary and conversational opening, "I might very well say now." Crusoe is better suited to plodding everyday life than to dramatic sublimity. Even when events call for drama, Crusoe seems to do all he can to make them humdrum. This emphasis on the ordinary was a new trend in English literature and is a major characteristic of the novel, a form that Defoe helped invent.

I was born in the year 1632, in the city of York, of a good family, though not of that country, my father being a foreigner of Bremen who settled first at Hull. He got a good estate by merchandise and, leaving off his trade, lived afterward at York, from whence he had married my mother whose relations were named Robinson, a very good family in that country, and from whom I was called Robinson Kreutznaer;

but by the usual corruption of words in England we are called, nay, we call ourselves, and write our name "Crusoe," and so my companions always called me.

Location: Chapter I
Speaker: Crusoe
Context: Crusoe introduces his family

"O drug!" said I aloud, "what art thou good for? Thou art not worth to me, no, not the taking off of the ground; one of those knives is worth all this heap; I have no manner of use for thee; e'en remain where thou art and go to the bottom as a creature whose life is not worth saving." However, upon second thoughts, I took it away.

Location: Chapter VI
Speaker: Crusoe
Context: Crusoe has found gold

My island was now peopled, and I thought myself very rich in subjects; and it was a merry reflection, which I frequently made, how like a king I looked. First of all, the whole country was my own mere property, Baso that I had an undoubted right of dominion. Secondly, my people were perfectly subjected. I was absolute lord and lawgiver, they all owed their lives to me, and were ready to lay down their lives, if there had been occasion of it, for me.

Location: Chapter XXV
Speaker: Crusoe
Context: Crusoe reflects on his dominion

ROMEO AND JULIET

William Shakespeare

Two children of rival families marry in secret but die tragically, reconciling their families.

THE LIFE OF WILLIAM SHAKESPEARE

William Shakespeare, the most influential writer in all of English literature, was born in 1564 to a successful middle-class glove-maker in Stratford-upon-Avon, England. Shakespeare's formal education did not progress beyond grammar school. In 1582, he married an older woman, Anne Hathaway. His union with Anne produced three children. Around 1590, Shakespeare left his family behind and traveled to London to work as an actor and playwright. He quickly earned public and critical acclaim, and eventually became the most popular playwright in England and a part-owner of the Globe Theater. Shakespeare's career bridged the reigns of Elizabeth I (ruled 1558–1603) and James I (ruled 1603–1625), and he was a favorite of both monarchs. James paid Shakespeare's company a great compliment by giving its members the title of King's Men. Shakespeare retired to Stratford a wealthy and renowned man, and died in 1616 at the age of fifty-two. At the time of Shakespeare's death, literary luminaries such as Ben Jonson hailed his works as timeless.

Shakespeare's works were collected and printed in various editions in the century following his death, and by the early eighteenth century his reputation as the greatest poet ever to write in English was well established. The unprecedented regard in which Shakespeare's works were held led to a fierce curiosity about his life, but many details of Shakespeare's personal history are unknown or shrouded in mystery. Some people have concluded from this lack of information and from Shakespeare's modest education that Shakespeare's plays were actually written by someone else—Francis Bacon and the Earl of Oxford are the two most popular candidates—but the support for this claim is overwhelmingly circumstantial, and the theory is not taken seriously by many scholars.

Shakespeare is generally thought to be the author of the thirty-eight plays (two of them possibly collaborations) and 154 sonnets that bear his name. The legacy of this body of work is immense. A number of Shakespeare's plays seem to have transcended even the category of brilliance, influencing the course of Western literature and culture.

ROMEO AND JULIET IN CONTEXT

Shakespeare did not invent the story of *Romeo and Juliet*. He did not, in fact, even introduce the story into the English language. A poet named Arthur Brooks first brought the story of *Romeus and Juliet* to an English-speaking audience in a long and plodding poem. Brooks' work was an adaptation of adaptations that stretched across nearly a hundred years and two languages. Many of the details of Shakespeare's plot are lifted directly from Brooks's poem, including the meeting of Romeo and Juliet at the ball, their secret marriage, Romeo's fight with Tybalt, the sleeping potion, and the timing of the lovers' eventual suicides.

Despite its many sources, Shakespeare's play distinguishes itself from its predecessors in several important aspects: the subtlety and originality of its characterization (Shakespeare almost wholly created Mercutio); the intense pace of its action, compressed into four frenetic days; a powerful enrichment of the story's thematic aspects; and, above all, an extraordinary use of language.

Romeo and Juliet is also similar in plot and themes to the story of Pyramus and Thisbe, which appears in Ovid's *Metamorphoses*. Shakespeare was certainly aware of the Pyramus and Thisbe story: *Romeo and Juliet* contains a reference to Thisbe. Moreover, the story of Pyramus and Thisbe is presented as the comically awful play-within-a-play put on by Bottom and his friends in *A Midsummer Night's Dream*, which Shakespeare wrote around the same time he was composing *Romeo and Juliet*. Indeed, one can look at the play-within-a-play in *A Midsummer Night's Dream* as parodying the very story that Shakespeare seeks to tell in *Romeo and Juliet*. Shakespeare wrote *Romeo and Juliet* in full knowledge that the story he was telling was old, clichéd, and an easy target for parody. In writing *Romeo and Juliet*, Shakespeare, then, implicitly set himself the task of telling a love story despite the considerable forces he knew were stacked against its success. Through the incomparable intensity of his language, Shakespeare succeeded in this effort, writing a play that is universally accepted in Western culture as the preeminent, archetypal story of tragic love.

ROMEO AND JULIET: KEY FACTS

Full Title: The Most Excellent and Lamentable Tragedy of Romeo and Juliet

Time and place written: London; mid-1590s

Date of first publication: 1597 (First Quarto, incomplete and likely unauthorized); 1599 (Second Quarto)

Genre: Tragedy

Setting (time): Renaissance (fourteenth or fifteenth century)

Setting (place): Italy: Verona and Mantua

Protagonist: Romeo, Juliet

Antagonist: The Montague-Capulet feud, Tybalt, fate

Major conflict: Lovers Romeo and Juliet struggle to be together despite their families' feud

ROMEO AND JULIET: PLOT OVERVIEW

In the streets of Verona, a brawl breaks out between the servants of the feuding noble families of Capulet and Montague. Benvolio, a Montague, tries to stop the fighting, but is himself embroiled when the rash Capulet, Tybalt, arrives on the scene. After citizens outraged by the constant violence beat back the warring factions, Prince Escalus, the ruler of Verona, attempts to prevent any further conflicts between the families by decreeing death for any individual who disturbs the peace in the future.

Romeo, the son of Montague, runs into his cousin Benvolio, who had earlier seen Romeo moping in a grove of sycamores. After some prodding by Benvolio, Romeo confides that he is in love with Rosaline, a woman who does not return his affections. Benvolio counsels him to forget this woman and find another, more beautiful one, but Romeo remains despondent.

Meanwhile, Paris, a kinsman of the Prince, seeks Juliet's hand in marriage. Her father Capulet, though happy at the match, asks Paris to wait two years, since Juliet is not yet even fourteen. Capulet dispatches a servant with a list of people to invite to a masquerade and feast he traditionally holds. He invites Paris to the feast, hoping that Paris will begin to win Juliet's heart.

Romeo and Benvolio, still discussing Rosaline, encounter the Capulet servant bearing the list of invitations. Benvolio suggests that they attend, since that will allow Romeo to compare his beloved to other beautiful women of Verona. Romeo agrees to go with Benvolio to the feast, but only because Rosaline, whose name he reads on the list, will be there.

In Capulet's household, young Juliet talks with her mother, Lady Capulet, and her nurse about the possibility of marrying Paris. Juliet has not yet considered marriage but agrees to look at Paris during the feast to see if she thinks she could fall in love with him.

The feast begins. A melancholy Romeo follows Benvolio and their witty friend Mercutio to Capulet's house. Once inside, Romeo sees Juliet from a distance and instantly falls in love with her; he forgets about Rosaline completely. As Romeo watches Juliet, entranced, a young Capulet, Tybalt, recognizes him and is enraged that a Montague would sneak into a Capulet feast. He prepares to attack, but Capulet holds him back. Soon, Romeo speaks to Juliet, and the two experience a profound attraction. They kiss, not even knowing each other's names. When he finds out from Juliet's nurse that she is the daughter of Capulet, his family's enemy, he becomes distraught. When Juliet learns that the young man she has just kissed is the son of Montague, she grows equally upset.

As Mercutio and Benvolio leave the Capulet estate, Romeo leaps over the orchard wall into the garden, unable to leave Juliet behind. From his hiding place, he sees Juliet in a window above the orchard and hears her speak his name. He calls out to her, and they exchange vows of love.

Romeo hurries to see his friend and confessor Friar Lawrence, who, though shocked at the sudden turn of Romeo's heart, agrees to marry the young lovers in secret, since he sees in their love the possibility of ending the age-old feud between Capulet and Montague. The following day, Romeo and Juliet meet at Friar Lawrence's cell and are married. The Nurse, who is privy to the secret, procures a ladder, which Romeo will use to climb into Juliet's window for their wedding night.

The next day, Benvolio and Mercutio encounter Tybalt, Juliet's cousin. Tybalt, still enraged that Romeo attended Capulet's feast, has challenged Romeo to a duel. Romeo appears. Now Tybalt's kinsman by marriage, Romeo begs the Capulet to hold off the duel until he understands why Romeo does not want to fight. Disgusted with this plea for peace, Mercutio says that he will fight Tybalt himself. The two begin to duel. Romeo tries to stop them by leaping between the combatants. Tybalt stabs Mercutio under Romeo's arm, and Mercutio dies. Romeo, in a rage, kills Tybalt. Romeo flees from the scene. Soon after, the Prince declares him forever banished from Verona for his crime. Friar Lawrence arranges for Romeo to spend his wedding night with Juliet before he has to leave for Mantua the following morning.

In her room, Juliet awaits the arrival of her new husband. The Nurse enters and, after some confusion, tells Juliet that Romeo has killed Tybalt. Distraught, Juliet suddenly finds herself married to a man who has killed her kinsman. But she resettles herself and realizes that her duty belongs with her love: to Romeo.

Romeo sneaks into Juliet's room that night, and at last they consummate their marriage and their love. Morning comes, and the lovers bid farewell, unsure when they will see each other again. Juliet learns that her father, affected by the recent events, now intends for her to marry Paris in just three days. Juliet is unsure of how to proceed. She is unable to reveal to her parents that she is married to Romeo, but unwilling to marry Paris now that she is Romeo's wife. She asks her Nurse for advice. The Nurse counsels Juliet to proceed as if Romeo were dead and to marry Paris, who is a better match anyway. Disgusted with the Nurse's disloyalty, Juliet disregards her advice and hurries to Friar Lawrence. He concocts a plan to reunite Juliet with Romeo in Mantua. The night before her wedding to Paris, Juliet must drink a potion that will make her appear to be dead. After she is laid to rest in the family's crypt, the Friar and Romeo will secretly retrieve her, and she will be free to live with Romeo, away from their parents' feuding.

Juliet returns home to discover the wedding has been moved ahead one day, and she is to be married tomorrow. That night, Juliet drinks the potion, and the Nurse discovers her, apparently dead, the next morning. The Capulets grieve, and Juliet is entombed according to plan. But Friar Lawrence's message explaining the plan to Romeo never reaches Mantua. Its bearer, Friar John, gets confined to a quarantined house. Romeo learns only of Juliet's death and decides to kill himself rather than live without her. He buys a vial of poison from a reluctant Apothecary, then speeds back to Verona to take his own life at Juliet's tomb. Outside the Capulet crypt, Romeo comes upon Paris, who is scattering flowers on Juliet's grave. They fight, and Romeo kills Paris. He enters the tomb, sees Juliet's inanimate body, drinks the poison, and dies by her side. Just then, Friar Lawrence enters and realizes that Romeo has killed Paris and himself. At the same time, Juliet awakes. Friar Lawrence hears the coming of the watch. When Juliet refuses to leave with him, he flees alone. Juliet sees her beloved Romeo and realizes he has killed himself with poison. She kisses his poisoned lips, and when that does not kill her, buries his dagger in her chest, falling dead upon his body.

The watch arrives, followed closely by the Prince, the Capulets, and Montague. Montague declares that Lady Montague has died of grief over Romeo's exile. Seeing their children's bodies, Capulet and Montague agree to end their long-standing feud and to raise gold statues of their children side by side in a newly peaceful Verona.

CHARACTERS IN *ROMEO AND JULIET*

THE CAPULETS

Capulet The patriarch of the Capulet family, father of Juliet, husband of Lady Capulet, and enemy, for unexplained reasons, of Montague. He truly loves his daughter, though he is not well acquainted with Juliet's thoughts or feelings and seems to think that what is best for her is a "good" match with Paris. Often prudent, he commands respect and propriety, but he is liable to fly into a rage when either is lacking.

Lady Capulet Juliet's mother, Capulet's wife. A woman who herself married young (by her own estimation, she gave birth to Juliet at close to the age of fourteen), she is eager to see her daughter marry Paris. She is an ineffectual mother, relying on the Nurse for moral and pragmatic support.

Juliet The daughter of Capulet and Lady Capulet. A beautiful thirteen-year-old girl, Juliet begins the play as a naïve child who has thought little about love and marriage, but she grows up quickly upon falling in love with Romeo, the son of her family's great enemy. Because she is a girl in an aristocratic family, she has none of the freedom Romeo has to roam around the city, climb over walls in the middle of the night, or get into swordfights. Nevertheless, she shows amazing courage in trusting her entire life and future to Romeo, even refusing to believe the worst reports about him after he kills her cousin Tybalt. Juliet's closest friend and confidant is her Nurse, though she's willing to shut the Nurse out of her life the moment the Nurse turns against Romeo.

The Nurse Juliet's nurse, the woman who breast-fed Juliet when she was a baby and has cared for Juliet her entire life. A vulgar, longwinded, and sentimental character, the Nurse provides comic relief with her frequently inappropriate remarks and speeches. Until a disagreement near the play's end, the Nurse is Juliet's faithful confidante and loyal intermediary in Juliet's affair with Romeo. She provides a contrast with Juliet, given that her view of love is earthy and sexual, whereas Juliet is idealistic and intense. The Nurse believes in love and wants Juliet to have a nice-looking husband, but the idea that Juliet would want to sacrifice herself for love is incomprehensible to her.

Peter A Capulet servant who invites guests to Capulet's feast and escorts the Nurse to meet with Romeo. He is illiterate and a bad singer.

Sampson and Gregory Two servants who, like their master, hate the Montagues. At the outset of the play, they successfully provoke some Montague men into a fight.

Tybalt Juliet's cousin on her mother's side. Vain, fashionable, supremely aware of courtesy and the lack of it, he becomes aggressive, violent, and quick to draw his sword when he feels his pride has been injured. Once drawn, his sword is something to be feared. He loathes Montagues.

THE MONTAGUES

Abram Montague's servant, who fights with Sampson and Gregory in the first scene of the play.

Balthasar Romeo's dedicated servant, who brings Romeo the news of Juliet's death, unaware that her death is a ruse.

Benvolio Montague's nephew, Romeo's cousin and thoughtful friend, he makes a genuine effort to defuse violent scenes in public places, though Mercutio accuses him of having a nasty temper in private. He spends most of the play trying to help Romeo get his mind off Rosaline, even after Romeo has fallen in love with Juliet.

Montague Romeo's father, the patriarch of the Montague clan and bitter enemy of Capulet. At the beginning of the play, he is chiefly concerned about Romeo's melancholy.

Lady Montague Romeo's mother, Montague's wife. She dies of grief after Romeo is exiled from Verona.

Romeo The son and heir of Montague and Lady Montague. Romeo is handsome, intelligent, and sensitive. Though impulsive and immature, his idealism and passion make him an extremely likable character. He lives in the middle of a violent feud between his family and the Capulets, but he is not at all interested in violence. His only interest is love. At the beginning of the play, he is madly in love with a woman named Rosaline, but the instant he lays eyes on Juliet, he falls in love with her and forgets Rosaline. Thus, Shakespeare gives us every reason to question how real Romeo's new love is, but Romeo goes to extremes to prove the seriousness of his feelings. He secretly marries Juliet, the daughter of his father's worst enemy; he happily takes abuse from Tybalt; and he would rather die than live without his beloved. Romeo is also an affectionate and devoted friend to Benvolio, Mercutio, and Friar Lawrence.

ADDITIONAL CHARACTERS

The Apothecary An apothecary in Mantua. Had he been wealthier, he might have been able to afford to value his morals more than money and refused to sell poison to Romeo.

The Chorus A character, developed in Greek drama, whose function is to comment on the play's plot and themes.

Friar Lawrence A Franciscan friar, friend to both Romeo and Juliet. Kind, civic-minded, a proponent of moderation, and always ready with a plan, Friar Lawrence secretly marries the impassioned lovers in hopes that the union might eventually bring peace to Verona. As well as being a Catholic holy man, Friar Lawrence is an expert in the use of seemingly mystical potions and herbs.

Friar John A Franciscan friar charged by Friar Lawrence with taking the news of Juliet's false death to Romeo in Mantua. Friar John is held up by a quarantine, and the message never reaches Romeo.

Mercutio A kinsman to Prince Escalus, and Romeo's close friend. One of the most extraordinary characters in all of Shakespeare's plays, Mercutio overflows with imagination, wit, and at times a strange, biting satire and brooding fervor. Mercutio loves wordplay, especially sexual double entendres. He can be quite hotheaded and hates people who are affected, pretentious, or obsessed with the latest fashions. He finds Romeo's romanticized ideas about love tiresome and tries to convince Romeo to view love as a simple matter of sexual appetite.

Paris A kinsman of Prince Escalus, and the suitor of Juliet whom Capulet most preferred. Once Capulet has promised him he can marry Juliet, he behaves very presumptuously toward her, acting as if they are already married.

Prince Escalus The Prince of Verona. A kinsman of Mercutio and Paris. As the seat of political power in Verona, he is concerned about maintaining the public peace at all costs.

Rosaline The woman with whom Romeo is infatuated at the beginning of the play. Rosaline never appears onstage, but it is said by other characters that she is very beautiful and has sworn to live a life of chastity.

THEMES IN *ROMEO AND JULIET*

THE POWER OF LOVE In *Romeo and Juliet*, love is a violent, ecstatic, overpowering force that supersedes all other values, loyalties, and emotions. In the course of the play, the young lovers are driven to defy their entire social world: families ("Deny thy father and refuse thy name," Juliet asks, "Or if thou wilt not, be but sworn my love, / And I'll no longer be a Capulet"); friends (Romeo abandons Mercutio and Benvolio after the feast in order to go to Juliet's garden); and ruler (Romeo returns to Verona for Juliet's sake after being exiled by the Prince on pain of death in II.i.76–78). Love in *Romeo and Juliet* is a brutal, powerful emotion that captures individuals and catapults them against their world and at times against themselves.

Love's strength and power is evidenced by the way descriptions of love consistently fail to capture its entirety. At times love is described in the terms of religion, as in the fourteen lines when Romeo and Juliet first meet. At others it is described as a sort of magic: "Alike bewitchèd by the charm of looks" (II.Prologue.6). Juliet, perhaps, most perfectly describes her love for Romeo by refusing to describe it: "But my true love is grown to such excess / I cannot sum up some of half my wealth" (III.i.33–34). Love, in other words, resists any single metaphor because it is too powerful to be so easily contained or understood.

LOVE LEADS TO VIOLENCE Romeo and Juliet's love is linked with death from the moment of its inception: Tybalt notices that Romeo has crashed the feast and determines to kill him just as Romeo catches sight of Juliet and falls instantly in love with her. From that point on, love seems to push the lovers closer to violence, not farther from it. Romeo and Juliet are plagued with thoughts of suicide and a willingness to experience it: in III.iii, Romeo brandishes a knife in Friar Lawrence's cell and threatens to kill himself after he has been banished from Verona and his love. Juliet also pulls a knife in order to take her own life in Friar Lawrence's presence just three scenes later. After Capulet decides that Juliet will marry Paris, Juliet says, "If all else fail, myself have power to die" (III.v.242). Finally, each imagines that the other looks dead the morning after their first and only sexual experience ("Methinks I see thee," Juliet says, "… as one dead in the bottom of a tomb" (III.v.242; III.v.55–56). This theme continues until its inevitable conclusion: double suicide. This tragic choice is the highest, most potent expression of love that Romeo and Juliet can make. It is only through death that they can preserve their love, and their love is so profound that they are willing to end their lives in its defense. In the play, love emerges as an amoral thing, leading as much to destruction as to happiness.

THE TENSION BETWEEN SELF AND SOCIETY Much of *Romeo and Juliet* involves the lovers' struggles against public and social institutions that either explicitly or implicitly oppose their love. Such structures range from the concrete to the abstract: families and the placement of familial power in the father; law and the desire for public order; religion; and the social importance placed on masculine honor. These institutions often come into conflict with each other. The importance of honor, for example, time and again results in brawls that disturb the public peace.

Romeo and Juliet may be viewed as a battle between the responsibilities and actions demanded by social institutions and those demanded by the private desires of the individual. Romeo and Juliet's appreciation of night, with its darkness and privacy, and their renunciation of their names, with its attendant loss of obligation, make sense in the context of individuals who wish to escape the public world. But the lovers cannot stop the night from becoming day, and Romeo cannot cease being a Montague simply because he wants to; the rest of the world will not let him. The lovers' suicides can be understood as the ultimate night, the ultimate privacy.

SYMBOLS IN *ROMEO AND JULIET*

THUMB-BITING In I.i, the buffoonish Samson begins a brawl between the Montagues and Capulets by flicking his thumbnail from behind his upper teeth, an insulting gesture known as biting the thumb. He engages in this juvenile and vulgar display because he wants to get into a fight with the Montagues but doesn't want to be accused of starting the fight by making an explicit insult. Because of his timidity, he settles for being annoying rather than challenging. Biting the thumb, a silly gesture, represents the foolishness of the Capulet-Montague feud.

QUEEN MAB In I.iv, Mercutio delivers a dazzling speech about the fairy Queen Mab, who rides through the night on her tiny wagon bringing dreams to sleepers. The dreams she brings do not bring out the best sides of the dreamers; rather, they confirm their vices—greed, violence, lust. The description of Mab and her carriage goes to extravagant lengths to emphasize how tiny and insubstantial she and her accoutrements are. Queen Mab and her carriage symbolize the power of waking fantasies, daydreams, and desires. Through the Queen Mab imagery, Mercutio suggests that all desires and fantasies are as nonsensical and fragile as Mab. This point of view contrasts starkly with that of Romeo and Juliet, who see their love as real and ennobling.

IMPORTANT QUOTATIONS FROM *ROMEO AND JULIET*

But soft, what light through yonder window breaks?
It is the east, and Juliet is the sun.
Arise, fair sun, and kill the envious moon,
Who is already sick and pale with grief
That thou, her maid, art far more fair than she.. . . .
The brightness of her cheek would shame those stars
As daylight doth a lamp; her eye in heaven
Would through the airy region stream so bright
That birds would sing and think it were not night.

Location: II.i.44-64
Speaker: Romeo
Context: After Capulet's dance, Romeo hides in the Capulet orchard and glimpses Juliet at her window

Juliet's beauty makes Romeo imagine that she is the sun, transforming the darkness into daylight. Romeo likewise personifies the moon, calling it "sick and pale with grief" at the fact that Juliet, the sun, is far brighter and more beautiful. Romeo then compares Juliet to the stars, claiming that she eclipses the stars as daylight overpowers a lamp. Her eyes alone shine so brightly that they will convince the birds to sing at night as if it were day. The passage introduces one of the play's most beautiful and famous sequences and plays with the light/dark imagery that peppers the play.

> *O Romeo, Romeo,*
> *Wherefore art thou Romeo?*
> *Deny thy father and refuse thy name,*
> *Or if thou wilt not, be but sworn my love,*
> *And I'll no longer be a Capulet.*

Location: II.i.74–78
Speaker: Juliet
Context: Unaware that Romeo is hiding in the orchard, Juliet declares her love for him

Juliet asks why (wherefore) Romeo must be Romeo—why he must be a Montague, the son of her family's greatest enemy. Still unaware of Romeo's presence, she asks him to deny his family for her love. She adds, however, that if he will not, she will deny her family in order to be with him if he merely tells her that he loves her.

The tension between social and family identity (represented by one's name) and personal identity is one of the important themes explored in the play. Juliet thinks of Romeo in individual terms, and thus her love for him overrides her family's hatred for the Montague name. She says that if Romeo were not called "Romeo" or "Montague," he would still be the person she loves. "What's in a name?" she asks. "That which we call a rose / By any other word would smell as sweet" (II.i.85–86).

> *O, then I see Queen Mab hath been with you.. . . .*
> *She is the fairies' midwife, and she comes*
> *In shape no bigger than an agate stone*
> *On the forefinger of an alderman,*
> *Drawn with a team of little atomi*
> *Athwart men's noses as they lie asleep.*

Location: I.iv.53–59
Speaker: Mercutio
Context: Mercutio tries to mock Romeo into coming to the Capulet feast

---

> *From forth the fatal loins of these two foes*
> *A pair of star-crossed lovers take their life,*
> *Whose misadventured piteous overthrows*
> *Doth with their death bury their parents' strife.. . . .*

Location: Prologue.5–8
Speaker: Chorus
Context: The Chorus summarizes the action of the play

> *O, I am fortune's fool!*

Location: III.i.131
Speaker: Romeo
Context: Romeo has just killed Tybalt, hours after marrying Tybalt's cousin Juliet

A ROOM OF ONE'S OWN

Virginia Woolf

An anonymous novelist surveys the history of women writers and analyzes their recent efforts.

THE LIFE OF VIRGINIA WOOLF

Virginia Woolf was born on January 25, 1882, to Leslie Stephen and Julia Duckworth Stephen. She was one of four children. Woolf's mother died in 1895, triggering Woolf's first mental breakdown. For weeks after Julia's death, Sir Leslie groaned, threw tantrums, wept, and refused to eat. George Duckworth, Woolf's twenty-seven-year-old half brother, began sexually abusing the grieving thirteen-year-old Woolf, secretly fondling her. Woolf took refuge from harassment and depression in her father's vast library. Sir Leslie remarked that he had never seen anyone "gobble up" books like Woolf did.

Woolf's half-sister, Stella Duckworth, died during emergency surgery when Woolf was fifteen. Seven years after Stella's death, Sir Leslie died after a long bout with cancer. Woolf suffered a breakdown and attempted to commit suicide by jumping out of a window. The Stephen children moved to Bloomsbury, a seedy but still elegant neighborhood in London. A group of intellectual, liberal young men and women met regularly in their house. They called their circle "Bloomsbury," and are known historically as the Bloomsbury Group.

After a trip to Greece, Woolf's brother Thoby died of typhoid fever. Woolf was devastated and never truly recovered from the loss of her older brother, whom she adored. She memorialized him in her novel *Jacob's Room* (1922) and as Percival in *The Waves* (1931).

In 1912, Woolf married Leonard Woolf. It was a fortunate match. Leonard was a nurturing caretaker, which was a blessing for Woolf. The possibility of professional failure so terrified Woolf that she had to be hospitalized before the publication of her first novel, *The Voyage Out*. After returning home, she attempted suicide with sleeping pills. Her fears proved unfounded, however. Critics greeted *The Voyage Out* with enthusiasm, praising it for being "recklessly feminine" and for exhibiting "something startlingly like genius."

World War I (1914–1918) erupted. Although air warfare was in its infancy, raids over London sometimes occurred. In 1917, a year before the end of the war, Leonard and Woolf moved to a home in the suburbs, bought a printing press, and launched their own printing company, Hogarth Press. The company soon became profitable, publishing works by T. S. Eliot, Maxim Gorky, Katherine Mansfield, and Sigmund Freud.

Woolf succumbed to another bout of depression after finishing *Jacob's Room* in 1922. She began thinking about Clarissa Dalloway, the heroine of her next novel. Three years later, *Mrs. Dalloway* was published to ecstatic reviews. Critical, popular, and financial success followed. Still, Woolf lapsed into months of depression and illness. Woolf's health eventually improved because of her deep friendship and love affair with Vita Sackville-West (1892–1962). Vita was an author, outstanding gardener, and figurehead for feminists—although she abhorred labels like "feminist."

Woolf entered a particularly productive period, completing *To the Lighthouse* (1927) and beginning *The Waves*. Critics began to consider her a novelist of the first rank, a major British writer who had dusted off old forms and established new novelistic conventions. In 1927, happy with life and grateful for Vita's love, Woolf began *Orlando* (1928), a tongue-in-cheek fantasy about a boy who becomes a woman.

During World War II, bombs destroyed the Woolfs' home while they were at their residence in Sussex. Desperate to sustain her mental health, Virginia Woolf continued writing. By early March 1941, she feared she was slipping into a deep mental illness from which she would never recover. She began hearing voices. On March 28, Woolf wrote farewell notes to Leonard and her sister Vanessa, expressing her certainty that she would not recover, and set out across a meadow toward the River Ouse. There, she placed a large stone in her coat pocket and walked or jumped into the river, where she drowned.

A ROOM OF ONE'S OWN IN CONTEXT

Virginia Woolf began working on *A Room of One's Own* in October 1928, when she was invited to deliver lectures on the topic of women and fiction at Newnham College and Girton College. At that time, Newnham and Girton were the only women's colleges at Cambridge University, which, along with Oxford University, was one of the oldest and most respected educational institutions in the world. Compared to the men's colleges at Cambridge, some of which had been in existence since the thirteenth century, the women's colleges were relatively new: Girton had opened in 1869 and Newnham in 1871. In Woolf's time, the women's colleges were underfunded, and their students and faculty lacked power in the larger University. However, the colleges did provide a happy environment for female students, where intellectual women could feel that they truly belonged—an option that had not been available to Virginia Woolf when she was a young woman. Despite imperfections, the fact that female students had penetrated Cambridge and Oxford, traditionally male bastions of learning, was a remarkable accomplishment.

The turn of the twentieth century had seen the rise of the women's suffrage movement in England. In 1903, "suffragettes" began to use drastic measures to win women the right to vote. They smashed windows, went on hunger strikes, and held mass demonstrations. World War I provided new opportunities for women, who had a chance to work at traditionally male jobs while men were away at war. In 1918, women over thirty were granted suffrage (voting age for men was twenty-one), partially in recognition of their valuable contributions to the war effort.

When women got the right to vote, many people—women among them—believed the goal of feminism had been met. But opportunities for women remained extremely limited. Women still had few work or educational opportunities. It is this sense of complacency that Woolf protests against in *A Room of One's Own*.

Woolf's personal experiences influenced her arguments in *A Room of One's Own*. Although she came from an educated family, she was not given a formal education because her parents didn't consider it necessary. After her parents' death, Woolf was able to pursue an intellectual career with the help of an inheritance from her aunt and an understanding husband who gave her all the room she needed. As a writer, Woolf attempted to practice what she preached in *A Room of One's Own*, writing novels concerned with the female experience.

After she delivered her lectures at Girton and Newnham, Woof revised and added to them, printing them as an essay in 1929. The title *A Room of One's Own* has become a cliché in our culture, a fact that testifies to the book's importance and its enduring influence.

A ROOM OF ONE'S OWN: KEY FACT

Time and place written: 1928; England

Date of first publication: 1929

Publisher: Hogarth Press in the United Kingdom, Harcourt Brace & Company in the United States

Type of work: Essay

Genre: Literary criticism; literary theory; feminist theory; essay

Language: English

Setting (time): 1929

Setting (place): England

Tense: Present

Tone: Persuasive, elaborately surprised, steely

Narrator: A nameless woman, narrating in the first person; she is a writer and an intellectual who lives on an inheritance from her aunt

Point of view: The narrator's

Protagonist: The narrator

Antagonist: The forces that oppress women

A ROOM OF ONE'S OWN: PLOT OVERVIEW

In her essay, Woolf takes on the persona of a nameless woman—"Mary Beton, Mary Seton, Mary Carmichael or . . . any name you please"—who has concluded that "a woman must have money and a room of her own if she is to write fiction." In the essay, the narrator explains how she came to this conclusion.

The narrator begins her investigation at Oxbridge College, where she reflects on women's lack of access to the education and money men enjoy. She spends a day in the British Library perusing the scholarship on women, all of which has written by men and all of which has been written in anger. Turning to history, she finds so little data about the everyday lives of women that she decides she must reconstruct their existence imaginatively. She wonders what would have happened if William Shakespeare had had a brilliant sister, and concludes this sister would have been mocked, abused, and ignored.

The narrator considers the achievements of the major women novelists of the nineteenth century and reflects on the importance of tradition to an aspiring writer. A survey of the current state of literature follows. The narrator examines the first novel of "Mary Carmichael" and finds it excellent, considering that Carmichael was "an unknown girl writing her first novel in a bed-sitting room, without enough of those desirable things, time, money, and idleness." Woolf closes the essay by exhorting women to write.

CHARACTERS IN *A ROOM OF ONE'S OWN*

Mr. A An imagined male author. Mr. A's work is overshadowed by his self-consciousness and petulant assertiveness.

The Beadle An Oxbridge security official who reminds the narrator that women are not permitted on the grass.

Mary Beton The narrator's aunt. Mary Beton leaves her niece five hundred pounds a year, securing her niece's financial independence. ("Mary Beton" is also one of the names Woolf assigns to her narrator.)

Mary Carmichael A fictitious novelist. The narrator of the essay analyzes Mary Carmichael's novel, which she thinks has "broke[n] the sentence . . . broken the sequence," and changed the course of women's writing.

The Narrator The fictionalized narrator of the essay. Like Woolf, the narrator is a writer who lives on an inheritance.

Mary Seton A student at Fernham College. Mary Seton is a friend of the narrator.

Judith Shakespeare The imagined sister of William Shakespeare. Judith Shakespeare suffers greatly and eventually commits suicide because she can find no socially acceptable outlets for her genius.

THEMES IN *A ROOM OF ONE'S OWN*

THE MUTUAL EXCLUSIVITY OF POVERTY AND CREATIVITY Woolf's central contention is a revolutionary one because it contradicts what was then a common assumption: that women are inherently stupider than men. Woolf argues that there are so few great women writers not because women are less creative and intelligent than men, but because the economic conditions of their lives make writing impossible. In order to write, Woolf says, people need leisure, privacy, and financial independence—all things that have been denied to women throughout history. Not all men enjoyed these conditions, but all upper-class men did, as did many middle-class and some talented lower-class men. Certainly no men were expected to tend babies or clean houses. For women, even wealthy women, achieving leisure, privacy, and financial independence was almost always impossible.

With this argument, Woolf debunks the notion that artists live in a dream world, hardly noticing what they eat or where they live because they are so obsessed with their creations. On the contrary, she points out, artists can only ignore their surroundings when they are comfortable ones. When Woolf's narrator visits the underfunded women's college at Oxbridge, she notes the bad food and unpleasant décor, elements that inspire anxiety in the students. She also notes that the women who work at the college are constantly worrying about funding and so are unable to devote themselves to loftier concerns.

THE DAMAGING EFFECT OF INSTITUTIONALIZED SEXISM Women need a literal room of their own: a place to write and the time to write in it. They also need a metaphorical room of their own: intellectual and educational freedom, and a respected spot in the world of literature. The people in charge of centers of learning like libraries and universities must recognize that women belong there and that they have as much right to knowledge as men do. When Woolf's narrator visits Oxbridge, a fictional amalgam of Oxford and Cambridge, the two great English universities, she is treated like a second-class citizen because she is a woman. She is not allowed to walk on the lawn, which is reserved for male Fellows and Scholars of the college. She is not allowed to enter the university library by herself. In general, she is shown that Oxbridge does not respect women or believe that they should be part of intellectual discourse. Woolf suggests that this attitude damages budding women writers, forcing them to navigate a morass of sexist rules when they should be navigating their own writing in peace.

THE INCOMPATIBILITY OF RAGE AND GREAT LITERATURE Woolf thinks that the best literature comes from writers whose incandescent minds burn away the writer's personal biases and resentments in the purifying flame of creativity. She argues that authors should not have a personal agenda when they write, and their novels should not contain any traces of protest, complaint, or vengefulness. This objectivity is difficult for all writers to achieve, but for women writers it is almost impossible. Financial security and physical comfort allow men writers to lose themselves and their petty concerns as they work, but women writers are constantly interrupted and threatened by poverty, lack of privacy, limited access to education, and contempt and condescension. These factors make it nearly impossible for them to forget their own lives as they write. Also, they are constantly aware that as women writers, they are bizarre creatures in the eyes of men writers. They constantly feel that they have something to prove, which causes resentment, self-righteousness, and insecurity to seep into their writing. As an example, Woolf holds up Charlotte Brontë, whom she considers a genius, but whose writing she thinks is marred by Brontë's passionate outrage at the oppression of women. Of Brontë, she writes, "she will never get her genius expressed whole and entire. Her books will be deformed and twisted. She will write in a rage where she should write calmly. She will write foolishly where she should write wisely. She will write of herself where she should write of her characters. She is at war with her lot. How could she help but die young, cramped, and thwarted?"

SYMBOLS IN *A ROOM OF ONE'S OWN*

THE TURF AT OXBRIDGE The plot of grass that the narrator walks on before being chased back onto the path by a wildly gesticulating beadle symbolizes the intellectual territory forbidden to women. Oxbridge is an ancient bastion of male learning that has produced hundreds of brilliant writers and intellectuals, and it is loathe to accept women. Its sanctity as a male institution is guarded so closely that a woman can't even stray onto its grass without fear of punishment. The narrator's reception at Oxbridge suggests the general reception of women by academia.

THE BRITISH MUSEUM In English literary culture, the British Museum symbolizes truth, fairness, and easy access to knowledge. When Woolf goes there to research women and fiction, however, she finds that the British Museum is full of books that perpetuate lies about women's writing and women's history. In *A Room of One's Own*, the British Museum symbolizes not truth but the way fiction frequently masquerades as fact.

IMPORTANT QUOTATIONS FROM *A ROOM OF ONE'S OWN*

> [F]iction is like a spider's web, attached ever so lightly perhaps, but still attached to life at all four corners. Often the attachment is scarcely perceptible; Shakespeare's plays, for instance, seem to hang there complete by themselves. But when the web is pulled askew, hooked up at the edge, torn in the middle, one remembers that these webs are not spun in mid-air by incorporeal creatures, but are the work of suffering human beings, and are attached to grossly material things, like health and money and the houses we live in.

Location: Chapter 3
Speaker: The narrator
Context: The narrator speaks of the relationship between art and the everyday

In this passage, Woolf explains how easy it is to forget that fiction does not exist separately from the sordid details of everyday life. Shakespeare's masterpieces seem to hang "complete by themselves" like a spider web—a totally false illusion that is the goal of art. We forget about the circumstances that make this illusion possible: access to education, the ability to pursue theatrical ambitions without harassment or molestation, the chance to earn a living by writing, and the funds to pay for a place to write. Writers become great and produce seemingly freestanding work only when they have material comforts. Yet when we read great writing, we do not consider that it is only great because the writer had the time and resources he needed. Woolf suggests that women will be able to produce masterpieces that seem to float above everyday life only when their minds are freed from worry about "health and money and the houses we live in."

All women together ought to let flowers fall on the tomb of Aphra Behn, which is, most scandalously but rather appropriately, in Westminster Abbey, for it was she who earned them the right to speak their minds.

Location: Chapter 4
Speaker: The narrator
Context: Woolf writes of Behn's contribution

In Chapter 4, Woolf describes the progress made by women writers since the seventeenth century. Until Aphra Behn, Woolf says, English women wrote with a certain degree of shame, not wanting to publish or to be known as women authors. Writing was thought of as a "sign of folly and a distracted mind," or at best a frivolous pastime. Behn, a middle-class woman, made a living by publishing her writing and selling her plays for production. The fact that she made money with her writing proved its worth in the eyes of some. Because of Behn, writing became a viable profession for women, and publishing became more common.

Woolf believes a female literary tradition is of crucial importance. Behn, among other writers mentioned in Chapter 4, has done an immeasurable service for the women who came after her. The "foremothers" of Woolf and her contemporaries provide not only literary models, but spiritual ones: they show exemplary disdain for social and financial barriers. Woolf says that Behn earned "all women," not just women writers, the right to speak their minds. Woolf's inclusion of "all women" in the group that Behn has liberated suggests that women who write fiction are in some way speaking for all the women in the world. As Woolf states in other parts of the essay, women experience life differently from men, and so fiction by men writers cannot describe the female experience. In writing and publishing fiction, women writers are enriching literature with the female experience, "speaking the minds" of generations of silent women.

A woman must have money and a room of her own if she is to write fiction.

Location: Chapter One
Speaker: The narrator
Context: Woolf articulates her primary argument

Of the two—the vote and the money—the money, I own, seemed infinitely the more important.

Location: Chapter Two
Speaker: The narrator
Context: The narrator talks about the vote and her inheritance

She wrote as a woman, but as a woman who has forgotten that she is a woman, so that her pages are full of that curious sexual quality which comes only when sex is unconscious of itself.

Location: Chapter 5
Speaker: The narrator
Context: Woolf describes the style of Mary Carmichael, a fictional contemporary novelist

THE SCARLET LETTER

Nathaniel Hawthorne

A married woman living in Puritan Boston has an affair with a preacher, which leads to her public disgrace and his death.

THE LIFE OF NATHANIEL HAWTHORNE

Nathaniel Hawthorne was born in Salem, Massachusetts, in 1804. His family descended from the earliest settlers of the Massachusetts Bay Colony. Among his forebears was John Hathorne (Hawthorne added the "w" to his name when he began to write), one of the judges at the 1692 Salem witch trials. Throughout his life, Hawthorne was both fascinated and disturbed by his kinship with John Hathorne. Hawthorne's father died when Hawthorne was two. His widowed mother raised him on a lonely farm in Maine. Hawthorne attended Bowdoin College, where he met two people who were to have great impact upon his life: Henry Wadsworth Longfellow, who would later become a famous poet, and Franklin Pierce, who would later become president of the United States.

After college, Hawthorne tried his hand at writing, producing historical sketches and an anonymous novel, *Fanshawe*, that detailed his college days rather embarrassingly. He also held positions as an editor and as a customs surveyor. He was part of the intellectual circle that included Ralph Waldo Emerson and Margaret Fuller, an association that led him to abandon his customs post for the utopian experiment at Brook Farm, a commune designed to promote economic self-sufficiency and transcendentalist principles.

After marrying fellow transcendentalist Sophia Peabody in 1842, Hawthorne left Brook Farm and moved into the Old Manse, a home in Concord where Emerson had once lived. In 1846, he published *Mosses from an Old Manse*, a collection of essays and stories that earned him the attention of the literary establishment. America was trying to establish cultural independence to complement its political independence, and Hawthorne's collection of stories displayed both a stylistic freshness and an interest in American subject matter. Herman Melville, among others, hailed Hawthorne as the "American Shakespeare."

In 1845, Hawthorne again went to work as a customs surveyor, this time, like the narrator of *The Scarlet Letter*, at a post in Salem. In 1850, after having lost the job, he published *The Scarlet Letter* to enthusiastic, if not widespread, acclaim. His other major novels include *The House of the Seven Gables* (1851), *The Blithedale Romance* (1852), and *The Marble Faun* (1860). In 1853, Hawthorne's college friend Franklin Pierce, now president, appointed Hawthorne a United States consul. Hawthorne spent the next six years in Europe. He died in 1864, a few years after returning to America.

THE SCARLET LETTER IN CONTEXT

The Scarlet Letter, like the majority of Hawthorne's work, takes America's Puritan past as its subject. The Puritans were a group of religious reformers who arrived in Massachusetts in the 1630s under the leadership of John Winthrop, whose death is recounted in Hawthorne's novel. Puritans were known for their intolerance of ideas and lifestyles different from their own. In *The Scarlet Letter*, Hawthorne suggests that the repressive, judgmental Puritans are like humankind in general. The Puritans' reaction to Hester, Dimmesdale, and Chillingworth is a universal statement about the way all societies react to that which they fear or secretly desire.

THE SCARLET LETTER: KEY FACTS

Time and place written: Late 1840s; Salem and Concord, Massachusetts

Date of first publication: 1850

Publisher: Ticknor, Reed, and Fields

Type of work: Novel

Genre: Allegory

Language: English

Setting (time): Mid-seventeenth century

Setting (place): Boston, Massachusetts

Tense: Past, occasionally present

Tone: Contemplative, bitter, straightforward, ironic

Narrator: An omniscient, unnamed customhouse surveyor in the first person, who writes some two hundred years after the events he describes took place

Point of view: The narrator's

Protagonist: Hester Prynne

Antagonist: The community

THE SCARLET LETTER: PLOT OVERVIEW

The Scarlet Letter opens with a long explanation of how the book came to be written. The nameless narrator explains that he used to work as the surveyor of a customhouse in Salem, Massachusetts. In the customhouse's attic, he discovered a number of documents, among them a manuscript bundled with a scarlet, gold-embroidered patch of cloth in the shape of an A. The manuscript, the work of a past surveyor, details events that occurred about two hundred years before the narrator's time. When the narrator lost his customs post, he decided to write a fictional account of the events recorded in the manuscript. *The Scarlet Letter* is that fictional account.

The story begins in seventeenth-century Boston, then a Puritan settlement. A young woman, Hester Prynne, is led from the town prison with her infant daughter, Pearl, in her arms and the scarlet letter A on her breast. A man in the crowd tells an elderly onlooker that Hester is being punished for adultery. Hester's husband, a scholar much older than she is, sent her ahead to America, but he never arrived in Boston. People assume he has been lost at sea. In her husband's absence, Hester had an affair and gave birth to a child. She will not reveal her lover's identity, and the scarlet letter is her punishment for sinning and keeping a secret. Hester is now led to the town scaffold and harangued by the town fathers, but she still refuses to identify her child's father.

The elderly onlooker is Hester's missing husband, who is now practicing medicine and calling himself Roger Chillingworth. He settles in Boston, intent on revenge. He reveals his true identity to no one but Hester, and swears her to secrecy. Several years pass. Hester supports herself by working as a seamstress, and Pearl grows into a willful, impish child. Shunned by the community, they live in a small cottage on the outskirts of Boston. Community officials attempt to take Pearl away from Hester, but Hester fends them off with the help of Arthur Dimmesdale, a young minister, and mother and daughter manage to stay together.

Dimmesdale, who suffers from mysterious heart trouble, appears to be wasting away. Chillingworth attaches himself to the ailing minister and eventually moves in with him so that he can provide his patient with round-the-clock care. Chillingworth suspects a connection between the minister's torments and Hester's secret, and he begins to test Dimmesdale to see what he can learn. One afternoon, while the minister sleeps, Chillingworth discovers a mark on the man's breast (the details of which are kept from the reader), which convinces him that his suspicions are correct. Dimmesdale's psychological anguish deepens, and he invents new tortures for himself.

Hester's charitable deeds and quiet humility have earned the approval of the community. One night, when Pearl is about seven years old, she and her mother are returning home from a visit to a deathbed when they encounter Dimmesdale atop the town scaffold, trying to punish himself for his sins. Hester and Pearl join him, and the three link hands. Pearl asks Dimmesdale to acknowledge her publicly the next day. He refuses, and a meteor marks a dull red A in the night sky. Hester can see that the minister's condition is worsening, and she resolves to intervene. She goes to Chillingworth and asks him to stop adding to Dimmesdale's self-torment. Chillingworth refuses.

Hester and Dimmesdale meet in the forest and decide to flee to Europe, where they can live with Pearl as a family. They will leave in four days. Both feel a sense of release, and Hester removes her scarlet letter and lets down her hair. Pearl, playing nearby, does not recognize her mother without the letter. The day before the ship is set to sail, the townspeople gather for a holiday, and Dimmesdale preaches his most eloquent sermon ever. Hester has learned that Chillingworth knows of their plan and has booked passage on the same ship. Dimmesdale, leaving the church after his sermon, sees Hester and Pearl standing before the town scaffold. He impulsively mounts the scaffold with his lover and daughter, and confesses publicly, exposing a scarlet letter seared into the flesh of his chest. He falls dead as Pearl kisses him.

Frustrated in his revenge, Chillingworth dies a year later. Hester and Pearl leave Boston. Many years later, Hester returns alone, still wearing the scarlet letter, to live in her old cottage and resume her charitable work. She receives occasional letters from Pearl, who has married a European aristocrat and established a family of her own. When Hester dies, she is buried next to Dimmesdale. The two share a single tombstone, which bears a scarlet A.

CHARACTERS IN *THE SCARLET LETTER*

Governor Bellingham A wealthy, elderly gentleman who resembles a traditional English aristocrat. Bellingham tends to adhere strictly to rules, but he is easily swayed by Dimmesdale's eloquence.

Roger Chillingworth Hester's husband in disguise. Chillingworth takes deep pleasure in discovering and tormenting Hester's lover. He is self-absorbed and both physically and psychologically monstrous.

Reverend Arthur Dimmesdale Hester's lover. Dimmesdale achieved fame in England as a theologian and then emigrated to America. He is an intelligent and emotional man, and his sermons are masterpieces of eloquence and persuasiveness. His commitment to his congregation constantly conflicts with his guilt and need to confess.

Mistress Hibbins A widow who lives with her brother, Governor Bellingham, in a luxurious mansion. As everyone but Governor Bellingham knows, Mistress Hibbins is a witch who ventures into the forest at night to ride with the "Black Man."

Narrator The unnamed narrator of the story. He is a rather high-strung man who feels guilty about his writing career. He writes because he is interested in American history and because he believes that America needs to understand its religious and moral heritage.

Pearl Hester's illegitimate daughter. Pearl is moody and mischievous. She quickly perceives secrets. The townspeople say she hardly seems human, and they spread rumors that the Devil fathered her.

Hester Prynne The novel's protagonist. Hester is passionate and strong, patiently enduring years of shame and scorn. She equals both her husband and her lover in intelligence. Her alienation distances her from the community and enables her to make acute observations about it, particularly about its treatment of women.

Reverend Mr. John Wilson Boston's elder clergyman. Reverend Wilson is scholarly and grandfatherly, a stereotypical Puritan father. Like Governor Bellingham, Wilson follows the community's rules strictly but can be swayed by Dimmesdale's eloquence. Unlike Dimmesdale, his junior colleague, Wilson preaches hellfire and damnation, and advocates harsh punishment of sinners.

THEMES IN *THE SCARLET LETTER*

THE BENEFITS OF SIN Sin and knowledge are linked in the Judeo-Christian tradition. The story of Hester and Dimmesdale recalls the story of Adam and Eve, who were expelled from the Garden of Eden because they sinned by eating from the tree of knowledge. Once expelled, they were forced to toil and to procreate—two labors that define the human condition. For Hester and Dimmesdale, as for Adam and Eve, sin results in expulsion and suffering, but also in knowledge. For Hester, the scarlet letter is a "passport into regions where other women dared not tread." Wearing it alienates her from the townspeople, leading her to "speculate" about her society and herself more "boldly" than anyone else in New England. Sin also makes Hester and Dimmesdale better people. The "burden" of sin gives Dimmesdale "sympathies so intimate with the sinful brotherhood of mankind." His sin makes him an effective preacher, inspiring him to give eloquent and powerful sermons. Most members of Puritan society hide their sins or convince themselves that they are sinless, which makes them pinched, judgmental, and cruel. Because Hester and Dimmesdale are forced to admit to their sins, they become humble and empathetic, as Puritans are supposed to be.

THE NATURE OF EVIL Hawthorne argues that evil is extremely confusing because it is not, as many people assume, the polar opposite of good. Instead, evil springs from the combination of hate and love. As the narrator points out in the novel's concluding chapter, both emotions depend upon "a high degree of intimacy and heart-knowledge; each renders one individual dependent . . . upon another." Chillingworth exemplifies the evil that results from love and hate. He first loves Hester and then comes to hate her after discovering her adultery, a combination that perverts him and inspires him to plot a careful, poisonous revenge. Because it is not the product of mixed hate and love, Hester and Dimmesdale's lovemaking is not evil. For the same reason, the cruel ignorance of the Puritan fathers is unfortunate rather than evil.

IDENTITY AND SOCIETY Hester insists on determining her own identity instead of letting others determine it for her. This is why she stays in Boston even after the townspeople publicly shame her and force her to wear a badge of humiliation. Leaving Boston would allow her to remove the scarlet letter and resume a normal life, but she feels that leaving would be an acknowledgment of society's power over her, an admission that the letter has succeeded in chastening her. By staying and doing charitable works, she tells the public that she has sinned, she has made the sin part of her identity, and she is a good person despite their expectations. Dimmesdale also struggles to resist society's defining impulses. As the community's minister, he is more symbol than human being. Except for Chillingworth, everyone ignores Dimmesdale's obvious anguish, misinterpreting it as holiness. But Dimmesdale never learns what Hester does: that sinning does not mean you must reject your identity wholesale, merely that you must redefine it.

SYMBOLS IN *THE SCARLET LETTER*

THE SCARLET LETTER The scarlet letter symbolizes different things for different characters. For the townspeople, it symbolizes Hester's shame. For Hester, it becomes a powerful symbol of identity. The letter's meaning shifts as time passes. Originally intended to mark Hester as an adulterer, the A eventually stands for "Able." The Native Americans who come to watch the Election Day pageant think it marks Hester as a person of importance. Like Pearl, the letter functions as a physical reminder of Hester's affair with Dimmesdale. But, compared with a human child, the letter seems insignificant and underlines the ultimate meaninglessness of the community's system of judgment and punishment.

PEARL Although Pearl is a complex character, she functions primarily as a symbol. Only after Dimmesdale admits that he is Pearl's father can Pearl can become fully human. Until then, she symbolizes unsolved mystery and sin. Pearl is a living version of Hester's scarlet letter, the physical consequence of sexual sin and the indicator of a transgression. Yet, even as a reminder of Hester's "sin," Pearl is more than a mere punishment to her mother: she is also a blessing. She represents not only sin but the vital spirit and passion that inspired Hester's adultery. Pearl gives her mother reason to live, bolstering her spirits when she is tempted to give up.

IMPORTANT QUOTATIONS FROM *THE SCARLET LETTER*

"A writer of story-books! What kind of a business in life,—what mode of glorifying God, or being serviceable to mankind in his day and generation,—may that be? Why, the degenerate fellow might as well have been a fiddler!" Such are the compliments bandied between my great-grandsires and myself, across the gulf of time! And yet, let them scorn me as they will, strong traits of their nature have intertwined themselves with mine.

Location: The introduction
Speaker: The narrator
Context: The narrator worries that writing, his avocation, is frivolous

The narrator descended from the original Puritan settlers of Massachusetts, so his interest in Hester Prynne's story is personal for that reason. Like Hester, the narrator both affirms and resists Puritan values. He is driven to write, yet the Puritan in him sees the frivolity in such an endeavor, worrying that his work does nothing to benefit God or society. His anxiety about the conflict between individual impulses and social codes is the same anxiety that haunts Hester's story. The narrator finds Hester Prynne compelling because she represents America's past, but also because her experiences reflect his own dilemmas. Thus, for the narrator, writing about Hester is a way of understanding himself and his social context.

But Hester Prynne, with a mind of native courage and activity, and for so long a period not merely estranged, but outlawed, from society, had habituated herself to such latitude of speculation as was altogether foreign to the clergyman. She had wandered, without rule or guidance, in a moral wilderness. . . . The scarlet letter was her passport into regions where other women dared not tread. Shame, Despair, Solitude! These had been her teachers,—stern and wild ones,—and they had made her strong, but taught her much amiss.

Location: Chapter XVIII, "A Flood of Sunshine"
Speaker: The narrator
Context: Hester and Dimmesdale decide to run away to Europe together

During their first significant conversation in many years, Hester and Dimmesdale decide to run away to Europe together. This decision shocks the minister, but Hester accepts it with relative equanimity. One result of her "sin" has been her profound alienation from society—she has been forced into the role of philosopher, and the idea of leaving the society she has observed with dispassion does not shock her as it does Dimmesdale, who has none of her distance or objectivity. It is ironic that Hester's punishment, which was intended to make her apologetic, conventional, and eager to follow society's rules, has instead led her into a "moral wilderness" devoid of "rule or guidance."

"Mother," said little Pearl, "the sunshine does not love you. It runs away and hides itself, because it is afraid of something on your bosom.. . . It will not flee from me, for I wear nothing on my bosom yet!"
"Nor ever will, my child, I hope," said Hester.
"And why not, mother?" asked Pearl, stopping short.. . . "Will it not come of its own accord, when I am a woman grown?"

Location: Chapter XVI, "A Forest Walk"
Speaker: The narrator
Context: Pearl innocently, or perhaps with intentional cruelty, asks her mother about the scarlet letter

---

"Mother," said [Pearl], "was that the same minister that kissed me by the brook?"
"Hold thy peace, dear little Pearl!" whispered her mother. "We must not always talk in the market-place of what happens to us in the forest."

Location: Chapter XXII
Speaker: The narrator
Context: Pearl sees Dimmesdale walk by

But there was a more real life for Hester Prynne here, in New England, than in that unknown region where Pearl had found a home. Here had been her sin; here, her sorrow; and here was yet to be her penitence. She had returned, therefore, and resumed,—of her own free will, for not the sternest magistrate of that iron period would have imposed it,—resumed the symbol of which we have related so dark a tale. Never afterwards did it quit her bosom. But . . . the scarlet letter ceased to be a stigma which attracted the world's scorn and bitterness, and became a type of something to be sorrowed over, and looked upon with awe, and yet with reverence, too.

Location: The final chapter
Speaker: The narrator
Context: Hester's letter becomes a symbol of redemption rather than a symbol of sin

SENSE AND SENSIBILITY

Jane Austen

Two sisters mature and find husbands.

THE LIFE OF JANE AUSTEN

Jane Austen, whom some critics consider England's best novelist, was born in 1775 in Steventon, a small town in the southwest of England. The seventh of eight children, she lived with her family for her entire life, first in Steventon and later in Bath, Southampton, and Chawton. Her father was a parish rector. Although not wealthy, Austen's family was well connected and well educated. Austen briefly attended boarding school in Reading but received the majority of her education at home. According to rumor, she had a brief love affair when she was twenty-five, but it did not lead to a marriage proposal. Two years later, she accepted and then quickly rejected a proposal. She never married. In 1817, Austen died of what was probably Addison's disease, at age forty-one.

Austen began writing stories at a very young age and completed her first novel in her early twenties. However, she did not publish until 1811, when *Sense and Sensibility* appeared anonymously, followed by *Pride and Prejudice* (1813) and *Mansfield Park* (1814). *Emma*, published in 1816, was the last novel published during Austen's lifetime. (*Northanger Abbey* and *Persuasion* appeared posthumously.)

Austen's novels received little critical or popular recognition during her lifetime, and her identity as a novelist was not revealed until after her death. She wrote during the Romantic period, but her satirical novels have little to do with the passionate intensity and individuality that interested the Romantics. Critics have pointed out that the Romantics were almost exclusively male, and women with literary ambitions were excluded from the movement. While male writers such as Percy Bysshe Shelley and Lord Byron were free to promote their own individuality through wide travel and sexual and military adventurism, women were largely denied these freedoms. For women, the penalty for excessive freedom was social ostracism and poverty.

In this social context, Austen's commitment to reason and moderation can be seen as feminist and progressive rather than conservative. With intelligence and resourcefulness, her heroines push the limits of their constricted world of courtship and marriage.

SENSE AND SENSIBILITY IN CONTEXT

Austen always had trouble finding a publisher for her novels. She paid to print *Sense and Sensibility*, her first novel, at considerable financial risk. Luckily, the novel was successful, and Austen made 140 pounds from its publication.

Sense and Sensibility is unique among Austen's novels for its direct engagement with Romanticism, the movement that dominated Austen's era. In creating the character of Marianne Dashwood, a near-parody of a Romantic heroine, Austen displays a thorough understanding of Romantic literature, values, and aesthetics. She warns against the excesses of the movement, which advocated individual freedom, passion, and intensity, and allies herself with the values of the eighteenth century, otherwise known as the Age of Reason, when literature glorified wit, poise, and propriety.

SENSE AND SENSIBILITY: KEY FACTS

Time and place written: 1797–1798, 1809–10; Steventon and Chawton

Date of first publication: 1811

Publisher: Thomas Egerton

Type of work: Novel

Genre: Satire

Language: English

Setting (time): The end of the eighteenth century

Setting (place): England, in Devonshire and London

Tone: Dry, ironic, detached

Tense: Past

Narrator: Anonymous, omniscient narrator in the third person

Point of view: The narrator's

Protagonist: Elinor Dashwood

Antagonist: Extreme romanticism and hasty judgment

SENSE AND SENSIBILITY: SUMMARY

When Mr. Henry Dashwood dies, leaving all his money to John Dashwood, his son by his first wife, his second wife and her three daughters are left with no permanent home and very little income. John promised his father to provide for them, but he quickly justifies giving them very little after the death of Mr. Dashwood. Mrs. Dashwood and her daughters Elinor, Marianne, and Margaret are invited to stay with their distant relations, the Middletons, at Barton Park. Elinor is sad to leave their home at Norland. She has grown close to Edward Ferrars, the brother-in-law of her half-brother John Dashwood.

At Barton Park, Elinor and Marianne make many new acquaintances, including the retired officer and bachelor Colonel Brandon and the gallant and impetuous John Willoughby, who rescues Marianne after she twists her ankle. Willoughby openly courts Marianne, and together the two flaunt their attachment to one another. One day, Willoughby suddenly announces that he must go to London on business, leaving Marianne lovesick and miserable. Anne and Lucy Steele, two recently discovered relations of Lady Middleton's mother, Mrs. Jennings, arrive at Barton Park as guests of the Middletons. Lucy ingratiates herself to Elinor and informs her that she (Lucy) has been secretly engaged to Mr. Ferrars for a year. Elinor initially assumes that Lucy is referring to Edward's younger brother, Robert, but is shocked and pained to learn that Lucy is actually referring to her own beloved Edward.

In Volume II of the novel, Elinor and Marianne travel to London with Mrs. Jennings. Colonel Brandon informs Elinor that everyone in London is talking of an engagement between Willoughby and Marianne, although Marianne has not announced any engagement. Marianne is anxious to be reunited with Willoughby, but when she sees him at a party in town, he cruelly rebuffs her and then sends her a letter denying that he ever had feelings for her. Colonel Brandon tells Elinor that Willoughby has a history of callousness and debauchery. Mrs. Jennings says that Willoughby, having squandered his fortune, has become engaged to the wealthy heiress Miss Grey.

In Volume III, Lucy's older sister inadvertently reveals that Lucy is engaged to Edward Ferrars. Outraged at the news, Edward's mother disinherits him, promising his fortune to Robert. The Dashwood sisters visit family friends at Cleveland on their way home from London. At Cleveland, Marianne develops a severe cold while taking long walks in the rain and falls deathly ill. After hearing of her illness, Willoughby comes to visit, attempting to explain his misconduct. Elinor pities him, and Marianne realizes that she behaved imprudently with Willoughby and could never have been happy with him. Mrs. Dashwood and Colonel Brandon arrive at Cleveland and are relieved to learn that Marianne has begun to recover.

The Dashwoods return to Barton. Edward Ferrars visits and explains that Lucy was only interested in his money and has decided to marry his brother Robert. Edward proposes to Elinor. Not long after, Marianne and Colonel Brandon become engaged. The couples live together at Delaford and remain in close touch with their mother and younger sister at Barton Cottage.

CHARACTERS IN *SENSE AND SENSIBILITY*

Colonel Brandon A retired officer and friend of Sir John Middleton. Colonel Brandon falls in love with Marianne Dashwood. He always treats the Dashwoods kindly, honorably, and graciously.

Elinor Dashwood The protagonist of the novel. Elinor is the nineteen-year-old eldest daughter of Mr. and Mrs. Henry Dashwood. She is composed but affectionate, both when she falls in love with Edward Ferrars and when she comforts and supports her younger sister Marianne.

Fanny Dashwood John Dashwood's wife. Fanny is selfish, snobbish, and manipulative. She is the sister of Edward and Robert Ferrars.

Henry Dashwood The father of John Dashwood and, by his second marriage, of Elinor, Marianne, and Margaret Dashwood. He dies in the opening chapter of the novel, bequeathing his estate at Norland to his son.

John Dashwood Henry Dashwood's son. John is weak-minded and money-grubbing. Heeding the advice of his wife, Fanny, he disobeys the promise he made to his father on his deathbed and gives almost no money to his late father's wife and daughters.

Margaret Dashwood The youngest daughter of Mr. and Mrs. Henry Dashwood. Margaret, a good-humored thirteen-year-old, shares Marianne's romantic tendencies.

Marianne Dashwood The second daughter of Mr. and Mrs. Henry Dashwood. Marianne is seventeen years old. Her spontaneity, excessive sensibility, and romantic idealism lead her to fall in love with John Willoughby. After her spurns her, she marries her admirer, Colonel Brandon.

Mrs. Dashwood The kind and loving mother of Elinor, Marianne, and Margaret. Mrs. Dashwood is Henry Dashwood's second wife. She wants the best for her daughters and shares Marianne's romantic sensibilities.

Mrs. Ferrars The mother of Edward and Robert. Mrs. Ferrars is a wealthy, manipulative woman who disinherits Edward when he refuses to marry a rich heiress.

Edward Ferrars The older brother of Fanny Dashwood and Robert Ferrars. Edward, a sensible and friendly man, proposes to Elinor after he is freed from a four-year engagement to Lucy Steele.

Robert Ferrars The younger brother of Edward and Fanny. Robert is a conceited coxcomb. At the end of the novel, he marries Lucy Steele.

Miss Sophia Grey The wealthy heiress whom Willoughby marries after abandoning Marianne.

Mrs. Jennings Lady Middleton's mother. Mrs. Jennings, a gossipy but well-intentioned woman, invites the Dashwood sisters to stay with her in London and makes it her "project" to marry them off as soon as possible.

Lady Middleton A distant relation of the Dashwoods. Lady Middleton lives at Barton Cottage with her husband, Sir John Middleton, and their four spoiled children.

Sir John Middleton A distant relation of the Dashwoods. A jovial but vulgar man, he invites Mrs. Dashwood and her daughters to stay at Barton Cottage after Mr. and Mrs. John Dashwood inherit Norland, leaving the women homeless.

Mr. Thomas Palmer Mrs. Palmer's gruff, unemotional husband.

Mrs. Charlotte Palmer Mrs. Jennings's daughter. Mrs. Palmer, a talkative and foolish woman, invites the Dashwood sisters to stay at her home in Cleveland on their way from London to Barton.

Anne Steele Lucy Steele's older, unmarried sister. Anne accidentally reveals her sister's secret engagement to Edward Ferrars.

Lucy Steele Mrs. Jennings's cousin. Lucy is a sly, selfish, insecure young woman. She breaks her secret, four-year engagement to Edward Ferrars after Edward is disinherited, and instead marries his brother, Robert.

John Willoughby An attractive but deceitful young man. Willoughby wins Marianne Dashwood's heart but then abandons her for the wealthy Miss Sophia Grey.

THEMES IN *SENSE AND SENSIBILITY*

THE IMPORTANCE OF BALANCING SENSE AND SENSIBILITY   Although Austen seems to favor sense (calm and wisdom, as embodied by Elinor) over sensibility (excess feeling and sentimentality, as embodied by Marianne and her mother), she warns against succumbing to an excess of either. By satirizing the impractical dreams and ludicrous pronouncements of Romantic characters like Marianne and Willoughby, Austen criticizes the Romantic movement that they represent. Marianne refuses to understand the practical, material aspects of life, insisting on the existence of perfect romance. This insistence blinds her to Willoughby's flaws and Colonel Brandon's virtues. Her stereotypically romantic love of rambling through sublime natural landscapes results in injury and even life-threatening illness. In the end, Marianne discovers that prudence and self-restraint are as important as expressing one's emotions and observing glorious landscapes.

Although Austen criticizes Marianne, she does not denounce her. Marianne is a genuinely goodhearted, loving person, and although her emotions are exaggerated, they are also authentic. Austen criticizes characters with an overly pragmatic attitude as much as, if not more than, she criticizes characters with too much sensibility. John Dashwood and his wife, for example, place too much emphasis on material, practical matters and not enough on emotion or sentimentality. Their obsession with money and their lack of sympathy for their relatives makes them ridiculous figures. Elinor's common sense and restraint is a little excessive, but even she does not lack sensibility. She appreciates nature and art, and her emotions are as powerful as any romantic heroine's—she just knows how to control them. Eventually, both sisters learn to balance sense with sensibility.

THE DANGER OF LEAPING TO CONCLUSIONS   Much of the plot of *Sense and Sensibility* revolves around misunderstandings. At the beginning of the novel, everyone assumes that Elinor and Edward are engaged. Later, everyone assumes that Marianne and Willoughby are engaged, or will be very soon. There is confusion about which Ferrars brother Lucy Steele has married, and there are a variety of misunderstandings about Colonel Brandon's intentions toward Elinor and Marianne. Many of these misunderstandings result when people make hasty judgments based on appearances instead of waiting patiently to find out the truth. Such hasty judgments, especially of character, are almost always erroneous. Marianne instantly judges Willoughby a passionate but faithful lover, while based on first impressions she dismisses Colonel Brandon for his age and Edward for his stodginess. After time passes, however, she reverses her judgments of all three men. Austen suggests that the best method is Elinor's, which requires waiting and observing before drawing conclusions.

THE INANE BEHAVIOR OF IDLE PEOPLE   *Sense and Sensibility* contains a good deal of social satire, much of it directed at the leisure classes living in the English countryside. When they move to Barton Cottage, the cultured Dashwood sisters are not entertained by their new neighbors despite the kind intentions of Sir Middleton and Mrs. Jennings. Most of the people they encounter have nothing to talk about. Sir Middleton talks exclusively about hunting, Lady Middleton talks only about her children, and Mrs. Jennings does nothing but tease the girls about getting married. The limited nature of the conversations reflects the idleness of the characters' lives: they have no employment or financial worry to occupy their time, so they fill it with idle chatter. Elinor and Marianne, though their social circles are as limited as the Middletons' or the Palmers', manage to avoid this inanity, possibly because they have less economic security than those families do. Elinor's precarious financial situation has forced her to become practical and sensible, and both Dashwood sisters manage to avoid idleness, choosing to occupy themselves with art and music instead of domestic prattle.

SYMBOLS IN *SENSE AND SENSIBILITY*

LOCKS OF HAIR   The lock of hair that Marianne gives to Willoughby symbolizes the danger of rushing headlong into love affairs. In Austen's day, giving a man a lock of hair was an intimate act, appropriate only if the woman was engaged to the man. By giving Willoughby a lock of hair, Marianne makes an implicit commitment to a man she does not really know. The locks of hair also symbolize the danger of judging by appearances. Marianne assumes that Edward's lock of hair belongs to his sister, when it actually belongs to Lucy. The Dashwoods assume that Marianne gave her lock of hair to Willoughby because they are engaged.

TREES In *Sense and Sensibility*, trees and shrubs symbolize the Romantic ideal. Romantic poets and painters identified strongly with the natural world and frequently depicted enchanted groves and awe-inspiring forests in their work. A character's attitudes toward trees—and nature in general—reveals how much his or her personality is dominated by sensibility. Marianne's worshipful attitude toward the trees at Norland reflects her passionate adherence to the Romantic movement. Elinor's more restrained appreciation for nature suggests her more balanced character. For the mercenary John and Fanny Dashwood, trees are not sacred at all, but simply possessions that can be cut down or moved around at will.

IMPORTANT QUOTATIONS FROM *SENSE AND SENSIBILITY*

The necessity of concealing from her mother and Marianne, what had been entrusted in confidence to herself, though it obliged her to unceasing exertion, was no aggravation of Elinor's distress. On the contrary it was a relief to her, to be spared the communication of what would give such affliction to them, and to be saved likewise from hearing that condemnation of Edward, which would probably flow from the excess of their partial affection for herself, and which was more than she felt equal to support.

Location: Chapter 23
Speaker: The narrator
Context: The narrator describes Elinor's relief at concealing her knowledge of Lucy Steele's engagement to Edward Ferrars

In this passage, Elinor is the extreme embodiment of "sense." She is relieved that a promise prevents her from telling her family about her troubles, a reaction that shows how different she is from Marianne, who makes her emotions known to almost anyone who will listen. On most occasions when Austen contrasts Elinor's behavior with Marianne's, Elinor's reason and restraint come off as more desirable qualities than Marianne's tendency to impulsively follow her emotions and proclaim her romantic ideals from the rooftops. Austen wants us to admire Elinor's restraint here too. Elinor remains calm even when she feels unhappy and betrayed. Many women would be happy to hear their mothers and sisters abuse a man who has misled them, but Elinor recognizes that Edward is a good man in an awkward situation and does not want to hear anything negative about him. She also wants to spare her family any unnecessary discomfort.

At the same time, this passage marks one of the few places in the novel where Austen suggests that Elinor has slightly too much sense for her own good. Understandably, Elinor does not feel "equal to support" her mother's and sister's condemnation of Edward, but we get the sense that neither is she equal to their "excess of emotion." Her desire for calm and privacy, even at the cost of keeping a painful secret and rejecting comfort from her family, suggests that Elinor might not be able to deal with strong emotions at all. Elinor is learning, painfully, how to allow sensibility into her life, just as Marianne must learn how to allow a little more sense into hers.

"Two thousand a-year"; and then working himself up to a pitch of enthusiastic generosity, he added, "Elinor, I wish, with all my heart, it were twice as much, for your sake."

Location: Chapter 33
Speaker: John Dashwood
Context: John thinks Elinor is going to marry Colonel Brandon and expresses his happiness about the riches the marriage will bring her

John Dashwood's statement exemplifies the unseemly practicality that results when a character lacks any sensibility or finer feeling. John's assumption—that money always equals happiness, that more money always equals more happiness, and that all a woman needs to know about her husband is that he is wealthy—is as naïve as Mrs. Dashwood's and Marianne's assumption that money and other practical concerns have no bearing on a woman's happiness. Throughout the novel, John's bald materialism and lack of empathy for his half-sisters makes him a ridiculous and unlikable character. Here he emphasizes his obliviousness by assuming that his past emotional and financial neglect of his sisters will be erased with one generous statement: that he wishes Elinor had four thousand pounds a year.

The character of John Dashwood also exemplifies the subtlety of Austen's satire. Austen wants the reader to laugh at John and feel contempt for him, but at the same time does not reduce him to a one-dimensional character. John does not have a strong personality, and so he has allowed his incredibly materialistic wife, Fanny, to influence him in all things, but he is not a terrible person. Most of his more callous statements and greedy actions stem from Fanny. He internalizes her beliefs so deeply that he forgets that they are her beliefs and assumes he has always held them himself. Some glimmer of nobler feelings remain, however: John did feel guilty for going against his father's wishes and failing to provide for his sisters, and he is genuinely happy to imagine that Elinor will be taken care of. He has accepted his wife's materialism so far, however, that the only way he can express that happiness is by congratulating Elinor on her future wealth.

And you, ye well-known trees! — but you will continue the same. — No leaf will decay because we are removed, nor any branch become motionless although we can observe you no longer! — No; you will continue the same; unconscious of the pleasure or the regret you occasion, and insensible of any change in those who walk under your shade! — But who will remain to enjoy you?

Location: Chapter 5
Speaker: Marianne
Context: Marianne prepares to leave her beloved childhood home

---

I have not wanted syllables where actions have spoken so plainly. Has not his behavior to Marianne and to all of us, for at least the last fortnight, declared that he loved and considered her as his future wife, and that he felt for us the attachment of the nearest relation? Have we not perfectly understood each other?

Location: Chapter 15
Speaker: Mrs. Dashwood
Context: Mrs. Dashwood asserts her confidence in Willoughby

[N]or could he even be brought to acknowledge the simple proposition of its being the finest child in the world.

Location: Chapter 36
Speaker: The narrator
Context: Mr. Palmer refuses to bend to the affectionate hysteria of his wife and mother-in-law

A SEPARATE PEACE

John Knowles

A private school student injures his best friend, whom he both loves and envies.

THE LIFE OF JOHN KNOWLES

John Knowles was born in 1926 in Fairmont, West Virginia. He attended Phillips Exeter Academy, an exclusive boarding school located in New Hampshire. After graduating from Exeter in 1945, he spent eight months as an Air Force cadet before enrolling at Yale University. After earning a bachelor's degree in 1949, Knowles spent seven years working as a journalist and freelance writer, traveling in Europe and publishing a number of short stories. He befriended the noted playwright Thornton Wilder, a fellow Yale alumnus, who encouraged him to write. In 1957, Knowles landed a job as an associate editor at *Holiday* magazine. Two years later, he published his first novel, *A Separate Peace*, to overwhelmingly favorable reviews. The commercial success of the book allowed him to devote himself to writing full time. Since 1960, he has published eight other novels, including *Peace Breaks Out*, the companion volume to *A Separate Peace*, and a number of stories. None has garnered the acclaim or audience that *A Separate Peace* enjoyed and continues to enjoy today. Knowles has served as a writer-in-residence at Princeton University and at the University of North Carolina, and he continues to lecture widely.

A SEPARATE PEACE IN CONTEXT

The plot and setting of *A Separate Peace* were largely inspired by Knowles's experiences at Exeter. Like Gene Forrester, one of the novel's two principal characters, Knowles was a student from the South studying in New Hampshire during World War II. Also like his characters, Knowles attended two summer sessions in 1943 and 1944, and even participated in a club whose new initiates had to jump out of a tall tree into a river—a club much like the "Super Suicide Society of the Summer Session" founded by Gene and his friend Finny in *A Separate Peace*. Knowles has told interviewers that he modeled Finny on a member of this club named David Hackett, who later served under Robert F. Kennedy in the Department of Justice.

Yet while much of the novel is inspired by Exeter, Knowles has always emphatically noted that his own high-school years, unlike his characters', were not plagued by envy, violence, or alienation. He has written that he thoroughly enjoyed his time at the school and sought to convey his love and appreciation for it in *A Separate Peace*. It is true that despite its dark tone and pessimistic view of the human condition, the novel paints a positive and even nostalgic portrait of boarding-school life. Unlike other accounts of boarding-school culture, such as *Dead Poets Society* and *Scent of a Woman*, which have portrayed the educational system itself as an oppressive force, Knowles blames his characters, not their school, for their difficulties.

A SEPARATE PEACE: KEY FACTS

Time and place written: 1957–58; New England	
Date of first publication: 1959	
Publisher: Macmillan	
Type of work: Novel	
Genre: Bildungsroman	
Language: English	
Setting (time): The story begins in 1958 but quickly flashes back to the years 1942–43	
Setting (place): The Devon School, an exclusive New England academy	
Tense: Past	

Tone: Nostalgic, brooding, melancholy

Narrator: Gene Forrester in the first person

Point of view: Gene's

Protagonist: Gene

Antagonist: Gene's resentment

A SEPARATE PEACE: PLOT OVERVIEW

Gene Forrester is a quiet, intellectual student at Devon School in New Hampshire. During the summer session of 1942, he becomes close friends with his daredevil roommate Finny, whose charisma allows him to get away with mischief. Finny prods Gene into making a dangerous jump from a tree into a river, and the two start a secret society based on this ritual. Finny has astonishing athletic abilities—he breaks a school swimming record on his first try. Gene envies Finny's athleticism and thinks that Finny, in turn, envies his own superior academic achievements. He suspects Finny has been trying to distract him from his studies. Gene's suspicions turn into resentful hatred, but he carefully pretends that he still likes Finny.

One day, Finny expresses a sincere desire to see Gene succeed, and Gene realizes that the rivalry between them existed only in his own imagination. While still in a state of shock from the force of this realization, he accompanies Finny to the tree for their jumping ritual. When Finny reaches the edge of the branch, Gene's knees bend, shaking the branch and causing Finny to fall to the bank and shatter his leg. The tragedy is generally considered an accident, and no one thinks to blame Gene—especially not Finny. But when the doctor tells Gene that Finny's athletic days are over, Gene feels piercing guilt. He goes to see Finny and begins to admit his part in Finny's fall, but the doctor interrupts him, and Gene does not confess.

The summer session ends, and Gene goes home to the South for a brief vacation. On his way back to school, he stops by Finny's house and explains to his friend that he shook the branch on purpose. Finny refuses to listen to him, and Gene takes back his confession and continues on to school. Gene tries to avoid actual athletic activity by becoming assistant manager of the crew team, but he feuds with the crew manager and quits. World War II is in full swing, and the boys at Devon are all eager to enlist in the military. Brinker Hadley, a prominent class politician, suggests to Gene that they enlist together, and Gene agrees. That night, however, he finds Finny has returned to school. He consequently abandons his plans to enlist, as does Brinker. Finny expects Gene to take his place as the school's sports star now that he is injured. When Gene protests that sports don't seem important in the midst of a war, Finny says the war is nothing but a conspiracy to keep young men from eclipsing the older authorities.

Finny tells Gene that he once had aspirations to go to the Olympics, and Gene agrees to train for the 1944 Olympics in his place. All the boys are surprised when a gentle, nature-loving boy named Leper Lepellier becomes the first one in their class to enlist in the war effort. Gene and Finny go on training. During a winter carnival, which Finny has organized, a telegram arrives for Gene from Leper, saying that he has "escaped" and desperately needs Gene to visit him in Vermont. Gene goes to Vermont and finds that Leper has gone slightly mad. Leper, who was present at Finny's accident, reveals that he knows the truth about what happened. Leper's ranting frightens Gene and makes him anxious about how he himself might react to military life. He goes back to Devon. When Brinker hears of what has happened to Leper, he laments in front of Finny that Devon has already lost two of its potential soldiers—Leper and the crippled Finny. Gene, afraid that Finny will be hurt by this remark, tries to raise his spirits by getting him to discuss his conspiracy theory again, but Finny now denies the war only ironically.

Brinker, who suspects that Gene might have been partly responsible for Finny's accident, organizes a tribunal of schoolboys and has Gene and Finny summoned without warning. The boys on the tribunal question the two about the fall. Finny's perceptions of the incident are so blurred that he cannot speak conclusively on the matter, and Gene says he doesn't remember the details. The boys bring in Leper, who begins to implicate Gene. Finny declares that he does not care about the facts and rushes out of the room. Hurrying on the stairs, he falls and breaks his leg again.

Gene sneaks over to the school's infirmary that night to see Finny, who angrily sends him away. Gene wanders the campus until he falls asleep under the football stadium. The next morning, he goes to see Finny again, takes full blame for the tragedy, apologizes, and tries to explain that his action did not arise from hatred. Finny accepts these statements and the two are reconciled. Later, as the doctor is operating on Finny's leg, some marrow detaches from the bone and enters Finny's bloodstream, going directly to his heart and killing him. Gene receives the news with relative tranquility. He feels that he has become a part of Finny and will always be with him. The rest of the boys graduate and enlist in relatively safe branches of the military. Gene reflects on the constant hostility that plagues the human heart—a curse from which he believes only Finny was immune.

CHARACTERS IN *A SEPARATE PEACE*

Chet Douglass Gene's main rival for the position of class valedictorian. Chet is an excellent tennis and trumpet player who sincerely loves learning.

Finny Gene's classmate and best friend. Finny is honest, handsome, self-confident, disarming, extremely likable, and incredibly athletic. According to Gene, Finny never perceives anyone as an enemy or strives to defeat others. Finny relishes pure achievement rather than competition. He makes the dangerous assumption that everyone is as kind and generous as he is.

Gene Forrester The narrator and protagonist of the novel. Gene is thoughtful, intelligent, and competitive. He alternately adores and envies Finny. He often wants to let go of his own identity and live as a part of Finny. Gene often proves a reticent and unreliable narrator when it comes to his own emotions.

Brinker Hadley A charismatic class politician. Brinker is straight-laced, organized, and conservative. He has complete confidence in his own abilities and carries out his ideas with startling efficiency—at times even with ruthlessness. As opposed to Finny, who delights in innocent anarchy, Brinker believes in justice and order.

Leper Lepellier A classmate of Gene's and Finny's. Leper is a mild, gentle boy from Vermont who loves nature. He is not popular at Devon, which doesn't seem to bother him. He is the first boy from Gene's class to enlist in the army, but military life proves too much for him, and he suffers hallucinations and a breakdown.

Mr. Ludsbury The master in charge of Gene's dormitory. A stern disciplinarian, Mr. Ludsbury thrives on the unquestioning obedience of schoolboys.

Mr. Patch-Withers The substitute headmaster of Devon during the summer session.

Cliff Quackenbush The manager of the crew team. The boys at Devon have never liked Quackenbush, which has made him quick to anger.

Dr. Stanpole Devon's resident doctor. Dr. Stanpole operates on Finny. He is a caring man who laments the troubles of Gene's generation.

THEMES IN *A SEPARATE PEACE*

THE THREAT OF CODEPENDENCY TO IDENTITY Finny's and Gene's friendship shifts over the course of the novel, changing from one fueled by envy and resentment to one fueled by codependency. Early in the novel, Gene is jealous of Finny, trying to match Finny's physical prowess with academic excellence. After indulging these bitter feelings by making Finny fall from the tree, Gene ceases to envy his crippled friend. The two boys, now made more equal because of Gene's act of violence, begin to resemble each other. Immediately after the fall, Gene dresses in Finny's clothes and thinks that he looks exactly like Finny. With Finny's encouragement, Gene starts imitating Finny's old existence, playing sports because Finny cannot. Finny enjoys living vicariously through Gene, and Gene enjoys subsuming his own identity in Finny's. Although the boys fulfill each other, their codependency also prevents them from growing up and developing their own ambitions. They concoct a private illusion that World War II is a mere conspiracy and delude themselves that Gene will go to the Olympics. When Finny dies, Gene feels like Finny's funeral is his own. Only when he realizes that Finny never wished anyone ill, a quality few people have, does Gene understand that he is not the same person as Finny—he is, by his own reckoning, a different and inferior one.

THE CREATION OF ENEMIES A *Separate Peace* takes place during wartime and is a novel about war—and yet not a single shot is fired in the course of the story, no one dies in battle, and only the unfortunate Leper even joins the military before graduation. Knowles focuses on personal, internal wars that have little to do with armed conflict. He suggests that every human being goes to war when he or she realizes that the world is a fundamentally hostile place containing some created or ready-made enemy who must be destroyed. The novel implies that at the moment a boy realizes the necessity of personal war, his childhood innocence shatters and his adulthood begins. For most of Gene's classmates, World War II sparks this realization, and each boy reacts to it in his own way—Brinker with bravado, for example, and Leper with a descent into madness. Gene states that he fought his own war while at Devon and killed his enemy there. Perhaps by this he means that Finny was his enemy. Perhaps he means that his own resentful, envious nature was his enemy, which he "killed" either by knocking Finny from the tree or by obtaining forgiveness from Finny for doing so. Only Finny refuses to go to war, insisting that he has no enemies. In part because of this refusal, Finny's death is inevitable: his innocence makes him too good for the rest of the war-torn world.

THE DANGER OF TRANSFORMATION A *Separate Peace* features a number of significant transitions, none of them positive. Finny is transformed from a healthy athlete into a cripple. Gene is partially transformed into an athlete. These developments are part of the broader process by which Gene's identity blurs into Finny's. The summer session at Devon, a time of peace and carefree innocence, transforms into the winter session, during which friendships sour and the darkness of the war encroaches on Devon. In a broad sense, the novel is about the transformation of boys into men. The horrifying visions of transformation that drive Leper from the army—men turning into women, men's heads on women's bodies—stand for the anxieties that plague all of his classmates as they deal with the joint onset of war and adulthood.

SYMBOLS IN *A SEPARATE PEACE*

THE SUMMER AND WINTER SESSIONS AT DEVON The summer session at Devon symbolizes innocence and youth. It is a time of anarchy and freedom, when the teachers are lenient and Finny's enthusiasm and clever tongue let him get away with anything. The winter session symbolizes adulthood. It is dark, disciplined, and filled with difficult work. Together, the two sessions represent the shift from carefree youth to somber maturity.

FINNY'S FALL Finny's fall, the climax of the novel, symbolizes the universal fall from innocence. His fall ends the summer session—the period of carefree innocence—and ushers in the darker winter session. His fall also shows Gene that resentment, envy, and half-subconscious violence can have serious consequences.

IMPORTANT QUOTATIONS FROM *A SEPARATE PEACE*

He had never been jealous of me for a second. Now I knew that there never was and never could have been any rivalry between us. I was not of the same quality as he. I couldn't stand this.. . . Holding firmly to the trunk, I took a step toward him, and then my knees bent and I jounced the limb. Finny, his balance gone, swung his head around to look at me for an instant with extreme interest, and then he tumbled sideways, broke through the little branches below and hit the bank with a sickening, unnatural thud. It was the first clumsy physical action I had ever seen him make. With unthinking sureness I moved out on the limb and jumped into the river, every trace of my fear of this forgotten.

Location: Chapter 4
Speaker: Gene
Context: Gene realizes that Finny is not competing with him and makes Finny fall off the branch

In the moments leading up to this scene, Gene's notion of mutual enmity and competition between himself and Finny breaks down. He realizes that Finny has never wanted to compete with anyone—certainly not with him. Gene suddenly perceives his own moral inferiority to his best friend, and his anguish at this realization ("I couldn't stand this") is the only explanation offered for the events on the tree. Gene describes his violent act in a detached tone, without explaining what he is thinking when he bends his legs and shakes the limb. Gene leaves the question of his intentions up in the air—perhaps because he himself is not sure about the degree of his guilt. Finny's slip from the branch is "the first clumsy physical action [Gene] had ever seen him make." The clumsy slip is the first sign of Finny's mortality we have seen. It also suggests that Finny's charm and grace come from the conviction that everyone is as loving as he is. When faced with proof that other people are violent and cruel, Finny's grace slips away.

Fear seized my stomach like a cramp. I didn't care what I said to him now; it was myself I was worried about. For if Leper was psycho it was the army which had done it to him, and I and all of us were on the brink of the army.

Location: Chapter 10
Speaker: Gene
Context: Gene worries that he, like Leper, could go mad

While visiting Leper in Vermont, Gene listens to the story of Leper's training camp madness and grows distraught—not for Leper's sake, but for his own. Leper's transformation from gentle nature-lover into "psycho" shatters the illusion, promoted by Finny, that adulthood can be staved off forever. Before, Gene and his classmates celebrated imagined heroics performed by Leper, trying to cover up their own insecurities about military service by pretending that their meek classmate was succeeding mightily as a soldier. But faced with proof that war has demented Leper, Gene can no longer pretend. In the minds of Gene and the rest of the boys, Leper's madness transforms the war from a distant threat into an immediate reality.

I found it. I found a single sustaining thought. The thought was, You and Phineas are even already. You are even in enmity. You are both coldly driving ahead for yourselves alone.. . . I felt better. Yes, I sensed it like the sweat of relief when nausea passes away; I felt better. We were even after all, even in enmity. The deadly rivalry was on both sides after all.

Location: Chapter 4
Speaker: Gene
Context: Gene convinces himself that Finny shares his competitive feelings

---

"Listen, pal, if I can't play sports, you're going to play them for me," and I lost part of myself to him then, and a soaring sense of freedom revealed that this must have been my purpose from the first: to become a part of Phineas.

Location: Chapter 6
Speaker: Gene
Context: Gene and Finny talk on the phone

I never killed anybody and I never developed an intense level of hatred for the enemy. Because my war ended before I ever put on a uniform; I was on active duty all my time at school; I killed my enemy there. Only Phineas never was afraid, only Phineas never hated anyone.

Location: The end of the novel
Speaker: Gene
Context: Gene reflects on his personal war

SIDDHARTHA

Hermann Hesse

A man searches for the truth and for knowledge of himself, living many different kinds of lives in the process and ultimately becoming a Buddha.

THE LIFE OF HERMANN HESSE

Hermann Hesse was born on July 2, 1877, in Calw, a town in the Black Forest region of Germany. Hesse's mother was born in India. His maternal grandfather, Hermann Gundert, had been a missionary in India for more than twenty years and was fluent in at least three Indian languages. Hesse's family subscribed to Pietism, a Protestant religion that emphasizes devotion and charitable activity rather than dogma. Hesse was sent to a monastery but left after a year.

As a youth, Hesse read voraciously and decided to become a writer. After years of struggling to publish his work, he gained acclaim with his novel *Peter Camenzind* (1904). The royalties from the novel allowed Hesse to quit his job as a bookseller and devote himself to writing full time. They also allowed him to support his new wife, Maria Bernoulli, whom he had married in 1904.

Increasingly restless with his life in Gaienhofen, Germany, Hesse took to traveling. In 1911, he made his first trip to India. He later commented that India did not afford the immediate spiritual transformation for which he had hoped. Instead, it convinced him that the East is nothing but a representation of the qualities that each man must find within himself. This trip eventually inspired Hesse to write *Siddhartha* (1922).

After returning from India, Hesse moved to Switzerland. When World War I broke out, he volunteered for military service, but was turned down. He later become a vocal pacifist and renounced his German citizenship. While living in Switzerland, Hesse grew increasingly interested in Jungian psychoanalysis and attempted to plumb his own subconscious. In the following years, Hesse's marriage and mental health fluctuated, but his career thrived. The 1922 publication of *Siddhartha* brought him fame, as did *Steppenwolf* (1927) and *Narcissus and Goldmund* (1930). Hesse's primary influences in these novels were German Romanticism, late-nineteenth-century aestheticism, and Indian and Chinese religious philosophy. The lives of Hesse's characters are generally uncomfortable, but his prose lends romance to their suffering.

Hesse struggled with alcoholism, bringing it under control in 1926 and retiring to his country retreat in Montagnola. The popularity of Hesse's work has always waxed and waned. His outspokenly pacifist novels were banned in Nazi Germany but celebrated after World War II. In America, the Beat generation of the 1950s and the hippies of the 1960s enthusiastically embraced Hesse's blend of Eastern philosophy and existentialism. Today, Hesse is considered one of the most influential German authors of the twentieth century. Hesse's efforts earned him the Nobel Prize for Literature in 1946. He died in 1962 at his home in Switzerland.

SIDDHARTHA IN CONTEXT

Siddhartha's careful structure parallels the spiritual journey of its protagonist. It is formally divided into two parts, but in fact it has a strict tripartite structure that corresponds to the three stages Siddhartha passes through on his path to enlightenment: the stage of the mind, which corresponds to walking with the ascetics and listening to the Buddha; the stage of the flesh, which corresponds to tutelage in the arts of love with Kamala and the arts of commerce with Kamaswami; and the stage of transcendence, which corresponds to the epiphany by the river and a father's lesson in love. Some critics argue that Siddhartha is projected into three possibilities of being: Govinda, Gotama, and Vasudeva. Even sentences, clauses, and phrases have a tripartite structure.

SIDDHARTHA: KEY FACTS

Time and place written: 1919–1922; Montagnola, Switzerland

Date of first publication: 1922	
Publisher: S. Fischer (Berlin)	
Type of work: Novel	
Genre: Parable, allegory	
Language: German	
Tense: Past	
Tone: Calm, insightful	
Setting (time): Fifth to sixth century B.C.	
Setting (place): India	
Narrator: Anonymous, third-person narrator	
Point of view: Siddhartha's	
Protagonist: Siddhartha	
Antagonist: The obstacles to self-realization	

SIDDHARTHA: PLOT OVERVIEW

In his youth, Siddhartha, a handsome Brahmin, occupies himself with gods, sacrifices, and the sacred teachings. Leaving these behind, he sets out with his childhood friend, Govinda, to lead a life of harsh asceticism with the Samanas. Although he learns to conquer his body and senses, he still feels that he has learned nothing. Siddhartha and Govinda go in search of Gotama Buddha, whose teachings are wondrous. Govinda stays and becomes a follower of Gotama, and Siddhartha continues on alone. He crosses a river and comes to Samsara, a lush land. He spends twenty years in Samsara, enjoying the pleasures of the flesh and the concerns of the secular world. He learns the arts of love (but not love itself) from the courtesan Kamala and the secrets of money-making from the businessman Kamaswami. In the beginning, this existence is an amusing game, but over the years it turns into an overwhelming, disgusting occupation. When Siddhartha dreams that a bird in Kamala's golden cage is dead and that he must throw out its dead body with everything good that is inside him, he decides to leave Samsara for good.

Siddhartha goes back to the river he crossed and falls into a deep sleep. Govinda, now a monk, guards Siddhartha from snakes while he sleeps, but does not recognize his old friend. Siddhartha wakes. He studies ferrying and listening to the secrets of the river with the ferryman Vasudeva, who lives by the river. Together, the two old men grow very wise. One day, eleven years later, Kamala crosses the river with the son she had by Siddhartha, in search of the dying Gotama Buddha. A snake bites Kamala and she dies in front of the ferrymen. She dies at peace because she has looked at the face of a buddha after all—Siddhartha. Siddhartha cares for his son, but the boy is spoiled and unhappy, and eventually runs away. Heartbroken, Siddhartha gives chase but cannot catch his son. Finally, he knows what it is to love. He returns to the river, whose plentiful voices sing the word of perfection: "Om." Siddhartha learns that there is only the present, that the past and future are shadows, and that it is fruitless to worry about the cycle of life. This lesson readies him to be a ferryman alone, and Vasudeva leaves him and goes to the woods to find death. Years later, Govinda comes in search of the fabled Buddha of the river. The Buddha is Siddhartha, but Govinda does not recognize him. When he kisses Siddhartha on the forehead, he has a vision of a stream of infinite faces that fills him with love and admiration for this Buddha.

Siddhartha uses the world of thought and the world of action until he can gain no more from them, and then he goes beyond them to reach the realm of the soul. In this realm, he lives in accord with himself and life. After each momentous encounter, Siddhartha casts a world behind him—after the Buddha, the world of the mind; after Kamala, the world of the flesh; after the ferryman and his son, he departs from himself altogether, emerging a transfigured man.

CHARACTERS IN *SIDDHARTHA*

Gotama A wise man from the race of Sakya. Everyone believes that Gotama, who is also called the Illustrious One and the Buddha, has achieved Nirvana and left the cycle of reincarnation. Gotama has a radiant and peaceful smile, and glows with knowledge.

Govinda The eternal follower of Siddhartha. Govinda is a perpetual seeker who has great difficulty recognizing that which is right in front of him. He fails to recognize his own best friend, Siddhartha, first when Siddhartha is a businessman and again when Siddhartha is a Buddha. Govinda never finds satisfaction because he relies on doctrine instead of thought, trusting that dogma will show him the truth without his really looking for the truth on his own.

Kamala A beautiful courtesan. Kamala's name derives Kama, the Hindu god of love and desire. Kamala teaches Siddhartha until he becomes the best lover she has ever had.

Kamaswami A well-to-do businessman. Kamaswami's name translates roughly into "master of love." He takes Siddhartha as his apprentice, giving him food, clothing, lodging, and business duties until Siddhartha learns to earn them for himself. Kamaswami takes gains and losses very seriously, which Siddhartha does not. The two men constantly disagree about what is valuable. The day that Siddhartha turns into a double of Kamaswami, fat with wealth and rank with vices, is the day he leaves his life in Samsara.

Siddhartha The protagonist of the novel. "Siddhartha," the name of the historical Buddha during his secular life, translates roughly as "he who finds the goal." When the novel begins, Siddhartha is a handsome, clever, superior young Brahmin. As he ages, he becomes a bearded, long-haired ascetic, an opulently dressed businessman, and finally a simple ferryman. These stages correspond to the stage of the mind, the stage of the senses, and finally enlightenment.

Vasudeva The god Krishna. "Vasudeva," one of Krishna's many names, means "the one who abides in all things and to whom all things abide." Vasudeva, a kind, wise man, mentors Siddhartha, working by his side as a ferryman. He voices what is in Siddhartha's mind and what Siddhartha knows to be the truth. Vasudeva is an exceptional listener who makes people feel as if he understands and absorbs everything even as he keeps silent. Siddhartha equates Vasudeva with the river of life from which he learns the unity of all things.

THEMES IN *SIDDHARTHA*

THE SEARCH FOR THE SELF Almost every action Siddhartha undertakes springs from his desire to find himself. In the first pages of the novel, he muses, "To pierce there, to the self, to myself, to Atman—was there any other path worth seeking?" The strength of his desire to seek this path consumes him for the rest of his life, inspiring him to leave behind the luxurious life of a Brahmin (an Indian of high status) and set out to seek enlightenment. Occasionally, Siddhartha loses sight of his goal, as when he spends time with Kamaswami and Kamala, and indulges in worldly pleasures. But later he derides himself for wasting time this way. The part of Siddhartha's philosophy that demands self-realization is distinctly Hindu. Buddhist philosophy holds that no human has a self or a soul, a belief that, if Siddhartha held it, would negate his search.

THE UNIVERSALITY OF THE HUMAN EXPERIENCE With the story of Siddhartha, Hermann Hesse makes a broad statement about life in general. Siddhartha stands for all people, and his quest to find himself stands for the universal project. The breadth of his experience makes him a believable stand-in for humanity in general. At different points, he is rich and poor, famous and anonymous, obsessed with his mind and obsessed with his body, joyful and crushed by pain, a child and an old man. Intense curiosity about the self is the constant quality that underpins all of these variable experiences.

THE MIDDLE PATH In the beginning, Siddhartha thinks that taking intense, extreme measures is the only way he will be able to answer his questions. He renounces the extreme wealth of his family in favor of extreme poverty, and then returns to extreme wealth. In the course of his spiritual experiments, he fasts for days and meditates for hours. Then he abandons bodily pain and pursues bodily pleasure to the exclusion of all else. Although Siddhartha probably does not know it, the Buddha he encounters once embraced extremes as Siddhartha does. Eventually, the Buddha decided on a "middle path." He neither starves himself nor overeats, neither deprives himself of comfort nor lounges in the lap of luxury. By the end of his life, Siddhartha too finds a middle path, living on the river with Vasudeva and listening to the water. He sleeps, but not excessively. He eats, but not gluttonously. This outer balance parallels the inner balance that Siddhartha has found in his mind. He has no need to search for peace anymore, because he has found it. He has learned to unite the life of the mind with the life of the body.

SYMBOLS IN *SIDDHARTHA*

THE RIVER   The first time Siddhartha crosses the river, it symbolizes the divide between mind and body. Siddhartha crosses it in attempt to flee his unsatisfying mental life as an ascetic and live a mundane life of the body with Kamala. When Siddhartha returns to the river after many years of hedonism, the river still represents the space between mind and body, but Siddhartha no longer treats it as a divide to be conquered. Now wise enough to find the unity between mind and body, Siddhartha recognizes the river as his middle path and dwells there comfortably for the last years of his life. Thus, the river ultimately symbolizes om, or enlightenment. The river also symbolizes the present. Like the present, the river contains both past and future. It is always moving, always new, yet always the same. Finally, the river symbolizes Vasudeva. Both are constant, soothing, silent, dark, and deep.

KAMALA'S BIRD   In her "pleasure garden," Kamala shows Siddhartha the "ways of love." This pleasure garden is excessively opulent, and among its treasures is a "small, rare songbird in a gold cage." After many years of companionship with Kamala, Siddhartha dreams that he has found this bird dead in its cage. The bird represents his life as a bodily being. His riches and sensual pleasures are lovely, like the gold cage, but they hold him captive.

IMPORTANT QUOTATIONS FROM *SIDDHARTHA*

"Om is bow, the arrow is soul,
Brahman is the arrow's goal
It must be struck unswervingly."

Location: Part I
Speaker: Siddhartha
Context: Young Siddhartha repeats an old poem that will guide his spiritual journey

As a child, Siddhartha recites this short poem as part of a religious ritual. The verses characterize the arrow's journey as a linear one. They call up an image of a determined soul striking out for Brahman, or the one essence of life, never swerving, stopping, or straying from its course. As a young man, Siddhartha imagines that his search for Brahman will mimic the determined, unwavering flight of the arrow described in the poem. However, he realizes that the poem is mistaken. Enlightenment does not move in a neat forward trajectory from start to finish, but in a swirling scribble of setbacks, false steps, and confusion. As Vasudeva knows, and as the doctrine of karma holds, people and things move in complicated, intertwining circles. Siddhartha does not start on one side of the river, cross the river, and end up in the promised land. He wanders on one side of the river, crosses it and wanders on the other side, gives up the search altogether for a time, and contemplates suicide before finally finding peace.

Yes, strange was his fate! Things were going downhill for him, and now he stood again empty and naked and foolish in the world. Yet he could feel no grief, no, he actually felt like laughing, laughing at himself, laughing at this strange and stupid world.

Location: Part II
Speaker: The narrator
Context: Siddhartha has been saved from a suicidal episode

Siddhartha returns to the river with no possessions and nothing concrete to show for his life of spiritual struggle. Crushed by the realization that he has not found the answers he sought as a young Brahmin, he considers ending his life by drowning himself in the river. The river saves him by speaking to him and causing him to repeat the holy word "om." After this crisis, Siddhartha falls into a deep, refreshing sleep. When he wakes, his old friend Govinda is watching over him. Govinda's presence reminds Siddhartha of the interdependence of all beings and of the transient, impermanent nature of life. He feels able to love the things around him. He realizes that the loss of his possessions is not necessarily a disaster. At least it enables him to make a clean start. In a small epiphany, he realizes that he does not care at all about his lost wealth and dignity, and that in fact he has the ability to laugh "at this strange and stupid world."

"Whether the world is good or evil, whether life in it is sorrow or joy, no matter—it may even be unessential. But the unity of the world, the coherent togetherness of all events, the enfolding of everything, big or little, in the same river, in the same law of cause and effect, of becoming and dying: all this shines brightly from your sublime teaching, O Perfect One.... But there is one thing that the so clear, so venerable Teaching does not contain: it does not contain the secret of what the Sublime One himself has experienced, he alone among the hundreds of thousands.... That is why I am resuming my wandering—not to seek a different, a better teaching, for I know that there is none; but to leave all teachings and all teachers and to reach my goal alone or die."

Location: Part I
Speaker: Siddhartha
Context: After hearing the Buddha give a sermon, Siddhartha tells the Buddha about his own spiritual quest

---

Kamaswami conducted his business with care and often with passion, but Siddhartha treated it all as a game, whose rules he strove to learn precisely, but whose content did not touch his heart.

Location: Part II
Speaker: The narrator
Context: Siddhartha participates in business without caring too much about it

---

"It was the river that taught me how to listen; you too will learn how from the river. The river knows everything, one can learn everything from it."

Location: Part II
Speaker: Vasudeva
Context: Vasudeva explains the importance of the river to Siddhartha

SILAS MARNER

George Eliot

A benumbed, alienated man finds happiness after adopting a young girl.

THE LIFE OF GEORGE ELIOT

George Eliot was the pseudonym of Mary Ann Evans, who was born in 1819 at the estate of her father's employer in Chilvers Coton, Warwickshire, England. At boarding school, Eliot was deeply influenced by the evangelical preacher Rev. John Edmund Jones and developed a strong religious faith. After her mother's death, Eliot moved with her father to the city of Coventry. There she met Charles and Caroline Bray, progressive intellectuals who led her to question her faith. In 1842, she stopped going to church, which put a strain on her relationship with her father.

Eliot traveled to Geneva and then to London, where she worked as a freelance writer. She met George Lewes, who could not marry her because he had an estranged wife, but who became her husband for all intents and purposes. In 1857, Eliot published her first collection of stories under her male pseudonym. The stories won immediate acclaim from critics as prestigious as Charles Dickens and William Thackeray, and inspired a great deal of speculation about the identity of the mysterious George Eliot. After the publication of *Adam Bede* (1859), Eliot's first novel, a number of impostors claimed authorship. In response, Eliot identified herself as the true author, causing quite a stir in a society that regarded women as incapable of serious writing.

In 1860, Eliot published *The Mill on the Floss*, which she followed with *Silas Marner* (1860). Her best-known work is *Middlemarch* (1871–1872). Lewes died in 1878, and in 1880, Evans married a banker named John Walter Cross, who was twenty-one years her junior. She died the same year.

Eliot's novels are deeply philosophical. In exploring the inner workings of her characters and their relationship to their environments, she draws on influences that include the English poet William Wordsworth, the Italian poet Dante, the English art critic John Ruskin, and the Portuguese-Dutch philosopher Baruch Spinoza, whose work Eliot translated into English. The philosophical concerns and references found in her novels—and the refusal to provide happy endings—struck some contemporary critics as unbecoming in a lady novelist. Eliot's detailed and insightful psychological portrayals of her characters, as well as her exploration of the complex ways these characters confront moral dilemmas, decisively broke from the plot-driven domestic melodrama that previously characterized the Victorian novel. Eliot's break from tradition inspired the modern novel.

SILAS MARNER IN CONTEXT

Silas Marner is the tale of a lonely, miserly village weaver transformed by the love of his adopted daughter. Many of the novel's themes and concerns stem from Eliot's own experiences. Silas's loss of religious faith recalls Eliot's own struggle with her faith, and the novel's setting in the vanishing English countryside reflects Eliot's concern that England was fast becoming industrialized and impersonal.

SILAS MARNER: KEY FACTS

Full title: Silas Marner: The Weaver of Raveloe
Time and place written: 1860–61; London
Date of first publication: 1861
Publisher: William Blackwood and Sons
Type of work: Novel
Genre: Novel of ideas; pastoral
Language: English

Setting (time): Early nineteenth century

Setting (place): Raveloe, a fictional village in the English countryside

Tense: Past

Tone: Morally uncompromising, slightly condescending, sympathetic

Narrator: Anonymous omniscient narrator in the third person

Point of view: Shifts

Protagonist: Silas Marner

Antagonist: Silas Marner's lack of faith and human connection

SILAS MARNER: PLOT OVERVIEW

Silas Marner is the weaver in the English countryside village of Raveloe. Like many weavers of his time, he is an outsider. His special skills make him an object of suspicion, as does the fact that he has moved to Raveloe from elsewhere. The villagers thinks Silas is especially odd because of the curious cataleptic fits he occasionally suffers. Silas has ended up in Raveloe because the members of his religious sect in Lantern Yard, an insular neighborhood in a large town, falsely accused him of theft and excommunicated him.

Much shaken by the accusation, Silas loses his faith and falls into a numbing routine of solitary work. His one attempt at neighborliness backfires: when an herbal remedy he suggests for a neighbor's illness works, he is rumored to be a sort of witch doctor. With little else to live for, Silas becomes obsessed with money, hoarding it and living off as little as possible. Every night, he pulls his gold from its hiding place beneath his floorboards to count it. Fifteen years pass.

Squire Cass, the wealthiest man in Raveloe, has two sons named Godfrey and Dunstan, nicknamed Dunsey. Dunsey is greedy and cruel. He enjoys tormenting Godfrey, his older brother. Godfrey is good-natured but weak-willed. Though secretly married to the opium addict Molly Farren, he is in love with Nancy Lammeter. Dunsey talked Godfrey into the marriage to Molly and repeatedly blackmails him with threats to reveal the marriage to their father. Godfrey gives Dunsey 100 pounds of the rent money paid to him by one of their father's tenants. Dunsey insists that Godfrey pay the rent himself and threatens to reveal Godfrey's marriage. After some arguing, he offers to sell Godfrey's prize horse, Wildfire, to repay the loan.

The next day, Dunsey meets with some friends and negotiates the sale of the horse. Dunsey decides to go hunting with his friends before finalizing the sale. During the hunt, Dunsey has a riding accident and his horse dies. Dunsey schemes to intimidate Silas Marner, who is rumored to have a hoard of wealth, into lending him money. Finding Silas's cottage empty, Dunsey steals the money. Silas returns from an errand to find his money gone. Overwhelmed by the loss, he runs to the local tavern for help and announces the theft to a sympathetic audience of tavern regulars. The theft becomes the talk of the village, and a theory arises that the thief might have been a peddler who came through the village some time before.

Dunsey has not come home. Godfrey decides to tell his father about the money, though not about his marriage. The Squire flies into a rage at the news, but does not do anything drastic to punish Godfrey.

Silas, utterly disconsolate at the loss of his gold, numbly continues his weaving. Some of the townspeople stop by to offer their condolences and advice. One of these visitors, Dolly Winthrop, is especially gentle and sympathetic. Like many of the visitors, she encourages Silas to go to church, which he has not done since he was banished from Lantern Yard.

Nancy Lammeter arrives at Squire Cass's famed New Year's dance resolved to reject Godfrey's advances because of his unsound character. However, Godfrey is more direct and insistent than he has been in a long time, and Nancy finds herself exhilarated. Meanwhile, Molly, Godfrey's secret wife, is making her way to the Casses' house to reveal the secret marriage. She has their daughter, a toddler, in her arms. Tiring after her long walk, Molly takes a draft of opium and passes out by the road. Seeing Silas's cottage and drawn by the light of the fire, Molly's little girl wanders through the open door and falls asleep at Silas's hearth.

Silas is having one of his fits and does not notice the little girl enter his cottage. When he comes to, he is shocked to see her asleep on his hearth. Silas traces the girl's footsteps outside and finds Molly's body lying in the snow. He goes to the Squire's house to find the doctor, causing a stir at the dance by arriving with the baby girl in his arms. Godfrey, recognizing his daughter, accompanies the doctor to Silas's cottage. When the doctor declares Molly dead, Godfrey realizes that his secret is safe. He does not claim his daughter, and Silas adopts her.

Silas grows increasingly attached to the child, whom he names Eppie, after his mother and sister. With Dolly Winthrop's help, Silas raises the child lovingly. Eppie begins to serve as a bridge between Silas and the rest of the villagers, who offer him help and advice, and begin to think of him as an exemplary person because of what he has done. Eppie also brings Silas out of his benumbed state. In his newfound happiness, Silas begins to explore long-repressed memories of his past.

The novel jumps ahead sixteen years. Godfrey has married Nancy, and Squire Cass has died. Godfrey has inherited his father's house, but he and Nancy have no children. Their one daughter died at birth, and Nancy has refused to adopt. Eppie has grown into a pretty and spirited young woman, and Silas a contented father. The stone-pit behind Silas's cottage is drained to water neighboring fields, and Dunsey's skeleton is found at the bottom, along with Silas's gold. The discovery frightens Godfrey, who becomes convinced that his own secrets will be uncovered. He confesses to Nancy, telling her about Molly and Eppie. Nancy is regretful, saying that they could have adopted Eppie legitimately if Godfrey had told her earlier.

That evening, Godfrey and Nancy visit Silas's cottage and tell Silas and Eppie the truth about Eppie's lineage. They claim her as their daughter. However, after the story, Eppie says she would rather stay with Silas than live with her biological father. Godfrey and Nancy leave, resigning themselves to helping Eppie from afar. The next day, Silas visits Lantern Yard to see if he was ever cleared of the theft of which he was accused years before. The town has changed almost beyond recognition, and Silas's old chapel has been torn down to make way for a factory. Silas realizes that his questions will never be answered, but he is content with the faith he has regained through his life with Eppie. That summer, Eppie marries Aaron Winthrop, Dolly's son. Aaron comes to live in Silas's cottage, which has been expanded and refurbished at Godfrey's expense.

CHARACTERS IN *SILAS MARNER*

Bryce A friend of Godfrey's and Dunsey's. Bryce arranges to buy Wildfire, Godfrey's horse.

Dunstan Cass One of Squire Cass's sons. Dunsey, as he is usually called, is a cruel, lazy, unscrupulous man who loves gambling and drinking.

Godfrey Cass The eldest son of Squire Cass. Godfrey is good-natured but selfish and weak-willed.

Squire Cass The wealthiest man in Raveloe. The Squire is lazy, self-satisfied, and short-tempered.

William Dane Silas's proud and priggish best friend from childhood. William Dane frames Silas for theft in order to disgrace him, then marries Silas's fiancée, Sarah.

Mr. Dowlas The town farrier. Mr. Dowlas shoes horses and tends to general livestock diseases. He is a fierce contrarian.

Eppie A girl whom Silas Marner eventually adopts. Eppie is the biological child of Godfrey Cass and Molly Farren, Godfrey's secret wife. She is pretty, spirited, and loving.

Molly Farren Godfrey's secret wife and Eppie's mother. Once pretty, Molly has been destroyed by her addictions to opium and alcohol.

Misses Gunn Sisters from a large nearby town who come to the Squire's New Year's dance. The Gunns look down on Raveloe's rustic ways. Nancy Lammeter's beauty impresses them.

Mr. Kimble Godfrey's uncle and Raveloe's doctor. Mr. Kimble is an animated conversationalist and joker who gets irritable when he plays cards. He has no medical degree and inherited the position of village physician from his father.

Mr. Lammeter Nancy's and Priscilla's father. Mr. Lammeter is a proud, morally uncompromising man.

Nancy Lammeter The object of Godfrey's affection and his eventual wife. Nancy is pretty, caring, and stubborn. She lives by a code that sometimes seems arbitrary and uncompromising.

Priscilla Lammeter Nancy's homely and plainspoken sister.

Mr. Macey Raveloe's parish clerk. Mr. Macey is opinionated and smug, but he means well.

Silas Marner The protagonist of the novel. Silas is a simple, honest, and kindhearted weaver. After losing faith in God and his fellow man, Silas lives for fifteen years as a solitary miser. After his money is stolen, his faith and trust are restored by his adopted daughter, Eppie.

Sally Oates Silas's neighbor and the cobbler's wife. Silas eases the pain of Sally's heart disease and dropsy with a concoction he makes out of foxglove.

The peddler A suspect in the theft of Silas's gold because of his gypsylike appearance.

Jem Rodney A somewhat disreputable character and a poacher. Silas accuses Jem of stealing his gold.

Sarah Silas's fiancée in Lantern Yard. Sarah is put off by Silas's strange fits and marries William Dane after Silas is disgraced.

Mr. Snell The landlord of the Rainbow, a local tavern. By nature a conciliatory person, Mr. Snell always tries to settle arguments.

Aaron Winthrop Dolly's son and Eppie's eventual husband.

Dolly Winthrop The wheelwright's wife. Dolly helps Silas with Eppie and later becomes Eppie's godmother and mother-in-law. She is kind, patient, and devout.

THEMES IN *SILAS MARNER*

THE INDIVIDUAL IN THE COMMUNITY   Much of the novel's dramatic force is generated by the tension between Silas and the society of Raveloe. In the early nineteenth century, a person's village or town was all-important, providing the sole source of material and emotional support. Eliot emphasizes the interconnectedness of a village, writing about the parish's charitable allowance for the crippled, the donation of leftovers from the Squire's feasts to the village's poor, and the kindness of the villagers to Silas after he is robbed and after he adopts Eppie. The community also gives its members a structured sense of identity. In Raveloe's public gatherings, interaction is ritualized through a shared understanding of each person's social class and place in the community. As an outsider, Silas initially lacks an identity because he has no defined place in the community. To be outside the community is to be something unnatural, even otherworldly—Silas is compared to an apparition when he shows up at the Rainbow and the Red House. Though it takes fifteen years, Silas eventually establishes his place in Raveloe. In large part, he establishes his place involuntarily. First Dunsey robs him, then Eppie shows up in his cottage. Eliot suggests that the interconnectedness of community is unavoidable.

CHARACTER AS DESTINY   Eliot gives each character his or her just deserts: Dunsey dies, the Squire's lands are divided, Godfrey wins Nancy but ends up childless, and Silas lives happily ever after with Eppie as the most admired man in Raveloe. The tidiness of the novel's resolution may or may not be entirely believable, but it is a central part of Eliot's goal to present the universe as a morally ordered place. Fate, defined as a higher power rewarding and punishing each character's actions, is a central force in the novel. Eliot suggests that who we are determines not only what we do, but also what is done to us. Nearly any character in the novel could serve as an example of this moral order, but perhaps the best illustration is Godfrey. Godfrey usually means well, but he is unwilling to make sacrifices for what he knows is right. His constant hemming and hawing back him into tight corners and make him panicky. At one point, he finds himself wishing for Molly's death. However, Eliot makes it clear that Godfrey is not a bad person—he has simply been compromised by his inaction. Godfrey ends up with a similarly compromised destiny: he marries Nancy thinking that is what he wants, only to realize that it is not what he wants after all.

THE INTERDEPENDENCE OF FAITH AND COMMUNITY   *Silas Marner* is the story of Silas's loss and regaining of faith. It is also the story of Silas's rejection and embrace of his community. Eliot links faith and community, suggesting that they are intertwined human necessities. The community of Lantern Yard is united by religious faith, and Raveloe is united by its shared set of superstitious beliefs. Eliot also associates faith in a higher being with faith in one's fellow man. In fact, Silas's regained faith could be defined as faith in the godliness of other people. In Lantern Yard, he trusted in God absolutely, choosing not to defend himself against a false charge of thievery because he believed that a just God would clear his name. In Raveloe, Silas finds a faith that is not even explicitly Christian. Silas bases his faith on the strength of his and Eppie's commitment to each other, saying, "since . . . I've come to love her . . . I've had light enough to trusten by; and now she says she'll never leave me, I think I shall trusten till I die."

SYMBOLS IN *SILAS MARNER*

SILAS'S LOOM   Silas's loom embodies many of the novel's major themes. On a literal level, the loom is Silas's livelihood and source of income. The extent to which Silas's obsession with money deforms his character is symbolized by Silas's bent frame and damaged eyesight, which result from so many hours spent at the loom. The loom, a machine, also foreshadows the coming of industrialization. The loom, constantly in motion but never going anywhere, also stands for the unceasing, unchanging nature of Silas's work and life. Finally, the process of weaving functions as a metaphor for the creation of a community, with its many interwoven threads, and suggests the way Silas will bring together the village of Raveloe.

THE HEARTH   The hearth represents the comforts of home and family. When Godfrey dreams of a life with Nancy, he sees himself "with all his happiness centred on his own hearth, while Nancy would smile on him as he played with the children." Initially, Silas shares his hearth with no one, which suggests his lack of family. The two intruders who change his life, first Dunsey and then Eppie, are drawn out of inclement weather by the inviting light of Silas's fire. In the end, Godfrey is childless and has no family to collect around his hearth, while Silas is warmed by Eppie's love.

IMPORTANT QUOTATIONS FROM *SILAS MARNER*

To have sought a medical explanation for this phenomenon would have been held by Silas himself, as well as by his minister and fellow-members, a willful self-exclusion from the spiritual significance that might lie therein.

Location: Chapter 1
Speaker: The narrator
Context: The narrator describes the reaction of Silas's religious sect to Silas's cataleptic fits

The worshippers in Silas's chapel insist on believing that Silas's fits are divinely inspired, a sort of holy trance. Eliot suggests that the sect members' faith in the "spiritual significance" of Silas's fits requires them to turn a blind eye to other possible explanations. Their beliefs rule out complexity, ambiguity, and rigorous inquiry. Eliot does not hesitate, in this chapter and elsewhere, to label this sort of belief primitive. There is a note of condescension in Eliot's description, a wink at her contemporary readers, for these simple folk from the past who ascribe supernatural causes to anything the least bit unusual. She writes as someone who once believed passionately in similar teachings but had since broken from them. She has both experienced and rejected comforts and tenets similar to the ones Silas's sect embraces.

Strangely Marner's face and figure shrank and bent themselves into a constant mechanical relation to the objects of his life, so that he produced the same sort of impression as a handle or a crooked tube, which has no meaning standing apart. The prominent eyes that used to look trusting and dreamy, now looked as if they had been made to see only one kind of thing that was very small, like tiny grain, for which they hunted everywhere; and he was so withered and yellow, that, though he was not yet forty, the children always called him "Old Master Marner."

Location: Chapter 2
Speaker: The narrator
Context: The narrator describes the effect of work and greed on Silas

This passage describes the dehumanizing effect labor has on Silas, whose mechanical way of life and love of money make him into an almost grotesque parody of Karl Marx's theoretical worker. For Marx, industrialization dehumanizes workers, reducing them to nothing more than the amount of money their labor is worth. In this passage, Silas is described as a disconnected, machine-like being. He is prematurely aged, "withered and yellow," and has shrunk and bent to fit to his loom—so much so that he looks like a part of the loom, "a handle or a crooked tube, which has no meaning standing apart." Eliot emphasizes the fact that Silas's labor has overtaken his humanity. Silas's inability to see things that are far away takes on metaphorical overtones. He can see only "one kind of thing that was very small, for which [his eyes] hunted everywhere"—that is, gold. Here, as elsewhere, Silas's physical deterioration parallels his spiritual decline.

This strangely novel situation of opening his trouble to his Raveloe neighbours, of sitting in the warmth of a hearth not his own, and feeling the presence of faces and voices which were his nearest promise of help, had doubtless its influence on Marner, in spite of his passionate preoccupation with his loss. Our consciousness rarely registers the beginning of a growth within us any more than without us: there have been many circulations of the sap before we detect the smallest sign of the bud.

Location: Chapter 7
Speaker: The narrator
Context: Silas goes to the Rainbow and finds himself in a community for the first time since his banishment from Lantern Yard

---

Godfrey was silent. He was not likely to be very penetrating in his judgments, but he had always had a sense that his father's indulgence had not been kindness, and had had a vague longing for some discipline that would have checked his own errant weakness and helped his better will.

Location: Chapter 9
Speaker: The narrator
Context: Godfrey weathers a severe tongue-lashing from his father, Squire Cass, after confessing that he lent Dunsey a tenant's money

---

I can't say what I should have done about that, Godfrey. I should never have married anybody else. But I wasn't worth doing wrong for—nothing is in this world. Nothing is so good as it seems beforehand—not even our marrying wasn't, you see.

Location: Chapter 18
Speaker: Nancy
Context: Godfrey has confessed that he is Eppie's father

SIR GAWAIN AND THE GREEN KNIGHT

Anonymous

King Arthur's nephew accepts the challenge of a mysterious Green Knight, even though it will likely cost him his life.

THE WRITER IN CONTEXT

The alliterative poem *Sir Gawain and the Green Knight*, likely written in the mid- to late fourteenth century, survives in a late-fourteenth-century manuscript with three other poems—"Pearl," "Purity," and "Patience"—by the same author. Very little is known about the author of these poems, but most scholars believe that he was a university-trained clerk or the official of a provincial estate. Though it cannot be said with certainty that one person wrote all four poems, some shared characteristics point toward common authorship and also suggest that the Gawain-poet may have written another poem, "St. Erkenwald," that exists in a separate manuscript. All the poems except *Sir Gawain and the Green Knight* deal with overtly Christian subject matter. It remains unclear why *Sir Gawain*, an Arthurian romance, was included in an otherwise religious manuscript.

SIR GAWAIN AND THE GREEN KNIGHT IN CONTEXT

Sir Gawain and the Green Knight is written in a Middle English dialect that links it with Britain's Northwest Midlands, probably the county of Cheshire or Lancashire. The English provinces of the late fourteenth century, although they did not have London's economic, political, and artistic dominance, were not necessarily less culturally active than London, where Geoffrey Chaucer and William Langland were writing at the time. In fact, the works of the Gawain-poet belong to a movement traditionally known as the Alliterative Revival, usually associated with northern England.

Sir Gawain and the Green Knight's adapted Old English meter tends to connect the two halves of each poetic line through alliteration, or repetition of consonants. The poem also uses rhyme to structure its stanzas, and each group of long alliterative lines concludes with a word or phrase containing two syllables and a quatrain—known together as the "bob and wheel." The bobs and wheels in *Sir Gawain and the Green Knight* provide commentaries on what has just happened, create suspense or resolution, and serve as transitions to the next scene or idea.

Told in four "fitts," or parts, the poem weaves together at least three separate narrative strands commonly found in medieval folklore and romance. The first plot, the beheading game, appears in ancient folklore and may derive from pagan myths related to the cycle of planting and harvesting crops. The second and third plots concern the exchange of winnings and the hero's temptation, both of which derive from medieval romances and dramatize tests of the hero's honesty, loyalty, and chastity.

A larger story that frames the narrative is about Morgan le Faye, half-sister of King Arthur and a powerful sorceress. Traditionally, Morgan le Faye hates Arthur and his court, called Camelot. Medieval readers knew of Morgan's role in the destined fall of Camelot, the perfect world depicted in *Sir Gawain and the Green Knight*.

The poem's second frame is a historical one. The poem begins and ends with references to the myth of Britain's lineage. According to the myth, Brutus, a man from the ancient city of Troy, founded Britain. These references root the Arthurian romance in the tradition of epic literature, a tradition that was older and more elevated than the tradition of courtly literature. They also link fourteenth-century England to Rome, which was also founded by a Trojan (Aeneas). Thus, *Sir Gawain and the Green Knight* presents us with a version of *translatio imperii*—a Latin phrase meaning the transfer of culture from one civilization (classical antiquity, in this case) to another (medieval England). The Gawain-poet adopts an ironic tone at times, but he is also deeply invested in elevating his country's legends, history, and literary forms by relating them directly to classical antiquity.

SIR GAWAIN AND THE GREEN KNIGHT: KEY FACTS

Author: Anonymous; referred to as the Gawain-poet or the Pearl-poet

Time and place written: c. 1340–1400; West Midlands, England

Publisher: The original work circulated for an unknown length of time in manuscript format. It now exists as MS Cotton Nero A.x, fols. 91r–124v, held at the British Library. Many different modern English and original language editions exist

Type of work: Alliterative poem

Genre: Romance, Arthurian legend

Language: Middle English

Tense: Past

Tone: Admiring, ironic, nostalgic, critical

Setting (time): The mythical past of King Arthur's court (sometime after Rome's fall, but before recorded history)

Setting (place): Camelot; the wilderness; Bertilak's castle; the Green Chapel

Narrator: Third-person omniscient

Point of view: Gawain's

Protagonist: Sir Gawain

Antagonist: The Green Knight

SIR GAWAIN AND THE GREEN KNIGHT: PLOT OVERVIEW

During a New Year's Eve feast at King Arthur's court, a strange figure, referred to only as the Green Knight, pays the court an unexpected visit. He challenges the group's leader or anyone else to a game. The Green Knight says he will allow whomever accepts the challenge to strike him with his own axe, on condition that the challenger find him in exactly one year to receive a blow in return.

Stunned, Arthur hesitates to respond, but when the Green Knight mocks Arthur's silence, the king steps forward to take the challenge. As soon as Arthur grips the Green Knight's axe, Sir Gawain leaps up and asks to take the challenge himself. In one deadly blow, he cuts off the knight's head. To the amazement of the court, the Green Knight survives and picks up his severed head. Before riding away, the head reiterates the terms of the pact, reminding the young Gawain to seek him in a year and a day at the Green Chapel. The company returns to its festival, but Gawain is uneasy.

Time passes, and autumn arrives. On the Day of All Saints, Gawain prepares to leave Camelot and find the Green Knight. He puts on his best armor, mounts his horse, Gringolet, and starts off toward North Wales, traveling through the wilderness of northwest Britain. Gawain encounters all sorts of beasts, suffers from hunger and cold, and grows more desperate as the days pass. On Christmas Day, he prays to find a place to hear Mass, then looks up and sees a castle shimmering in the distance. The lord of the castle welcomes Gawain warmly, introducing him to his lady and to the old woman who sits beside her. For amusement, the host (whose name is later revealed to be Bertilak) strikes a deal with Gawain: the host will go out hunting with his men every day, and when he returns in the evening, he will exchange his winnings for anything Gawain has managed to acquire by staying behind at the castle. Gawain happily agrees to the pact and goes to bed.

The first day, the lord hunts a herd of does, while Gawain sleeps late. The lord's wife sneaks into Gawain's chambers and attempts to seduce him. Gawain puts her off, but before she leaves she steals one kiss from him. That evening, when the host gives Gawain the venison he has captured, Gawain kisses him in return. The second day, the lord hunts a wild boar. The lady again enters Gawain's chambers, this time kissing Gawain twice. That evening Gawain gives the host the two kisses in exchange for the boar's head.

The third day, the lord hunts a fox, and the lady kisses Gawain three times. She also asks him for a love token such as a ring or a glove. Gawain refuses to give her anything and refuses to take anything from her, until the lady mentions her girdle. The green silk girdle she wears around her waist is no ordinary piece of cloth, the lady claims, but possesses the magical ability to protect its wearer from death.

Intrigued, Gawain accepts the cloth. When it comes time to exchange his winnings with the host, Gawain gives the three kisses but does not mention the green girdle.

New Year's Day arrives. Gawain dons his armor, including the girdle, and sets off with Gringolet to seek the Green Knight. A guide accompanies him out of the estate grounds. When they reach the border of the forest, the guide says he would not tell anyone if Gawain decided to give up the quest. Gawain refuses to give up. Eventually, he comes to a kind of crevice in a rock. He hears the whirring of a grindstone, confirming his suspicion that this strange cavern is the Green Chapel. Gawain calls out, and the Green Knight emerges to greet him. Intent on fulfilling the terms of the contract, Gawain presents his neck to the Green Knight, who proceeds to feign two blows. On the third feint, the Green Knight nicks Gawain's neck, barely drawing blood. Angered, Gawain shouts that their contract has been met. The Green Knight merely laughs.

The Green Knight reveals that he is the lord of the castle where Gawain recently stayed. Because Gawain did not honestly exchange all of his winnings on the third day, Bertilak drew blood on the third blow. Nevertheless, Gawain has proven himself a worthy knight without equal in all the land. When Gawain questions Bertilak further, Bertilak explains that the old woman at the castle is really Morgan le Faye, Gawain's aunt and King Arthur's half-sister. She sent the Green Knight on his original errand, using her magic to change his appearance. Relieved to be alive but extremely guilty about his sinful failure to tell the whole truth, Gawain wears the girdle on his arm as a reminder of his own failure. He returns to Arthur's court, where all the knights wear girdles on their arms to show their support for Gawain.

CHARACTERS IN *SIR GAWAIN AND THE GREEN KNIGHT*

King Arthur The king of Camelot. During the time when *Sir Gawain* takes place, Arthur is young, and his court is in its golden age. With the confusion of a young man, Arthur is stunned by the Green Knight's offer, but he proves his mettle by recovering and stepping forward to meet the challenge.

Bertilak of Hautdesert/The Green Knight The sturdy, good-natured lord of the castle where Gawain spends Christmas, and the man who Morgan le Faye turns into the Green Knight. The Gawain-poet associates Bertilak with the natural world—his beard resembles a beaver, his face a fire—but also with the courtly behavior of an aristocratic host. Lord Bertilak is boisterous, powerful, brave, and generous. As the Green Knight, he is huge, wild-looking, and green complexioned.

Bertilak's Wife The lady who regularly attempts to seduce Gawain during his stay at the castle. Bertilak's wife is a very clever debater and an astute reader of Gawain's responses. Like her husband, she turns out to be a pawn in Morgan le Faye's plot.

Morgan le Faye A powerful sorceress trained by Merlin, and King Arthur's half sister. Not until the last one hundred lines of the poem do we discover that the old woman at the castle is Morgan le Faye and that she has controlled the poem's entire action from beginning to end. As she often does in Arthurian literature, Morgan appears here as an enemy of Camelot.

Sir Gawain The poem's protagonist. Gawain is Arthur's nephew and one of his most loyal knights. Gawain has a reputation as a great knight and courtly lover. He prides himself on observing the five points of chivalry in every aspect of his life. Gawain is a pinnacle of humility, piety, integrity, loyalty, and honesty. His only flaw is his willingness to lie in order to protect himself. Gawain leaves the Green Chapel penitent and changed.

Gringolet Gawain's horse.

Queen Guinevere Arthur's wife. The beautiful young Guinevere of *Sir Gawain and the Green Knight* has little in common with the one of later Arthurian legend. She is a silent, objectified presence in the midst of the knights of the Round Table.

THEMES IN *SIR GAWAIN AND THE GREEN KNIGHT*

THE NATURE OF CHIVALRY The world of *Sir Gawain and the Green Knight* is governed by well-defined codes of behavior. The code of chivalry, in particular, shapes the characters. The ideals of chivalry derive from the Christian concept of morality, and the proponents of chivalry seek to promote spiritual ideals in a spiritually fallen world. The ideals of Christian morality and knightly chivalry are brought together in Gawain's symbolic shield. The pentangle represents the five virtues of knights: friendship, generosity, chastity, courtesy, and piety. Gawain's adherence to these virtues is tested throughout the poem, but the poem examines more than Gawain's personal virtue: it asks whether heavenly virtue is realistic in a fallen world. What is really being tested in *Sir Gawain and the Green Knight* might be the chivalric system itself, symbolized by Camelot.

Arthur's court depends heavily on the code of chivalry, and *Sir Gawain and the Green Knight* gently criticizes the fact that chivalry values appearances and symbols over truth. Arthur is introduced as the "most courteous of all," indicating that the members of his court are ranked according to their mastery of a certain code of behavior and good manners—or perhaps that Arthur is automatically said to be the most courteous simply because he is king. When the Green Knight challenges the court, he mocks its members for being so afraid of mere words, suggesting that words and appearances hold too much power over the company. The members of the court never reveal their true feelings, instead choosing to seem exclusively beautiful, courteous, and fair-spoken.

In the forest, Gawain must abandon the codes of chivalry and admit that he needs physical comfort. Once he admits weakness and prays for help, he is rewarded by the appearance of a castle. The inhabitants of Bertilak's castle teach Gawain about a kind of chivalry that is more firmly based in truth and reality than that of Arthur's court. These people are connected to nature, as their hunting and even the way the servants greet Gawain by kneeling on the "naked earth" suggest. As opposed to the courtiers at Camelot, who celebrate with no understanding of how unusually rich they are, Bertilak's courtiers joke self-consciously about the excessive lavishness of their feast.

The poem does criticize the codes of chivalry. Gawain's adherence to them is what keeps him from sleeping with his host's wife. The lesson Gawain learns as a result of the Green Knight's challenge is that he is just a physical being who is mainly concerned with his own life. Chivalry provides a valuable set of ideals toward which to strive, but people must not forget their own mortality and weakness. Gawain's time in the wilderness, his flinching at the Green Knight's axe, and his acceptance of the lady's green girdle teach him that though he may be the most chivalrous knight in the land, he is nevertheless human and capable of error.

THE LETTER OF THE LAW   Though the Green Knight refers to his challenge as a "game," he uses the language of the law to bind Gawain into an agreement with him. He repeatedly uses the word "covenant," meaning a set of laws, a word that evokes the two covenants represented by the Old and the New Testaments. The Old Testament describes the covenant made between God and the people of Israel through Abraham, and the New Testament describes a new covenant between Christ and his followers. In 2 Corinthians 3:6, Paul writes that Christ has "a new covenant, not of letter but of spirit; for the letter kills, but the Spirit gives life." The "letter" to which Paul refers here is the legal system of the Old Testament. From this statement comes the Christian belief that the literal enforcement of the law is less important than serving the spirit of the law.

Throughout most of the poem, the covenant between Gawain and the Green Knight refers to the literal kind of legal enforcement that medieval Europeans might have associated with the Old Testament. The Green Knight at first seems concerned solely with the letter of the law. Even though he has tricked Gawain into their covenant, he expects Gawain to follow through on the agreement. And Gawain, though he knows that following the letter of the law means death, is determined to see his agreement through to the end because he sees this as his knightly duty.

At the end of the poem, the covenant takes on a new meaning, resembling the less literal, more merciful New Testament covenant between Christ and his Church. In a Christian gesture, the Green Knight absolves Gawain because Gawain has confessed his faults. To remind Gawain of his weakness, the Green Knight gives him a penance in the form of the wound on his neck. The Green Knight punishes Gawain for breaking his covenant to share all his winnings with his host, but he does not follow to the letter his promised punishment. Instead of chopping Gawain's head off, Bertilak spares Gawain. Ultimately, Gawain clings to the letter of the law. He cannot accept his sin and absolve himself of it the way Bertilak has, and he continues to do penance by wearing the girdle for the rest of his life.

SYMBOLS IN *SIR GAWAIN AND THE GREEN KNIGHT*

THE PENTANGLE   According to the Gawain-poet, King Solomon originally designed the pentangle, a five-pointed star, as his own magic seal. A symbol of truth, the star has five points that link and lock with each other, forming what is called the endless knot. Each line of the pentangle passes over one line and under one line, and joins the other two lines at its ends. The pentangle symbolizes the virtues to which Gawain aspires: to be faultless in his five senses; never to fail in his five fingers; to be faithful to the five wounds that Christ received on the cross; to be strengthened by the five joys that the Virgin Mary had in Jesus (the Annunciation, Nativity, Resurrection, Ascension, and Assumption); and to possess brotherly love, courtesy, piety, and chastity. The side of the shield facing Gawain has an image of the Virgin Mary to make sure that Gawain never loses heart.

THE GREEN GIRDLE   The meaning of the host's wife's girdle changes over the course of the narrative. The girdle is made out of green silk and embroidered with gold thread, colors that link it to the Green Knight. The host's wife claims it possesses the power to keep its wearer from harm, but in Part 4 it is revealed that the girdle has no magical properties. After the Green Knight explains that he is the host, Gawain curses the girdle as a symbol of cowardice and an excessive love of mortal life. He wears it from then on as a badge of his sinfulness.

IMPORTANT QUOTATIONS FROM *SIR GAWAIN AND THE GREEN KNIGHT*

There hurtles in at the hall-door an unknown rider,
One the greatest on ground in growth of his frame:
From broad neck to buttocks so bulky and thick,
And his loins and his legs so long and so great,
Half a giant on earth I hold him to be,
But believe him no less than the largest of men,
And the seemliest in his stature to see, as he rides,
For in back and in breast though his body was grim,
His waist in its width was worthily small,
And formed with every feature in fair accord

was he.
Great wonder grew in hall
At his hue most strange to see,
For man and gear and all
Were green as green could be.

Location: Lines 136–150
Speaker: The narrator
Context: The Green Knight arrives in Arthur's court

The Gawain-poet describes the mysterious visitor to King Arthur's court as an incredibly large being, "[h]alf a giant on earth." The poet's comparison of the Green Knight to a half-giant may be an allusion to a passage in Genesis just before the story of Noah that claims that fallen angels and human women mated together to produce superhuman, wicked children, precipitating God's punishment in the form of the flood (Gen. 6:1–4). But the poet goes on to reassure his audience that the Green Knight is in fact a human being, and an extremely good-looking one. With fair features and a form composed of clean lines (broad shoulders tapering into a thin waist), the Green Knight cuts a beautiful figure. In this passage the bob and wheel creates tension, snaking us through a lengthy description before the wheel announces its surprise: this beautiful knight is green.

Sir, if you be Gawain, it seems a great wonder—
A man so well-meaning, and mannerly disposed,
And cannot act in company as courtesy bids,
And if one takes the trouble to teach him, 'tis all in vain.
That lesson learned lately is lightly forgot,
Though I painted it as plain as my poor wit allowed."

"What lesson, dear lady?" he asked all alarmed;
"I have been much to blame, if your story be true."
"Yet my counsel was of kissing," came her answer then,
"Where favor has been found, freely to claim
As accords with the conduct of courteous knights."

Location: Lines 1481–1491
Speaker: The narrator
Context: Gawain and the host's wife talk on the second morning of Gawain's game

The lady plays on the tension between courtesy and chastity in an attempt to get what she wants. She begins by challenging Gawain's name and reputation, claiming that her guest cannot be the real Gawain, because that famous knight would not forget to be "gracious." She likens him to an errant student who has forgotten his lesson from the day before, and herself to his teacher. In doing so, she calls upon a long history of cultural imagery from the courtly love and classical traditions. In the courtly love tradition, the beloved lady is an erotic teacher, instructing the lover in proper spiritual comportment as well as in the courtly "art of love." She is supposed to ennoble her knight by teaching him how to be a proper lover and a better man. At the same time, the host's wife evokes the classical tradition of education, in which female allegorical figures such as Lady Grammar and Lady Philosophy are responsible for the education of boys and men.

Gawain was glad to begin those games in hall,
But if the end be harsher, hold it no wonder,
For though men are merry in mind after much drink,
A year passes apace, and proves ever new:
First things and final conform but seldom.

Location: Lines 495–499
Speaker: The narrator
Context: The narrator describes the passage of time

[T]here hoved a great hall and fair:
Turrets rising in tiers, with tines at their tops,
Spires set beside them, splendidly long,
With finials well-fashioned, as filigree fine.
Chalk-white chimneys over chambers high
Gleamed in gay array upon gables and roofs;
The pinnacles in panoply, pointing in air,
So vied there for his view that verily it seemed
A castle cut of paper for a king's feast.
The good knight on Gringolet thought it great luck
If he could but contrive to come there within
To keep the Christmas feast in that castle fair
and bright.

Location: Lines 794–806
Speaker: The narrator
Context: Gawain sees the host's castle for the first time

But if a dullard should dote, deem it no wonder,
And through the wiles of a woman be wooed into sorrow,
For so was Adam by one, when the world began,

And Solomon by many more, and Samson the mighty—
Delilah was his doom, and David thereafter
Was beguiled by Bathsheba, and bore much distress;
. . . .

For these were proud princes, most prosperous of old,
Past all lovers lucky, that languished under heaven,
> > *bemused.*
> > *And one and all fell prey*
> > *To women they had used;*
> > *If I be led astray,*
> > *Methinks I may be excused.*

Location: Lines 2414–2419, 2422–2428
Speaker: Gawain
Context: Gawain compares himself to biblical figures who were led astray by deceitful women

SLAUGHTERHOUSE-FIVE

Kurt Vonnegut

A veteran of World War II remembers being in Dresden during the firebombing and describes his postwar existence.

THE LIFE OF KURT VONNEGUT

Kurt Vonnegut, Jr., was born in Indianapolis in 1922. His father was an architect, and his mother was a noted beauty. Both spoke German fluently but decided not to teach Kurt the language because of widespread anti-German sentiment following World War I. Vonnegut's two siblings attended private schools, but the Great Depression hit hard in the 1930s, and the Vonneguts sent Kurt to public school and moved to more modest accommodations. Vonnegut attended college at Cornell for a little over two years. In 1943, he enlisted in the U.S. Army. In 1944, his mother committed suicide, and Vonnegut was taken prisoner in the Ardennes Forest of Belgium following the Battle of the Bulge.

After the war, Vonnegut married, and he entered a master's degree program in anthropology at the University of Chicago. He also worked as a reporter for the Chicago City News Bureau. His master's thesis, titled *Fluctuations Between Good and Evil in Simple Tales*, was rejected. He departed for Schenectady, New York, to take a job in public relations at a General Electric research laboratory.

Vonnegut left GE in 1951 to devote himself full time to writing. *Player Piano*, his first novel, appeared in 1952. *Sirens of Titan* was published in 1959, followed by *Mother Night* (1962), *Cat's Cradle* (1963), *God Bless You, Mr. Rosewater* (1965), and *Slaughterhouse-Five* (1969), his most highly praised work. Vonnegut continues to write prolifically.

SLAUGHTERHOUSE-FIVE IN CONTEXT

Slaughterhouse-Five treats one of the most horrific massacres in European history—the World War II Allied firebombing of Dresden, a city in eastern Germany, on February 13, 1945—with mock-serious humor and clear antiwar sentiment. More than 130,000 civilians died in Dresden, roughly the same number of deaths that resulted from the Allied bombing raids on Tokyo and from the atomic bomb dropped on Hiroshima, both of which also occurred in 1945. Inhabitants of Dresden were incinerated or suffocated in the firestorm in a matter of hours.

The novel is based on Kurt Vonnegut's own experience in World War II. Like his protagonist Billy Pilgrim, Vonnegut was in Dresden as a prisoner of war during the firebombing. He only survived because he happened to be confined in a meat locker beneath a slaughterhouse. Vonnegut's surviving captors put him to work finding, burying, and burning bodies. His task continued until the Russians came and the war ended. Vonnegut has said that he wanted to write about the experience but could not for more than twenty years. He also found he could not describe what happened in a linear fashion, so he wrote about it in a shifting, jumbled, nonlinear way.

Slaughterhouse-Five was published in 1969, when the United States was in the midst of the Vietnam War. Vonnegut was an outspoken pacifist and critic of the conflict, and his novel made a forceful statement about the campaign in Vietnam, a war in which incendiary technology was once more being employed against nonmilitary targets in the name of a dubious cause.

SLAUGHTERHOUSE-FIVE: KEY FACTS

Full title: Slaughterhouse-Five; or, The Children's Crusade: A Duty-Dance with Death

Time and place written: Approximately 1945–1968; United States

Date of first publication: 1969

Publisher: Dell Publishing

Type of work: Novel

Genre: War novel; historical fiction; science fiction; semi-autobiographical fiction

Language: English

Tense: Past, occasionally present and future

Tone: Familiar, ironic, darkly humorous, absurd

Setting (time): Mainly 1944–1945, also 1920s–1976

Setting (place): Germany, Luxembourg, New York, the planet Tralfamadore

Narrator: An anonymous narrator in the third and first person

Point of view: Billy Pilgrim's

Protagonist: Billy Pilgrim

Antagonist: War

SLAUGHTERHOUSE-FIVE: PLOT OVERVIEW

Note: *Billy Pilgrim, the novel's protagonist, is "unstuck in time." He travels between periods of his life, unable to control which period he lands in. As a result, the narrative jumps back and forth in time and place. This summary describes Billy's life chronologically.*

Billy Pilgrim is born in 1922. He grows up in Ilium, New York. A funny-looking, weak youth, he does reasonably well in high school, enrolls in night classes at the Ilium School of Optometry, and is drafted into the army during World War II. He trains as a chaplain's assistant in South Carolina, where an umpire officiates during practice battles. Billy's father dies in a hunting accident shortly before Billy ships overseas to join an infantry regiment in Luxembourg. Billy is thrown into the Battle of the Bulge in Belgium and immediately taken prisoner behind German lines. Just before his capture, he sees the entirety of his life in one sweep.

Billy is transported in a crowded railway boxcar to a POW camp in Germany. Upon his arrival, he and the other privates are treated to a feast by a group of fellow prisoners, English officers who were captured earlier in the war. Billy has a breakdown and gets a shot of morphine that makes him time-trip. Soon he and the other Americans are moved to the beautiful city of Dresden where the prisoners must work at various tasks, including the manufacture of a nutritional malt syrup. Their camp is in a former slaughterhouse.

One night, Allied forces carpet bomb the city, then drop incendiary bombs. The resulting firestorm sucks most of the oxygen into the blaze, asphyxiating or incinerating roughly 130,000 people. Billy and his fellow POWs survive in an airtight meat locker. They emerge to find a moonscape of destruction. They are forced to excavate corpses from the rubble. Several days later, Russian forces capture the city, and Billy's involvement in the war ends.

Billy returns to Ilium and finishes optometry school. He gets engaged to Valencia Merble, the obese daughter of the school's founder. After having a nervous breakdown, Billy commits himself to a veterans' hospital and receives shock treatments. A fellow patient in the mental ward introduces Billy to the science-fiction novels of a writer named Kilgore Trout. After his recuperation, Billy gets married. His wealthy father-in-law sets him up in the optometry business, and Billy and Valencia raise two children and grow rich. Billy acquires the trappings of the suburban American dream: a Cadillac, a stately home with modern appliances, a bejeweled wife, and the presidency of the Lions Club. At his eighteenth wedding anniversary party, the sight of a barbershop quartet triggers a memory of Dresden, and Billy breaks down.

The night after his daughter's wedding in 1967, as he later reveals on a radio talk show, Billy is kidnapped by Tralfamadorians, two-foot-high aliens who resemble upside-down toilet plungers. They take him in their flying saucer to the planet Tralfamadore, where they put him in a zoo and mate him with a movie actress named Montana Wildhack. The Tralfamadorians explain to Billy that for them, time exists in its entirety in the fourth dimension. When someone dies, that person is simply dead at a particular time. Somewhere else and at a different time, he or she is alive and well. Tralfamadorians prefer to focus on life's nicer moments.

When he returns to Earth, Billy initially says nothing of his experiences. In 1968, he gets on a chartered plane to go to an optometry conference in Montreal. The plane crashes into a mountain, and only Billy survives. A brain surgeon operates on him in a Vermont hospital. On her way to visit him there, Valencia dies of accidental carbon monoxide poisoning after crashing her car. Back in Ilium, Billy's daughter places Billy under the care of a nurse. Billy has foreseen this moment while time-tripping and knows that his message will eventually be accepted. He sneaks off to New York City, where he goes on a radio talk show. Shortly thereafter, he writes a letter to the local paper. His daughter is at her wit's end and does not know what to do with him. Billy makes a tape recording of his account of his death, which he predicts will occur in 1976 after Chicago has been hydrogen-bombed by the Chinese. He knows exactly how it will happen: a vengeful man he knew in the war will hire someone to shoot him. Billy adds that he will experience the violet hum of death and then will skip back to some other point in his life. He has seen it all many times.

CHARACTERS IN *SLAUGHTERHOUSE-FIVE*

Billy's Mother A woman "trying to construct a life that made sense from things she found in gift shops." Billy's mother visits Billy in the mental hospital. Her presence embarrasses Billy, making him feel that he is an ungrateful son because of his indifference to life.

Billy's Father Billy's father throws his son into the YMCA pool to teach him how to swim. Billy prefers the bottom of the pool, but he is rescued unwillingly from drowning after he loses consciousness.

Howard W. Campbell, Jr. An American who has become a Nazi. Campbell speaks to the prisoners in the slaughterhouse and tries to recruit them for the "Free American Corps," a German army unit that he is forming to fight the Russians.

Edgar Derby Another survivor of Dresden's incineration. After the firebombing, Derby is sentenced to die by firing squad for plundering a teapot from the wreckage. His death is anticlimactic, since Billy views it as an inevitability.

Werner Gluck A young German guard at the slaughterhouse. Gluck gets his first glimpse of a naked woman alongside Billy. Their shared interest in the naked female body unites these two men.

Paul Lazzaro The POW responsible for Billy's death. Lazzaro, a ruffian with criminal tendencies, arranges for Billy's assassination to avenge Roland Weary's death.

Valencia Merble Billy's pleasant, fat wife. Valencia loves Billy dearly.

Barbara Pilgrim Billy's daughter. Barbara marries at age twenty-one and is soon faced with the sudden death of her mother and the apparent mental breakdown of her father.

Billy Pilgrim The protagonist of the novel. Billy is a World War II veteran, POW survivor of the firebombing of Dresden, prospering optometrist, and good husband and father. He believes he has "come unstuck in time."

Robert Pilgrim Billy's son. Robert is a failure and a delinquent in school, but he cleans up his life enough to become a Green Beret in the Vietnam War. Billy cannot communicate with or relate to his own son.

Eliot Rosewater A war veteran who occupies the bed near Billy in the mental ward of a veterans' hospital. Rosewater helps Billy find escape in the science-fiction novels of Kilgore Trout.

Bertram Copeland Rumfoord A Harvard history professor and the official U.S. Air Force historian. Rumfoord is laid up by a skiing accident in the same Vermont hospital as Billy after his plane crash. He is reluctant to believe that Billy was present during the Dresden raid.

Lily Rumfoord Rumfoord's young trophy wife and research assistant. Lily Rumfoord is frightened of Billy.

Tralfamadorians Aliens shaped like toilet plungers, each with one hand containing an eye. The novel's narrative mimics the Tralfamadorians' philosophies of time, which they perceive as an assemblage of moments existing simultaneously rather than as a linear progression. Their acceptance of death, which Billy embraces, leads the narrator to remark simply "So it goes" at each mention of death.

Kilgore Trout A bitter, unappreciated author of several cleverly ironic science-fiction novels. Trout, who appears in many of Vonnegut's works, functions as Vonnegut's alter ego.

Kurt Vonnegut The novel's author and a minor character in *Slaughterhouse-Five*. Vonnegut periodically inserts himself in the narrative, as when he becomes the incontinent soldier in the latrine in the German prison camp.

Roland Weary A stupid, cruel soldier taken prisoner by the Germans along with Billy. Unlike Billy, who is totally out of place in the war, Weary is a deluded glory-seeker who fancies himself part of the Three Musketeers and saves Billy's life out of a desire to be heroic.

Wild Bob An army colonel in the German rail yard. Wild Bob has lost his mind. He dies an arbitrary death.

Montana Wildhack A nubile young actress who is kidnapped by the Tralfamadorians to be Billy's mate inside the zoo. Billy wins Montana's trust and love, and fathers a child by her in Tralfamadore. Billy's relationship with Montana may a delusion triggered by a visit to an adult bookstore in Times Square, where he sees her videos and a headline claiming to reveal her fate.

THEMES IN *SLAUGHTERHOUSE-FIVE*

THE DESTRUCTIVENESS OF WAR The catastrophic firebombing of the German town of Dresden during World War II is the lynchpin of the narrative. In his swimming lessons at the YMCA, his speeches at the Lions Club, and his captivity in Tralfamadore, Billy Pilgrim always returns to the meat locker in Dresden, where he very narrowly survived asphyxiation and incineration. Billy's experiences in Dresden shape the rest of his life. Although he seems very successful in his postwar life—he is president of the Lions Club, works as a prosperous optometrist, lives in a comfortable modern home, and fathers two children—he is sleepwalking through his existence. His father-in-law got him his job. He realizes he is a stranger to his son. He does not have a real relationship with his wife. Perhaps he hallucinates about the Tralfamadorians as a way to escape a world he cannot understand.

THE ILLUSION OF FREE WILL The Tralfamadorians live with the knowledge of the fourth dimension, which, they say, contains all moments of time occurring and reoccurring endlessly and simultaneously. Because they believe that all moments of time have already happened (since all moments repeat themselves endlessly), they accept their fates calmly, knowing that they are powerless to change them. Only on Earth, according to the Tralfamadorians, is there talk of free will, since humans mistakenly think of time as a linear progression. Billy thinks of his life as a series of proofs that free will does not exist. He would like to drown on the bottom of the pool, but he is rescued against his will. He is drafted into the war against his will. It becomes clear that surviving a war is a matter of chance, and that no amount of the will to live can help.

THE IMPORTANCE OF SIGHT In several ways, Billy feels it is his mission to correct the world's sight. Most literally, his work as an optometrist involves correcting the vision of his patients. His knowledge of the fourth dimension leads him to believe he should help the world understand the nonlinear nature of time. However, it is also possible to argue that Billy has lost true sight and lives in a world of hallucination and self-doubt. After witnessing the horrors of war, he becomes mentally unstable. He has a shaky grip on reality and at random moments experiences overpowering flashbacks to other parts of his life. His conviction that aliens have captured him and kept him in a zoo before sending him back to Earth may be the product of an overactive imagination.

SYMBOLS IN *SLAUGHTERHOUSE-FIVE*

THE BIRD WHO SAYS "POO-TEE-WEET?" The jabbering bird symbolizes the impossibility of speaking intelligently about war. After the massacre, birdsong rings out alone in the silence, and "*Poo-tee-weet?*" seems an appropriately meaningless response, since no words can describe the horror of the Dresden firebombing. The bird sings outside Billy's hospital window and again in the last line of the book, asking a question which we can't understand and can't answer.

BLUE AND IVORY On various occasions in *Slaughterhouse-Five*, Billy's bare feet are described as blue and ivory, as when Billy writes a letter in his basement in the cold and when he waits for the flying saucer to kidnap him. These cold, corpselike hues suggest the fragility of the membrane between life and death, between worldly and otherworldly experience.

IMPORTANT QUOTATIONS FROM *SLAUGHTERHOUSE-FIVE*

Billy had a framed prayer on his office wall which expressed his method for keeping going, even though he was unenthusiastic about living. A lot of patients who saw the prayer on Billy's wall told him that it helped them to keep going, too. It went like this: "God grant me the serenity to accept the things I cannot change, courage to change the things I can, and wisdom always to tell the difference." Among the things Billy Pilgrim could not change were the past, the present, and the future.

Location: Chapter 3
Speaker: The narrator
Context: Billy has been kidnapped and taken to Tralfamadore, where he sees this inscription on a locket around Montana's neck

The saying Billy keeps on his wall is much darker to Billy than it is to his patients. His patients imagine that if they have courage, they can make changes that will affect the present and the future. Billy, who believes that time is not linear, believes that he is powerless to change anything.

Billy answered. There was a drunk on the other end. Billy could almost smell his breath—mustard gas and roses. It was a wrong number. Billy hung up.

Location: Chapter 4
Speaker: The narrator
Context: Vonnegut calls Billy

The night after his daughter's wedding, Billy cannot sleep and gets out of bed. He knows that the flying saucer will come for him soon. He wanders into his daughter's empty bedroom, and the phone rings. We recognize this drunk from Chapter 1: he is the author, Kurt Vonnegut, who in his middle age has a tendency to make late-night, drunken phone calls to old girlfriends, his breath stinking of mustard gas and roses. Vonnegut's characterization of his breath as a combination of mustard gas, often used as a chemical weapon, and roses, a symbol of romance, suggests that the war has infected every corner of his life, poisoning his relationships and fond memories.

It is so short and jumbled and jangled, Sam, because there is nothing intelligent to say about a massacre. Everybody is supposed to be dead, to never say anything or want anything ever again. Everything is supposed to be very quiet after a massacre, and it always is, except for the birds. And what do the birds say? All there is to say about a massacre, things like "Poo-tee-weet?"

Location: Chapter 1
Speaker: Kurt Vonnegut
Context: Vonnegut addresses his publisher

"If I hadn't spent so much time studying Earthlings," said the Tralfamadorian, "I wouldn't have any idea what was meant by 'free will.' I've visited thirty-one inhabited planets in the universe, and I have studied reports on one hundred more. Only on Earth is there any talk of free will."

Location: Chapter 4
Speaker: A Tralfamadorian
Context: One of Billy's captors tells him about the true nature of time

There isn't any particular relationship between the messages, except that the author has chosen them carefully, so that, when seen all at once, they produce an image of life that is beautiful and surprising and deep. There is no beginning, no middle, no end, no suspense, no moral, no causes, no effects. What we love in our books are the depths of many marvelous moments seen all at one time.

Location: Chapter 5
Speaker: A Tralfamadorian
Context: Billy's captors explain the Tralfamadorian novel to him

SONG OF SOLOMON

Toni Morrison

A spoiled young man changes after learning about his family history.

THE LIFE OF TONI MORRISON

Toni Morrison was born Chloe Anthony Wofford on February 18, 1931, in Lorain, Ohio, a small steel-mill city west of Cleveland. She was the second of four children. Her parents were George Wofford, who worked as a shipyard welder, and Rahmah Willis Wofford, whose parents had been sharecroppers.

Morrison excelled in high school and, in 1949, became the first woman in her family to go to college. She matriculated at Howard University, the esteemed, predominantly black institution in Washington, D.C. Morrison joined the college's drama club and during the summers traveled with the club throughout the South, performing for all-black audiences. At this time, Morrison began calling herself Toni, a shortened version of her middle name, Anthony.

After graduating from Howard with a bachelor's degree in English literature in 1953, Morrison earned a master's degree in English from Cornell University. In 1955, Morrison accepted her first teaching job at Texas Southern University, a predominantly black institution. Morrison has said that Texas Southern University instilled in her a sense of "black culture as a subject, an idea, as a discipline." She left Texas Southern after two years and returned to Howard University to join its English faculty. In Washington, she met Harold Morrison, a Jamaican architect, and married him in 1958. Three years later, she gave birth to their first son, Harold Ford.

Morrison did not take an active part in the Civil Rights movement, which had electrified the Howard campus by the early 1960s. She was uncomfortable with the movement's philosophy of integration; she believed that integration would come only through the kind of black solidarity she had found at Texas Southern.

After the birth of their second son, Morrison and her husband divorced. Morrison took a job as a textbook editor at a subsidiary of Random House in Syracuse, New York. Eventually she became a senior editor at Random House's New York City headquarters. She worked there for eighteen years, specializing in the literary works of black authors and collaborating on *The Black Book* (1974), a groundbreaking scrapbook of sorts that included photographs, documents, and articles collected from 300 years of African-American history and culture. Her goal as an editor was to help create a canon of African-American literature.

In the late 1960s, as Morrison's prominence as an editor grew, her literary career also began to flourish. Before leaving Syracuse, she had shown a short story to Alan Rancler, an editor, who encouraged her to expand the story into a full-length novel. Rancler published the resulting novel, *The Bluest Eye*, in 1970. Morrison's second novel, *Sula* (1973), was nominated for the National Book Award for Fiction in 1975. Her third novel, *Song of Solomon* (1977), which won the National Book Critics Circle Award, was the breakthrough work that made Morrison a household name in America. Morrison's other works include *Tar Baby* (1981), *Jazz* (1992), *Paradise* (1998), and *Beloved* (1987), which won the Pulitzer Prize in Fiction in 1988. In 1993, Morrison won the Nobel Prize in Literature, becoming the eighth woman and the first black woman to receive the honor.

SONG OF SOLOMON IN CONTEXT

Song of Solomon, Morrison's third novel, was popular with both critics and readers. In 1978, the novel won the National Critics Circle Award and the Letters Award. 570,000 paperback copies are currently in print.

Morrison drew on her own life in creating the characters in *Song of Solomon*. Jake (also known as Macon Dead I) has experiences similar to those of Morrison's beloved grandfather, John Solomon Willis. After Willis lost his land and was forced to become a sharecropper, he grew disillusioned by the unfulfilled promises of the Emancipation Proclamation, Abraham Lincoln's 1865 document freeing black slaves. The character Heddy may have been modeled on Morrison's Native American great-grandmother. Guitar is a composite character, a reflection of many of Morrison's family and friends whose lives were destroyed by racism. Milkman's journey to uncover his roots can be compared to Morrison's own. Like Milkman's, Morrison's creative life began after age thirty and has been grounded in the African-American experience.

Song of Solomon reflects Morrison's desire to preserve African-American folklore, art, music, and literature. She has said in interviews that she opposed desegregation in the early 1960s despite her awareness of its terrible effects. She worried that the excellent historically black schools and universities would disappear and that African-American cultural life would grow diffuse. While *Song of Solomon* explores the different experiences of white people and black people, almost all of the action occurs in an African-American world.

SONG OF SOLOMON: KEY FACTS

Time and place written: 1977; United States

Date of first publication: 1977

Publisher: Penguin Books

Type of work: Novel

Genre: Adventure story, quest, bildungsroman

Language: English

Tense: Past

Tone: Dramatic, portentous

Setting (time): 1931–1963, with occasional flashbacks

Setting (place): An unnamed city in Michigan (probably Detroit), Pennsylvania, Virginia

Narrator: Limited omniscient narrator in the third person

Point of view: Varies

Protagonist: Milkman Dead

Antagonist: Wealth, ignorance

SONG OF SOLOMON: PLOT OVERVIEW

Robert Smith, an insurance agent in an unnamed Michigan town, stands on the roof of Mercy Hospital wearing blue silk wings and claiming that he will fly to the opposite shore of Lake Superior. Mr. Smith leaps off the roof and plummets to his death. The next day, Ruth Foster Dead, the daughter of the first black doctor in town, gives birth to the first black child born in Mercy Hospital: Milkman Dead.

After discovering, at age four, that humans cannot fly, Milkman loses all interest in himself and others. He grows up nourished by the love of his mother and his aunt, Pilate. His sisters, First Corinthians and Magdalene (called Lena), take care of him. His lover and cousin, Hagar, adores him. Milkman, a bored and privileged boy, does not reciprocate their kindness. In his lack of compassion, Milkman resembles his father, Macon Dead II, a ruthless landlord interested only in the accumulation of wealth.

Milkman is afflicted with a genetic malady, an emotional disease that has its origins in oppression endured by past generations and passed on to future ones. Milkman's grandfather, Macon Dead, received his odd name when a drunk Union soldier misheard him. Macon was killed while defending his land. His two children, Macon Jr. and Pilate, witnessed the murder, which permanently scarred them. They are estranged from each other. Pilate is now a poor but strong woman, the matriarch of a family that includes her daughter, Reba, and her granddaughter, Hagar. Macon Jr. is reviled by his family and his tenants.

By the time Milkman reaches the age of thirty-two, he feels stifled living with his parents. Macon Jr. tells Milkman that Pilate may have millions of dollars in gold wrapped in a green tarp. With the help of his best friend, Guitar Bains, whom he promises a share of the loot, Milkman robs Pilate. The green tarp holds only rocks and a human skeleton. We later learn that the skeleton is Milkman's grandfather's, Macon Dead I. Guitar wanted the gold to help carry out his mission for the Seven Days, a secret society that avenges injustices committed against African Americans by murdering innocent whites.

Thinking that the gold might be in a cave near Macon's old Pennsylvania farm, Milkman heads south, promising Guitar a share of whatever gold he finds. Before he leaves, Milkman severs his romantic relationship with Hagar, who goes mad and tries to kill Milkman. After arriving in Montour County, Pennsylvania, Milkman discovers that there is no gold to be found. He looks for his long-lost family history rather than for gold. Milkman meets Circe, an old midwife who helped deliver Macon Jr. and Pilate. Circe explains that Macon's original name was Jake and that he was married to an Indian girl, Sing.

Encouraged by his findings, Milkman heads south to Shalimar, his grandfather's ancestral home in Virginia. Guitar secretly follows Milkman, convinced that Milkman has cheated him out of his share of the gold and planning to kill him. Milkman initially feels uncomfortable in the small town of Shalimar, but he grows to love it as he uncovers clues about his family history. Milkman discovers that Jake's father, his great-grandfather, was the legendary flying African, Solomon, who escaped slavery by flying back to Africa. Although Solomon's flight was miraculous, it left a scar on his family that has lasted for generations because in order to leave, Solomon had to abandon his wife, Ryna, and their twenty-one children. Ryna went insane. Jake was raised by Heddy, an Indian woman whose daughter, Sing, Jake married.

Milkman's findings make him joyful and give him a sense of purpose. He becomes a compassionate, responsible adult. After surviving an assassination attempt at Guitar's hands, Milkman returns home to Michigan to tell Macon Jr. and Pilate about his discoveries. At home, he finds that Hagar has died of a broken heart. Milkman accompanies Pilate back to Shalimar, where they bury Jake's bones on Solomon's Leap, the mountain from which Solomon's flight to Africa began. Immediately after Jake's burial, Pilate is struck dead by a bullet that Guitar intended for Milkman. Milkman calls out Guitar's name and leaps off the mountain toward him.

CHARACTERS IN *SONG OF SOLOMON*

Guitar Bains Milkman's best friend. Guitar was impoverished after his father died in a factory accident. He hates white people and blames them for all of the evil in the world. Guitar's murders of white people neither combat racism nor help the African-American community.

Circe A maid and midwife who worked for the wealthy Butler family. Circe delivered Macon Jr. and Pilate. In her encounter with Milkman, Circe plays the same role as her namesake in Homer's *Odyssey*, giving the hero crucial information.

First Corinthians Dead Milkman's worldly sister. First Corinthians was educated at Bryn Mawr and in France. Her name comes from a New Testament book in which the apostle Paul seeks to mend the disagreements within the early Christian church. First Corinthians's passionate love affair with a yardman, Henry Porter, crosses class boundaries.

Macon Dead I Macon Jr.'s father and Milkman's grandfather. Macon Dead I is also known as Jake. He was abandoned in infancy when his father, Solomon, flew back to Africa, and his mother, Ryna, went insane.

Milkman Dead The protagonist of the novel, also known as Macon Dead III. Raised in a sheltered, privileged world, Milkman is egotistical, uncompassionate, and alienated from the African-American community. He changes after his discovery of his family history gives his life purpose.

Pilate Dead Macon Jr.'s younger sister, Reba's mother, and Hagar's grandmother. Pilate is a fearless mother who is selflessly devoted to others. She protects Milkman.

Ruth Foster Dead Macon Jr.'s wife and the mother of Milkman, First Corinthians, and Lena. Ruth feels that only her deceased father, Dr. Foster, loves her. It is possible that she had an incestuous affair with Dr. Foster.

Dr. Foster The first black doctor in the novel's Michigan town. Dr. Foster is an arrogant, self-hating racist who calls fellow African-Americans "cannibals."

Freddie A janitor employed by Macon Jr., Freddie, the town gossip, coins the nickname "Milkman" for Ruth's son after seeing Milkman nursing as a young boy.

Michael-Mary Graham The Michigan poet laureate. Graham is a liberal who writes sentimental poetry and hires First Corinthians as a maid.

Hagar Pilate's daughter and Milkman's lover. Hagar devotes herself to Milkman. Like her biblical namesake—a servant who bears Abraham's son and is thrown out of the house by his barren wife, Sarah—Hagar is used and abandoned.

Macon Jr. Milkman's father and Ruth's husband, also known as Macon Dead II. Macon Jr. is money-hungry and emotionally dead.

Henry Porter   First Corinthians's lover and a member of the Seven Days vigilante group. Porter is a yard-man.

Reba   Pilate's daughter and Hagar's mother. Reba, also known as Rebecca, is attracted to abusive men. She has an uncanny ability to win contests.

Ryna   Milkman's great-grandmother and Solomon's wife.

Sing   Milkman's grandmother and Macon Dead I's wife. Sing is an Indian woman also known as Singing Bird.

Robert Smith   An insurance agent and member of the Seven Days vigilante group. Smith kills himself by attempting to fly off of the roof of Mercy Hospital.

Solomon   Milkman's great-grandfather. Solomon supposedly flew back to Africa but dropped his son Jake shortly after taking off.

Sweet   A prostitute with whom Milkman has a brief affair. Unlike Milkman's affairs with other women, his relationship with Sweet is mutually respectful and entirely reciprocal.

THEMES IN *SONG OF SOLOMON*

FLIGHT AS A MEANS OF ESCAPE   While flight is an escape from constricting circumstances, it is also a selfish act that scars those who are left behind. Solomon's flight allowed him to escape slavery in the Virginia cotton fields, but it also meant abandoning his wife, Ryna, with twenty-one children, an abandonment that drove her mad. Milkman's flight from Michigan frees him from his oppressive, familiar surroundings, but it also causes Hagar to die of heartbreak. Morrison suggests that women have an easier time balancing responsibility and freedom. As Milkman notes, Pilate is able to fly without lifting her feet from the ground, managing to be free of subjugation without leaving anyone behind. Many of the characters in *Song of Solomon* treat flight as a realistic possibility for humans. The residents of Shalimar, Virginia, think that Solomon's flight is a historical fact, not a myth. For the long period of time during which Milkman doubts the possibility of human flight, he remains abnormal in the eyes of his community. Only when he begins to believe in the reality of flight does he cease to feel alienated.

THE DOUBLE BURDEN OF WOMEN   In *Song of Solomon*, black women must carry a double burden: they are oppressed not only by racism, but also by their own men. Guitar tells Milkman that black men are the unacknowledged workhorses of humanity, but the novel's events suggest that it is black women who fit this description. Men bear responsibility only for themselves, but women are responsible for themselves, their families, and their communities. Solomon flies home to Africa, and Ryna must stay enslaved in Virginia with her twenty-one children. Rubbing salt in the wound, the community refuses to recognize the plight of women. Although Solomon abandoned his family, people remember him as the brave patriarch of the whole community and name a scenic mountain peak after him. In contrast, people remember Ryna as a woman who went mad because she was too weak to do everything on her own, and they name a dark gulch after her.

THE ALIENATING EFFECTS OF RACISM   Racism and oppression are the central causes of suffering in the novel. Slavery poisons generation after generation of the novel's central family, causing Solomon to flee toward freedom and end his marriage to Ryna, a flight that begets a legacy of trauma. Other characters are similarly oppressed. The knowledge that his father died because of his white employers' negligence makes Guitar keenly sensitive to the injustices perpetrated against African Americans. Emmett Till's murder and the Birmingham Church bombing remind Guitar of his own tragedy, transforming him into a ruthless, vengeful murderer. Guitar's story shows how racism alienates its victims from their native communities and causes them to lose touch with their own humanity.

SYMBOLS IN *SONG OF SOLOMON*

WHITE   White symbolizes violence and evil. After Guitar's father is cut in half during a sawmill accident, the mill's white foreman offers the family almost no sympathy or financial support. Circe's wealthy white employers, the Butlers, are murderers. A white bull causes Freddie's mother to go into labor and die. The white peacock that makes Guitar and Milkman infatuated with the pursuit of wealth stands for the corrupting influence of the rich.

ARTIFICIAL ROSES   The artificial roses that First Corinthians and Lena make symbolize the stifling life of the upper class and the oppression of women. The roses do not bring in much money. The girls make them as a mindless distraction from their boredom.

IMPORTANT QUOTATIONS FROM *SONG OF SOLOMON*

He didn't mean it. It happened before he was through. She'd stepped away from him to pick flowers, returned, and at the sound of her footsteps behind him, he'd turned around before he was through. It was becoming a habit—this concentration on things behind him. Almost as though there were no future to be had.

Location: Chapter 2
Speaker: The narrator
Context: Milkman hears Lena and turns, accidentally urinating on her

This passage emphasizes Milkman Dead's alienation from the world and from himself. At a young age, Milkman has inherited Macon Jr.'s mistrustful attitude and spiritual deadness. Milkman is six years old, but he acts like a world-weary man. Unlike most children, who think about the future, Milkman concentrates "on things behind him," which Morrison signals by having Milkman literally look behind him. When Milkman turns "at the sound of . . . footsteps behind him," it suggests that his father, who fled Pennsylvania after killing a man, has passed on to his son the mentality of a hunted man. Milkman's childhood is warped by events that took place before his birth. It is as if he is unknowingly looking behind himself at his family's past.

This passage also suggests Milkman's poor treatment of women. He urinates on Lena by accident, but urination becomes a metaphor for his treatment of women. Milkman is so concerned with his own problems that he does not even notice the love showered on him by the women in his life. He may not mean to metaphorically urinate on them, but that does not excuse him.

"Gold," he whispered, and immediately, like a burglar on his first job, stood up to pee.

Life, safety, and luxury fanned out before him like the tailspread of a peacock, and as he stood there trying to distinguish each delicious color, he saw the dusty boots of his father standing just on the other side of the shallow pit.

Location: Chapter 7
Speaker: The narrator
Context: After killing a white man, Macon Jr. discovers gold in a cave

This quotation describes a crucial turning point in Macon Jr.'s life. Before his father is murdered and before he attempts to kill the white man, Macon Jr. is a simple, kindhearted farm boy. But with the murder of his father, Macon Jr.'s idyllic childhood ends. When he finds gold, he believes he has stumbled upon a resolution to all of his recent traumas. Even when he sees the dusty boots of his father standing on the other side of the treasure pit, Macon Jr. does not shift his focus from the treasure. Gold becomes more important than Macon Jr.'s love for the man he cares about most. The moment Macon Jr. discovers gold is the moment when he begins his transformation from hardworking farm boy to soulless landlord.

The singing woman . . . had wrapped herself up in an old quilt instead of a winter coat. Her head cocked to one side, her eyes fixed on Mr. Robert Smith, she sang in a powerful contralto.

Location: Chapter 1
Speaker: The narrator
Context: Pilate sings about Sugarman as Robert Smith prepares to jump off the roof of Mercy Hospital

---

Milkman closed his eyes and opened them. The street was even more crowded with people, all going in the direction he was coming from. All walking hurriedly and bumping against him. After a while he realized that nobody was walking on the other side of the street.

Location: Chapter 3
Speaker: The narrator
Context: Distraught about his parents' relationship, Milkman wanders the streets

---

O Solomon don't leave me here
Cotton balls to choke me
O Solomon don't leave me here
Buckra's arms to yoke me

Solomon done fly, Solomon done gone
Solomon cut across the sky, Solomon gone home.

Location: Chapter 12
Speaker: Shalimar children
Context: Milkman hears the children singing a song about his family

THE SOUND AND THE FURY

William Faulkner

A Southern family on the decline crumbles completely when one of its members has a child out of wedlock.

THE LIFE OF WILLIAM FAULKNER

William Faulkner was born in New Albany, Mississippi, on September 25, 1897, the oldest of four sons in a southern family descended from the great Civil War soldier, statesman, and railroad builder Colonel William Clark Falkner. A number of his ancestors were involved in the Mexican-American War, the Civil War, and the Reconstruction, and were part of the local railroad industry and political scene. Faulkner showed signs of artistic talent from a young age, but became bored with his classes and never finished high school.

Faulkner grew up in the town of Oxford, Mississippi, and eventually returned there in his later years and purchased his famous estate, Rowan Oak. Oxford and the surrounding area were Faulkner's inspiration for the fictional Yoknapatawpha County, Mississippi, and its town of Jefferson. These locales became the setting for a number of his works. Faulkner's "Yoknapatawpha novels" include *The Sound and the Fury* (1929), *As I Lay Dying* (1930), *Light in August* (1932), *Absalom, Absalom!* (1936), *The Hamlet* (1940), and *Go Down, Moses* (1942), and they feature some of the same characters and locations.

Faulkner was particularly interested in the decline of the Deep South after the Civil War. Many of his novels explore the deterioration of the Southern aristocracy after the destruction of its wealth and way of life during the Civil War and Reconstruction. Faulkner populates Yoknapatawpha County with the skeletons of old mansions and the ghosts of great men, patriarchs and generals from the past whose aristocratic families fail to live up to their family legacies. These families try to cling to old Southern values, codes, and myths that are corrupted and out of place in the reality of the modern world. The families in Faulkner's novels are populated by failed sons, disgraced daughters, and smoldering resentments between whites and blacks.

Faulkner's reputation as one of the greatest novelists of the twentieth century is largely due to his highly experimental style. Faulkner was a pioneer in literary modernism, dramatically diverging from the forms and structures traditionally used in novels before his time. Faulkner often employs stream-of-consciousness narrative, non-chronological order, multiple narrators, shifts between the present and past tense, and impossibly long and complex sentences. Not surprisingly, these stylistic innovations make some of Faulkner's novels challenging to the reader. However, these bold innovations had a deep impact on literature.

Although eventually he found critical success, Faulkner did not fare well financially. He was forced to work as a screenwriter in Hollywood to supplement his dwindling income. His fortunes were revived with the 1946 publication of *The Portable Faulkner*, which featured a large and varied selection of his writings. He was awarded the Nobel Prize in Literature in 1950. A pair of Pulitzer Prizes followed in 1955 and 1962. Faulkner continued to write until his death in 1962.

THE SOUND AND THE FURY IN CONTEXT

First published in 1929, *The Sound and the Fury* is recognized as one of the most successfully innovative and experimental American novels of its time, as well as one of the most challenging to interpret. The novel concerns the downfall of the Compsons, who have been a prominent family in Jefferson, Mississippi, since before the Civil War. Faulkner represents the human experience by portraying events and images subjectively through several different characters' memories of childhood. The novel's stream-of-consciousness style is frequently opaque, and events are often deliberately obscured and narrated out of order. Despite its formidable complexity, *The Sound and the Fury* is an overpowering and deeply moving novel. It is generally regarded as Faulkner's most important and remarkable literary work.

THE SOUND AND THE FURY: KEY FACTS

Time and place written: 1928; Oxford, Mississippi

Date of publication: 1929

Publisher: Jonathan Cape and Harrison Smith

Type of work: Novel

Genre: Modernist novel

Language: English

Setting (time): Easter weekend, 1928, and June 1910

Setting (place): Jefferson, Mississippi, and Cambridge, Massachusetts

Tense: Present and past

Tone: Varies by narrator

Narrator: Benjy, Quentin, Jason, and an omniscient, third-person narrator

Point of view: Varies

Protagonist: The four Compson children

Antagonist: The struggle to live up to the past

THE SOUND AND THE FURY: PLOT OVERVIEW

The first three chapters of the novel consist of the convoluted thoughts, voices, and memories of the three Compson brothers. The brothers are Benjy, a severely retarded thirty-three-year-old man, speaking in April, 1928; Quentin, a young Harvard student, speaking in June, 1910; and Jason, a bitter farm-supply store worker, speaking in April, 1928. The fourth chapter, which is narrated in the third person, focuses on Dilsey, the Compson family's devoted "Negro" cook. Faulkner focuses on a single symbolic moment to forecast the decline of the once prominent Compson family and to examine the deterioration of the Southern aristocratic class since the Civil War.

The Compsons are one of several prominent families in the town of Jefferson, Mississippi. Their ancestors helped settle the area and defended it during the Civil War. Since the war, the Compsons have gradually seen their wealth, land, and status crumble away. Mr. Compson is an alcoholic. Mrs. Compson is a self-absorbed hypochondriac who depends on Dilsey, the cook, to raise her four children. Quentin, the oldest child, is a sensitive bundle of neuroses. Caddy is stubborn, loving, and compassionate. She is also a mother figure for Benjy and Quentin. Jason has been difficult and mean-spirited since birth and the other children spurn him. Benjy is severely mentally disabled, an "idiot" with no understanding of time or morality.

As the children grow older, Caddy begins to behave promiscuously, which torments Quentin and sends Benjy into fits of moaning and crying. Mr. Compson sells a large portion of the family land to raise money for Quentin's Harvard tuition. Caddy loses her virginity and gets pregnant. She is unable or unwilling to name the father of the child. The father is probably Dalton Ames, a boy from town.

Caddy's pregnancy shatters Quentin. Later he thinks he should have lied to his father that he (Quentin) fathered Caddy's child. Caddy quickly marries Herbert Head, a banker she met in Indiana. But when Herbert realizes that Caddy is pregnant, he immediately divorces her and rescinds a job offer he had made to Jason. Quentin, still despairing over Caddy's sin, commits suicide by drowning himself in the Charles River just before the end of his first year at Harvard.

The Compsons disown Caddy but take in her newborn daughter, Miss Quentin. Dilsey raises Miss Quentin. Mr. Compson dies of alcoholism roughly a year after Quentin's suicide. As the oldest surviving son, Jason becomes the head of the Compson household. While working at a menial job in the local farm-supply store, Jason devises an ingenious scheme to steal the money Caddy sends to support Miss Quentin's upbringing.

Miss Quentin grows up to be an unhappy, rebellious, and promiscuous girl, constantly in conflict with her overbearing and vicious uncle Jason. On Easter Sunday, 1928, Miss Quentin steals several thousand dollars from Jason and runs away with a man from a traveling show. While Jason fruitlessly chases after Miss Quentin, Dilsey takes Benjy and the rest of her family to Easter services at the local church.

CHARACTERS IN *THE SOUND AND THE FURY*

Dalton Ames A local Jefferson boy. Dalton probably fathered Caddy's child.

Uncle Maury Bascomb Mrs. Compson's brother. Bascomb lives off his brother-in-law's money.

Gerald Bland A swaggering Harvard student. Quentin fights with Gerald because he reminds him of Dalton Ames.

Mrs. Bland Gerald Bland's boastful Southern mother.

Charlie One of Caddy's first suitors.

Benjy Compson The youngest of the Compson children and the narrator of the novel's first chapter. Benjy is severely mentally retarded.

Caddy Compson The second Compson child. Caddy is very close to her brother Quentin.

Caroline Compson Mr. Compson's wife and mother of the four Compson children. Mrs. Compson is a self-pitying, self-absorbed hypochondriac who does not pay attention to her children.

Jason Compson III The head of the Compson household until his death from alcoholism in 1912.

Jason Compson IV The second youngest of the Compson children and the narrator of the novel's third chapter. Jason is mean-spirited, petty, and cynical.

Quentin Compson The oldest of the Compson children and the narrator of the novel's second chapter. A sensitive and intelligent boy, Quentin is preoccupied with his love for Caddy and his idea of the Compson family's honor. He commits suicide at Harvard.

Damuddy The Compson children's grandmother.

Deacon A black man in Cambridge, Massachusetts, to whom Quentin gives his suicide notes.

Dilsey The Compsons' cook. Dilsey is a pious, strong-willed, protective woman who stabilizes the Compson family.

Earl The owner of the farm-supply store where Jason works. Earl puts up with Jason because he feels some loyalty toward Mrs. Compson.

Frony Dilsey's daughter. Frony is Luster's mother and works in the Compsons' kitchen.

Sydney Herbert Head The prosperous banker whom Caddy marries.

Uncle Job A black man who works with Jason at Earl's store.

Julio The brother of an Italian girl who attaches herself to Quentin in Cambridge.

Lorraine Jason's mistress. Lorraine is a prostitute who lives in Memphis.

Luster Frony's son and Dilsey's grandson.

Shreve MacKenzie Quentin's roommate at Harvard. A young Canadian man, Shreve reappears in *Absalom, Absalom!*, which he and Quentin narrate from their dorm room at Harvard.

The Man With the Red Tie The mysterious man with whom Miss Quentin allegedly elopes.

Mr. and Mrs. Patterson The Compsons' next-door neighbors. Uncle Maury has an affair with Mrs. Patterson.

Roskus Dilsey's husband and the Compsons' servant. Roskus suffers from severe rheumatism.

Reverend Shegog A pastor at the black church in Jefferson.

Spoade A Harvard senior from South Carolina.

T.P. One of Dilsey's sons.

Miss Quentin   Caddy's illegitimate daughter. Miss Quentin is rebellious, promiscuous, and a miserably unhappy girl.

Versh   One of Dilsey's sons.

THEMES IN *THE SOUND AND THE FURY*

THE CORRUPTION OF SOUTHERN ARISTOCRATIC VALUES   Because of the Civil War and Reconstruction, once great families like the Compsons have lost touch with reality and sunk into self-absorption. Traditional values have been lost. Aristocratic Southern men were once expected to display courage, moral strength, perseverance, and chivalry. Women were expected to be models of feminine purity, grace, and virginity until it came time for them to provide children to inherit the family legacy. Everyone was expected to care about the family name. But as *The Sound and the Fury* unfolds, it becomes clear that these values have been corrupted. In the Compson family, Mr. Compson has a vague notion of family honor—something he passes on to Quentin—but alcoholism distracts him, and he maintains a fatalistic belief that he cannot control the events that befall his family. Mrs. Compson wallows in hypochondria and self-pity. Quentin's obsession with old Southern morality paralyzes him and makes his family's mistakes seem cataclysmic. Caddy tramples on the Southern notion of feminine purity, as does her daughter. Jason wastes his cleverness on self-pity and greed. Benjy is the physical manifestation of the Compsons' decline.

RESURRECTION AND RENEWAL   Three of the novel's four sections take place on or around Easter, 1928, a time associated with Christ's crucifixion on Good Friday and resurrection on Easter Sunday. A number of symbolic events in the novel could be likened to the death of Christ: Quentin's death, Mr. Compson's death, Caddy's loss of virginity, and the decline of the Compson family in general.

Some critics have characterized Benjy as a Christ figure, since Benjy was born on Holy Saturday and is thirty-three when the novel takes place, the same age as Christ at the crucifixion. Interpreting Benjy as a Christ figure has a variety of implications. Benjy may represent the impotence of Christ in the modern world and the need for a new Christ figure to emerge. Alternatively, Faulkner may be implying that the modern world has failed to recognize Christ in its midst.

Easter weekend is a reminder of death, but also of renewal and resurrection. Though the Compson family has fallen, Dilsey is a source of hope. Dilsey is also a Christ figure. A spiritual descendent of the suffering servant of the Bible, Dilsey has endured hardship throughout her long life of service to the disintegrating Compson family. Christlike, she has patiently borne Mrs. Compson's self-pity, Jason's cruelty, and Benjy's frustrating incapacity. While the Compsons crumble around her, Dilsey maintains the values that the Compsons have long abandoned—hard work, endurance, love of family, and religious faith.

THE FAILURE OF LANGUAGE AND NARRATIVE   Faulkner said he could never satisfactorily convey the story of *The Sound and the Fury* through any single narrative voice. His decision to use four different narrators highlights the subjectivity of each narrative and casts doubt on the ability of language to convey truth or meaning. Benjy, Quentin, and Jason have vastly different views on the Compson tragedy, none of which seem more valid than the others. As each new angle emerges, more details and questions arise. Even the final section, with its omniscient third-person narrator, does not tie up all of the novel's loose ends. In interviews, Faulkner lamented the imperfection of the final version of the novel, which he termed his "most splendid failure."

SYMBOLS IN *THE SOUND AND THE FURY*

WATER   Water symbolizes cleansing and purity, especially in relation to Caddy. Playing in the stream as a child, Caddy suggests purity and innocence, although she muddies her underclothes, which foreshadows her later promiscuity. Benjy gets upset when he first smells Caddy wearing perfume. Caddy washes the perfume off, symbolically washing away her sin. After Benjy catches her with Charlie, she washes her mouth out with soap.

QUENTIN'S WATCH   Quentin's watch is a gift from his father, who hopes that it will alleviate Quentin's obsession with watching time. But the watch, because it once belonged to Mr. Compson, constantly reminds Quentin of his family's glorious heritage. The watch's incessant ticking symbolizes the constant, inexorable passage of time. Quentin attempts to escape time by breaking the watch, but it continues to tick even without its hands.

IMPORTANT QUOTATIONS FROM *THE SOUND AND THE FURY*

If I'd just had a mother so I could say Mother Mother[.]

Location: June Second, 1910
Speaker: Quentin
Context: Quentin thinks about his mother's neglect

During the last hours of his life, Quentin repeats this sentence several times. The fact that just before his death he focuses on his mother's neglect shows how damaging Mrs. Compson's failure has been to her children. Consumed by self-absorption and insecurities about her family name, Mrs. Compson showed affection for Jason alone. Quentin and Caddy formed a close bond as neglected, unloved outsiders, but Quentin's attachment to his sister turns out to be dangerous. He cannot bear to think of her promiscuity, and his despair over it leads to his suicide.

I wouldn't lay my hand on her. The bitch that cost me a job, the one chance I ever had to get ahead, that killed my father and is shortening my mother's life every day and made my name a laughing stock in the town. I wont do anything to her.

Location: April Eighth, 1928
Speaker: Jason
Context: In conversation with the sheriff, Jason sarcastically pretends he has no reason to hurt Miss Quentin

The sarcasm and self-pity that drip from this passage are typical of Jason. Always a victim, in his own eyes at least, Jason interprets every event through a lens of self-absorption. He understands Caddy's divorce as an insult to him, not as a stroke of bad luck his desperate sister could not control. He understands Miss Quentin's departure as a wrong done to him, not as an understandable flight away from the uncle who had been stealing all of her money. Jason blames his failure on everyone but himself, when it is his own sourness and whininess that ensure he will always be unsuccessful. Like his mother, Jason is drowning in self-absorption.

Caddy smells like trees.

Location: April Seventh, 1928
Speaker: Benjy
Context: Benjy describes his sister

Whoever God is, He would not permit that. I'm a lady. You might not believe that from my offspring, but I am.

Location: April Eighth, 1928
Speaker: Mrs. Compson
Context: Mrs. Compson dismisses the notion that Miss Quentin has killed herself

I seed de beginnin, en now I sees de endin.

Location: April Eighth, 1928
Speaker: Dilsey
Context: During the Easter church service, just after learning that Miss Quentin has left, Dilsey makes
this pronouncement

THE STRANGER

Albert Camus

A disaffected young man kills an Arab man on the beach and is sentenced to death.

THE LIFE OF ALBERT CAMUS

Albert Camus was born on November 7, 1913, in French colonial Algeria. In 1914, his father was killed in World War I, at the Battle of the Marne. Camus, his mother, and his brother shared a two-bedroom apartment with Camus's maternal grandmother and a paralyzed uncle. Despite his family's extreme poverty, Camus was able to attend the University of Algiers by working a series of odd jobs. One of several severe attacks of tuberculosis forced him to drop out of school.

Camus worked at an anti-colonialist newspaper, writing extensively about poverty in Algeria. From 1935 to 1938, Camus ran a theater company that attempted to attract working-class audiences to performances of great dramatic works. During World War II, Camus went to Paris and became a leading writer for the anti-German resistance movement. He was also the editor of *Combat*, an important underground newspaper.

In wartime Paris, Camus developed his philosophy of the absurd, which holds that life has no rational or redeeming meaning. The experience of World War II led many other intellectuals to similar conclusions. But Camus's absurdist philosophy is not a cynical one. It says that humans should react to the knowledge that life has no meaning by living passionate, dignified lives.

In 1942, Camus published a novel, *The Stranger*, and a philosophical essay on the absurd, *The Myth of Sisyphus*. These two works helped establish Camus's reputation as a brilliant and important literary figure. Camus went on to produce many novels, plays, and essays. Among his most notable novels are *The Plague* (1947) and *The Fall* (1956). His best-known philosophical essay, second to *The Myth of Sisyphus*, is *The Rebel*. Camus was awarded the Nobel Prize for Literature in 1957. He died in an automobile accident just three years later at age forty-seven.

THE STRANGER IN CONTEXT

The Stranger is both a brilliantly crafted story and an illustration of Camus's absurdist worldview. Published in 1942, the novel tells the story of an emotionally detached, amoral young man named Meursault. Only when Meursault accepts the "gentle indifference of the world" does he finds peace with himself and with the society that persecutes him.

The Stranger is often described as an "existential" novel, but this description is not necessarily accurate. "Existentialist" is a broad classification that is often misapplied or overapplied. As it is most commonly used, existentialism refers to the idea that there is no higher meaning to the universe or to man's existence, and no rational order to the events of the world.

Some ideas in *The Stranger* fit with this working definition of existentialism, but the novel does not subscribe to every tenet of the philosophy of existentialism. Camus himself rejected the idea that *The Stranger* is an existentialist novel. Rather, it is an absurdist novel, a philosophy Camus developed himself.

THE STRANGER: KEY FACTS

Time and place written: Early 1940s; France	
Date of first publication: 1942	
Publisher: Librairie Gallimard, France	
Type of work: Novel	
Genre: Existential novel; crime novel	
Language: French	
Setting (time): Just before World War II	

Setting (place): Algeria

Tense: Shifts between immediate past (or real-time narration) and more distant past

Tone: Detached, sober, plain, subtly ironic

Narrator: Meursault in the first person

Point of view: Meursault's

Protagonist: Meursault

Antagonist: Society

THE STRANGER: PLOT OVERVIEW

Meursault, the narrator, is a young man living in Algiers. After receiving a telegram informing him of his mother's death, he takes a bus to Marengo, where his mother had been living in an old persons' home. The director of the home asks Meursault if he would like to see his mother's body, but Meursault declines.

That night, Meursault keeps vigil over his mother's coffin. The talkative caretaker stays with him the whole time. Meursault smokes a cigarette, drinks coffee, and dozes off. The next morning, the director informs him that Thomas Perez, an old man who was very close to Meursault's mother, will attend the funeral service. The funeral procession heads for the small local village. Perez faints from the heat. Meursault reports that he remembers little of the funeral. That night, he arrives back in Algiers.

The next day, Meursault goes to the public beach for a swim. There, he runs into Marie Cardona, a former co-worker. The two make a date to see a comedy at the movie theater that evening. After the movie they spend the night together. When Meursault wakes up, Marie is gone. He stays in bed until noon and then sits on his balcony until evening, watching people pass on the street.

The following day, Monday, Meursault returns to work. That night, he runs into Salamano, an old man who lives in his building and owns a mangy dog. Meursault also runs into his neighbor, Raymond Sintes, who is widely rumored to be a pimp. Raymond invites Meursault over for dinner. Raymond says he recently beat up his mistress after he discovered that she had been cheating on him. As a result, he got into a fight with her brother. Raymond now wants to torment his mistress even more, so he asks Meursault to write a letter luring his mistress back to him. Meursault does as he asks.

The following Saturday, Marie visits Meursault at his apartment. She asks Meursault if he loves her, and he replies that he probably does not. They hear shouting and go out into the hall. A policeman arrives, slaps Raymond, and says he will be summoned to the police station for beating up his mistress. Later, Raymond asks Meursault to testify on his behalf, and Meursault agrees. That night, Raymond runs into Salamano, who laments that his dog has run away.

Marie asks Meursault if he wants to marry her. Indifferent, he says they can if she wants to, so they become engaged. The following Sunday, Meursault, Marie, and Raymond go to a beach house owned by Masson, one of Raymond's friends. They swim happily in the ocean and then have lunch. That afternoon, Masson, Raymond, and Meursault run into two Arabs on the beach, one of whom is the brother of Raymond's mistress. A fight breaks out and Raymond is stabbed. After tending his wounds, Raymond returns to the beach with Meursault. They find the Arabs at a spring. Raymond considers shooting them, but Meursault talks him out of it and takes his gun away. Later, Meursault returns to the spring and, for no apparent reason, shoots Raymond's mistress's brother.

Meursault is arrested and jailed. Meursault's lack of remorse disgusts his lawyer. Meursault meets with the examining magistrate, who cannot understand Meursault's actions. The magistrate brandishes a crucifix and demands that Meursault put his faith in God. Meursault refuses, saying he does not believe in God. Frightened by Meursault's lack of belief, the magistrate dubs him "Monsieur Antichrist."

One day, Marie visits Meursault in prison. She expresses hope that Meursault will be acquitted and that they will get married. As he awaits his trial, Meursault slowly adapts to prison life. His isolation from nature, women, and cigarettes torments him at first, but after a time he does not even notice their absence.

On the morning of Meursault's trial, spectators and members of the press fill the courtroom. The subject of the trial quickly shifts away from the murder to a general discussion of Meursault's character, and of his reaction to his mother's death in particular. The director and several other people testify to Meursault's lack of grief. Marie reluctantly testifies that the day after his mother's funeral, Meursault took her to see a comedic movie. During his summation the following day, the prosecutor calls Meursault a monster and says that his lack of moral feeling threatens all of society. Meursault is found guilty and sentenced to death by beheading.

Meursault returns to prison to await his execution. He has trouble accepting the inevitability of his fate. He imagines escaping or filing a successful legal appeal. One day, the chaplain comes to visit against Meursault's wishes. He urges Meursault to turn to God, but Meursault refuses. Like the magistrate, the chaplain cannot believe that Meursault does not long for faith and the afterlife. Enraged, Meursault grabs the chaplain and shouts at him, saying the world truly is meaningless. For the first time, Meursault fully embraces the idea that human existence has no meaning. He abandons all hope for the future and accepts the "gentle indifference of the world." This acceptance makes Meursault happy.

CHARACTERS IN *THE STRANGER*

The Arab The brother of Raymond's mistress. The Arab's mysteriousness as a character makes it all the more difficult to understand why Meursault kills him.

Marie Cardona Meursault's girlfriend. Marie is young, beautiful, and high-spirited. She loves swimming and the outdoors. Marie does not understand Meursault, but she is drawn to his peculiarities.

The Caretaker A worker at the old persons' home. The caretaker sits with Meursault by his mother's coffin, drinking coffee and smoking cigarettes with him. Later, this incident is taken as evidence of Meursault's monstrous indifference to his mother's death.

Celeste The proprietor of a café where Meursault frequently eats lunch. During the trial, Celeste loyally testifies to Meursault's honesty and decency.

The Chaplain A priest who attends to the religious needs of condemned men. The chaplain's nervous insistence that Meursault turn to God catalyzes Meursault's psychological and philosophical development, inspiring him to understand that life is meaningless and that all men are condemned to die.

The Director The manager of the old persons' home.

The Examining Magistrate The man who questions Meursault several times after his arrest. The magistrate is deeply disturbed by Meursault's apparent lack of grief over his mother's death. He says that the meaning of his own life is threatened by Meursault's lack of belief.

Masson One of Raymond's friends. Masson is a vigorous, contented man. He testifies to Meursault's good character.

Madame Meursault Meursault's mother. Toward the end of the novel, Meursault decides that his mother, in her old age, must have embraced a meaningless universe and lived for the moment, just as he does.

Meursault The protagonist and narrator of *The Stranger*. Meursault is detached and emotionless. He refuses to adhere to the moral order of society. Meursault's atheism and atypical behavior threaten society. Meursault finds peace by accepting the world's meaninglessness.

Thomas Perez One of the elderly residents of the old persons' home. Madame Meursault and Perez shared a deep, perhaps romantic, attachment. Their relationship is one of the few genuine emotional attachments in the novel.

The Prosecutor A lawyer who characterizes Meursault as a cool, calculating monster. The prosecutor demands the death penalty for Meursault not because of the crime he committed, but because Meursault's moral indifference threatens society.

Salamano One of Meursault's neighbors. Salamano curses and beats his old dog, but when the animal disappears, Salamano weeps and longs for its return.

Raymond Sintes A local pimp and Meursault's neighbor. Out of indifference, Meursault does whatever Raymond asks him to do. Raymond tries to help Meursault with his testimony during the trial.

THEMES IN *THE STRANGER*

THE IRRATIONALITY OF THE UNIVERSE As a work of fiction, *The Stranger* examines Camus's philosophical notion of absurdity as it applies to one man. In his essays, Camus asserts that human existence has no rational meaning or order, and that people cannot accept this and try to create meaning. Absurdity results from humanity's futile attempt to find rational order where none exists. The events of Meursault's life fit this theory. Neither the external world in which Meursault lives nor the internal world of his thoughts has any rational order. Meursault acts without reason, agreeing to marry Marie and killing the Arab without explanation. Society searches for rational explanations for Meursault's irrational actions, unable to accept the idea that he acts without reason. The trial represents society's attempt to manufacture rational order. The prosecutor and Meursault's lawyer offer explanations for Meursault's crime that are based on logic, reason, and the concept of cause and effect. But these explanations have no basis in fact. They are simply attempts to defuse the frightening idea that the universe is irrational. The trial itself is an absurdity, an instance of humankind's futile attempt to impose rationality on an irrational universe.

THE MEANINGLESSNESS OF HUMAN LIFE A second major component of Camus's absurdist philosophy is the idea that human life has no meaning. Camus argues that the only certain thing in life is the inevitability of death. Because all humans will die, all lives are all equally meaningless. Meursault gradually moves toward this realization throughout the novel, but he does not fully grasp it until after his argument with the chaplain in the final chapter. Meursault at last realizes that the universe is indifferent to him just as he is indifferent to the universe. Like all people, Meursault has been born, will die, and will cease to matter.

Paradoxically, this seemingly dismal realization makes Meursault happy. When he fully comes to terms with the inevitability and meaning of death, he understands that it does not matter whether he dies by execution or of old age. This understanding enables Meursault to put aside his fantasies of escaping or filing a successful legal appeal. He realizes that these illusory hopes, which had previously preoccupied his mind, would do little more than give him the false sense that death is avoidable. Meursault sees that his hope for sustained life has been a burden. His liberation from this false hope means he is free to live life for what it is, and to make the most of his remaining days.

THE IMPORTANCE OF THE PHYSICAL WORLD Meursault is far more interested in the physical aspects of the world around him than in its social or emotional aspects. The focus of his attention is correct. Since no higher meaning exists, people should focus on the life they are living and its details. Meursault's narration centers on his body, his physical relationship with Marie, the weather, and other physical elements of his surroundings. The heat during the funeral procession causes Meursault far more pain than the thought of burying his mother. The sun on the beach torments Meursault, and during his trial Meursault momentarily identifies his suffering under the sun as the reason he killed the Arab. The style of Meursault's narration also reflects his interest in the physical. Though he offers terse, plain descriptions of emotional or social situations, his descriptions become more vivid when he discusses topics such as nature and the weather.

SYMBOLS IN *THE STRANGER*

THE COURTROOM The court symbolizes society. In the courtroom, the law stands for the will of the people, and the jury sits in judgment on behalf of the entire community. Nearly every one of the minor characters from the first half of the novel reappears in the courtroom, strengthening the symbolism of the court as a microcosm of society. The court's attempts to construct a logical explanation for Meursault's crime symbolize humanity's attempts to find rational explanations for the irrational events of the universe.

THE CRUCIFIX The crucifix that the examining magistrate waves at Meursault symbolizes Christianity, which stands in opposition to Camus's absurdist world view. Whereas absurdism is based on the idea that human life is irrational and purposeless, Christianity conceives of a rational universe based on God's creation, and invests human life with higher metaphysical meaning. The crucifix also symbolizes rationality in general. The chaplain's insistence that Meursault turn to God does not necessarily represent a desire that Meursault accept Christian beliefs so much as a desire that he embrace the principle of a meaningful universe.

IMPORTANT QUOTATIONS FROM *THE STRANGER*

Maman died today. Or yesterday maybe, I don't know. I got a telegram from the home: "Mother deceased. Funeral tomorrow. Faithfully yours." That doesn't mean anything. Maybe it was yesterday.

Location: The first lines of the novel
Speaker: Meursault
Context: Meursault gets word of his mother's death

The first words of the novel immediately introduce Meursault's emotional indifference. Meursault does not say that the news of his mother's death caused him any grief. He merely reports the fact of her death in a plain and straightforward manner. His chief concern is the precise day of his mother's death—a seemingly trivial detail. Mersault's comment "That doesn't mean anything," has at least two possible meanings. It could mean that the telegram does not reveal any meaningful information about the date of his mother's death. It could also mean that her death does not mean anything. This reading introduces the idea of the meaninglessness of human existence, a theme that resounds throughout the novel.

I said that people never change their lives, that in any case one life was as good as another and that I wasn't dissatisfied with mine here at all.

Location: Part One, Chapter 5
Speaker: Meursault
Context: Meursault describes his response to his boss's offer of a position in Paris

Meursault's statement shows his belief that human existence, in all its various permutations, is essentially the same for everyone. His comment that "one life was as good as another" suggests that although details may change, one's life is essentially constant, and no one's life is better or worse than anyone else's. At this point in the novel, Meursault offers no explanation for his belief in the interchangeability of human lives. In the novel's final chapter, he identifies death as the force that makes all lives equal, for all lives end in death. A comparison of this quotation to Meursault's ideas following his death sentence shows how much Meursault's understanding of the human condition deepens as a result of his experiences.

She said, "If you go slowly, you risk getting sunstroke. But if you go too fast, you work up a sweat and then catch a chill inside the church." She was right. There was no way out.

Location: Part One, Chapter 1
Speaker: Meursault
Context: The nurse describes the weather

A minute later she asked me if I loved her. I told her it didn't mean anything but that I didn't think so.

Location: Part One, Chapter 4
Speaker: Meursault
Context: Meursault relates Marie's question

As if that blind rage had washed me clean, rid me of hope; for the first time, in that night alive with signs and stars, I opened myself to the gentle indifference of the world. Finding it so much like myself—so like a brother, really—I felt that I had been happy and that I was happy again. For everything to be consummated, for me to feel less alone, I had only to wish that there be a large crowd of spectators the day of my execution and that they greet me with cries of hate.

Location: The last lines of the novel
Speaker: Meursault
Context: Meursault describes his meeting with the chaplain

A STREETCAR NAMED DESIRE

Tennessee Williams

An aging Southern belle clashes with her immigrant brother-in-law and retreats into her fantasies.

THE LIFE OF TENNESSEE WILLIAMS

Tennessee Williams was born in Columbus, Mississippi, in 1911. His given name was Thomas Lanier Williams III. In college, his classmates nicknamed him "Tennessee" because of his Southern accent and his father's home state. The Williams family produced several illustrious Tennessee politicians, but Williams's grandfather squandered the family fortune. Williams's father, C. C. Williams, was a traveling salesman and a heavy drinker. Williams's mother, Edwina, was the daughter of a Mississippi clergyman and prone to hysterical attacks. The young Williams, always shy and fragile, was ostracized at school. During his school years, he became extremely close to Rose, his older sister.

In high school, Williams turned to the movies and writing for solace. When he was sixteen, he won five dollars in a national competition for his answer to the question "Can a good wife be a good sport?" The next year, he published a horror story in a magazine called *Weird Tales*, and the year after that he entered the University of Missouri as a journalism major. While there, he wrote his first plays. When Williams failed a required ROTC program course, his father forced him to withdraw from school and go to work at the same shoe company where he himself worked.

After working at the shoe factory for three years, Williams suffered a minor nervous breakdown. When he recovered, he returned to college, this time at Washington University in St. Louis. While he was studying there, a St. Louis theater group produced his plays *The Fugitive Kind* and *Candles to the Sun*. Personal problems led Williams to drop out of Washington University and enroll in the University of Iowa. While he was in Iowa, his sister, Rose, had a prefrontal lobotomy (an intensive brain surgery). Despite this trauma, Williams finally graduated in 1938. In the years that followed, he lived a bohemian life, working menial jobs, wandering from city to city, and writing. During the early years of World War II, Williams worked in Hollywood as a scriptwriter.

The Glass Menagerie (1944), a highly personal, explicitly autobiographical play, earned Williams fame, fortune, critical respect, and a Drama Critics' Circle Award. He won another Drama Critics' Circle Award and a Pulitzer Prize for *A Streetcar Named Desire*. In 1955, he won the same two prizes again, for *Cat on a Hot Tin Roof*.

The impact of success on Williams's life was colossal and detrimental. Alcoholism, depression, thwarted desire, loneliness in search of purpose, and insanity plagued Williams. He was gay, and homosexuality was not accepted in his era and culture. He referred to the 1960s as his "stoned age." He suffered a period of intense depression after the death of his longtime partner in 1961 and, six years later, entered a psychiatric hospital in St. Louis. He continued to write, but most critics agree that the quality of his work diminished in his later life. His life's work adds up to twenty-five full-length plays, five screenplays, over seventy one-act plays, hundreds of short stories, two novels, poetry, and a memoir. Five of his plays were made into movies. Williams died from choking in a drug-related incident in 1983.

A STREETCAR NAMED DESIRE IN CONTEXT

Set in the postwar South, *A Streetcar Named Desire* chronicles the decline and fall of fading Southern belle Blanche DuBois. Much of the pathos of this and other Williams works was mined from Williams's own life, from his experiences with depression, thwarted desire, loneliness, alcoholism, and insanity. In particular, he was influenced by his experiences as an openly gay man in the early twentieth century. Williams's most memorable characters, many of them female, were based in part on himself, his mother and his sister. Stanley Kowalski and other vulgar, ruthless male characters find echoes in Williams's father.

NOTE ON THE EPIGRAPH

The epigraph to *A Streetcar Named Desire* is a stanza from "The Broken Tower" by American poet and Williams's hero, Hart Crane. Like Williams, Crane was an alcoholic homosexual writer looking for means of self-expression in a heterosexual world. Unlike Williams, Crane succumbed to his demons and drowned himself in 1932 at the age of thirty-three. Williams was influenced by Crane's imagery and attentiveness to metaphor. The epigraph's description of love as only an "instant" and as a force that precipitates "each desperate choice" recalls Blanche and her struggles.

A STREETCAR NAMED DESIRE: KEY FACTS

Time and place written: Late 1940s; New Orleans	
Date of publication: 1947	
Publisher: New Directions	
Type of work: Play	
Genre: Southern literature	
Language: English	
Setting (time): 1940s	
Setting (place): New Orleans	
Tone: Ironic and sympathetic	
Protagonist: Blanche DuBois	
Antagonist: Stanley Kowalski; the decline of the Old South; the harsh reality of unrealized desires	

A STREETCAR NAMED DESIRE: PLOT OVERVIEW

SCENES I AND II

Blanche DuBois, a schoolteacher from Laurel, Mississippi, arrives at the New Orleans apartment of her sister, Stella Kowalski. The sisters have been out of touch, but Blanche has come to stay, armed with a large trunk. Blanche tells Stella that she lost Belle Reve, their ancestral home, after the death of all their remaining relatives. She also mentions that she has taken a leave of absence from teaching because of bad nerves.

Blanche has little money, but disdains the Kowalskis' cramped two-room apartment and their noisy, working-class neighborhood. Stella and her husband Stanley, a Polish auto-parts supplier, have a gratifying sex life, and Stella is pregnant with their first baby. Stanley takes an instant dislike to Blanche. In particular, he suspects that Blanche has cheated Stella out of a share of their inheritance. Blanche finally reveals that the mortgage on Belle Reve was foreclosed. Blanche tries to conceal her heavy drinking from Stella and Stanley.

SCENE III

At a drunken poker game between Stanley and his friends, Blanche gets under Stanley's skin, especially when he sees his close friend Mitch attracted to her. When Mitch speaks to Blanche in the bedroom, Stanley erupts in anger and throws the radio out of the window. When Stella defends Blanche, he beats her. His friends pull him off, and Blanche and Stella escape to their upstairs neighbor Eunice's apartment. Later in the evening, Stanley, full of remorse, cries up to Stella to forgive him. To Blanche's alarm, Stella goes down to Stanley and embraces him passionately. Mitch meets Blanche outside the Kowalski flat and comforts her.

SCENE IV, V, AND VI

The next day, Blanche tries to convince Stella to leave Stanley for someone of a better social status. When Stella laughs at her, Blanche reveals that she is completely broke. Stanley walks in and overhears

Blanche making fun of him. Later, he drops threatening hints that he has heard rumors of Blanche's disreputable past. She is visibly dismayed.

While Blanche is alone in the apartment one evening, waiting for Mitch to pick her up for a date, a teenage boy comes by to collect money for the newspaper. Blanche flirts with him and kisses him lustfully. After their date, Blanche reveals to Mitch the greatest tragedy of her past: years ago, her young husband committed suicide after she discovered that he was gay. Mitch describes his own loss of a former love and tells Blanche that they need each other.

SCENE VII

A month later, Stella is preparing Blanche's birthday dinner—Mitch is expected—when Stanley comes in and announces that he found out about Blanche's sordid past. After losing the DuBois mansion, Blanche moved into a fleabag motel from which she was eventually evicted because of her numerous sexual liaisons. She was fired from her teaching job after having an affair with a teenage student. Stanley has shared these stories with Mitch.

SCENE VIII

The birthday dinner comes and goes, but Mitch never arrives. Stanley indicates to Blanche that he is aware of her past. For a birthday present, he gives her a one-way bus ticket back to Laurel. Stella is disturbed by Stanley's cruelty, but goes into labor before a real argument breaks out.

SCENE IX

Several hours later, Blanche, drunk, sits alone in the apartment. Mitch, also drunk, arrives and confronts Blanche with what he has heard from Stanley. Eventually, Blanche confesses that Stanley's stories are true, saying that she was very lonely after her husband's death. Mitch tells Blanche that he can never marry her. He tries to have sex with Blanche, but she attracts the attention of passersby and forces him to leave.

SCENE X

Stanley returns from the hospital to find Blanche even more drunk. She tells him that she will soon be leaving New Orleans with her former suitor Shep Huntleigh who is now a millionaire. Happy about his baby, Stanley proposes they each celebrate their good fortune. Blanche spurns Stanley's invitation, and the situation turns ugly. Stanley blocks Blanche's way to the exit. Terrified, she smashes a bottle on the table. Stanley grabs Blanche, carries her to the bed, and forces her to have sex with him.

SCENE XI

Weeks later, Stella and Eunice pack Blanche's bags: a doctor will soon take her to an insane asylum. Blanche is taking a bath, convinced that she will soon join her millionaire. Stanley is playing poker with his buddies in the front room. Stella confesses to Eunice that she cannot allow herself to believe Blanche's assertion that Stanley raped her. When Blanche emerges from the bathroom, her deluded talk makes it clear that she has lost touch with reality.

The doctor arrives with a nurse, and Blanche initially panics and struggles when they try to take her away. Stanley and his friends subdue her while Eunice keeps Stella from interfering. Mitch begins to cry. Finally, the doctor speaks to Blanche gently, and she allows him to lead her away. Her baby in her arms, Stella sobs. Stanley comforts her.

CHARACTERS IN *A STREETCAR NAMED DESIRE*

STELLA'S RELATIVES

Blanche DuBois Stella's thirty-something older sister. Blanche comes from an impoverished Southern aristocratic family and still plays the Southern belle. She prefers to live in her imaginative fantasies rather than face reality. Blanche has strong sexual urges and has had many lovers—sometimes in exchange for money, Williams implies. She lost her job teaching high school English in Laurel, Mississippi, after having an affair with a student.

Stanley Kowalski Stella's husband; a Polish auto-parts salesman and World War II veteran. Loyal to his friends, passionate to the point of violence with his wife, and cruel to Blanche, Stanley embodies virility and survival. He represents the new robust, multicultural America. Practical and strong, Stanley has no patience for Blanche's fantasies and genteel pretensions.

Stella Kowalski, née DuBois Blanche's younger sister; Stanley's pregnant wife. Stella's union with Stanley is robustly sexual and sometimes violent. Throughout the play, Stella is torn between her husband and her sister; her husband ultimately wins.

NEIGHBORS AND FRIENDS

Pablo Gonzales Stanley's brutish poker buddy. Pablo's Hispanic background emphasizes the culturally diverse nature of their neighborhood.

Eunice Hubbell Stella's landlady and upstairs neighbor. Eunice and her husband Steve represent the low-class, carnal life that Stella has chosen. Like Stella, Eunice stays with and loves her husband despite his occasional outbursts of violence—and advises Stella to do the same.

Steve Hubbell Stanley's poker buddy; Eunice's husband. Like Stanley, Steve is a brutish, hot-blooded, strong male and an abusive husband.

Harold "Mitch" Mitchell Stanley's army friend, coworker, and poker buddy. Mitch courts Blanche until he finds out about her sordid past. Although clumsy and unrefined, Mitch is more sensitive and polite than his friends. He lives with his dying mother.

Young Collector A teenager who collects money for the newspaper. He is bewildered when Blanche flirts with him and kisses him. He embodies Blanche's obsession with youth and is a stand-in for her teenage love Allan Grey.

MINOR CHARACTERS

Doctor An insane asylum doctor. In gently leading Blanche away at the play's finale, the doctor conforms to the role of the chivalric Southern gentleman who will bring salvation.

Mexican Woman A vendor of funeral decorations who frightens Blanche with her plaintive "Flores para los muertos" ("Flowers for the dead").

Negro Woman A neighbor who laughs when Stanley throws meat at Stella, which is an overtly sexual gesture. The Negro Woman is seen rifling through the prostitute's bag before Stanley rapes Blanche.

Nurse (Matron) A severe, unfeminine insane asylum nurse who accompanies the doctor to pick up Blanche.

Prostitute She is glimpsed being pursued by a drunkard moments before Stanley rapes Blanche, evoking Blanche's predicament.

OFFSTAGE CHARACTERS

Allan Grey Blanche's young poet husband, long dead. He shot himself after she discovered that he was gay and expressed her disgust. His death marked the end of Blanche's sexual innocence.

Shep Huntleigh Blanche's former suitor, who has become wealthy. She imagines that he will come and sweep her away.

Shaw Stanley's supply man, who tells Stanley about Blanche's unsavory past.

THEMES IN *A STREETCAR NAMED DESIRE*

REALITY TRIUMPHANT OVER FANTASY   The antagonism between Blanche and Stanley is a struggle between fantasy and reality. Frail, romantic Blanche fibs in order to escape the difficulties of her life. Practical Stanley, a virile laborer grounded in the physical world, resents Blanche's fabrications (as well as her snobbery) and tries to unravel them. Ultimately, Stanley wins; he proves stronger in both body (as he rapes Blanche, as his child is born) and spirit (as Blanche breaks down).

Williams uses the set of the Kowalski apartment and the surrounding street to explore the boundary between the exterior and interior and to symbolize the struggle between reality and fantasy. The open apartment expresses the notion that the home is not a sanctuary; external real life necessarily intrudes on the fantasies hiding inside. This idea crystallizes in Scene Ten: just before Stanley rapes Blanche, the apartment's back wall becomes transparent to show street scuffles and foreshadow the violation inside the house.

DEATH AS NATURAL RESULT OF UNHEALTHY SEXUAL DESIRE   Blanche tries to stave off death and aging by repeatedly asserting her sexuality. She ultimately fails and is expulsed from society to an insane asylum, just as she is evicted from Belle Reve, fired from the teaching job, and ostracized in Laurel. Indeed, in the play, sex and sexual desire, especially what is perceived as unhealthy sexual desire, leads to death. Her husband kills himself after she discovers that he is gay. Blanche is haunted by the deaths of her ancestors and troubled by their "epic fornications."

Blanche arrives at the Kowalski residence on streetcars named Desire and Cemeteries, and gets off at a street named Elysian Fields. This journey is an allegory for the trajectory of Blanche's life. The sexual desire of her unsavory life in Laurel has brought her to cemeteries and Elysian Fields—the land of the dead in Greek mythology.

OLD SOUTH GIVING WAY TO NEW AMERICA   The DuBois and Kowalski families demonstrate the evolution of Southern society over the first half of the twentieth century. The DuBois, especially Blanche, represents the nineteenth-century Southern aristocracy of plantation owners. Stanley Kowalski, the son of Polish immigrants, is one of the emerging class of new Southerners. His factory job, made possible by industrial revolution, contributes to the demise of the agrarian society in which Blanche and Stella were raised. Blanche cannot cope with the demise of the Old South and retreats into fantasy; Stella turns her back on her family, marrying a man beneath her social standing.

Stanley, strong and violent, is well adapted for survival in a urban center of the New South such as New Orleans. Stella and Stanley's newborn child, a mixture of immigrant American and Southern aristocracy, represents the future of the South.

SYMBOLS IN *A STREETCAR NAMED DESIRE*

LIGHT   Light is a symbol of real life in all its clarity, both beautiful and ugly. Blanche avoids appearing in direct light to hide her age: she covers the exposed light bulb in the Kowalski apartment with a Chinese paper lantern and refuses to see Mitch during the day or in well-lit locations. Through these evasions, she obscures reality with dreams and illusions. As Mitch confronts her about her past in Scene Nine, he forces her to stand under the light, her age and secrets exposed. In Scene Six, Blanche tells Mitch that falling in love with Allan Grey was like turning on a "blinding light"—a light that has been extinguished after his suicide, as she has withdrawn deeper and deeper into fantasy.

THE VARSOUVIANA POLKA   Blanche and her young husband danced to the Varsouviana polka tune when she last saw him alive. Having recently discovered that he was gay, she told him on the dance floor that he "disgusted" her; he committed suicide. The polka music plays several times throughout the play, whenever Blanche feels remorse for Allen's death. It represents Blanche's loss of innocence, and signals Blanche's psychological deterioration.

IMPORTANT QUOTATIONS FROM *A STREETCAR NAMED DESIRE*

There are thousands of papers, stretching back over hundreds of years, affecting Belle Reve as, piece by piece, our improvident grandfathers and father and uncles and brothers exchanged the land for their epic fornications—to put it plainly! . . . The four-letter word deprived us of our plantation, till finally all that was left—and Stella can verify that!—was the house itself and about twenty acres of ground, including a graveyard, to which now all but Stella and I have retreated.

Location: Scene Two
Speaker: Blanche to Stanley
Context: In answering Stanley's accusations that she swindled Stella out of her inheritance, Blanche situates herself in a long line of ancestors who have had to pay for their sexual desires

Blanche attributes her family's decline in fortune to the debauchery of its male members. She herself is one of many ancestors who have been unable to express their sexual desire in a healthy way. Sexual depravity has led Bell Reve ("beautiful dream") and the family to ruin and the "graveyard."

Whoever you are—I have always depended on the kindness of strangers.

Location: Scene Eleven; Blanche's last words
Speaker: Blanche to the doctor
Context: Blanche agrees to leave with the doctor

Blanche's comment is ironic in several ways. First, the doctor is not the gentleman rescuer that she perceives him to be. Second, Blanche's dependence on the kindness of strangers is an exaggeration; Williams implies that strangers have been kind to her in exchange for sex. Her final comment poignantly expresses her ultimate detachment from reality, and signals the effective end of her life.

They told me to take a street-car named Desire, and transfer to one called Cemeteries, and ride six blocks and get off at—Elysian Fields!

Location: Beginning of Scene One
Speaker: Blanche
Context: Blanche has just arrived at the Kowalski apartment, to which desire has led her

---

Oh, I guess he's just not the type that goes for jasmine perfume, but maybe he's what we need to mix with our blood now that we've lost Belle Reve.

Location: Scene Two
Speaker: Blanche to Stella
Context: Discovering that Stella is pregnant, Blanche remarks that, now that the South's heyday has passed, uncouth immigrants may give fallen aristocrats some sorely needed survival skills

I am not a Polack. People from Poland are Poles, not Polacks. But what I am is a one hundred percent American, born and raised in the greatest country on earth and proud as hell of it, so don't ever call me a Polack.

Location: Scene Eight

Speaker: Stanley to Blanche

Context: Stanley situates himself as representative of the new American society of upwardly mobile immigrants

THE SUN ALSO RISES

Ernest Hemingway

A young American veteran of World War I lives in Paris and travels with his friends and the woman he loves.

THE LIFE OF ERNEST HEMINGWAY

Ernest Hemingway was born in Oak Park, Illinois, in the summer of 1899. He later described his middle-class parents in harsh terms, condemning them for their conventional morality and values. As a young man, he left home to become a newspaper writer in Kansas City. Early in 1918, he joined the Italian Red Cross. He served as an ambulance driver in Italy during World War I, in which the Italians allied with the British, French, and Americans against Germany and Austria-Hungary. During his time abroad, Hemingway had two experiences that affected him profoundly and that would later inspire one of his most celebrated novels, *A Farewell to Arms*. The first occurred on July 8, 1918, when a trench mortar shell struck him as he crouched beyond the front lines with three Italian soldiers. Hemingway embellished the story over the years, so the actual facts are difficult to ascertain, but it is certain that he was transferred to a hospital in Milan, where he fell in love with a Red Cross nurse named Agnes von Kurowsky. Scholars are divided over Agnes's role in Hemingway's life and writing, but there is little doubt that his relationship with her informed the relationship between Lieutenant Henry and Catherine Barkley in *A Farewell to Arms*.

After his recovery, Hemingway spent several years as a reporter, during which time he honed the clear, concise, and emotionally evocative writing style that generations of authors after him would imitate. In September 1921, he married and settled in Paris, where he made valuable connections with American expatriate writers like Gertrude Stein and Ezra Pound. Hemingway's landmark collection of stories, *In Our Time*, introduced Nick Adams, one of the author's favorite protagonists, whose difficult road from youth into maturity he chronicled. Hemingway's reputation as a writer was most firmly established by the publication of *The Sun Also Rises* in 1926 and *A Farewell to Arms* in 1929.

Most critics maintain that Hemingway's writing fizzled after World War II, when his physical and mental health declined. Despite fantastic bouts of depression, Hemingway did muster enough energy to write *The Old Man and the Sea*, one of his most beloved stories, in 1952. This novella earned him a Pulitzer Prize, and three years later Hemingway was awarded the Nobel Prize in Literature. Still, not even these accolades could soothe the devastating effects of a lifetime of debilitating depression. On July 2, 1961, Hemingway killed himself in his home in Ketchum, Idaho.

THE SUN ALSO RISES IN CONTEXT

The Sun Also Rises portrays the so-called Lost Generation, the group of men and women whose early adulthood was consumed by World War I. This horrific conflict, also referred to as the Great War, shattered many people's ideas about decency and manhood. Robbed of their convictions, members of the generation that fought and worked in the war felt aimless. Although the characters in *The Sun Also Rises* rarely mention the war directly, its effects haunt everything they do and say.

THE SUN ALSO RISES: KEY FACTS

Time and place written: Mid-1920s; Paris	
Date of first publication: 1926	
Publisher: Charles Scribner's Sons	
Type of work: Novel	
Genre: Modernist novel; travelogue; novel of disillusionment	
Language: English	

Setting (time): 1924

Setting (place): Paris, France; Pamplona, Spain; Madrid, Spain

Tense: Past

Tone: Somber, detached, ironic, nostalgic

Narrator: Jake Barnes in the first person

Point of view: Jake's

Protagonist: Jake

Antagonist: Jake's impotence and loyalty

THE SUN ALSO RISES: PLOT OVERVIEW

The narrator, Jake Barnes, is a veteran of World War I who now works as a journalist in Paris. His friend Robert Cohn is a rich Jewish American writer who lives in Paris with his controlling girlfriend, Frances Clyne. Cohn is restless of late. One afternoon, he comes to Jake's office to try to convince Jake to go with him to South America. Jake refuses and tries to get rid of Cohn. That night at a dance club, Jake runs into Lady Brett Ashley, a divorced socialite and the love of Jake's life. Brett is a free-spirited and independent woman who can be very selfish. She and Jake met in England during World War I, when Brett treated Jake for a war wound. During Jake and Brett's conversation, it is subtly implied that Jake's injury rendered him impotent. Although Brett loves Jake, she hints that she is unwilling to give up sex and so does not want to commit to a relationship with him.

The next morning, Jake and Cohn have lunch. Cohn, who is taken with Brett, gets angry when Jake tells him that Brett plans to marry Mike Campbell, a heavy-drinking Scottish war veteran. That afternoon, Brett stands Jake up. That night she arrives unexpectedly at his apartment with Count Mippipopolous, a rich Greek expatriate. After sending the count out for champagne, Brett tells Jake that she is leaving for San Sebastian, in Spain, saying it will be easier on both of them to be apart.

Several weeks later, while Brett and Cohn are away, one of Jake's friends, a fellow American war veteran named Bill Gorton, arrives in Paris. Bill and Jake make plans to go to Spain to do some fishing and attend the fiesta at Pamplona. Jake also makes plans to meet Cohn on the way to Pamplona. Jake runs into Brett and Mike, her fiancé. They ask if they may join Jake in Spain, and he politely says they may. When Mike leaves for a moment, Brett tells Jake that she was in San Sebastian with Cohn.

Bill and Jake take a train from Paris to Bayonne, in the south of France, where they meet Cohn. The three men travel together to Pamplona. They planned on meeting Brett and Mike that night, but the couple does not show up. Bill and Jake decide to leave for a small town called Burguete to fish, but Cohn chooses to stay and wait for Brett. In the Spanish countryside, Bill and Jake check into a small, rural inn. They spend five pleasant days fishing, drinking, and playing cards. Eventually, Jake receives a letter from Mike, who writes that he and Brett will be arriving in Pamplona shortly. Jake and Bill leave on a bus that afternoon to meet the couple. After arriving in Pamplona, Jake and Bill check into a hotel owned by Montoya, a Spanish bullfighting expert who likes Jake for his earnest interest in the sport. Jake and Bill meet up with Brett, Mike, and Cohn, and the whole group goes to watch the bulls being unloaded in preparation for the bullfights. Mike mocks Cohn for following Brett around when he is not wanted.

After a few more days of preparation, the fiesta begins, consuming the city with dancing, drinking, and general debauchery. At the first bullfight, Pedro Romero, a nineteen-year-old prodigy, distinguishes himself from the other bullfighters. Despite its violence, Brett cannot take her eyes off the bullfight, or Romero. A few days later, Jake and his friends are at the hotel dining room, and Brett notices Romero at a nearby table. She persuades Jake to introduce her to him. Mike verbally abuses Cohn, and they almost come to blows before Jake defuses the situation. Later that night, Brett asks Jake to help her find Romero, with whom she says she has fallen in love. Jake agrees to help, and Brett and Romero spend the night together.

Jake meets up with Mike and Bill, who are both extremely drunk. Cohn soon arrives, demanding to know where Brett is. After an exchange of insults, Cohn attacks Mike and Jake, knocking them both out. When Jake returns to the hotel, he finds Cohn lying face down on his bed and crying. Cohn begs Jake's forgiveness, and Jake reluctantly grants it. The next day, Jake learns that Cohn beat up Romero when he discovered the bullfighter with Brett. Cohn later begged Romero to shake hands with him, but Romero refused.

At the bullfight that afternoon, Romero fights brilliantly, dazzling the crowd by killing a bull that had gored a man to death in the streets. Afterward, he cuts off the bull's ear and gives it to Brett. After this final bullfight, Romero and Brett leave for Madrid together. Cohn has left that morning, so only Bill, Mike, and Jake remain as the fiesta draws to a close.

The next day, the three men rent a car and drive to Bayonne, where they go their separate ways. Jake heads back to San Sebastian, where he plans to spend several quiet days relaxing. But he soon receives a telegram from Brett asking him to come meet her in Madrid. He boards an overnight train. Jake finds Brett alone in a Madrid hotel room. She has broken with Romero, fearing that she would ruin him and his career. She says she wants to return to Mike. Jake books tickets for them to leave Madrid. As they ride in a taxi through the Spanish capital, Brett says she and Jake could have had a wonderful time together. Jake says, "Yes, isn't it pretty to think so?"

CHARACTERS IN *THE SUN ALSO RISES*

Lady Brett Ashley A beautiful British socialite. Though she loves Jake, Brett does not want to give up sex. She has difficulty committing to any of the men with whom she has affairs.

Jake Barnes The narrator and protagonist of the novel. Jake is an American veteran of World War I working as a journalist in Paris, where he and his friends have a life full of drinking and parties. Jake is the most stable of his friends, but he struggles with his love for Lady Brett Ashley, his impotence, and the emotional aftermath of the war. Jake rarely speaks directly about himself, but his descriptions of other people and events reveals his own thoughts and feelings.

Belmonte A bullfighter. In his early days, Belmonte was a skilled and popular bullfighter. When he came out of retirement, he found he could never live up to the legends that had grown around him. A bitter, purposeless, and dejected man, he stands for the Lost Generation.

Mike Campbell A drunken, bankrupt Scottish war veteran. Mike has a terrible temper, which his drinking exacerbates. He reacts to Brett's sexual promiscuity with self-pity and anger.

Frances Clyne Cohn's girlfriend at the beginning of the novel. A manipulative status-seeker, Frances persuaded Cohn to move to Paris. As her looks begin to fade, she becomes increasingly possessive and jealous.

Robert Cohn A wealthy American writer living in Paris. Cohn stands apart from his friends because he had no direct experience of World War I and because he is Jewish. Jake and his friends treat Cohn cruelly because of these differences. Cohn holds on to romantic prewar ideals of love and fair play—values that seem tragically absurd in the devastating aftermath of World War I.

Georgette A prostitute. Georgette is beautiful but somewhat thick-witted. Jake picks her up and takes her to dinner, but quickly grows bored of her superficial conversation and abandons her in a club.

Bill Gorton A heavy-drinking war veteran. Bill uses humor to deal with the emotional and psychological fallout of World War I. Their status as American veterans gives Bill and Jake a strong bond. Their friendship is one of the few genuine emotional connections in the novel.

Count Mippipopolous A wealthy Greek count and a veteran of seven wars and four revolutions. Count Mippipopolous becomes infatuated with Brett, but, unlike most of Brett's lovers, he is not jealous or controlling. As opposed to Jake's careless, amoral pleasure-seeking crowd, the count is stable and sane.

Montoya A bullfighting expert and the owner of a Pamplona inn. Montoya believes bullfighting is sacred, and he respects and admires Jake for his genuine enthusiasm about bullfighting. Montoya takes a paternal interest in the gifted young bullfighter Pedro Romero and seeks to protect him from the corrupting influences of tourists and fame.

Pedro Romero A beautiful, nineteen-year-old bullfighter. Romero's talents in the ring charm spectators. He differs from Jake and his friends in many ways: he carries himself with dignity and confidence at all times, his passion for bullfighting gives his life meaning and purpose, and he is a figure of honesty, purity, masculinity, and strength.

Harvey Stone A drunken expatriate gambler who is perpetually out of money. Harvey is intelligent and well read, but excessive drinking and gambling torment him. Like many of Jake's friends, he is prone to petty cruelty toward Cohn.

Wilson-Harris A British war veteran. Jake and Bill befriend Wilson-Harris while fishing in Spain. Harris, as Jake and Bill call him, is a kind, friendly person.

THEMES IN *THE SUN ALSO RISES*

THE AIMLESSNESS OF THE LOST GENERATION World War I called into question accepted notions of morality, faith, and justice. No longer able to rely on the traditional beliefs that gave life meaning, the men and women who experienced the war became psychologically and morally lost, wandering aimlessly in a world that appeared meaningless. Jake, Brett, and their acquaintances typify the Lost Generation. Because they no longer believe in anything, their lives are empty. They fill their time with inconsequential and escapist activities, such as drinking, dancing, and debauchery.

Hemingway never explicitly states that Jake and his friends' lives are aimless, or that war caused this aimlessness, but his portrayal of the characters' barren emotional and mental lives makes his point clear. Although Jake and his friends constantly carouse, they are not happy. At best, their drinking and partying temporarily blunts their self-knowledge and memories of the war.

MALE INSECURITY World War I forced a radical reevaluation of what it meant to be masculine. The prewar ideal of the brave, stoic soldier had little relevance in the context of brutal trench warfare and the knowledge that survival was a matter of luck, not bravery. Jake, who was made impotent by a war injury, literally embodies the emasculating effect of war. He cannot escape the feeling that he has lost his manliness, that he is inadequate—a worry confirmed by Brett's refusal to have a relationship with him.

Jake's condition is the most explicit example of weakened masculinity in the novel, but many other examples exist. All of the veterans feel insecure in their manhood and attempt to reassure themselves by abusing Cohn, whose non-veteran status makes him an easy target. In many ways, Brett is more tradition-ally masculine than the men in the book. She refers to herself as a "chap," she has a short, masculine haircut and a masculine name, she is strong and independent, and she enjoys sex with multiple partners. The men's collective longing for Brett may contain an element of envy for her easy masculinity.

THE DESTRUCTIVENESS OF SEX Sex is a powerful and destructive force in *The Sun Also Rises*. Sexual jealousy leads Cohn to violate his code of ethics and attack Jake, Mike, and Romero. The desire for sex prevents Brett from entering into a relationship with Jake, although she loves him. Brett is closely associated with the negative consequences of sex. She is a liberated woman, sleeping with multi-ple men and feeling no compulsion to commit to any of them, but her carefree sexuality makes Jake and Mike miserable and drives Cohn to acts of violence. In Brett, Hemingway may be expressing his own anxieties about strong, sexually independent women.

SYMBOLS IN *THE SUN ALSO RISES*

BULLFIGHTING The bullfighting episodes in *The Sun Also Rises* are rich in symbolic possibilities. Nearly every episode involving bulls or bullfighting parallels an episode that either has occurred, or will soon occur, among Jake and his friends. For example, the killing of the steer by the bull at the start of the fiesta may prefigure Mike's assault on Cohn, or Brett's destruction of Cohn and his values. The bullfight-ing episodes nearly always function from two symbolic viewpoints: Jake's perspective and the perspective of postwar society. For instance, from Jake's point of view, just as Cohn, Mike, and Jake all once com-manded Brett's affection, Belmonte once commanded the affection of the crowd. But in a larger context, Belmonte symbolizes the entire Lost Generation, which has been left behind. On still another level, Hemingway uses bullfighting to develop the theme of the destructiveness of sex. The language Heming-way employs to describe Romero's bullfighting is almost always sexual. Romero's killing of the bull is described as a seduction, linking sex to violence.

IMPORTANT QUOTATIONS FROM *THE SUN ALSO RISES*

Robert Cohn was once middleweight boxing champion of Princeton. Do not think I am very much impressed by that as a boxing title, but it meant a lot to Cohn. He cared nothing for boxing, in fact he disliked it, but he learned it painfully and thoroughly to counteract the feeling of inferiority and shyness he had felt on being treated as a Jew at Princeton.

Location: The first lines of the novel
Speaker: Jake
Context: Jake briefly sketches Robert Cohn's biography

This passage presents many of the novel's key themes and motifs, such as competitiveness, resentment between men, and insecurity. Cohn has an intense need to be accepted. Although he dislikes boxing, he perfects it in order to better his social position at Princeton. This need for acceptance proves harmful to Cohn in his relationships with Jake and Brett, who cannot stomach his insecurities. Jake describes Cohn condescendingly. As the novel progresses, this condescension turns into outright hostility and antagonism toward Cohn. Cohn feels insecure because he is a Jew surrounded by Gentiles. His insecurities are well-founded, as the characters' abuse of Cohn proves, but nearly all the male characters in the novel feel insecure about something. For example, Jake's hostile and skeptical attitude toward Cohn is bound up with jealousies and insecurities of his own. In typical fashion, Hemingway suggests a great deal of meaning with a brief, indirect passage.

"Couldn't we live together, Brett? Couldn't we just live together?"
"I don't think so. I'd just tromper you with everybody."

Location: Chapter VII
Speaker: Jake and Brett
Context: Brett has shown up at Jake's house with Count Mippipopolous

This exchange has to do with the central conflict of the novel, a conflict that is never directly expressed. While little is said here, much is communicated. Jake begs Brett to be with him, but she replies that she would always "tromper" him, a French word here meaning "to commit adultery." A wound Jake received during the war rendered him impotent, and thus he cannot satisfy Brett's need for sex. Brett is telling Jake that she would have to be with other men behind Jake's back, which she knows he would not be able to stand. This central, intractable emotional conflict is at the center of the novel's action.

"I can't stand it to think my life is going so fast and I'm not really living it."
"Nobody ever lives their life all the way up except bull-fighters."

Location: Chapter II
Speaker: Cohn and Jake
Context: Cohn worries about the purpose of his life

You can't get away from yourself by moving from one place to another.

Location: Chapter II
Speaker: Jake
Context: Cohn tries to convince Jake to travel with him to South America

---

"Oh, Jake," Brett said, "we could have had such a damned good time together."
Ahead was a mounted policeman in khaki directing traffic. He raised his baton. The car slowed suddenly pressing Brett against me.

"Yes," I said. *"Isn't it pretty to think so?"*

Location: The final lines of the novel
Speaker: Jake
Context: Jake and Brett take a taxi

A TALE OF TWO CITIES

Charles Dickens

During the French Revolution, a woman's love turns a selfish man into a hero.

THE LIFE OF CHARLES DICKENS

Charles Dickens was born on February 7, 1812. He spent the first ten years of his life in Kent, a marshy region by the sea in the east of England. Dickens was the second of eight children. His father, John Dickens, was kind and likable, but fiscally irresponsible. His huge debts caused tremendous strain on his family.

When Dickens was ten, his family moved to London. Two years later, his father was arrested and thrown in debtors' prison. Dickens's mother moved into the prison with seven of her children. Charles tried to earn money for the struggling family. For three months, he worked with other children pasting labels on bottles in a blacking warehouse. Dickens found the three months he spent apart from his family highly traumatic. Not only was the job itself miserable, but he considered himself too good for it, earning the contempt of the other children. His experiences at this warehouse inspired passages of *David Copperfield*.

An inheritance gave John Dickens enough money to free himself from his debt and from prison. Dickens attended Wellington House Academy for two years. He became a law clerk, then a newspaper reporter, and finally a novelist. His first novel, *The Pickwick Papers* (1837), met with huge popular success. Dickens was a literary celebrity in England for the rest of his life.

Dickens's work includes *Oliver Twist* (1837–1839), *Nicholas Nickelby* (1838–1839), and *A Christmas Carol* (1843). Perhaps his best known novel, *Great Expectations* (1860–1861) shares many thematic similarities with *David Copperfield*. Dickens died in Kent on June 9, 1870, at the age of fifty-eight.

A TALE OF TWO CITIES IN CONTEXT

A Tale of Two Cities was originally published serially in a magazine called *All the Year Round*, which Dickens had created after a falling-out with his regular publishers. The novel was inspired by a play by Wilkie Collins entitled *The Frozen Deep*, which Dickens starred in. (He also fell in love with an actress in the play, precipitating the effective end of his twenty-three-year marriage to Catherine Hogarth.) In the play, Dickens played the part of a man who sacrifices his own life so that his rival may have the woman they both love. The love triangle in the play became the basis for the complex relations between Charles Darnay, Lucie Manette, and Sydney Carton in *A Tale of Two Cities*. Dickens also appreciated the play for its treatment of redemption and rebirth, love and violence. He decided to transpose these themes onto the French Revolution. In order to make his novel historically accurate, Dickens turned to Thomas Carlyle's account of the revolution, which was then considered definitive.

Dickens had forayed into historical fiction only once before with *Barnaby Rudge* (1841), and *A Tale of Two Cities* proved a difficult undertaking. The vast scope and the gravity of his historical subject forced Dickens largely to abandon the outlandish and often comical characters that had come to define his writing. Although Jerry Cruncher and Miss Pross have some typically Dickensian qualities—exaggerated mannerisms, idiosyncratic speech—they play only minor roles in the novel. More experimental than the novels that precede it, *A Tale of Two Cities* shows its author in transition. Dickens would emerge from this transition as a mature artist, ready to write *Great Expectations* and *Our Mutual Friend* (1864–1865).

A TALE OF TWO CITIES: KEY FACTS

Time and place written: 1859; London

Date of first publication: Published in weekly serial form between April 20, 1859, and November 26, 1859

Publisher: Chapman and Hall

Type of work: Novel

Genre: Historical fiction

Language: English

Setting (time): 1775–1793

Setting (place): London and its outskirts; Paris and its outskirts

Tense: Past

Tone: Sentimental, sympathetic, sarcastic, horrified, grotesque, grim

Narrator: Anonymous, omniscient narrator in the third person

Point of view: Varies

Protagonist: Charles Darnay or Sydney Carton

Antagonist: Bloodthirstiness

A TALE OF TWO CITIES: PLOT OVERVIEW

The year is 1775, and social ills plague France and England. Jerry Cruncher, an odd-job-man who works for Tellson's Bank, stops the Dover mail-coach with an urgent message for Jarvis Lorry. The message instructs Lorry to wait at Dover for a young woman. Lorry responds with the cryptic words, "Recalled to Life." At Dover, Lorry is met by Lucie Manette, a young orphan whose father, a once-eminent doctor whom she supposed dead, has been discovered in France. Lorry escorts Lucie to Paris, where they meet Defarge, a former servant of Doctor Manette who has kept Manette safe in a garret. Driven mad by eighteen years in the Bastille, Manette spends all of his time making shoes, a trade he learned while in prison. Lorry assures Lucie that her love and devotion can recall her father to consciousness, and he is right.

In 1780, Charles Darnay stands accused of treason against the English crown. A bombastic lawyer named Stryver pleads Darnay's case, but it is not until his drunk, good-for-nothing colleague, Sydney Carton, assists him that the court acquits Darnay. Carton clinches his argument by pointing out that he himself bears an uncanny resemblance to the defendant, which undermines the prosecution's assertion that Darnay is truly the spy the authorities spotted. Lucie and Doctor Manette watched the court proceedings. That night, Carton escorts Darnay to a tavern and asks how it feels to have the sympathy of a woman like Lucie. Carton despises and resents Darnay because he reminds him of what he might have been.

In France, the cruel Marquis Evrémonde runs down a plebian child with his carriage. In typical aristocratic fashion, the Marquis curses the peasantry and hurries home to his chateau, where he awaits the arrival of his nephew Darnay from England. When Darnay arrives, he curses his uncle and the French aristocracy for their abominable treatment of the people. He renounces his identity as an Evrémonde and announces his intention to return to England. That night, the Marquis Evrémonde is murdered. The murderer leaves a note signed with the nickname adopted by French revolutionaries: "Jacques."

A year passes, and Darnay asks Manette for permission to marry Lucie. He says that if Lucie accepts, he will reveal his true identity to Manette. Carton also pledges his love to Lucie, saying that his life is worthless, but she has helped him dream of a better, more valuable existence. On the streets of London, Jerry Cruncher gets swept up in the funeral procession for a spy named Roger Cly. Later that night, he demonstrates his talents as a "Resurrection-Man," sneaking into the cemetery to steal and sell Cly's body.

In Paris, an English spy known as John Barsad drops into Defarge's wine shop. Barsad hopes to turn up evidence concerning the mounting revolution. Madame Defarge sits in the shop knitting a secret registry of those whom the revolution seeks to execute. Back in London, Darnay, on the morning of his wedding, keeps his promise to Manette and reveals his true identity. That night, Manette relapses into his old prison habit of making shoes. After nine days, Manette regains his presence of mind and soon joins the newlyweds on their honeymoon. Upon Darnay's return, Carton pays him a visit and asks for his friendship. Darnay assures Carton that he is always welcome in his home.

The year is now 1789. The peasants in Paris storm the Bastille and the French Revolution begins. The revolutionaries murder aristocrats in the streets, and Gabelle, a man charged with the maintenance of the Evrémonde estate, is imprisoned. Three years later, he writes to Darnay, asking to be rescued. Despite the danger to himself, Darnay departs immediately for France.

As soon as Darnay arrives in Paris, the French revolutionaries arrest him as an emigrant. Lucie and Manette make their way to Paris in hopes of saving him. Darnay remains in prison for a year and three months before receiving a trial. In order to help free him, Manette uses his considerable influence with the revolutionaries, who sympathize with him because he served time in the Bastille. Darnay is acquitted, but that same night he is arrested again. This time, the charges come from Defarge and his vengeful wife. Carton arrives in Paris with a plan to rescue Darnay and obtains the help of John Barsad, who turns out to be Solomon Pross, the long-lost brother of Miss Pross, Lucie's loyal servant.

At Darnay's trial, Defarge produces a letter that he discovered in Manette's old jail cell in the Bastille. The letter explains the cause of Manette's imprisonment. Years ago, the brothers Evrémonde (Darnay's father and uncle) enlisted Manette's medical assistance. They asked him to tend to a woman, whom one of the brothers had raped, and her brother, whom the same brother had stabbed fatally. Fearing that Manette might report their misdeeds, the Evrémondes had him arrested. After hearing this story, the jury condemns Darnay for the crimes of his ancestors and sentences him to die within twenty-four hours.

That night, at the Defarge's wine shop, Carton overhears Madame Defarge plotting to have Lucie and her daughter executed. It turns out that Madame Defarge is the surviving sibling of the man and woman killed by the Evrémondes. Carton arranges for the Manettes' immediate departure from France. He then visits Darnay in prison, tricks him into changing clothes with him, and, after dictating a letter of explanation, drugs his friend, making him fall unconscious. Barsad carries Darnay, now disguised as Carton, to an awaiting coach, while Carton, disguised as Darnay, awaits execution. As Darnay, Lucie, their child, and Dr. Manette speed away from Paris, Madame Defarge arrives at Lucie's apartment, hoping to arrest her. There she finds the supremely protective Miss Pross. A scuffle ensues, and Madame Defarge dies by a bullet from her own gun. Sydney Carton meets his death at the guillotine. The narrator Carton dies with the knowledge that he has finally imbued his life with meaning.

CHARACTERS IN *A TALE OF TWO CITIES*

John Barsad A British spy. Barsad falsely claims to be a virtuous man of upstanding reputation.

Sydney Carton One of the protagonists of the novel. In the beginning, Carton is insolent, indifferent, and alcoholic. His love for Lucie eventually transforms him into a man of profound merit. At first the polar opposite of Darnay, Carton morally surpasses him in the end.

Roger Cly A British spy. Cly swears that patriotism alone inspires all of his actions. He feigns honesty but constantly participates in conniving schemes.

Jerry Cruncher An odd-job-man for Tellson's Bank. Cruncher is gruff, short-tempered, superstitious, and uneducated. He supplements his income by working as a "Resurrection-Man," one who digs up dead bodies and sells them to scientists.

Charles Darnay One of the protagonists of the novel. A French aristocrat by birth, Darnay chooses to live in England because he cannot bear to be associated with the cruel injustices of the French social system. Darnay is virtuous, honest, and courageous.

Madame Defarge The sister of a man and woman cruelly mistreated by Darnay's uncle and father. A cruel revolutionary whose hatred of the aristocracy fuels her tireless crusade, Madame Defarge spends a good deal of the novel knitting a register of everyone who must die for the revolutionary cause. Unlike her husband, she is unrelentingly bloodthirsty.

Monsieur Defarge A wine-shop owner and revolutionary in the poor Saint Antoine section of Paris. Monsieur Defarge formerly worked as a servant for Doctor Manette. Defarge is an intelligent and committed revolutionary leader.

Marquis Evrémonde Charles Darnay's uncle. The Marquis Evrémonde is a French aristocrat who typifies an inhumanly cruel caste system.

Gabelle The man charged with keeping up the Evrémonde estate after the Marquis's death. Gabelle is imprisoned by the revolutionaries.

Jarvis Lorry   An elderly businessman who works for Tellson's Bank. Mr. Lorry is a business-oriented bachelor with a strong moral sense and a good, honest heart.

Doctor Manette   Lucie's father and a brilliant physician. Doctor Manette spent eighteen years as a prisoner in the Bastille. At first demented by his incarceration, he proves to be a kind, loving father who prizes his daughter's happiness above all things.

Lucie Manette   A young French woman who grew up in England. Lucie was raised as a ward of Tellson's Bank. She is an archetype of compassion whose love transforms those around her, revitalizing her father and turning Sydney Carton from a "jackal" into a hero.

Miss Pross   The servant who raised Lucie. Miss Pross is brusque, tough, and fiercely loyal to her mistress. The personification of order and loyalty, she is the foil to Madame Defarge, who epitomizes the violent chaos of the revolution.

Mr. Stryver   An ambitious lawyer. Stryver dreams of climbing the social ladder. Unlike his associate, Sydney Carton, Stryver is bombastic, proud, and foolish.

THEMES IN *A TALE OF TWO CITIES*

THE POSSIBILITY OF RESURRECTION   With *A Tale of Two Cities*, Dickens asserts his belief in the possibility of resurrection and transformation, both on a personal level and on a societal level. Doctor Manette is spiritually dead after his imprisonment in the Bastille, but the love of his daughter recalls him to life. Although Carton spends most of the novel wallowing in indolence and apathy, the supreme selflessness of his final act speaks to a human capacity for change. By delivering himself to the guillotine, Carton becomes a Christ figure whose death saves the lives of others. His own existence thus gains meaning and value. Dickens suggests that Carton, like Christ, will be resurrected—reborn in the hearts of those he has died to save. Dickens also implies that the death of the old regime in France prepares the way for the beautiful and renewed Paris that Carton envisions from the guillotine. Although the novel explores the atrocities committed both by the aristocracy and by the outraged peasants, it ultimately expresses the belief that this violence will give way to a new and better society.

THE NECESSITY OF SACRIFICE   Dickens argues that sacrifice is necessary to achieve happiness. The revolutionaries show that a new, egalitarian French republic can come about only if personal loves and loyalties are sacrificed for the good of the nation. When Darnay is arrested for the second time, the guard who seizes him reminds Manette that state interests are more important than personal loyalties. Madame Defarge gives her husband a similar lesson when she chastises him for his devotion to Manette. In her opinion, this kindness only clouds her husband's obligation to the revolutionary cause. Most important, Carton's transformation into a man of moral worth depends upon his sacrifice of his former self and his very life.

THE VIOLENCE OF REVOLUTIONARIES   Dickens approaches his historical subject with some ambivalence. While he supports the revolutionary cause, he often points to the evil of the revolutionaries themselves. Dickens deeply sympathizes with the plight of the French peasantry and emphasizes their need for liberation. The several chapters that deal with the Marquis Evrémonde, for example, paint a picture of a vicious aristocracy that shamelessly exploits and oppresses the nation's poor. But although Dickens condemns this oppression, he also condemns the peasants' strategies of overcoming it. In fighting cruelty with cruelty, the peasants only perpetuate the violence they themselves have suffered. Dickens makes his stance clear in his suspicious, cautionary depictions of mobs. The scenes in which the people sharpen their weapons at the grindstone and dance the grisly Carmagnole are deeply macabre. Dickens's most concise description of revolution comes in the final chapter, in which he notes the link between the oppressed and the oppressor: "Sow the same seed of rapacious license and oppression over again, and it will surely yield the same fruit according to its kind."

SYMBOLS IN *A TALE OF TWO CITIES*

MADAME DEFARGE'S KNITTING   Madame Defarge's knitting is a symbol she creates, a secret list of people condemned to die in the name of a new republic. Her knitting also represents the stealthy, cold-blooded vengefulness of the revolutionaries. As Madame Defarge sits quietly knitting, she appears harmless, but she is calming and methodically sentencing people to death. Similarly, the French peasants may look like simple and humble figures, but they rise up to massacre their oppressors. Greek mythology often links weaving to vengefulness and fate. The Fates, three sisters who control human life, spin, measure, and cut the web of life. Madame Defarge's knitting links her to these three women.

THE MARQUIS The Marquis Evrémonde is less a believable character than a symbol of an evil and corrupt social order. He is incredibly self-indulgent and completely indifferent to the lives of the peasants whom he exploits, scorning the father of the child he has trampled to death.

IMPORTANT QUOTATIONS FROM *A TALE OF TWO CITIES*

> *The wine was red wine, and had stained the ground of the narrow street in the suburb of Saint Antoine, in Paris, where it was spilled. It had stained many hands, too, and many faces, and many naked feet, and many wooden shoes. The hands of the man who sawed the wood, left red marks on the billets; and the forehead of the woman who nursed her baby, was stained with the stain of the old rag she wound about her head again. Those who had been greedy with the staves of the cask, had acquired a tigerish smear about the mouth; and one tall joker so besmirched, his head more out of a long squalid bag of a night-cap than in it, scrawled upon a wall with his finger dipped in muddy wine-lees—blood.*

Location: Book the First, Chapter 5
Speaker: The narrator
Context: A wine cask has broken outside Defarge's wine-shop

This passage, which opens the novel's examination of Paris, acts as a potent depiction of the peasants' hunger. These oppressed people are not only physically starved—they are willing to slurp wine from the city streets—but spiritually starved for a new world order, for justice and freedom. In this passage, Dickens foreshadows the lengths to which the peasants' desperation will take them. The desperate, gluttonous drinking of the wine is echoed later in the novel when the revolutionaries, smeared with red blood, gather around the grindstone to sharpen their weapons. The reference to staining the scrawling of the word "blood," and the appearance of the wood-sawyer foreshadow the coming bloodbath.

> *I see a beautiful city and a brilliant people rising from this abyss, and, in their struggles to be truly free, in their triumphs and defeats, through long years to come, I see the evil of this time and of the previous time of which this is the natural birth, gradually making expiation for itself and wearing out.. . .*
>
> *I see that child who lay upon her bosom and who bore my name, a man winning his way up in that path of life which once was mine. I see him winning it so well, that my name is made illustrious there by the light of his.. . .*
>
> *It is a far, far better thing that I do, than I have ever done; it is a far, far better rest I go to than I have ever known.*

Location: The final chapter
Speaker: Carton
Context: Carton awaits his execution

This passage, which occurs in the final chapter, prophesies two resurrections: one personal, the other national. In a novel that examines the nature of revolution, the struggles of France and of Sydney Carton parallel each other. Here, Dickens articulates the outcome of those struggles: just as Paris will "ris[e] from [the] abyss" of the French Revolution's chaotic and bloody violence, Carton will be reborn into glory after a virtually wasted life. In the prophecy that Paris will become "a beautiful city" and that Carton's name will be "made illustrious," we see evidence of Dickens's faith in the essential goodness of humankind. The last thoughts attributed to Carton, in their lyricism and calm, register this faith as a calm and soothing certainty.

It was the best of times, it was the worst of times, it was the age of wisdom, it was the age of foolishness, it was the epoch of belief, it was the epoch of incredulity, it was the season of Light, it was the season of Darkness, it was the spring of hope, it was the winter of despair, we had everything before us, we had nothing before us, we were all going direct to Heaven, we were all going direct the other way . . .

Location: The first lines of the novel
Speaker: The narrator
Context: The narrator puts his story in context

A wonderful fact to reflect upon, that every human creature is constituted to be that profound secret and mystery to every other. A solemn consideration, when I enter a great city by night, that every one of those darkly clustered houses encloses its own secret; that every room in every one of them encloses its own secret; that every beating heart in the hundreds of thousands of breasts there, is, in some of its imaginings, a secret to the heart nearest it! Something of the awfulness, even of Death itself, is referable to this.

Location: Book the First, Chapter 3
Speaker: The narrator
Context: Jerry Cruncher has delivered a cryptic message to Jarvis Lorry

Along the Paris streets, the death-carts rumble, hollow and harsh. Six tumbrels carry the day's wine to La Guillotine. All the devouring and insatiate Monsters imagined since imagination could record itself, are fused in one realization, Guillotine. And yet there is not in France, with its rich variety of soil and climate, a blade, a leaf, a root, a sprig, a peppercorn, which will grow to maturity under conditions more certain than those that have produced this horror. Crush humanity out of shape once more, under similar hammers, and it will twist itself into the same tortured forms. Sow the same seed of rapacious license and oppression over again, and it will surely yield the same fruit according to its kind.

Location: The final chapter
Speaker: The narrator
Context: Dickens describes the revolutionaries

THE TEMPEST

William Shakespeare

A powerful magician who used to be the Duke of Milan causes his enemies to wash up on his island, then uses his magic to reconcile with them and regain his dukedom.

THE LIFE OF WILLIAM SHAKESPEARE

William Shakespeare, the most influential writer in all of English literature, was born in 1564 to a successful middle-class glove-maker in Stratford-upon-Avon, England. Shakespeare's formal education did not progress beyond grammar school. In 1582, he married an older woman, Anne Hathaway. His union with Anne produced three children. Around 1590, Shakespeare left his family behind and traveled to London to work as an actor and playwright. He quickly earned public and critical acclaim, and eventually became the most popular playwright in England and a part-owner of the Globe Theater. Shakespeare's career bridged the reigns of Elizabeth I (ruled 1558–1603) and James I (ruled 1603–1625), and he was a favorite of both monarchs. James paid Shakespeare's company a great compliment by giving its members the title of King's Men. Shakespeare retired to Stratford a wealthy and renowned man and died in 1616 at the age of fifty-two. At the time of Shakespeare's death, literary luminaries such as Ben Jonson hailed his works as timeless.

Shakespeare's works were collected and printed in various editions in the century following his death, and by the early eighteenth century his reputation as the greatest poet ever to write in English was well established. The unprecedented regard in which Shakespeare's works were held led to a fierce curiosity about his life, but many details of Shakespeare's personal history are unknown or shrouded in mystery. Some people have concluded from this lack of information and from Shakespeare's modest education that Shakespeare's plays were actually written by someone else—Francis Bacon and the Earl of Oxford are the two most popular candidates—but the support for this claim is overwhelmingly circumstantial, and the theory is not taken seriously by many scholars.

Shakespeare is generally thought to be the author of the thirty-eight plays (two of them possibly collaborations) and 154 sonnets that bear his name. The legacy of this body of work is immense. A number of Shakespeare's plays seem to have transcended even the category of brilliance, influencing the course of Western literature and culture.

THE TEMPEST IN CONTEXT

The Tempest probably was written in 1610–1611, and was first performed at court by the King's Men in the fall of 1611. It was performed again in the winter of 1612–1613 during the festivities in celebration of the marriage of King James's daughter Elizabeth. *The Tempest* is most likely the last play written entirely by Shakespeare, and it is remarkable for being one of only two plays by Shakespeare (the other being *Love's Labor's Lost*) whose plot is entirely original. The play does, however, draw on travel literature of its time—most notably the accounts of a tempest off the Bermudas that separated and nearly wrecked a fleet of colonial ships sailing from Plymouth to Virginia. The English colonial project seems to be on Shakespeare's mind throughout *The Tempest*, as almost every character, from the lord Gonzalo to the drunk Stefano, ponders how he would rule the island on which the play is set if he were its king. Shakespeare seems also to have drawn on Montaigne's essay "Of the Cannibals," which was translated into English in 1603. The name of Prospero's servant-monster, Caliban, may be an anagram or derivative of "Cannibal."

The Tempest includes stage directions for a number of elaborate special effects. The many pageants and songs accompanied by ornately costumed figures or stage-magic—for example, the banquet in Act III, scene iii, and the wedding celebration for Ferdinand and Miranda in Act IV, scene i—give the play the feeling of a masque, a highly stylized form of dramatic, musical entertainment popular among the aristocracy of the sixteenth and seventeenth centuries. It is perhaps the tension between simple and elaborate stage effects that gives the play its eerie, dreamlike quality. *The Tempest* is rich and complex even though it is one of Shakespeare's shortest, most simply constructed plays.

It is tempting to think of *The Tempest* as Shakespeare's farewell to the stage because one of its characters is a great magician giving up his art. Indeed, we can interpret Prospero's reference to the dissolution of "the great globe itself" (IV.i.153) as an allusion to Shakespeare's theatre. However, Shakespeare is known to have written at least two other plays after *The Tempest*: *The Two Noble Kinsmen* and *Henry VIII* in 1613, both possibly written with John Fletcher. A performance of the latter was, in fact, the occasion for the actual dissolution of the Globe. A cannon fired during the performance accidentally ignited the thatch, and the theater burned to the ground.

THE TEMPEST: KEY FACTS

Full title: The Tempest

Time and place written: 1610–1611; England

Date of first publication: 1623

Genre: Romance

Setting (time): The Renaissance

Setting (place): An island in the Mediterranean sea, probably off the coast of Italy

Protagonist: Prospero

Major conflict: Prospero seeks to use his magic to make Antonio and Alonso repent and restore him to his rightful place

THE TEMPEST: PLOT OVERVIEW

A storm strikes a ship carrying Alonso, Ferdinand, Sebastian, Antonio, Gonzalo, Stefano, and Trinculo, who are on their way to Italy after coming from the wedding of Alonso's daughter, Claribel, to the prince of Tunis in Africa. The royal party and the other mariners, with the exception of the unflappable Boatswain, begin to fear for their lives. Lightning cracks, and the mariners cry that the ship has been hit. Everyone prepares to sink.

The next scene begins much more quietly. Miranda and Prospero stand on the shore of their island, looking out to sea at the recent shipwreck. Miranda asks her father to do anything he can to help the poor souls in the ship. Prospero assures her that everything is all right and then informs her that it is time she learned more about herself and her past. He reveals to her that he orchestrated the shipwreck and tells her the lengthy story of her past, a story he has often started to tell her before but has never finished. The story goes that Prospero was the Duke of Milan until his brother Antonio, conspiring with Alonso, the King of Naples, usurped his position. With the help of Gonzalo, Prospero was able to escape with his daughter and with the books that are the source of his magic and power. Prospero and his daughter arrived on the island where they remain now and have been for twelve years. Only now, Prospero says, has Fortune at last sent his enemies his way, and he has raised the tempest in order to make things right with them once and for all.

After telling this story, Prospero charms Miranda to sleep and then calls forth his familiar spirit Ariel, his chief magical agent. Prospero and Ariel's discussion reveals that Ariel brought the tempest upon the ship and set fire to the mast. He then made sure that everyone got safely to the island, though they are now separated from each other into small groups. Ariel, who is a captive servant to Prospero, reminds his master that he has promised Ariel freedom a year early if he performs tasks such as these without complaint. Prospero chastises Ariel for protesting and reminds him of the horrible fate from which he was rescued. Before Prospero came to the island, a witch named Sycorax imprisoned Ariel in a tree. Sycorax died, leaving Ariel trapped until Prospero arrived and freed him. After Ariel assures Prospero that he knows his place, Prospero orders Ariel to take the shape of a sea nymph and make himself invisible to all but Prospero.

Miranda awakens from her sleep, and she and Prospero go to visit Caliban, Prospero's servant and the son of the dead Sycorax. Caliban curses Prospero, and Prospero and Miranda berate him for being ungrateful for what they have given and taught him. Prospero sends Caliban to fetch firewood. Ariel, invisible, enters playing music and leading in the awed Ferdinand. Miranda and Ferdinand are immediately smitten with each other. He is the only man Miranda has ever seen, besides Caliban and her father. Prospero is happy to see that his plan for his daughter's future marriage is working, but decides that he must upset things temporarily in order to prevent their relationship from developing too quickly. He accuses Ferdinand of merely pretending to be the Prince of Naples and threatens him with imprisonment. When Ferdinand draws his sword, Prospero charms him and leads him off to prison, ignoring Miranda's cries for mercy. He then sends Ariel on another mysterious mission.

On another part of the island, Alonso, Sebastian, Antonio, Gonzalo, and other miscellaneous lords give thanks for their safety but worry about the fate of Ferdinand. Alonso says that he wishes he never had married his daughter to the prince of Tunis because if he had not made this journey, his son would still be alive. Gonzalo tries to maintain high spirits by discussing the beauty of the island, but his remarks are undercut by the sarcastic sourness of Antonio and Sebastian. Ariel appears, invisible, and plays music that puts all but Sebastian and Antonio to sleep. These two then begin to discuss the possible advantages of killing their sleeping companions. Antonio persuades Sebastian that the latter will become ruler of Naples if they kill Alonso. Claribel, who would be the next heir if Ferdinand were indeed dead, is too far away to be able to claim her right. Sebastian is convinced, and the two are about to stab the sleeping men when Ariel causes Gonzalo to wake with a shout. Everyone wakes up, and Antonio and Sebastian concoct a ridiculous story about having drawn their swords to protect the king from lions. Ariel goes back to Prospero while Alonso and his party continue to search for Ferdinand.

Caliban, meanwhile, is hauling wood for Prospero when he sees Trinculo and thinks he is a spirit sent by Prospero to torment him. He lies down and hides under his cloak. A storm is brewing, and Trinculo, curious about but undeterred by Caliban's strange appearance and smell, crawls under the cloak with him. Stefano, drunk and singing, comes along and stumbles upon the bizarre spectacle of Caliban and Trinculo huddled under the cloak. Caliban, hearing the singing, cries out that he will work faster so long as the "spirits" leave him alone. Stefano decides that this monster requires liquor and attempts to get Caliban to drink. Trinculo recognizes his friend Stefano and calls out to him. Soon the three are sitting up together and drinking. Caliban quickly becomes an enthusiastic drinker, and begins to sing.

Prospero puts Ferdinand to work hauling wood. Ferdinand finds his labor pleasant because it is for Miranda's sake. Miranda, thinking that her father is asleep, tells Ferdinand to take a break. The two flirt with one another. Miranda proposes marriage, and Ferdinand accepts. Prospero has been on stage most of the time, unseen, and he is pleased with this development.

Stefano, Trinculo, and Caliban are now drunk and raucous and are made all the more so by Ariel, who comes to them invisibly and provokes them to fight with one another by impersonating their voices and taunting them. Caliban grows more fervent in his boasts that he knows how to kill Prospero. He even tells Stefano that he can bring him to where Prospero is sleeping. He proposes that they kill Prospero, take his daughter, and set Stefano up as king of the island. Stefano thinks this a good plan, and the three prepare to set off to find Prospero. They are distracted, however, by the sound of music that Ariel plays on his flute and tabor-drum, and they decide to follow this music before executing their plot.

Alonso, Gonzalo, Sebastian, and Antonio grow weary from traveling and pause to rest. Antonio and Sebastian secretly plot to take advantage of Alonso and Gonzalo's exhaustion, deciding to kill them in the evening. Prospero, probably on the balcony of the stage and invisible to the men, causes a banquet to be set out by strangely shaped spirits. As the men prepare to eat, Ariel appears like a harpy and causes the banquet to vanish. He then accuses the men of supplanting Prospero and says that it was for this sin that Alonso's son, Ferdinand, has been taken. He vanishes, leaving Alonso feeling vexed and guilty.

Prospero now softens toward Ferdinand and welcomes him into his family as the soon-to-be-husband of Miranda. He sternly reminds Ferdinand, however, that Miranda's "virgin-knot" (IV.i.15) is not to be broken until the wedding has been officially solemnized. Prospero then asks Ariel to call forth some spirits to perform a masque for Ferdinand and Miranda. The spirits assume the shapes of Ceres, Juno, and Iris and perform a short masque celebrating the rites of marriage and the bounty of the earth. A dance of reapers and nymphs follows but is interrupted when Prospero suddenly remembers that he still must stop the plot against his life.

He sends the spirits away and asks Ariel about Trinculo, Stefano, and Caliban. Ariel tells his master of the three men's drunken plans. He also tells how he led the men with his music through prickly grass and briars and finally into a filthy pond near Prospero's cell. Ariel and Prospero then set a trap by hanging beautiful clothing in Prospero's cell. Stefano, Trinculo, and Caliban enter looking for Prospero and, finding the beautiful clothing, decide to steal it. They are immediately set upon by a pack of spirits in the shape of dogs and hounds, driven on by Prospero and Ariel.

Prospero uses Ariel to bring Alonso and the others before him. He then sends Ariel to bring the Boatswain and the mariners from where they sleep on the wrecked ship. Prospero confronts Alonso, Antonio, and Sebastian with their treachery, but tells them that he forgives them. Alonso tells him of having lost Ferdinand in the tempest and Prospero says that he recently lost his own daughter. Clarifying his meaning, he draws aside a curtain to reveal Ferdinand and Miranda playing chess. Alonso and his companions are amazed by the miracle of Ferdinand's survival, and Miranda is stunned by the sight of people unlike any she has seen before. Ferdinand tells his father about his marriage.

Ariel returns with the Boatswain and mariners. The Boatswain tells a story of having been awakened from a sleep that had apparently lasted since the tempest. At Prospero's bidding, Ariel releases Caliban, Trinculo and Stefano, who then enter wearing their stolen clothing. Prospero and Alonso command them to return it and to clean up Prospero's cell. Prospero invites Alonso and the others to stay for the night so that he can tell them the tale of his life in the past twelve years. After this, the group plans to return to Italy. Prospero, restored to his dukedom, will retire to Milan. Prospero gives Ariel one final task—to make sure the seas are calm for the return voyage—before setting him free. Finally, Prospero delivers an epilogue to the audience, asking them to forgive him for his wrongdoing and set him free by applauding.

CHARACTERS IN *THE TEMPEST*

Alonso   The King of Naples and the father of Ferdinand. Alonso helped Antonio unseat Prospero twelve years before. He is acutely aware of the consequences of his actions, and blames the death of his son on his own decision to marry his daughter to the Prince of Tunis. He also regrets his role in the usurping of Prospero.

Antonio   Prospero's brother. Antonio is power-hungry and foolish.

Ariel   Prospero's spirit helper. Most critics refer to Ariel as "he," but his gender and physical form are ambiguous. Rescued by Prospero from a long imprisonment at the hands of the witch Sycorax, Ariel is Prospero's servant until Prospero decides to release him. He is mischievous and ubiquitous, able to traverse the length of the island in an instant and to change shape at will.

Boatswain   A shipman. The boatswain is vigorous and good-natured. He is competent and almost cheerful in the shipwreck scene, demanding practical help rather than weeping and prayer. He seems surprised but not stunned when he awakens from a long sleep at the end of the play.

Caliban   Another of Prospero's servants. Caliban, the son of the deceased witch Sycorax, acquainted Prospero with the island when Prospero arrived. Caliban believes that the island rightfully belongs to him and has been stolen by Prospero. His speech and behavior is sometimes coarse and brutal, as in his drunken scenes with Stefano and Trinculo, and sometimes eloquent and sensitive, as in his rebukes of Prospero and his description of the eerie beauty of the island.

Ferdinand   Alonso's son and heir. In some ways, Ferdinand is as pure and naïve as Miranda. He falls in love with her at first sight and happily submits to servitude in order to win her father's approval.

Gonzalo   An old, honest lord. Gonzalo helped Prospero and Miranda to escape after Antonio usurped Prospero's title. Gonzalo's speeches provide commentary on the events of the play.

Miranda   Prospero's daughter. Miranda was brought to the island at an early age and has never seen anyone other than her father and Caliban, although she dimly remembers being cared for by female servants as an infant. Miranda's perceptions of other people tend to be naïve and non-judgmental. She is compassionate, generous, and loyal to her father.

Prospero   The play's protagonist, and Miranda's father. Twelve years before the events of the play, Prospero was the Duke of Milan. His brother, Antonio, in concert with Alonso, king of Naples, usurped him, forcing him to flee in a boat with his daughter. Prospero has spent twelve years on the island refining his magic.

Sebastian   Alonso's brother. Like Antonio, Sebastian is both aggressive and cowardly. He is easily persuaded to kill his brother, and he tells a ridiculous story about lions when Gonzalo catches him with his sword drawn.

Trinculo & Stefano   A jester and a drunken butler. Trinculo and Stefano are a comic foil to the other, more powerful pairs of Prospero and Alonso and Antonio and Sebastian. Their drunken boasting and petty greed reflect and deflate the quarrels and power struggles of Prospero and the other noblemen.

THEMES IN *THE TEMPEST*

THE ILLUSION OF JUSTICE *The Tempest* tells a fairly straightforward story about the usurpation of Prospero's throne by his brother, and Prospero's quest to reestablish justice by restoring himself to power. However, the ideal of justice that motivates Prospero is highly subjective. Prospero presents himself as a victim working to right the wrongs that have been done to him, but his ideas of justice and injustice are somewhat hypocritical: he is furious with his brother for taking over his power and domain, but he has no qualms about enslaving Ariel and Caliban on their own territory. Because Prospero is often sinister, and because the play offers no notion of higher order or justice to supersede Prospero's interpretation of events, *The Tempest* is morally ambiguous.

However, if we think of Prospero as an author creating a story, his sense of justice begins to seem, if not perfect, at least sympathetic, for authors have no choice but to impose their own morality on their fictional worlds. Like a writer, Prospero tries to show others the way he views the world. By using magic and tricks that echo the special effects and spectacles of the theater, Prospero gradually persuades the other characters and the audience of the rightness of his case. As he does so, the ambiguities surrounding his methods slowly resolve themselves. Prospero forgives his enemies, releases his slaves, and relinquishes his magic power. At the end of the play, he is only an old man whose work has given the audience pleasure. The establishment of Prospero's idea of justice becomes less a commentary on justice in life than on the nature of morality in art. Happy endings are possible, Shakespeare seems to say, because the creativity of artists can create them, even if the moral values that establish the happy ending originate from nowhere but the imagination of the artist.

THE DIFFICULTY OF DISTINGUISHING NATURE FROM NURTURE Upon seeing Ferdinand for the first time, Miranda says that he is "the third man that e'er I saw" (I.ii.449). The other two are, presumably, Prospero and Caliban. In their first conversation with Caliban, however, Miranda and Prospero say very little that suggests they consider Caliban a human. Miranda reminds Caliban that before she taught him language, he gabbled "like / A thing most brutish" (I.ii.59–60) and Prospero says that he gave Caliban "human care" (I.ii.349), implying that this was something Caliban did not deserve. Caliban's exact nature continues to be ambiguous later. In Act IV, scene i, Prospero refers to Caliban as a "devil, a born devil, on whose nature / Nurture can never stick" (IV.i.188–189). Miranda and Prospero think that their education has lifted Caliban from his brutish status, but they simultaneously think that his inherent brutishness can never be eradicated.

The audience is left to decide whether Caliban is inherently brutish or made brutish by oppression. Caliban claims he was kind to Prospero, but Prospero repaid that kindness by imprisoning him; Prospero claims he stopped being kind to Caliban after Caliban tried to rape Miranda. Our determination of who is telling the truth depends on our interpretation of Caliban's character. Caliban's behavior clarifies nothing. He alternates eloquent speeches with the most degrading kind of drunken, servile behavior.

THE ALLURE OF RULING A COLONY The nearly uninhabited island presents the sense of infinite possibility to almost everyone who lands there. In its isolation, Prospero has found it an ideal place to school his daughter. Sycorax, Caliban's mother, worked her magic there after she was exiled from Algeria. Caliban laments losing control of the island. As he attempts to comfort Alonso, Gonzalo imagines ruling over a utopian society on the island. Stefano imagines killing Prospero and ruling himself, saying to Caliban, "Monster, I will kill this man. His daughter and I will be King and Queen—save our graces!—and Trinculo and thyself shall be my viceroys" (III.ii.101–103). Stefano particularly looks forward to taking advantage of the spirits that make "noises" on the isle; they will provide music for his kingdom for free. All of these characters envision the island as a place where they could rule well.

Shakespeare does not support the ambitions of these would-be colonizers. Gonzalo's utopian vision is undercut by a sharp retort from the usually foolish Sebastian and Antonio. When Gonzalo says there would be no commerce or work or "sovereignty" in his society, Sebastian says sarcastically, "yet [Gonzalo] would be king on't," and Antonio adds, "The latter end of his commonwealth forgets the beginning" (II.i.156–157). Sebastian and Antonio criticize Gonzalo for suggesting that a society could be utterly free when a tyrant rules it. Their criticism is humorous in this context, but it applies in a serious way to Prospero's delusions.

SYMBOLS IN *THE TEMPEST*

THE TEMPEST The tempest that begins the play and puts all of Prospero's enemies at his disposal symbolizes the suffering Prospero endured and the suffering he wants to inflict on others. All of those shipwrecked are put at the mercy of the sea, just as Prospero and his infant daughter were twelve years ago. The tempest also symbolizes Prospero's magic and the frightening, potentially malevolent side of his power.

THE GAME OF CHESS The chess game that Prospero arranges between Miranda and Ferdinand symbolizes the entire story he has created. The object of chess is to capture the king, which is what Prospero does by catching Alonso and reprimanding him for his treachery. Prospero manipulates people, even people he loves, like inanimate chess pieces, arranging things so that Alonso's son and Prospero's daughter marry, thus solidifying Prospero's hold on power (Alonso will have no interest in upsetting a dukedom to which his own son is heir).

Caught up in their game, Miranda and Ferdinand also symbolize something ominous about Prospero's power. For a few moments, they do not even notice the others staring at them, so perfect is the tableau that Prospero has arranged. "Sweet lord, you play me false," Miranda says, and Ferdinand assures her that he "would not for the world" do so (V.i.174–176). Miranda does not realize that her father is playing her as if she is a chess piece, and Ferdinand has nothing to do with it.

IMPORTANT QUOTATIONS FROM *THE TEMPEST*

[I weep] at mine unworthiness, that dare not offer
What I desire to give, and much less take
What I shall die to want. But this is trifling,
And all the more it seeks to hide itself
The bigger bulk it shows. Hence, bashful cunning,
And prompt me, plain and holy innocence.
I am your wife, if you will marry me.
If not, I'll die your maid. To be your fellow
You may deny me, but I'll be your servant
Whether you will or no.

Location: III.i.77–86
Speaker: Miranda
Context: Miranda declares her undying love for Ferdinand

Miranda does not so much propose marriage as insist on it. This is one of two times in the play that Miranda seems to break out of the passivity she has developed under the influence of her father's magic. As in Act I, scene ii, when she scolds Caliban, here Miranda expresses her desires in forthright language. The naïve girl who can hardly hold still long enough to hear her father's long story in Act I, scene ii, and who is charmed asleep and awake as though she were a puppet, seems to turn into a stronger, more mature woman at this moment. Not only does Miranda make her intentions clear, she does so in boldly sexual language, using a metaphor that suggests both an erection and pregnancy (she compares her love to the "bigger bulk" trying to hide itself).

At the same time, the last three lines somewhat undercut the power of this speech. Miranda characterizes herself as a slave to her desires, pledging to follow Ferdinand no matter what the cost to herself, and no matter what Ferdinand wants. This self-effacing language makes Miranda sound like Caliban, who uses similar words as he abases himself before Stefano.

Be not afeard. The isle is full of noises,
Sounds, and sweet airs, that give delight and hurt not.
Sometimes a thousand twangling instruments

Will hum about mine ears, and sometime voices
That, if I then had waked after long sleep
Will make me sleep again; and then in dreaming
The clouds methought would open and show riches
Ready to drop upon me, that when I waked
I cried to dream again.

Location: III.ii.130–138
Speaker: Caliban
Context: Caliban explains the mysterious musicto Stefano and Trinculo

Though Caliban claims that the chief virtue of his newly learned language is that it allows him to curse, here he uses language in the most sensitive and beautiful fashion. This speech is generally considered one of the most poetic in the play, and that Shakespeare puts it in the mouth of the drunken man-monster suggests that Caliban has depths Prospero and Miranda do not see.

It is unclear whether the "noises" Caliban speaks of are the noises of the island itself or noises, like the music of the invisible Ariel, created by Prospero's magic. Caliban himself does not seem to know where these noises come from. His speech conveys the wondrous beauty of the island and the strength of his attachment to it, as well as a certain amount of respect and love for Prospero's magic, and for the possibility that he creates the "[s]ounds and sweet airs that give delight and hurt not."

You taught me language, and my profit on't
Is I know how to curse. The red plague rid you
For learning me your language!

Location: I.ii.366–368
Speaker: Caliban
Context: Miranda has scolded Caliban for his ingratitude; Calib an responds to Prospero and Miranda

---

There be some sports are painful, and their labour
Delight in them sets off. Some kinds of baseness
Are nobly undergone, and most poor matters
Point to rich ends. This my mean task
Would be as heavy to me as odious, but
The mistress which I serve quickens what's dead
And makes my labours pleasures.

Location: III.i.1–7
Speaker: Ferdinand
Context: Ferdinand expresses his willingness to perform the task Prospero has set him to, for Miranda's sake

---

Our revels now are ended. These our actors,
As I foretold you, were all spirits, and
Are melted into air, into thin air;
And, like the baseless fabric of this vision,
The cloud-capped towers, the gorgeous palaces,
The solemn temples, the great globe itself,
Yea, all which it inherit, shall dissolve;
And, like this insubstantial pageant faded,
Leave not a rack behind. We are such stuff

As dreams are made on, and our little life
Is rounded with a sleep.

Location: IV.i.148–18158
Speaker: Prospero
Context: Prospero has remembered the plot against his life

TESS OF THE D'URBERVILLES

Thomas Hardy

The life of an impoverished girl is ruined when a sinister man impregnates her.

THE LIFE OF THOMAS HARDY

Thomas Hardy was born on June 2, 1840, in a rural region of southwestern England. The son of a builder, Hardy was apprenticed at the age of sixteen to John Hicks, an architect who lived in the city of Dorchester, which would later serve as the model for Hardy's fictional Casterbridge. Although Hardy gave serious thought to attending university and then entering the church, a struggle he dramatized in his 1895 novel *Jude the Obscure*, his religious skepticism and lack of money led him to pursue a career in writing instead. Hardy spent nearly a dozen years toiling in obscurity and producing unsuccessful novels and poetry. *Far from the Madding Crowd*, published in 1874, was his first critical and financial success. Hardy married Emma Lavinia Gifford later that year.

Hardy considered poetry his calling and novels his way of earning a living. In many respects, he was caught between the nineteenth and twentieth centuries, between Victorian and modern sensibilities, and between tradition and innovation.

Hardy accepted Charles Darwin's theory of evolution. He also studied the works of the German philosopher Arthur Schopenhauer, who described an "Immanent Will," a blind force that drives the universe. Though his novels often end in crushing tragedies that reflect Schopenhauer's philosophy, Hardy described himself as a *meliorist*, one who believes that the world tends to become better and that people aid in this betterment. Hardy died in 1928 at his estate in Dorchester. His heart was buried in his wife's tomb.

TESS OF THE D'URBERVILLES IN CONTEX

Tess of the d'Urbervilles stirred up controversy by ascribing the problems of Tess, a lower class woman, to the self-righteous rigidity and sexual hypocrisy of English society. The novel also appalled conservative, status-conscious Britons with its scorn for the aristocracy. Hardy portrays Tess's family, with its fantasies about belonging to an ancient and aristocratic line, as a bunch of fools who do not realize that such a family history is not only meaningless but also utterly undesirable.

TESS OF THE D'URBERVILLES: KEY FACTS

Time and place written: 1880s; England

Date of first publication: 1891

Publisher: Random House

Type of work: Novel

Genre: Victorian

Language: English

Setting (time): 1880s and 1890s

Setting (place): Wessex, in the southwest of England

Tense: Past

Tone: Realistic, pessimistic

Narrator: Anonymous, omniscient narrator in the third person

Point of view: Tess's

Protagonist: Tess Durbeyfield

Antagonist: Alec d'Urberville

TESS OF THE D'URBERVILLES: PLOT OVERVIEW

A poor peddler, John Durbeyfield, is stunned to learn that he is the descendent of an ancient noble family, the d'Urbervilles. Tess, his eldest daughter, joins the other village girls in the May Day dance, where she exchanges glances with a young man. Mr. Durbeyfield and his wife decide to send Tess to the d'Urberville mansion, where they hope Mrs. d'Urberville will give Tess a fortune. In reality, Mrs. d'Urberville is not related to Tess at all: her husband, the merchant Simon Stokes, changed his name to d'Urberville after he retired. The lascivious Alec d'Urberville, Mrs. d'Urberville's son, gets Tess a job tending fowls on the d'Urberville estate.

Tess spends several months at this job, resisting Alec's repeated attempts to seduce her. Finally, Alec and Tess have sex in the woods one night after a fair. It is unclear whether Alec has raped Tess. Tess, who does not love Alec, becomes pregnant. She returns home to her family to give birth to Alec's child, a boy Tess christens Sorrow. Sorrow soon dies, and Tess spends a miserable year at home before deciding to seek work elsewhere. She finally accepts a job as a milkmaid at the Talbothays Dairy.

Tess is happy at Talbothays. She befriends three of the milkmaids—Izz, Retty, and Marian—and meets a man named Angel Clare, who turns out to be the man from the May Day dance at the beginning of the novel. Tess and Angel slowly fall in love, and Tess accepts Angel's proposal of marriage. Tess, troubled by her conscience, feels she should tell Angel about her past. She writes him a confessional note and slips it under his door, but it slides under the carpet and Angel never sees it.

After their wedding, Angel and Tess confess to indiscretions: Angel tells Tess about an affair he had with an older woman in London, and Tess tells Angel about her history with Alec. Tess forgives Angel, but Angel cannot forgive Tess. He gives her some money and boards a ship bound for Brazil, where he thinks he might establish a farm. He tells Tess he will try to accept her past but warns her not to try to join him until he comes for her.

Tess struggles. She has a difficult time finding work and is forced to take a job at an unpleasant farm. She tries to visit Angel's family but leaves after overhearing Angel's brothers talk about his unfortunate marriage. She stops to hear a wandering preacher speak and is stunned to discover that he is Alec d'Urberville, who has been converted to Christianity by Angel's father, the Reverend Clare. Both Alec and Tess are shaken by their encounter. Alec begs Tess never to tempt him again. Soon after, however, he turns his back on his religious ways and begs Tess to marry him.

Tess learns from her sister, Liza-Lu, that her mother is near death. Tess returns home to take care of her. Her mother recovers, but her father unexpectedly dies. The Durbeyfields are evicted from their home. Alec offers help, but Tess refuses his offer, knowing that he only wants her to be under an obligation to him.

At last, Angel decides to forgive his wife. He leaves Brazil, desperate to find her. Tess's mother tells him that Tess has gone to a village called Sandbourne. There, Angel finds Tess in an expensive boarding-house called The Herons, where he tells her he has forgiven her and begs her to take him back. Tess tells him he has come too late: she was unable to resist and went back to Alec d'Urberville. Angel leaves in a daze. Tess, heartbroken to the point of madness, goes upstairs and stabs Alec to death. When the landlady finds Alec's body, she raises an alarm, but Tess has already fled to find Angel.

Angel agrees to help Tess. He does not quite process the fact that she murdered Alec. They hide out in an empty mansion for a few days, then move on. They come to Stonehenge. Tess falls asleep, and in the morning a search party discovers them. Tess is arrested and sent to jail. Angel and Liza-Lu watch as a black flag is raised over the prison, signaling Tess's execution.

CHARACTERS IN TESS OF THE D'URBERVILLES

Mercy Chant Cuthbert Clare's fiancée.

Angel Clare Tess's true love. Angel is an intelligent young man who has decided to become a farmer in order to escape the pressures of city life. Angel's father and two brothers are respected clergymen, but Angel's religious doubts have kept him from joining the ministry.

Mrs. Clare Angel's mother. Mrs. Clare is a loving, snobbish woman who wants Angel to marry well. Initially she looks down on Tess as a "simple" and impoverished girl, but later grows to appreciate her.

Reverend Clare Angel's father. Reverend Clare is a principled but somewhat intractable clergyman in the town of Emminster. He considers it his duty to convert the populace.

Reverend Cuthbert Clare Angel's brother. Cuthbert is a classical scholar and dean at Cambridge.

Reverend Felix Clare Angel's brother. Felix is a village curate.

Eliza Louisa Durbeyfield Tess's younger sister. Tess believes Liza-Lu has all of Tess's good qualities and none of her bad ones. She encourages Angel to look after and even marry Liza-Lu after Tess dies.

Mr. John Durbeyfield Tess's father. Mr. Durbeyfield is a lazy peddler who hates work despite his natural quickness.

Mrs. Joan Durbeyfield Tess's mother. Mrs. Durbeyfield has a strong sense of propriety and very particular hopes for Tess's life. She is continually disappointed and hurt by Tess's experiences, but her simple-mindedness and charity make her unable to remain angry with Tess—particularly once Tess becomes her primary means of support.

Tess Durbeyfield The novel's protagonist. Tess is a beautiful, loyal, and impoverished young woman whose inexperience and imperfect upbringing leave her extremely vulnerable.

Alec d'Urberville The handsome, amoral son of a wealthy merchant. Alec is a manipulative, sinister young man who seduces the inexperienced Tess. He does try to help Tess after impregnating her.

Mrs. d'Urberville Alec's mother, and the widow of Simon Stokes. Mrs. d'Urberville is blind and often ill. She cares more for animals than she does for her maid, her son, or Tess.

Marian, Izz Huett, and Retty Priddle Milkmaids at the Talbothays Dairy. Marian, Izz, and Retty, Tess's friends, are all in love with Angel and are devastated when he chooses Tess over them: Marian turns to drink, Retty attempts suicide, and Izz nearly runs off to Brazil with Angel when he leaves Tess. Nevertheless, they remain helpful to Tess. Marian helps her find a job, and Marian and Izz write Angel a plaintive letter encouraging him to give Tess another chance.

Sorrow Tess's son with Alec d'Urberville. Sorrow dies in early infancy. Tess christens him and buries him herself.

THEMES IN *TESS OF THE D'URBERVILLES*

THE INJUSTICE OF EXISTENCE Hardy suggests that for the Durbeyfields, as for all people except the very wealthy, life is unfair from beginning to end. Tess is punished for her poverty, punished when Alec takes advantage of her, punished for her honesty to Angel, and punished for her anger at the man who ruined her life. Nor does Hardy suggest, as Christianity does, that heaven will dole out justice to those who suffered in life. The only truly devout Christian in the novel is Angel's father, Reverend Clare, who has no need of heavenly justice because he has a happy life. Mrs. Durbeyfield never mentions otherworldly rewards. During his religious period, Alec preaches heavenly justice for earthly sinners, but his shallow, insincere faith does more to cast doubt on this promise than to strengthen it. Generally, the moral atmosphere of the novel is not Christian at all, but pagan. The forces that rule human life in *Tess of the d'Urbervilles* are absolutely unpredictable and not concerned with our well-being. Hardy emphasizes the pagan nature of the world by bookending his novel with pre-Christian rituals practiced by farm workers and with Tess's final rest at Stonehenge. Hardy concludes the novel by making sarcastic reference to earthly justice: "'Justice' was done, and the President of the Immortals (in the Aeschylean phrase) had ended his sport with Tess." We believe in justice to keep sane, but Hardy reminds us that what passes for justice is actually one of the pagan gods enjoying a bit of "sport," or a frivolous game.

CHANGING IDEAS OF SOCIAL CLASS IN VICTORIAN ENGLAND The social esteem in which the Durbeyfields are held suggests that Victorians do not judge class as people did in the Middle Ages—that is, by blood alone, with no attention paid to fortune or worldly success. The Durbeyfields do come from the pure d'Urberville line, but no one cares. Their lineage amounts to nothing more than a piece of genealogical trivia. For their fellow Victorians, cash matters more than lineage. Hardy emphasizes the new aristocracy of money by giving us Simon Stokes, who buys the d'Urberville name and prestige with his large fortune. The d'Urbervilles pass for what the Durbeyfields truly are—authentic nobility—because definitions of class have changed.

MEN DOMINATING WOMEN Some men in the novel dominate women in full knowledge of what they are doing—Alec, for example, who acknowledges how bad he was to seduce Tess for his own momentary pleasure. Alec's act of abuse, which ultimately ruins Tess's life, is the most serious instance of male domination in the novel. But there are other, less obvious examples. Angel seems to dominate Retty and Marian unintentionally. His stated preference for Tess causes Retty to attempt suicide and Marian to become an alcoholic. These girls are utterly dominated by a man who, the narrator tells us explicitly, does not even realize that they are interested in him. This sort of unconscious male domination of women is almost more unsettling than Alec's outward and self-conscious cruelty, because it seems less preventable. Even Angel's love for Tess, as pure and gentle as it seems, dominates her in a dangerous way. Angel substitutes an idealized picture of Tess as a pure country girl for the real-life woman that he continually refuses to get to know. When Angel calls Tess names like "Daughter of Nature" and "Artemis," he denies her true self in favor of a mental image that he prefers. When she forces him to see her true identity and experiences, he is shocked by the disconnect between his fanciful version of her and the truth. The pattern of male domination is finally reversed with Tess's murder of Alec, which marks the first time in the novel that a woman takes active steps against a man. Hardy suggests that while Tess's aggression is heroic, women who buck the system are doomed: Tess's act only engenders even greater suppression of a woman by men, as symbolized by the crowd of male police officers that arrests Tess at Stonehenge.

SYMBOLS IN *TESS OF THE D'URBERVILLES*

PRINCE When Tess dozes off in the wagon and loses control, the Durbeyfield's horse, Prince, dies. Prince's name and fate symbolize Tess's own claims to aristocracy. Like the horse, Tess has a high-class name but is doomed to a lowly life of physical labor. Tess has been dreaming of meeting a prince just before her own Prince dies, and with him her family's only means of financial sustenance. This sequence of events foreshadows her own story in which she dies, and with her the Durbeyfields' only means of support.

THE D'URBERVILLE FAMILY VAULT The vault symbolizes both the glory of life and the end of life, both the grandeur and the hollowness of an aristocratic family name. Since Tess herself moves from passivity to active murder by the end of the novel, attaining personal grandeur even as she brings death to others and to herself, the double symbolism of the vault makes it a powerful site for the culminating meeting between Alec and Tess. Alec brings Tess both his lofty name and, indirectly, her own death. The vault that sounds so glamorous when John Durbeyfield rhapsodizes over it eventually seems strangely hollow and meaningless. When Alec stomps on the floor of the vault, it produces only a hollow echo. When Tess is executed, the narrator says that her ancestors are snoozing in their crypts, as if bored by the fate of a member of their own majestic family.

IMPORTANT QUOTATIONS FROM *TESS OF THE D'URBERVILLES*

Clare came close, and bent over her. "Dead, dead, dead!" he murmured. After fixedly regarding her for some moments with the same gaze of unmeasurable woe he bent lower, enclosed her in his arms, and rolled her in the sheet as in a shroud. Then lifting her from the bed with as much respect as one would show to a dead body, he carried her across the room, murmuring, "My poor poor Tess, my dearest darling Tess! So sweet, so good, so true!" The words of endearment, withheld so severely in his waking hours, were inexpressibly sweet to her forlorn and hungry heart. If it had been to save her weary life she would not, by moving or struggling, have put an end to the position she found herself in. Thus she lay in absolute stillness, scarcely venturing to breathe, and, wondering what he was going to do with her, suffered herself to be borne out upon the landing. "My wife—dead, dead!" he said.

Location: Chapter XXXVII
Speaker: The narrator
Context: In his sleep, Angel thinks Tess is dead

Angel Clare begins to sleepwalk on the third night of his estrangement from Tess, having rejected her as his wife because she slept with Alec and had his child. Like Lady Macbeth's sleepwalking, Angel's sleepwalking reveals an inner conflict in a character who, awake, seems in control, inflexible, and utterly convinced of the justness of one course. Awake, Angel insists that Tess is bad, corrupt, and unforgivable. Asleep, he reveals the tender love and moral respect for her ("so good, so true!") that exist buried inside him. This revelation foreshadows his final, tardy realization that he can forgive Tess. Angel's words "dead, dead, dead" foreshadow Tess's death.

"Justice" was done, and the President of the Immortals (in Aeschylean phrase) had ended his sport with Tess. And the d'Urberville knights and dames slept on in their tombs unknowing. The two speechless gazers bent themselves down to the earth, as if in prayer, and remained there a long time, absolutely motionless: the flag continued to wave silently. As soon as they had strength they arose, joined hands again, and went on.

Location: Chapter LIX
Speaker: The narrator
Context: Tess has been executed

The tired, unimpassioned tone of this passage suggests the narrator's weariness with the world, and his conviction that life always unfolds this way. The novel refuses to end on a note of transcendence. Liza-Lu and Angel just go on, as life will go on in its usual unfair way. No understanding is achieved. Instead, ignorance rules: the d'Urberville ancestors who cause the tragedy are not moved from their slumber, blithely unaffected by the agony and death of one of their own line. The passage reminds us that while we may have been moved by Tess's story, it is just one more humdrum affair, another tale typical of the world we live in.

"Don't you really know, Durbeyfield, that you are the lineal representative of the ancient and knightly family of the d'Urbervilles, who derive their descent from Sir Pagan d'Urberville, that renowned knight who came from Normandy with William the Conqueror, as appears by Battle Abbey Roll?"
    "Never heard it before, sir!"

Location: Chapter I
Speaker: The narrator
Context: The local parson tells Mr. Durbeyfield about his grand lineage

---

Under the trees several pheasants lay about, their rich plumage dabbled with blood; some were dead, some feebly twitching a wing, some staring up at the sky, some pulsating quickly, some contorted, some stretched out—all of them writhing in agony except the fortunate ones whose tortures had ended during the night by the inability of nature to bear more. With the impulse of a soul who could feel for kindred sufferers as much as for herself, Tess's first thought was to put the still living birds out of their torture, and to this end with her own hands she broke the necks of as many as she could find, leaving them to lie where she had found them till the gamekeepers should come, as they probably would come, to look for them a second time. "Poor darlings—to suppose myself the most miserable being on earth in the sight o' such misery as yours!" she exclaimed, her tears running down as she killed the birds tenderly.

Location: Chapter XLI
Speaker: The narrator
Context: Tess stumbles upon dying birds

As soon as she drew close to it she discovered all in a moment that the figure was a living person; and the shock to her sense of not having been alone was so violent that she was quite overcome, and sank down nigh to fainting, not however till she had recognized Alec d'Urberville in the form. He leapt off the slab and supported her. "I saw you come in," he said smiling, "and got up there not to interrupt your meditations. A family gathering, is it not, with these old fellows under us here? Listen." He stamped with his heel heavily on the floor; whereupon there arose a hollow echo from below. "That shook them a bit, I'll warrant," he continued. "And you thought I was the mere stone reproduction of one of them. But no. The old order changeth. The little finger of the sham d'Urberville can do more for you than the whole dynasty of the real underneath.. . . Now command me. What shall I do?"

Location: Chapter LII
Speaker: The narrator
Context: Tess comes upon Alec in her family's tomb

THEIR EYES WERE WATCHING GOD

Zora Neale Hurston

After two marriages to oppressive men, a woman finds temporary happiness with a husband twelve years her junior.

THE LIFE OF ZORA NEALE HURSTON

Zora Neale Hurston was born on January 7, 1891, in Notasulga, Alabama, to John Hurston, a carpenter and Baptist preacher, and Lucy Potts Hurston, a former schoolteacher. Hurston was the fifth of eight children. When she was a toddler, her family moved to Eatonville, Florida, the first all-black town in the United States, where John Hurston served several terms as mayor. In 1917, Hurston enrolled in Morgan Academy in Baltimore.

Hurston earned an associate degree from Howard University. In 1925, she moved to New York and became a significant figure in the Harlem Renaissance. A year later, Hurston, Langston Hughes, and Wallace Thurman organized the journal *Fire!*, considered one of the defining publications of the era.

She also enrolled in Barnard College and studied anthropology with Franz Boas, arguably the greatest anthropologist of the twentieth century. Hurston's life in Eatonville and her extensive anthropological research on rural black folklore greatly influenced her writing.

In 1937, Hurston published *Their Eyes Were Watching God*. She wrote prolifically, both fiction and anthropology, and won a Guggenheim Fellowship. Still, Hurston fell into obscurity. By the late 1940s, she was having increasing difficulty getting her work published. By the early 1950s, she was forced to work as a maid. In the 1960s, when the counterculture revolution disdained any literature that was not overtly political, Hurston's writing continued to be ignored.

A stroke in the late 1950s forced Hurston to enter a welfare home in Florida. She died penniless on January 28, 1960, and was buried in an unmarked grave. Alice Walker, another prominent African-American writer, rediscovered her work in the late 1960s. In 1973, Walker traveled to Florida to place a marker on Hurston's grave that read "A Genius of the South." Walker's 1975 essay "In Search of Zora Neale Hurston," published in *Ms.* magazine, propelled Hurston's work back into the limelight. Since then, Hurston's opus has been published and republished many times.

THEIR EYES WERE WATCHING GOD IN CONTEXT

Their Eyes Were Watching God is often associated with the Harlem Renaissance, but it was published in 1937, long after the heyday of the Renaissance. With the 1930s came the Depression and the end of the cultural openness that had allowed the Harlem Renaissance to flourish. As the Depression worsened, political tension ratcheted up in the United States. Social realism, a gritty, political style, dominated culture. Proponents of social realism felt that art should be political and concerned with exposing social injustice. They dismissed much of the Harlem Renaissance as bourgeois, devoid of artistic merit because it was devoid of important political content. The influential and highly political black novelist Richard Wright, then an ardent communist, wrote a scathing review of *Their Eyes Were Watching God* upon its publication, claiming that it was not "serious fiction" and that it "carrie[d] no theme, no message, no thought."

Hurston's work fits into a number of different American literary traditions. Although published after the Harlem Renaissance, it speaks to that movement's concerns. It is also in the tradition of American Southern literature. *Their Eyes Were Watching God*, with its rural Southern setting and its focus on the relationship between man and nature, the dynamics of human relationships, and a hero's quest for independence, is a descendent of such works as Mark Twain's *The Adventures of Huckleberry Finn* and William Faulkner's *The Sound and the Fury*. The novel carries on the tradition of novels such as Kate

Chopin's *The Awakening*. Zora Neale Hurston is often viewed as the first in a succession of great American black women writers that includes Alice Walker, Toni Morrison, and Gloria Naylor.

THEIR EYES WERE WATCHING GOD: KEY FACTS

Time and place written: 1937; Haiti	
Date of first publication: 1937	
Publisher: J.B. Lippincott, Inc.	
Type of work: Novel	
Genre: Bildungsroman; southern novel	
Language: English	
Setting (time): Probably the 1920s or 1930s	
Setting (place): Rural Florida	
Tense: Past	
Tone: Sympathetic, affirming	
Narrator: Anonymous, omniscient narrator in the third person	
Point of view: Janie's	
Protagonist: Janie	
Antagonist: Conventional values	

THEIR EYES WERE WATCHING GOD: PLOT OVERVIEW

Janie Crawford, an attractive, confident, middle-aged black woman, returns to Eatonville, Florida, after a long absence. The black townspeople gossip about her and speculate about where she has been and what has happened to her young husband, Tea Cake. They interpret her confidence as aloofness. Janie's friend Pheoby Watson visits Janie. Their conversation frames the story that Janie tells.

Janie explains that her grandmother raised her after her mother ran off. Nanny loves Janie, but her life as a slave and her experience with her own daughter has warped her worldview. She wants to marry Janie off, as soon as possible, to a man who can give her security and social status. She insists that Janie marry Logan Killicks, a farmer much older than her.

Janie is miserable with Logan, who pampers her for a year and then starts treating her like a pack mule. One day, Joe Starks, a smooth-talking, ambitious man, ambles by the farm. He and Janie flirt in secret for a couple weeks before she runs off and marries him. Janie and Jody, as she calls him, travel to all-black Eatonville, where Jody hopes to have a "big voice." A consummate politician, Jody soon becomes the mayor and postmaster of Eatonville. He also owns a store and becomes the biggest landlord in town. Janie grows disenchanted with the monotonous, stifling life that she shares with Jody. She wishes she could take part in the rich social life in town, but Jody doesn't allow her to interact with "common" people. Jody sees Janie as a fitting ornament to his wealth and power, and he tries to shape her into his vision of what a mayor's wife should be. On the surface, Janie silently submits to Jody, but secretly she remains passionate and full of dreams.

After almost twenty years of marriage, Janie finally asserts herself. When Jody insults her appearance, Janie attacks him in front of the townspeople, telling them all how ugly and impotent he is. In retaliation, he beats her savagely. Their marriage breaks down, and Jody falls ill. Months pass, and Janie finally visits Jody on his deathbed. As she berates him for the way he treated her, he dies.

Janie feels free for the first time in years. She rebuffs various suitors because she loves her newfound independence. Then she meets and begins dating Tea Cake, a man twelve years her junior. To the shock of the townspeople, Janie marries Tea Cake nine months after Jody's death, sells Jody's store, and leaves town to go to Jacksonville with Tea Cake.

Tea Cake and Janie have a difficult first week together. Tea Cake steals Janie's money and leaves her alone one night. Janie worries that Tea Cake only married her for her money. But he returns, explaining that he never meant to leave her and that his theft occurred in a moment of weakness. They promise to share all their experiences and opinions with each other. They move to the Everglades, where they work during the harvest season and socialize during the summer off-season. Tea Cake's quick wit and friendliness make their shack the center of social life.

A terrible hurricane hits the Everglades two years into Janie and Tea Cake's marriage. As they desperately flee the rising waters, a rabid dog bites Tea Cake. Three weeks later, Tea Cake falls ill. During a rabies-induced bout of madness, Tea Cake becomes convinced that Janie is cheating on him. He fires a pistol at her, and Janie is forced to kill him to save her life. She is tried for murder, but the all-white, all-male jury finds her not guilty. She returns to Eatonville, where her former neighbors are ready to spread malicious gossip about her. They assume Tea Cake left her and took her money. Pheoby is greatly impressed by Janie's experiences. Back in her room that night, Janie feels at one with Tea Cake and at peace with herself.

CHARACTERS IN *THEIR EYES WERE WATCHING GOD*

Janie Mae Crawford The protagonist of the novel. Janie defies gender conventions, insisting on independence. She is curious, confident, and generous.

Tea Cake Janie's third husband and first real love. Tea Cake has a quick wit and a zest for living. He also respects and understands Janie. He does steal from her once and beat her, but on the whole he is a good man.

Leafy Crawford Janie's mother. Leafy ran away after giving birth to Janie.

Nanny Crawford Janie's grandmother. Nanny was once a slave. She believes in the importance of financial security, respectability, and upward mobility. Although Janie's independence and restlessness clash with Nanny's values, eventually Janie respects these values and believes they were well intended.

Amos Hicks A resident of Eatonville, Florida, tries unsuccessfully to lure Janie away from Jody.

Logan Killicks Janie's first husband. Nanny arranges Janie's marriage to Logan because he seems respectable and financially secure. Feeling used and unloved, Janie leaves Logan for Jody Starks.

Hezekiah Potts The delivery boy and assistant shopkeeper at Jody's store.

Jody Starks Janie's second husband. Jody is a consummate politician and businessman. He treats Janie as an object rather than a person, and their marriage deteriorates.

Motor Boat One of Tea Cake and Janie's friends in the Everglades.

Nunkie A girl in the Everglades who flirts relentlessly with Tea Cake. After Tea Cake reassures Janie that Nunkie means nothing to him, Nunkie disappears from the novel.

Dr. Simmons A friendly white doctor.

Annie Tyler A wealthy widow who lived in Eatonville. Annie's much younger fiancé, Who Flung, took her money and fled at the first opportunity.

Johnny Taylor A young man whom Janie kisses at age sixteen. Because of the kiss, Nanny forces Janie to marry the more socially respectable Logan Killicks.

Mr. and Mrs. Turner Everglades residents who run a small restaurant. Mrs. Turner prides herself on her Caucasian features and disdains anyone with a more African appearance. She worships Janie because of her Caucasian features.

Mr. and Mrs. Washburn Nanny's employers after she became a free woman. The Washburns helped raise Janie with their own children.

Pheoby Watson Janie's best friend in Eatonville. Pheoby is the audience for Janie's story. Her presence is occasionally felt in the colloquial speech that the narrator mixes in with a more sophisticated narrative style.

Sam Watson Pheoby's husband. In response to Eatonville residents resentful of Jody, Sam acknowledges that Jody can be overbearing and commanding but points out that he has made many improvements to the town.

THEMES IN *THEIR EYES WERE WATCHING GOD*

THE ILLUSION OF POWER Both Jody and Tea Cake believe in their own infallible power, and both are eventually disillusioned. Jody attempts to achieve fulfillment through the exertion of power. He tries to purchase and control everyone and everything around him, as if he can subordinate the world. Tea Cake believes his skill makes him impervious to natural forces. He thinks he will easily survive the hurricane. Both men come to understand the limits of their power. Jody realizes that he is not all-powerful when disease sets in. The loss of authority over Janie furthers his disillusionment. Tea Cake realizes he is not infallible when the hurricane forces him to flee and the floods force him to struggle for his life.

THE NON-NECESSITY OF RELATIONSHIPS Hurston does not portray men as no-good, oppressing misogynists. She depicts successful relationships involving the acceptance of gender differences. In such successful relationships, the woman balances out the man with qualities he does not possess, and vice versa. Janie's marriage to Tea Cake succeeds because the partners in it respect each other and view their relationship as reciprocal. At the same time, Hurston suggests that relationships are not necessary for happiness or fulfillment. At the end of the novel, Janie is alone but seems content. She has liberated herself from her unpleasant and unfulfilling marriages to Logan and Jody. She has enjoyed a mostly happy marriage to Tea Cake. She has turned into a person she respects and likes. Her happiness is complete without a man.

THE FOLKLORIC QUALITY OF RELIGION As the title indicates, God is a presence in the novel. However, the God Hurston depicts is not a Judeo-Christian one. She depicts a God that is not a single entity but a diffuse force. His or her presence can be felt in nature, in the sun, moon, sky, sea, and horizon. Janie's quest is a spiritual one not because she seeks the Judeo-Christian God, but because she wants to find her place in the world—which is, in Hurston's novel, suffused with God. Except for one brief reference to church in Chapter 12, organized religion never appears in the novel. Rather, the characters enjoy a spirituality rooted in folklore and mythology. As an anthropologist, Hurston studied the rural mythology and folklore of black people in America and the Caribbean. Many visions of mysticism that appear in her novel—her haunting personification of Death, the idea of a sun-god, the horizon as a boundary at the end of the world—are likely culled directly from these sources.

SYMBOLS IN *THEIR EYES WERE WATCHING GOD*

HAIR Janie's hair has a number of symbolic meanings. First, it symbolizes her rebelliousness. The townspeople consider it undignified for a woman of Janie's age to wear her hair down, but Janie refuses to change her hair. It also symbolizes phallic power. Hurston repeatedly describes Janie's braid in phallic terms, suggesting Janie's masculine power and potency and blurring gender lines. Finally, it symbolizes whiteness. Mrs. Turner worships Janie because of her straight hair and her other Caucasian characteristics.

THE PEAR TREE The pear tree represents Janie's idealized view of nature. Janie considers the bees' interaction with pear tree flowers a perfect moment full of erotic energy, passionate connection, and blissful harmony. She chases after this ideal throughout the rest of the novel.

IMPORTANT QUOTATIONS FROM *THEIR EYES WERE WATCHING GOD*

[Janie] was stretched on her back beneath the pear tree soaking in the alto chant of the visiting bees, the gold of the sun and the panting breath of the breeze when the inaudible voice of it all came to her. She saw a dust-bearing bee sink into the sanctum of a bloom; the thousand sister-calyxes arch to meet the love embrace and the ecstatic shiver of the tree from root to tiniest branch creaming in every blossom and

frothing with delight. So this was a marriage! She had been summoned to behold a revelation. Then Janie felt a pain remorseless sweet that left her limp and languid.

Location: Chapter 2
Speaker: Janie watches a bee pollinate a flower
Context: Janie has a spiritual and sexual awakening

This passage uses the meeting of bee and flower as an explicit metaphor for sex. Hurston emphasizes the power of Janie's epiphany by using language that suggests Janie herself is having sex. Janie "stretch[es] on her back," and after watching the consummation, goes "limp and languid." The incident enlightens Janie to the delights of sex, but it also gives her an abstract idea of love as mutual, reciprocal fulfillment. The bee goes to the flower, the flower arches to meet the bee, and both enjoy an ecstatic encounter. Janie takes this meeting between bee and flower as her ideal and searches for a reciprocal relationship.

"Listen, Sam, if it was nature, nobody wouldn't have tuh look out for babies touchin' stoves, would they? 'Cause dey just naturally wouldn't touch it. But dey sho will. So it's caution."

"Naw it ain't, it's nature, cause nature makes caution. It's de strongest thing dat God ever made, now. Fact is it's de onliest thing God ever made. He made nature and nature made everything else."

Location: Chapter 6
Speaker: Lige Moss and Sam Watson
Context: The men debate nature versus nurture

As Lige Moss and Sam Watson sit on the porch of Jody's store, they debate man's relationship to nature. Lige believes that people must be taught everything they know, that no innate instinct protects them from the dangers of the world. Sam believes that people are born with some innate instincts, caution among them.

Ships at a distance have every man's wish on board. For some they come in with the tide. For others they sail forever on the horizon, never out of sight, never landing until the Watcher turns his eyes away in resignation, his dreams mocked to death by Time. That is the life of men.

Now, women forget all those things they don't want to remember, and remember everything they don't want to forget. The dream is the truth. Then they act and do things accordingly.

Location: The opening passage of the novel
Speaker: The narrator
Context: The narrator theorizes about a basic difference between men and women

---

It was inevitable that she should accept any inconsistency and cruelty from her deity as all good worshippers do from theirs. All gods who receive homage are cruel. All gods dispense suffering without reason. Otherwise they would not be worshipped. Through indiscriminate suffering men know fear and fear is the most divine emotion. It is the stones for altars and the beginning of wisdom. Half gods are worshipped in wine and flowers. Real gods require blood.

Location: Chapter 16
Speaker: The narrator
Context: The narrator describes Mrs. Turner's religion

The wind came back with triple fury, and put out the light for the last time. They sat in company with the others in other shanties, their eyes straining against crude walls and their souls asking if He meant to measure their puny might against His. They seemed to be staring at the dark, but their eyes were watching God.

Location: Chapter 18
Speaker: The narrator
Context: Janie, Tea Cake, and Motor Boat seek refuge from the storm

THINGS FALL APART

Chinua Achebe

A Nigerian clan leader, terrified of being weak like his father was, brings destruction and tragedy on himself and his family.

THE LIFE OF CHINUA ACHEBE

Albert Chinualumogu Achebe was born on November 16, 1930, in Ogidi, a large village in Nigeria. His upbringing was multicultural. He was the child of a Protestant missionary and received his early education in English, but he absorbed the traditional Igbo culture of Ogidi. Achebe attended the Government College in Umuahia from 1944 to 1947. He graduated from University College, Ibadan, in 1953. In college, Achebe studied history and theology. He also developed an interest in indigenous Nigerian cultures. He rejected his Christian name, Albert, in favor of his indigenous one, Chinua.

In the 1950s, Achebe and others began a Nigerian literary movement that drew upon the traditional oral culture of indigenous people. In 1959, he published *Things Fall Apart* as a response to novels like Joseph Conrad's *Heart of Darkness*, which treats Africa as a primordial and cultureless foil for Europe. Tired of reading white men's accounts of how primitive, socially backward, and language-less native Africans were, Achebe sought to give voice to an underrepresented and exploited group by depicting one African culture.

Achebe is now internationally renowned as a father of modern African literature. He is also an essayist and a professor of English literature at Bard College in New York. Achebe is prominent in Nigeria's academic culture and in its literary and political institutions. He worked for the Nigerian Broadcasting Company for over a decade and later became an English professor at the University of Nigeria. He has also been influential in the publication of new Nigerian writers. In 1967, he cofounded a publishing company with Nigerian poet Christopher Okigbo, and in 1971, he began editing *Okike*, a journal of Nigerian writing. In 1984, he founded *Uwa ndi Igbo*, a bilingual magazine. He has been active in Nigerian politics since the 1960s, and many of his novels address the postcolonial social and political problems that Nigeria still faces.

THINGS FALL APART IN CONTEXT

Things Fall Apart, set in the 1890s, portrays the clash between Nigeria's white colonial government and the traditional culture of the indigenous Igbo people. Achebe portrays the complex, advanced social institutions and artistic traditions of Igbo culture prior to its contact with Europeans. He also portrays Europeans as a multifaceted group whose members range from benevolent to zealous to ruthless.

Achebe's decision to write *Things Fall Apart* in English was a political one. He wanted his novel to respond to earlier colonial accounts of Africa in a way that English-speaking readers could understand. Unlike some later African authors who chose to revitalize native languages as a form of resistance to colonial culture, Achebe wanted to achieve cultural revitalization within and through English.

THINGS FALL APART: KEY FACTS

Time and place written: 1959; Nigeria	
Date of first publication: 1959	
Publisher: Heinemann Educational Books	
Type of work: Novel	
Genre: Postcolonial literature	
Language: English	
Setting (time): 1890s	

Setting (place): Lower Nigerian villages	
Tense: Past	
Tone: Ironic, tragic, satirical, fablelike	
Narrator: Anonymous, omniscient narrator in the third person	
Point of view: Varies	
Protagonist: Okonkwo	
Antagonist: The new customs of the whites, the memory of Okonkwo's father	

THINGS FALL APART: PLOT OVERVIEW

Okonkwo is a wealthy and respected warrior of the Umuofia clan, a lower Nigerian tribe that is one of nine connected villages. Okonkwo is haunted by the memory of Unoka, his cowardly and spendthrift father. Unoka died in disrepute, leaving many village debts unsettled. Okonkwo became a clansman, warrior, farmer, and family provider. He has a twelve-year-old son named Nwoye whom he considers lazy. Okonkwo worries that Nwoye will turn into a failure like Unoka.

In a settlement with a neighboring tribe, Okonkwo wins a virgin and a fifteen-year-old boy for the tribe. Okonkwo is entrusted with the boy, Ikemefuna. Nwoye forms a strong attachment to Ikemefuna, and Okonkwo considers Ikemefuna an ideal son. Ikemefuna begins to call Okonkwo "father," but despite this and despite his affection for the boy, Okonkwo does not let himself show any emotion. During the Week of Peace, Okonkwo accuses his youngest wife, Ojiugo, of negligence. He severely beats her, breaking the peace of the sacred week. He makes some sacrifices to show his repentance, but his community remains shocked.

Ikemefuna stays with Okonkwo's family for three years. Nwoye looks up to him as an older brother and, much to Okonkwo's pleasure, becomes more masculine. One day, locusts come to Umuofia. The village excitedly collects the locusts, which are good to eat when cooked. Ogbuefi Ezeudu, a respected village elder, privately informs Okonkwo that the Oracle has said that Ikemefuna must be killed. He tells Okonkwo that because Ikemefuna calls him "father," Okonkwo should not take part in the boy's death. Okonkwo lies to Ikemefuna, telling him that they must return him to his home village.

The men of Umuofia, including Okonkwo, walk with Ikemefuna. Okonkwo's clansmen attack the boy with machetes. Ikemefuna runs to Okonkwo for help, but Okonkwo, not wanting to look weak in front of his fellow tribesmen, cuts the boy down. In the days after the killing, Okonkwo sinks into a depression, unable to sleep or eat. He visits his friend Obierika and begins to feel a little better. Okonkwo's daughter Ezinma falls ill and recovers.

Ogbuefi Ezeudu dies. Okonkwo feels guilty about disregarding Ezeudu's warning against taking part in Ikemefuna's death. At Ogbuefi Ezeudu's large and elaborate funeral, the men beat drums and fire their guns. Okonkwo accidentally shoots Ogbuefi Ezeudu's sixteen-year-old son. Because killing a clansman is a crime against the earth goddess, Okonkwo and his family must go into exile for seven years and atone. They go to Okonkwo's mother's village, Mbanta.

Okonkwo's kinsmen, especially his uncle, Uchendu, receive him warmly. Although he is bitter about his misfortune, Okonkwo reconciles himself to his new life. During the second year of Okonkwo's exile, Obierika brings several bags of cowries (shells used as currency) that he has made by selling Okonkwo's yams. Obierika also brings the bad news that Abame, a village, has been destroyed by the white men.

Six missionaries travel to Mbanta. Through an interpreter, the missionaries' leader, Mr. Brown, tells the villagers that their gods are false and that worshipping more than one God is idolatrous. Mr. Brown does not allow his followers to antagonize the clan. Mr. Brown falls ill, and Reverend James Smith, an intolerant and strict man, replaces him. A zealous convert, Enoch, dares to unmask an *egwugwu* during a ceremony, an act equivalent to killing an ancestral spirit. The next day, the *egwugwu* burn Enoch's compound and Reverend Smith's church to the ground.

The District Commissioner requests a meeting with the leaders of Umuofia. They comply, but the meeting is a setup. The leaders are handcuffed and thrown in jail, where they suffer insults and physical abuse. After the prisoners are released, the clansmen hold a meeting during which five court messengers approach and order the clansmen to desist. Expecting his fellow clan members to join him, Okonkwo kills their leader with his machete. When the crowd allows the other messengers to escape, Okonkwo realizes that his clan is not willing to go to war.

The District Commissioner arrives at Okonkwo's compound and finds that Okonkwo has hanged himself. Obierika explains that suicide is a grave sin. According to custom, none of Okonkwo's clansmen may touch his body. The commissioner, who is writing a book about Africa, believes that the story of Okonkwo's rebellion and death will make for an interesting paragraph or two. He has already chosen the book's title: *The Pacification of the Primitive Tribes of the Lower Niger*.

CHARACTERS IN *THINGS FALL APART*

Akunna　A clan leader of Umuofia. Akunna and Mr. Brown discuss their religious beliefs peacefully. Akunna formulates an articulate, rational defense of his religious system and draws striking parallels between his worship and Christian worship.

Mr. Brown　The first white missionary to travel to Umuofia. Mr. Brown institutes a policy of compromise, understanding, and nonaggression between his flock and the clan. He becomes friends with prominent clansmen and builds a school and a hospital in Umuofia.

Chielo　A priestess in Umuofia who is dedicated to the Oracle of the goddess Agbala. Chielo is a widow with two children. At one point, she carries Ezinma on her back for miles in order to purify her and appease the gods.

The District Commissioner　An authority figure in the white colonial government in Nigeria. The prototypical racist colonialist, the District Commissioner thinks that he understands everything about native African customs and cultures, none of which he respects.

Ekwefi　Okonkwo's second wife. Ekwefi ran away from her first husband to live with Okonkwo. Ekwefi had nine children who died in infancy. Only Ezinma survives.

Enoch　A fanatical convert to the Christian church in Umuofia. Mr. Brown keeps Enoch in check in the interest of community harmony, but Reverend Smith approves of his zealotry.

Ogbuefi Ezeudu　The oldest man in the village and one of the most important clan elders and leaders. Ogbuefi Ezeudu was a great warrior in his youth and now delivers messages from the Oracle.

Ezinma　The only child of Okonkwo's second wife, Ekwefi. Ekwefi treats Ezinma as her equal. Ezinma is Okonkwo's favorite child because she understands him and because she reminds him of Ekwefi when Ekwefi was the village beauty. Okonkwo wishes that Ezinma were a boy, because she would have been the perfect son.

Ikemefuna　A boy given to Okonkwo by a neighboring village. Ikemefuna grows close to Nwoye and Okonkwo.

Mr. Kiaga　A native-turned-Christian missionary. In Mbanta, Mr. Kiaga converts Nwoye and many others.

Maduka　Obierika's son. Maduka is promising and manly.

Nwakibie　A wealthy clansmen. Nwakibie takes a chance and lends Okonkwo a large number of seed yams, a gesture that helps Okonkwo build up the beginnings of his personal wealth, status, and independence.

Nwoye　Okonkwo's oldest son. Okonkwo continually beats Nwoye, whom he considers weak and lazy. Because he questions some of the laws and rules of his tribe, Nwoye eventually converts to Christianity, an act that Okonkwo criticizes as "effeminate."

Obiageli　The daughter of Okonkwo's first wife.

Obierika　Okonkwo's close friend. Obierika looks out for Okonkwo, making sure he has enough money and comforting him when he is depressed. Like Nwoye, Obierika questions some of the tribe's strictures.

Ojiugo　Okonkwo's third and youngest wife.

Okonkwo　An influential clan leader in Umuofia. Since early childhood, Okonkwo's scorn for his lazy, squandering, effeminate father, Unoka, has driven him to succeed. Okonkwo's terror of turning into his father results in trouble and sorrow.

Reverend James Smith The missionary who replaces Mr. Brown. Reverend Smith, the stereotypical white colonialist, is an uncompromising, strict man who shows no respect for indigenous customs or culture. He intentionally provokes his congregation, inciting it to anger.

Uchendu Okonkwo's uncle. Like Okonkwo, Uchendu has suffered—all but one of his six wives are dead and he has buried twenty-two children—but unlike Okonkwo, he is a peaceful, compromising man.

Unoka Okonkwo's father. By the standards of the clan, Unoka was a coward and a spendthrift. He never took a title, he borrowed money from his clansmen, he rarely repaid his debts, and he never became a warrior because he feared the sight of blood. But Unoka was also a talented musician and a gentle, if idle, man.

Okagbue Uyanwa A famous medicine man.

THEMES IN *THINGS FALL APART*

THE CONFLICT BETWEEN CHANGE AND TRADITION Characters often cling to tradition or embrace change not for idealistic, abstract reasons, but for personal ones. Okonkwo resists the new political and religious orders because he is obsessed with manliness, and he feels the new orders are not manly. Okonkwo also resists cultural change because he fears losing social status. He has always judged himself, and expected others to judge him, by the traditional standards of his village. If those standards change, Okonkwo will be at sea. Many members of the clan embrace Christianity for similarly personal reasons. Long-scorned outcasts find a social refuge in Christianity, the adoption of which gives them a more elevated status than they have ever enjoyed before.

THE MISINTERPRETATION OF MASCULINITY Okonkwo's interpretation of masculinity puts him at odds with his village. He associates masculinity with aggression and believes that anger is the only emotion that he should display. For this reason, he frequently beats his wives, even threatening to kill them from time to time. He does not think things through, and he acts rashly and impetuously. Achebe contrasts Okonkwo's behavior with that of other villagers who manage to be both masculine and nonviolent. Obierika, for example, is "a man who thought about things." In order to embody his own perverse definition of masculinity, Okonkwo must ignore the wishes of his village. When Okonkwo insists on joining the party that will execute his surrogate son out of a misplaced conviction that to do so is manly, he intentionally flouts the ruling of a respected village elder. Even after the disastrous execution, Okonkwo cannot change his conception of manliness. During his seven-year exile from his village, he ignores his uncle's advice to appreciate his mother's land and reflect on his mother's ancestors. Instead, he spends his exile reminding himself that his maternal kinsmen are not as warlike and fierce as the villagers of Umuofia. He faults them for what he considers their feminine preference for negotiation, compliance, and avoidance over anger and bloodshed.

LANGUAGE AS A SIGN OF CULTURAL DIFFERENCE By showing the imaginative, often formal language of the Igbo, Achebe emphasizes that Africa is not the silent or incomprehensible country that white novelists think it is. He includes translated proverbs, folktales, and songs, conveying the rhythms, structures, and cadences of the Igbo language. Achebe also points out the linguistic variations in Africa that utterly escape colonialist writers. The villagers of Umuofia, for example, make fun of Mr. Brown's translator because his language is slightly different from their own. On a broader level, Achebe makes a point by writing *Things Fall Apart* in English, indicating that the novel should be read by Westerners.

SYMBOLS IN *THINGS FALL APART*

LOCUSTS The locusts that descend on the village symbolize the white settlers who feast on and exploit the Igbo. The Igbo who eat these locusts as if they are not harmful stand for the Igbo who convert to Christianity with a light heart. The locusts are so heavy that they break the tree branches, which suggests the way white culture fractures and destroys Igbo traditions. In Chapter Fifteen, Achebe makes the connection explicit: "the Oracle . . . said that other white men were on their way. They were locusts."

FIRE   Fire symbolizes Okonkwo's anger. Fire, like Okonkwo's anger, destroys everything it consumes. Okonkwo is physically destructive—he kills Ikemefuna and Ogbuefi Ezeudu's son. He is also emotionally destructive—he hides his fondness for Ikemefuna and Ezinma, and treats them coldly. In the end, Okonkwo allows his anger to destroy himself.

IMPORTANT QUOTATIONS FROM *THINGS FALL APART*

Among the Igbo the art of conversation is regarded very highly, and proverbs are the palm-oil with which words are eaten.

Location: Chapter One
Speaker: The narrator
Context: The narrator explains Unoka's conversation skill

Unoka was a master at calmly interacting with someone to whom he owed money. As the narrator explains, the Igbo practice rhetoric as an art. Their brand of conversation clashes with the European style of talking. Where the Igbo are subtle and complex, the Europeans are efficient and direct.

"Does the white man understand our custom about land?"
"How can he when he does not even speak our tongue? But he says that our customs are bad; and our own brothers who have taken up his religion also say that our customs are bad. How do you think we can fight when our own brothers have turned against us? The white man is very clever. He came quietly and peaceably with his religion. We were amused at his foolishness and allowed him to stay. Now he has won our brothers, and our clan can no longer act like one. He has put a knife on the things that held us together and we have fallen apart."

Location: Chapter Twenty
Speaker: Obierika and Okonkwo
Context: Obierika sees the demise of his people

Upset that the white men have no regard for Igbo ideas of justice, Obierika points to the absurdity of denigrating customs without knowing anything about them, reflexively putting them down simply because they are Igbo, not European. Yet Obierika does not lay the blame wholly on the white men. He blames the Umuofians who have converted to Christianity for consciously turning their backs on their own "brothers." Here, as elsewhere, Achebe paints a nuanced portrait of the relationship between the colonialists and the villagers. Religion and tradition are the threads that hold the clan together, but religion is flawed and tradition is vulnerable in ways that have nothing to do with white men.

Turning and turning in the widening gyre
The falcon cannot hear the falconer;
Things fall apart; the center cannot hold;
Mere anarchy is loosed upon the world.

Location: The epigraph
Speaker: The narrator of William Butler Yeats's poem "The Second Coming"
Context: Achebe gestures at the chaos and collapse his novel will chronicle

And at last the locusts did descend. They settled on every tree and on every blade of grass; they settled on the roofs and covered the bare ground. Mighty tree branches broke away under them, and the whole country became the brown-earth color of the vast, hungry swarm.

Location: Chapter Seven
Speaker: The narrator
Context: The locusts descend on the village

He had already chosen the title of the book, after much thought: The Pacification of the Primitive Tribes of the Lower Niger.

Location: The last sentence of the novel
Speaker: The narrator
Context: The narrator satirizes the idiocy of the colonialists

THE THINGS THEY CARRIED

Tim O'Brien

A soldier looks back on his days in Vietnam.

THE LIFE OF WILLIAM TIMOTHY O'BRIEN

William Timothy O'Brien was born on October 1, 1946, to an insurance salesman and an elementary school teacher in Austin, Minnesota. He was raised in Worthington, a small town in southern Minnesota that he later described as what one would find "in a dictionary under the word boring." As a child, the overweight and introspective O'Brien spent his time practicing magic tricks and making pilgrimages to the public library. His father's *New York Times* accounts of fighting in Iwo Jima and Okinawa during World War II inspired O'Brien to consider a career in writing. Two weeks after graduating summa cum laude and Phi Beta Kappa from Macalester College, O'Brien was drafted to fight in Vietnam.

O'Brien reported for basic training despite his strong opposition to the war. He served in the Fifth Battalion of the 46th Infantry, 198th Infantry Brigade, American Division. He was eventually wounded and returned home with a Purple Heart, a Bronze Star for Valor, and a Combat Infantry Badge. He also returned with an endless supply of guilt and observations that would later comprise his memoir *If I Die in a Combat Zone, Box Me Up and Ship Me Home* (1973). O'Brien began graduate studies and then abandoned them for a career as a national affairs reporter for the *Washington Post*. In 1975, he published *Northern Lights*, an account of two brothers in rural Minnesota. *Going After Cacciato*, O'Brien's account of a platoon forced to chase one of its AWOL soldiers, won the National Book Award in 1979.

After publishing *The Nuclear Age* (1985), a home-front comedy, O'Brien wrote the first short story, "Speaking of Courage," in what would eventually become *The Things They Carried* (1990), a sequence of lyrical and interrelated stories that has been heralded as one of the finest works of fiction about the Vietnam War.

THE THINGS THEY CARRIED IN CONTEXT

O'Brien draws heavily on his own experiences in *The Things They Carried*, although elements of fiction blend with the mostly factual narrative. The narrator and protagonist of the short-story collection is named Tim O'Brien. Like the author, the fictional O'Brien grew up in Worthington, Minnesota, attended Macalester College, and has written stories and novels about his experiences in Vietnam. Unlike the author, the fictional O'Brien killed a man while at war, and he has children.

The Things They Carried was a finalist for both the Pulitzer Prize and the National Book Critics Circle Award. O'Brien is often compared to Stephen Crane and Kurt Vonnegut. Crane's *The Red Badge of Courage* (1895) chronicles the experience of a Union regiment in the Civil War, specifically one recruit who, like the protagonist in *The Things They Carried*, struggles to be brave. Vonnegut's 1969 novel *Slaughterhouse-Five* is about a World War II draftee taken prisoner during the Battle of the Bulge. Like Vonnegut, O'Brien inserts himself into his stories.

THE THINGS THEY CARRIED: KEY FACTS

Time and place written: Late 1980s; Massachusetts	
Date of first publication: 1990	
Publisher: Houghton Mifflin / Seymour Lawrence	
Type of work: Interconnected short stories	
Genre: War stories; bildungsroman	

Language: English

Setting (time): Late 1960s and late 1980s

Setting (place): Vietnam and Massachusetts

Tense: Past

Tone: Introspective, self-conscious

Narrator: Tim O'Brien in the first person

Point of view: O'Brien's

Protagonist: Tim O'Brien

Antagonist: The Vietnam War

THE THINGS THEY CARRIED: PLOT OVERVIEW

In the story "The Things They Carried," the protagonist, who is named Tim O'Brien, catalogs the variety of things his fellow soldiers in the Alpha Company brought on their missions. These things range from the intangible, including guilt and fear, to the physical, including matches, morphine, M-16 rifles, and M&M's.

The first member of the Alpha Company to die was Ted Lavender, a "grunt," or low-ranking soldier, who dealt with his anxiety about the war by taking tranquilizers and smoking marijuana. Lavender was shot in the head on his way back from the bathroom. His superior, Lieutenant Jimmy Cross, had been thinking of Martha, a college crush, when Lavender was shot. He blamed himself for the tragedy.

In "Love," we learn that Cross's feelings for Martha were never reciprocated, and that twenty years after the war, he still feels guilty about Lavender's death. In "On the Rainy River," O'Brien explains the series of events that led him to Vietnam. He received his draft notice in June 1968 and contemplated fleeing to Canada. Sitting in a rowboat with the proprietor of the Tip Top Lodge, where he was staying, O'Brien decided that his guilt about avoiding the war and his fear of disappointing his family were more important than his political convictions.

A few other members of the Alpha Company were killed during their mission overseas, including Curt Lemon, who died playing catch with a grenade. In "The Dentist," O'Brien tells a story of Lemon at the dentist. After fainting before a routine checkup with an army-issued dentist, Lemon tried to save face by insisting that the dentist pull a perfectly good tooth. Lee Strunk, another member of the company, stepped on a landmine and died. In "Friends," O'Brien remembers that before Strunk was fatally hurt, Strunk and Dave Jensen made a pact that if either man were irreparably harmed, the other man would make sure he was killed quickly. However, when Strunk was actually hurt, he begged Jensen to spare him, and Jensen complied. News of his friend's swift death en route to treatment relieved Jensen.

Kiowa was a much-loved member of the Alpha Company and one of O'Brien's closest friends. In "Speaking of Courage," Norman Bowker remembers Kiowa's death. Years after the war, Bowker drives around a lake in his Iowa hometown and thinks about failing to save Kiowa, who was killed when a mortar round hit and caused him to sink headfirst into a marshy sewage field. In "Notes," O'Brien realizes that he and Norman Bowker dealt differently with their guilt over Kiowa's death. Just before the end of the war, O'Brien received a long letter from Bowker saying he has not found a way to make life meaningful after the war. O'Brien resolved to tell Bowker's story and the story of Kiowa's death in order to negotiate his own feelings of guilt and hollowness.

In "The Man I Killed" and "Ambush," O'Brien confronts his guilt about killing a man with a grenade outside the village of My Khe. In "The Man I Killed," O'Brien imagines the life of his victim, from his childhood to the way things would have turned out for him had O'Brien not spotted him on a path and thrown a grenade at his feet. In "Ambush," O'Brien imagines how he might tell the story of the man he killed to his nine-year-old daughter, Kathleen. In this second story, O'Brien provides more details of the actual killing—including the sound of the grenade and his own feelings—and explains that he still has not finished sorting out the experience.

In the last story, "The Lives of the Dead," O'Brien explains that his imagination allowed him to handle his guilt and confusion over the death of his fourth-grade love, Linda.

CHARACTERS IN *THE THINGS THEY CARRIED*

Azar A soldier in the Alpha Company. Azar is one of the few unsympathetic characters in the work. He tortures Vietnamese civilians and pokes fun at the dead, enemy and fellow soldier alike. In a moment of remorse, he helps unearth Kiowa's body from the muck of the sewage field.

Mary Anne Bell Mark Fossie's high-school sweetheart. Mary Anne arrives in Vietnam full of innocence, but she gains respect for death and the darkness of the jungle where, according to legend, she disappears.

Elroy Berdahl The proprietor of the Tip Top Lodge near the Canadian border. Kind, quiet Berdahl is a father figure for O'Brien, spending six days with him after he receives his draft notice.

Norman Bowker A soldier in the Alpha Company. Bowker, a quiet and unassuming man, suffers greatly because of Kiowa's death.

Jimmy Cross The lieutenant of the Alpha Company. Cross has good intentions, but he does not know how to lead his men. He is wracked with guilt because he believes his preoccupation with an old crush and his tendency to follow orders against his better judgment caused the deaths of Ted Lavender and Kiowa.

Henry Dobbins The platoon's machine gunner. Henry Dobbins, a gentle giant, is profoundly decent.

Mark Fossie A medic on Rat Kiley's previous assignment. Fossie loses his innocence when he realizes that his girlfriend, Mary Anne, would rather be out on ambush with Green Berets than home planning a wedding.

Dave Jensen A minor character whose guilt over his injury of Lee Strunk causes him to break his own nose.

Bobby Jorgenson The medic who replaces Rat Kiley. The second time O'Brien is shot, Jorgenson's incompetence infuriates O'Brien.

Kathleen O'Brien's daughter. Kathleen's youth and innocence force O'Brien to gain new perspective on his war experience.

Bob "Rat" Kiley The platoon's medic. O'Brien has great respect for Kiley's medical prowess. Though levelheaded and kind, Kiley eventually blows off his toe so that he will be forced to leave his post.

Kiowa O'Brien's closest friend. Kiowa is a model of quiet, rational morality amid the atrocities of war. His death, which results when the company mistakenly camps in a sewage field, is the focal point of three stories.

Ted Lavender A young, frightened soldier in the Alpha Company. Lavender pops tranquilizers to calm himself.

Curt Lemon A childish and careless member of the Alpha Company. O'Brien did not particularly like Lemon, but he continually contemplates Lemon's death with sadness and regret.

Linda O'Brien's first love. Linda died of a brain tumor in the fifth grade.

Tim O'Brien The narrator and protagonist of the collection of stories. O'Brien is a pacifist who contends with his guilt and confusion about Vietnam by writing.

Mitchell Sanders One of the most likable soldiers in the stories. Sanders is kind and devoted, and he has a strong sense of justice. His ability to tell stories and to discuss their nuances makes a profound impression on O'Brien.

Lee Strunk Another soldier in the platoon. He breaks his nose while struggling with Dave Jensen over a jackknife.

THEMES IN *THE THINGS THEY CARRIED*

PHYSICAL AND EMOTIONAL BURDENS O'Brien's characters carry literal and figurative burdens. They carry both heavy physical loads and heavy emotional loads of grief, terror, love, and longing. Each man's physical burden underscores his emotional burden. Henry Dobbins carries his girlfriend's pantyhose and a longing for love and comfort. Jimmy Cross carries compasses and maps and the responsibility for the men in his charge. After the war, the men continue to carry the psychological burdens picked up during the war. Those who survive carry guilt, grief, and confusion. In "Love," Jimmy Cross confides to O'Brien that he has never forgiven himself for Ted Lavender's death. Norman Bowker's grief and confusion are such a heavy weight on his shoulders that he hangs himself in a YMCA. The burdens are heaviest, O'Brien suggests, when they are carried alone. Bowker carried his psychological burdens alone, but O'Brien shares the things he carries, his war stories, with us. By writing down his stories, he asks his readers to help carry the burden of the Vietnam War as part of their collective past.

THE UNFORTUNATE INFLUENCE OF SOCIAL PRESSURE O'Brien illustrates the power of social pressure, pointing out that it does not recede into the background during wartime. In "On the Rainy River," O'Brien explains that although he deeply disapproved of the war, he did not want people to think him a coward. He decided to report for basic training not because of patriotism, but because he worried that his family and community would disapprove of him if he dodged the draft. In Vietnam, social pressures persisted. The immediacy of death and the necessity of group unity do not stop the characters from engaging in absurd or dangerous actions because of worry about what their friends will think. Curt Lemon, humiliated that he fainted at the dentist, insists on having a perfectly good tooth pulled in an effort to impress his friends. Jimmy Cross went to war only because his friends did, and in Vietnam he is a confused and uncertain leader who endangers the lives of his soldiers. The men in O'Brien's company commit brutalities and murder not because they are manly or brave, but because they do not want to embarrass themselves.

THE SUBJECTION OF TRUTH TO STORYTELLING O'Brien intentionally blends fact and fiction, making the point that the technical facts about an individual event are less important than the overarching, subjective truth of what the war meant to soldiers and how it changed them. The different storytellers in *The Things They Carried*, particularly Rat Kiley, Mitchell Sanders, and O'Brien, lay out truths about war so profound and ugly that they require neither facts nor long explanations. Such statements as "This is true," which opens "How to Tell a True War Story," do not claim that the events recounted in the story actually occurred. Rather, they claim that the stylistic and thematic content of the story is true to the experience the soldiers had in the war. This truth is often unpleasant and brutal in contrast to the ideas of glory and heroism associated with war before Vietnam.

SYMBOLS IN *THE THINGS THEY CARRIED*

THE YOUNG VIETNAMESE SOLDIER O'Brien's guilt over killing the young soldier symbolizes humankind's collective guilt about war. The fact that he is not sure whether he actually threw a grenade and killed a man makes the symbolism stronger, suggesting that even those not directly involved in war are responsible for its atrocities.

KATHLEEN Kathleen represents the reader. O'Brien gains a new perspective on his experiences in Vietnam when he thinks about how he should explain them to his impressionable young daughter, just as he thinks about his experiences differently when telling them to a reader in mind. Kathleen's reactions suggest the gap between the storyteller and the listener. When O'Brien takes Kathleen to Vietnam, she can only notice the stink of the muck and the strangeness of the land. She has no sense of the place's emotional significance to O'Brien.

IMPORTANT QUOTATIONS FROM *THE THINGS THEY CARRIED*

He was a slim, dead, almost dainty young man of about twenty. He lay with one leg bent beneath him, his jaw in his throat, his face neither expressive nor inexpressive. One eye was shut. The other was a star-shaped hole.

Location: "The Man I Killed"
Speaker: O'Brien
Context: O'Brien describes the man he killed with a grenade

"The Man I Killed" is narrated from a third-person perspective. It is largely a series of unconnected observations and fantasies about the dead soldier. In this passage, O'Brien describes the corpse of the young Vietnamese soldier in concrete, blunt terms. His matter-of-factness wipes away sentimentality and melodrama. O'Brien captures the unreality of the moment, the inability to believe that the soldier is really dead. He lists the soldier's qualities as if describing a young man at a party: "slim, dead, almost dainty." O'Brien uses the word "dead" as he might use the word "debonair." The jarring incongruity captures O'Brien's youthful refusal to realize that he is looking at a corpse. O'Brien's description of the star-shaped hole in the boy's eye is both a means of detaching himself and a way of seeing death as mystical and beautiful.

By telling stories, you objectify your own experience. You separate it from yourself. You pin down certain truths. You make up others. You start sometimes with an incident that truly happened, like the night in the shit field, and you carry it forward by inventing incidents that did not in fact occur but that nonetheless help to clarify and explain.

Location: "Notes"
Speaker: O'Brien
Context: O'Brien reflects on storytelling

After Norman Bowker sends O'Brien a letter, O'Brien reflects on his own storytelling. Bowker asks O'Brien for a story, saying he wants to explain his feelings of frustration and disillusionment but doesn't know what to say. The letter inspires O'Brien to consider storytelling as a means for coping with his traumatic experiences. This particular passage is one of several that support O'Brien's contention that in storytelling, objective truth is not as important as a truthful representation of emotion. Later, in "Good Form," O'Brien says that the stories he tells may be entirely made up, forcing us to wonder whether his characters and contentions would lose some of their power and validity if we thought they were an invention.

They carried the soldier's greatest fear, which was the fear of blushing. Men killed, and died, because they were embarrassed not to. It was what had brought them to the war in the first place, nothing positive, no dreams of glory or honor, just to avoid the blush of dishonor. They died so as not to die of embarrassment.

Location: "The Things They Carried"
Speaker: O'Brien
Context: O'Brien discusses the reason he and his comrades killed

I'd come to this war a quiet, thoughtful sort of person, a college grad, Phi Beta Kappa and summa cum laude, all the credentials, but after seven months in the bush I realized that those high, civilized trappings had somehow been crushed under the weight of the simple daily realities. I'd turned mean inside.

Location: "The Ghost Soldiers"
Speaker: O'Brien
Context: O'Brien concedes that his desire to get revenge on Bobby Jorgensen is irrational

---

[S]ometimes I can even see Timmy skating with Linda under the yellow floodlights. I'm young and happy. I'll never die. I'm skimming across the surface of my own history, moving fast, riding the melt beneath the blades, doing loops and spins, and when I take a high leap into the dark and come down thirty years later, I realize it is as Tim trying to save Timmy's life with a story.

Location: "The Lives of the Dead"
Speaker: O'Brien
Context: O'Brien writes that memory and storytelling comfort the mourning

TO KILL A MOCKINGBIRD

Harper Lee

A girl confronts evil as her father unsuccessfully defends an innocent black man accused of raping a white woman.

THE LIFE OF HARPER LEE

Nelle Harper Lee was born on April 28, 1926, in Monroeville, Alabama. Her father was a lawyer, as is her character Atticus in *To Kill a Mockingbird*, and Truman Capote was one of her childhood friends. Capote later earned fame as a writer, and Lee used him as the model for her character Dill in *To Kill a Mockingbird*. Lee earned her bachelor's degree from the University of Alabama and then enrolled in the University of Alabama law school, although she left the program a few months short of graduation.

In 1950, Lee moved to New York City, where she worked at an airline. In 1960, she published *To Kill a Mockingbird*. Despite the mixed critical response the novel received, it became an enormous popular success, winning the Pulitzer Prize in 1961 and selling over fifteen million copies. Two years after the novel's publication, an Academy Award–winning film version of the novel, starring Gregory Peck as Atticus Finch, was produced. Lee retreated from the public eye, avoiding interviews, declining to write the screenplay for the film version, and publishing only a few short magazine articles after 1961. Lee eventually returned to Monroeville, where she lives today.

TO KILL A MOCKINGBIRD IN CONTEXT

Despite the many similarities between *To Kill a Mockingbird* and Lee's personal life, Lee maintains that the novel portrays a nonspecific Southern town, not her own childhood town. "People are people anywhere you put them," she declared in a 1961 interview.

Yet the book's setting and characters are not the only aspects of the story shaped by events that occurred during Lee's childhood. In 1931, when Lee was five, nine young black men were accused of raping two white women near Scottsboro, Alabama. After a series of lengthy, highly publicized, and often bitter trials, five of the nine men were sentenced to long prison terms. Many prominent lawyers and other American citizens believed that the sentences were motivated by racial prejudice. Many people suspected that the women were lying about the rapes. Over the course of numerous appeals, their claims seemed increasingly dubious. The Scottsboro Case, as the trials of the nine men came to be called, likely inspired the fictional trial that stands at the heart of Lee's novel.

In 1993, Lee wrote a brief foreword to her book, asking that future editions of *To Kill a Mockingbird* be spared critical introductions. "*Mockingbird*," she writes, "still says what it has to say; it has managed to survive the years without preamble." The book remains a staple of high school and college reading lists.

TO KILL A MOCKINGBIRD: KEY FACTS

Time and place written: 1950s (completed in 1957); New York City	
Date of first publication: 1960	
Publisher: J. B. Lippincott	
Type of work: Novel	
Genre: Courtromm drama; social protest novel; southern novel	
Language: English	
Tense: Past	
Tone: Childlike, humorous, nostalgic, innocent, dark, foreboding	

Setting (time): 1933–1935

Setting (place): The fictional town of Maycomb, Alabama

Narrator: Scout Finch in the first person

Point of view: Scout's

Protagonist: Scout

Antagonist: Bob Ewell, Scout's teachers, and racism

TO KILL A MOCKINGBIRD: PLOT OVERVIEW

Scout Finch lives with her brother, Jem, and their widowed father, Atticus, in the sleepy Alabama town of Maycomb. The Great Depression has hit Maycomb hard, but Atticus is a prominent lawyer, and the Finch family is reasonably well off. One summer, Jem and Scout befriend a boy named Dill who has come to live in their neighborhood for the summer. Dill is fascinated with the spooky house on their street called the Radley Place. The house is owned by Mr. Nathan Radley, whose brother, Arthur (nicknamed Boo), lives there and never comes outside.

Scout goes to school for the first time that fall and detests it. She and Jem find gifts apparently left for them in a knothole of a tree on the Radley property. Dill returns the following summer, and he, Scout, and Jem act out the story of Boo Radley. Atticus puts a stop to their antics, urging the children to try to see life from another person's perspective before making judgments. On Dill's last night in Maycomb, the three sneak onto the Radley property, where Nathan Radley shoots at them. Jem loses his pants as the children scramble to escape. When he returns for them, he finds them mended and hung over the fence. The next winter, Jem and Scout find more presents in the tree, presumably left by the mysterious Boo. Nathan Radley eventually plugs the knothole with cement. A fire breaks out in another neighbor's house, and as Scout watches the blaze, someone slips a blanket onto her shoulders. Convinced that Boo did it, Jem tells Atticus about the mended pants and the presents.

To the consternation of Maycomb's racist white community, Atticus agrees to defend a black man named Tom Robinson who has been accused of raping a white woman. Because of Atticus's decision, children abuse Jem and Scout. Calpurnia, the Finches' black cook, takes them to the local black church, where the warm and close-knit community embraces the children.

Atticus's sister, Alexandra, comes to live with the Finches the next summer. Dill, who is supposed to live with his "new father" in another town, runs away and comes to Maycomb. Tom Robinson's trial begins. When Robinson is placed in the local jail, a mob gathers to lynch him. Atticus faces the mob down the night before the trial. Jem and Scout, who have sneaked out of the house, join him. Scout recognizes one of the men as the father of one of her classmates, and her polite inquiries after his son shames him into dispersing the mob.

At the trial, Jem and Scout sit in the "colored balcony" with the town's black citizens. Atticus provides clear evidence that the accusers, Mayella Ewell and her father, Bob, are lying. The truth is that Mayella propositioned Tom Robinson, and when her father caught her, she accused Tom of rape to cover her shame and guilt. Atticus suggests that Mayella's face is marked because her father, not Tom, beat her. Despite the significant evidence pointing to Tom's innocence, the all-white jury convicts him. Tom later tries to escape from prison and is shot to death. Jem's faith in justice is badly shaken, and he lapses into despondency and doubt.

Despite the verdict, Bob Ewell feels that Atticus and the judge made a fool of him, and he vows revenge. He menaces Tom Robinson's widow, tries to break into the judge's house, and finally attacks Jem and Scout as they walk home from a Halloween party. Boo Radley intervenes, saving the children and killing Ewell in the struggle. After carrying the wounded Jem home and sitting with Scout for a while, Boo disappears once more into the Radley house. Scout thinks she can finally imagine what life is like for Boo. She embraces her father's advice to practice sympathy and understanding.

CHARACTERS IN *TO KILL A MOCKINGBIRD*

Aunt Alexandra Atticus's sister. Alexandra is a strong-willed woman, fiercely devoted to her family and committed to propriety and tradition.

Miss Maudie Atkinson The Finches' neighbor. Miss Maudie is a sharp-tongued widow almost the same age as Atticus's younger brother, Jack. She shares Atticus's passion for justice and is the children's closest adult friend.

Calpurnia The Finches' black cook. Calpurnia, a stern disciplinarian, introduces Jem and Scout to her own black community.

Mr. Walter Cunningham A poor farmer. Cunningham, part of the mob that seeks to lynch Tom Robinson, backs down in the face of Scout's politeness.

Walter Cunningham Mr. Walter Cunningham's son. Walter is one of Scout's classmates.

Link Deas Tom Robinson's employer. Deas praises Tom in court.

Mrs. Henry Lafayette Dubose An elderly, ill-tempered, racist woman who lives near the Finches. Atticus admires Mrs. Dubose for the courage with which she battles her morphine addiction.

Bob Ewell A drunken, usually unemployed member of Maycomb's poorest family. Ewell wrongfully accuses Tom Robinson of raping his daughter. He is ignorant and hateful.

Mayella Ewell Bob Ewell's abused, lonely, unhappy daughter.

Atticus Finch Scout and Jem's father. Atticus, a widower lawyer with a dry sense of humor, has a strong sense of morality and justice.

Jean Louise "Scout" Finch The narrator and protagonist of the novel. Scout is intelligent, tomboyish, and combative. The events of the novel test her basic faith in the goodness of people.

Jeremy Atticus "Jem" Finch Scout's brother. Four years older than Scout, Jem gradually separates himself from her games, but remains her close companion and protector.

Charles Baker "Dill" Harris Jem and Scout's summer neighbor and friend. Dill is a diminutive, confident boy with an active imagination.

Arthur "Boo" Radley Jem and Scout's reclusive neighbor. Boo was an intelligent child but emotionally damaged by his cruel father. He is one of the novel's mockingbirds, a good person injured by the evil of mankind.

Nathan Radley Boo Radley's older brother. Nathan seems similar to his and Boo's deceased father: cruel and impatient.

Mr. Dolphu Raymond A wealthy white man. Raymond pretends to be a drunk so that the people of Maycomb will be able to explain the fact that he lives with his black mistress and mulatto children. He dislikes white society's hypocrisy.

Tom Robinson A black field hand. Tom is a generous man who is accused of rape.

Heck Tate The sheriff of Maycomb. Heck, who is a major witness at Tom Robinson's trial, is a decent man who tries to protect the innocent.

Mr. Underwood The publisher of Maycomb's newspaper. Mr. Underwood respects Atticus.

THEMES IN *TO KILL A MOCKINGBIRD*

THE ABILITY TO FEND OFF CYNICISM *To Kill a Mockingbird* explores the moral nature of human beings, asking whether people are essentially good or essentially evil. Lee approaches this question by dramatizing Scout and Jem's transition from childhood innocence, a time when they assume that people are good because they have never seen evil, to young adulthood, when they have seen evil and must incorporate it into their worldviews. Atticus Finch, the moral voice of the novel, has managed to experience and understand evil without losing his faith in the human capacity for goodness. He tries to teach his children that by understanding that most people are basically good but struggle with evil tendencies, it is possible to live a moral life without losing hope or becoming cynical. For example, Atticus admires Mrs. Dubose's courage even while deploring her racism. Atticus's children have varying degrees of success in maintaining an optimistic outlook. Scout loses her innocence without becoming jaded. Jem becomes disillusioned. But the ability to avoid cynicism, the task that preoccupies the main characters, is an academic question for most. Atticus, Scout, and Jem are essentially detached observers of evil, but people like Tom Robinson and Boo Radley are real victims of evil. For them, the struggle to avoid disillusionment is totally irrelevant. Some people may be good, or some people may be partly good, but it doesn't really matter. Enough evil exists in humanity to destroy Tom and Boo.

THE MORAL EDUCATION OF CHILDREN Lee suggests that the moral education of children is at least as important as their academic education. She contrasts Atticus's patient, kind, moral education of his children with that provided by the teachers at Scout's school, who are either frustratingly unsympathetic or morally hypocritical. Atticus gets through to Scout and Jem by putting himself in their shoes, while teachers like Miss Caroline alienate their students by sticking rigidly to certain educational techniques, even those that are ineffectual. Lee concludes that learning sympathy and understanding from a sympathetic, understanding teacher is far more important than learning algebra from a tyrant.

THE IRRATIONALITY OF THE CLASS SYSTEM Lee suggests that social hierarchies such as Maycomb's are irrational. The relatively well-off Finches stand near the top of Maycomb's social hierarchy, with most of the townspeople beneath them. Ignorant country farmers like the Cunninghams come next, followed by trashy families like the Ewells. The black community is at the bottom of the heap. Lee emphasizes the illogic of forcing an entire group of people into the lowest social stratum simply because of their race. Under this system, a nasty, uneducated man like Bob Ewell can persecute a kind, responsible man like Tom Robinson without cause, simply because he is white and his victim is black. Lee also emphasizes the way people living in a stratified system eventually equate economic status with worth. For example, Scout's Aunt Alexandra refuses to let Scout associate with Walter Cunningham because he is poor. Scout and Jem are constantly baffled by the rules that govern society. With their bafflement, Lee points out that rules adults accept as absolute are actually relative and probably silly.

SYMBOLS IN *TO KILL A MOCKINGBIRD*

MOCKINGBIRDS In the novel, mockingbirds symbolize innocence, so to kill a mockingbird is to destroy innocence. Jem, Tom Robinson, Dill, Boo Radley, and Mr. Raymond are mockingbirds—innocents who have been injured or destroyed through contact with evil. As Miss Maudie says, "Mockingbirds don't do one thing but . . . sing their hearts out for us. That's why it's a sin to kill a mockingbird." After Tom Robinson is shot, Mr. Underwood compares his death to "the senseless slaughter of songbirds." At the end of the novel, Scout thinks that hurting Boo Radley would be like "shootin' a mockingbird." Jem and Scout's last name, Finch (another type of small bird), emphasizes their innocence.

BOO RADLEY Boo Radley stands for the children's development from innocence to adulthood. At the beginning of the novel, Boo interests the children for his strangeness and creepiness. He gradually becomes increasingly real to them, leaving them presents and mending pants. By the end of the novel, he has become fully human to Scout, which suggests that she has become a sympathetic and understanding individual.

IMPORTANT QUOTATIONS FROM *TO KILL A MOCKINGBIRD*

Maycomb was an old town, but it was a tired old town when I first knew it. In rainy weather the streets turned to red slop . . . bony mules hitched to Hoover carts flicked flies in the sweltering shade of the live oaks on the square. Men's stiff collars wilted by nine in the morning. Ladies bathed before noon, after their three-o'clock naps, and by nightfall were like soft teacakes with frostings of sweat and sweet talcum.. . . There was no hurry, for there was nowhere to go, nothing to buy and no money to buy it with, nothing to see outside the boundaries of Maycomb County. But it was a time of vague optimism for some of the people: Maycomb County had recently been told that it had nothing to fear but fear itself.

Location: Chapter 1
Speaker: Scout
Context: Scout describes Maycomb

Scout describes her hometown as a slow, old-fashioned, slightly backwards place. The tone of the passage tells us that Scout is telling her story as an adult looking back on her childhood experiences. The description of Maycomb provides clues about the story's chronological setting, making reference to mule-driven Hoover carts, dirt roads, and the widespread poverty of the town, implying that Maycomb is suffering during the Great Depression. Scout alludes to the words "We have nothing to fear but fear itself," the most famous line from Franklin Delano Roosevelt's first inaugural speech, made after the 1932 presidential election. It is reasonable to infer that the action of the story opens in the summer of 1933, an assumption that subsequent historical clues support. The defeat of the National Recovery Act in the Supreme Court in 1935, for instance, is mentioned in Chapter 27 of the novel, when Scout is eight—about two years after the start of the novel.

"When they finally saw him, why he hadn't done any of those things . . . Atticus, he was real nice.. . ."
His hands were under my chin, pulling up the cover, tucking it around me.
  "Most people are, Scout, when you finally see them." He turned out the light and went into Jem's
room. He would be there all night, and he would be there when Jem waked up in the morning.

Location: Chapter 31
Speaker: Scout
Context: Scout talks to Atticus before falling asleep

These words conclude the novel. As Scout falls asleep, she tells Atticus about the events of *The Gray Ghost*, a book in which one of the characters is wrongly accused of committing a crime and considered dangerous. The wronged hero of the story suggests both Tom Robinson and Boo Radley. Atticus gently reminds Scout that most people are good, if misunderstood. This exchange is a reminder of the novel's themes of innocence, persecution, and empathy. The passage also emphasizes Atticus's strength and tenderness. He tucks Scout in, then goes to sit by Jem's bedside all night long. Through Atticus's strength, the tension and danger of the previous chapters are resolved, and the novel ends on a note of security and peace.

"You never really understand a person until you consider things from his point of view . . . until you
climb into his skin and walk around in it."

Location: Chapter 3
Speaker: Atticus
Context: Atticus explains his philosophy to Scout

"Remember it's a sin to kill a mockingbird." That was the only time I ever heard Atticus say it was a sin
to do something, and I asked Miss Maudie about it.
  "Your father's right," she said. "Mockingbirds don't do one thing but make music for us to enjoy . . .
but sing their hearts out for us. That's why it's a sin to kill a mockingbird."

Location: Chapter 10
Speaker: Scout
Context: Scout relates her father's strong words about the evil of harming the innocent

---

A boy trudged down the sidewalk dragging a fishing pole behind him. A man stood waiting with his
hands on his hips. Summertime, and his children played in the front yard with their friend, enacting a
strange little drama of their own invention. It was fall, and his children fought on the sidewalk in front of
Mrs. Dubose's.. . . Fall, and his children trotted to and fro around the corner, the day's woes and
triumphs on their faces. They stopped at an oak tree, delighted, puzzled, apprehensive. Winter, and his

children shivered at the front gate, silhouetted against a blazing house. Winter, and a man walked into the street, dropped his glasses, and shot a dog. Summer, and he watched his children's heart break. Autumn again, and Boo's children needed him. Atticus was right. One time he said you never really know a man until you stand in his shoes and walk around in them. Just standing on the Radley porch was enough.

Location: Chapter 31
Speaker: Scout
Context: Scout imagines the world from Boo's perspective

TO THE LIGHTHOUSE

Virginia Woolf

A family visits its summerhouse, enduring drastic change between visits.

THE LIFE OF VIRGINIA WOOLF

Virginia Woolf was born on January 25, 1882, to Leslie Stephen and Julia Duckworth Stephen. She was one of four children. Woolf's mother died in 1895, triggering Woolf's first mental breakdown. For weeks after Julia's death, Sir Leslie groaned, threw tantrums, wept, and refused to eat. George Duckworth, Woolf's twenty-seven-year-old half brother, began sexually abusing the grieving thirteen-year-old Woolf, secretly fondling her. Woolf took refuge from harassment and depression in her father's vast library. Sir Leslie remarked that he had never seen anyone "gobble up" books like Woolf did.

Woolf's half-sister, Stella Duckworth, died during emergency surgery when Woolf was fifteen. Seven years after that, Sir Leslie died after a long bout with cancer. Woolf suffered a breakdown and attempted to commit suicide by jumping out of a window. The Stephen children moved to Bloomsbury, a seedy but still elegant neighborhood in London. A group of intellectual, liberal young men and women met regularly in their house. They called their circle "Bloomsbury," and are known historically as the Bloomsbury Group.

After a trip to Greece, Woolf's brother Thoby died of typhoid fever. Woolf was devastated and never truly recovered from the loss of her older brother, whom she adored. She memorialized him in her novel *Jacob's Room* (1922) and as Percival in *The Waves* (1931).

In 1912, Woolf married Leonard Woolf. It was a fortunate match. Leonard was a nurturing caretaker, which was a blessing for Woolf. The possibility of professional failure so terrified Woolf that she had to be hospitalized before the publication of her first novel, *The Voyage Out*. After returning home, she attempted suicide with sleeping pills. Her fears proved unfounded, however. Critics greeted *The Voyage Out* with enthusiasm, praising it for being "recklessly feminine" and for exhibiting "something startlingly like genius."

World War I (1914–1918) erupted. Although air warfare was in its infancy, raids over London sometimes occurred. In 1917, a year before the end of the war, Leonard and Woolf moved to a home in the suburbs, bought a printing press, and launched their own printing company, Hogarth Press. The company soon became profitable, publishing works by T. S. Eliot, Maxim Gorky, Katherine Mansfield, and Sigmund Freud.

Woolf succumbed to another bout of depression after finishing *Jacob's Room* in 1922. She began thinking about Clarissa Dalloway, the heroine of her next novel. Three years later, *Mrs. Dalloway* was published to ecstatic reviews. Critical, popular, and financial success followed. Still, Woolf lapsed into months of depression and illness. Woolf's health eventually improved because of her deep friendship and love affair with Vita Sackville-West (1892–1962). Vita was an author, outstanding gardener, and figurehead for feminists—although she abhorred labels like "feminist."

Woolf entered a particularly productive period, completing *To the Lighthouse* (1927) and beginning *The Waves*. Critics began to consider her a novelist of the first rank, a major British writer who had dusted off old forms and established new novelistic conventions. In 1927, happy with life and grateful for Vita's love, Woolf began *Orlando* (1928), a tongue-in-cheek fantasy about a boy who becomes a woman.

During World War II, bombs destroyed the Woolfs' home while they were at their residence in Sussex. Desperate to sustain her mental health, Virginia Woolf continued writing. By early March 1941, she feared she was slipping into a deep mental illness from which she would never recover. She began hearing voices. On March 28, Woolf wrote farewell notes to Leonard and her sister Vanessa, expressing her certainty that she would not recover, and set out across a meadow toward the River Ouse. There, she placed a large stone in her coat pocket and walked or jumped into the river, where she drowned.

TO THE LIGHTHOUSE IN CONTEXT

To the Lighthouse (1927), one of Woolf's most experimental works, unfolds according to the conscious-nesses of the characters. Woolf devotes more than half the novel to the events of a single afternoon and a few dozen pages to the events of the following ten years. Compared with the plot-driven novels standard in the Victorian era, *To the Lighthouse* has little in the way of obvious action. Almost all of the events of the novel take place in the characters' minds.

Woolf conceived of *To the Lighthouse* as partly autobiographical. She drew on memories from her childhood when creating characterization and plot. In her diary, Woolf wrote that she wanted to call the book an elegy rather than a novel. She thought of *To the Lighthouse* as a memory piece about the past, specifically about deceased members of her family such as her mother, father, brother Thoby, and half-sister Stella. Woolf, concerned that the work might be "sentimental," experimented with fresh tech-niques that would distance her from the emotion she felt when, for example, a family member died. The story of *To the Lighthouse* came to her quickly. She decided that the first segment would deal with one day in the life of a family of eight children, like the one in which she grew up. The father would be bril-liant, tyrannical, and dependent on his wife's care—like Woolf's father. The mother would be beautiful and sensitive to the needs of others—like Woolf's mother. From the year of Woolf's birth to the year before her mother's death, the Stephen family had spent all of their summers in Talland House in Corn-wall. A similar summerhouse is the setting for most of *To The Lighthouse*.

TO THE LIGHTHOUSE: KEY FACTS

Time and place written: 1926; London	
Date of first publication: 1927	
Publisher: Hogarth Press	
Type of work: Novel	
Genre: Modern novel	
Language: English	
Setting (time): The years immediately preceding and following World War I	
Setting (place): The Isle of Skye, in the Hebrides (a group of islands west of Scotland)	
Tense: Past	
Tone: Elegiac, poetic, rhythmic	
Narrator: An anonymous, omniscient narrator in the third person	
Point of view: Varies	
Protagonist: Mrs. Ramsay, Lily Briscoe	
Antagonist: The chaos of life	

TO THE LIGHTHOUSE: PLOT OVERVIEW

"The Window" opens just before the start of World War I. Mr. Ramsay and Mrs. Ramsay bring their eight children to their summerhouse in the Hebrides. Six-year-old James Ramsay desperately wants to go to the lighthouse across the bay, and Mrs. Ramsay promises they will go the next day if the weather permits. Mr. Ramsay tells James coldly that the weather will be bad. James believes his father enjoys being cruel to James and his siblings.

The Ramsays host a number of guests at their summerhouse, including the dour Charles Tansley, who admires Mr. Ramsay's work as a metaphysical philosopher. Another guest is Lily Briscoe, a young painter who begins a portrait of Mrs. Ramsay. Mrs. Ramsay wants Lily to marry William Bankes, an old friend of the Ramsays, but Lily resolves to remain single. Mrs. Ramsay schemes to create a romance between Paul Rayley and Minta Doyle, two of her acquaintances.

During the afternoon, Paul proposes to Minta, Lily begins her painting, Mrs. Ramsay soothes the resentful James, and Mr. Ramsay frets over his shortcomings as a philosopher, periodically turning to Mrs. Ramsay for comfort. That evening, the Ramsays host a dinner party. Paul and Minta are late return-ing from their walk on the beach with two of the Ramsay children. Lily bristles at the outspoken comments of Charles Tansley, who suggests that women can neither paint nor write. Mr. Ramsay reacts rudely when Augustus Carmichael, a poet, asks for a second plate of soup. As the night draws on, however, these awkward moments smooth over.

As Mrs. Ramsay leaves her guests in the dining room, she reflects that the event has already slipped into the past. Later, she joins her husband in the parlor. Mrs. Ramsay can tell that her husband wants her to declare her love for him. Mrs. Ramsay is not one to make such pronouncements, but she tells him he was right earlier—the weather will be too rough for a trip to the lighthouse the next day. Mr. Ramsay takes these words as a declaration of love.

The "Time Passes" segment beings, and the narration speeds up. War breaks out across Europe. Mrs. Ramsay dies suddenly one night. Andrew Ramsay, the oldest Ramsay son, is killed in battle. His sister Prue dies from an illness related to childbirth. The family no longer vacations at its summerhouse, which falls into a state of disrepair. Weeds take over the garden, and spiders nest in the house. Ten years pass before the family returns. Mrs. McNab, the housekeeper, and a few other women set the house in order.

In "The Lighthouse" segment, the narration returns to its original pace. Lily Briscoe comes to the summerhouse. Mr. Ramsay declares that he, James, and his daughter Cam will journey to the lighthouse. On the morning of the voyage, delays irk him. He appeals to Lily for sympathy. Lily realizes it is women's social duty to soothe men, but she has a difficult time comforting Mr. Ramsay. The Ramsays set off for the lighthouse, and Lily takes her place on the lawn, determined to complete the painting she abandoned on her last visit. James and Cam bristle at their father's bluster and self-pity. Still, as the boat reaches its destination, they feel a fondness for him. When Mr. Ramsay praises James, James feels happy despite himself. Across the bay, Lily puts the finishing touch on her painting. Finally having achieved her vision, she puts down her brush.

CHARACTERS IN *TO THE LIGHTHOUSE*

William Bankes A botanist and old friend of the Ramsays. Bankes is a kind, mellow man. He and Lily do not marry, as Mrs. Ramsay hoped they would, but they are close friends.

Lily Briscoe A young, single painter. Like Mr. Ramsay, Lily is plagued by fears that her work lacks worth. She does not wish to marry, a position that shocks conventional people.

Augustus Carmichael A poet. Carmichael, an opium user, languishes in literary obscurity until his verse becomes popular during the war.

Minta Doyle A flighty young woman. Because of Mrs. Ramsay's machinations, Minta marries Paul Rayley.

Mrs. McNab An elderly woman. Mrs. McNab restores the Ramsays' house after they abandon it for ten years.

Macalister A fisherman. Macalister accompanies the Ramsays to the lighthouse, telling Mr. Ramsay stories of shipwrecks and maritime adventure, and complimenting James on his handling of the boat.

Andrew Ramsay The oldest of the Ramsay sons. Andrew is a competent, independent young man.

Cam Ramsay One of the Ramsay daughters. Cam is torn between loyalty to James and to her father.

James Ramsay The Ramsays' youngest son. James loves his mother deeply and hates his father, with whom he must compete for Mrs. Ramsay's love. By the end of the novel, James has grown into a willful and moody young man who has much in common with his father.

Jasper Ramsay One of the Ramsay sons. Jasper enjoys shooting birds.

Mr. Ramsay Mrs. Ramsay's husband. Mr. Ramsay, a prominent metaphysical philosopher, loves his family but bullies them. His personal and professional anxieties make him selfish and harsh.

Mrs. Ramsay Mr. Ramsay's wife. A beautiful and loving woman, Mrs. Ramsay takes pride in being a wonderful hostess. She lavishes special attention on her male guests, whom she believes have delicate egos and need constant support and sympathy. A dutiful and loving wife, she struggles to accommodate her husband's difficult moods and selfishness.

Nancy Ramsay One of the Ramsays' daughters. Nancy accompanies Paul Rayley and Minta Doyle on their trip to the beach. Like her brother Roger, Nancy is adventurous.

Prue Ramsay The oldest Ramsay girl. Prue, a beautiful young woman, dies in childbirth.

Roger Ramsay One of the Ramsays' sons. Roger is wild and adventurous, like his sister Nancy.

Rose Ramsay One of the Ramsays' daughters. Rose has a talent for generating beauty. She arranges the fruit for her mother's dinner party and picks out her mother's jewelry.

Paul Rayley A young friend of the Ramsays. Paul is a kind, impressionable young man who follows Mrs. Ramsay's wishes and proposes to Minta Doyle.

Charles Tansley A young philosopher and pupil of Mr. Ramsay. Tansley is a prickly, unpleasant, insecure man. He often insults other people, particularly women such as Lily, whose talent and accomplishments worry him.

THEMES IN *TO THE LIGHTHOUSE*

THE TRANSIENCE OF LIFE AND WORK   Mr. Ramsay relies on his intellect, while Mrs. Ramsay depends on her emotions. But they dread mortality with equal passion. Mr. Ramsay reflects that even the most enduring of reputations, such as Shakespeare's, are doomed to eventual oblivion. Mrs. Ramsay's mind seizes on the lack of "reason, order, justice" in the world. She realizes that happiness is fleeting and ephemeral, and her awareness of death makes these rare happy moments precious to her. Unlike Mr. Ramsay, Mrs. Ramsay is able to move beyond the "treacheries" of the world by accepting their existence. Mr. Ramsay is so mired in the horror of his own mortality that he is rendered helpless and dependent upon his wife.

ART AS A MEANS OF PRESERVATION   Mr. Ramsay, Mrs. Ramsay, and Lily Briscoe make three distinct attempts to harness the chaos of life and make it meaningful. Mr. Ramsay's attempt is intellectual; Mrs. Ramsay's, social; and Lily's, artistic. Only Lily's attempt succeeds. Mr. Ramsay fails to progress to the end of human thought, that elusive letter Z that he believes represents the ultimate knowledge of life. Mrs. Ramsay, although she succeeds in fashioning graceful moments out of small ones, does not create anything lasting. Only Lily's attempt at artistic order succeeds, and it does so with grace and power. Lily has a "vision" that enables her to bring the separate, conflicting objects of her composition—"hedges and houses and mothers and children"—into harmony. This synthesizing impulse balances the narrative fragmentation of the novel as well as the competing worldviews of the characters. Lily's painting represents a single instant lifted out of the flow of time and made permanent. Art is the only hope of permanence in a world destined to change. Lily reflects that "nothing stays, all changes; but not words, not paint."

THE SUBJECTIVE NATURE OF REALITY   Toward the end of the novel, Lily reflects that in order to see Mrs. Ramsay clearly—to understand her character completely—she would need at least fifty pairs of eyes. The truth, Woolf suggests, lies in the accumulation of different, even opposing perspective. Following this precept, Woolf narrates her novel through multiple pairs of eyes, creating a portrait of the world that consists of the various private perceptions of her characters. To try to imagine *To the Lighthouse* told from a single character's perspective or—in the tradition of the Victorian novelists—from the author's perspective is to realize the radical scope and difficulty of Woolf's project.

SYMBOLS IN *TO THE LIGHTHOUSE*

THE LIGHTHOUSE   The lighthouse, which means something different and intimately personal to each character, is inaccessible, illuminating, and infinitely interpretable. It symbolizes the irreducible complexity of life. James concludes that the lighthouse can be two contradictory things at once—both a relic of his childhood fantasy and a stark, somewhat banal structure. He realizes that the lighthouse, like everything in life, is not dominated by one meaning. The world cannot be reduced or simplified. Contradictory meanings exist everywhere, and they are all correct.

THE SEA   Broadly, the ever-changing, ever-moving waves symbolize the constant forward movement of time and the changes it brings. Woolf describes the sea lovingly and beautifully, but her most evocative depictions of it point to its violence. As a force that destroys, has the power to decimate islands, and, as

Mr. Ramsay reflects, "eats away the ground we stand on," the sea symbolizes the impermanence and delicacy of human life and accomplishments.

IMPORTANT QUOTATIONS FROM *TO THE LIGHTHOUSE*

It partook . . . of eternity . . . there is a coherence in things, a stability; something, she meant, is immune from change, and shines out (she glanced at the window with its ripple of reflected lights) in the face of the flowing, the fleeting, the spectral, like a ruby; so that again tonight she had the feeling she had had once today, already, of peace, of rest. Of such moments, she thought, the thing is made that endures.

Location: "The Window," Chapter XVII
Speaker: The narrator
Context: Mrs. Ramsay reflects on the meaning of her successful dinner party

Mrs. Ramsay's dinner party is a microcosm of the novel, paralleling the novel's movement from chaos to order, from obscurity to clarity. The dinner party begins badly. Not all of the guests have arrived, Charles Tansley makes hostile comments to Lily, and Augustus Carmichael offends Mr. Ramsay. But as darkness descends outside and the candles are lit, the evening rights itself. Everyone is content. Mrs. Ramsay hopes that the rare, peaceful moment will survive permanently in the minds of her guests. However, by the end of the novel, it is clear that such moments are beautiful but not permanent. They do not endure, as Mrs. Ramsay hopes. Art, not lovely dinner parties, is what lasts.

The Lighthouse was then a silvery, misty-looking tower with a yellow eye, that opened suddenly, and softly in the evening. Now—James looked at the Lighthouse. He could see the white-washed rocks; the tower, stark and straight; he could see that it was barred with black and white; he could see windows in it; he could even see washing spread on the rocks to dry. So that was the Lighthouse, was it?

No, the other was also the Lighthouse. For nothing was simply one thing. The other Lighthouse was true too.

Location: "The Lighthouse," Chapter VIII
Speaker: The narrator
Context: James struggles to understand the lighthouse

As the Ramsays' boat approaches the lighthouse, James reflects on images of the edifice that are competing in his mind. The first is from his childhood, when the lighthouse looked to him like a "silvery, misty-looking tower." The second image, formed as he sails closer, is stripped of shadows and romance. The lighthouse now looks hard, plain, and real, a prosaic structure surrounded by laundry. James's first inclination is to banish one of these pictures from his mind and grant the other sovereignty, but he corrects himself, realizing that the lighthouse is both what it was then and what it is now. James forces himself to gather the competing images of the lighthouse into one truth. This challenge is the same one that Lily faces at the end of the novel, when she must reconcile her competing feelings of adoration and disenchantment with Mrs. Ramsay. Woolf applauds James's and Lily's willingness to face the complex, even contradictory, nature of all things.

Who shall blame him? Who will not secretly rejoice when the hero puts his armour off, and halts by the window and gazes at his wife and son, who, very distant at first, gradually come closer and closer, till lips and book and head are clearly before him, though still lovely and unfamiliar from the intensity of his isolation and the waste of ages and the perishing of the stars, and finally putting his pipe in his pocket and bending his magnificent head before her—who will blame him if he does homage to the beauty of the world?

Location: "The Window," Chapter VI
Speaker: The narrator
Context: Mr. Ramsay strolls across the lawn and catches sight of Mrs. Ramsay and James

---

Could loving, as people called it, make her and Mrs. Ramsay one? for it was not knowledge but unity that she desired, not inscriptions on tablets, nothing that could be written in any language known to men, but intimacy itself, which is knowledge, she had thought, leaning her head on Mrs. Ramsay's knee.

Location: "The Window," Chapter IX
Speaker: The narrator
Context: Lily thinks about love and knowledge

[S]he could not say it.. . . [A]s she looked at him she began to smile, for though she had not said a word, he knew, of course he knew, that she loved him. He could not deny it. And smiling she looked out of the window and said (thinking to herself, Nothing on earth can equal this happiness)—
"Yes, you were right. It's going to be wet tomorrow. You won't be able to go." And she looked at him smiling. For she had triumphed again. She had not said it: yet he knew.

Location: "The Window," Chapter XIX
Speaker: The narrator
Context: Mrs. Ramsey conveys her love for her husband without actually articulating it

THE ADVENTURES OF TOM SAWYER

Mark Twain

Two boys growing up in Missouri have a variety of adventures, thwart a murderer, and find gold.

THE LIFE OF MARK TWAIN

Mark Twain was born Samuel Langhorne Clemens in Florida, Missouri, in 1835. At the age of four, he moved with his family to Hannibal, a town on the Mississippi River. Twain's father was a prosperous man who owned a number of household slaves. He died when Twain was twelve. Twain left school and worked as a printer, finding work in numerous American cities, including New York and Philadelphia. In his early twenties, Clemens found work on the Mississippi riverboats. Eventually, he became a riverboat pilot. The river inspired his pen name; "Mark Twain" means a river depth of two fathoms. Life on the river also gave Twain material for several of his novels, including the raft scenes of *The Adventures of Huckleberry Finn*.

During the Civil War, Twain joined a Confederate cavalry division. His division deserted en masse, and Twain made his way west with his brother, working first as a silver miner in Nevada and then as a journalist. In 1863, he began signing articles with the name Mark Twain. Twain's writing—articles, stories, memoirs, and novels characterized by unique humor and a deft ear for language—made Twain incredibly famous. In 1876, *The Adventures of Tom Sawyer* was published to wild national acclaim, cementing Twain's position as a behemoth of American literature. Book sales made him wealthy enough to build a large house in Hartford, Connecticut, for himself and his wife Olivia, whom he had married in 1870.

In the early 1880s, the hopefulness of the post–Civil War years began to fade. Reconstruction, the political program designed to reintegrate the defeated South into the Union, was failing. Southern states and individuals oppressed the black men and women that the war had freed.

Meanwhile, Clemens's personal life began to collapse. His wife was sickly, and the couple's first son died when he was nineteen months old. Because of an investment gone wrong, Clemens found himself mired in debilitating debt. As his fortune dwindled, he continued to write. Drawing on his personal plight and the troubles of nation, he finished a draft of his masterpiece, *The Adventures of Huckleberry Finn*, in 1883. In 1884, when it was published, the novel met with great public and critical acclaim.

Over the next ten years, Clemens continued to write. He published two more popular novels, *A Connecticut Yankee in King Arthur's Court* (1889) and *Pudd'nhead Wilson* (1894). After that, he went into an artistic decline and never again published work up to the standards of *Huck Finn* or even *Pudd'nhead*. His finances burdened him, and his wife and two daughters died over the course of a few years. Clemens's writing from this period until the end of his life reflects depression and righteous rage at the injustices of the world. Despite his feelings of alienation, Twain's literary reputation was stellar, and he was in continual demand as a public speaker until his death in 1910.

THE ADVENTURES OF TOM SAWYER IN CONTEXT

While *The Adventures of Tom Sawyer* retains some of the fragmented, episodic qualities of Twain's earlier, shorter pieces, the novel is a significant literary departure for Twain. *The Adventures of Tom Sawyer* tones down the large-scale social satire that characterized many of Twain's earlier works, instead chronicling the development of one character.

Twain based *The Adventures of Tom Sawyer* largely on his boyhood in Hannibal in the 1840s. In his preface to the novel, he states, "[m]ost of the adventures recorded in this book really occurred," and calls Tom Sawyer "a combination . . . of three boys whom I knew." Indeed, nearly every figure in the novel comes from the young Twain's village experience: Aunt Polly shares many characteristics with Twain's mother, Mary is based on Twain's sister Pamela, and Sid resembles Twain's younger brother, Henry.

Huck Finn, the Widow Douglas, and even Injun Joe also have real-life counterparts, although the actual Injun Joe was a harmless drunk.

Unlike Twain's later masterpiece, *The Adventures of Huckleberry Finn*, *The Adventures of Tom Sawyer* is mostly concerned with painting an idyllic picture of life along the Mississippi River. Though Twain satirizes adult conventions throughout the novel, he does not touch certain difficult issues broached in *The Adventures of Huckleberry Finn*: racism, slavery, and xenophobia, for example. Because it avoids these issues, the novel has largely escaped the controversy over race and language that has surrounded *The Adventures of Huckleberry Finn* in the twentieth and twenty-first centuries.

THE ADVENTURES OF TOM SAWYER: KEY FACTS

Time and place written: 1874–1875; Hartford, Connecticut	
Date of first publication: 1876	
Publisher: Chatto and Windus (England), American Publishing Company (America)	
Type of work: Novel	
Genre: Bildungsroman; picaresque; frontier literature	
Language: English	
Setting (time): Not specified, but probably around 1845	
Setting (place): The fictional town of St. Petersburg, Missouri	
Tense: Past	
Tone: Satirical, nostalgic	
Narrator: Anonymous adult in the third-person	
Point of view: The narrator's	
Protagonist: Tom Sawyer	
Antagonist: Injun Joe	

THE ADVENTURES OF TOM SAWYER: PLOT OVERVIEW

An imaginative and mischievous boy named Tom Sawyer lives with his Aunt Polly and his half-brother, Sid, in the Mississippi River town of St. Petersburg, Missouri. After playing hooky from school and dirtying his clothes in a fight, Tom is made to whitewash the fence as punishment. He tricks his friends into giving him small treasures for the privilege of doing his work. He trades these treasures for tickets given out in Sunday school for memorizing Bible verses and uses the tickets to claim a Bible as a prize. He loses face when he incorrectly states that the first two disciples were David and Goliath.

Tom falls in love with Becky Thatcher, a new girl in town, and persuades her to get engaged to him. Their romance collapses when Becky learns that Tom has been engaged before, to a girl named Amy Lawrence. One night, Tom accompanies Huckleberry Finn, the son of the town drunk, to the graveyard to try out a cure for warts. At the graveyard, they see the Native American "half-breed" Injun Joe murder young Dr. Robinson. Scared, Tom and Huck run away and swear a blood oath not to tell anyone what they have seen. Injun Joe blames his companion, Muff Potter, a hapless drunk, for the crime. Potter is wrongfully arrested, and Tom feels guilty.

Tom, Huck, and Tom's friend Joe Harper run away to an island to become pirates. On the island, they realize that the community is searching the river for their bodies. Tom sneaks back home one night to observe the commotion. After a brief moment of remorse at the suffering of his loved ones, Tom is struck by the idea of appearing at his funeral and surprising everyone. He persuades Joe and Huck to do the same. Their return is met with great rejoicing, and they become the envy of their friends.

Tom wins back Becky's affection. Muff Potter's trial begins, and Tom, overcome by guilt, testifies against Injun Joe. Potter is acquitted, but Injun Joe flees the courtroom through a window. Summer arrives, and Tom and Huck go hunting for buried treasure in a haunted house. Venturing upstairs, they hear a noise below. Peering through holes in the floor, they see Injun Joe enter the house disguised as a deaf, mute Spaniard. He and his companion, an unkempt man, plan to bury some stolen treasure of their own. By an amazing coincidence, Injun Joe and his partner find a buried box of gold themselves. When they see Tom and Huck's tools, they become suspicious that someone is sharing their hiding place and carry off the gold instead of reburying it.

Huck shadows Injun Joe every night, watching for an opportunity to nab the gold. Tom goes on a picnic to McDougal's Cave with Becky and their classmates. That night, Huck hears Injun Joe and his partner making plans to attack the Widow Douglas, a kind resident of St. Petersburg. By running to fetch help, Huck forestalls the violence and becomes an anonymous hero.

Tom and Becky get lost in the cave. The next morning, their absence is noticed, and the men of the town search for them. Tom and Becky run out of food and candles, and begin to weaken. Tom, looking for a way out of the cave, happens upon Injun Joe, who is using the cave as a hideout. Eventually, just as the searchers are giving up, Tom finds a way out. The town celebrates. Becky's father, Judge Thatcher, locks up the cave. Injun Joe, trapped inside, starves to death.

A week later, Tom takes Huck to the cave and they find the gold, which is invested for them. The Widow Douglas adopts Huck. Huck attempts to escape civilized life, but Tom promises him that if he returns to the widow, he can join Tom's robber band. Reluctantly, Huck agrees.

CHARACTERS IN *THE ADVENTURES OF TOM SAWYER*

Mr. Dobbins The schoolmaster. Mr. Dobbins's ambition to become a doctor has been thwarted. He is a heavy drinker and the butt of schoolboy pranks.

Huckleberry Finn The son of the town drunk. Respectable society shuns Huck, but local boys adore him. Like Tom, Huck is highly superstitious and adventurous.

Joe Harper Tom's "bosom friend" and frequent playmate. As the novel progresses, Huck assumes Joe's place as Tom's companion.

Jim Aunt Polly's young slave.

Injun Joe A violent, villainous man. Half Native American and half Caucasian, Injun Joe has been excluded by society and commits crimes because he wants revenge.

Mr. Jones A Welshman who lives with his sons near the Widow Douglas's house. Mr. Jones treats Huck kindly.

Amy Lawrence Tom's former love. Tom abandons Amy when Becky Thatcher comes to town.

Mary Tom's sweet, almost saintly cousin. Mary has a soft spot for Tom.

Aunt Polly Tom's aunt and guardian. Aunt Polly is a simple, kindhearted woman who struggles to balance her love for her nephew with her duty to discipline him.

Muff Potter A hapless drunk and friend of Injun Joe. Potter is kind and grateful to Tom and Huck, who bring him presents after he is wrongly jailed for Dr. Robinson's murder.

Dr. Robinson A respected local physician. On the night of his murder, Dr. Robinson hires Injun Joe and Muff Potter to dig up Hoss Williams's grave so he can use the corpse for medical experiments.

Ben Rogers One of Tom's friends.

Tom Sawyer The novel's protagonist. Tom is mischievous and imaginative. He has a good heart and a strong moral conscience.

Sid Tom's half-brother. Sid is a goody-goody who enjoys getting Tom into trouble. He hides his mean-spiritedness with a show of good behavior.

Mr. Sprague The minister of the town church.

Alfred Temple A well-dressed new boy in town. Becky pretends to like Alfred in order to make Tom jealous.

Becky Thatcher Judge Thatcher's pretty, yellow-haired daughter. Naïve at first, Becky soon matches Tom as a romantic strategist.

Judge Thatcher Becky's father and the county judge. A local celebrity, Judge Thatcher inspires the respect of the townspeople and takes responsibility for community issues.

Mr. Walters The Sunday school superintendent.

Widow Douglas A kindhearted, pious resident of St. Petersburg.

THEMES IN *THE ADVENTURES OF TOM SAWYER*

SOCIETY'S HYPOCRISY   Twain satirizes the hypocrisy—and often the essential childishness—of public opinion and social institutions such as school, church, and the law. He suggests that society is often dangerously indulgent. Parents like Aunt Polly, for example, might attempt to restrain and punish their children, but in the end they always go soft. The community in general is too quick to forgive. In its relief that Tom and his friends are safe, it ignores their bad behavior and fails to prevent them from behaving more dangerously in the future. The community also forgives the villainous Injun Joe after his death for no better reason than sentimentality.

SOCIETY'S TOLERANCE   Even though St. Petersburg is an insular community in which outsiders are easily identified, it is also a tolerant one. The people of St. Petersburg endure Muff Potter, a drunken but harmless rascal. They protect Huck, a motherless boy whose drunken father has more or less abandoned him. They completely exclude Injun Joe from the community, but they manage to tolerate him in some sense after his death, when they manipulate his memory to weave him into the fabric of St. Petersburg lore.

SUPERSTITION IN AN UNCERTAIN WORLD   Superstition informs most of Huck's and Tom's decisions. Conveniently, the boys have so many superstitious beliefs, and these beliefs are so endlessly interpretable, that Tom and Huck can pick and choose whichever belief suits their needs at a given moment. The humorousness of the boys' obsession with witches, ghosts, and graveyards masks, to some extent, the real horror of the what the boys witness and experience: grave digging, murder, starvation, and attempted mutilation. The boys negotiate these terrifying experiences by existing in a world suspended somewhere between reality and make-believe. Their fear of death is real and pervasive, but they do not really understand death and all of its ramifications.

SYMBOLS IN *THE ADVENTURES OF TOM SAWYER*

THE STORM   The storm on Jackson's Island symbolizes the dangerousness of the boys' removal from society. It is part of an interruptive pattern in the novel, in which periods of relative peace and tranquility alternate with episodes of high adventure or danger. Later, when Tom is sick, he believes that God directed the storm at him personally. The storm thus becomes an external symbol of Tom's conscience.

THE VILLAGE   Many readers have interpreted the small village of St. Petersburg as a microcosm of the United States or of society in general. All major social institutions are present on a small scale in the village, and all are susceptible to Twain's comic treatment.

IMPORTANT QUOTATIONS FROM *THE ADVENTURES OF TOM SAWYER*

I ain't doing my duty by that boy, and that's the Lord's truth, goodness knows. Spare the rod and spile the child, as the Good Book says. I'm a-laying up sin and suffering for us both, I know. He's full of the Old Scratch, but laws-a-me! he's my own dead sister's boy, poor thing, and I ain't got the heart to lash him, somehow. Every time I let him off, my conscience does hurt me so, and every time I hit him my old heart most breaks.

Location: Chapter 1
Speaker: Aunt Polly
Context: Tom has escaped his aunt's wrath once again

Aunt Polly's mixture of amusement and frustration at Tom's antics is characteristic of her good humor. She attempts to discipline Tom because she feels it is her duty to keep him in line, not because his bad behavior makes her angry. In fact, she often seems to admire Tom's cleverness and vivacity.

In addition to its distinctive idiom and accent, Aunt Polly's speech is peppered with clichés and folk wisdom, mixing Scripture and local sayings. Such faithful re-creation of regional dialects is a distinctive element of Twain's fiction. Twain studied the speech of his local Missouri community and experimented with different ways of rendering it in writing. He closely attended to the internal variations in speech even within such a small town as Hannibal (rendered in his fiction as St. Petersburg), capturing the differences between the language of rich and poor, black and white.

Tom was a glittering hero once more — the pet of the old, the envy of the young. His name even went into immortal print, for the village paper magnified him. There were some that believed he would be President, yet, if he escaped hanging.

Location: Chapter 24
Speaker: The narrator
Context: Tom has testified against Injun Joe

The community's assessment of Tom implicitly acknowledges the close relationship between misbehavior and heroism. If Tom had not sneaked out to carouse in the cemetery with Huck, he would not have been present to witness Dr. Robinson's murder, and consequently he would not have been able to clear Muff's name. Tom's behavior is risky and officially unacceptable, but it puts him in a position to do real good. The extremity of Tom's character will certainly lead either to greatness or to ignominy; as some say, Tom will either become president or hang.

"Oh come, now, you don't mean to let on that you like it?"

The brush continued to move.

"Like it? Well I don't see why I oughtn't to like it. Does a boy get a chance to whitewash a fence every day?"

That put the thing in a new light. Ben stopped nibbling his apple. Tom swept his brush daintily back and forth — stepped back to note the effect — added a touch here and there — criticized the effect again — Ben watching every move and getting more and more interested, more and more absorbed. Presently he said: "Say, Tom, let me whitewash a little."

Location: Chapter 2
Speaker: The narrator
Context: Ben Rogers watches Tom whitewash the fence, a task he has been assigned to do as punishment

---

Mr. Walters fell to "showing off," with all sorts of official bustlings and activities.. . . . The librarian "showed off" — running hither and thither with his arms full of books.. . . The young lady teachers "showed off".. .. .. The young gentlemen teachers "showed off".. . . The little girls "showed off" in various ways, and the little boys "showed off" with such diligence that the air was thick with paper wads and the murmur of scufflings. And above it all the great man sat and beamed a majestic judicial smile upon all the house, and warmed himself in the sun of his own grandeur — for he was "showing off," too.

Location: Chapter 4
Speaker: The narrator
Context: Twain gently satirizes the universal human desire to impress

---

Huck Finn's wealth and the fact that he was now under the Widow Douglas's protection introduced him into society — no, dragged him into it, hurled him into it — and his sufferings were almost more than he could bear. The widow's servants kept him clean and neat, combed and brushed.. . . He had to eat with knife and fork; he had to use napkin, cup, and plate; he had to learn his book, he had to go to church; he had to talk so properly that speech was become insipid in his mouth; whithersoever he turned, the bars and shackles of civilization shut him in and bound him hand and foot.

Location: Chapter 35
Speaker: The narrator
Context: Huck chafes under the civilized ideas of the Widow Douglas

THE TURN OF THE SCREW

Henry James

A governess believes that the children in her care are in league with two ghosts.

THE LIFE OF HENRY JAMES

Henry James was born into a wealthy New York family in 1843. His father was a scholar of philosophy and was friends with such luminaries as Henry David Thoreau and Ralph Waldo Emerson. His brother William James later became an eminent philosopher. James's childhood was spent traveling in Europe. James briefly enrolled in Harvard Law school, but withdrew to pursue a writing career. James frequently traveled to Europe before moving to Paris. In 1876, he moved to London in order to pursue writing opportunities.

Many of James's novels, among them *The American* (1877), *Daisy Miller* (1879), and *The Portrait of a Lady* (1881), describe the encounter between innocent, sometimes uncultured America and urbane, refined Europe. For several years, James attempted to become a playwright. He wrote twelve plays, but they were not well-received. James wrote many of his most celebrated novels later in his career, including *What Maisie Knew* (1897) and *The Turn of the Screw* (1898). His late works are considered his most masterful efforts. They include *The Wings of the Dove* (1902), *The Ambassadors* (1903), and *The Golden Bowl* (1904).

James also wrote travel narratives, articles, literary criticism, short stories, and introductions to his own novels. He is famous for the complexity of his prose, which resulted from his desire to capture the complexity of human thought and emotion.

James never married. His relationships with both men and women seem to have been asexual, although some scholars believe he was a homosexual. He died on February 28, 1916.

THE TURN OF THE SCREW IN CONTEXT

The Turn of the Screw has many characteristics of Gothic literature, such as an ominous atmosphere, an investigation of the gruesome aspects of human nature, and a challenge to the reader's ideas about reality. However, the novel is far more sophisticated than most Gothic tales. James is less concerned with creating the kind of dark, supernatural world popular in Gothic literature than he is with exploring the human capacity to do evil. He is also less explicit about the precise terms of his mystery than are many Gothic novelists. Perversities are hinted at but never fully explained. Sexual deviancy seethes through the narrative but is never examined head-on. James creates a psychological riddle by telling his story from the point of view of the unreliable, perhaps insane governess. *The Turn of the Screw* never solves its mystery for readers or reaches a moment of moral closure. Instead, it remains ambiguous to the last and endlessly interpretable.

THE TURN OF THE SCREW: KEY FACTS

Time and place written: 1897; London	
Date of first publication: 1898	
Publisher: Collier's Weekly magazine	
Type of work: Novella	
Genre: Gothic fiction; frame story; ghost story	
Language: English	
Setting (time): Late nineteenth century	

Setting (place): England, on the rural estate of Bly

Tense: Past

Narrator: The governess in the first person

Tone: Ominous, oppressive, mysterious

Point of view: The governess's

Protagonist: The governess

Antagonist: Either the governess or the ghosts that plague the governess

THE TURN OF THE SCREW: PLOT OVERVIEW

At a party one night, a man named Douglas speaks of his sister's governess. The governess died twenty years ago, but before she passed away she sent him a manuscript detailing her experiences with one family. Douglas explains that this governess, when she was a young woman, met a dashing young man who was the guardian of two young children, Flora and Miles. She agreed to become governess to these children, despite the man's admission that the previous governess had died and his condition that she never bother him about anything. The novella consists of the governess's manuscript, which Douglas reads aloud.

In Bly, England, the governess is greeted by Mrs. Grose, the housekeeper, and Flora, the most beautiful, charming child the governess has ever seen. Miles, who has been dismissed from school, is also incredibly beautiful and has a "fragrance of purity." The governess spends the summer enjoying the children's enchanting company and dreaming her employer. One evening, she sees a man looking at her from a tower. She returns to the house, where Mrs. Grose seems relieved to see her. The governess does not mention the man for fear of frightening Mrs. Grose.

One day, the governess sees the man again and describes him to Mrs. Grose, who says he sounds like Peter Quint, the master's deceased former valet. The governess believes Quint is after Miles. Mrs. Grose says Quint was "much too free" with Miles, whom he liked to play with and spoil. The governess resolves to protect the children from Quint's ghost and begins to watch them "in a stifled suspense."

One afternoon at the lake, the governess sees a woman dressed in black watching them from the other side of the lake. Flora seems not to see the figure, but the governess thinks she is pretending. The governess believes the figure was Miss Jessel, the children's former governess. Mrs. Grose tells the governess "there was everything between" Miss Jessel and Peter Quint, who "did what he wished with them all." The governess weeps and says the children are lost. Mrs. Grose says that Miles had an inappropriately close alliance with Peter Quint.

The governess occasionally sees the ghosts. One night she sees Flora staring out the window, face to face with the female ghost. She sneaks out of the room without disturbing Flora and sees a person standing in the tower and Miles standing outside on the lawn. The governess learns that Miles and Flora planned the whole night because Miles wanted the governess to think he was bad. The governess starts to believe that the children's unearthly beauty and unnatural goodness is a fraudulent game and that they are under the spell of the ghosts of Peter Quint and Miss Jessel. The governess feels that the children are aware of her thoughts about them and are watching her.

One day while strolling to church, Miles addresses the governess as "my dear" and asks when he is returning to school. He says he cannot be in a lady's company every hour even if she is a "jolly, perfect lady." The governess asks why he was bad on that night, and Miles says he merely wanted to show her that he could be, adding that he can do it again. Miles implies that he will persuade his uncle to visit and take charge of the situation.

The governess reluctantly decides to leave Bly immediately. She rushes to the schoolroom to collect her belongings, but she comes upon the ghost of Miss Jessel sitting at the table. The ghost stands and vanishes. The governess tells Mrs. Grose that Miss Jessel wants Flora to share the torments of the damned with her. The governess decides to write to her employer. That night, Miles says he has been thinking about the way she is bringing him up and "all the rest." He says she knows "what a boy wants." Miles says that she must tell his uncle everything and asks her to leave him alone.

The next morning, the children show special affection for the governess. The governess loses track of Flora. Before hurrying out to find her, she leaves her letter on a table for a servant to post. Mrs. Grose and the governess find Flora next to the lake. She smiles silently and strangely at them. The governess asks where Miss Jessel is. The governess suddenly points across the lake, where she sees Miss Jessel standing. Mrs. Grose sees nothing. Flora declares that she sees nothing and never has. She bursts into tears and throws herself into Mrs. Grose's arms, demanding to be taken away from the governess.

In the morning, Mrs. Grose reports that Flora has a high fever and worries that the governess will come after her. The governess orders Mrs. Grose to take Flora to London to her uncle. She hopes to win Miles over to her side. The housekeeper informs the governess that Flora has accused her of "things" — what things, she does not say. Mrs. Grose says that she still believes in the governess's sightings.

Mrs. Grose reports that the governess's letter to the children's uncle is missing and suggests that Miles took it. The governess resolves to get a confession out of him and save him. Mrs. Grose kisses her and says that she will save her even if Miles turns against her. At dinner, Miles accuses the governess of staying at Bly only because she wants him to tell her something. The governess admits that he is right and presses him to confess immediately. She asks if he took the letter. She springs forward to catch Miles, but stumbles when she sees Peter Quint glaring through the window behind him. Struggling with her fear, she resolves to prevent Miles from seeing him. He admits that he took the letter and read it because he wanted to know what she said about him.

The governess asks why he was expelled, and Miles confesses that he "said things" to "[t]hose [he] liked." The governess demands that he tell her exactly what he said. Miles tries to dart away, but the governess catches him. She shrieks at Quint while pressing the boy to her body. Miles asks if Peter Quint is there. The governess says Quint has lost him forever and tells Miles to look at the window. He jerks around but sees nothing. He cries out and falls. His heart has stopped beating.

CHARACTERS IN *THE TURN OF THE SCREW*

Douglas One of the holiday guests in the Prologue. Douglas reads the manuscript, which comprises the bulk of the novel. The governess, the author of the manuscript, was the governess of Douglas's sister.

Flora The orphaned eight-year-old niece of the governess's employer. Flora possesses an unearthly, angelic beauty.

The Governess The writer of the manuscript. As Flora's and Miles's twenty-year-old governess, she becomes convinced that she is seeing ghosts. It is possible that she kills Miles by suffocating him.

Mr. Griffin One of the holiday guests in the Prologue. His story about a boy visited by a ghost prompts Douglas to mention the governess's manuscript.

Mrs. Griffin One of the holiday guests in the Prologue. She suggests that Douglas was in love with the governess.

Mrs. Grose The housekeeper at Bly. It is implied that Mrs. Grose has feelings of a romantic nature for the governess. She professes to believe the governess's stories about the ghosts of Peter Quint and Miss Jessel.

Miss Jessel The children's deceased former governess. There are hints that Miss Jessel became pregnant by Peter Quint and that she might have drowned herself in the lake at Bly.

The Master The uncle of Flora and Miles, who are orphans. A dashing, charming man, the master asks the governess to assume complete responsibility for running Bly and to refrain from contacting him for any reason.

Miles The orphaned ten-year-old nephew of the governess's employer. Miles is expelled from school, perhaps because he engaged in homosexual conduct with some classmates or imparted inappropriate sexual knowledge to them. It is also implied that Quint either sexually molested Miles or gave him information about sex. Miles is an extraordinarily beautiful, clever child. He grows uncomfortable with the governess's attentions. It is possible that the governess smothers him to death.

The Narrator A member of the holiday gathering in the Prologue.

Peter Quint The deceased valet of the governess's employer. It is implied that Peter Quint impregnated Miss Jessel and had a close, perhaps sexual relationship with Miles. Peter Quint died after slipping and injuring his head on the roads near Bly.

THEMES IN *THE TURN OF THE SCREW*

THE TERROR OF THE UNRELIABLE NARRATOR *The Turn of the Screw* derives its atmosphere of horror primarily from its ambiguity. We must rely on the governess's version of events, but the governess is an unreliable narrator—isolated, fervent, and possibly mad. As she becomes increasingly convinced of her own uprightness and of the ghosts' evil, she seems less and less reasonable. Because the governess is an unreliable narrator, we cannot readily believe her interpretation of events and must ferret out meaning on our own. This necessity increases the terror of the story: instead of understanding one meaning provided by the author, we are free to consider multiple frightening meanings. We never find out definitively whether the governess is mad, whether Mrs. Grose truly believes in the visions the governess claims to see, whether Flora and Miles are actually conspiring with the ghosts of Peter Quint and Miss Jessel, whether Mrs. Grose is in league with the children and the demons, or whether the governess kills Miles. Furthermore, we are forced to imagine the details of Flora's and Miles's bad behavior, and of the characters' various deviant thoughts or possible sexual perversions, because the governess refuses to spell them out. Thus we become complicit in the moral crimes the governess thinks she observes.

THE POSSIBILITY OF PERVERSION Intimations of sexual perversion fill *The Turn of the Screw*, although James never confirms the suspicions he arouses. The governess falls in love with her employer and, unable to act on her feelings for him, displaces them onto his nephew, Miles. She grows obsessed with Miles. Miles, in turn, sometimes talks to his governess as an adult man would to his lover. It is possible that Miles was expelled from school because of homosexual activity with his classmates, and it is strongly hinted that he and Peter Quint had a homosexual relationship before Quint's death. The lake where the governess spots Miss Jessel is described in highly sexualized terms and almost explicitly likened to a vagina. As Flora plays on the banks of the lake, she inserts a "piece of wood" into a hole, consciously or unconsciously playing a sexualized game. The governess and Mrs. Grose are physically affectionate with each other, and the governess bullies Mrs. Grose as a domineering husband might his wife.

James makes these sexual combinations disturbing by merely hinting at them, as if suggesting that the truth about them is too horrible to face. He also leaves open the possibility that the governess is imagining perversion where none exists, perhaps because she is sexually repressed, perhaps because she is mad, or perhaps because she cannot acknowledge her own illicit longings and so projects them onto other people.

THE PRESENCE OF EVIL James explicitly connects Miles and Flora to Adam and Eve. Both pairs are innocent, both live in an idyllic place, and both are threatened by evil. However, the specific terms of the metaphor are debatable. The governess becomes convinced that evil, in the form of Quint and Miss Jessel, has corrupted the children, just as the snake corrupted Adam and Eve. But it is possible that the ghosts of Quint and Miss Jessel do not exist outside of the governess's maddened mind. In that case, the evil force that damages the children is the governess, who kills Miles just as the snake symbolically killed Adam, turning humans from immortal beings into mortal ones.

SYMBOLS IN *THE TURN OF THE SCREW*

THE SCREW The screw of James's title has several symbolic meanings. First, it suggests a thumbscrew used as an instrument of torture. Second, it refers to the piece of hardware which can be screwed into place. Finally, it suggests the slang expression "to screw," meaning to copulate. Each of these symbolic meanings are important to the novella, which is concerned with sexual repression and a demanding, deeply inquisitive governess.

THE GOVERNESS The governess symbolizes either savior or inquisitor. She fancies herself a spiritual savior to the children, believing that she has the power to save them from evil. In Chapter 17, she says, "'Dear little Miles . . . I just want you to help me to save you!'" These words take on a sinister meaning, however, if the governess is not a savior but a misguided inquisitor. The title of the novella suggests the thumbscrew, and many of the governess's questioning techniques remind us of an inquisitor's.

IMPORTANT QUOTATIONS FROM *THE TURN OF THE SCREW*

Here at present I felt afresh—for I had felt it again and again—how my equilibrium depended on the success of my rigid will, the will to shut my eyes as tight as possible to the truth that what I had to deal with was, revoltingly, against nature. I could only get on at all by taking "nature" into my confidence and my account, by treating my monstrous ordeal as a push in a direction unusual, of course, and unpleasant, but demanding after all, for a fair front, only another turn of the screw of ordinary human virtue.

Location: Chapter 22
Speaker: The governess
Context: The governess and Miles sit down to dinner

This passage exemplifies the governess's image of herself as a valiant moral crusader. She glories in her own strength and ability to handle a "monstrous ordeal." James leaves it to us to decide whether she is truly a crusader against evil or a crazed woman made dangerous by her unshakable self-confidence. The passage is also typical of the novella's multiple meanings and ambiguities. The governess refers to something disgustingly unnatural, which could mean any number of things. It could mean Miles's homosexuality, or Quint's homosexuality, or Quint's pedophilia, or the children's devilish natures, or the governess's lust for Miles.

"It's HE?"

I was so determined to have all my proof that I flashed into ice to challenge him. "Whom do you mean by 'he'?"

"Peter Quint—you devil!" His face gave again, round the room, its convulsed supplication. "WHERE?"

They are in my ears still, his supreme surrender of the name and his tribute to my devotion. "'What does he matter now, my own?—what will he EVER matter? I have you," I launched at the beast, "but he has lost you forever!" Then, for the demonstration of my work, "There, THERE!" I said to Miles.

Location: Chapter 24
Speaker: The governess
Context: Just before Miles's death, the governess believes she has won Miles back from Quint

The meaning of this disturbing scene changes drastically depending on whether we believe the governess or Miles. If we believe the governess, this encounter is the moment when Miles at last stops pretending to know nothing of ghosts. By speaking the name "Peter Quint," which he has never done before, he justifies the governess's suspicions and admits that he is conspiring with Quint's ghost. By capitulating to the governess and speaking Quint's name, Miles also gives up his allegiance with Quint's ghost and returns to his governess's protection. Perhaps he also returns her sexual love in some way or at least she thinks he does: "I have you . . . but he has lost you forever!" If we believe Miles, however, this encounter is terrifying proof of the governess's madness. He does not suspect that his governess thinks he has been conspiring with Quint's ghost, so her enraged questioning—"Whom do you mean by 'he'?"—is baffling.

I scarce know how to put my story into words that shall be a credible picture of my state of mind; but I was in these days literally able to find a joy in the extraordinary flight of heroism the occasion demanded of me. . . . I saw my response so strongly and so simply.

Location: Chapter 4
Speaker: The governess
Context: The governess has seen Quint for the first time

She had picked up a small flat piece of wood, which happened to have in it a little hole that had evidently suggested to her the idea of sticking in another fragment that might figure as a mast and make the thing a boat. This second morsel, as I watched her, she was very markedly and intently attempting to tighten in its place.

Location: Chapter 6
Speaker: The governess
Context: The governess has seen Miss Jessel across the lake, but Flora seems oblivious as she plays with the wood she has found

---

That she now saw—as she had not, I had satisfied myself, the previous time—was proved to me by the fact that she was disturbed neither by my reillumination nor by the haste I made to get into slippers and into a wrap. Hidden, protected, absorbed, she evidently rested on the sill—the casement opened forward—and gave herself up. There was a great still moon to help her, and this fact had counted in my quick decision. She was face to face with the apparition we had met at the lake, and could now communicate with it as she had not then been able to do.

Location: Chapter 10
Speaker: The governess
Context: The governess sees Flora communing with Miss Jessel

ULYSSES

James Joyce

Gripped by pride and insecurities, a man finds a spiritual father in someone who is exiled from home while his wife entertains her lover.

THE LIFE OF JAMES JOYCE

James Joyce was born on February 2, 1882, in Dublin, Ireland, into a Catholic middle-class family that soon became poverty-stricken because of its patriarch's financial irresponsibility. Despite this impoverishment, Joyce received the best education available to someone of his station. He attended Jesuit schools, followed by University College in Dublin, where he began publishing essays and writing lyric poetry. After graduating in 1902, Joyce went to Paris, where he devoted all of his time to writing poetry, stories, and theories of aesthetics. Joyce returned to Dublin the following year upon learning that his mother was seriously ill. After his mother's death, Joyce stayed in Dublin, where eventually he met his future wife, Nora Barnacle, a chambermaid at Finn's Hotel.

Nora and Joyce left Dublin in1904. They spent most of the next eleven years living in Rome and Trieste, Italy, where Joyce taught English. He and Nora had two children, Giorgio and Lucia. Joyce's first book of poems, *Chamber Music*, was published in 1907. In 1914, he published both a book of short stories, *Dubliners*, and a serialized autobiographical novel, *A Portrait of the Artist as a Young Man*.

Joyce began writing *Ulysses* in 1914. When World War I broke out, he moved his family to Zurich, Switzerland, where his fortunes improved. His talent attracted several wealthy patrons, including Harriet Shaw Weaver. He published *Portrait* in book form (1916), a play, *Exiles* (1918), and the first episodes of *Ulysses* in *The Little Review* (1918). In 1919, the Joyces moved back to Trieste, but in 1920, at Ezra Pound's urging, they moved to Paris. *Ulysses* was published in Paris in book form in 1922, causing an international scandal with its frank sexual content and revolutionary prose style. In 1923, with his eyesight quickly diminishing, Joyce began working on what became *Finnegans Wake* (1939). Joyce died in 1941.

ULYSSES IN CONTEXT

Initially conceived as a short story for *Dubliners*, *Ulysses* evolved into a long tome, a sequel to *A Portrait of the Artist as a Young Man*. It picks up Stephen Dedalus's life more than a year after he leaves for Paris at the end of *Portrait*. The novel introduces two other main characters, Leopold and Molly Bloom, and takes place in Dublin on a single day, June 16, 1904.

Ulysses achieves a new kind of realism by rendering the thoughts and actions of its main characters—both trivial and significant—in a scattered and fragmented form that strives to evoke the way thoughts, perceptions, and memories actually appear in our minds. At the same time, *Ulysses* also works on a mythic level through a series of parallels with Homer's *Odyssey*. Bloom, Molly, and Stephen correspond respectively to Odysseus (or Ulysses), his wife Penelope, and son Telemachus; each of the novel's eighteen episodes corresponds to an adventure from the *Odyssey*.

Ulysses has become particularly famous for Joyce's stylistic innovations and technical experimentation. In *Portrait*, Joyce worked with both interior monologue and evolving narrative styles—the narrative voice changes as Stephen matures. In *Ulysses*, Joyce uses interior monologue extensively; instead of employing one narrative voice, he radically shifts narrative style with each new episode of the novel. Its multivoiced narration, textual self-consciousness, mythic framework, and thematic focus on life in a modern metropolis situate *Ulysses* as a seminal modern work among texts such as *The Waste Land* (1922), T. S. Eliot's mythic poem, and *Mrs. Dalloway* (1925), Virginia Woolf's stream-of-consciousness novel. Joyce's final work, *Finnegans Wake*, bridges the gap between modernism and postmodernism. A novel only in the loosest sense, *Finnegans Wake* looks forward to postmodern texts in its playful celebration (rather than lamentation) of the fragmentation of experience and the decentered nature of identity, as well as in its examination of language as an unreliable medium.

Although Joyce, like many other modernists, wrote in self-imposed exile in urban Europe, his work is set in Ireland and is strongly tied to Irish political and cultural history. In 1922—the year *Ulysses* was published as a novel—Ireland finally gained independence from Britain after a bloody civil war. Several late nineteenth-century attempts to grant Ireland some political independence within Great Britain had failed—in part because of the downfall of the Irish MP Charles Stewart Parnell, who was publicly persecuted by the Irish church and the populace in 1889 for conducting a long-term adulterous affair with Kitty O'Shea. Joyce saw this persecution as a hypocritical betrayal of Ireland by the Irish.

ULYSSES: KEY FACTS

Time and place written: 1914–21; Trieste (Italy), Zurich, and Paris

Date of publication: 1922. Partially serialized in the U.S. journal *The Little Review* 1918–20

Publisher: Shakespeare & Company (Sylvia Beach's bookstore), Paris

Type of work: Novel

Genre: Modernist novel; quest novel

Language: English

Setting (time): June 16, 1904 (from 8:00 a.m. to approximately 3 a.m.)

Setting (place): Dublin and suburbs

Tense: Present

Tone, narrator, and point of view: Vary

Episodes 1–2: Anonymous third-person narrator

Episode 3: Stephen's interior monologue

Episodes 4–8: Anonymous third-person narrator

Episodes 9–11: Anonymous third-person narrator; self-conscious and playful

Episode 12: Anonymous first-person narrator; hyperbolic and belligerent

Episode 13: Anonymous third-person narrator, Gerty McDowell's interior monologue, and Bloom's interior monologue; sentimental

Episode 14: Series of narrators evoking prose styles of historical English authors in chronological order; tone varies, including pious, sensational, and satiric

Episode 15: Play-script

Episode 16: Anonymous third-person narrator; exhausted

Episode 17: Anonymous third-person narrator; objective and scientific

Episode 18: Molly's interior monologue

Protagonist: Stephen Dedalus, Leopold Bloom, Molly Bloom

Antagonist: Blazes Boylan; Molly's infidelity; Stephen's hyper–self-consciousness and inability to love

ULYSSES: PLOT OVERVIEW

PART I, EPISODE 1: TELEMACHUS 8 A.M.

Stephen Dedalus spends the early morning hours of June 16, 1904, resenting his mocking friend Buck Mulligan and Buck's English acquaintance, Haines. As Stephen leaves for work, Buck tells him to leave his house key and meet them at a pub at 12:30 p.m.

PART I, EPISODE 2: NESTOR 10 A.M.

Stephen teaches a history class at Garrett Deasy's boys' school. After class, Stephen receives his wages from Deasy, who narrow-mindedly lectures him on life. Stephen agrees to take Deasy's editorial letter about cattle disease to acquaintances at the newspaper.

PART I, EPISODE 3: PROTEUS 11 A.M.

Stephen walks alone on Sandymount Strand, thinking critically about perception and about recent events, including his time in Paris, and his mother's death. He composes a poem and jots it down on a scrap torn from Deasy's letter.

PART II, EPISODE 4: CALYPSO 8 A.M.

Leopold Bloom makes breakfast. He brings his wife her mail and breakfast in bed. One of her letters is from Molly's concert tour manager, Blazes Boylan—also Molly's lover—who will visit at four this afternoon. Downstairs, Bloom reads a letter from their daughter Milly, then goes to the outhouse.

PART II, EPISODE 5: LOTUS EATERS 10 A.M.

Bloom picks up a tepid love letter at the post office—he is corresponding with a Martha Clifford under the pseudonym Henry Flower. He ducks briefly into a church, then orders Molly's lotion from the pharmacist. He runs into Bantam Lyons, who misinterprets Bloom's comment and thinks that Bloom gives him a tip on the afternoon's Gold Cut horse race.

PART II, EPISODE 6: HADES 11 A.M.

Bloom feels out of place sharing a ride with Simon Dedalus (Stephen's father), Martin Cunningham, and Jack Power on the way to Paddy Dignam's funeral. At the funeral, Bloom thinks about the deaths of his son and his father.

PART II, EPISODE 7: AEOLUS 12 P.M.

Bloom negotiates a newspaper ad for Keyes, a liquor merchant, in the offices of the *Freeman*. Several men, including the editor, Myles Crawford, are idling in the office and discussing political speeches. Bloom leaves to secure the ad with Keyes. Stephen arrives with Deasy's letter. He and the other men leave for the pub just as Bloom is returning. On his way out, Crawford dismisses Bloom's ad negotiation.

PART II, EPISODE 8: LESTRYGONIANS 1 P.M.

Bloom runs into Josie Breen, an old flame. They discuss Mina Purefoy, who is giving birth at the hospital. Bloom stops in Burton's restaurant but decides to move on to Davy Byrne's for a light lunch. He remembers an intimate afternoon with Molly on Howth. On his way to the National Library, Bloom spots Boylan on the street and hides in the National Museum.

PART II, EPISODE 9: SCYLLA AND CHARYBDIS 2 P.M.

In the National Library, Stephen talks to the poet A. E., the essayist John Eglinton, and two librarians. He explains to them his theory about Shakespeare, which he has come up with by inferring biographical information about Shakespeare from patterns in his plays. A. E. dismisses Stephen's theory and leaves. Buck enters and jokingly scolds Stephen for standing him and Haines up at the pub. On the way out, Buck and Stephen pass Bloom, who has come to obtain a copy of Keyes's ad.

PART II, EPISODE 10: SIRENS 4 P.M.

Simon Dedalus, Ben Dollard, Lenehan, and Blazes Boylan converge at the Ormond Hotel bar. Bloom has followed Boylan's car to the bar. Boylan soon leaves for his appointment with Molly. Bloom sits morosely in the Ormond restaurant, briefly mollified by Dedalus and Dollard's singing. Bloom writes a reply to Martha and leaves for the post office.

PART II, EPISODE 11: CYCLOPS 5 P.M.

Bloom arrives at Barney Kiernan's pub to meet Martin Cunningham about the Dignam family finances. The citizen, a belligerent Irish nationalist, becomes increasingly drunk and begins attacking Bloom for being Jewish. Bloom answers with an appeal for peace and love over xenophobia and violence. Cunningham's carriage carries Bloom away just as the altercation turns ugly.

PART II, EPISODE 12: NAUSICAA SUNSET

Having visited Mrs. Dignam, Bloom relaxes on Sandymount Strand. Gerty MacDowell notices Bloom watching her from across the beach. She reveals more of her legs while Bloom surreptitiously masturbates. Gerty leaves, and Bloom dozes.

PART II, EPISODE 13: OXEN OF THE SUN 10:00 P.M.

Bloom checks on Mina Purefoy at the maternity hospital, where Stephen and his medical student friends are drinking and joking about sex, pregnancy, and birth. Though Bloom disapproves of their revelry, he agrees to join them. Buck arrives, and everyone proceeds to Burke's pub. At closing time, Stephen convinces his friend Lynch to go to the brothels. Bloom follows, feeling protective.

PART II, EPISODE 14: CIRCE

Bloom finally locates Stephen and Lynch at Bella Cohen's brothel. Drunk, Stephen imagines that he sees the ghost of his mother; full of rage, he shatters a lamp with his walking stick. Bloom finds Stephen in an argument with a British soldier who knocks him out.

PART III, EPISODE 15: EUMAEUS

Bloom revives Stephen and takes him for coffee at a cabman's shelter to sober up. He invites Stephen back to his house.

PART III, EPISODE 16: ITHACA

Stephen and Bloom arrive at Bloom's house. They drink cocoa and talk about their lives. Bloom asks Stephen to stay the night. Stephen politely refuses. Bloom sees him out and comes back in to find evidence of Boylan's visit. Feeling peaceful nevertheless, Bloom climbs into bed, tells Molly about his day, and requests breakfast in bed the next morning.

PART III, EPISODE 17: PENELOPE

Surprised by Bloom's self-assurance, Molly stays up after Bloom falls asleep. Her mind wanders to her childhood in Gibraltar, her afternoon with Boylan, her singing career, Stephen Dedalus. Her interior monologue ends with memories of his marriage proposal at Howth, an unqualified positive affirmation.

CHARACTERS IN *ULYSSES*

LEOPOLD BLOOM AND FAMILY

Leopold Bloom, 38 One of the novel's protagonists; an advertising canvasser for the *Freeman*. Throughout the novel, Bloom's thoughts return to his wife Molly, her infidelity, and their dead son Rudy. Bloom's deep compassion and an extraordinary ability to empathize with many creatures—animals, blind men, women in labor—make him the novel's true and unironic hero. He was raised in Dublin by his Hungarian Jewish father Rudolph and his Irish Catholic mother Ellen.

Marion Bloom (Molly), 33 Leopold Bloom's wife; a professional singer. Plump, pretty, and flirtatious, Molly is clever and opinionated, if not well educated. Molly is impatient with Bloom, especially his refusal to sleep with her ever since the death of their son Rudy eleven years ago. She grew up in Gibraltar with her father, Major Brian Tweedy.

Millicent Bloom (Milly), 15 Molly and Leopold Bloom's daughter, who recently moved to Mullingar to study photography. Blond and pretty, Milly is dating Alec Bannon. She does not appear in *Ulysses*.

Rudy Bloom Leopold and Molly Bloom's dead son.

STEPHEN DEDALUS AND FAMILY

Boody, Dilly, Katey, and Maggy Dedalus Stephen's younger sisters, who struggle with running the household after their mother's death.

May Dedalus Stephen's dead mother; a devout Catholic. Despite her pleas, Stephen refused to pray on her deathbed and is now paralyzed by guilt.

Simon Dedalus Stephen's father. A good singer, Simon has driven the family to poverty through bad money management and heavy drinking. Stephen's sense that Simon Dedalus has failed him as a father precipitates Stephen's search for a spiritual father in Shakespeare and in Bloom.

Stephen Dedalus One of the novel's protagonists; an aspiring poet in his early twenties. Intelligent and extremely well read but profoundly lonely, Stephen struggles with insecurities and arrogance that make it impossible for him to commune with other people. He grew up devoutly Catholic and is crippled by guilt about his mother's recent death.

MORE DUBLINERS

A. E. (George Russell) A poet and, historically, the central figure of the Irish Literary Revival. Stephen disdains A. E.'s focus on national literature, as opposed to literature in general, but resents being ostracized from his literary circles.

Hugh "Blazes" Boylan Molly's well-liked, sleazy concert manager and lover.

Richard Best A National Library librarian, enthusiastic if not a visionary.

Edy Boardman Gerty MacDowell's friend, who is annoyed by Gerty's uppity demeanor.

Denis Breen Josie Breen's mentally unstable and paranoid husband.

Josie Breen, née Powell Bloom's former sweetheart. Josie has grown haggard taking care of her "dotty" husband Denis.

Cissy Caffrey Gerty MacDowell's close friend. A frank tomboy, Cissy babysits her brothers, Jacky and Tommy.

Jacky and Tommy Caffrey Cissy Caffrey's toddler brothers.

The Citizen An older Irish patriot. A former national athlete, the citizen is belligerent and xenophobic.

Martha Clifford A woman with whom Bloom corresponds under the pseudonym Henry Flower. Her letter is full of spelling mistakes and her innuendo is hackneyed.

Bella Cohen A large, conniving brothel madame. One of her customers pays her son's Oxford tuition.

Martin Cunningham A leader in Bloom's circle of casual friends. Martin Cunningham sticks up for Bloom but also treats him as an outsider.

Garrett Deasy Headmaster of the boy's school where Stephen teaches. A Protestant from the north, Deasy respects the English rule in Ireland. His overwrought letter to the editor of the *Freeman* to the editor about foot-and-mouth disease becomes an object of mockery.

Patrick Dignam (Paddy) Bloom's acquaintance, recently dead from drink. Bloom attends his funeral at 11 a.m.

Mrs. Dignam Paddy Dignam's wife, left poor after his death because he used his life insurance to pay off debts.

Patrick Dignam, Jr. Paddy Dignam's son.

Ben Dollard A down-and-out Dubliner with a superior bass voice.

John Eglinton An essayist who listens to Stephen's theory about Shakespeare with skepticism, affronted by Stephen's youthful self-confidence.

Haines An Englishman studying Irish culture at Oxford who has been staying with Buck and Stephen at the Martello tower. Often unwittingly condescending, Haines reminds Stephen of Britain's control of Ireland.

Zoe Higgins An outgoing prostitute at Bella Cohen's brothel.

Joe Hynes Freeman reporter who owes Bloom three pounds.

Richie Goulding Stephen's uncle (mother's brother). A law clerk, Richie suffers from a bad back.

Sara Goulding (Sally) Richie Goulding's wife.

Walter Goulding Richie and Sally Goulding's "skeweyed," stuttering son.

Corny Kelleher Undertaker's assistant.

Mina Kennedy A golden-haired barmaid at the Ormond Hotel bar.

Lydia Douce A bronze-haired barmaid at the Ormond Hotel bar. Miss Douce has a crush on Blazes Boylan.

Ned Lambert Simon Dedalus's jolly friend. Ned works in a seed and grain warehouse downtown.

Lenehan *Freeman* editor. Sceptre, Lenehan's tip for the Gold Cup horse race, loses.

Lynch Stephen's longtime medical student friend. Lynch often listens to Stephen's theorizing on aestheticism. He is seeing Kitty Ricketts.

Thomas W. Lyster National Library librarian; a Quaker.

Gerty MacDowell A young working-class woman whom Bloom glimpses on the beach. Lame because of a childhood accident, Gerty fastidiously attends to her clothing and personal beauty regimen.

John Henry Menton Solicitor who employed Paddy Dignam; Bloom's rival for Molly years ago.

Narrator of Episode 12 Currently a debt collector, he keeps up with city gossip.

City Councillor Nannetti MP and the *Freeman's* head printer.

J. J. O'Molloy An unemployed lawyer who futilely tries to borrow money from his friends.

Malachi Mulligan (Buck) Stephen's medical student friend and roommate at the Martello tower. Plump, well read, and well liked, Buck ridicules everything with bawdy humor. Stephen intensely resents Buck's ease with people and comfort with his life.

Jack Power Simon Dedalus's and Martin Cunningham's friend.

Kitty Ricketts Prostitute at Bella Cohen's brothel. Thin and well dressed, Kitty spends part of the day with Lynch.

Florry Talbot Prostitute at Bella Cohen's brothel. Florry is plump and slow.

THEMES IN *ULYSSES*

THE QUEST FOR A FATHER On a straightforward level, *Ulysses* tells the story of Stephen's search for a father figure and Bloom's search for a son. The plot parallels Telemachus and Odysseus searching for each other in the *Odyssey*. Stephen feels that his biological father, Simon Dedalus, has failed him as a father because he has ruined the family financially, because he has given Stephen little intellectually, and because he has never appreciated what Stephen sees as his own sensitive, artistic nature. Stephen wants a father who will enable him to be an artist, to father art himself. Preoccupied with his search, Stephen contemplates the Trinity in an attempt to reconcile Church doctrine that propounds the unity of God the father and God the son (Jesus) with heretical writings that argue that God the father created the other two parts of the Trinity—God the son and God the holy spirit—and is therefore inherently different from them. Stephen's search also fuels his theory about Shakespeare: he sees himself as the disenfranchised Hamlet, creative heir of Shakespeare who had cast himself as Hamlet's ghost-father in writing his play. Shakespeare, in translating his life into his art, became the father-creator of his own father, of his own life, and "of all his race." Stephen's quest culminates in Bloom's kitchen as Bloom recognizes "the future" in Stephen and Stephen recognizes "the past" in Bloom.

REMORSE OF CONSCIENCE   Stephen, tormented by guilt over his mother's death, remembers the religious phrase *agenbite of inwit* ("remorse of conscience") again and again throughout the day. Bloom too feels guilt about his rupture from family and traditions—an alienation associated with modernity. Episode 15, "Circe," dramatizes this remorse as Bloom's "Sins of the Past" rise up and confront him one by one. Stephen's guilt and remorse have a paralyzing effect, but they also demonstrate a self-awareness that is the hallmark of an ethical being.

THE HOME USURPED (SYMBOL: MISSING HOUSE KEYS)   In the *Odyssey*, while Odysseus is away from Ithaca, his household is usurped by would-be suitors of his wife Penelope. In the *Ulysses* parallel, Bloom's home has been usurped by Blazes Boylan, who comes and goes at will and has sex with Molly in Bloom's absence. Stephen feels that his home too —the Martello tower, for which he pays rent—has been usurped by Buck, especially as Buck demands Stephen's key. Stephen dramatizes his situation as a replay of Claudius's usurpation of Gertrude and the throne in *Hamlet*. Stephen's and Bloom's lack of house keys during the day thematically unites them and symbolizes these usurpations.

SYMBOLS IN *ULYSSES*

PLUMTREE'S POTTED MEAT   In Episode 5, Bloom reads an ad in his newspaper: "What is home without / Plumtree's Potted Meat? / Incomplete. / With it an abode of bliss." Bloom immediately thinks that the ad is poorly placed—directly below the obituaries, suggesting an infelicitous relation between dead bodies and "potted meat." Subconsciously, Plumtree's Potted Meat comes to stand for Bloom's anxieties about Boylan usurping his wife and home. The image of meat inside a pot crudely suggests Boylan and Molly's sexual relations. Indeed, Bloom later finds crumbs of the potted meat that Boylan and Molly shared earlier in his own bed. The ad gives voice to Bloom's fears of inadequacy—he worries that he is not the head of an "abode of bliss" but rather a servant in a home "incomplete."

THE GOLD CUP HORSERACE   In Episode 5, Bantam Lyons mistakenly thinks that Bloom has given him a tip to bet on Throwaway, the dark horse with a long-shot chance to win the Gold Cup. Throwaway does end up winning the race, notably ousting Sceptre, the favorite horse with the phallic name, backed by Boylan and Lenehan. This underdog victory represents Bloom's eventual understated triumph over Boylan to win the "Gold Cup" of Molly's heart.

IMPORTANT QUOTATIONS FROM *ULYSSES*

Amor matris: subjective and objective genitive.

Location: Episode 2
Speaker: Stephen Dedalus (interior monologue)
Context: Tutoring Sargent after school, Stephen thinks that Sargent has a face only a mother could
   love—and remembers his guilt over his own mother's death

Obsessed with thoughts of his mother, Stephen necessarily interprets the world through that lens: seeing Sargent dirty and disheveled, he thinks that Sargent's mother nevertheless loves him. Throughout *Ulysses*, Stephen contrasts the visceral *amor matris* ("mother love") to the disconnected, tension-ridden relation between a father and a child. In Episode 9, he refers to mother love as "the only true thing in life" and skeptically calls paternity "a legal fiction." The qualification "subjective and objective genitive" refers to the ambiguity in translation: *amor matris* can mean either a mother's love for her child (mother as subject) or the child's love for its mother (mother as object). Confusion about the role of the word *matris* recalls Stephen's struggle in deciding whether to approach life actively or passively. This is the choice he refers to in Episode 9's "Act. Be acted on."

History, Stephen said, is a nightmare from which I am trying to awake.

Location: Episode 2
Speaker: Stephen (indirect discourse) to Mr. Deasy
Context: Stephen responds to Deasy's remark that Jews, who "sinned against the light," are condemned to wander the earth

Stephen's comment is both an explicit challenge to Deasy's belief that history is moving toward a single goal (the manifestation of God) and an implicit challenge to Haines's view that history is impersonal and cut off from the present ("It seems history is to blame," Episode 1). Stephen sees history, Irish history in particular, as marked by frequent violence. Both Deasy's perspective (excluding Jews from the historical narrative) and Haines's perspective (absolving perpetrators from blame by moving on and forgetting) enable that violence. Stephen is also struggling to overcome his own personal history, including his upbringing and his mother's death.

He [Shakespeare] found in the world without as actual what was in his world within as possible. Maeterlinck says: If Socrates leave his house today he will find the sage seated on his doorstep. If Judas go forth tonight it is to Judas his steps will tend. Every life is many days, day after day. We walk through ourselves, meeting robbers, ghosts, giants, old men, young men, wives, widows, brothers-in-love, but always meeting ourselves.

Location: Episode 9
Speaker: Stephen Dedalus
Context: At the National Library, Stephen presents his theory of Shakespeare, which is grounded in the idea that people, in their daily lives, focus on those aspects of the world that echo their own thoughts

---

. . . each contemplating the other in both mirrors of the reciprocal flesh of theirhisnothis fellowfaces.

Location: Episode 17
Speaker: The narrator
Context: Stephen and Bloom share a wordless moment of connection in Bloom's garden just before Stephen leaves

---

. . . and then he asked me would I yes to say yes my mountain flower and first I put my arms around him yes and drew him down to me so he could feel my breasts all perfume yes and his heart was going like mad and yes I said yes I will Yes.

Location: Episode 18 (last words of novel)
Speaker: Molly Bloom (interior monologue)
Context: In an unqualified affirmation of life and of physical and emotional love, Molly remembers agreeing to marry Bloom at Howth

UNCLE TOM'S CABIN

Harriet Beecher Stowe

A pious, kind slave endures terrible mistreatment but never loses his faith in God.

THE LIFE OF HARRIET BEECHER STOWE

Harriett Beecher Stowe was born in 1811 into an eccentric, intellectual Connecticut family. Her father was an eminent New England preacher. Before she was ten years old, Stowe had learned Latin and written a children's geography book. Throughout her life, she was deeply involved in religious movements, feminist causes, and the most divisive political and moral issue of her time: the abolition of slavery.

Stowe grew up in the Northeast. She lived for a time in Cincinnati, which was evenly divided for and against abolition. Stowe often wrote pieces under pseudonyms and in contrasting styles. She absorbed a great deal of information about slavery during her Cincinnati years and conducted extensive research before writing *Uncle Tom's Cabin* (1851–52), writing to Frederick Douglass and others for help in creating a realistic picture of slavery in the Deep South. Her black cook and household servants also helped by telling her stories of their slave days.

Stowe wrote a great deal after the publication of *Uncle Tom's Cabin*, but nothing approached its success. She died in 1896.

UNCLE TOM'S CABIN IN CONTEXT

Upon meeting Harriet Beecher Stowe for the first time, Abraham Lincoln reportedly said, "So this is the little lady who made this big war." Stowe's *Uncle Tom's Cabin* was one of the most widely read and influential books of its time. It sold hundreds of thousands of copies and was translated into numerous languages. Many historians have credited the novel with hastening the outbreak of the Civil War.

Stowe wanted *Uncle Tom's Cabin* to convince Northerners of the necessity of ending slavery. Most immediately, the novel was a response to the Fugitive Slave Act of 1850, which made it illegal to give aid or assistance to a runaway slave. In her novel, Stowe exposed the horrors of Southern slavery.

Uncle Tom's Cabin was published in episodes in the *National Era* in 1851 and 1852, then in its entirety on March 20, 1852. It sold 10,000 copies in its first week and 300,000 by the end of the year, astronomical numbers for the mid-nineteenth century.

UNCLE TOM'S CABIN: KEY FACTS

Full title: Uncle Tom's Cabin or, Life Among the Lowly

Time and place written: 1850–1851; Brunswick, Maine

Date of first publication: 1851

Publisher: The National Era (serial publication)

Type of work: Novel

Genre: Social protest novel

Language: English

Setting (time): Around the early 1850s

Setting (place): Kentucky, Louisiana, Ohio and several Northern Quaker settlements, Canada

Tense: Past

Tone: Lecturing, subjective

Narrator: Omniscient narrator in the third and second person

Point of view: The slaves'

Protagonist: Uncle Tom

Antagonist: Slavery

UNCLE TOM'S CABIN: PLOT OVERVIEW

A Kentucky farmer named Arthur Shelby has run up large debts and faces the prospect of losing everything. He decides to raise money by selling two of his slaves to Mr. Haley, a coarse slave trader. The slaves in question are Uncle Tom, a middle-aged man with a wife and children on the farm, and Harry, the son of the maid, Eliza. When Shelby tells his wife, Emily, about his agreement with Haley, she is appalled. She had promised Eliza that Shelby would not sell Harry.

Eliza overhears the conversation between Haley and his wife and, after warning Uncle Tom and his wife, Aunt Chloe, she takes Harry and flees to the North, hoping to find freedom with her husband, George, in Canada. Haley pursues her, but Eliza miraculously evades capture by crossing the half-frozen Ohio River, the boundary separating Kentucky from the North. Haley hires a slave hunter named Loker to bring Eliza and Harry back to Kentucky. Eliza and Harry make their way to a Quaker settlement, where the Quakers agree to help transport them to safety. George joins them at the settlement.

Meanwhile, Uncle Tom sadly leaves his family and Mas'r George, Shelby's young son. Haley takes Tom and heads to the slave market. On a boat on the Mississippi, Tom meets an angelic little white girl named Eva, who quickly befriends him. When Eva falls into the river, Tom dives in to save her, and her father, Augustine St. Clare, gratefully agrees to buy Tom from Haley. Tom travels with the St. Clares to their home in New Orleans, where he grows invaluable to the St. Clare household and increasingly close to Eva, with whom he shares a devout faith in God.

Up North, George and Eliza continue to run from Loker and his men. When Loker attempts to capture them, George shoots him in the side, and the other slave hunters retreat. Eliza convinces George and the Quakers to bring Loker to the next settlement, where he can be healed. In New Orleans, St. Clare discusses slavery with his cousin Ophelia, who opposes slavery as an institution but is deeply prejudiced against blacks. St. Clare, by contrast, feels no hostility toward blacks but tolerates slavery because he feels powerless to change it. To help Ophelia overcome her bigotry, he buys Topsy, a young black girl who was abused by her past master, and arranges for Ophelia to educate her.

After Tom has lived with the St. Clares for two years, Eva grows ill and dies. Her death has a profound effect on everyone who knew her: Ophelia resolves to love the slaves, Topsy learns to trust others, and St. Clare decides to set Tom free. But before St. Clare can free Tom, he is stabbed to death while trying to settle a brawl. As he dies, he finds God and goes to be with his mother in heaven.

St. Clare's cruel wife, Marie, sells Tom to a vicious plantation owner named Simon Legree. Tom is taken to rural Louisiana with a group of new slaves, including Emmeline, whom the demonic Legree has purchased to use as a sex slave. When Tom refuses to whip a fellow slave as ordered, Legree beats him severely and resolves to crush his faith in God. Tom meets Cassy and hears her story. After being separated from her daughter by slavery, she became pregnant again and killed the child because she could not stand to have it taken from her.

Around this time, with the help of Tom Loker—now a changed man after being healed by the Quakers—George, Eliza, and Harry cross over into Canada from Lake Erie and obtain their freedom. In Louisiana, Tom's faith is severely tested by his hardships, and he nearly ceases to believe. He has two visions, however—one of Christ and one of Eva—which renew his spiritual strength and give him the courage to withstand Legree's torments. He encourages Cassy to escape. She does so, taking Emmeline with her. When Tom refuses to tell Legree where Cassy and Emmeline have gone, Legree orders his overseers to beat him. Tom, near death, forgives Legree and the overseers. George Shelby arrives with money in hand to buy Tom's freedom, but he is too late. He can only watch as Tom dies a martyr's death.

Taking a boat toward freedom, Cassy and Emmeline meet George Harris's sister and travel with her to Canada, where Cassy realizes that Eliza is her long-lost daughter. The newly reunited family travels to France and decides to move to Liberia, the African nation created for former American slaves. George Shelby returns to the Kentucky farm, where, after his father's death, he sets all the slaves free in honor of Tom's memory. He urges them to think about Tom's sacrifice every time they look at his cabin and to follow Tom's example and lead a pious Christian life.

CHARACTERS IN *UNCLE TOM'S CABIN*

Senator and Mrs. Bird Mrs. Bird is a virtuous woman. Senator Bird is well-meaning and sympathetic to the abolitionist cause, but complacent nevertheless.

Cassy Legree's former sex slave and Eliza's mother. Cassy is a proud, intelligent woman.

Aunt Chloe Uncle Tom's wife and the Shelbys' cook. Chloe often acts like a jovial simpleton around the Shelbys to mask her true feelings.

Mr. Haley A slave trader. Haley presents himself as a kind individual who treats his slaves well, but actually he violently mistreats his slaves.

Eliza Harris Mrs. Shelby's maid, George's wife, and Harry's mother. Eliza is an intelligent, beautiful, and brave young slave. Eliza's escape, during which she crosses the Ohio River on patches of ice, is the novel's most famous scene.

George Harris Eliza's husband. George is an intellectually curious man who loves his family deeply. He does not hesitate to shoot the slave hunter Tom Loker when he imperils George's family.

Harry Harris Eliza and George's young son.

Simon Legree Tom's ruthlessly evil master on the Louisiana plantation. Legree is a vicious, barbaric, loathsome man.

Tom Loker A slave hunter. Tom Loker is a gruff, violent man at first, but after George shoots him and the Quakers heal him, he transforms and joins the Quakers.

Miss Ophelia St. Clare's cousin from Vermont. Ophelia opposes slavery in the abstract, but she is prejudiced against slaves. Stowe hoped her Northern audience might recognize itself in Ophelia and reconsider its views on slavery.

Arthur Shelby Uncle Tom's owner in Kentucky. Although he is an educated and kind man, Shelby tolerates and perpetuates slavery. Stowe uses him to show how slavery makes villains of all its practitioners—not just the most cruel masters.

Emmeline A young and beautiful slave girl whom Legree buys for himself. Emmeline has been raised as a pious Christian.

Emily Shelby Mr. Shelby's wife. Emily Shelby is a loving, Christian woman who does not believe in slavery. She is one of the novel's many morally virtuous and insightful female characters.

George Shelby The Shelbys' goodhearted son. After his father dies, George resolves to free all the slaves on the family farm.

Augustine St. Clare Tom's master in New Orleans and Eva's father. St. Clare is a flighty, romantic man. He does not believe in God, and he drinks every night. Although he dotes on his daughter and treats his slaves with compassion, St. Clare shares the hypocrisy of Mr. Shelby: he sees the evil of slavery but nonetheless tolerates and practices it.

Evangeline (Eva) St. Clare St. Clare and Marie's angelic daughter. Stowe presents Eva as a completely moral being and an unimpeachable Christian. Eva laments the existence of slavery and sees no difference between blacks and whites.

Marie St. Clare's wife. Petty, whining, and foolish, Marie is the opposite of the many idealized woman in the novel.

Uncle Tom The protagonist of *Uncle Tom's Cabin*. Even under the worst conditions, Uncle Tom maintains his faith in God.

The Quakers A Christian group that arose in mid-seventeenth-century England. The Quakers dedicated themselves to understanding God without the use of creeds, clergy, or rites. The Quakers have a long history of contribution to social reform and peace efforts. In *Uncle Tom's Cabin*, many Quaker characters help slaves.

Topsy A wild and uncivilized slave girl. Topsy gradually learns to love and respect others by following Eva's example.

THEMES IN *UNCLE TOM'S CABIN*

THE EVIL OF SLAVERY   In *Uncle Tom's Cabin*, Stowe attacks slavery and the Fugitive Slave Act of 1850, which made it illegal for anyone in the United States to offer aid or assistance to a runaway slave. Each of Stowe's scenes, while fleshing out characters and advancing plot, also persuades the reader that slavery is evil, un-Christian, and intolerable in a civil society. Stowe uses a carefully plotted method, first deflating the pro-slavery reader by showing the evil of the "best" kind of slavery, and then showing the shocking wickedness of slavery at its worst. Many people in Stowe's day claimed that slavery benefited the slaves because most masters acted in their slaves' best interest. Stowe refutes this argument, insisting that the slaves' best interest is freedom and that even conscientious masters are ultimately evil. Though Shelby and St. Clare are kind and intelligent, their ability to tolerate slavery turns them into morally weak hypocrites. Slaves suffer even under the kindest masters, as Tom does under Shelby. In the final third of the book, Stowe depicts slavery in its most naked and hideous form. The barbaric Legree plantation, on which slaves suffer beatings, sexual abuse, and even murder, uses the power of shock to further Stowe's argument. If slavery is wrong in the best of cases, it is nightmarish and inhuman in the worst of cases.

THE INCOMPATIBILITY OF SLAVERY AND CHRISTIAN VALUES   With her predominantly Protestant audience in mind, Stowe takes great pains to point out that slavery and Christianity oppose each other. No Christian, she insists, should be able to tolerate slavery. Throughout the novel, the more religious a character is, the more he or she objects to slavery. Eva, the most morally perfect white character in the novel, cannot understand why anyone perceives a difference between blacks and whites. The morally revolting, nonreligious Legree practices slavery as a policy of deliberate blasphemy and evil. Stowe argues that Christianity, which advocates universal love, can be used to fight slavery. Uncle Tom triumphs over slavery by loving his enemy, as Christ commanded, and refusing to compromise his faith. He dies forgiving his murderers, becoming a Christian martyr and a model for the other characters.

THE MORAL POWER OF WOMEN   *Uncle Tom's Cabin* anticipates the widespread growth of the women's rights movement in the late 1800s, portraying women as morally conscientious, committed, and courageous. Stowe implies a parallel between the oppression of blacks and the oppression of women, although she shows that women can exert influence on their oppressors. They can also use their influence to convince their husbands—the people with voting rights—of the evil of slavery. Throughout the novel, Stowe idealizes mothers and wives who attempt to save their morally inferior husbands or sons.

SYMBOLS IN *UNCLE TOM'S CABIN*

UNCLE TOM'S CABIN   Uncle Tom's cabin symbolizes the suffering Tom experienced as a slave. It also symbolizes Uncle Tom's willingness to be beaten and even killed rather than harm or betray his fellow slaves—his willingness to suffer and die rather than go against the Christian values of love and loyalty.

GEOGRAPHY   Stowe uses the North to represent freedom and the South to represent slavery and oppression. Eliza and George flee northward to Canada. Tom, against his will, moves southward, dying in rural Louisiana. This geographical split represents the wide gulf between freedom and slavery.

IMPORTANT QUOTATIONS FROM *UNCLE TOM'S CABIN*

"Mas'r, if you was sick, or in trouble, or dying, and I could save ye, I'd give ye my heart's blood; and, if taking every drop of blood in this poor old body would save your precious soul, I'd give 'em freely, as the

Lord gave his for me. Oh, Mas'r! don't bring this great sin on your soul! It will hurt you more than't will me! Do the worst you can, my troubles'll be over soon; but, if ye don't repent, yours won't never end!"

Location: Chapter XL
Speaker: Tom
Context: Tom refuses to tell Legree about Cassy's escape

Tom asks Legree not to beat him for refusing to divulge information about Cassy's escape. Tom urges Legree to reconsider, not for Tom's sake, but for Legree's. Tom explains that his own "troubles" will soon end (that is, he will die and go to heaven), but the damage Legree does to his own soul will lead to his eternal damnation. The quotation reveals the extent of Tom's piety and selflessness. Threatened with pain and death by a man who torments him, Tom's first thought is for his oppressor's soul. He even tells Legree that he would give his "heart's blood" to save him. In these lines and elsewhere, Tom embodies the Christian injunction to "love thine enemy." Because he continues to love Legree, Tom ultimately defeats him, even in death.

"Witness, eternal God! Oh, witness that, from this hour, I will do what one man can to drive out this curse of slavery from my land!"

Location: Chapter XLI
Speaker: George Shelby
Context: George vows to work against slavery

This quotation exemplifies Stowe's most sentimental, melodramatic style. It also explains her position on the problem of how one person can possibly hope to stop slavery. Men like George's father and St. Clare can see the evil of slavery but continue to tolerate and practice it. St. Clare says that he does so because there is nothing one man can do to change an entire system. But Stowe advocates acting on one's own conscience in accordance with one's personal relationship to God, suggesting that this approach can change a system. If every individual refused to tolerate oppression, as George does, slavery would cease to exist.

"You ought to be ashamed, John! Poor, homeless, houseless creatures! It's a shameful, wicked, abominable law, and I'll break it, for one, the first time I get a chance; and I hope I shall have a chance, I do! Things have got to a pretty pass, if a woman can't give a warm supper and a bed to poor, starving creatures, just because they are slaves, and have been abused and oppressed all their lives, poor things!"

"But, Mary, just listen to me. Your feelings are all quite right, dear . . . but, then, dear, we mustn't suffer our feelings to run away with our judgment; you must consider it's not a matter of private feeling,—there are great public interests involved,—there is a state of public agitation rising, that we must put aside our private feelings."

"Now, John, I don't know anything about politics, but I can read my Bible; and there I see that I must feed the hungry, clothe the naked, and comfort the desolate; and that Bible I mean to follow."

Location: Chapter IX
Speaker: Senator and Mrs. Bird
Context: Mrs. Bird insists on helping Eliza

"I looks like gwine to heaven," said the woman; "an't thar where white folks is gwine? S'pose they'd have me thar? I'd rather go to torment, and get away from Mas'r and Missis."

Location: Chapter XVIII
Speaker: Prue
Context: Tom tries to convince Prue to find God, but Prue says she would rather go to hell than share heaven with white people

---

"It was on his grave, my friends, that I resolved, before God, that I would never own another slave, while it is possible to free him; that nobody, through me, should ever run the risk of being parted from home and friends, and dying on a lonely plantation, as he died. So, when you rejoice in your freedom, think that you owe it to that good old soul, and pay it back in kindness to his wife and children. Think of your freedom, every time you see UNCLE TOM'S CABIN; and let it be a memorial to put you all in mind to follow in his steps, and be as honest and faithful and Christian as he was."

Location: Chapter XLIV
Speaker: George Shelby
Context: George endows Uncle Tom's cabin with symbolic meaning

WAITING FOR GODOT

Samuel Beckett

To men wait for a third man, who never comes.

THE LIFE OF SAMUEL BECKETT

Samuel Barclay Beckett was born in 1906 in a suburb of Dublin to a family of middle-class Protestants. After a pleasant, sheltered childhood, Beckett attended Dublin's Trinity College, where he studied French and Italian, and discovered modernist French writers such as Marcel Proust and Andre Gide. In 1928, he took a two-year teaching fellowship at the Ecole Normale Superieure in Paris. In Paris, he began writing seriously and befriended the celebrated Irish author James Joyce. In 1933, he suffered a nervous breakdown after witnessing his father die from a heart attack. He spent a few years drifting around Europe, spending three years in London and a year in Germany. His first book of short stories, *More Pricks than Tricks* (1934), was banned in Ireland, and Beckett vowed to spend less than a month each year there. He finally settled in Paris in 1937.

In Paris, Beckett grew close with Suzanne Deschevaux-Dumesnil, who would later become his wife. During the German occupation, Beckett and Suzanne joined the French Resistance movement but were discovered and had to escape to the south of France. After the war, Beckett began writing in French. Between 1947 and 1950, he wrote prolifically, including his now-famous trilogy—*Molloy* (1951), *Malone Dies* (1951), and *The Unnamable* (1953)—and *Waiting for Godot* (1952), his most famous work. *Waiting for Godot* was produced to great public acclaim in 1953, effectively inaugurating the Theatre of the Absurd.

Throughout the 1950s and 1960s, Beckett continued to write plays, including *Endgame* (1958) and *Krapp's Last Tape* (1959). He was often very involved in their productions and wrote several experimental plays such as *Breath* (1969), a thirty-second play. In 1969 he received the Nobel Prize for Literature. This was a mixed blessing. Beckett did not appreciate the public attention, and some sources report that he gave the prize money away. He died in 1989, a few months after his wife.

WAITING FOR GODOT IN CONTEXT

Waiting for Godot proved to be the benchmark play of the Theater of the Absurd, one of the most significant twentieth-century theatrical movements. Absurdist theater rejects conventional dramatic elements such as plot and setting, and uses language to confuse meaning rather than to clarify in order to emphasize the meaninglessness of life and the absence of objective truth. Like Beckett, other absurdist playwrights, including Eugene Ionesco and Arthur Adamov, had left their native countries to live in Paris after World War II. Their work reflects the disillusionment of many Europeans after living through the senseless atrocities of the war. Although Beckett did not associate himself with the existentialists, the Theater of the Absurd was greatly influenced by existentialist philosophy. *Waiting for Godot* explores several existentialist themes, such as the human search for meaning, the need for distractions from the emptiness of life, and the paralysis precipitated by having to make choices.

In his playful use of language, Beckett was influenced by his friend and fellow Irishman James Joyce, whose experiments with language paved the way for *Waiting for Godot*'s obscure dialogue. The play also leans on the American vaudeville tradition, especially as brought to the screen by American silent film comedians such as Buster Keaton and Charlie Chaplin. Their scrappy tramps in bowler hats prefigure Vladimir and Estragon. Humor is an important element in Beckett's work: although Vladimir and Estragon are tragic figures, the absurdity of their lives is laughable; the realization that we are laughing at their plight renders their tragedy even more acute.

Shortly after moving to Paris in the late 1930s, Beckett was stabbed, almost to death, by a Parisian pimp. When Beckett later asked the man why he had stabbed him, the man replied "Sir, I don't even know"—a reaction reminiscent of Vladimir and Estragon's belief that there is "nothing to be done" but wait for Godot and try to pass the time.

WAITING FOR GODOT: KEY FACTS

Time and place written: 1948–1949; Paris

Date of publication: 1952

Publisher: Editions de Minuit

First performance: January 5, 1953, at the Théâtre de Babylone in Paris

Type of work: Play

Genre: Existential play

Language: French (English translation by the author)

Setting (time): Evening

Setting (place): "A country road. A tree."

Tone: Objective and distant; keenly aware of the meaninglessness of the characters' repetitive lives

Narrator: Narrative presence conveyed through minutely detailed stage directions

Protagonist: Vladimir, or Vladimir and Estragon

Antagonist: Pozzo; Godot's continual failure to show up; a meaningless world

WAITING FOR GODOT: PLOT OVERVIEW

ACT I

Vladimir and Estragon, two vagabonds, meet near a tree. Vladimir examines his hat while Estragon struggles with his boot. They discuss different versions of the gospels story of the two thieves hanged next to Jesus. Estragon wants to leave, but Vladimir says that they must wait for Godot. Estragon falls asleep, but Vladimir wakes him because he feels lonely. They consider parting, argue, and conciliate.

Pozzo enters, driving his slave Lucky by a rope around his neck. During their conversation, Vladimir explodes with anger at Pozzo's cruel treatment of Lucky. Estragon wonders why Lucky does not put down his heavy bags. Pozzo says that he plans to sell Lucky at the fair, after almost sixty years of service. Pozzo commands Lucky to entertain Vladimir and Estragon by dancing and thinking. Lucky thinks aloud in a long, convoluted monologue. Pozzo and Lucky leave.

Vladimir and Estragon argue about whether Pozzo and Lucky have changed. A boy timidly enters with a message from Mr. Godot. Estragon verbally bullies the boy. The boy tells Vladimir that Mr. Godot will not come this evening, but that he will surely come tomorrow. Vladimir asks him questions about Mr. Godot. Night falls. Vladimir and Estragon decide to go to a shelter together. As the curtain falls, they remain still.

ACT II

At the same time and place the following evening, Vladimir and Estragon meet again. They wonder why they keep returning to each other, since each is happier alone. Estragon does not remember the previous day's events, even when Vladimir reminds him about Pozzo and Lucky. Vladimir notices that the tree now has several leaves. They discuss Estragon's boots, and fall asleep. Vladimir has a nightmare and wakes up. Vladimir and Estragon switch off putting on Lucky's hat. Vladimir plays Lucky and instructs Estragon how to play Pozzo. They insult each other, then make up and embrace.

Pozzo and Lucky come in. Pozzo is blind and cries for help when he falls down. Vladimir welcomes their arrival, since it will help pass the time. Eventually, Vladimir and Estragon try to help Pozzo, but end up on the ground as well. They doze off. When Pozzo answers to both "Abel" and "Cain," Estragon concludes that Pozzo is all of humanity. Vladimir and Estragon get up, this time easily, and help Pozzo. Lucky is asleep, and Estragon kicks him to wake him up. Vladimir wants Lucky to entertain them, but Pozzo says that Lucky is mute. Pozzo and Lucky leave.

Vladimir wakes Estragon because he is lonely. Estragon dozes off again after unsuccessfully struggling with his boots. The boy returns. Vladimir knows what the boy is going to say before he says it. They establish that the boy was not there yesterday, and that he has a message from Mr. Godot: Godot will not come tonight, but definitely tomorrow. Vladimir asks the boy questions about Godot. They boy leaves. The sun sets. Estragon wakes up and wants to leave. Vladimir replies that they cannot go far because they must return to meet Godot tomorrow. They discuss hanging themselves from the tree, but they have no rope. They decide to go, but do not move as the curtain falls.

CHARACTERS IN *WAITING FOR GODOT*

The Boy Godot's messenger. He appears at the end of both acts to inform Vladimir that Godot will not be coming that night. Both times, he insists that he was not there the previous night.

Estragon (Gogo) One of the play's two main characters. Weak and helpless, he seeks Vladimir's protection. In Act II, he has forgotten the events of Act I.

Godot Someone with answers and opinions whom Vladimir and Estragon await in vain. Godot is often thought to stand in for God. He never appears in the play.

Lucky Pozzo's slave, who carries Pozzo's bags and stool. In Act I, he entertains by dancing and thinking aloud. In Act II, he is mute.

Pozzo Lucky's master. He and Lucky pass by and help Vladimir and Estragon pass the time in both acts. In Act I, Pozzo is on his way to sell Lucky at the fair. In Act II, Pozzo is blind and does not remember the previous evening's events.

Vladimir (Didi, Mr. Albert) One of the play's two main character. He is more contemplative than Estragon and has some authority over him. Because he voices the play's ideas more explicitly, he may be seen as the protagonist.

THEMES IN *WAITING FOR GODOT*

MAN'S SEARCH FOR MEANING IN A MEANINGLESS WORLD The play's main characters long for direction, clarity, and meaning. Estragon and, especially, Vladimir frequently struggle to make sense of something such as the conflicting accounts of the four gospels and Lucky's acquiescence to his miserable life. The questions have no answers, and the absurdities have no explanations, but the characters continue to try to figure them out. This need for meaning is one of the reasons Vladimir and Estragon continue to wait for Godot: they cling to the hope that he will explain what they should do. Because the characters stand in for all of humanity, their quest represents the human quest for meaning, which can take many forms: philosophy, religion, childrearing. Even though we, as readers or viewers of a play, expect to be able to interpret the actions and words of the characters, this play's events and dialogue make little sense. As we read or watch the play, we too search for meaning in meaninglessness, sharing in the characters' quest.

THE PARALYZING EFFECTS OF ROUTINE Beckett's work often explores the human reliance on routines and the paralyzing effect these routines on human lives. The play's characters lead repetitive lives: they do and say the same things every day and often repeat one another's words and actions. Act II echoes Act I in structure, content, and dialogue. Vladimir and Estragon's comments—they "came here yesterday," Estragon was beaten up by "the same lot as usual"—suggest that they have been living the same day for a long time. These routines are reassuring and give structure to their lives. At the same time, Vladimir and Estragon have repeated the same actions and the same phrases so many times that the actions and phrases have lost all meaning. They no longer remember why they do what they do; often they forget that they have done something before. Their reliance on routine renders them powerless to break the repetitive cycle of their existence.

HUMAN COMPANIONSHIP Despite the fact that both Vladimir and Estragon claim to be happier alone, they are dependent on each other. Estragon depends on Vladimir for food—carrots and turnips—and guidance. Vladimir is often lonely without Estragon, and his insistence that Estragon needs him suggests that he is afraid of being deserted. Their codependence represents the human need for companionship, but at the same time, it is part of their paralyzing routine and prevents them from altering their lives.

Their mutual dependence has been interpreted as the codependence of the mind (Vladimir) and the body (Estragon). In this interpretation, their struggles represent the internal struggles of a single human being. Just as Vladimir and Estragon sometimes long to be free of each other, humans sometimes long to be unfettered by the influence of either the body or the mind. Just as human beings are forced to accept the realities of both spiritual and physical pain, so Vladimir and Estragon are forced to accept each other's companionship.

SYMBOLS IN *WAITING FOR GODOT*

GODOT Despite Beckett's resistance to analysis of his play, the figure of Godot has been interpreted by many readers as representing God. Mysterious and elusive, Godot does play a Godlike role for Vladimir and Estragon. They wait and hope for him as a distant, improbable solution to their problems. Although he never comes, the wait alone gives purpose and structure to their meaningless lives.

LUCKY'S BAGS The heavy bags that Lucky carries around symbolize the burden of life and its crippling routines. Lucky carries his bags out of habit, fear, and hope that Pozzo will let him stay. Even when resting, he does not set them down. Life's burden's are ours to bear.

IMPORTANT QUOTATIONS FROM *WAITING FOR GODOT*

Astride of a grave and a difficult birth. Down in the hole, lingeringly, the grave-digger puts on the forceps. We have time to grow old. The air is full of our cries. (He listens) *But habit is a great deadener.* (He looks again at Estragon) *At me too someone is looking, of me too someone is saying, He is sleeping, he knows nothing, let him sleep on.* (Pause.) *I can't go on!* (Pause.) *What have I said?*

Location: End of Act 2
Speaker: Vladimir
Context: For a brief moment, Vladimir realizes that life is meaningless; this marks the climax of the play

Vladimir realizes that all of life's events, all communications and protests ("our cries"), are merely ways to "pass the time." The only real goal of life is death. He recognizes that he and Estragon have been coping with this knowledge: "habit is a great deadener." Vladimir has caught a glimpse of the meaning in his meaningless life, realizing that there is no meaning to anything. Something in him rebels against this lack of meaning, but a moment later he is already confused about what he has said. The meaninglessness is too horrible to bear, and he and Estragon turn back to live out their routines.

. . . that man in short that man in brief in spite of the strides of alimentation and defecation wastes and pines wastes and pines and concurrently simultaneously what is more for reasons unknown in spite of the strides of physical culture the practice of sports such as tennis football running cycling swimming flying floating riding gliding . . . for reasons unknown but time will tell fades away.. . .

Location: Act 1 (Lucky's long speech)
Speaker: Lucky
Context: Ordered to entertain the others by "thinking," Lucky describes how humans try to forget their mortality and the meaninglessness of their existence with various activities

Having lost hope in their minds and souls, humans turn to the physical world for reassurance and meaning. However, despite its reliable "strides of alimentation and defecation," the human body inevitably betrays the human. Life ends, for unknown reasons, in a lingering, unspectacular way—it "fades away." As is typical of *Waiting for Godot*, Lucky's morbid speech has humorous elements. The list of leisure activities goes into a surprising amount of detail, and the juxtaposition of the thematic grandeur (God has deserted humanity, death is inevitable) and the quotidian activities is absurd. The references to respectable bourgeois activities such as tennis show that the diversions of the general public are as absurd and meaningless as the bizarre diversions that Vladimir and Estragon engage in to pass the time.

Nothing to be done.

Location: First line of Act 1
Speaker: Estragon
Context: The line, repeated several times in the play, sets up many of the play's important themes: paralysis, boredom, the meaninglessness of existence

---

ESTRAGON: *Let's go.*
VLADIMIR: *We can't.*
ESTRAGON: *Why not?*
VLADIMIR: *We're waiting for Godot.*

Location: Beginning of Act 1
Speaker: Estragon and Vladimir
Context: This exchange is repeated several times throughout the play

---

Don't touch me! Don't question me! Don't speak to me! Stay with me!

Location: Beginning of Act 2
Speaker: Estragon to Vladimir
Context: Estragon has found Vladimir singing happily alone, which brings his own misery and loneliness into sharp relief

WALDEN

Henry David Thoreau

A man recounts the time he spent living a life of simplicity near Walden Pond.

THE LIFE OF HENRY DAVID THOREAU

Henry David Thoreau was born in Concord, Massachusetts, on July 12, 1817, to John Thoreau and Cynthia Dunbar Thoreau. The freethinking and cultured Thoreaus were poor, making their living by the modest production of homemade pencils. Henry received a top-notch education, first at Concord Academy and then at Harvard College. After college, Thoreau met Ralph Waldo Emerson, a prominent American philosopher, essayist, and poet who had recently moved to Concord. The following June, Thoreau founded a small, progressive school that emphasized intellectual curiosity over rote memorization. His brother, John, joined the venture.

Thoreau was exposed to the transcendentalist movement, which Emerson headed. Transcendentalism saw self-reliance not just as an economic virtue but also as a whole philosophical and spiritual basis for existence. It also sanctioned the rejection of any social norms that contradict one's personal vision. With his unorthodox manners and irreverent views, Thoreau quickly made a name for himself among Emerson's followers and began to enjoy modest success as a writer. Ellen Sewall rejected Thoreau's marriage proposal in 1840 (as she had turned down his brother, John, before him) because her family considered the Thoreaus financially unstable and suspiciously radical.

During the early 1840s, Thoreau lived as a pensioner at the Emerson address. It was on Emerson's land at Walden Pond that Thoreau, inspired by the experiment of his Harvard classmate, Charles Stearns Wheeler, erected a small dwelling in order to live closer to nature. On July 4, 1845, Thoreau moved to the woods by Walden Pond. He spent the next two years there drafting *A Week on the Concord and Merrimack Rivers* (1849) and *Walden; or, Life in the Woods* (1854). Thoreau's isolation during this period is sometimes exaggerated. He lived within easy walking distance of Concord and received frequent visitors in his shack.

In 1846, a constable imprisoned Thoreau for refusing to pay a tax because it supported a nation endorsing slavery. Thoreau defended his actions in a lecture to the Concord Lyceum. Later he revised and published this lecture under the title "Civil Disobedience," a work that inspired such prominent social thinkers as Leo Tolstoy and Mahatma Gandhi.

After a rift in his friendship with Emerson, Thoreau returned to his family home, where he remained for the rest of his life, and resumed work in the pencil business. In the 1850s, Thoreau took on a vocal role in the burgeoning abolitionist movement. He assisted fugitive slaves on the Underground Railroad and took an unpopular stand by supporting John Brown, who had sought to incite a slave rebellion in Harper's Ferry, Virginia. Thoreau died of tuberculosis in Concord on May 6, 1862, at the age of forty-four.

WALDEN IN CONTEXT

Although today Thoreau is held in great esteem, his work was not lauded during his lifetime, and a considerable number of his neighbors held him in contempt. Thoreau had to pay to publish his first book, *A Week on the Concord and Merrimack Rivers*. Published in an edition of 1,000, only around 300 copies of this book sold. Even *Walden* was met with scant interest. Not until the twentieth century was Thoreau's extraordinary impact on American culture felt. In the upsurge in counterculture sentiment during the Vietnam War and the Civil Rights era, *Walden* and "Civil Disobedience" inspired many young Americans to vocally disavow official U.S. policies. *Walden*'s critique of consumerism and capitalism appealed to the hippies and others who wanted to drop out of consumer society and pursue greater aims. Thoreau politicized the American landscape and nature itself, articulating a liberal view on the environment that influenced the Sierra Club and the Green Party. Finally, Thoreau gave generations of American writers a distinctive style to emulate: a combination of homey folksiness and erudite allusions.

WALDEN: KEY FACTS

Full title: Walden; or, Life in the Woods; Thoreau abbreviated the title to *Walden* for the second edition

Time and place written: 1845–1854; Walden Pond, near Concord, Massachusetts

Date of first publication: 1854

Publisher: Ticknor and Fields, Boston

Type of work: Essay

Genre: Autobiography; essay; social protest literature

Language: English

Setting (time): One summer in the 1840s

Setting (place): Walden Pond

Tense: Past and present

Tone: Mystical, lyrical, hardheaded, practical, observational, didactic

Narrator: Henry David Thoreau in the first person

Point of view: Thoreau's

Protagonist: Henry David Thoreau

Antagonist: Civilized American life

WALDEN: PLOT OVERVIEW

Thoreau begins *Walden* by explaining that he spent two years at Walden Pond, living a simple life supported by no one. He now resides among the civilized again. Thoreau contradicts the Concordians, who believe that society is the only place to live. He writes that he borrowed or found most of the materials and tools he used to build his home. In order to make a little money, Thoreau cultivates a modest bean-field. He reserves his afternoons and evenings for contemplation, reading, and walking around the countryside. Thoreau contrasts his own freedom with the imprisonment of others who devote their lives to material prosperity.

Despite his isolation, Thoreau feels the presence of society around him. The Fitchburg Railroad rushes past Walden Pond, forcing Thoreau to contemplate the power of technology. He talks with the occasional peasant farmer, railroad worker, or visitor to Walden. Thoreau describes a Canadian-born woodcutter, Alex Therien, who is grand and sincere if not intellectual. Thoreau makes frequent trips into Concord to see his longtime friends and conduct business. On one such trip, he spends a night in jail for refusing to pay a poll tax.

Thoreau describes nature, the passing of the seasons, and the creatures of the woods. He recounts the habits of many animals, some of which he endows with larger meaning. For instance, the hooting loon that plays hide and seek with Thoreau becomes a symbol of nature's playfulness and amusement at human endeavors. An ant war prompts Thoreau to meditate on human warfare.

As autumn turns to winter, Thoreau prepares for the arrival of the cold. The squirrel, the rabbit, and the fox gather food. Thoreau watches the migrating birds and welcomes the pests that infest his cabin as they escape the cold. By day, Thoreau studies the snow and ice. By night, he listens to the wind as it whips and whistles outside his door. Thoreau occasionally sees ice-fisherman come to cut out huge blocks that will be shipped to cities. Friends such as William Ellery Channing or Amos Bronson Alcott sometimes visit Thoreau, but for the most part he is alone. In one chapter, he imagines earlier residents of Walden Pond long dead and largely forgotten, including poor tradesmen and former slaves. Thoreau prefers to see himself in their company rather than amid the cultivated and wealthy classes.

Thoreau finds that Walden Pond is no more than a hundred feet deep, refuting common folk wisdom that it is bottomless. He meditates on the pond as a symbol of infinity that people need in their lives. Eventually, winter gives way to spring, and the ice of Walden Pond begins to melt and hit the shore. In lyric imagery echoing the biblical description of Judgment Day, Thoreau describes the coming of spring as a vast transformation of the face of the world, a time when all sins are forgiven.

Thoreau says he returned to civilized life on September 6, 1847. In the last chapter of *Walden*, Thoreau's observations give way to direct sermonizing about the untapped potential of humanity. In visionary language, Thoreau exhorts us to "meet" our lives and exist fully.

CHARACTERS IN *WALDEN*

Amos Bronson Alcott A noted educator and social reformer, and the father of Louisa May Alcott. Alcott founded the Temple School in Boston, a noted progressive school that spawned many imitators. Alcott also had a hand in the utopian communities Brook Farm and Fruitlands.

William Ellery Channing Thoreau's closest friend. Channing was an amateur poet and a Transcendentalist.

Henry Clay A prominent Whig senator from Kentucky. Clay is known as "the Great Compromiser" for his role in the Missouri Compromise and the Compromise of 1850. Thoreau was a staunch critic of Clay and of the expansionism Clay advocated.

Confucius A Chinese sage of the sixth century B.C. His teachings form a secular religion known as Confucianism, which served as a model for the Chinese government. Confucius's writings had a significant effect on the transcendentalist movement. He was one of Thoreau's favorite authors.

Lidian Emerson Emerson's second wife. During Ralph Waldo Emerson's tours of Europe, Thoreau stayed with Lidian, and the two developed a close friendship.

Ralph Waldo Emerson An essayist, poet, and leading figure of transcendentalism. Emerson's ideas, especially the doctrine of self-reliance, pervade Thoreau's work. However, Emerson and Thoreau often disagreed on the necessity of following some public conventions. Thoreau devotes minimal attention to Emerson in *Walden*, failing to mention that Emerson owns the land he lives on and treating him indifferently when he visits.

John Field A poor Irish-American laborer. John Field lives with his wife and children just outside of Concord. Thoreau uses Field as an example of an "honest, hard-working, but shiftless man," someone who lacks unusual natural abilities or social position. Thoreau heatedly advises Field to cut down on coffee and meat consumption, and concludes that Field has inherited Irish laziness. The conversation is an uncomfortable reminder that Thoreau's ideas and convictions set him apart from the poor people he idealizes.

James Russell Lowell A lawyer and later an author. Lowell was a professor of modern languages at Harvard and the first editor of the *Atlantic Monthly*.

Mencius A Chinese sage of the fourth century B.C. and a disciple of Confucius. Mencius was a powerful influence on Thoreau.

Alex Therien A laborer in his late twenties who works near Thoreau's dwelling. Thoreau says it would be difficult to find a more simple or natural human being than Therien, who is conversant and intelligent although he is not a reader. Therien appeals to Thoreau as an untutored backwoods sage. Thoreau compares him to Walden Pond itself, saying both possess hidden depths.

Henry David Thoreau The narrator and protagonist of *Walden*. Thoreau, an amateur naturalist, essayist, lover of solitude, and poet, believed in the perfectibility of mankind through education, self-exploration, and spiritual awareness.

John Thoreau Henry David Thoreau's elder brother. Henry and John oversaw and taught at the Concord Academy, a progressive independent school, from 1838 to 1841. John Thoreau died in 1842 from complications related to lockjaw.

THEMES IN *WALDEN*

THE IMPORTANCE OF SELF-RELIANCE Thoreau's living experiment can be interpreted as the practice of the philosophical ideals Ralph Waldo Emerson explained in his enormously influential essay "Self-Reliance." In *Walden*, Thoreau suggests that in matters of friendship and finance, independence is better than neediness. Thoreau dwells on the contentment of his solitude, assuring us that he finds entertainment in the laugh of the loon and the march of the ants rather than in balls, marketplaces, or salons. He does not disdain human companionship—in fact, he values it highly when it comes on his own terms—but he refuses to need it. He also values economic independence, detailing the way he supports himself through his own labor, producing more than he consumes and producing a profit. As Emerson's essay details, self-reliance is also spiritual. In transcendentalist thought, the self is the center of reality. Self-reliance thus means not just taking care of one's own needs, but understanding that the natural world and humankind exist because of the self.

THE VALUE OF SIMPLICITY   Simplicity is not just a mode of life for Thoreau, it is a philosophical ideal. In "Economy," Thoreau writes that people can resolve their dissatisfaction with their possessions either by acquiring more or by reducing their desires. His fellow Concord residents take the first path, making mortgage payments and buying the latest fashions. Thoreau prefers to take the second path, radically minimizing his consumer activity. He patches his clothes instead of buying new ones and dispenses with unnecessary accessories. He builds his own shack instead of getting a bank loan to buy one. Thoreau points out that those who want impressive possessions actually have fewer possessions than he does, since he owns his house outright, while theirs are technically held by mortgage companies. He argues that the simplification of one's lifestyle does not hinder such pleasures as owning one's residence, but actually facilitates them.

THE ILLUSION OF PROGRESS   Thoreau's society is fascinated by the idea of technological, economic, and territorial advances, but Thoreau is stubbornly skeptical that any outward improvement of life can bring the inner peace and contentment he craves. In an era of capitalist expansion, Thoreau is doggedly anti-consumption. In a time of pioneer migrations, he lauds the pleasures of staying put. In a century notorious for its smug dismissal of all that preceded it, Thoreau points out that stifling conventionality and constraining labor conditions made nineteenth-century progress possible.

Thoreau's attitude toward the train typifies his feeling about technology. Throughout Europe and America, the train symbolized the wonders and advantages of technological progress, but Thoreau sees it as a false idol of social progress. He questions the value of moving people quickly from one point to another. "Have not men improved somewhat in punctuality since the railroad was invented?" he asks with irony, as if punctuality were the greatest improvement progress can provide. People "talk and think faster in the depot" than they did earlier in stagecoach offices, but Thoreau wonders why we should prefer speedy talk and quick thinking to thoughtful speech and deep thinking. Trains, like all technological "improvements," give people the illusion of heightened freedom, but in fact represent a new servitude, making people subservient to fixed schedules and routes. The train chugs along on its fixed path and makes us believe that our lives must progress in the same unthinking, preordained fashion.

SYMBOLS IN *WALDEN*

WALDEN POND   Walden Pond symbolizes almost everything Thoreau holds dear spiritually, philosophically, and personally. The pond symbolizes the alternative to social conventions and obligations. It also symbolizes the vitality and tranquility of nature. The pond becomes a metaphor for spiritual belief when Thoreau wonders why people want to believe that the pond is bottomless and concludes that humans need to believe in infinity. Walden Pond becomes a symbol of heavenly purity on earth when Thoreau describes the pond reflecting heaven and making the swimmer's body pure white.

ICE   Ice, the only useful product of Walden Pond, symbolizes the social use and importance of nature and the exploitation of natural resources. The ice-cutters, the only group Thoreau describes, represent society in miniature, and their encounter with the pond becomes a symbolic microcosm of the confrontation of society and nature. At first glance it seems that society gets the upper hand. The frozen pond is chopped up, disfigured, and robbed of ten thousand tons of its contents. But nature triumphs in the end, since less than twenty-five percent of the ice ever reaches its destination. The rest melts and evaporates en route, making its way back to Walden Pond. This process suggests that humankind's efforts to exploit nature are in vain.

IMPORTANT QUOTATIONS FROM *WALDEN*

The mass of men lead lives of quiet desperation.

Location: "Economy"
Speaker: Thoreau
Context: Thoreau analyzes modern life

This sentence, perhaps the most famous in *Walden*, suggests Thoreau's prophetic ability. Thoreau was not just a nature writer living in isolation, but a deeply social and moral writer with an ardent message for the masses. His use of the word *desperation* instead of a milder word like *discontentment* or *unhappiness* underlines the grimness of his vision of the mainstream American lifestyle. Thoreau believes that the monomaniacal pursuit of success and wealth has paradoxically cheapened the lives of those engaged in it, making people unable to appreciate the simple pleasures enumerated in *Walden*. But the unpleasantness of American life, according to Thoreau, is not just financial or economic—it is spiritual. "Desperation" is a word with deep religious connotations. It means the "lack of hope" that comes with alienation from God. *The Pilgrim's Progress*, John Bunyan's Protestant spiritual classic and a bestseller in the New England of Thoreau's day, features a hero who passes through a bleak lowland called the Slough of Despair on his way to meet God. By asserting that most humans live in despair, Thoreau suggests that their lives are preventing them from finding redemption.

So that all the pecuniary outgoes, excepting for washing and mending, which for the most part were done out of the house, and their bills have not yet been received . . . were

House, $28 12 ¢
Farm one year, 14 72 ¢
Food eight months, 8 74
Clothing &c., eight months, 8 40 ¢
Oil, &c., eight months, 2 00
In all, $61 99 ¢

Location: "Economy"
Speaker: Thoreau
Context: Thoreau includes a bit of bookkeeping

One of several bookkeeping excerpts included in *Walden*, this passage from the chapter "Economy" shows that, as the chapter's title indicates, Thoreau is not a free spirit fleeing social realities, but a responsible man with a sharp eye for financial matters. Many first-time readers of *Walden* are surprised to find so much minute financial detail in what they expect to be inspirational nature writing. But this is Thoreau's point: the true inspiration of the spirit does not entail financial failure, and economic and spiritual well-being are two sides of the same coin. Thoreau is not escaping the world of human values at all. He defines his success in his Walden project not solely in terms of his own spiritual development but also in economic terms—he seeks to live without incurring debt. Money defines his freedom as much as spiritual transcendence does.

At the same time, Thoreau's account-keeping reveals the amateur nature of his project and confirms the feeling that he is a Harvard man slumming temporarily in the woods rather than a truly needy person struggling to make ends meet. Thoreau fails to include his laundry bills in his grand total on the frivolous grounds that they have not come in yet. He lists a year's rent on the farm, but only eight months' expenditures on food and clothing. The sloppiness of this bookkeeping suggests that choice, not necessity, compels Thoreau's economizing.

I went to the woods because I wished to live deliberately, to front only the essential facts of life, and see if I could not learn what it had to teach, and not, when I came to die, discover that I had not lived.

Location: "Where I Lived, and What I Lived For"
Speaker: Thoreau
Context: Thoreau answers the question posed by his chapter title

A field of water betrays the spirit that is in the air. It is continually receiving new life and motion from above. It is intermediate between land and sky.

Location: "The Ponds"
Speaker: Thoreau
Context: Thoreau compares the pond to the human soul, which exists between heaven and earth

It is not worth the while to go round the world to count the cats in Zanzibar.

Location: "Context"
Speaker: Thoreau
Context: Thoreau scoffs at physical travel

WAR AND PEACE

Leo Tolstoy

Russian families endure Napoleon's invasion and their own private troubles.

THE LIFE OF LEO TOLSTOY

Lev (Leo) Nikolaevich Tolstoy was born into a large and wealthy Russian landowning family in 1828. Tolstoy's mother died when he was only two years old, and he idealized her throughout his life. When Tolstoy was nine, his family moved to Moscow. Shortly afterward, Tolstoy's father was murdered while traveling. Although Tolstoy was an intelligent child, he had little interest in academics. He failed his university entrance exam on his first attempt. Finally, he entered Kazan University at age sixteen and studied law and language. He developed an interest in the grand heroic cultures of Persia, Turkey, and the Caucasus—an interest that persisted throughout his life. Tolstoy was not popular at the university. In 1847, he left school without a degree.

After visiting his brother in the Russian army, Tolstoy decided to enlist. He served in the Crimean War (1854–1856), an experience he drew on to write *Sevastopol Stories* (1855). During his stint in the army, Tolstoy found time to write, producing a well-received autobiographical novel, *Childhood* (1852), followed by two others, *Boyhood* (1854) and *Youth* (1857).

In 1862, Tolstoy married Sofya Andreevna Behrs. He devoted most of the next two decades to raising a large family, managing his estate, and writing his two greatest novels, *War and Peace* (1865–1869) and *Anna Karenina* (1875–1877). Just before he married, Tolstoy had visited western Europe, partly to observe educational methods abroad. Upon returning, he founded schools for his peasants. Tolstoy came to believe that peasants possessed morality and camaraderie lacking in the upper classes.

Tolstoy lived during a period of intense development in Russia. By the time of his death in 1910, Russia had changed from an agricultural country to a major industrialized world power. The Slavophiles and the Westernizers, two intellectual groups, argued about Russia's direction. The Slavophiles believed Russia should reject modernization and cherish the traditional, Asiatic elements of its culture. The Westernizers believed Russia should join Europe in its march toward secular values and scientific thought. Political debates also raged in Russia, as a series of authoritarian tsars angered liberal and radical intellectuals who wanted constitutional rights.

By the 1890s, Tolstoy's reputation as a prophet of social thought had attracted disciples to his estate at Yasnaya Polyana. In 1898, Tolstoy published a radical essay called *What Is Art?* in which he argues that moral instruction is the sole aim of great art, and that by that standard Shakespeare's plays and Tolstoy's own novels are artistic failures. Frustrated by the disconnect between his philosophy and his wealth, and by his frequent quarrels with his wife, Tolstoy stole away from his estate in November 1910, at the age of eighty-two. Several days later, he died of pneumonia in a faraway railway station.

WAR AND PEACE IN CONTEXT

War and Peace reflects many of Tolstoy's personal beliefs. In it, Tolstoy celebrates the morality, camaraderie, and joie de vivre of the peasantry. He also criticizes the superficiality of upper-class Russians, particularly in his portrait of the Kuragin family. The character Nicholas Rostov, who dismisses modern Western farming techniques and practices a distinctly Russian style of land management, reveals Tolstoy's belief that Russia should resist secularization and modernization. Tolstoy's critical portrayal of leadership in *War and Peace* owes its bite to the Russian liberals' attack on authoritarian politics. *War and Peace* also illustrates Tolstoy's turn toward religion. The character Pierre embodies Tolstoy's belief that moral commitment to humanity should transcend class and nationality.

WAR AND PEACE: KEY FACTS

Time and place written: 1863–1869; the estate of Yasnaya Polyana, near Moscow

Date of first publication: 1865–1869 (serial publication)

Publisher: M. N. Katkov	

Publisher: M. N. Katkov

Type of work: Novel

Genre: Historical novel; epic novel; novel of ideas

Language: Russian

Setting (time): 1805–1820

Setting (place): Various locations in Russia and eastern Europe

Tense: Past

Tone: Impersonal, sympathetic, philosophical

Narrator: An unnamed, omniscient, third-person narrator

Point of view: Varies

Protagonist: Pierre Bezukhov; Andrew Bolkonski; Natasha Rostova; General Kutuzov; Mary Bolkonskaya; Nicholas Rostov

Antagonist: Napoleon's French forces

WAR AND PEACE: PLOT OVERVIEW

It is 1805 in the Russian city of St. Petersburg. Napoleon has conquered western Europe. A society lady hosts a party that is attended by, among others, Pierre Bezukhov, the awkward, likeable, illegitimate son of a rich count, and Andrew Bolkonski, the intelligent and ambitious son of a retired military commander. Tolstoy introduces the sneaky and shallow Kuragin family, including the wily father Vasili, the fortune-hunting son Anatole, and the ravishing daughter Helene. He also introduces the Rostovs, a noble Moscow family, including the lively daughter Natasha, the quiet cousin Sonya, and the impetuous son Nicholas, who has just joined the army led by the old General Kutuzov.

The Russian troops, in alliance with the Austrian empire, mobilize to resist Napoleon's onslaught. Both Andrew and Nicholas go to the front. Andrew is wounded at the Battle of Austerlitz. Pierre inherits his father's fortune and marries Helene Kuragina in a daze. Helene cheats on Pierre, who nearly kills her lover in a duel. Andrew returns to his estate, much to the shock of his family, who thought he was dead. His wife, Lise, dies in childbirth, leaving Andrew's devout sister Mary to raise the son. Meanwhile, Pierre, disillusioned by married life, leaves his wife and gets involved with the spiritual practice of Freemasonry. He attempts to apply Freemason principles to his estate management. He also tells his skeptical friend Andrew about Freemasonry.

The Rostovs' fortunes are failing, partly because of Nicholas's gambling debts. The Rostovs consider selling their beloved family estate, Otradnoe. Nicholas had promised to marry Sonya, but he is encouraged to marry a rich heiress instead. His army career continues, and he witnesses the great peace between Napoleon and Tsar Alexander. Natasha grows up, attends her first ball, and falls in love with various men before becoming seriously attached to Andrew. Andrew's father objects to the marriage and insists that Andrew wait a year before wedding Natasha. Natasha reluctantly submits to this demand, and Andrew goes off to travel.

Andrew's father begins to be irritable and cruel to his daughter Mary. She accepts this bad treatment with Christian forgiveness. Natasha decides that she loves Anatole and wants to elope with him, but the plan fails. Andrew comes home and rejects Natasha because of her involvement with Anatole. Pierre consoles Natasha and feels attracted to her. Natasha falls ill.

In 1812, Napoleon invades Russia, and Tsar Alexander reluctantly declares war. Andrew returns to active military service. Pierre develops the insane conviction that he must assassinate Napoleon. The French approach the Bolkonski estate. Mary's father dies just as the French troops arrive. Mary, finally forced to leave her estate, finds the local peasants hostile. Nicholas happens to ride by and save her. Mary and Nicholas feel the stirrings of romance.

At Borodino, the smaller Russian army inexplicably defeats the French forces, much to Napoleon's dismay. In St. Petersburg, life in high society continues almost unaffected by the occupation of Moscow. Helene seeks an annulment of her marriage to Anatole in order to marry a foreign prince. Distressed by this news, Pierre becomes deranged and flees his companions, wandering alone through Moscow.

The Rostovs pack up their belongings, preparing to evacuate, but in the end they generously give up the carts they were using for their possessions to soldiers in need of transport. Natasha's younger brother Petya joins the army. On the way out of the city, the Rostovs take the wounded Andrew with them. Pierre, still wandering half-crazed in Moscow, sees anarchy, looting, fire, and murder. Still obsessed with killing Napoleon, he saves a girl from a fire but is apprehended by the French authorities on suspicion of espionage. Pierre witnesses the execution of several of his prison mates and bonds with a wise peasant named Platon Karataev.

Nicholas's aunt tries to arrange a marriage between Nicholas and Mary, but Nicholas resists, remembering his commitment to Sonya. Mary visits the Rostovs to see the wounded Andrew, and Natasha and Mary grow closer. Andrew forgives Natasha, declaring his love for her before he dies. General Kutuzov leads the Russian troops back toward Moscow, which the French have finally abandoned after their defeat at Borodino. The French force the Russian prisoners of war, including Pierre, to march with them. On the way, Platon falls ill and is shot for straggling. The Russians follow the retreating French, and small partisan fighting ensues. Petya is shot and killed.

Pierre, after being liberated, falls ill for three months. Upon recovering, he realizes that he loves Natasha. Pierre and Natasha marry in 1813 and eventually have four children. Natasha grows into a solid, frumpy Russian matron. Nicholas weds Mary, resolving his family's financial problems. He also rebuilds Mary's family's estate, which had been damaged in the war. Despite some tensions, Nicholas and Mary enjoy a happy family life.

CHARACTERS IN *WAR AND PEACE*

A NOTE ON RUSSIAN NAMES:

Russians have three names: a first name, a patronymic, and a surname. The patronymic is the father's first name with a suffix meaning "son of" or "daughter of": for example, Kyril Vladimirovich (son of Vladimir), or Anna Mikhaylovna (daughter of Mikhail). In formal address, people are called by both their first names and their patronymics (Pierre Bezukhov). In informal address, people are sometimes called by nicknames, or diminutives. For instance, Natalya Rostova is called Natasha (the diminutive of Natalya). Surnames reflect gender. For example, Andrew's surname is Bolkonski, while his sister Mary's surname is Bolkonskaya.

Bagration   A Russian military commander.

Pierre Bezukhov   The illegitimate son of an old Russian grandee. Pierre is large-bodied, ungainly, and socially awkward, but his unexpected inheritance of a large fortune makes him desirable. The fortune-hunting Helene Kuragina snares Pierre and then betrays him. Pierre's mistreatment at Helene's hands leaves him depressed and confused, spurring a spiritual odyssey that spans the novel. Pierre eventually marries Natasha Rostova.

Lise Bolkonskaya   Andrew's angelic wife. Lise dies in childbirth.

Mary Bolkonskaya   Prince Bolkonski's daughter. Princess Mary is lonely, plain, and long-suffering. She cares for her father, calmly enduring his cruel treatment. Nicholas Rostov eventually weds Mary, saving her from unhappy solitude.

Andrew Bolkonski   Son of the retired military commander Prince Bolkonski. Andrew is intelligent, disciplined, ambitious, and cold. He falls in love with Natasha after the death of his wife, Lise, but is unable to forgive her momentary passion for Anatole.

Prince Bolkonski   Andrew and Mary's father. A stodgy, old-fashioned recluse, Prince Bolkonski is cynical, stern, and sometimes cruel to Mary.

Mademoiselle Bourienne   Princess Mary's French companion. Mademoiselle Bourienne becomes the object of Prince Bolkonski's affections shortly before his death.

Denisov   Nicholas's army friend. Denisov is short, hairy, and good-looking. He falls for Sonya and eventually faces a court-martial for seizing army food provisions to feed his men.

Princess Anna Mikhaylovna Drubetskaya An impoverished noblewoman. Anna Mikhaylovna longs to secure a good future for her son, Boris. She makes Vasili Kuragin promise to help Boris get an officer's position in the army.

Boris Drubetskoy Anna Mikhaylovna's son and Nicholas Rostov's friend. Boris is poor but ambitious, intelligent, and talented. Eventually he marries an heiress.

Dolokhov A handsome Russian army officer and friend of Nicholas. After having an affair with Helene, Dolokhov almost dies in a duel with Pierre.

Julie Karagina Mary's friend and pen pal. Julie, an heiress, lives in Moscow and eventually marries Boris Drubetskoy.

Anatole Kuragin Vasili's son. Anatole is a roguish, spendthrift man on the hunt for a rich wife. He falls for Natasha Rostova at the opera, causing her rift with Andrew Bolkonski.

Hippolyte Kuragin Vasili's son. Hippolyte is ugly and undistinguished.

Vasili Kuragin A Russian nobleman. Vasili, an artificial, untrustworthy man, is a special friend of Anna Pavlovna. He continually tries to maneuver his children into lucrative marriages.

Helene Kuragina Vasili's daughter. Helene is cold, imperious, and beautiful. After seducing Pierre into marriage, she immediately takes up with Dolokhov. People consider Helene witty, but she is actually stupid and shallow.

General Kutuzov An old, one-eyed general. Kutuzov leads the Russians to military success at Borodino, but falls from favor toward the end of his life. His spirituality and humility contrast sharply with Napoleon's vanity and logic.

Napoleon The French emperor and military leader. Napoleon, a small, plump, arrogant man, embodies self-serving rationalization and vainglory.

Count Ilya Rostov A nobleman. Rostov is a loving, friendly, financially carefree man who lives with his large family at Otradnoe. The old count lives beyond his means, eventually depriving his children of their inheritance—a failing for which he seeks his children's forgiveness before he dies.

Nicholas Rostov The eldest Rostov son. Nicholas spends much of the novel on the front. He accumulates gambling debts that burden his family, but after his father dies, he supports his mother and cousin Sonya on his meager salary while continuing to pay off the family's debts. Nicholas eventually marries the heiress Mary Bolkonskaya, saving his family from financial ruin.

Petya Rostov The youngest Rostov son. Petya, who is close to Natasha and beloved by his mother, is killed in partisan fighting after the French begin their withdrawal from Moscow.

Countess Natalya Rostova Count Rostov's wife. Like her husband, the countess maintains fiscally irresponsible standards of luxury. The death of her youngest son, Petya, sinks the countess into a permanent gloom.

Natasha Rostova The younger Rostov daughter. Natasha, a lively and irrepressible girl, charms everyone she meets. After a series of romantic entanglements, Natasha marries Pierre and becomes a stout, unkempt matron.

Sonya Rostova The humble cousin of Natasha and Nicholas. Sonya lives with the Rostovs as a ward. Sonya generously gives up Nicholas, her childhood sweetheart, so that he can marry a rich woman and save the Rostov finances.

Vera Rostova The eldest Rostov daughter. Vera is cold and unpleasant. Her only proposal of marriage comes from the officer Berg, who candidly admits that he needs her dowry.

Anna Pavlovna Scherer A wealthy St. Petersburg society hostess and matchmaker for the Kuragin family. Anna Pavlovna's party opens the novel.

Speranski A brilliant liberal advisor to the tsar. Until his fall from grace, Speranski attempts to reform and modernize the Russian state.

THEMES IN *WAR AND PEACE*

THE IRRATIONALITY OF HUMAN MOTIVES Tolstoy constantly emphasizes the irrationality that motivates human behavior in both peace and war. He defines wisdom not as the ability to reason, but as the ability to accept the fact that our actions are mysterious, even to ourselves. Tolstoy emphasizes that even war should not revolve around strategy or sensible reasoning. General Kutuzov emerges as a great leader not because he develops a logical plan and demands that everyone follow it, but because he is willing to adapt to unexpected events and think on his feet. In love as well as in war, characters behave irrationally. Nicholas suddenly decides to wed Mary after resolving to go back to Sonya. Natasha marries Pierre unexpectedly. Yet almost all the irrational actions in the novel turn out successfully, which suggests Tolstoy's belief that instinct is more reliable than reason.

THE SEARCH FOR THE MEANING OF LIFE In *War and Peace*, Tolstoy explores the way people think about the meaning of life and the varying ways they try to give their lives meaning. Andrew comprehends the absurdity of life after his near-death experience at Austerlitz. Pierre begins to think about the meaning of life after marrying an unkind woman. He spends most of the novel wondering why his existence is so empty and artificial, and why humans were put on Earth. Tolstoy suggests that of the many ways people try to imbue their lives with meaning, only love works. Pierre tries to find meaning in the mystical practice of Freemasonry, but eventually he grows bored with the Masons and dissatisfied with their passivity. He also tries to find meaning by immersing himself in politics, but eventually his interest morphs into obsession and he develops a crazy fixation on assassinating Napoleon. What finally gives meaning to Pierre's life is the experience of real love with Natasha.

THE LIMITS OF LEADERSHIP Tolstoy creates a cynical, humorous picture of great men. By exploring the full range of society, from peasants to tsars, from servants to emperors, he shows us how Napoleon and Alexander compare to society in general. The comparison is not flattering. Tolstoy presents the supposed giants of history as fretful, ordinary little men not very different from the peasants they terrify. Nicholas is surprised to find that Alexander is just an average man. We are surprised to watch Napoleon in his bathroom getting his plump little body rubbed down. Tolstoy's depiction of these men fits with his philosophy of history. He sees history not as a creation of great men, but as the result of millions of individual chains of cause and effect too small to be controlled or analyzed independently. Emperors may imagine they rule the world, but they too are caught in these innumerable chains.

SYMBOLS IN *WAR AND PEACE*

THE BATTLE OF BORODINO The Battle of Borodino symbolizes the superiority of Russian spirit to European reason. The French are confident that they will win because of their logical advantages and careful planning. The Russians, in contrast, follow more instinctive and less rational principles. Tolstoy depicts the Russian victory at Borodino as a kind of minor miracle, and proof of the triumph of spirit.

THE FRENCH OCCUPATION OF MOSCOW Tolstoy makes the French occupation of Moscow into a symbol of the European cultural invasion of Russia, using it to criticize dependency on foreign styles and institutions wrongly deemed superior to native Russian ones. *War and Peace* opens with a conversation between two Russians chatting in French—proof that the Russian nobility is closer to French aristocrats than to their own Russian peasantry. The answer to the French occupation, Tolstoy implies, is greater appreciation of native Russians.

IMPORTANT QUOTATIONS FROM *WAR AND PEACE*

> "Well, Prince, so Genoa and Lucca are now just family estates of the Buonapartes. But I warn you, if you don't tell me that this means war, if you still try to defend the infamies and horrors perpetrated by that Antichrist—I really believe he is Antichrist—I will have nothing more to do with you.. . ."

Location: Book One, Chapter 1
Speaker: Anna Pavlovna
Context: At her party, Anna talks politics

These words, which open War and Peace, establish a dual focus on wartime aggression and peacetime conversation. They immediately suggest, as the novel's title does, that war and peace will be constantly interwoven in the story, just as military maneuvers go hand in hand with socializing. We might expect a socialite like Anna Pavlovna to live an insular existence, but here she demonstrates a surprising fluency in current events. The Italian principalities of Genoa and Lucca are far from St. Petersburg, yet Anna Pavlovna has a global view of their importance. Her toughness in addressing the prince with threatening phrases such as "I warn you" and "I will have nothing more to do with you" suggests her willingness to act like a general—a trait we also see in the dictatorial way she runs her party. Moreover, Anna Pavlovna shows a diplomat's sensitivity to the political subtleties of language, calling Napoleon by his Italian name, Buonaparte, rather than his French name, Bonaparte, thereby insulting Napoleon's non-French background.

Anna Pavlovna's conversation also reveals how arbitrary and absurd people's understanding of war often is. Her declaration that Napoleon is the Antichrist seems exaggerated and ridiculous even before we encounter Tolstoy's portrait of the French emperor as a silly, vainglorious, and deluded little man. Napoleon may be dangerous, but he is hardly evil incarnate. Similarly, Anna Pavlovna's threats to the prince are social games not intended seriously or taken seriously. Her mock-serious flirtation suggests that most talk of war in higher state circles may be similarly blustery and hollow. Anna Pavlovna may be feigning an interest in the war to appear current and informed. We do not detect much real emotion in what she says, even though the war may threaten her own country's well-being. Reason and clear judgment appear to have little place in discussions about war, as Tolstoy repeatedly shows throughout the novel.

> This black-eyed, wide-mouthed girl, not pretty but full of life . . . ran to hide her flushed face in the lace of her mother's mantilla—not paying the least attention to her severe remark—and began to laugh. She laughed, and in fragmentary sentences tried to explain about a doll which she produced from the folds of her frock.

Location: Book One, Chapter 5
Speaker: The narrator
Context: Tolstoy introduces the major female character of the novel, Natasha Rostova

Tolstoy's introduction of twelve-year-old Natasha Rostova reveals much of her symbolic importance. While almost all the other main characters are introduced by name before they are physically described, Natasha is left nameless for some time. The impression is less of an individual human being than of a mythic presence, an embodiment of vital girlhood. Natasha's wide mouth suggests a readiness to feed on experience and an eagerness to express herself fully, though not necessarily in a rational way. Natasha's inability to "explain" her doll suggests that she is emotional rather than analytical. She may express herself through laughter or other nonverbal means better than she does through reasoned speech. The emotional extravagance and rational limitation evidenced in our first view of Natasha continue through her life, as when she submits to the seductive Anatole and plans a madcap elopement with him.

Natasha's bold and even rebellious spirit comes through in her indifference to her mother's stern remarks. This rebellion later leads to unhappiness when Natasha incurs Sonya's criticism and her family's disapproval by planning to elope with Anatole. Despite its downfalls, rebelliousness leads Natasha to a deeper wisdom than a scrupulous rule-follower like Sonya could ever attain. Finally, Natasha's beloved doll foreshadows her ultimate role as mother of four. She hides in her mother's mantilla while holding her imagined child, suggesting a bond between grandmother, mother, and child that underscores the values of the Rostov family and the continuity of their line.

Pierre, who from the moment Prince Andrew entered the room had watched him with glad, affectionate eyes, now came up and took his arm. Before he looked round Prince Andrew frowned again, expressing his annoyance with whoever was touching his arm, but when he saw Pierre's beaming face he gave him an unexpectedly kind and pleasant smile.

Location: Book One, Chapter 1
Speaker: The narrator
Context: Pierre and Andrew meet

When everything was ready, the stranger opened his eyes, moved to the table, filled a tumbler with tea for himself and one for the beardless old man to whom he passed it. Pierre began to feel a sense of uneasiness, and the need, even the inevitability, of entering into conversation with this stranger.

Location: Book Five, Chapter 1
Speaker: The narrator
Context: Pierre waits at the Torzhok station for a connection on his way to St. Petersburg

---

When he related anything it was generally some old and evidently precious memory of his "Christian" life, as he called his peasant existence. The proverbs, of which his talk was full, were . . . those folk sayings which taken without a context seem so insignificant, but when used appositely suddenly acquire a significance of profound wisdom.

Location: Book Twelve, Chapter 3
Speaker: The narrator
Context: The narrator describes the peasant Platon Karataev

THE WOMAN WARRIOR

Maxine Hong Kingston

A Chinese American woman tells the story of her life.

THE LIFE OF MAXINE HONG KINGSTON

Maxine Hong Kingston was born in 1940 in Stockton, California. She was the oldest of six children. Her parents, Tom and Ying Lan Hong, operated a laundry. In 1962, Kingston graduated from the University of California at Berkeley and married actor Earll Kingston. After participating in the antiwar protests of the late 1960s, the Kingstons moved to Hawaii, where Kingston taught English and wrote two memoirs, *The Woman Warrior* (1976) and *China Men* (1980). She published her first novel, *Tripmaster Monkey: His Fake Book* (1988) after returning to California with her husband. In 1990, Kingston began teaching at Berkeley.

Some have criticized Kingston for purporting to represent the "typical" Chinese American experience and for changing traditional material to suit her needs. For instance, in the "White Tigers" section of *The Woman Warrior*, Kingston reworks the story of Fa Mu Lan, a traditional Chinese myth about a girl who takes her father's place in battle. But Kingston says that she never intended such stories to be either representative or accurate. She also says she is attempting to tell only her story, not the story of all Chinese Americans.

THE WOMAN WARRIOR IN CONTEXT

The Woman Warrior, which won the 1976 National Book Critics Circle Award for nonfiction, fits into many genres. It tells a story of cultural displacement and alienation using postmodern techniques of autobiography. Though *The Woman Warrior* can stand on its own, Kingston did intend it to be read in conjunction with *China Men*, which focuses on Kingston's father. Kingston has said that she considers *China Men* a more accomplished work than *The Woman Warrior*. Still, it is the first memoir that usually appears on high-school and college syllabi and in anthologies.

The Woman Warrior explores issues of gender, especially regarding the role of women in traditional Chinese society. The character Brave Orchid has an archetypal Chinese attitude of self-denial and self-abnegation for the good of the community—the same qualities that "No-Name Woman" lacks. Kingston's memoir is full of references to the subjugation of women in Chinese culture and tradition. *The Woman Warrior* chronicles Kingston's search for voice and strength within a society that considers it "better to have geese than girls."

THE WOMAN WARRIOR: KEY FACTS

Full title: The Woman Warrior: Memoirs of a Girlhood Among Ghosts
Time and place written: 1973–1975; Hawaii
Date of first publication: 1976
Publisher: Alfred A. Knopf
Type of Work: Memoir
Genre: Autobiography
Language: English
Setting (time): 1924–1975
Setting (place): China, Canton, and California

Tense: Immediate past, present	
Tone: Angry, childlike, ironic	
Narrator: Kingston in the first person	
Point of view: Kingston's	
Protagonist: Kingston and Brave Orchid	
Antagonist: Brave Orchid	

THE WOMAN WARRIOR: PLOT OVERVIEW

The Woman Warrior tells the stories of five women: Kingston's long-dead aunt, "No-Name Woman"; a mythical female warrior, Fa Mu Lan; Kingston's mother, Brave Orchid; Kingston's aunt, Moon Orchid; and Kingston herself. The five chapters of the memoir combine Kingston's narration with a series of her mother's talk-stories—spoken stories that combine Chinese history, myths, and beliefs.

The first chapter, "No-Name Woman," begins with a talk-story about an aunt Kingston never knew she had. After disgracing her family by having an illegitimate child, this aunt killed herself and her baby by jumping into the family well in China. Kingston's mother tells her this story as a warning and forbids Kingston to mention her aunt aloud again. Kingston decides to create a history of her aunt in her memoir. She imagines how her aunt attracted a suitor, comparing her aunt's quiet rebellion to her own rebellion. Kingston imagines her aunt giving birth in a pigsty. She thinks of her aunt's ghost walking around with no one to give it gifts, as was Chinese custom. In the end, Kingston does not know whether she is doing justice to her aunt's memory or just serving her own needs.

"White Tigers" is based on a talk-story about the mythical female warrior Fa Mu Lan. Fa Mu Lan, whose story Kingston tells in the first person, begins training to become a warrior at age seven. Pretending to be a man, she leads an army in battle against a corrupt baron and emperor. After her battles are over, she becomes a wife and mother. Kingston contrasts Fa Mu Lan's life to her own in America, where she can hardly stand up to her racist bosses. Kingston realizes that words are her weapons.

In "Shaman," Kingston tells the story of her mother, Brave Orchid, and her life in China. In her village, Brave Orchid was a powerful doctor, midwife, and destroyer of ghosts. As a girl, Kingston found the story of her mother's life astounding and terrifying. Many of the images from that story—Chinese babies left to die, slave girls bought and sold, a woman stoned to death by villagers—haunt Kingston's dreams for years. At the end of the chapter, Maxine visits her mother after a separation of many years. The two women end many years of disagreement and conflict by coming to an understanding. Brave Orchid is warm and affectionate toward her daughter for the first time in the memoir.

The title of "At the Western Palace" refers to Brave Orchid's talk-story about an emperor who had four wives. The story is an allegory about Brave Orchid's sister, Moon Orchid. Moon Orchid's husband left her behind in China, remarried in America, and became a successful doctor. Brave Orchid urges her sister to come to America and confront her errant husband. The confrontation is disastrous, and Moon Orchid, who does not speak a word of English, is left to fend for herself in America. She goes crazy and dies in a California state mental asylum.

The final chapter of the memoir, "A Song for a Barbarian Reed Pipe," tells the story of Kingston's childhood and teenage years. Kingston spent the early part of her life angry and frustrated by trying to express herself and please an unappreciative mother. A number of characters in the chapter reflect Kingston's own characteristics, including a silent Chinese girl whom Kingston torments as a little girl. Kingston eventually erupts at her mother, letting loose a torrent of complaints and criticisms. Later in her life, however, Kingston appreciates her mother and her talk-stories. At the end of the chapter, she tells one of her own: the story of Ts'ai Yen, a warrior poetess captured by barbarians who returns to the Chinese with songs from another land.

CHARACTERS IN THE WOMAN WARRIOR

Brave Orchid Kingston's mother. Brave Orchid's talk-stories about Chinese life and traditions haunt Kingston and make up a large part of her memoir. Brave Orchid is a proud and intelligent woman who is both gentle and cruel.

Maxine Hong Kingston The author and narrator of *The Woman Warrior*. Kingston's memories of her own life do not figure prominently until the final chapter, "A Song for a Barbarian Reed Pipe," in which she shakes off the frustrations of her childhood and finds her own voice.

Fa Mu Lan A heroic female warrior from a traditional Chinese legend. Fa Mu Lan represents both the female ideal of motherhood and the male ideal of power and independence.

Moon Orchid Brave Orchid's sister. At Brave Orchid's urging, Moon Orchid comes to America in the 1960s to find her estranged husband, who left China thirty years earlier. Moon Orchid is timid and incapable.

Moon Orchid's Husband A successful doctor in Los Angeles.

No-Name Woman Kingston's unnamed aunt. No-Name Woman kills herself and her illegitimate child in China. Kingston imagines a history for her aunt, portraying her as a timid woman who gave in to a forbidden passion and was then driven to suicide by the condemnation of her village.

The Old Couple An elderly couple in the legend of Fa Mu Lan. The old couple train Fa Mu Lan in martial arts and survival skills on top of the mountain. The old couple are quasi-deities.

The Silent Girl A classmate of Kingston's. Like Kingston, the silent girl is quiet and unpopular. Kingston torments the girl because she hates being reminded of her own weaknesses.

Ts'ai Yen A Chinese poet born in 175 A.D. After barbarians captured Ts'ai Yen and forced her to fight their battles, she brought her people, the Han, a song called "Eighteen Stanzas for a Barbarian Reed Pipe." Ts'ai Yen's song from a savage land is a metaphor for Kingston's memoir.

THEMES IN *THE WOMAN WARRIOR*

THE TYRANNY OF WOMEN Kingston suggests that even if patriarchy is to blame for oppressing women, it is women, not men, who enthusiastically continue the tradition of oppression. Women say things like "better to have geese than girls," women destroy the house of No-Name Woman, girls torment each other on the playground. Brave Orchid tells stories of female swordswomen and shamans, and is herself an accomplished, intelligent doctor, but she also reinforces the notion that girls are always disappointments to their parents, no matter how much they accomplish. As a little girl, Kingston is haunted by the ghosts of Chinese girls whose parents left them to die because they wanted sons instead of daughters. With the story of Fa Mu Lan, Kingston suggests that refusing to belong entirely to the gender is the only way to resolve the dilemma. Fa Mu Lan manages to be both man and woman, leading her people to victory in battle and then becoming a wife and mother.

SILENCE AND VOICE Kingston stresses the importance of silence in the first words of her memoir: "You must not tell anyone." The importance of silence may seem counterintuitive at first. Memoirs themselves exist to break silence, to tell an important story to as many people as possible. Also, Brave Orchid continually gives voice to Chinese customs, traditions, and ghosts. But silence does pervade the Chinese emigrant community Kingston portrays. Often, the emigrants' children bear the burden of the community's silence. Kingston, who is quiet and socially awkward as a girl, chronicles her battle against silence in *The Woman Warrior*. Brave Orchid helps her and hinders her in this battle. She says she cut Kingston's tongue in order to help her talk more, although Kingston believes she did it to silence her. Despite her own natural reticence and the dubious influence of Brave Orchid, Kingston eventually begins to tell talk-stories herself. The existence of the memoir testifies to her success at finding her voice.

THE DIFFICULTIES OF THE FIRST GENERATION Although Kingston has said she did not intend her memoir to be "representative," *The Woman Warrior* does speak to the widespread displacement and frustration Kingston perceives in the Chinese American community. Especially for the first generation born in America, Kingston suggests, it is difficult to reconcile the heavy-handed and often restrictive expectations of parents with the relative freedom and laxity of life in America. Being Chinese American often means being torn between two worlds without feeling like a part of either. Kingston feels as different from her own relatives as she does from her American classmates. Many of the typical traits of Chinese women, such as a loud speaking voice, are not considered "American-feminine," which leads to confusion. Women and men of the first generation must contend with a cultural heritage that is always secondhand, filtered through the lens—or talk-story—of a parent. *The Woman Warrior* is largely about Kingston's attempt to understand what is Chinese, what is peculiar to her family, what is real, and what is just "the movies."

SYMBOLS IN *THE WOMAN WARRIOR*

BIRDS In "White Tigers," the bird that guides seven-year-old Fa Mu Lan up the mountain to meet her mentors symbolizes the fantastical possibility of a girl literally rising above her station in life to become a great leader. In the story of the death of Kingston's Fourth Uncle, birds symbolize death. This dark symbolism disturbs Kingston, who thinks of the happy symbolism of birds in Fa Mu Lan's story and worries that the talk-stories are contradicting themselves. In "Shaman," birds symbolize luck. A sea bird is painted on the side of Brave Orchid's boat to Canton, possibly warding off the pirates who board the very next ship. Birds might also represent fortune in the literal sense. When Brave Orchid goes to the market to shop, her wallet unfolds "like wings."

CIRCLES In "No-Name Woman," the circle symbolizes the Chinese belief in community, family kinship, and law. The Chinese family is like a circle: people have children to look after them when they get old, and then the dead look after the family. It is also a closed circle, shut off to everyone outside it. Any interruption in the circle has profound effects. No-Name Woman's transgression has such dire consequences because it breaks her family circle.

IMPORTANT QUOTATIONS FROM *THE WOMAN WARRIOR*

> *"See here. We know his address. He's living in Los Angeles with his second wife, and they have three children. Claim your rights. Those are your children. He's got two sons, You have two sons. You take them away from her. You become their mother."*
>
> *"Do you really think I can be a mother of sons? Don't you think they'll be loyal to her, since she gave birth to them?"*
>
> *"The children will go to their true mother—you," said Brave Orchid. "That's the way it is with mothers and children."*

Location: "At the Western Palace"
Speaker: Brave Orchid and Moon Orchid
Context: Brave Orchid urges her sister to confront her husband and his children

Brave Orchid has grand illusions that her sister will confront her estranged husband and be welcomed into his new home. So confident is Brave Orchid in this outcome that she has convinced Moon Orchid to sell her apartment and move to America for good. This exchange illustrates the extent of Brave Orchid's delusions about how emigrant Chinese behave in America. She assumes that the old traditions will carry over in the new country and asserts, without hesitation, that the children will renounce their own mother. Theoretically, Brave Orchid should know more about America than her sister does, but it is Moon Orchid who provides the voice of reason. She points out what everyone but Brave Orchid understands, foreshadowing the disaster of the eventual confrontation. The fact that Brave Orchid is so misguided here raises the possibility that she has misinterpreted other Chinese traditions.

> Be careful what you say. It comes true. It comes true. I had to leave home in order to see the world logically, logic the new way of seeing. I learned to think that mysteries are for explanation. I enjoy the simplicity. Concrete pours out of my mouth to cover the forests with freeways and sidewalks. Give me

plastics, periodical tables, TV dinners with vegetables no more complex than peas mixed with diced carrots. Shine floodlights into dark corners: no ghosts.

Location: "A Song for a Barbarian Reed Pipe"
Speaker: Kingston
Context: Kingston writes about leaving home

In this passage, Kingston explains the clarity she felt after leaving home. Away from her mother, she could tell real from false and find sense where before there was only confusion. She found that she could Americanize herself, turn herself into a woman of plastic and TV dinners. Kingston is ambivalent about this change. She urges us to "be careful" what we say, as if she wishes she had not longed for logic, clarity, and Americanization. Kingston characterizes herself as an American ruining the natural world, likening her literary output to concrete poured over forests. The implicit and unfavorable comparison is to her mother's talk-stories, populated by mythical places and people—the kind of mysterious forests Kingston now destroys. Still, Kingston admits that Americanization has its pleasures. She enjoys "the simplicity" of her new self.

"You must not tell anyone," my mother said, "what I am about to tell you. In China your father had a sister who killed herself. She jumped into the family well. We say that your father has all brothers because it is as if she had never been born."

Location: The opening passage of "No-Name Woman"
Speaker: Brave Orchid
Context: Brave Orchid tells Kingston about her disgraced aunt

---

The swordswoman and I are not so dissimilar. May my people understand the resemblance soon so that I can return to them. What we have in common are the words at our backs. The idioms for revenge are "report a crime" and "report to five families." The reporting is the vengeance—not the beheading, not the gutting, but the words. And I have so many words—"chink" words and "gook" words too—that they do not fit on my skin.

Location: The end of "White Tigers"
Speaker: Kingston
Context: Kingston compares herself to Fa Mu Lan

To make my waking life American-normal, I turn on the lights before anything untoward makes an appearance. I push the deformed into my dreams, which are in Chinese, the language of impossible stories. Before we can leave our parents, they stuff our heads like the suitcases which they jam-pack with homemade underwear.

Location: "Shaman"
Speaker: Kingston
Context: Kingston reflects on the anguish of combining cultures

WUTHERING HEIGHTS

Emily Brontë

A mistreated man robbed of his true love tries to revenge himself on his abusers.

THE LIFE OF EMILY BRONTË

Emily Brontë was born in Yorkshire, England, in 1818 to Maria Branwell and Patrick Brontë. When Brontë was three, her mother died. In 1824, Brontë and three of her sisters—Maria, Elizabeth, and Charlotte—were sent to Cowan Bridge, a school for clergymen's daughters. Maria and Elizabeth died of tuberculosis, and Emily and Charlotte were brought home.

Under Charlotte's direction, the Brontë sisters founded a school. The venture was unsuccessful, but the sisters' literary projects flourished. Charlotte, Anne, and Emily collaborated on a book of poems, publishing under male pseudonyms: Charlotte was Currer Bell, Emily was Ellis Bell, and Anne was Acton Bell. When the poetry volume received little public notice, the sisters decided to work on separate novels, still using their pseudonyms. Anne and Emily produced their novels in 1847 (*Agnes Grey* and *Wuthering Heights* respectively). Charlotte never found a publisher for her first novel, *The Professor*, but her second novel, *Jane Eyre*, became one of the most successful of its era, both critically and commercially.

Emily Brontë died in 1848 at age thirty.

WUTHERING HEIGHTS IN CONTEXT

Wuthering Heights, which has long been one of the most popular novels in English literature, went almost unnoticed when it was published in 1847. It sold very poorly and received only a few mixed reviews. Victorian readers found the novel shocking in its depiction of passionate, ungoverned love and cruelty (despite the fact that the novel portrays no sex or bloodshed), and the work was virtually ignored. Even Charlotte Brontë, who wrote about Gothic love and desolate landscapes, was ambivalent about the unapologetic intensity of her sister's novel. In a preface to the novel, which she wrote shortly after Emily Brontë's death, Charlotte Brontë stated, "Whether it is right or advisable to create beings like Heathcliff, I do not know. I scarcely think it is."

Today, *Wuthering Heights* has a secure position in the canon of world literature, and Emily Brontë is revered as one of the finest writers—male or female—of the nineteenth century. Like Charlotte Brontë's *Jane Eyre*, *Wuthering Heights* is based partly on the Gothic tradition of the late eighteenth century, a style of literature that featured supernatural encounters, crumbling ruins, moonless nights, and grotesque imagery. But *Wuthering Heights* transcends its genre with sophisticated observation and artistic subtlety.

WUTHERING HEIGHTS: KEY FACTS

Time and place written: 1846–7; Haworth, Yorkshire

Date of first publication: 1847

Publisher: Thomas C. Newby

Type of work: Novel

Genre: Gothic novel; frame story

Language: English

Setting (time): The 1770s–1802

Setting (place): Two houses on the Yorkshire moors

Tense: Past

Tone: Melodramatic

Narrator: Lockwood in the first person and in Nelly's voice

Point of View: Nelly's

Protagonist: Heathcliff, Catherine

Antagonist: Heathcliff's need for revenge

WUTHERING HEIGHTS: PLOT OVERVIEW

In the late winter months of 1801, a man named Lockwood rents a manor house called Thrushcross Grange in the isolated moor country of England. His landlord is a dour, wealthy man named Heathcliff who lives in the ancient manor of Wuthering Heights, four miles away from the Grange. In this wild, stormy countryside, Lockwood asks his housekeeper, Nelly Dean, to tell him the story of Heathcliff and the people of Wuthering Heights. Nelly consents, and Lockwood writes down his recollections of her tale in his diary. These written recollections form the main part of *Wuthering Heights.*

Nelly remembers her childhood. As a young girl, she works as a servant at Wuthering Heights for the owner of the manor, Mr. Earnshaw, and his family. One day, Mr. Earnshaw goes to Liverpool and returns home with an orphan boy whom he plans to raise with his own children. At first, the Earnshaw children—a boy named Hindley and his younger sister Catherine—detest the dark-skinned Heathcliff. But Catherine soon comes to love him, and the two grow inseparable. After his wife's death, Mr. Earnshaw grows to prefer Heathcliff to his own son, and when Hindley continues to treat Heathcliff cruelly, Mr. Earnshaw sends Hindley away to college, keeping Heathcliff nearby.

Three years later, Mr. Earnshaw dies, and Hindley inherits Wuthering Heights. He returns with a wife, Frances, and immediately seeks revenge on Heathcliff, forcing him to work in the fields like a common laborer. Heathcliff continues his close relationship with Catherine, however. One night they wander to Thrushcross Grange, hoping to tease Edgar and Isabella Linton, the cowardly, snobbish children who live there. A dog bites Catherine, and she must stay at the Grange for five weeks, recuperating. Mrs. Linton tries to turn Catherine into a proper young lady. Catherine returns home infatuated with Edgar Linton.

When Frances dies after giving birth to a baby boy named Hareton, Hindley descends into alcoholism and behaves even more cruelly and abusively toward Heathcliff. Eventually, Catherine's desire for social advancement prompts her to get engaged to Edgar Linton, despite her overpowering love for Heathcliff. Heathcliff leaves Wuthering Heights.

Three years later, after Catherine's marriage to Edgar, Heathcliff returns, determined to take revenge on all who have wronged him. Now vastly and mysteriously wealthy, he lends money to the drunken Hindley, knowing that Hindley will only increase his debts. When Hindley dies, Heathcliff inherits the manor. He also places himself in line to inherit Thrushcross Grange by marrying Isabella Linton, whom he treats cruelly. Catherine becomes ill, gives birth to a daughter, and dies. Heathcliff begs her spirit to remain on Earth. He says she may haunt him or drive him mad as long as she does not leave him alone. Shortly thereafter, Isabella flees to London and gives birth to Heathcliff's son, Linton.

Thirteen years pass. Nelly Dean works as nursemaid to Catherine's daughter at Thrushcross Grange. Young Catherine is beautiful and headstrong like her mother, but she has some of her father's gentleness. Young Catherine grows up at the Grange with no knowledge of Wuthering Heights until she discovers it one day while wandering through the moors. She meets Hareton, Hindley's son, and plays with him. Isabella dies, and Linton comes to live with Heathcliff. Heathcliff treats his sickly, whining son even more cruelly than he treated the boy's mother.

Three years later, young Catherine meets Heathcliff on the moors and visits Wuthering Heights to meet Linton. She and Linton begin a secret romance conducted entirely through letters. When Nelly destroys Catherine's collection of letters, the girl begins sneaking out at night to spend time with her frail young lover. However, it quickly becomes apparent that Linton is pursuing Catherine only because Heathcliff is forcing him to. Heathcliff hopes that a marriage between Catherine and Linton would solidify his legal claim on Thrushcross Grange. One day, with Edgar Linton near death, Heathcliff lures Nelly and Catherine back to Wuthering Heights and holds them prisoner until Catherine marries Linton. Edgar dies, and soon Linton dies too. Heathcliff now controls both Wuthering Heights and Thrushcross Grange. He forces Catherine to live at Wuthering Heights as a servant.

Nelly's story ends as she reaches the present. Lockwood, appalled, ends his tenancy at Thrushcross Grange and returns to London. Six months later, he pays a visit to Nelly and learns of further developments in the story. Although Catherine originally mocked Hareton's ignorance and illiteracy (in an act of retribution, Heathcliff ended Hareton's education after Hindley died), she grows to love Hareton as they live together at Wuthering Heights. Heathcliff becomes more and more obsessed with the memory of the elder Catherine and begins speaking to her ghost. Shortly after a night spent walking on the moors, Heathcliff dies. Hareton and young Catherine inherit Wuthering Heights and Thrushcross Grange and plan to marry on the next New Year's Day. After hearing the end of the story, Lockwood goes to visit the graves of Catherine and Heathcliff.

CHARACTERS IN *WUTHERING HEIGHTS*

THE FIRST GENERATION

Mr. Earnshaw Catherine and Hindley's father. Mr. Earnshaw adopts Heathcliff and comes to love him more than Hindley. Nevertheless, he bequeaths Wuthering Heights to Hindley.

Mrs. Earnshaw Catherine and Hindley's mother. Mrs. Earnshaw dislikes and distrusts Heathcliff. She dies shortly after Heathcliff's arrival.

Mr. Linton Edgar and Isabella's father. Mr. Linton owns Thrushcross Grange when Heathcliff and Catherine are children.

Mrs. Linton Mr. Linton's snobbish wife. Mrs. Linton does not like her children, Edgar and Isabella, to associate with Heathcliff. She instills social ambitions in Catherine.

THE SECOND GENERATION

Catherine One of the novel's protagonists. Catherine, Mr. Earnshaw's daughter, falls powerfully in love with Heathcliff. However, her desire for social advancement motivates her to marry Edgar Linton. Catherine is free-spirited, beautiful, spoiled, and often arrogant. She brings misery to both of the men who love her.

Frances Earnshaw Hindley's simpering, silly wife. Frances dies shortly after giving birth to Hareton.

Hindley Earnshaw Catherine's brother, and Mr. Earnshaw's son. Hindley resents Heathcliff's presence at Wuthering Heights. After his father dies and he inherits the estate, Hindley abuses Heathcliff, terminating his education and forcing him to work in the fields. When Hindley's wife, Frances, dies shortly after giving birth to their son Hareton, Hindley lapses into alcoholism and dissipation.

Heathcliff One of the novel's protagonists. An orphan adopted by Mr. Earnshaw, Heathcliff falls intensely in love with Mr. Earnshaw's daughter, Catherine. After Catherine marries Edgar Linton, Heathcliff's humiliation and misery sour him. He spends most of the rest of his life seeking revenge on Hindley, his beloved Catherine, and their respective children (Hareton and young Catherine). Heathcliff is a powerful, fierce, and often cruel man.

Edgar Linton Isabella Linton's brother. Well-bred but rather spoiled as a boy, Edgar Linton grows into a tender, constant, but cowardly man. He is an almost ideal gentleman, but he is no match for Heathcliff, who gains power over Edgar's wife, sister, and daughter.

Isabella Linton Edgar Linton's sister. Isabella falls in love with Heathcliff, whom she sees as a romantic figure, like a character in a novel. Heathcliff marries her because she is a useful tool in his quest for revenge on the Linton family.

THE THIRD GENERATION

Catherine Catherine's daughter. Like her mother, Catherine is headstrong, impetuous, and occasionally arrogant. However, Edgar's influence has made young Catherine a gentler and more compassionate woman than her mother.

Hareton Earnshaw The son of Hindley and Frances Earnshaw, and Catherine's nephew. After Hindley's death, Heathcliff forced Hareton to be an uneducated field worker, just as Hindley did to Heathcliff himself. Illiterate and quick-tempered, Hareton is easily humiliated, but he has a good heart and a deep desire to improve himself. At the end of the novel, he and young Catherine fall in love.

Linton Heathcliff Heathcliff's son by Isabella. Weak, sniveling, demanding, and constantly ill, Linton does not meet his father until he is thirteen years old. Heathcliff despises Linton, treats him contemptuously, and, by forcing him to marry the young Catherine, uses him to cement his control over Thrushcross Grange after Edgar Linton's death. Linton himself dies not long after this marriage.

OTHERS

Ellen (Nelly) Dean The chief narrator of the novel. A sensible, intelligent, and compassionate woman, Nelly grew up as a servant alongside Hindley and Catherine.

Mr. Green Edgar Linton's lawyer. Mr. Green arrives too late to hear Edgar change his will in order to prevent Heathcliff from obtaining control over Thrushcross Grange.

Joseph An elderly servant at Wuthering Heights. Joseph is longwinded, fanatically religious, stubborn, and unkind.

Lockwood A gentleman who rents Thrushcross Grange. Lockwood's narration forms a frame around Nelly's. A somewhat vain and presumptuous gentleman, Lockwood occasionally misunderstands the events of the story.

Zillah The housekeeper at Wuthering Heights during the later stages of the narrative.

THEMES IN *WUTHERING HEIGHTS*

THE DESTRUCTIVENESS OF UNCHANGING LOVE Brontë neither condemns Catherine and Heathcliff nor idealizes them as romantic heroes. She does make it clear, however, that they are doomed to be unhappy because of their inability to change. After falling in love as children, Catherine and Heathcliff freeze emotionally. Catherine marries Edgar, but she refuses to sacrifice Heathcliff or love Edgar. In Chapter XII, she says she longs to return to the moors of her childhood. Heathcliff has an almost superhuman ability to maintain the same passion and to nurse the same grudges for years and years. Part of their inability to change, Brontë suggests, comes from their conviction that they are one person. To let go of each other or allow their passion to cool would be to let go of themselves. Catherine declares, famously, "I *am* Heathcliff." Heathcliff wails that he cannot live without his "soul," meaning Catherine. Because Catherine and Heathcliff refuse to change, their tragedies are overcome not by some climactic reversal, but by the inexorable passage of time and the rise of a new generation.

THE PRECARIOUSNESS OF SOCIAL CLASS Brontë portrays members of the gentry (the upper-middle class) as anxious about their place in society. Unlike aristocrats, the gentry did not have titles to formally solidify their status. They were considered more or less gentlemanly depending on the amount of land they owned, the number of tenants and servants they kept, their manner of speaking, their ability to afford horses and a carriage, and the provenance of their money. The gentry in *Wuthering Heights* go to great lengths to prove that their position in the gentry is solid. Catherine marries Edgar so that she will be "the greatest woman of the neighbourhood." The Lintons take pains to flaunt their status. The Earnshaws, who do not have a carriage, much land, or a grand house, struggle to maintain their place. A large part of Heathcliff's revenge involves turning himself from a common laborer into a landed, wealthy gentleman. Even when he succeeds, the status-conscious Lockwood remarks that Heathcliff is only a gentleman in "dress and manners."

THE CONFLICT BETWEEN NATURE AND CULTURE *Wuthering Heights* can be interpreted as an allegory for the corruption of culture by nature. The Earnshaw family, Catherine and Heathcliff in particular, represent nature. Earnshaws act on their passions, not on their sober reflections. The Linton family represents culture, refinement, and convention. When Catherine is brought into Thrushcross

Grange, nature and culture are set on a collision course. The Linton family gets involved in the dramas of the Earnshaw family, and tragedy results.

SYMBOLS IN *WUTHERING HEIGHTS*

MOORS Moors—wide, wild expanses, high and soggy—symbolize the danger of nature. Moors cannot be cultivated. People get lost on them and drown in them. Catherine and Heathcliff play on the moors as children, and the moors come to symbolize the dangerous, wild nature of their love.

GHOSTS Brontë is ambiguous about whether the ghosts of *Wuthering Heights* are real or imagined. Either way, they symbolize the potent power of memory.

IMPORTANT QUOTATIONS FROM *WUTHERING HEIGHTS*

[Mr. Heathcliff] is a dark-skinned gypsy in aspect, in dress and manners a gentleman, that is, as much a gentleman as many a country squire: rather slovenly, perhaps, yet not looking amiss with his negligence, because he has an erect and handsome figure—and rather morose. Possibly, some people might suspect him of a degree of under-bred pride; I have a sympathetic chord within that tells me it is nothing of the sort: I know, by instinct, his reserve springs from an aversion to showy displays of feeling—to manifestations of mutual kindliness. He'll love and hate, equally under cover, and esteem it a species of impertinence to be loved or hated again—No, I'm running on too fast—I bestow my own attributes overliberally on him.

Location: Chapter I
Speaker: Lockwood
Context: Lockwood tries to puzzle out Heathcliff's character

This is the first of many attempts to explain the character and motivations of the mysterious Heathcliff. For Lockwood, the question of Heathcliff's social position—is he a gentleman or a gypsy?—causes particular confusion. The reader, just entering the story of *Wuthering Heights*, is reliant on Lockwood for information. Already, however, Lockwood seems to be an untrustworthy narrator. He freely admits projecting his "own attributes" onto the fascinating Heathcliff. His claim to recognize Heathcliff as a kindred soul whom he can understand "by instinct" later seems absurd. The gossipy, vain Lockwood does not resemble Heathcliff in the least. Lockwood's many misjudgments and blunders reveal how easy it is to misinterpret Heathcliff's complex character. They also serve as a warning to readers not to trust either Lockwood or their own instincts too far.

The ledge, where I placed my candle, had a few mildewed books piled up in one corner; and it was covered with writing scratched on the paint. This writing, however, was nothing but a name repeated in all kinds of characters, large and small—Catherine Earnshaw, here and there varied to Catherine Heathcliff, and then again to Catherine Linton. In vapid listlessness I leant my head against the window, and continued spelling over Catherine Earnshaw—Heathcliff—Linton, till my eyes closed; but they had not rested five minutes when a glare of white letters started from the dark, as vivid as spectres—the air swarmed with Catherines; and rousing myself to dispel the obtrusive name, I discovered my candle wick reclining on one of the antique volumes, and perfuming the place with an odour of roasted calf-skin.

Location: Chapter III
Speaker: Lockwood
Context: Lockwood reads and dreams

Lockwood describes the first of the troubling dreams he has in Catherine's old bed. The quotation emphasizes Lockwood's role as stand-in for the reader of *Wuthering Heights*. Like that reader, Lockwood is a perplexed outsider determined to discover the secrets of Heathcliff and Catherine. Catherine first appears to Lockwood, as she does to readers, as a written word—her name is scratched into paint. When Lockwood reads over the scraped letters, they take on a ghostly power, just as Brontë's characters rise off the page and take on larger meaning in her readers' minds. What gives the Catherine spectres their swarming, ghostly power is the reader, Lockwood. By reading Catherine's names and thinking about them, he imbues them with meaning, just as the reader imbues *Wuthering Heights* with meaning.

This passage also indicates the difficulty of classifying *Wuthering Heights*. The novel often straddles two genres: the Gothic, a genre popular in the late eighteenth century featuring ghosts, gloom, and demonic heroes, and the socially conscious realistic novel, a genre on the ascent when Brontë wrote *Wuthering Heights*. In this passage, as in many others, Gothic and realistic elements exist simultaneously. The ghosts can be interpreted from a Gothic stance as physical beings no less real than the other characters, but they can also be interpreted from a realistic stance as nightmares springing from the tormented psyches of the characters who see them.

It would degrade me to marry Heathcliff now; so he shall never know how I love him; and that, not because he's handsome, Nelly, but because he's more myself than I am. Whatever our souls are made of, his and mine are the same, and [Edgar's] is as different as a moonbeam from lightning, or frost from fire.

Location: Chapter IX
Speaker: Catherine
Context: Catherine explains the nature of her love for Heathcliff

---

". . . I got the sexton, who was digging Linton's grave, to remove the earth off her coffin lid, and I opened it. I thought, once, I would have stayed there, when I saw her face again—it is hers yet—he had hard work to stir me; but he said it would change, if the air blew on it, and so I struck one side of the coffin loose, and covered it up—not Linton's side, damn him! I wish he'd been soldered in lead—and I bribed the sexton to pull it away, when I'm laid there, and slide mine out too. I'll have it made so, and then, by the time Linton gets to us, he'll not know which is which!"

Location: Chapter XXIX
Speaker: Heathcliff
Context: Heathcliff describes looking at Catherine's corpse

That, however, which you may suppose the most potent to arrest my imagination, is actually the least, for what is not connected with her to me? and what does not recall her? I cannot look down to this floor, but her features are shaped on the flags! In every cloud, in every tree—filling the air at night, and caught by glimpses in every object by day, I am surrounded with her image! The most ordinary faces of men and women—my own features—mock me with a resemblance. The entire world is a dreadful collection of memoranda that she did exist, and that I have lost her!

Location: Chapter XXXIII
Speaker: Heathcliff
Context: Heathcliff explains how the memory of Catherine torments him

APPENDIX I: TITLES LISTED BY AUTHOR

Achebe, Chinua	*Things Fall Apart*
Aeschylus	*Agamemnon*
Alcott, Louisa May	*Little Women*
Alighieri, Dante	*Inferno*
Angelou, Maya	*I Know Why the Caged Bird Sings*
Anonymous	*Beowulf*
	Epic of Gilgamesh, The
	Sir Gawain and the Green Knight
Atwood, Margaret	*Handmaid's Tale, The*
Austen, Jane	*Emma*
	Pride and Prejudice
	Sense and Sensibility
Beckett, Samuel	*Waiting for Godot*
Bolt, Robert	*Man for All Seasons, A*
Bradbury, Ray	*Farenheit 451*
Bronte, Charlotte	*Jane Eyre*
Bronte, Emily	*Wuthering Heights*
Buck, Pearl	*Good Earth, The*
Burgess, Anthony	*Clockwork Orange, A*
Camus, Albert	*Plague, The*
	Stranger, The
Carroll, Lewis	*Alice in Wonderland*
Cather, Willa	*My Antonia*
Cervantes, Miguel de	*Don Quixote*
Chaucer, Geoffrey	*Canterbury Tales, The*
Chopin, Kate	*Awakening, The*
Cisneros, Sandra	*House on Mango Street, The*
Conrad, Joseph	*Heart of Darkness*
Cooper, James Fenimore	*Last of the Mohicans, The*
Crane, Stephen	*Red Badge of Courage, The*
Defoe, Daniel	*Robinson Crusoe*
Dickens, Charles	*Christmas Carol, A*
	David Copperfield
	Great Expectations
	Hard Times
	Oliver Twist
	Tale of Two Cities, A
Dostoevsky, Fyodor	*Brothers Karamazov*
	Crime and Punishment
Douglass, Frederick	*Narrative of the Life of Frederick Douglass*
Dumas, Alexandre	*Count of Monte Cristo, The*
Eliot, George	*Silas Marner*
Ellison, Ralph	*Invisible Man*
Euripides	*Medea*
Faulkner, William	*As I Lay Dying*
	Light in August

	Sound and the Fury, The
Fitzgerald, F. Scott	*Great Gatsby, The*
Flaubert, Gustave	*Madame Bovary*
Forster, E.M.	*Passage to India*
Frank, Anne	*Diary of a Young Girl, The*
Gardner, John	*Grendel*
Golding, William	*Lord of the Flies, The*
Hansberry, Lorraine	*Raisin in the Sun, A*
Hardy, Thomas	*Far from the Madding Crowd*
	Mayor of Casterbridge, The
	Tess of the D'Urbervilles
Hawthorne, Nathaniel	*House of Seven Gables*
	Scarlet Letter, The
Heller, Joseph	*Catch-22*
Hemingway, Ernest	*Farewell to Arms, A*
	Old Man and the Sea, The
	Sun Also Rises, The
Hesse, Hermann	*Siddhartha*
Hinton, S.E.	*Outsiders, The*
Homer	*Iliad, The*
	Odyssey, The
Hugo, Victor	*Les Miserables*
Hurston, Zora Neale	*Their Eyes Were Watching God*
Huxley, Aldous	*Brave New World*
Ibsen, Henrik	*Doll House, The*
	Hedda Gabler
James, Henry	*Turn of the Screw, The*
Joyce, James	*Dubliners*
	Portrait of the Artist as a Young Man, A
	Ulysses
Kafka, Franz	*Metamorphosis*
Kerouac, Jack	*On the Road*
Kesey, Ken	*One Flew Over the Cuckoo's Nest*
Kingston, Maxine Hong	*Woman Warrior*
Knowles, John	*Separate Peace, A*
Lee, Harper	*To Kill a Mockingbird*
London, Jack	*Call of the Wild*
Machiavelli, Niccolo	*Prince, The*
Marlowe, Christopher	*Doctor Faustus*
Marquez, Gabriel Garcia	*One Hundred Years of Solitude*
Melville, Herman	*Billy Budd*
	Moby Dick
Miller, Arthur	*Crucible, The*
	Death of a Salesman
Milton, John	*Paradise Lost*
Morrison, Toni	*Beloved*
	Song of Solomon
Nabokov, Vladimir	*Lolita*
O'Brien, Tim	*Things They Carried, The*
Orwell, George	*1984*
	Animal Farm
Paton, Alan	*Cry, the Beloved Country*
Plath, Sylvia	*Bell Jar, The*

Plato	*Plato's Republic*
Potok, Chaim	*Chosen, The*
Rand, Ayn	*Fountainhead, The*
Remarque, Erich Maria	*All Quiet on the Western Front*
Rostand, Edmond	*Cyrano*
Salinger, J.D.	*Catcher in the Rye, The*
Shakespeare, William	*Hamlet*
	Julius Caesar
	King Lear
	Macbeth
	Merchant of Venice, The
	Midsummer Night's Dream, A
	Much Ado About Nothing
	Othello
	Romeo & Juliet
	Tempest, The
Shaw, George Bernard	*Pygmalion*
Shelley, Mary	*Frankenstein*
Sinclair, Upton	*Jungle, The*
Solzhenitsyn, Aleksandr	*One Day in the Life of Ivan Denisovich*
Sophocles	*Oedipus Rex*
Steinbeck, John	*Grapes of Wrath, The*
	Of Mice and Men
	Pearl, The
Stevenson, Robert Louis	*Dr. Jekyll and Mr. Hyde*
Stoker, Bram	*Dracula*
Stowe, Harriet Beecher	*Uncle Tom's Cabin*
Swift, Jonathan	*Gulliver's Travels*
Tan, Amy	*Joy Luck Club, The*
Thoreau, Henry David	*Walden*
Tolkien, J.R.R.	*Hobbit, The*
Tolstoy, Leo	*Anna Karenina*
	War and Peace
Twain, Mark	*Huckleberry Finn, The Adventures of*
	Tom Sawyer, The Adventures of
Virgil	*Aeneid, The*
Voltaire	*Candide*
Vonnegut, Kurt	*Slaughterhouse Five*
Walker, Alice	*Color Purple, The*
Wharton, Edith	*Ethan Frome*
Wiesel, Eli	*Night*
Wilde, Oscar	*Importance of Being Earnest, The*
	Picture of Dorian Gray, The
Wilder, Thornton	*Our Town*
Williams, Tennesse	*Glass Menagerie, The*
	Streetcar Named Desire, A
Woolf, Virginia	*Mrs. Dalloway*
	Room of One's Own, A
	To the Lighthouse
Wright, Richard	*Black Boy*
	Native Son

APPENDIX II: TITLES LISTED BY DATE OF PUBLICATION

If published in serial form, date of first appearance in serial publication is given.

Gilgamesh	between 1300 and 1000 B.C.
Iliad, The	unknown; after 750 B.C., when it was written
Odyssey, The	unknown; after 700 B.C., when it was written
Agamemnon	around 458 B.C.
Medea	431 B.C.
Oedipus Rex	unknown; probably around the fifth century B.C.
Plato's Republic	unknown; after 380 B.C., when it was written
Aeneid, The	after 19 B.C.
Beowulf	around 1000
Inferno	1314
Sir Gawain and the Green Knight	around 1340–1400
Canterbury Tales, The	early fifteenth century
Prince, The	1532
Romeo & Juliet	1597
Merchant of Venice, The	1600
Midsummer Night's Dream, A	1600
Much Ado About Nothing	1600
Hamlet	1603
Don Quixote	1604 (First part)
	1614 (Second part)
Doctor Faustus	1604
Othello	1622
Julius Caesar	1623
King Lear	1623
Macbeth	1623
Tempest, The	1623
Paradise Lost	1667 (First Edition, ten books)
	1674 (Second Edition, twelve books)
Gulliver's Travels	1726
Candide	1759
Sense and Sensibility	1811
Pride and Prejudice	1813
Emma	1816
Frankenstein	1818
Last of the Mohicans, The	1826
Oliver Twist	1837
Christmas Carol, A	1843
Count of Monte Cristo, The	1844
Narrative of the Life of F.D.	1845
Jane Eyre	1847
Wuthering Heights	1847

David Copperfield	1849
Scarlet Letter, The	1850
House of Seven Gables	1851
Moby Dick	1851
Uncle Tom's Cabin	1851
Hard Times	1854
Walden	1854
Madame Bovary	1857
Tale of Two Cities, A	1859
Great Expectations	1860
Silas Marner	1861
Les Miserables	1862
Alice in Wonderland	1865
War and Peace	1865
Crime and Punishment	1866
Little Women	1868
Far from the Madding Crowd	1874
Anna Karenina	1875
Tom Sawyer	1876
Brothers Karamazov	1879
Doll House, The	1879
Huckleberry Finn	1885
Dr. Jekyll and Mr. Hyde	1886
Mayor of Casterbridge, The	1886
Hedda Gabler	1890
Picture of Dorian Gray, The	1890
Tess of the D'Urbervilles	1891
Red Badge of Courage, The	1895
Dracula	1897
Cyrano	1897 (performance)
Turn of the Screw, The	1898
Awakening, The	1899
Heart of Darkness	1899
Importance of Being Earnest, The	1899
Call of the Wild	1903
Jungle, The	1906
Ethan Frome	1911
Pygmalion	1913
Dubliners	1914
Metamorphosis	1915
Portrait of the Artist as a Young Man, A	1916
My Antonia	1918
Siddhartha	1922
Ulysses	1922
Billy Budd	1924
Passage to India	1924
Great Gatsby, The	1925
Mrs. Dalloway	1925
Sun Also Rises, The	1926
To the Lighthouse	1927
All Quiet on the Western Front	1928
Farewell to Arms, A	1929
Room of One's Own, A	1929

Sound and the Fury, The	1929
As I Lay Dying	1930
Good Earth, The	1931
Brave New World	1932
Light in August	1932
Hobbit, The	1937
Of Mice and Men	1937
Our Town	1938
Grapes of Wrath, The	1939
Native Son	1940
Stranger, The	1942
Fountainhead, The	1943
Black Boy	1945
Glass Menagerie, The	1945
Pearl, The	1945
Animal Farm	1946
Diary of a Young Girl, The	1947
Plague, The	1947
Streetcar Named Desire, A	1947
Cry, the Beloved Country	1948
1984	1949
Death of a Salesman	1949
Catcher in the Rye, The	1951
Invisible Man	1952
Old Man and the Sea, The	1952
Waiting for Godot	1952
Crucible, The	1953
Farenheit 451	1953
Robinson Crusoe	1953
Lord of the Flies, The	1954
Lolita	1955
On the Road	1957
Night	1958
Raisin in the Sun, A	1959
Separate Peace, A	1959
Things Fall Apart	1959
Man for All Seasons, A	1960
To Kill a Mockingbird	1960
Catch-22	1961
Clockwork Orange, A	1962
One Day in the Life of I.D.	1962
One Flew Over the Cuckoo's Nest	1962
Bell Jar, The	1963
Chosen, The	1967
One Hundred Years of Solitude	1967
Outsiders, The	1967
I Know Why the Caged Bird Sings	1969
Slaughterhouse Five	1969
Grendel	1971
Woman Warrior	1976
Song of Solomon	1977
Color Purple, The	1982
House on Mango Street, The	1984

Handmaid's Tale, The	1986
Beloved	1987
Joy Luck Club, The	1989
Their Eyes Were Watching God	1990
Things They Carried, The	1990

APPENDIX III: TITLES LISTED BY GENRE

ADVENTURE LITERATURE

Call of the Wild
Candide
Count of Monte Cristo, The
Heart of Darkness
Last of the Mohicans, The
Moby-Dick
Robinson Crusoe
Song of Solomon

ALLEGORICAL LITERATURE

Animal Farm
Billy Budd
Crucible, The
Fountainhead, The
Inferno
Lord of the Flies, The
Moby-Dick
One Flew Over the Cuckoo's Nest
Pearl, The
Scarlet Letter, The
Siddhartha

AUTOBIOGRAPHICAL LITERATURE

Bell Jar, The
Black Boy
Diary of a Young Girl, The
Great Expectations
House on Mango Street, The
I Know Why the Caged Bird Sings
My Antonia
Narrative of the Life of Frederick Douglass
Night
Portrait of the Artist as a Young Man, A
Slaughterhouse Five
Walden
Woman Warrior

BILDUNGSROMAN

Bell Jar, The
Black Boy
Candide
Catcher in the Rye, The
Chosen, The
David Copperfield
Great Expectations
House on Mango Street, The
Huckleberry Finn
Invisible Man
Jane Eyre

Light in August
Little Women
Mayor of Casterbridge, The
Narrative of the Life of Frederick Douglass
Outsiders, The
Portrait of the Artist as a Young Man, A
Separate Peace, A
Song of Solomon
Things They Carried, The
Tom Sawyer

CASTAWAY LITERATURE

Lord of the Flies
Robinson Crusoe
Tempest, The

COMEDIES (DRAMA)

Cyrano de Bergerac
Importance of Being Earnest, The
Pygmalion

COMEDIES OF MANNERS (DRAMA)

Importance of Being Earnest, The

COURTROOM DRAMAS

Crucible, The
Cry, the Beloved Country
To Kill a Mockingbird

DIARIES

Diary of a Young Girl, The

DYSTOPIAN LITERATURE

1984
Animal Farm
Brave New World
Clockwork Orange, A
Handmaid's Tale, The

EPIC POEMS

Aeneid, The
Beowulf
Gilgamesh
Iliad, The
Inferno
Odyssey, The
Paradise Lost

EPIC LITERATURE

Hobbit, The
Les Misérables
Moby-Dick
War and Peace

EPISTOLARY LITERATURE

Color Purple, The
Frankenstein

ESSAYS

Room of One's Own, A
Walden

EXISTENTIAL LITERATURE

Black Boy
Invisible Man, The

Plague, The
Stranger, The
Waiting for Godot

FANTASIES

Alice in Wonderland
Inferno
Hobbit, The

FRAME STORIES

Heart of Darkness
Turn of the Screw, The
Wuthering Heights

GHOST STORIES

Beloved
Christmas Carol, A
Hamlet
Turn of the Screw, The

GOTHIC LITERATURE

Christmas Carol, A
Dr. Jekyll and Mr. Hyde
Dracula
Frankenstein
Jane Eyre
Picture of Dorian Gray, The
Turn of the Screw, The
Wuthering Heights

HISTORICAL LITERATURE

All Quiet on the Western Front
Julius Caesar
Les Misérables
Man for All Seasons, A
Slaughterhouse Five
Tale of Two Cities, A
War and Peace

KUNSTLERROMAN

Awakening, The
House on Mango Street, The
On the Road
Portrait of the Artist as a Young Man, A

MAGICAL REALISM

One Hundred Years of Solitude

MEMOIRS

Black Boy
Narrative of the Life of Frederick Douglass
Night

NOVELS/DRAMAS OF IDEAS

Anna Karenina
Brothers Karamazov
Crime and Punishment
Doll's House, A
Fountainhead, The
Hedda Gabler
Silas Marner
War and Peace

NOVELLAS

Awakening, The
Christmas Carol, A
Heart of Darkness
Metamorphosis
Turn of the Screw, The
Old Man and the Sea, The

PARABLES

Good Earth, The
Old Man and the Sea, The
Pearl, The
Siddhartha

PARODIES

Don Quixote
Neal Pollack

PASTORALS

Far from the Madding Crowd
Silas Marner

PICARESQUE LITERATURE

Candide
Don Quixote
Huckleberry Finn
On the Road
Tom Sawyer

PLAYS

Agamemnon
Crucible, The
Cyrano de Bergerac
Death of a Salesman
Doctor Faustus
Doll's House, A
Glass Menagerie, The
Hamlet
Hedda Gabler
Importance of Being Earnest, The
Julius Caesar
King Lear
Macbeth
Man for All Seasons, A
Medea
Merchant of Venice, The
Midsummer Night's Dream, A
Much Ado About Nothing
Oedipus Rex
Othello
Our Town
Pygmalion
Raisin in the Sun, A
Romeo & Juliet
Streetcar Named Desire, A
Tempest, The
Waiting for Godot

POETRY

Aeneid, The

Canterbury Tales, The
Cyrano de Bergerac
Gilgamesh
Hamlet
Julius Caesar
King Lear
Macbeth
Merchant of Venice, The
Midsummer Night's Dream, A
Much Ado About Nothing
Oedipus trilogy
Othello
Romeo & Juliet
Sir Gawain and the Green Knight
Tempest, The

POLITICAL TREATISES

Plato's Republic
Prince, The

PRISON LITERATURE

One Day in the Life of Ivan Denisovich

QUEST LITERATURE

Cry, the Beloved Country
Hobbit, The
Moby-Dick
Odyssey, The
Song of Solomon
Ulysses

ROMANCES

Count of Monte Cristo, The
Cyrano de Bergerac
Don Quixote
Last of the Mohicans, The
Les Miserables
Sir Gawain and the Green Knight

SATIRES

Animal Farm
Candide
Canterbury Tales, The
Catch-22
Emma
Gulliver's Travels
Hard Times
Huckleberry Finn
Importance of Being Earnest, The
Pride and Prejudice
Sense and Sensibility

SCIENCE FICTION

Dr. Jekyll and Mr. Hyde
Farenheit 451
Frankenstein
Slaughterhouse Five

SHORT STORIES

Dubliners

House on Mango Street, The

SOCIAL PROTEST LITERATURE

All Quiet on the Western Front
Cry, the Beloved Country
Death of a Salesman
Doll's House, A
Grapes of Wrath, The
Great Expectations
Hard Times
Hedda Gabler
Hobbit, The
Invisible Man, The
Jane Eyre
Jungle, The
Narrative of the Life of Frederick Douglass
Native Son
Oliver Twist
One Day in the Life of Ivan Denisovich
One Flew Over the Cuckoo's Nest
Pygmalion
To Kill a Mockingbird
Uncle Tom's Cabin
Walden

SOUTHERN LITERATURE

As I Lay Dying
Glass Menagerie, The
Light in August
Streetcar Named Desire, A
Their Eyes Were Watching God
To Kill a Mockingbird

SURREALIST LITERATURE

Metamorphosis

TRAGEDIES (DRAMA)

Crucible, The
Death of a Salesman
Doctor Faustus
Hamlet
Julius Caesar
King Lear
Macbeth
Medea
Oedipus Rex
Othello
Romeo & Juliet

UTOPIAN LITERATURE

Republic, The

WAR NOVELS

All Quiet on the Western Front
Catch-22
Farewell to Arms, A
Red Badge of Courage, The
Slaughterhouse Five
Things They Carried, The

GLOSSARY

AESTHETICISM (Movement; 1835–1910): A late nineteenth-century literary movement that believed in art for art's sake, rejecting the idea that art had to posses a higher moral or political quality.
Ex: Oscar Wilde, William Pater
Ex: The Picture of Dorian Grey

ALLEGORY (Genre): A narrative whose literal elements, both characters and events, correspond clearly and directly to abstract ideas and theories.
Ex: The narrator's journey in Dante's Inferno is an allegory for his—and all humankind's—search for meaning and divine grace. Animal Farm allegorically depicts the rise of Soviet communism and oppression.

ALLITERATION (Figurative Language/sound): The repetition of initial consonant sounds in nearby words for poetic effect.
Ex: Beowulf bode in the burg

ALLUSION (Literary Technique): An implicit reference to a historical, literary, or biblical character, event, or element. The title of Faulkner's The Sound and the Fury alludes to a line from Shakespeare's Macbeth: "[Life] is a tale told by an idiot / Full of sound and fury signifying nothing." Captain Ahab's name in Melville's Moby-Dick is a running allusion to the wicked and idolatrous biblical king Ahab. Allusions add symbolic weight by making subtle connections with other works.

ANAPHORA (Figurative Language/phrase structure): Deliberate repetition of the phrase structure for effect.

ANTAGONIST (Story Elements/character): The entity that acts to frustrate the goals of the protagonist. The antagonist is usually another character but may also be a non-human force.
Ex: The antagonist to Hamlet is Claudius; the antagonist to Yossarian in Joseph Heller's Catch-22 is the military bureaucracy.

ANTHROPOMORPHISM (Figurative Language/imagery): The attribution of human characteristics to animals, things, or ideas.

ANTIHERO (Story Elements/character type): A protagonist who lacks the traditional attributes of an admirable hero, or who challenges our notions of what is admirable.

ANTITHESIS (Figurative Language/phrase structure): The juxtaposition of two contradictory ideas in similar grammatical structures. Also used to refer to the second of such ideas.

ANTONYM (Words): A word that means the opposite of another word.
Ex: "High" and "low" are antonyms.

APHORISM (Literary Form): A concise expression of an insight into worldly wisdom. See also epigram.
Ex: "The vanity of others offends our taste only when it offends our vanity," Friedrich Nietzsche

APOSTROPHE (Literary Technique/narration): A direct address to an object, to an idea, or to an absent or dead person.
Ex: Shakespeare uses apostrophe in Juliet's soliloquy as she impatiently awaits her wedding night and addresses the night directly: "Come, civil night, / Thou sober-suited matron, all in black, / And learn me how to lose a winning match, / Played for a pair of stainless maidenhoods" (R&J, III.ii).

ASSONANCE (Figurative Language/sound): The repetition of similar vowel sounds in a sequence of nearby words, especially in stressed syllables.

ASYNDETON (Figurative Language/phrase structure): The omission of conjunctions for a cumulative, list-like effect. The opposite of asyndeton is **polysyndeton**.
Ex: "I came, I saw, I conquered."

AUTOBIOGRAPHY (Genre): A story of the author's life, organized into a narrative. Autobiographies are usually, though not always, narrated in the first person.
Ex: Narrative of the Life of Frederick Douglass.

BEAT GENERATION (Movement/group; 1950s–1960s; American): 1950s–1960s American writers rebelling against the bourgeois values of the prosperous post-World War II era. They valued anti-intellectualism, unmediated experience, marginalized groups (such as "bums"), jazz music, and minor drugs.
Ex: Allen Ginsberg, Jack Kerouac, William S. Burroughs
Ex: On the Road

BILDUNGSROMAN (Genre): A novel chronicling the intellectual, spiritual, or moral development of a young protagonist; also known as a **coming-of-age** novel.
Ex: J. D. Salinger's Catcher in the Rye; *James Joyce's* A Portrait of the Artist as a Young Man; *Charles Dickens's* David Copperfield; *Gustave Flaubert's* A Sentimental Education

BLACK COMEDY (Genre): Disturbing or absurd material presented in a humorous manner, usually with the intention to confront uncomfortable truths.
Ex: Catch-22

BLANK VERSE (Poetry/poetic form): Unrhymed iambic pentameter. Most of Shakespeare's verse work is in iambic pentameter.

BLOOMSBURY GROUP (Movement/group; 1910s–1930s; England): 1910s–1930s group of intellectuals who met in the Bloomsbury district of London. They challenged what they saw as Victorian hypocrisy in art, religion, human interaction, and sexual politics; eventually they became influential and well-known as elitist aesthetes.
Ex: E. M. Forster, Virginia Woolf, sometimes T. S. Eliot
Ex: Mrs. Dalloway, A Room of One's Own, To the Lighthouse, A Passage to India

CASTAWAY NOVEL (Genre): A novel chronicling the adventures and ingenuity of characters shipwrecked (or plane-wrecked) on a desert island.
Ex: Daniel Defoe's Robinson Crusoe *is the classic castaway novel. Others include William Golding's* Lord of the Flies *and Jules Verne's* The Mysterious Island.

CHARACTER (Story Elements): Any person, animal, or other being who plays a role in a story.

CHIASMUS (Figurative Language/phrase structure): A criss-crossing effect, whether lexical or syntactical.
Ex: Lexical: "The spectacle of power and the power of spectacle." Syntactical: "I love too much and too little hate."

CHORUS (Drama/stock character): In Greek drama, a group of singers and dancers who filled in plot points or provided commentary on the action. A solitary chorus figure sometimes recited the prologue, epilogue, and inter-act commentary in Elizabethan drama, including some of Shakespeare's plays.
Ex: Shakespeare's Romeo and Juliet *begins with summary of the action delivered by a chorus: "Two houses, both alike in dignity . . ."*

CLIMAX (Story Elements/plot): In a narrative, the moment at which the conflict comes to a head. This moment usually coincides with the *dramatic climax*, the moment of highest dramatic tension, when the reader is most emotionally invested in the story.

COMEDY (Genre/drama): A play written to amuse the audience. In the middle ages, the term "comedy" referred to a poetic work with a happy ending, like Dante's *Divine Comedy*. Later it extended to dramatic works as well. Shakespearean comedies are light in tone and end in marriage. There are many types of comedy, including the **comedies of manners**.

COMEDY OF MANNERS (Genre/drama): A comedy, often satirical, that revolves around the social customs of sophisticated society. Common character types of this genre include clandestine lovers, jealous husbands, foolish dandies, and witty observers.
Ex: *Oscar Wilde's* The Importance of Being Earnest *and other works; works by Moliere; works by Noel Coward.*

COMING-OF-AGE NOVEL (Genre): *See* **bildungsroman**.

CONCEIT (Figurative Language/imagery): An elaborate parallel between two seemingly dissimilar objects or ideas.

CONNOTATION (Words): The figurative meanings and associations of a word. Contrasted with **denotation**.

CONSONANCE (Figurative Language/sound): The repetition of consonant sounds in nearby words, especially of final sounds.

COUPLET (Poetry/Stanza Form): Two consecutive rhyming lines of verse. *See also* **heroic couplet**.

DENOTATION (Words): The literal, dictionary meaning of a word. Contrasted with **connotation**, the figurative and associative meanings.
Ex: *The denotation of the word "diamond" is "an extremely hard carbon compound"; the connotations of "diamond" range from engagement rings to love to two months' salary.*

DEUX EX MACHINA (Literary Technique/plot): The use of a forced, unexpected event to resolve the conflicts in a story.
Ex: *Fortinbras's appearance at the end of* Hamlet *is a* deux ex machina *that assures the succession to the Danish thone.*

DOPPELGANGER (Literary Technique/stock character): A mysterious figure, often haunting, who is in some way the double of another character.

DRAMATIC IRONY (Literary Technique/plot): Any situation in which the audience understands more about the characters' words or actions than the characters do themselves.

DYSTOPIAN NOVEL (Genre; 20th century): A novel set in an imagined future society that purports to be utopian but is revealed as terrifyingly restrictive and inhuman. The intent is usually to warn contemporary readers that their own society is in danger of turning into this horrifying future world.
Ex: *Seminal works include Aldous Huxley's* Brave New World *and George Orwell's* 1984; *also Margaret Atwood's* The Handmaid's Tale, *Anthony Burgess's* A Clockwork Orange, *and George Orwell's* Animal Farm.

ELIZABETHAN SONNET (Poetry/Poetic Form): *See* **Shakespearean sonnet**.

END RHYME (Poetry/Rhyme): Rhyme between the ends of two lines. When thinking about whether a poem rhymes, most people think of end rhyme first.

END-STOP (Poetry/Rhythm & Meaning): The completion of the thought and the grammatical construction (sentence or clause) at the end of a line of verse. An end-stopped line usually ends in a comma, a semicolon, or a period.

ENGLISH SONNET (Poetry/Poetic Form): *See **Shakespearean sonnet**.*

ENJAMBMENT (Poetry/Rhythm & Meaning): The continuation of a grammatical construction (sentence or clause) of a line of verse into the next line. Enjambment stands in opposition to an **end-stop**. It creates a sense of suspense and excitement, and emphasizes the last word of the enjambed line. It also adds emphasis to the word at the end of the line.
Ex: *John Keats's "Ode to a Nightingale": "Thy plaintive anthem fades / Past the near meadows, over the still stream."*

ENLIGHTENMENT (Movement; 1660–1790; France): A 17th-century intellectual movement in France and throughout Europe that emphasized reason, progress, liberty, and rationality. Sometimes called the Age of Reason, the Englightenment is primarily associated with nonfiction works such as essays and philosophical treatises.
Ex: *Thomas Hobbes, John Locke, Jean-Jacques Rousseau, René Descartes, Thomas Paine*
Ex: Gulliver's Travels, Candide

EPIC (Genre): A lengthy narrative chronicling the deeds of a heroic figure—often a figure of national or cultural importance—in elevated language. Taken narrowly, the term applies only to verse narratives, but it also is used to describe other works of similar scope.
Ex: *the* Epic of Gilgamesh, *by an anonymous writer;* Beowulf, *by an anonymous writer; the* Iliad *and the* Odyssey, *by Homer; the* Aeneid, *by Virgil; and* Paradise Lost, *by John Milton are among the best-known examples.*

EPIGRAM (Literary Form): A succint, pithy saying. Unlike **aphorisms**, epigrams are usually humorous.
Ex: *Oscar Wilde is known for his epigrams: "Bigamy is having one wife too many. Monogamy is the same." "I am not young enough to know everything."*

EPIGRAPH (Publishing): A short quotation that introduces a novel or a chapter.
Ex: *"No man is an island... therefore ask not for whom the bell tolls. It tolls for thee."* For Whom the Bell Tolls, *Hemingway*

EPIPHANY (Literary Technique): A sudden, powerful, and often spiritual or life-changing realization that a character reaches in an otherwise ordinary or everyday moment.
Ex: *Many of the short stories in James Joyce's* Dubliners *involve moments of epiphany.*

EPISTOLARY NOVEL (Genre): A novel whose story is told through letters exchanged by its characters. This form was especially popular in the 1700s.
Ex: *Samuel Richardson's* Clarissa; *Alice Walker's* The Color Purple

EXISTENTIALISM (Movement; mid-20th century; France): A postwar European philosophical movement. Faced with the isolation and meaninglessness of individual lives in a hostile global context, existentialists argued that individuals must take responsibility for the consequences of their actions.
Ex: *Jean-Paul Sartre, Albert Camus, Simone de Beauvoir, Dostoyevsky, Franz Kafka, Samuel Beckett, Eugene Ionesco*
Ex: The Stranger, The Plague

FABLIAU (PL. FABLIAUX) (Genre; Middle Ages; French): A comical and often grotesque verse tale; its plots often hinge on the comical treatment of bodily functions—sex, flatulence, diarrhea, etc.
Ex: *"The Miller's Tale" and other stories from* The Canterbury Tales

FEMININE ENDING (Poetry/Meter): An extrametrical unstressed syllable added to an **iamb** or an **anapest**.

FIGURE OF SPEECH (Figurative Language): Any expression that stretches the meaning of words beyond their literal meaning.

FIN DE SIECLE (Movement/era; 1890s; Europe): Last decade of the nineteenth century. The art of this period is decadent, realistic, and nontraditional.

FIRST FOLIO (Publishing/Shakespeare; 1623): The first (almost complete) publication of Shakespeare's collected works, and the major primary source for many of his plays.

FIRST-PERSON NARRATION (Story Elements/narration): The narrator tells the story from his or her own point of view, referring to himself or herself as "I." The narrator may be an active participant in the story or just an observer. The narrator may be a character in the story or a personified narrative presence. The narrator may be closely identified with the author or a distinct entitity. *See also **unreliable narrator.***
Ex: *Miguel de Cervantes's* Don Quixote, *F. Scott Fitzgerald's* Great Gatsby.

FLASHBACK (Literary Technique/plot): Any presentation of material that happens before the opening scene. Flashbacks are most often narrated as memories or stories told by characters.

FOIL (Story Elements/character): A character who, by comparison, brings the characteristics of another character (often, a major character) into relief.
Ex: *Laertes, quick to act and slow to think, is a foil for Hamlet. In* The Awakening, *Adele, a committed mother, is a foil for Edna.*

FOLIO (Publishing): A standard sheet of paper folded in half; also, a book made up of folio sheets. Most of Shakespeare's plays appear in the 1623 First Folio publication.

FOOT (Poetry/Meter): In verse, a unit of rhythm, usually with at least one accented syllable. **Iamb, trochee, anapest, dactyl, amphibrach**, and **spondee** are all types of feet.

FORESHADOWING (Literary Technique/plot): Any clue or hint of future events in a literary work.
Ex: *The yellow fever is mentioned several times in* Daisy Miller *before the title character becomes sick.*

FRAME STORY (Genre): A narrative that consists of or connects several otherwise unrelated stories. The term "frame story," or sometimes "**framework story**" can also refer to any story-within-a-story narrative.
Ex: *Geoffrey Chaucer's* Canterbury Tales; *Bocaccio's* The Decameron; *Shakespeare's* The Taming of the Shrew; *Joseph Conrad's* Heart of Darkness; *Emily Bontë's* Wuthering Heights

FRAMEWORK STORY (Genre): See **frame story.**

FREE INDIRECT DISCOURSE (Story Elements/narration): A character's inner thoughts are conveyed through third-person narration. Free indirect discourse ("She would buy the flowers herself") is different from indirect discourse ("She decided to buy the flowers herself"). This style was pioneered by Gustave Flaubert in *Madame Bovary.*
Ex: *Jane Austen's* Emma: *"it darted through her with the speed of an arrow that Mr. Knightley must marry no one but herself!"*

FREE VERSE (Poetry/poetic form): Verse that does not conform to any fixed meter or rhyme scheme. Less evident rhythmic patterns are present in free verse to give the poem shape.
Ex: *Walt Whitman's "Leaves of Grass" is a seminal work of free verse.*

GENRE: A catergory of literary works, determined based on themes, literary techniques, or, sometimes, era of composition.

GOTHIC NOVEL (Genre; c. 1764–1820): A genre of literature popular in late 18th-century England. Gothic ficton features remote landscapes, medieval castles, and supernatural experiences, all of which seek to create an atmosphere of suspense and fear. Gothic fiction influenced what we now call "horror stories."
Ex: *Mary Shelley's* Frankenstein; *Charlotte Brontë's* Jane Eyre; *Edgar Allan Poe's short stories*

GREEK CHORUS (Drama/stock character): *See* **chorus**.

HARLEM RENAISSANCE (Movement; c. 1918–1930; American (NYC)): The flowering of African-American literature, art, and music in 1920s New York City. The movement was anticipated by W.E.B. DuBois's *The Souls of Black Folk.*
Ex: *Zora Neale Hurston, Alain Locke, Langston Hughes (poet), Countee Cullen (poet)*
Ex: *Their Eyes Were Watching God*

HERO, HEROINE (Story Elements/character type): The main character of a literary work. The terms "hero" and "heroine" are often synonymous with **protagonist**, but sometimes they are reserved for admirable protagonists and contrasted with **antihero**.

HEROIC COUPLET (Poetry/stanza form): Two rhyming lines of iambic pentameter. A **Shakespearean sonnet** ends with a heroic couplet.
Ex: *"The time is out of joint: O cursed spite, / That ever I was born to set it right!" (Hamlet)*

HISTORY PLAY (Genre/drama; late 16th century; England): A genre of Elizabethan drama that loosely depicts historical events, often surrounding the reign of a single king. These plays were based on contemporary historical chronicles, which were sometimes tweaked to suit the dramatic structure. Patriotic in spirit and massive in cast size, they featured sensational scenes such as coronations and battles.
Ex: *Shakespeare wrote ten history plays, from the forgettable* 1 Henry VI *to the iconic* Richard III.

HOMONYM (Words): A word that sounds the same as another word but has a different meaning.
Ex: *"Know" and "no" are homonyms, as are "leaves" (form of "to leave") and "leaves" (plural of "leaf").*

HUBRIS (Literary Technique/character): Excessive pride that leads to the **protagonist**'s downfall.

HYPERBOLE (Figurative Language/degree): Any kind of exaggeration, including for humor or effect.

IAMB (Poetry/Meter: foot type): A disyllabic foot: one unstressed syllable and one stressed syllable.
Ex: *behold*

IAMBIC PENTAMETER (Poetry/Meter): Each line of verse has five **iambic** feet (unstressed syllable followed by stressed syllable). Iambic pentameter is one of the most popular metrical schemes in English poetry. Most of Shakespeare's work is in iambic pentameter.
Ex: *The meter of "When* **I** *| do* **count** *| the* **clock** *| that* **tells** *| the* **time**" *(Sonnet 12) is perfect iambic pentameter.*

IN MEDEA RES (Literary Technique/plot): The technique of beginning a story in the middle of the action, with background information given later in **flashbacks**. *In media res* is Latin for "in the middle of things."

INTERIOR MONOLOGUE (Literary Technique/narration): A record of a character's thoughts and impressions; a technique for presenting the character's **stream of consciousness**. The term "interior monologue" may be used as a synonym for "stream of consciousness," but is often restricted to refer to a more structured sequence of rational thoughts.

INTERNAL RHYME (Poetry/Rhyme): Rhyme between two or more words within a single line of verse.
Ex: *"And all is seared with trade; bleared, smeared with toil."*

INTRUSIVE NARRATOR (Story Elements/narration): An omniscient narrator who interrupts the action to provide commentary.

IRONY (Literary Technnique): The use of detachment to draw awareness to the discrepancy between the apparent literal meaning of words and their intended implication, between the stated and the actual. See also *dramatic irony.*

ITALIAN SONNET (Poetry/Poetic Form): See *Petrarchan sonnet.*

KUNSTLERROMAN (Genre): A novel portraying the artistic realization or development of a maturing protagonist. A type of **bildungsroman**.
Ex: *James Joyce's* A Portrait of the Artist as a Young Man; *Marcel Proust's* Remembrance of Things Past

LEGEND (Genre): A story about a heroic figure, derived from oral tradition and based partly on fact and partly on fiction. The terms legend and **myth** are sometimes used interchangeably, but legends are typically rooted in historical events, whereas myths are primarily supernatural.
Ex: *The stories about King Arthur and Robin Hood*

LIMITED OMNISCIENT NARRATOR (Story Elements/narration): A narrator who knows the actions, feelings, and motivations of only one character or a few characters.
Ex: *The narrator of Lewis Carroll's* Alice In Wonderland *knows only Alice's thoughts and feelings.*

LITOTES (Figurative Language/degree): Understatement expressed through negating the opposite.
Ex: *"She's no fool."*

LOCAL COLOR NOVEL (Genre): A work that incorporates cultural details of a particular region— dialect, mannerisms, thought patterns—to portray a community, often sentimentally. Frequently includes eccentric characters.
Ex: *Kate Chopin's* The Awakening; *Toni Morrison's* Beloved.

LOST GENERATION (Movement/group; 1920s–1930s; American): A group of American writers, many of them soldiers, who came of age during World War I.
Ex: *F. Scott Fitzgerald, Ernest Hemingway, John Dos Passos*
Ex: *Hemingway's* The Sun Also Rises *embodies the Lost Generation's sense of disillusionment.*

LYRIC POETRY (Poetry/genre): A short poetic composition that describes the thoughts of a single speaker. Most modern poetry is lyrical (as opposed to dramatic or narrative). The **ode** and the **sonnet** are types of lyric poetry.
Ex: *Shakespeare's sonnets; John Keat's "Ode on a Grecian Urn"*

MAGICAL REALISM (Movement; 20th century; Latin America): A style of literature in which fantastical or dreamlike elements exist in a realistic framework.
Ex: *Gabriel Garcia Marquez, Jorge Luis Borges, Italo Calvino, Umberto Eco, Salman Rushdie, Thomas Pynchon, Zadie Smith*

MEDIEVAL ROMANCE (Genre; Middle Ages): A tale about knights and ladies incorporating courtly love themes. Standard narrative elements include knights rescuing maidens, embarking on quests, and forming bonds with kings, queens, and other knights.

Ex: *Stories of King Arthur, his queen Guinevere, and his "knights of the round table," including Launcelot. The Knight's Tale, the Miller's Tale, and the Wife of Bath's Tale of the* Canterbury Tales *all include elements of medieval romance.* Don Quixote *looks back on medieval romances with both ridicule and homage.*

MEIOSIS (Figurative Language/degree): Intentional understatement used for ironic effect. **Litotes** is a type of **meiosis**.

Ex: *In Act III of* Romeo and Juliet, *the mortally wounded Mercutio insists that his wound is merely "a scratch" (R&J III.i.98).*

MELODRAMA (Genre): A work that uses sentimentality, gushing emotion, or sensational action and plot twists to provoke a response. Popular in Victorian England, melodrama is now often derided it as manipulative and hokey.

Ex: Charles Dickens's The Old Curiosity Shop

METAPHOR (Figurative Language/imagery): A comparison of two things that does not use the words "like" or "as." Colloquially, the word "metaphor" is often used to refer to any kind of imaginative comparison, including **simile**.

Ex: *"Life is but a walking shadow; a poor player / That struts and frets his hour upon the stage / And then is head no more" (*Macbeth, V.v.23–25).

METONYMY (Figurative Language/imagery): The substitution of one term for another closely associated term; for example, calling businessmen "suits." **Synecdoche** is a type of metonymy.

Ex: *In "Uneasy lies the head that wears the crown" (*2 Henry IV, III.i.31*), "wear[ing] the crown" implies "being a king."*

MIXED METAPHOR (Figurative Language/imagery): A combination of metaphors that produces a confused or contradictory image.

Ex: *"The collapse of the movie studio left mountains of debt in its wake."*

MODERNISM (Movement; 1890s–1940s): A literary and artistic movement that represented a radical break with traditional modes of Western art, thought, religion, social conventions, and morality. Modernist writers explored ideas of fragmentation and discontinuity in both subject matter and stylistic form, focusing more on how people look at the world than on what they actually see.

The term **high modernism** refers to the 1920s golden age of modernist literature, the period of publication of James Joyce's *Ulysses*, T.S. Eliot's *The Waste Land*, Virginia Woolf's *Mrs. Dalloway*, and Marcel Proust's *Remembrance of Things Past*.

Ex: *Virginia Woolf, James Joyce, Marcel Proust, T.S. Eliot, William Faulkner*

MONOLOGUE (Drama): A speech of a single character. If the character is alone on stage, the monologue is often called a **soliloquy**, although the term "monologue" is usually reserved to represent words spoken to a listener, even if none is present. In contrast, a **soliloquy** is meant to represent a character's thoughts.

Ex: *Mark Antony's "Friends, Romans, countrymen, lend me your ears; / I come to bury Caesar, not to praise him" (*Julius Caesar III.ii*) is a monologue.*

MORALITY PLAY (Genre/drama; 15th–16th centuries): A play that presents an **allegory** of the Christian struggle for salvation.

MOTIF (Thematic Meaning): A recurring object, phrase, idea, emotion, or other device that develops or informs a work's major themes.

MYTH (Genre): A narrative that explains the origins of a culture's beliefs or practices, usually derived from oral tradition and set in an imagined supernatural past. *See also* **legend**.
Ex: *Homer's* Iliad, *Homer's* Odyssey, *Ovid's* Metamorphoses

NARRATIVE (Story Elements): A sequence of events told by a **narrator** in story form.

NARRATOR (Story Elements): Anyone who tells the story. The narrator may or may not be a **character** in the narrative. In careful speech or writing, the narrator is always present, explicitly or implicitly; the narrator is a presence distinct from the author. *See also* **first-person narration, third-person narration, omniscient narrator, limited omniscient narrator, unreliable narrator, intrusive narrator, point of view.**

NATURALISM (Movement; 1865–1900; France, America): A literary movement that used detailed (and often unpleasant) realism to portray social conditions, heredity, and environment as inescapable forces that shape human character.
Ex: *Émile Zola, Theodore Dreiser, George Eliot, Thomas Hardy, Stephen Crane*
Ex: *Theodore Dreiser's* Sister Carrie

NEOCLASSICISM (Movement; c. 1660–1798; England): A movement inspired by the rediscovery of classical works of ancient Greece and Rome and influenced by Greco-Roman values: reason, self-control, moderation, restraint, clarity, unity and balance of form. Most neoclassical works are letters, essays, or parodies. Neoclassicism roughly coincided with the **Enlightenment.**
Ex: *Samuel Johnson, Alexander Pope, Jonathan Swift*
Ex: *Jonathan Swift's* Gulliver's Travels

NOVEL OF IDEAS (Genre): A novel used as a platform for discussing ideas. Character and plot are of secondary importance.
Ex: *Ayn Rand's* The Fountainhead, *George Eliot's* Middlemarch

NOVELLA (Genre): A shorter work of prose fiction, often divided into a few chapters.
Ex: *Joseph Conrad's* Heart of Darkness; *Kate Chopin's* The Awakening; *Henry James's* Daisy Miller

OBJECTIVISM (Movement): Most generally, any doctrine that holds that all knowledge comes from observing an objective reality. Objectivism also refers to the philosophy of Ayn Rand, who believed ideal society is achieved when everyone acts in his or her own best interest—what may be called moral capitalism.
Ex: *Ayn Rand's* The Fountainhead, *Ayn Rand's* Atlas Shrugged

OBLIQUE RHYME (Poetry/rhyme): Imperfect rhyme of similar but not identical syllables, as between "port" and "heart." Also known as **off rhyme** and slant rhyme. Modern poets often use oblique rhyme as a subtler alternative to perfect rhyme.

ODE (Poetry/Poetic Form): A serious lyric poem, often of significant length, that usually conforms to an elaborate metrical structure.
Ex: *William Wordsworth's* "Ode: Intimations of Immortality."

OEDIPUS COMPLEX (Literary Technique/character): In psychoanalysis, the (subconsciously sexual) attachment of a young boy to his mother.

OFF RHYME (Poetry/rhyme): *See* **oblique rhyme**.

OMNISCIENT NARRATOR (Story Elements/narration): A narrator who knows all of the actions, feelings, and motivations of the story's characters. *See also* **limited omniscient narrator**.
Ex: *The narrator of Leo Tolstoy's* Anna Karenina *is omniscient.*

ONOMATOPOEIA (Figurative Language/sound & sense): The effect produced by a word whose sound evokes its meaning.

Ex: *"Meow," "buzz," "murmur," and "moan" are onomatopoeic.*

OXYMORON (Figurative Language/imagery): The association of two conflicting terms, as in the word "bittersweet" or the expression "same difference."

Ex: *In Romeo and Juliet, Romeo's melodramatic outburst: "O brawling love, O loving hate, / O anything of nothing first create! / O heavy lightness, serious vanity, / Misshapen chaos of well-seeming forms! / Feather of lead, bright smoke, cold fire, sick health, / Still-waking sleep, that is not what it is." (R&J I.i.169-174)*

PARABLE (Genre): A short narrative that illustrates a moral by means of **allegory**.

PARODY (Genre): A humorous, often satirical imitation of the style or a particular work of another author.

Ex: *Henry Fielding's* Shamela *is a parody of Samuel Richardson's* Pamela.

PASTORAL (Genre): A celebration of the simple, rustic life of shepherds and farmers, often written by a sophisticated urban author. The lonely farmer or shepherd who longs to wed, like Farmer Oak from *Far From the Madding Crowd*, is a typical hero of the genre.

Ex: *Thomas Hardy's* Far from the Madding Crowd; *Shakespeare's* As You Like It *contains pastoral elements.*

PENTAMETER (Poetry/meter: length): Five feet per line of verse.

PERSONIFICATION (Figurative Language/imagery): The attribution of personal characteristics to animals, things, or ideas. **Anthropomorphism**—attribution of specifically human emotions and characteristics—is a type of personification.

Ex: *In Sonnet 65, Shakespeare personifies death as an attacking enemy.*

PETRARCHAN SONNET (Poetry/poetic form): A sonnet composed of an eight-line **octave** with the **rhyme scheme** *abbaabba* followed by a six-line **sestet** rhyming *cdecde* or *cdccdc*. The octave poses a problem that the sestet answers. This form was developed by the Italian Renaissance poet Petrarch; it is also known as the Italian sonnet.

PHILOSOPHICAL NOVEL (Genre): A novel serving as a vehicle to explore philosophical ideas.

PICARESQUE (Genre): Originally, a realistic novel detailing the exploits of a scoundrel. The term now refers to any novel with a colorful, loosely structured, episodic plot that revolves around the adventures of a central character from a low social class.

Ex: *Miguel de Cervantes's* Don Quixote; *Mark Twain's* Huckleberry Finn

PLOT (Story Elements): The arrangement of events in a narrative, including their order, their relative emphasis, and the implied causal connections between them.

POINT OF VIEW (Story Elements/perspective): The perspective from which the story is being told; the relationship of the narrator to his narrative.

Ex: The Great Gatsby *is told from the point of view of Nick Carraway. Nick narrates from a first-person point of view.*

POLYSYNDETON (Figurative Language/phrase structure): The repetition of conjunctions where they would not normally be used. The opposite of polysyndeton is **asyndeton**.

POSTMODERNISM (Movement; c. 1945–present): A notoriously ambiguous term that usually refers to post–World War II literature characterized by a disjointed, fragmented pastiche of high and low culture that reflects the absence of tradition and structure from a world driven by technology and consumerism. Postmodernism can be seen as a response to the elitism of **high modernism**, to the horrors of World War II, and to the emptiness of postwar prosperity.

Ex: *Vladimir Nabokov, Salman Rushdie, Don DeLillio, Julian Barnes, Kurt Vonnegut, Thomas Pynchon, Tom Stoppard (playwright), Harold Pinter (playwright)*

Ex: *Vladimir Nabokov's* Lolita

PRE-RAPHAELITES (Movement/group; 1848–1870; England): The literary arm of a late nineteenth-century artistic movement that drew inspiration from Italian artists working before Raphael (1483–1520). The Pre-Raphaelites combined sensuousness and religiosity through archaic poetic forms and medieval settings.

Ex: *William Morris, Christina Rossetti, Dante Gabriel Rossetti, Charles Swinburne*

PROBLEM PLAY (Genre/drama): A term sometimes used to refer to three or four of Shakespeare's plays that do not comfortably fit into a traditional genre—plays that present a classification problem. Like the comedies, they end in or revolve around marriage, but the circumstances and the dark tone leave audiences uneasy. At the same time, the characters are not treated with enough dignity for tragedy. The three problem plays are *All's Well that Ends Well, Troilus and Cressida,* and *Measure for Measure; The Merchant of Venice* is occasionally cited as well.

The term is also used to describe modern plays that confront a contemporary social problem with the intent of influencing public opinion. Problem plays in this sense were developed and popularized by Henrik Ibsen in works such as *A Doll's House* and *Hedda Gabler.* George Bernard Shaw continued the tradition.

PROTAGONIST (Story Elements/character): The main character in a literary work. Typically, the protagonist undergoes some kind of change or development over the course of the story. *See also **antagonist.***

PSYCHOLOGICAL NOVEL (Genre): A novel whose primary focus is on the characters' emotions and internal motivations as they respond to external events.

Ex: *Fyodor Dostoyevsky's* Crime and Punishment; Portrait of a Lady *and other novels by Henry James*

QUARTO (Publishing): A standard sheet of paper folded into quarters; also a book made up of quarto sheets. Eighteen of Shakespeare's plays appeared in one or more quarto editions before the publication of the **First Folio** in 1623.

REALISM (Movement; 1830–1900; France, England, America): A loose term that can refer to any work that aims at honest portrayal over sensationalism, exaggeration, or melodrama. Technically, realism refers to a late-19th-century literary movement that aimed at accurate and detailed portrayal of ordinary, contemporary life. **Naturalism** (see above) can be seen as an intensification of realism.

Ex: *Many of the 19th century's greatest novelists, such as Honoré de Balzac, Charles Dickens, George Eliot, Gustave Flaubert, and Leo Tolstoy, are realists.*

REIFICATION (Figurative Language/imagery): Referring to an abstract concept as a concrete thing.

Ex: *In Sonnet 65, Shakespeare reifies coffins as "Time's chest."*

RENAISSANCE (Movement; 14th–16th centuries; Western Europe): The revival of the art and learning of antiquity that accompanied the transition between the Middle Ages and the modern world. The Renaissance spread throughout Europe after beginning in Italy in the fourteenth century.

Ex: *Dante, Shakespeare, Marlowe*

RHYME (Poetry): Similarity of endings of stressed syllables in words, often in corresponding positions of lines of verse. "Summer" and "drummer" rhyme, as do "say" and "away." *See also* **end rhyme, internal rhyme, masculine rhyme, feminine rhyme, oblique rhyme.**

RHYME SCHEME (Poetry): The pattern of **end rhymes** in a **stanza**. Rhyme scheme is usually notated with a letter of the alphabet for each similar end sound.
Ex: *"Roses are red; / Violets are blue. / You are so sweet / That I love you" has the rhyme scheme* abcb.

RHYTHM (Poetry): The recurring pattern of stressed and unstressed syllables, especially in verse.

ROMAN À CLEF (Genre): A novel in which historical people and events are represented as fictional. The *clef* ("key") is the key to unlocking the correpondence between the novel and real life.
Ex: *Jack Kerovac's* On the Road; *Ernest Hemingway's* The Sun Also Rises

ROMAN À THÈSE (Genre): *See* **thesis novel**.

ROMANCE (Genre): A nonrealistic story, in verse or prose, that features idealized characters, improbable adventures, and exotic settings. Although love often plays a significant role, the association of the word "romance" with love is a modern phenomenon. Romances were particularly popular in the Middle Ages and during the Renaissance. *See also* **medieval romance**.
Ex: The Winter's Tale, The Tempest, Pericles, Cymbeline, *Edmund Spenser's* The Faerie Queene

ROMANTICISM (Movement; c. 1798–1832; France, England, America): A literary and artistic movement that reacted against the restraint and universalism of the Enlightenment. The Romantics celebrated spontaneity, imagination, subjectivity, and the purity of nature.
Ex: *English Romantic writers: Jane Austen, William Blake, Lord Byron, Samuel Taylor Coleridge, John Keats, Percy Bysshe Shelley, and William Wordsworth. American Romantic writers: Nathaniel Hawthorne, Edgar Allan Poe, William Cullen Bryant, and John Greenleaf Whittier.*

SATIRE (Genre): A work that exposes to ridicule the shortcomings of individuals, institutions, or society, often to make a political point.
Ex: Gulliver's Travels *is one of the most famous satires in English literature.*

SCIENCE FICTION (Genre; from late 19th century): Fiction set in an alternative, technologically advanced reality. The genre traces its roots to the works of Jules Verne and H.G. Wells in the late 1800s.
Ex: Fahrenheit 451 *and other works by Ray Bradbury; works by Isaac Asimov, Stanislav Lem*

SETTING (Story Elements): The time and place of a narrative. Setting may be very specific historically or geographically, as in the ancient Rome of Robert Graves's *I, Claudius*; or it may be vague and imaginary, as in the Neverland of J.M. Barrie's *Peter Pan*.

SHAKESPEAREAN SONNET (Poetry/poetic form): A sonnet composed of three rhyming quatrains and a **heroic couplet**; the usual rhyme scheme is *abab cdcd efef gg*. This form was popularized by Shakespeare during the rule of Queen Elizabeth. It is also known as the Elizabethan sonnet or the English sonnet.

SHORT STORY (Genre): A short work of prose fiction, rarely longer than forty pages.
Ex: *"The Dead" and other stories in* Dubliners, *Ernest Hemingway's "A Clean, Well-Lighted Place" and "Hills Like White Elephants," and Katherine Mansfield's "The Garden Party."*

SIMILE (Figurative Language/imagery): A comparison of two things using "like" or "as."
Ex: *The expressions "cool as a cucumber," "happy as a clam," "sick as a dog" are all similes.*

SLANT RHYME (Poetry/rhyme): *See* **oblique rhyme**.

SLICE OF LIFE (Genre): A term referring to the realistic presentation of quotidian daily events. Originally coined to describe the works of the nineteenth-century French naturalists.

Ex: *James Joyce's* Dubliners

SOCIAL PROTEST NOVEL (Genre): A novel that aims to illuminate and draw attention to contemporary social problems with the goal of inciting change for the better.

Ex: *Classic examples inclue Harriet Beecher Stowe's* Uncle Tom's Cabin; *Upton Sinclair's* The Jungle; *John Steinbeck's* The Grapes of Wrath.

SONNET (Poetry/poetic form): A single-stanza **lyric poem** of fourteen lines of equal length. In English, sonnets are in **iambic pentameter**. There are two major sonnet types: the **Petrarchan sonnet** (also known as Italian sonnet), and the **Shakespearean sonnet** (also known as English sonnet or Elizabethan sonnet). The Italian sonnet is divided into a problem-posing **octave** and a resolving **sestet**. The Shakespearean sonnet is divided into three **quatrains** and a **couplet**.

SPEECH ACT (Theory & Criticism): An utterance that performs an action in a particular context. For example, the words "I promise" perform the act of promising when they are spoken.

Ex: *"Hail!" is a speech act that appears frequently in Shakespeare's plays.*

STANZA (Poetry): A group of two or more lines of verse whose metrical form and rhyme scheme may be repeated in other stanzas of a peom.

STOCK CHARACTER (Story Elements/character): A character type that recurs throughout literature, or throughout a literary genre. Notable examples include the witty servant, the scheming villain, and the femme fatale. The fairy godmother is a stock character of fairy tales.

STREAM OF CONSCIOUSNESS (Literary Technique/narration): The thoughts and awarenesses of a character. A character's stream of consciousness could be reported directly in first person or through **free indirect discourse**. It could be represented as a sequence of rational thoughts or as a less articulate stream of words and images. *See also* **interior monologue**. James Joyce is famous for his stream-of-consciousness style in *Ulysses*.

Ex: *James Joyce (direct); Virginia Woolf (indirect)*

SUBPLOT (Story Elements/plot): A secondary plot. A subplot serves as a point of contrast or comparison to the main plot.

Ex: *In* King Lear, *Gloucester's conflicts with his sons form a subplot that comments on the main plot about Lear and his daughters.*

SURREALISM (Movement; 1920s–1930s; France): An avant-garde movement that sought to break down the boundaries between rational and irrational, conscious and unconscious, through a variety of literary and artistic experiments. The surrealist poets, such as André Breton and Paul Eluard, were not as successful as their artist counterparts, who included Salvador Dalí, Joan Miró, and René Magritte.

SYMBOL (Thematic Meaning/object): An object, character, image or another element that represents an abstract idea or concept. Symbols may be universal or take on different meanings in different contexts.

Ex: *A red rose is associated with romantic love. The fork in the road in Robert Frost's poem "The Road Not Taken" symbolizes the choice between two paths in life.*

SYMBOLISM (Movement; 1870s–1890s; France): A poetic movement that reacted against realism with a poetry of suggestion based on private symbols, engendering new poetic forms such as **free verse** and the **prose poem**. The symbolists were influenced by Charles Baudelaire. In turn, they had a seminal influence on early 20th century modernist poetry.

Ex: *Stéphane Mallarmé, Arthur Rimbaud, Paul Verlaine*

SYNECDOCHE (Figurative Language/imagery): A form of **metonymy** in which a part is used to refer to the whole (as in "my wheels" instead of "my car"), or the whole is used to refer to a part (as in "the U.S. won the cup" instead of "the U.S. sailing team won the cup").

Ex: *In "Uneasy lies the head that wears the crown" (2 Henry IV, III.i.31), having a head implies being a person.*

SYNONYM (Words): A word that has the same or a similar meaning as a different word.

Ex: *"Raise" and "elevate" are synonyms.*

TERZA RIMA (Poetry/poetic form): A systems of interlaced **tercets** linked by common rhymes: *aba bcb cdc,* etc. The form was pioneered by Dante in *The Divine Comedy.* The form is tricky to maintain in English, although there are some notable exceptions, such as Percy Bysshe Shelley's "Ode to the West Wind."

TETRALOGY (Publishing): Four works grouped together.

Ex: *Eight of Shakespeare's history plays form two tetralogies:* Richard II, 1 Henry IV, 2 Henry IV, *and* Henry V; *and* 1 Henry VI, 2 Henry VI, 3 Henry VI, *and* Richard III.

THEATER OF THE ABSURD (Movement/drama; 1930s–70s; France): A movement that responded to the apparent illogicality and purposelessness of human life with works marked by a lack of clear narrative, understandable psychological motives, or emotional catharsis. Absurdist theater rejects conventional dramatic elements and uses language to confuse meaning rather than to clarify in order to emphasize the absence of objective truth.

Ex: *Samuel Beckett, Eugene Ionesco, Arthur Adamov; sometimes Albert Camus (in literature)*

Ex: *Beckett's* Waiting for Godot *is the semial play of the theater of the absurd.*

THEME (Thematic Meaning/story): A fundamental and universal idea explored in a literary work.

THESIS (Thematic Meaning/story): The central argument that an author tries to make in a work. The term is primarily associated with nonfictional literature, but can also apply to fiction.

Ex: *In* The Prince *Niccolò Machiavelli argues that rulers should be guided by pragmaticism, not morals. The thesis of Upton Sinclair's* The Jungle *is that Chicago meatpacking plants subject poor immigrants to horrible, unjust working conditions, and that the government must do something to address the problem*

THESIS NOVEL (Genre): A novel that presents problems and argues in favor of a solution. *See also novel of ideas.*

Ex: *Harriet Beecher Stowe's* Uncle Tom's Cabin; *Charles Dickens's* Hard Times

THIRD-PERSON NARRATION (Story Elements/narration): The narrator remains outside of the story and refers to its characters by their names and by the third-person pronouns "he," "she," "it," and "they."

TONE (Story Elements/perspective): The attitude of the author or the narrator toward the narrative or the reader; the atmosphere conveyed by the work.

TRAGEDY (Genre/drama): A serious play that ends unhappily for the protagonist.

Ex: *Euripedes'* Medea; *Shakespeare's* King Lear

TRAGIC FLAW (Literary Technique/character): In critical theory, the flaw that leads to the downfall of a tragic hero. In *Othello,* jealousy is Othello's tragic flaw.

TRANSCENDENTALISM (Movement; c. 1835–1860; America): An New England–based American philosophical and spiritual movement that focused on the primacy of the individual conscience and rejected materialism in favor of closer communion with nature.
Ex: Ralph Waldo Emerson, Henry David Thoreau
Ex: Henry David Thoreau's Walden

TRILOGY (Publishing): Three works grouped together.
Ex: Shakespeare's Henry VI is a trilogy. Jules Verne's adventure tales The Children of Captain Grant, The Mysterious Island, and Twenty Thousand Leagues Under the Sea form a trilogy, although they do not happen consecutively.

TROPE (Figurative Language): A category of figures of speech that extend the literal meanings of words by inviting a comparison to other words, things, or ideas. **Metaphor**, **metonymy**, and **simile** are three common tropes.

UNRELIABLE NARRATOR (Story Elements/narration): A narrator who, over time, is revealed to be an untrustworthy source of information.
Ex: Humbert in Vladimir Nabokov's Lolita and Stevens in Kazuo Ishiguro's The Remains of the Day

UTOPIAN FICTION (Genre): A work describing an imaginary ideal society that has eliminated worldly evils such as hatred and pain. The term comes from Sir Thomas More's Utopia (1516), whose name is a pun on Greek and Latin constructions that mean "good place" and "no place."
Ex: Plato's Republic is the earliest utopian work.

VICTORIAN AGE (Movement/era; c. 1832–1901; England): The **peroid** that roughly coincided with the reign of Queen Victoria (ruled 1837–1901). Though remembered for strict social, political, and sexual conservatism and frequent clashes between religion and science, the period also saw prolific literary activity and significant social reform and criticism.
Ex: Notable Victorian novelists include the Brontë sisters, Charles Dickens, George Eliot, William Makepeace Thackeray, Anthony Trollope, and Thomas Hardy. Prominent poets include Matthew Arnold; Robert and Elizabeth Barrett Browning; Gerard Manley Hopkins; Alfred, Lord Tennyson; and Christina Rossetti. Notable Victorian nonfiction writers include Walter Pater, John Ruskin, and Charles Darwin.

VILLAIN   (Story Elements/character type): The evil character who opposes the **hero**. A villain is an **antagonist** who has been judged as evil.